The One Show

Judged To Be Advertising's Best Print, Radio, TV. Volume 10
A Presentation of The One Club for Art & Copy

Published by Rotovision S.A. Geneva

The One Club For Art & Copy

Allan Beaver
PRESIDENT

Angela Dominguez
EXECUTIVE DIRECTOR

Carolyn Dempsey
MEMBERSHIP COORDINATOR/
ASSISTANT EDITOR

Robert Reitzfeld
DESIGNER

Ryuichi Minakawa
ART DIRECTOR

Izabella Piestrzynska
EDITOR

Robert Ammirati (Cover)
Angela Dominguez (Interior)
PHOTOGRAPHERS

Keefe & Associates, Inc.
(Using Apple Mac II, Quark Express 2.0)
TYPESETTING

PUBLISHED AND DISTRIBUTED BY
RotoVision SA
Route Suisse 9
CH-1295 Mies
Switzerland
Telephone: 22-55 30 55
Telex: 419 246 rovi ch
Fax: 22-55 40 72

From April 1989:
Telephone: 22-755 30 55
Fax: 22-755 40 72

IN ASSOCIATION WITH
The One Club for Art & Copy, Inc.
3 West 18th Street
New York, NY 10011
(212) 255-7070
(FAX 212-633-6950)

First Printing.
ISBN 0-929837-00-2
ISSN 0273-2033

Printed in Hong Kong by Everbest Printing Co., Ltd.

Contents

The Board of Directors

President's Message

As Madison Avenue moves downtown, and we try to figure out who merged with whom and which acquisition is American, or English, or French, this 1988 One Show Award Book reflects a lot of what is happening in this business of Advertising today.

The procedure we used to judge this year's Show was developed because of Advertising's global attitude and was unique for an American award show. We traveled to London with fifteen American judges and invited six English creative directors to join their American colleagues in choosing the finalists. Then, the One Club invited the English to join us in New York to select the medal winners.

The procedure was not without some interesting controversy.

Can the separate cultures understand each other's communication?

Is the English use of typographic leading, interesting graphically–or just bad typography?

Can the English find the Lexington Avenue subway? Would they want to?

Will nationalism become more convincing than good professional judgement?

Can the Americans adjust to tea at 4 p.m.?

I believe we have survived the controversy and are the better for it. Today's advertising industry is reflective of the world we live in and that world is shrinking.

We are now much closer (more than just geographically) to our colleagues in Europe, and throughout the world. In fact, this year's One Show was selected from over 10,000 entries worldwide, not only from England and France, but places like Australia, New Zealand, Denmark, Japan, Trinidad, Hong Kong, Taiwan, Canada, Brazil, Iceland, Scotland, Wales, and Singapore.

So it seems to me it makes sense to increase the dialogue between our colleagues here and abroad.

George Bernard Shaw said: "America and Britain are two nations divided by a common language."

But today, tea and crumpets at 4:00 in the afternoon isn't so crazy after all and MacDonald's has been accepted in Piccadilly Circus.

This collection of extraordinary work from all over the world is proof that the times have indeed changed.

Allan Beaver

Judges Panel

Ralph Ammirati
Co-Chairman/Director of Creative Services
Ammirati & Puris (New York)

Tony Angotti
Executive Vice President/Creative Director
Hill Holliday Connors Cosmopulos (New York)

Ron Berger
Partner
Messner Vetere Berger Carey (New York)

Neil Calet
Co-Chairman/Executive Creative Director
Calet Hirsch & Spector (New York)

Tim Delaney
Chairman/Creative Director
Leagas Delaney Partnership (London)

Amil Gargano
Chairman
Ally & Gargano (New York)

Paul Garrett
Creative Director
WCRS Mathews Marcantonio (London)

Roy Grace
Chairman
Grace and Rothschild (New York)

Derrick Hass
Creative Director
Ogilvy & Mather (London)

Bob Kuperman
Senior Vice President/Creative Director
Chiat/Day (Venice, CA)

Andrew J. Langer
President/Creative Director
Lowe Marschalk (New York)

Bob Levenson
Vice Chairman
Scali McCabe Sloves (New York)

James Lowther
Joint Creative Director
Saatchi & Saatchi (London)

Rob Morris
Joint Creative Director
Coleman RSCG (London)

John O'Donnell
Creative Director
Collett Dickenson Pearce (London)

Joe O'Neill
Executive Vice President/Creative Director
Hill Holliday Connors Cosmopulos (New York)

Steve Penchina
Chairman/Creative Director
Penchina Selkowitz (New York)

Hal Riney
Chairman/Chief Executive Officer
Hal Riney & Partners (San Francisco)

Phyllis Robinson
President
Phyllis K. Robinson Inc. (New York)

Diane Rothschild
President
Grace and Rothschild (New York)

Sam Scali
Vice Chairman/Creative Director US
Scali McCabe Sloves (New York)

Martin Solow
Chairman
Durfee & Solow (New York)

One Club Members

Mike Abadi
Jeffrey Abbott
Francine Abdow
Debbie Adelman
Robin Albin
Gregory Alderisio
Carl Ally
Hal Altman
David Altschiller
Lawrence Ancona
Susan Andreasen
Anthony Angotti
Jeffrey Antman
Nadine Appel
Sharon Appleman
Brian Arcarese
Arnold Arlow
Craig Astler
Thomas Augusta
Don Austen
Ellen Azorin

Kate Bahlke
Bob Barrie
Brenda Basken
Allan Beaver
Lisa Becker
Elisabeth Bell
Ron Berger
Eric Berkeley
Rose Bernatovich
David Bernstein
George Betsis
Jack Bloom
Chris Bodden
Karen Booney
Kate Borman
Michael Borst
Kathy Botas
Doreen Bowens
Harry Braver
Bill Brokaw
David Bromberg
Jennifer Brooke
Toni Courtney Brown
Matthew Brownell
Amy Bryant
Cindy Bruckner
Florence Buchanan
Bryan Buckley
Richard Buckley
Mary Ann Bunda
Ron Burkhardt
Ed Butler
John Butler

John Caceres
Larry Cadman
Jerry Caggiano
Nando Caldarone
Neil Calet
Maryann Camarda
Dale Campbell
John Caples
Vito Caramia
Patricia Cardello
Bob Carducci
Patrick Carella
Leynete Cariapa
David Carlin
Michele Carlo
Barbara Carmack
Dina Carpenter
Marie Carroll
Susan Carroll
Earl Carter
Earl Cavanah
Heidi Cervenka
Ronald Cesark
Larry Chase
Vincent Chieco
Linda Chirby
Marcia Christ
Shelly Chung
Tom Chung
Ed Cicale
Lisa Ciocci
John Clapps
Eric Claussen
Andrew Cohen
Dale Cohen
Deanna Cohen
Nick Cohen
James Colasurdo
Adrienne Collier
John Colquhoun
Jerry Confino
Tad Consani
Allison Constantine
Tom Cook
Lynn Corley
David Corr
Rachel Couillard
Robert Cox
Cheryl Crain
Scott Croce
Amy Cryer-Hassett
Bob Culver
Linda Cummings
Ellen Curtis
Lisa Cushman

James Dale
Boris Damast
Kristine D'Amico
Gregory Davis
Heather Davis
Robin Pato Davis
Sarah Defty
Rena De-Levie
Scott Dell
Jerry Della Femina
Craig Demeter
Cynthia Derosier
Yvonne DeSanti
John Dillon
Deborah Dilworth
Simon Dixon
Kevin Donovan
Penny Dorrance
Kevin Drexler
Mark Driscoll
Lorraine Duffy
Rosalyn Dunham
Laurence Dunst
Jim Durfee

Charles Eaton
Phoebe Eaton
Vickery Eckhoff
Michael Edelstein
Shannon Edwards
Victoria Eichinger
Neil Eichner
Arthur Einstein
Mitchell Eisenman
Michael Eldred
Leslie Eskildsen

Timothy Fahey
Gene Federico
Oksana Fedorenko
Doug Feinstein
Deborah Feit
Jeremy Feldman
Steve Feldman
Stefani Feller

Bernadette Ferrara
Sal Finazzo
Carole Anne Fine
Michael Fine
Kevin Finn
Toby Finneman
Janice Fitzgibbon
Daniel Flamberg
Daniel Flynn
John Follis
Rosemarie Fontana
Kevin Foreman
Joseph Forte
David Freedman

Harvey Gabor
Bob Gage
Jim Garaventi
Alison Gardner
Amil Gargano
Rich Garramone
Lisa Garrone
Karen Gedney
Judith Gee
Richard Gee
Robert Gerardi
Dona Gibbs
Ed Giddens
Keith Gillespie
Scott Gilliam
Frank Ginsberg
Sharon Glazer
Robert Gloddy
Barry Gloffke
Jeff Goldberg
Patti Goldberg
Phyllis Goldberg
Charles Goldman
Jo Ann Goldsmith
Adam Goldstein
Mark Goldstein
Susan Goodell
William Gordon
Milt Gossett
Gary Graf
Stella Grafakos
John Grant
Liz Gravitz
David Green
Donald Green
Paula Green

Rosalind Greene
Christopher Gregor
Dick Grider
Josclynne Grier
Dina Grossman
Susan Grube
Elizabeth Gummere

David Hackett
Heidi Hake
Jim Hallowes
Ellen Halper
Barbara Hamilton
Alton Hansley
Kirsten Hanson
Sally Harley
Cabell Harris
Joel Harrison
Paul Hartzell
Takeshi Hayakawa
Giichi Hayami
Juliet Heeg
William Heinrich
Roy Herbert
Rony Herz
Stephen Herz
Heather Higgins
Elizabeth Hinton
Peter Hirsch
Jacqueline Ho
Bernie Hogya
Barri Lynn Hollander
Julia Hopkins
Nancy Ellis Horowitz
Paul Horscroft
Hugh Hough
Mike Hughes
Neal Hughlett
Lisa Hurwitz

Karl Iglesias

George Jaccoma
Richard Jackson
Ellen Jacobs
Harry Jacobs Jr.
Corrin Jacobsen
Brian Johnson
Gary Johnson
Raymond Johnson
James Johnston

Caroline Jones

Paul Kane
Gloria Kapral
Ken Karsen
Sheryl Katz
Paul Kaufman
Talo Kawasaki
Nancy Keating
Steven Keltz
Karen Kliewe
Gregory Knox
Julian Koenig
Daren Koniuk
Gary Kopervas
Lois Korey
Ronni Korn
Renee Korus
Jonathan Krevolin
Debra Krinick
Bjarni Kristinsson
Helmut Krone
David Kronheim
Shep Kurnit
Henry Kwok
Eleanor Kyle

Dane LaChiusa
Michele Laddin
Larry Laiken
Andrew Langer
Patricia Sutula Langer
James Lansbury
Anthony LaPetri
Karen Larson
Ali Lasky
Doris Latino
Mary Wells Lawrence
Bruce Lee
Dany Lee Lennon
Margaret Leonard
Mike Lescarbeau
Diane Letulle
Robert Levenson
Ilysse Leventhal
Meg Levine
Sharron Lewisy
Susan Lieber
Krista Light Hiser
Fred Lind
David Lindberg

Peter Lish
Wallace Littman
Margaret Livingston
Roger Livingston
George Lois
Cecile Lozano
Margaret Lubalin
Peter Lubalin
Marcia Luce
Alden Ludlow III
David Luhn
Lisa Lurie
John Lyons

Kevin McAllister
Ed McCabe
Ruth McCarthy
Lisa McComsey
Shelia McCreven
Bill McCullam
Wilma McDaniel
Tom McDonnell
Tom McElligott
Thomas McLoughlin
Gerard McMahon
Michael McNulty

Tony Macchia
Thomas Madeo
Ira Madris
Maria Maestre
David Maisel
Michael Mangano
Howard Margulies
Richard Marino
John Mariucci
Donald Marner
Paul Marro
Hillary Martin
Lou Martin
Rodd Martin
Nelson Martinez
Mary Means
Leslie Stokes Mechanic
Bill Meinel
Roberto Mendoza
Mario Messina
Tom Messner
David Metcalf
Lyle Metzdorf
Lou Miano

Harold Michelson
Mark Millar
Don Miller
Jim Millman
John Mims
Jonathan Mindell
Erik Mintz
Vera Ann Mioli
Patrick Miranda
Robert Mizrahi
Thomas Monahan
Jeffrey Moore
John Morrison
Syl Morrone
Dina Morrongiello
Roger Mosconi
Norman Muchnick
Tammy Muse

Ernest Nargi
Thomas Nathan
Bruce Nelson
Jeff Nelson
Steve Nicholas
Bruce Nilson
Jennifer Noble
Eileen Norton

Dick O'Brien
Sharon Occhipinti
Rafe Offer
David Ogilvy
Steve Ohman
Vicky Oliver
Joe O'Neill
Donald Ong
Curvin O'Rielly
Roberta Orshan
Cathy Ouchterloney

Maxine Paetro
Stephen Pardee
Donald Parker
Sheri Pasetsky
Joanne Pateman
Andrew Payton
Jon Pearce
Sue Peckar
Anthony Pepitone
Ellen Perless
Earl Place Peterson

John Petruney
Randy Petschauer
Lynn Piasecki
David Piatkowski
Kate Pickman
Susan Picking
Dallene Pierce
Derek Pierce
Darlene Pike
Larry Plapler
Paul Plastaras
Angelo Pocchia
Robin Pollak
Chris Pollock
Shirley Polykoff
Diana Poulos

Elissa Querze
Brian Quinn
Elissa Quinn

Douglas Raboy
Richard Raboy
Radhika Radhakrishnan
Jose Ramirez
Jim Raniere
Chris Ransick
Michael Reid
Kevin Reilly
Dean Victoria Reilly
Robert Reitzfeld
Harry Remer
Donn Resnick
Robert Resnick
Kathryn Rice
Nancy Rice
Judy Rifkin
Jim Ritterhoff
Nancy Robbins
Phyllis Robinson
Jonathan Rodgers
Lynne Rose
Ron Rosenfeld
Robert Rosenthal
Stuart Rosenwasser
Tom Rost
David Rothberg
Mark Rothenberg
Carolyn Amorosi Rothseid
M. Susan Roy
Joanne Rudden

John Russo
Mike Rylander

Paul Safsel
Laurie Salzberg
Kenneth Sandbank
Laird Sanders
Jon Sandhaus
Harry Sandler
Luis Santana
Neil Sanzari
Ernie Schenck
Glenn Scheuer
Joyce Schnaufer
John Schmidt
Sy Schreckinger
Jay Schulberg
Jamie Scott
Susannah Sculco
Norb Seufert
Ted Shaine
John Shammas
Jason Shaw
Tim Shaw
Laurie Shea
Regina Sheahan
Joe Sherlock
Brett Shevack
Carole Shiber
David Shih
Jon Shoates
Constantine Shoukas
Scott Shulim
Virgil Shutze
John Siddall
Evan Silberman
Jon Sills
Jorge Silva
Mark Silveira
Alan Silver
Ann Silvi
Susan Simmons
Leonard Sirowitz
Mike Slosberg
Robert Slosberg
Hillary Smith
Jo Smith
Priscilla Smith
James Snedeker
Alan Solomon
Richard Solomon

Martin Solow
John Soltez
Dennis Soohoo
Stephanie Sorine
Blair Sorrel
Kayvan Sotoodeh
Kirk Souder
Cheri Soukup
Hazel Spector
Mark Spector
Helayne Spivak
Timothy Spoleti
Andrew St. Angelo
Paige St. John
Scott Stefan
Dean Stefanides
Elaine Stein
Deborah Steiner
Jillian Stern
Fred Stesney
Stan Stoj
Donna Strauss
Ira Sturtevant
Pamela Sullivan
Anna Suplina
Leslie Sweet
Regina Sweeney
John Swieter

Judy Tabak
George Tatarinow
William Taylor
Donna Tedesco/Hartmann
Judy Teller
Mike Tesch
Tom Thomas
Deepak Thosar
Bill Tomlinson
Stephen Touhill
William Troncone
Peter Trondsen
Anne Tum Suden
Bill Tsapalas
Mylene Turek
Carol Turturro

Rodney Underwood
Ben Urman

Sally Van Devanter
William Vartorella

David Vawter
Annette Vendryes
June Vidart

Ronald Wachino
Nina Wachsman
Marvin Waldman
Teri Walker
Laura Walsh
Matt Warhaftig
Jane Warrick
Jane Warshaw
Bruce Wartman
Peter Watson
Denise Webber
Karen Weber
John Weber
Johann Wechter
Kevin Weidenbacher
Pamela Weiler
Mitchell Wein
Carol Weinfeld
Riva Weinstein
Mimi Weisbond
Ron Weissman
David Wheeler
Thomas White
Anne Whitney
Bob Whitworth
Renee Wightman
Richard Wilde
Kathy Wilder
Kurt Willinger
Cindy Wojdyla
David Wojdyla
Paul Wolfe
Amelia Woodbridge
Grace Wong
Tracy Wong
Brian Wright
Carolyn Wyman
Elizabeth Wynn

Tom Yablonski
Eric Yadven
Terri Yenko

Joe Zagorski
Leah Zennario
Charles Ziga
Karen Zohar

Gold, Silver & Bronze Awards

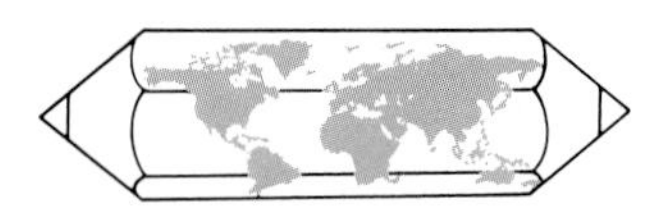

Gold, Silver & Bronze Awards

Consumer Newspaper Over 600 Lines: Single

1 GOLD

ART DIRECTOR
Ken Grimshaw

WRITER
John Donnelly

PHOTOGRAPHER
Gary Redmore

CLIENT
Volvo

AGENCY
Abbott Mead Vickers/
SMS - London

2 SILVER

ART DIRECTOR
Logan Wilmont

WRITER
Mike Court

PHOTOGRAPHER
Andreas Heumann

CLIENT
Mates Healthcare

AGENCY
Still Price Court Twivy
D'Souza/London

3 BRONZE

ART DIRECTOR
Bob Brihn

WRITER
George Gier

PHOTOGRAPHER
Jim Arndt

CLIENT
Federal Express

AGENCY
Fallon McElligott/
Minneapolis

THANKS TO VOLVO, THE OWNER DIDN'T HIT THE ROOF.

On Friday last, Jane Asher's brand new Volvo 240 Estate fell foul of the freak weather conditions in London.

A tree blew down right on top of it.

The Volvo, although only suffering a slight dent, couldn't be moved.

But Miss Asher's routine wasn't disturbed in the slightest.

Volvo's new Careline service ensured that she was furnished with a hire car (paid for by us) within hours.

The RAC stood by to take her Estate to the nearest Volvo dealer (again free of charge) as soon as it was out from under.

Come Hell, High Water or even Hurricane you get more than just a car when you buy a new Volvo. **VOLVO CARELINE**

1 GOLD

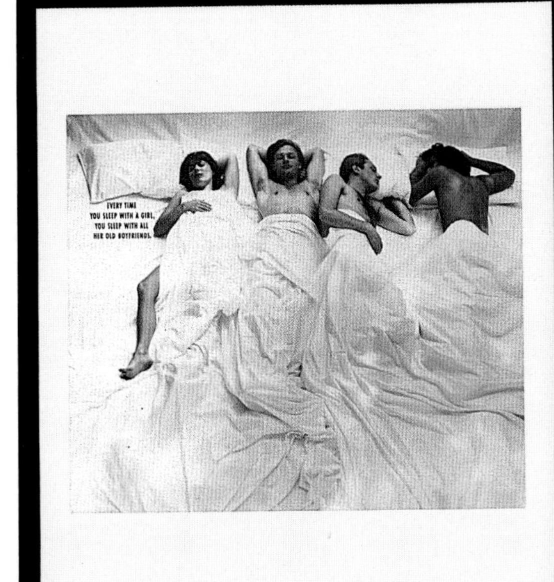

These days you can't be too careful.

You see, sexually transmitted diseases aren't that fussy. They don't care whether you're male or female, straight or gay, promiscuous or choosy.

On average, you're likely to have six sexual relationships in your life. So, if you sleep with six other average people you are actually part of a chain of contacts that totals a staggering 46,656 people. No wonder AIDS is spreading.

Already a person dies of the disease every day, and the British Medical Association figures suggest that by 1991, some 100,000 people in Britain will be affected.

And, with the virus itself changing five times faster than other viruses, hope of a cure seems distant. It's terrifying news. But there is something you can do to protect yourself. Use a condom.

Because it's been shown that condoms help prevent the transfer of the virus (they'll also reduce the risk of VD, cervical cancer and unwanted pregnancy).

Mates condoms are just as reliable and just as sensitive as other brands. The range includes Ribbed Mates, Natural Mates and Coloured Mates – all of which carry the BSI Kite-mark.

They're widely available in pubs, newsagents, clubs, record stores, garages, chemists and supermarkets.

They're made by one of the world's largest manufacturers. Yet they cost less than other condoms.

And all profits from Mates Healthcare Ltd are going to help fight AIDS. We'll be producing leaflets, videos and information packs to educate people in 'Safer Sex' techniques.

Because prevention is better than cure.

We also plan to give money to hospices and counselling services for those dying of the disease.

So when you use a Mates condom, you won't have to worry about the present and you'll also be helping to safeguard everyone's future.

MATES. YOU MAKE LOVE. THEY MAKE SENSE.

These days you can't be too careful.

You see, sexually transmitted diseases aren't that fussy. They don't care whether you're male or female, straight or gay, promiscuous or choosy.

On average, you're likely to have six sexual relationships in your life. So, if you sleep with six other average people you are actually part of a chain of contacts that totals a staggering 46,656 people. No wonder AIDS is spreading.

Already a person dies of the disease every day, and the British Medical Association figures suggest that by 1991, some 100,000 people in Britain will be affected.

And, with the virus itself changing five times faster than other viruses, hope of a cure seems distant. It's terrifying news. But there is something you can do to protect yourself. Use a condom.

Because it's been shown that condoms help prevent the transfer of the virus (they'll also reduce the risk of VD, cervical cancer and unwanted pregnancy).

Mates condoms are just as reliable and just as sensitive as other brands. The range includes Ribbed Mates, Natural Mates and Coloured Mates – all of which carry the BSI Kite-mark.

They're widely available in pubs, newsagents, clubs, record stores, garages, chemists and supermarkets.

They're made by one of the world's largest manufacturers. Yet they cost less than other condoms.

And all profits from Mates Healthcare Ltd are going to help fight AIDS. We'll be producing leaflets, videos and information packs to educate people in 'Safer Sex' techniques.

Because prevention is better than cure.

We also plan to give money to hospices and counselling services for those dying of the disease.

So when you use a Mates condom, you won't have to worry about the present and you'll also be helping to safeguard everyone's future.

MATES. YOU MAKE LOVE. THEY MAKE SENSE.

2 SILVER

BOLT
XPRESS
AirWing
DELIVERY
UNFORTUNATELY, THIS IS WHAT MOST AIR EXPRESS COMPANIES MEAN WHEN THEY SAY DOOR-TO-DOOR SERVICE.
When you call your air express company they may tell you they offer door-to-door service, but what they don't tell you is whose door they deliver it to.
In many cases, it's to the door of another air express company.
It seems the only way they can ship your package to the United States, is by giving it to someone else to deliver.
But that means more people will have to handle your package. And too many people handling your package allows for too many opportunities for something to go wrong. And if something were to go wrong, it can be extremely difficult to locate the problem, let alone your package.
Fortunately there is an alternative. You can call Federal Express.
When we pick up your package in Toronto for delivery in Chicago, for example, we handle it all the way. Which means, the only place your package can be, is on one of our trucks, or on one of our planes.
And with our COSMOS tracking system, getting information on the status of your package is just a phone call away.
Because of this complete control, you can expect reliability. And we stand behind it with this guarantee – if we deliver a shipment late (even just 60 seconds late) you can request your money back.
So next time, call Federal Express. We won't call anyone else.
For a free international starter kit call 897-9322, outside the metro area, 1-800-387-5982.
WORLDWIDE SERVICE FROM FEDERAL EXPRESS.

3 BRONZE

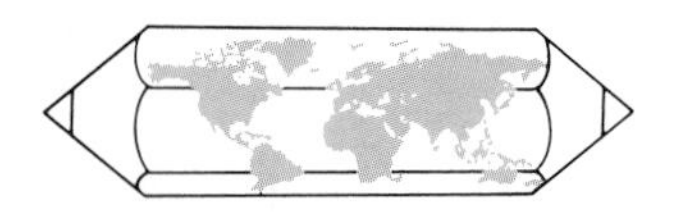

Gold, Silver & Bronze Awards

Consumer Newspaper Over 600 Lines: Campaign

4 GOLD

ART DIRECTOR
Jordin Mendelsohn

WRITERS
Jordin Mendelsohn
Perrin Lam

CLIENT
Southern California
Acura Dealers

AGENCY
Mendelsohn/Zien -
Los Angeles

BMW SPENDS MILLIONS TELLING YOU THEY'RE THE ULTIMATE DRIVING MACHINE.

BUT ACCORDING TO THIS TEST, THEY SHOULD PUT THEIR MONEY INTO THEIR ENGINES AND TRANSMISSIONS.

For years now, BMW has told you they're "The Ultimate Driving Machine." And to be honest, for years they were. No automobile, with the possible exception of Mercedes and Porsche, could match BMW's precision. Speed. Sheer power and engineering prowess.

Until recently.

Just last year, the Acura Legend was found to be as good or better than the prestigious BMW 735 1.7. A car costing double what the Legend cost. And those findings weren't in just one category. Or two. But in an eye-opening thirteen areas of comparison. According to Ward's Auto World's thorough evaluation study.

You would think a car twice the Legend's price would have an engine twice as good. But, on a scale of one to ten, Ward's Auto World ranked both a ten. And the same results occurred in the crucial ride/suspension category. Even BMW's famous anti-lock braking system scored no better than the Acura's.

So where was the justification of BMW's $40,000 plus price tag? Were their expertly engineered transmissions superior to Acura's?

According to the findings, the answer was no again.

Not only did BMW fail to win in this category, but they failed to even tie. Acura Legend won by a 10-9 margin. Nowhere did the BMW ever show itself to be worth as much as $2,000 more than the Legend. Let alone $20,000. Not in the engine. Not in the transmission. Not in fit and finish. And as you can see in the chart above, not even in styling.

As a matter of fact, according to the judges, "The Ultimate Driving Machine" ultimately scored lower than the Acura Legend when all points were totalled.

So to us, the picture is clear. Unless BMW has reduced their car's price by half, and as of today they haven't, they should spend more money making their car better. A lot better.

Of course, the other alternative is to double the price of today's Legend. Or triple it. Because in that same test the '86 Legend also beat, by a six point margin, the '86 Mercedes 560 SEC. A car almost three times the Legend's price.

Now you know why we say we're not just a good car for the money. We'd be a good car for a lot more money.

WARD'S AUTO WORLD IMPORT EVALUATION SCOREBOARD

ACURA
Southern California Dealers

SEE ANY ONE OF THE SOUTHERN CALIFORNIA ACURA DEALERS LISTED BELOW.

4 GOLD

THE ACURA LEGEND WOULD COMPARE EQUALLY TO A MERCEDES 560 SEC IF ONLY IT WASN'T MISSING A $40,000 PART.

There they were. The facts, spelled out in black and white, for the entire world to see. In a whopping fourteen categories that included everything from engine performance to luggage room, Ward's Auto World had made its evaluations.

The $62,500 Mercedes 560 SEC was scored on the same ten point scale as the $21,000 Acura Legend. Initial impressions of the cars? Ten each. Engine and transmission? Ten for the Acura Legend, nine for a car that's advertised to be "engineered like no other car in the world". And a car three times the Legend's base price. But let's get on with the evaluation. Surely the ride and suspension category must have been dominated by the 560 SEC? Wrong. Another ten to nine victory for the Legend.

In category after category, both cars were neck and neck. Except one. Perhaps the most important category of all. Price.

And that's how we arrived at the conclusion that, all things being about equal, that innocuous little hood emblem on the Mercedes 560 SEC must be worth about $40,000.

BUY AN ACURA. BECAUSE NOW BMW AND MERCEDES-BENZ STAND BEHIND IT.

It's true. In the most recently conducted, highly acclaimed J. D. Power Customer Satisfaction Index, both Mercedes and BMW are rated behind Acura. Significantly behind. In fact, the twenty thousand people surveyed put Acura ahead of Mercedes. Not by a mere 5 percentage points. Or 10. But by a whopping 19. As for BMW's "Ultimate Driving Machines" they ultimately proved an astonishing 40 percentage points less satisfying to owners than Acura did.

1987 J.D. POWER CUSTOMER SATISFACTION INDEX

Acura	146
Mercedes-Benz	127
Cadillac	111
Jaguar	110
BMW	106

Industry Average Points 104

But what's more remarkable is the fact that the survey was completed in 1987. Acura's second year in business. So victory was all the more sweet, considering the losers have had nearly a hundred years to practice the art of engineering fine cars and satisfying customers.

You ask, what happened to Mercedes and BMW? Did they get sloppy? Or did they just lower their standards? On the contrary, these fine German masterpieces remained at the top of the survey. In fact, they finished 3rd and 11th respectively. And that's why we're so delighted. You see, the 1987 Customer Satisfaction Index clearly states, "It's not that Mercedes-Benz did anything wrong…it's just that Acura did much better."

So if you're looking for a luxury car that's 19 to 40 percentage points more satisfying than the best Germany has to offer, at a price often half of what Germany's best go for,* consider an Acura.

ACURA
Southern California Dealers

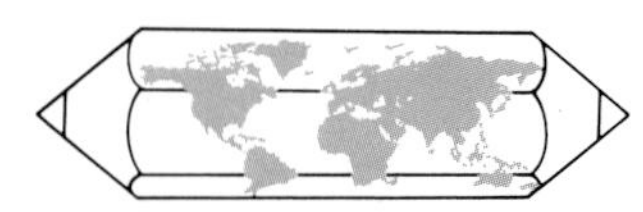

Gold, Silver & Bronze Awards

Consumer Newspaper Over 600 Lines: Campaign

5 SILVER

ART DIRECTOR
Robb Armstrong

WRITER
Kelly Simmons

DESIGNER
Lewis Gilman & Kynett

CLIENT
The Philadelphia Inquirer & Daily News

AGENCY
The Philadelphia Inquirer & Daily News In-House

"Yeah? Well I don't need you or your lousy diamond!"

DURAN, Howard Jones, Phils
ERS, Europe, Psych. Furs
FIRST ROW TICKETS
90 555-9000

ESIS Floor & Section 216
For both nites 555-8491

GENESIS TICKETS
field. 555-6838

SIS TICKETS - Both Shows
seats 555-4409

I have a steady job, a drivers
and social security number,
finance you in a
NEW CAR
or
PICKUP
ust have no credit or limited
credit. Interested? Please call
00

TREASURE - I search
l detector for lost valuables
rings, jewelry etc]. 555-7107

ce Furniture Equipment

$150,000
SED EXECUTIVE FURN.
Desks, Credenzas, Tables
Lateral Files, Chairs, etc.
555-7997

9165 Facsim ansceiver
es & sends i up 1, 2 or 3
Call 555

ED OFFICE
etc. Must sell

ERENCE TA
airs, 1 Exc. chair
555-9252

UTIVE office furniture, desk
2", credenza & hi-back chair
old orig. list $2,600, must sell
or Best Offer. 555-2694

FURN/EQUIPT-New & Used
ercial and Domestic 555-3737

SAVE UP TO 60%
MODELING SHOWROOM
Exec. Desks & Credenzas
Sect'l Work Stations
ck. Low Back & Sect'l Chairs
Lateral & Vertical Files
Computer Furniture
ood Book Cases. All sizes.
onference Tables & Chairs
veseat. Lamps. Prints, etc.
Everything Must Go!!!
555-9741

MACY Shelving & counter
its with drawers. White, clean
ng. For details call 555-8009

★

ROOM FURNITURE

ent cond. Sofa, chair, coffee
end table, and lamp. Like
Hardly used! All for one low,
ce. $175. 555-1573 or 555-9479

★

INER Great shape! Tan &
$150 OBO 555-4633 aft6pm.

ESTAURANT EQUIPMENT
hape. All stainless steel. Re-
tors. Freezers. Deep fryer.
erie hold 25 chicken. Tables,
& misc. Reas. Best offer for
sale. Call 555-2157

& Loveseat, Hunter Green,
& lamps. walnut all-wood
n hulch, odd all-wood bdrm
books & clothing + miscell
Moving, must sell. 555-8565

Modern, Beige. Good cond.
555-4296 eves. & wknds

BED, Queen great cond, $75
Call 555-2387

Custom made Electric Blue
& Leather Burgundy Lounge
Best offer. 555-1492

Loveseat, Chrs, 2 cocktail
2 barcolounge chrs, kit set,
antiques, bkcase 555-1515

E DRESSER Fr Prov. Hen-
Exc cd. $300 Firm 555-1934

FURNISHINGS, 2 tan chairs,
om, kitchen, odd household
best offer 555-3899

ER, dryer,

Machinery & Tools

ALIGNMENT EQUIP Lite Align,
snap on rack. $550. 555-7783

FORK LIFT-PETTIBONE, GMC diesel, 4 Whl Drive, 4 whl, steering 6
masonry forks. Lifts 25'. Cap. 25T,
vy gd tires. Paint tight. Mdl No.
6531. Pd $14,000. Must sell; will ac-
cept $12,000. 555-8868 betw 10 & 7.

ROLLER-General 1½ T, like new.
Asking $2800. 555-8774

Building Materials

Boa

1982 30ft MARTINI Cigarette type
canvas, teak swim platform, many
555-0989
(215) 55 / 4074

AQUASPORT '74 24' 6" Cuddy,
T/115 Evinrudes. $5900. Call (215)
555-5799 4-7 pm;

Aristocraft '79 19' 120 hp inb-
d/outbrd, am/fm cass, water skiis,
new parts & extras $5000. 555-5721

BAYINER '86 14 ft. w/150 HP motor
& galv. trailer. Div. pltfrm, AM-FM
radio cass player plus acces. Used
for 2 hrs. $4900. Call 555-3204

BAYLINER '79 27.5, Volvo I/O, low
hours. Loaded. Excellent condition.
$16,000 555-2342

BAYLINER '84 19' Bayrider, 125
Volvo I/O, all canvases, trlr, exc
cond. $6850. 555-8201 day;
555-4570 eves/wknds.

BAYLINER '84 16' Cuddy, 85hp
O/B. Good cond. Lo hrs. Many
xtras. $6000 or B.O. 555-7582 aft 6pm

BAYLINER '86 14' Capri Bow-
rider- 50 HP w/trailer - amfm cass,
coast guard pkg, CB, LCR 2000
Depthfinder, Great fish/Ski boat!
$4300. Call 555-9778

BOSTON Whaler '85 17' Montauk,
like new, loaded. $12,000. 555-5266

BOWRIDER 16' 85hp Johnson, full
cov, trlr. Make offer. 555-4636 aft 5.

CENTURY '72 17' 78 235 Evin-
rude. Trailer, Cover. Fish/ski/go
fast. $2950. Call 555-4086

CHAPARREL '84 235XL, 24', 350
merc cruiser, Loadrite trailer.
Many, many extras. Must Sell.
Make Offer. 555-9794 aft 6 pm.

CHRIS CRAFT 55' Motor Yacht-
Constellation. Always shed kept in
fresh water. Lo time diesels, new
gen., new decor. Positively beautiful inside & out. Only 3 owners since
built in '59. Bought larger yacht.
555-2178

CHRIS CRAFT '76 30 ft. TF. T/250
FWC. O/R, Loran, DF, VHF, ex
cd. Must Sell $34,000/BO. days. 555-
6835, eves. 555-7941

CHRIS CRAFT '78 25' Slps 4,
equipped for fishing. Good cond.
Asking $10,500. 555-5815 days.

CHRIS CRAFT '68 30 ft. Cavalier,
wood. Twin 185 HP, CB, DF, sleeps
6, very gd cond. $7500 555-0936 aft 4

CHRIS-CRAFT, Scorpian 210
260hp, easy, load, gal. trlr. Excel
cond. 555-0564

CHRIS CRAFT Connie '63, 34'
Good Condition. Call 555-6030

CHRYSLER Outboard 100HP. Exc.
Cond. $1000. Call 555-4746

CIGARETTE 20' 350 Chevy $11,000
CHECKMATE 13'

rude, galv. trlr, P/W. $5000. 555-5141

CRUISER Inc. '78-21' cuddy cabin,
225 OMC io VHF DF trimtabs port-
a-potty, S/S prop. $7800 Must Sell
555-4588

CRUISER Inc. '84. 22' Cuddy, swim
platform, VHF radio, 260 i/o df,
many extras $15K 555-4043; 555-0447

CRUSADER Marine Engine
270hp cw, tot rblt, new manifolds,
risers, f/w system, trans compl
rblt. Eng compl. Just drop in boat.

EGG HARBOR
3KW gen, h/w, shower, slps
555-0384 aft 6 wk or 555-4425

work. $1000. Call 555-6841

Still under fa warranty. Paid
000. Must 182,500.
1350 or 555-8061

$12,500 B/O. 555-2631, 555-6526

FOUR WINNS '85 21ft. Liberator,
300HP, Merc. I/O, 5+ MPH, 2
seasons, $15,500 Exc cond. 555-5954

GRADY WHITE '84
20 ft. overnighter. w/trlr, less than
50 hrs. Must see to appreciate!
Call Ed 555-2565

GRADYWHITE 240 Off-shore, '85
Twin 120 Evinrudes. Warr. till 8/88.
w/trlr, Askg $27,000. 555-2738

HOUSEBOAT - 28'. Nauta-Line,
slps 6, dual voltage, i/o, stern pwr,
stern drive, Chrys 225hp eng, fully
eqpd. Gd running cond. Make offer.
Box 291.

HOUSEBOAT 35', 1973. 35' long
Driftacruz, sleeps 8. Exc cond.
Ready for the season. 555-2565

JERSEY 40' 80 3208T Cats, tower,
chair, new int'r fully eqpd. EXCEL
cond. $135,000. 555-1039

JET BOAT/RALLY SPORT mod-
el blue metal-flake with white int.
455 Olds. motor w/Berkley jet drive
and Jet/A/Vator. With trailer, ex.
water ski boat w/excess. Make offer. 555-3769

LUHRS '67, 24', 10½ ft beam, re-
powr'd, '78 Chevy eng, fully equip.
for fishing. $2000. 555-2382

MAKO 17', '75 engine, 70hp Evin.,
new battery. D/F, & CB, '85 trailer.
$3300 555-1583

MAKO 228 walk-a-round cutty
cabin 1984 excel cond aux. eng. & all
electronics w/Sea Isle City slip for
season. Call 555-1000, ext 231 or
aft 6pm. 555-4377

MAKO 23' Inboard. Large B top,
teak cover boards, fish box, O/R,
trailer, loaded. $15,000.
555-3482 or 555-1020

MAKO '78 21' 1982 200hp Merc.
T-top, trlr, loran, VHF, recorder,
etc. New Boat in! Must Sell! $10,500
or B.O.! 555-1166 or 555-0539

MANATEE 18 ft. center console, 85
HP Mercury, galvanized trlr, chart
recorder, CB. $5250. Call 555-3688

MARATHON 22' '84, 140hp I/O,
U.S.C.G. pkg, ready to go, priced to
sell. 555-6288 eves.

MARK TWAIN 1976 17' Deep V
1979 Johnson 135 hp O/B mtr. 1985
E-Z loader trlr. Runs great. Incl
everything nec to pass Coast Guard
insp. Plus ski equip & plenty other
of access. $3895. 555-8292

McDANIEL '76 18' 85hp mer
motor, low hrs.
w elect

attachments, 3 radios, D/F & Loran, including all safety equip. Boat
in Cape May water $13,500. Firm.
Eve 555-6157 or 555-7184

For Sale

ND. Westinghouse
$150. Emerson Quiet
TU. $125. 555-7311

ICKET. One way to Los
ay 18, $75. 555-4056

ANDERSEN Windows & Doors &
Atrium Doo 0% Off. 555-0205

ATTENTION izens of Phila.
ONZE BELL.
2" base. 25" high.
5-2933

Outside Lift for
WHEELCHAIR. Exc cd. 555-8682

BUS STATION Shelter Like new
ass walls and skylight

ts, novelties, notions, fix.
entory 6-10pm, 555-5161

CASH REGISTER
In carton. Sacrific

ic New
55-1480

CERAMIC GREENWARE
819 Creek Rd.
555-3090

COMPUTER, IBM port, w/dual
360K dr, built in monitor 640K ram
$799; IBM-PC w/(1) 360K floppy (1)
ten meg hard drive, 256K ram &
IBM mono monitor $850. 555-4810

CUTTING TABLES (2) 4x15-ft; 7
misc. tables 8x132 ft, suitable for any
use.
BEST OFFER 555-898

SLIGHTLY USED DIAMOND.
Call 555-3857, ask for Darla.

DISHWASHER Caloric, excel

DRAFTING Tables lg quantity &
variety. 25% of new. 555-1315

DRY CLEANER-TAILOR, Drop
Store. All equip for sale. Retiring
Make offer Call 555-1170

DRY Cleaning Machines, 2 Speed
Queen Coin-Op. Very gd cond. Very
Reas. Call 9-5 Mon-Fri 555-6312

FILES. 2,3,4 Drawer $15 up. Black
or tan, A-1 cond 555-7282

FILES $25 Up. Desks, chairs, Vi-
sa/MC 224 N. 13th St 555-6552

FILES, Desks, Chairs & Systems
Furniture. Must see. 555-1315

FORMICA/WILSONART 50¢ & 80¢
ft. Huge stock 151 N. 3rd 555-3424

GOLF CLUBS Taylor-Medes 3-9. &
PW. 1-3-5 metal woods, bag, head
covers. Used 3x paid $300 want $195
cash only! 555-6879

GOLF-Drivers $30, balls $4 dz, variety. Used, exc. 555-3800

HAMILTON Arch. drafting table, 2
way adj, outlets. Ask $900. 555-9415

HELICOPTER-Radio Controlled
w/gas engine. $350. 555-9358

HENNY PENNY, FRYERS (4),
Garland stoves (4) $150 each. Mis-
cellaneous other restaurant equipment. Call 555-3069

HOSPITAL BED - Elec., w/side
rails, like new orig., $1800
ASK $400 555-1210

LAWNMOWERS, gas $59, elect $65,
hand $22. 555-5123

LAWNMOWER - Gilson Riding 38"
cut brand new, never used, $1199
555-5200 day, 555-0210 eve. Andy

LAWN MOWERS.
gang,

INQUIRER/DAILY NEWS
CLASSIFIED

When you want something taken off your hands, just take two: Two lines, two papers, one week, only $15. The Philadelphia Inquirer and Daily News Classified. We'll get your ad into more people's hands than any single newspaper. Call 563-5000.

2 lines, 2 papers, one week, only $15.

Private Parties Only. Some Classifications Excluded.

5 SILVER

"Mom, I think Fred's pregnant again."

CRAFT '78 25' Slps 4, ed for fishing. Good cond. $10,500. 555-5815 days.

CRAFT '68 30 ft, Cavalier, Twin 185 HP, CB, DF, sleeps gd cond. $7500 555-0936 aft 4

-CRAFT Scorpian 210 easy load, gd trlr. Excel 555-0564

S CRAFT Connie '63, 34' Condition. Call 555-6030

LER Outboard 100HP. Exc. $1000. Call 555-4746

ETTE 20' 350 Chevy $11,000 KMATE 13' 65hp Merc. 555-0025

'82, 16' 60hp Johnson, trail-ly extras. $5000. 555-8926

'84 19 ft CUDDY 140 Merc

EBOAT 35', 1973. 35' long cruz, sleeps 8. Exc cond. for the season. 555-2565

Y 40' 80 3208T Cats, tower, new Int'r fully eqpd. EXCEL $135,000 555-1039

BOAT/RALLY SPORT mod- metal-flake with white int. ds, motor w/Berkley jet drive et/A/Vator. With trailer, ex. ski boat w/excess. Make of- 5-3769

'67, 24', 10½ ft beam, re- '78 Chevy eng, fully equip. ing. $2000 555-2382

17', '75 engine. 70hp Evin., attery, D/F & CB. '85 trailer. 555-1583

228 walk-a-round cutty 984 excel cond aux. eng. & all nacs w/Sea Isle City slip for Call 555-1000, ext 231 or n, 555-4377

23' Inboard. Large B top. over boards, fish box. O/R. loaded. $15,000 82 or 555-1020

'78 21' 1982 200hp Merc. trlr, loran, VHF, recorder. w Boat in! Must Sell! $10,500 555-1166 or 555-0539

TEE 18 ft. center console, 85 ercury, galvanized trlr, chart CB. $5250. Call 555-3688

THON 22' '84, 140hp I/O, pkg, ready to go, priced to 5-6288 eves.

TWAIN 1976 17' Deep V ohnson 135 hp O/B mtr. 1985 ader trlr. Runs great. Incl ing nec to pass Coast Guard lus ski equip & plenty other ss. $3895. 555-8292

NIEL '76 18' 85hp merc low hrs. of use. Sealion trlr ct. winch & other extras. Call 555-3005 aft 6pm.

RCRAFT 16½' Fiberglass Skis & all access. Johnson quiet 45HP (needs work) Call 555-2382

OARD- 40 HP Johnson, Gd 16' Boat Trailer. 555-6430

MAKER '76 26' Sport Fish- slps 4, UHF, VHF, outrig- ow hours. 225 Chrysler. Mint 555-1231, 9-5

MAKER '73-74 DC 36' all f/g 6.5 gen f/b $35k priv. owner

extras. $8000. Call 555-2514

POST '79 Spt Fish. 671 Diesels. Fresh water boat. $165k. 555-2664 wkdays, wkends 555-5382

REGAL 28' 277XL '85, twin 190 Mercs, 100 hrs, fully eqpd, in water. Ready to Go! Like new! Call: 215-555-0443 or 555-5510

REGAL '86, 195 Seabring Cuddy. 205 Hp, V6, Full top, used 7 times. Load Rite trlr w/brakes. Must sell. $13,500, B/O. 555-0533 anytime

REINELL '73 19ft 6in bow rider, tri hull, 270 Volvo eng. IO galvanized tandem trlr, good cond. $2875 or BO. Must sell. Call 555-8677

RENKEN '86, 20'Bowrider, 140hp, OMC I/O, w/galv trailer. Full canvas run'g cover, cass dk w/Jensen

Birds

YELLOW Nape Amazon, talks, sings, whistles, 2 yrs old, 1 bird too many. 555-5208 anytime

Cats

HIMALAYAN, CFA

HIMALAYAN Kittens - CFA Family raised. Little "Teddy Bears" Call aft 6pm: 555-3954

HIMALAYAN KITTENS, CFA
The perfect Mother's Day gift. F. Seal pt. 10 wks, shots. 555-2836

HIMALAYAN KITTEN
also adlt M CFA 555-6622

HIMALAYAN Kittens - CFA reg. Blue points. Please call 555-6369

Himalayan Kits M., sealpoint, shots, CFA, $250. 555-7429

HIMALAYAN PERSIAN KITS for Mothers Day. CFA 555-6346

KITTENS - Siamese & Linx, M/F, Purebred. No papers. $80. 555-5461

MAINE COON kittens, CFA & CFF reg. Lg bone lg hair. 555-9709

PERSIAN, blue male, 9 mo. no papers, declawed, $100. 555-2922

PERSIAN HIMALAYAN Kittens Male Seal Point. Beautiful. 555-5570 555-0684

SIAMESE. Female, 1 yr. old $85. 555-2345

SIAMESE KITTENS CFA Excellent lineage. 555-5092 aft 6pm

SIAMESE KITTENS
8 wks old $85. 555-4950

SIAMESE Kittens - Sealpoint, 9 wks old. $125, w/Papers. 555-0563

SIAMESE kittens, seal pt, 8 wks, pure bred. $75 555-5382

SIAMESE Kittens, 8 wks. first shots, adorable, 555-3269

SIAMESE kittens, 8 wks., M&F, seal pt. w/shots. $80-100. 555-3184

Pets

Dogs

AIRDALE. AKC pups, ch bldlines. Call early AM or aft 5 PM. 555-1430

AIREDALE TERRIERS
Male 6 mos. old. Excellent lines, excel temperment. Will be kept if not sold. Please call 555-9605

AKITA outstanding Male pup, champion parents. 555-0107

AKITA Pups, 1M & 5F. AKC

BOUVIER DesFLANDRES AKC puppies $300. 555-3322

BOXER PUPS - born 3/23, AKC, parents on prem, fawn w/blk mask & fawn & wht. 555-5112 anytime

BRITTANY PUPS. AKC, W&L, bred for hunting. 555-5266

BRITTANY SPANIEL PUPS, AKC, shots, exc hunting stock, ideal family pet. 555-2659

BRITTANY SPANIELS, AKC, 7 wks old, good hunting stock. Shots & wormed. $110. Call 555-3420

CAIRN TERRIER - 2 years old. Excellent watch dog. 555-1564

CHIHUAHUA PUPS - AKC reg. Males. Long coat. Deposit OK.

CHINESE SHAR-PEI, 3M-2F, red-fawn, superb champ sired litter.

CHINESE Shar Pei pup. Blk. horse coat female. Res. 555-0471

COLLIE PUPS AKC Regis'd. wormed, markings

DALMATION PUPS-3 males left. Call 555-5035, or eve aft 5, 555-0493

DOBERMAN-M pup, big boned, champ. AKC papers. 555-3984

DOBERMAN PUPS - 5 wks old. AKC regis'd. Father champion 555-8775

DOBERMANS & ROTTWEILLERS several outstanding show quality litters available. Champions at stud. 555-3600

DRAHTHAARS Pups - For hunters only. $300-$400. 555-1531

ENGLISH SETTERS for the serious hunter. Finest gun dog blood line. Brainy, birdy & beaut. 555-7142

ENGLISH SPRINGER Spaniels
Pups. AKC, shots, dewclaws, liver & wht, blk & wht, 8 wks 555-7075

GENUINE GERMAN shep pups $150. 555-4783

GERMAN SHEP. Pups, AKC, ready to go, extr Lge bone. $200 14 gen ped 555-1823

GERMAN Shepherd puppies M&F, AKC reg. $150. 555-1288

GERMAN Shep AKC, Fem, 3 mos. Blk tan $150 555-7902

GERMAN Shorthair Pointers-(2) Fully trained for hunting in Missouri. Excellent registered bloodlines. Relocating must sell. BO 555-6777

GERMAN short haired pointer pups, 7 wks. Champion lines. Field & show. Call 555-7981 after 7 PM.

GERM Shep Pups, AKC, females. Exc lrg boned. Champ sired. $350 555-0388

Germ Sheps-wht 6 wks, AKC, m&f, parents premises. $250. 555-0246

GOLDEN RETRIEVER PUPS-AKC. Champ lione. Parents X-rayed & on premises. Male $250. Female $275. Ready w/shots. May 16. 555-3000, eve. 555-3205

GOLDEN RETRIEVER PUPS
AKC papers. Gold-Rush Line 555-0722 after 4pm

GOLDEN RETRIEVERS-Males 7 wks. AKC reg'd. Champion lines, raised w/TLC. $250. 555-8174

GOLDEN RETRIEVER - 2 yrs., male. $100. AKC. 555-0475 after 5

GOLDEN RETRIEVER PUPS
ACK, males, shots, 555-7846

GOLDEN Retriever [illegible] wormed

LAB BLACK AKC $150
Call aft 3:30 pm, 555-0949

LAB PUPS - Yellow/Creme, English Champ lines. $359. 555-0273

LAB RETRIEVER PUPS - Champ. lines. Hips & Eyes clear. Yellow & blk. Call Eves Wknds. 555-5569

LAB RETRIEVERS - Top quality AKC Black pups, M & F, ready 5/20/87 555-7378

LABS. Blk & yel. AKC, Champ. sired. Good looking, working stock, shots & wormed. Call 555-4179

LABS. Yellow, AKC, 5 M., 1 F., Ready to sell May 15. Asking $200 555-6911

LHASA APSO 11 wks old fem., ACK reg. 1st shots & wormed. 555-0161 days, 555-9721 eves

LHASA APSO Pups, 8 wks old, M only. Shots wormed. $135

shots. Ask $100. 555-5676

ST. BERNARD PUPPIES - AKC

VIZSLA PUPS - AKC
Exc. Bloodlns. 555-9017 aft 5.

WEIMARANER pups, AKC reg. Good pets & hunters. Ready to go Call 555-3162

WOLF, Hybrid pups, M&F, reg. $275 to $375. 555-5238

Fish

FISH TANK - 26 gal octagon w/stand Wood grain finish 555-7918

Other Pets

MONKEY - 9mth old male, domestically bred Capuchin. Vet checked & shots. Starter cage included. $2200 Firm. Serious inquiries only. Leave name & number 555-2045

Pets For Adoption

FREE 10 mo old Golden Lab needs warm fun loving home. Call 555-6854 before 12 noon

GERMAN SHEPHERD 5 yrs old with papers. FREE TO GOOD HOME. Call 555-3611

GERMAN SHEPHERD PUP. Free to good home. Call 555-[illegible]

KITTENS [illegible] wks old. Black 555-6472

FREE KITTENS.
Call 555-2102 anytime!

KITTENS - Male. Free [illegible]

LAB MIX, 2 yers, housebroken, good w/kids. Free to good home Call 555-1028 aft 5PM

RETRIEVER/MIX - Black Female, 1 yr old, hsebrkn, spayed, all shots, playful dogs who needs outdoor space to run, fenced yd a must 555-2638, 555-5222

SIAMESE CATS two Blue Point Beautiful 16 mos old, free to gd home, fiance allergic 555-1125, eves

Pet Services & Supplies

DACHSHUND - Miniature, long-haired Male, 21 mos. AKC, wants to breed w/same. 555-8439

MINIATURE Schnauzer at stud. Grandson of national ch jester 555-9722

WANTED-Stud Service for Fem Chiquaqua in N.E. Phila. Pref. male to be brown, wht or choc. 555-6060

Pets Wanted

WANTED German shepherd dog. Gd home w/lrg fnc'd yd.

ARABIAN /Crabbet Rea

ARABIAN SADDLE w/G match. $450; mal. $45; Both

BOOTS Cust $225

BREEDINGS Egyptian Ara payments ok

DAPPLE G Gentle, will $1500, B/O 55

GELDING, C Eng & West. $

HALF ARAB will sell open time payments

HORSE, 11 y ners horse $45

JOG CART J Offer.

MARE 4yr. Q quiet. $2000

MUST SELL yrs jumps 3' best ofr, also '8

PAINT, Arab reg'd & qu

PONY Palim sire Roadste

QUARTER chestnut, rid- Quarter Hor rides quiet, 2 Trailer, like br 555-0484 or 5

QUARTER 5 yrs, 14.3H, best offer

QUARTERHO bay, 15.2, 5 horse mare

SHOW ARAB sell by 6/15. ings. MD line

McQUERRY Trailer, excel paint $1500, 5

PAINT, Arab reg'd & quiet

QUARTER 17h, ch. g, 9 jumping 2ft, horse. $3500

QUARTER h 15.1H, 7 yrs. Call before 10

SHOW ARAB sell by 6/15. ings. 555-065

T.B. GELDIN confirmation &

THOR - (2) 16. ea. 555-0388

WELSH ARA old. Rides E manners. Goo aft 4pm. 555-

Persona

A. Baker, B.

AIR. CONC 555-7572

AIRLINE A BUYI

AIR LINE T Palm Beach Less than 1/2

DATI SINGLE WI

BRYAN AD TICKETS COSTA

INQUIRER/DAILY NEWS
CLASSIFIED

When you want to find a good home, you'll find it faster when you take two: Two lines, two papers, one week, only $15. The Philadelphia Inquirer and Daily News Classified. We reach more good homes than any single newspaper. Call 563-5000.

2 lines, 2 papers, one week, only $15.

Private Parties Only. Some Classifications Excluded.

"Look, either that motorcycle goes... or I do!"

betw. 6-9pm 555-8458

Ave 4200 blk, bright studio, rm, ei kit $275 includs utils. ndent on premises 555-0184

1st. 2 rm effic & bth, view $245+utils+dep. 555-1124

2ND-Spac Studio, 1,2 BR, m $350. 555-4606

h, renov effcys, $270 mo. elev bldg. 555-9190

TON VILLAGE 1 brm firs incls h.w. & elec $425 555-1128 9-5pm

ON VILLAGE. 2 - 3 stu- share a spacious 1BR in a Historic Victorian. Ldry- $500. 555-0204 lev msg.

S PL. 22XX. 2 BR, W/D, el & gas. 6/1. 555-7182

& 2nd - 1 & 2BR. Lrg Sun- W/D. On Septa. 5min to nding & I95. $424/mo incl 55-7677

VIC. 21ST & PINE
1 br. $415+ util. Avail rent btw. 5/16 & 5/31. 0116 or 555-5975

& 21ST

21st Effc

& 23rd Effcys, lg closets Fr $325+. 555-7488

& 23rd. Newly renov G/D, W/D in bldg. $445 555-6800

at 23rd. Studio, Hrdwd ath. A/C. $325 555-4200

SHINGTON SQ WEST
R, w/w crpt, G/D, A/C, laundry on premises. No 0 + elec. Day 555-4285, ends 555-4545

West. Very small Historic lg kit, G/D, 3 sml brs, 2 A/C, garden, parkg avail ys 555-8888 eve 555-8813

st. 2BR 2 bth trinity in pvt W/D, C/A, G/H. $675+ 555-4200

2 br quiet tree-lined st d/w, c/a. $650+ 555-0866

Rent—ter City Furnished

ne. Furn Studio or 1BR apt ht & hot wtr incld Call 555-1335

Rent—West Phila.

ne 3rd fl furn'd Effic 2 rms 5+util. 1mo sec. 555-1457

1st St-Newly decor'd effcy bath $225/mo 555-7467

50TH - Spacious sunny 3 350 + util. 555-5566

R & 47th-2BR, lrg fp. $450 + utils. 1BR, huge fp, new. $400 + utils. 00. 555-4775

7th-2 BR, sep. util's. $350. 555-2300

Ave-Small 1 bedrm, kit & e furn. incl. 555-1886

T - 48th. Spacious wshr/dry facil. HBO gd Secur. Lv msg 555-0204

1 4700 blk. 2 rms. kitchen- children. Secure. 555-9272

Apts. Sr citizens pref. sec wed. $300-$375. 555-3535 ts. wkdays 9-5, Sat. 9-12

Rent—versity City

furn. apt on Best Block, w/w crpt. oversize equip. kit, sunny DR, frpl BQ, patio, 5 min. walk to bus to C.C. stops at cor. to $750. Avail June. Ideal e. Call 555-4266

RACE - 1 BR	$465
OSAGE - Eff	$285
PINE - 3 BR	$650
SPRINGFIELD - 1 BR	$395

555-5457

Walnut, 1 br, w/w cpt, ex + elect. 555-8827

Chestnut nr D

4045 BALTIMORE AVE
Bright spac studio apt w/separate dressing area, tile bth, cptg. Avail immed. $295+ utils 555-2697

40th & Baltimore, 4 BR, 2 b, quiet street. Possible indoor prkg. $925 inclds ht. Avail 6-1. 555-4137

40th & Walnut Vic. Attn: Students, great loc, renov bldgs, ht inc Eff. 1 & 2 br start'g $265. Eves 555-1999

40TH-45TH, Chestnut to Baltimore

NOW RENTING FOR SEPT '87
Ideal locations for students. Effcy. 1 to 4 BR apts. firs, tile bth, many porches. Rentals as low as effcys, $160 per person in bdrm apts. Call now for best selection! 555-2986, 10-6

42ND &

5br house $395/mo

43rd & Avail 6-1

TH & WALNUT

46TH CHESTER 2nd flr, 2br, hrdwd $450+, ref. req. 555-6311 aft. 7pm

48TH & Pine - Beaut 6/1 fr $450 + utils.

48th St. 800 blk S. heat incl'd

BALT. Ave Area - 4700 Hazel Ave Clean, bright effic. Hrdwd flrs. $250+ elec. & gas. Call 555-2150

BALTIMORE - 4815. 1 bdr apts. $220 & $250/mo. Call 555-5690 aft 4pm

BALTIMORE Ave vic newly renov. 1-2 BR apt $275 up. 555-5600

CEDAR Pk-Lg 1 BR. 1st flr. Fenced rear yd, full bsmt. $325+. 555-0899

CHESTER AVENUE
Luxurious renovation of sunny 1BR apts. Central heat, s/c, hdwd flrs, intercom system, laundry on premises. All new bath & kitchen including d/w, g/d & European-style cabinets. From $325 + utils. Call anytime 555-7317

CHESTER LYNNE 4619 Chester Renov studios. New kits & bths. lndry facil. Elev bldg. #13 trolley at door. Affordably priced. 555-2500

CHESTNUT 4039. Fine, secure elev bldg. 2 rm avail. Application taken. Ideal for prof & career people. 555-5775

CHESTNUT AT 39TH - Renov hi rise bldg. 1 BRs avail for May, June & July occup. Beginning at $485 inclds all utils, A/C, 24 hr security. 555-3350

CLARK PARK vic. 1BR apt. on 2 flrs. Sunny loc, quiet st. $425 incls utils. 555-5202

CLOSE to U of P, spac lux 2 BR, ultra mod kit & bth, D/W, G/D, hdwd flrs. $550 incl ht. 555-5069

LANCASTER & 35th, Quaker Building. Lge 1 BR w/loft. New appls, micro, d/w, W&D. Rent negotiable. Avail mid June. 555-4156

LARCHWOOD at 45th. Huge renovated convt. 2 bdrm, dshwhr, w/w carpts, wshr/dryer facilties, encl porch. $565+. Lv Msg. 555-0204

LOCUST & 40TH Vic - Spac 2 BR apt + pvt garden. Avail Immd. Asking $650 incl ht & hw. 555-4200 Mon-Fri

MARKET & 40th 1 BR unfurn. For more info, betw. 6-9pm 555-8458

Osage Ave 4200 blk, bright studio, dressing rm, ei kit $275 includs utils. Superintendent on premises 555-0184

PINE & 51st. 2 rm effic & bth, view of park. $245+utils+dep. 555-1124

PINE & 42ND-Spac Studio, 1,2 BR, New. From $350. 555-4606

PINE 45th, renov effcys, $270 mo. utils incl, elev bldg. 555-9190

POWELTON VILLAGE 1 brm apt, hdwd flrs incls h.w.

POWELTON VILLAGE. 2 - 3 students can share a spacious 1BR in a restored Historic Victorian. Ldry- facl. & A/C. $500. 555-0204 lev msg.

REFURBISHED efficiency & 1 BR unit $240-$350 555-2403

SOUTH ST. & 27th

2BR Student Apts
Short walk to Penn - Spme 2 bth. Pvt ent. Tri-level. Park'g avail. All new A/C, D/W, GD, W/W & Cable. Short lease avail. Start at $625.

Call 555-6006

SPRINGFIELD/49th 2 BR.

Spring Gdn at 34th. Effcy $235, 1 BR $295 incldg ht. 555-9416

W. POWELTON-5br hse. New

renov. $420+. 555-8484

Apts. Rent—Wynnefield

$290 incl heat. Cooking gas & electric extra. Immediate occupancy. 555-1636

Apts. Rent— Wynnefield Hgts.

BALWYNNE PARK $450+ 2 BR duplex apt. Avail May 15th. Call today for appt! 555-1272

BALWYNNE PARK
Lovely 2 BR apts. immed occup. 1st & 2nd flrs. From $425 + utils. 555-1636

54th/Wynnefield vic. 3 rm & bth apt in pvt home for 1 mature adult. $375 incl all utils. 555-5368 bet 7-9pm

Apts. Rent—Overbrook

63rd ST STUDIO $275 incl heat, hot water & gas, elec. extra 555-3602

CITY Ave & 63rd-Spac effic & 1 BR Clean, great loc 555-7202, 555-8859

LOVELY Studios & 1 bedrm apts. From $285 + electric. Corner of Sherwood & Lancaster 555-8261 555-1636

Apts. Rent— Southwest Phila.

Chester/51st. 2br-1st fl. W/D, back yd. $300+elec. Heat free 555-6875

KINGSESSING sm 1 rm efficiency $55/wk+. 2 wks secur. gd for sgl pers or woman w/infant 555-0547

PENROSE PK mod. 2 br in duplex $485/mo. + utils. 555-1434

WOODLAND Ave (5715)- 1Bd $230 + util. No credit chk but must be working. Call 555-0791

Apts. Rent—South Phila.

13th & Fed, Lg 1br, mod tile bth, sml yrd conv to CC $375+. 555-5003

SNYDER 16XX blk-Lg. 1 BR, crpt, full kit. $400 mo 555-8802 9am-3pm

Tasker nr 7th. 2nd fl, 3 rms & bth. $295 + utils. Avail now. 555-2980

Apts. Rent—North Phila.

BROAD & ALLEGHENY. Effic & 1 BR apts avail. $260-$360. References reqd. Laundry facil & elevator. Several floorplans to choose from. Call 555-0674

Apartments Wanted

W. or S.W. Ph

Call Mark 555-0100 dy, 555-6236 ev

Prof'l Male seeks affordable apt. in priv. home in Del Co or Mont Co. for Oct. occupancy. 555-7985

BENSALEM Female prof'l to share 2 BR/2Bth Apt. $300/mo + 555-1564 eves & wknds.

Apts. Wanted To Share

BENSALEM
Straight young male Professional has new 4 Bedrm home in a lovely country setting. Convenient location. Only incls utils. Call 555-6595

CITY-Male 50 share 2 female. low rent for student or young person just starting out. Call eves. only 555-1898

Executive seeks to share his res. & lifestyle w/white fem in 20's in exchange for general duties 555-2931

FEMALE wanted to share spac. 3 br twnhs. 9th & Lombard sts. W/D, lrg bkyrd. $216 Mo. Call 555-0788

GRAD Student looking for roommate Art Mus area 2 br 2 bth. rent negotiable. 555-1808

HOUSE to Share for female prof'l. Non-smoker. 555-0253

ITALIAN MARKET 3 Story house. Natural wd. flrs. W&D. your own pvt fl. w/2 adjoining rms. Share rest of house. View of city skyline. Women only. $275/mo 555-9656

K. OF P. Prof'l female mid 30's seeks same to share lrg. 2BR apt. Day 555-4500

Man seeks responsible female to share a 2 br apt. in NE Phila. $325 inclds all util. Close to shop. & trans. 555-8668 days. 555-0077 aft. 3pm.

N.E. Phila.-Older man seeking

ROOMMATE WANTED.
Call 555-1630

ROOMMATE WANTED

3BR 2½ bth twnhse. Art Museum area. Excel. neigh. w/d, beautiful & modern house. Live w/2 young prof'ls. $260/mo + utils. call aft 6pm or wknds 555-5742

Roommate Wanted Now!
N.E. Male/Female to share 3 Bedrm house. furn. $200 mo. + utils. ref. req. 555-6642

ROOMMATE wanted for So. Phila. house, working person. $150/mo + ½ utils. 555-9788

YOUNG PROF'L FEM. seeks young prof'l to share CC Apt. $305 incl all. exc location. 555-0009

R.E. Sale—Center City

NORT. LIB., 1039 N. 3rd, shell - 2 lots, zoned 2 family. + CO. 555-

PENNSPORT QUALITY DUPLEX Perfect 1 BR each. Ultra kitch. W/W carpet, new bath, separate utils, perfect location. $95,000 555-4400

R.E. Sale—West Phila.

55TH NR MEDIA 4 BR $20,000

R.E. Sale—Kensington

B&Leh

R.E. Sale

4949 N. 7th Porch, 3 br bath, mod kit

OLNEY-157 W Nr 2nd St. Cash needed yd, mostly

MT. AIRY-W take back negotiable 55

RUGBY ST. $3900 neede

SYDNEY ST Call Mon-Thu

WEST Mt. A DR. fplc. w vices, exc co

R.E. Sale

ACADEMY-C Townhouse mod kitch. F

ACADI

Blvd & F furn

BLVD VIC-F Little

Bridesburg

BURHOLME

BUSTLETON

BUSTLETON

R.E. Sale

TYSON dupl

R.E. Sale Temple

ANDREWS

R.E. Sale

2 story 4 BR

R.E. Sale

BLVD/FRONT

R.E. Sale

BRYN MAWR

INQUIRER/DAILY NEWS
CLASSIFIED

When you find yourself with a vacancy, you'll fill it faster when you take two: Two lines, two papers, one week, only $15. The Philadelphia Inquirer and Daily News Classified. We reach more people than any single newspaper. Call 563-5000.

2 lines, 2 papers, one week, only $15.

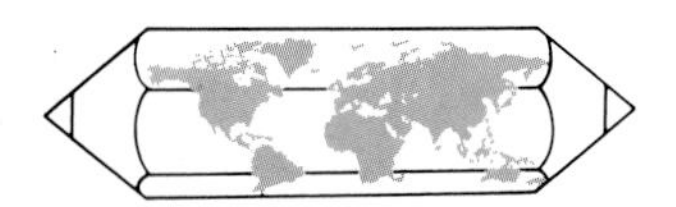

Gold, Silver & Bronze Awards

Consumer Newspaper Over 600 Lines: Campaign

6 BRONZE

ART DIRECTOR
Mike Chandler

WRITER
Wayne Garland

DESIGNER
Mike Chandler

CLIENT
Australian Defense Force Academy

AGENCY
The Ball Partnership/
North Sydney

Field Marshal Erwin Rommel, one of the most respected, formidable, yet honourable soldiers in history. His career started in World War I, where he was awarded the "Pour le Merit" for outstanding bravery.
At the start of World War II he led the 7th Panzer Division during the 1940 Battle for France.
Promoted to Lieutenant General, he commanded all German troops in Libya and from here made his name and reputation as the commander of the brilliant Afrika Korps.

Major General Leslie Morshead, one of the most outstanding Australian Army officers of modern times.
An unashamedly strict disciplinarian, he believed that battles and campaigns were won by leadership and discipline, and above all, by sheer bravery.
It was under his leadership and command that the might of the German Army under Rommel was thwarted in its push across North Africa in the epic siege of Tobruk.

Could you have matched wits with Rommel and his crack Afrika Korps in the epic siege of Tobruk?

Early in 1941, the Allied armies, fleeing ignominiously before the forces of the brilliant German desert commander, Erwin Rommel, suddenly turned on their pursuers at the former Italian fortress of Tobruk.

There they made their stand.

They fought back for nearly eight months, and tied up the Axis army so effectively that Rommel was prevented from taking his attack into Egypt and was denied a most vital base in the Eastern Mediterranean.

What did the Australian commander, Major General Morshead, have that stopped Rommel in his tracks and thwarted his push across North Africa? Why was he so successful?

What moved Churchill to say "... *the whole Empire is watching your steadfast and spirited defence with gratitude and admiration*?"

The Profession of Arms.

Morshead was a *leader of men*.

Right now, The Royal Military College, Duntroon is looking for good men and women to follow in this tradition.

We want them to train as officers.

To become leaders.

We only want the very best this country has to offer.

We want young men and women who thrive on challenge and responsibility.

The ethic we adhere to is demanding.

Not many can meet the challenge.

Those who do, go on to rewarding careers. Duntroon graduates and their achievements line the pages of Australia's military history books.

And after successful military careers, many have gone on to careers as historians, barristers, politicians, engineers, senior public servants and in commerce and industry.

What is Duntroon?

Alongside Sandhurst and West Point, the Royal Military College, Duntroon is recognised as one of the finest officer training establishments in the world.

It is also recognised as one of the most demanding tests of one's mental and physical capabilities.

It has to be if you are going to become a true leader.

Founded in 1911, Duntroon is Australia's only officer training and commissioning establishment for the Regular Army.

Here one takes the first steps in learning the finest and highest order of skills needed to become proficient in *The Profession of Arms*.

It is a rigorous, 18-month course in leadership, management and military skills.

These skills include tactics, field training, weapons handling, administration, military history and strategic studies, instructional techniques and logistics.

It's tough, but it's not all spit and polish.

Duntroon is not a military version of a university.

Life there is tough and disciplined.

But that discipline is sensible.

Your life is not regimented to extremes.

You will have your own room, you can have your own car, and go out for drinks with friends.

You are granted leave most weekends and you're paid from the time you join.

In 18 months we take you from a raw cadet and turn you into a regimental officer.

Along the way you learn to command and manage men and women.

And if you can last the distance, you graduate after a year and a half as a Lieutenant commanding up to 30 soldiers in your own platoon or troop.

Appointed to one of the 14 different Corps, such as Armour, Artillery or Engineers, that form the major part of the Australian Army.

Ready to follow in the footsteps of success enjoyed by many Duntroon graduates.

Could you get into Duntroon?

Of course, not everyone who joins Duntroon becomes a Brigadier or General.

Hopefully, battles like Tobruk are a thing of the past.

However, uncertainties in the world today demand that Australia has men and women who are highly proficient in *The Profession of Arms.*

If you are aged from 18 to under 23 on entry (or a graduate up to 25), have completed Year 12 or equivalent, and are of above-average physical ability, you have the basic requirements to be considered for entering Duntroon.

You may not have previously considered a career as an Army officer.

But life in the Army as a Duntroon graduate can give you, at a very early age, higher level executive and command responsibilities than most people achieve in a lifetime.

You could find yourself as part of a United Nations Peacekeeping Force ensuring peace in a troubled part of the world; or leading a platoon into unknown country for several weeks, with their total welfare your sole responsibility.

Or handling the logistics of moving 500 soldiers and their equipment across an entire continent.

But before that happens, find out what it would have been like matching wits with the Desert Fox himself, Rommel, in these five crucial episodes of the siege of Tobruk.

Could you have matched wits with Rommel? Take this quick test and find out for yourself.

(The answers are to be found at the bottom of the page.)

Question 1.

When Rommel arrived in Africa, the Italian Army had been forced back to Tripoli.

They were demoralised and the only German troops immediately available were the 5th Light Division.

But the crack German 15th Panzer Division was expected soon.

British morale was high but they were overextended.

What would you have done if you were Rommel?

First strengthened the defences around Tripoli and secured this area as a base before planning to attack?

Postponed operations until the crack 15th Panzer Division arrived and then prepared to attack?

Conducted a "reconnaissance in force" operation only, at this stage, to assess the British strength?

Surprised the British and attacked immediately with only the 5th Light Division?

Question 2.

The British position at Mersa Brega was flanked by the sea and a marsh.

Rommel's basic alternatives were a frontal assault or an amphibious operation.

He lacked the naval support for an amphibious operation.

A frontal assault could mean heavy casualties.

Rommel's Chief of Staff recommended that Rommel delay any attack until mid-May, when his Afrika Korps would be at full strength.

Yet an immediate attack just might win through because it would be so unexpected.

It would be a big risk should it fail, and the British counter-attacked.

If you were Rommel what would you do?

Accept the considered and professional advice of the Chief of Staff and delay till mid-May?

Take the calculated gamble and attack immediately hoping that boldness and surprise would win out?

Question 3.

When Rommel moved out from Mersa Brega to Benghazi and Derna, he did something quite inexplicable.

He had three routes to choose from.

The main road, via Balbia towards Benghazi. The north-east route via the oases Msus and Merchili. The eastern inland route through the desert to bypass the Green Mountains.

The first route was the easiest but very exposed to the enemy. The second was longer, yet far safer. And the third, very dangerous but by far the fastest.

What would you have done?

Question 4.

Rommel knew that eliminating the garrison at Tobruk was the key to taking Egypt and securing North Africa.

But his men were exhausted from the incredible rigours of their successful desert campaign.

They had pushed the British back hundreds of miles in a series of brilliant tactical moves.

Conventional military thinking argued that his army needed rest and re-equipment before another major attack.

Similarly, it was argued that Tobruk's defences needed careful reconnaissance before committing his men.

On the other hand, improbable audacity had already won Rommel a string of victories against the odds. Could he pull it off again?

Could his exhausted Afrika Korps be called on for yet another unreasonable effort?

If luck was with him and his exhausted men succeeded, Egypt could soon be his.

What would you have done?

Question 5.

Rommel lost the first battle of El Alamein.

He realised his situation was critical.

The British were being re-equipped at a rapid rate. But because of British air superiority and Rommel's long line of resupply, his situation was deteriorating.

He had three choices:

Wait for the British to attack with overwhelming strength and hope that he would hold them off.

Withdraw now, accepting that North Africa would eventually be lost.

Attack, aware that his forces would probably lose, but in the heat of battle they just might pull off another unexpected victory.

What would you have done?

Enquire now for further details.

If you've read this far and would like to know more about becoming an Army Officer, phone now or complete the coupon details below and mail it to Defence Force Recruiting, or Army Careers Information Centre in your State.

Applications for the January 1988 intake close September 18, 1987.

Maybe you will be one of those who could have matched wits with Rommel.

For more information, post this coupon to an Army Officer Careers Advisor, Freepost 2600A, Box XYZ in your capital city.

Or telephone capital cities: Sydney 219 5550, Melbourne 697 9717, Brisbane 226 2759, Adelaide 212 1455, Perth 325 6222, Canberra 57 2311, Hobart 34 7077.

Other areas: Albury 21 8277, Ballarat 31 1240, Bendigo 43 8008, Bundaberg 73 1152, Geelong 21 1588, Launceston 31 1005, Lismore 21 6111, Newcastle 26 3011, Parramatta 633 4031, Townsville 72 4566, Wagga Wagga 21 1282, Wollongong 28 1855.

TOLL FREE SERVICE — Country Residents Only: N.S.W. 008 422 177, NTH. QLD. 008 015 150. STH. QLD. 008 777 531, VIC. 008 136 377, S.A. (Reverse Charges) 08 212 1455. W.A. 008 199 018.

Name ....
Sex .... Date of Birth ....
Address ....
.... Postcode .... Phone ....
Highest Education Standard ....

All enquiries treated in the strictest confidence.
Authorised by the Department of Defence.

ROYAL MILITARY COLLEGE
DUNTROON
ONE OF THE FINEST OFFICER TRAINING ESTABLISHMENTS IN THE WORLD

The Australian Light Horse. Somewhere they still ride on.

The time was 1917. The place was the burning desert of Sinai. The objective, to take the crucially important village of Beersheba.

The Australian Light Horsemen against the might of the Turkish Army.

In modern warfare terms it seemed madness.

Mounted infantry moving across five kilometres of open ground against a dug-in enemy supported by aircraft, artillery and machine guns. But what the enemy did not know was what they were facing.

The greatest cavalry force of modern times.

The 40,000 Light Horsemen from Down Under.

They fought and suffered to emerge triumphant in a battle that is now part of military folklore.

Under the command of Lieutenant-General Sir Harry Chauvel, the Desert Mounted Corps rode into history.

What did Chauvel and the men he led have that proved so invincible that crucial day at Beersheba?

"Defeat be damned!"

Chauvel was a leader of men.

Right now The Royal Military College, Duntroon, is looking for good men and women to follow in this tradition.

We want them to train as officers. To become leaders.

We only want the very best this country has to offer.

We want young men and women who thrive on challenge and responsibility.

The ethic we adhere to is demanding. Not many can meet the challenge. Those who do, go on to rewarding careers.

Duntroon graduates and their achievements line the pages of Australia's military history books.

And after successful military careers, many have gone on to careers as historians, barristers, politicians, engineers, senior public servants and in commerce and industry.

What is Duntroon?

Alongside Sandhurst and West Point, Duntroon is recognised as one of the finest training establishments for army officers in the world.

It is also recognised as one of the most demanding tests of one's mental and physical abilities.

It has to be if you are going to become a true leader.

Founded in 1911, Duntroon is Australia's only training and commissioning establishment for the Regular Army.

Here one takes the first steps in learning the finest and highest order of skills in becoming proficient and highly skilled in *The Profession of Arms.*

It is a rigorous, 18-month course in leadership, management and military skills.

These skills include tactics, field training, weapons handling, administration, military history and strategic studies, instructional techniques and logistics.

Lieutenant-General Sir Harry Chauvel, the brilliant leader of the famed 40,000 Horsemen. Under his command they rode to victory and into history at Gaza, Damascus and Beersheba. He was a true "commander from the front."

It's tough, but it's not all spit and polish.

Duntroon is not a university, nor a military version of one.

Life there is tough and disciplined. But that discipline is sensible. Your life is not regimented to extremes.

You will have your own room, you can have your own car, go out for drinks with friends and go on leave at night. You are granted leave most weekends and you're paid from the time you join.

In 18 months we take you from a raw cadet and turn you into a regimental officer.

Along the way you learn to command and manage men and women.

And if you can last the distance, you graduate after a year-and-a-half on a salary in the vicinity of $26,000 p.a., as a Lieutenant commanding up to 30 soldiers in your own platoon or troop in one of the 14 different Corps such as Infantry, Armour, Artillery, or Engineers that comprise the major part of the Australian Army.

Ready to follow in the footsteps of success enjoyed by many Duntroon graduates.

Could you get into Duntroon?

Of course, not everyone who joins Duntroon becomes a Brigadier or General.

Or is plunged into situations like Beersheba.

However, strategic uncertainties in the world today demand that Australia has men and women who are highly proficient in *The Profession of Arms.* If you are aged between 18 to under 23 on entry (or are a graduate up to age 25), have completed Year 12 or equivalent, and are of above average physical ability, you have the basic requirements to be considered for entering Duntroon.

You may not have previously considered a career as an Army officer. But life in the Army as a Duntroon graduate can give you, at a very early age, higher level executive and command responsibilities than most people achieve in a lifetime.

You could find yourself as part of a United Nations Peacekeeping Force ensuring peace in a troubled part of the world or leading a platoon into unknown country for several weeks with their total welfare your sole responsibility.

Or handling the logistics of moving 500 soldiers and their equipment across an entire continent.

But before that happens, find out what it would have been like that fateful day in 1917 in the burning desert of the Sinai.

Could you have led The Light Horse?

In August 1917, the gifted Australian Light Horse Commander, Harry Chauvel, was promoted to Lieutenant-General to command what was now known as the Desert Mounted Corps – one of the largest bodies of cavalry ever assembled in war.

The British Prime Minister instructed Allenby to capture Jerusalem by Christmas.

But the Gaza-Beersheba line was now formidably defended.

Von Kressenstein, the German Commander in charge of the 8th Turkish Army, which was thought to consist of "*46,000 rifles, 2,800 sabres and 200 guns.*"

The only gap in the Turkish line lay between Qawuka and Beersheba – a distance of about 13 kilometres.

At Beersheba, although the frontal defences were well developed, those to the east were not so formidable.

But the harsh waterless desert east of the town was a dreadful obstacle to man and beast alike.

Question 1.

(Answers can be found at the bottom of the page.)

If you had been Allenby, what plan of attack would you have chosen?

Another frontal assault on Gaza?

A thrust through the Qawuka-Beersheba gap to isolate Beersheba and cut off Gaza from the rear?

An attack on Beersheba with a feint attack on Gaza?

Question 2.

On October 10, 1917 a Turkish patrol spotted a lone enemy horseman in no man's land about halfway between Gaza and Beersheba.

They gave chase.

When the enemy horseman stopped and fired at them from a range of about 600 metres they returned fire and tried to gallop him down.

He was then seen to remount hurriedly, but seemed to have been hit. Nevertheless he escaped.

The patrol found a bloodstained rifle, binoculars, a water bottle and haversack.

Inside the haversack the Turks found: a packed lunch, 20 pounds in notes, and a much folded and creased letter from the enemy officer's wife, describing in very emotional words their newly born son.

The Turks also found the following items.

A copy of a signal to the Desert Mounted Corps advising that an officer from headquarters would be passing through their area.

Documents showing there would be a feint attack on Beersheba to cover a third attack on Gaza.

A letter from a fellow officer criticising this plan for a third attack on Gaza and arguing that a full scale attack on Beersheba would have been better.

If you had been Von Kressenstein, would you have:

Dismissed these documents as a planted fake?

Treated them as an intelligence coup because of how they were obtained and such persuasive details as the money and the letter from the officer's wife?

Question 3.

Beersheba, meaning "*Well of the Oath*" was a small frontier town on the edge of the desert, dating back to biblical times. Its plentiful water wells and railway station made it strategically important.

It was defended by a garrison of about 5,000 Turks with 28 field guns. There were two lancer regiments and five infantry regiments, one of which was a regiment of crack storm troops.

The garrison commander was Lieutenant Colonel Ismet Dey, a highly competent and experienced officer. Sceptical of the "haversack intelligence", he improved his defences on all flanks.

The central problem to attacking the town was water.

Water was so limited in the flanking desert that Allenby's predecessors had considered an attack from that direction was impossible.

But Allenby, fresh from the horrors of the Western Front, wanted to avoid relying solely on another meat-grinder frontal assault.

He would have liked to hook Harry Chauvel's Light Horsemen round through the desert to attack from the east and cut off the Turkish withdrawal. But was this just a pipe dream?

Chauvel calculated there was just enough water in the desert wells for an initial approach march by two of his divisions. But they would then have to face a gruelling 43 kilometre last ride without water to attack Beersheba.

If the attack failed, or was too slow, and the Turks had time to destroy the wells, thousands of horses might die of thirst.

If you were Allenby, what would you have done?

Reluctantly decided the risk of losing two divisions of cavalry from thirst wasn't worth it?

Trusted Chauvel and his Australian Light Horsemen to manage somehow?

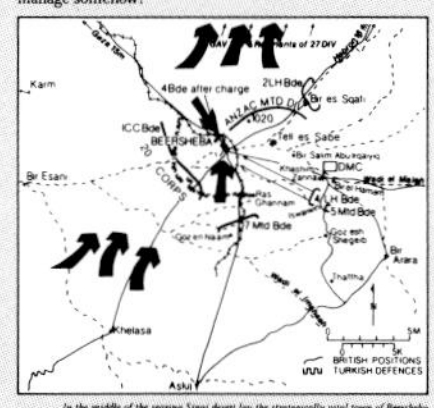

In the middle of the searing Sinai desert lay the strategically vital town of Beersheba defended by "46,000 rifles, 2,800 sabres and 200 guns." But, they didn't know they faced The 40,000 Horsemen from Down Under.

Question 4.

Allenby decided to send two divisions of Chauvel's Desert Mounted Corps through the desert to attack from the east – the Anzac Mounted Division and the Australian Mounted Division.

They began advancing late on October 28, and arrived in position to attack early in the morning of October 31.

Some horses had to ride as far as 56 kilometres on the last night without water.

The corps of infantry commanded by the English general, Chetwode, was to attack Beersheba from the southwest, while Chauvel's two divisions of Light Horse attacked from the southeast.

Chauvel sited his headquarters seven kilometres from Beersheba on a hill which gave him a panoramic view of the battle.

Chauvel's men had to overcome two key strong points about seven kilometres east of Beersheba before the town itself could be captured.

These were Telle es Sabe and Bir es Sqati, the linch-pins in a crescent of outer Turkish defensive works.

It was tough, slow going, requiring final dismounted assaults. These were not completed by the Anzac Division till after 3.00 pm. By then most horses had not had water for 32 hours. Some had been without for 48 hours.

At this rate of advance Chauvel's men would not be able to take the Beersheba wells before nightfall. The nearest alternative water was 12 hours away. The Light Horse could soon be defeated by thirst.

Chauvel called up the senior officers of his reserve, the Australian Mounted Division, and explained the situation.

Brigadier Grant of the 4th Brigade, a swashbuckling, impulsive officer, said he thought he could capture the town with a cavalry attack.

Brigadier Fitzgerald, commanding the British 5th Yeomanry, countered that his men would be better suited for the job because they had swords.

However, they were a mile further back than Grant's brigade.

If you had been Chauvel, which brigade would you have chosen?

The closer 4th Brigade of Australians, minus swords?

The further away Yeomanry with their swords?

Question 5.

At 4.30 pm only 20 minutes before sunset the 4th Light Horse Brigade moved off, initially at a walk.

The 4th Regiment was on the right. The 12th Regiment was on the left. The 11th Regiment was in Reserve.

With about 800 horsemen in charge formation, the pace quickened to a trot.

The Light Horsemen were heading straight for Beersheba into the setting sun. Grasping their bayonets like swords, they quickened the pace again.

It seemed madness in modern warfare – mounted infantry moving across five kilometres of open ground against a dug-in enemy supported by aircraft, artillery and machine guns.

It was three kilometres to the first Turkish trenches. An eye witness said, "The enemy trenches were outlined in fire by the flashes of their rifles … beyond, blazed the bigger, deeper flashes of their field guns …"

The Turks identified the horsemen as mounted infantry and expected them to dismount for the final assault.

Three batteries of Turkish artillery opened fire and caused extensive casualties.

If you had been leading the Light Horsemen at this point, what would you have done?

Dismounted according to customary mounted infantry tactics and closed in for the kill on foot?

Galloped on, hoping speed and shock effect would carry the day?

Enquire now for further details.

If you've read this far and would like to know more about becoming an Army Officer, phone now or complete the coupon details below and mail it to Defence Force Recruiting, or Army Careers Information Centre in your State.

Applications for the January 1988 intake close September 18, 1987. Maybe you will be one of those who could have matched wits with Rommel.

For more information, post this coupon to an Army Officer Careers Advisor, Freepost 2600A, Box XYZ in your capital city.

Or telephone capital cities: Sydney 219 5550, Melbourne 697 9717, Brisbane 226 2759, Adelaide 212 1455, Perth 325 6222, Canberra 57 2311, Hobart 34 7077.

Other areas: Albury 21 8277, Ballarat 31 1240, Bendigo 43 8008, Bundaberg 73 1152, Geelong 21 1588, Launceston 31 1005, Lismore 21 6111, Newcastle 26 3011, Parramatta 633 4031, Townsville 72 4566, Wagga Wagga 21 1282, Wollongong 28 1855.

TOLL FREE SERVICE – Country Residents Only: N.S.W. 008 422 177, NTH. QLD. 008 015 150. STH. QLD. 008 777 531, VIC. 008 136 377, S.A. (Reverse Charges) 08 212 1455. W.A. 008 199 018.

Name

Sex Date of Birth

Address

Postcode Phone

Highest Education Standard

All enquiries treated in strictest confidence. Authorised by the Department of Defence.

How many of us could get all these "Heat of the Battle" decisions exactly right?

(Smith & Townsend did.)

In Harry Smith's own words "*... everything went mad.*"

His 100-man company, deployed by the battalion commander Colin Townsend, was ambushed by an entire Viet Cong regiment of 2,500 soldiers.

When the battle was over however, history had been made.

Eighteen Australian soldiers had died displaying a performance of duty of the highest order.

Not only had annihilation been averted, but the Viet Cong had been defeated at their own game, jungle warfare.

How did Smith and Townsend and the men they led do it?

What thoughts ran through their minds that fateful day?

And what enabled them to prevail against the odds?

The Profession of Arms.

Smith and Townsend were *leaders of men.*

Right now, the Royal Military College, Duntroon, is looking for good men and women to follow in this tradition.

We want them to train as officers.

To become leaders.

We only want the very best this country has to offer.

We want young men and women who thrive on challenge and responsibility.

The ethic we adhere to is demanding.

Not many can meet the challenge.

Those who do, go on to rewarding careers.

Duntroon graduates and their achievements line the pages of Australia's military history books.

And after successful military careers, many have gone on to careers as historians, barristers, politicians, engineers, senior public servants and in commerce and industry.

What is Duntroon?

Alongside Sandhurst and West Point, Duntroon is recognised as one of the finest training establishments for army officers in the world.

It is also recognised as one of the most demanding tests of one's mental and physical abilities. *It has to be* if you are going to become a true leader.

Founded in 1911, Duntroon is Australia's only training and commissioning establishment for the Regular Army.

Here one takes the first steps in learning the finest and highest order of skills in becoming proficient in *The Profession of Arms.*

It is a rigorous, 18-month course in leadership, management and military skills.

These skills include tactics, field training, weapons handling, administration, military history and strategic studies, instructional techniques and logistics.

It's tough, but it's not all spit and polish.

Duntroon is not a university, nor a military version of one.

Life there is tough and disciplined.

But that discipline is sensible.

Your life is not regimented to extremes.

You will have your own room, you can have your own car, go out for drinks with friends and go on leave at night.

You are granted leave most weekends and you're paid from the time you join.

In 18 months we take you from a raw cadet and turn you into a regimental officer.

Along the way you learn to command and manage men and women.

And if you can last the distance, you graduate after a year and a half on a salary in the vicinity of $26,000 p.a. as a Lieutenant commanding up to 30 soldiers in your own platoon or troop in one of the 14 different Corps, such as Infantry, Armour, Artillery, or Engineers that comprise the major part of the Australian Army.

Ready to follow in the footsteps of success enjoyed by many Duntroon graduates.

Could you get into Duntroon?

Of course, not everyone who joins Duntroon becomes a Brigadier or General.

Or is plunged into situations like Long Tan.

However, strategic uncertainties in the world today demand that Australia has men and women who are highly proficient in *The Profession of Arms.*

If you are aged between 18 and 23 on entry (or are a graduate up to age 25), have completed Year 12 or equivalent, and are of above-average physical ability, you have the basic requirements to be considered for entering Duntroon.

You may not have previously considered a career as an Army officer.

But life in the Army as a Duntroon graduate can give you, at a very early age, higher level executive and command responsibilities than most people achieve in a lifetime.

You could find yourself as part of a United Nations Peacekeeping Force ensuring peace in a troubled part of the world, or leading a platoon into unknown country for several weeks, with their total welfare your sole responsibility. Or handling the logistics of moving 500 soldiers and their equipment across an entire continent.

But before that happens, find out what it would have been like that fateful day in 1966 being suddenly ambushed by an overwhelming force of the Viet Cong.

Could you have made the correct battlefield decisions that fateful day in August 1966, in the middle of the jungle, under intense fire with 100 men depending on your leadership!

(The answers are to be found at the bottom of the page.)

By August 1966, the Australians had dramatically altered the balance of power in Phuoc Tuy province of South Vietnam. The Viet Cong had to do something.

In the early hours of the morning, they bombarded the Australian camp with heavy mortar and rifle fire.

The next day the Australians searched and found the Viet Cong firing positions.

Major Harry Smith's D Company, 6th Battalion, found tracks going left, right and centre.

He followed the centre tracks, going east into the Long Tan rubber plantation.

After about 500 metres, the company encountered a small force of the Viet Cong and fighting broke out.

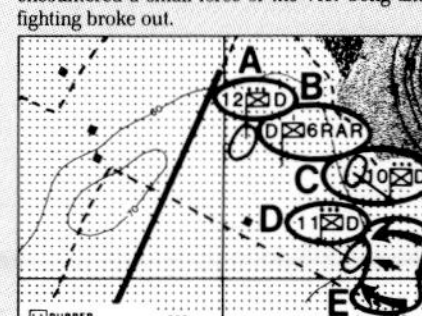

LEGEND: A. 12 Platoon, D Company. B. D Company Headquarters, 6th Battalion, Royal Australian Regiment. C. 10 Platoon. D. 11 Platoon. E. Viet Cong Battalions.

Question 1.

If you had been Smith, having found the Viet Cong, would you have:

Advanced further into the enemy area?

Stayed put, reporting back to base and calling for reinforcements?

Question 2.

Smith's company was advancing through an unnatural silence, the air sticky with imminent monsoon rain.

Suddenly, the Viet Cong opened fire.

"*In the next 10 minutes everything went mad,*" Smith said. "*11 Platoon was being surrounded and over-run... the whole company under fire from mortars, rifles and machine guns.*"

Torrential rain began to fall. Smith called for artillery and air support, but because of the rain, the pilots could not see his position.

No air strike.

If you were Smith, knowing you were greatly outnumbered, what would you have tried to do?

Send your other two platoons to the rescue of 11 Platoon?

Leave 11 Platoon to extricate themselves while forming the remaining platoons and company HQ into a tight defensive perimeter and fight on?

Reluctantly leave 11 Platoon and try to break away back to base camp?

Question 3.

Lieutenant Colonel Colin Townsend had been following the battle closely on the radio.

At an early stage he alerted another company to join with a troop of Armoured Personnel Carriers (APCs) to be ready to go as a relief force if necessary.

At 5.45 he ordered them to go. However, two broke down.

Should the APC troop commander:

Return to camp?

Wait for reinforcements?

Go on to assist the beleaguered infantry?

Question 4.

The relief force ran into a Viet Cong company about 1000 metres from the battle.

A platoon dismounted and attacked the Viet Cong, supported by machine gun fire from the APCs.

The Viet Cong took about 15 casualties then broke and ran.

Another 300 metres on, the relief force met a second group of Viet Cong.

They killed and wounded about 50 Viet Cong and pressed on.

At 7.10 pm, just as it was turning dark, Townsend and the relief column reached the edge of the D Company position.

The Viet Cong were massing for a final all-out attack to overrun the D Company survivors, down to about 70 since 17 had been killed and 21 wounded.

If you had been Townsend, what would you have done at this stage?

Halted the relief column at the edge of the battle and then carried out a reconnaissance to decide what to do next? That is a frontal assault or a flank assault.

Halted the column outside of the enemy encirclement and then given Smith fire support to help him achieve a breakout?

Crashed on through, to reinforce D Company?

Crashed on through and when the enemy broke, followed them up in hot pursuit?

Enquire now for further details.

If you've read this far and would like to know more about becoming an Army Officer, phone during business hours or complete the coupon details below and mail it to Defence Force Recruiting, or Army Careers Information Centre in your State.

Applications for the January 1988 intake close September 18, 1987.

Maybe you will be one of those who could have made the right "heat of the battle" decisions that day at Long Tan.

For more information, post this coupon to: Army Officer Careers Advisor, Freepost 2600A, Box XYZ in your capital city or telephone during business hours.

Capital cities: Sydney 219 5550, Melbourne 696 2677, Brisbane 226 2759, Adelaide 212 1455, Perth 325 6222, Canberra 57 2311, Hobart 34 7077.

Other areas: Albury 21 8277, Ballarat 31 1240, Bendigo 43 8008, Bundaberg 73 1152, Geelong 21 1588, Launceston 31 1005, Lismore 21 6111, Newcastle 26 3011, Parramatta 633 4031, Townsville 72 4566, Wagga Wagga 21 1282, Wollongong 28 1855.

TOLL FREE SERVICE – Country Residents Only: N.S.W. 008 422 177, VIC. 008 136 377, NTH. QLD. 008 015 150. STH. QLD. 008 777 531, W.A. 008 199 018. S.A./N.T. 008 888 554.

Name

Sex Date of Birth

Address

Postcode Phone

Highest Education Standard

All enquiries treated in strictest confidence. Authorised by the Department of Defence.

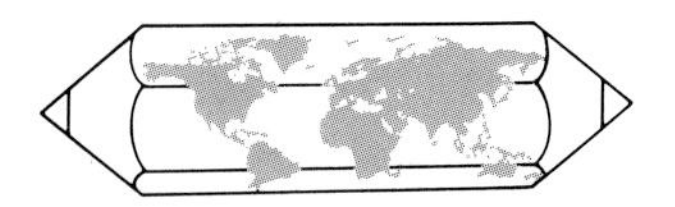

Gold, Silver & Bronze Awards

Consumer Newspaper 600 Lines Or Less: Single

7 GOLD
ART DIRECTOR
Roy Grace
WRITER
Diane Rothschild
PHOTOGRAPHER
Carl Furuta
CLIENT
Range Rover of North America
AGENCY
Grace and Rothschild

8 SILVER
ART DIRECTOR
Coby Neill
WRITER
Todd Tilford
CLIENT
Kwik-Kopy Printing
AGENCY
Valentine-Radford/ Kansas City, MO

9 BRONZE
ART DIRECTOR
Michael Vaughan
WRITER
Constantin Cotzias
DESIGNER
Michael Vaughan
CLIENT
Filomena's
AGENCY
Chinnici & Vaughan

PLEASE BUCKLE UP FOR SECURITY. © 1987 RANGE ROVER OF NORTH AMERICA, INC.

We brake for fish.

Would you like to experience a Range Rover under optimum conditions?

Just add water.

A Range Rover can hold its own in water deep enough for a boat.

At the same time, it reaches speeds of roughly 90 knots on the test track.

And provides you with the luxury you'd expect in a luxury car.

So why not consider a Range Rover?

And convert your money into a liquid asset?

RANGE ROVER

7 GOLD

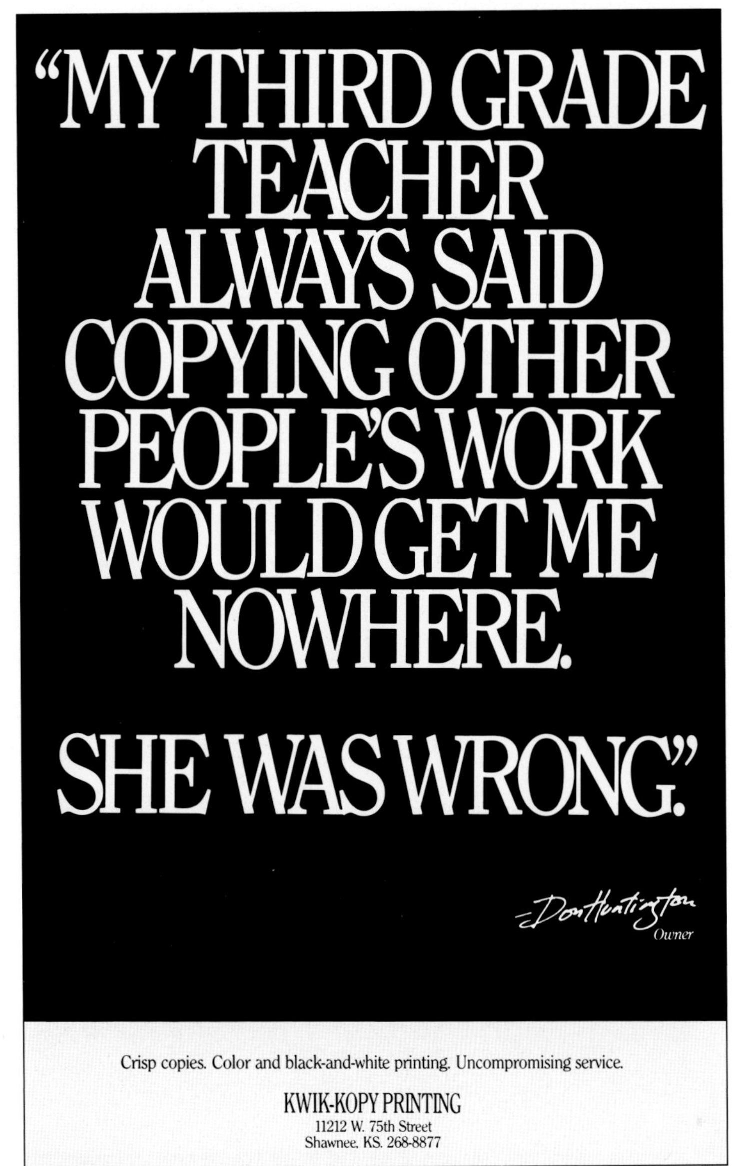

"MY THIRD GRADE TEACHER ALWAYS SAID COPYING OTHER PEOPLE'S WORK WOULD GET ME NOWHERE.
SHE WAS WRONG."
Owner
Crisp copies. Color and black-and-white printing. Uncompromising service.
KWIK-KOPY PRINTING
11212 W. 75th Street
Shawnee, KS. 268-8877

8 SILVER

FILOMENA. BORN IN ITALY. NOT ON MADISON AVENUE.

Filomena is not a figment of some advertising person's imagination.

She's real, and so is her tomato sauce. It's made with a recipe that dates back farther than most families.

With no added preservatives.

With no added salt.

With no expensive marketing.

With no slick advertising campaign.

Filomena's. Made by members of the family, not members of a corporation.

9 BRONZE

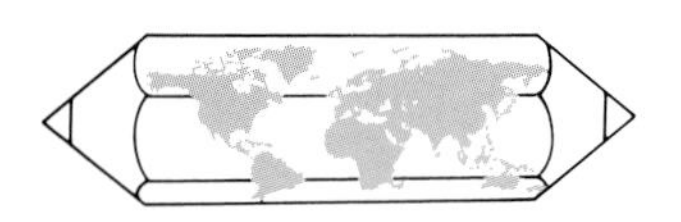

Gold, Silver & Bronze Awards

Consumer Newspaper 600 Lines Or Less: Campaign

10 GOLD
ART DIRECTOR
John Strohmeyer
WRITER
Stephen Fechtor
PHOTOGRAPHER
Charles Purvis
CLIENT
Parker Pen USA
AGENCY
Lowe Marschalk/
Cleveland, OH

10 GOLD

YOU LIVE IN A COUNTRY WHERE THE TAX FORMS ARE EXACTLY 5 MILES LONG, AND BY LAW, CANNOT BE TYPED.

HERE'S WHY YOU DON'T MIND.

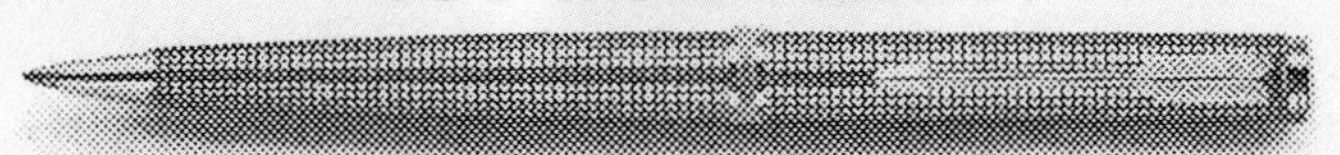

So there you are. Living in a land where the mangos grow wild, myna birds call you by name, and it rains 12½ minutes a year.

It's as close to paradise as one can get. Except, of course, for that quirky old tax form.

Luckily, you have the perfect answer: The Parker Premier Sterling Ball Pen featured above.

Its stainless steel, medium point writes up to five miles between refills. And is much more durable than the brass and nickel silver points commonly found in ordinary pens.

Making it the obvious choice for tax forms of great length, in countries such as yours.

THERE ARE TIMES WHEN IT HAS TO BE PARKER.

PARKER

Every Parker pen comes with a lifetime guarantee. For more information, call 1-800-BEST PEN.

YOU'RE AT A WASHINGTON COCKTAIL PARTY, AND THE CONVERSATION SUDDENLY TURNS TO NIB GRINDING.

HERE'S WHY YOU'RE THE EXPERT.

There you are, hobnobbing with the intelligentsia and literati of the Washington scene, when someone casually mentions how difficult it is to find a good nib-grinder these days.

Conversation stops.

You, being the owner of the fine writing instrument featured above (the Parker Premier Gold Plate and Laque fountain pen), slide into action.

You explain that the nibs of each Parker are precision-ground, to allow them to conform to your own particular style and angle of writing.

You demonstrate the exquisitely smooth writing flow and feel.

And finally, having gained everyone's attention, you take this rare opportunity to share a pet theory of yours: That Shakespeare was actually the pseudonym of a washerwoman named Flo.

THERE ARE TIMES WHEN IT HAS TO BE PARKER.

PARKER

Every Parker pen comes with a lifetime guarantee. For more information, call 1-800-BEST PEN.

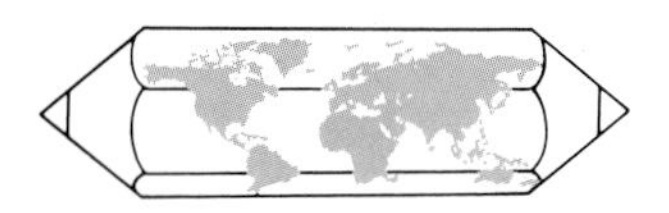

Gold, Silver & Bronze Awards

Consumer Newspaper 600 Lines Or Less: Campaign

11 SILVER

ART DIRECTOR
Paul Cournoyer

WRITER
Michele McKenna

PHOTOGRAPHER
Bruce Wilson

CLIENT
Diet Center

AGENCY
Cole & Weber/
Seattle

"I was tired of living in a tent."

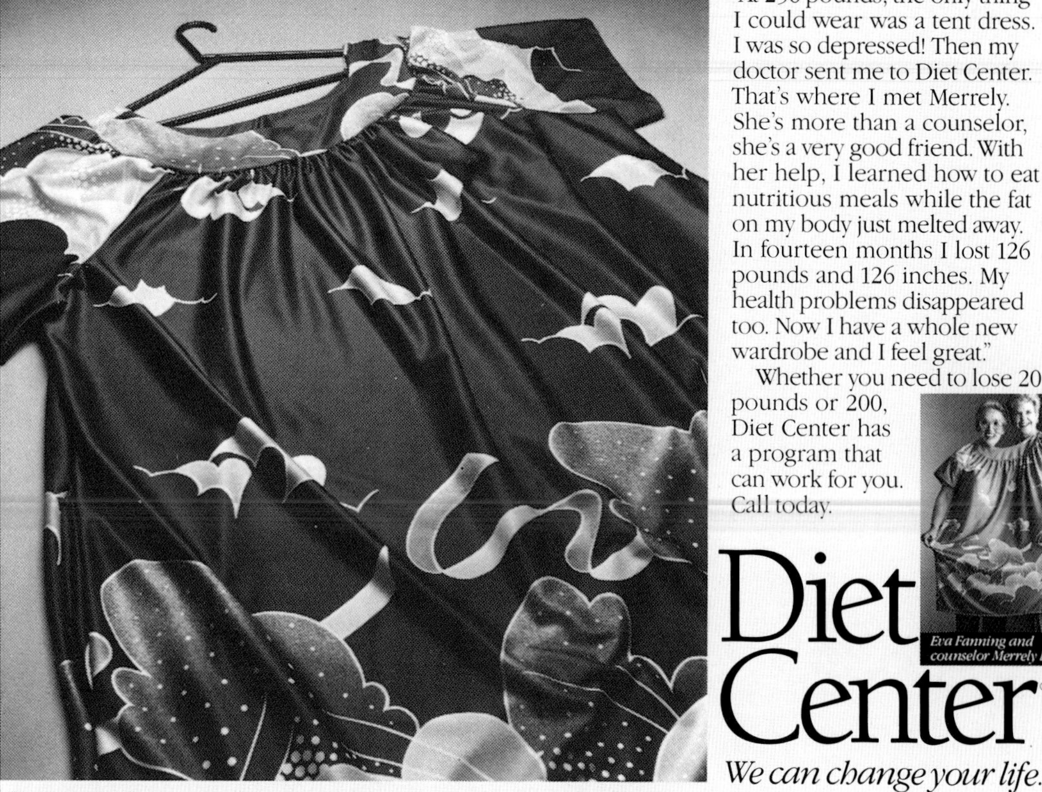

"At 256 pounds, the only thing I could wear was a tent dress. I was so depressed! Then my doctor sent me to Diet Center. That's where I met Merrely. She's more than a counselor, she's a very good friend. With her help, I learned how to eat nutritious meals while the fat on my body just melted away. In fourteen months I lost 126 pounds and 126 inches. My health problems disappeared too. Now I have a whole new wardrobe and I feel great."

Whether you need to lose 20 pounds or 200, Diet Center has a program that can work for you. Call today.

Eva Fanning and counselor Merrely Bantell

Diet Center®

We can change your life.

11 SILVER

"I was a big embarrassment to my kids."

"When my weight reached 262 pounds, I broke down and cried. I felt I was an embarrassment to my family and myself. But at Diet Center I got the support I needed to lose weight without feeling hungry or depressed. I lost 141 pounds in 12 months — and I've never gained it back. Now I'm a much happier size 5. And my kids say they have the prettiest mom at school."

If you want to lose weight fast and keep it off, call the Diet Center nearest you.

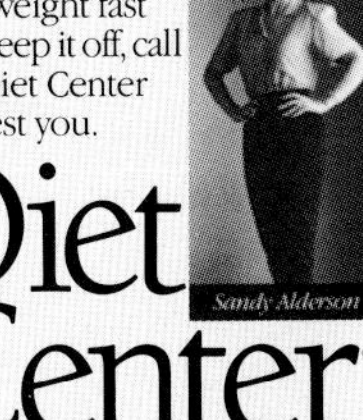

Diet Center®

We can change your life.

"I was too big to fly."

"Two years ago you couldn't get me on an airplane. I was so big, I could barely squeeze down the aisle of a bus or drive a car. When I began the Diet Center program I weighed 290 pounds. I lost 123 pounds in 14 months. I feel as if a whole new world has opened up for me. I'm healthier and more energetic. I really have to give all the credit to Diet Center."

Find out how you can lose weight fast — without fad diets or gimmicks — and lead a healthier, happier life. Call Diet Center today.

Diet Center®

We can change your life.

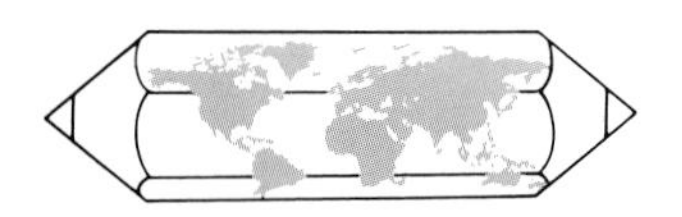

Gold, Silver & Bronze Awards

Consumer Newspaper 600 Lines Or Less: Campaign

12 BRONZE

ART DIRECTOR
Mark Wolf

WRITER
Mike Smith

DESIGNER
Mark Wolf

CLIENT
JoEllen Housecleaning Service

AGENCY
Creswell Munsell Fultz & Zirbel/ Cedar Rapids, IA

"I *know more about scrubbing up than most doctors*"

Jo Ellen Smith

Jo's House Cleaning 492-9002

12 BRONZE

"I've *come clean more often than* Richard Nixon"

Jo Ellen Smith

Jo's House Cleaning 492-9002

"I've *dusted more fingerprints than the* FBI"

Jo Ellen Smith

Jo's House Cleaning 492-9002

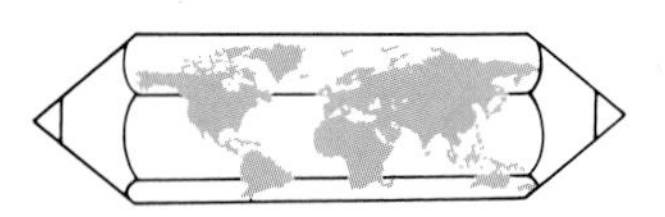

Gold, Silver & Bronze Awards

Consumer Magazine B/W: 1 Page Or Spread Including Magazine Supplements

13 GOLD
ART DIRECTOR
Randall Saitta
WRITER
Charles Borghese
PHOTOGRAPHER
David Burnett
CLIENT
International Center of Photography
AGENCY
Lowe Marschalk

14 SILVER
ART DIRECTOR
Nancy O'Neal
WRITER
Billings Fuess
PHOTOGRAPHER
Tom Berthiaume
CLIENT
International Paper
AGENCY
Ogilvy & Mather

15 BRONZE
ART DIRECTOR
Sig Gross
WRITER
David Corr
CLIENT
WWOR-TV
AGENCY
Hill Holliday Connors Cosmopulos

AT THE GENEVA SUMMIT
THIS PHOTOGRAPH DID ALL THE TALKING.

It took an incredible eye. An eye that instinctively knew what moment in time would sum up the entire event. A photograph is often the vital link we all need to understand the full story. And there's an organization that wants outstanding photojournalism exposed to as many people as possible. It's the International Center of Photography. And when you become a member of the ICP, your contribution will help us put together exhibits like the one in which this photograph was first seen. Of course, you'll also receive special invitations to previews of our exhibits, discounts on lectures and instructional classes and catalogs for discounts at our Museum Shop. For more information on how to join, call (212) 860-1781. Or write to: Membership, ICP, 1130 Fifth Avenue, New York, N.Y. 10128.

INTERNATIONAL CENTER OF PHOTOGRAPHY

13 GOLD

How to write a personal letter

by Garrison Keillor

International Paper asked Garrison Keillor, author of the best-selling books, Happy to Be Here and Lake Wobegon Days, to tell you how to write a letter that will bring joy into the life of someone you love.

We shy persons need to write a letter now and then, or else we'll dry up and blow away. It's true. And I speak as one who loves to reach for the phone, dial the number, and talk. I say, "Big Bopper here—what's shakin', babes?" The telephone is to shyness what Hawaii is to February, it's a way out of the woods, *and yet:* a letter is better.

Such a sweet gift

Such a sweet gift—a piece of handmade writing, in an envelope that is not a bill, sitting in our friend's path when she trudges home from a long day spent among wahoos and savages, a day our words will help repair. They don't need to be immortal, just sincere. She can read them twice and again tomorrow: *You're someone I care about, Corinne, and think of often and every time I do you make me smile.*

We need to write, otherwise nobody will know who we are. They will have only a vague impression of us as A Nice Person, because frankly, we don't shine at conversation, we lack the confidence to thrust our faces forward and say, "Hi, I'm Heather Hooten, let me tell you about my week." Mostly we say "Uh-huh" and "Oh really." People smile and look over our shoulder, looking for someone else to talk to.

So a shy person sits down and writes a letter. To be known by another person—to meet and talk freely on the page—to be close despite distance. To escape from anonymity and be our own sweet selves and express the music of our souls.

Same thing that moves Bruce Springsteen to sing his heart out in front of 123,000 people moves us to take ballpoint in hand and write a few lines to our dear Aunt Eleanor. *We want to be known.* We want her to know that we have fallen in love, that we quit our job, that we're moving to New York, and we want to say a few things that might not get said in casual conversation: *thank you for what you've meant to me, I am very happy right now.*

Skip the guilt

The first step in writing letters is to get over the guilt of *not* writing. You don't "owe" anybody a letter. Letters are a gift. The burning shame you feel when you see unanswered mail makes it harder to pick up a pen and makes for a cheerless letter when you finally do. *I feel bad about not writing, but I've been so busy,* etc. Skip this. Few letters are obligatory, and they are *Thanks for the wonderful gift* and *I am terribly sorry to hear about George's death* and *Yes, you're welcome to stay with us next month,* and not many more than that. Write those promptly if you want to keep your friends. Don't worry about the others, except love letters, of course. When your true love writes *Dear Light of My Life, Joy of My Heart, O Lovely Pulsating Core of My Sensate Life,* some response is called for.

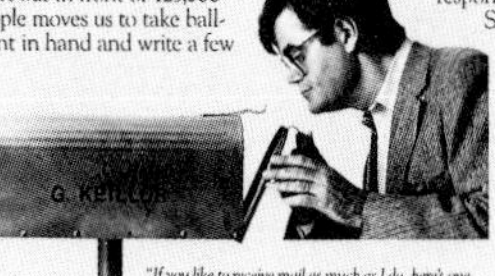

"If you like to receive mail as much as I do, here's one infallible rule: To get a letter, you've got to send a letter."

Some of the best letters are tossed off in a burst of inspiration, so keep your writing stuff in one place where you can sit down for a few minutes and *Dear Roy, I am in the middle of an essay for International Paper but thought I'd drop you a line. Hi to your sweetie too* dash off a note to a pal. Envelopes, stamps, address book, everything in a drawer so you can write fast when the pen is hot.

A blank white 8" x 11" sheet can look as big as Montana if the pen's not so hot—try a smaller page and write boldly. Or use a note card with a piece of fine art on the front; if your letter ain't good, at least they get the Matisse. Get a pen that makes a sensuous line, get a comfortable typewriter, a friendly word processor—whichever feels easy to the hand.

"Outrage, confusion, love—whatever is in your mind, let it find a way to the page."

Sit for a few minutes with the blank sheet in front of you, and meditate on the person you will write to, let your friend come to mind until you can almost see her or him in the room with you. Remember the last time you saw each other and how your friend looked and what you said and what perhaps was unsaid between you, and when your friend becomes real to you, start to write.

Tell us what you're doing

Write the salutation—*Dear* You—and take a deep breath and plunge in. A simple declarative sentence will do, followed by another and another and another. Tell us what you're doing and tell it like you were talking to us. Don't think about grammar, don't think about lit'ry style, don't try to write dramatically, just give us your news. Where did you go, who did you see, what did they say, what do you think?

If you don't know where to begin, start with the present moment: *I'm sitting at the kitchen table on a rainy Saturday morning. Everyone is gone and the house is quiet.* Let your simple description of the present moment lead to something else, let the letter drift gently along.

Take it easy

The toughest letter to crank out is one that is meant to impress, as we all know from writing job applications; if it's hard work to slip off a letter to a friend, maybe you're trying too hard to be terrific. A letter is only a report to someone who already likes you for reasons other than your brilliance. Take it easy.

Don't worry about form. It's not a term paper. When you come to the end of one episode, just start a new paragraph. You can go from a few lines about the sad state of rock 'n roll to the fight with your mother to your fond memories of Mexico to your cat's urinary tract infection to a few thoughts on personal indebtedness to the kitchen sink and what's in it. The more you write, the easier it gets, and when you have a True True Friend to write to, a *compadre,* a soul sibling, then it's like driving a car down a country road, you just get behind the keyboard and press on the gas.

Don't tear up the page and start over when you write a bad line—try to write your way out of it. Make mistakes and plunge on. Let the letter cook along and let yourself be bold. Outrage, confusion, love—whatever is in your mind, let it find a way to the page. Writing is a means of discovery, always, and when you come to the end and write *Yours ever* or *Hugs and Kisses,* you'll know something you didn't when you wrote *Dear Pal.*

An object of art

Probably your friend will put your letter away, and it'll be read again a few years from now—and it will improve with age. And forty years from now, your friend's grandkids will dig it out of the attic and read it, a sweet and precious relic of the ancient Eighties that gives them a sudden clear glimpse of you and her and the world we old-timers knew. You will then have created an object of art. Your simple lines about where you went, who you saw, what they said, will speak to those children and they will feel in their hearts the humanity of our times.

You can't pick up a phone and call the future and tell them about our times. You have to pick up a piece of paper.

Garrison Keillor

Today, the printed word is more vital than ever. Now there is more need than ever for all of us to *read* better, *write* better and *communicate* better. International Paper offers this series in the hope that, even in a small way, we can help.

If you'd like to share this article with others, we'll gladly send you free reprints. So far we've sent out over 30 million reprints of the series in response to requests from people everywhere. Doubleday has now published 13 of the articles in a book, titled: *How to Use the Power of the Printed Word.* For the paperback version, send us a check for $5.95 made out to Doubleday. Write: International Paper Co., Dept. 16G, P.O. Box 954, Madison Sq. Sta., N.Y., NY 10010.

INTERNATIONAL PAPER COMPANY
We believe in the power of the printed word.

14 SILVER

Coffee grinds and eggshells are one thing. Infectious waste is an entirely different matter.

But many local hospitals aren't making the distinction. They're dumping things like used hypodermic needles and AIDS contaminated body parts in plastic bags with the regular trash.

Which means they could be spreading the same diseases they're supposed to be containing.

What hospitals are guilty? We'll find out tonight as Bob Gilmartin begins this alarming special investigative report.

SPECIAL REPORT: WASTE NOT
TONIGHT 10PM.

15 BRONZE

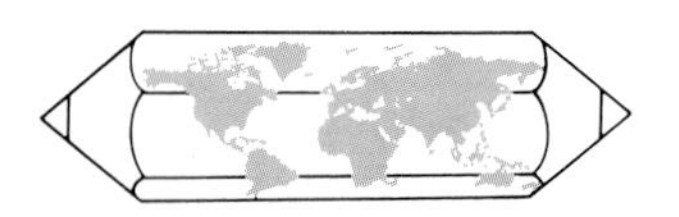

Gold, Silver & Bronze Awards

Consumer Magazine Color: 1 Page Or Spread Including Magazine Supplements

16 GOLD
ART DIRECTOR
Steve Dunn
WRITER
Tim Delaney
PHOTOGRAPHER
Graham Cornthwaite
CLIENT
Linguaphone
AGENCY
Leagas Delaney Partnership/London

17 SILVER
ART DIRECTOR
Andy Arghyrou
WRITER
Lynda Richardson
PHOTOGRAPHER
Steve Cavalier
CLIENT
Cow & Gate
AGENCY
Abbott Mead Vickers/ SMS - London

18 BRONZE
ART DIRECTOR
Steve Dunn
WRITER
Tim Delaney
PHOTOGRAPHER
Graham Cornthwaite
CLIENT
Linguaphone
AGENCY
Leagas Delaney Partnership/London

16 GOLD

You wouldn't do it to your baby. We wouldn't do it to our babyfood.

The make-up on this little girl's face contains no less than 100 chemicals.

It seems outrageous to do such a thing to her delicate baby skin. (And of course we didn't. We re-touched the photograph.)

But what about her delicate baby stomach?

It's quite within the law to add some 4,000 artificial additives to baby foods.

When you think about it, that's even more outrageous.

Young babies are particularly vulnerable to the adverse effects of artificial additives.

Because the mechanisms which provide protection against these substances are not fully developed.

For that reason, we'd like to tell you what we don't put in any Cow & Gate babyfood. Or juice. Or rusk. Or yogurt.

No artificial colouring.

Since when did a baby complain that our Vegetable Casserole and Pasta looked a bit on the pale and pasty side?

Or our Strawberry Fool looked a trifle dull?

The value of artificial colouring is purely cosmetic. And you all know what we think about that.

No artificial flavouring.

When we first mixed up our Lamb Dinner, we decided it wasn't as tasty as it could be.

But the last thing we thought of adding was artificial flavouring.

We simply added a few carrots.

That way we improved both the taste, and nutritional value. And that's the way we make all our babyfoods.

No artificial preservatives.

Many manufacturers go along with adding artificial preservatives. Granted, that's one way of doing it.

We prefer to employ some 400 people checking, sterilising or pasteurising, double-checking, then vacuum sealing.

We even put a 'safety button' on baby-

meal jars. So you can check that the food is in perfect condition.

No added salt.

Young babies don't have fully matured kidneys. If they are over-loaded with too much salt, it can build up in their blood.

Besides that, the foods we use naturally contain any salt a baby needs.

So salt is one thing you'll never find on our tables.

No need to guess.

We want you to know exactly what goes into our babyfoods.

On every Cow & Gate label there's a complete list of ingredients. Plus nutritional information.

In addition, the 'tick' system means each item can be checked for additives, at a glance.

If you'd like a leaflet that goes into even more detail, write to Consumer Affairs (G.N.), Cow & Gate, Trowbridge, Wiltshire BA14 8YX.

- ✔ NO ADDED SUGAR
- GLUTEN FREE
- ✔ NO ARTIFICIAL COLOURING
- ✔ NO ADDED PRESERVATIVES
- ✔ NO ARTIFICIAL FLAVOURING
- ✔ NO ADDED SALT
- ✔ ADDED VITAMIN C

Clearly, we shy away from the use of anything artificial. Only adding Vitamin C to our drinks. Or a tiny sprinkling of sugar to some of our fruit puddings. But only enough to overcome the natural tartness of the fruit.

So when you pop Cow & Gate food into a baby's mouth, you can be sure it's as natural as we can possibly make it.

Babies being babies, they may end up with their faces covered in food. But at least you know it's not covered in artificial chemicals.

Cow & Gate

Babymeals. Baby Juices. Liga Rusks.

17 SILVER

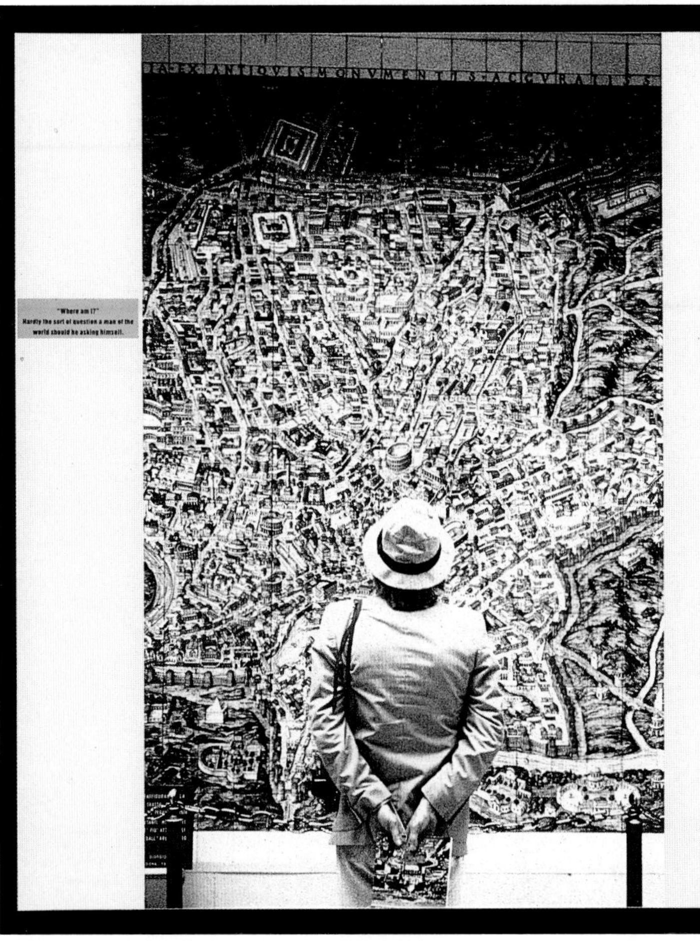

"Where am I?"
Hardly the sort of question a man of the world should be asking himself.

Are you a man of the world until you travel abroad?

As you go about your daily business you are, no doubt, accorded the respect due to a person of your standing.

Yet merely by transporting yourself across a frontier or two, this situation can quickly change.

Your PhD means very little to a grumpy Parisian taxi-driver.

Your recent elevation to the Board is of supreme irrelevance to the customs man in Milan.

Why, even your collection of metallic-coloured credit cards can be reduced to worthless plastic by the shrug of a waiter's shoulders in Rio de Janeiro.

Of course, if you could understand and talk to people when you were abroad, your self-esteem would not be put in such jeopardy.

At Linguaphone, we've spent the last 60 years helping people talk to each other. In fact, since we began, our courses have enabled over 5 million people to learn another language.

You start by listening to native speakers in life-like situations. Then you follow illustrations of objects you know coupled with names you don't.

Very quickly, you are able to imitate the words that describe the pictures. It is not long before you can actually converse.

As you probably don't recall, you learned your very first words using this method. Indeed, it could be said that we are all walking advertisements for its effectiveness.

The Linguaphone method is used to teach 30 different languages in 101 countries.

No fewer than 27 British universities use it. As do many of the biggest companies in the world, including BP, Unilever and Ford.

If you would like to take one of our language courses, just fill in the coupon below.

Alternatively, you could visit the new Linguaphone Language Centre in Brompton Road, opposite Harrods.

Then, when next you find yourself in foreign climes, you may rest assured that your credentials as a man of the world will go unchallenged.

LINGUAPHONE

Dear Linguaphone, my self-esteem is very important to me. Please send me details of your language courses. Please specify language.

Linguaphone, Freepost, Linguaphone House, London W6 9BR. Call 0800-400485 anytime (no charge).

Mr Mrs Miss Ms ____

Address ____

____ Postcode ____ Language ____

18 BRONZE

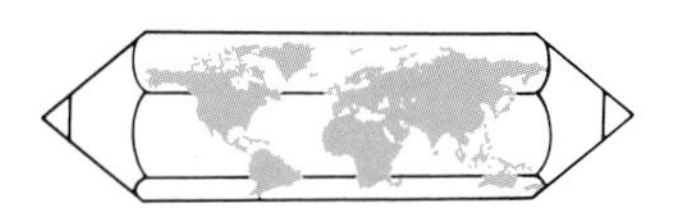

Gold, Silver & Bronze Awards

Consumer Magazine B/W: Campaign Including Magazine Supplements

19 GOLD

ART DIRECTOR
Mark Johnson

WRITERS
Tom McElligott
Bruce Bildsten

PHOTOGRAPHERS
Herman Wong
Angela Fisher
Thomas L. Kelly

CLIENT
Bloomingdale's

AGENCY
Fallon McElligott/
Minneapolis

There are 5 million people and 60 thousand factories in Hong Kong.

But we were there to meet only one man, who still made jewelry that was simply one-of-a-kind.

To reach him we would have to go to the much less populous New Territories.

Where, thanks to a typhoon in the South China Sea, roads were rivers.

Fortunately, at Bloomingdale's, to find truly unique merchandise we're not only prepared to travel halfway around the world.

We're quite willing to get our feet wet.

"Where is the man who makes this jewelry?" I said.

"Not far," answered my guide, "but the roads are a bit wet this time of year."

bloomingdale's
No one goes as far as we do.

19 GOLD

A six-thousand mile airplane ride to Casablanca.

A seven-hour Land Rover ride to Marakkech.

And we still had a three-hour camel ride before those remarkable Moroccan rugs would be ours.

We not only go out of our way to find the unique, we go to the ends of the earth.

"This rug is beautiful. Where can I find more?" I said.

"Have you ever ridden a camel?" He replied.

bloomingdale's

No one goes as far as we do.

Napkin rings—that's all they were. But each was a work of art.

One of our buyers discovered them on his annual trip to Delhi, India in a street bazaar.

But to get enough of the rings to stock our store he would have to go to the people who made them, in Kashmir, several hours away in the Himalaya Mountains.

He wasn't surprised when an April blizzard stranded his guide's Jeep along the way. But he was surprised by what came to their rescue: a Himalayan limousine, of sorts. A Yak. Led, oddly enough, by the very men who made the napkin rings.

Thankfully, the napkin rings were well worth the journey. But, of course, this wasn't the first high adventure one of our buyers had experienced. Nor would it be the last.

Because, at Bloomingdale's, to find truly unique goods, we're quite willing to travel the world. By air. By land. By sea. And even, upon occasion, by yak.

"I must have those napkin rings," I exclaimed, "but can we reach their village in such weather?"

"Don't worry," my guide replied, "they will send their limousine for us."

bloomingdale's

No one goes as far as we do.

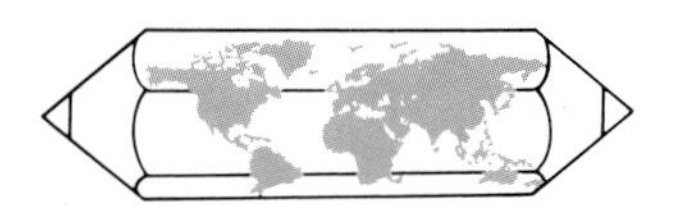

Gold, Silver & Bronze Awards

Consumer Magazine B/W: Campaign Including Magazine Supplements

20 SILVER

ART DIRECTOR
Bob Brihn

WRITERS
Jamie Barrett
George Gier

PHOTOGRAPHERS
Rick Dublin
Craig Perman

CLIENT
WFLD

AGENCY
Fallon McElligott/
Minneapolis

SIT BACK AND WATCH A WOODY ALLEN MOVIE.

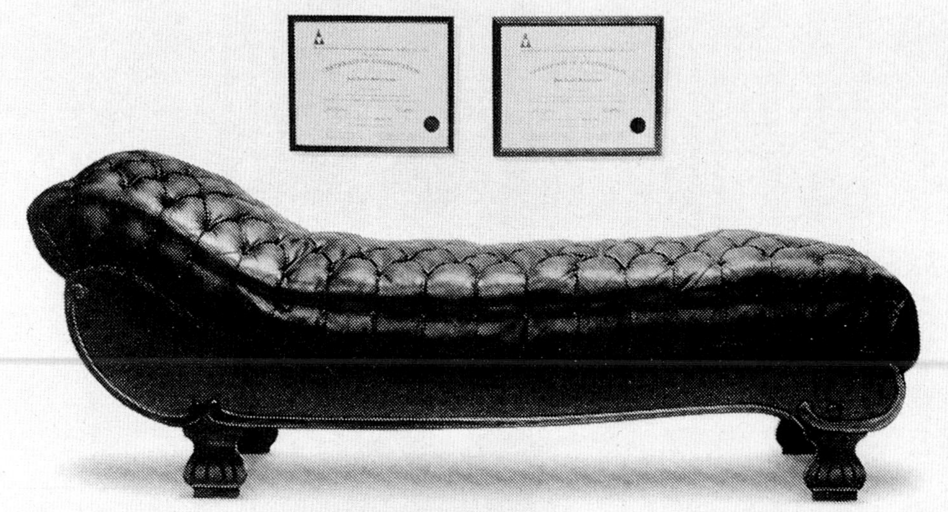

"Broadway Danny Rose," Wednesday at 7 PM.

32
WFLD

20 SILVER

JET GOES DOWN IN NEW YORK. FILM AT 7:00.

Tuesday, see the classic musical of two rival gangs, the Jets and the Sharks.

"WEST SIDE STORY"

32
WFLD

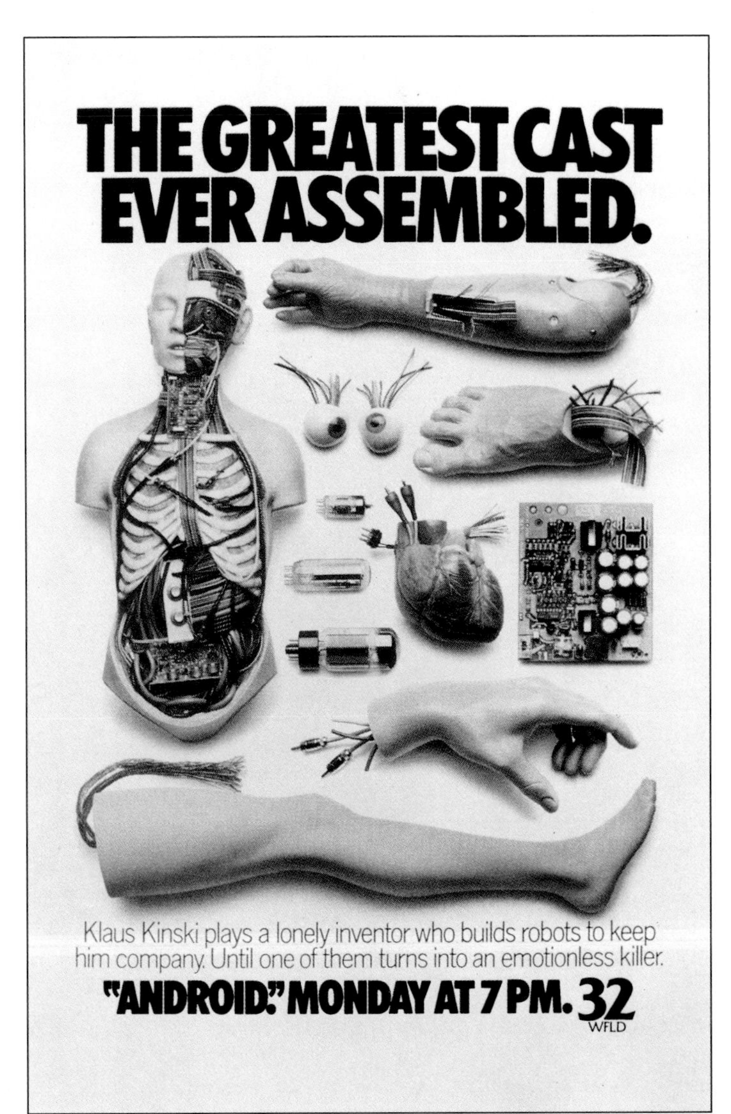

THE GREATEST CAST EVER ASSEMBLED.
Klaus Kinski plays a lonely inventor who builds robots to keep him company. Until one of them turns into an emotionless killer.
"ANDROID." MONDAY AT 7 PM. 32
WFLD

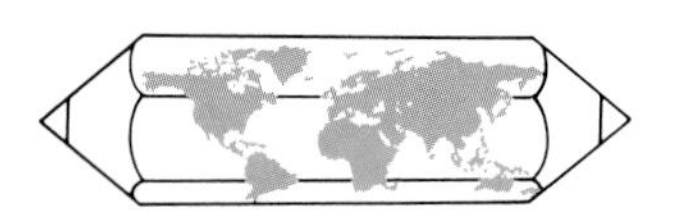

Gold, Silver & Bronze Awards

Consumer Magazine Color: Campaign Including Magazine Supplements

21 GOLD

ART DIRECTOR
Steve Dunn

WRITER
Tim Delaney

PHOTOGRAPHER
Graham Cornthwaite

CLIENT
Linguaphone

AGENCY
Leagas Delaney
Partnership/London

Are you a man of the world until you travel abroad?

As you go about your daily business you are, no doubt, accorded the respect due to a person of your standing.

Yet merely by transporting yourself across a frontier or two, this situation can quickly change.

Your PhD means very little to a grumpy Parisian taxi-driver.

Your recent elevation to the Board is of supreme irrelevance to the customs man in Milan.

Why, even your collection of metallic-coloured credit cards can be reduced to worthless plastic by the shrug of a waiter's shoulders in Rio de Janeiro.

Of course, if you could understand and talk to people when you were abroad, your self-esteem would not be put in such jeopardy.

At Linguaphone, we've spent the last 60 years helping people talk to each other. In fact, since we began, our courses have enabled over 5 million people to learn another language.

You start by listening to native speakers in life-like situations. Then you follow illustrations of objects you know coupled with names you don't.

Very quickly, you are able to imitate the words that describe the pictures. It is not long before you can actually converse.

As you probably don't recall, you learned your very first words using this method. Indeed it could be said that we are all walking advertisements for its effectiveness.

The Linguaphone method is used to teach 30 different languages in 101 countries.

No fewer than 27 British universities use it. As do many of the biggest companies in the world, including BP, Unilever and Ford.

If you would like to take one of our language courses, just fill in the coupon below.

Alternatively, you could visit the new Linguaphone Language Centre in Brompton Road, opposite Harrods.

Then, when next you find yourself in foreign climes, you may rest assured that your credentials as a man of the world will go unchallenged.

LINGUAPHONE

Mr/Mrs/Miss/Ms
Address
Postcode Language

21 GOLD

Even being fluent in sign language doesn't get you very far.

Travel is supposed to broaden the mind not render it useless.

Can you remember when you first saw the Eiffel Tower? Or St. Peter's? Or the Pyramids?

Do you recall how personal the wonder felt? How you marvelled at Man's ability to transcend the physical in the pursuit of the spiritual?

Of course you do.

It is this very feeling that has given travel such a good name over the years.

Unfortunately, in this age of visual saturation even wonders of the world can appear common place.

Which is why many people who travel regularly find their stimulation in the nuances of a culture, the idiosyncracies of a place.

And how, you may ask, does one do this? One obvious way is to be able to speak to the people.

At Linguaphone, we've spent the last 60 years helping people talk to each other.

In fact, since we began, our courses have enabled over 5 million people to learn another language. No doubt you've spotted some of them on your travels.

They're the ones who found the little restaurant you passed by on your last day, on their first day.

Who chatted-up the fishermen and got their langouste fresher and cheaper than everyone else.

And who cajoled the old boatman into taking them to a beach that wasn't even on the map.

But isn't it difficult to learn a language? Not if you use our method.

You start by listening to native speakers in life-like situations. Then you follow illustrations of objects you know coupled with names you don't.

Very soon, you are able to imitate the words that describe the pictures. Not long after, you can actually converse.

The Linguaphone method is used to teach 30 different languages in 101 countries.

No fewer than 27 British universities use it. As do many of the biggest companies in the world, including BP, Unilever and Ford.

If you would like to take one of our language courses, just fill in the coupon below. And you may never have to engage in mindless conversations again. (See pictures left.)

LINGUAPHONE

Linguaphone, Freepost, Linguaphone House, London W6 9BR. Call 0800-400485 anytime (no charge).

Mr/Mrs/Miss/Ms

Address

Postcode Language

The world is shrinking. Shouldn't your vocabulary be expanding?

According to official figures, more than 24 million British people have travelled abroad in the past 12 months alone.

Yet statistics from the boys at the Education Ministry show that our interest in learning languages is actually falling.

Which must mean that more and more of us who arrive in other countries are reduced to communicating in language equivalent to baby talk.

For tourists this is, of course, all part of the 'fun.' For businessmen and women, however, it represents that deadliest of all the commercial sins.

It's uncompetitive.

Not surprisingly, large numbers of people with business interests abroad are now turning to Linguaphone for help. And with good reason.

Our method is based on two simple principles. One: people learn more quickly when they're enjoying themselves. And two: they learn more easily when they have listened to a language *before* reading about it.

Now we know that business people don't always have time to spend on immersion courses.

So our Minilab course gives you the freedom to learn when and where you like, and at a pace you find comfortable.

We can't claim it's easy. We wish we could. Having said that, the Linguaphone method is used to teach 30 different languages in over 100 countries.

No fewer than 27 British universities employ it. As do many of the biggest companies in the world. Ford, Unilever, BP, American Express and British Airways among them.

If your firm is expanding its overseas operations, ring Karina Mellinger, our Business Sales Manager, on 01-741 1655.

And if you doubt the importance of learning another language, she might well invoke the success of another island about the size of ours.

It's called Japan.

LINGUAPHONE

Linguaphone, Freepost, Linguaphone House, London W6 9BR. Call 0800-400485 anytime (no charge).

Mr/Mrs/Miss/Ms

Address

Postcode Language

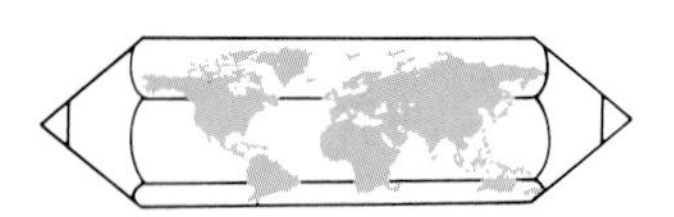

Gold, Silver & Bronze Awards

Consumer Magazine Color: Campaign Including Magazine Supplements

22 SILVER

ART DIRECTOR
Parry Merkley

WRITER
Gordon Bowen

PHOTOGRAPHER
Annie Leibovitz

CLIENT
American Express

AGENCY
Ogilvy & Mather

Tip O'Neill. Cardmember since 1973.

Membership has its privileges.℠

Don't leave home without it.℠

Call 1-800-THE CARD to apply.

22 SILVER

Wilt Chamberlain. Cardmember since 1976.
Willie Shoemaker. Cardmember since 1966.

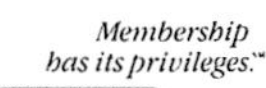

Don't leave home without it.℠
Call 1-800-THE CARD to apply.

Elmore Leonard. Cardmember since 1961.

Membership has its privileges.℠

Don't leave home without it.℠
Call 1-800-THE CARD to apply.

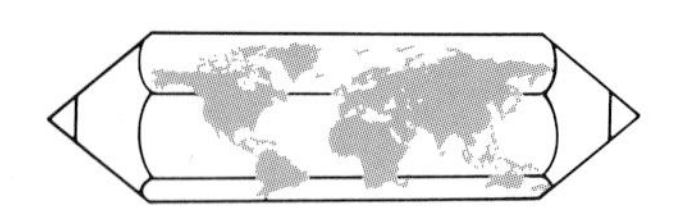

Gold, Silver & Bronze Awards

Consumer Magazine Color: Campaign Including Magazine Supplements

23 BRONZE

ART DIRECTORS
Tom Lichtenheld
Rob Dalton

WRITERS
Jamie Barrett
George Gier

PHOTOGRAPHER
Dennis Manarchy

CLIENT
Lee Jeans

AGENCY
Fallon McElligott/
Minneapolis

There are approximately 19,000 women models in the U.S. These jeans are designed for the 100,000,000 women who aren't.

So maybe you're not a model.
That doesn't mean you can't look great in a pair of jeans.
At Lee, we design our Relaxed Rider jeans to bring out the best in every woman.
Because, while some jean makers cut their material on a straight line, Relaxed Riders are cut on a curve, which means they conform to the natural contours of a woman's body.
And since our jeans are made of soft, stone-washed denim, they feel as good as they fit.
The next time you're looking for jeans, try on a pair of Relaxed Riders.
We think you'll like your body a lot more.
And maybe hate models a little bit less.

Relaxed Riders 

23 BRONZE

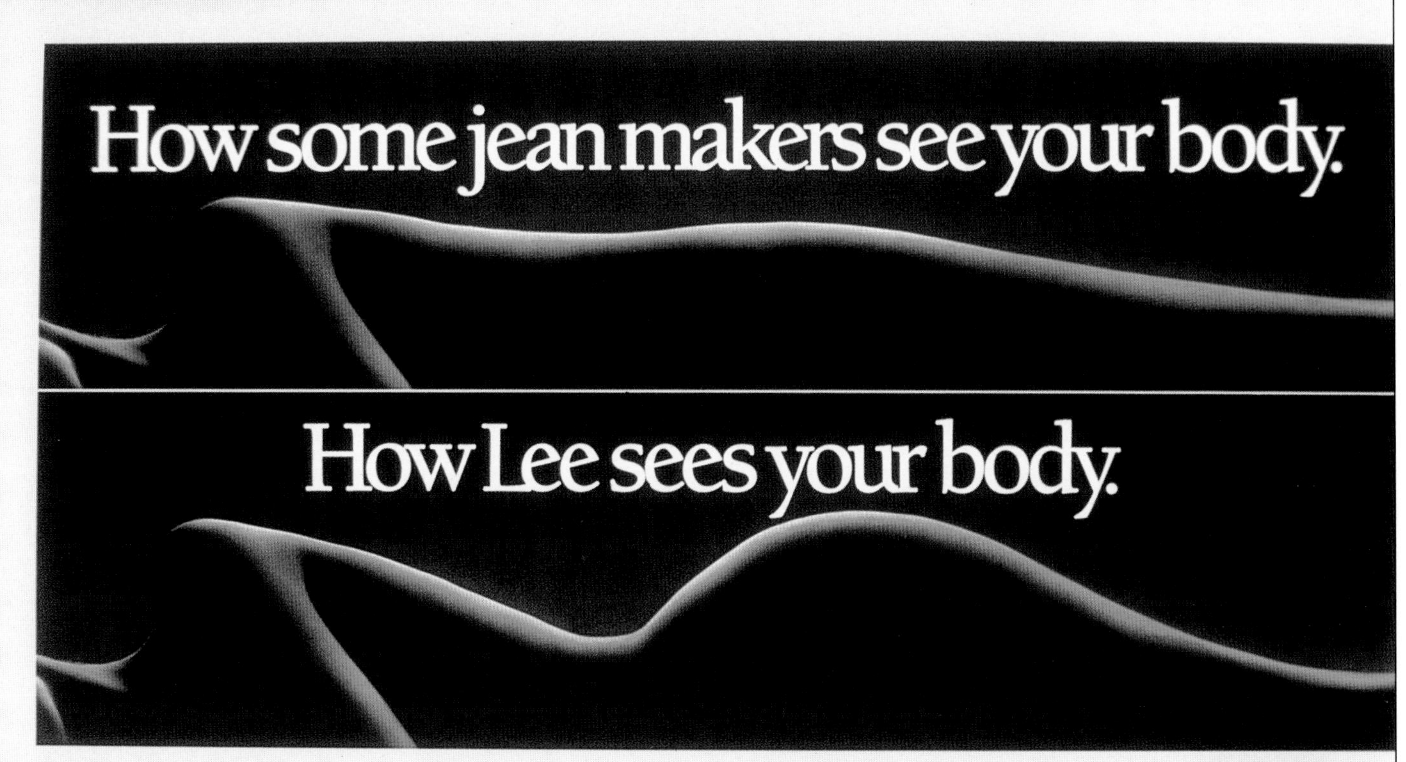

How some jean makers see your body.
How Lee sees your body.

Unlike some jeans, Relaxed Riders are designed to flatter your form. We use a special cut that follows the contours of your body. So where you curve, Relaxed Riders curve right along with you.

Relaxed Rider® jeans from Lee® Try on a pair. We think you'll begin to see your body in a whole new way.

Relaxed Riders Lee

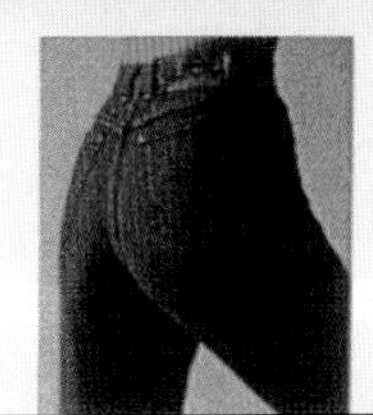

Maybe it's not a better body you need. Maybe it's better jeans.

All women are not created equal. But all women are created with curves.

The funny thing is, many jeans are cut on a straight line. Which may help explain why so many women blame their own bodies when they can't find jeans that fit.

At Lee, we don't think your body should have to fit your jeans. We think your jeans should fit you. When we make Relaxed Rider jeans, we cut them to conform to the natural contours of your body. So where you curve, your jeans curve along with you.

And since they're made of soft, stonewashed denim, they feel just as good as they fit.

Lee® Relaxed Rider® jeans.
Your body is fine. It's your jeans that need changing.

Relaxed Riders

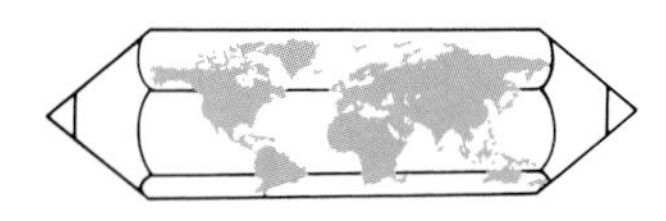

Gold, Silver & Bronze Awards

Consumer Magazine Less Than A Page B/W Or Color: Single

24 GOLD
ART DIRECTOR
Paul Federico
WRITER
Rich Pels
CLIENT
WWOR-TV
AGENCY
Hill Holliday Connors Cosmopulos

Consumer Magazine Less Than A Page B/W or Color: Campaign

25 GOLD
ART DIRECTORS
Mike Shine
Bryan Buckley
WRITERS
Bryan Buckley
Mike Shine
PHOTOGRAPHER
Earl Culberson
CLIENT
Sara Lee
AGENCY
Chiat/Day

ONLY ONE THING'S AS SCARY AS SOMEONE RAPING YOUR DAUGHTER. SOMEONE RAPING YOUR SON.

A shocking number of men are victims of a crime thought only to attack women. Rape. What are its emotional and physical effects? Share the horror of men who have personally experienced its devastation.

PEOPLE ARE TALKING • LIVE TODAY 11AM

24 GOLD

Ever wonder why France was invaded seven times?
Sara Lee

Manufacturer's coupon. Expires 9/30/88.

Save 20¢ on any Sara Lee L'Original Croissant.

GROCER: This coupon good only on purchase of product indicated. LIMIT ONE COUPON PER PURCHASE. Reimbursement is at the coupon face value 1/20¢. Mail to: Kitchens of Sara Lee, P.O. Box 9210, Newport Beach, CA 92658. FRAUD CLAUSE: Redeemable from retail customer only, any other use constitutes fraud. Proof-of-purchase of sufficient stock may be required.
8713

Manufacturer's coupon. Expires 9/30/88.

Save 30¢ on any Sara Lee Le San★wich® Croissant.

GROCER: This coupon good only on purchase of product indicated. LIMIT ONE COUPON PER PURCHASE. Reimbursement is at the coupon face value 1/20¢. Mail to: Kitchens of Sara Lee, P.O. Box 9210, Newport Beach, CA 92658. FRAUD CLAUSE: Redeemable from retail customer only, any other use constitutes fraud. Proof-of-purchase of sufficient stock may be required.
8805

25 GOLD

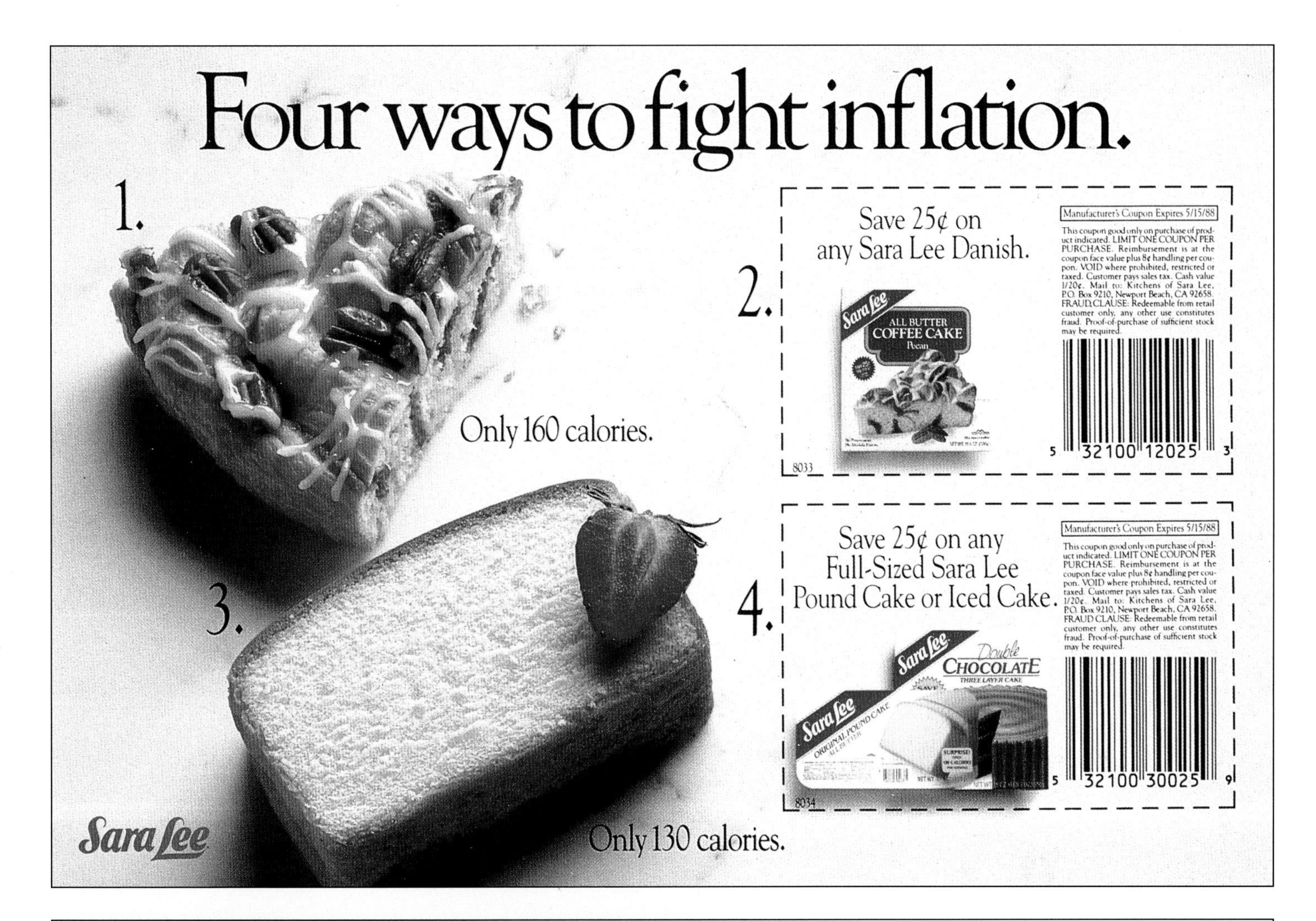

We've made cherry pie
even harder to resist.

Save 25¢ on any
Chef Pierre pie.

This coupon good only on purchase of product indicated. LIMIT ONE COUPON PER PURCHASE. Reimbursement is at the coupon face value plus 8¢ handling per coupon. VOID where prohibited, restricted or taxed. Customer pays sales tax. Cash value 1/20¢. Mail to: Kitchens of Sara Lee, P.O. Box 9210, Newport Beach, CA 92658. FRAUD CLAUSE: Redeemable from retail customer only, any other use constitutes fraud. Proof-of-purchase of sufficient stock may be required.

8931

Manufacturer's Coupon Expires 5/15/88

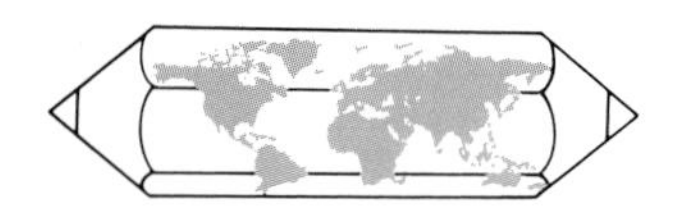

Gold, Silver & Bronze Awards

Consumer Magazine Less Than A Page B/W or Color: Campaign

26 SILVER

ART DIRECTOR
Bob Phillips

WRITER
Tom Thomas

PHOTOGRAPHER
Cailor/Resnick

CLIENT
Austin Nichols - Wild Turkey Bourbon

AGENCY
Angotti Thomas Hedge

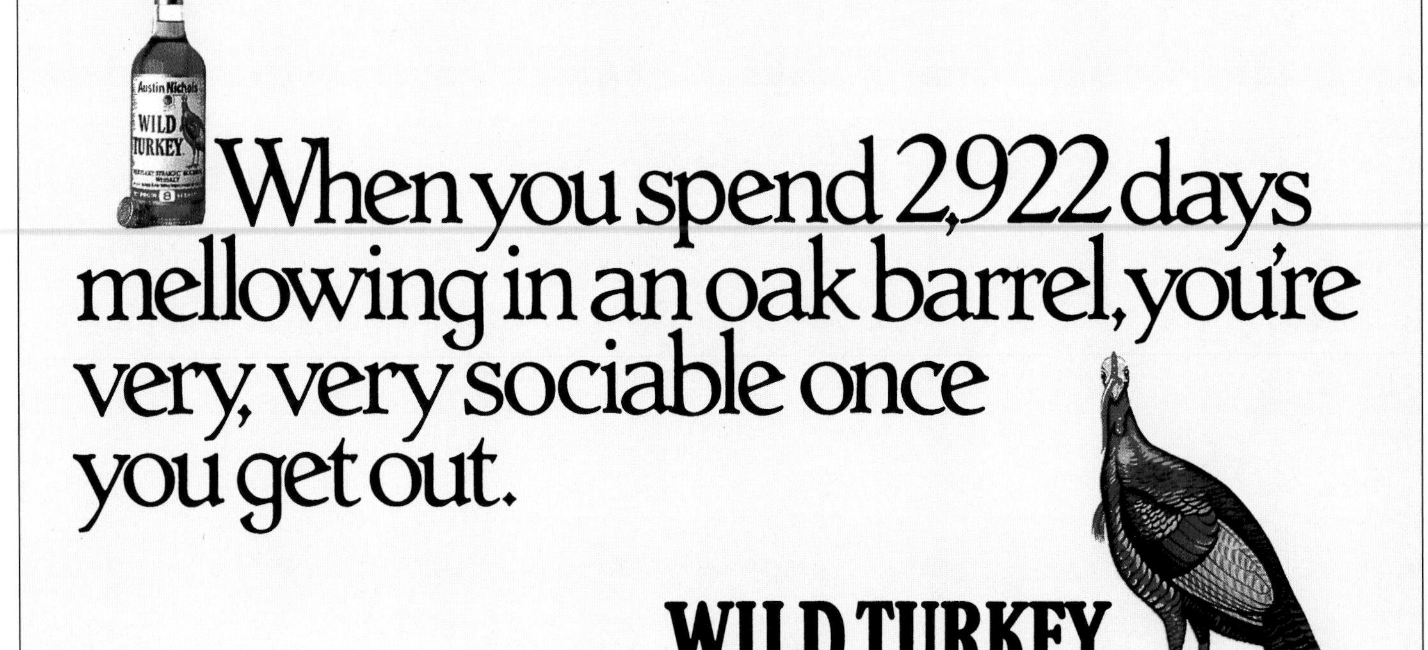

26 SILVER

There are less expensive bourbons. There are also thinner steaks and smaller cars.

WILD TURKEY

8 years old, 101 proof, pure Kentucky.

TO SEND A GIFT OF WILD TURKEY®/101 PROOF ANYWHERE* CALL 1-800-CHEER UP. *EXCEPT WHERE PROHIBITED. KENTUCKY STRAIGHT BOURBON WHISKEY. ALC. BY VOL. 50.5%. AUSTIN NICHOLS DISTILLING CO., LAWRENCEBURG, KY © 1988.

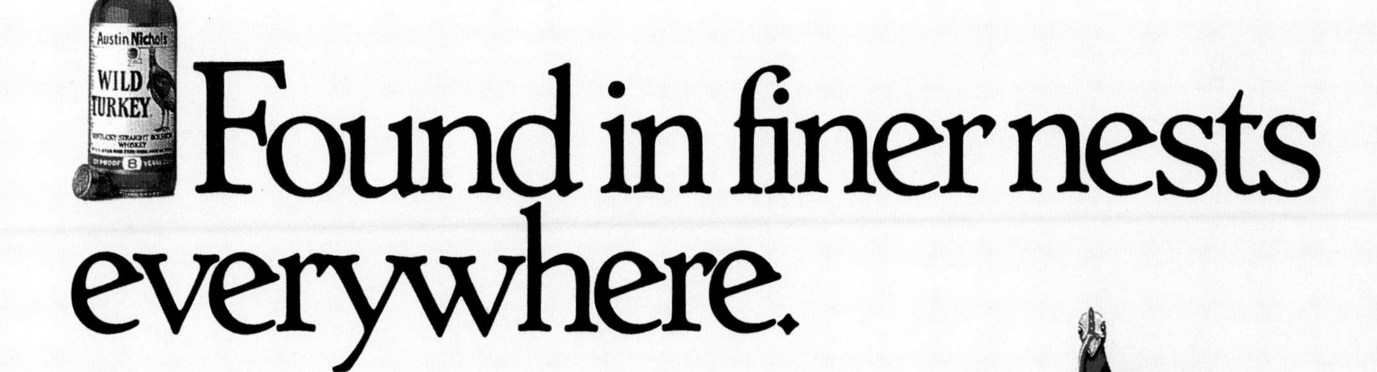

WILD TURKEY

8 years old, 101 proof, pure Kentucky.

TO SEND A GIFT OF WILD TURKEY®/101 PROOF ANYWHERE* CALL 1-800-CHEER UP. *EXCEPT WHERE PROHIBITED. KENTUCKY STRAIGHT BOURBON WHISKEY. AUSTIN NICHOLS DISTILLING CO., LAWRENCEBURG, KY © 1986.

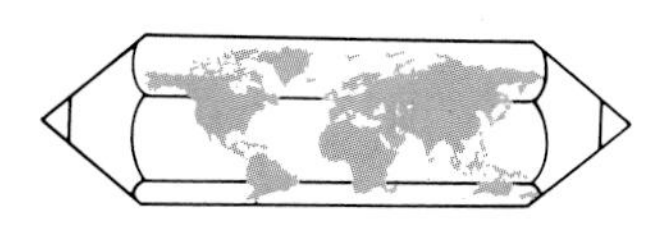

Gold, Silver & Bronze Awards

Consumer Magazine Less Than A Page B/W or Color: Campaign

27 BRONZE

ART DIRECTOR
Frank Haggerty

WRITER
Jack Supple

PHOTOGRAPHER
Marvy!

CLIENT
Blue Fox Tackle Company

AGENCY
Carmichael Lynch/ Minneapolis

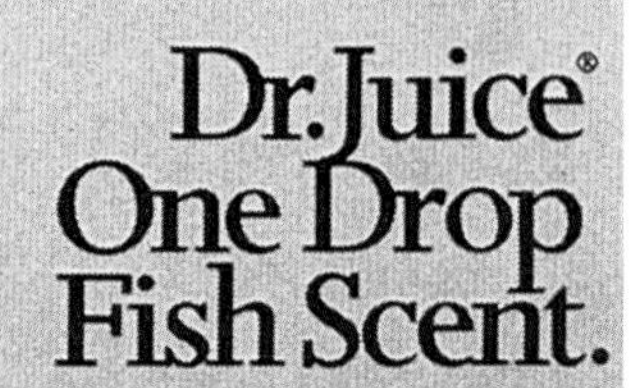

Blue Fox® Tackle Co., 645 N. Emerson, Cambridge, MN 55008

27 BRONZE

©1988 Blue Fox Tackle Co.

Dr. Juice
WALLEYE
SCENT

1,800 Walleyes In Two Months.

900 in the 5-10 lb. range.
Capt. Dick Thompson and customers.
Procaster Charters, Southington, OH.

Dr. Juice® One Drop Fish Scent.

Blue Fox® Tackle Co., 645 N. Emerson, Cambridge, MN 55008

©1988 Blue Fox Tackle Co.

13 lb. 1 oz. Bass.
Caught by Roland Martin.
Largest bass of his TV career.
Nov. 20, 1986. Tampa, Fla.
Dr. Juice
Dr. Juice® One Drop Fish Scent.
Blue Fox® Tackle Co., 645 N. Emerson, Cambridge, MN 55008

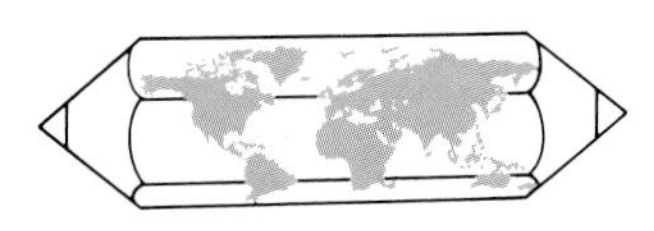

Gold, Silver & Bronze Awards

Trade B/W: 1 Page Or Spread

28 GOLD

ART DIRECTOR
Gail Bartley

WRITER
Tom Thomas

PHOTOGRAPHER
John Alcorn

CLIENT
Barron's

AGENCY
Angotti Thomas Hedge

29 SILVER

ART DIRECTOR
Tim O'Connell

WRITER
Gary Lennox

PHOTOGRAPHERS
Bob Jackson
Frazer Douglas

CLIENT
Nikon Canada

AGENCY
SMW Advertising/Toronto

30 BRONZE

ART DIRECTOR
Neil Leinwohl

WRITER
Kevin McKeon

PHOTOGRAPHER
Earl Culberson

CLIENT
Savin

AGENCY
Korey Kay & Partners

Millionaires aren't a dime a dozen. Actually, they run about 2¢ each.

The exact figure is 2.41 cents for every millionaire we deliver.

Which, as a little comparison shopping will show, is well below the going rate for the rich.

Barron's offers a lower cost per thousand—and per millionaire—than Business Week, Forbes or Fortune. And they're available in quantities considerably larger than a dozen. Or a hundred. Or a hundred thousand.

In fact, 37% of Barron's readers are millionaires. And that just includes their own household assets.

They also control or influence millions more in corporate assets. Because Barron's readers represent a greater concentration of highly paid decision-makers than any other major business or financial magazine.

Of course, you can still reach such people through those other magazines. All it takes is a willingness to pay more for them.

Which is definitely not the recommended way to become a millionaire—or to buy one.

HOW THE SMART MONEY GETS THAT WAY.

Sources: *Survey of Adults and Markets of Affluence*, 1986, Mendelsohn Media Research, Inc. CPMs are based on 7" x 10" black and white units for all publications.

28 GOLD

No, he wouldn't.

Which is why Nikon invented the F3 High Eyepoint.

The Nikon F3HP is equipped with a high eyepoint viewfinder that acts virtually like an action finder.

So whether you're wearing glasses or not, you can see 100% of what's happening right through the lens, with full field, full information display.

Only Nikon can promise this degree of viewing capability, durable reliability, technical sophistication and simplicity of use all in one camera.

The F3HP is also backed by the great array of Nikon system accessories and the high benefit Nikon Professional Services – an exclusive for professionals only.

Now there can be only one thing between you and the world's greatest pictures.

The Nikon F3HP.

Nikon

We take the world's greatest pictures.

Call Nikon Professional Services for more information at 416-625-9910. Nikon Canada Inc., 1366 Aerowood Drive, Mississauga, Ontario L4W 1C1.

29 SILVER

We wanted to compare our Savin 7065 to a Xerox 1065. But we couldn't afford one.

The new Savin 7065. $17,290.

The new Xerox 1065. $24,895.

We were curious. We heard the Xerox 1065 could turn out 62 copies a minute. Just like the Savin 7065.

And that it would hand you your first copy in 7.6 seconds. Which isn't *that* much slower than the 4.0 clocking of our 7065.

Of course, the Xerox copier *is* rumored to have only two modes of reduction, and one mode of enlargement. Which doesn't really compare to Savin's four and three.

And we did read that their copier can't copy from two-sided originals, the way our 7065 can.

But Xerox is a nice company. So we thought we'd give them the benefit of the doubt, put the two copiers side by side, and compare them ourselves.

Then we learned that the Xerox 1065 costs almost $8,000 more than the Savin 7065.

So we called the whole thing off.

It's nothing personal against Xerox. But if we start buying copiers at those prices, before long, we'd have to start charging more for our own.

Savin Corporation, 335 Bishop Hollow Road, Newtown Square, PA 19073.

I'm interested in learning more about the Savin 7065.

Name ________ Title ________
Company ________
Address ________
City ________ State ________
Zip ________ Telephone ( ) ________

MZ FO09147

savin

Follow the leaders.

Suggested retail prices include copier with 20-bin sorter.

Xerox® and 1065 are trademarks of Xerox Corporation.

30 BRONZE

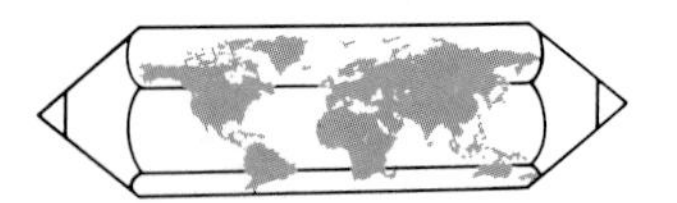

Gold, Silver & Bronze Awards

Trade Color: 1 Page Or Spread

31 GOLD

ART DIRECTOR
Sal DeVito

WRITER
Sal DeVito

PHOTOGRAPHER
Cailor/Resnick

CLIENT
Cailor/Resnick Studio

AGENCY
Levine Huntley Schmidt & Beaver

32 SILVER

ART DIRECTOR
Mitch Gordon

WRITER
Steve Silver

ARTIST
Leonard Morgan

PHOTOGRAPHER
Dave Jordano

CLIENT
Nichols-Homeshield

AGENCY
Zechman & Associates/ Chicago

33 BRONZE

ART DIRECTOR
John Merriman

WRITER
Paul Weinberger

PHOTOGRAPHER
Richard Cooke

CLIENT
Mobil Oil

AGENCY
Lowe Howard-Spink/ London

31 GOLD

How to sustain a direct blow to the head from a blunt instrument.

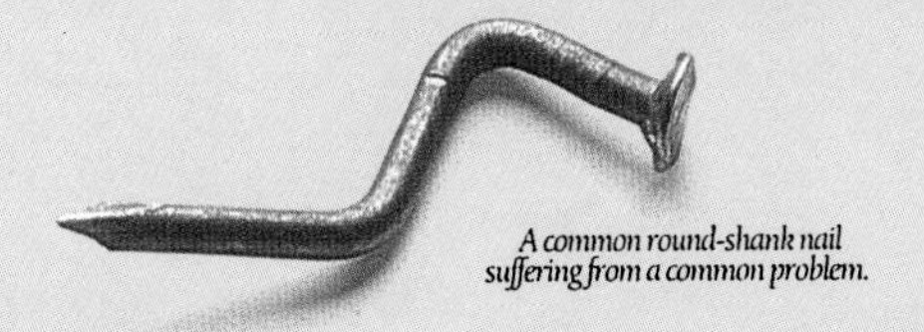

A common round-shank nail suffering from a common problem.

It's a crime.

Too many nails buckle at the knees as soon as they're tapped on the cranium.

So to prevent further headaches, we at Nichols-Homeshield took up our notepads, picked up our hammers, and walloped all sorts of nails at all sorts of angles.

This is what we found out. Bending doesn't occur at the head of the nail, even though that's where the blow falls. The problem lies in the mid-section.

So we redesigned it.

Introducing the world's first trim nail whose shank isn't round, as dictated by tradition: It's triangular.

Without going into the laws of physics, suffice it to say this triangular shape provides three walls of support.

The result is a stronger nail, which in turn means you can work faster with less waste.

Appropriately enough, we've named it the new Bend-Less Aluminum Nail.

It's available to match our eight colors of soffit, rainware and trim finishes, and like other aluminum nails, it's corrosion resistant and economical (about three times as many as steel in every pound). So call us at 1-800-323-2512 (in Illinois, call 1-312-851-5430) for samples, and we'll rush them right out to you. After all, for over 80 years we've bent over backwards just to make sure your nails won't.

The new triangular-shank nail. Uncommonly strong.

The New Bend-Less Aluminum Nail.

homeshield

NICHOLS · HOMESHIELD

©Nichols-Homeshield, 1987

32 SILVER

Nigel insists on our oil when he's cooking.

Down into second for the new chicane.

The needle whips violently to a whining 12,500 revs.

Through third into fourth as Woodcote bend unfolds. The straight beckons ahead.

Fifth. Sixth.

The faces in the Silverstone crowd hurtle backwards in a 200 mph blur.

Inside the engine of the Williams Honda the heat is intense.

In the sump it is 150°C. At the mouth of the twin turbos it is a blistering 1100°C.

Yet Nigel Mansell's oil shows no signs of degrading.

It is Mobil synthetic, conceived inside the laboratory for the ultimate demands of the race track.

So advanced is the chemical composition of our oil that it will protect and lubricate even at the extremes of temperature.

Remarkably, it also reduces friction, leading to an increase in power.

(The Williams team tested it between 10,000 and 11,000 revs. The result was an extra thirteen bhp.)

Fortunately, our synthetic oil technology is not the exclusive preserve of the racing professional.

It is also available to you, as Mobil One Rally Formula.

It, too, will give you the benefits of extra power and high temperature protection.

It will keep your turbo cleaner, longer.

It is, as Nigel Mansell will certainly tell you, hot stuff.

Mobil 1 Rally Formula

The world's most advanced motor oil.

33 BRONZE

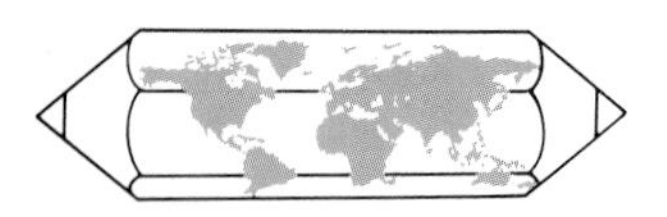

Gold, Silver & Bronze Awards

Trade Less Than A Page B/W Or Color: Single

34 GOLD
ART DIRECTOR
Jim Mountjoy
WRITER
Ed Jones
PHOTOGRAPHER
Bettman Archives
CLIENT
JTA Talent
AGENCY
Loeffler Ketchum Mountjoy/Charlotte, NC

35 SILVER
ART DIRECTOR
Lloyd Wolfe
WRITER
Mark Deschenes
PHOTOGRAPHER
Mark Alexander
CLIENT
Lloyd Wolfe
AGENCY
Lloyd Wolfe/Overland Park, KS

36 BRONZE
ART DIRECTOR
Larry Jarvis
WRITER
Glen Wachowiak
CLIENT
Portfolio Center
AGENCY
Bozell Jacobs Kenyon & Eckhardt/Minneapolis

THE WRONG TALENT CAN RUIN A GREAT CONCEPT.
Call JTA Talent • 704-377-5987

34 GOLD

Hire A Terrific Art Director And Get
A Mediocre Copywriter Absolutely Free.

I'm an Art Director and I wrote most of the headlines in my book.

That's not the way advertising is supposed to work. (Imagine if copywriters did all the layouts.)

I'm looking for a place where I can work with good writers and do great work.

If I were working with a good writer right now, he'd probably know how to end this.

Lloyd Wolfe

3639 Monteith Avenue/Cincinnati, Ohio 45208/(513) 321-6427

35 SILVER

FINALLY, A SCHOOL THAT TEACHES YOU HOW TO CONCEIVE.

Behind every great ad there's a great idea.
Why not go to a school that recognizes that?

PORTFOLIO CENTER

125 Bennet St. N.W., Atlanta, GA 30309. (404) 351-5055

36 BRONZE

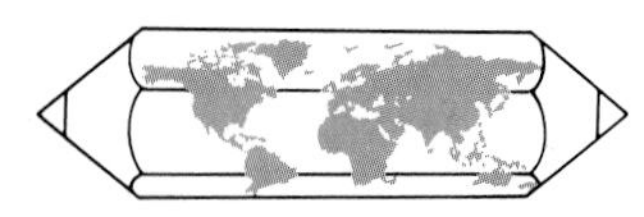

Gold, Silver & Bronze Awards

Trade Any Size B/W Or Color: Campaign

37 GOLD

ART DIRECTOR
Bob Phillips

WRITER
Tom Thomas

ARTIST
Ron Barrett

PHOTOGRAPHERS
John Alcorn
Robert Ammirati

CLIENT
Barron's

AGENCY
Angotti Thomas Hedge

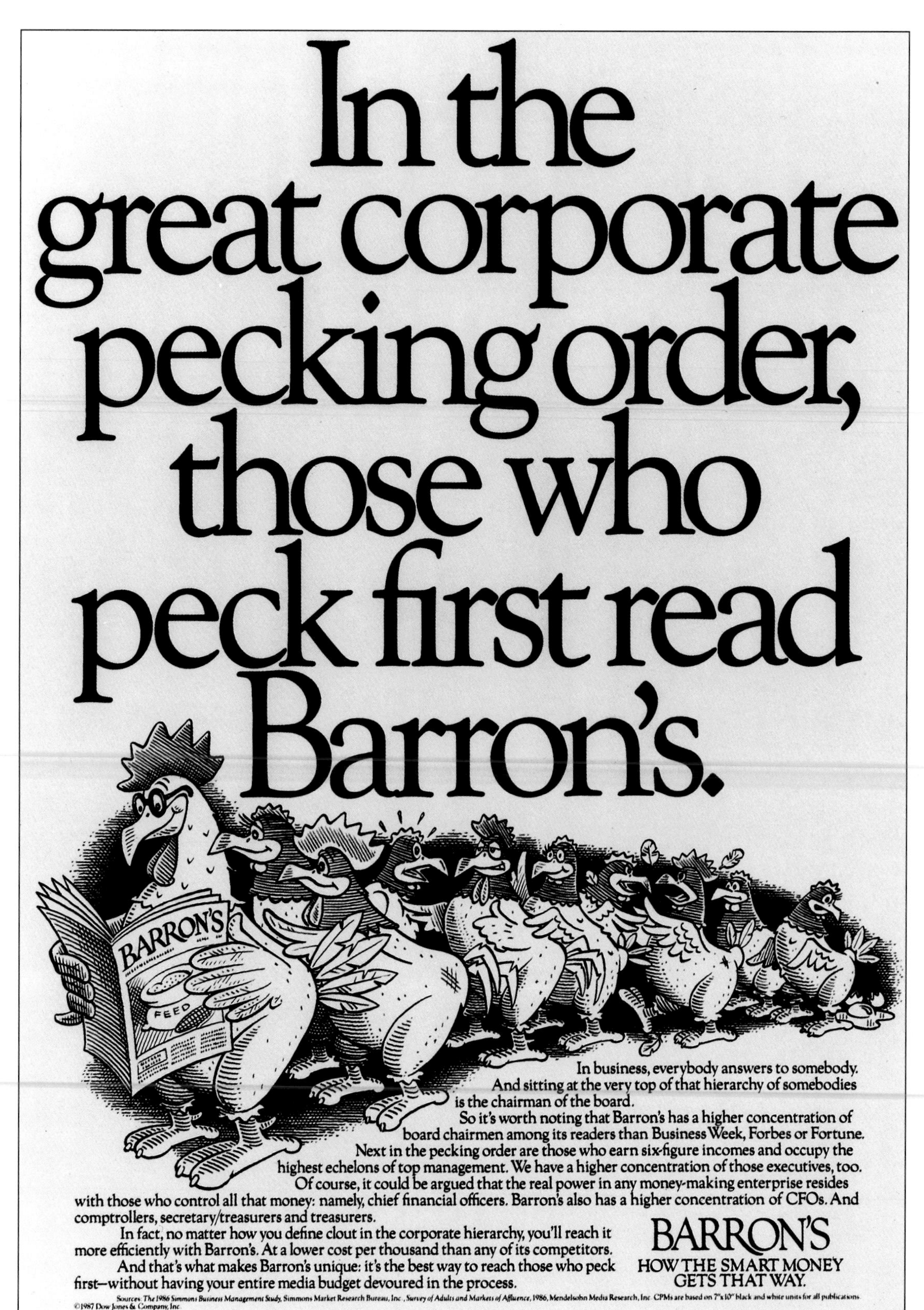

37 GOLD

Millionaires aren't a dime a dozen. Actually, they run about 2¢ each.

The exact figure is 2.41 cents for every millionaire we deliver.

Which, as a little comparison shopping will show, is well below the going rate for the rich.

Barron's offers a lower cost per thousand—and per millionaire—than Business Week, Forbes or Fortune. And they're available in quantities considerably larger than a dozen. Or a hundred. Or a hundred thousand.

In fact, 37% of Barron's readers are millionaires. And that just includes their own household assets.

They also control or influence millions more in corporate assets. Because Barron's readers represent a greater concentration of highly paid decision-makers than any other major business or financial magazine.

Of course, you can still reach such people through those other magazines. All it takes is a willingness to pay more for them.

Which is definitely not the recommended way to become a millionaire—or to buy one.

HOW THE SMART MONEY GETS THAT WAY.

Sources: Survey of Adults and Markets of Affluence, 1986, Mendelsohn Media Research, Inc. CPMs are based on 7" x 10" black and white units for all publications. © DOW JONES & COMPANY, INC

Breakfast Of Millionaires.

You're familiar with what's called the coffee table magazine.

Barron's is something else: a breakfast table magazine.

Every Saturday morning, Barron's reaches the rich and powerful all over America. In fact, an astonishing 37% of all Barron's readers are millionaires.

And unlike magazines that sit on coffee tables and are read with no special urgency (if at all), Barron's is read only hours after it's published.

Eighty-six percent of Barron's readers who go out and buy it on newsstands read it the weekend it appears. For an average of *two* hours an issue.

The importance of all this for advertisers is clear—especially if you've ever suspected that your advertising is languishing somewhere in dens, magazine racks and waiting rooms.

The way to a millionaire's heart may or may not be through his stomach. But the way to his mind is definitely through Barron's.

BARRON'S
HOW THE SMART MONEY GETS THAT WAY.

Sources: Survey of Adults and Markets of Affluence, 1986, Mendelsohn Media Research, Inc.; Portrait of the Inner Circle, Erdos and Morgan, 1985. © 1987 Dow Jones & Company, Inc.

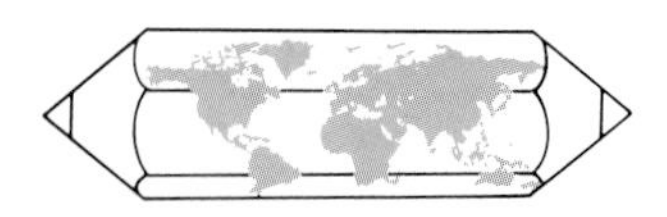

Gold, Silver & Bronze Awards

Trade Any Size B/W Or Color: Campaign

38 SILVER

ART DIRECTOR
Rich Silverstein

WRITER
David Fowler

PHOTOGRAPHER
Mark Hauser

CLIENT
Communication Arts Magazine

AGENCY
Goodby Berlin & Silverstein/San Francisco

"WHY DOESN'T ANYBODY STEAL THE MAGAZINES I DESIGN?"
ROGER BLACK
ART DIRECTOR
TRIPS MAGAZINE
SAN FRANCISCO
The New York Times Magazine
Lennon
Newsweek
YES, THERE ARE SNAPPIER PUBLICATIONS. BUT WHEN WAS THE LAST TIME YOU ROOTED THROUGH YOUR PARTNER'S OFFICE TO FIND ONE? SUBSCRIBE VIA MARY AT (415) 326-6040.
COMMUNICATION ARTS

38 SILVER

"This is my complete collection. Minus the ones Gorman, Johns, and Hayden stole."
Lee Clow, President
Executive Creative Director
Chiat/Day
Los Angeles
FOR 30 YEARS, GOOD PEOPLE HAVE TAKEN CA. MAYBE IT'S TIME A FEW MORE OF THEM SUBSCRIBED.
MARY, OUR SUBSCRIPTION WHIZ, STANDS READY AT (415) 326-6040.
COMMUNICATION ARTS

"Eddie here understands very clearly that the agency copy always comes to me first."
Phil Dusenberry
Chairman
Chief Creative Officer
BBDO
New York
Eddie Hooper
Mailroom Clerk
BBDO
New York
IF YOU THINK THE AGENCY COPY WILL EVENTUALLY TURN UP, THERE ARE A LOT OF PEOPLE WAY AHEAD OF YOU.
TO AVOID THE LINE, SUBSCRIBE VIA MARY, AT (415) 326-6040.
COMMUNICATION ARTS

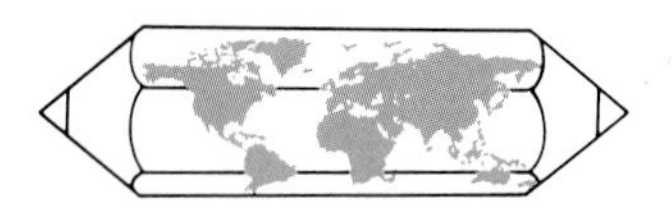

Gold, Silver & Bronze Awards

Trade Any Size B/W Or Color: Campaign

39 BRONZE

ART DIRECTOR
Bob Barrie

WRITER
Jarl Olsen

DESIGNER
Bob Barrie

PHOTOGRAPHER
Rick Dublin

CLIENT
Hush Puppies Shoe Company

AGENCY
Fallon McElligott/ Minneapolis

Sophisticated Hush Puppies.
Supple leather with the look of reptile. For those with a nose for the finer things.

39 BRONZE

Casual Hush Puppies.
These comfortable leather shoes are as laid-back as a Saturday afternoon.
Perfect for shopping, errands or just hanging out.

Old Yeller
Old Yeller
F. Gipson
Classic Hush Puppies.
We have all our favorites leather bound.

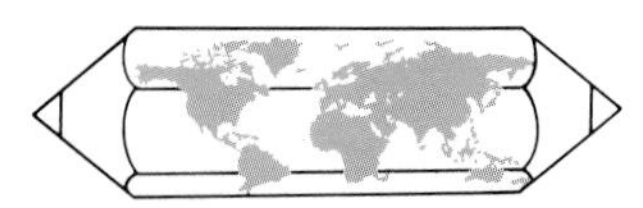

Gold, Silver & Bronze Awards

Collateral Brochures Other Than By Mail: Single

40 GOLD

ART DIRECTORS
Nancy Rice
Nick Rice

WRITER
Jim Newcombe

DESIGNERS
Roger Christensen
Great Faces

PHOTOGRAPHER
Marvy!

CLIENT
The One Show

AGENCY
Rice & Rice/Minneapolis

41 SILVER

ART DIRECTOR
Bob Brihn

WRITER
Jamie Barrett

PHOTOGRAPHER
Mark LaFavor

CLIENT
Hush Puppies Shoe Company

AGENCY
Fallon McElligott/Minneapolis

42 BRONZE

ART DIRECTOR
Clive Jackson

WRITER
Simon Linton

DESIGNER
Clive Jackson

PHOTOGRAPHER
John Claridge

CLIENT
Midwales Development

AGENCY
Garratt Baulcombe/FCB - Nottingham

Welcome to another evening of whining and dining.

40 GOLD

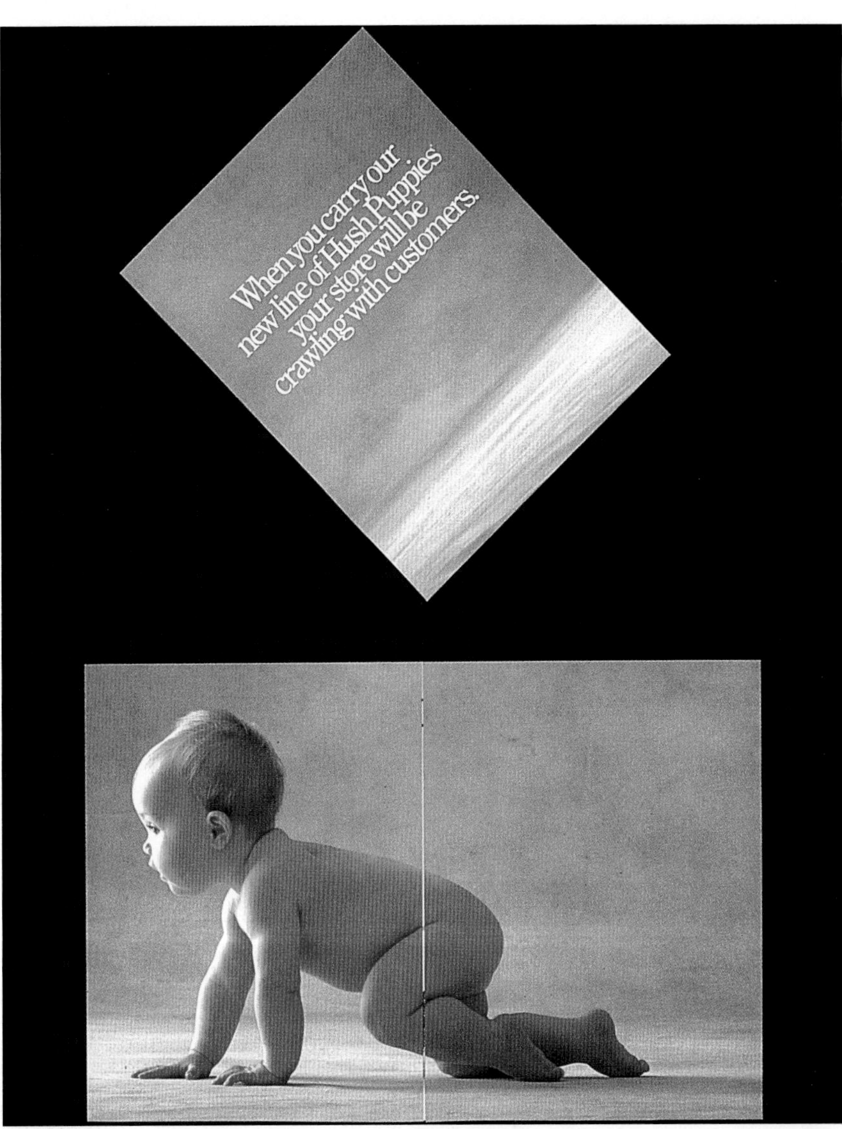

41 SILVER

42 BRONZE

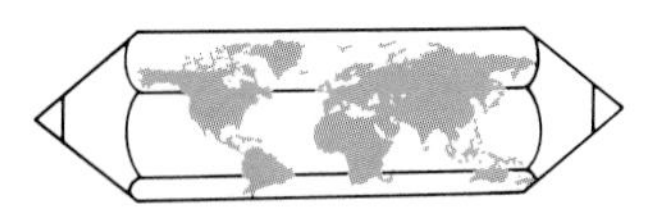

Gold, Silver & Bronze Awards

Collateral Sales Kits: Single

43 GOLD

ART DIRECTOR
Mark Johnson

WRITER
Tom McElligott

PHOTOGRAPHER
Dan Lamb

CLIENT
Hush Puppies Shoe Company

AGENCY
Fallon McElligott/ Minneapolis

44 SILVER

ART DIRECTOR
Frank Schulwolf

WRITER
Arthur Low

ARTISTS
Mark English
James Dietz
Ted Lodigensky

PHOTOGRAPHER
George Schiavone

CLIENT
Ryder System Aviation Leasing & Services

AGENCY
Susan Gilbert & Company/ Coral Gables, FL

45 BRONZE

ART DIRECTOR
Frank Schulwolf

WRITER
Arthur Low

ARTISTS
John Mattos
Paul Salmon
Ted Lodigensky

PHOTOGRAPHER
George Schiavone

CLIENT
Ryder System Aviation Leasing & Services

AGENCY
Susan Gilbert & Company/ Coral Gables, FL

For years, Hush Puppies® has led the shoe industry in brand awareness. However, when people think of us, most still think of the original suede Hush Puppies® shoe we first sold in 1958.
But that's all about to change.
In the fall, our new advertising campaign will break in national magazines like Time, People, US, Newsweek, and Life. Full color spreads of the Hush Puppies celebrities will show off this year's line. Which has been updated and now contains over 130 attractive styles for men, women and children.
Plus, we're supporting our advertising efforts with an excit-
Sweepstakes that will really drive our message home.
to help you keep up with the demand, we'll give you
so you can restock immediately anytime of
stock up on Hush Puppies, America's best loved
and your store will make a great pair.
call (616)874-8448 and ask for: John
VP, Men's shoes or Ray Sessa, VP, General
Match the faces to the Hush Puppies.

43 GOLD

44 SILVER

45 BRONZE

Gold, Silver & Bronze Awards

Collateral Sales Kits: Campaign

46 GOLD

ART DIRECTOR
Frank Schulwolf

WRITER
Arthur Low

ARTISTS
Mark English
James Dietz
Ted Lodigensky
John Mattos
Paul Salmon

CLIENT
Ryder System Aviation Leasing & Services

AGENCY
Susan Gilbert & Company/
Coral Gables, FL

46 GOLD

Brits
Brits
B4863

THE
Boche

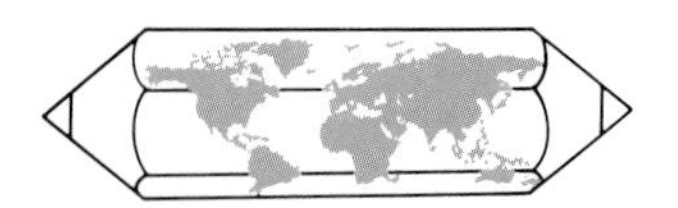

Gold, Silver & Bronze Awards

Collateral Direct Mail: Single

47 GOLD

ART DIRECTORS
Nancy Rice
Nick Rice

WRITER
Jim Newcombe

DESIGNERS
Roger Christensen
Great Faces

PHOTOGRAPHER
Marvy!

CLIENT
The One Show

AGENCY
Rice & Rice/Minneapolis

48 SILVER

ART DIRECTOR
Terrell Daniels

WRITER
Virg Viner

PHOTOGRAPHER
Jim Williams

CLIENT
Campbell-Mithun

AGENCY
Campbell-Mithun/
Minneapolis

49 BRONZE

ART DIRECTOR
Frank Schulwolf

WRITER
Arthur Low

ARTISTS
Mark English
James Dietz
Ted Lodigensky

CLIENT
Ryder System Aviation
Leasing & Services

AGENCY
Susan Gilbert & Company/
Coral Gables, FL

47 GOLD

48 SILVER

49 BRONZE

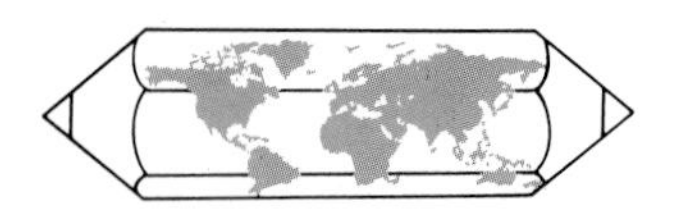

Gold, Silver & Bronze Awards

Collateral Direct Mail: Campaign

50 GOLD

ART DIRECTOR
Frank Schulwolf

WRITER
Arthur Low

CLIENT
Ryder System Aviation Leasing & Services

AGENCY
Susan Gilbert & Company/
Coral Gables, FL

50 GOLD

FRENCHY

The Boche

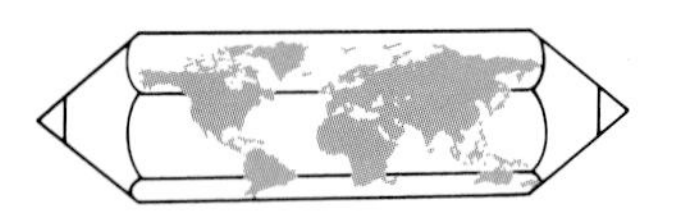

Gold, Silver & Bronze Awards

Collateral Direct Mail: Campaign

51 SILVER

ART DIRECTOR
Billy Wilson

WRITERS
Don Jeffries
Joann Jeffries

PHOTOGRAPHER
Roger Ball

CLIENT
Rebound, Christian Rehabilitation Center

AGENCY
Wray/Ward Advertising - Charlotte, NC

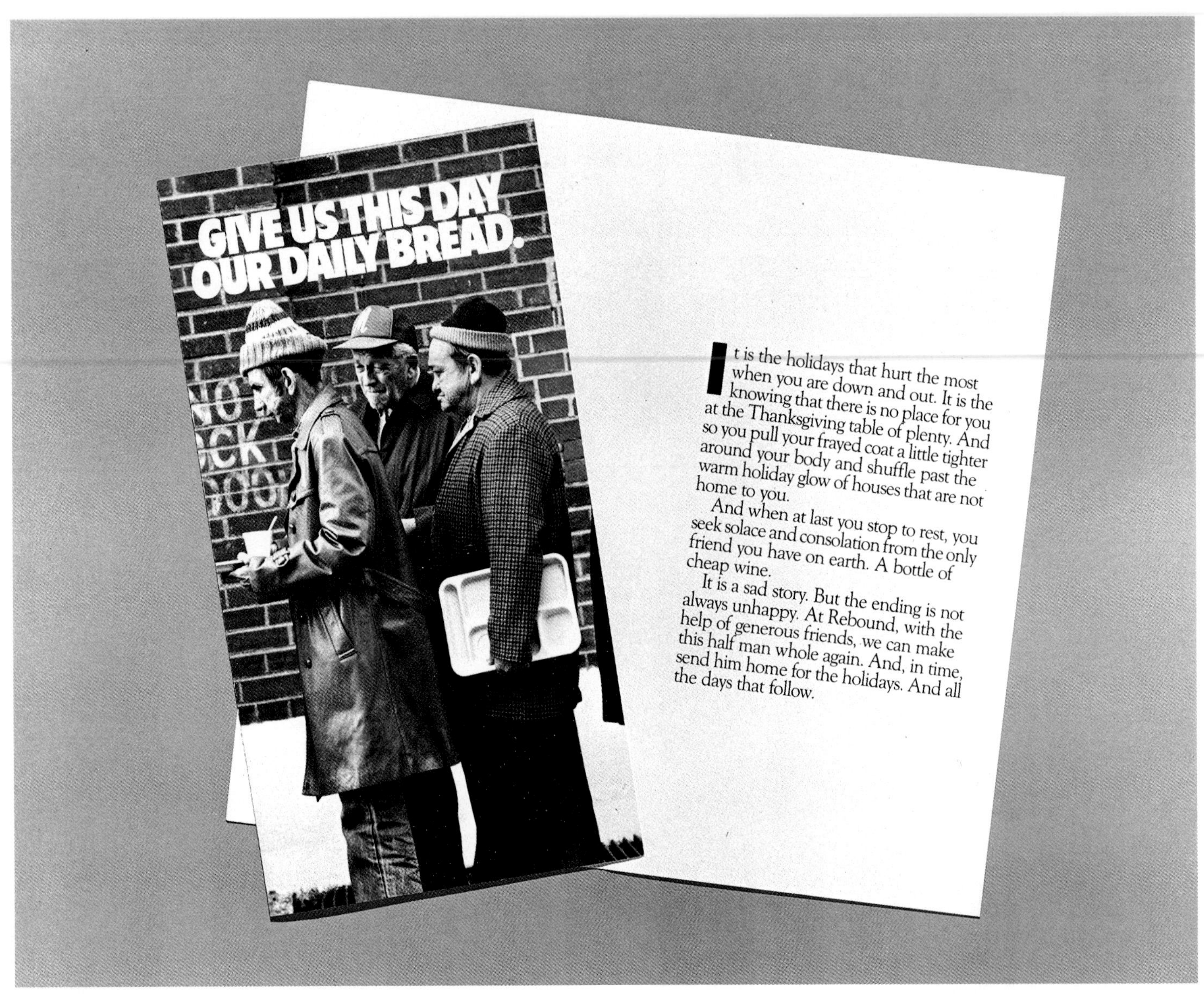

GIVE US THIS DAY OUR DAILY BREAD.
It is the holidays that hurt the most when you are down and out. It is the knowing that there is no place for you at the Thanksgiving table of plenty. And so you pull your frayed coat a little tighter around your body and shuffle past the warm holiday glow of houses that are not home to you.
And when at last you stop to rest, you seek solace and consolation from the only friend you have on earth. A bottle of cheap wine.
It is a sad story. But the ending is not always unhappy. At Rebound, with the help of generous friends, we can make this half man whole again. And, in time, send him home for the holidays. And all the days that follow.

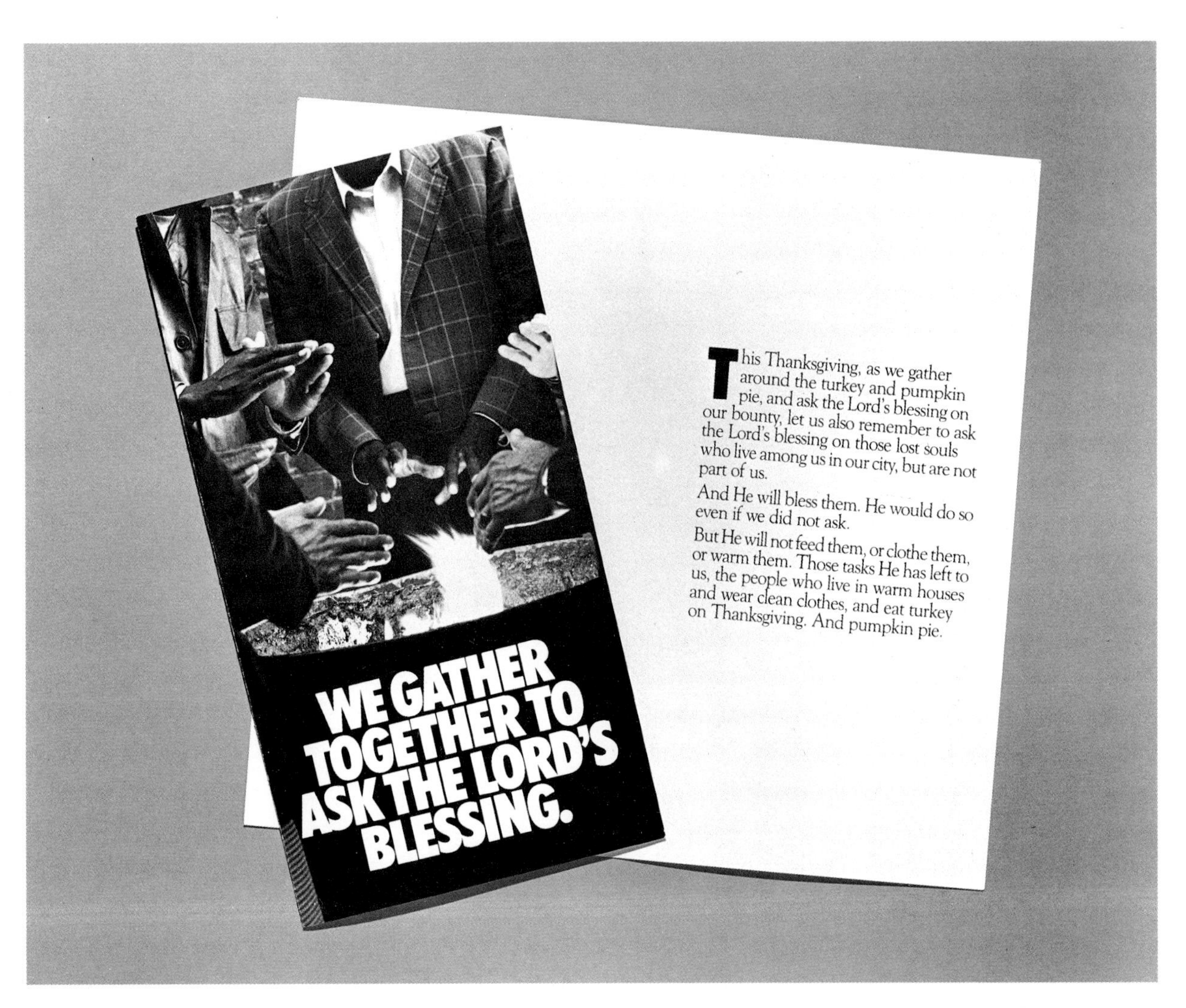
WE GATHER TOGETHER TO ASK THE LORD'S BLESSING.
This Thanksgiving, as we gather around the turkey and pumpkin pie, and ask the Lord's blessing on our bounty, let us also remember to ask the Lord's blessing on those lost souls who live among us in our city, but are not part of us.
And He will bless them. He would do so even if we did not ask.
But He will not feed them, or clothe them, or warm them. Those tasks He has left to us, the people who live in warm houses and wear clean clothes, and eat turkey on Thanksgiving. And pumpkin pie.

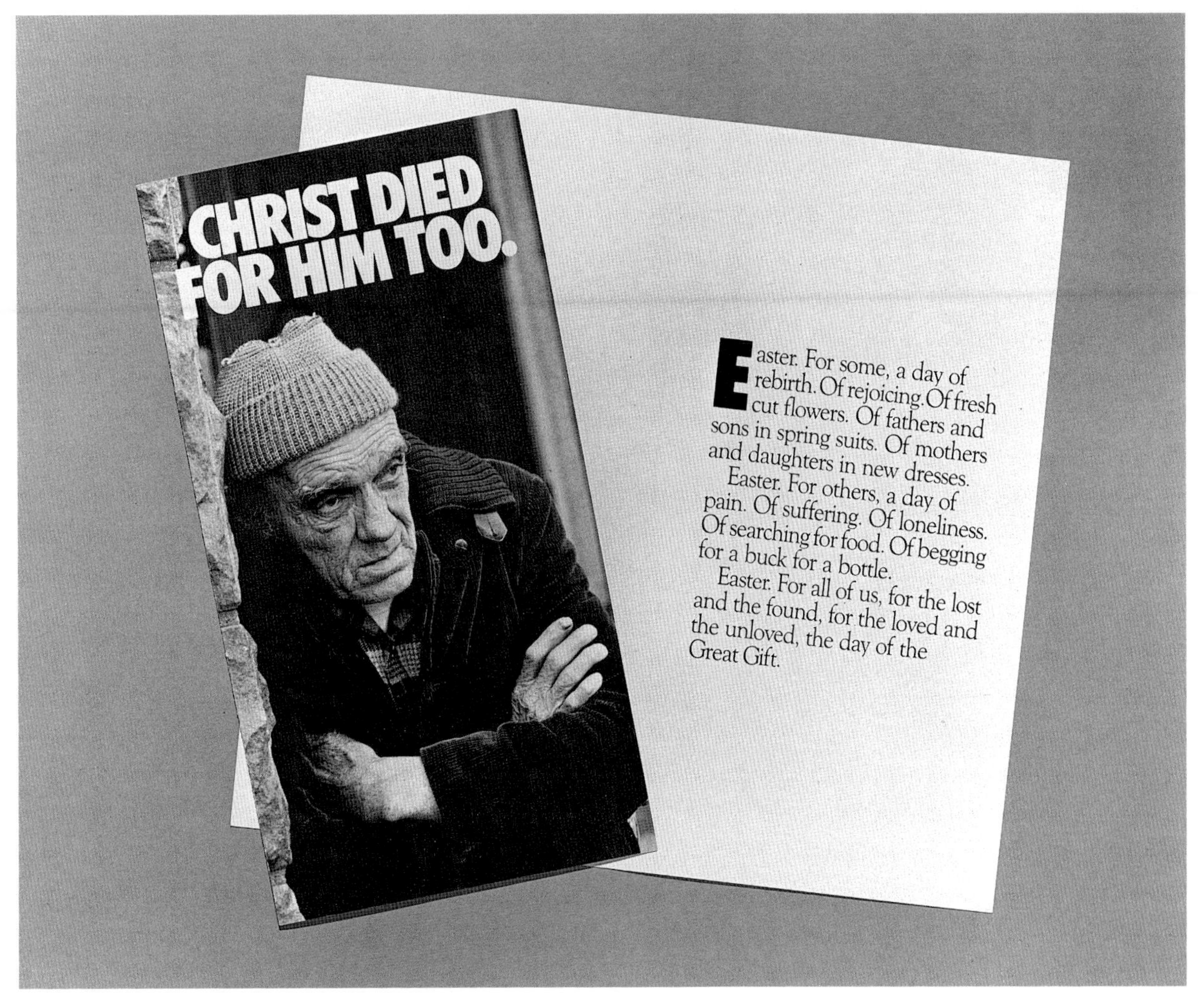
CHRIST DIED FOR HIM TOO.
Easter. For some, a day of rebirth. Of rejoicing. Of fresh cut flowers. Of fathers and sons in spring suits. Of mothers and daughters in new dresses.
Easter. For others, a day of pain. Of suffering. Of loneliness. Of searching for food. Of begging for a buck for a bottle.
Easter. For all of us, for the lost and the found, for the loved and the unloved, the day of the Great Gift.

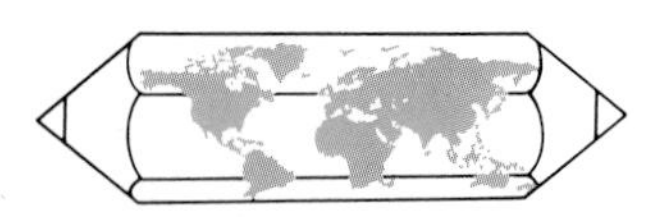

Gold, Silver & Bronze Awards

Collateral Direct Mail: Campaign

52 BRONZE

ART DIRECTOR
Craig Hadorn

WRITER
Craig Jackson

CLIENT
Price/McNabb

AGENCY
Price/McNabb - Raleigh, NC

52 BRONZE

WHAT GOES BEST WITH A KOSHER GHERKIN?

UNORTHODOX ADVERTISING.

What it does for a gherkin it'll do for any pickle. Call Price/McNabb, Raleigh at 872-8180 and ask for Ron Campana.

HOW'D YOU LIKE TO CLIMB ALL OVER MT. OLIVE?

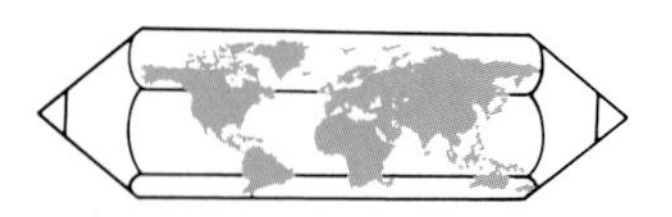

Gold, Silver & Bronze Awards

Collateral
P.O.P

53 GOLD

ART DIRECTORS
Nancy Rice
Nick Rice

WRITER
Jim Newcombe

DESIGNERS
Roger Christensen
Great Faces

PHOTOGRAPHER
Marvy!

CLIENT
The One Show

AGENCY
Rice & Rice/Minneapolis

54 SILVER

ART DIRECTOR
Chuck Anderson

WRITER
Jarl Olsen

PHOTOGRAPHER
Rick Dublin

CLIENT
Harry Singh's

AGENCY
Fallon McElligott/
Minneapolis

55 BRONZE

ART DIRECTOR
Bob Barrie

WRITER
Jarl Olsen

DESIGNER
Bob Barrie

PHOTOGRAPHER
Rick Dublin

CLIENT
Hush Puppies Shoe
Company

AGENCY
Fallon McElligott/
Minneapolis

Announcing another evening of whining and dining.

ONE SHOW AWARD

The level of complaints can tell you a lot about the level of quality at an awards show. The One Show is no exception. However, one thing no one can complain about is this year's party. It's at the Palladium. (Which is about the only place harder to get into than the One Show.) Compared to years past, there'll be less sitting down. And more getting down. But this year, don't come as you are. Come as you want to be. Dressed in gold, silver or bronze. The One Show. Where the whine list is sure to be longer than the winners list.

Thursday, June 4, 1987 • The Palladium, 14th Street at Irving Place • Cocktails and food, 5:30 to 7:00 • Awards presentation, 7:30 to 9:30 • Party, 9:30 on • $110 per person

Separations: Weston Engraving • Type: Great Faces • Keyline: Production Artists • Printing: Process Displays • Photography: Marvy Photography

53 GOLD

The hottest dishes in town.
HARRY SINGH'S
CARIBBEAN RESTAURANT
611 W. Lake St., Minneapolis/Lake at Lyndale.

54 SILVER

Corporate Hush Puppies.
Dress Lites with our super-lightweight soles. They'll make someone at the office drool.

55 BRONZE

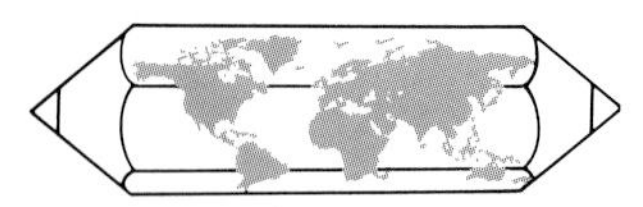

Gold, Silver & Bronze Awards

Outdoor: Single

56 GOLD
ART DIRECTOR
Larry Corby
WRITER
Peter Angelos
PHOTOGRAPHER
Patrice Meigneux
CLIENT
Sunkist Growers
AGENCY
Foote Cone & Belding/ Los Angeles

57 SILVER
ART DIRECTOR
Andy Dijak
WRITER
Bill Stenton
PHOTOGRAPHER
Jeffrey Zwart
CLIENT
Porsche Cars North America
AGENCY
Chiat/Day - Venice, CA

58 BRONZE
ART DIRECTORS
Ted Shaine
Alain Briere
WRITER
Helayne Spivak
PHOTOGRAPHER
Roy Volkman
CLIENT
Club Med
AGENCY
Ammirati & Puris

Outdoor: Campaign

59 GOLD
ART DIRECTORS
Ted Shaine
Alain Briere
WRITER
Helayne Spivak
PHOTOGRAPHERS
Roy Volkman
Stephen Frink
CLIENT
Club Med
AGENCY
Ammirati & Puris

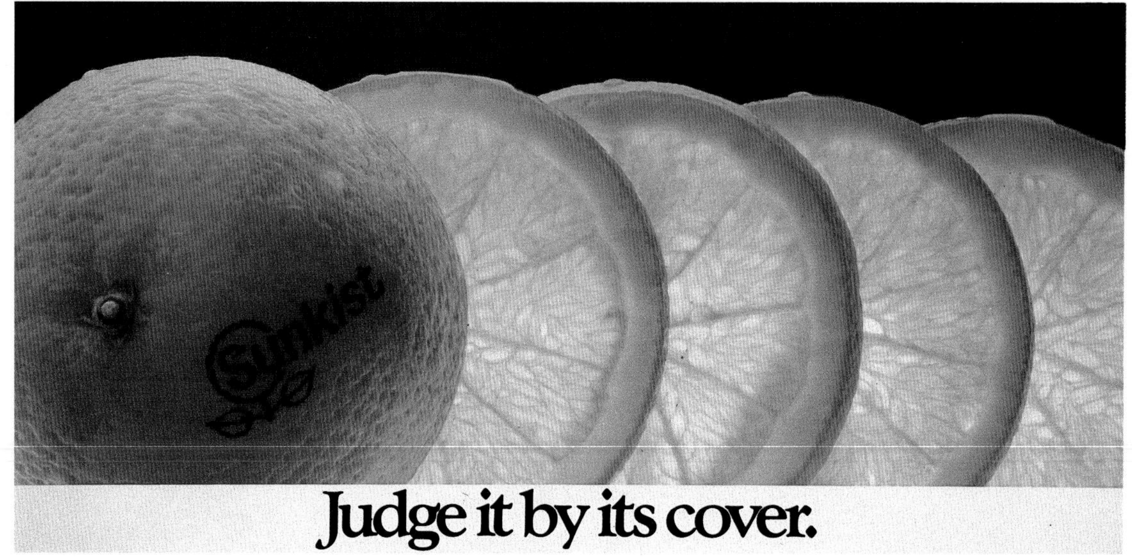

56 GOLD

In Germany there are no getaway cars.
POLIZEI
(Dealer Name)
©1987 Porsche Cars North America, Inc.

57 SILVER

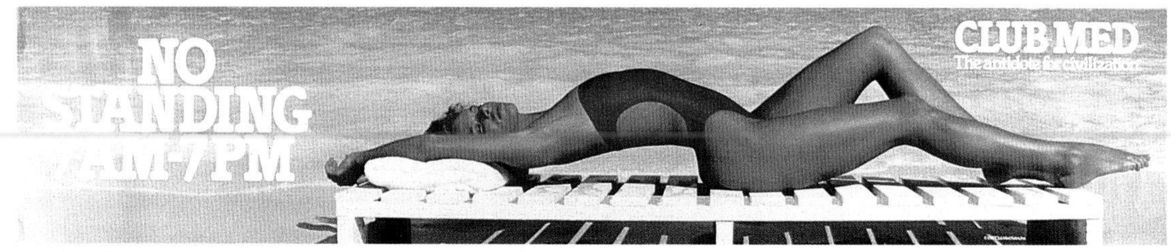

58 BRONZE

NO
STANDING
7 AM-7 PM
CLUB MED
The antidote for civilization.

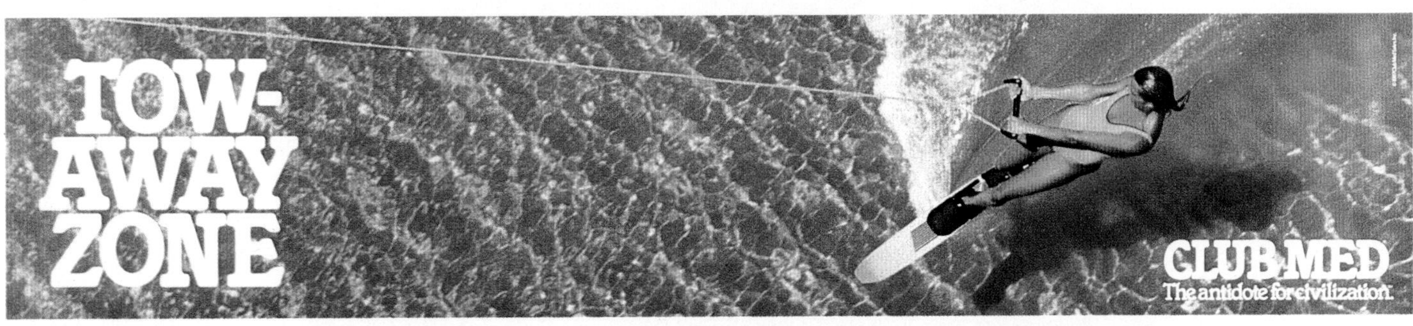
TOW-
AWAY
ZONE
CLUB MED
The antidote for civilization.

CLUB MED
The antidote for civilization.
SCHOOL
CROSSING

59 GOLD

Gold, Silver & Bronze Awards

Outdoor: Campaign

60 SILVER
ART DIRECTOR
Steve Sweitzer
WRITER
Jarl Olsen
PHOTOGRAPHER
Ben Saltzman
CLIENT
Ben Saltzman Photography
AGENCY
Fallon McElligott/
Minneapolis

60 SILVER

© 1987
Ben Saltzman
Photographer

© 1987
Ben Saltzman
Photographer

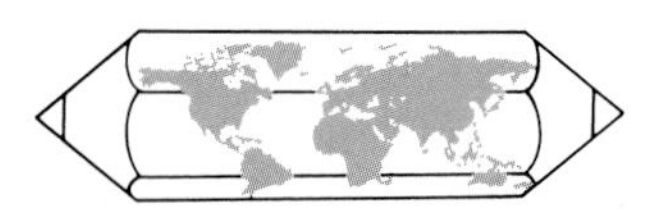

Gold, Silver & Bronze Awards

Outdoor: Campaign

61 BRONZE

ART DIRECTOR
Tom Lichtenheld

WRITER
Rod Kilpatrick

ARTIST
Art Simons

PHOTOGRAPHERS
Kent Severson
Steve Umland

CLIENT
The Wall Street Journal

AGENCY
Fallon McElligott/
Minneapolis

What's the matter, don't you get it?

To subscribe to The Wall Street Journal, call 800-453-6606.

61 BRONZE

Read all about it.

To subscribe to The Wall Street Journal, call 800-453-6606.

The Wall Street Journal.
The daily diary of the American dream.

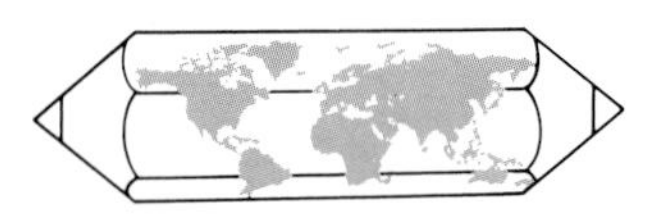

Gold, Silver & Bronze Awards

Public Service Newspaper Or Magazine: Single

62 GOLD
ART DIRECTOR
Wayne Gibson
WRITER
Luke Sullivan
CLIENT
People for the Ethical Treatment of Animals
AGENCY
The Martin Agency/ Richmond, VA

63 SILVER
ART DIRECTOR
Wayne Gibson
WRITER
Luke Sullivan
CLIENT
People for the Ethical Treatment of Animals
AGENCY
The Martin Agency/ Richmond, VA

64 BRONZE
ART DIRECTOR
Wayne Gibson
WRITER
Luke Sullivan
CLIENT
People for the Ethical Treatment of Animals
AGENCY
The Martin Agency/ Richmond, VA

Imagine having your body left to science while you're still in it.

Three animals die every second in U.S. laboratories.

The monkey pictured here was surgically crippled and then forced to use his deadened arm.

Other animals, including rabbits, dogs, and cats are routinely blinded, shocked, mutilated, decapitated and force-fed poisons in tests which could easily be replaced with modern and more reliable alternative tests.

These sadistic animal tests are being conducted by the government, universities, medical associations, and profit-making corporations.

And always behind closed, locked doors. Pigs, rats, chickens, horses and other laboratory animals suffer by the millions.

The cost to U.S. taxpayers, however, is in the billions.

If you think these kinds of cruel experiments have no place in the 20th century, please join us: People for the Ethical Treatment of Animals.

PETA is America's leading animal rights organization. By working with medical and legal professionals, the media, members of Congress, and people like you, PETA has been able to stop some of the most horrifying animal experiments, including the one pictured here.

Even as you read this ad, there are thousands more lab experiments being conducted without your knowledge, *but with your tax dollars.*

So please join us today.

Yes, I want to help stop the abuse of animals in experiments.

Name ______
Address ______
City ______ State ______ Zip ______
Please accept my tax-deductible contribution of: $15 ______
$25 ______ $50 ______ $100 ______ other ______

Contributors of $15 or more receive a free copy of the book *Animal Liberation.*

People For The Ethical Treatment Of Animals

P.O. Box 42516 Washington, D.C. 20015 (202) 726-0156

62 GOLD

If you can't look at these pictures, look at the coupon.

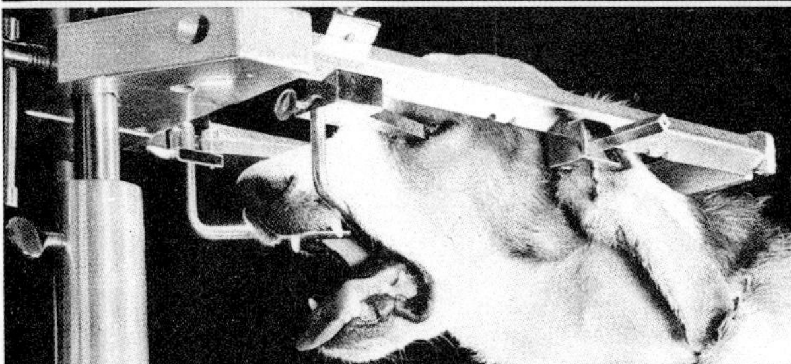

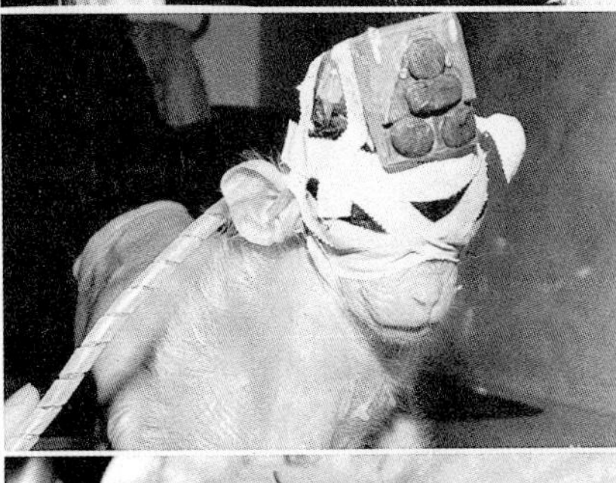

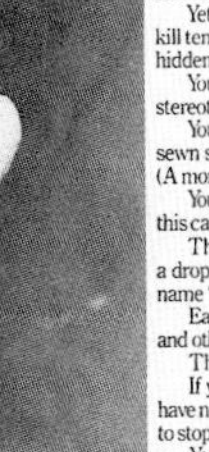

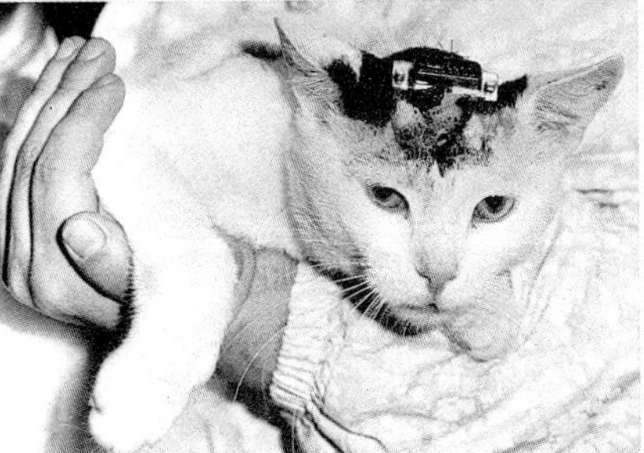

Animal experiments are crude, cruel and scientifically unnecessary.

Yet, each year $4 billion in our taxes helps kill tens of millions of animals in laboratories hidden all across the country.

Your taxes paid to put this dog in a painful stereotaxic device, after which he was killed.

Your taxes paid to have this monkey's eyes sewn shut and electrodes sunk into her brain. (A monkey we later managed to save.)

Your taxes paid to have electrodes sunk into this cat's brain. (We managed to save her, too.)

The few atrocities you've read here are just a drop in the bucket of blood that goes by the name "animal research" in America today.

Each year, cats, dogs, pigs, rats, monkeys and other animals suffer and die by the millions.

The cost to taxpayers is in the *billions*.

If you believe these kinds of experiments have no place in the 20th century, please help us to stop them.

Your tax-deductible donation can help us to stop this barbaric and useless cruelty.

People for the Ethical Treatment of Animals (PETA) is America's number one organization supporting the rights of animals.

By working with the media, medical and legal professionals, members of Congress and people like you, PETA has been able to halt funding to some of the country's most sadistic and horrifying animal experiments.

But, even as you read this ad, thousands of atrocities are still being conducted.

Please join us today.

Yes, I want to help stop the abuse of animals in experiments.

Name ______

Address ______

City ______ State ______ Zip ______

Please accept my tax deductible contribution of: $15 ______

$25 ______ $50 ______ $100 ______ other ______

Contributors of $15 or more receive a free copy of the book *Animal Liberation*.

People For The Ethical Treatment Of Animals

P.O. Box [illegible] Washington, D.C. [illegible]

63 SILVER

These animals aren't being tortured in the name of science. It's in the name of a new shampoo.

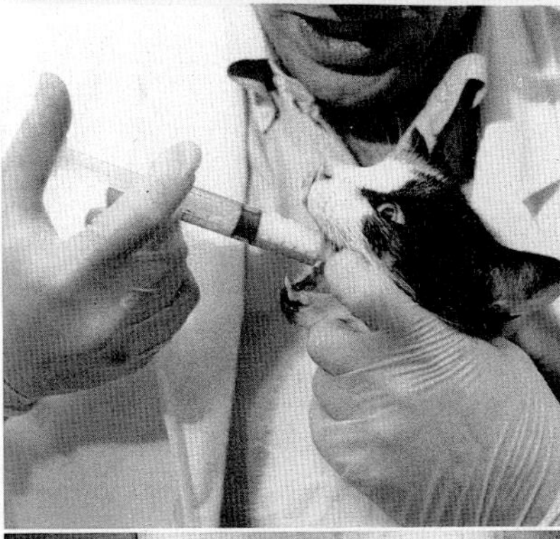

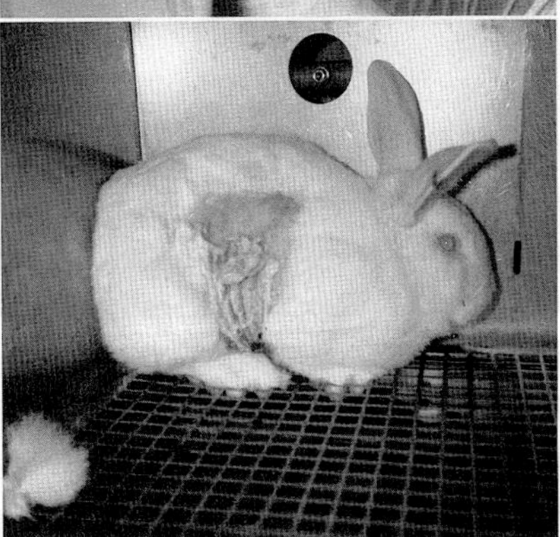

Each year, millions of animals are slaughtered in U.S. laboratories.

At least 70% of them suffer and die in archaic *non*-medical experiments— to test cosmetics, gasoline, detergents and oven cleaners.

Yet scientists know that the amount of detergent it takes to kill a cat has nothing to do with the amount that it would take to kill a human being.

Toxic ingredients affect different species differently.

If the results of animal experiments don't help protect the health of people, *why* do corporations conduct them?

Because these tests allow them to hide behind the claim that their product has been "safety-tested" if they are sued for damages caused by their product.

But there are products which have never caused any animal to suffer.

More than 100 U.S. companies have shunned all animal experiments.

They use ingredients which are already known to be safe and effective. Won't you help these companies grow?

We can supply you with a list of "cruelty-free" products.

We're called People for the Ethical Treatment of Animals.

We work with medical and legal professionals, the media, members of Congress and people like you to expose this animal abuse and tax waste in the animal experimentation industry.

We've brought an end to a lot of these horror stories but thousands of other cruel experiments are being conducted even as you read this ad.

Please join us today. And thank you.

Please send me information on "Cruelty-Free" products.

Name ______

Address ______

City ______ State ______ Zip ______

Please accept my tax-deductible contribution of: $15 ______

$25 ______ $50 ______ $100 ______ other ______

Contributors of $15 or more receive a free copy of the book *Animal Liberation*.

People For The Ethical Treatment Of Animals

P.O. Box [illegible] Washington, D.C. [illegible]

64 BRONZE

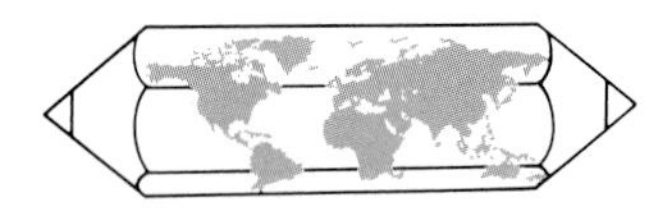

Gold, Silver & Bronze Awards

Public Service Newspaper Or Magazine: Campaign

65 GOLD

ART DIRECTOR
Wayne Gibson

WRITER
Luke Sullivan

CLIENT
People for the Ethical Treatment of Animals

AGENCY
The Martin Agency/ Richmond, VA

Imagine having your body left to science while you're still in it.

Three animals die every second in U.S. laboratories.

The monkey pictured here was surgically crippled and then forced to use his deadened arm.

Other animals, including rabbits, dogs, and cats are routinely blinded, shocked, mutilated, decapitated and force-fed poisons in tests which could easily be replaced with modern and more reliable alternative tests.

These sadistic animal tests are being conducted by the government, universities, medical associations, and profit-making corporations.

And always behind closed, locked doors. Pigs, rats, chickens, horses and other laboratory animals suffer by the millions.

The cost to U.S. taxpayers, however, is in the billions.

If you think these kinds of cruel experiments have no place in the 20th century, please join us: People for the Ethical Treatment of Animals.

PETA is America's leading animal rights organization. By working with medical and legal professionals, the media, members of Congress, and people like you, PETA has been able to stop some of the most horrifying animal experiments, including the one pictured here.

Even as you read this ad, there are thousands more lab experiments being conducted without your knowledge, *but with your tax dollars.*

So please join us today.

Yes, I want to help stop the abuse of animals in experiments.

Name ______

Address ______

City ______ State ______ Zip ______

Please accept my tax-deductible contribution of: $15 ______

$25 ______ $50 ______ $100 ______ other ______

Contributors of $15 or more receive a free copy of the book *Animal Liberation.*

People For The Ethical Treatment Of Animals

P.O. Box 42516 Washington, D.C. 20015 (202) 726-0156

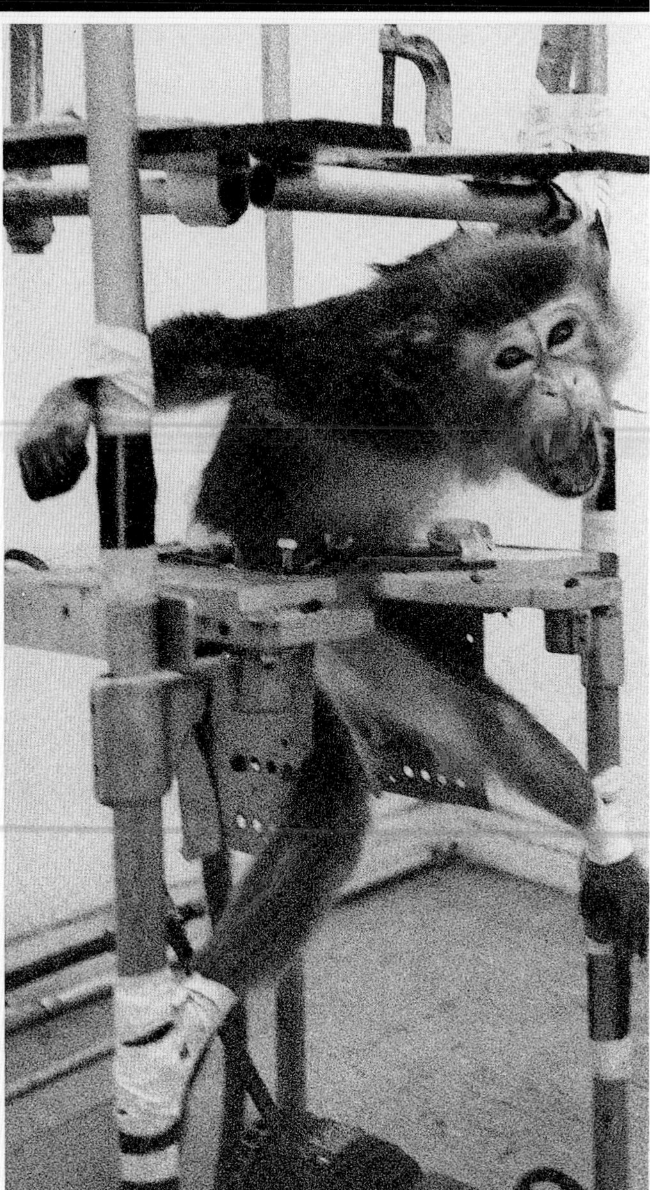

Thanks to a $12 million government grant, scientists have conclusive proof that monkeys die when their skulls are crushed.

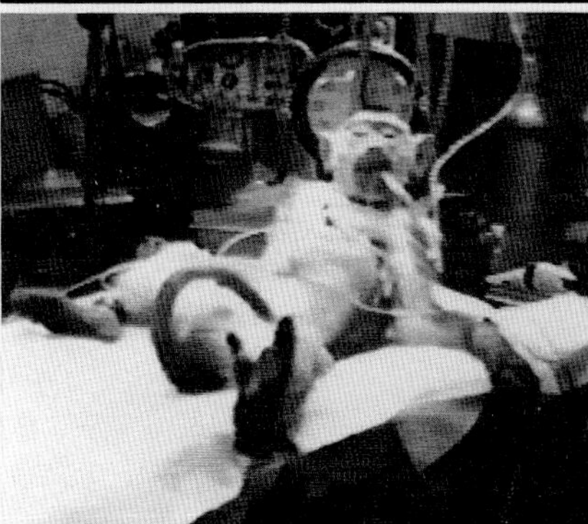

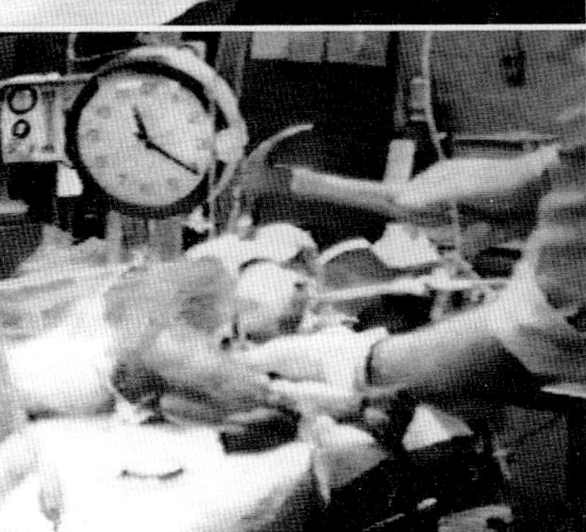

Did you know what other "experiments" that you've helped underwrite with your hard-earned tax dollars?

You paid to have a group of grown men keep a group of cats awake for a week straight.

Cats that were then placed on floating pieces of wood to see how long the cats' fear of falling in would keep them awake. Proving exactly what? Anything?

Care for another? To test the effectiveness of the Heimlich maneuver (already well-documented as effective), another federally-funded lab wanted to drown some dogs.

Fortunately, the scientists were drowned with letters instead (thanks to an effort by our organization) and the experiment was called off.

That experiment isn't the only one we've managed to have had scrapped.

We helped raise such an outroar over the head-injury research on the monkeys you see in these pictures, that it was closed down.

But for every sadistic and scientifically worthless experiment we've shut down, there are literally thousands we haven't.

People For The Ethical Treatment Of Animals (PETA) works with medical and legal professionals, the media, members of Congress, and people like you to help expose animal abuse and tax waste in this horrible animal experimentation industry.

We've brought an end to many horror stories, but thousands of cruel experiments are being conducted even as you read this ad.

That's why we're asking for your help. Because our opponents don't listen to moral arguments or pleas of mercy.

They have to be pinned down in court.

So please, send us your tax-deductible contribution today. And thank you.

Yes, I want to help stop the abuse of animals in experiments.

Name ______

City ______ State ______ Zip ______

Please accept my tax deductible contribution of: $15 ______

People For The Ethical Treatment Of Animals

If you liked pulling the wings off flies as a kid, you may be cut out for a career in animal experimentation.

Think of the cruelest thing you can do to an animal and you may qualify for a big government grant.

Think that's an exaggeration? Well, here are just a few of the experiments your tax dollars paid for recently:

Surgically crippled monkeys (one of the monkeys is pictured here) were burned and electro-shocked in a Maryland lab to force them to use their deadened arms.

This experiment cost taxpayers $1.5 million. Until we stopped it.

Conscious, unanaesthetized baboons had their heads locked into a hydraulic device at the University of Pennsylvania. At the flip of a switch, these baboons had their brains scrambled.

This cost U.S. taxpayers $12 million, for almost a dozen years. Until we stopped it.

Immobilized dogs were scheduled to be shot at close range in a Washington, D.C. military test.

It would've cost taxpayers $1.1 million. But we stopped it.

The few atrocities you've read here are just a drop in the bucket of blood that goes by the name "animal research."

Each year, cats, monkeys, dogs, pigs, rats and other lab animals suffer and die by the millions in American laboratories.

The cost to taxpayers is in the *billions.*

If you think these kinds of experiments have no place in the 20th century, please help us stop them.

People for the Ethical Treatment of Animals (PETA) works with medical and legal professionals, the media, members of Congress, and people like you to expose animal abuse and tax waste in the animal experimentation industry.

We've brought an end to many horror stories, but there are thousands of other cruel experiments being conducted even as you read this ad.

So please join us today.

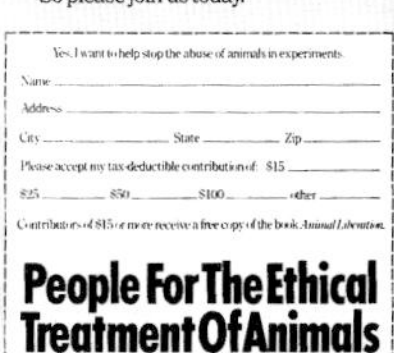

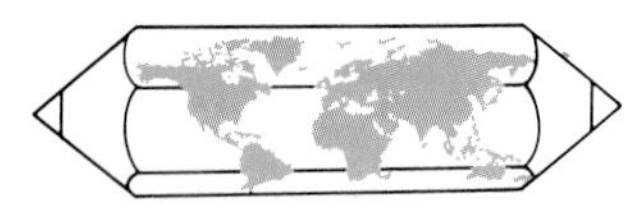

Gold, Silver & Bronze Awards

Public Service Newspaper Or Magazine: Campaign

66 SILVER

ART DIRECTOR
Tom Schwartz

WRITER
Dean Hacohen

PHOTOGRAPHER
Larry Sillen

CLIENT
Partnership for a Drug-Free America

AGENCY
DDB Needham Worldwide

66 SILVER

PARTNERSHIP FOR A DRUG-FREE AMERICA
COCAINE
©1987 DDB Needham Worldwide Inc.

PARTNERSHIP FOR A DRUG-FREE AMERICA
COCAINE
©1987 DDB Needham Worldwide Inc.

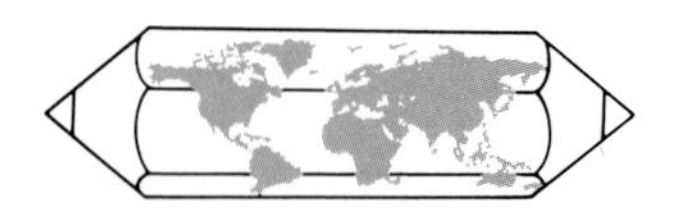

Gold, Silver & Bronze Awards

Public Service Newspaper Or Magazine: Campaign

67 BRONZE

ART DIRECTOR
Tom Bleakly

WRITER
Tim Pegors

DESIGNER
Tom Bleakly

CLIENT
St. John's Lutheran Church

AGENCY
Blaisdell & Westlie/
St. Paul, MN

Anyone Who Believes In Jesus Christ Should Be Committed.

We're committed to our beliefs at St. John's Lutheran. Join us this Sunday.

67 BRONZE

Don't Let Your Kids Grow Up Thinking God's Last Name Is Damn.

Does it seem that your efforts to teach values to your children have been in vain?
At St. John's, we take Christian Education seriously. Visit us this Sunday.

If Jesus Could Rise From The Dead, Surely You Can Get Up For The 11:00 a.m. Service.

For some people, getting up early on the weekend requires an almost superhuman effort.
At St. John's we make it worth your while. So, rise to the occasion and visit us this Sunday.

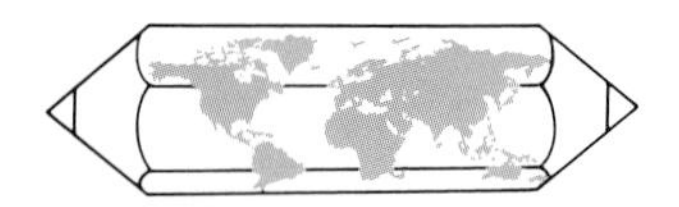

Gold, Silver & Bronze Awards

Public Service Outdoor: Single

68 GOLD

ART DIRECTOR
Wayne Gibson

WRITER
Luke Sullivan

CLIENT
People for the Ethical Treatment of Animals

AGENCY
The Martin Agency/ Richmond, VA

69 SILVER

ART DIRECTOR
Janet Guillet

WRITER
Kenneth Sandbank

CLIENT
Reader's Digest

AGENCY
Da Vinci Einstein

70 BRONZE

ART DIRECTOR
Kirk Souder

WRITER
Martin Canellakis

DESIGNER
Kirk Souder

ARTIST
Kirk Souder

CLIENT
Reader's Digest

AGENCY
Homer & Durham

Imagine having your body left to science while you're still in it.
Please join us today: write People For The Ethical Treatment Of Animals, Box 42516, Washington, D.C. 20015. Or call (202) 726-0156.

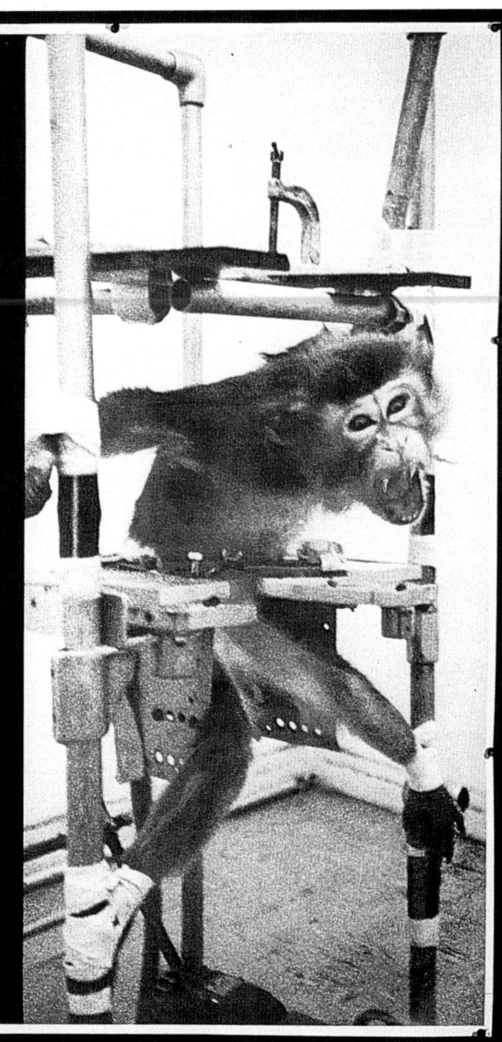

68 GOLD

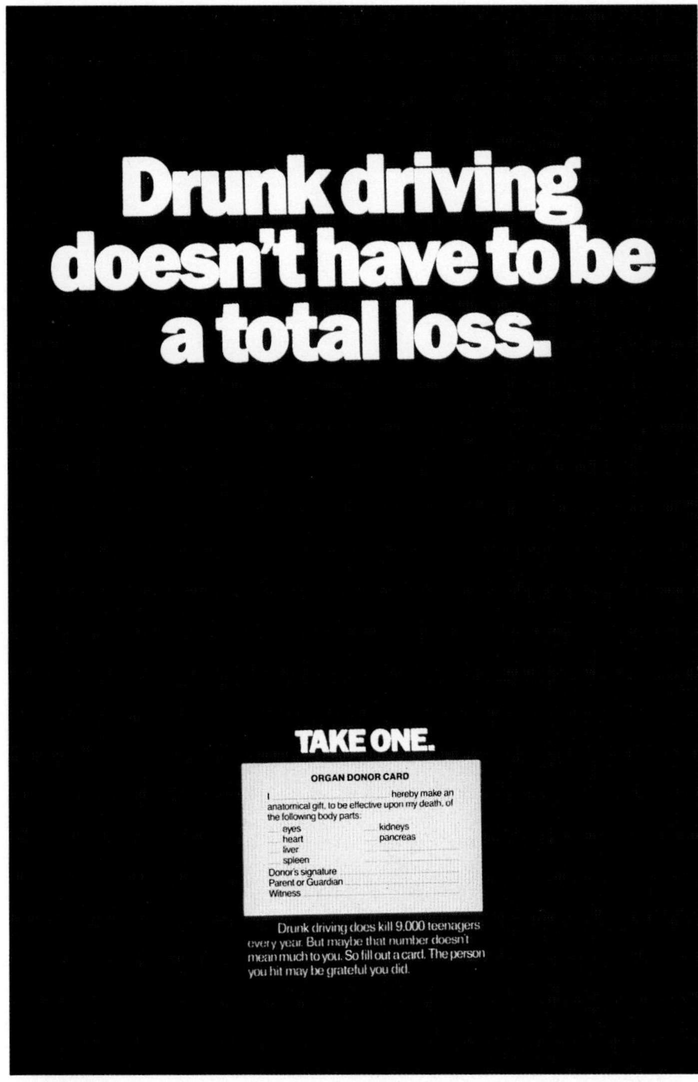

69 SILVER

70 BRONZE

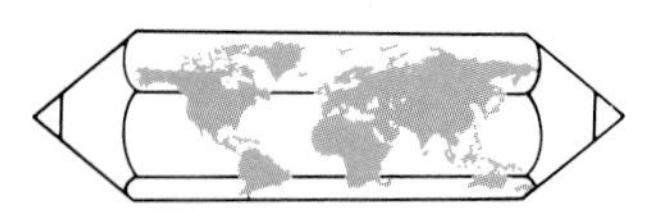

Gold, Silver & Bronze Awards

Political Newspaper Or Magazine: Single

71 GOLD
ART DIRECTOR
David Peterson
WRITER
Carl Pfirman
PHOTOGRAPHER
Jim Arndt
CLIENT
PAL
AGENCY
Campbell-Mithun/
Minneapolis

72 SILVER
ART DIRECTORS
Ron Anderson
Larry Jarvis
WRITER
Bert Gardner
CLIENT
Freespeech Committee
AGENCY
Bozell Jacobs Kenyon &
Eckhardt/Minneapolis

CARS AREN'T THE ONLY THINGS SOLD FOR THEIR PARTS.

If your dog or cat gets picked up by the pound, they'll hold it for five days. After that, they can sell it to a research laboratory.

And with 26 different pounds in the Twin Cities, that doesn't give you much time to find your pet. If you ever do.

In February, your state legislature will vote on a bill that would prevent pounds from selling private pets to laboratories. So please show your support. Call your state legislators now. Or call PAL at: 521-5332, 824-8742, or 724-8633. Or write: PAL, P.O. Box 11557, St. Paul, MN 55111.

Because loose pets aren't just getting picked up. They're getting picked apart.

PAL
Minnesota Pet Owners Association

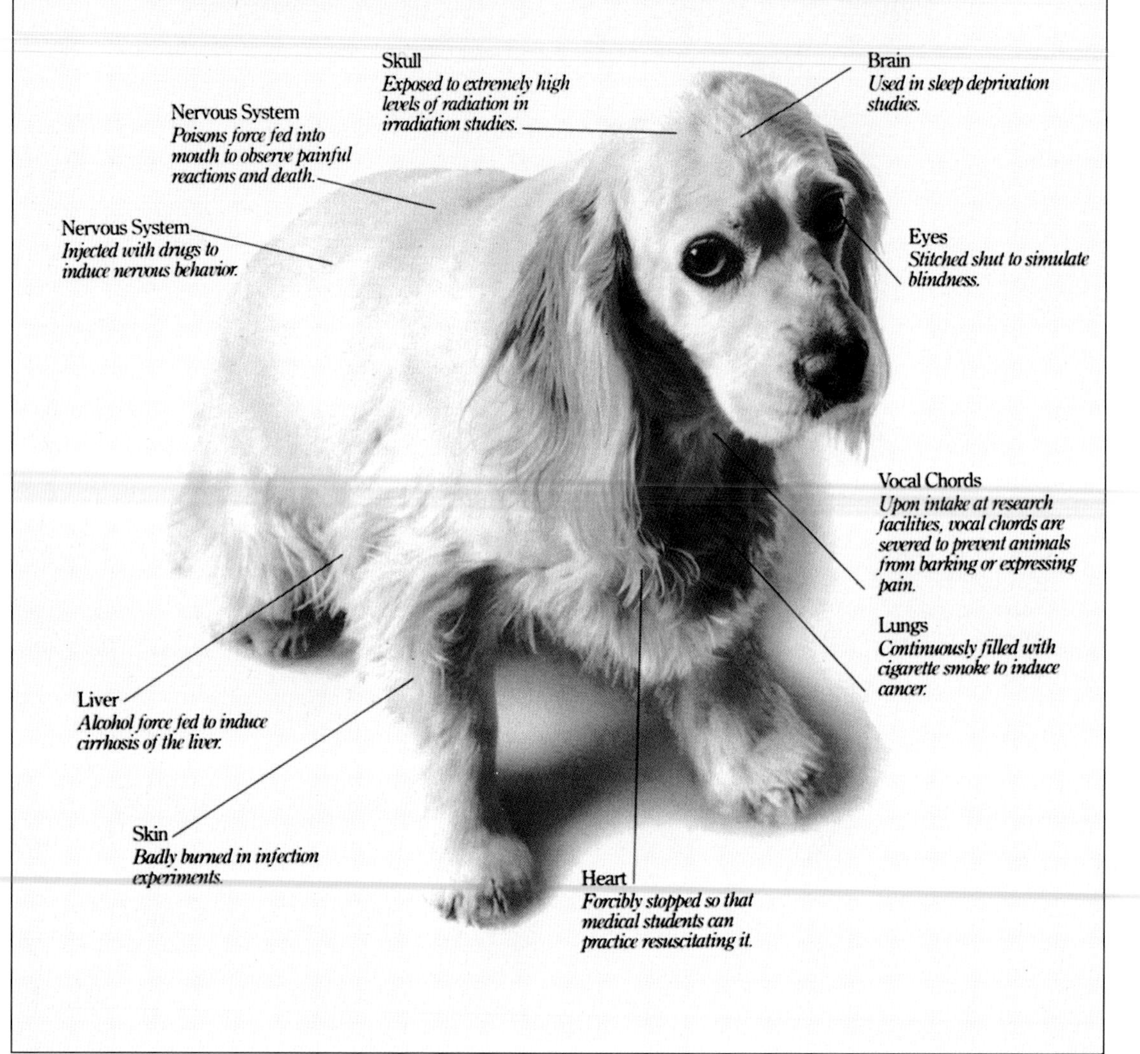

Skull
Exposed to extremely high levels of radiation in irradiation studies.
Brain
Used in sleep deprivation studies.
Nervous System
Poisons force fed into mouth to observe painful reactions and death.
Nervous System
Injected with drugs to induce nervous behavior.
Eyes
Stitched shut to simulate blindness.
Vocal Chords
Upon intake at research facilities, vocal chords are severed to prevent animals from barking or expressing pain.
Lungs
Continuously filled with cigarette smoke to induce cancer.
Liver
Alcohol force fed to induce cirrhosis of the liver.
Skin
Badly burned in infection experiments.
Heart
Forcibly stopped so that medical students can practice resuscitating it.

71 GOLD

Everything he is today he owes to a free press.

The Watergate scandal could never have happened in Russia.

Oh, the actual events might have occurred. Russian officials are just as human as American officials.

But Russia has no free press. So there would have been no investigation. No news reports. No trials.

But despite such recent proof of its importance, people still don't agree on just how free the press should be. In a 1986 poll, 75% of Minnesotans said that the government has the right to prohibit the distribution of information it considers damaging to national security.

But such a right, unrestricted, would have allowed the government to suppress the Watergate story.

We should be concerned about our changing attitudes towards America's basic freedoms. And speak up for The First Amendment. Because the best way to prevent scandals is to allow them to happen.

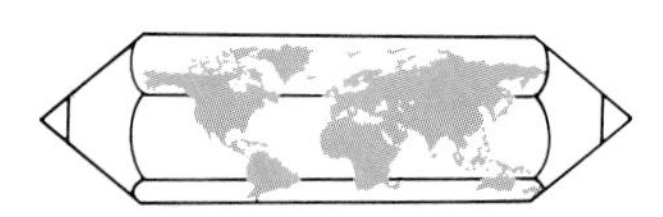

Gold, Silver & Bronze Awards

Political Newspaper Or Magazine: Campaign

73 SILVER

ART DIRECTORS
LeeAnn Heltzel
Ron Anderson
Larry Jarvis

WRITER
Bert Gardner

PHOTOGRAPHER
Rick Dublin

CLIENT
Freespeech Committee

AGENCY
Bozell Jacobs Kenyon & Eckhardt/Minneapolis

The pen is mightier than the sword. But what about scissors?

Today, only a small minority of the world's 5 billion inhabitants enjoy the benefits associated with freedom of the press.

And many of the fortunate few who *do* enjoy such benefits live in America – land of the free and home of The First Amendment.

But even though The First Amendment clearly states that Congress shall make no law abridging the freedom of the press, not everyone agrees as to just *how* free the press should be.

For example, in a 1986 poll of Minnesotans, 75% of them said the government has the right to prohibit distribution of information it considers damaging to national security.

If this right is exercised without restraint, it could lead to a society where no news is good news. If you believe that no news is *bad* news, you can help protect your right to be informed.

By speaking up for The First Amendment.

Freespeech

73 SILVER

Everything he is today he owes to a free press.

The Watergate scandal could never have happened in Russia.

Oh, the actual events might have occurred. Russian officials are just as human as American officials.

But Russia has no free press. So there would have been no investigation. No news reports. No trials.

But despite such recent proof of its importance, people still don't agree on just how free the press should be. In a 1986 poll, 75% of Minnesotans said that the government has the right to prohibit the distribution of information it considers damaging to national security.

But such a right, unrestricted, would have allowed the government to suppress the Watergate story.

We should be concerned about our changing attitudes towards America's basic freedoms. And speak up for The First Amendment. Because the best way to prevent scandals is to allow them to happen.

Freespeech

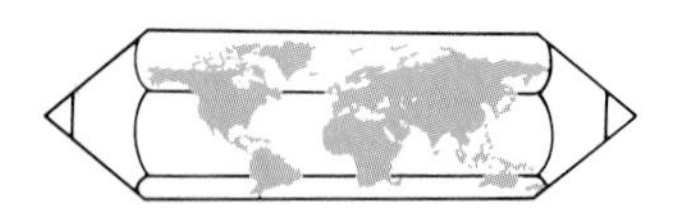

Gold, Silver & Bronze Awards

Political Newspaper Or Magazine: Campaign

73 SILVER

ART DIRECTORS
LeeAnn Heltzel
Ron Anderson
Larry Jarvis

WRITER
Bert Gardner

PHOTOGRAPHER
Rick Dublin

CLIENT
Freespeech Committee

AGENCY
Bozell Jacobs Kenyon & Eckhardt/Minneapolis

The pen is mightier than the sword. But what about scissors?

Today, only a small minority of the world's 5 billion inhabitants enjoy the benefits associated with freedom of the press.

And many of the fortunate few who *do* enjoy such benefits live in America – land of the free and home of The First Amendment.

But even though The First Amendment clearly states that Congress shall make no law abridging the freedom of the press, not everyone agrees as to just *how* free the press should be.

For example, in a 1986 poll of Minnesotans, 75% of them said the government has the right to prohibit distribution of information it considers damaging to national security.

If this right is exercised without restraint, it could lead to a society where no news is good news. If you believe that no news is *bad* news, you can help protect your right to be informed.

By speaking up for The First Amendment.

Freespeech

73 SILVER

Everything he is today he owes to a free press.

The Watergate scandal could never have happened in Russia.

Oh, the actual events might have occurred. Russian officials are just as human as American officials.

But Russia has no free press. So there would have been no investigation. No news reports. No trials.

But despite such recent proof of its importance, people still don't agree on just how free the press should be. In a 1986 poll, 75% of Minnesotans said that the government has the right to prohibit the distribution of information it considers damaging to national security.

But such a right, unrestricted, would have allowed the government to suppress the Watergate story.

We should be concerned about our changing attitudes towards America's basic freedoms. And speak up for The First Amendment. Because the best way to prevent scandals is to allow them to happen.

The only thing that scares a politician more is premature baldness.

Any politician knows that the most effective public watchdog around is a free press.

Without one, we cannot be an informed citizenry.

That's why our right to know the facts is guaranteed by The First Amendment.

Unfortunately, we seem to be changing our attitude toward the basic freedoms upon which America was built.

For example, in a 1986 poll, 75% of Minnesotans said that the government has the right to prohibit the distribution of information it considers damaging to national security.

But this right, unrestricted would have kept us from knowing anything about Watergate.

If you would like to help protect America's freedom of expression, we suggest you use it.

And speak up for The First Amendment.

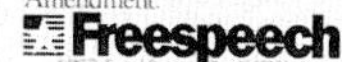

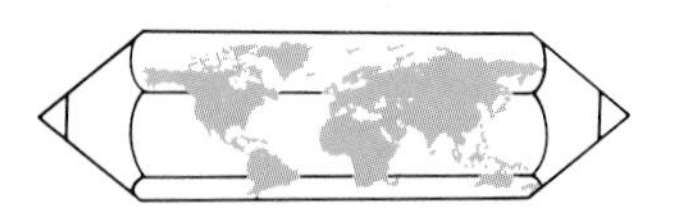

Gold, Silver & Bronze Awards

Political Newspaper Or Magazine: Campaign

74 BRONZE

ART DIRECTORS
Ron Anderson
Larry Jarvis

WRITER
Bert Gardner

CLIENT
Freespeech Committee

AGENCY
Bozell Jacobs Kenyon & Eckhardt/Minneapolis

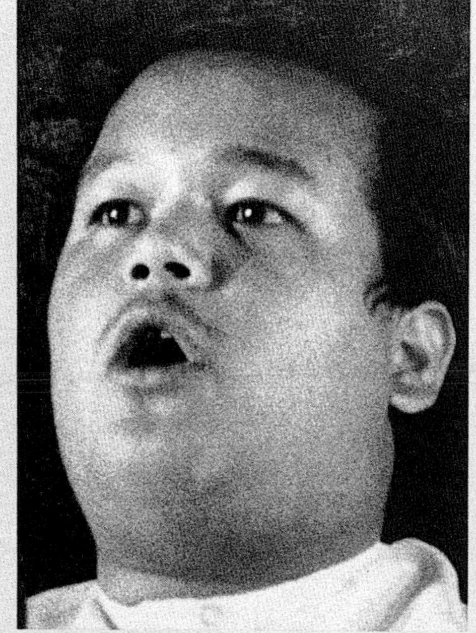

Just how strong is your belief in religious freedom?

It is no accident that the first words of The First Amendment to the U.S. constitution are these:

"Congress shall make no law respecting an establishment of religion, or prohibiting the free exercise thereof...."

Because the founding fathers were well aware that wherever religion was established, some form of religious intolerance, oppression or persecution was likely to follow.

Even so, not everyone agrees as to how much The First Amendment restricts government involvement in religious matters.

For example, in a 1986 poll of Minnesotans, 77% of them believed the government has the right to monitor certain religious groups if they are thought to be doing something illegal.

Obviously, no one has a right to break the law. But the question still arises: who would monitor the government monitors?

One of the best ways to protect your rights under the law is to exercise them.

So if you want to speak up for The First Amendment, feel free.

Freespeech

74 BRONZE

Some people think the only way to make their voice heard is by taking away everyone else's.

As a U.S. citizen, your right to speak your mind is guaranteed by The First Amendment, which says in no uncertain terms that Congress shall make no law abridging the freedom of speech.

Unfortunately, a surprising number of people want to add a lot of ifs, ands, or buts.

For example, in a 1986 poll of Minnesotans, 40% of them said government should prohibit expression of views that might lead people to commit undesirable or violent acts.

Trouble is, if someone else's right to express an unpopular view is ignored today, your right to express a different view may be ignored tomorrow.

One of the best ways to protect your freedom of expression is to use it.

By speaking up for The First Amendment.

Freespeech

You have the right not to remain silent.

As a U.S. citizen, your right to speak your mind is guaranteed by The First Amendment, which says in no uncertain terms that Congress shall make no law abridging the freedom of speech.

Unfortunately, a surprising number of people want to add a lot of ifs, ands, or buts.

For example, in a 1986 poll of Minnesotans, 40% of them said government should prohibit expression of views that might lead people to commit undesirable or violent acts.

Trouble is, if someone else's right to express an unpopular view is ignored today, your right to express a different view may be ignored tomorrow.

One of the best ways to protect your freedom of expression is to use it.

By speaking up for The First Amendment.

Gold, Silver & Bronze Awards

Consumer Radio: Single

75 GOLD

WRITERS
Dick Orkin
Haris Orkin
Julie Prendiville
Christine Coyle

AGENCY PRODUCER
Wally Lawrence

CLIENT
Adweek Magazine

AGENCY
Adweek In-House

76 SILVER

WRITER
Al Lowe

CLIENT
Blue Cross/Blue Shield of Rhode Island

AGENCY
Pagano Schenck & Kay/ Providence, RI

77 BRONZE

WRITER
Margaret Wilcox

AGENCY PRODUCER
Lisa Page

CLIENT
The Boston Globe

AGENCY
Hill Holliday Connors Cosmopulos/Boston

75 GOLD

ED: Hi. I'm Ed, vice president of the agency.

DICK: Hello.

ED: This is Dave, the writer.

DAVE: I'm the writer.

ED: And may I say, our agency is very pleased to be here.

TINKY: Thank you. I'm Mr Tinky and I'm very keen to see the campaign your shop is proposing for Tinky's Frozen Quiches.

DAVE: F . . . Frozen quiches?

TINKY: Uh-huh.

DAVE: I thought it was Tinky Tractors.

ED: Farm Tractors.

TINKY: We used to make tractors.

ED & DAVE: Oh, no . . .

TINKY: We're entirely into frozen quiches now. The story was in *Adweek*. I thought you ad people loved *Adweek*?

ED: Uh . . . yes . . . well . . . See, we've been so busy putting this pitch together that we . . . uh . . .

TINKY: Well, if you're not ready . . .

ED: No, no. Just a few adjustments and it'll work. Dave, why don't you tell Mr Tinky the slogan.

DAVE: Why didn't we just read *Adweek* . . .

ED: Dave, the slogan.

DAVE: Nothing feels the same after you sit on . . . a Tinky Frozen Quiche.

TINKY: No, I don't like it.

ED: Dave, maybe you should try the jingle. Dave . . .

DAVE: But I can't . . .

ED: The jingle!

DAVE & ED (TO "MARY HAD A LITTLE LAMB"): If you sit on a quiche for pay, a Tinky Quiche feels good all day.

TINKY: No, I don't like it, I just don't . . .

ED: Well, we'll try it again. You like our agency, right?

TINKY: Not really. I don't like your agency.

ED & DAVE (SINGING): If you want a quiche that's green, that hauls and plows . . .

(SFX: FADE OUT)

ANNCR: If you're in the ad game, it may seem once in a while no one likes you. Not true. *Adweek* likes ad people.

76 SILVER

(MUSIC: "FANFARE FOR THE COMMON MAN")

VO: Competing in the Olympics isn't just the ultimate test of the human spirit, it's also the ultimate test of the human body. Consider, for instance, that a person jumping off a ninety-meter ski jump will fall a distance equivalent to the height of a thirty-story building . . .

(SFX: CROWD; SKI JUMP WHOOSH)

VO: . . . and that during a cross country ski race, the heart of the average participant will pump more than twenty-five quarts of blood per minute, over six times the normal rate . . .

(SFX: FAST, LOUD HEART PUMPING; HEAVY BREATHING; CROSS- COUNTRY SKIS SLIDING)

VO: . . . and that while twisting and turning a mere two inches above glare ice, a bobsledder will be going at speeds of up to ninety miles an hour . . .

(SFX: SOUND OF BOBSLED AND CREW-RUNNERS ON ICE, BOUNCING OFF WALLS)

VO: . . . and while you're watching some of the most incredible athletes in the world subject themselves to some of the most incredible stresses and dangers a body can endure, you might also consider that the health plan the International Olympic Committee has chosen to protect them is Blue Cross and Blue Shield. No one protects you better.

77 BRONZE

(SFX: HOSPITAL SOUNDS)

ANNCR: I'd like to introduce you to an AIDS patient. His name is Jeffrey. He's too sick to live at home. So he lives down the hall here in the AIDS ward. And he's not alone. The ward is full of AIDS patients. And the number keeps growing. In fact, the amount of cases is predicted to skyrocket in the next few years. Because most people just aren't taking the warnings of AIDS seriously. They still think that as long as you're not a drug user or a homosexual, you're safe. Not true. This Sunday, May 17, *The Boston Globe* will include a special insert called "Living with AIDS." It'll give you the facts. Like how you can and can't get AIDS. How hard AIDS is going to hit Massachusetts. How to talk to your children about it. And most importantly, who can get AIDS. Well here we are. This is Jeffrey's room.

(SFX: DOOR OPENING AND BABY CRYING)

ANNCR: And as you can hear, he's awake. Now if you're one of those people who still believes AIDS can only be caught by drug users and homosexuals, answer this. Which is he?

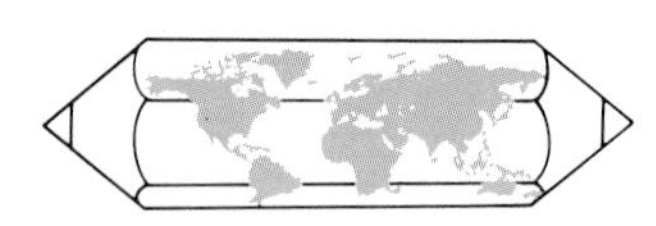

Gold, Silver & Bronze Awards

Consumer Radio: Campaign

78 GOLD

WRITERS
Dick Orkin
Haris Orkin
Julie Prendiville
Christine Coyle

AGENCY PRODUCER
Wally Lawrence

CLIENT
Adweek Magazine

AGENCY
Adweek In-House

79 SILVER

WRITERS
David Fowler
Thomas Hripko

AGENCY PRODUCER
Lisa Dee

CLIENT
Motel 6

AGENCY
The Richards Group/Dallas

78 GOLD

ED: Hi. I'm Ed, vice president of the agency.

DICK: Hello.

ED: This is Dave, the writer.

DAVE: I'm the writer.

ED: And may I say, our agency is very pleased to be here.

TINKY: Thank you. I'm Mr Tinky and I'm very keen to see the campaign your shop is proposing for Tinky's Frozen Quiches.

DAVE: F . . . Frozen quiches?

TINKY: Uh-huh.

DAVE: I thought it was Tinky Tractors.

ED: Farm Tractors.

TINKY: We used to make tractors.

ED & DAVE: Oh, no . . .

TINKY: We're entirely into frozen quiches now. The story was in *Adweek*. I thought you ad people loved *Adweek*?

ED: Uh . . . yes . . . well . . . See, we've been so busy putting this pitch together that we . . . uh . . .

TINKY: Well, if you're not ready . . .

ED: No, no. Just a few adjustments and it'll work. Dave, why don't you tell Mr Tinky the slogan.

DAVE: Why didn't we just read *Adweek* . . .

ED: Dave, the slogan.

DAVE: Nothing feels the same after you sit on . . . a Tinky Frozen Quiche.

TINKY: No, I don't like it.

ED: Dave, maybe you should try the jingle. Dave . . .

DAVE: But I can't . . .

ED: The jingle!

DAVE & ED (TO "MARY HAD A LITTLE LAMB"): If you sit on a quiche for pay, a Tinky Quiche feels good all day.

TINKY: No, I don't like it, I just don't . . .

ED: Well, we'll try it again. You like our agency, right?

TINKY: Not really. I don't like your agency.

ED & DAVE (SINGING): If you want a quiche that's green, that hauls and plows . . .

(SFX: FADE OUT)

ANNCR: If you're in the ad game, it may seem once in a while no one likes you. Not true. *Adweek* likes ad people.

78 GOLD

(SFX: FOOTSTEPS)

FRED: Hi, Jerry.

JERRY: Oh, hi, Fred . . . Listen, have you seen Bob Gurzinsky?

FRED: Why?

JERRY: Today's our agency's ad presentation.

FRED: He's in Tahiti. Finishing his screenplay.

JERRY: Screenplay?

FRED: Yeah, based on his creative for the Binker Birdseed campaign.

JERRY: What?

FRED: It was in *Adweek*. Didn't you see it?

JERRY: I . . . no . . . wow . . . I guess I'll just make the presentation to Stinkerman's Sticky Deodorant Stick's alone.

FRED: We lost that account.

JERRY: Lost . . . when?

FRED: Two weeks ago. It was in *Adweek*.

JERRY: It was?

FRED: Don't you read *Adweek*?

JERRY: I'm always too busy.

FRED: That's why I read *Adweek*. It's concise, snappy, easy-to-read.

JERRY: Boy, you know that account is gonna break Greg Norberg's heart.

FRED: Jerry, Greg resigned last week to go into show business full time.

JERRY: What?

FRED: Yeah. He decided he liked being a name better than a creative director.

JERRY: I didn't know . . .

FRED: It was in *Adweek*.

ANNCR: Every once in a while, you may have a day when nothing is going your way and you need a pal. You've got one in Adweek.

JERRY: Boy, I've got to start reading *Adweek*.

FRED: Keeps me on top.

JERRY (LAUGHING): I mean I could have been fired and not know 'cuz I haven't been reading *Adweek*.

(BEAT)

(FRED: THROAT CLEAR.)

JERRY: Oh, no . . .

ANNCR: *Adweek* likes ad people.

78 GOLD

TED: Want another beer, Wally?

WALLY: Ted?

TED: Yeah, Wally.

WALLY: How in the heck do you do it?

TED: Order beers?

WALLY: You're so darn popular and successful . . .

TED: Not really.

WALLY: Hey . . . You've only been with our ad agency for a year . . .

TED: Nine months!

WALLY: You've had three promotions!

TED: Four!

WALLY: The president of the agency knows your first name.

TED: I had a date with his daughter last night.

WALLY: How do you do it?

TED: Well, Wally, in the ad game, you've just got to know what's happening . . .

GLORIA: Hello, Teddy. Nice job on the Bushmacher account.

TED: Hi, Gloria, wanna meet my pal Wally?

GLORIA: No.

WALLY: See what I mean . . .

TED: Wally, you know what this is?

WALLY: *Adweek Magazine*?

TED: *Adweek Magazine*. And I'm never without *Adweek*. You know why?

PHIL: Hi, Teddy.

TED: Hi, Phil. Because *Adweek* keeps me on top. It's concise, compact, written for busy ad people.

JILL: Hi, Ted. Your kitty litter commercials are awesome!

TED: Thanks, Jill. Wanta say hi to my friend Wally?

JILL: No.

WALLY: See, people just don't . . .

TED: A lot of people like you, Wally.

WALLY: Who?

TED (BEAT): Just . . . try and read *Adweek*.

WALLY: You're trying to tell me if I read *Adweek*, I'll be popular, just like you?

TED: Get serious, Wally. I'm six foot two, good looking. You're dumpy, unkempt, and wear ugly plaid coats . . .

WALLY: Right, I didn't think just reading *Adweek* would do it . . . (ETC. . . . FADE)

ANNCR: You see—even when it seems no one likes you, *Adweek* likes ad people.

79 SILVER

ANNCR: Hi. Tom Bodett for Motel 6 with a few words about roughin' it. Well, when you stay at Motel 6 you'll have to turn the bed down all by yourself, and go without that little piece of chocolate those fancy hotels leave on your pillow. Well, I know it's a lot to ask, but for around twenty bucks, the lowest prices of any national chain, well you can't expect the moon now can you? After all, you do get a clean comfortable room, free T.V., movies and local calls. And no service charge on long distance calls. No, we won't bring meals to your room on a silver cart, but that doesn't mean you can't get room service. Since local calls are free, just look up a pizza joint that delivers and give 'em a buzz. They'll bring that large pepperoni pineapple right to your door. So if you can tough it out all in the name of savin' a few bucks, well Motel 6 is where you oughta stay. We've got over 420 locations coast to coast. Just call 505-891-6161 for reservations. I'm Tom Bodett for Motel 6 and we'll leave the light on for you.

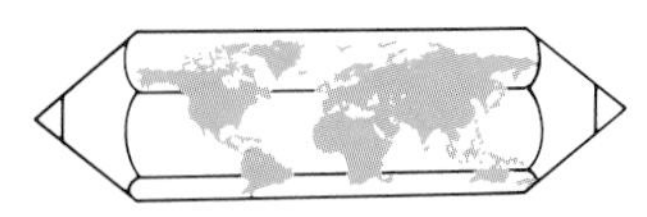

Gold, Silver & Bronze Awards

Consumer Television Over :30 (:45/:60/:90) Single

80 GOLD
ART DIRECTOR
Gerald Andelin
WRITERS
Dan Mountain
Peter Murphy
Sally Gill
AGENCY PRODUCER
Sue Rugtiv
PRODUCTION CO.
PYTKA
DIRECTOR
Joe Pytka
CLIENT
The Perrier Group
AGENCY
Hal Riney & Partners/
San Francisco

81 SILVER
ART DIRECTOR
Gerald Andelin
WRITERS
Dan Mountain
Peter Murphy
Sally Gill
AGENCY PRODUCER
Sue Rugtiv
PRODUCTION CO.
PYTKA
DIRECTOR
Joe Pytka
CLIENT
The Perrier Group
AGENCY
Hal Riney & Partners/
San Francisco

82 BRONZE
ART DIRECTOR
Logan Wilmont
WRITER
Mike Court
AGENCY PRODUCER
Debbie Court
PRODUCTION CO.
Sid Roberson
DIRECTOR
Simon Delaney
CLIENT
Mates Healthcare
AGENCY
Still Price Court Twivy
D'Souza/London

80 GOLD

(MUSIC: UNDER)

ANNCR VO: If the Earth had been tilted a little more to the left, it probably wouldn't have happened.
If the continents had waited a day or two to start drifting, it's doubtful.
And if the rain hadn't fallen that day, or the moon hadn't been full . . . who knows.
There might not be a town called Vergeze, or a spring called Perrier.
But luckily, everything happened just right.
It's perfect. It's Perrier.

81 SILVER

ANNCR VO: Maybe it's because meteors fell from the sky that night.
Or because a day is only twenty-four hours long.
Or could it be because air turned out lighter than water?
All we know is, whatever had to happen happened just right.
In a town called Vergeze. At a spring called Perrier.
It's perfect. It's Perrier.

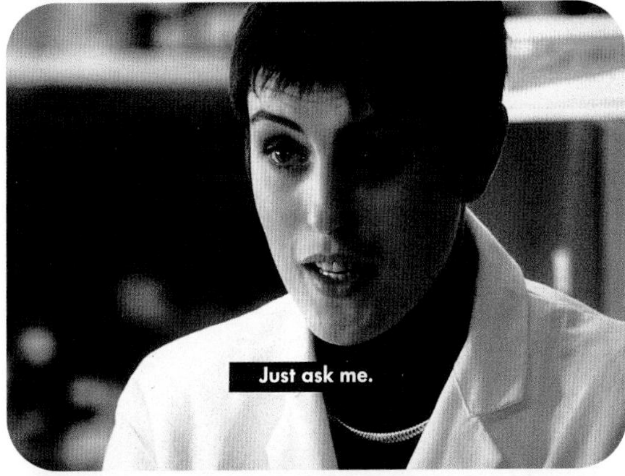

82 BRONZE

(SFX: HALF-SECOND SILENCE; SHOP DOORBELL)

ASSISTANT: Hello.

BOY: Yes . . . er . . . I'd er . . . well . . .
(SUBTITLE: OH, NO! IT'S A WOMAN)

ASSISTANT: Yes?
(SUBTITLE: HE WANTS SOME CONDOMS)

BOY: I want some co . . . cotton wool.
(SUBTITLE: I REALLY WANT SOME CONDOMS)

ASSISTANT: Of course, will there be anything else?
(SUBTITLE: SILLY QUESTION)

(SFX: CASH REGISTER RING)

BOY: Yeah. Have you got a packet of . . . tissues?
(SUBTITLE: JUST ASK HER)

ASSISTANT: Man-size tissues. Is that all?
(SUBTITLE: JUST ASK ME)

(SFX: CASH REGISTER RING)

MVO: Mates are a new range of condoms. Like other condoms, they're reliable. But they're cheaper. She sells hundreds of packets. She's not embarrassed. So why should you be?

BOY: And a packet of Mates Condoms, please.

ASSISTANT: Of course.
(SUBTITLE: AT LAST)

(SUBTITLE: NO SWEAT)

ASSISTANT (TO BACK ROOM): Mr Williams, how much are these Mates Condoms?

MVO: Mates. You make love. They make sense.

Gold, Silver & Bronze Awards

Consumer Television Over :30 (:45/:60/:90) Campaign

83 GOLD

ART DIRECTOR
Gerald Andelin

WRITERS
Dan Mountain
Peter Murphy
Sally Gill

AGENCY PRODUCER
Sue Rugtiv

PRODUCTION CO.
PYTKA

DIRECTOR
Joe Pytka

CLIENT
The Perrier Group

AGENCY
Hal Riney & Partners/
San Francisco

83 GOLD

(MUSIC: UNDER)

ANNCR VO: What if an ancient wind had blown north instead of south?
Or the glaciers had melted on Tuesday instead of Thursday?
Suppose Jupiter had never aligned with Mars?
There may never have been a place called Vergeze, or a spring called Perrier.
But luckily, everything happened just right.
It's perfect. It's Perrier.

83 GOLD

(MUSIC: UNDER)

ANNCR VO: If the Earth had been tilted a little more to the left, it probably wouldn't have happened.
If the continents had waited a day or two to start drifting, it's doubtful.
And if the rain hadn't fallen that day, or the moon hadn't been full . . . who knows.
There might not be a town called Vergeze, or a spring called Perrier.
But luckily, everything happened just right.
It's perfect. It's Perrier.

83 GOLD

ANNCR VO: Maybe it's because meteors fell from the sky that night.
Or because a day is only twenty-four hours long.
Or could it be because air turned out lighter than water?
All we know is, whatever had to happen happened just right.
In a town called Vergeze. At a spring called Perrier.
It's perfect. It's Perrier.

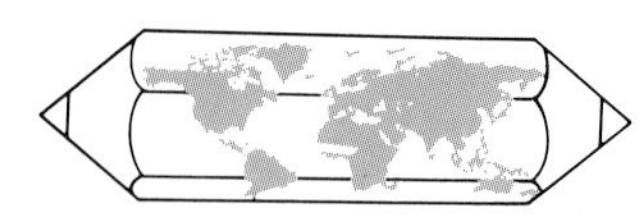

Gold, Silver & Bronze Awards

Consumer Television Over :30 (:45/:60/:90) Campaign

84 SILVER

ART DIRECTORS
Logan Wilmont
Nick Scott

WRITERS
Mike Court
Richard Spencer

AGENCY PRODUCER
Debbie Court

PRODUCTION CO.
Sid Roberson

DIRECTOR
Simon Delaney

CLIENT
Mates Healthcare

AGENCY
Still Price Court Twivy D'Souza/London

Consumer Television Over :30 (:45/:60/:90) Campaign

85 BRONZE

ART DIRECTOR
Ivan Horvath

WRITERS
Ken Segall
Michael Baldwin

AGENCY PRODUCERS
Paul Gold
Trish Reeves

PRODUCTION CO.
PYTKA

DIRECTOR
Joe Pytka

CLIENT
Apple Computer

AGENCY
BBDO

84 SILVER

MAN: I'll get it.
(SUBTITLE: THIS'LL IMPRESS HER)

GIRL: No, you always pay.
(SUBTITLE: HE ISN'T MADE OF MONEY)

MAN: I insist.
(SUBTITLE: OR DO I?)

MAN: Are you sure?
(SUBTITLE: PHEW!)

GIRL: It's eight each.
(SUBTITLE: AND WORTH EVERY PENNY)

MAN: Ooooops!
(SUBTITLE: AAAAAARRRRRRGGGGGGHHHHHH!)

(SUBTITLE: ¡#*!)

GIRL: I think you've dropped something.
(SUBTITLE: BET HE FEELS AN IDIOT)

MAN: Er, I don't know what to say.
(SUBTITLE: WHAT AN IDIOT!)

GIRL: Don't say anything.
(SUBTITLE: I THINK YOU'RE VERY SENSIBLE)

GIRL: Shall we go?

MVO: Mates are a new range of condoms. Like other condoms, they're reliable. But they're cheaper. It doesn't matter who carries them as long as one of you does.

MAN: Thanks for a lovely evening.
(SUBTITLE: SHAME I RUINED IT)

GIRL: Thank you.
(SUBTITLE: SHAME IT'S OVER)

MAN: See you again next week?
(SUBTITLE: HARDLY WORTH ASKING)

GIRL: Of course.
(SUBTITLE: I THOUGHT HE'D NEVER ASK)

MVO: Mates. You make love. They make sense.

85 BRONZE

JOEY: Hey, Baldwin, how you doin'?

BALDWIN: Pretty good, Joey. How are you?

SAL: Ah, finished already.

WOMAN: Hey, I thought we were supposed to be doing this in-house.

BALDWIN: That's right. Pass the salt, would you?

SAL: Hey, your group did this?

BALDWIN: New computer. The salt?

SAL: Quintile analysis? Gimme a break.

BALDWIN: Well, Segall did that.

SAL: I thought he was in the LA office.

BALDWIN: So's Edwards—she did the graphics.

SAL: The market projections?

BALDWIN: Garnett. Chicago.

SAL: How'd you get everybody together in the same place?

BALDWIN: I told you. New computer.

SAL: What kind of system can do that?

BALDWIN (UNINTELLIGABLY): Mcntsh.

SAL: What?

BALDWIN: Mcntsh.

SAL: Pardon me?

SUPER: MACINTOSH. THE POWER TO BE YOUR BEST.

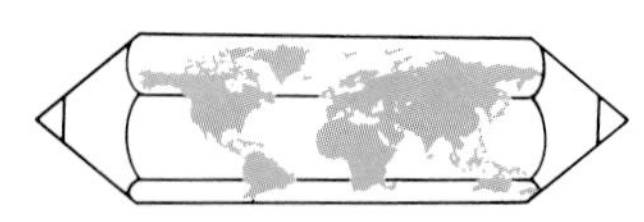

Gold, Silver & Bronze Awards

Consumer Television :30 Single

86 GOLD
ART DIRECTOR
Tom Stoneham
WRITER
Tim O'Leary
AGENCY PRODUCER
Larry Asher
PRODUCTION CO.
Charles Samuel Productions
DIRECTOR
Chuck East
CLIENT
King County Medical Blue Shield
AGENCY
Borders Perrin & Norrander/Seattle

87 SILVER
ART DIRECTOR
Michael Lawlor
WRITER
Charlie Breen
AGENCY PRODUCER
Andy Cornelius
PRODUCTION CO.
Image Point
CLIENT
Hyundai Motor America
AGENCY
Backer Spielvogel Bates

88 BRONZE
ART DIRECTOR
Marty Weiss
WRITER
Robin Raj
AGENCY PRODUCERS
Mark Sitley
Steve Amato
PRODUCTION COS.
Directing Artists
Fernbach Productions
DIRECTORS
Kevin Godley
Lol Creme
Alex Fernbach
CLIENT
NYNEX
AGENCY
Chiat/Day

86 GOLD

(MUSIC: CLASSICAL THEME THROUGHOUT)

ANNCR: We'd like to remind you about something the U.S. Olympic Team already knows. It's not whether you win or lose. It's whether you have a good health plan.
King County Medical Blue Shield.

87 SILVER

(SFX: TIRES SCREECH)

(MUSIC: UP AND UNDER)

(SFX: HURRIED FOOTSTEPS)

ANNCR VO: For less than the average price of a new car, you can get two new Hyundai Excels. They're both dependable, have front wheel drive, room for five, and more standard features than any cars in their class.
The only problem is . . . getting them home.
Hyundai. Cars that make sense.

(MUSIC: OUT)

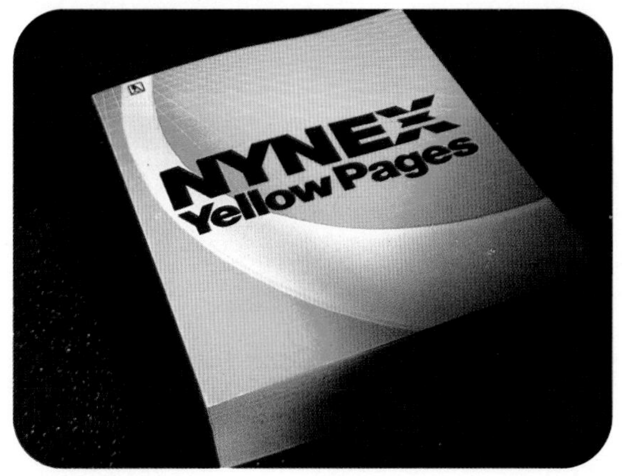

88 BRONZE

(SFX: OPENING CHIME; AS LIGHTS GO DOWN, STRIPPER MUSIC BEGINS; CLAPPING; WHISTLING)

(SFX: MUSIC AND CROWD NOISE CONTINUE)

(SFX: MUSIC AND CROWD NOISE CONTINUE; SOUND OF SPRINGS POPPING OFF)

(SFX: MUSIC AND CROWD NOISE CONTINUE)

VO: If it's out there, it's in here . . .

(SFX: CAT CALL WHISTLE)

The NYNEX Yellow Pages.

(SFX: BOOK SLAMS SHUT)

Why would anyone need another?

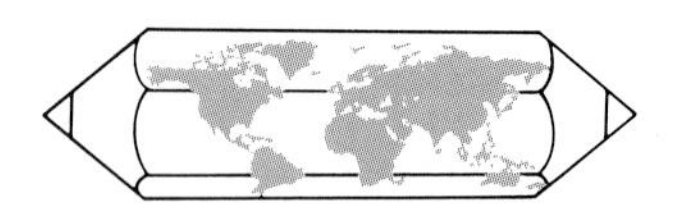

Gold, Silver & Bronze Awards

Consumer Television :30 Campaign

89 GOLD

ART DIRECTOR
Marty Weiss

WRITER
Robin Raj

AGENCY PRODUCERS
Mark Sitley
Steve Amato

PRODUCTION COS.
Directing Artists
Fernbach Productions

DIRECTORS
Kevin Godley
Lol Creme
Alex Fernbach

CLIENT
NYNEX

AGENCY
Chiat/Day

90 SILVER

ART DIRECTORS
Steve Miller
John Colquhoun
Frank Todaro

WRITERS
Jane King
Arthur Bijur
Rick Lemoine

AGENCY PRODUCER
Steve Friedman

PRODUCTION CO.
Story Piccolo Guliner

DIRECTOR
Mark Story

CLIENT
North American Philips

AGENCY
Cliff Freeman & Partners

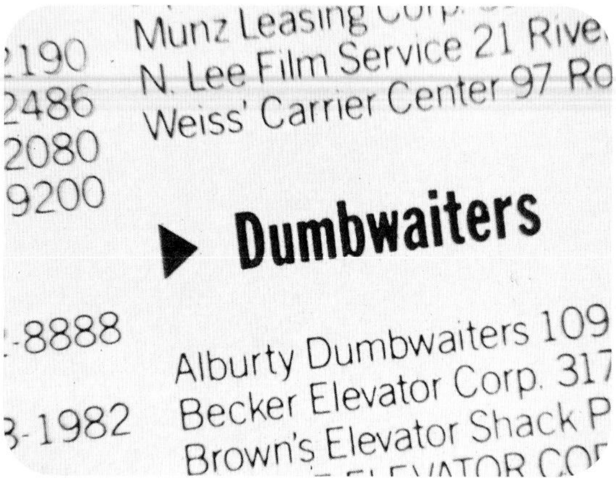

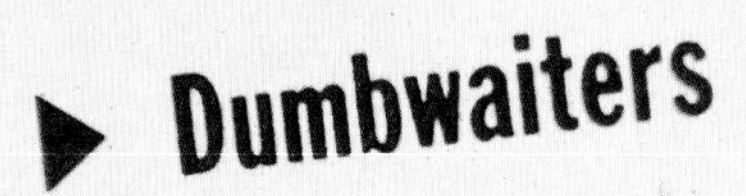

89 GOLD

(SFX: OPENING CHIME; RESTAURANT SOUNDS)

MVO: Excuse me . . .

WAITER: Sir!

MVO: What are your specials today?

WAITER: I don't know.

FVO: Do your entrees come with salad?

WAITER: I don't know.

MVO: Do you have escargots?

WAITER: Escargots? (PAUSE) I don't know.

FVO: May we see a menu?

WAITER (CONFUSED): Yes! No! I don't know.

VO: If it's out there, it's in here . . .

(SFX: PLATES BREAKING)

VO :The NYNEX Yellow Pages.

(SFX: BOOK SLAMS SHUT)

VO :Why would anyone need another?

89 GOLD

(SFX: OPENING CHIME; SOUND OF MARCHING)

OFF-CAMERA SERGEANT (YELLING): Attend Hut! Funky Chicken.

(SFX: MILITARY SNARE DRUM THROUGHOUT)

SARGE: Duckwalk! . . . Moonwalk! . . . Disco! . . . Windmill! . . . Air Guitar! . . . James Brown!

SOLDIERS (YELLING TOGETHER): Huh!

SARGE: Jimi plays Monterey!

VO: If it's out there, it's in here . . . The NYNEX Yellow Pages.

(SFX: BOOK SLAMS SHUT)

VO: Why would anyone need another?

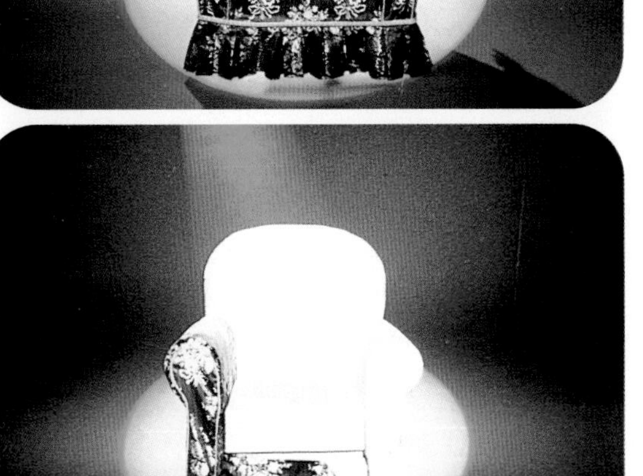

89 GOLD

(SFX: OPENING CHIME; AS LIGHTS GO DOWN, STRIPPER MUSIC BEGINS; CLAPPING; WHISTLING)

(SFX: MUSIC AND CROWD NOISE CONTINUE)

(SFX: MUSIC AND CROWD NOISE CONTINUE; SOUND OF SPRINGS POPPING OFF)

(SFX: MUSIC AND CROWD NOISE CONTINUE)

VO: If it's out there, it's in here . . .

(SFX: CAT CALL WHISTLE)

The NYNEX Yellow Pages.

(SFX: BOOK SLAMS SHUT)

Why would anyone need another?

90 SILVER

MAN: Hey, get a load of this.
Lord Klempston gazed upon Lucretia's loveliness. Her milky white shoulders were ablaze in the moonlight. Lord Klempston approached her and wrapped his thickly-muscled arms around her delicate waist.
He then whispered into her ear . . .

(SFX: BULB BLOWS)

MAN: . . . I can't see!

MAN #2: Lord Klempston was blind?!

ANNCR: It's time to change your bulb to Philips.
Philips Longer Life square bulbs.
Last thirty-three percent longer than ordinary bulbs.

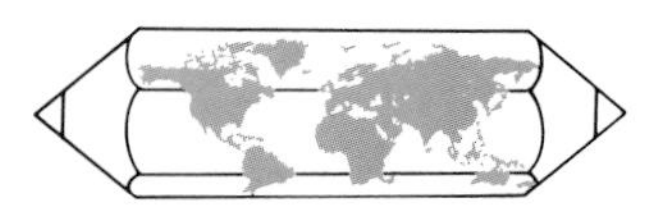

Gold, Silver & Bronze Awards

Consumer Television :30 Campaign

91 BRONZE

ART DIRECTOR
Ted Shaine

WRITER
Helayne Spivak

AGENCY PRODUCER
Ozzie Spenningsby

PRODUCTION CO.
Spots Films/New York

DIRECTOR
David Cornell

CLIENT
Club Med

AGENCY
Ammirati & Puris

Consumer Television Over :10 But Under :30 Single

92 GOLD

ART DIRECTORS
Cathi Mooney
Ken Mandelbaum

WRITERS
Ken Mandelbaum
Cathi Mooney

AGENCY PRODUCER
Betsy Flynn

PRODUCTION CO.
Ampersand

DIRECTOR
Elbert Budin

CLIENT
New Zealand Kiwifruit Authority

AGENCY
Hal Riney & Partners/San Francisco

93 SILVER

ART DIRECTOR
Mike Thomas

WRITER
John Allen

AGENCY PRODUCER
Lisa Ristuccia

PRODUCTION CO.
Ian MacDonald Productions

DIRECTOR
Ian MacDonald

CLIENT
Hoover Brush Vac

AGENCY
Clemenger/Sydney

94 BRONZE

ART DIRECTOR
Steve Miller

WRITER
Jane King

AGENCY PRODUCER
Steve Friedman

PRODUCTION CO.
Story Piccolo Guliner

DIRECTOR
Mark Story

CLIENT
North American Philips

AGENCY
Cliff Freeman & Partners

91 BRONZE

VO: The world news Club Med style.
Oil spills along the coast.
Foreign relations improving.
Gold plunges overseas.
Border dispute settled.
Tensions ease in Gulf.
And that's the way it is.
At Club Med.

92 GOLD

ANNCR VO: In California, it seems like people will eat just about anything.
And you're afraid to try a kiwifruit?

SUPER: NEW ZEALAND KIWIFRUIT.

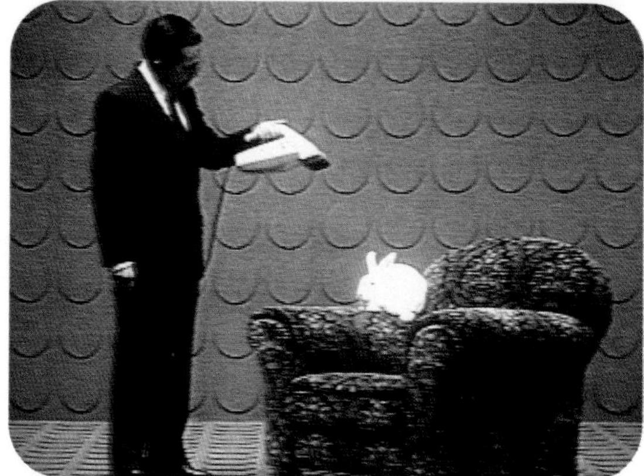

93 SILVER

(SFX: BRUSH VAC MOTOR)

DAVID: The Hoover Brush Vac has a motor-driven brush in its cleaning head, so it can easily pick up hard-to-pick-up items . . .

(SFX: BRUSH VAC)

DAVID: . . . like pet hairs.

(SFX: POP)

DAVID VO: That's why Hoover is ahead of the rest.

94 BRONZE

WOMAN: The magic's gone.
The minute the lights go out you fall asleep.

(SFX: SPOON DROPPING; MAN'S HEAD FALLING INTO SOUP; MAN SNORES INTO SOUP)

ANNCR: It's time to change your bulb to Philips. Philips Longer Life square bulbs.

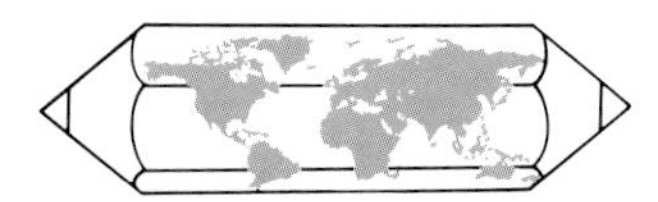

Gold, Silver & Bronze Awards

Consumer Television Over :10 But Under :30 Campaign

95 GOLD

ART DIRECTOR
Peter Cohen

WRITER
Larry Spector

AGENCY PRODUCER
Rachel Novak

PRODUCTION CO.
Story Piccolo Guliner

DIRECTOR
Mark Story

CLIENT
Good Sense

AGENCY
Levine Huntley Schmidt & Beaver

95 GOLD

MAN: When Good Sense asked me to sit under their bag filled with fifty-eight pounds of elephant fertilizer . . .
I said no.
Then they said it was made of super-tough plastic. Obviously that took a load off my mind.

ANNCR: Good Sense. The best things you'll ever throw out.

(SFX: BAG DROPPING)

SUPER: THE BEST THINGS YOU'LL EVER THROW OUT.

95 GOLD

MAN: Unlike paper plates, Good Sense plastic plates never go limp or weak.

(SFX: WHOOSH)

MAN: So you can go back for seconds.

(SFX: WHOOSH)

MAN: By the way, we also make plastic cups.

(SFX: SPLASH)

ANNCR: Good Sense. The best things you'll ever throw out.

95 GOLD

MAN: When Good Sense asked me to sit under their bag filled with fifty-eight pounds of kitty litter . . . I said no.
Then they said it was made of super-tough plastic.
Obviously that took a load off my mind.

ANNCR: Good Sense. The best things you'll ever throw out.

(SFX: BAG DROPPING)

SUPER: THE BEST THINGS YOU'LL EVER THROW OUT.

Gold, Silver & Bronze Awards

Consumer Television :10 Single

96 GOLD
ART DIRECTOR
Earl Cavanah
WRITER
Larry Cadman
AGENCY PRODUCER
Jaki Keuch
PRODUCTION CO.
Sandbank Films
DIRECTOR
Henry Sandbank
CLIENT
Volvo
AGENCY
Scali McCabe Sloves

97 SILVER
ART DIRECTOR
Dean Hanson
WRITER
Phil Hanft
AGENCY PRODUCER
Char Loving
PRODUCTION CO.
Sandbank Films
DIRECTOR
Henry Sandbank
CLIENT
Conran's
AGENCY
Fallon McElligott/
Minneapolis

Public Service Television: Single

98 GOLD
ART DIRECTOR
Logan Wilmont
WRITER
Mike Court
AGENCY PRODUCER
Debbie Court
PRODUCTION CO.
Sid Roberson
DIRECTOR
Simon Delaney
CLIENT
Mates Healthcare
AGENCY
Still Price Court Twivy
D'Souza/London

96 GOLD

(MUSIC: THROUGHOUT)

(SFX: CLICK)

ANNCR VO: How well does your car stand up to heavy traffic?

(MUSIC: OUT)

97 SILVER

VO: At Conran's, we don't believe beautifully-designed furniture . . . should be so expensive . . . you're afraid to even sit on it.

(SFX: BURP)

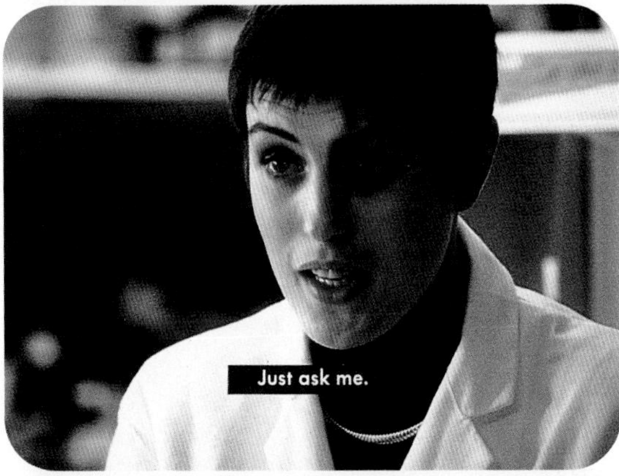

98 GOLD

(SFX: HALF-SECOND SILENCE; SHOP DOORBELL)

ASSISTANT: Hello.

BOY: Yes . . . er . . . I'd er . . . well . . .
(SUBTITLE: OH, NO! IT'S A WOMAN)

ASSISTANT: Yes?
(SUBTITLE: HE WANTS SOME CONDOMS)

BOY: I want some co . . . cotton wool.
(SUBTITLE: I REALLY WANT SOME CONDOMS)

ASSISTANT: Of course, will there be anything else?
(SUBTITLE: SILLY QUESTION)

(SFX: CASH REGISTER RING)

BOY: Yeah. Have you got a packet of . . . tissues?
(SUBTITLE: JUST ASK HER)

ASSISTANT: Man-size tissues. Is that all?
(SUBTITLE: JUST ASK ME)

(SFX: CASH REGISTER RING)

MVO: Mates are a new range of condoms. Like other condoms, they're reliable. But they're cheaper. She sells hundreds of packets. She's not embarrassed. So why should you be?

BOY: And a packet of Mates Condoms, please.

ASSISTANT: Of course.
(SUBTITLE: AT LAST)

(SUBTITLE: NO SWEAT)

ASSISTANT (TO BACK ROOM): Mr Williams, how much are these Mates Condoms?

MVO: Mates. You make love. They make sense.

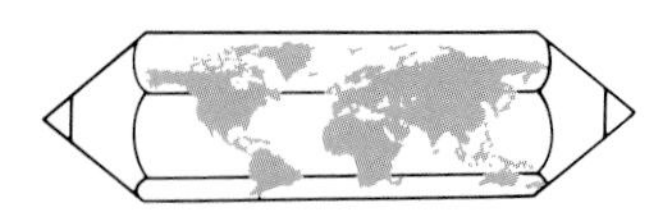

Gold, Silver & Bronze Awards

Public Service Television: Single

99 SILVER
ART DIRECTOR
Derrick Hass
WRITER
Howard Fletcher
AGENCY PRODUCER
Ros McClellan
PRODUCTION CO.
Spots Films/London
DIRECTOR
David Brown
CLIENT
Royal National Institute for the Deaf
AGENCY
Ogilvy & Mather/London

100 BRONZE
ART DIRECTOR
Ann Rhodes
WRITER
Steve Sandoz
PRODUCTION CO.
Noren Productions
DIRECTOR
Bob Peterson
CLIENT
Harbor View Injury Prevention Center
AGENCY
Worthy Cause Advertising/ Mercer Island, WA

Public Service Television: Campaign

101 GOLD
ART DIRECTOR
Mark Shap
WRITER
Veronica Nash
AGENCY PRODUCER
Tina Raver
PRODUCTION CO.
Petermann/Dektor
DIRECTOR
Leslie Dektor
CLIENT
Partnership for a Drug-Free America
AGENCY
Ogilvy & Mather

YOU GOT A SCREW LOOSE?

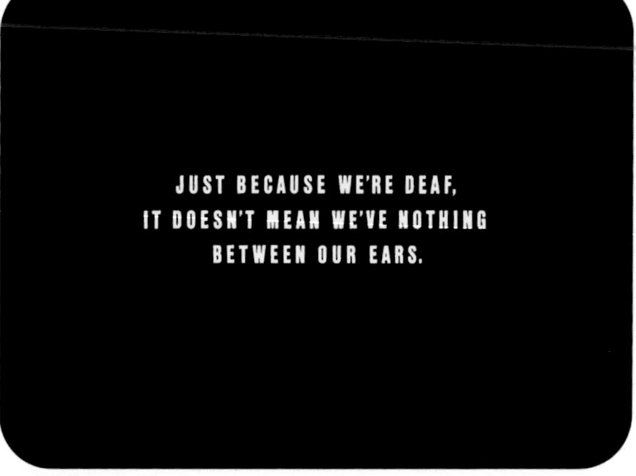
JUST BECAUSE WE'RE DEAF,
IT DOESN'T MEAN WE'VE NOTHING
BETWEEN OUR EARS.

99 SILVER

SUBTITLES: SIGN LANGUAGE FOR THE DEAF.
A PUBLIC INFORMATION FILM.
FOR PETE'S SAKE LISTEN.
I MIGHT AS WELL TALK TO MYSELF.
WASH YOUR BLEED'N EARS OUT.
IS HE A FOREIGNER OR WHAT?
YOU GOT A SCREW LOOSE?
GET LOST.
JUST BECAUSE WE'RE DEAF, IT DOESN'T MEAN WE'VE NOTHING BETWEEN OUR EARS.
SO PLEASE DON'T TREAT US LIKE IDIOTS.
THE ROYAL NATIONAL INSTITUTE FOR THE DEAF.

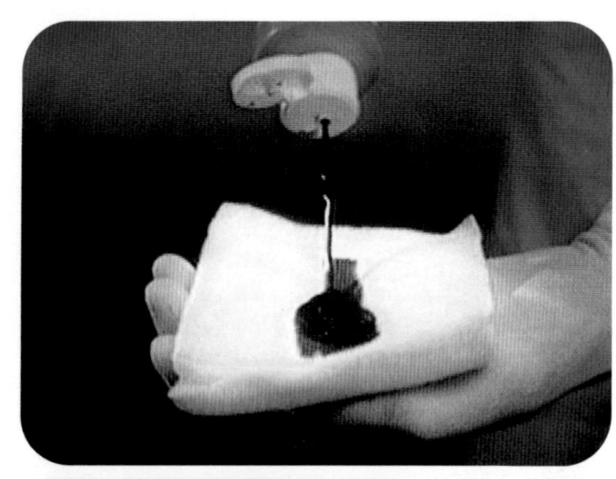

100 BRONZE

(MUSIC: SOLO PIANO UP AND UNDER)

ANNCR: If you're ever caught in a serious house fire, these things can save your life.
This is a debridement kit. It removes dead tissue from your burns.
This is betadine solution. It's used to scrub your burns twice a day.
This is a Pagget Dermatome. It removes healthy skin for grafts.
This is a PCA pump. It gives you morphine to control the pain.
And this is a smoke alarm. Use it and we may never have to use any of this other equipment on you.

101 GOLD

GIRL: Hi, Richie, I really need to talk to you.

DEALER: Yeah, yeah, I got you covered.

GIRL: I only want a little—come on.

DEALER: Sure, I understand.

GIRL: Just a couple of hits. I don't have any money—please.

DEALER: You mean you bring me out here for nothin'! That's a no-no, you understand? What, are you stupid? What do I look like . . .

GIRL: Richie, I just gave you a hundred dollars!

DEALER: That's got nothin' to do with now!

GIRL: Richie, please!

DEALER: Listen to me: no money, no candy, no crack, you understand? Now dissolve, lose yourself.

GIRL: Richie, come on, don't leave, please!

DEALER: Listen, shh, shh—that girl you're gonna get—that little red-headed girl and the both of yous are gonna come over to my crib . . .

GIRL: Charlotte?

DEALER: That's right. Go to a nice little party, understand me? Then I'll take care of ya.

SUPER: KIDS. IT'S YOU AGAINST THEM.

101 GOLD

DEALER (SLAMS ROOF OF CAR WITH TEENAGERS INSIDE): Creeps—I don't believe it! Driving in from the suburbs in their daddy's car to score and then trying to beat me down on the price . . . I don't cut my price for anybody . . . (SCREAMS) . . . 'specially for these rich creeps.
I got good stuff—you want good stuff—you gonna pay for it.

DEALER #2: They'll be back.

DEALER: Trying to tell me they can take it or leave it. Did you see those little punks, man?

DEALER #2: You're gonna be the first one to take it or leave it.

DEALER: Yeah, drivin' their daddy's big car. You know what I'd like to do to them? I'd like to rub their faces . . .

DEALER #2: You know, they're so stupid, they deserve to be burned.

DEALER: They're good for nothing, man . . .

DEALER #2: They're good for something . . . They're good for taking money off of.

DEALER #3 (WAVES CRACK AT CAR WITH KIDS): Hey, man, got some good crack . . . what do you need?

SUPER: KIDS. IT'S YOU AGAINST THEM.

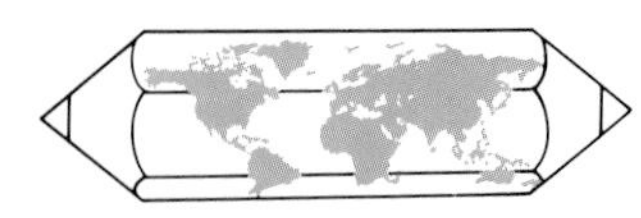

Gold, Silver & Bronze Awards

Public Service Television: Campaign

101 GOLD

ART DIRECTOR
Mark Shap

WRITER
Veronica Nash

AGENCY PRODUCER
Tina Raver

PRODUCTION CO.
Petermann/Dektor

DIRECTOR
Leslie Dektor

CLIENT
Partnership for a Drug-Free America

AGENCY
Ogilvy & Mather

Public Service Television: Campaign

102 SILVER

ART DIRECTOR
Logan Wilmont

WRITER
Mike Court

AGENCY PRODUCER
Debbie Court

PRODUCTION CO.
Sid Roberson

DIRECTOR
Simon Delaney

CLIENT
Mates Healthcare

AGENCY
Still Price Court Twivy D'Souza/London

103 BRONZE

ART DIRECTOR
Lionel Sosa

WRITERS
Lionel Sosa
Kathy Pena

AGENCY PRODUCERS
Deann Bostic
Lyn Nettleship

PRODUCTION CO.
Ashe-Bowie

DIRECTOR
Mike Bowie

CLIENT
Centers for Disease Control

AGENCY
Sosa & Associates/ San Antonio, TX

101 GOLD

(SFX: TRAFFIC NOISE)

MAN: You know, kid, all you gotta do is be cool. You just give the stuff to your best buddies.You take it to a party. Tell your friends it's a great high. They should just try it. Tell them it can't hurt them.

KID: I can do that.

MAN: Yeah, it's easy. Those kids are going to be a pushover, 'cause they like you. You're a hot shot, right? They'll love you for it.

KID: So how much do I charge?

MAN: Right now, nothing.

KID: Nothing?

MAN: Just give it away. Let 'em have a free taste. Then you watch. You watch and you see who comes back for more.

KID: And then I start charging.

MAN: You're a smart kid. You have a good day at school, Billy Boy.

(SFX: TRAFFIC NOISE)

SUPER: KIDS. IT'S YOU AGAINST THEM.

102 SILVER

(SFX: HALF-SECOND SILENCE; SHOP DOORBELL)

ASSISTANT: Hello.

BOY: Yes . . . er . . . I'd er . . . well . . .
(SUBTITLE: OH, NO! IT'S A WOMAN)

ASSISTANT: Yes?
(SUBTITLE: HE WANTS SOME CONDOMS)

BOY: I want some co . . . cotton wool.
(SUBTITLE: I REALLY WANT SOME CONDOMS)

ASSISTANT: Of course, will there be anything else?
(SUBTITLE: SILLY QUESTION)

(SFX: CASH REGISTER RING)

BOY: Yeah. Have you got a packet of . . . tissues?
(SUBTITLE: JUST ASK HER)

ASSISTANT: Man-size tissues. Is that all?
(SUBTITLE: JUST ASK ME)

(SFX: CASH REGISTER RING)

MVO: She sells hundreds of packets. She's not embarrassed. So why should you be?

BOY: And a packet of condoms, please.

ASSISTANT: Of course.
(SUBTITLE: AT LAST)

(SUBTITLE: NO SWEAT)

ASSISTANT (TO BACK ROOM): Mr Williams, how much are these condoms?

MVO: Condoms. It goes without saying they make sense.

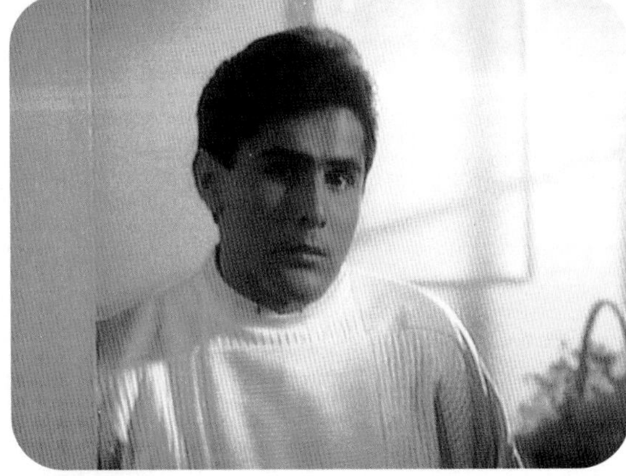

103 BRONZE

ALEJANDRO PAREDES: Do I look like someone who has AIDS?
Of course not.
I finished school. I have a good job. I help support my family. My kind of guy doesn't get AIDS, right? Well, I have AIDS. And I don't mind telling you . . . it's devastating.

VO: One Hispanic dies of AIDS every four hours.
Don't be one of them.
Be informed.
Call 1-800-342-AIDS.

ALEJANDRO: If I had a second chance, I'd be better informed.
Believe me.

Gold, Silver & Bronze Awards

Political Television: Single

104 GOLD
ART DIRECTOR
Judy Penny
WRITER
Sueanne Peacock
AGENCY PRODUCER
Beth Herscott
PRODUCTION CO.
Century III
CLIENT
Emerson College
AGENCY
Hill Holliday Connors Cosmopulos/Boston

105 SILVER
ART DIRECTORS
Randall Saitta
Scott Sorokin
WRITERS
Charles Borghese
Nancy Librett
AGENCY PRODUCER
Cynthia Woodward
PRODUCTION CO.
Associates & Nadel & Butler
DIRECTOR
Charlie Cole
CLIENT
Amnesty International USA
AGENCY
Lowe Marschalk

106 BRONZE
ART DIRECTOR
Ted Charron
WRITER
Ted Charron
AGENCY PRODUCER
Marge Charron
PRODUCTION CO.
Big City Films
CLIENT
Amnesty International USA
AGENCY
Theodore J. Charron Advertising

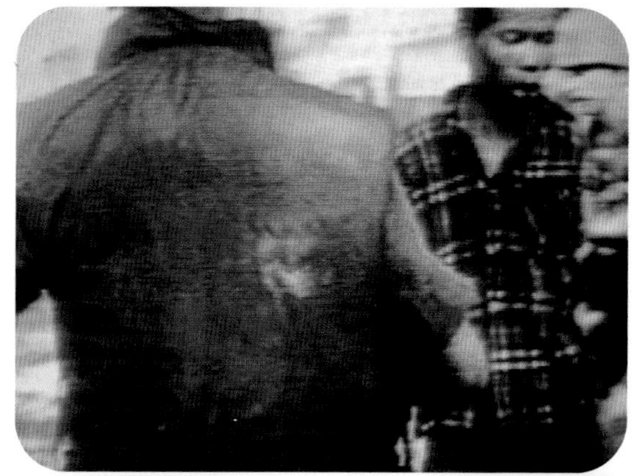

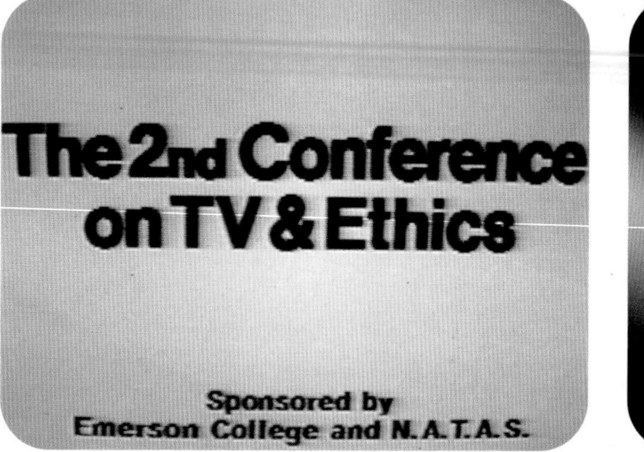

104 GOLD

VO: When do you turn the cameras off?
. . . And when do you show the truth?
When do you protect the viewers?
. . . And when are you keeping them in the dark?
When are you influencing history?
. . . And when are you making it?
The Second Conference on T.V. and Ethics.
You can call now for reservations . . .
Or you can close your eyes.

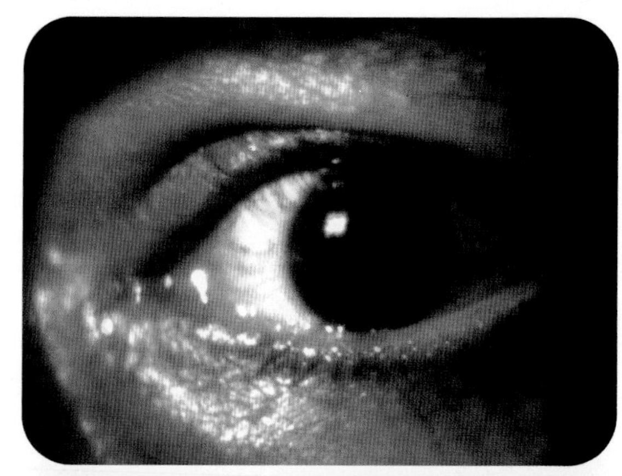

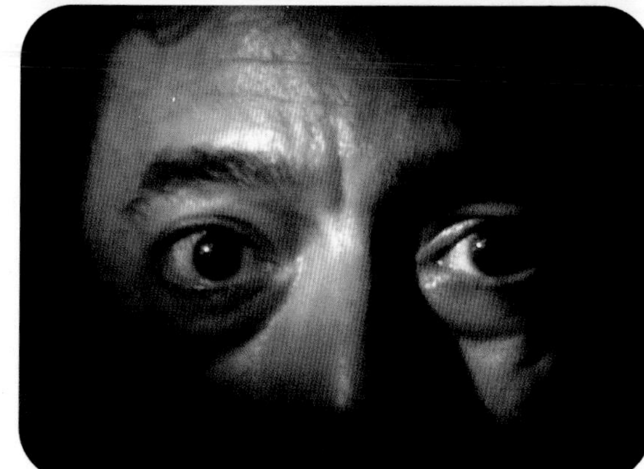

105 SILVER

(MUSIC & SFX: UP AND UNDER)

ANNCR: A student in South Africa.
A journalist in Chile
A dissident in the Soviet Union.
Prisoners of conscience.
Silenced without reason,
perhaps never to be heard
from again.
They need your voice.
We need your help.

Amnesty International USA
P.O. Box 37137
Washington, D.C. 20013

106 BRONZE

(SFX: SYNTHESIZER TONES; SUSPENSE, TERROR, PANIC)

VO: In certain countries a police interrogation can be rather relentless. In fact, they don't even give you a moment to catch your breath. Torture hurts everyone. To stop it, write: Amnesty International USA.

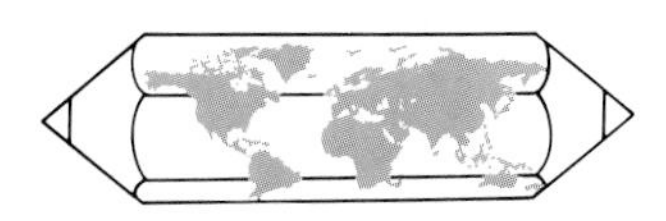

Gold, Silver & Bronze Awards

College Competition

Assignment: PAND (Performing Artists for Nuclear Disarmament)

107 GOLD
ART DIRECTOR
Barney Goldberg
WRITER
Barney Goldberg
SCHOOL
Virginia Commonwealth University/Richmond, VA

108 SILVER
ART DIRECTOR
Barney Goldberg
WRITER
Barney Goldberg
SCHOOL
Virginia Commonwealth University/Richmond, VA

109 BRONZE
ART DIRECTOR
Maryann Overath
WRITER
Maryann Overath
SCHOOL
University of Texas at Austin

A NUCLEAR WAR WOULD BRING PEOPLE A LOT CLOSER.

The truth is, a nuclear war would kill or maim almost everyone involved. Fortunately PAND, a group of performing artists, is working to eliminate nuclear weapons. If you would like to join our group or support the cause, contact PAND. Otherwise, prepare to join the group in the photo.

PERFORMING ARTISTS FOR NUCLEAR DISARMAMENT
Attn: Barbara Kopit 225 Lafayette St. New York, NY 10012, (212) 431-7921

107 GOLD

Save This Photo In Case Of A Nuclear War.
It'll Remind You Of What The Earth Looked Like.

Most everyone takes trees, grass and blue skies for granted. But after a nuclear war, these things will be just a memory. That's why PAND, a group of performing artists, have joined together to eliminate nuclear weapons. If the thought of nuclear war alarms you, contact PAND. If not, you better get out your scissors.

PERFORMING ARTISTS FOR NUCLEAR DISARMAMENT
Attn: Barbara Kopit 225 Lafayette St. New York, NY 10012, (212) 431-7921

108 SILVER

Nuclear war will destroy priceless works of art.

Performing Artists for Nuclear Disarmament want everyone to get in on the act. Please help.
For information, write PAND 225 Lafayette St. New York, NY 10012

109 BRONZE

The Gold Award Winners On The Gold Award Winners

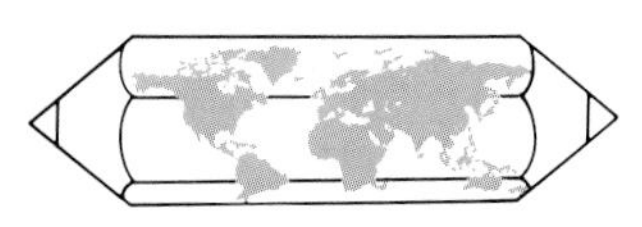

The Gold Award Winners on The Gold Award Winners

Consumer Newspaper
Over 600 Lines: Single

AGENCY: Abbott Mead Vickers/SMS - London
CLIENT: Volvo

16th October, 1987
4:00 am: Hurricane weather hits southern England.
11:00 am: Avoiding fallen trees, we finally make it into the agency.
1:00 pm: Volvo get in touch with Account man, Mike Turnbull. Turnbull rushes up to Creative floor with news of a car under a tree.
1:10 pm: Call photographer.
1:15 pm: Photographer departs for location.
1:30 pm: Write ad.
2:00 pm: Write better ad.
3:00 pm: Turnbull gets approval from Volvo over the phone.
3:15 pm: Arrange typesetting.
3:30 pm: Photography arrives.
3:45 pm: Organise print and retouching.
4:00 pm: Have lunch.
5:00 - 10:00 pm: Anxiously wait for everything.
10:20 pm: We arrive at setting house.
10:30 - 12:00 pm: Put mechanical together.
12:15 am: Artwork and mechanical biked to *The Observer* newspaper.
(Phew!)

John Donnelly
Ken Grimshaw

1 GOLD

Consumer Newspaper Over 600 Lines: Campaign

AGENCY: Mendelsohn/Zien - Los Angeles
CLIENT: Southern California Acura Dealers

A sincere thanks to Mercedes and BMW.

Jordin Mendelsohn
Perrin Lam

4 GOLD

Consumer Newspaper 600 Lines Or Less: Campaign

AGENCY: Lowe Marschalk/Cleveland, OH
CLIENT: Parker Pen USA

We couldn't come up with any original ideas for this campaign.
So we drew from our actual, real-life experiences.

Stephen Fechtor
John Strohmeyer

10 GOLD

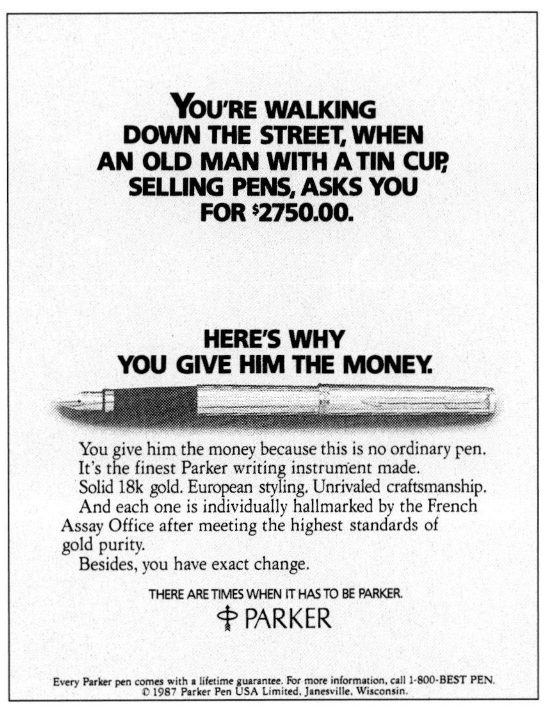

The Gold Award Winners on The Gold Award Winners

Consumer Magazine B/W: 1 Page Or Spread Including Magazine Supplements

AGENCY: Lowe Marschalk
CLIENT: International Center of Photography

'I'm worried.'
'Why?'
'You know, they're having another summit.'
'So?'
'Our ad hasn't run yet.'
'So?'
'So what if they get along this time?'

Charles Borghese
Randall Saitta

13 GOLD

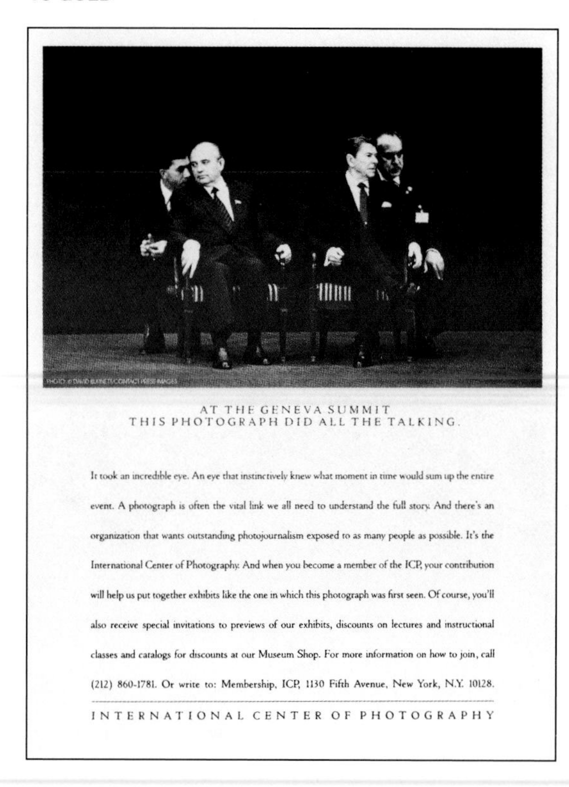

Consumer Magazine Color: 1 Page Or Spread Including Magazine Supplements

AGENCY: Leagas Delaney Partnership/London
CLIENT: Linguaphone

Who said 'Truth in Advertising' was dead?
We wrote that ad in a taxi.

Tim Delaney
Steve Dunn

16 GOLD

Travel is supposed to broaden the mind not render it useless.
LINGUAPHONE

Consumer Magazine
Color: Campaign
Including Magazine
Supplements

AGENCY: Leagas Delaney Partnership/London
CLIENT: Linguaphone

Have you ever tried to ask an Italian waiter to "hold the mango"?
Told a Spanish taxi driver to "hang in there"?
Wondered why a German Fraülein wouldn't "come across"?
You have?
Then you know exactly how easy it was to write these ads.

Tim Delaney
Steve Dunn

21 GOLD

Consumer Magazine
Less Than A Page
B/W Or Color: Single

AGENCY: Hill Holliday Connors Cosmopulos
CLIENT: WWOR-TV

If it's possible to make a soap interesting, it's essential to make a special about rape seem extremely vivid.

But try to keep that in mind during "sweeps" week, when there are as many as forty ads due by Friday.

We were enlisted by David Corr and Sig Gross (who have a bronze WWOR ad in this book) to do, oh, about ten of these along with whatever else we had to do that week.

And then there was the client. Believe it or not, not just any client will buy a frank, even shocking line about rape. WWOR justified a lot of late nights and weekends by signing off on ads like these.

Rich Pels
Paul Federico

24 GOLD

The Gold Award Winners on The Gold Award Winners

Consumer Magazine Less Than A Page B/W Or Color: Campaign

AGENCY: Chiat/Day
CLIENT: Sara Lee

As usual, the client gave us the great headlines, but this time we stuck them in the coupons.

Bryan Buckley
Mike Shine

25 GOLD

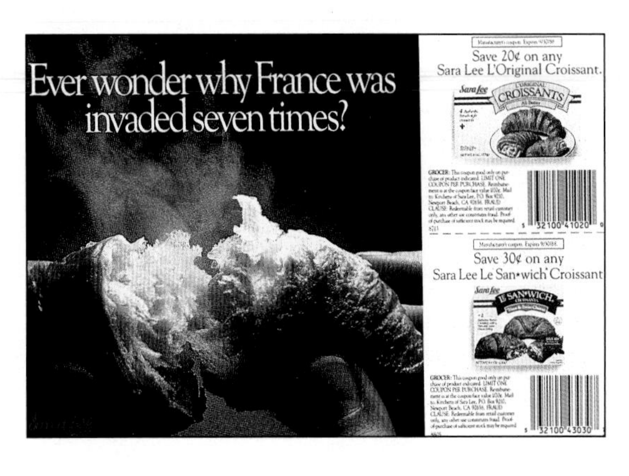

Trade B/W: 1 Page Or Spread

AGENCY: Angotti Thomas Hedge
CLIENT: Barron's

This ad owes as much to math as it does to marketing.

When we first got the *Barron's* trade business, we waded into the sea of numbers that media accounts seem to generate. We came across an amazing fact: almost a third of all *Barron's* readers were millionaires. Using that number, and relating it to the magazine's cost-per-thousand, we worked out how much it costs to reach each one of them. That led to an ad that made its way into these pages last year ("Lowest cost per millionaire"), and led to this one as well.

The resulting ad had the weight of fact instead of claim, and approached readers with the truth instead of an advertiser's self-serving version of it.

And if it's written and illustrated with a certain wit, that's because we let copywriters and art directors–and not accountants–create advertising.

Tom Thomas
Gail Bartley

28 GOLD

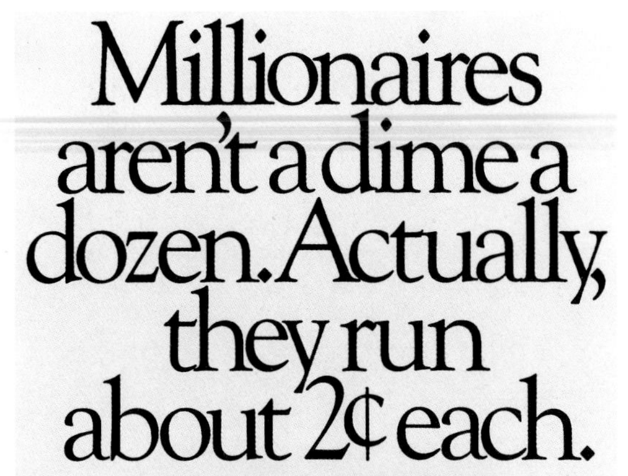

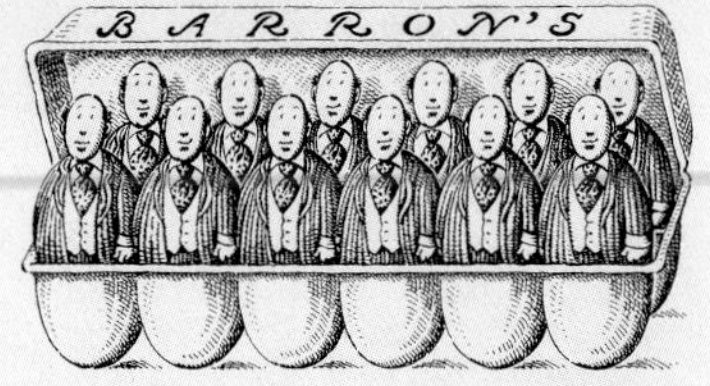

The exact figure is 2.41 cents for every millionaire we deliver.
Which, as a little comparison shopping will show, is well below the going rate for the rich.
Barron's offers a lower cost per thousand—and per millionaire—than Business Week, Forbes or Fortune. And they're available in quantities considerably larger than a dozen. Or a hundred. Or a hundred thousand.
In fact, 37% of Barron's readers are millionaires. And that just includes their own household assets.
They also control or influence millions more in corporate assets. Because Barron's readers represent a greater concentration of highly paid decision-makers than any other major business or financial magazine.
Of course, you can still reach such people through those other magazines. All it takes is a willingness to pay more for them.
Which is definitely not the recommended way to become a millionaire—or to buy one.

HOW THE SMART MONEY GETS THAT WAY.

Trade Color: 1 Page Or Spread

AGENCY: Levine Huntley Schmidt & Beaver
CLIENT: Cailor/Resnick Studio

It's Basic Advertising 101. Show a product benefit in an interesting way.

Sal DeVito

31 GOLD

Trade Less Than A Page B/W Or Color: Single

AGENCY: Loeffler Ketchum Mountjoy/Charlotte, NC
CLIENT: JTA Talent

We'd like to thank the night watchman at the Watergate for making this concept possible.

Jim Mountjoy
Ed Jones

34 GOLD

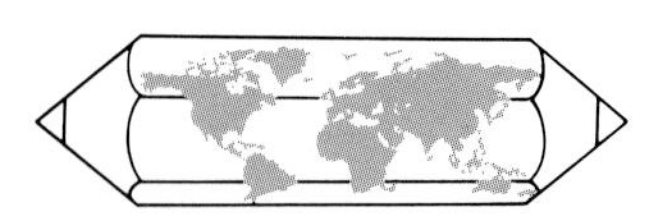

The Gold Award Winners on The Gold Award Winners

Trade Any Size B/W Or Color: Campaign

AGENCY: Angotti Thomas Hedge
CLIENT: Barron's

In agency media departments, *Barron's* is sometimes dismissed (mainly by people who don't read it) as a financial-only publication for a financial-only audience.

Not true. Real human beings, including at least one creative director, read it faithfully.

The campaign simply portrays *Barron's* as the best way of reaching those human beings–the rich and powerful kind–no matter what they do for a living. The objective is to get *Barron's* on the media shopping lists it should be on, to sell not just mutual funds, but expensive cars, computers or anything else real people with real money might buy.

Which is why the ads don't look like tombstones, and why they're written in English instead of Financialese.

Tom Thomas
Bob Phillips

37 GOLD

In the great corporate pecking order, those who peck first read Barron's.

In business, everybody answers to somebody.
And sitting at the very top of that hierarchy of somebodies is the chairman of the board.
So it's worth noting that Barron's has a higher concentration of board chairmen among its readers than Business Week, Forbes or Fortune.
Next in the pecking order are those who earn six-figure incomes and occupy the highest echelons of top management. We have a higher concentration of those executives, too.
Of course, it could be argued that the real power in any money-making enterprise resides with those who control all that money: namely, chief financial officers. Barron's also has a higher concentration of CFOs. And comptrollers, secretary/treasurers and treasurers.
In fact, no matter how you define clout in the corporate hierarchy, you'll reach it more efficiently with Barron's. At a lower cost per thousand than any of its competitors.
And that's what makes Barron's unique: it's the best way to reach those who peck first–without having your entire media budget devoured in the process.

BARRON'S
HOW THE SMART MONEY GETS THAT WAY.

Collateral Brochures Other Than By Mail: Single

AGENCY: Rice & Rice/Minneapolis
CLIENT: The One Show

After the photo session, we had to send the medal back. It was nice to be able to get one we could keep.

Nancy Rice
Nick Rice
Jim Newcombe

40 GOLD

Collateral
Sales Kits:
Campaign

AGENCY: Susan Gilbert & Company/Coral Gables, FL
CLIENT: Ryder System Aviation Leasing & Services

The Red Baron may have won the Blue Max and a chest full of other medals, decorations and ribbons.
But a Gold Pencil was to forever elude him.

Frank Schulwolf
Arthur Low

46 GOLD

Collateral
Direct Mail:
Single

AGENCY: Rice & Rice/Minneapolis
CLIENT: The One Show

The only thing that's more fun than getting to do a poster for The One Show is getting a gold medal for it.

Nancy Rice
Nick Rice
Jim Newcombe

47 GOLD

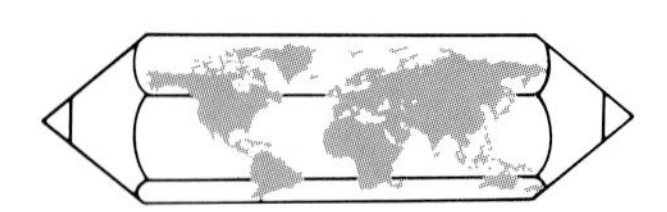

The Gold Award Winners on The Gold Award Winners

Collateral Direct Mail: Campaign

AGENCY: Susan Gilbert & Company/Coral Gables, FL
CLIENT: Ryder System Aviation Leasing & Services

The enemy swirling about probing for a weakness; nerves stretched to the breaking point; the cold, icy fingers of fear clutching at your bowels; your good friends going down in flames and the constant awareness that every day could be your last, too.
So who said advertising was going to be a picnic?

Frank Schulwolf
Arthur Low

50 GOLD

Collateral P.O.P.

AGENCY: Rice & Rice/Minneapolis
CLIENT: The One Show

The headline was easy. We just thought about what we'd be doing if we didn't win anything this year.

Nancy Rice
Nick Rice
Jim Newcombe

53 GOLD

Outdoor: Single

AGENCY: Foote Cone & Belding/Los Angeles
CLIENT: Sunkist Growers

We were at an oddball birthday party when a large, bald man, dressed in a white suit, jumped out of the cake and said, 'Slice the orange, fan it out and backlight the essentials.' Before we could ask for the headline, he was gone.

Peter Angelos
Larry Corby

56 GOLD

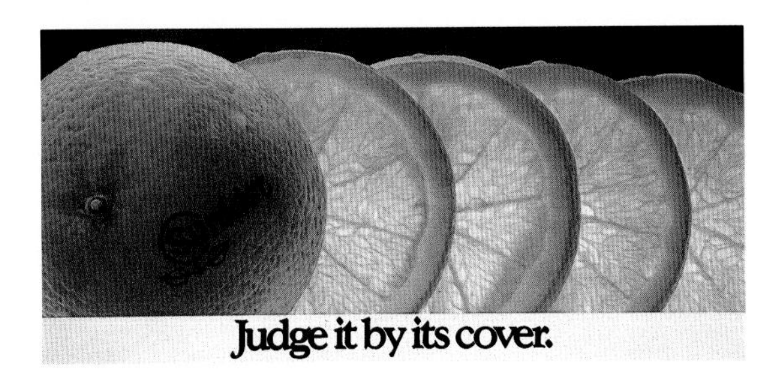

Outdoor: Campaign

AGENCY: Ammirati & Puris
CLIENT: Club Med

Ted thought of one of them. I thought of two. Ted may remember it differently.

Helayne Spivak
Ted Shaine

59 GOLD

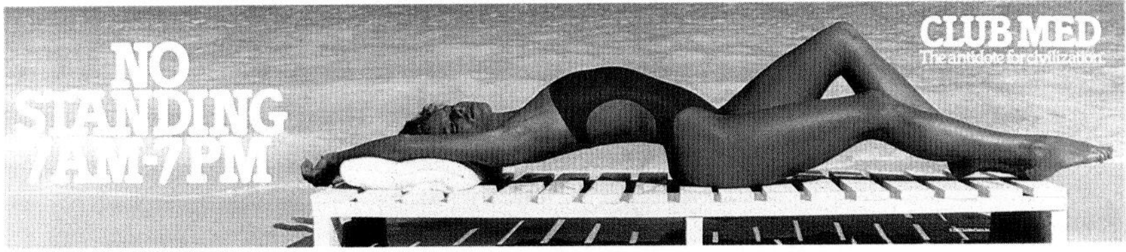

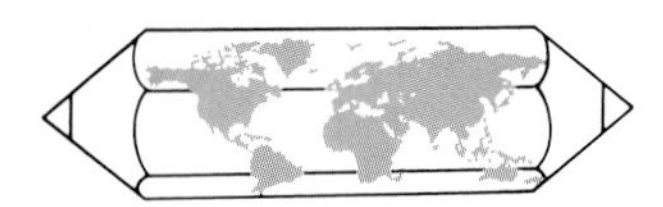

Public Service Newspaper Or Magazine: Single

AGENCY: The Martin Agency/Richmond, VA
CLIENT: People for the Ethical Treatment of Animals

When the Lord said man has dominion over the animals, did that include the right to test new drain openers by pouring them into an animal's eyes?
Thank you for the Gold Medal.

Luke Sullivan
Wayne Gibson

62 GOLD

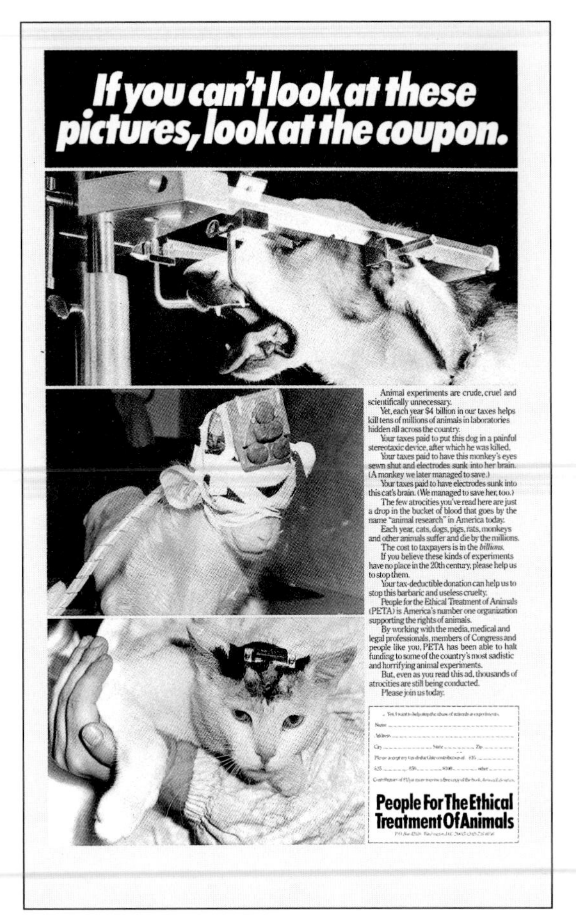

Public Service Newspaper Or Magazine: Campaign

AGENCY: The Martin Agency/Richmond, VA
CLIENT: People for the Ethical Treatment of Animals

In the past ten years, the National Institutes of Health and agencies of its like have spent billions (yes, billions) of your tax dollars granting money to "scientific" experiments that have included: sewing two rats together, sewing a baby monkey's eyes shut, pouring oven cleaner into the eyes of rabbits, decapitating dogs and monkeys to see how long the heads can be kept alive, sewing the head of one German Shepherd onto the neck of another one, shooting laser beams into the eyes of monkeys until they sizzle and burst, electrifying a baby monkey's food bowl, sinking electrodes into the brains of turtles to determine "if turtles dream," and cutting off the front paws of mice "to see how they'll groom." Given such input from the client, it was easy to do these ads.
People for the Ethical Treatment of Animals can be reached by writing PETA, Box 41526, Washington, DC 20015.

Luke Sullivan
Wayne Gibson

65 GOLD

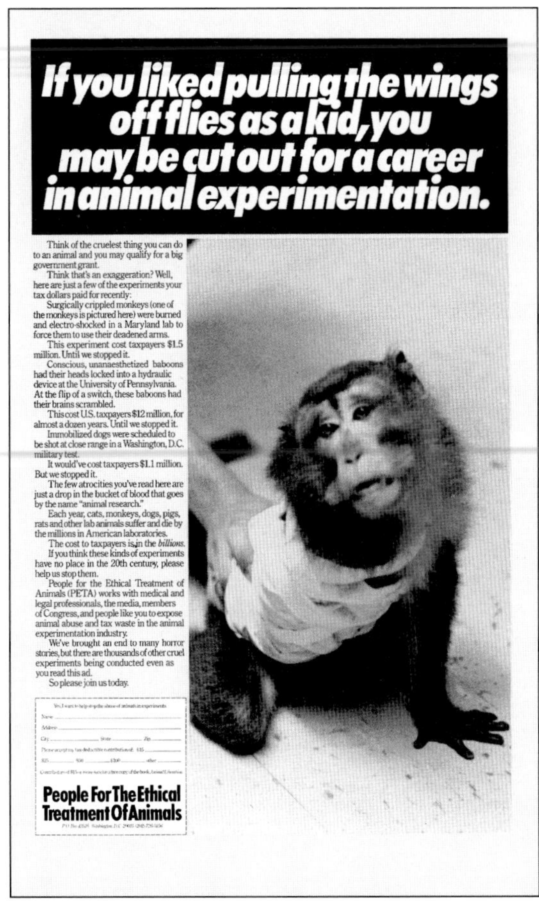

Public Service Outdoor: Single

AGENCY: The Martin Agency/Richmond, VA
CLIENT: People for the Ethical Treatment of Animals

We'd like to say that doing good work for a cause like this is as easy as shooting fish in a barrel, but our client's against that too.

Luke Sullivan
Wayne Gibson

68 GOLD

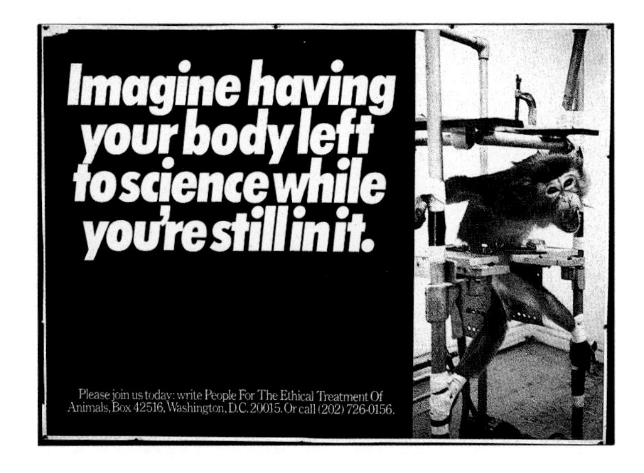

Political Newspaper Or Magazine: Single

AGENCY: Campbell-Mithun/Minneapolis
CLIENT: PAL

The tiny staff of the Minnesota Pet Owners Association received an overwhelming number of supportive letters and phone calls after running this ad. Of course, we were pretty overwhelmed when we got your phone call, too.

Carl Pfirman
David Peterson

71 GOLD

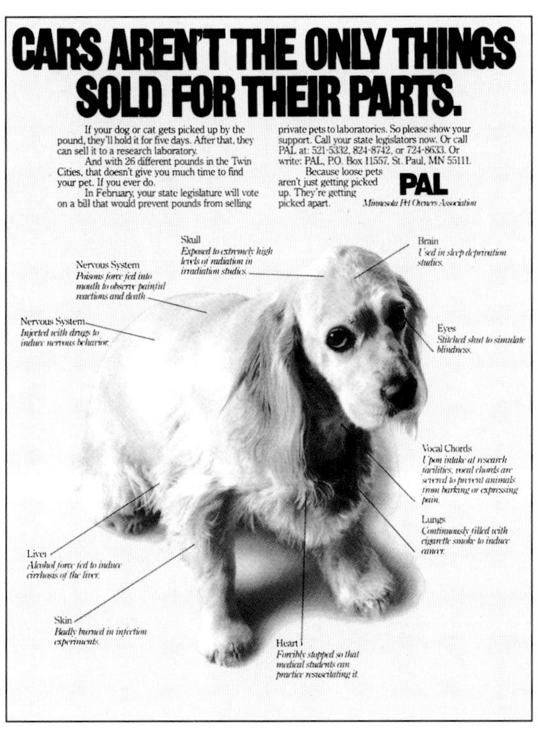

The Gold Award Winners on The Gold Award Winners

Consumer Radio: Single and Consumer Radio: Campaign

AGENCY: Adweek In-House
CLIENT: Adweek Magazine

We asked ourselves what creative approach the best Advertising Agencies would take. After we came up with it, we did just the opposite.

Dick Orkin
Chris Coyle
Haris Orkin

SEE GOLD AWARD WINNERS 75 AND 78

Consumer Television Over :30 (:45/:60/:90) Single and Consumer Television Over :30 (:45/:60/:90) Campaign

AGENCY: Hal Riney & Partners/San Francisco
CLIENT: The Perrier Group

There aren't too many times you can say 'everything happened just right' and have it stick, to a product or anything else. We thought we could say it for Perrier. The fun part was figuring out what the "everythings" were.

Dan Mountain

80 GOLD and 83 GOLD

Consumer Television
:30 Single

AGENCY: Borders Perrin & Norrander/Seattle
CLIENT: King County Medical Blue Shield

This is the perfect example of a window of opportunity. When we learned our client was helping to provide medical coverage for the U.S. Olympic team, a testimonial seemed only natural.

If you can crash-test cars, we figured why not. Take the idea a step further with crash-tested insurance. It was simple except for one thing: stock footage.

Anybody who's ever tried to pry the stuff loose, much less find it, is in for the real thrill of victory and agony of defeat.

Luckily we scored. Thanks to the athletes and a client who showed some guts, we got all the impact we hoped for. When the groans of the One Show Awards audience drowned out the announcer on the spot, it was music to our ears.

Tim O'Leary
Tom Stoneham
Larry Asher

86 GOLD

Consumer Television
:30 Campaign

AGENCY: Chiat/Day
CLIENT: NYNEX

Oh, let's think back now.

Dinner with our phone books. Pasta, we think it was. At Pete's Tavern.

It started with three simple observations.

Our yellow pages is full of weird stuff. We're awfully tired of big, overblown productions. And it's late. So we ate and talked it over. However, we kept getting interrupted by this really dumb waiter.

Robin Raj
Marty Weiss

89 GOLD

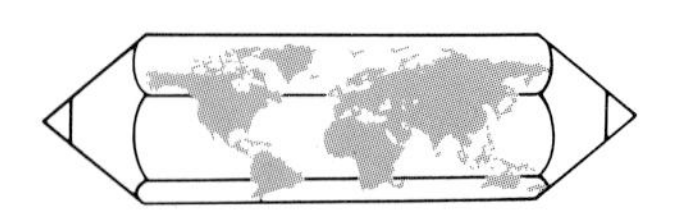

The Gold Award Winners on The Gold Award Winners

Consumer Television
Over :10 But Under :30
Single

AGENCY: Hal Riney & Partners/San Francisco
CLIENT: New Zealand Kiwifruit Authority

Everybody at Hal Riney & Partners thought we were incredibly daring to do a commercial and not hire Hal to do the voice-over

Ken Mandelbaum
Cathi Mooney
(formerly of Hal Riney & Partners)

92 GOLD

Consumer Television
Over :10 But Under :30
Campaign

AGENCY: Levine Huntley Schmidt & Beaver
CLIENT: Good Sense

When you're dealing with fifty-eight pounds of elephant manure in a garbage bag, you don't want it to breakthrough.

Thankfully, the judges at The One Show thought it did.

Peter Cohen
Larry Spector

95 GOLD

Consumer Television
:10 Single

AGENCY: Scali McCabe Sloves
CLIENT: Volvo

Earl Cavanah was doodling one day and idly drew a picture of a Volvo with a truck on top. At the time neither of us thought much about it.

Several weeks later however, I was rifling through our scrap pile of ideas to see if there was anything we'd missed. I ran across the drawing.

I wrote the line on the spot. The client liked the idea, both as a T.V. commercial and as a print ad, and it got produced.

The moral of the story is: it's not over 'till the fat lady empties your wastebasket.

Larry Cadman

96 GOLD

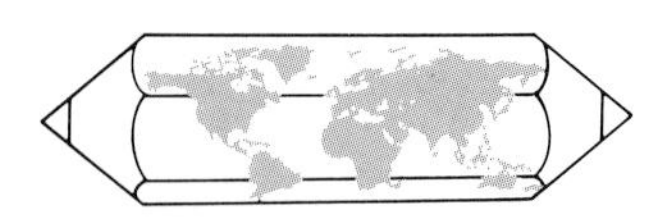

The Gold Award Winners on The Gold Award Winners

Public Service Television: Single

AGENCY Still Price Court Twivy D'Souza/London
CLIENT: Mates Healthcare

We painstakingly crafted the work for months.
(We had the idea at 5:00 am. The morning of the pitch.)
We talked to all the leading directors in London.
(But ended up using Simon Delaney.)
We threw money at the script.
(We eked out a tiny budget.)
We are absolutely delighted we won.
(We are absolutely delighted we won.)

Logan Wilmont
Mike Court

98 GOLD

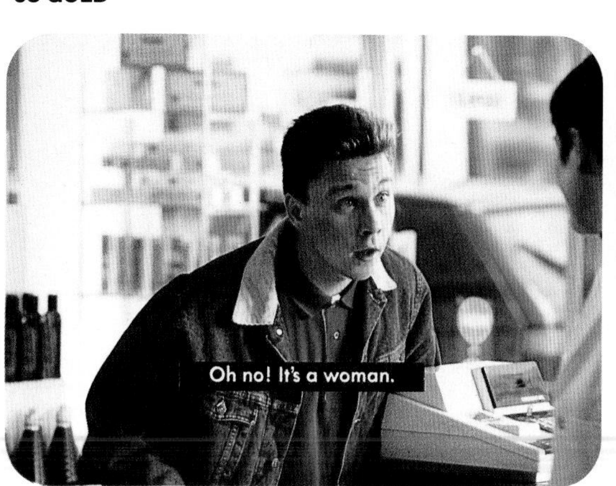

Public Service Television: Campaign

AGENCY: Ogilvy & Mather
CLIENT: Partnership for a Drug-Free America

How often has someone at a cocktail party said, 'You're in advertising? How can you live with yourself? Trying to *sell* stuff to people! Ugh!'

We realized that today's drug dealers are very smart salesmen. And if we exposed that, people might hate them. Almost as much as they hate us.

Veronica Nash

101 GOLD

Political Television: Single

AGENCY: Hill Holliday Connors Cosmopulos/Boston
CLIENT: Emerson College

No time. No money. Demonstrate the influence and responsibility of T.V. over the decades in thirty seconds. No–less. There's a phone number. We chose a powerful execution. Literally. It was that or nothing. So we used *both* to show the two sides of the issue. And made a moment in commercials hopefully as impactful as that moment on national news.

Sueanne Peacock
Judy Penny

104 GOLD

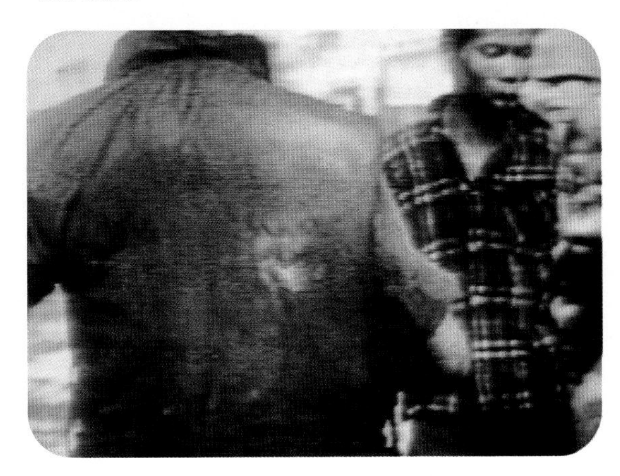

Print Finalists

Consumer Newspaper Over 600 Lines: Single

110
ART DIRECTORS
Tom McConnaughy
Brian Kelly
WRITER
James Schmidt
PHOTOGRAPHER
Tony D'Orio
CLIENT
HealthChicago
AGENCY
McConnaughy Barocci Brown/Chicago

111
ART DIRECTOR
Doug Lew
WRITER
Bill Johnson
CLIENT
Minneapolis Institute of Arts
AGENCY
Ruhr/Paragon - Minneapolis

112
ART DIRECTOR
Jordin Mendelsohn
WRITERS
Jordin Mendelsohn
Perrin Lam
CLIENT
Southern California Acura Dealers
AGENCY
Mendelsohn/Zien - Los Angeles

113
ART DIRECTOR
Jordin Mendelsohn
WRITERS
Jordin Mendelsohn
Perrin Lam
PHOTOGRAPHER
Jay Ahrend
CLIENT
Southern California Acura Dealers
AGENCY
Mendelsohn/Zien - Los Angeles

She Has A Head Full Of Kidney Stones.

It sounds ridiculous, doesn't it? But the sad fact is, it's true.

Each year, thousands of people complain of physical ailments that in reality are caused by emotional stress or trauma.

They visit doctors and check into hospitals, but in the end no physical problem is ever found.

So they visit even more doctors and on and on it goes.

The effect of all this on an individual can, as you might imagine, be devastating.

Equally devastating can be the effect on medical costs.

The fact is, those suffering from such psychosomatic ailments have 14 times the average cost for outpatient care. Six times the average for inpatient care. And nine times the average for total health expenditures.

How can such personal and financial troubles be avoided?

By offering people a health plan that not only provides comprehensive medical care, but one that provides comprehensive psychiatric care as well.

A plan, not so coincidentally, like that of HealthChicago.

At HealthChicago, all our psychiatric care is handled through the Northwestern Memorial Institute of Psychiatry. One of the most esteemed in the country.

The Institute provides HealthChicago and our doctors with a network of many of the finest psychiatrists and clinical psychologists in the Chicagoland area.

A group of experienced professionals who, in consultation with our doctors, are able to provide patients with precise diagnosis and treatment.

Such expertise ensures that our members receive the appropriate level of care.

And that our member companies receive benefits that indeed help them solve all of their health care problems.

It's this dedicated approach to psychiatric care that has led Dr. Harold Visotsky, Chairman of Psychiatry at Northwestern, to call our program, "...the best around. One that is constantly looking for new and innovative ways to provide its members with the finest in health care."

And it's this approach that has no doubt contributed to the fact that HealthChicago is the fastest growing health plan in the area.

With 40,000 new members in the last year alone.

For more information on HealthChicago, just call Karey McGowan at 1-800-345-1175. After all, shouldn't your employees have a health plan that treats their minds as well as it treats their bodies?

HealthChicago
GALANOS MARK
001 3465205 06
J C DARROW MD
0013 V2 E1

It's The Most Important Card You Can Carry.

110

WHO WAS THAT MASKED MAN?

AN ASSEMBLAGE OF SPIRITS: IDEA AND IMAGE IN NEW IRELAND / NOW THROUGH JANUARY 3.
Discover the true identity of the people behind the mask. When The Minneapolis Institute of Arts presents 50 rare carvings from the South Pacific. Organized by The Minneapolis Institute of Arts, this exhibition was made possible in part by grants from the National Endowment for the Arts and the National Endowment for the Humanities. Come see it at The Minneapolis Institute of Arts, 2400 Third Avenue South, Minneapolis, Minnesota.

The Minneapolis Institute of Arts

111

TWO OF THE TOP THREE LUXURY CARS IN THE COUNTRY HAVE TERRIBLE SLIPPAGE PROBLEMS.

A curious thing happened to Mercedes' and BMWs recently. They've started slipping. But this slippage has nothing to do with either automobile's excellent transmission or anti-lock brake system. Which is somewhat unfortunate. Because those problems can be easily fixed.

The slippage problem we're referring to is more complicated. And is caused by something a lot more serious.

A decline in customer satisfaction.

You see, it all started with this year's highly respected J. D. Power Customer Satisfaction Index. What the J. D. Power survey does is ask a lot of questions. Of lots of drivers.

Questions like: How many problems has your car had while under warranty? How many times has it needed fixing after it was fixed the first time? And were there even parts to fix it with?

After reading through all the responses, there emerged a very clear picture of what it's like to own a Mercedes. A BMW. And an Acura.

1987 J.D. POWER CUSTOMER SATISFACTION INDEX

Industry Average Points 104

Source: 1987 CSI

But something else emerged, too.

Mercedes-Benz wasn't on top of the list. No, not this year. This year, Mercedes slipped to an unprecedented third place.

And BMW, an embarrassing eleventh.

The car that came in first, by 19 percentage points better than Mercedes and a whopping 40 points better than BMW, was the Acura Legend.

Which should really come as no surprise.

After all, since its introduction in '86, Acura has been compared equal to or better than both Mercedes' and BMWs on numerous occasions. Why this year alone, it won Motor Trend's import car of the year award.

So if you're thinking of buying a Mercedes or a BMW, think again. You could be making a major slip-up.

ACURA
Southern California Dealers

WE HAVE TWO WORDS TO SAY TO CAR MAGAZINES WHO PUT US INTO UNFAIR COMPARISONS.

THANK YOU.

Frankly, the comparisons have been a bit embarrassing.

Not to the Acura Legend, but to the automobiles it's been compared to. Cars $5,000, $10,000, even $30,000 more.

Ward's Auto World compared the Acura Legend, a car that sells for about $21,000, against no less than 12 expensive European competitors. A full range of luxury motorcars. Luxury sport GT's. And midrange sedans. In 14 different categories such as engine, interior styling, ride/suspension and handling, everyone was graded on a scale of 1 to 10 and 140 points meant a perfect score.

Import Evaluation Scoreboard	Manufacturer Suggested Retail	Exterior Styling	Engine	Ride/Suspension	Fit/Finish	Final Impression	Other	Total Score
Acura Legend	$21,000	10	10	10	10	10	84	134
BMW 735 L7	44,000	7	10	10	10	9	83	129
BMW 325 ES	23,600	7	10	9	9	9	81	125
Mercedes 300E	36,700	10	10	10	10	10	86	136
Mercedes 190 16V	36,800	8	10	8	9	9	80	124
Mercedes 560 SEC	62,100	9	9	9	10	9	82	128

Source: Ward's Auto World, May 1986

The Acura Legend got 134. Five points higher than BMW's $44,000 735. Nine points higher than a $23,000 325. Against Mercedes, the Legend scored high enough to beat two of them. And lost to a third by just two points. The third was the 300E. A car almost twice as expensive as the Acura Legend.

Ward's Auto World wasn't alone. Car and Driver claimed that the Acura Legend was a better value than the Mercedes 300E. And had a better ride than the Cadillac Seville. Motor Trend went so far as to say, "...the Legend is a better BMW!"

The results are unanimous. Not only is the Acura Legend a good car for the money, it would be a good car for a lot more money.

ACURA
Southern California Dealers

Pricing and comparison information is published in Ward's Auto World, May 1986, Car and Driver, August 1986 and Motor Trend, April 1986. * Manufacturer's suggested retail price for the 5-speed Acura Legend is $20,767, September 1987.

Consumer Newspaper Over 600 Lines: Single

114

ART DIRECTOR
Daniel Russ

WRITER
Cabell Harris

PHOTOGRAPHER
Jim Erickson

CLIENT
Barnett Banks

AGENCY
The Martin Agency/
Richmond, VA

115

ART DIRECTORS
Kathy Izard
Jim Mountjoy

WRITERS
Ed Jones
Steve Lasch

PHOTOGRAPHER
Ron Chapple

CLIENT
Orthopaedic Hospital of Charlotte

AGENCY
Loeffler Ketchum Mountjoy/Charlotte, NC

116

ART DIRECTOR
Tim Sprague

WRITER
Betsy Wells

PHOTOGRAPHER
Gene Dwiggins

CLIENT
Providence Journal Bulletin

AGENCY
Duffy & Shanley/
Providence, RI

117

ART DIRECTOR
Carolyn Tye

WRITER
Kerry Feuerman

PHOTOGRAPHER
Jamie Cook

CLIENT
Crestar Bank

AGENCY
Ford & Westbrook/
Richmond, VA

"WE'RE THE NEW STANDARD FOR BANKING SERVICES IN ATLANTA. THAT'S A PROMISE."

We know you've heard all of this before. We know you have a hard time believing any of it, or even understanding why a bank would bother saying it.

So many banks make monumental, chest-beating claims, then turn out to be just like all the other banks.

So when we make a claim, we're going to give you a reason to believe it. First things first. First National Bank of Cobb County is now Barnett Bank. It's the same people, with a new name.

Okay, here's the first promise. Barnett will offer you a unique range of products. Here's your reason to believe it. Premier Account. You get your own Personal Banker: one individual who will handle all your banking needs. A CreditLine account from $5,000 to $90,000 accessible simply by writing a check. And you get our Premier VISA® with a minimum credit line of $5,000. All for less than you'd normally pay for a gold card alone.

You can give our Customer Service Center a call at (404) 429-3802 if you have questions about the merger or the new services you'll receive as a customer of Barnett.

We want to be your bank in a big way. But we know you're skeptical. So for now we'll keep the promise we've made and earn your trust. And one day, we'll earn your business.

Barnett Bank

We'll Keep Our Promises.

114

We're Providing Relief To Some Of The World's Most Troubled Spots.

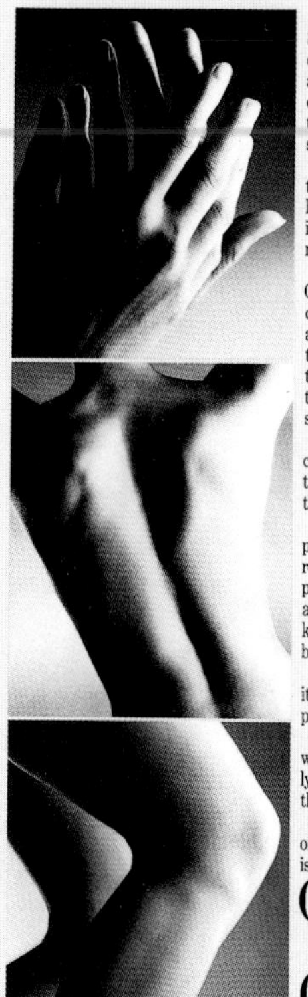

Inflamed hands, feet and joints. Severe back pains that flare up without provocation. A recurring ache in a hip, knee, shoulder or elbow. If one of these spots spells trouble for you these days, the sooner you get to the source of the pain, the better.

And that could mean getting to the Orthopaedic Hospital of Charlotte. Because we offer truly specialized care for problems of the joints, muscles and skeleton.

Take our staff, for example. At Orthopaedic Hospital, you have access to six specialists of the hands alone. Another eighteen concentrate on disorders of joints, such as the hips and knees. While an additional twenty-three devote themselves to problems of the back.

More than a few of these physicians are nationally recognized for the contributions they have made to their specialties.

Just as important, they are supported by a nursing and operating room staff expertly trained in orthopedic care. We even assign a personal nurse to each patient to allow a keener first-hand knowledge and better responsiveness.

And finally, our orthopedic facilities are designed solely for the purpose of solving problems like yours.

All of which may help explain why our average stay is substantially shorter than for other hospitals in the region.

Call the Orthopaedic Hospital of Charlotte. Because getting relief is less trouble than you think.

Orthopaedic Hospital Of Charlotte
1-800-942-6222
Call For Physician Referral • 1901 Randolph Road

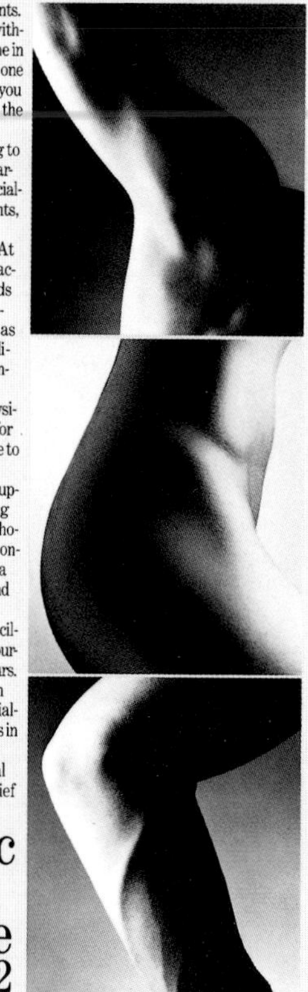

115

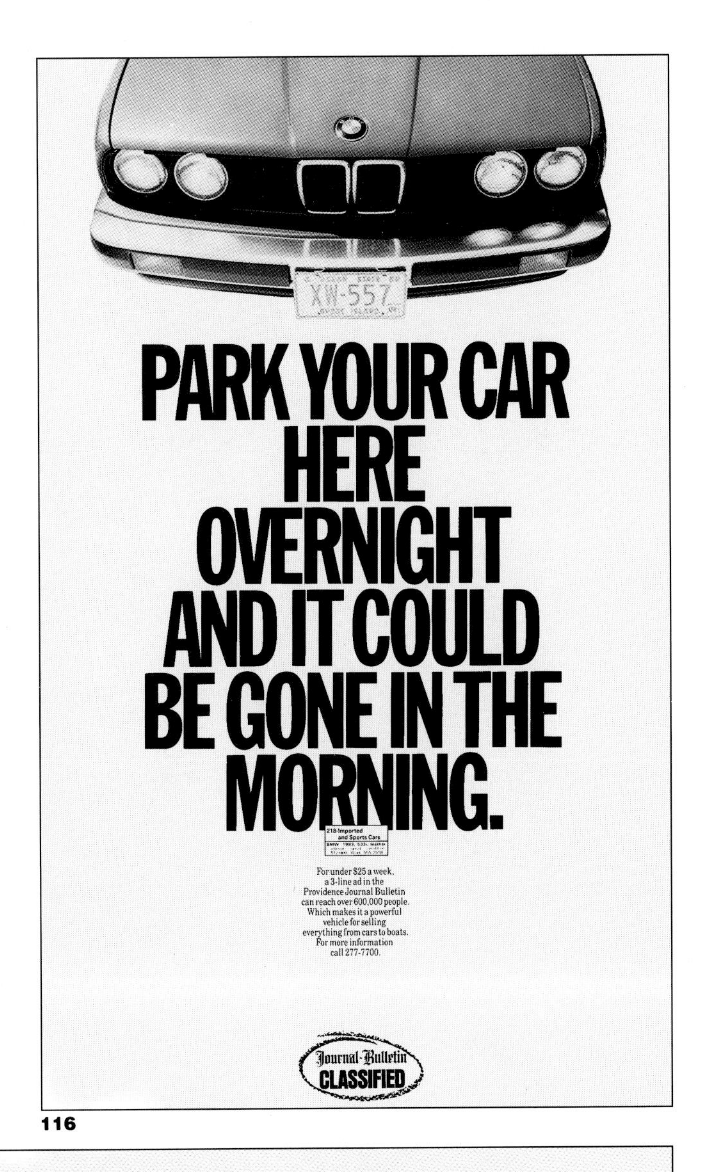
XW-557
RHODE ISLAND
PARK YOUR CAR HERE OVERNIGHT AND IT COULD BE GONE IN THE MORNING.
218-Imported and Sports Cars
BMW 1983, 533i, leather
For under $25 a week, a 3-line ad in the Providence Journal Bulletin can reach over 600,000 people. Which makes it a powerful vehicle for selling everything from cars to boats. For more information call 277-7700.
Journal-Bulletin
CLASSIFIED

116

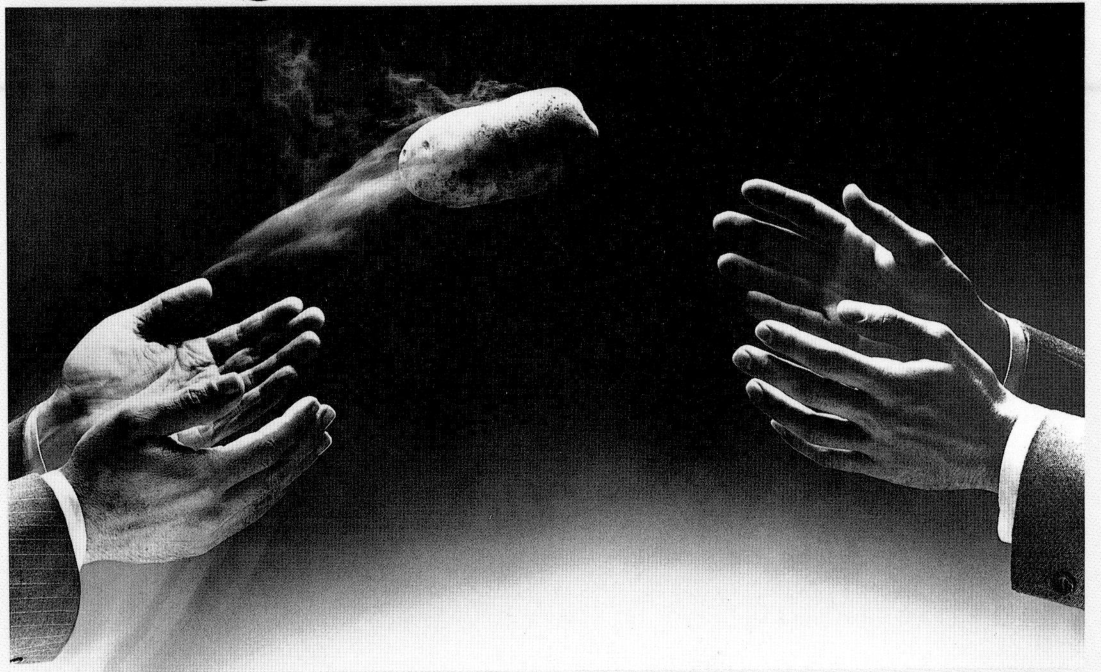
These people work for your bank.
That thing in the middle is your problem.
If your bank handles your problems like hot potatoes, don't talk to another teller. Don't talk to another branch manager. Don't talk to another vice president. Talk to another bank.
When you call Crestar with a problem, the person who answers, no matter who it is, is responsible for your problem. If they can't solve it, they'll connect you with the person who can. And they'll follow-up to make sure the problem was taken care of.
Personal contact is just one more way we're giving banking a better name. At Crestar we believe that when you call your bank, it should be the end of your problems. Not the beginning.
CRESTAR
We're out to give banking a better name.

117

Consumer Newspaper Over 600 Lines: Single

118
ART DIRECTOR
Mark Fuller
WRITER
Bill Westbrook
PHOTOGRAPHER
Dean Hawthorne
CLIENT
Office America
AGENCY
Ford & Westbrook/
Richmond, VA

119
ART DIRECTOR
Richard Ostroff
WRITERS
Alison Grant
Alan Chalfin
PHOTOGRAPHERS
Jerry Friedman
Satoshi
CLIENT
Changing Times Magazine
AGENCY
Levine Huntley Schmidt &
Beaver

120
ART DIRECTOR
Jim Mountjoy
WRITER
Ed Jones
CLIENT
McLeod
AGENCY
Loeffler Ketchum
Mountjoy/Charlotte, NC

121
ART DIRECTOR
Lloyd Wolfe
WRITER
Chris Wigert
PHOTOGRAPHER
Mark Alexander
CLIENT
Community Hospital
Indianapolis
AGENCY
Lawler Ballard/
Cincinnati, OH

Caution: Electrical Office Equipment Can Cause Sticker Shock.

118

119

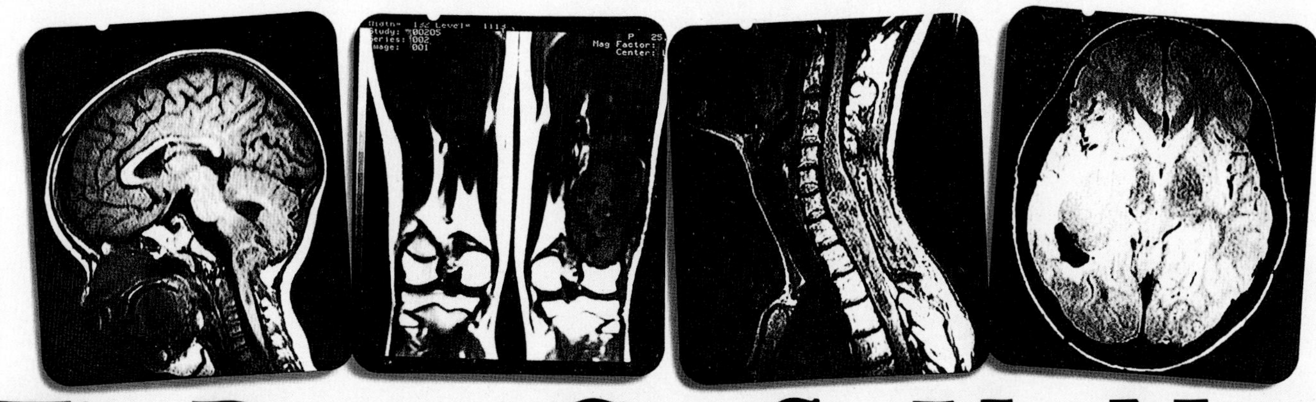

The Doctor Can See You Now.

Thanks to revolutionary technology at McLeod, doctors can now see inside the human body with unprecedented clarity.

The technology is called Magnetic Resonance Imaging or MRI. Many experts consider it to be the most dramatic advancement in medicine since the X-ray.

How dramatic? Consider this: while X-rays and the CAT scan enable us to see such bony structures as the skull and spine, MRI allows us to actually peer *behind* those structures into the soft tissue underneath.

That, of course, has staggering implications. For instance, multiple sclerosis, tumors, infections, and cancers of almost every form can be detected earlier. Consequently, in many cases, exploratory surgery is eliminated. More accurate diagnoses of various illnesses can be made. And ultimately, many more lives may be saved.

Those, however, aren't the only significant benefits of MRI. For instance, since MRI uses no radiation like X-rays, as many images of the patient may be taken as are necessary. And unlike X-ray technology, MRI produces views of the body from any angle.

Finally, MRI is painless. In fact, many patients find the procedure so comfortable they fall asleep on the MRI table during the study.

McLeod is proud to be the only hospital in the region to offer this revolutionary technology. But that isn't so unusual. We've been the area's leader in technological advances in health care for years.

So call (803) 667-2572 if you'd like to know more.

We'll be happy to share our exciting new insights into the diagnosis and cure of disease.

McLeod
MAGNETIC RESONANCE IMAGING CENTER
555 East Cheves Street • Florence, South Carolina 29501

120

Eenie, Meenie, Miney, Moe.

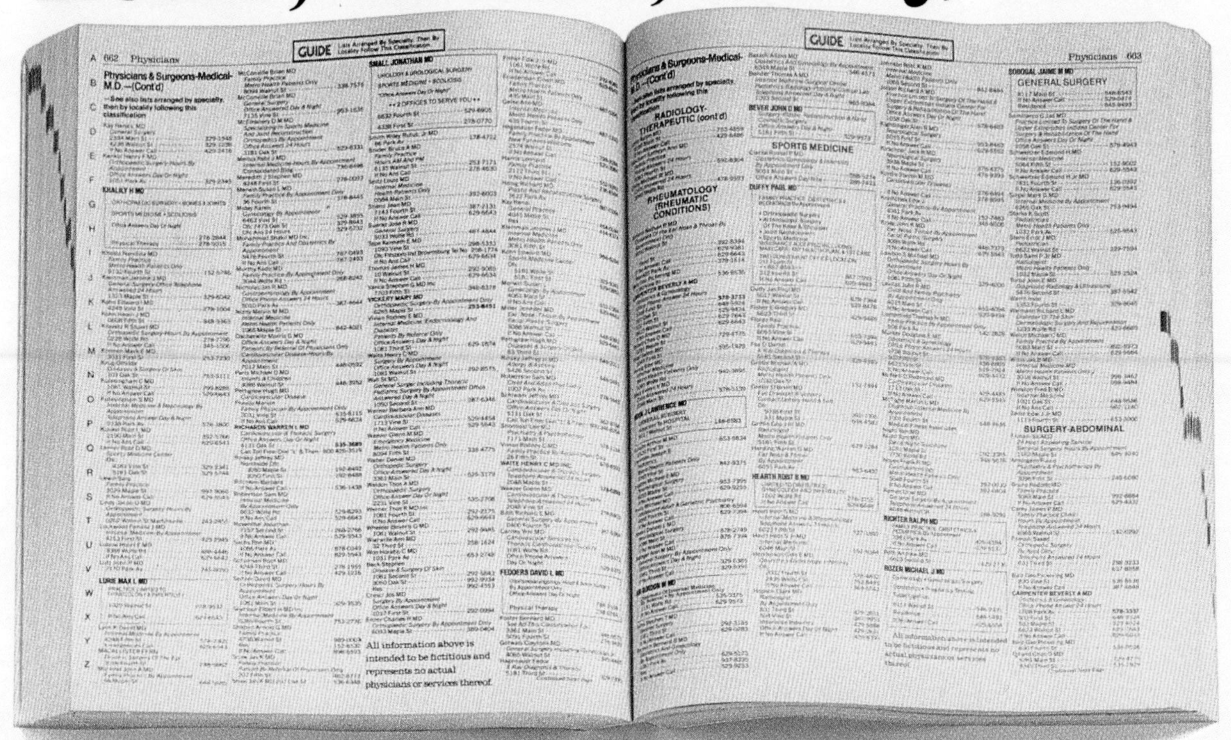

Suppose you need a family doctor who has evening hours and takes Visa® cards.

Or suppose you want a female obstetrician, preferably 40, who offers same-day appointments.

Where would you look? In the Yellow Pages? With 46 pages of doctors' names, addresses and phone numbers, the Yellow Pages might be a good place to start.

But who knows how many phone calls it will take you before you find exactly what you need.

With Physician Referral, One Call Can Do It All.

Wouldn't it be nice if you could find the kind of doctor you're looking for with just one phone call? Well now you can. With Physician Referral from Community Hospitals.

Our operators have instant access to the information you need.

Finding the doctor who meets your particular needs is now as easy as dialing 353-5491. You just call us at that number and tell us your specific needs.

You see, our computerized physician referral system contains extensive information to simplify and speed up your search.

Not just specialties, addresses and phone numbers. But also age, years in practice, medical school, office hours, payment procedures, insurance plan information, and special interests like sports medicine or the health needs of older adults.

Or even which doctors offer a free get-acquainted visit which gives you a chance to sit down and get to know one another before you decide.

We'll even help you set up the appointment, if you like. Because at Community Hospitals, we're here to help you.

So if you're looking for a doctor call Physician Referral at 353-5491.

Physician Referral
Community Hospitals Indianapolis
16th and Ritter Avenue, 82nd and Shadeland Avenue.

121

Consumer Newspaper Over 600 Lines: Single

122

ART DIRECTOR
Michael Vitiello

WRITER
Lee Garfinkel

CLIENT
Subaru of America

AGENCY
Levine Huntley Schmidt & Beaver

123

ART DIRECTOR
Bill Schwartz

WRITER
Joyce Spetrino

DESIGNER
Bill Schwartz

ARTIST
Janet Stuchlak

PHOTOGRAPHER
Martin Reuben

CLIENT
St. John Hospital

AGENCY
Meldrum and Fewsmith/Cleveland, OH

124

ART DIRECTORS
Bob Crantz
Max Fujishima

WRITER
Bonni Benstock Intall

PHOTOGRAPHER
Hashi

CLIENT
Canon USA

AGENCY
DCA Advertising

125

ART DIRECTOR
Patti Powell

WRITERS
DeWitt Long
Patti Powell

PHOTOGRAPHER
Mike Granberry

CLIENT
Desert Hospital

AGENCY
MediMarketing/Atlanta

OUR CARS WON'T PUT YOU THROUGH HELL BECAUSE THEY'VE ALREADY BEEN THERE.

All car companies test their cars. This is nothing new. In fact, over the years, you've probably seen hundreds of commercials with cars being driven on every kind of test track imaginable.

And while this kind of testing looks good, at Subaru we think it's rather unrealistic. Taking cars from the laboratory to the test track isn't enough.

So we take our cars one step further. Into the real world.

MANY OF OUR TEST AREAS HAVE NO TEST TRACKS. MANY HAVE NO ROADS.

We abuse our cars. Load them beyond capacity. Slam doors. Bang them around. And then abuse them some more.

Then the punishment begins. We drive our cars 24 hours a day, 6 days a week for up to 120,000 miles. Until every feature and function either survives, or is improved.

Cars are driven up and down mountains, around icy curves, through mud holes, blizzards, hail and rainstorms. On paved roads, back roads and no roads. They're subjected to constant braking, erratic acceleration and intense shifting. A testing schedule designed to achieve in a short period of time the kind of actual driving cars would get in 5 to 10 years of ownership.*

We also have a range of drivers testing our cars. Drivers with different temperaments and different driving styles. For example, heavy set drivers are even used to test seats, upholstery and interior room. In fact, the entire testing procedure is so draining, many of our drivers wear out before our cars do.

THE REAL WORLD PROVIDES REAL PUNISHMENT.

From the icy thin atmosphere of the high Sierras to the frozen northernmost regions of Canada, where temperatures can dip to −20° F, every Subaru function is tested and expected to perform as if these were everyday conditions.

And when we say we put our cars through hell, we mean it. During the summer we test in Death Valley. Relentlessly. In temperatures that could easily make an ordinary car overheat.

EXHAUSTIVE TESTING DOESN'T END WITH OUR CARS.

We want our accessory parts to be as reliable as our cars. So they're tested the equivalent of 5 years in pressurized salt baths. Here we make sure they're every bit as corrosive-resistant as our cars.

HIGH TECH ADDS TO OUR LOW MAINTENANCE.

In addition to some of the toughest testing done to any cars, Subaru technology adds a lot to our cars' reliability. For example, the electronic components in the Subaru engine are every bit as sophisticated as those in high performance cars costing two or three times as much. And since electronics work without moving parts, they can last a lot longer.

WHAT DOES ALL THIS INTENSE TESTING AND ENGINEERING MEAN TO YOU?

When Subaru says our cars are built to last, it's not just sales talk. The facts speak for themselves. 92% of all Subarus registered since 1978 are still on the road.** For the last 5 years, we've been one of the highest rated cars in customer satisfaction.***

And speaking of satisfaction, Subaru has a line of cars priced under $10,000!

What's more, to further satisfy your needs we are offering up to $2,000 cash back†† on selected Subaru models.

WE'RE TOUGH ON OUR CARS, SO THEY WON'T BE TOUGH ON YOU.

Perhaps no car sold in America is tested quite as fanatically as a Subaru. And our testing doesn't end with just one model. Every model we build no matter how similar or different is put through hell and treated almost fiendishly. With cruel and unusual punishment. So at times it even seems like we hate them.

Which is probably why our customers love them so much.

SUBARU.
We built our reputation by building a better car.

122

Only one was diagnosed as having Alzheimer's, but both will suffer from it.

It used to be diagnosed as premature senility until someone gave it a name. Alzheimer's disease.

Although, unfortunately, there is no cure for the disease, at St. John Hospital we offer counseling to help the family cope with Alzheimer's and other aging problems.

Because the day-to-day reality of caring for someone with complicated medical or psychological ailments places heavy responsibilities on the family.

Too much emotional and physical stress to be handling alone.

St. John Hospital was among the first to recognize, diagnose and treat the special medical problems of seniors.

Through our Senior Health Connection, we offer a network of the finest, most comprehensive geriatric programs in the city, if not the entire country.

Besides the doctors and nurses who specialize in gerontology, other health professionals, whose disciplines range from social work and psychiatry to family counseling and nutrition, are involved in the patient's treatment plan.

In our outpatient assessment center, we do a complete physical examination of the patient and evaluate physical functioning.

Review medications for any incompatibilities or problems.

Look for causes of pain and recommend treatments, especially physical therapy to help relieve, or manage, pain.

We evaluate mental status, and look for signs of depression in the patient. Not eating, for example.

And we consider the health and well-being of the family as well, through our family support groups and educational programs.

With our *Refresh* program, guests enjoy a home away from home while the family pursues vacation or personal plans without worry, for two days up to three weeks.

For the homebound patient, we offer Mobile Medical Care, with visits from a doctor and nurse.

Established in 1890, St. John is a 225-bed hospital on Detroit Avenue at West 80th Street, and co-owner of St. John & West Shore Hospital in Westlake.

Serving midwest Cleveland, St. John is minutes from most major thoroughfares, including I-71, I-77, I-90 and the West Shoreway.

For more information, call 651-9440. St. John Hospital.

Because it's not just extending life that's important, it's improving its quality.

ST. JOHN HOSPITAL
Enlightened medicine since 1890.
7911 Detroit Avenue

A Sisters of Charity of St. Augustine Hospital

123

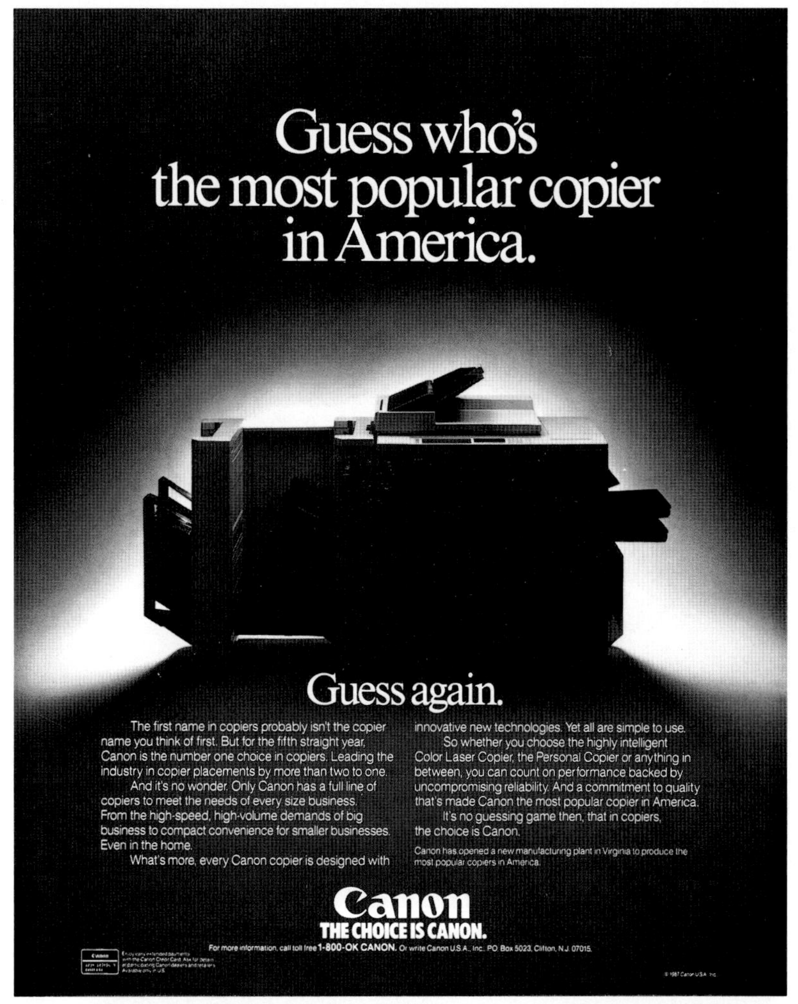

Guess who's
the most popular copier
in America.
Guess again.
The first name in copiers probably isn't the copier name you think of first. But for the fifth straight year, Canon is the number one choice in copiers. Leading the industry in copier placements by more than two to one.
And it's no wonder. Only Canon has a full line of copiers to meet the needs of every size business. From the high-speed, high-volume demands of big business to compact convenience for smaller businesses. Even in the home.
What's more, every Canon copier is designed with innovative new technologies. Yet all are simple to use.
So whether you choose the highly intelligent Color Laser Copier, the Personal Copier or anything in between, you can count on performance backed by uncompromising reliability. And a commitment to quality that's made Canon the most popular copier in America.
It's no guessing game then, that in copiers, the choice is Canon.
Canon has opened a new manufacturing plant in Virginia to produce the most popular copiers in America.
Canon
THE CHOICE IS CANON.
For more information, call toll free 1-800-OK CANON. Or write Canon U.S.A., Inc., P.O. Box 5023, Clifton, N.J. 07015.
© 1987 Canon U.S.A. Inc.

124

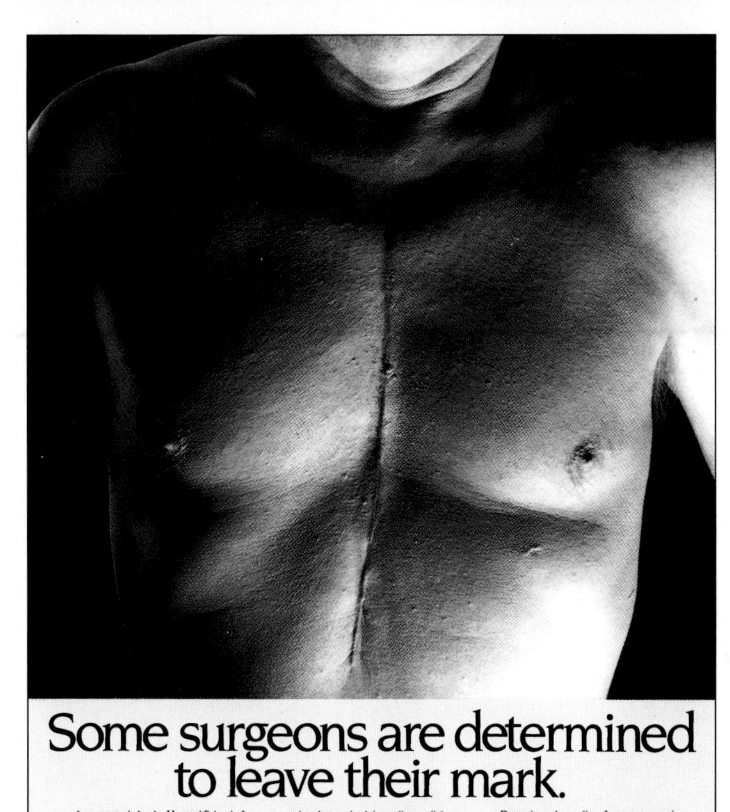

Some surgeons are determined to leave their mark.

A recent study by the Harvard School of Public Health estimates that up to half of all heart bypass surgeries performed each year are unnecessary.

That's up to 100,000 men and women who, last year, endured needless risk, trauma and expense.

Why?

Have some surgeons become so intent on building their professional reputations that they're endangering the well-being of patients in the process?

It's a sobering thought. But then, so is needless bypass surgery.

We don't ask the question lightly. We ask it in the hope that you'll ask questions, too.

You see, at Desert Hospital, we're committed to putting the *care* back in cardiac medicine.

We believe appropriate exercise and a change in diet is, over time, as potent a weapon as some patients will ever need in fighting heart disease. For others, carefully monitored medication produces remarkable results with minimum risk.

When intervention is indicated, a procedure called angioplasty can, in some cases, be every bit as effective as bypass surgery, and much less disruptive.

There are times, however, when bypass surgery is necessary. At Desert Hospital, it is a therapy that is recommended only after every alternative has been thoroughly explored. Because our cardiologists, cardiac anesthesiologists and surgeons have extensive experience in prestigious university settings, the emphasis at Desert is on the quality of care, not quantity of surgeries.

So, we ask you to be cautious if you've been told you need bypass surgery. Investigate your options. Call us at 323-6187 and we'll send you a copy of the Harvard study published in the Journal of the American Medical Association.

Then call Desert Hospital for a second opinion. Because these days, the cutting edge of cardiac care isn't always a knife.

DESERT HOSPITAL

A second opinion on cardiac care.

1150 N. Indian Avenue • Palm Springs, CA 92263 • 619/323-6187

125

Consumer Newspaper Over 600 Lines: Single

126
ART DIRECTOR
Lee St. James
WRITERS
Lee St. James
Daryl Travis
PHOTOGRAPHER
Craig Guyon
CLIENT
Blue Cross/Blue Shield
AGENCY
Arian Lowe & Travis/
Louisville, KY

127
ART DIRECTOR
Robert Cramer
WRITER
Kevin Mooney
DESIGNER
Robert Cramer
CLIENT
Olive Branch Bookstore
AGENCY
Ads "R" US East/
Bellmore, NY

128
ART DIRECTOR
Tom Stoneham
WRITER
Tom Molitor
PHOTOGRAPHER
Bruce Wilson
CLIENT
King County Medical Blue Shield
AGENCY
Borders Perrin &
Norrander/Seattle

129
ART DIRECTOR
Jeff France
WRITER
Ken Hines
CLIENT
Wake Medical Center
AGENCY
Lawler Ballard/
Richmond, VA

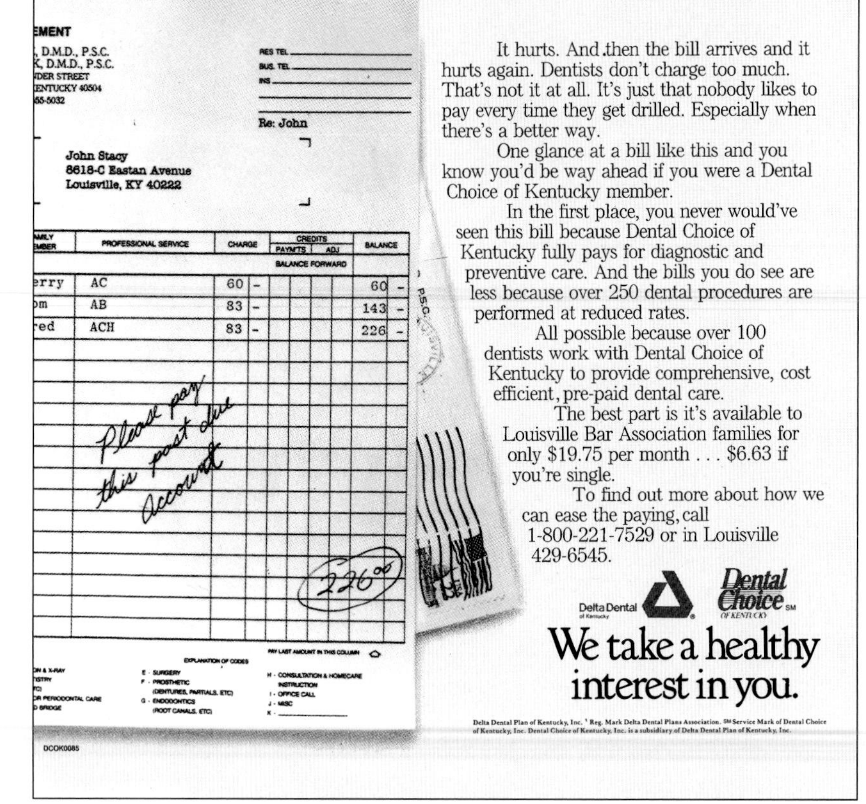

If you got crowned the last time you visited the dentist, we can ease the pain.
It hurts. And then the bill arrives and it hurts again. Dentists don't charge too much. That's not it at all. It's just that nobody likes to pay every time they get drilled. Especially when there's a better way.
One glance at a bill like this and you know you'd be way ahead if you were a Dental Choice of Kentucky member.
In the first place, you never would've seen this bill because Dental Choice of Kentucky fully pays for diagnostic and preventive care. And the bills you do see are less because over 250 dental procedures are performed at reduced rates.
All possible because over 100 dentists work with Dental Choice of Kentucky to provide comprehensive, cost efficient, pre-paid dental care.
The best part is it's available to Louisville Bar Association families for only $19.75 per month . . . $6.63 if you're single.
To find out more about how we can ease the paying, call 1-800-221-7529 or in Louisville 429-6545.
Delta Dental
Dental Choice
We take a healthy interest in you.
John Stacy
8618-C Eastan Avenue
Louisville, KY 40222
Please pay this past due account
226.00

126

If morals and business don't mix, we're in big trouble.

You're probably wondering what exactly a book, music and gift store with morals sells. Very simply, we only sell products we wouldn't mind having in our own homes.

Not the same old books.

Being an inspirational book, music and gift store, we obviously sell Bibles and study guides. But we also sell everything from children's books to romance novels.

Yet there's a definite difference between the books we sell and those you'd find in most bookstores.

For example, unlike many other romance novels, those we sell don't depend on sex and violence to keep your attention. We carry romance novels that rely on something unique to make them interesting—romance.

Another example are the books we sell in our children's section. Each of our children's books emphasize the positive aspects of life. We only sell these types of books because we understand that children are very impressionable. And we feel they'll get enough exposure to the down side of life without our help.

Is rock music evil?

Far be it from us to stand in judgement of different kinds of music. We know that music is purely a subjective art form. Which is why we sell all kinds of music, from choir music to rock and roll.

The difference in our music lies in the words. Again we prefer the music we sell to dwell on God and the joy of life, rather than on its hardships.

Movies we're not ashamed of.

We live in this neighborhood. We may even know some of you. So we're not about to sell movies we're ashamed of.

The movies we sell are the kind you could watch with your children. Movie videos of today's top Christian musicians, exercise videos, and dramas like "The Hiding Place" are just a few examples of the movies you'll find here.

To keep from starving.

Right about now you're no doubt saying to yourself "Who are they kidding, nobody is that nice." Well you're right.

You see, we have to run our store this way. We're Christians. Which means we have to live by a certain set of rules.

But don't get us wrong, we want to make money. After all, we don't want to give up eating.

We honestly think that there is a need in our neighborhood for a store like ours. Whether we're right or not, only time will tell.

The Olive Branch
Inspirational Book, Music and Gift Store

928 Hillside Ave. New Hyde Park. Just east of Lakeville Road. (516)775-7040 or (718)343-7040

127

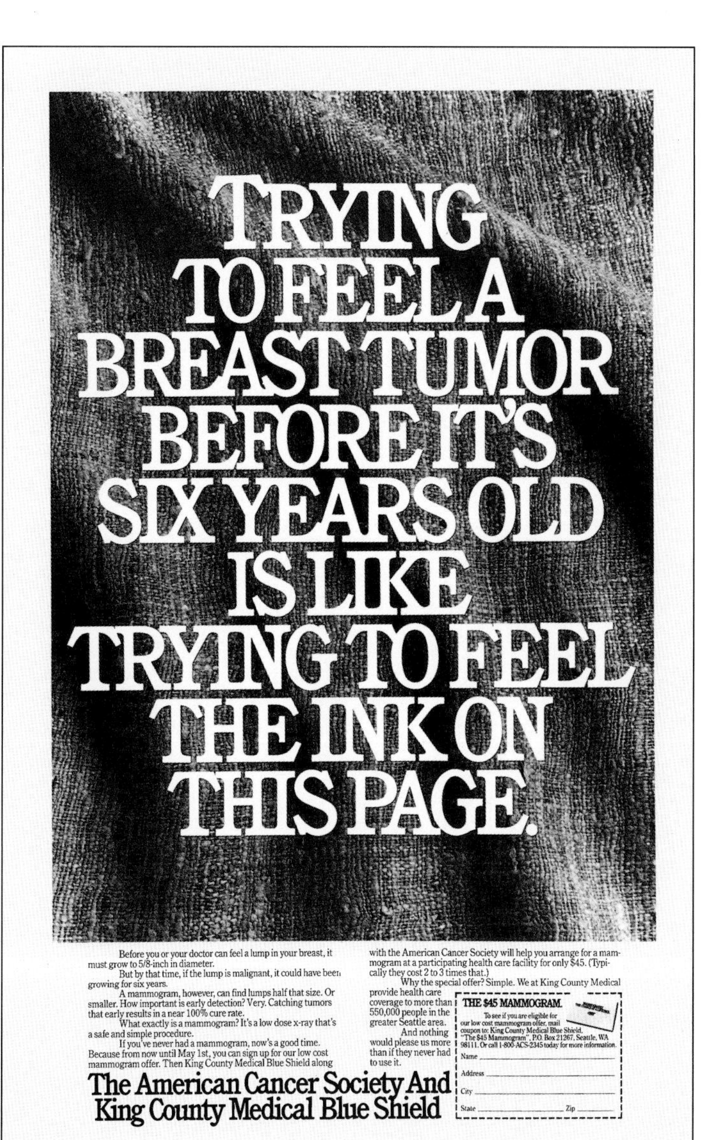
TRYING
TO FEEL A
BREAST TUMOR
BEFORE IT'S
SIX YEARS OLD
IS LIKE
TRYING TO FEEL
THE INK ON
THIS PAGE.
Before you or your doctor can feel a lump in your breast, it must grow to 5/8-inch in diameter.
But by that time, if the lump is malignant, it could have been growing for six years.
A mammogram, however, can find lumps half that size. Or smaller. How important is early detection? Very. Catching tumors that early results in a near 100% cure rate.
What exactly is a mammogram? It's a low dose x-ray that's a safe and simple procedure.
If you've never had a mammogram, now's a good time. Because from now until May 1st, you can sign up for our low cost mammogram offer. Then King County Medical Blue Shield along with the American Cancer Society will help you arrange for a mammogram at a participating health care facility for only $45. (Typically they cost 2 to 3 times that.)
Why the special offer? Simple. We at King County Medical provide health care coverage to more than 550,000 people in the greater Seattle area.
And nothing would please us more than if they never had to use it.
THE $45 MAMMOGRAM.
To see if you are eligible for our low cost mammogram offer, mail coupon to: King County Medical Blue Shield, "The $45 Mammogram", P.O. Box 21267, Seattle, WA 98111. Or call 1-800-ACS-2345 today for more information.
Name
Address
City
State
Zip
The American Cancer Society And King County Medical Blue Shield

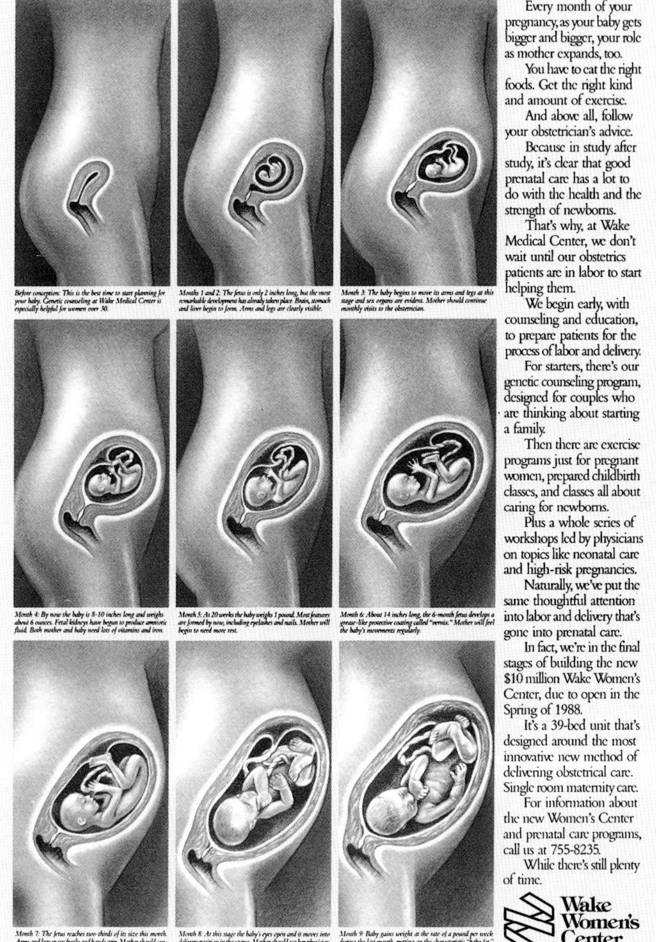
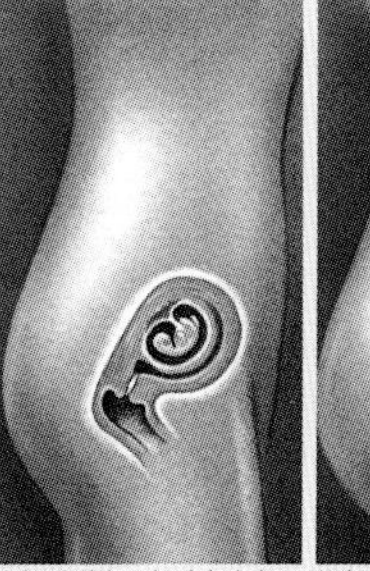
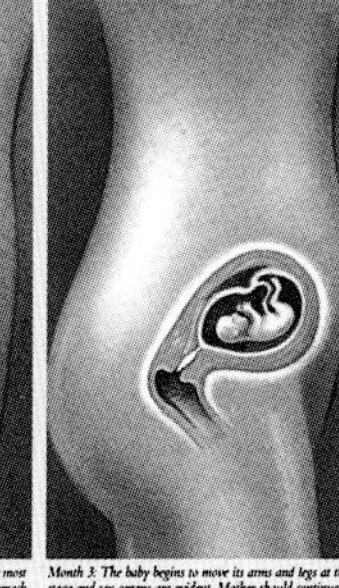

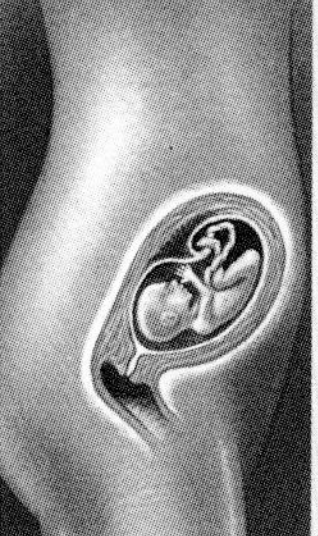
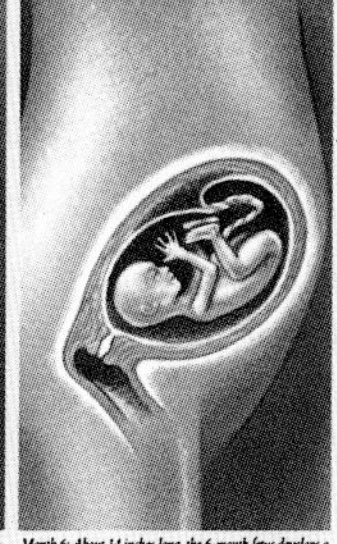
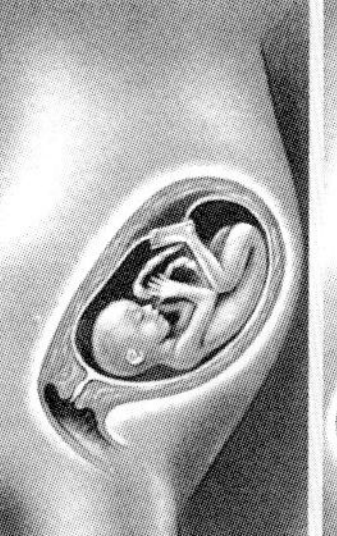
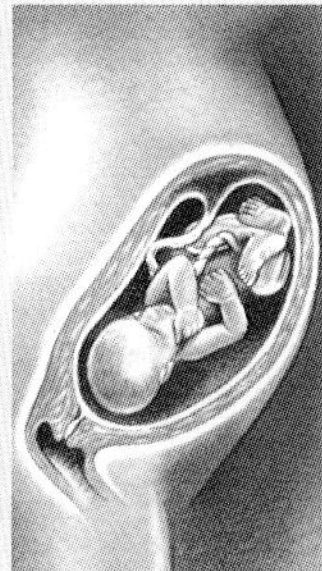
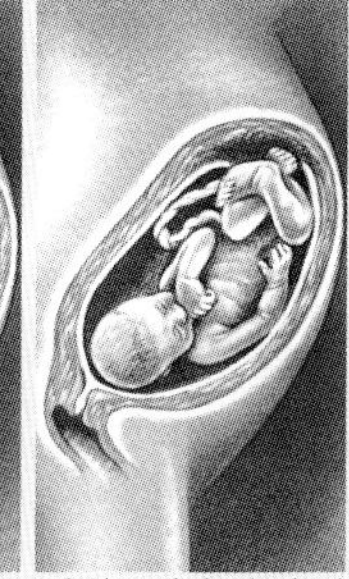

It's Never Too Early To Be A Good Mother.
Before conception: This is the best time to start planning for your baby. Genetic counseling at Wake Medical Center is especially helpful for women over 30.
Months 1 and 2: The fetus is only 2 inches long, but the most remarkable development has already taken place. Brain, stomach and liver begin to form. Arms and legs are clearly visible.
Month 3: The baby begins to move its arms and legs at this stage and sex organs are evident. Mother should continue monthly visits to the obstetrician.
Month 4: By now the baby is 8-10 inches long and weighs about 6 ounces. Fetal kidneys have begun to produce amniotic fluid. Both mother and baby need lots of vitamins and iron.
Month 5: At 20 weeks the baby weighs 1 pound. Most features are formed by now, including eyelashes and nails. Mother will begin to need more rest.
Month 6: About 14 inches long, the 6-month fetus develops a grease-like protective coating called "vernix." Mother will feel the baby's movements regularly.
Month 7: The fetus reaches two-thirds of its size this month. Arms and legs move freely and hands grip. Mother should continue light exercise.
Month 8: At this stage the baby's eyes open and it moves into delivery position in the uterus. Mother should see her physician every other week in months 7 and 8.
Month 9: Baby gains weight at the rate of a pound per week during the last month, putting on the characteristic "baby fat." Your obstetrician will see you weekly until delivery.
Every month of your pregnancy, as your baby gets bigger and bigger, your role as mother expands, too.
You have to eat the right foods. Get the right kind and amount of exercise.
And above all, follow your obstetrician's advice.
Because in study after study, it's clear that good prenatal care has a lot to do with the health and the strength of newborns.
That's why, at Wake Medical Center, we don't wait until our obstetrics patients are in labor to start helping them.
We begin early, with counseling and education, to prepare patients for the process of labor and delivery.
For starters, there's our genetic counseling program, designed for couples who are thinking about starting a family.
Then there are exercise programs just for pregnant women, prepared childbirth classes, and classes all about caring for newborns.
Plus a whole series of workshops led by physicians on topics like neonatal care and high-risk pregnancies.
Naturally, we've put the same thoughtful attention into labor and delivery that's gone into prenatal care.
In fact, we're in the final stages of building the new $10 million Wake Women's Center, due to open in the Spring of 1988.
It's a 39-bed unit that's designed around the most innovative new method of delivering obstetrical care. Single room maternity care.
For information about the new Women's Center and prenatal care programs, call us at 755-8235.
While there's still plenty of time.
Wake Women's Center

Consumer Newspaper Over 600 Lines: Single

130

ART DIRECTORS
Craig Hadorn
Jeff France

WRITER
Ken Hines

PHOTOGRAPHER
Pat Edwards

CLIENT
Wake Medical Center

AGENCY
Lawler Ballard/
Richmond, VA

131

ART DIRECTOR
Tom Perkins

WRITER
Joe Anson

CLIENT
Grand Union Supermarkets

AGENCY
Anson-Stoner/
Winter Park, FL

132

ART DIRECTOR
Tom Kelly

WRITER
Greg Eiden

PHOTOGRAPHER
Pete Stone

CLIENT
Blue Cross/Blue Shield of Oregon

AGENCY
Borders Perrin & Norrander/Portland, OR

133

ART DIRECTOR
Sharon Harms

WRITERS
Tom Amico
Jim Proimos

DESIGNER
Sharon Harms

ARTISTS
Janet Stuchlak
Ruth Diener
M&F

PHOTOGRAPHER
Hunter Freeman

CLIENT
Academy of Medicine of Cleveland

AGENCY
Meldrum and Fewsmith/
Cleveland, OH

Until Now, Infertility Treatments Haven't Been Very Productive.

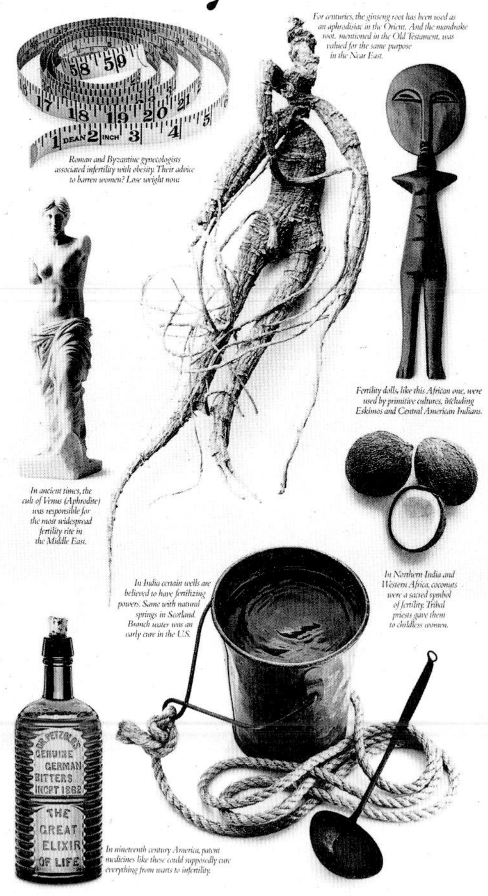

Few areas of medical research have been as fruitful as reproductive medicine.

In less than a decade, physicians have developed a handful of reliable new techniques.

The most promising one of all is *in vitro* fertilization.

And here in Raleigh, only one hospital is involved with it.

The one that's delivered breakthroughs in medicine time and again.

Wake Medical Center.

We're teaming up with the renowned *in vitro* program at the University of North Carolina Medical Center in Chapel Hill.

Which means our patients will have access to a first rate program. Right here at home.

It works like this.

After a detailed evaluation at UNC, the patients are sent to us for the initial stimulation phase.

With hormone therapy, we increase the chances of "harvesting" more than one mature egg.

Then, at just the right moment, we send our patients to Chapel Hill.

Where eggs are carefully retrieved, fertilized and implanted in the uterus.

Back home, our patients receive the most thorough follow-up care available.

And the reassurance of knowing that nobody in Raleigh handles high risk pregnancies the way we do.

To make sure it stays that way, we're building a new $10 million center for obstetrics and gynecology.

For more details about *in vitro* fertilization or any of the other programs at Wake Medical Center, call us at 755-8235.

We want to turn infertile couples into something they thought they'd never be.

Parents.

130

Our fried chicken may not be world-famous, but it's the best in these parts.

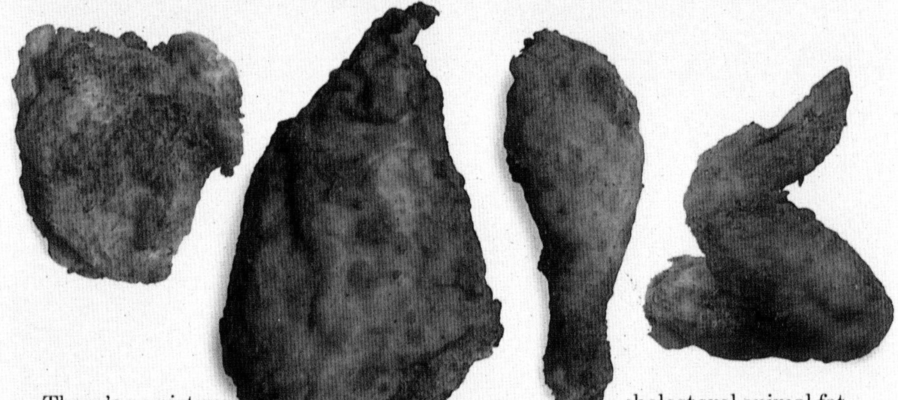

There's no picture of the Colonel on the take-out package. And not a drive-thru lane in sight.

But oooh the fried chicken!

This is Grade A fresh, cooked-to-order, fried-to-perfection chicken.

Chicken that's dipped in our own marinade and breading mix.

Chicken that's fried in low cholesterol vegetable oil instead of high cholesterol animal fat.

Chicken that's on special right now.

Pick up some parts soon at the Grand Union deli.

GRAND UNION

131

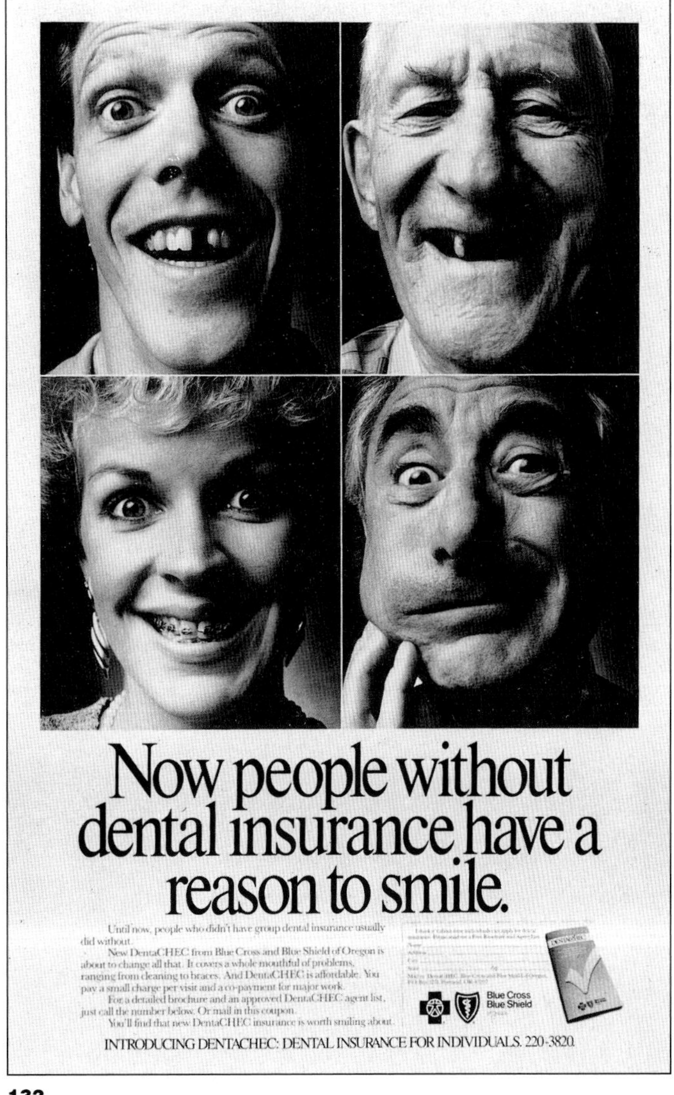

Now people without dental insurance have a reason to smile.
Until now, people who didn't have group dental insurance usually did without.
New DentaCHEC from Blue Cross and Blue Shield of Oregon is about to change all that. It covers a whole mouthful of problems, ranging from cleaning to braces. And DentaCHEC is affordable. You pay a small charge per visit and a co-payment for major work.
For a detailed brochure and an approved DentaCHEC agent list, just call the number below. Or mail in this coupon.
You'll find that new DentaCHEC insurance is worth smiling about.
Blue Cross
Blue Shield
INTRODUCING DENTACHEC: DENTAL INSURANCE FOR INDIVIDUALS. 220-3820.

132

The Soviet Press Has Described AIDS As Runaway Biological Warfare Created By The Pentagon.

That Would Make The Condom The Cheapest, Most Sensible, Lifesaving Defense Weapon This Country Has Ever Produced.

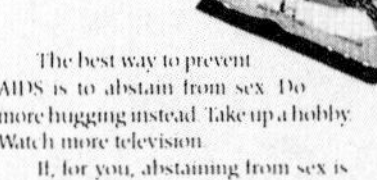

The best way to prevent AIDS is to abstain from sex. Do more hugging instead. Take up a hobby. Watch more television.

If, for you, abstaining from sex is unrealistic, don't abstain from thinking. Use a condom when having sex. Always. Especially if your partner has not been tested for the AIDS virus.

When used correctly, condoms are highly effective in preventing the spread of AIDS. And, right now, that's the best defense there is.

For more answers, call the AIDS hot line at 216-651-4611. Or just talk to your doctor.

IT WON'T KILL YOU TO ASK YOUR DOCTOR ABOUT AIDS.

133

Consumer Newspaper Over 600 Lines: Single

134

ART DIRECTOR
David Fox

WRITER
Joe Alexander

CLIENT
Cleveland Metro General Hospital

AGENCY
Clarity Coverdale Rueff/ Minneapolis

135

ART DIRECTOR
Rick Carpenter

WRITER
Jaci Sisson

PHOTOGRAPHER
Craig Takahashi

CLIENT
CooperVision

AGENCY
Della Femina Travisano & Partners/Los Angeles

136

ART DIRECTOR
Alan Chalfin

WRITER
Michael Lichtman

ARTIST
Bryan Sauriol

CLIENT
Subaru of America

AGENCY
Levine Huntley Schmidt & Beaver

137

ART DIRECTOR
Mike Preston

WRITER
Simon Connolly

PHOTOGRAPHER
Simon Crossett

CLIENT
Sony

AGENCY
SSB Advertising/ Potts Point, Australia

134

135

WE'RE KNOWN
FOR FOUR WHEEL DRIVE.
BUT OUR TECHNOLOGY
EXTENDS TO PARTS
UNKNOWN.
HI
HEAT
LO
BILEV
INT
A/C MAX
OFF
OFF
EEM
Subaru has more 4-wheel drive cars on the road than all others combined! But 4-wheel drive is only one part of our story.
All our parts reveal our state-of-the-art technology. And it's their sum that makes us unequalled.
Vented disc brakes, for example, may not seem that unusual. But they are unusual within Subaru's price range. And they're totally unknown in the $5,866 range of our new Justy.
The same can be said for everything else on this page. It's either exclusive to Subaru. Or found in cars costing 2 or 3 times as much.
In fact, it's these 'unknown' parts that make us what we are known for: reliability, longevity and value.
So if your present car is a stranger in these parts, it's time you got acquainted with Subaru.
SUBARU.
We built our reputation by building a better car.

136

The circuitry in here means exceptionally good hi-fi sound.
Three colour filters for perfect colour reproduction.
Play back through electronic viewfinder. (Lets you see what you just shot.)
All operation functions and warning conditions displayed through viewfinder.
Zoom lens.
Auto focus.
The tape records three hours of video.
Automatic white balance. (Means you don't have to worry if the light changes.)
Video 8 format instead of VHSC. (The latest technology instead of an outdated compromise.)
Back light switch compensates for the bright sunlight common to Australia.
'Flying erase' head. (In plain English, fault-free editing.)
Plays back direct through a TV. (No need for a VCR or cassette adaptor.)
Large CCD microchips here mean a better picture.
SONY
AF
Video 8
Handycam
If it had any more features we'd have to make it bigger.
At around $2600 the Sony V30 has got more features for the price than any other camera you can buy. Yet it weighs little more than a kilogram and is little bigger than the size of your hand.
SONY.

137

Consumer Newspaper Over 600 Lines: Single

138
ART DIRECTOR
Michael Vitiello
WRITER
Lee Garfinkel
CLIENT
Subaru of America
AGENCY
Levine Huntley Schmidt & Beaver

139
ART DIRECTOR
Larry Bennett
WRITER
Odette Embert Arnold
PHOTOGRAPHER
Jim Erickson
CLIENT
Piedmont Airlines
AGENCY
McKinney & Silver/ Raleigh, NC

140
ART DIRECTORS
John Loper
Jeff Kaumeyer
WRITER
Mitch Wein
CLIENT
KCET
AGENCY
Della Femina Travisano & Partners/Los Angeles

141
ART DIRECTOR
Bryan Lahr
WRITER
Joey Reiman
CLIENT
Days Inns of America
AGENCY
Babbit & Reiman/Atlanta

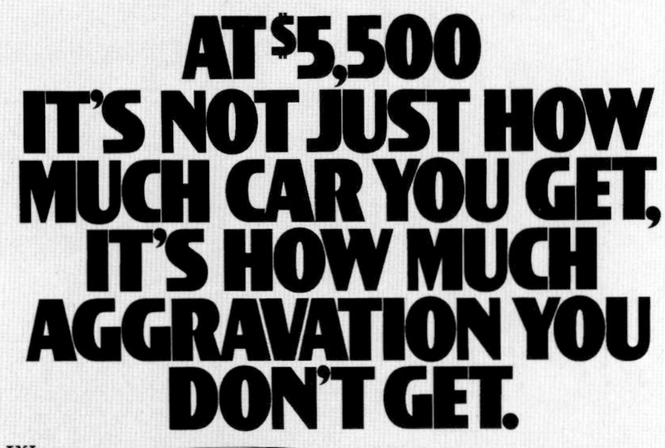

AT $5,500 IT'S NOT JUST HOW MUCH CAR YOU GET, IT'S HOW MUCH AGGRAVATION YOU DON'T GET.

When you buy a car for $5,500,* it can be a very scary experience.

After all, many of the cars in that price range were virtually unknown in the U.S. one or two years ago. And if spending $11,000 on a car doesn't insure you against headaches, what can you expect from a car that costs half as much.

Fortunately, there is one car company that doesn't think you should settle for less of a car just because you spent less on it.

91% OF ALL SUBARUS REGISTERED SINCE 1976 ARE STILL ON THE ROAD.**

This impressive statistic proves people not only drive our cars hard, but they hold up year after year.

At Subaru, dependability is a standard feature built into every one of our cars.

What's more, while every car company likes to brag about customer satisfaction, not every car company has the facts to back it up.

Subaru, on the other hand, has been in the top 10 in customer satisfaction for over 5 years. And for 2 straight years, we were second only to Mercedes Benz in customer satisfaction.***

As you can see, Subaru has a well-deserved reputation for building inexpensive cars that last.

HOW CAN THE JUSTY GIVE YOU SO MUCH AND STILL COST SO LITTLE?

Despite its low price, the Justy contains the same quality engineering as Subaru's more expensive models. And it has more state-of-the-art features than any car in its class.

How can this be true? There's no magic about it.

It's all the result of advanced engineering and cost-efficient manufacturing—taking out the fluff, while putting in substantial value.

For example, instead of the usual 4 cylinders, the Justy has a unique 9 valve, 3 cylinder overhead cam engine that's as powerful as it is economical (38 mpg city, 41 mpg highway).***** And in all honesty, to sell the Justy at a sticker price of $5495, we make less money on each car we sell.

But the bottom line is, even though everything about the car is new, it still has good old-fashioned Subaru dependability. In fact, the Justy is the result of 3 years of road testing in America and 2 million test miles.

YOU CAN'T GET SOMETHING FOR NOTHING. BUT YOU CAN GET A LOT FOR NEXT TO NOTHING.

The Justy doesn't cost a lot, but it does give you a lot. Including: front wheel drive; 5-speed transmission; 4-wheel fully independent suspension; variable ratio Rack & Pinion steering; vented front disc brakes; an electronically controlled carburetor; and more interior/cargo space than you have a right to expect in a car this size.

Of course, we wouldn't be doing the car justice if we left out another reason to own one: the Justy is truly fun to drive.

So think about it. Why spend your disposable income on a disposable car, when you can put your money into a much more lasting investment, the new Subaru Justy.

SUBARU.
Inexpensive. And built to stay that way.

138

NOW YOU CAN FLY FIRST CLASS FOR THE SAME REASON YOU'VE BEEN FLYING COACH.

If you've been flying coach because it's economical, you can now fly First Class.

Because it's economical.

On Piedmont, you can upgrade to First Class for as little as $20 over full-fare coach.

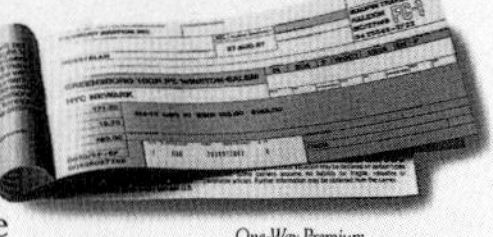

Miles Traveled	One-Way Premium Over Full-Fare Coach
500 miles or less	$20
501-1000 miles	$40
1001 miles or more	$60

Sorry, prices do not apply to our transatlantic service.

Without giving up any of the reasons you've always wanted to fly First Class.

We've designed a First Class with service that will truly pamper you on all Piedmont flights, whether you're on the plane for 30 minutes or for three hours.

You'll relax in a spacious seat that lets you stretch out while you're living it up.

On longer flights you'll be served gourmet meals, with fine wines and fresh flowers in crystal vases.

You'll enjoy the advantage of having your luggage loaded last, so it comes off the plane first. And in many airports, the ease of separate check-in facilities.

Plus, through the month of September, our double mileage offer will earn you a minimum of 3000 bonus miles every time you fly First Class.

So call your travel agent or call Piedmont Airlines.

If you've been looking for an excuse to fly First Class, we've just given you the reason you need.

PIEDMONT

139

Tonight, see what it was like to be one of The Chosen People.

Shoah evokes the horror of the concentration camps unlike any other documentary.

There's not a single frame of archival footage. Instead there's an astonishing collection of interviews with Jewish survivors, former SS officers, Polish eyewitnesses, and former freedom fighters that brings the past back to us with a devastating clarity.

Watch this unforgettable masterpiece by award winning filmmaker Claude Lanzmann.

There are six million reasons why you should.

KCET/28

Shoah. Witness The Holocaust Monday-Thursday, 8 P.M.

140

LATELY, WE'VE HAD A BUSY HOLIDAY SCHEDULE.

Holiday Inn® Williamsburg, VA	**Converted to Days Inn®** April 11, 1986
Holiday Inn Point South, SC	**Converted to Days Inn** April 29, 1986
Holiday Inn Springfield, OH	**Converted to Days Inn** May 6, 1986
Holiday Inn Edwardsville, IL	**Converted to Days Inn** June 18, 1986
Holiday Inn Indianapolis, IN	**Converted to Days Inn** June 25, 1986
Holiday Inn Alexandria, VA	**Converted to Days Inn** August 8, 1986
Holiday Inn Menands, NY	**Converted to Days Inn** October 14, 1986
Holiday Inn Allentown, PA	**Converted to Days Inn** November 11, 1986
Holiday Inn Ashville, NC	**Converted to Days Inn** November 26, 1986
Holiday Inn Framingham, MA	**Converted to Days Inn** January 13, 1987
Holiday Inn Jesup, GA	**Converted to Days Inn** January 14, 1987
Holiday Inn Wheeling, WV	**Converted to Days Inn** January 15, 1987
Holiday Inn Salem, [illegible]	**Converted to Days Inn** February 24, 1987
Holiday Inn Columbia, MO	**Converted to Days Inn** March 2, 1987
Holiday Inn Des Moines, IA	**Converted to Days Inn** March 2, 1987
Holiday Inn Ottumwa, IA	**Converted to Days Inn** March 2, 1987
Holiday Inn Superior, WI	**Converted to Days Inn** March 2, 1987
Holiday Inn Richmond, VA	**Converted to Days Inn** April 1, 1987
Holiday Inn Scottsboro, AL	**Converted to Days Inn** April 1, 1987
Holiday Inn Springfield, MO	**Converted to Days Inn** April 2, 1987

Not only have a large number of former Holiday Inn Hotels converted to Days Inn® Hotels recently, but a long list of others have joined our growing family as well.

In fact, a record 264 franchise agreements were executed in the past twelve months.

If you'd like to be added to this year's schedule, call us at Days Inns–(404) 728-4145. You'll find out why we've been so busy lately.

DAYS INN
We're Right Where America Wants Us.

DAYS INN.® ALL OTHERS ARE OUT.

This offering is made only by the offering circular. Holiday Inn is a registered service mark of Holiday Inns, Inc.

141

Consumer Newspaper Over 600 Lines: Single

142

ART DIRECTOR
John Vitro

WRITER
John Robertson

ARTIST
Amy Miyano

PHOTOGRAPHER
Paul Gersten

CLIENT
Foster Farms

AGENCY
Chiat/Day - Los Angeles

143

ART DIRECTORS
Bryan Buckley
Mike Shine

WRITERS
Mike Shine
Bryan Buckley

CLIENT
NYNEX

AGENCY
Chiat/Day

144

ART DIRECTOR
Rod Smith

WRITER
Fred Bertino

DESIGNER
Rod Smith

PHOTOGRAPHER
Linc Cornell

CLIENT
James Brown Paint

AGENCY
Smith Bertino/Boston

145

ART DIRECTOR
Michael Vaughan

WRITER
Constantin Cotzias

DESIGNER
Michael Vaughan

PHOTOGRAPHER
David D'Amico

CLIENT
Filomena's

AGENCY
Chinnici & Vaughan

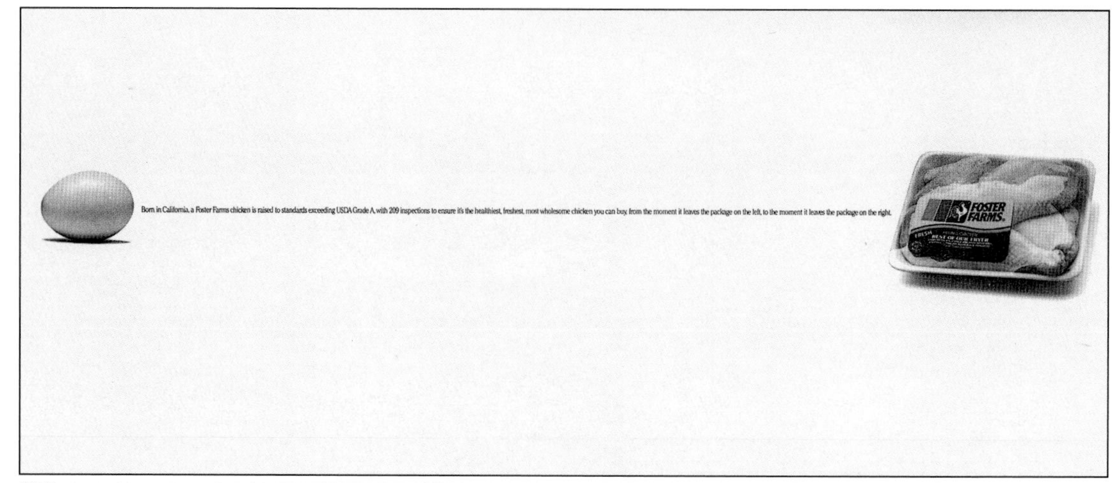

142

DINOSAUR TRACKS FOUND IN STAMFORD.

STAMFORD–You'll find things in the new NYNEX Yellow Pages that you can't find in your present yellow pages. Because we've gathered information from many different towns and put it into one book.

Now you can find listings five blocks away, or five towns away.

And if we could find fossilized Anomoepus tracks at the Stamford Museum and Nature Center, just imagine what you'll be able to find.

The NYNEX Yellow Pages for Stamford/Norwalk.

143

AFTER YOU BUY OUR PAINT, WE'LL GIVE YOU THE BRUSH OFF.

From now until August 1, when you buy 2 gallons or more of any kind of paint in our store, we'll give you 50% off any kind of brush in our store. Now that's a deal that should get you stirring.

JAMES BROWN PAINT
The Paint Store Of A Different Color.

Located in the College Plaza, New Haven 624-5846.

144

ONLY ONE OF THESE PEOPLE WASN'T CREATED BY AN AD AGENCY.

Advertising agencies don't only come up with ads, they sometimes come up with the products they do the ads for.

They first build an image, and then a product is made up to fit it.

At Filomena's we decided to do it backwards.

We took our 92 year old Italian grandmothers recipe, cooked it up, and put it in a mason jar.

And since it's her recipe, we put her name on it. As a result, she's real, and so is her sauce.

It's a sauce that contains ingredients that only a grandmother would serve her family. Choice peeled tomatoes, freshly chopped garlic, and special herbs and spices.

Try Filomena's. It's the homemade Italian spaghetti sauce that isn't pretending to be one.

FILOMENA'S
Born in Italy.
Not on Madison Avenue.

145

Consumer Newspaper Over 600 Lines: Single

146
ART DIRECTOR
Tom Roth
WRITER
Steve Trygg
DESIGNER
Mary Ellen Butkus
PHOTOGRAPHER
Michael O'Neil
CLIENT
Corporate Class Software
AGENCY
Anderson & Lembke/
Stamford, CT

147
ART DIRECTOR
Larry Phillips
WRITER
Jim Mott
DESIGNER
Larry Phillips
PHOTOGRAPHER
Joel Becker
CLIENT
Children's Hospital of the King's Daughters
AGENCY
Davis & Phillips/
Norfolk, VA

148
ART DIRECTOR
Steven Feldman
WRITER
Patrick Hanlon
DESIGNER
Steven Feldman
PHOTOGRAPHER
Steve Bronstein
CLIENT
Carillon Importers
AGENCY
TBWA

149
ART DIRECTOR
Jerry Gentile
WRITER
Barbara DeSantis
CLIENT
Adventist Health Systems
AGENCY
DDB Needham Worldwide/
Los Angeles

WHEN I TOLD MY FRIENDS ABOUT THIS AD THEY SAID, DON'T DO IT, BOB.

C. Robert Tully, for 15 years a vice president and chief financial officer, Celanese Corporation, New York.

What drives a man at the height of his career to risk his reputation on a new product from a start-up venture firm in a business probably more competitive than most?

What would it take to make you do it?

In Bob Tully's case it was simple. Bob Tully, a 15-year vice president and chief financial officer of the $3 billion Celanese Corporation, recently assumed the position of chairman of Corporate Class Software.

He took the job after having witnessed a dramatic change in white-collar productivity within Celanese brought on by Corporate Class Software's new product.

In plain numbers, the efficiency of Celanese's financial analysis and reporting had improved by 50 percent. Fifty percent! Reports that used to take two to three days to consolidate were now done in hours—with more accurate content. Year-end reports normally available in early April, prior to the annual meeting, were now ready in February. All thanks to a new type of computer software that is likely to change the way we think about financial software.

Bob Tully believes you could achieve the same improvements in your corporation, no matter what systems or software you use today.

In this ad, he explains how and why.

Bob Tully's corner office on the Avenue of the Americas in midtown Manhattan gives visitors one immediate impression: This is a place of hard work. Most of the desk space is taken up by everyday tools such as an IBM personal computer, an Epson printer and double calculators. Hard, smart work is Bob Tully's trademark.

PROBLEMS, PROBLEMS, PROBLEMS.

"Some people will tell you that I like to take risks," says Bob Tully. "But that's not really so.

"I have, for instance, never invested in stock except in companies I've worked for. I like to know what I'm getting into and be very unemotional about it. Corporate Class Software is a good example of that.

"It all started a few years back. To be frank, I was not satisfied with the way things were done in Celanese at the time. I had just come from the Ford Motor Company after 15 years and had been spoiled with the systems and tools for financial analysis there. At one time we actually controlled half of England's computer power outside the government.

"At Celanese, my financial staff was creating corporate reports based on data from our departments, divisions, and subsidiaries throughout the world. The problem was that each of these groups used different hardware and software. The information came to us in different formats and it was extremely difficult to integrate the data."

A SEARCH IN VAIN.

"It was obvious Celanese needed a new system for information gathering, analysis, and reporting.

"The system had to be efficient and easy to use for both periodic and ad hoc work. It had to standardize the way we handled financial information throughout the corporation, and it also had to take foreign currency conversion rates into consideration.

"But—and this was important—I didn't want to get tangled up in custom programming and hours of maintenance work. Our corporate structure changes constantly through acquisitions, mergers, and joint ventures. If the system couldn't cope with this, it wasn't for us.

"To make a long story short, we ended up having to develop this software product ourselves. Off-the-shelf software could only solve basic financial applications, and advanced applications meant more programming and maintenance than we were prepared to put up with.

"Our new software system got the name FASTAR—short for Financial Application Solution to Analysis and Reporting. It is now up and running in Celanese and has brought dramatic gains in productivity.

"I think you could achieve the same, and I'll tell you why."

THE PRODUCT THAT ALMOST DEFIES DESCRIPTION.

"FASTAR is very simple to work with—analysts without computer training can run it. And it's also very flexible, despite the fact that it's a packaged application. Very different Fortune 500 companies use it today. None of them needed more than three days to adapt the program to their corporate needs.

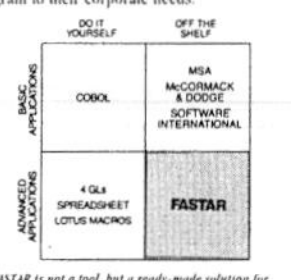

FASTAR is not a tool, but a ready-made solution for advanced financial applications, including financial consolidation and management reporting.

"What is FASTAR in a word? It's difficult to say since the product has created a whole new software category in itself: The *packaged* solution for *advanced* financial applications. You could say that FASTAR blends the volume, speed and security of mainframe software with the ease of use and flexibility of PC software.

"Of course, there are other ways to solve advanced needs. A fourth generation language can do it on your mainframe—but at three to four times the cost of FASTAR and with plenty of custom programming and maintenance. Microcomputer applications could also be used, if you've got users willing to spend months building their macros and then keeping up with them."

KEEP EVERYTHING YOU HAVE AND JUST ADD FASTAR.

"FASTAR has no problem accepting data from fourth generation language products and database management systems, as well as from microcomputer applications. In particular Lotus 1-2-3.

FASTAR is the packaged solution to advanced financial applications that can provide quantitative and qualitative improvements in your company's financial analyses.

"All this financial information goes into an end-user database, where your analysts share the data. Everybody works with *the same numbers*, picking out the pieces they need for the job at hand.

"Unlike traditional spreadsheets that organize data into two categories, FASTAR arranges them four ways: By financial schedule (income statements, etc.), entity (divisions, etc.), period (day, week, month, etc.) and type (any fourth type of data you choose such as actual, budget or forecast.)

"The result is twofold. With FASTAR, the amount of work needed to put together a certain report goes down, while the quality of what's in the report goes up.

"Now, your MIS manager may say that a packaged solution to advanced applications is an impossibility. After all, there hasn't been one before FASTAR.

"We met this same skepticism from an MIS manager at another billion dollar company. Finally, he let us try and watched the results very closely for some months.

"That same MIS manager has today installed FASTAR *in his own department* to manage and analyze information from more than ten cost centers."

ENOUGH TALK.

"Are you still with me? Fine.

"Then I'll add just one more thing. Behind Corporate Class Software stand the resources of its parent company. Two years of additional R&D work went into FASTAR before taking it to market. And the development of a second product is well under way. In my opinion, the company is bound for success.

"If you want to know more about FASTAR, just call 212-719-8209 for a brochure that shows in detail what the system could do for you. I know the people at Corporate Class Software will also gladly set up a live demonstration in your own office. Call or ask your secretary to send in the coupon."

CORPORATE CLASS
SOFTWARE, INC.
1211 Avenue of the Americas, 23rd floor New York, NY 10036 (212) 719-8209
A subsidiary of Hoechst Celanese Corporation

To: Mr. Richard J. Lyons President and Chief Executive Officer,
CORPORATE CLASS SOFTWARE, INC., 1211 Avenue of the Americas,
23rd floor, New York, NY 10036

☐ Please send me your FASTAR brochure.
☐ Please send me PC World's review of FASTAR.
☐ Please call me for a demonstration.

Name ______
Position ______
Company ______
Street ______
City/State/Zip ______
Phone ______

Anderson & Lembke

146

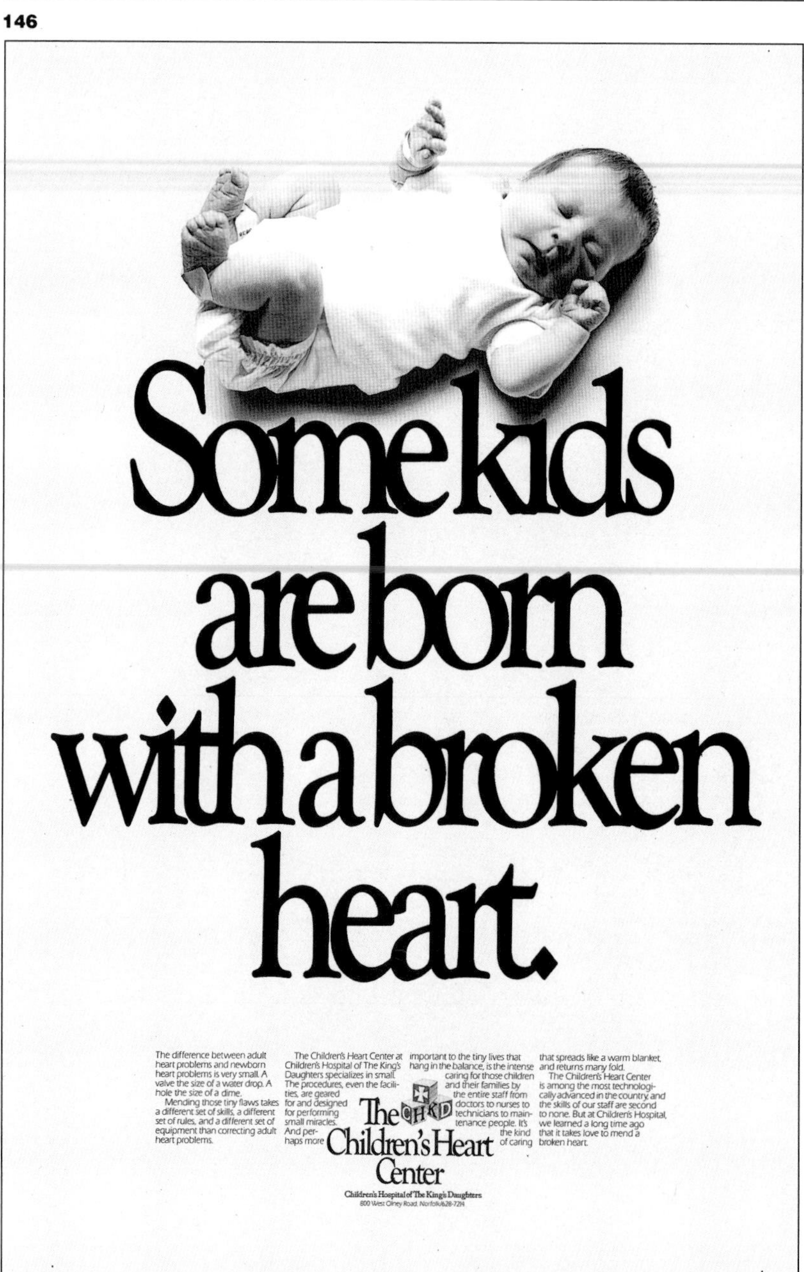

147

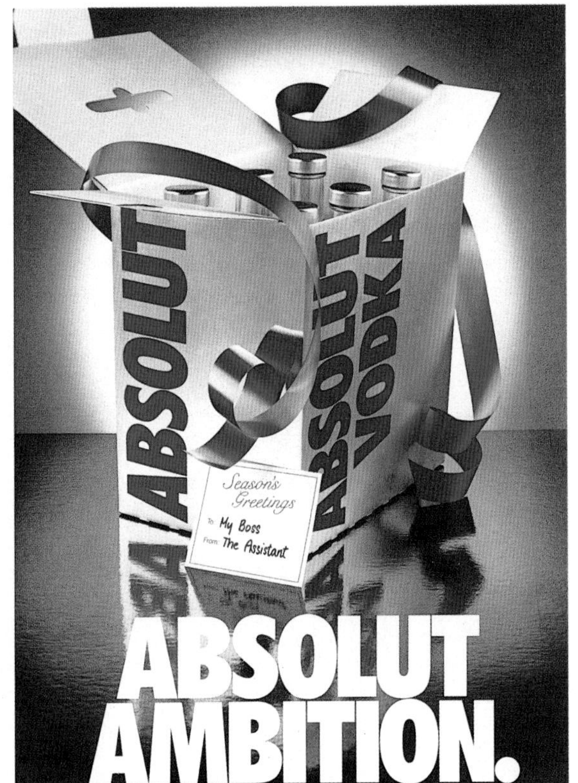

148

How can I tell if a wound is infected?

What is "normal" hair loss?

What foods have "good" cholesterol?

Can I breastfeed my adopted baby?

Does stress cause asthma?

Which mushrooms are poisonous?

Is it okay to give aspirin to a baby?

Where can I learn CPR?

Can I eat sushi while I'm pregnant?

Where can I learn to examine my breasts?

Is ice or butter better for a burn?

What's a good source of calcium?

Is marijuana addictive?

What should my target heart rate be?

Are steroids safe?

What is safe sex?

What are the warning signs of cancer?

Should I take the baby to the emergency room?

Are vaccinations dangerous?

Could my daughter be anorexic?

Should I induce vomiting?

Could I be having a heart attack?

What are the symptoms of glaucoma?

Can coffee cause headaches?

Are dental x-rays dangerous?

How long should I breastfeed?

How can I tell if my child has allergies?

Is it worth it to quit smoking after 15 years?

How often do I need a tetanus shot?

How much sun is too much?

Do I need a stress test before I begin exercising?

Can I take these two medications together?

What does poison ivy look like?

What's a safe, natural laxative?

Can you take too many vitamins?

What's the best way to lift something heavy?

Are my daughter's measles still contagious?

How can I tell if my son is on drugs?

What's the best way to remove a splinter?

What's a normal temperature for a baby?

What shots do I need to go overseas?

What should my blood pressure be?

Where can I get orthopedic shoes?

How often do I need a Pap smear?

How can I treat diaper rash?

How much fiber do I need?

Where can I find an obstetrician? Pediatrician? Family doctor? Doctor who speaks Spanish?

How much should I weigh?

What does chicken pox look like?

Where can I go for kidney dialysis?

When should I start brushing my baby's teeth?

Will drinking affect my blood pressure?

Where can I get a yearly physical?

How can I tell if my spouse is an alcoholic?

Who can help me with my allergies?

Where can I find a home health nurse?

How can I find out about Alzheimer's disease?

Should I wear special stockings for my varicose veins?

Are high heels bad for my feet?

Will tight clothes affect my circulation?

How much sleep do babies need?

What's the best way to clean dentures?

How can I tell what foods I'm allergic to?

Who can I see about Parkinson's disease?

Should I have my son circumcised?

Who can help me stop drinking?

Where can I buy a wheelchair?

How dangerous is secondhand smoke?

What's a good source of niacin?

How do I child-proof my house?

Can I catch a disease from a public phone?

Will spicy food give me ulcers?

Will warmed milk help me sleep?

What's the safest way to clean my ears?

What are the four food groups?

Is butter more fattening than margarine?

How do I make a tourniquet?

Is flossing really important?

Will cracking my knuckles give me arthritis?

Who should I see about my back pain?

Is it safe to give blood?

Does swimming after eating cause cramps?

Can aspirin upset my stomach?

What is aerobic exercise?

Who do I see about tennis elbow?

What's good for sports injuries—heat or ice?

What can I do about my child's bedwetting?

Can you have arthritis when you're young?

What causes shingles?

Will this pill make me drowsy?

What's an ultrasound?

Is barbecueing safe?

Can kidney stones be removed without surgery?

Are home pregnancy tests reliable?

Can I get rabies from an animal bite?

Can alcohol affect an unborn child?

Can I be allergic to myself?

How many calories will I burn if I run?

How can I cut my sodium intake?

WHAT YOU DON'T KNOW CAN HURT YOU.

Let's face it: when it comes to the subject of health, most of us could use a lot more information.

Information that could keep us healthy. Help us when we're sick. Or even save our lives in an emergency.

Fortunately, there is a way to get those facts without going to a lot of time, trouble or expense. It's called Ask-A-Nurse.SM

Ask-A-Nurse is a professional health care information and referral service staffed by registered nurses. It's confidential, free of charge, and available 24 hours a day. And in addition to answering your health care questions, we can give you personalized doctor referrals, fill you in on health care programs in your community—even assess your symptoms and help you determine what to do about them. For more information about your health, give us a call. It couldn't hurt.

ASK·A·NURSE

149

Consumer Newspaper Over 600 Lines: Single

150
ART DIRECTOR
Anne Baylor Oakley
WRITER
Mabon Childs
CLIENT
Norwegian Cruise Lines
AGENCY
McKinney & Silver/
Raleigh, NC

151
ART DIRECTOR
Jerry Gentile
WRITER
Barbara DeSantis
PHOTOGRAPHER
Ron Krisel
CLIENT
Adventist Health Systems
AGENCY
DDB Needham Worldwide/
Los Angeles

152
ART DIRECTOR
Michael Vitiello
WRITER
Lee Garfinkel
CLIENT
Subaru of America
AGENCY
Levine Huntley Schmidt &
Beaver

153
ART DIRECTOR
Mark Fuller
WRITER
Bill Westbrook
PHOTOGRAPHER
Dean Hawthorne
CLIENT
Office America
AGENCY
Ford & Westbrook/
Richmond, VA

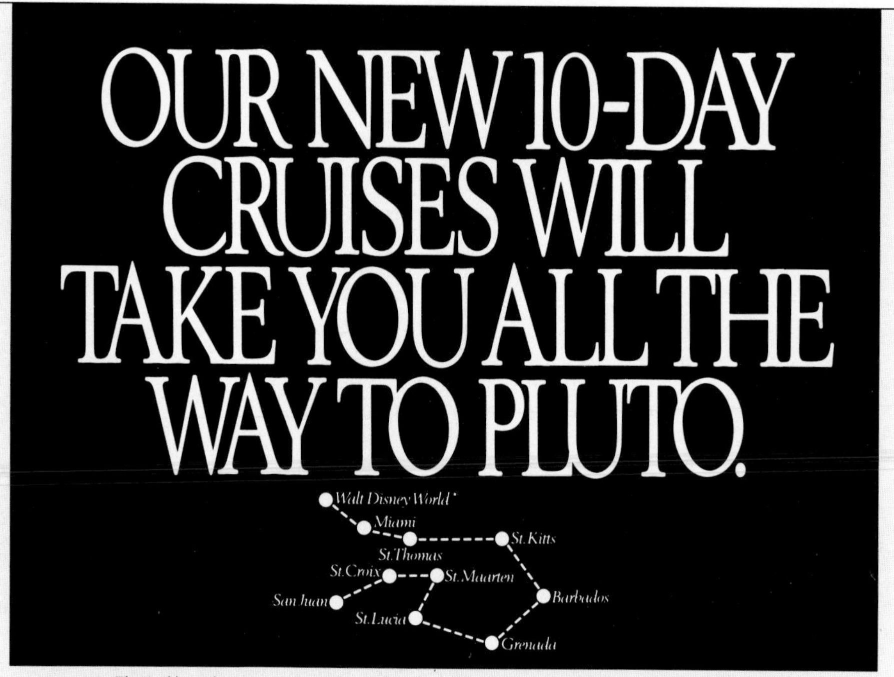

150

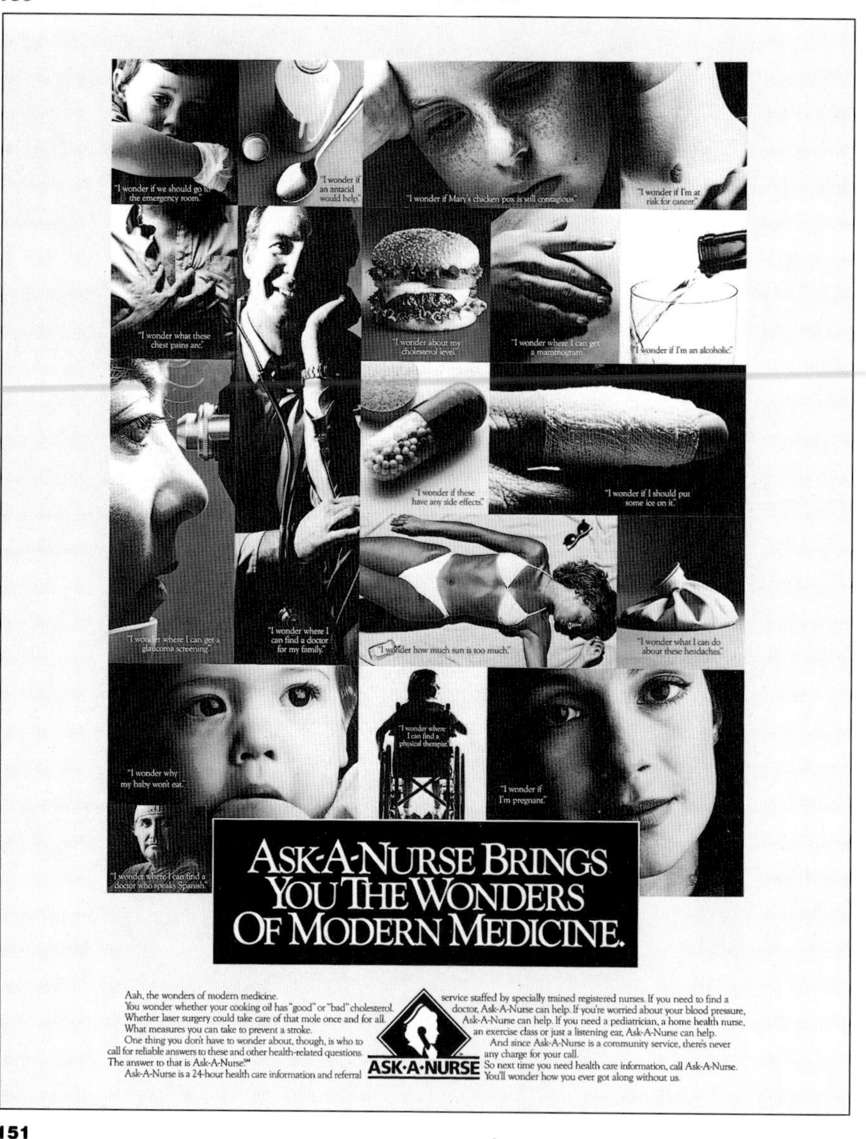

151

THE FOUR WHEEL DRIVE CAR THAT GOT THE AUTOMOTIVE INDUSTRY OFF ITS REAR.

Today the automotive industry is virtually inundated with front wheel drive cars. Well, this wasn't always the case. There was a time when practically every car in America was stuck with rear-wheel drive technology.

Fortunately, in 1969, Subaru introduced the first cars designed around the concept of front wheel drive. And we didn't do it just to be different. We did it because it made sense. Front wheel drive improves a car's stability and traction.

And in the last 19 years Subaru has consistently improved and refined front wheel drive. Making it one of the most advanced systems on the road.

1970 FWD SEDAN

WE'VE TAKEN FRONT WHEEL DRIVE TO ITS ULTIMATE CONCLUSION: 4-WHEEL DRIVE.

In 1975 Subaru introduced the first passenger cars with an On Demand™ 4-wheel drive system. Simply put, this system lets drivers shift from front to 4-wheel drive whenever weather or road conditions take a turn for the worse.

You see, 4-wheel drive gives power to all four wheels at the same time. Thus greatly increasing a car's handling ability, traction and safety.

And if you've ever experienced a loss of traction due to a sudden shower or loose gravel, you can see the wisdom of 4-wheel drive.

If you've ever been stuck in snow or mud, you can see the necessity of it.

Yet, despite these obvious benefits, for years Subaru was the only company that offered passenger cars with 4-wheel drive.

Now, 13 years later other car makers are finally "discovering" 4-wheel drive. It makes you wonder if they finally noticed the weather. Or us.

YOU DON'T HAVE TO REFINANCE YOUR HOUSE TO FINANCE YOUR CAR.

A Subaru is built to be as easy on your pocket as it is on the road.

In fact, we have an entire line of cars under $10,000.†

Like our DL XT, Wagon, 3-Door Coupe, Sedan or the Justy, the most inexpensive 4-wheel drive car sold in America.

You see, at Subaru we strongly believe that even if you have a budget that's limited, your choice of cars doesn't have to be.

NO OTHER CAR MAKER HAS SUCH A FIRM GRIP ON 4-WHEEL DRIVE TECHNOLOGY.

Even though Subaru pioneered 4-wheel drive, our accomplishments aren't limited to the past. This year, for example, we're offering Full-Time 4-wheel drive with a 4-speed electronic automatic transmission.

This system reacts automatically to any sudden loss of traction—from bad roads, bad weather or just simple cornering or braking.

1975 4WD WAGON

It's so advanced, no car sold in America has anything like it.

Of course, as important as 4-wheel drive is for keeping your car on the road, Subaru also believes your car should last down the road.

So Subaru cars are tested extensively in America and throughout the world...for reliability, performance and safety. And our testing doesn't end on the test track. We also test our cars in the real world. With real punishment. On roads you drive on. And on roads you would never even think of driving on. At Subaru, we're tough on our cars so they won't be tough on you.

91% OF ALL SUBARUS REGISTERED SINCE 1976 ARE STILL ON THE ROAD.*

In addition to this impressive statistic, Subaru has consistently been in the top 10 in customer satisfaction for over 5 years.

And for 2 straight years, we were second only to Mercedes Benz in customer satisfaction.**

BUY A SUBARU. OR GET STUCK WITH SOMETHING ELSE.

Since 1969, Subaru has been building front wheel drive cars that are reliable, durable and built to last.

And for 13 years, we've been committed to building 4-wheel drive cars with the same high standards.

As a result Subaru has more 4-wheel drive passenger cars on the road than all other car makers combined.* So before you buy your next car, think about this. Would you rather buy one from the company that pioneered front wheel drive and 4-wheel drive. Or from a company that was content to sit on its rear.

1988 XT WITH FULL-TIME 4WD

SUBARU.
We built our reputation by building a better car.

152

Before You Send Another Business Letter, Check The Margins.

Our chrome Cross fountain pen is $26.84. Pay $37.50 at LOPC and you'll have to treat it like gold.

Our Panasonic recorder is $42.99. Atlantic's price: $74.95.

Our typewriter elements are $13.99. IBM's elements from Richmond Office Supply: $25.00.

Our #10 envelopes are $5.99 per 500. The Quill discount catalog price is $9.66.

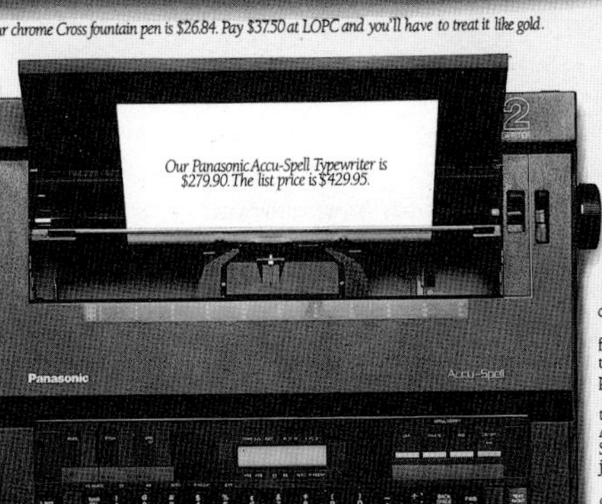

Our Panasonic Accu-Spell Typewriter is $279.90. The list price is $429.95.

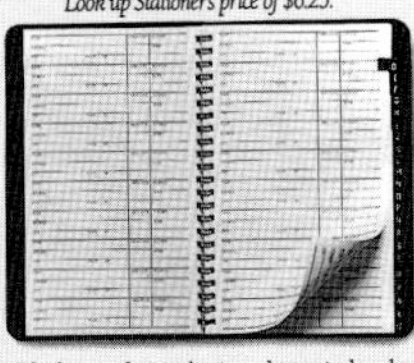
Our Guilford address book is $3.65. Look up Stationer's price of $6.25.

Our ribbons for the IBM Selectric II are $8.49 for six. Ginn's price: $17.95.

The bottom line on business letters is that they cost more than you think.

Unless, of course, you buy your office supplies from Office America. We sell dictating equipment, typewriters, copiers, paper, pens and 3000 other products at 30%-50% off.

That's because we buy our products direct from the manufacturer and eliminate the middleman. And we buy boxcars of everything instead of boxes. So you get the benefit of mass buying even if you're just buying a single item.

Come by our warehouse store in the 8000 block of West Broad Street in the Westland Shopping Center weekdays 8 a.m. to 9 p.m. and Saturdays 9 a.m. to 6 p.m. Or call 273-0900 to open an account and receive a free catalog in the mail.

Office America. Because you shouldn't have to sign a note just to send a letter.

OFFICE AMERICA

No one sells more office supplies for less.

Consumer Newspaper Over 600 Lines: Single

154
ART DIRECTOR
Mike Preston
WRITER
Simon Connolly
ARTIST
Greg McAlpine
CLIENT
John Fairfax
AGENCY
SSB Advertising/
Potts Point, Australia

155
ART DIRECTOR
Bart Cleveland
WRITER
Ernie Mosteller
DESIGNER
Bart Cleveland
ARTIST
Bart Cleveland
PHOTOGRAPHER
Curtis Graham
CLIENT
Publix Super Markets
AGENCY
Benito Advertising/
Tampa, FL

156
ART DIRECTOR
Pam Randall
WRITER
David Housewright
CLIENT
Starkey Hearing Aids
AGENCY
Blaisdell & Westlie/
St. Paul, MN

157
ART DIRECTOR
Sophie Howland
WRITERS
Deborah McAdam
Sophie Howland
CLIENT
Ansett Air Freight
AGENCY
DDB Needham Worldwide/
Sydney

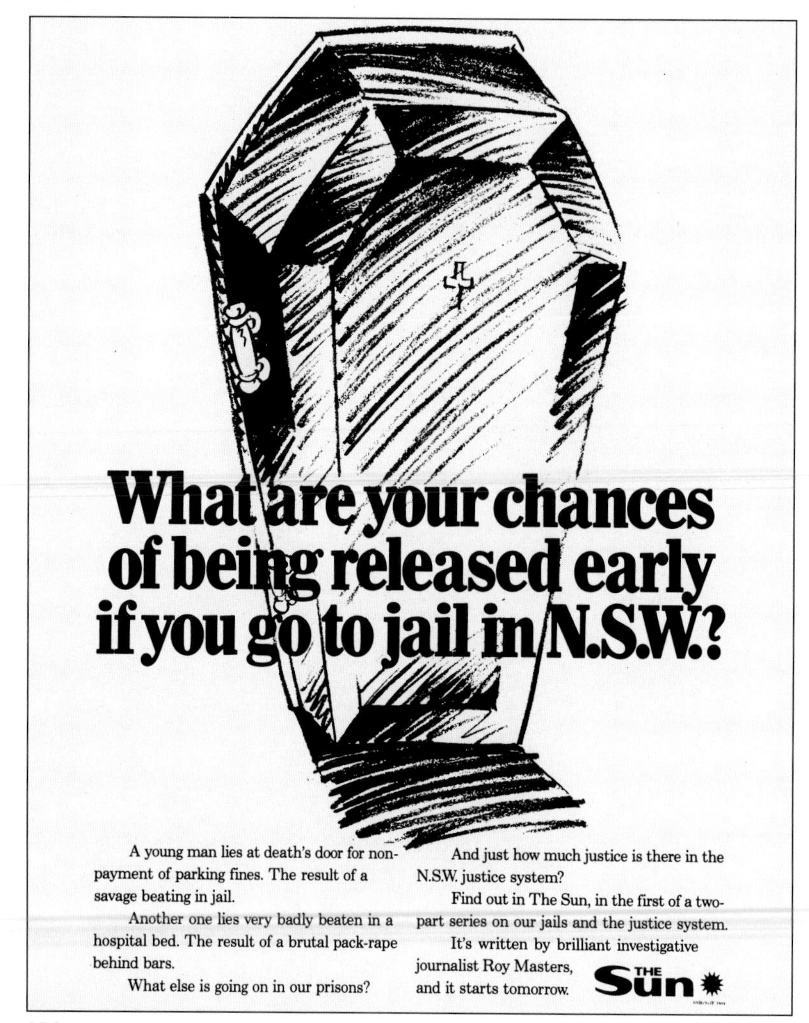

154

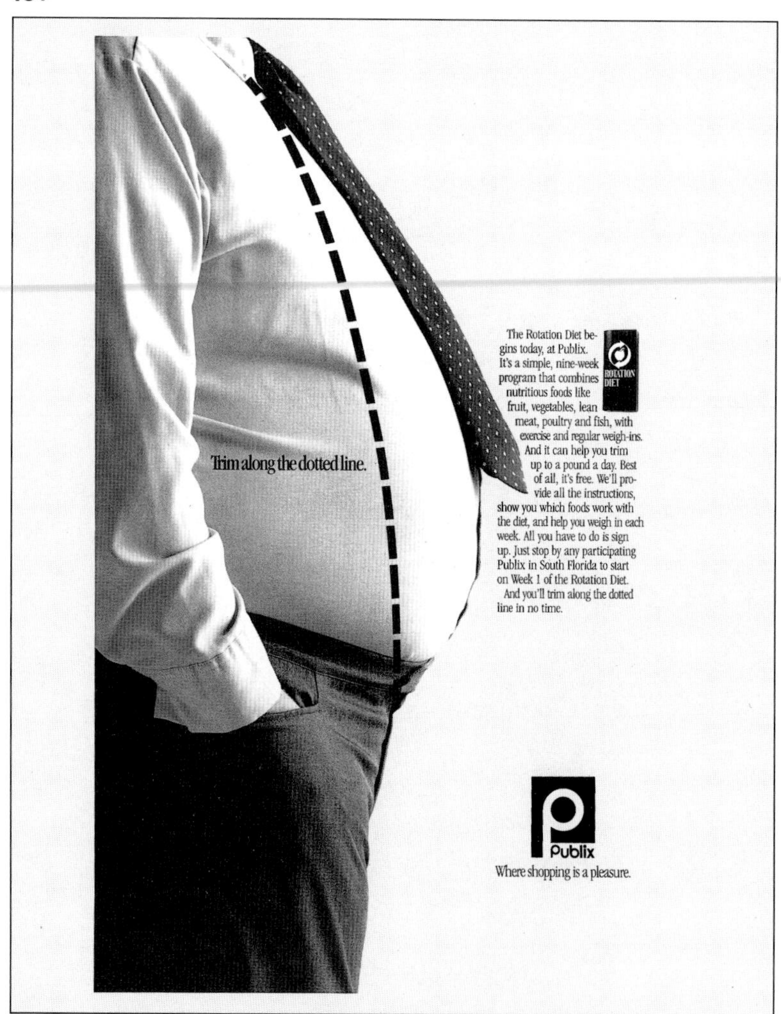

Trim along the dotted line.
The Rotation Diet begins today, at Publix. It's a simple, nine-week program that combines nutritious foods like fruit, vegetables, lean meat, poultry and fish, with exercise and regular weigh-ins. And it can help you trim up to a pound a day. Best of all, it's free. We'll provide all the instructions, show you which foods work with the diet, and help you weigh in each week. All you have to do is sign up. Just stop by any participating Publix in South Florida to start on Week 1 of the Rotation Diet.
And you'll trim along the dotted line in no time.
ROTATION DIET
Publix
Where shopping is a pleasure.

155

If You Haven't Seen Our Hearing Aids Yet, We're Not Surprised.

(Actual Size)

Wear the Audibel Intra Ear Hearing Aid.

Then sit back and see if anyone notices. Odds are they won't.

That's because the Audibel Intra Ear Hearing Aid is so small and compact, it hides neatly in your ear. Even the people closest to you will have trouble seeing it. The Audibel Intra Ear Hearing Aid lets you clearly hear everything that's going on around you—not just a few disjointed words.

And it eliminates the frustration of pretending to hear when you can't.

So come in and try our Audibel Intra Ear Hearing Aid. It might be the only time you'll see one.

APOLOGY

The ad booked to appear here didn't arrive in time. It was sent the normal way. However, for around the same cost they could have sent it air freight with Ansett's new *Parcelfast*. Delivery is guaranteed within 48 hours. So if you want to avoid making apologies phone Ansett Air Freight on 216301.

Consumer Newspaper
Over 600 Lines: Single

158
ART DIRECTORS
Suzanne Dashiell
Bob Shira
Jessica Welton
WRITER
Tommy Thompson
DESIGNER
Suzanne Dashiell
PHOTOGRAPHER
Tony Sylvestro
CLIENT
Potomac Mills Mall
AGENCY
Siddall Matus & Coughter/
Richmond, VA

159
ART DIRECTOR
Jac Coverdale
WRITER
Jerry Fury
PHOTOGRAPHER
Jim Arndt
CLIENT
St. Paul Pioneer Press
Dispatch
AGENCY
Clarity Coverdale Rueff/
Minneapolis

160
ART DIRECTORS
Chas Ardley
Jo Moore
WRITER
Simon Silvester
PHOTOGRAPHER
Derek Seagrim
CLIENT
William Grant and Sons
AGENCY
Delaney Fletcher Delaney/
London

161
ART DIRECTOR
Carolyn Tye
WRITER
Bill Westbrook
PHOTOGRAPHER
Richmond Newspapers
CLIENT
Ukrop's Supermarkets
AGENCY
Ford & Westbrook/
Richmond, VA

158

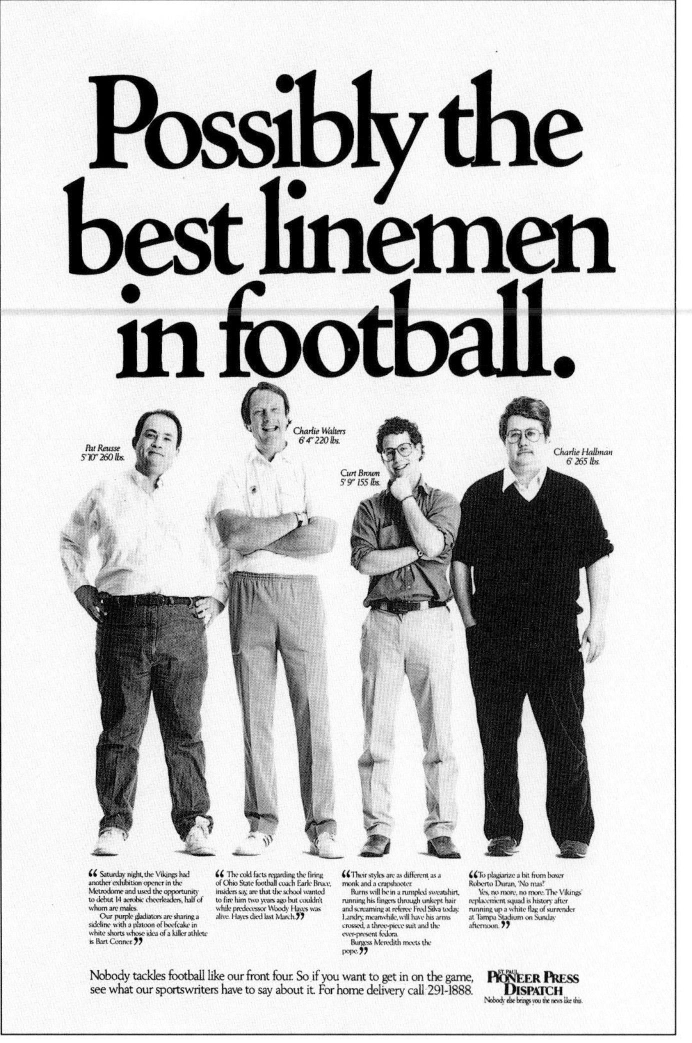

159

HELP US TO GIVE 20p TO CHARITY AND GET A NICE WARM FEELING INSIDE.

Belstead Arms
Radcliffe Drive, Ipswich

Black Horse
Black Horse Lane, Ipswich

Bristol Arms
Bristol Hill, Shotley, Ipswich

Brook
Washbrook, Ipswich

Canes
13/15 St. Margarets Plain, Ipswich

Case is Altered
341/3 Woodbridge Road, Ipswich

Cock and Pye
Upper Brook Street, Ipswich

Compasses
Ipswich Road, Holbrook, Ipswich

Cross Inn
Church Street, Woodbridge

Dales
Dales Road, Ipswich

Douglas Bader
The Square, Martlesham Heath
Ipswich

Gainsborough
Sandy Hill Lane, Ipswich

Golden Lion Hotel
Cornhill, Ipswich

Golf
Foxhall Road, Ipswich

Grosvenor
Ranelagh Road, Felixstowe

Halberd
15 Northgate Street, Ipswich

Inkerman
197 Norwich Road, Ipswich

Lions Head
213/215 Cauldwell Hall Road
Ipswich

TOLLY·COBBOLD

Live and Let Live
357/363 Wherstead Road, Ipswich

Man on the Moon
86 Palmcroft Road, Ipswich

Margaret Catchpole
Cliff Lane, Ipswich

Maybush
Cliff Road, Waldringfield
Woodbridge

Maypole
Old Norwich Road, Ipswich

Mulberry Tree
5 Woodbridge Road, Ipswich

Old Times
324 Spring Road, Ipswich

Ostrich Inn
Bourne End, Wherstead, Ipswich

Queens Head
Station Road, Stowmarket

Royal George
Colchester Road, Ipswich

Royal Oak
175 Felixstowe Road, Ipswich

Salutation
67 Carr Street, Ipswich

Shepherd and Dog
Felixstowe Road, Nacton Road
Ipswich

Spread Eagle
1/3 Fore Street, Ipswich

Station Hotel
Burrell Road, Ipswich

Swan Inn
9 King Street, Ipswich

Swan
Main Road, Westerfield, Ipswich

Wild Man
Bramford Road, Sproughton
Ipswich

When you hand in this coupon at any of the Tolly Cobbold pubs listed opposite, you will receive a free miniature of Glenborough, and William Grant and Sons will make a 20p donation to this year's Mayor's Charity Fund, on your behalf.

Customers are allowed just one free 40ml miniature each and, of course, this offer is only open to those aged 18 or over on the day of application. Since the offer is limited to 150 people per pub, if you want that nice warm feeling inside, you'd better get yourself into one of the listed Tolly Pubs.

I DECLARE THAT I AM OVER 18

Name ....

Address ....

THIS OFFER IS ONLY AVAILABLE ON FRIDAY 13th NOVEMBER 1987

ACTUAL SIZE.

GLENBOROUGH. SCOTCH AND BOURBON MATURED WITH WALNUT

160

Ukrop's supermarket invented Farm Aid when Willie Nelson was nine.

Shuts Store to Aid Farmer

Associated Press Photo

SEVEN MORE FARM HANDS—Joe Ukrop, Richmond grocer, not only has announced that his grocery store would be closed every Wednesday afternoon but that he and his wife and the store's five employes would spend the half "holidays" helping farmers harvest their crops. "The farmer can't get help," Ukrop said, "so we are going to try to help out"

The year was 1942, and young men by the hundreds of thousands left America for the distant shores of war.

They left their cities and towns and their women and children.

And, of course, great numbers of them left the farms.

It was a time of commitment. No less so for a small grocery store on Hull Street in Richmond, Virginia named Ukrop's.

Every Wednesday afternoon during harvest season Joe Ukrop, his wife and the store's five employees closed the doors and drove out to the country to help the farmers. The corn they harvested would have spoiled in the fields without them.

There may not have been enough labor to go around back in those days. But there was enough love.

In the years since, Ukrop's has supported just about every civic project and charity imaginable. Yes, we've grown from one location to 18. And our selection of groceries is probably 100 times as large as the original store's.

But the family that opens the doors every morning is the same family that closed them every Wednesday. Now that we've turned 50 it's good to look back every now and then.

To make sure we're going ahead in the right direction.

Ukrop's 50th Anniversary

161

Consumer Newspaper Over 600 Lines: Single

162

ART DIRECTORS
Pam Stern
Teri Koles

WRITERS
Pam Stern
Teri Koles

CLIENT
Pyramid Companies

AGENCY
Messner Vetere Berger Carey

163

ART DIRECTOR
Bob Barrie

WRITER
Jarl Olsen

DESIGNER
Bob Barrie

PHOTOGRAPHER
Rick Dublin

CLIENT
Hush Puppies Shoe Company

AGENCY
Fallon McElligott/ Minneapolis

164

ART DIRECTORS
Julius Weil
Rick Paynter

WRITERS
Leland Rosemond
Ray Palletier

PHOTOGRAPHER
Michael Somoroff

CLIENT
American International Group

AGENCY
Bozell Jacobs Kenyon & Eckhardt

165

ART DIRECTOR
Rob Oliver

WRITER
David Rossiter

PHOTOGRAPHER
John Parker

CLIENT
Sainsbury's

AGENCY
Abbott Mead Vickers/ SMS - London

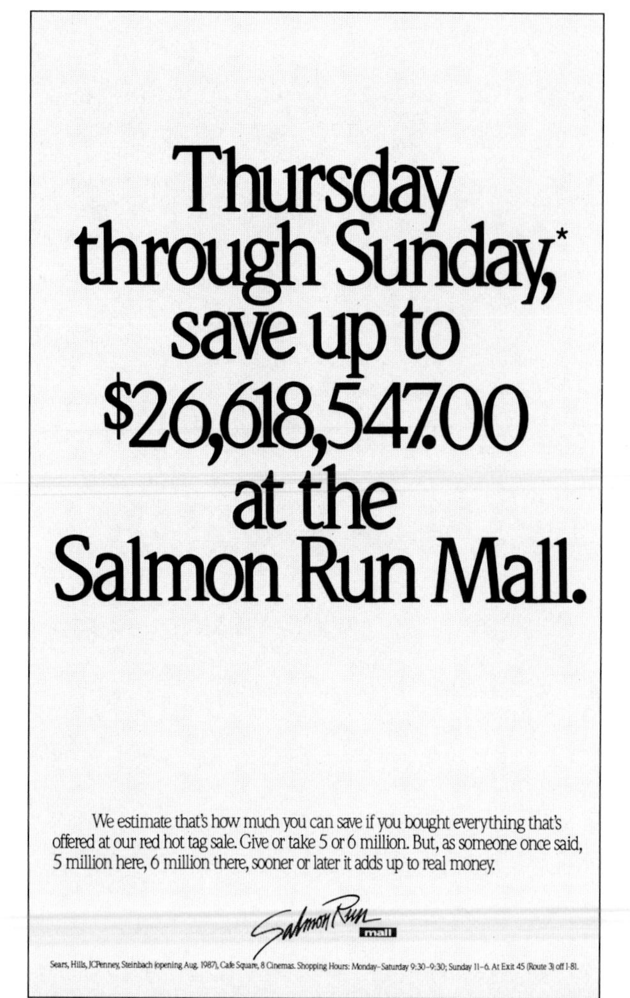

162

163

Sometimes the best way to stand out is to blend in.
It's a very important lesson we learned early in our 65-year history.
Leadership in the worldwide insurance industry isn't won by imposing our corporate culture on local operations. It's won by becoming part of the social, cultural and moral fabric of the countries in which we do business.
That idea is one reason for our current success in providing a broad range of commercial and personal insurance to businesses and individuals around the world. To learn more, contact AIG, Dept. A, 70 Pine St., N.Y., N.Y. 10270.
Thinking more like our customers than other insurance companies is how we won our stripes.
Insurance Companies That Don't Think Like Insurance Companies.
AIG

164

SAINSBURY'S BOOK OF
WINE
OZ CLARKE
Sainsbury's latest offering.
Once you pick it up, you won't want to lay it down.
Why were the cellarmen in Rheims apt to suffer from arthritis of the wrist?
How could the 1920 vintage be both a washout and pretty good?
How can you know, without tasting it, what to expect of a young Zinfandel from America?
The answers to all three questions are printed below but be warned.
They'll probably leave you thirsting to know more.
In which case, you'll just have to buy the new Sainsbury's Book of Wine.
And even if you knew the answers without looking, you'd still be well-advised to get hold of a copy.
For in our humble opinion, it's not only the most informative but also the most enjoyable book on
Good food costs less at Sainsbury's.

165

Consumer Newspaper Over 600 Lines: Single

166
ART DIRECTOR
Jac Coverdale
WRITER
Jerry Fury
CLIENT
St. Paul Pioneer Press Dispatch
AGENCY
Clarity Coverdale Rueff/ Minneapolis

167
ART DIRECTOR
Carl Warner
WRITER
Ross Myers
DESIGNER
Carl Warner
CLIENT
Sebastian's Closet
AGENCY
The Richards Group/Dallas

168
ART DIRECTOR
Joe Shyllit
WRITER
Jerry Kuleba
PHOTOGRAPHER
Colin Fraser
CLIENT
Suzuki Canada
AGENCY
Laser Kuleba Shyllit/ Ontario

169
ART DIRECTOR
Bob Brihn
WRITER
George Gier
PHOTOGRAPHER
Mark LaFavor
CLIENT
Federal Express
AGENCY
Fallon McElligott/ Minneapolis

Two of our most popular writers once suffered from writer's block.

See all the red ink on this page?

That's the kind of writer's block Joe Soucheray and Nick Coleman suffered from when they worked on the other side of the river. Soften

In fact, sometimes, even though they knew what they wanted to say, they just couldn't express themselves. So they left to find freedom of the Press. Too controversial!!

The Pioneer Press Dispatch.

Now no one dictates their style and no subject is too controversial. No!!

All we ask is that they each write four columns a week. Rewrite

Joe Soucheray and Nick Coleman. Read 'em the way they should be read. In the St. Paul Pioneer Press Dispatch. *For home delivery call 291-1880.*

ST. PAUL PIONEER PRESS DISPATCH

Nobody else brings you the news like this.

166

This Is How It Felt In Our Old Store.

Racks bulged with suits from Europe's most respected designers. Shelves strained under the weight of the finest collection of handmade shirts. And tables overflowed with classic cotton and cashmere sweaters. What's more, our mall location kept us from opening early or staying late when you needed us to. Quite simply, our old place didn't fit our needs any longer.

Sebastian's Closet

This Is How It Feels In Our New Store.

Now there's a wealth of room and an abundance of natural light all in a comfortable atmosphere. At The Village On The Parkway, we even have the freedom to extend our hours at your request. Now you can browse through a larger, more complete collection of European men's wear in a setting as impressive as the clothes themselves. We couldn't feel more at home.

Sebastian's Closet

Village on the Parkway, 5100 Belt Line, Suite 540. 214-387-0888.

167

Our competition is 100% behind us.

You don't often see other motorcycle companies get behind a competitor.

But they have been with Suzuki.

Have a look. Last year, Michel Mercier riding on a Suzuki won more races in the Canada Pro Open Class and ended up being the 1986 Superbike Champion.

In the Pro 750 Superbike Championship, Gary Goodfellow and his Suzuki cleaned up there.

And the beat goes on.

This year after 3 races* Suzuki once again has beaten everyone.

In today's world, the competition usually knocks you.

But we're real proud that race after race our competition is right there behind us. If not 100% of the time, at least 95% of the time.

And we plan to keep it that way.

Be a professional. Take a Canada Council Motorcycle Rider Training Course. See your Suzuki Dealer.

*The 1987 Motoplan Castrol National Pro 750 Superbike Championship Series.

168

AVOID AN INTERNATIONAL INCIDENT.

When you have an important package to be sent out of the country, don't trust it to just any air express company. Choose the one that invented the business—Federal Express.

Federal Express can ship packages up to 150 pounds to thousands of cities in over 85 countries. And only Federal has the COSMOS tracking system, that can trace international shipments within hours.

We also have one of the best reliability rates in the business. A fact we stand behind with this guarantee—if we deliver a shipment late (even just 60 seconds late), you can request your money back.

So next time, call Federal Express. And avoid an international incident. For a free international starter kit, call us at 1-800-238-5355.

WORLDWIDE SERVICE FROM FEDERAL EXPRESS.

169

Consumer Newspaper
Over 600 Lines: Single

170
ART DIRECTOR
Dean Hanson
WRITER
Phil Hanft
PHOTOGRAPHER
Rick Dublin
CLIENT
Conran's
AGENCY
Fallon McElligott/
Minneapolis

171
ART DIRECTORS
Nancy Rice
Nick Rice
WRITER
Jim Newcombe
DESIGNERS
Roger Christensen
Great Faces
ARTIST
Jack Krough
PHOTOGRAPHER
Marvy!
CLIENT
WCCO Radio
AGENCY
Rice & Rice/Minneapolis

172
ART DIRECTOR
Frank Haggerty
WRITER
Kerry Casey
DESIGNER
Frank Haggerty
CLIENT
Minnesota Zoo
AGENCY
Carmichael Lynch/
Minneapolis

173
ART DIRECTORS
Rob Rich
Woody Kay
WRITER
Ernie Schenck
DESIGNER
Judy Maddock
CLIENT
Vanderbilt Rehabilitation Center
AGENCY
Pagano Schenck & Kay/
Providence, RI

170

171

Which Would You Rather Watch This Summer?

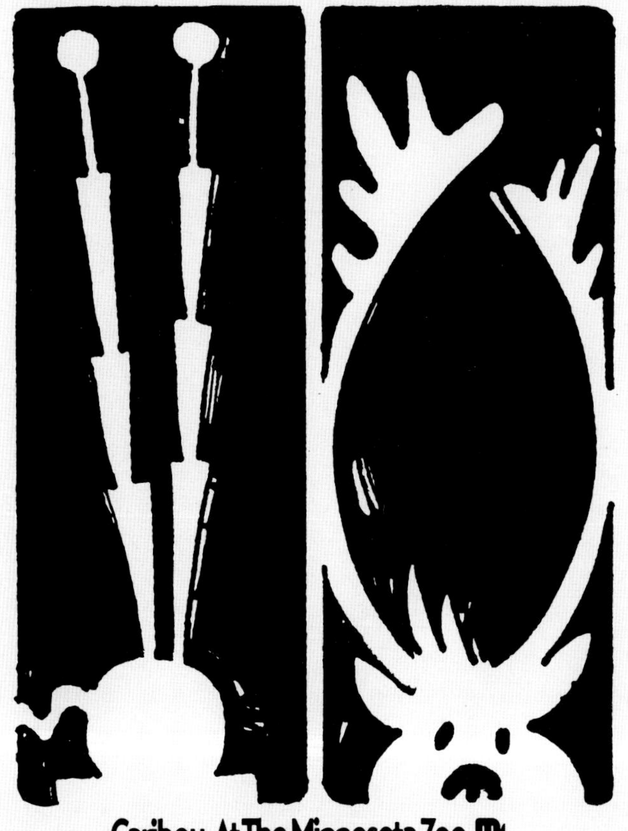

Caribou. At The Minnesota Zoo.

Exhibit's major corporate sponsor is the Star and Tribune

172

If A Spinal Cord Injury Puts You In A Wheelchair, Even A Curbstone Looks Different.

A six-inch slab of granite can seem like the Great Wall of China. Just climbing into a bathtub can make you feel like you're climbing Mt. Everest.

What once were simple things you took for granted suddenly turn into massive, insurmountable obstacles.

At the Vanderbilt Rehabilitation Center, we know a challenge like that takes time. It takes guts. And it takes some very specialized care.

Which is why our programs are designed to cover every aspect of a patient's recovery. From medical evaluation and goal-setting to physical rehabilitation and community reintegration.

All within a warm, compassionate atmosphere where each and every patient is treated on a personal basis.

As part of Newport Hospital's long-standing commitment to providing the best medical care possible, the Vanderbilt Rehabilitation Center offers a broad range of physician-supervised rehabilitation services including speech and hearing therapy, psychological and family support, and our Back Care program.

Call our Rehabilitation Program Coordinator at (401) 846-6400, extension 1852. Life in a wheelchair may be different. But it's nothing you can't get over.

VANDERBILT REHABILITATION CENTER

At Newport Hospital

173

Consumer Newspaper Over 600 Lines: Single

174
ART DIRECTOR
Grant Richards
WRITER
Glenn Gill
PHOTOGRAPHER
Gordon Willis
CLIENT
Flowers To Go
AGENCY
The Richards Group/Dallas

175
ART DIRECTORS
Ivan Horvath
Marten Tonnis
WRITERS
Steve Hayden
Laurie Brandalise
DESIGNER
Gina Norton
PHOTOGRAPHER
Bo Hylen Studios
CLIENT
Apple Computer
AGENCY
BBDO

176
ART DIRECTORS
Nancy Rice
Nick Rice
WRITER
Jim Newcombe
DESIGNERS
Roger Christensen
Great Faces
ARTIST
Jack Krough
PHOTOGRAPHER
Jim Arndt
CLIENT
WCCO Radio
AGENCY
Rice & Rice/Minneapolis

177
ART DIRECTOR
Bob Brihn
WRITER
George Gier
PHOTOGRAPHER
Jim Arndt
CLIENT
Federal Express
AGENCY
Fallon McElligott/
Minneapolis

Stop By Flowers To Go Or There May Be Another St. Valentine's Day Massacre.

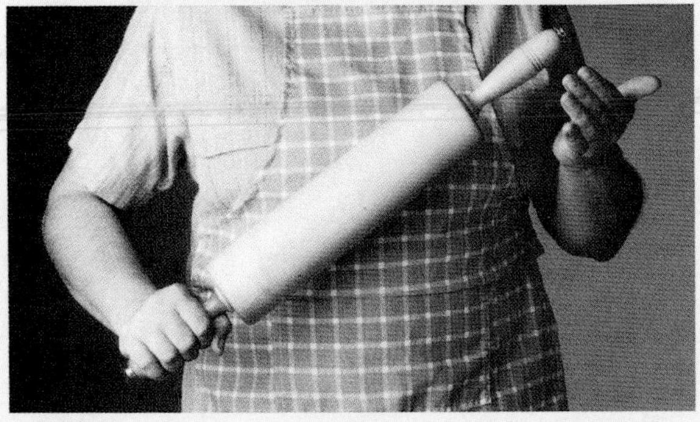

Failing to receive flowers on Valentine's Day has been known to bring out the worst in many a sweetheart. So, Flowers To Go is providing this subtle reminder.

We have a dozen red, yellow or white long stemmed roses for $34.95 wrapped. And $44.95 with vase. Without a doubt, the best deal in town. Or if she'd prefer exotic and fresh cut flowers, a potted

plant or an original arrangement, we have those, too. Flowers To Go can take your order right now, if you call **525-8111**. And in case you were wondering, we do deliver.

But place that order today to insure yourself a happy, as well as healthy Valentine's Day.

Flowers To Go

San Pedro at Rector/Perrin Beitel at Naco Perrin/S. W. Military at Tacoma, near I-35/Broadway at Pershing
San Pedro at Chula Vista/Bandera at Poss/Fredericksburg at Mockingbird/Blanco at Lockhill Selma.

174

Macintosh makes the financial page.

It also changes the weather. Pinpoints trouble spots. Displays baseball scores. And just generally covers the planet daily in a hundred different ways.

For publications ranging from Gannett's USA TODAY to the Denver Post to Knight-Ridder Newspapers.

In fact, every U.S. newspaper with a circulation of over 500,000 has given the Macintosh™ personal computer a job in their newsrooms. Because they've found it's the most cost efficient way to create sophisticated graphics for fast-breaking stories.

And to share them electronically, and instantly, news desk to news desk, city to city, anywhere in the world.

All this may come as news to a lot of business people who thought Apple® Desktop Publishing was just merely a good way to save money on printed fliers.

With a Macintosh and a LaserWriter® printer, your company can design, assemble and print everything from technical manuals to major presentations to, yes, newspapers—at a fraction of what it would cost to send them out.

In fact, you can afford to "publish" every document in your office, from internal memos to formal presentations. In hundreds of type styles and sizes and handsomely illustrated with Macintosh graphics.

But there's much more to Macintosh than looking good on paper. It can handle hundreds of other routine business tasks simply and professionally, with all the latest, and most advanced business software available.

Including powerful spreadsheets with built-in business graphics and macros. Project management programs that help organize and manage highly complex jobs. And data communications tools that allow Macintoshes to communicate with each other, IBM PCs, and mainframes.

And just as importantly, Macintosh goes about its business with the lowest training cost per desktop of any personal computer.

Because, unlike ordinary computer programs, every Macintosh program works precisely the same way—with simple point-and-click commands, windows, and consistent pull-down menus.

Which could very well be why a growing number of the Fortune 500 are turning to Macintosh computers for real productivity gains. In fact, in an in-depth analysis of seven Macintosh installations in large manufacturing companies, users all reported productivity gains of 25% or more.

So the next time you open up your newspaper, don't be too surprised if you see Macintosh making an appearance on the financial page.

And maybe even in the headlines.

The power to be your best.™

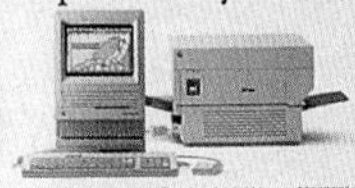

175

Traffic is a battle.
We provide the air cover.
5th St
If you're fighting traffic, WCCO Radio is a strong ally. We start bright and early every morning, and don't get home until you do. From high above the Twin Cities, John Lundell reports the changing traffic situation. Dean Spratt supplies timely ground support. And no other station has them. Together, they give you the ammunition you need to triumph over traffic. WCCO Radio. For traffic reports, we're the Twin Cities' greatest air power.
WCCO
RADIO 8·3·0

176

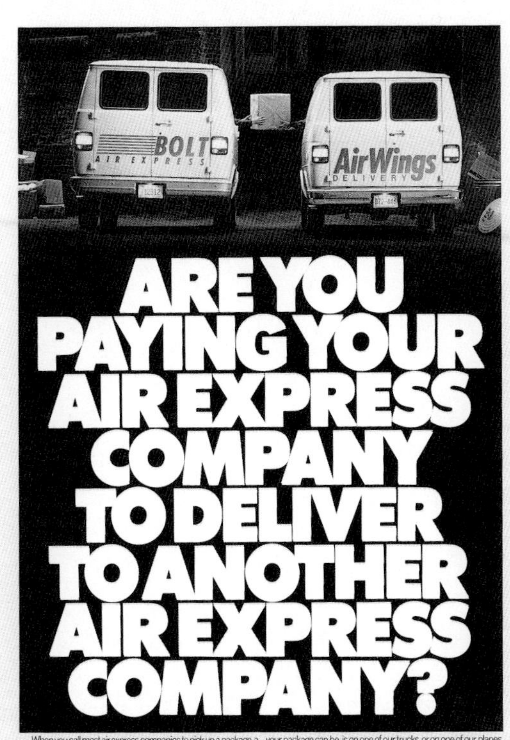
BOLT
AIR EXPRESS
AirWings
DELIVERY
ARE YOU PAYING YOUR AIR EXPRESS COMPANY TO DELIVER TO ANOTHER AIR EXPRESS COMPANY?
When you call most air express companies to pick up a package, a funny thing happens-they call another air express company to deliver it.
While this may be the way they ship your package to the United States, and to the rest of the world, it certainly isn't the best way.
Too many people handling your package allows for too many opportunities for something to go wrong. And if something were to go wrong, it can be extremely difficult to locate the problem, let alone your package.
Fortunately, there is an alternative. You can call Federal Express.
For example, when we pick up your package in Toronto for delivery in New York, we handle it all the way. Which means, the only place your package can be, is on one of our trucks, or on one of our planes.
And with our COSMOS tracking system, getting information on the status of your package is just a phone call away.
Because of this complete control, you can expect reliability. And we stand behind it with this guarantee—if we deliver a shipment late (even just 60 seconds late) you can request your money back. So next time, call Federal. And your package won't end up in the wrong hands. For a free international starter kit call 897-9322, outside the metro area, 1-800-387-5982.
WORLDWIDE SERVICE FROM FEDERAL EXPRESS.

177

Consumer Newspaper Over 600 Lines: Single

178

ART DIRECTOR
Dean Hanson

WRITER
Phil Hanft

PHOTOGRAPHER
Rick Dublin

CLIENT
Conran's

AGENCY
Fallon McElligott/
Minneapolis

179

ART DIRECTORS
Nancy Rice
Nick Rice

WRITER
Jim Newcombe

DESIGNERS
Roger Christensen
Great Faces

ARTIST
Jack Krough

PHOTOGRAPHER
Marvy!

CLIENT
WCCO Radio

AGENCY
Rice & Rice/Minneapolis

180

ART DIRECTOR
Felix Burgos

WRITER
Margaret Mandell

PHOTOGRAPHER
Clint Clemens

CLIENT
Lotus Cars USA

AGENCY
McCann-Erickson

181

ART DIRECTOR
Tom Lichtenheld

WRITER
Rod Kilpatrick

PHOTOGRAPHER
Jim Arndt

CLIENT
The Wall Street Journal

AGENCY
Fallon McElligott/
Minneapolis

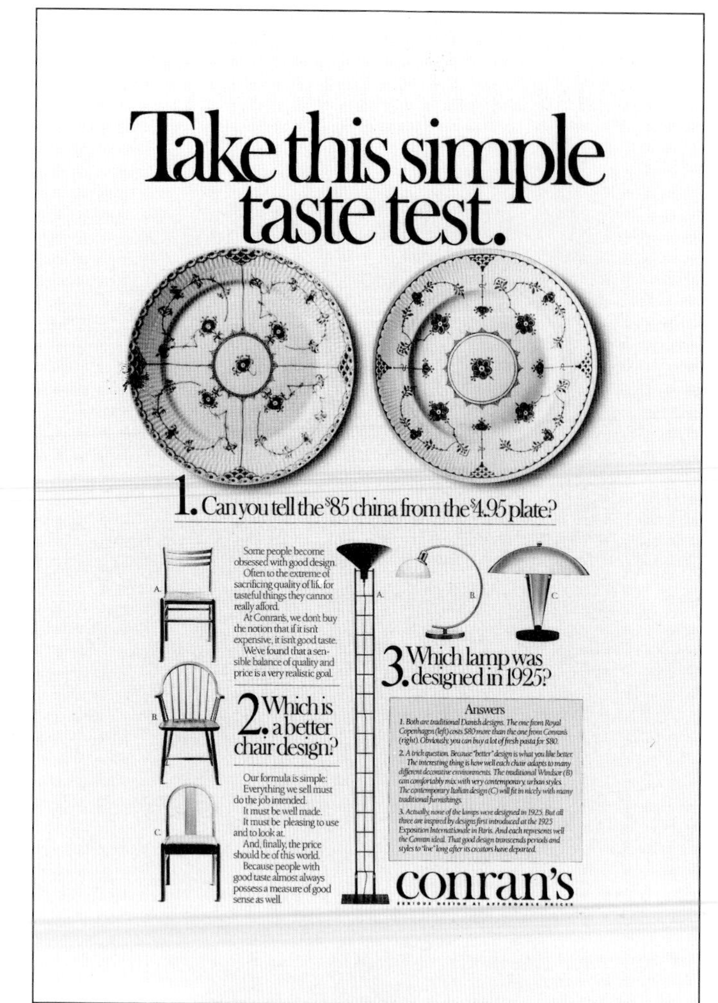

178

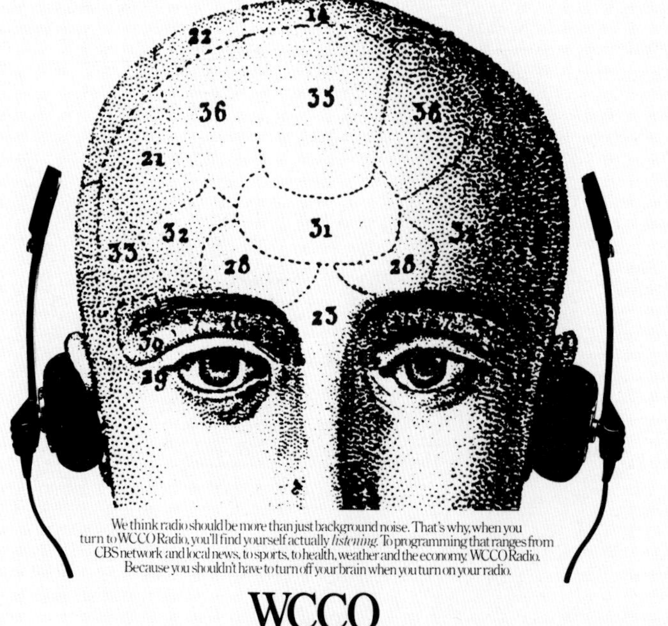

179

The People Who Drive Lotus
Aren't Mass-Produced Either.
Admittedly, the Lotus® Turbo Esprit is not for everyone. (Last year, a record 200 cars were produced for this country.)
After all, not everybody will appreciate the subtleties of a handcrafted car—solidly constructed to be as trustworthy as it is thrilling to drive.
features found on any car today, it also comes equipped with one of the most extensive warranties available.
In fact, no other car in its class has a warranty that outperforms it: a two-year unlimited mileage, limited warranty plus eight years' anticorrosion coverage on the chassis—testimony to our confidence in the Turbo Esprit's durability and reliability. (See your Lotus Dealer for details.)
Leasing A Lotus Has Never Made So Much Sense.
Although not everyone will recognize the value of this unique offer, to the few who know the difference, we present the opportunity of a lifetime.
Now you can lease a Lotus Turbo Esprit for only $870* a month.
Your participating dealer will be pleased to provide you with all the details, including the full range of leasing programs and advantageous financing plans available to fit your specific needs.
Of course, should you decide to purchase a Lotus, you can now do so at the very favorable retail rate of only 7.95% APR.**
A Warranty That's Unsurpassed In Its Class.
The 1987 Turbo Esprit offers the kind of performance that excels down the road, as well as on it.
It not only comes equipped with some of the most unique and revolutionary design
On The Road Is More Thrilling Than On The Page.
Words alone cannot begin to describe the Lotus experience.
Therefore, we invite you to test-drive this remarkable automobile built in the tradition of the world's most celebrated racing machines.
Only then can you start to understand what sets the Turbo Esprit apart.
And the people who drive it.
LOTUS
LOTUS
For The Few Who Know The Difference.
T U R B O E S P R I T

Do you have what it takes to be president?
They say that anyone with brains, talent and ambition can become president. But in 1988, a few million dollars in campaign funds wouldn't hurt, either.
The complicated economics of campaigning is but one of the issues that will be investigated in "Politics: A Wall Street Journal Special Report."
The Journal's report will consider the legacy of the Reagan years, and examine the implications for a country poised on the brink of change.
It will discuss the role of the media, lay out a complete schedule of the political year, and even look ahead to the turn of the new century.
And last, but certainly not least, it will be included in The Journal on Friday, December 4. Or you can receive a complimentary copy of the report by calling 800-841-1212, extension 977.
Either way, you'll find "Politics: A Special Report" to be extremely valuable. Because while you still may not have what it takes to be president, at least you'll have what it takes to vote for one.
Politics. A Wall Street Journal Special Report.

Consumer Newspaper Over 600 Lines: Single

182
ART DIRECTOR
Michael Hampton
WRITER
Cynthia Beck
CLIENT
NYNEX
AGENCY
Young & Rubicam

183
ART DIRECTOR
Dean Hanson
WRITER
Bruce Bildsten
PHOTOGRAPHER
Rick Dublin
CLIENT
The Wall Street Journal
AGENCY
Fallon McElligott/
Minneapolis

184
ART DIRECTOR
Howard Brody
WRITER
Cynthia Beck
CLIENT
US Postal Service-Express
Mail
AGENCY
Young & Rubicam

185
ART DIRECTOR
Mark Johnson
WRITER
Tom McElligott
CLIENT
Porsche Cars North
America
AGENCY
Fallon McElligott/
Minneapolis

Chances are we're holding up your bank.

We don't mean to boast. But of the top ten U.S. banks, eight are NYNEX customers.

Of the top ten diversified financial institutions, nine are NYNEX customers.

So are over half of all *Fortune* 500 companies.

NYNEX is upholding these giants in lots of ways. We've given most of them their data-capable phone systems, and many of them their computers and software as well.

Now, as you know, we're not exactly the only people in the world who offer telecommunications and information systems. So why are so many financial leaders choosing NYNEX?

One clue is our hot technology. Recently, for example, a worldwide bank needed help tracking their customer liability. And NYNEX gave them a software package that issues worldwide reports on who's naughty, who's nice.

The NYNEX family of information companies would like to work with you, too. Besides our two phone companies, we have nine companies in information and office systems, business support and publishing.

To learn more about why NYNEX is the answer for your business, call us at 1 800 535-1535.

We suspect you'll like our bids as much as our technology. At NYNEX we understand that our customers—even the top banks—are not made of money.

182

Is It The Light At The End Of The Tunnel,
Or Is It Another Train?

If you don't know exactly what's coming next in the stock market, you're not alone.

But if you want to know precisely what has happened, what it means, and most important, what could happen next, you do have a place to turn.

The Wall Street Journal.

In The Journal, you'll not only get a complete picture of all the markets, you'll also get a clear picture. Facts instead of rumors. And insights instead of hindsights.

So you'll not only learn how the market is affecting America's investors, but also how it's affecting America's businesses—your job as well as your portfolio.

And since the last thing you need in a market with such dramatic daily changes is weekly news, you can have The Journal delivered where you work or where you live every working day.

All of which makes this a remarkably opportune time to invest in a subscription. To order yours, simply call **800-841-8000.**

We may not be able to tell you exactly what's at the end of the tunnel, but at least we can help keep you on the right track.

The Wall Street Journal.
The daily diary of the American dream.

183

If there's one time late ain't great, it's Valentine's Day. But lover, don't fret. Express Mail® service from your post office can deliver your sweet nothings, your chocolates, your rubies and pearls, overnight. All at the sweetest prices–$10.75 for our 2-Pound Pak, $12.85 for up to five pounds. And you can send your package from any Express Mail post office or collection box, or give it to any letter carrier.

So don't just love 'em tender. Love 'em economically. And love 'em on time.

EXPRESS MAIL.

When we say overnight, we mean overnight.

184

At 107% resale value it performs on the same track with Matisse, Persian rugs and condos in Vail.

Normally, when one thinks of Porsche performance, names like Nurburgring, LeMans and Paris-to-Dakar come to mind.

And why not, after all? In the world of auto racing, no marque has been more honored, more often than Porsche. But while speed, endurance and state-of-the-art engineering have become legendary yardsticks of Porsche performance, there are other ways to measure it.

Over the years, for example, older Porsches (as most people know) and even many newer Porsches (as most people don't know) have actually risen in value.

Take the 1986 911 Carrera. Today, just two years after purchase, it is worth a remarkable 106.8%* of its original selling price.

So if you've postponed buying a Porsche in order to invest your money on, ahem, faster tracks, perhaps it's time to visit your local authorized Porsche dealer.

And invest in the car that may look as attractive in your portfolio as it does in your garage.†

PORSCHE

The Porsche experience begins with your authorized Porsche dealer.

185

Consumer Newspaper Over 600 Lines: Single

186
ART DIRECTOR
Steve Dunn
WRITER
Tim Delaney
PHOTOGRAPHER
John Serginson
CLIENT
Nationwide Anglia Building Society
AGENCY
Leagas Delaney Partnership/London

187
ART DIRECTOR
Vince Squibb
WRITER
Gerard Edmondson
PHOTOGRAPHER
Rolph Gobits
CLIENT
London Life
AGENCY
Still Price Court Twivy D'Souza/London

188
ART DIRECTORS
Greg Harrison
Rick Cohn
WRITER
Joe Lovering
CLIENT
Bay State Gas
AGENCY
Rizzo Simons Cohn/Boston

189
ART DIRECTOR
Vince Squibb
WRITER
Gerard Edmondson
PHOTOGRAPHER
Andreas Heumann
CLIENT
Mates Healthcare
AGENCY
Still Price Court Twivy D'Souza/London

If you want to find out how banks became the richest, most powerful institutions in the world, go into the red one day.

Banks have not always been as big and profitable as they are today.

Believe it or not, all the big boys on the High Street were small businesses once.

(In 1955, Barclays only made just over £2½ million profit.)

How then, did the High Street banks achieve the status they enjoy today?

and, most important of all, easily understood.

Of course, the reverse is true with most bank current accounts.

Which is no doubt why they have Hollywood-style adverts telling customers how much they care for them.

At Nationwide Anglia, we believe in deeds not words.

You simply ring one phone number and punch in your personal code. Then, by pressing a few more buttons, you can pay your bills.

Or, just as easily, get instant confirmation of your balance or order a full statement.

From any telephone in the world, at any time day or night. And all in return for a £10 deposit, which is refundable.

COMMISSION
OVERDRAFT ADMIN £26.00
****

Innovative ideas? Hardly. The first cheque was issued in 1659.

Dynamic management? You have called your bank manager a lot of things in your time, we bet 'dynamic' isn't one of them.

Customer satisfaction, then? No comment.

No.

Quite simply, it is you, dear reader, who have made the banks so rich and powerful.

You, and millions of people like you, who over the years have put your hard earned money into their coffers and received little in return.

Indeed, when you have had the temerity to go into the red, you have paid dearly for it.

Thankfully, there is now an alternative to a bank current account.

Nationwide Anglia's FlexAccount.

An account based on a very simple idea: that it is your money and we should not forget the fact.

So if you go into the red with a FlexAccount you don't start attracting mysterious 'service charges'.

You won't suddenly find yourself having to pay for standing orders and direct debits for a whole three month period when you have only slipped into the red for one day. And we won't slap in a bill, sorry, 'arrangement fee' just for discussing and sorting out an overdraft.

All we ask of you is interest on the money you borrow until you're in the black.

We think this is reasonable, straightforward

So we pay FlexAccount holders interest on the money in their current account.

Not just to people with lots of money in their account, mind.

Every FlexAccount holder gets 2% net per annum on anything up to £99. 3% interest on sums between £100 and £499. And 4% when you're £500 or more in credit.

(Both the higher rates are paid on the whole balance, not just the amount over £100 or £500.)

All calculated daily and paid into your account annually.

This is the interest the High Street banks have traditionally believed is theirs.

Somewhat strange logic as it is your money that earns it.

Isn't there anything good about a bank current account?

Of course there is.

Cheque books, cheque guarantee cards and cash cards. Not forgetting other services like standing orders and direct debits.

All excellent facilities.

Which is why they are all available to FlexAccount holders.

But that's not all.

Being rather keen on new ideas, we also offer our customers something called a Home Banking Unit.

Which works like an unusually helpful, round-the-clock counter clerk.

Not everyone will want one, we know. But that's not the point.

It's another expression of our philosophy.

Another way of helping people manage their money and, ultimately, get more from it.

Does all this sound too good to be true? It shouldn't. It is, after all, common sense.

Which is no doubt why Channel Four television's 'Money Spinner' programme singled it out as being a service "which High Street banks would do well to take notice of."

So far they haven't. Just check your last statement.

If you went into the red, you'll find a deduction has been duly made.

No information about how it's computed. No breakdown. No nothing.

Is it really the best way to treat a customer?

We don't think so. Maybe that's because we are not one of the richest, most powerful institutions in the world.

For further information, just call into your local Nationwide Anglia branch.

Or write now to Claire Adams, Nationwide Anglia Building Society, Chesterfield House, Bloomsbury Way, London WC1V 6PW.

We always remember whose money it is.

186

When an insurance salesman sells you a policy, whose retirement is he thinking of?

The gentleman here has to sell you a pension to earn his daily crust. The larger the policy, the bigger his slice.

But at London Life, we pay each of our advisors a salary. So whether they sell you a pension or not, they still eat. Allow us to explain.

With no thoughts of commission to cloud their judgement, they can take time to assess your long term financial needs.

After all, taking the wrong decision now can seriously affect your wealth when you come to retire.

Through our unique Pensions Advice Service, they'll then prepare the best plan for you. One which you can peruse at your leisure.

They won't bully, cajole or plead with you to make a decision. Nor will they vanish from the face of the earth once they've sold you a policy.

We've been in business since 1806, and have never been in better health.

What's more, our advisors will always be on hand to answer any problems that may crop up.

But, in the unlikely event that they can't be reached, we've set up a telephone helpline to deal with queries that just can't wait.

If you'd like to know how we can help you with your retirement plans, simply call Roberta Owen, on Freefone 0800 717111. We're quite sure you'll find that we're anything but retiring.

LONDON LIFE

HONESTY'S THE BEST POLICY.

187

NOT ALL HEAT RISES.

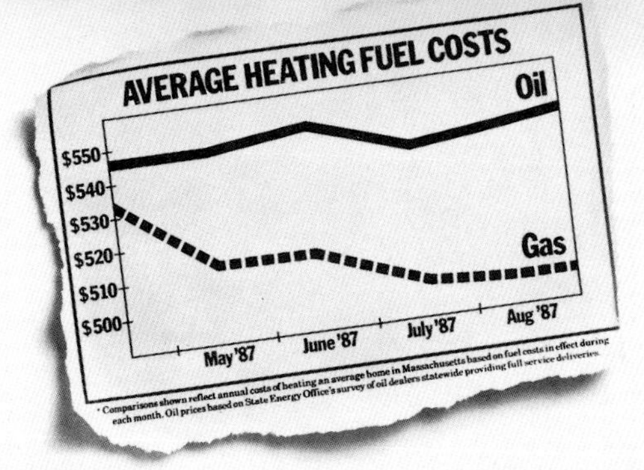

While the price of oil has been going up, the price of natural gas has been falling. But that's hardly unusual.

For eight of the past 10 years, gas has cost less than oil. So much less, you would have saved over $1,000 if you'd been heating your home with it.

You're not too late.

Right now, Bay State Gas will install a gas line and convert your oil furnace to gas. In most cases, absolutely free.

Call our Residential Sales Department for details.

With oil prices likely to keep rising, you'll want to have gas for the Fall.

NATURAL GAS THE MODERN ALTERNATIVE

Bay State Gas
1-800-242-0940

188

"I EXPECT TO GET THROUGH 50 GROSS IN THE NEXT FEW MONTHS."
Mates
R. DONALDSON

A rather extravagant claim, you'd be forgiven for thinking.

But having fun has become a serious business in the last year or so. And AIDS is the culprit.

In New York, it's already the biggest killer of women aged between 25 and 35.

And in Britain, it now claims one life each day. By 1991, BMA figures suggest that up to 100,000 people may have the virus.

Heterosexuals and homosexuals alike.

And given the speed with which the virus is changing, the chances of finding an effective cure are remote.

However bleak the outlook, it is possible to guard against it.

Using a condom will greatly reduce the risk of contracting AIDS, as well as cervical cancer and other sexually transmitted diseases. Of that, there's no doubt.

Hence the recent appearance of Mates Healthcare on the condom market.

Mates are made by one of the World's leading manufacturers.

The range includes Natural Mates, Ribbed Mates and Coloured Mates. All of which carry the official BSI Kite-mark.

They're just as reliable and sensitive as other condoms. But they cost less.

So they're easier on the pocket too. We've been joined in the protection business by pubs, newsagents, clubs, record shops, garages, chemists and supermarkets. Thanks to them, Mates are far more widely available.

What's more, though they cost less than other brands, Mates Healthcare Ltd. should still make a healthy profit.

That profit will chiefly be used for education programmes in 'Safer Sex' for the young.

We also plan to give money to hospices and counselling services for those dying of the disease.

All in all, it's our avowed aim to help stop the spread of AIDS. So spread the word.

MATES. YOU MAKE LOVE. THEY MAKE SENSE.

189

Consumer Newspaper Over 600 Lines: Single

190

ART DIRECTOR
Kirk Mosel

WRITER
Ty Montague

CLIENT
Champion

AGENCY
Scali McCabe Sloves

191

ART DIRECTOR
Logan Wilmont

WRITER
Mike Court

PHOTOGRAPHER
Andreas Heumann

CLIENT
Mates Healthcare

AGENCY
Still Price Court Twivy D'Souza/London

192

ART DIRECTOR
Bob Brihn

WRITER
George Gier

PHOTOGRAPHER
Jim Arndt

CLIENT
Federal Express

AGENCY
Fallon McElligott/ Minneapolis

193

ART DIRECTOR
Steve Dunn

WRITER
Tim Delaney

PHOTOGRAPHER
John Claridge

CLIENT
Nationwide Anglia Building Society

AGENCY
Leagas Delaney Partnership/London

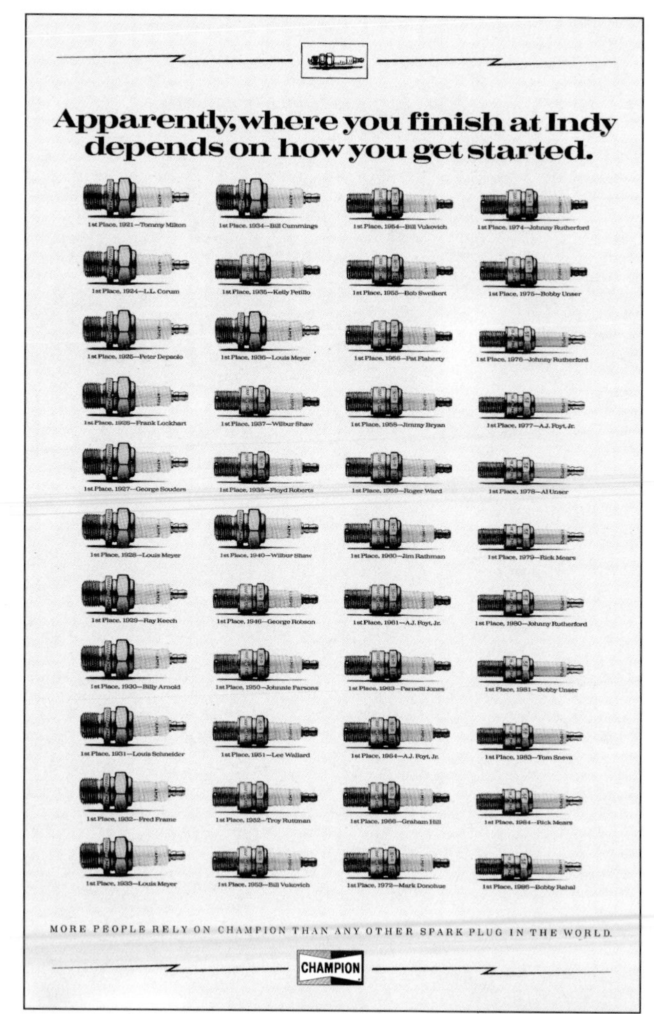

Apparently, where you finish at Indy depends on how you get started.
MORE PEOPLE RELY ON CHAMPION THAN ANY OTHER SPARK PLUG IN THE WORLD.
CHAMPION

190

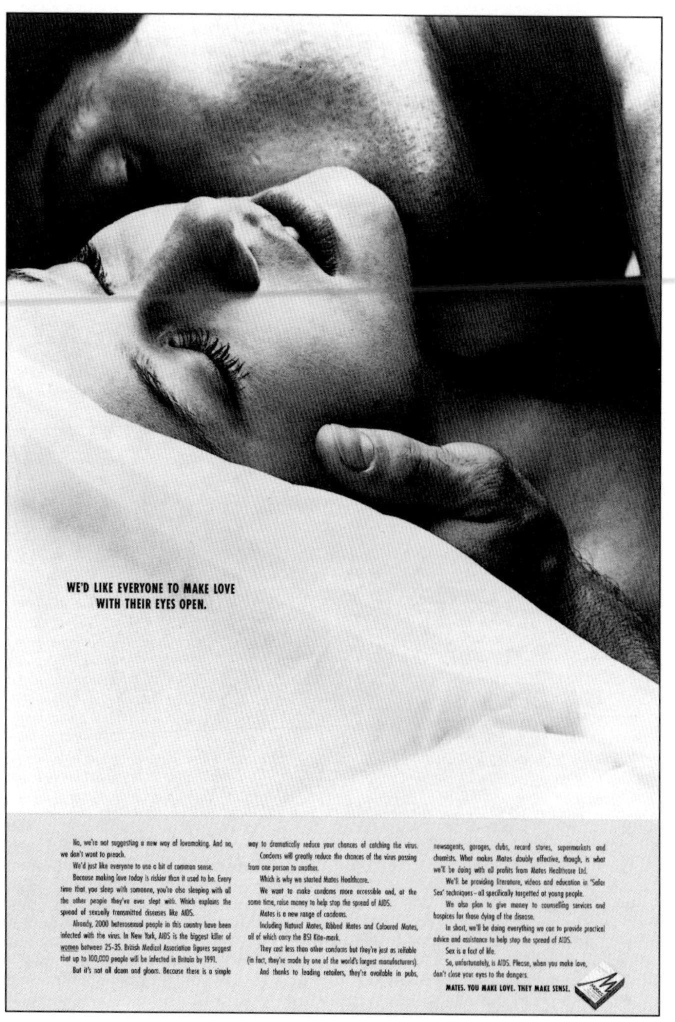

WE'D LIKE EVERYONE TO MAKE LOVE WITH THEIR EYES OPEN.
No, we're not suggesting a new way of lovemaking. And no, we don't want to preach.
We'd just like everyone to use a bit of common sense.
Because making love today is riskier than it used to be. Every time that you sleep with someone, you're also sleeping with all the other people they've ever slept with. Which explains the spread of sexually transmitted diseases like AIDS.
Already, 2000 heterosexual people in this country have been infected with the virus. In New York, AIDS is the biggest killer of women between 25-35. British Medical Association figures suggest that up to 100,000 people will be infected in Britain by 1991.
But it's not all doom and gloom. Because there is a simple way to dramatically reduce your chances of catching the virus.
Condoms will greatly reduce the chances of the virus passing from one person to another.
Which is why we started Mates Healthcare.
We want to make condoms more accessible and, at the same time, raise money to help stop the spread of AIDS.
Mates is a new range of condoms.
Including Natural Mates, Ribbed Mates and Coloured Mates, all of which carry the BSI Kite-mark.
They cost less than other condoms but they're just as reliable (in fact, they're made by one of the world's largest manufacturers).
And thanks to leading retailers, they're available in pubs, newsagents, garages, clubs, record stores, supermarkets and chemists. What makes Mates doubly effective, though, is what we'll be doing with all profits from Mates Healthcare Ltd.
We'll be providing literature, videos and education in 'Safer Sex' techniques – all specifically targetted at young people.
We also plan to give money to counselling services and hospices for those dying of the disease.
In short, we'll be doing everything we can to provide practical advice and assistance to help stop the spread of AIDS.
Sex is a fact of life.
So, unfortunately, is AIDS. Please, when you make love, don't close your eyes to the dangers.
MATES. YOU MAKE LOVE. THEY MAKE SENSE.

191

"Dear Miss Dixon, we'd like £7.50 to bounce your £4 cheque."

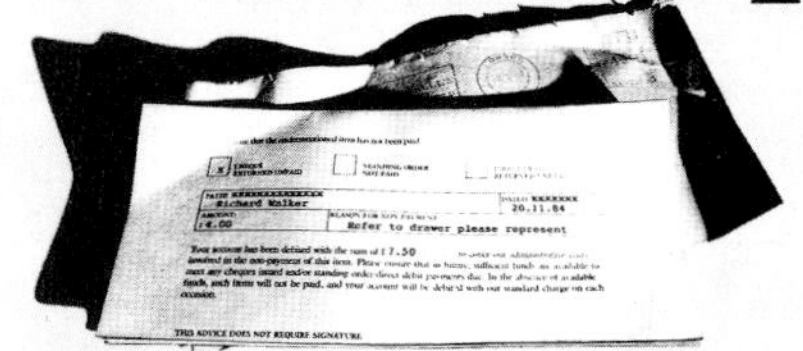

It sounds like something out of a TV comedy show doesn't it?

Like a lot of sitcoms, it is based on real life.

In fact only the unfortunate customer's name has been changed. Of course a bank should tell a customer that he or she is overdrawn.

But is it necessary to come down like a ton of bricks on someone who's only £4 in the red?

And then proceed to charge for every cheque, standing order and direct debit for the next 3 months?

Perhaps after all these years of virtual monopoly, the banks need a bit of healthy competition. (Their customers will certainly welcome it, even if they don't.)

Competition in the shape of a Nationwide FlexAccount, the first real alternative to the bank current account. Admittedly, if you reel off the facilities that come with a FlexAccount, they sound distinctly familiar.

Cheque book, cheque card, cashcard, salary credits, standing orders, direct debits and the rest.

But the resemblance is only superficial.

For example, there are absolutely no charges on a FlexAccount. Letters, stopped cheques, duplicate statements and standing orders are all free.

Even if you write a cheque, use your cashcard or request a duplicate statement while you're in the red, it won't cost you a penny.

Naturally, going into the red is something we don't encourage our customers to do.

But if you do need an overdraft we'll begin, not by sending the standard threatening letter, but by discussing with you what your needs are, how much you want to borrow and for how long.

Then, all you owe us is interest on the amount outstanding.

No "arrangement fees," no hidden extras.

It follows that when you get your FlexAccount monthly statement you'll know exactly where you stand. There'll be no nasty surprises lurking under the all-purpose, all-encompassing heading of "Bank Charges."

So much for the unwanted things we've got rid of. What, then, does a FlexAccount offer that the traditional bank current account doesn't?

Interest, for a start. To be exact, with up to £99 in your account, you get 2% interest net per annum. On sums between £100 and £499, 3.5%. And when you're £500 or more in credit, 5%.

(Both the higher interest rates are paid on the whole balance, not just the amount over £100 or £500.) All this is calculated daily, and paid out annually.

And on the subject of paying out, you can withdraw (or deposit) cash, get a mini-statement and even pay your bills 24 hours a day from our cash machines.

You can also withdraw cash anytime of the day or night from over 800 other places, wherever you see LINK, the sign of the national cash network.

More convenient still, a FlexAccount gives you the option of Home Banking. This amazing new development actually enables you to check your balance or request statements over your own telephone. Soon you'll be able to pay bills too.

Behind all these details lies a philosophy which amounts to nothing more than financial common sense. Instead of behaving like over-strict parents, at Nationwide we treat our customers as responsible adults.

We try to make money the approachable subject it should be.

Having encouraged you to tell us exactly what facilities you need, we set up a made-to-measure account which provides them.

How can we afford to be so flexible, to waive charges and pay interest, yet still compete with the banks? Unlike them, we don't have to make profits for shareholders.

Nationwide Building Society was established for the mutual benefit of people who want to save, and people who want to buy houses.

In effect, our shareholders are our customers.

And who in their right minds would charge a shareholder £7.50 to bounce a £4 cheque?

For further information, call into your local Nationwide branch. Or write to Claire Adams, Nationwide Building Society, New Oxford House, High Holborn, London WC1V 6PW.

FLEXACCOUNT

We always remember whose money it is.

Consumer Newspaper Over 600 Lines: Single

194

ART DIRECTOR
Roy Freemantle

WRITER
John Young

CLIENT
Volvo

AGENCY
Scali McCabe Sloves

195

ART DIRECTOR
Dean Hanson

WRITER
Bruce Bildsten

PHOTOGRAPHER
Rick Dublin

CLIENT
First Tennessee Bank

AGENCY
Fallon McElligott/
Minneapolis

196

ART DIRECTOR
Barbara Schubeck

WRITER
Sharon Vanderslice

PHOTOGRAPHER
Leon Kuzmanoff

CLIENT
WNBC-TV

AGENCY
Lord Geller Federico
Einstein

197

ART DIRECTOR
Rob Dalton

WRITER
Rod Kilpatrick

PHOTOGRAPHER
Kent Severson

CLIENT
The Wall Street Journal

AGENCY
Fallon McElligott/
Minneapolis

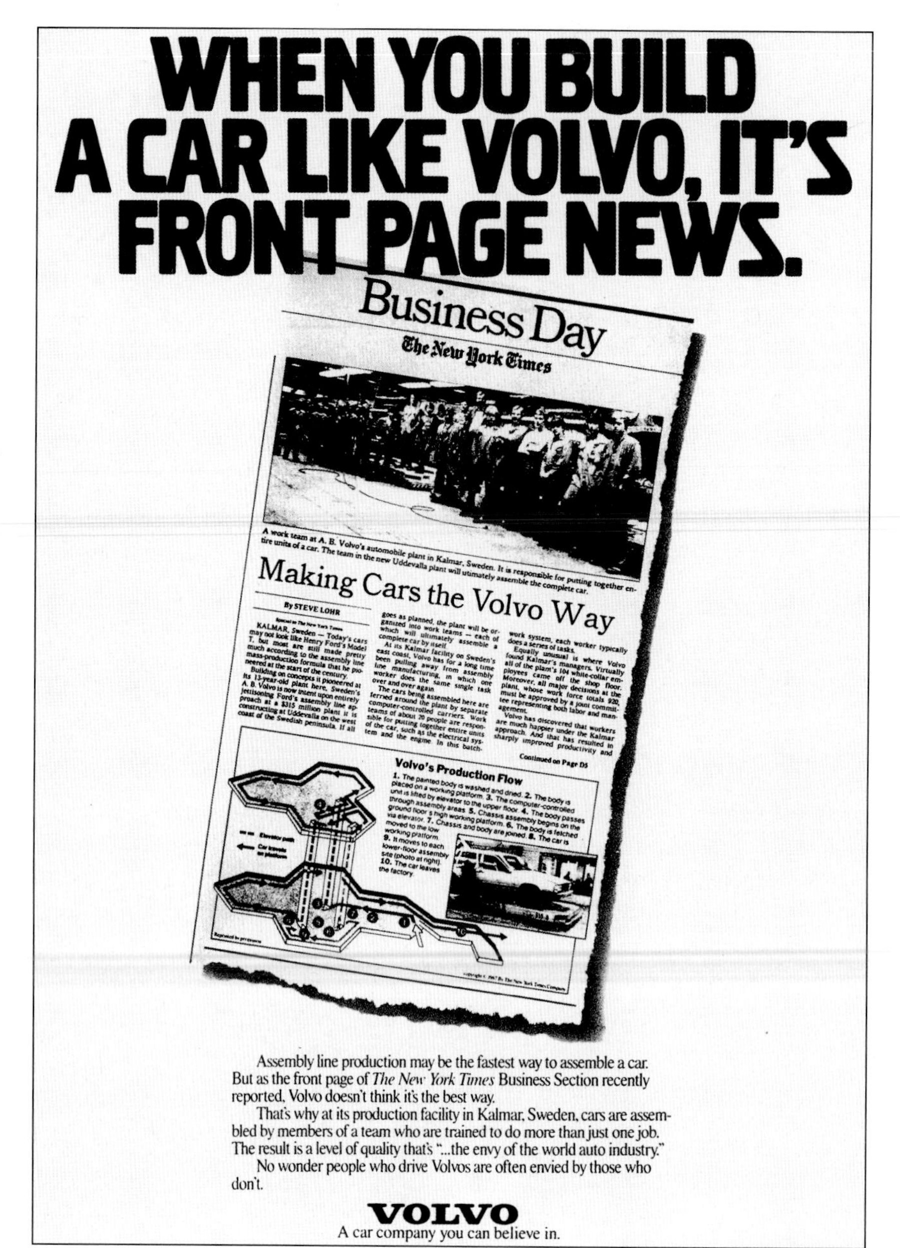

Business Day

The New York Times

A work team at A. B. Volvo's automobile plant in Kalmar, Sweden. It is responsible for putting together entire units of a car. The team in the new Uddevalla plant will utimately assemble the complete car.

Making Cars the Volvo Way

By STEVE LOHR

Special to The New York Times

KALMAR, Sweden — Today's cars may not look like Henry Ford's Model T, but most are still made pretty much according to the assembly line mass-production formula that he pioneered at the start of the century.

Building on concepts it pioneered at its 13-year-old plant here, Sweden's A. B. Volvo is now intent upon entirely jettisoning Ford's assembly line approach at a $315 million plant it is constructing at Uddevalla on the west coast of the Swedish peninsula. If all goes as planned, the plant will be organized into work teams — each of which will ultimately assemble a complete car by itself.

At its Kalmar facility on Sweden's east coast, Volvo has for a long time been pulling away from assembly line manufacturing, in which one worker does the same single task over and over again.

The cars being assembled here are ferried around the plant by separate computer-controlled carriers. Work teams of about 20 people are responsible for putting together entire units of the car, such as the electrical system and the engine. In this batch-work system, each worker typically does a series of tasks.

Equally unusual is where Volvo found Kalmar's managers. Virtually all of the plant's 104 white-collar employees came off the shop floor. Moreover, all major decisions at the plant, whose work force totals 920, must be approved by a joint committee representing both labor and management.

Volvo has discovered that workers are much happier under the Kalmar approach. And that has resulted in sharply improved productivity and

Continued on Page D5

Volvo's Production Flow

1. The painted body is washed and dried. **2.** The body is placed on a working platform. **3.** The computer-controlled unit is lifted by elevator to the upper floor. **4.** The body passes through assembly areas. **5.** Chassis assembly begins on the ground floor's high working platform. **6.** The body is fetched via elevator. **7.** Chassis and body are joined. **8.** The car is moved to the low working platform. **9.** It moves to each lower-floor assembly site (photo at right). **10.** The car leaves the factory.

Elevator path
Car travels on platform

194

It's As Easy To Burn Money With The Book On The Right As The Book On The Left.

Few things burn through money faster than the service charges and fees on the average checking account.

But for just $1 a month with our special introductory offer, you can get all the banking services you need, all in one simplified account with First Tennessee All-In-One checking.

Open your account by June 30th, and for just $1 a month you'll get unlimited free check writing.

You'll also get free personalized checks, a free Money/Belt℠ card, a Visa® or MasterCard® at no annual fee (with approval), free traveler's checks and free money orders. Plus five free stop-payments and five free returned checks every year.

All-In-One checking is so complete, you'll even get a discount rate on installment loans and a free $25,000 accidental death insurance policy.

Best of all, it requires no minimum balance. In fact, if your balance stays above $600 you'll even earn interest.

So the choice is simple. You can get all the banking services you need for just $1 a month.

Or you can keep getting burned.

195

Not all political prisoners are behind bars.
There are over 900,000 of them in the New York City public schools. They're pawns in a political game played by school officials– some of whom are more interested in the advancement of their careers than in the advancement of their students.
Watch Gabe Pressman's special report on "The Politics of Education." This week at 6 on Channel 4.
WNBC·TV NEWS 4 NEW YORK
Is there any reason to watch anyone else?

196

Don't go to work in the dark.

THE WALL STREET JOURNAL.

Upward Mobility
Many Wine Makers In France Are Striving To Improve Quality

What's News—

Business and Finance

World-Wide

Weekly Earnings

Business Bulletin

Warning Signs
HMO Insurance Plans Face Some Threats To Own Good Health

Now, with early-morning delivery, you can get The Journal when you really need it: First thing in the morning.

Thanks to The Journal's highly organized format, you can be briefed on the day's most significant developments before you've even finished your first cup of coffee. Then you can follow up with the more detailed reports on the inside pages.

You can absorb the practical insights of our in-depth analytical pieces, and consider what the news means to you in nuts-and-bolts terms. You can reap the benefits of our regular columns on taxes, personal finance, small business, real estate and other vital topics.

In short, you can stop going to work in the dark. And start going to work prepared.

If you already subscribe, we'll convert your subscription to early-morning delivery as soon as possible.

If you don't, we'll be happy to start your 13-week introductory subscription for just $29.50. Mail the coupon, or call 800-523-2004 ext. 517.

So if you want to get out of the dark, all you have to do is pick up the phone. And maybe a flashlight.

Early-Morning Delivery. 800-523-2004, ext. 517.

To subscribe, call 800-523-2004, ext. 517.
Or send coupon to: The Wall Street Journal, 200 Burnett Road, Chicopee, Mass. 01020.

Name
Address Apt./Suite
City State Zip

197

Consumer Newspaper Over 600 Lines: Single

198

ART DIRECTOR
Greg Campbell

WRITER
Jon Jackson

PHOTOGRAPHER
Norman Seef

CLIENT
Hospital Corporation of America

AGENCY
Ogilvy & Mather

199

ART DIRECTOR
Art Webb

WRITER
Tom Townsend

PHOTOGRAPHER
Steve Umland

CLIENT
St. John's Mercy Medical Center

AGENCY
Gardner Advertising/ St. Louis

200

ART DIRECTOR
Peggy Fields

WRITER
Barbara Hamilton

CLIENT
Perdue

AGENCY
Scali McCabe Sloves

201

ART DIRECTOR
Paul Blade

WRITER
Larry Hampel

DESIGNER
Paul Blade

PHOTOGRAPHER
Buddy Endress

CLIENT
Volvo

AGENCY
Scali McCabe Sloves

I told myself, "She's my daughter."
I told myself, "She's only 15."
But when I realized I'd started to hate her
I knew both of us needed help.

Are you worried about a teenager in your family? I know what you're going through.

For many years, I was raising a teenager in trouble, myself.

She'd fail in school, and I'd tell myself, "Well, the kid's under a lot of pressure. There are worse things in life than flunking eighth grade."

She'd run off with the car for a joy ride, and I'd think, "Well, teenagers are *supposed* to rebel."

Then it was drugs. That was a hard one. But you tell yourself all kids experiment with drugs these days. As you try not to worry to death.

"She'll grow out of it," I'd say.

And I'd think, "If she's like this now, what's it going to be like when she's 21? And on her own?"

Then one night six months ago, I really got scared. She disappeared. For three whole days. I thought, "Please—keep her safe." There she was, out on the streets by herself. And a lot can happen to a kid on the streets these days.

Well—that whole nightmare turned out to be a blessing in disguise. Because I finally did what I should have done in the first place. I picked up the phone and got some help.

When they suggested hospitalization, I panicked all over again. But they said it was the only right thing to do.

And when I got her in, and saw the hate in her eyes, I thought I'd lost her forever. *But I was wrong.*

She slowly learned how to control herself. Without "Mommy" there to watch her every step.

As for me—I got a lot of help, too.

We both had sessions that showed us where our family was going wrong. And what we could do about it.

And I discovered I was not alone. I met a lot of mothers who were going through just what I was. You'd be surprised how we help each other cope.

Yes, it was a real relief. And a whole new start.

I'm not going to tell you it's been easy. But today, six months later, my daughter and I are closer than we've ever been in our entire lives.

And so far (knock on wood) no more drugs.

If you're going through what I did—please—don't wait as long as I did before you get some help. And if you don't know where to get it, phone the number at the bottom of this page. They know the good programs in this area. Including ones that are covered by insurance.

If we could do it, you can do it. I'm praying for you—and wishing you and your family the best.

SPONSORED IN THE PUBLIC INTEREST BY THE HCA FAMILY OF HOSPITALS

HCA Rockford Center
(302) 652-3892

198

The Most Intelligent Species On Earth Is Also The Slowest To Grow Up.

Living up to the words "most intelligent species" is a pretty tall order for a newborn boy or girl. That's a title you have to grow into. So every step of the way, St. John's Child Health Center is right here to help.

1-3 Months *Already they're showing their temperament. Some babies are calm and quiet, others are loud and irritable. It's good that they're telling you so early on, so you can get used to your child's disposition. But that's about all they're telling you. Even early arrivals, like the premature babies in our Neonatal Intensive Care Unit, aren't necessarily saying anything about how punctual they'll be later in life.*

3-5 Months *Your child's finding new things to do with his energy. Quite literally, he shakes rattles and rolls; grasping toys, rolling over, and entertaining himself. Not all babies reach such milestones at the same time, however. If your child is late, don't be alarmed. But when you do have concerns, your pediatrician is there to help.*

5-8 Months

8-15 Months

15 Months-3 Years

3-7 Years

7-10 Years *By now, baby teeth are disappearing to make room for permanent ones. That's a cue to the mouth to start finding space for 32 teeth where there once were 20. In some mouths, the extra teeth aren't worth the crowding. Ask your dentist. Then rest assured that our oral surgeons at St. John's have special training for the mouths of children. But they know how to put smiles on a parent's face, too.*

10-13 Years

13-18 Years *They're too old to be children, and too young to be adults. Their parents think they're growing up too fast, they think they're not growing up fast enough. Sometimes that paradox alone causes frustration that leads to the breakdown of otherwise healthy family relationships. To us, where there's a sick or troubled child, there's a sick or troubled family. While our care is highly individualized to the patient, it's also oriented to the family. That point of view, along with our specialists in adolescent psychiatry, has helped us help families through times like these.*

The pediatricians and pediatric specialists at St. John's can tell you a lot about childhood. They'll talk of growing pains, preventative medicine and how to grow up as painlessly as possible.

But a boy or girl will tell you something else. They'll talk of how being grown up isn't everything. Getting there is half the fun.

St. John's Child Health Center
at St. John's Mercy Medical Center, 615 South New Ballas Road
St. Louis, MO 63141 314/569-6000

A member of the Sisters of Mercy Health System—St. Louis

199

WHY BUY A TURKEY FROM A CHICKEN MAN?

Frank Perdue has spent years finding ways to perfect his Perdue chickens. And now he's using what he learned to perfect another bird. The Perdue Turkey.

For one thing, Perdue's chickens taught him that a bird is only as good as its upbringing. So while other people who sell turkeys buy them fully grown from practically anyone, every Perdue turkey is raised by Perdue.

To make his turkeys good eating, he makes sure they eat good. He feeds them a special blend of only the finest foods, so they get all the daily nutritional requirements a growing turkey needs.

Perdue raises his turkeys in roomy, custom-built houses. They're specially designed to reduce stress, so his birds grow up healthy and relaxed. Each house has luxuries like air conditioning for the summer, and extra insulation for the winter. They have giant picture windows for sunlight. And even curtains that can be drawn if it begins to get too warm.

With such a pampered life, Perdue turkeys always turn out naturally tender, juicy and delicious. And they're also endowed with more breast meat than rival birds.

To ensure your turkey's as perfect coming out of your oven as it is going in, every Perdue turkey has a pop-up timer that lets you know when your turkey's done.

And carving's easier, because Perdue's removed the leg tendons.

Like Perdue chickens, Perdue turkeys have to meet standards that are even higher than the USDA's Grade A standards. In fact, Perdue puts his turkeys through more inspections than the government calls for. Making sure they're clean of scrapes, bruises and pinfeathers.

And while some people just sell their turkeys and run, Perdue stands behind every turkey he sells with a money-back guarantee.

When you have a turkey as good as Perdue's, there's no reason to be chicken.

PERDUE
FRESH
Young Turkey

200

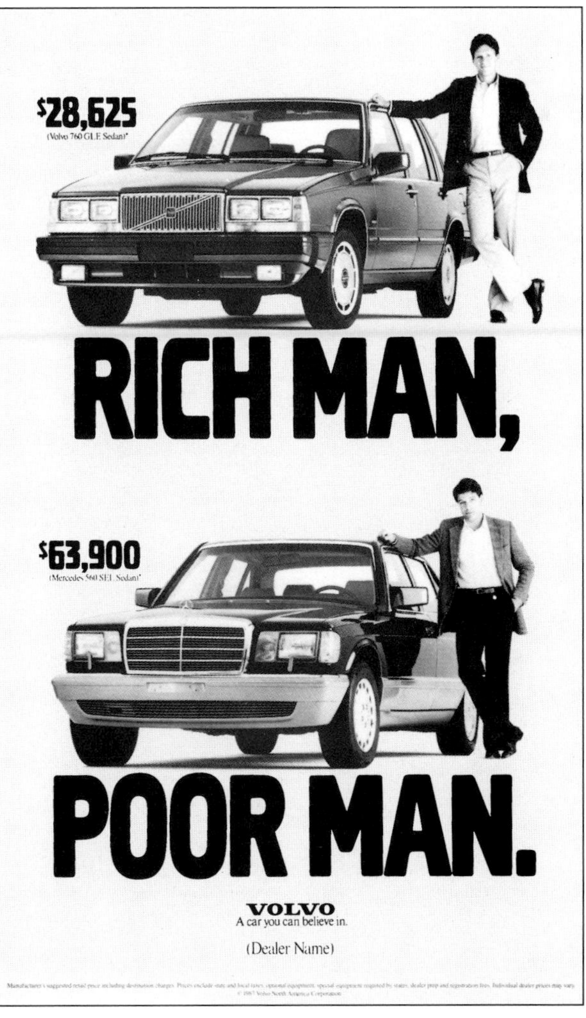

$28,625
(Volvo 760 GLE Sedan)*
RICH MAN,
$63,900
(Mercedes 560 SEL Sedan)*
POOR MAN.
VOLVO
A car you can believe in.
(Dealer Name)

201

Consumer Newspaper
Over 600 Lines: Single

202
ART DIRECTOR
Joanne Pateman
WRITER
Peter Swerdloff
CLIENT
The Wall Street Journal
AGENCY
Lord Geller Federico Einstein

203
ART DIRECTOR
Bill Murphy
WRITER
Margaret Wilcox
PHOTOGRAPHER
Michael Pierce
CLIENT
The Boston Globe
AGENCY
Hill Holliday Connors Cosmopulos/Boston

204
ART DIRECTORS
Ivan Horvath
John Morrison
WRITER
Ken Segall
DESIGNER
Gina Norton
PHOTOGRAPHER
Bo Hylen Studios
CLIENT
Apple Computer
AGENCY
BBDO

205
ART DIRECTOR
Jeff Terwilliger
WRITER
Bert Gardner
CLIENT
Star Tribune
AGENCY
Bozell Jacobs Kenyon & Eckhardt/Minneapolis

WATCH THE BEARS AND RAIDERS THIS WEEKEND.

The Wall Street bears, that is. And the corporate raiders. On The Wall Street Journal Report. The weekend television show that chronicles the game that never goes on strike.

You'll see the kind of coverage The Wall Street Journal's known for. Consuelo Mack, the editor and anchor, is one of the most respected journalists on television.

You'll see the Journal writers you've been reading. And you'll meet the newsmakers you've read about.

True, you won't see all the moves you're used to seeing on a Sunday. On the other hand, you may see plays that you can use on Monday.

So tune in this weekend. Check your local listings for the time and channel. Catch the big game for a change.

THE WALL STREET JOURNAL REPORT ON TELEVISION

© 1987 Dow Jones & Company, Inc.

Sponsored in part by MCDONNELL DOUGLAS

202

What will it be going out as this Halloween?

An apple? A brownie? A candy bar? Or will someone think of a brand new way to disguise it and cut short your children's fun?

This Halloween, we want parents everywhere to get scared. And not just about razor blades. About pins. Pills. And any other trick someone might dress up as a treat for your kids.

Look over all your children's candy carefully. Very carefully. It's easy to miss a slit or a pin hole. Remember, when in doubt throw it out. And make sure your kids don't run into one Halloween disguise they'll never forget. The Boston Globe

203

The best seller. The sequel.

Macintosh Plus.

Macintosh SE.

File this under nonfiction:

The Macintosh® Plus personal computer now tops the best seller list in business.

That is to say, in retail business sales, Macintosh Plus is currently out-performing computers of every name. And letter.

Of course, none of this should come as too big a surprise. After all, with our Macintosh technology, we created an entirely new set of standards for what a personal computer can do.

From Apple® Desktop Publishing and Desktop Communications to next-generation software like Microsoft's best-selling spreadsheet, Excel.

And as more businesses decide to go with Macintosh, they're making some rather spectacular gains in productivity. According to one recent multi-industry study, an increase as high as 24%.

All this at a substantially lower cost than with conventional computers.

The fact is, today you'd have to go a long way to find a more powerful computer for business.

At least a page.

And now the plot thickens.

Enter the new Macintosh SE:

The first computer to combine the business power of the best seller to your left with the added power of expandability.

Inside the SE, there's a slot where you can plug in some potent options.

Like a card that connects you to an Ethernet network, or a mainframe. A card that lets you add a disk drive for using documents created on IBM or compatible PCs. An accelerator card that can take you through the most complex spreadsheets posthaste. Or other cards yet to be invented.

And, we're pleased to report, we've also done a bit of expanding elsewhere.

Along with its built-in 800K floppy disk drive, the SE comes with an internal 20-megabyte hard disk that can store 10,000 pages of information. Or, if you prefer, a second built-in floppy drive.

In addition, you can use the SE with either of two new keyboards. One of which has 15 function keys for special applications.

We must stress, however, that for many people in business, the Macintosh Plus continues to offer more than enough power.

It's for those who need more than more-than-enough, that we suggest the Macintosh SE. Which can easily meet far greater business demands, and still give you all the benefits of the best seller.

Including the happy ending.

The power to be your best.

204

Our New Columnist Knows
More About Foreign Affairs Than
Ronald Reagan Has Forgotten.

We are proud to welcome our new Washington Bureau Chief, Pulitzer Prize winner William Beecher.

205

Consumer Newspaper Over 600 Lines: Campaign

206

ART DIRECTORS
Tom McConnaughy
Brian Kelly

WRITER
James Schmidt

PHOTOGRAPHERS
Dave Jordano
Tony D'Orio

CLIENT
HealthChicago

AGENCY
McConnaughy Barocci Brown/Chicago

207

ART DIRECTOR
Mark Fuller

WRITERS
Bill Westbrook
Robin Konieczny

PHOTOGRAPHERS
Dean Hawthorne
Bob Jones Jr.

CLIENT
Office America

AGENCY
Ford & Westbrook/Richmond, VA

She Has A Head Full Of Kidney Stones.

It sounds ridiculous, doesn't it? But the sad fact is, it's true.

Each year, thousands of people complain of physical ailments that in reality are caused by emotional stress or trauma.

They visit doctors and check into hospitals, but in the end no physical problem is ever found.

So they visit even more doctors and on and on it goes.

The effect of all this on an individual can, as you might imagine, be devastating.

Equally devastating can be the effect on medical costs.

The fact is, those suffering from such psychosomatic ailments have 14 times the average cost for outpatient care. Six times the average for inpatient care. And nine times the average for total health expenditures.

How can such personal and financial troubles be avoided?

By offering people a health plan that not only provides comprehensive medical care, but one that provides comprehensive psychiatric care as well.

A plan, not so coincidentally, like that of HealthChicago.

At HealthChicago, all our psychiatric care is handled through the Northwestern Memorial Institute of Psychiatry. One of the most esteemed in the country.

The Institute provides HealthChicago and our doctors with a network of many of the finest psychiatrists and clinical psychologists in the Chicagoland area.

A group of experienced professionals who, in consultation with our doctors, are able to provide patients with precise diagnosis and treatment.

Such expertise ensures that our members receive the appropriate level of care.

And that our member companies receive benefits that indeed help them solve all of their health care problems.

It's this dedicated approach to psychiatric care that has led Dr. Harold Visotsky, Chairman of Psychiatry at Northwestern, to call our program, "...the best around. One that is constantly looking for new and innovative ways to provide its members with the finest in health care."

And it's this approach that has no doubt contributed to the fact that HealthChicago is the fastest growing health plan in the area.

With 40,000 new members in the last year alone.

For more information on HealthChicago, just call Karey McGowan at 1-800-345-1175. After all, shouldn't your employees have a health plan that treats their minds as well as it treats their bodies?

HealthChicago
GALANOS MARK
001 3465205 06
J C DARROW MD
0013 V2 E1

It's The Most Important Card You Can Carry.

It's A Bitter Pill To Swallow.

ASPIRIN

$2.00. The average price hospitals charge for an aspirin.

Consider, if you will, the plight of the average company when it comes to health care.

Not only must it worry about the hospitals, who these days charge an arm and a leg to take care of an arm or a leg.

But it must worry about its bottom line as well. And how it's affected by such costs.

Plus, on top of that dilemma, it must also be concerned with keeping its many employees happy. Or it could be faced with very long lines outside the Benefits Manager's office.

It's obviously a complex problem.

But one with a simple, innovative solution: managed health care.

The kind provided so expertly by HealthChicago.

(A 97% reenrollment rate and over 44,000 new members in the last year alone, we believe, qualify us as experts.)

Our managed care begins, quite naturally, with preventive care.

After all, the best way to keep hospital costs down is to keep people out of the hospital.

But no matter how much preventive care is given, people are going to get sick now and then.

And may require hospitalization.

If they do, our Quality Assurance and Utilization Team will be put on the case the minute the doctor notifies us of the impending hospitalization.

Our team—comprised of a HealthChicago Medical Director and group of registered nurses—will check the patient's progress daily and conduct a concurrent review (along with the hospitals) to ensure the patient receives care that is not only appropriate, but is of the highest quality as well.

They'll also assist in discharge planning—a key to effective managed care. And will even set up a home care program if the doctor recommends it.

(Home care isn't only financially beneficial, statistic after statistic shows that people generally recover quicker in familiar surroundings.)

At HealthChicago, our entire managed health care program is governed by the tenet that care should be given not because it's demanded, but because it's needed.

It's the kind of approach a hypochondriac might find a bit frustrating.

But it's one that has allowed us to keep our premium increases at only 4-6%. Well below the current 7.9% of the medical price index.

And our number of hospital days at only 340 per 1000 members. Lowest in the state last year and less than half the norm of 700. For more information about HealthChicago and everything it has to offer, just phone Karey McGowan at 1-800-345-1175.

Because when it comes to health care, we can offer immediate relief from some major headaches.

HealthChicago
GALANOS MARK
001 3465205 06
J C DARROW MD
0013 V2 E1

It's The Most Important Card You Can Carry.

What We Look For In A HealthChicago Member.

At HealthChicago, we look for members who recognize, as we do, the foolishness of leaving their health to chance.

Members who, wanting to avoid the maladies listed on this page, appreciate a health plan that covers such routine care as checkups, inoculations and well-child care.

We look for members who want to carry a card (the one you've no doubt noticed just a few lines below) that gives them access to many of the finest doctors and hospitals in the Chicagoland area.

Members who'd rather not have to deal with any medical bills. Or be bothered with any paperwork.

Finally, we look for members who understand what it means when a health plan adds 44,000 new members in the last year alone. And can claim a reenrollment rate of 97%.

And now that we've told you what we look for in a member, we hope you have a much better idea of what you should be looking for in a company health plan.

For more information on HealthChicago, and all it has to offer, just phone Karey McGowan at 1-800-345-1175.

HealthChicago
GALANOS MARK
001 3465205 06
J C DARROW MD
0013 V2 E1

It's The Most Important Card You Can Carry.

Before You Send Another Business Letter, Check The Margins.
The bottom line on business letters is that they cost more than you think.
Unless, of course, you buy your office supplies from Office America. We sell dictating equipment, typewriters, copiers, paper, pens and 3000 other products at 30%-50% off.
That's because we buy our products direct from the manufacturer and eliminate the middleman. And we buy boxcars of everything instead of boxes. So you get the benefit of mass buying even if you're just buying a single item.
Come by our warehouse store in the 8000 block of West Broad Street in the Westland Shopping Center weekdays 8 a.m. to 9 p.m. and Saturdays 9 a.m. to 6 p.m. Or call 273-0900 to open an account and receive a free catalog in the mail.
Office America. Because you shouldn't have to sign a note just to send a letter.
OFFICE AMERICA
No one sells more office supplies for less.

Caution: Electrical Office Equipment Can Cause Sticker Shock.
People are amazed at how much office machines cost at most stores. And, conversely, how little they cost at Office America.
That's because Office America sells typewriters, shredders, calculators, copiers and 3500 other office products at 30% to 50% off. We simply eliminate the middleman and buy directly from the manufacturer.
We also buy boxcars of everything instead of boxes. So you get the benefit of mass buying even if you're just buying a single item.
Come by our warehouse store in the 8000 block of West Broad Street in the Westland Shopping Center any weekday 8 a.m. to 9 p.m. and Saturdays 9 a.m. to 6 p.m. Or you can call 273-0900 to open an account and receive a free Office America catalogue.
After all, why risk being shocked by an office machine before you've even plugged it in?
OFFICE AMERICA
No one sells more office supplies for less.

Take Away The Padding And Office Furniture Gets A Lot More Comfortable.
Our price, $159.99; list price, $273.00
Our price is $99.99 list price is $189.00
Furnishing an office is expensive. And when you consider the mark-up at most office furniture stores, it gets downright painful.
But not at Office America.
Office America is an office furniture and supplies warehouse store. Our prices are 30% to 50% lower than you'll find at any office supply store in town. And while our prices are small, our inventory is huge.
We have secretary chairs, executive chairs, and everything in between. We have pens, paper, paperclips. In all, over 2,500 items from file folders to filing cabinets, calculators to copiers. We even sell the most beloved office machine in America today: the microwave oven.
You save 30% to 50% because we eliminate the middleman and buy directly from the manufacturer. At prices like ours, your company could save thousands of dollars a year. And we're sure you won't have a problem finding a use for money like that.
Office America. We're located in the Westland Shopping Center in the 8000 block of West Broad Street. Whether you're setting up a business or home office, or simply need paperclips, come see us. Or call 273-0900 to set up an account or arrange delivery at a small extra charge.
Office America. We have all of the office supplies you need.
At prices that won't put you out of business.
OFFICE AMERICA
No one sells more office supplies for less.

Consumer Newspaper Over 600 Lines: Campaign

208

ART DIRECTOR
Brian Fandetti

WRITER
Edward Boches

ARTIST
Mark Wilson

PHOTOGRAPHER
Myron

CLIENT
Worcester Telegram & Gazette

AGENCY
Mullen Advertising/
S. Hamilton, MA

209

ART DIRECTOR
Michael Vitiello

WRITER
Lee Garfinkel

CLIENT
Subaru of America

AGENCY
Levine Huntley Schmidt & Beaver

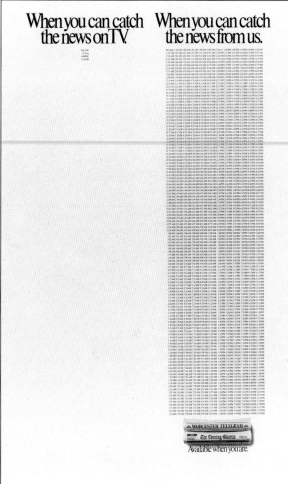

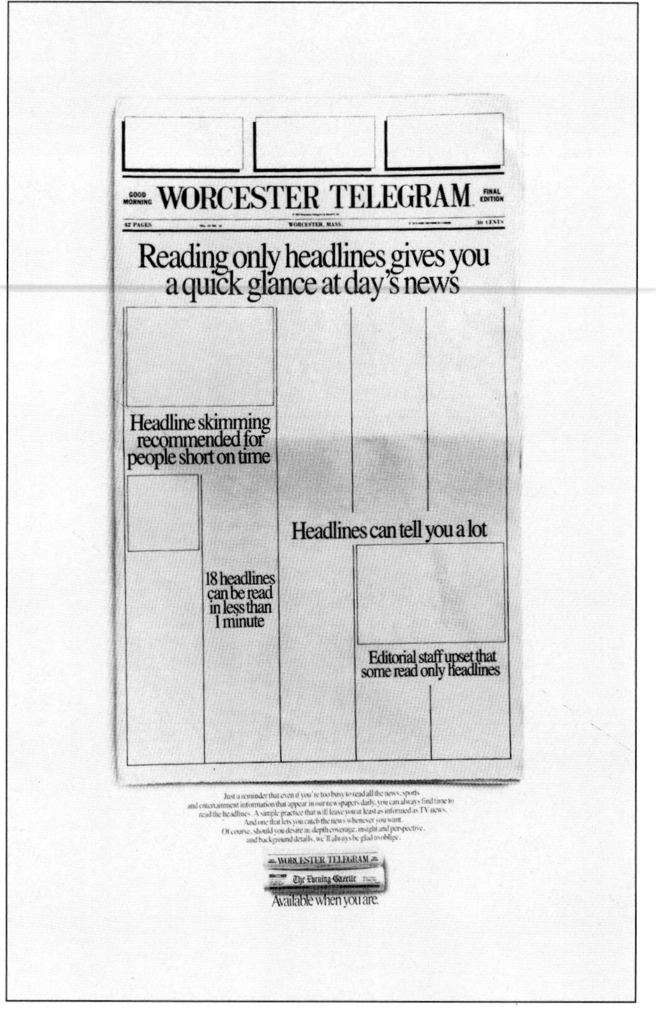

OUR CARS WON'T PUT YOU THROUGH HELL BECAUSE THEY'VE ALREADY BEEN THERE.

All car companies test their cars. This is nothing new. In fact, over the years, you've probably seen hundreds of commercials with cars being driven on every kind of test track imaginable.

And while this kind of testing looks good, at Subaru we think it's rather unrealistic. Taking cars from the laboratory to the test track isn't enough.

So we take our cars one step further. Into the real world.

MANY OF OUR TEST AREAS HAVE NO TEST TRACKS. MANY HAVE NO ROADS.

We abuse our cars. Load them beyond capacity. Slam doors. Bang them around. And then abuse them some more.

Then the punishment begins. We drive our cars 24 hours a day, 6 days a week for up to 120,000 miles. Until every feature and function either survives, or is improved.

Cars are driven up and down mountains, around icy curves, through mud holes, blizzards, hail and rainstorms. On paved roads, back roads and no roads. They're subjected to constant braking, erratic acceleration and intense shifting. A testing schedule designed to achieve in a short period of time the kind of actual driving cars would get in 5 to 10 years of ownership.*

We also have a range of drivers testing our cars. Drivers with different temperaments and different driving styles. For example, heavy set drivers are even used to test seats, upholstery and interior room. In fact, the entire testing procedure is so draining, many of our drivers wear out before our cars do.

THE REAL WORLD PROVIDES REAL PUNISHMENT.

From the icy thin atmosphere of the high Sierras to the frozen northernmost regions of Canada, where temperatures can dip to −20° F, every Subaru function is tested and expected to perform as if these were everyday conditions.

And when we say we put our cars through hell, we mean it. During the summer we test in Death Valley. Relentlessly. In temperatures that could easily make an ordinary car overheat.

EXHAUSTIVE TESTING DOESN'T END WITH OUR CARS.

We want our accessory parts to be as reliable as our cars. So they're tested the equivalent of 5 years in pressurized salt baths. Here we make sure they're every bit as corrosive-resistant as our cars.

HIGH TECH ADDS TO OUR LOW MAINTENANCE.

In addition to some of the toughest testing done to any cars, Subaru technology adds a lot to our cars' reliability. For example, the electronic components in the Subaru engine are every bit as sophisticated as those in high performance cars costing two or three times as much. And since electronics work without moving parts, they can last a lot longer.

WHAT DOES ALL THIS INTENSE TESTING AND ENGINEERING MEAN TO YOU?

When Subaru says our cars are built to last, it's not just sales talk. The facts speak for themselves. 92% of all Subarus registered since 1978 are still on the road.** For the last 5 years, we've been one of the highest rated cars in customer satisfaction.***

And speaking of satisfaction, Subaru has a line of cars priced under $10,000.†

What's more, to further satisfy your needs we are offering up to $2,000 cash back†† on selected Subaru models.

WE'RE TOUGH ON OUR CARS, SO THEY WON'T BE TOUGH ON YOU.

Perhaps no car sold in America is tested quite as fanatically as a Subaru. And our testing doesn't end with just one model. Every model we build no

matter how similar or different is put through hell and treated almost fiendishly. With cruel and unusual punishment. So at times it even seems like we hate them.

Which is probably why our customers love them so much.

SUBARU.

We built our reputation by building a better car.

AT $5,500 IT'S NOT JUST HOW MUCH CAR YOU GET, IT'S HOW MUCH AGGRAVATION YOU DON'T GET.

When you buy a car for $5,500,* it can be a very scary experience.

After all, many of the cars in that price range were virtually unknown in the U.S. one or two years ago. And if spending $11,000 on a car doesn't insure you against headaches, what can you expect from a car that costs half as much.

Fortunately, there is one car company that doesn't think you should settle for less of a car just because you spent less on it.

91% OF ALL SUBARUS REGISTERED SINCE 1976 ARE STILL ON THE ROAD.**

This impressive statistic proves people not only drive our cars hard, but they hold up year after year.

At Subaru, dependability is a standard feature built into every one of our cars.

What's more, while every car company likes to brag about customer satisfaction, not every car company has the facts to back it up.

Subaru, on the other hand, has been in the top 10 in customer satisfaction for over 5 years. And for 2 straight years, we were second only to Mercedes Benz in customer satisfaction.***

As you can see, Subaru has a well-deserved reputation for building inexpensive cars that last.

HOW CAN THE JUSTY GIVE YOU SO MUCH AND STILL COST SO LITTLE?

Despite its low price, the Justy contains the same quality engineering as Subaru's more expensive models. And it has more state-of-the-art features than any car in its class.

How can this be true? There's no magic about it.

It's all the result of advanced engineering and cost-efficient manufacturing—taking out the fluff, while putting in substantial value.

For example, instead of the usual 4 cylinders, the Justy has a unique 9 valve, 3 cylinder overhead cam engine that's as powerful as it is economical (38 mpg city, 41 mpg highway).***** And in all honesty, to sell the Justy at a sticker price of $5495, we make less money on each car we sell.

But the bottom line is, even though everything about the car is new, it still has good old-fashioned Subaru dependability. In fact, the Justy is the result of 3 years of road testing in America and 2 million test miles.

YOU CAN'T GET SOMETHING FOR NOTHING. BUT YOU CAN GET A LOT FOR NEXT TO NOTHING.

The Justy doesn't cost a lot, but it does give you a lot. Including: front wheel drive; 5-speed transmission; 4-wheel fully independent suspension; variable ratio Rack & Pinion steering; vented front disc brakes; an electronically controlled carburetor; and more interior/cargo space than you have a right to expect in a car this size.

Of course, we wouldn't be doing the car justice if we left out another reason to own one: the Justy is truly fun to drive.

So think about it. Why spend your disposable income on a disposable car, when you can put your money into a much more lasting investment, the new Subaru Justy.

SUBARU.

Inexpensive. And built to stay that way.

THE FOUR WHEEL DRIVE CAR THAT GOT THE AUTOMOTIVE INDUSTRY OFF ITS REAR.

Today the automotive industry is virtually inundated with front wheel drive cars. Well, this wasn't always the case. There was a time when practically every car in America was stuck with rear-wheel drive technology.

1970 FWD SEDAN

Fortunately, in 1969, Subaru introduced the first cars designed around the concept of front wheel drive. And we didn't do it just to be different. We did it because it made sense. Front wheel drive improves a car's stability and traction.

And in the last 19 years Subaru has consistently improved and refined front wheel drive. Making it one of the most advanced systems on the road.

WE'VE TAKEN FRONT WHEEL DRIVE TO ITS ULTIMATE CONCLUSION: 4-WHEEL DRIVE.

In 1975 Subaru introduced the first passenger cars with an On Demand™ 4-wheel drive system. Simply put, this system lets drivers shift from front to 4-wheel drive whenever weather or road conditions take a turn for the worse.

You see, 4-wheel drive gives power to all four wheels at the same time. Thus greatly increasing a car's handling ability, traction and safety.

And if you've ever experienced a loss of traction due to a sudden shower or loose gravel, you can see the wisdom of 4-wheel drive.

If you've ever been stuck in snow or mud, you can see the necessity of it.

Yet, despite these obvious benefits, for years Subaru was the only company that offered passenger cars with 4-wheel drive.

Now, 13 years later other car makers are finally "discovering" 4-wheel drive. It makes you wonder if they finally noticed the weather. Or us.

YOU DON'T HAVE TO REFINANCE YOUR HOUSE TO FINANCE YOUR CAR.

A Subaru is built to be as easy on your pocket as it is on the road.

In fact, we have an entire line of cars under $10,000.†

Like our DL XT, Wagon, 3-Door Coupe, Sedan or the Justy, the most inexpensive 4-wheel drive car sold in America.

You see, at Subaru we strongly believe that even if you have a budget that's limited, your choice of cars doesn't have to be.

NO OTHER CAR MAKER HAS SUCH A FIRM GRIP ON 4-WHEEL DRIVE TECHNOLOGY.

Even though Subaru pioneered 4-wheel drive, our accomplishments aren't limited to the past. This year, for example, we're offering Full-Time 4-wheel drive with a 4-speed electronic automatic transmission.

This system reacts automatically to any sudden loss of traction—from bad roads, bad weather or just simple cornering or braking.

1975 4WD WAGON

It's so advanced, no car sold in America has anything like it.

Of course, as important as 4-wheel drive is for keeping your car on the road, Subaru also believes your car should last down the road.

So Subaru cars are tested extensively in America and throughout the world...for reliability, performance and safety. And our testing doesn't end on the test track. We also test our cars in the real world. With real punishment. On roads you drive on. And on roads you would never even think of driving on. At Subaru, we're tough on our cars so they won't be tough on you.

91% OF ALL SUBARUS REGISTERED SINCE 1976 ARE STILL ON THE ROAD.*

In addition to this impressive statistic, Subaru has consistently been in the top 10 in customer satisfaction for over 5 years.

And for 2 straight years, we were second only to Mercedes Benz in customer satisfaction.**

BUY A SUBARU. OR GET STUCK WITH SOMETHING ELSE.

Since 1969, Subaru has been building front wheel drive cars that are reliable, durable and built to last.

And for 13 years, we've been committed to building 4-wheel drive cars with the same high standards.

As a result Subaru has more 4-wheel drive passenger cars on the road than all other car makers combined.* So before you buy your next car, think about this. Would you rather buy one from the company that pioneered front wheel drive and 4-wheel drive. Or from a company that was content to sit on its rear.

1988 XT WITH FULL-TIME 4WD

SUBARU.

We built our reputation by building a better car.

Consumer Newspaper Over 600 Lines: Campaign

210

ART DIRECTORS
Bryan Buckley
Mike Shine

WRITERS
Mike Shine
Bryan Buckley

CLIENT
NYNEX

AGENCY
Chiat/Day

211

ART DIRECTOR
Carolyn Tye

WRITER
Bill Westbrook

PHOTOGRAPHERS
Ukrop's Supermarkets
Richmond Newspapers

CLIENT
Ukrop's Supermarkets

AGENCY
Ford & Westbrook/
Richmond, VA

KILLER BEES FOUND IN WEST SYRACUSE.

SYRACUSE–You'll find more things in the new NYNEX Yellow Pages than ever before. Because each of the new NYNEX Yellow Pages now covers a much wider area.

So you can find listings five blocks away, or five towns away.

And if we could find the movie, "The Bees," at the TV Factory video shop on West Genesee Street, just imagine what you'll be able to find.

The NYNEX Yellow Pages for Onondaga County.

NYNEX Yellow Pages

GIANT SQUID FOUND NEAR SHORES OF RARITAN RIVER.

SCOTCH PLAINS–You'll find things in the new NYNEX Yellow Pages that you can't find in your present yellow pages. Because we've gathered information from many different towns and put it into one book.

Now you can find listings five blocks away, or five towns away.

And if we could find fresh squid at Scotch Plains Fish Market, just imagine what you'll be able to find.

The NYNEX Yellow Pages for Union, Middlesex, and Eastern Somerset Counties.

NYNEX Yellow Pages

DINOSAUR TRACKS FOUND IN STAMFORD.

STAMFORD–You'll find things in the new NYNEX Yellow Pages that you can't find in your present yellow pages. Because we've gathered information from many different towns and put it into one book.

Now you can find listings five blocks away, or five towns away.

And if we could find fossilized Anomoepus tracks at the Stamford Museum and Nature Center, just imagine what you'll be able to find.

The NYNEX Yellow Pages for Stamford/Norwalk.

NYNEX Yellow Pages

Our Vice President was picky about produce at the ripe age of six.

When Bobby Ukrop got his start in the grocery business, labor was a little short in more ways than one. After school he could often be found sitting in the corner of the family store, culling produce from one basket to the next until the place closed.

It was a humble beginning, but auspicious. In the years that followed he continued to look for bad apples wherever he could find them, even in the grapes and melons and artichokes.

That attention to quality is evident in Ukrop's produce selection today. That's why, for example, our cucumbers are never too big (too many seeds), our eggplants never too heavy (too many seeds), nor our carrots too thick (no seeds, but too fibrous). We pick through all of our produce so you don't have to.

We're particularly finicky about what goes into our salad bar. Obviously, we know everything is fresh because all of it comes from you-know-where. But we go the extra step to cut all our fruit into bite-sized pieces and try to remove all the seeds (seeds again) from the watermelon. The trouble with being picky is that it never ends.

We're pleased to report, however, that after 50 years of hard work Ukrop's produce department has been rated No. 1 in the Richmond area. No one knows better than our Vice President what it's taken to get us there.

When he says he started on the ground floor, he really did.

Ukrop's 50th Anniversary

Ukrop's supermarket invented Farm Aid when Willie Nelson was nine.

Shuts Store to Aid Farmer

SEVEN MORE FARM HANDS—Joe Ukrop, Richmond grocer, not only has announced that his grocery store would be closed every Wednesday afternoon but that he and his wife and the store's five employes would spend the half "holidays" helping farmers harvest their crops. "The farmer can't get help," Ukrop said, "so we are going to try to help out."

Associated Press Photo

The year was 1942, and young men by the hundreds of thousands left America for the distant shores of war.

They left their cities and towns and their women and children.

And, of course, great numbers of them left the farms.

It was a time of commitment. No less so for a small grocery store on Hull Street in Richmond, Virginia named Ukrop's.

Every Wednesday afternoon during harvest season Joe Ukrop, his wife and the store's five employees closed the doors and drove out to the country to help the farmers. The corn they harvested would have spoiled in the fields without them.

There may not have been enough labor to go around back in those days. But there was enough love.

In the years since, Ukrop's has supported just about every civic project and charity imaginable. Yes, we've grown from one location to 18. And our selection of groceries is probably 100 times as large as the original store's.

But the family that opens the doors every morning is the same family that closed them every Wednesday. Now that we've turned 50 it's good to look back every now and then.

To make sure we're going ahead in the right direction.

Ukrop's 50th Anniversary

Everyone at Ukrop's goes through a long training program. This, for example, is our president.

At Ukrop's, we take the view that learning never stops. Of course, the earlier you get started, the better.

For example, Jim Ukrop started delivering groceries in the truck with his father practically before he could walk. (It must have been good training because 25 years later he was in the driver's seat of the company.)

Even our courtesy clerks study and take tests before they come to work. We send our people to the dairy farms in Wisconsin, the lettuce fields in California, the citrus groves in Texas and enroll them in fish school in Boston. We also hold regular refresher meetings so that store personnel can relay customer comments and suggestions.

We think our program is working. An independent survey rated Ukrop's No. 1 in friendly personnel. No. 1 in fast checkout. Even No. 1 in the arrangement of items on the shelf.

Interestingly enough, Ukrop's also rated at the top of the list for "good values." After 50 years in the grocery business, that last survey item was particularly gratifying. Not only do those values represent what's inside our stores. They tell you a lot about what's inside our people, too.

Ukrop's 50th Anniversary

Consumer Newspaper Over 600 Lines: Campaign

212

ART DIRECTOR
Jac Coverdale

WRITER
Jerry Fury

PHOTOGRAPHERS
Paul Sinkler
Jim Arndt

CLIENT
St. Paul Pioneer Press Dispatch

AGENCY
Clarity Coverdale Rueff/ Minneapolis

213

ART DIRECTORS
Craig Hadorn
Jeff France

WRITER
Ken Hines

PHOTOGRAPHER
Pat Edwards

CLIENT
Wake Medical Center

AGENCY
Lawler Ballard/ Richmond, VA

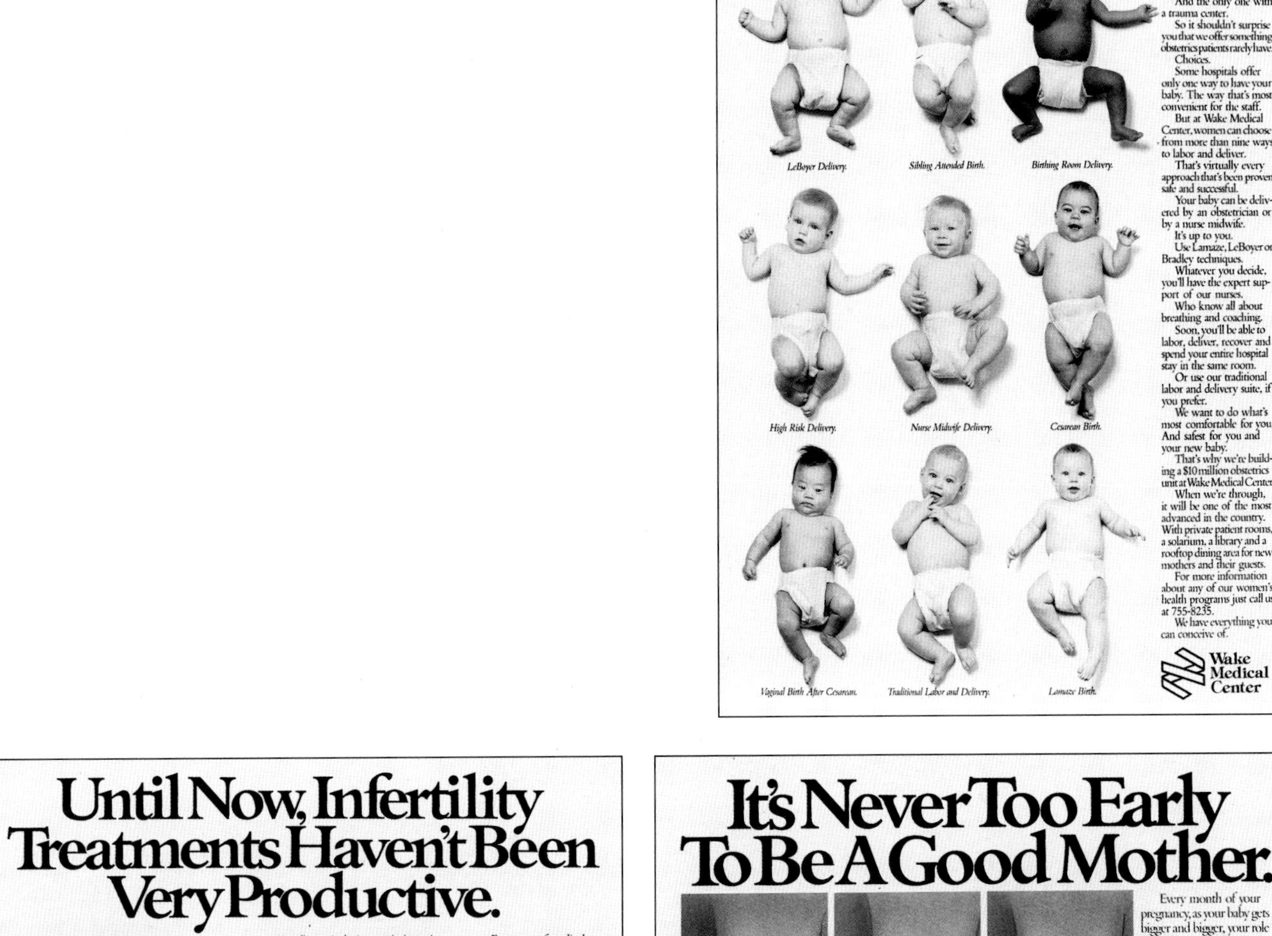

No Other Hospital Gives You All These Methods Of Birth Control.
LeBoyer Delivery.
Sibling Attended Birth.
Birthing Room Delivery.
High Risk Delivery.
Nurse Midwife Delivery.
Cesarean Birth.
Vaginal Birth After Cesarean.
Traditional Labor and Delivery.
Lamaze Birth.
Here at Wake Medical Center we've delivered one medical breakthrough after another to Raleigh.
Ours was the first hospital with a cardiac cath lab and CAT scans.
And the only one with a trauma center.
So it shouldn't surprise you that we offer something obstetrics patients rarely have.
Choices.
Some hospitals offer only one way to have your baby. The way that's most convenient for the staff.
But at Wake Medical Center, women can choose from more than nine ways to labor and deliver.
That's virtually every approach that's been proven safe and successful.
Your baby can be delivered by an obstetrician or by a nurse midwife.
It's up to you.
Use Lamaze, LeBoyer or Bradley techniques.
Whatever you decide, you'll have the expert support of our nurses.
Who know all about breathing and coaching.
Soon, you'll be able to labor, deliver, recover and spend your entire hospital stay in the same room.
Or use our traditional labor and delivery suite, if you prefer.
We want to do what's most comfortable for you. And safest for you and your new baby.
That's why we're building a $10 million obstetrics unit at Wake Medical Center.
When we're through, it will be one of the most advanced in the country. With private patient rooms, a solarium, a library and a rooftop dining area for new mothers and their guests.
For more information about any of our women's health programs just call us at 755-8235.
We have everything you can conceive of.
Wake Medical Center

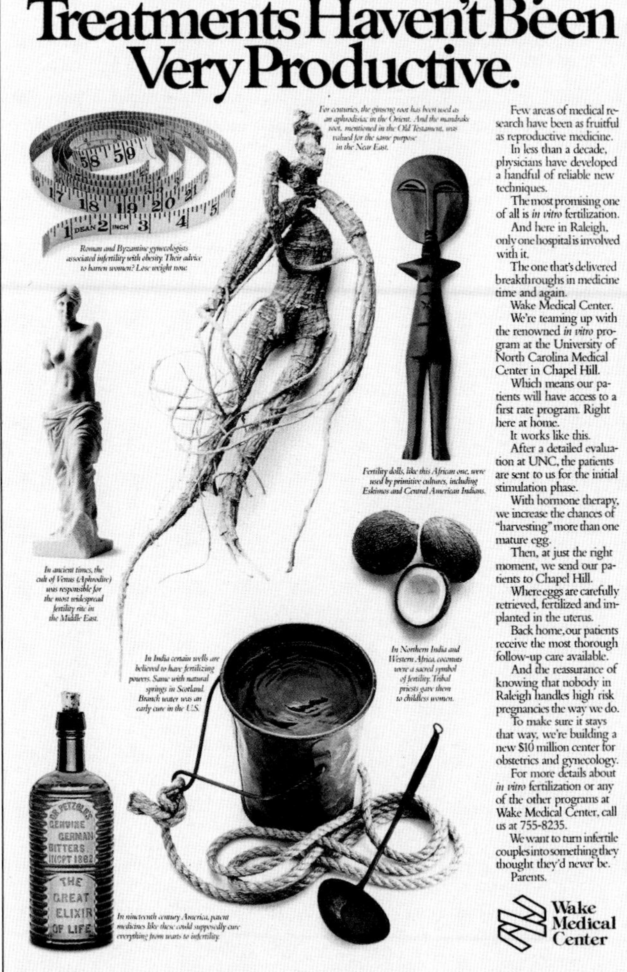

Until Now, Infertility Treatments Haven't Been Very Productive.
Roman and Byzantine gynecologists associated infertility with obesity. Their advice to barren women? Lose weight now.
For centuries, the ginseng root has been used as an aphrodisiac in the Orient. And the mandrake root, mentioned in the Old Testament, was valued for the same purpose in the Near East.
In ancient times, the cult of Venus (Aphrodite) was responsible for the most widespread fertility rite in the Middle East.
Fertility dolls, like this African one, were used by primitive cultures, including Eskimos and Central American Indians.
In India certain wells are believed to have fertilizing powers. Same with natural springs in Scotland. Branch water was an early cure in the U.S.
In Northern India and Western Africa, coconuts were a sacred symbol of fertility. Tribal priests gave them to childless women.
In nineteenth century America, patent medicines like these could supposedly cure everything from warts to infertility.
Few areas of medical research have been as fruitful as reproductive medicine.
In less than a decade, physicians have developed a handful of reliable new techniques.
The most promising one of all is in vitro fertilization.
And here in Raleigh, only one hospital is involved with it.
The one that's delivered breakthroughs in medicine time and again.
Wake Medical Center.
We're teaming up with the renowned in vitro program at the University of North Carolina Medical Center in Chapel Hill.
Which means our patients will have access to a first rate program. Right here at home.
It works like this.
After a detailed evaluation at UNC, the patients are sent to us for the initial stimulation phase.
With hormone therapy, we increase the chances of "harvesting" more than one mature egg.
Then, at just the right moment, we send our patients to Chapel Hill.
Where eggs are carefully retrieved, fertilized and implanted in the uterus.
Back home, our patients receive the most thorough follow-up care available.
And the reassurance of knowing that nobody in Raleigh handles high risk pregnancies the way we do.
To make sure it stays that way, we're building a new $10 million center for obstetrics and gynecology.
For more details about in vitro fertilization or any of the other programs at Wake Medical Center, call us at 755-8235.
We want to turn infertile couples into something they thought they'd never be.
Parents.
Wake Medical Center

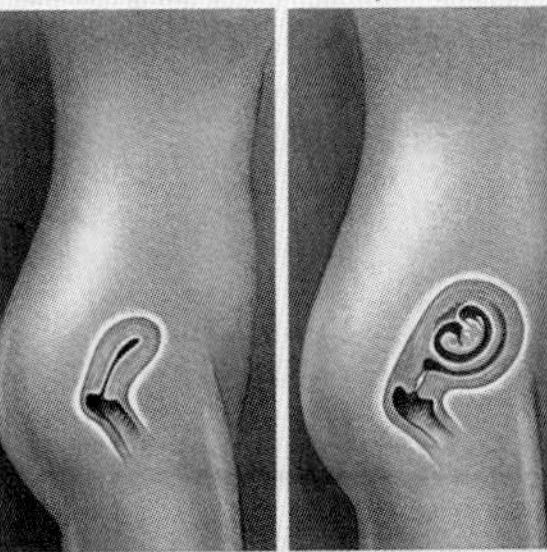
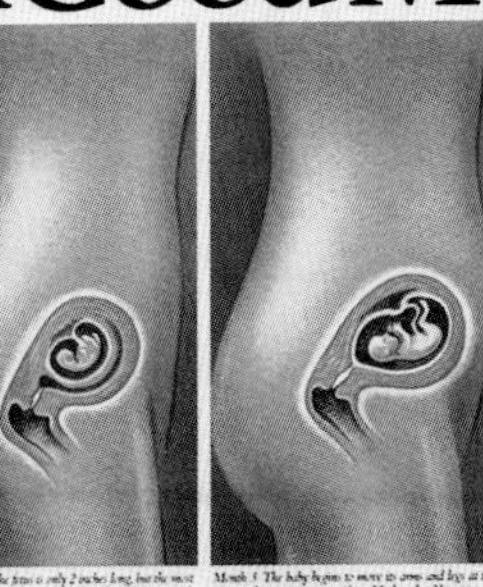
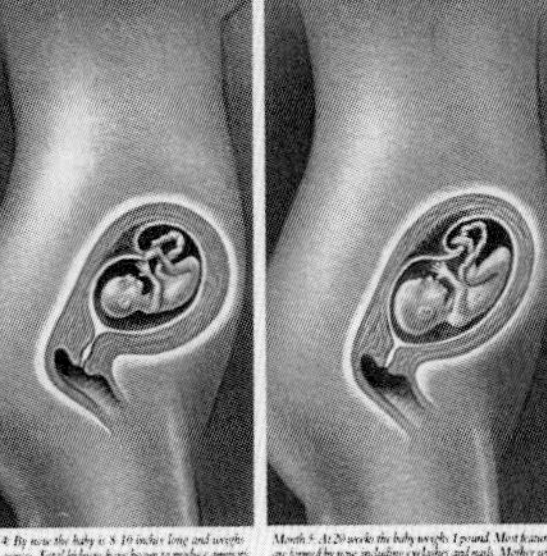
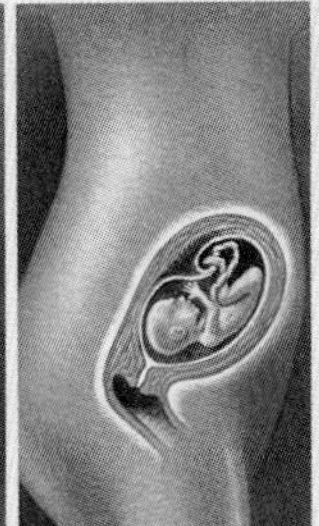
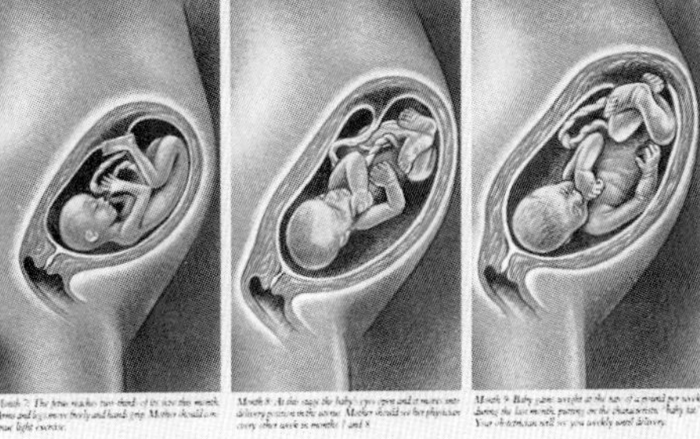
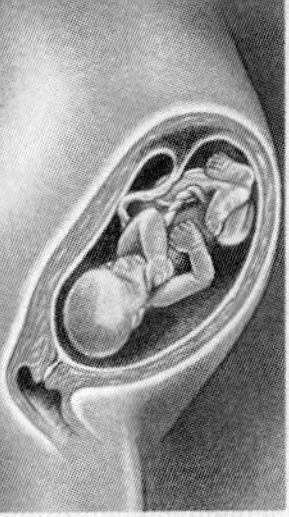
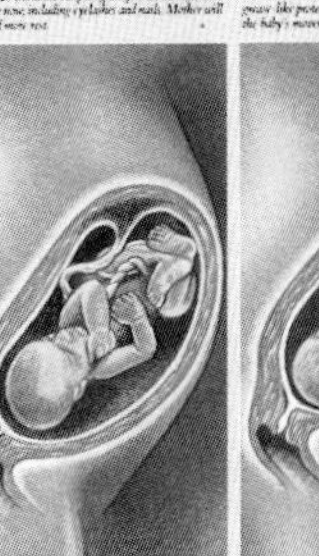
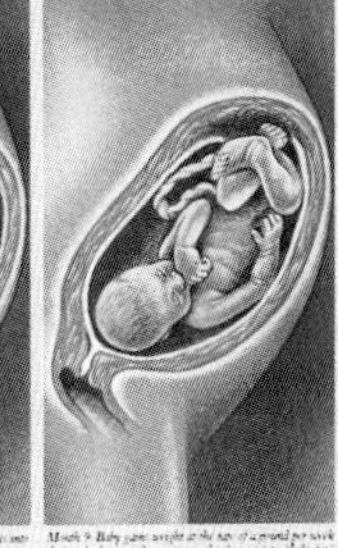

It's Never Too Early To Be A Good Mother.
Every month of your pregnancy, as your baby gets bigger and bigger, your role as mother expands, too.
You have to eat the right foods. Get the right kind and amount of exercise.
And above all, follow your obstetrician's advice.
Because in study after study, it's clear that good prenatal care has a lot to do with the health and the strength of newborns.
That's why, at Wake Medical Center, we don't wait until our obstetrics patients are in labor to start helping them.
We begin early, with counseling and education, to prepare patients for the process of labor and delivery.
For starters, there's our genetic counseling program, designed for couples who are thinking about starting a family.
Then there are exercise programs just for pregnant women, prepared childbirth classes, and classes all about caring for newborns.
Plus a whole series of workshops led by physicians on topics like neonatal care and high-risk pregnancies.
Naturally, we've put the same thoughtful attention into labor and delivery that's gone into prenatal care.
In fact, we're in the final stages of building the new $10 million Wake Women's Center, due to open in the Spring of 1988.
It's a 39-bed unit that's designed around the most innovative new method of delivering obstetrical care. Single room maternity care.
For information about the new Women's Center and prenatal care programs, call us at 755-8235.
While there's still plenty of time.
Wake Women's Center

Consumer Newspaper Over 600 Lines: Campaign

214

ART DIRECTOR
Bob Pendleton

WRITERS
Jim Johnston
Paul Keye
Tom McElligott
Allen Rosenshine

PHOTOGRAPHERS
Pete Tangen
Henry Wolf
William Coupon

CLIENT
The Wall Street Journal

AGENCY
Jim Johnston Advertising

215

ART DIRECTOR
Nick Scott

WRITER
Richard Spencer

PHOTOGRAPHERS
Geoff Senior
Robert Dowling

CLIENT
P&O Canberra Cruises

AGENCY
Still Price Court Twivy D'Souza/London

Allen Shines.

Allen Rosenshine. Once a copywriter, still a strategist, he's the architect of the cosmic tri merger that united BBDO with Doyle Dane Bernbach and Needham Harper to form Omnicom. Paradoxically intellectual and pragmatic, intense and selfless, publicized but publicity-shy, he leads a goliath that's one of the industry's most talked about topics. Here, from a recent conversation, are his thoughts on advertising and the agency business, now—and in the years to come.

On beginnings:
I'm a New Yorker, through and through. Born here, I grew up here and went on to graduate from high school and college in New York City. While the city has changed enormously, it's still incredibly dynamic, with more energy, more opportunity per square foot than anywhere. Where else could you start out as a writer on business-to-business accounts in a small agency, and wind up as senior management with a global giant? That's how I began; writing industrial ads in a small agency. And when I began at BBDO, that was still my specialty. Then we had a problem on a consumer account, and *everyone* got a crack at it. Jim Jordan liked what I did. He told me, "Allen, you belong on consumer business—that's where you work from now on." He gave me my start and a lot of support.

On the team:
This is a business where people work with people, where you need other people to help you do your best. Enhancing the BBDO reputation for creativity—and making it worldclass—has been a team effort, and I'm proud I've played a role. I am not a superb creative person, not in the sense of execution. Phil Dusenberry and Keith Reinhard know that side far better than I do. I believe my strength is as a creative *strategist*. You need both—strategy and execution. That's why Phil and I have been a good team, and why Keith and I are working well together.

On the role of the global agency:
The global agency makes good sense because marketing opportunities don't stop at national borders. Think how globalization can apply—should apply—to the *positioning* of a product. Many people confuse global *positioning* with global *execution*. They aren't the same. Rarely will globalization mean that the same execution—of a TV commercial or a print ad—can be used all around the world. But positioning can and often does work across national borders, in totally different cultures. The real strength of a global agency is the ability to provide *network resources* wherever a client has markets.

On making a global agency work:
Omnicom's management heritage—which for me is the BBDO corporate culture—has long emphasized a lean and trim management structure. In the days when Tom Dillon and then Bruce Crawford headed the company, BBDO was a very large and growing agency. But it was never fat or top-heavy. In Bruce's era, no more than six or seven people, here and overseas, ran the entire agency. Then, and now, there was a premium put on agility, flexibility, and the ability to move quickly. Bruce had no tolerance for committees, memos, detailed plans. Decisions were reached on the basis of experience, instinct and common sense and the process had just three steps. Oral discussion. Agreement in principle. Then *do it*. The process forced people to talk to each other, to form real *working* relationships. That's paid large dividends. The relationship between Willi Schalk and me began years ago—and it was a key in turning the concept of Omnicom into a *reality*. The same kind of *relationships* are critical in making a global agency work. A global agency must be far more than offices and billings and clients. It begins with people who can make a global business work—because they can work together, no matter where they're located.

On the most important word in advertising:
There is nothing more critical in our business than *relevance*. To consumers, it's relevance of your brands, of your marketing, of your advertising. To all advertising agencies, it's relevance of what we do and how we do it; of being relevant to our clients. Too much of advertising isn't simply *bad*, it's simply irrelevant.

On the client challenge:
Clients—not simply ours, but all clients—are demanding more cost-effective service. As everyone knows, client companies are under tremendous cost control pressures themselves. And now they're beginning to look at their marketing and advertising budgets. And they're looking at their advertising agencies as a resource that must be operated in the most cost-effective manner possible. So every agency is being scrutinized. Clients are asking the questions they ought to be asking: "What are we getting for what we're paying?" That's fair. Responsible clients are *not* saying, "We want everything we got last year but we want to pay you less." What they are saying is, "Let's look more carefully at what we're paying and what we're getting. Do we really need everything we're getting? Are we getting what we need in the most usable way?" The issue is value. Increased value is an absolute requirement. Clients are demanding it—and they're going to keep demanding it. Agencies must respond.

On fat agencies:
Too many agencies have made the mistake of *looking* fat—in terms of travel, entertainment, life style; perhaps the inherent insecurities in the business create a need to *feel* important. Beyond *perception*, the reality of agency fat results from the inability to measure productivity. How do you measure the productivity of a person who produces *ideas*? Staffs grow and people stay because it's tough to measure value in a business built on ideas. When management does set out to cut staff, no one wants to do it. Manufacturing management may view staff-cutting as a rational step. In the agency business, it's an emotional experience. You must sit down across the table from people you know and like, and tell them they've lost their job. So we avoid the trauma, and fail to fire people who should be fired. Then a crisis occurs—a lost account, budget cuts—and it simply must be done. That's why agencies wind up firing 50 people all at once. In any business, there's a need for prudent management and continuous attention to costs and profits. But it's not easy in the agency business.

On agency compensation:
The 15% commission is still to the advantage of many clients. Obviously, it's no longer a given. In our agencies, we have all kinds of compensation systems, and I'm sure that's equally true of every major agency. But the issue isn't 15%—it's what's in the best interest of both client and agency. In some instances, the specific services a specific agency delivers to a specific client are worth even more than the 15%. The issue isn't price. The issue is *value*.

On creativity:
Agencies are moving—and strongly—toward a new role as creative *resources*. But that isn't a role that's limited to copy, layouts, story-boards. There's a need to be more creative in media, in research, in how we handle accounts, in everything we do. Surveys show clients select agencies on the basis of "creativity." Isn't that a bit like the surveys that show people saying they prefer to buy a detergent *without* phosphates rather than one *with* phosphates? The answer is self-evident; how many people want to say they're polluting fools? But after they buy a non-phosphate detergent and find it doesn't clean as well, they return to the phosphate detergent they used before. So while clients say creativity is the most important factor, creativity *alone* isn't enough. You have to provide a set of services. I wouldn't want to be in this business if creative wasn't critical. It will always be the most important characteristic that distinguishes clients' brands and agencies from each other. But an agency that only promises "the best creative"—the best words, the best songs, the best pictures—is going to get killed, sooner or later. Significant clients demand agencies that understand and respect their businesses. That's particularly true among the global, multinational clients, and that's where the business is going. If you don't believe that, you're heading for a fall. If you want to do what we're trying to do, then remember you're talking about a business relationship that goes far beyond awards and whether or not people like your advertising.

On The Wall Street Journal:
I've been reading The Journal since I began in this business. Sure, you'll find the big stories in other publications. But until I read The Journal story, I'm never sure I have the real story. There's a variety of factors involved. The Journal's understanding of business, and the world beyond business. The style, the prose, the understanding of the reporter, the sensitivity of the editor, the information in a story. Put them all together and that's how The Journal goes far beyond any other daily in the world. Most importantly, The Journal does it with *relevance*. People in business lack the time or the patience to try to understand the esoteric, to relate a printed story to the real world. The Journal makes that connection; quickly, lucidly, effortlessly. It *is* unique. Because The Journal is unique, being in it makes the advertiser look unique. That's a strong reason for advertising in The Journal that goes beyond demography, beyond circulation. Someone *might* replicate demographics and reach. But they couldn't replicate the ambiance of The Wall Street Journal.

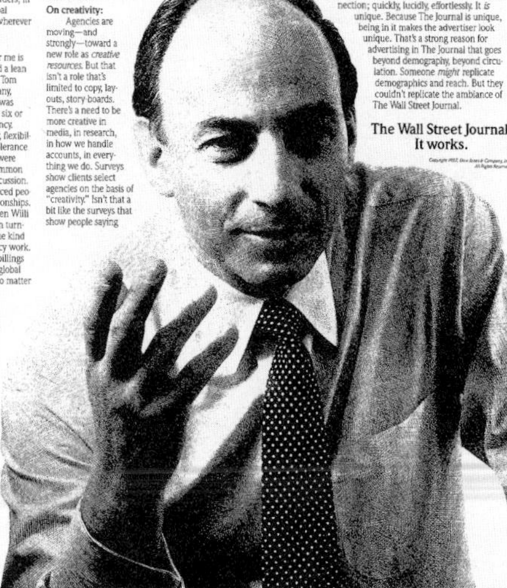

The Wall Street Journal.
It works.

keye. rhymes with high.

Paul Keye. Writer, account executive, with agencies as diverse as Ogilvy & Mather and Papert Koenig Lois; co-founder and creative leader of a lively Los Angeles agency, keye/donna/pearlstein. In a recent conversation, he shared his thoughts on advertising, California and the high-flying agency he heads.

On beginnings:
My father was a Navy surgeon and a family doctor. I was born in San Diego and grew up in a little farm town on the Mexican border, El Centro. Then we moved to Beverly Hills, of all places. My older brother, John, was a really good student. Most of my time in school was spent under house arrest. I graduated from Duke, which was not then the Serious University it is today. I joined the Marine Corps during the Korean War. If you were a college grad, it was: Parris Island, Quantico, 38th Parallel—and, yes, young man, you're a platoon leader. It wasn't much of a war, but it was the only one we had.

On getting into advertising:
I came back to Southern California and got a job at a TV station. It *sounded* creative, but was very process-oriented. I began noticing these critters from somewhere called "advertising agencies," so I followed one of them back to his office and got a job as an account executive. It was an archetypal 50s agency: Lots of service. (Make lunch dates, not waves.) We worried about the clients a lot, what they liked and didn't like. I don't remember anyone getting excited about the ads. I liked being an account executive. They got to talk in meetings.

On New York:
I headed East in the early 60s. I interviewed at Ogilvy. Writers had very recently come into fashion, so I told them I was a writer. Thus began the longest year of my life. I was put into a room with a typewriter and a pile of blank paper. No one talked to me. No meetings. If that was what writers did, I wanted to be an account executive. I went to Papert Koenig Lois where I worked on Seagrams, *The Herald-Tribune*, and Xerox. I also handled Jacob Javits's re-election campaign. It was a wild, magical place—inmates did indeed run the asylum. Think what could happen to an impressionable young man whose authority figures were Fred Papert, Julian Koenig, George Lois and Carl Ally. That's what happened to me. No wonder I grew up funny.

On being an accidental proprietor:
After four mad, marvelous years at PKL, I returned to California to become the third partner in a new agency—Faust/Day—mostly involved in technical, business-to-business advertising. Then Mario Donna and I started what Mario *thought* was a creative service; I *thought* it was an advertising agency. (So much for the prenuptial agreements.) Six months later, when Leonard Pearlstein arrived from Carson/Roberts we were still arguing the point.

On getting real:
Sometimes I worry about the visibility keye/donna/pearlstein has today. (Actually, I think the whole agency business is going through a mild seizure of over-reportage.) But I rationalize all the attention by remembering the Invisible Years. When you start as we did, with nothing—no accounts—you need time and a highly plastic ego. Someone would see a Peace Corps ad or a Lone Star commercial or find out who perpetrated the International Imitation Hemingway Contest for Harry's Bar (budget: $40,000 annually), and we'd have our random moment of visibility. But it was Continental Airlines—a big, tough, hyperactive account that rescued us from oblivion. They were hardly a dream client. Continental was on the glide path to bankruptcy. Every time we went to a meeting there was someone new in charge of marketing. We ended up with a very small pile of not really wonderful work. But we gained some hard-earned maturity and a place on The Real Agencies list.

On ideas:
Too many ideas get squashed, pureed or killed by turf wars or hierarchy. Someone decides that only copywriters can have copy ideas, only account folk can have marketing ideas. Expensive, senior people's notions are treated more reverently than strong ideas from juniors. Too bad. Ideas don't know who their parents are.

On writing:
First, it's a set of muscles. Exercise them. Second, don't talk about writing. It takes the passion away and it angers The Word Fairy. And always, always remember: Writers and messiahs are generally self-appointed. No one else wants you to be a writer. They want you to get a job. How to write an interesting ad? Try this: "Hello, I want to tell you something important or interesting or useful or funny. It's about you. I won't take very long, and there's a prize if you stay till the very end."

On risk-taking:
There's so much talk about risk-taking today. It tells you what cautious times we're living through. (I don't think this is an advertising agency problem, by the way. I think it's much deeper than that.) So it's probably a good time to be on the lookout for the "Just-Fight-The-Big-Ones" syndrome. In a craft that considers which way the teddy bear ought to dance around the cereal box, there aren't any "Big Ones" in the Whoppingly Significant ethical sense of the word. All the more reason to swing for the fences. Great advertising doesn't cost any more than not-so-great advertising, and you sleep a lot better at night.

On New York vs. California:
In New York, there's a swifter dispatch of the Painfully Obvious. In California, there's a tendency to worry about people's sensibilities. Score one point for New York. But New York also has a hierarchy for *everything*. You can't buy a tie, try a lunch place or see a play until you check it with an Authority. In California, no one runs anything. It doesn't mean we're without opinions. It just means there are precious few style-masters. You're free to do what you want to do, the way you want to do it. I'd give the point to California. I love the sense of freedom or self-determination. But some folks find it absolutely terrifying.

On California advertising:
The idea of "California style" advertising is absurd. California advertising is created by New Yorkers like Jay Chiat or folks from the Northwest like Hal Riney. But there's a hilarious sidelight to all this. California—Los Angeles in particular—has gone from backwater to wellspring. I think that's funny.

On The Wall Street Journal:
Every time I've been on the *inside*, next to the texture and the detail of a company—so I *knew* the true story—I've been astonished at the accuracy and insight of The Journal. I like the writing, too. Words placed next to one another in a remarkable, memorable way. I think it's interesting that right smack in the middle of this High Concept, icon-drenched, post-literate society of ours someone's making money selling a couple pounds of high-fiber, fat-free, black and white words and numbers five days a week. No, it's more than interesting, it's amazing.

The Wall Street Journal.
It Works.

McElligott's got it.

Tom McElligott. Founder, creative leader of Fallon McElligott, the Minneapolis-based agency that's enjoyed meteoric success. Son of an Episcopal clergyman, he has preached and practiced the gospel of creative excellence from coast-to-coast, winning hundreds of awards and ever-larger clients. Here, from a recent conversation, are insights into the writer who's proved he's got what it takes.

On beginnings:
When I was a child, we moved from parish to parish, state to state. I went to high school in Fargo, North Dakota, where I was the underachiever of the century. Then came the Marine Corps, the University of Minnesota, marriage, family—and my first job, as a junior copywriter at Dayton's, a major department store in Minneapolis. The pay wasn't much—but it was a start.

On retailing:
There's no better place for a young writer than in retail advertising. You learn the limits of aesthetics. You discover the world has no time for self-indulgence. You have to write ad after ad, and meet deadlines that force you to be fast. And every ad is judged on the basis of sales—period. All this was true at Dayton's. But so were high standards in taste, ethics and style. Example: superlatives were a sin. You can't claim one thing is "best" today, and something else "best" tomorrow. Like other Dayton's rules, it wasn't just logical, but ethical: reflecting a philosophy that customers should be treated with honesty and respect. Writing a multimillion dollar campaign may seem far removed from writing retail ads. But advertising at any level should be measured by Dayton's standard: Is it *effective*? Is it *honest*?

On the early years:
After a year with a small agency, I joined Knox Reeves. The agency had lost its largest client, was in trouble with most of the others, and we were fighting just to survive. But as the staff grew smaller, I moved up—farther and faster than I ever dreamed possible. More important, I began working with Ron Anderson, and discovered two people together can do things neither could do alone. Eventually, Bozell & Jacobs bought the agency, stabilized the situation and gave us the chance to show what we could do.

On Lunch Hour, Ltd.:
At the same time Knox Reeves was struggling to stay alive, I started a free-lance business—called Lunch Hour, Ltd.—with Pat Fallon who was at Martin/Williams. Later, Ron Anderson joined us. We were picky about our clients, did work we could believe in and won quite a few awards. That led to more clients, more business, more work, more awards. From time to time, we'd talk about starting an agency. But we never all seemed to be in the mood at the same time. I finally told Pat: "Either we start or I'm gone." He agreed, and we were off and running minus Ron, who opted to stay at Bozell & Jacobs. We continued in our regular jobs for a year, while we put together our plan and recruited Fred Senn, Irv Fish and Nancy Rice. When we opened for business, all our key players were in place so I could focus on the things I do best—and stay clear of those I don't.

On the price of success:
Many people talk about—and perhaps envy—our growth. But I wonder if they understand how tough those first years were. We worked twelve hours a day, seven days a week; pushing to the edge of endurance and beyond. The toughest part was sticking to our creative principles. Remember, it was before creativity became chic again, and we were just an upstart agency without a track record. So any client that chose us was taking a big gamble. If we'd caved in on principles, it might have been easier—in the beginning. But we wouldn't have become what we are today. Thank heaven we believed in ourselves. Thank heaven we found clients who believed, too.

On quality control:
I really want to see *everything* that goes out of the agency. My name is on the door and reputation is on the line. So it may not be my ad, but it's my business. That said, I don't think any of our writers or art directors would accuse me of meddling in the creative process. It's not necessary—nor advisable. Not with our senior creative people—they're hired because they don't need supervision. And our junior people can learn more by working with our senior people than they ever could by listening to me talk.

On recruiting:
When we began to grow, we needed creative people. Sure, the top writers and art directors in town knew we were doing good work just as we had at Lunch Hour. But they wondered if we were for real. Once we proved we were in business to stay, they started calling—along with creative people from all over the country. It's an interesting twist. Now we know a dozen people we'd love to hire—if we had the business. Of course, Pat Fallon says he can solve *that* problem.

On the Minnesota advantage:
Three out of every four people on our staff are Minnesotans. It never occurred to us, but we are incredibly lucky to be in a market so loaded with good people. Why Minneapolis? I suppose it's a combination of things: good schools, cultural resources, quality of life. But I suspect the thing that makes our area different isn't what it *has*, but what it *doesn't have*. And that's cynicism. It's practically nonexistent in Minnesota. Oh, we're just as intense as New Yorkers, just as determined to win. But in the upper Midwest, you grow up believing nothing is impossible if you're willing to work harder and longer. So you put more trust in what you do than in who you know; more faith in sweat than in style. That must seem naive and unsophisticated to some. But if so, I think most American businesses could do with less sophistication and more work.

On awards:
Agencies don't sign ads. So it would be an anonymous business if it weren't for the award competitions. They give agencies, art directors and writers recognition—and that's a form of compensation as well as the strongest incentive to do the best work you can. Obviously, award-winning work tends to attract new business. But to keep the business, you need to make something happen in the marketplace. Are there too many competitions—too many awards? Well, never forget that we all crave recognition from our peers—and most of us like to see good work recognized. That's not simply true of advertising; it's true in sports, business, in every area of human activity.

On making ads:
When your agency is hot and you're flushed with the heat of sudden celebrity, you're flooded with invitations—to make speeches, to judge shows, to write articles. It happened to me. And I found myself drifting further and further away from my craft. To the point that I had to pull in the reins and remind myself, "Tom, you're a writer. And writers ought to spend a good chunk of their time writing." I have yet to meet an advertiser who wants to hire us so he can hear me *talk* about advertising.

On competition:
Client awareness of the need to break through the clutter has increased—and that's helped raise the creative level of advertising. There's not much doubt that today's advertising is far, far better—more interesting, involving, rewarding. I'd like to think we've been part of the trend. Ironically, the better most advertising becomes, the tougher it is for us to create work that will stand out, be seen, be heard. But that's good; competition can only make us better. Bland, boring advertising breeds complacency, and complacency is the enemy of excellence.

On selling ideas:
Selling is an act of passion. When you're passionate about an idea, it shows—and it's easy to sell it. If there's been a secret to our success, that's it. We truly believe in what we're doing and we believe *passionately*. I find it impossible to be cool and reserved—I won't present an ad or a campaign unless I really believe in it. And when I *believe*, I can be pretty persuasive.

On the future:
I never imagined we'd get so big, so fast. Our growth has been somewhat unreal; like a dream where you're afraid you might just wake up. That's a real fear—I've seen too many bubbles burst to take it all for granted. So what can we do to keep it going? In my mind, the thing we must do is avoid compromising our ideals. I was impressed when Jay Chiat said: "We want to see how big we can get before we get bad." Well, Chiat/Day has gotten much bigger—and stayed true to their creative standards. I hope people can say the same thing about us in five years.

On The Wall Street Journal:
As a reader, I've always treasured the quality of The Wall Street Journal, the excellence of Journal writing. As a writer, I've always appreciated the environment—a unique combination of topical urgency and thought-provoking insights that makes advertising work harder, work faster. When we pitched The Wall Street Journal's circulation account, I *knew* The Journal, and what makes it tick, and that helped us score our biggest win. At the time, we were a young, small, relatively untested Minneapolis agency competing with big, established New York agencies. So it wasn't simply another piece of business to us. After all, The Journal *is* the most respected publication in America. That respect hasn't just come from its size or financial success, but from its ability to meet a business need better than any other medium, print or broadcast. It's the same in our business. Agency success shouldn't be measured in terms of billings or growth, but in terms of the work the agency does. If we maintain our quality in what *we* do as well as The Journal does in what *it* does, we'll have achieved the only success that matters.

The Wall Street Journal.
It works.

THERE IS A CORNER OF A FOREIGN SEA THAT IS FOREVER ENGLAND.

From the Caribbean to the Mediterranean, from the Adriatic to the Fjords, a Canberra cruise is the perfect holiday for the Englishman (or Scots or Welshman) abroad.

How else can one enjoy a decent cuppa in the Azores? Or round off a lavish five-course meal with a fine piece of Stilton in Port Said? Where else could you see a musical in Marseilles and still understand it?

As well as the best of British, Canberra gives you the best of foreign holidays too.

P&O

You can enjoy five countries instead of just one, and mingle with the locals, knowing that civilisation awaits you back on board.

You're even safe from the perils of foreign exchange. The shipboard currency, as well as the service, is Sterling. Not that you'll need much of that with fares starting at a mere £868 for two weeks, all in.

It'll seem as if you've travelled the world without ever leaving home.

For further details phone 01-831 1407, see your local ABTA travel agent, or post the coupon to Canberra Brochure Services, PO Box 3, Eccles, Manchester M30 0NB.

Please rush me the 1988 Canberra brochure.
Name
Address
Postcode Tel
Tick if you've cruised before ☐ With Canberra ☐

CANBERRA
THE FIRST RESORT

ONE OF THE THINGS YOU'LL LIKE ABOUT CANBERRA IS THAT THE KIDS ARE TAKEN CARE OF. EVEN IF YOU HAVEN'T GOT ANY.

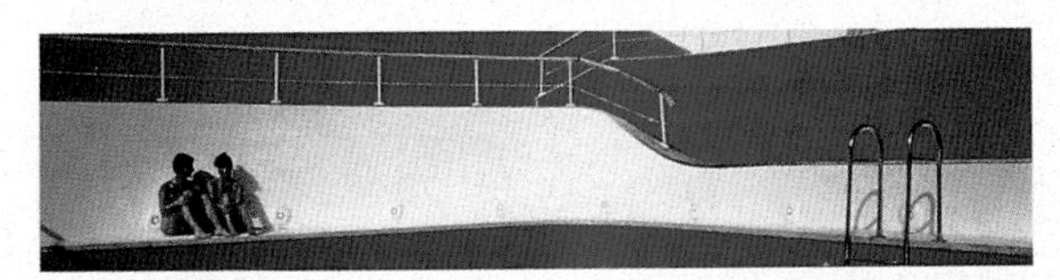

On Canberra we believe that children, as far as possible, should be neither seen nor heard. Especially if you've taken a romantic break where more than two is, most definitely, a crowd.

Which is why we keep them fully occupied in our Junior Club, with their own pool, their own entertainments and, best of all, no grown ups to spoil the fun.

And why we give them an early evening meal, so your quiet dinner for two is actually quiet (they wouldn't like smoked salmon anyway).

P&O

Of course, if you've brought the family along, you may actually want to see the kids. Fortunately they're never far from hand on Canberra even though it may seem they're a million miles away as you abandon yourself in the nightclub.

And with fares as low as £868 for two weeks, all in, and discounts of up to 85% for the kids, paying for a Canberra cruise is simply child's play.

For further details phone 01-831 1407, see your local ABTA travel agent, or post the coupon to Canberra Brochure Services, PO Box 3, Eccles, Manchester M30 0NB.

Please rush me the 1988 Canberra brochure.
Name
Address
Postcode Tel:
Tick if you've cruised before ☐ With Canberra ☐

CANBERRA
THE FIRST RESORT

IF THE PROMISE OF FOREIGN CLIMES, EXOTIC PORTS AND STRANGE CULTURES ISN'T ENOUGH TO TEMPT YOU, LET'S TALK MONEY.

Over £2 million to be precise. That's how much commission we expect to pay out to ABTA travel agents over the next year.

Canberra's equally good value for your customers too.

For example, a ten day cruise through the Azores can be theirs for as little as £490. If they still feel that's expensive, wait 'til they discover that the cost includes lavish five-course dinners, impeccable service and a dazzling array of entertainment.

P&O

Mention a range of ports as diverse as Oslo or Rio, Grenada or Haifa, and your customers will begin to wonder why they haven't been on a cruise before.

If they're still not convinced, we're producing 250,000 extra brochures to finally persuade them.

After that the sale, or sail, is as good as yours.

For further information ring Clive Swann at Canberra Sales on 01-831 1234.

CANBERRA
THE FIRST RESORT

Consumer Newspaper Over 600 Lines: Campaign

216

ART DIRECTOR
Gary Larsen

WRITER
Rick Colby

PHOTOGRAPHERS
Paul Sanders
After Image

CLIENT
Simi Valley Hospital

AGENCY
Larsen Colby Koralek/
Los Angeles

217

ART DIRECTORS
Nancy Rice
Nick Rice

WRITER
Jim Newcombe

DESIGNERS
Roger Christensen
Great Faces

ARTIST
Jack Krough

PHOTOGRAPHERS
Marvy!
Jim Arndt

CLIENT
WCCO Radio

AGENCY
Rice & Rice/Minneapolis

We go to market fifteen times a day.

Introducing the Wall Street Journal Report. Only on WCCO Radio. Fifteen times a day, we bring you up to the minute stock market reports and other fast breaking business news. Starting every morning at 5:20 a.m. and at 50 minutes past the hour, 5:50 a.m. to 6:50 p.m. weekdays. The Wall Street Journal Report, beginning January 4 on WCCO Radio. We cover business like nobody's business.

WCCO
RADIO 8·3·0

Radio that hits you right between the ears.

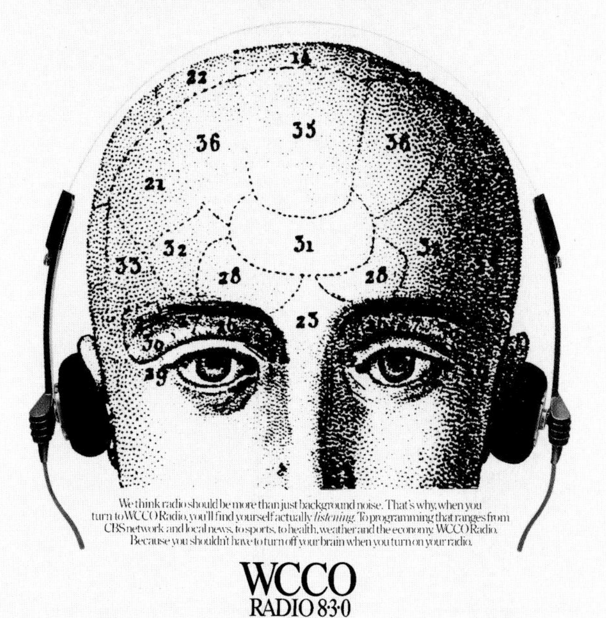

We think radio should be more than just background noise. That's why, when you turn to WCCO Radio, you'll find yourself actually *listening*. To programming that ranges from CBS network and local news, to sports, to health, weather and the economy. WCCO Radio. Because you shouldn't have to turn off your brain when you turn on your radio.

WCCO
RADIO 8·3·0

Traffic is a battle. We provide the air cover.

If you're fighting traffic, WCCO Radio is a strong ally. We start bright and early every morning, and don't get home until you do. From high above the Twin Cities, John Lundell reports the changing traffic situation. Dean Spratt supplies timely ground support. And no other station has them. Together, they give you the ammunition you need to triumph over traffic. WCCO Radio. For traffic reports, we're the Twin Cities' greatest air power.

WCCO
RADIO 8·3·0

Consumer Newspaper Over 600 Lines: Campaign

218

ART DIRECTOR
Bill Murphy

WRITER
Margaret Wilcox

CLIENT
Bildner's

AGENCY
Hill Holliday Connors Cosmopulos/Boston

219

ART DIRECTOR
Steve Dunn

WRITER
Tim Delaney

PHOTOGRAPHER
John Claridge

CLIENT
Nationwide Anglia Building Society

AGENCY
Leagas Delaney Partnership/London

"Dear Miss Dixon, we'd like £7.50 to bounce your £4 cheque."

It sounds like something out of a T.V comedy show doesn't it?

Like a lot of sitcoms, it is based on real life.

In fact only the unfortunate customer's name has been changed. Of course a bank should tell a customer that he or she is overdrawn.

But is it necessary to come down like a ton of bricks on someone who's only £4 in the red?

And then proceed to charge for every cheque, standing order and direct debit for the next 3 months?

Perhaps after all these years of virtual monopoly, the banks need a bit of healthy competition. (Their customers will certainly welcome it, even if they don't.)

Competition in the shape of a Nationwide FlexAccount, the first real alternative to the bank current account. Admittedly, if you reel off the facilities that come with a FlexAccount, they sound distinctly familiar.

Cheque book, cheque card, cashcard, salary credits, standing orders, direct debits and the rest.

But the resemblance is only superficial.

For example, there are absolutely no charges on a FlexAccount. Letters, stopped cheques, duplicate statements and standing orders are all free.

Even if you write a cheque, use your cashcard or request a duplicate statement while you're in the red, it won't cost you a penny.

Naturally, going into the red is something we don't encourage our customers to do.

But if you do need an overdraft we'll begin, not by sending the standard threatening letter, but by discussing with you what your needs are, how much you want to borrow and for how long.

Then, all you owe us is interest on the amount outstanding.

No "arrangement fees," no hidden extras.

It follows that when you get your FlexAccount monthly statement you'll know exactly where you stand. There'll be no nasty surprises lurking under the all-purpose, all-encompassing heading of "Bank Charges."

So much for the unwanted things we've got rid of. What, then, does a FlexAccount offer that the traditional bank current account doesn't?

Interest, for a start. To be exact, with up to £99 in your account, you get 2% interest net per annum. On sums between £100 and £499, 3.5%. And when you're £500 or more in credit, 5%.

(Both the higher interest rates are paid on the whole balance, not just the amount over £100 or £500.) All this is calculated daily, and paid out annually.

And on the subject of paying out, you can withdraw (or deposit) cash, get a mini-statement and even pay your bills 24 hours a day from our cash machines.

You can also withdraw cash anytime of the day or night from over 800 other places, wherever you see LINK, the sign of the national cash network.

More convenient still, a FlexAccount gives you the option of Home Banking. This amazing new development actually enables you to check your balance or request statements over your own telephone. Soon you'll be able to pay bills too.

Behind all these details lies a philosophy which amounts to nothing more than financial common sense. Instead of behaving like over-strict parents, at Nationwide we treat our customers as responsible adults.

We try to make money the approachable subject it should be.

Having encouraged you to tell us exactly what facilities you need, we set up a made-to-measure account which provides them.

How can we afford to be so flexible, to waive charges and pay interest, yet still compete with the banks? Unlike them, we don't have to make profits for shareholders.

Nationwide Building Society was established for the mutual benefit of people who want to save, and people who want to buy houses.

In effect, our customers are our customers.

And who in their right minds would charge a shareholder £7.50 to bounce a £4 cheque?

For further information, call into your local Nationwide branch. Or write to Claire Adams, Nationwide Building Society, New Oxford House, High Holborn, London WC1V 6PW.

Nationwide
FLEXACCOUNT
We always remember whose money it is.

This is a real letter from a real bank. Unreal isn't it?

One of the leading banks used to have a slogan which ran "Money is our business."

Perhaps they could explain the business logic behind the remarkable document reproduced here.

The sheer scale of manpower and resources in relation to the problem makes the process of cracking peanuts with sledgehammers look quite efficient.

If you allow half an hour of managerial, clerical and secretarial time at an average £5 an hour, it cost £2.50 to prepare the letter.

Add 18p for postage, and you get a grand total of £2.68.

In other words, sending this letter cost the bank over ten times as much as the overdraft that led to it!

Even more bizarre than the arithmetic is the tone of voice. Wouldn't an offer of advice be more appropriate than a threat?

It's common sense, isn't it?

At Nationwide we've applied a good deal of common sense to financial problems like these, and come up with the first real alternative to a bank account.

It's called the Nationwide FlexAccount.

At first glance it looks much like a bank account, with all the usual facilities like a cheque book, cheque card, cashcard, salary credits, standing orders and direct debits.

But there are more differences than similarities.

Interest for example, the last thing you'd expect on a current account.

With up to £99 in your account, you get 2% interest net per annum. On sums between £100 and £499, 3.5%. And when you're £500 or more in credit, 5%.

(Both the higher interest rates are paid on the whole balance, not just the amount over £100 or £500.)

All this is calculated daily, and paid out annually.

And on the subject of paying out, you can withdraw (or deposit) cash, get a mini-statement and even pay your bills 24 hours a day from our cash machines.

You can withdraw cash anytime of the day or night from over 800 other places, wherever you see LINK, the sign of the national cash network.

More convenient still, a FlexAccount gives you the option of Home Banking. This amazing new development actually enables you to check your balance or request statements over your own telephone. Soon you'll be able to pay bills too.

Another area in which FlexAccount differs radically from bank accounts is the vexed subject of charges. Quite simply, on a FlexAccount there aren't any.

Even if you write a cheque, use your cashcard or request a statement while you're overdrawn, we still won't charge you a penny.

Naturally we don't encourage our customers to go into the red.

But if you do need an overdraft we'll begin not by sending the standard threatening letter, but by discussing with you what your needs are, how much you want to borrow and for how long.

Then, all you owe us is interest on the amount outstanding. No "arrangement fee," no extras.

When there are no account charges, there's nothing to hide, either.

So we go out of our way to be open about money and make it the approachable subject it should be.

This is simply a reflection of the biggest difference between us and the banks.

Our philosophy.

In place of the 'take it or leave it' approach, a FlexAccount allows you to choose from a selection of different services to suit your needs. If you need advice we're always ready to talk to you, face to face.

Of course, we can't guarantee that you will never receive a letter from us.

But if you do, it will be rooted in something which others have apparently lost sight of. Reality.

For further information, call in at your local Nationwide branch. Or write to Claire Adams, Nationwide Building Society, New Oxford House, High Holborn, London WC1V 6PW.

Nationwide
FLEXACCOUNT
We always remember whose money it is.

If you want to find out how banks became the richest, most powerful institutions in the world, go into the red one day.

Banks have not always been as big and profitable as they are today.

Believe it or not, all the big boys on the High Street were small businesses once.

(In 1955, Barclays only made just over £2½ million profit.)

How then, did the High Street banks achieve the status they enjoy today?

And, most important of all, easily understood.

Of course, the reverse is true with most bank current accounts.

Which is no doubt why they have Hollywood-style adverts telling customers how much they care for them.

At Nationwide Anglia, we believe in deeds not words.

You simply ring one phone number and punch in your personal code. Then, by pressing a few more buttons, you can pay your bills.

Or, just as easily, get instant confirmation of your balance or order a full statement.

From any telephone in the world, at any time day or night. And all in return for a £10 deposit, which is refundable.

COMMISSION
OVERDRAFT ADMIN
**** £26.00

Innovative ideas? Hardly. The first cheque was issued in 1659.

Dynamic management? You have called your bank manager a lot of things in your time, we bet 'dynamic' isn't one of them.

Customer satisfaction, then? No comment.

No.

Quite simply, it is you, dear reader, who have made the banks so rich and powerful.

You, and millions of people like you, who over the years have put your hard earned money into their coffers and received little in return.

Indeed, when you have had the temerity to go into the red, you have paid dearly for it.

Thankfully, there is now an alternative to a bank current account.

Nationwide Anglia's FlexAccount.

An account based on a very simple idea: that it is your money and we should not forget the fact.

So if you go into the red with a FlexAccount you don't start attracting mysterious 'service charges.'

You won't suddenly find yourself having to pay for standing orders and direct debits for a whole three month period when you have only slipped into the red for one day. And we won't slap in a bill, sorry, 'arrangement fee' just for discussing and sorting out an overdraft.

All we ask of you is interest on the money you borrow until you're in the black.

We think this is reasonable, straightforward

So we pay FlexAccount holders interest on the money in their current account.

Not just to people with lots of money in their account, mind.

Every FlexAccount holder gets 2% net per annum on anything up to £99. 3% interest on sums between £100 and £499. And 4% when you're £500 or more in credit.

(Both the higher rates are paid on the whole balance, not just the amount over £100 or £500.)

All calculated daily and paid into your account annually.

This is the interest the High Street banks have traditionally believed is theirs.

Somewhat strange logic as it is your money that earns it.

Isn't there anything good about a bank current account?

Of course there is.

Cheque books, cheque guarantee cards and cash cards. Not forgetting other services like standing orders and direct debits.

All excellent facilities.

Which is why they are all available to FlexAccount holders.

But that's not all.

Being rather keen on new ideas, we also offer our customers something called a Home Banking Unit.

Which works like an unusually helpful, round-the-clock counter clerk.

Not everyone will want one, we know. But that's not the point.

It's another expression of our philosophy.

Another way of helping people manage their money and, ultimately, get more from it.

Does all this sound too good to be true? It shouldn't. It is, after all, common sense.

Which is no doubt why Channel Four television's 'Money Spinner' programme singled it out as being a service "which High Street banks would do well to take notice of."

So far they haven't. Just check your last statement.

If you went into the red, you'll find a deduction has been duly made.

No information about how it's computed. No breakdown. No nothing.

Is it really the best way to treat a customer?

We don't think so. Maybe that's because we are not one of the richest, most powerful institutions in the world.

For further information, just call into your local Nationwide Anglia branch.

Or write now to Claire Adams, Nationwide Anglia Building Society, Chesterfield House, Bloomsbury Way, London WC1V 6PW.

We always remember whose money it is.

Consumer Newspaper Over 600 Lines: Campaign

220

ART DIRECTOR
Roy Carruthers

WRITER
Steve Jeffery

ARTIST
Roy Carruthers

CLIENT
Seagrams/Glenlivet

AGENCY
Ogilvy & Mather

221

ART DIRECTOR
Bob Brihn

WRITER
George Gier

PHOTOGRAPHER
Jim Arndt

CLIENT
Federal Express

AGENCY
Fallon McElligott/
Minneapolis

TO SOME financial analysts, the recent growth in sales of THE GLENLIVET single malt Scotch whisky is extraordinary and totally inexplicable.

Why should the success of The Glenlivet be so mystifying and so unexpected? Is this phenomenon unique to The Glenlivet? And if so, what makes The Glenlivet unique?

To find the answer it is necessary to have an understanding of the difference between an unblended single malt Scotch whisky (The Glenlivet) and blended Scotch whisky (mass-market brands). One of the main problems in understanding the difference is due to a semantic illusion. Surely anything that is "blended" must be more complex, interesting, and special than something that is *un*blended. The negative prefix misleads us. And surely if The Glenlivet is a *single* malt Scotch whisky, then by inference mass-market brands must contain a blend of many different malts and that must be better, mustn't it? The answer, in a word, is "no." It takes a few more words to understand exactly why. Since any discussion of single malt Scotch begins and ends with The Glenlivet, we must go back to 1747.

"Any discussion of single malt Scotch begins and ends with The Glenlivet."

In 1747, when The Glenlivet was first distilled, there was no such thing as a mass-market blended Scotch whisky. When John Smith first made The Glenlivet, he did so illegally to avoid the King's taxes. He picked his barley and he soaked it in water to turn it into "malt." This he dried over fires of peat to give his Scotch a light distinctive smokiness. He then steeped the malted barley in water which he drew from a single spring known as Josie's Well. The result was an unblended single malt Scotch whisky which is made in the same way with the same water today.

Eventually John Smith's business was legalized. Very quickly The Glenlivet became famous. King George IV would drink nothing else. Sir Walter Scott wrote about it. Balladeers sang its praises.

Then in 1830, a certain Aeneas Coffee, an Irishman, invented a different kind of still which produced a cheaper, less flavorable spirit than its Highlands counterpart. Distillers began mixing the neutral grain spirit from this new still with traditional Highland malts.

While this new "blended whisky" was more affordable and quite pleasing to the taste, it lacked the character of The Glenlivet.

The ultimate test of character is the test of time. And today, over a century and a half later, The Glenlivet continues to set a standard of excellence to which others can only aspire.

In fact, The Glenlivet Distillery releases a limited part of its output to be incorporated into blended Scotches to enhance their quality. One might say incorporation is the sincerest form of flattery.

The Glenlivet is still made from a single malted barley, and steeped in the soft waters that spring from Josie's Well. In the words of one devotee, it has "a fine nose, extraordinarily subtle flavor notes; a smooth, mellow integration of peatiness, softness and subtle sweetness." In other words, The Glenlivet is unique. That could explain why The Glenlivet is enjoying its unique popularity.

For those fortunate enough to own a $20 bottle of The Glenlivet falls the problem of protecting it. And for those unfortunates who cannot afford to buy a bottle of their own, there's always the thrill of the hunt.

THE GLENLIVET. JUST SLIGHTLY OUT OF REACH.

©1987 Imported by The Glenlivet Distilling Company, New York, New York. 12-Year-Old Unblended Scotch Whisky. Eighty-six Proof. The Glenlivet is a registered trademark.

"IT HAS A FINE NOSE and some extraordinarily subtle flavor notes. A smooth, mellow integration of peatiness, softness and a subtle sweetness."

If you think that's no way to talk about a fine wine, you're right. But it is, increasingly, the way a growing and influential minority are referring to an unblended single malt Scotch whisky. Just as Middle America was beginning to grasp the curious semantics of wine appreciation, able to swap vintages with pious sommeliers, along comes what one commodities trader recently referred to as "a whole new ball game for the connoisseur."

But, while it can take a lifetime to acquire little more than a working knowledge of wine, an appreciation of single malt Scotch is far easier to come by. Instead of literally thousands of varieties, there are a mere 50 or so different brands of single malt Scotch available in the US. That's the first piece of good news. But the best news is that you don't have to taste all 50 to become well versed since there is one single malt Scotch by which all others are judged. That Scotch is THE GLENLIVET, the definitive single malt Scotch whisky.

"The Glenlivet is worth all the wines of France, and more cordial besides."

For the majority who think a Scotch is a Scotch is a Scotch, all this may seem irritatingly precious. But consider the following facts.

The Glenlivet has been made in exactly the same way, in the same area of the Scottish Highlands by members of the same family (for the most part) since 1747. When, in that year, John Smith started to distill The Glenlivet, there was no such thing as a mass-market Scotch. Indeed, for years Smith worked illegally, avoiding the unjust taxes of an unpopular King. Ironically, when Smith decided to legalize his operation, the new King George IV claimed that he drank "nothing else." In those days, we're up to 1824 or so, The Glenlivet was made only from the ripest barley, malted to perfection, dried over fires of peat and then mashed in water drawn from a single spring known, for reasons long forgotten, as Josie's Well. In the years that followed, while the development of mass markets led others to concentrate on the production of blended Scotch, the painstaking distillers of The Glenlivet stuck to their guns and their old ways.

Of course, others tried to imitate John Smith's methods and produce distinctive single malt Scotches in smaller quantities. But none of them could draw upon the soft pure waters of Josie's Well, credited by many to be at the heart of what makes The Glenlivet single malt Scotch whisky. The Glenlivet, outselling its nearest rival in the US by 2 to 1, arouses in its devotees passions and opinions that run as high as those to be found at any wine tasting. And remember that a fine wine worthy of hyperbole may cost perhaps twenty times as much as a mass-produced table wine. By contrast, at $20 or so, The Glenlivet really does seem to be ridiculously inexpensive.

With that in mind, let one of the memorable characters created by Sir Walter Scott have the final word. Of The Glenlivet he said, "It is worth all the wines of France, and more cordial besides."

At around $20 a bottle, The Glenlivet single malt Scotch whisky creates envy and desire among the have-nots and supreme satisfaction among the haves.

THE GLENLIVET. JUST SLIGHTLY OUT OF REACH.

©1987 Imported by The Glenlivet Distilling Company, New York, New York. 12-Year-Old Unblended Scotch Whisky. Eighty-six Proof. The Glenlivet is a registered trademark.

OBSERVERS OF the distilled spirits business have been increasingly puzzled by a phenomenon that seems to fly in the face of contemporary trends. Why should a college-educated stock analyst who contributes to his local radio station, owns a computer and sends flowers by wire suddenly develop a passion for a product that King George IV of England swore was the only thing he drank? The product in question is an unblended single malt Scotch whisky called THE GLENLIVET. Is this renewed passion another clichéd symptom of Yuppie over-achieving? Or is it truly a less self-conscious expression of the pursuit of excellence? Do people drink The Glenlivet single malt Scotch whisky to please themselves or impress their peers? To those who have never tasted a single malt Scotch, let alone The Glenlivet, the increasingly higher profile enjoyed by the 50 brands available now in the US is little short of mystifying. But a simple taste test reveals the answer.

The Glenlivet "is the only liquor fit for a gentleman to drink."

The unique softness, subtle flavor notes and gentle peatiness of The Glenlivet are far too elusive for those whose palates play second fiddle to their pretentions. Drinkers of The Glenlivet drink it because they love it. They are not drinking it to impress. Market researchers and behavioral analysts call this an "inner directed" characteristic. Certainly King George IV didn't feel the need to impress anybody but himself by declaring his passion for The Glenlivet. Indeed, it would have been foolish to publicize his enthusiasm for a product that at the time was produced illicitly in order to avoid the taxes levied by his own exchequer. It would seem that Britain, at least in those days, had an "inner directed" monarchy.

The intelligentsia soon followed suit. A character in the novel "St. Ronan's Well" by Sir Walter Scott was driven to declare of The Glenlivet: "It is the only liquor fit for a gentleman to drink... if he can have the good fortune to come by it...." Coming by it, then and now, has always been the problem.

In the very earliest days it was the law that made things difficult. John Smith, the first distiller of The Glenlivet, harvested his barley secretly, turned it into the finest malt and dried it over fires of peat that he would dig by hand from the glens. Then he would steep the malt in the pure, soft waters of a spring called Josie's Well. The very same well that his direct descendants still use today to make The Glenlivet. Today, the problem of coming by The Glenlivet has become a simple one of economics. At $20 or so a bottle, it is not something that all can enjoy. But for those who can, those darlings of market researchers, those racquet ball players and owners of VCRs, for those who can have it and don't need to flaunt it – to them belongs the rarest of pleasures.

And for those analysts and observers impervious to its appeal who are still puzzled by the phenomenal growth of The Glenlivet, maybe the words of Abraham Lincoln will have to provide the only other possible explanation. "People who like this sort of thing," said Mr. Lincoln, "will find this the sort of thing they like."

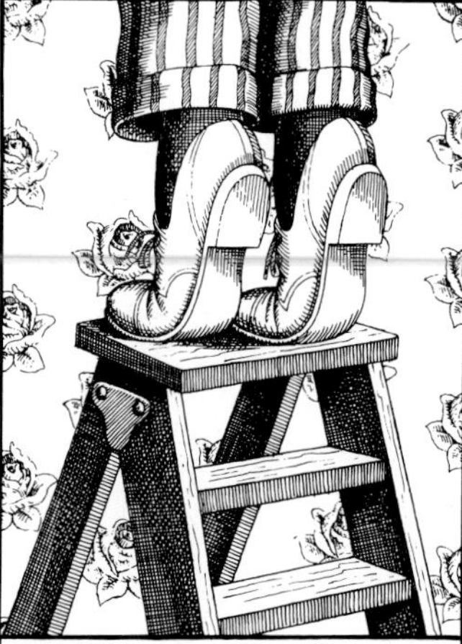

Think of it this way. If some things in life weren't worth reaching for, if all our desires were too easily gratified, the world would be a duller place. At $20 or so a bottle, most people find they can afford The Glenlivet, at a stretch.

THE GLENLIVET. JUST SLIGHTLY OUT OF REACH.

©1987 Imported by The Glenlivet Distilling Company, New York, New York. 12-Year-Old Unblended Scotch Whisky. Eighty-six Proof. The Glenlivet is a registered trademark.

BOLT
AIR EXPRESS
AirWings
DELIVERY
ARE YOU PAYING YOUR AIR EXPRESS COMPANY TO DELIVER TO ANOTHER AIR EXPRESS COMPANY?
When you call most air express companies to pick up a package, a funny thing happens-they call another air express company to deliver it.
While this may be the way they ship your package to the United States, and to the rest of the world, it certainly isn't the best way.
Too many people handling your package allows for too many opportunities for something to go wrong. And if something were to go wrong, it can be extremely difficult to locate the problem, let alone your package.
Fortunately, there is an alternative. You can call Federal Express.
For example, when we pick up your package in Toronto for delivery in New York, we handle it all the way. Which means, the only place your package can be, is on one of our trucks, or on one of our planes.
And with our COSMOS tracking system, getting information on the status of your package is just a phone call away.
Because of this complete control, you can expect reliability. And we stand behind it with this guarantee – if we deliver a shipment late (even just 60 seconds late) you can request your money back. So next time, call Federal. And your package won't end up in the wrong hands. For a free international starter kit call 897-9322, outside the metro area, 1-800-387-5982.
WORLDWIDE SERVICE FROM FEDERAL EXPRESS.

IRONICALLY, THE BIGGEST CHALLENGE FACING MOST AIR EXPRESS COMPANIES IS ON THE GROUND.

ADUANA
CUSTOMS
AVISO – ZONA PROHIBIDA

Getting a package overseas is quite a task. Unpredictable weather and vast distances are incredible obstacles.

But even the unfriendliest of skies isn't a match for what awaits an air express company on the ground – the challenge of getting your package through customs.

At Federal Express, we realize the ability to span the globe is only half the battle. The other half lies in getting your package through the varied rules and regulations that each country has established.

And no other air express company prepares itself better than Federal.

Our staff of experienced, multi-lingual personnel will assist you in any way possible. From advising on what documentation is required, to helping you fill out the necessary forms. Just call 1-800-238-5355 and ask for the international desk.

A Federal Express service agent will even review all the paperwork to help get your package through customs without a hitch.

Which brings us to an important point: with Federal, you get competitive prices, without hidden charges. There are no brokerage fees, no fees for document preparation, and no surcharges for handling dutiable shipments. All of which means no surprises. So next time, call Federal Express. We won't leave you up in the air.

For a free starter kit call 1-800-238-5355.

WORLDWIDE SERVICE FROM FEDERAL EXPRESS.

BOLT
XPRESS
AirWing
DELIVERY
UNFORTUNATELY, THIS IS WHAT MOST AIR EXPRESS COMPANIES MEAN WHEN THEY SAY DOOR-TO-DOOR SERVICE.
When you call your air express company they may tell you they offer door-to-door service, but what they don't tell you is whose door they deliver it to.
In many cases, it's to the door of another air express company.
It seems the only way they can ship your package to the United States, is by giving it to someone else to deliver.
But that means more people will have to handle your package. And too many people handling your package allows for too many opportunities for something to go wrong. And if something were to go wrong, it can be extremely difficult to locate the problem, let alone your package.
Fortunately, there is an alternative. You can call Federal Express.
When we pick up your package in Toronto for delivery in Chicago, for example, we handle it all the way. Which means, the only place your package can be, is on one of our trucks, or on one of our planes.
And with our COSMOS tracking system, getting information on the status of your package is just a phone call away.
Because of this complete control, you can expect reliability. And we stand behind it with this guarantee – if we deliver a shipment late (even just 60 seconds late) you can request your money back. So next time, call Federal Express. We won't call anyone else.
For a free international starter kit call 897-9322, outside the metro area, 1-800-387-5982.
WORLDWIDE SERVICE FROM FEDERAL EXPRESS.

Consumer Newspaper Over 600 Lines: Campaign

222

ART DIRECTORS
Woody Kay
Rob Rich

WRITER
Ernie Schenck

DESIGNER
Judy Maddock

PHOTOGRAPHER
Frank Foster

CLIENT
Vanderbilt Rehabilitation Center

AGENCY
Pagano Schenck & Kay/ Providence, RI

223

ART DIRECTOR
Logan Wilmont

WRITER
Mike Court

PHOTOGRAPHER
Andreas Heumann

CLIENT
Mates Healthcare

AGENCY
Still Price Court Twivy D'Souza/London

If A Spinal Cord Injury Puts You In A Wheelchair, Even A Curbstone Looks Different.

A six-inch slab of granite can seem like the Great Wall of China. Just climbing into a bathtub can make you feel like you're climbing Mt. Everest.

What once were simple things you took for granted suddenly turn into massive, insurmountable obstacles.

At the Vanderbilt Rehabilitation Center, we know a challenge like that takes time. It takes guts. And it takes some very specialized care.

Which is why our programs are designed to cover every aspect of a patient's recovery. From medical evaluation and goal-setting to physical rehabilitation and community reintegration.

All within a warm, compassionate atmosphere where each and every patient is treated on a personal basis.

As part of Newport Hospital's long-standing commitment to providing the best medical care possible, the Vanderbilt Rehabilitation Center offers a broad range of physician-supervised rehabilitation services including speech and hearing therapy, psychological and family support, and our Back Care program.

Call our Rehabilitation Program Coordinator at (401) 846-6400, extension 1852. Life in a wheelchair may be different. But it's nothing you can't get over.

VANDERBILT
REHABILITATION CENTER
At Newport Hospital
Powel Avenue, Newport, Rhode Island 02840

If He Isn't Careful, The Trash Won't Be The Only Thing He Throws Out.

The fact is, you can hurt your back as easily lifting a bag of garbage as you can a bag of cement.

At the Vanderbilt Rehabilitation Center, we know all about back problems and how painful they can be.

Which is why we offer some of the most specialized programs available for treating back pain.

Our Back School is devoted exclusively to teaching people how to reduce, possibly even eliminate, back pain.

And thanks to our Back Care Program, we're helping to prevent on-the-job back injuries from happening in the first place.

As part of Newport Hospital's long-standing commitment to providing the best medical care possible, the Vanderbilt Rehabilitation Center offers a broad range of physician-supervised rehabilitation services, from occupational, physical, speech and hearing therapy to computer-assisted memory retraining and psychological support.

If you think that we can help you, just call our Rehabilitation Program Coordinator at (401) 846-6400, extension 1852. And start putting your back problems behind you.

VANDERBILT
REHABILITATION CENTER
At Newport Hospital
Powel Avenue, Newport, Rhode Island 02840

With Some Speech Problems, You Know The Words. You Just Can't Get Them Out.

When you have a serious communication problem, it can change your whole life.

It can cause problems in school. It can affect your job. It can be as emotionally traumatic as anything you can possibly imagine.

At the Vanderbilt Rehabilitation Center, one of the most important things we do is help adults with speech, communication and hearing disorders.

Problems that range from slurred speech to a total inability to talk or understand as a result of a stroke or head injury.

As part of Newport Hospital's long-standing commitment to providing the best medical care possible, the Vanderbilt Rehabilitation Center offers a broad range of physician-supervised rehabilitation services from occupational and physical therapy to computer-assisted memory retraining and psychological and family support.

If you'd like to learn more, call our Rehabilitation Program Coordinator at (401) 846-6400, extension 1852.

Words can't describe what we can do for you.

VANDERBILT
REHABILITATION CENTER
At Newport Hospital
Powel Avenue, Newport, Rhode Island 02840

ANNOUNCING THE WORLD'S
MOST SENSITIVE CONDOM.

Mates are every bit as sensitive and reliable as other condoms.
They're just as effective at helping to prevent the transmission of cervical cancer, venereal diseases and even AIDS.
Yet they cost less than other condoms.
What makes them twice as sensitive though, is the fact that profits from Mates Healthcare Ltd. go to help the fight against AIDS.
AIDS is neither a gay plague, nor something that's going to go away if we ignore it.
In Africa, it's estimated that there are 10,000,000 carriers – men, women and children.
In New York, the disease is already the biggest single killer of women between the ages of 25-35. And in this country, it's estimated that up to 100,000 people will be infected by 1991.
Mates Healthcare Ltd. was set up with the dual aims of making condoms more widely available and acceptable, and of raising money to provide practical assistance, education and information about AIDS.
To make condoms more widely used, we're introducing a range. Including Coloured Mates, Natural Mates and Ribbed Mates, all of which carry the BSI Kite-mark.
And, thanks to many forward-thinking retailers, Mates are far more widely available. Mates Healthcare Ltd. will be using its profits to help educate people about 'Safer Sex' techniques. Providing educational videos, informative literature and practical advice.
We also plan to give money to counselling services and hospices for those dying of the disease.
In short, we want to provide as much money as we can where it will be the most use.
These days, it makes sense to use a condom. And we think it makes more sense to use Mates.
MATES. YOU MAKE LOVE. THEY MAKE SENSE.

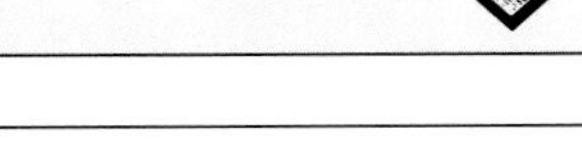

Consumer Newspaper 600 Lines or Less: Single

224
ART DIRECTORS
Bryan Buckley
Mike Shine
WRITERS
Mike Shine
Bryan Buckley
PHOTOGRAPHER
Cailor/Resnick
CLIENT
The Rockport Company
AGENCY
Chiat/Day

225
ART DIRECTOR
David Fox
WRITER
Jerry Fury
PHOTOGRAPHER
Rick Dublin
CLIENT
YMCA
AGENCY
Clarity Coverdale Rueff/
Minneapolis

226
ART DIRECTOR
Ron Lopez
WRITER
Donn Carstens
DESIGNER
David Bartels
CLIENT
Donn Carstens
AGENCY
Bartels & Carstens/
St. Louis

227
ART DIRECTOR
Stephanie Donath
WRITER
Travis Ashby
CLIENT
Mostly Seafood
AGENCY
AD-O-RAMA

CARRY LESS WEIGHT AT THE OFFICE.

The more you have on your mind, the less you should have on your feet. That's why we created DresSports.® Like other dress shoes, they look stylish. Unlike other dress shoes, they're lightweight, flexible, cushioned, and they actually feel good.

After all, your feet shouldn't slow you down on your way up.

Rockport®
Marlboro, Mass.

Dealer Imprint Here.

224

Lose your cookies.

Drop those wonderful little sweets off before they show up in places they shouldn't. Join the Downtown YMCA, only $20 a month.

YMCA

225

▪ FOR $350 I'LL ▪ SPEND A NIGHT WITH A BITCH

I'm a proven stud. Plenty of references, no complaints. My name's B.J. Honeycutt and I'm an AKC registered Old English Sheepdog with a line of champions in my blood that goes all the way back to King Henry VIII.

Send $1 and I'll send you a picture and papers. 425 Algonquin Pl., St. Louis, MO 63119

314-962-4386

▪ For Puppies You Can Be Proud Of. ▪

226

Fish so fresh, even their next of kin haven't been notified.

A Restaurant & Market

Republic Plaza Building 303 16th Street Denver, Colorado 80202 (303) 892-5999

227

Consumer Newspaper 600 Lines or Less: Single

228
ART DIRECTOR
Ronnie Holland
WRITER
Bill Loeffler
CLIENT
WJZY
AGENCY
Loeffler Ketchum Mountjoy/Charlotte, NC

229
ART DIRECTOR
Ron Rosen
WRITERS
Larry Silberfein
Craig Demeter
PHOTOGRAPHER
Clint Clemens
CLIENT
Range Rover of North America
AGENCY
Grace and Rothschild

230
ART DIRECTOR
Dan Ragland
WRITER
Kristy Meredith
PHOTOGRAPHER
Jan Oswald
CLIENT
Swedish Medical Center
AGENCY
Kuper-Finlon/Boulder, CO

231
ART DIRECTOR
Jerry Gentile
WRITER
Barbara DeSantis
PHOTOGRAPHER
Stuart Watson
CLIENT
Adventist Health Systems
AGENCY
DDB Needham Worldwide/Los Angeles

THE CHRISTIANS AND THE LIONS MEET AGAIN.

Notre Dame Vs. Penn State Today At Noon.

WJZY46 Charlotte

228

PLEASE BUCKLE UP FOR SECURITY. © 1987 RANGE ROVER OF NORTH AMERICA

Our service department drives people away.

Perhaps it's because we train our mechanics so well.
We send them to England for two grueling weeks. Where they do nothing but study the mechanics of a Range Rover. Everything from fuel injection to permanent 4-wheel drive to the intricacies of suspension and braking.
They even take Range Rover's V-8 engine apart. And reassemble it again. And again.
Then our mechanics return home, with as much skill as their British counterparts.
So, not only do you get superb performance from your Range Rover.
You get it from your mechanic too.

RANGE ROVER

229

TAKE THE PRESENTS.

When it comes to birthing and parenting information, you need something more reliable than old wives tales.

You need facts. And at Swedish Medical Center that's what we offer. For 20 years, we've been giving classes in everything from breastfeeding to understanding your newborn. From childbirth techniques to infant safety. And for those veteran parents who've already survived the terrible twos, we have courses on subjects like sibling rivalry and refresher Lamaze. There's even a class for first time parents over 30. And, since today's dads do more than pass out cigars, we offer a special class on fathering, taught by men who know their way around a playpen.

For registration, call 788-6578. And remember, the best thing about the gift of knowledge is you don't have to write a thank you note.

501 E. Hampden Avenue Englewood, CO 80110

230

Addiction to food can be every bit as devastating as addiction to alcohol or drugs. If you or someone close to you suffers from bulimia, compulsive overeating or anorexia, call our Eating Disorders Program at (800) 862-7575. We'll give you the help you've been starving for.

St. Helena Hospital
and Health Center of Napa Valley
Deer Park, CA 94576
800-862-7575

231

Consumer Newspaper 600 Lines or Less: Single

232
ART DIRECTOR
Bob Brihn
WRITER
Bruce Bildsten
PHOTOGRAPHER
Rick Dublin
CLIENT
First Tennessee Bank
AGENCY
Fallon McElligott/
Minneapolis

233
ART DIRECTOR
Pam Conboy
WRITER
Lee Schmidt
PHOTOGRAPHER
Rick Dublin
CLIENT
Skipper's Seafood
Restaurants
AGENCY
Martin/Williams -
Minneapolis

234
ART DIRECTORS
Mike Shine
Bryan Buckley
WRITERS
Bryan Buckley
Mike Shine
PHOTOGRAPHER
Cailor/Resnick
CLIENT
The Rockport Company
AGENCY
Chiat/Day

235
ART DIRECTOR
Tom Lichtenheld
WRITER
Rod Kilpatrick
ARTIST
Tom Lichtenheld
CLIENT
Fleetham
AGENCY
Fallon McElligott/
Minneapolis

232

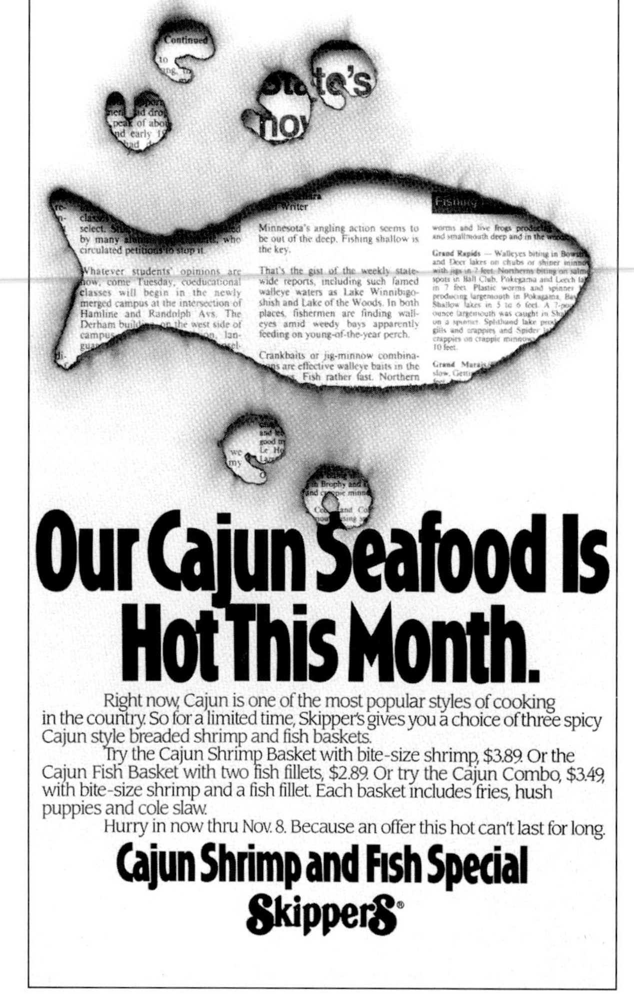

233

WALK AROUND TOPLESS.

Now women can go topless and still get the support they need. Because Sunlight® sandals have soft leather straps and cushioned soles that are shaped and contoured to feel even better than they look.

After all, who said support can't be beautiful?

Dealer Imprint Here.

234

Now you can afford that lamp you've always wanted.

Fleetham's 40th Anniversary Furniture Sale

235

Consumer Newspaper 600 Lines or Less: Single

236
ART DIRECTOR
Michael Ware
WRITER
Don Pogany
DESIGNER
Michael Ware
ARTIST
Suzanne Barnes
CLIENT
Woburn Supply Outlet
AGENCY
Ingalls Quinn and Johnson/ Boston

237
ART DIRECTOR
Bill Maddox
WRITER
Bob Sundland
PHOTOGRAPHER
D.J. Hawkins
CLIENT
San Diego Zoo
AGENCY
Phillips-Ramsey/ San Diego, CA

238
ART DIRECTOR
Michael Fazende
WRITER
Bruce Bildsten
PHOTOGRAPHER
Craig Perman
CLIENT
Kenwood Cyclery
AGENCY
Fallon McElligott/ Minneapolis

239
ART DIRECTOR
Chuck Anderson
WRITER
Jarl Olsen
PHOTOGRAPHER
Rick Dublin
CLIENT
Harry Singh's
AGENCY
Fallon McElligott/ Minneapolis

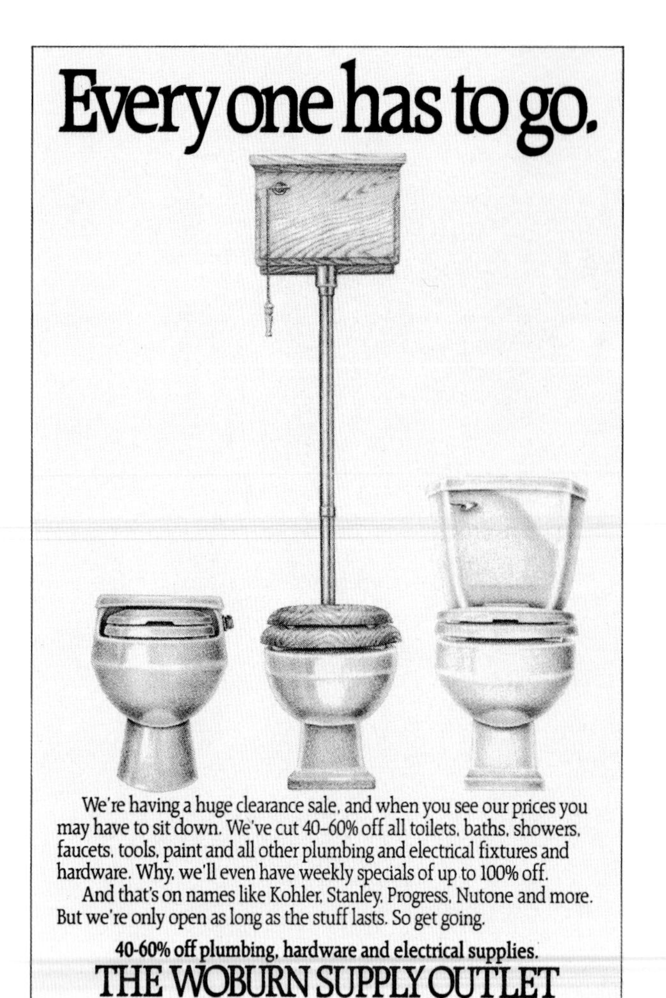

Every one has to go.
We're having a huge clearance sale, and when you see our prices you may have to sit down. We've cut 40-60% off all toilets, baths, showers, faucets, tools, paint and all other plumbing and electrical fixtures and hardware. Why, we'll even have weekly specials of up to 100% off.
And that's on names like Kohler, Stanley, Progress, Nutone and more. But we're only open as long as the stuff lasts. So get going.
40-60% off plumbing, hardware and electrical supplies.
THE WOBURN SUPPLY OUTLET
508 Main Street, Woburn. 935-6442. Open Wednesday through Saturday.

236

The Zoo's latest attraction was captured in the waters off Australia.

This Saturday only, see the America's Cup at the San Diego Zoo.
View the trophy won by San Diego's own "Stars & Stripes."
You don't have to be a member of the San Diego Yacht Club to see the Cup on Saturday. You just have to be in the Zoo.

The most famous prize in yachting will be on display from 9 a.m. to 4 p.m. for one day only, January 30th, by arrangement with the San Diego Yacht Club.
If you're here for the Super Bowl, you ought to see the Super Cup. The San Diego Zoo

237

The only fuel our exotic Italian road machines require.

Our handcrafted, precision Bianchi bicycles start at less than $350. Fuel not included.

KENWOOD CYCLERY

2123 W. 21st St., Mpls. 374-4042

238

239

Consumer Newspaper 600 Lines or Less: Single

240
ART DIRECTOR
Tom Lichtenheld
WRITER
Rod Kilpatrick
ARTIST
Tom Lichtenheld
CLIENT
Murray's
AGENCY
Fallon McElligott/ Minneapolis

241
ART DIRECTOR
Tim Parker
WRITER
Michael Farnam
DESIGNER
Tim Parker
ARTIST
Christine Nagel
PHOTOGRAPHER
Joel Conison
CLIENT
Jewish Hospital
AGENCY
Northlich Stolley LaWarre/ Cincinnati, OH

242
ART DIRECTOR
Ron Lopez
WRITER
Donn Carstens
DESIGNER
David Bartels
ARTIST
Bill Uuksanovica
CLIENT
Kaegel Drug Company
AGENCY
Bartels & Carstens/ St. Louis

243
ART DIRECTOR
Rob Dalton
WRITER
George Gier
PHOTOGRAPHERS
Eric Saulitis
Rick Dublin
CLIENT
Judith McGrann
AGENCY
Fallon McElligott/ Minneapolis

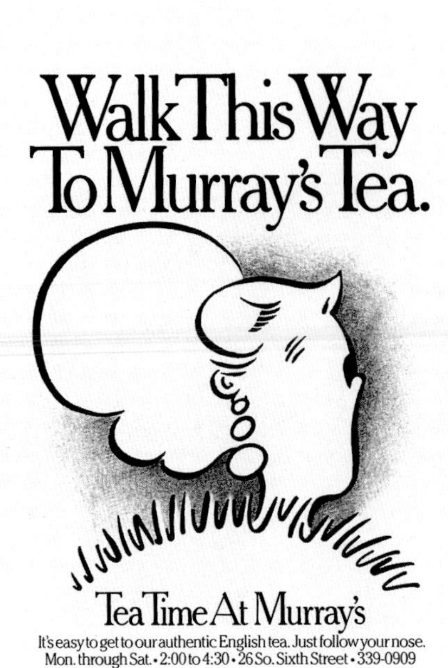

240

241

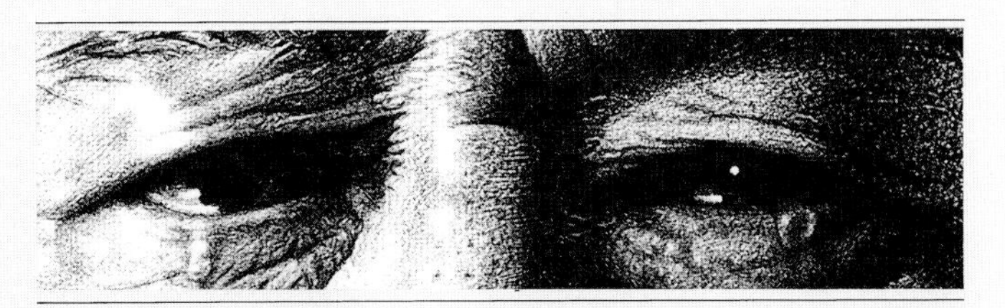

WHEN I WOKE UP THIS MORNING, I WAS 101.

Nothing seemed the same. My mind was saying one thing. My body another. My muscles ached right to the bones. When you're 101, a glassy film forms over your eyes such that everything you see, you see differently. Simple pleasures, like eating, become unpleasant. Turning a page, even turning on a television, is a chore too difficult to perform. You don't think about tomorrow. You think about the next minute. The next second. Memories crash through your mind. Anything to escape where you are. Others told you what it would be like. But you never fully understood. Then that question keeps creeping back into your mind: If you had it to do over again, would you do it all the same? Would you have worn your galoshes? Or at least a hat to protect you from the cold? Mother always told you to. It's too late to reflect on all that. Because here you are at 101. And about the only thing you can do is take a couple of Bayer, fall asleep and wait until you're back to 98.6 again.

Kaegel Drug Company · 8744 Big Bend Blvd. · 962-1020

242

The Pages Of This Book Are Blank. Yet They're Filled With Wonderful Stories.

Tucked away in a tiny village in the northwest corner of Vermont, David Goldberg puts the finishing touches on his latest book.

But it's not a best seller he is completing. It's a beautifully hand-crafted volume that will one day become someone's diary or journal. You see, David is a book maker, and each day he carries on the traditional art of book binding.

Beginning with thick paper stock from Germany, he slowly tears each sheet giving it a classic-looking rough edge. Then, carefully, he hand stitches them together with a linen thread that has been drawn through beeswax. (Beeswax is still the best method of preserving a book's binding from exposure.)

Now it's been said that you can't judge a book by its cover, but with David's books you can. He finishes each with hand made Italian cover stock, insurance that these books will hold their secrets for centuries.

David's books are just one of the wonderfully hand-crafted articles at Judith McGrann and Friends. In fact, you'll find everything we sell has a story of its own.

Hand crafted works from around the world.
3016 West 50th Street Minneapolis Phone 922-2971
Open 11:00 to 4:30 Tue.-Fri. 11:00 to 5:00 Sat. 1:00 to 4:00 Sun.

Consumer Newspaper 600 Lines or Less: Single

244
ART DIRECTOR
Michael Fazende
WRITER
John Stingley
CLIENT
Emmis Broadcasting
AGENCY
Fallon McElligott/
Minneapolis

245
ART DIRECTOR
Jillian Stern
WRITER
Evan Silberman
PHOTOGRAPHER
Randy Allbritton
CLIENT
BMW of North America
AGENCY
Ammirati & Puris

246
ART DIRECTOR
Ron Fisher
WRITER
Mark Slatko
CLIENT
Joe May Valet
AGENCY
HutchesonShutze/Atlanta

247
ART DIRECTOR
Rob Dalton
WRITER
George Gier
PHOTOGRAPHERS
Eric Saulitis
Rick Dublin
CLIENT
Judith McGrann
AGENCY
Fallon McElligott/
Minneapolis

DO SOMETHING ABOUT YOUR JOCK ITCH.

Introducing WFAN 1050 AM. The world's first 24-hour sports radio station. With enough results, live coverage and talk to soothe the fiercest itch for sports.

Get results and updates every 15 minutes. Live. From a worldwide network of reporters. Not stale, wire service reports.

Plus call-in talk shows with sports figures. Inside information on New York's professional athletes. Live coverage of the Mets. Historic moments in sports. Trivia. If it's happening in sports, we'll have it as it happens on WFAN.

Maybe we can't cure an infection. But we can treat an addiction.

WFAN
Sports Radio 1050

244

TEST DRIVE THE CAR THAT PERFORMS AS WELL ON PAPER AS IT DOES ON PAVEMENT.

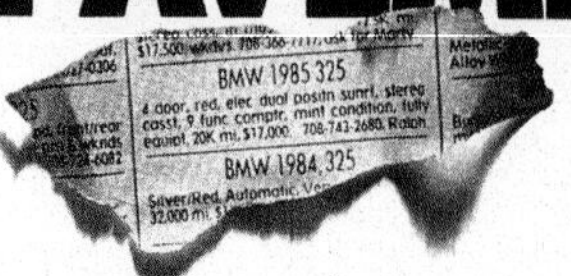

THE PROVEN INVESTMENT VEHICLE.
THE BMW 325.

You're looking at one of the daily testaments to the inherent worth of the BMW 325: the automobile classifieds.

Where, over the last five years, according to the NADA Used-Car Guide, the 3-Series BMW held its value better than 98% of the cars on the road.*

A not entirely surprising track record for the car whose 2.7-liter, six-cylinder Eta engine sounds, in the words of Car and Driver magazine "like an expensive aircraft engine."

Whose standard equipment includes a computerized anti-lock braking system so effective, it inspired the editors at Motor Trend to write "if ever there was a piece of safety equipment that should be mandatory, this is it."

And whose jewel-like finish, an achievement of a 40-stage, 10-hour, two-mile-long paint process, is guaranteed by no less than a 6-year limited warranty against rust perforation.**

But if all this hasn't convinced you to invest in the 325, perhaps this will: over the next five years, the Kelley Blue Book*** projects that the BMW 325 will once again retain a residual value better than 9 out of 10 cars sold this year.

A performance you'll find entirely predictable once you've test driven the 325 at your authorized BMW dealer.

THE ULTIMATE DRIVING MACHINE.

*Resale price based on average retail price according to August 1987 NADA Used Car Guide. Your selling price may vary according to the condition of your car and whether you sell it privately or to a dealer. **Warranty applies only to U.S. specification automobiles purchased from authorized U.S. BMW dealers. For details see the BMW warranty at your authorized U.S. BMW dealer. ***Comparison based on Kelley Blue Book Residual Guide, November/December 1987. Projected residual value after 5 years, of the 1987 BMW 325 vs. all other makes and models. Actual future value may vary. ©1987 BMW of North America, Inc. The BMW trademark and logo are registered.

YOUR AUTHORIZED BMW DEALERS:

City	City	City	City	City	City
DEALER NAME	**DEALER NAME**	**DEALER NAME**	**DEALER NAME**	**DEALER NAME**	**DEALER NAME**
Dealer Address	Dealer Address	Dealer Address	Dealer Address	Dealer Address	Dealer Address
Phone Number	Phone Number	Phone Number	Phone Number	Phone Number	Phone Number

245

OUT, OUT, DAMNED SPOT!

Begone ye irksome stains and wretched dirt.
Joe May Valet. Quality drycleaning since MCMXXXVI.

JOE MAY VALET

246

The Real Warmth From These Quilts Comes From The Women Who Make Them.

Long ago, in small towns and villages across America, women would gather in the afternoon at quilting bees to continue the ancient art of quilting.

These quilters believed that what they were making was more than just a blanket, it was a pronouncement of who they were. And they knew as these quilts would be handed down through the generations, a little of their legacy would go with them.

Many of these wonderful quilts have survived the years. All are originals. And all are hand-crafted with love.

At Judith McGrann & Friends we know the warmth a fine hand-worked artifact can add to your home. We have an exclusive collection of arts and crafts from around the world, and from many time periods.

Of course, you will also be able to find a variety of beautifully hand-made quilts. Which should leave you with a very warm feeling, inside and out.

Judith McGrann And Friends

Hand crafted works from around the world.

3016 West 50th Street. Minneapolis. Phone 922-2971.
Open 11:00 to 4:30 Tue.-Fri. 11:00 to 5:00 Sat. 1:00 to 4:00 Sun.

Consumer Newspaper 600 Lines or Less: Single

248

ART DIRECTOR
Curt Johnson

WRITER
Rob Wallace

CLIENT
Canterbury Downs

AGENCY
Ruhr/Paragon - Minneapolis

249

ART DIRECTOR
Ron Fisher

WRITER
Mark Slatko

CLIENT
Joe May Valet

AGENCY
HutchesonShutze/Atlanta

250

ART DIRECTOR
Frank Haggerty

WRITER
Kerry Casey

CLIENT
WCCO-Radio

AGENCY
Carmichael Lynch/
Minneapolis

THIS SATURDAY, BRING YOUR LITTLE ONES OUT TO MEET OURS.

Saturday is Jockey Day at Canterbury Downs. You'll get one FREE 18"x 24" color poster with your paid admission that features 22 of our jockeys, as well as Lost Code winning the St. Paul Derby. A $7.95 value courtesy of Fuji and Canterbury, it's only available while supplies last. Plus, the jockeys will be on hand to meet racing fans and sign autographs from 11 a.m. until 12:30 p.m.

There'll also be FREE pony and amusement rides, clowns, jugglers and face painters. Kids can get a FREE racing coloring book. Add 10 exciting Thoroughbred races and you have a whole day of family fun! General admission is just $3 for adults. Kids 17 and under get in FREE with parents. Gates open at 11 a.m., first race 1:30 p.m.

And don't forget our special Monday racing program August 10th. Gates open at 2 p.m., first race 3:30 p.m.

JOCKEY POSTER DAY. CANTERBURY DOWNS

248

SEE SPOT GO.

See beastly stains and doggone dirt go, too.
Joe May Valet. Quality drycleaning since 1936.

JOE MAY VALET

249

TWO WINTER LIES.

THERE'S A BETTER WEATHER STATION THAN WCCO.

YOUR TONGUE WON'T STICK TO THE FLAGPOLE.

Listen to WCCO Radio and stay in tune with the latest weather developments as they happen. We offer 24-hour coverage. Five meteorologists in the Weather Center. And a 30-year tradition of school closing announcements. So tune in. Or the weather may take you by storm.

WCCO Real Radio 8·3·0.

Consumer Newspaper 600 Lines or Less: Campaign

251
ART DIRECTOR
Robin Chrumka
WRITER
Mike Stocker
CLIENT
Complete Travel Services
AGENCY
Creative Outlet /Detroit

252
ART DIRECTOR
Cabell Harris
WRITER
Ken Hines
PHOTOGRAPHER
Pat Edwards
CLIENT
Under Where?
AGENCY
Lawler Ballard/
Richmond, VA

WE'VE HELPED A LOT OF SUCCESSFUL EXECUTIVES GET WHERE THEY ARE TODAY.

Fast, hassle-free travel reservations are just what today's busy executive needs. Call us at 649-1234 and we'll get you where you want to be in the business world.

Complete Travel Service Inc.
2075 W. Big Beaver Rd., Troy

FOR THE ULTIMATE EXOTIC VACATION, GO TO TROY, MICHIGAN.

Take a trip to Complete Travel Service in Troy and we'll show you the world. Then we'll plan your ultimate dream vacation. Now isn't that worth a trip to Troy?

Complete Travel Service Inc.
2075 W. Big Beaver Rd., Troy

GO AWAY.
There comes a time when everybody has to get away from it all. When it's your time, call Complete Travel Service at 649-1234. We promise to send you away happy.
Complete Travel Service Inc.
2075 W. Big Beaver Rd., Troy

Take our advice and try out some daring intimate apparel.
It'll help you keep the home fires burning.

Under Where?

5069 Forést Hill Ave., 9107 Quioccasin Rd., 10421 Midlothian Trnpk.

When it comes to bras, our store has a double-A rating.

Our stores have every bra imaginable, in every size made.
So whatever you need, you'll get our support.

Under Where?

5069 Forest Hill Ave., 9107 Quioccasin Rd., 10421 Midlothian Trnpk.

This Valentine's day, give your sweetheart the slip.

This year buy your Valentine an intimate gift from
Under Where. And show her your heart's in the right place.

Under Where?

5069 Forest Hill Ave., 9107 Quioccasin Rd., 10421 Midlothian Trnpk.

Consumer Newspaper 600 Lines or Less: Campaign

253

ART DIRECTORS
Michael Wilde
Jim Hill

WRITERS
Michael Wilde
Jim Hill

DESIGNER
Michael Wilde

PHOTOGRAPHER
Dick Dickinson

CLIENT
University of South Florida

AGENCY
Benito Advertising/
Tampa, FL

254

ART DIRECTORS
John Doyle
Margaret McGovern

WRITER
Paul Silverman

PHOTOGRAPHER
Peter Noel

CLIENT
Maserati

AGENCY
Mullen Advertising/
S. Hamilton, MA

SUPPLY.
DEMAND.
When several hundred college graduates are going after the same job, somebody's going to be left out. Improve your odds by signing up for USF Cooperative Education at SVC-243. Or call 974-2171. And get some real working experience before you go after the job.
USF COOPERATIVE EDUCATION

AN MBA DOESN'T GUARANTEE A BMW.

At one time, a college degree automatically put you on the road to success.

Today, things have become more competitive. Potential employers are looking for experience as well as a college education.

With USF's Cooperative Education, you'll get real working experience before you get out of school. You'll spend one year out of your college education working in your chosen field. You'll even get paid for it. And you'll become more valuable to your potential employers.

Sign up for USF's Cooperative Education at SVC-243. Or call 974-2171. And get more mileage out of your college education.

USF COOPERATIVE EDUCATION

REAL WORLD 101.

College graduates are realizing that it takes more than a degree to get a good paying job. It takes experience.

With USF's Cooperative Education, you'll get real working experience before you get out of school. You'll spend one year out of your college education working in your chosen field.

You'll even get paid for it. And you'll become more valuable to potential employers.

Sign up for Cooperative Education at SVC-243. Or call 974-2171. And find out about the real world before you get out of college.

USF COOPERATIVE EDUCATION

Oompah vs. Vivaldi.

There's a difference between a tuba and a violin, a fine beer and a fine wine, a BMW and a Maserati.

Consumer Newspaper 600 Lines or Less: Campaign

255

ART DIRECTOR
David Fox

WRITER
Jerry Fury

PHOTOGRAPHER
Rick Dublin

CLIENT
YMCA

AGENCY
Clarity Coverdale Rueff/ Minneapolis

256

ART DIRECTOR
Michael Fazende

WRITER
John Stingley

PHOTOGRAPHER
Steve Umland

CLIENT
Emmis Broadcasting

AGENCY
Fallon McElligott/ Minneapolis

Pay for your donuts at the YMCA.
By exercising, you don't have to worry about what donuts will cost you. So eat now and pay later.
Join Now And Get 50% Off All Joiners' Fees.
YMCA

DoveBar®
It's time to pay for your sins.
Start exercising regularly and you can enjoy the sweetest pleasures in life without feeling guilty. So join the Downtown YMCA, only $20 a month.
YMCA

OREO
Lose your cookies.
Drop those wonderful little sweets off before they show up in places they shouldn't. Join the Downtown YMCA, only $20 a month.
YMCA

DO SOMETHING ABOUT YOUR JOCK ITCH.

Introducing WFAN 1050 AM. The world's first 24-hour sports radio station. With enough results, live coverage and talk to soothe the fiercest itch for sports.

Get results and updates every 15 minutes. Live. From a worldwide network of reporters. Not stale, wire service reports.

Plus call-in talk shows with sports figures. Inside information on New York's professional athletes. Live coverage of the Mets. Historic moments in sports. Trivia. If it's happening in sports, we'll have it as it happens on WFAN.

Maybe we can't cure an infection. But we can treat an addiction.

WFAN
Sports Radio 1050

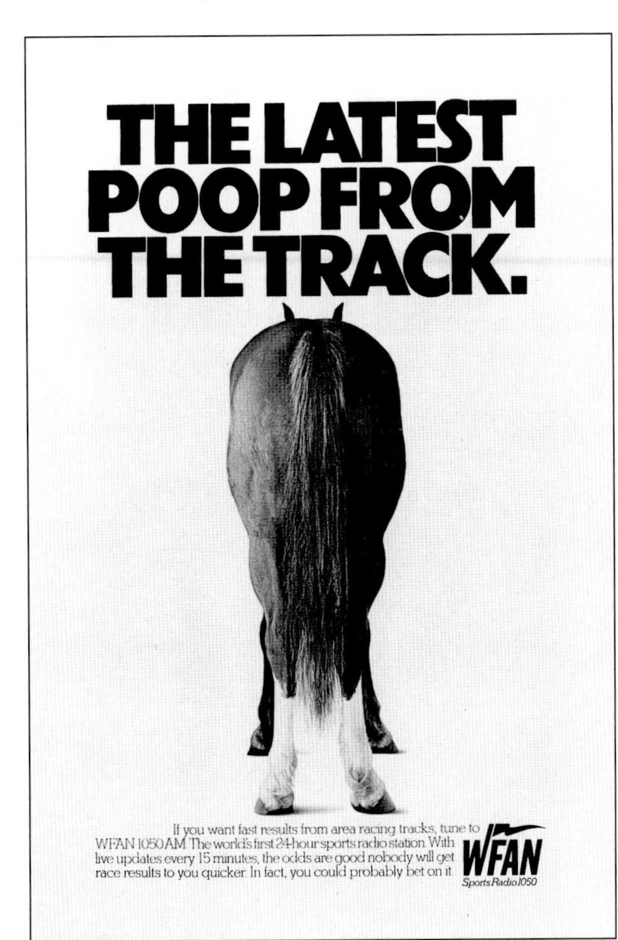

THE LATEST POOP FROM THE TRACK.
If you want fast results from area racing tracks, tune to WFAN 1050 AM. The world's first 24-hour sports radio station. With live updates every 15 minutes, the odds are good nobody will get race results to you quicker. In fact, you could probably bet on it.
WFAN
Sports Radio 1050

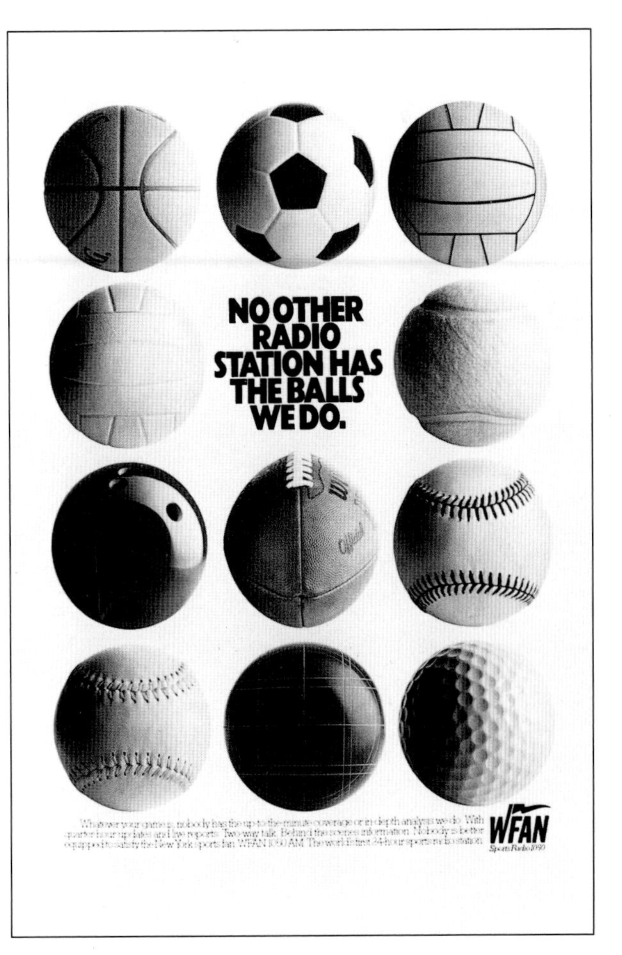

NO OTHER RADIO STATION HAS THE BALLS WE DO.
Whatever your game is, nobody has the up-to-the-minute coverage or in-depth analysis we do. With quarter-hour updates and live reports. Two-way talk. Behind the scenes information. Nobody is better equipped to satisfy the New York sports fan. WFAN 1050 AM. The world's first 24-hour sports radio station.
WFAN
Sports Radio 1050

Consumer Newspaper 600 Lines or Less: Campaign

257

ART DIRECTOR
Richard Crispo

WRITER
Scott Aal

PHOTOGRAPHER
Michael Justice

CLIENT
Los Angeles Herald Examiner

AGENCY
Ketchum/Los Angeles

258

ART DIRECTOR
David Fox

WRITER
Joe Alexander

PHOTOGRAPHER
Jim Arndt

CLIENT
YMCA

AGENCY
Clarity Coverdale Rueff/ Minneapolis

Get into heavy metal.

Want to crank it up in a 4x4? The Herald Examiner Classified Section can turn your heavy metal dreams into reality. It's also a great way to sell your truck. Three lines for seven days for just fifteen dollars.* Call (213) 744-8100 or 1-800-252-9393. MasterCard and Visa gladly accepted.

LOS ANGELES HERALD SUBSCRIBE: 1 800 HERALD-X

It's all over L.A.

*Private Party Rate

Kiss your grandfather goodbye.

GRANDFATHER CLOCK. Xlnt
GRANDFATHER CLOCK of the
rich & famous. This clock
GREAT GRANDFATHER
CLOCKS! You want one, we've
got one. Oak finish, great cond.
$600/obo. 213/555-9034 pp

If it's gotta go, it's gotta go. The Herald Examiner Classified Section is great for selling clocks and all kinds of furniture. A great place to find them, too. Three lines for seven days, only fifteen dollars.* Call (213) 744-8100 or 1-800-252-9393. MasterCard and Visa gladly accepted.

LOS ANGELES HERALD SUBSCRIBE: 1 800 HERALD-X

It's all over L.A.

*Private Party Rate

What to do if the Rabbit dies.

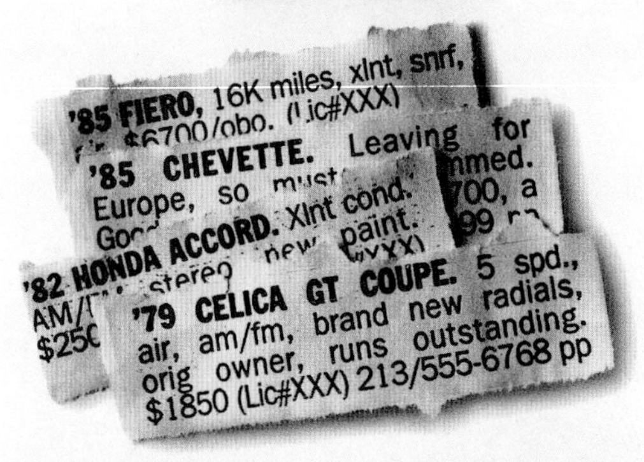

Don't panic. Just buy another car through the Herald Examiner Classified Section. It's a great vehicle for finding the one you want. And for selling the one you don't. Three lines for seven days, only fifteen dollars.* Call (213) 744-8100 or 1-800-252-9393. MasterCard and Visa gladly accepted.

LOS ANGELES HERALD SUBSCRIBE: 1 800 HERALD-X

It's all over L.A.

*Private Party Rate

257

Every now and then, kids deserve a good paddling.

When it comes to activities, YMCA Summer Camps go overboard. From canoes and horses to sailboats and backpacks. There are plenty of ways for your kids to get their feet wet.

Call The Summer Camp Hotline. 822-CAMP.

Phones answered Monday through Friday 8am to 8pm.

YMCA

Maybe it's time your child met a horse that didn't talk.

Horseback riding is just one of the activities kids talk about after experiencing a YMCA Summer Camp. So let your child see a horse from the saddle. Instead of the sofa.

Call The Summer Camp Hotline. 822-CAMP.

Phones answered Monday through Friday 8am to 8pm.

YMCA

Imagine life without your kids.

YMCA Summer Camps last from one to five weeks. So while your kids are sitting around a campfire, you'll have time to do some rekindling of your own.

Call The Summer Camp Hotline. 822-CAMP.

Phones answered Monday through Friday 8am to 8pm.

YMCA

Consumer Newspaper 600 Lines or Less: Campaign

259

ART DIRECTORS
Richard Foster
Dick Pantano

WRITERS
Rich Pels
Joe O'Neill

CLIENT
Hyatt Hotels & Resorts

AGENCY
Hill Holliday Connors Cosmopulos

260

ART DIRECTORS
Dick Pantano
Richard Foster

WRITERS
Joe O'Neill
Peter Nichols
Rich Pels
Wayne Winfield
Tim Bayless
Rochelle Klein

CLIENT
Hyatt Hotels & Resorts

AGENCY
Hill Holliday Connors Cosmopulos

TODAY'S BUSINESS STRATEGY:

The problem with being a martyr on a business trip is that your business may suffer more than you do.

For reservations at any of 87 Hyatt Hotels in North America or 44 Hyatt International Hotels, call **1-800-228-9000**, or your travel planner.

TODAY'S BUSINESS STRATEGY:

Lodging that's merely adequate should be reserved for employees who are.

For reservations at any of 87 Hyatt Hotels in North America or 44 Hyatt International Hotels, call **1-800-228-9000**, or your travel planner.

TODAY'S BUSINESS FINDING:

It's still possible to maintain your standards without violating your per diem.

For reservations at any of 87 Hyatt Hotels in North America or 44 Hyatt International Hotels, call **1-800-228-9000**, or your travel planner.

TODAY'S BUSINESS FINDING:

Accommodations that are undistinguished seem to inspire work of the same quality.

For reservations at any of 87 Hyatt Hotels in North America or 44 Hyatt International Hotels, call **1-800-228-9000**, or your travel planner.

TODAY'S BUSINESS FINDING:

When the enjoyment goes out of a business trip, the business usually follows.

For reservations at any of 87 Hyatt Hotels in North America or 44 Hyatt International Hotels, call **1-800-228-9000**, or your travel planner.

TODAY'S BUSINESS QUESTION:

Is it mere coincidence that a bad day with a client is often preceded by a bad night at a hotel?

For reservations at any of 87 Hyatt Hotels in North America or 44 Hyatt International Hotels, call **1-800-228-9000**, or your travel planner.

Consumer Magazine B/W: 1 Page Or Spread Including Magazine Supplements

261
ART DIRECTOR
Simon Bowden
WRITER
David Tessler
PHOTOGRAPHER
Cailor/Resnick
CLIENT
Volvo
AGENCY
Scali McCabe Sloves

262
ART DIRECTOR
Lou Carvell
WRITER
Abbie Simon
PHOTOGRAPHER
Gary Hanlon
CLIENT
Smith Corona
AGENCY
Rosenfeld Sirowitz
Humphrey & Strauss

263
ART DIRECTORS
Nancy Rice
Nick Rice
WRITER
Jim Newcombe
DESIGNERS
Roger Christensen
Great Faces
ARTIST
Jack Krough
PHOTOGRAPHER
Jim Arndt
CLIENT
WCCO Radio
AGENCY
Rice & Rice/Minneapolis

264
ART DIRECTOR
Bob Brihn
WRITER
Jarl Olsen
PHOTOGRAPHER
Rick Dublin
CLIENT
WFLD
AGENCY
Fallon McElligott/
Minneapolis

© 1987 Volvo North America Corporation

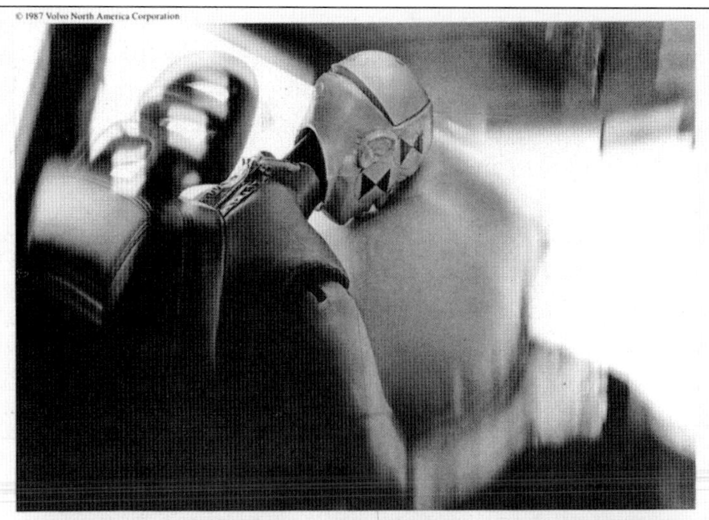

VOLVOS ARE NOW AVAILABLE WITH AN ADDITIONAL SHOCK ABSORBER.

Volvo presents cushioning designed to make you feel more relaxed—about driving.

It's the new Volvo Driver Side Supplemental Restraint System (SRS). And it's designed to increase protection to the driver in certain types of accidents, when used in conjunction with the three-point seat belt.

Perhaps best of all, it's included in a car that's already equipped with such safety features as a steel cage and rigid door reinforcements. All of which combine to comfort a portion of your anatomy most shock absorbers can't.

Namely, your mind.

VOLVO
A car you can believe in.

(Dealer Name)

261

IF YOU WEREN'T BORN WITH GREAT WRITING SKILLS, YOUR PARENTS CAN STILL GIVE THEM TO YOU.

Introducing the Grammar-Right™ System. It puts passion in your prose, life in your letters, dash in your documents.

What you didn't inherit from your parents in writing ability, we've more than made up for with technology.

It's the remarkable new Smith Corona XD 6700 with the Grammar-Right System. Step by step it can turn a boring writer into a born writer.

Press the Word Count feature and the XD 6700 will remind you that you've used a certain word too often on the page. The Thesaurus will then give you word options to make your sentences richer. Word Alert tells you when you're using a commonly confused term and lets you know how to use it right. So you won't type "exceptable" when you meant "acceptable."

The XD 6700 doesn't just help you become a better writer, it helps you to type more accurately, too. That's because it has the most advanced correction system you can find on any portable typewriter. The 75,000 word Spell-Right electronic dictionary catches spelling and typing errors before you can. WordFind® will locate the error quickly. Word-Right AutoSpell will show you the correct spelling and type it in for you. Word-Eraser correction takes out whole words at a touch.

These, plus a host of other super automatic features all give you letter-perfect typing plus the kind of prose your English teacher never could get out of you. Now that's a *writing* gift. The Smith Corona XD 6700, proudly made in the U.S.A.

MADE IN USA

For more information on this product, write to Smith Corona Corporation, 65 Locust Avenue, New Canaan, CT 06840

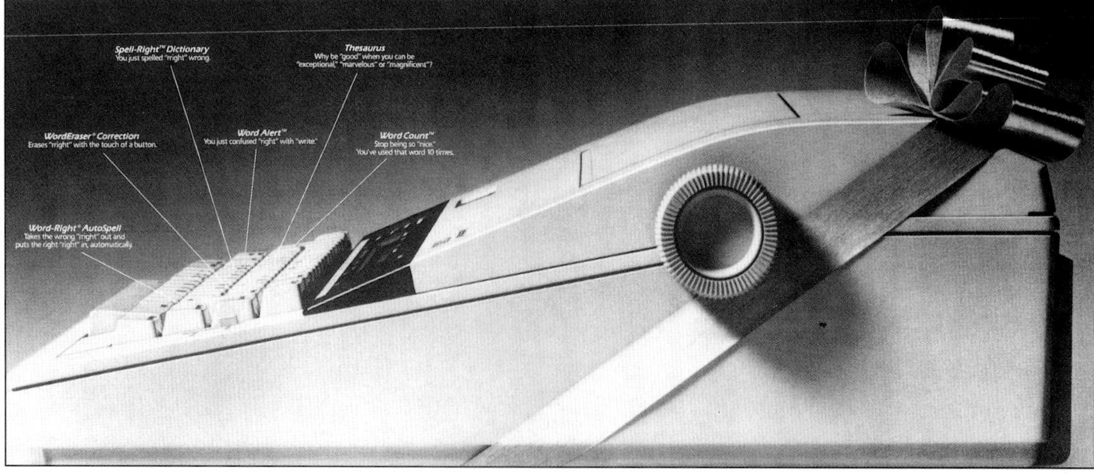

262

Traffic is a battle.
We provide the air cover.
5th St
If you're fighting traffic, WCCO Radio is a strong ally. We start bright and early every morning, and don't get home until you do. From high above the Twin Cities, John Lundell reports the changing traffic situation. Dean Spratt supplies timely ground support. Together, they give you the ammunition you need to triumph over traffic. WCCO Radio. For traffic reports, we're the Twin Cities' greatest air power.
WCCO RADIO 8·3·0

263

"Bachelor Party," starring Tom Hanks. Wednesday at 7PM.
32
WFLD

264

Consumer Magazine B/W: 1 Page Or Spread Including Magazine Supplements

265
ART DIRECTORS
Nancy Rice
Nick Rice
WRITER
Jim Newcombe
DESIGNER
Roger Christensen
Great Faces
ARTIST
Jack Krough
PHOTOGRAPHER
Marvy!
CLIENT
WCCO Radio
AGENCY
Rice & Rice/Minneapolis

266
ART DIRECTOR
Curt Johnson
WRITER
Dana Offerman
PHOTOGRAPHER
Jim Williams
CLIENT
WCCO T.V.
AGENCY
Ruhr/Paragon - Minneapolis

267
ART DIRECTOR
Bob Brihn
WRITER
Jamie Barrett
PHOTOGRAPHER
Craig Perman
CLIENT
WFLD
AGENCY
Fallon McElligott/ Minneapolis

268
ART DIRECTOR
Earl Cavanah
WRITER
Larry Cadman
CLIENT
Volvo
AGENCY
Scali McCabe Sloves

265

266

SIT BACK AND WATCH A WOODY ALLEN MOVIE.

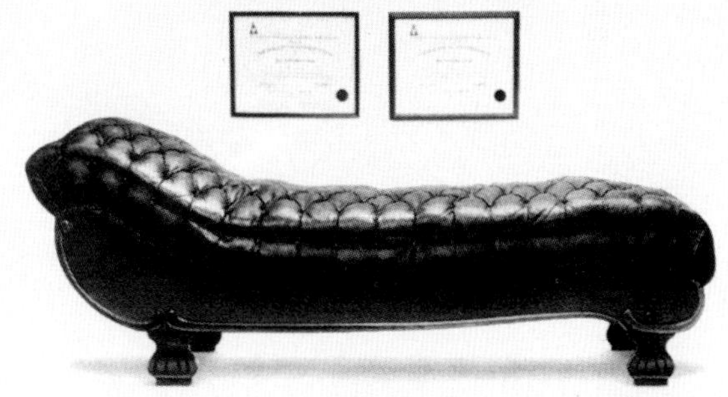

"Broadway Danny Rose," Wednesday at 7 PM.

32
WFLD

267

VOLVO'S 24 HOUR ROADSIDE ASSISTANCE PLAN NOW COVERS A FEW NEW CARS.

Last year Volvo introduced "On Call,"℠ an emergency roadside assistance plan to provide free towing and other services to the owners of new Volvos.

For 1987, we've extended it to the owners of all Volvos, no matter what the year. For only $69.95 a year, every Volvo owner can take advantage of the features of "On Call." (In addition to towing, these include re-imbursement for hotel accommodations if an accident hangs you up overnight. Free trip routing. Emergency cash privileges. Discounts on rental cars and travel packages, plus much more.)*

See your Volvo dealer for all the details.

At Volvo, we stand behind our cars long after they leave the showrooms. And we don't discriminate because of a little thing like age.

VOLVO
A car you can believe in.

℠ "On Call" is a service mark of Volvo North America Corporation, and is offered in cooperation with the Amoco Motor Club. *To find out more about the other valuable features of the "On Call" Plan, as well as any limitations or restrictions, see your local Volvo dealer. California residents who own 1985 and older Volvos are not eligible for the plan. © 1987 Volvo North America Corporation.

DEALER NAME

268

Consumer Magazine B/W: 1 Page Or Spread Including Magazine Supplements

269

ART DIRECTORS
Bob Brihn
Tom Lichtenheld

WRITERS
George Gier
Jamie Barrett

PHOTOGRAPHER
Rick Dublin

CLIENT
Continental Illinois

AGENCY
Fallon McElligott/
Minneapolis

270

ART DIRECTORS
Jim Hill
Jackie Warner

WRITERS
Jackie Warner
Jim Hill

PHOTOGRAPHER
Martin Fox

CLIENT
Dial Page/Communications
Properties

AGENCY
Price McNabb/
Asheville, NC

271

ART DIRECTOR
Bob Brihn

WRITER
Mike Lescarbeau

CLIENT
WFLD

AGENCY
Fallon McElligott/
Minneapolis

272

ART DIRECTOR
Sig Gross

WRITER
David Corr

CLIENT
WWOR-TV

AGENCY
Hill Holliday Connors
Cosmopulos

TC1810C
No one appreciates a good film more than we do.
Continental Illinois is proud to support this year's Chicago Film Festival.
Continental Illinois

269

You're listening to an actual demonstration
of just how quiet your pager can be.

If you didn't hear anything, you heard a Dial Page® silent pager.

It's a pager that alerts you to messages by softly vibrating–instead of annoying you with loud "beeps."

With the Dial Page silent pager, you're always in touch. Just give your pager number to anyone you want to keep in touch with–the office, clients or your family. Then, when you can't be reached by phone, all they have to do is call your pager number. Enter their phone number. And the easiest step of all, hang up.

Your pager then vibrates. Look at your pager display, and you'll see the phone number of who just called.

That's all there is to it. And a Dial Page silent pager can cost less than a dollar a day.

But of course, if you like the beeping, that's fine, too. With a flip of a switch, you can change your silent pager to beep when you have a message.

For more information on the complete line of pagers from the number one paging company in the Southeast, mail the coupon today. Or call your local Dial Page office or 1-800-845-PAGE. You'll hear a demonstration of just how helpful we can be.

☐ Yes, I'm interested in a Dial Page silent pager. Please send me more information on how a pager can help me.

Name_____

Company_____

Address_____

City_____ State_____ ZIP_____

Telephone (   )_____

The most convenient time to contact me is_____

DIAL PAGE®
In touch when you want to be.

P.O. Drawer 10767, Federal Station, Greenville, SC 29603-0767
1-800-845-PAGE

270

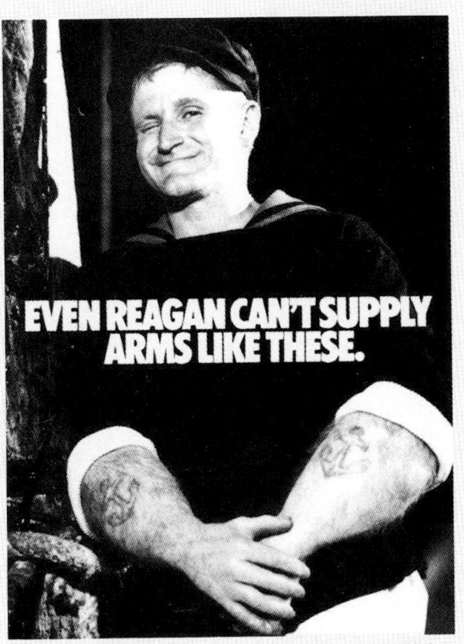
EVEN REAGAN CAN'T SUPPLY
ARMS LIKE THESE.

Robin Williams in "Popeye." Friday at 7 PM.

32
WFLD

271

YOU
HAVE THE
RIGHT
TO
REMAIN
HYSTERICAL.

BARNEY MILLER • WEEKNIGHTS 7:30PM.

WWOR-TV

272

Consumer Magazine B/W: 1 Page Or Spread Including Magazine Supplements

273
ART DIRECTOR
Bob Brihn
WRITER
Jamie Barrett
CLIENT
WFLD
AGENCY
Fallon McElligott/ Minneapolis

274
ART DIRECTOR
Kim Wong
WRITER
David Bernstein
CLIENT
Baileys
AGENCY
Backer Spielvogel Bates

275
ART DIRECTOR
Bob Brihn
WRITER
George Gier
PHOTOGRAPHER
Jim Arndt
CLIENT
WFLD
AGENCY
Fallon McElligott/ Minneapolis

276
ART DIRECTOR
Bob Brihn
WRITER
Jamie Barrett
CLIENT
WFLD
AGENCY
Fallon McElligott/ Minneapolis

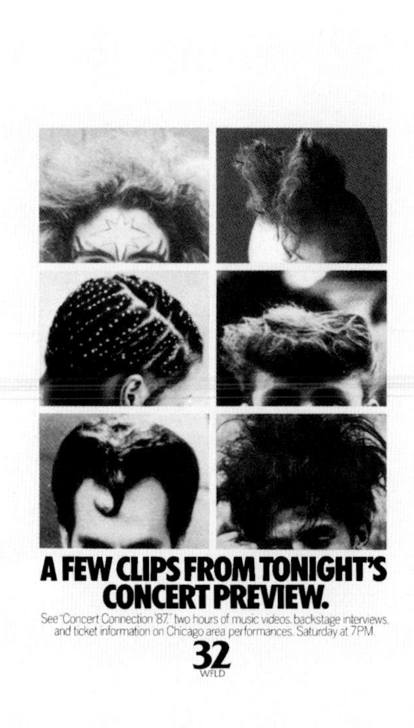

273

But today a Black woman named Alice Walker has won a Pulitzer Prize for literature.
One named Rose Mary Sanders has become a judge in the state of Alabama.
And yet another named Susan Taylor has been made editor in chief of a national magazine.
They and others like them have opened the doors to a multitude of careers for Black women.
And to celebrate their remarkable achievements, each has been honored by an award. An award given by the National Coalition of 100 Black Women and sponsored by Baileys Original Irish Cream.
It's called a Candace Award.
And this year, at the Metropolitan Museum of Art in New York, we'll be celebrating the careers of several more leaders.
Because thanks to them, the voice of a Black woman isn't heard only in the entertainment industry. It's heard in all industries.

BAILEYS® ORIGINAL IRISH CREAM® PRESENTS
The 1988 Candace Awards
SPONSORED BY THE NATIONAL COALITION OF 100 BLACK WOMEN

274

A FEW BARS FROM
ELVIS PRESLEY'S BIGGEST HIT.
When the King gets caught by the law he sings like a canary. Friday at 7PM.
"JAILHOUSE ROCK"
32
WFLD

275

SIX MEN WHO HAVE CHANGED HISTORY.

Christ Caesar Columbus

Napoleon Hitler Mel Brooks

"History of the World Part I," Wednesday at 7PM.

32
WFLD

276

Consumer Magazine B/W: 1 Page Or Spread Including Magazine Supplements

277
ART DIRECTOR
Tom Lichtenheld
WRITER
Rod Kilpatrick
ARTIST
Tom Lichtenheld
PHOTOGRAPHER
Lars Hansen
CLIENT
Fleetham
AGENCY
Fallon McElligott/
Minneapolis

Consumer Magazine Color: 1 Page Or Spread Including Magazine Supplements

278
ART DIRECTOR
Ron Arnold
WRITER
Jamie Seltzer
PHOTOGRAPHER
Terry Heffernan
CLIENT
Sara Lee
AGENCY
Chiat/Day

279
ART DIRECTOR
Michael Smith
WRITER
Jackie End
PHOTOGRAPHER
Cailor/Resnick
CLIENT
Arrow
AGENCY
Chiat/Day

280
ART DIRECTOR
Marty Weiss
WRITERS
Nat Whitten
Steve Salinaro
PHOTOGRAPHER
Dennis Manarchy
CLIENT
Reebok
AGENCY
Chiat/Day

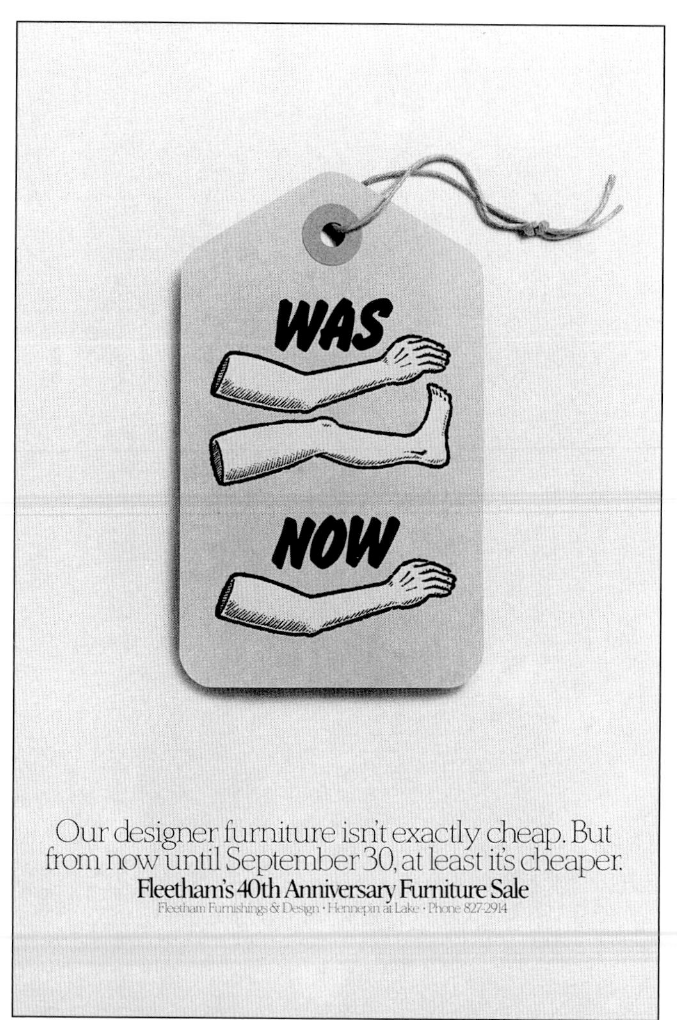

WAS
NOW
Our designer furniture isn't exactly cheap. But from now until September 30, at least it's cheaper.
Fleetham's 40th Anniversary Furniture Sale
Fleetham Furnishings & Design • Hennepin at Lake • Phone 827-2914

277

We think our incredible tasting cheesecake for 200 calories a slice is going to be very popular.
People are already showing some interest. Sara Lee
Light Classics: French Cheesecake, Strawberry French Cheesecake, Chocolate Mousse, Strawberry Mousse.

278

Starch.

No Starch.

Hasn't Arrow always made sure that you had the white shirt you needed to dress up in? Well, now you can loosen your collar, because that's what we've done to ours.

Arrow

279

280

Consumer Magazine Color: 1 Page Or Spread Including Magazine Supplements

281

ART DIRECTOR
Michael Smith

WRITER
Graham Turner

PHOTOGRAPHER
Steve Gross

CLIENT
Arrow

AGENCY
Chiat/Day

282

ART DIRECTOR
Marty Weiss

WRITER
Graham Turner

PHOTOGRAPHER
Dennis Manarchy

CLIENT
Reebok

AGENCY
Chiat/Day

283

ART DIRECTOR
Garrett Jewett

WRITER
Jim Walsh

PHOTOGRAPHER
Ibbetson Cherry

CLIENT
Colombian Coffee

AGENCY
DDB Needham Worldwide

284

ART DIRECTOR
Ron Arnold

WRITER
Nat Whitten

PHOTOGRAPHER
Dennis Chalkin

CLIENT
Reebok

AGENCY
Chiat/Day

We spent the last 75 years making shirts to be proud of.
We spent the last six months making something to cover them up.
To help make the holiday season a little warmer, we designed a bright new collection of sweaters. In 100% cotton and cotton/ramie blend. With strong, clean lines. Bold, vibrant colors. And the quality you'd expect from Arrow. We'd never cover our shirts with anything less.
Arrow

281

Body developed by Kathryn Hamerski, aerobic instructor, Minneapolis, Minnesota.
Foot Support developed by Reebok.
The new Aerobic 4000. With a raised Dynamic Cradle™ for mid and rear-foot stability. A new tubular outsole to cushion each point of impact. And polyurethane straps for lateral and medial forefoot control.
Exceptional comfort. Essential support.
Reebok

282

Colombian coffee is now being served
in the starboard lounge.
The richest coffee in the world.™

100% Colombian Coffee

283

110th and 3rd Avenue, New York City.
Reebok
Basketball
Stick
Midtown
Money
Johnny B.
Willie
King Neil

Consumer Magazine Color: 1 Page Or Spread Including Magazine Supplements

285
ART DIRECTOR
Tracy Wong
WRITER
David Apicella
PHOTOGRAPHER
Aaron Jones
CLIENT
Fibre Trim
AGENCY
Ogilvy & Mather

286
ART DIRECTOR
Leslie Sweet
WRITERS
Nat Whitten
Steve Salinaro
PHOTOGRAPHER
Raymond Meier
CLIENT
Reebok
AGENCY
Chiat/Day

287
ART DIRECTORS
Tod Seisser
Jay Taub
WRITERS
Jay Taub
Stephanie Arnold
PHOTOGRAPHER
Henry Sandbank
CLIENT
Maidenform
AGENCY
Levine Huntley Schmidt & Beaver

288
ART DIRECTOR
Marisa Acocella
WRITERS
Richard Kirshenbaum
Jon Bond
Jon Cranin
PHOTOGRAPHER
Geoff Spear
CLIENT
Personal Condoms
AGENCY
Kirshenbaum & Bond

EUROPEANS KNOW HOW TO LEAD US INTO TEMPTATION.

N E W

Europeans know good food.

They also know that you can't indulge in cakes and pastries if you want to stay on a diet and lose weight.

You have to resist temptation.

Turn away from bread and chocolate. Say "no" to crêpes and croissants.

It isn't easy, but for years Europeans have known that Fibre Trim* can help.

And now there is a new way to help lose weight. Not surprisingly, it's from Fibre Trim, and it's called Fibre Trim* Sparkling FruitTabs.

AND HELP DELIVER US FROM IT.

THE DELICIOUS WAY TO HELP YOU LOSE WEIGHT

Developed in Denmark, Fibre Trim Sparkling FruitTabs are effervescent tablets that make a great-tasting, sparkling clear beverage, in two flavors—orange and mixed berry.

Fibre Trim Sparkling FruitTabs contain fiber. Taken before meals, the fiber helps fill you up and makes you feel less hungry. So you can eat less, and lose weight.

CURB YOUR HUNGER AND EAT LESS

If between-meal hunger pangs plague you, carry Fibre Trim Sparkling FruitTabs with you to make a great-tasting drink — anytime, anywhere.

TAKE IT OFF AND HELP KEEP IT OFF

Fibre Trim Sparkling FruitTabs can help you keep the weight off once you've lost it. It's not magic, of course, but if you make them a part of a sensible diet plan, one that includes the right foods and exercise, you can lose weight. Gradually and safely – the best way to lose weight permanently.

And that, after all, is what dieting is all about.

FIBRE TRIM SPARKLING FRUITTABS

285

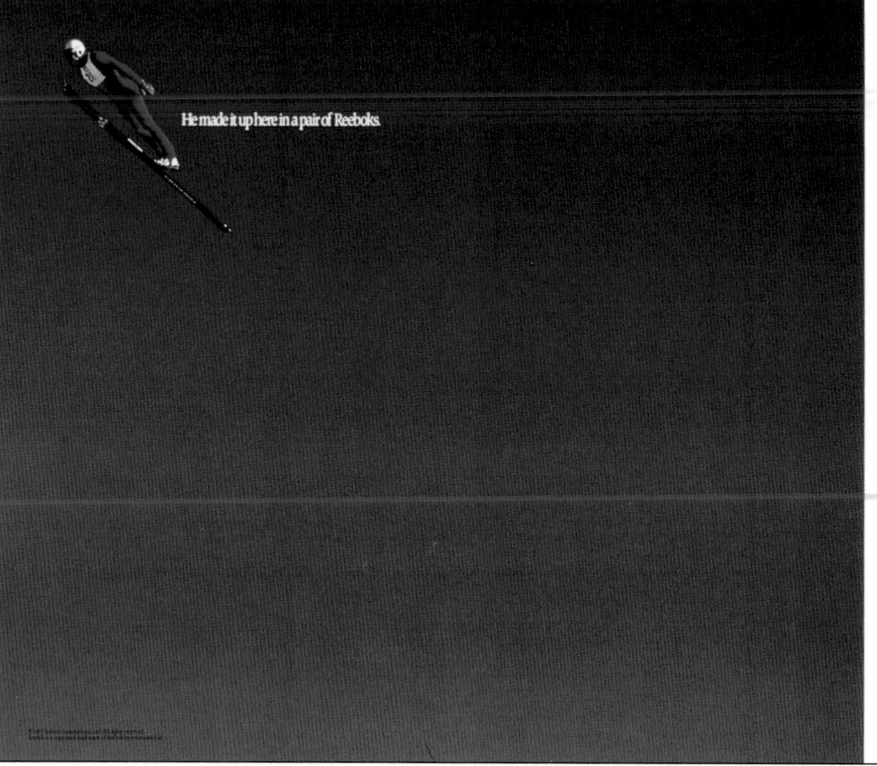

286

"Lingerie reveals more of a woman than just skin. When a woman wears beautiful lingerie it says she likes herself. I think that's sexy. To me, lingerie expresses how she feels. Playful. Romantic. Mysterious. The possibilities are always interesting."
Maidenform offers women over 150 ways to express themselves. Obviously, people are listening.
MAIDENFORM

287

WHO'S BETTER EQUIPPED THAN THE ITALIANS TO DESIGN THE WORLD'S BEST CONDOMS?
That's because Italians have always understood form and design. So it's only natural that they excel when it comes to something as sensitive as condoms. Introducing Personal, the #1 condom brand in Italy for 65 years. Now it's available here, in the United States, and in 7 different varieties including fashion colors.
© Imported by Razi Corporation (516) 932-2121. P.O. Box 755 Manhasset, NY 10030-1710
personal
anatomico
What they're wearing in Italy.

288

Consumer Magazine Color: 1 Page Or Spread Including Magazine Supplements

289
ART DIRECTOR
George Zipparo
WRITER
Carol Turturro
CLIENT
The Dannon Company
AGENCY
HDM

290
ART DIRECTOR
Jerry Torchia
WRITER
Mike Hughes
PHOTOGRAPHER
Scott Barrow
CLIENT
Virginia Division of Tourism
AGENCY
The Martin Agency/
Richmond, VA

291
ART DIRECTORS
Tod Seisser
Irv Klein
WRITERS
Jay Taub
Stephanie Arnold
PHOTOGRAPHER
Henry Sandbank
CLIENT
Maidenform
AGENCY
Levine Huntley Schmidt & Beaver

292
ART DIRECTOR
Mitch Gordon
WRITER
Steve Silver
ARTIST
Leonard Morgan
PHOTOGRAPHER
Dave Jordano
CLIENT
Nichols-Homeshield
AGENCY
Zechman & Associates/
Chicago

It's time we stop taking yogurt for granted. Because while we've been peacefully eating what we thought was completely pure and natural, some yogurt makers have been adding things, like artificial flavorings, artificial coloring, carageenan, modified food starch, sorbic acid, agar and guar gum.

Maybe it's time we start reading labels again.

NO ARTIFICIAL ANYTHING.™

289

This is an advertisement for a resort that's bigger than some states.

It's a place where backpacks and tuxedos are equally welcomed. A place where presidents, from George Washington on, have come to work and to play.

Like all good resorts, this one has swimming pools, tennis courts and world-famous golf courses.

There are, of course, quaint foot-trails here. But there's also the Skyline Drive and the Blue Ridge Parkway. Natural Bridge is here. And Daniel Boone's Wilderness Trail.

Other resorts would be proud to have five stars. This one has millions,

Air-conditioned rooms are available this summer in the Blue Ridge Mountains of Virginia.

all crystal clear in the cool night air.

No corporation owns and operates this resort: it's yours the minute you climb its mountains, walk its valleys or explore its caverns.

We're referring, of course, to the Blue Ridge Mountains and Shenandoah Valley of Virginia, a natural resort that stretches more than 200 miles through some of the most beautiful and historic land in America.

The inhabitants include more than 200 kinds of birds, more than 40 kinds of mammals, and some of the friendliest people on earth. People who speak a language that's basically English, but distinctly their own.

This year, when you consider vacations, consider this. At our unique resort, you'll picnic by gentle waterfalls and breathe in fresh mountain air. You'll be charmed by the hill country hospitality of Charlottesville and Lexington. You'll be captivated by the genius of Jefferson at Monticello and the University of Virginia. But you can't do all of this unless you come here, to the mountains and valleys of Virginia. Where your room is already waiting for you.

For all the facts about Virginia, including information about Mount Vernon, Virginia Beach and Colonial Williamsburg, call or write the Virginia Division of Tourism, Dept. K501, Richmond, VA 23219.

Virginia is for lovers

Discover a new world. Call 1-800-248-4833

290

"Lingerie does a lot for a woman. Not to mention what it does for a man. I love a woman who says how she feels. But I also love a woman who has secrets. In fact, it's what she keeps to herself that says the most about her.
Lingerie. That's a secret she doesn't share with the world. So sometimes you don't find out. But, then again, sometimes you do."
At Maidenform, we offer women over 150 ways to express themselves. Obviously, people are listening.
MAIDENFORM

291

How to sustain a direct blow to the head from a blunt instrument.

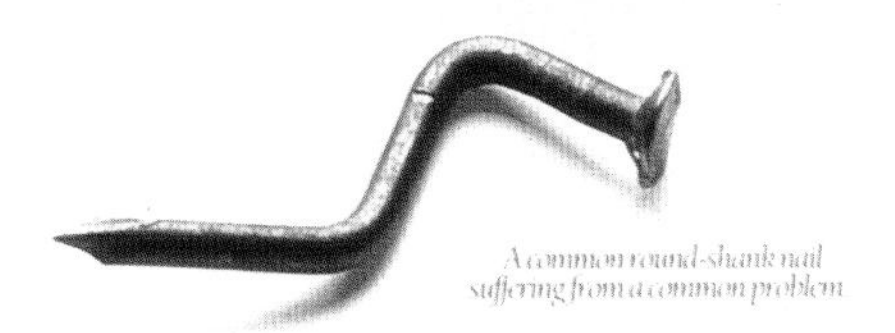

It's a crime.

Too many nails buckle at the knees as soon as they're tapped on the cranium.

So to prevent further headaches, we at Nichols-Homeshield took up our notepads, picked up our hammers, and walloped all sorts of nails at all sorts of angles.

This is what we found out. Bending doesn't occur at the head of the nail, even though that's where the blow falls. The problem lies in the mid-section.

So we redesigned it.

Introducing the world's first trim nail whose shank isn't round, as dictated by tradition: It's triangular.

Without going into the laws of physics, suffice it to say this triangular shape provides three walls of support.

The result is a stronger nail, which in turn means you can work faster with less waste.

Appropriately enough, we've named it the new Bend-Less Aluminum Nail.

It's available to match our eight colors of soffit, rainware and trim finishes, and like other aluminum nails, it's corrosion resistant and economical (about three times as many as steel in every pound). So call us at 1-800-323-2512 (in Illinois, call 1-312-851-5430) for samples, and we'll rush them right out to you. After all, for over 80 years we've bent over backwards just to make sure your nails won't.

The new triangular-shank nail. Uncommonly strong.

The New Bend-Less Aluminum Nail.

homeshield

292

Consumer Magazine Color: 1 Page Or Spread Including Magazine Supplements

293

ART DIRECTOR
Tom Kelly

WRITER
Bill Borders

CLIENT
Blitz-Weinhard Brewing

AGENCY
Borders Perrin & Norrander/Portland, OR

294

ART DIRECTOR
John Horton

WRITER
Tom Jenkins

PHOTOGRAPHER
Ken Griffiths

CLIENT
Volvo

AGENCY
Abbott Mead Vickers/ SMS - London

295

ART DIRECTORS
Jerry Whitley
Sherry Pollack

WRITER
Bill McCullam

PHOTOGRAPHER
Barney Edwards

CLIENT
Waterford Crystal

AGENCY
Ammirati & Puris

296

ART DIRECTOR
Ken Grimshaw

WRITER
John Donnelly

PHOTOGRAPHER
Geoff Senior

CLIENT
Volvo

AGENCY
Abbott Mead Vickers/ SMS - London

A LIGHT BEER DEDICATED TO THE GOOD OLD DAYS WHEN WATERING DOWN A BEER COULD GET YOU SHOT.

While the exact date and place have been lost to history, it is safe to assume that man experienced his first taste of light beer well over 100 years ago. He just didn't happen to know it at the time.

Back then, overly enterprising proprietors – knowing it was often a long time between beer deliveries – devised a way of "stretching their inventory." All it required was an inattentive customer, a partially filled mug of beer and an inconspicuous source of water. Suddenly, the mug would be full; but its contents would be less filling and vaguely less satisfying to the (hopefully) unsuspecting consumer.

THE PENALTY OF PROGRESS.

While this practice might make the modern beer lover wince, it should be pointed out that today's light beers unfortunately taste like they follow the same time-honored tradition all too closely. The chief difference

THE A.B.D.'S OF LIGHT BEER.

Too often, light beer is gulped down unceremoniously like a glass of water. A commentary, no doubt, on the way most light beers are made. And taste. A more revealing procedure is to pause first and sniff the aroma. It should be definite, not vague, with a subtle hop pungence. Next, hold the glass aloft towards a source of light and study the body visually. Look for clarity, but also a richness and only slightly lighter color than regular beer. Reject paleness. The final measure, of course, is drinkability. But sip first. And hold it in your mouth. There should be the true tang of beer, that marvelous hoppy character. With a lingering but not bitter aftertaste. And certainly no watery thinness to dilute your pleasure. Now then, gulp away.

being that the water isn't added behind the bar.

The end result, we believe, is still the same. A lager that is light in body and calories, yes. But one that is also lacking in the most essential quality of all, flavor.

So it is, that when we approached the task of creating a product for the light beer market, we chose not to follow the techniques of the chap standing to the left, but instead adhered to the principles of a more familiar gentleman.

MEET THE HENRY WEINHARD'S OF LIGHT BEERS.

When Henry established our brewery in 1856, he did so with rather definite ideas about the craft of making beer. We rely on these same guidelines in creating Henry's Light.

This means more time must be taken in the brewing, fermenting and ageing than is usual within the beer industry. It also means the ingredients used must be the finest, most costly obtainable: rich, two-row malting barley, and choice Cascade hops.

Additionally, to achieve real beer body, we employ approximately 30% more barley malt than other brewers. And, in order to achieve a richer flavor, our brewmaster adds hops not only during the traditional brewkettle stage but *also* during the leisurely ageing process. So as the beer matures, it acquires a greater presence of our famous Cascade hop. Which means more aroma, more tang, more real beer taste than other light beers.

True, this is all a great deal more painstaking than just adding extra water to a batch of regular Henry's, but the results are a great deal more impressive. And, this way, we are able to sleep nights.

THE ONLY DISAPPOINTMENT MAY BE IN TRYING TO FIND IT.

As with our original Henry's and Henry's Dark, we brew Henry's Light just 500 barrels at a time and only at our small Portland brewery. This results in many advantages regarding control and consistency but, alas, it occasionally results in one disadvantage: limited availability.

Still, while it may require a little extra effort on your part to find Henry's Light, once you do, your search for a beer that is legitimately less filling and fully rewarding will have ended. At which point you will also discover the considerable difference between simply making a good beer light and making a good light beer.

THE BLITZ-WEINHARD BREWERY OF PORTLAND, OREGON

293

CAPACITY: 75 CUBIST FEET.

THE VOLVO 740 TURBO ESTATE. £16,500.

294

At Waterford, we have the world's most advanced technology for making brilliant crystal.
For two centuries, Waterford® stemware has been acknowledged as the world's most brilliant.
Because for two centuries, each piece has been born from a unique mix of molten crystal that must be mouth-blown and cut by hand to bring out the special fire within.
An eight-hour process using iron blowing rods and tongs, pearwood molds, stone cutting wheels, and other tools so well adapted to their tasks that time has suggested few improvements.
It's quite a contrast to the soulless way other crystal is churned out by industrial robots.
And if one day you find yourself in the town of Waterford, we invite you to come by and watch us ply our craft.
WATERFORD
Steadfast in a world of wavering standards.

295

SECURITY EXPRESS
Nationwide Service
THE BANK WON'T BREAK THE VOLVO. AND VICE VERSA.
What you see above is no photographic trick.
The Volvo 740 GL Estate is actually supporting the full weight of a Security Express armoured vehicle – 3.5 tonnes.
The 740 GL's reinforced door pillars, roof bars and rigid steel safety cage can take the strain without so much as a buckle.
Even if the Security Express van was able to carry an extra 2.5 tonnes of gold bullion (worth about £24,000,000), the Volvo could take it.
Though at £13,075 the 740 GL is somewhat less of a financial burden.
In fact £1,065 less than the Audi Avant CC and a hefty £3,155 less than the Mercedes 200T.
A 5-speed gearbox, power steering, central locking, electric front windows and electric door mirrors are all there.
So you can be well equipped in the Volvo without sitting on a fortune.
Even when a fortune's sitting on you.
To: Volvo, Springfield House, Princess Street, Bristol BS3 4EF.
For a brochure, call 0800 400 430 free, or post the coupon.
Mr/Mrs/Miss
Address
Postcode
Tel:
VOLVO 740GL ESTATE. £13,075.

296

Consumer Magazine Color: 1 Page Or Spread Including Magazine Supplements

297
ART DIRECTOR
Jerry Whitley
WRITER
Bill McCullam
PHOTOGRAPHER
Barney Edwards
CLIENT
Waterford Crystal
AGENCY
Ammirati & Puris

298
ART DIRECTOR
Rod Smith
WRITER
Michael Ward
PHOTOGRAPHER
Myron
CLIENT
Foot-Joy
AGENCY
HBM/Creamer - Boston

299
ART DIRECTOR
Bob Phillips
WRITER
Tom Thomas
PHOTOGRAPHER
Cailor/Resnick
CLIENT
Austin Nichols - Wild Turkey Bourbon
AGENCY
Angotti Thomas Hedge

300
ART DIRECTORS
Clem McCarthy
Alain Briere
Arthur Vibert
WRITER
Paul Wolfe
PHOTOGRAPHER
Jeffrey Zwart
CLIENT
BMW of North America
AGENCY
Ammirati & Puris

297

298

There are less expensive bourbons. There are also thinner steaks and smaller cars.

WILD TURKEY

8 years old, 101 proof, pure Kentucky.

TO SEND A GIFT OF WILD TURKEY®/101 PROOF ANYWHERE* CALL 1-800-CHEER UP. *EXCEPT WHERE PROHIBITED. KENTUCKY STRAIGHT BOURBON WHISKEY ALC. BY VOL. 50.5%. AUSTIN NICHOLS DISTILLING CO. LAWRENCEBURG, KY © 1987

299

CIVILIZATION
HAS NEVER
ADVANCED
QUITE SO
RAPIDLY.

It coddles five passengers in an ambience of luxury, while assaulting the road with the ferocity of a race car.

Such is the scope of the BMW 535i.

A luxury sedan for those who've reached civilization's higher echelons with heart and spirit intact.

"To put it bluntly," wrote AutoWeek on the 535i, "this is a car that encourages you to drive the hell out of it."

The encouragement is provided by a race-bred, 3.5-liter, 182-horsepower engine that catapults the 535i from 0 to 60 in 7.4 seconds. Yet, the 535i exercises its power with such civility that, even at pulse-stirring speeds, "it feels stable, comfortable and quiet" (AutoWeek).

Such grace under velocity is technologically explained. Beginning with a widely-emulated, four-wheel independent, double-pivot suspension—now further enhanced by progressive rate springing and gas-pressure shock absorbers.

A microprocessor-based engine management system that couples optimum engine performance with peak fuel efficiency.*

Advanced anti-lock brakes that can mean the difference between having an accident and avoiding it.

And an interior environment that bestows on five adults the blessings of orthopedically-designed leather seats, a power sunroof, and an 8-speaker anti-theft stereo sound system.

Perhaps no greater tribute can be paid to one of the world's fastest sedans than Motor Trend's response: "We were completely won over by the car's charming manners, ease of operation and elegant comfort."

We invite you to share in that experience.

It would be uncivilized of us not to.

THE ULTIMATE DRIVING MACHINE.

*EPA estimated mpg, 28 highway manual transmission. Fuel efficiency figures are for comparison only. Actual mileage may vary, depending on speed, weather and trip length. Highway mileage may be lower. © 1987 BMW of North America, Inc. The BMW trademark and logo are registered.

Consumer Magazine Color: 1 Page Or Spread Including Magazine Supplements

301

ART DIRECTORS
Tony Angotti
Eric David

WRITERS
Mary Knox
Susan Cummings-Walder

PHOTOGRAPHER
Jerry Cailor

CLIENT
Springmaid Sheets

AGENCY
Hill Holliday Connors Cosmopulos

302

ART DIRECTOR
Grant Richards

WRITER
Grant Richards

PHOTOGRAPHER
Randy Miller

CLIENT
Phoenix Marine

AGENCY
The Richards Group/Dallas,

303

ART DIRECTORS
Tony Angotti
Eric David

WRITERS
Mary Knox
Susan Cummings-Walder

PHOTOGRAPHER
Jerry Cailor

CLIENT
Springmaid Sheets

AGENCY
Hill Holliday Connors Cosmopulos

304

ART DIRECTOR
Art Mszanski

WRITER
Neil Drossman

PHOTOGRAPHER
Tim Turner

CLIENT
Einstein Moomjy

AGENCY
Drossman Lehman Marino

301

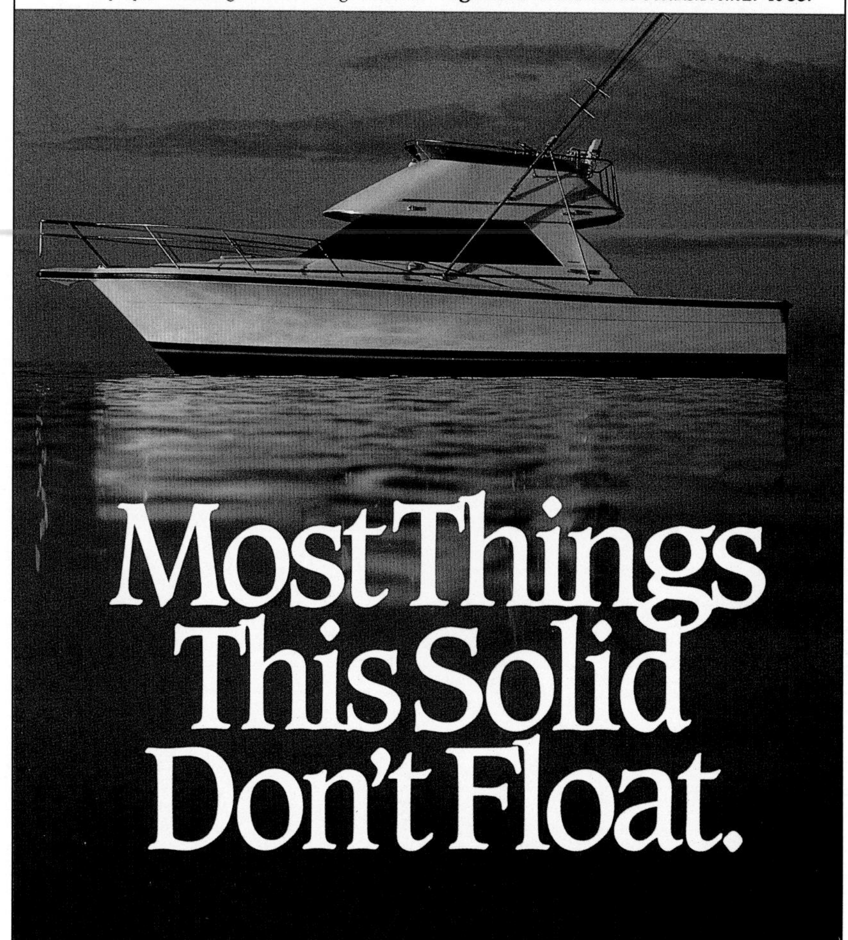

That's our way of saying the new Phoenix 33 is built like a rock. But not just any rock. This one skips across the surface at better than 30 knots.
The key to the Phoenix's rigidity is its patented, one-piece inner-liner, a marvel of engineering that runs the entire length of the boat. Where most builders bolt or glue their inner-liners together, Phoenix builds theirs in one piece, making it inherently stronger.
Every aspect of its construction is, of course, pure Phoenix. No compromises. No shortcuts. Every hatch, every switch, every cleat is precisely where it ought to be.
Up top, there's seating for five on a bridge whose size is unprecedented in a 33-foot sportfisherman. You'll also find 114 square feet of wide-open cockpit.
Add to that a giant galley, a convertible dinette, a spacious shower stall, and a luxurious master stateroom, and you've got 33 feet of solid value.
For more information on the 33 or any Phoenix boat, write Phoenix Marine Enterprises, Box M, 1775 W. Okeechobee, Hialeah, FL 33010, or call (305) 887-5625.
The Phoenix Fleet
Engineered For The World's Oceans. From 27' To 38'.
Most Things This Solid Don't Float.

302

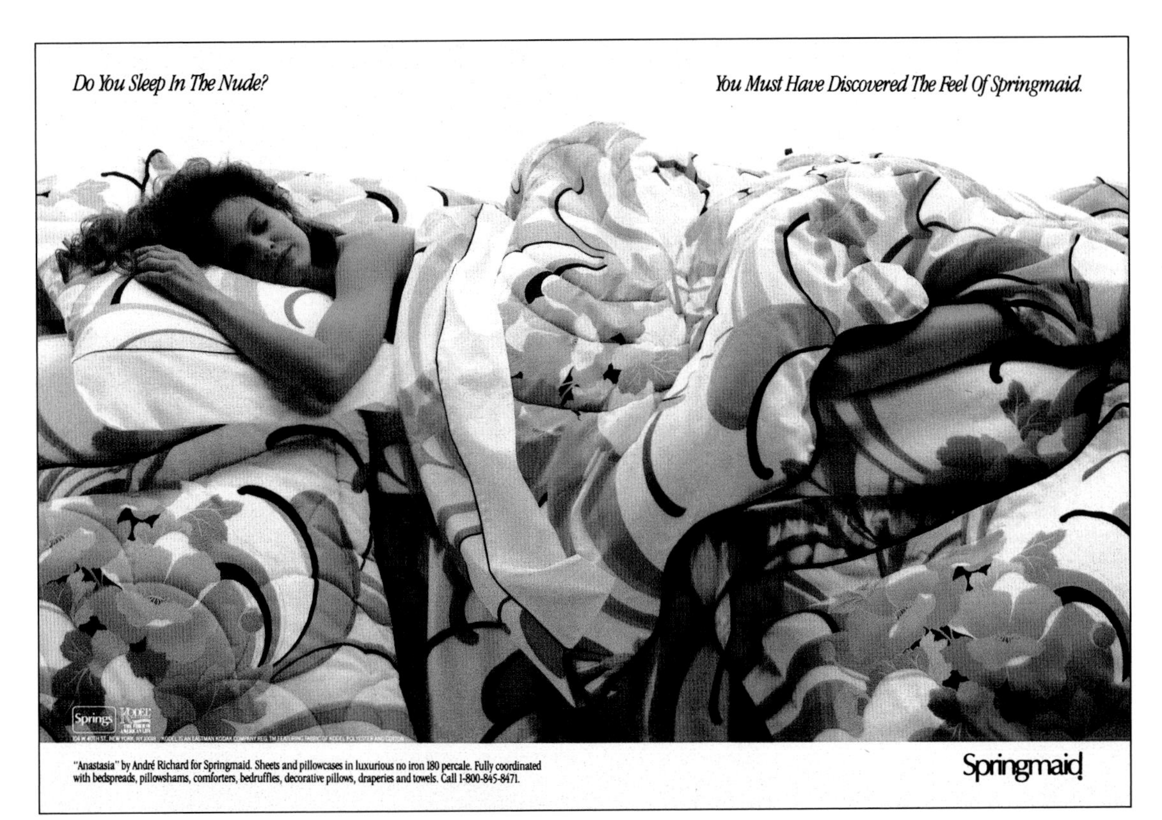
Do You Sleep In The Nude?
You Must Have Discovered The Feel Of Springmaid.
Springs
"Anastasia" by André Richard for Springmaid. Sheets and pillowcases in luxurious no iron 180 percale. Fully coordinated with bedspreads, pillowshams, comforters, bedruffles, decorative pillows, draperies and towels. Call 1-800-845-8471.
Springmaid

303

This Anso V Worry-Free™ Carpet Does Not Come in the Following Popular Colors.
It doesn't come in wine (1975 Bordeaux or any other year), chocolate syrup or mint chocolate chip.
In fact, it doesn't come in beer, blood or butter, sugar or chalk.
It doesn't even come in the old favorites like auto grease or lipstick, dirt or clay.
For this Anso V Worry-Free carpet contains a special built-in barrier that resists stains, soil and static.
So even though it may eat and drink as much as other carpet, it doesn't look it.
What it does look is beautiful. With a thick, plush, velvet Saxony finish you'll take a shimmer to.
Oh by the way, it does come in colors like café, bolder dust, bolero rose, burma beige, fawn, dusty coral and white wing (shown).
And while they may not be as popular as milk, mud or mayonnaise, they sure look a lot better.
So if you'd like a carpet you don't have to worry about, stop by Einstein Moomjy where the only thing you'll have to worry about is picking the right Anso V Worry-Free carpet out of our enormous Anso Collection.
Oh by the way, there's one more thing that won't stick to this carpet. The price. It's been reduced to $26.99 a sq. yd.* from $35.99.
Shoe polish and shortening not included.
Einstein Moomjy.
The Carpet Department Store®
*Padding and installation not included. New York and Whippany stores open Sunday Noon-5.
IN NEW YORK: 150 EAST 58TH ST., (BET. LEXINGTON & THIRD AVENUES) A&D BLDG., (212) 758-0900. STORE OPEN 9:30 AM TO 6:30 PM INCL. SAT., MON. & THURS. TILL 8 PM.
IN NEW JERSEY: PARAMUS, 526 ROUTE 17 (201) 265-1100. N. PLAINFIELD, 934 ROUTE 22 (201) 755-6800. WHIPPANY, 265 ROUTE 10 (201) 887-3600.
LAWRENCEVILLE, 2801 BRUNSWICK PIKE (ALT. U.S. 1) (609) 883-0700. ALL N.J. STORES OPEN DAILY TO 9 PM, SAT. TO 6 PM. WE ACCEPT VISA, MASTERCARD AND AMERICAN EXPRESS.
Anso V Worry-Free

304

Consumer Magazine
Color: 1 Page Or Spread
Including Magazine
Supplements

305
ART DIRECTOR
Larry Bennett
WRITER
John Russo
PHOTOGRAPHER
Randy Miller
CLIENT
Norwegian Cruise Lines
AGENCY
McKinney & Silver/
Raleigh,NC

306
ART DIRECTOR
David Page
WRITER
Joe Nagy
PHOTOGRAPHER
Dennis Manarchy
CLIENT
Harley-Davidson
AGENCY
Carmichael Lynch/
Minneapolis

307
ART DIRECTOR
Ian Potter
WRITER
Rob Janowski
CLIENT
Booker Health
AGENCY
FCO/London

308
ART DIRECTORS
Clem McCarthy
Marcus Kemp
William Hartwell
Alain Briere
WRITERS
Paul Wolfe
Rav Friedel
PHOTOGRAPHER
Jeffrey Zwart
CLIENT
BMW of North America
AGENCY
Ammirati & Puris

LIKE ALL GREAT CITIES, IT HAS THEATRE, RESTAURANTS AND SHOPPING. IT EVEN HAS STREETS AND TAXIS.

The Norway – as long as the Empire State Building is tall. And she stands just as tall when it comes to elegance and tradition.

The Grand Hotel of the Caribbean. See a show in our Saga Theatre. Shop. Stop by a neighborhood pub. Take a stroll down the beautiful boulevards which run the length of The Norway. One is called Fifth Avenue; the other is the Champs Elysées. Then, there are our playgrounds. With racquetball, aerobics, swimming, skeet shooting. Even a driving range. Ask your travel agent about our city on the sea.

Oh yes, the taxis. They'll take you from The Norway onto some beautiful Caribbean islands. And no, you don't even have to tip the drivers.

NORWEGIAN CRUISE LINE.
Name
Address
City
State
Zip
For a free cruise guide, just mail this coupon to NCL, P.O. Box 7715, Itasca, Illinois 60143. Ships' Registry: Bahamas.

305

The Less You Take With You, The More You Bring Back.

When it comes to building a touring motorcycle, most motorcycle manufacturers would have you believe that more is better. More cylinders. More computers. More gadgets.

Harley-Davidson® offers a simpler philosophy. It's based on the belief that complexity doesn't add to the touring experience. A great motorcycle does. A motorcycle, for example, like the Electra Glide® Classic.

It's built around 80 cubic inches of V² Evolution® engine. Its performance is complemented by superbly engineered braking and suspension systems. And enhanced with a comfortable seat, floorboards, and one of the best sound systems in motorcycling.

But the essence of a Harley-Davidson touring bike transcends the mere mechanical. When you ride one, you're part of an experience known only by other Harley® riders. And we'll make it official when you buy a new Harley-Davidson. You'll get a free one year membership to the Harley Owners Group.® As a member, you'll be invited to rides, rallies, and receptions all over the country. And you'll share an on-the-road camaraderie with over 70,000 other H.O.G.® members.

When you look at a Harley, you're looking beyond machinery. Underneath it all, and inside yourself, you will discover what it means to ride a Harley-Davidson. As far as gadgets go, you'll take less along. But no other motorcycle in the world lets you bring as much back.

Things Are Different On A Harley.

306

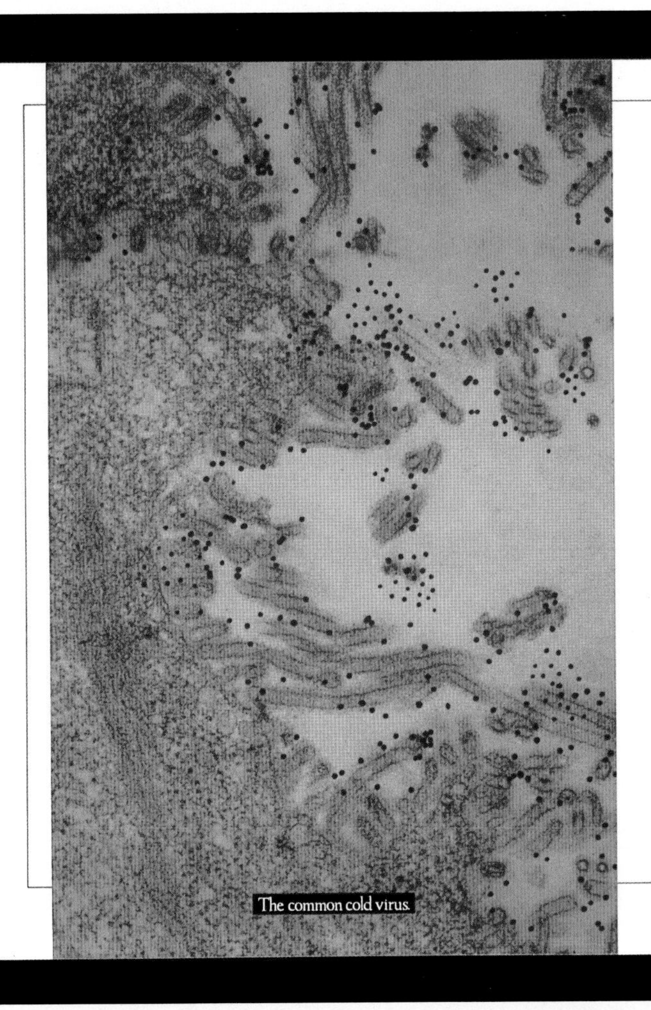
The common cold virus.

No wonder they say feed a cold, you're eating for 6 million.

Unfortunately Healthcrafts produce vitamins and minerals, not miracles.

There is no cure for the common cold. You just have to be patient while your natural antibodies fight the virus.

But even in a cold war the army marches on its stomach.

Your body needs the vitamin C in food to maintain its immune system, while vitamin A on the other hand, is essential for healthy skin including the lining of your nose and throat.

Normally you'd get sufficient amounts from your everyday diet, however a cold often means you lose your healthy appetite.

And aspirin, cough medicine and jugs of cordial aren't exactly brimming with vitamins.

So it's not surprising that more people are finding that Healthcrafts food supplements aren't to be sniffed at.

They're available from Holland & Barrett, good health food stores and leading chemists.

307

SCULPTED FROM THE LAWS OF PHYSICS, NOT THE WHIMS OF FASHION.
BMW

A perusal of the motorcycle world quickly reveals what the whims of fashion have wrought: mass-produced, look-alike machines, created as much to bolster the rider's self-image as to enhance the joy of riding.

The laws of physics, on the other hand, have produced something far rarer and far less transitory: the BMW K75S. A stunning European sport bike whose real beauty lies in the riding.

To that end, BMW engineers have perfected the K75S's liquid-cooled, fuel-injected 3-cylinder engine. A power source proclaimed by Motorcyclist to be "as smooth as anything on the market."

An engine whose broad power band makes touring equally easy, whether on the autobahn or in the Alps.

Meanwhile, the rider exercising this abundance of power is the beneficiary of a frame-mounted fairing whose design emerged from relentless hours in BMW's wind tunnel. A design that affords you a cool indifference to foul weather as well as an increase in the K75S's overall performance.

Finally, in experiencing the results of a taut sports suspension—a pure product of applied physics—he will see exactly why the editors of both Cycle and Motorcyclist call the K75S "the best-handling BMW ever."

All with something else not exactly fashionable in motorcycling: a 3-year, limited warranty—the longest in the industry.*

Which makes the decision to buy a K75S anything but a whim.

THE LEGENDARY MOTORCYCLES OF GERMANY.

308

Consumer Magazine Color: 1 Page Or Spread Including Magazine Supplements

309

ART DIRECTOR
Yvonne Sumter

WRITER
Boris Damast

PHOTOGRAPHER
Arthur Massey

CLIENT
Conga International Foods

AGENCY
Saatchi & Saatchi/
Melbourne

310

ART DIRECTORS
Clem McCarthy
Marcus Kemp
William Hartwell
Alain Briere

WRITERS
Paul Wolfe
Rav Friedel

PHOTOGRAPHER
Jeffrey Zwart

CLIENT
BMW of North America

AGENCY
Ammirati & Puris

311

ART DIRECTOR
Betsy Nathane

WRITERS
Theresa Aycock
Tim Braybrooks

PHOTOGRAPHER
Paul Sanders

CLIENT
VLI Corporation

AGENCY
keye/donna/pearlstein -
Los Angeles

312

ART DIRECTOR
Mark Johnson

WRITER
Bill Miller

PHOTOGRAPHER
Randy Miller

CLIENT
Lee Jeans

AGENCY
Fallon McElligott/
Minneapolis

As harsh as it sounds we have to
turn our back on the average olive.
OLIO SASSO
Olio Sasso from Italy. We've been turning olives into oil for one hundred and twenty years.
Saatchi BCG 006/DPS

309

310

CHANCES ARE YOU WEREN'T AN EXPERT WHEN YOU FIRST PICKED OUT YOUR CONDOM.

A little red-faced perhaps, but you went ahead and chose it.
You called it a rubber (or worse). And no teenage wallet was complete without one.
But you've changed a lot since then, and so has the condom.
The Today® condom is just what it says it is. A condom for today.
It's contoured, for comfort.
It's passed strength tests way beyond the accepted standards, for reliability.
It's ultra-thin, for sensitivity.
And it's available either non-lubricated, or with a standard or spermicidal lubricant.
Your old condom was fine, believe us.
But that was then.
And this is Today.
Today
Today
LUBRICATED

© 1987 VLI Corp. From the makers of the Today Sponge.

311

Be seen in all the right places.

No matter where you are, when you're wearing Lee® Leen Jeans, you'll be seen in all the right places. Fit tight, in stone washed or frosted indigo. You have nothing to hide. Leen Jeans Lee The brand that fits.

312

Consumer Magazine Color: 1 Page Or Spread Including Magazine Supplements

313

ART DIRECTOR
Frank Haggerty

WRITER
Kerry Casey

PHOTOGRAPHER
Marvy!

CLIENT
Normark/Rapala

AGENCY
Carmichael Lynch/
Minneapolis

314

ART DIRECTORS
John Cabalka
Mario Donna

WRITER
Paul Keye

ARTISTS
Margo Nahas Vigon
Bob Commander
Kirk Botero
James Henry
Roger Loveless
Scot Lowry
Kevin Hulsey
Lawrence Duke
Kim Whitesides
Dugald Stermer
Ken Rosenberg
Joyce Kitchey
Ellery Knight
Will Nelson
Jae Wagoner
Ron Sweet
Lisa French
Steve Jones

PHOTOGRAPHERS
Morton Beebe
Gary Sato
Jeffrey Nadler
David Leach
Michael Ruppert
Kathleen Norris Cook
Christopher Springman
Vince Streano
Larry Prosor
David Muench
Baron Wolman

CLIENT
State of California

AGENCY
keye/donna/pearlstein -
Los Angeles

315

ART DIRECTOR
Yvonne Sumter

WRITER
Boris Damast

PHOTOGRAPHER
Arthur Massey

CLIENT
Conga International Foods

AGENCY
Saatchi & Saatchi/
Melbourne

316

ART DIRECTOR
Doug Byrnes

WRITER
Mike Coulter

DESIGNER
Doug Byrnes

PHOTOGRAPHER
Jerry Oke

CLIENT
Oddbins

AGENCY
HDM Horner Collis &
Kirvan/London

©1988 Normark Corp.
Rapala
SHAD RAP
Landing net not included.
Six years ago, we introduced the Shad Rap to fishermen. "Expect big things," we told you.
To date, no lure ever introduced has sold faster. Which must mean you not only expect big
things from the Shad Rap, but you catch big things with it, too. Available in No. 5, 7, 8, 9.
Rapala
Normark

313

314

Many are picked.

Few are chosen.

Olio Sasso from Italy. We've been turning olives into oil for one hundred and twenty years.

Saatchi BCG 005/DPS

THEY'VE COME A LONG WAY.

Not so very long ago, Australian wines were virtually unknown in this country.

And those that were, could hardly be described as ripper, bonzer or beaut. In fact some were downright crook.

Consisting mainly of burly, thick-set reds known as 'Tonic Burgundies' and the odd fortified wine, their appeal was, shall we say, somewhat limited.

Yet, within the last two decades, Australian wines have improved in leaps and bounds.

New production methods, a shift to cooler growing areas, and the introduction of more noble grape varieties (such as Cabernet Sauvignon, Chardonnay, Riesling and Semillion,) has led to a radical change.

Creating fine wines in a host of styles.

Now, because of the comparative weakness of the Australian economy, Oddbins can offer you many of these sensational wines at prices you'll find more than fair dinkum.

So that's where Australians get the corks for their hats from.

At Oddbins we have over 25 different Australian wines. Here's just a taste.

Barossa Valley Estates Semillon/Chenin Blanc 1986 £2.69
'The citric bouquet and rich buttery-fruity palate is a delight. By rights Oddbins should sell their stock quickly.' Jane MacQuitty, The Times.

Barossa Valley Estates Shiraz/Cabernet 1984 £2.69
'Garnet red colour, and warm, spicy, cedary nose backed up by lots of soft fruit is a revelation.' The Times.

Seaview Chardonnay 1986 £3.49
'Given a little time in oak before bottling, this Chardonnay has a brilliant light colour, an attractive liveliness and bags of flavour. This will certainly find a place on my wine rack.' I. Vaughan-Hughes MW.

Koonunga Hill 1984 £3.89
'We liked its dark ruby colour and remarkably long berry finish, its soft tannin and definite structure.' P. Levy The Observer.

Orlando Chardonnay 1986 £3.99
'A remarkable wine - that consistently wins top trophies at the wine shows. The attractive aroma shows sweet toasted oak and ripe fruit, and has a lot of charm. Top class winemaking.' Tony Lord, Decanter Magazine.

"How they can ship these wines from Australia and still make a profit is a mystery."
Jane MacQuitty. The Times.

Let's all have a good wine.

Of course it should come as no surprise to find Australia's best wines prominently displayed at Oddbins. (It would be a shame to keep them outback.)

They exemplify our philosophy of offering great wines at affordable prices. From wherever they may come.

Those we've unearthed in Italy destroy once and for all its image as a plonk producing country.

Our wines from the sunny state of California have been showered with superlatives.

Not forgetting our unforgettable Bordeaux, Loire, Rioja and Port.

In all we have over 500 wines to offer.

And offers such as, buy 6 bottles get a 7th free on selected ranges.

What's more, we can arrange sale or return, account facilities and in some cases, free delivery.

We'll even help with your party planning.

Oddbins. It isn't a job, it's a vocation.

As you've probably gathered by now, the last thing Oddbins is, is an off-licence.

We're more, a de-snobbed wine merchant really.

Everyone gets the same welcome whether it's for a 4 pack of beer or a case of Krug.

At Oddbins, you'll find staff who are genuinely interested and knowledgeable.

(And well informed staff, tend to create well-informed customers.)

One of our vintage managers started as a customer and enthused so much about the wine he decided to join the company.

·THE·ODDBINS·OFFER·

Q: Why are Oddbins customers like Boomerangs?
A: Because they keep coming back. No wonder with offers like this. Buy the superb Aussie wines listed and get them for just £15.00. (Normal price £16.75) It's a marvellous introduction to the delights of down under. Offer subject to availability and must end 30th June 1987.

·MADE·IN·AUSTRALIA·

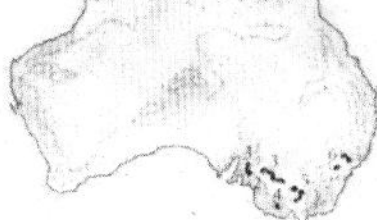

We're proud that over 60% of our managers have passed the Wine and Spirit Diploma which is one step below the coveted Master of Wine.

While all new staff are expected to attend and graduate from recognised wine courses.

(Employees at other places we could name often have only one qualification, nimble fingers on a cash till.)

Even the wine descriptions on our shelves are written by staff, with observations on each specific wine.

We also organise regular tastings for people on both sides of the counter.

When all's said and done, we believe Oddbins staff are one of our best products, and advertisements.

Come along and confirm this for yourself. You can also check out our current promotions on Australian wines.

You won't have to turn the place upside down to find them.

·O·D·D·B·I·N·S·

Consumer Magazine Color: 1 Page Or Spread Including Magazine Supplements

317
ART DIRECTOR
Ron Brown
WRITER
David Abbott
PHOTOGRAPHER
Steve Cavalier
CLIENT
Sainsbury's
AGENCY
Abbott Mead Vickers/ SMS - London

318
ART DIRECTOR
Gary Goldsmith
WRITER
Neal Gomberg
DESIGNER
Gary Goldsmith
PHOTOGRAPHER
Gil Cope
CLIENT
Knoll International
AGENCY
Goldsmith/Jeffrey

319
ART DIRECTOR
Michael McLaughlin
WRITER
Stephen Creet
PHOTOGRAPHER
Tim Saunders
CLIENT
Birks
AGENCY
MacLaren Advertising/ Toronto

320
ART DIRECTOR
David Page
WRITERS
Ron Sackett
Joe Nagy
PHOTOGRAPHER
Dennis Manarchy
CLIENT
Harley-Davidson
AGENCY
Carmichael Lynch/ Minneapolis

317

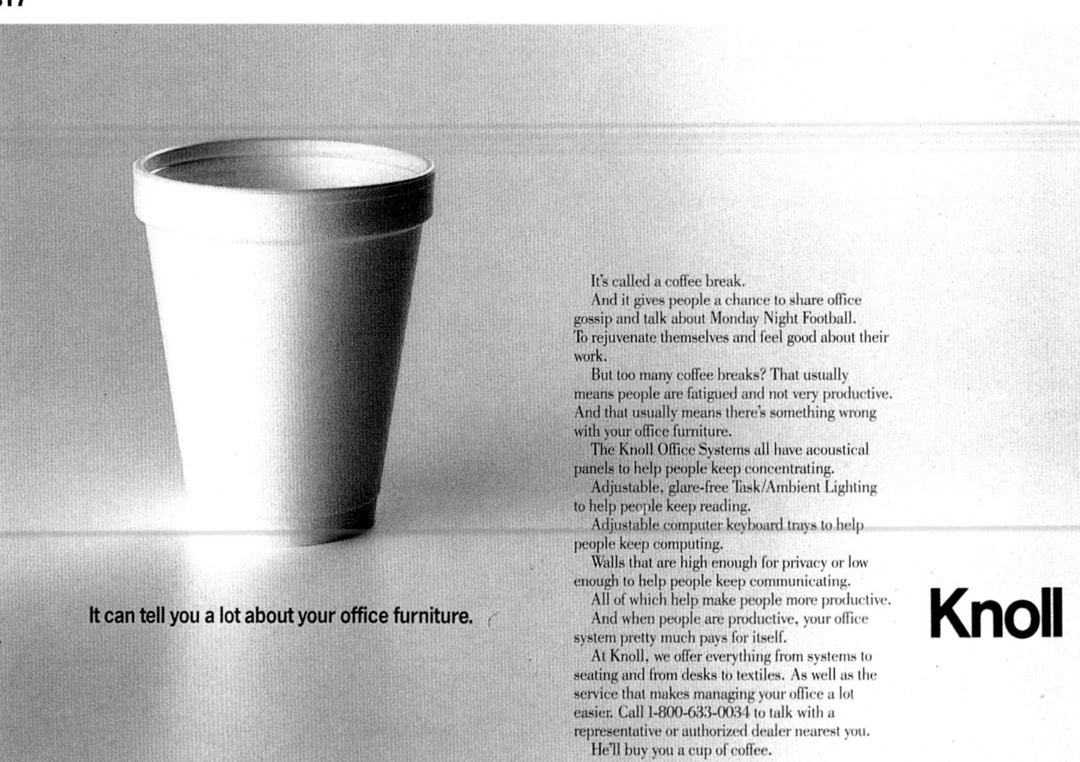

318

Birks Carries A Full Range Of Word Processing Equipment.

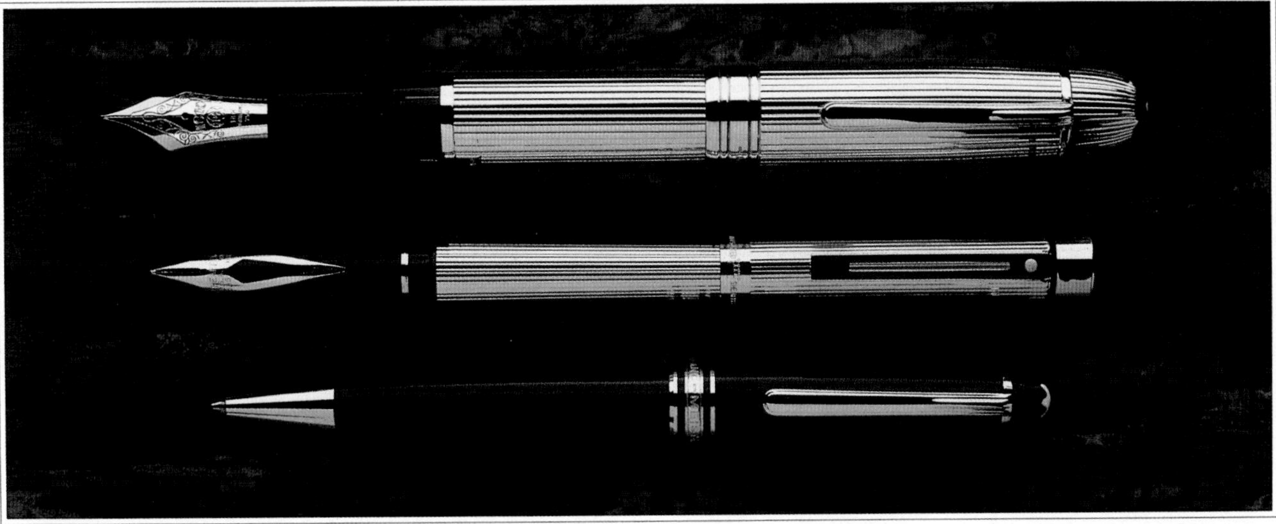

Birks has an impressive selection of compact format word processors. Or as they're ordinarily called: pens. However there's nothing ordinary about these finely crafted, beautifully balanced instruments for writing. Some are inlaid with gold, many are worth thousands of dollars, all are exquisite examples of the world's finest craftsmanship.

As with everything in Birks, they represent the ideal combination: contemporary design and traditional quality. So if you're lucky enough to get a pen or anything else from Birks, congratulations. You really have something to write home about.

Only at BIRKS

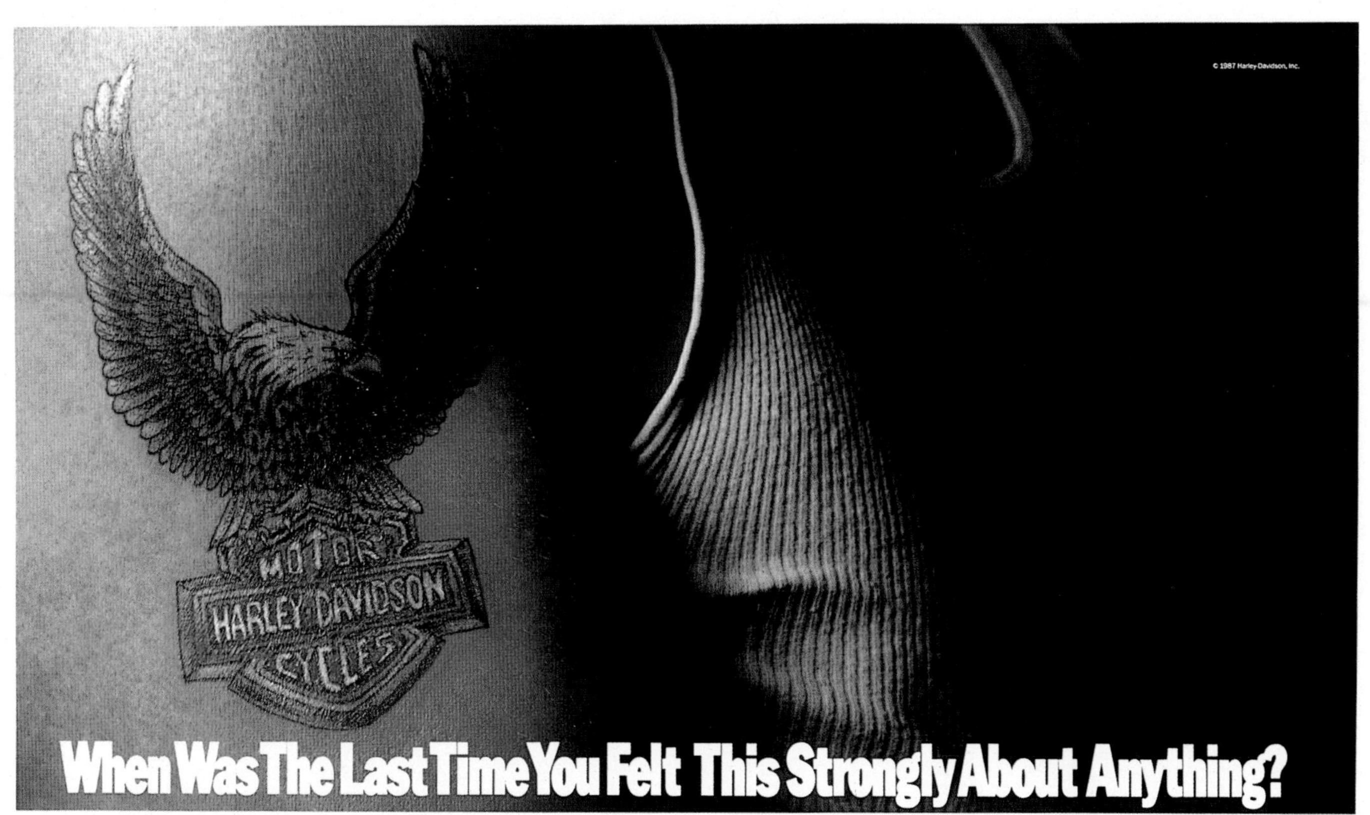

© 1987 Harley-Davidson, Inc.
MOTOR
HARLEY-DAVIDSON
CYCLES
When Was The Last Time You Felt This Strongly About Anything?

Wake up in the morning, and life picks up where it left off. You do what has to be done. Use what it takes to get there. And what once seemed exciting has now become part of the numbing routine. It all begins to feel the same.

Except when you've got a Harley-Davidson.* Something strikes a nerve. The heartfelt thunder rises up, refusing to become part of the background. Suddenly, things are different. Clearer. More real. As they should have been all along.

The feeling is personal. It affects everyone a little differently. For some, owning a Harley* is a statement of individuality. For others, owning one means being a part of a home-grown legacy that was born in a tiny Milwaukee shed in 1903. Regardless of the reason, more people are getting to know the feeling. Harley-Davidson has reemerged as the number one selling brand of super heavyweight motorcycles in the U.S.A.*

To the uninitiated, a Harley-Davidson motorcycle is often associated with a certain look, a certain sound. Anyone who owns one will tell you it's much more than that. Riding a Harley changes you from within.

The effect is permanent. Maybe it's time you started feeling this strongly.

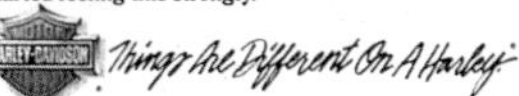

We support the AMA and recommend you wear a helmet and protective gear while riding.
*New motorcycle registrations over 850cc, as per R.L. Polk and Co., Sept. 1987 YTD.

Consumer Magazine Color: 1 Page Or Spread Including Magazine Supplements

321

ART DIRECTOR
Pat Burnham

WRITER
Bill Miller

PHOTOGRAPHERS
Craig Perman
Marvy!

CLIENT
Jack Daniels

AGENCY
Fallon McElligott/
Minneapolis

322

ART DIRECTOR
Mark Johnson

WRITERS
Tom McElligott
Bruce Bildsten

PHOTOGRAPHERS
Angela Fisher
Robert Ammirati

CLIENT
Bloomingdale's

AGENCY
Fallon McElligott/
Minneapolis

323

ART DIRECTOR
Frank Haggerty

WRITER
Kerry Casey

PHOTOGRAPHER
Rod Pierce

CLIENT
Normark/Rapala

AGENCY
Carmichael Lynch/
Minneapolis

324

ART DIRECTOR
Peter Sutherland

WRITER
Steve Dodds

CLIENT
DuPont

AGENCY
Young & Rubicam/Sydney

"Do you think Frank and Ed ever had a Tennessee Cooler?"
"Apparently not."
WITH ALL the coolers out there these days, things are getting a little crowded on the front porch. It's hard to tell the locals from the strangers.
We've been here since 1866. And if you want a taste of what life on the front porch is really all about, take a swallow of Jack Daniel's Tennessee Cooler.
This light, clean, carbonated concoction is Jack Daniel's answer when the back of your throat asks for something to wash down a long, hot day. Not too sweet. Not too tart.
Pop one open and take your first swallow.
Life isn't so hard after all.
JACK DANIEL'S TENNESSEE COOLER
JACK DANIEL'S
Tennessee
COOLER

321

A Moroccan tribesman labors for six to twelve months to make a rug. Unfortunately, we were about to learn, the task of acquiring one of them can be nearly as difficult.

We had dispatched a buyer to Marakkech, the heart of Morocco's rug trade, to find some very special rugs. After seeing almost 900, he had found scores of beautiful rugs. But no extraordinary ones.

He had no choice but to head straight for the source, across the desert by Land Rover to the tiny tribal villages in the High Atlas Mountains.

As it turned out, the rugs came to him.

In front of the Land Rover there suddenly appeared a mysterious Moroccan tribesman on a camel, his lap draped with what was perhaps the most remarkable rug our buyer had ever seen.

The tribesman had several more like it, but they were at his tent, which could only be reached by a bumpy three-hour camel ride into the Atlas foothills.

Fortunately, the rugs he found there were well worth the saddle sores. But, then again, going out of our way is nothing new to us at Bloomingdale's.

Because we believe that the only way to make our stores unique is to make our wares unique. Every buying trip we make is an adventure.

So you really shouldn't be surprised that after a dinner of lamb "mechoui" roasted over an open fire, and some rather heated haggling, those extraordinary rugs were finally ours.

However, we're sad to say, this story doesn't have a happy ending.

There was still a three-hour camel ride back to Marakkech ahead of him.

"This rug is beautiful. Where can I find more?" I said. "Have you ever ridden a camel?" He replied.

bloomingdale's
No one goes as far as we do.

322

How to get to a fish. One Shad Rap at a time.

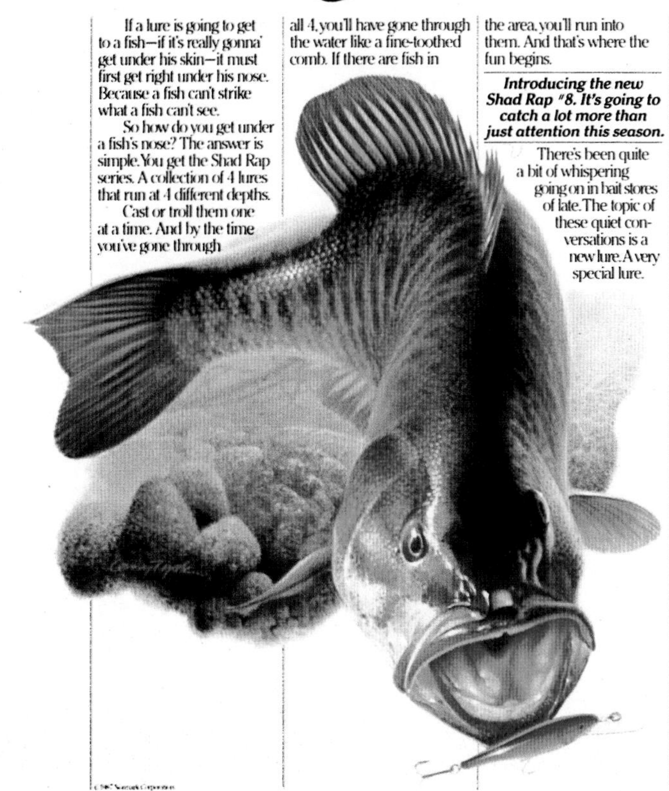

If a lure is going to get to a fish—if it's really gonna' get under his skin—it must first get right under his nose. Because a fish can't strike what a fish can't see.

So how do you get under a fish's nose? The answer is simple. You get the Shad Rap series. A collection of 4 lures that run at 4 different depths.

Cast or troll them one at a time. And by the time you've gone through all 4, you'll have gone through the water like a fine-toothed comb. If there are fish in the area, you'll run into them. And that's where the fun begins.

Introducing the new Shad Rap #8. It's going to catch a lot more than just attention this season.

There's been quite a bit of whispering going on in bait stores of late. The topic of these quiet conversations is a new lure. A very special lure.

Some say casting one is like casting a magic spell on a fish. While others dismiss all this chatter as just another fish story.

Well the rumors are true. This new lure has arrived. It's the Shad Rap #8. And in the tradition of the three Shad Raps that have preceded it, this one is destined for greatness.

So remember, if you're looking for a lazy afternoon of fishing, you should be looking for a different lure. If not, then by all means continue reading.

How to work 4 Shad Raps like a search party for fish.

When you're fishing, you can't wait for the fish to find you. Instead, you have to find the fish.

And now there's a complete line of lures designed to do just that. The Shad Rap series.

Begin by casting the #5. As you bring it in, you'll be working 6-8 feet of water.

If you don't move any fish there, tie on the #7. It swims at 8-10 feet. To go a little deeper, there's the new #8. It takes you down 10-12 feet. And finally, there's the #9. For those days when the fish are 12-14 feet deep.

How do we know the precise depth these lures run at? The answer is simple: we make a very precise lure.

Every Shad Rap is hand-tuned and tank-tested. And every Shad Rap is carefully designed for "neutral buoyancy." Which means the lure reaches its designed depth and then runs at that depth during the retrieve.

How to fish Shad Raps from top to bottom.

The #5 runs at 6-8 feet.

The #7 runs at 8-10 feet.

The NEW #8 runs at 10-12 feet.

The #9 runs at 12-14 feet.

Whereas most other crankbaits spend the majority of their retrieve either diving or rising.

If you don't have all 4 Shad Raps, you don't know what you're missing.

Without the complete line of Shad Raps, you may be missing that big bass in 8 feet of water. Or those walleyes over the rock pile at 14 feet.

You see, the Shad Rap series work through the water like a seine—each lure covering a certain depth. But without all 4 lures, there's a hole in your net. And the fish slips through unnoticed.

So get out to your favorite tackle store and pick up all 4 Shad Raps. And then, on one of those days when you can't find a fish to save your life, one of those lures is going to take you where the action is.

Please send me:
- ☐ How To Fish A Rapala By The Book: Secrets for taking more and bigger fish ($2.50)
- ☐ Rapala Fishing Guide ($3.95)
- ☐ How to Clean A Mess of Fish ($2.50)
- ☐ All of the above ($5)

Send to:
Normark Corporation
1710 East 78th Street
Minneapolis, MN 55423

Name
Address
City
State Zip

RAPALA
NORMARK

323

HOW MANY DRINKS DOES IT TAKE BEFORE YOUR CARPET TURNS UGLY?

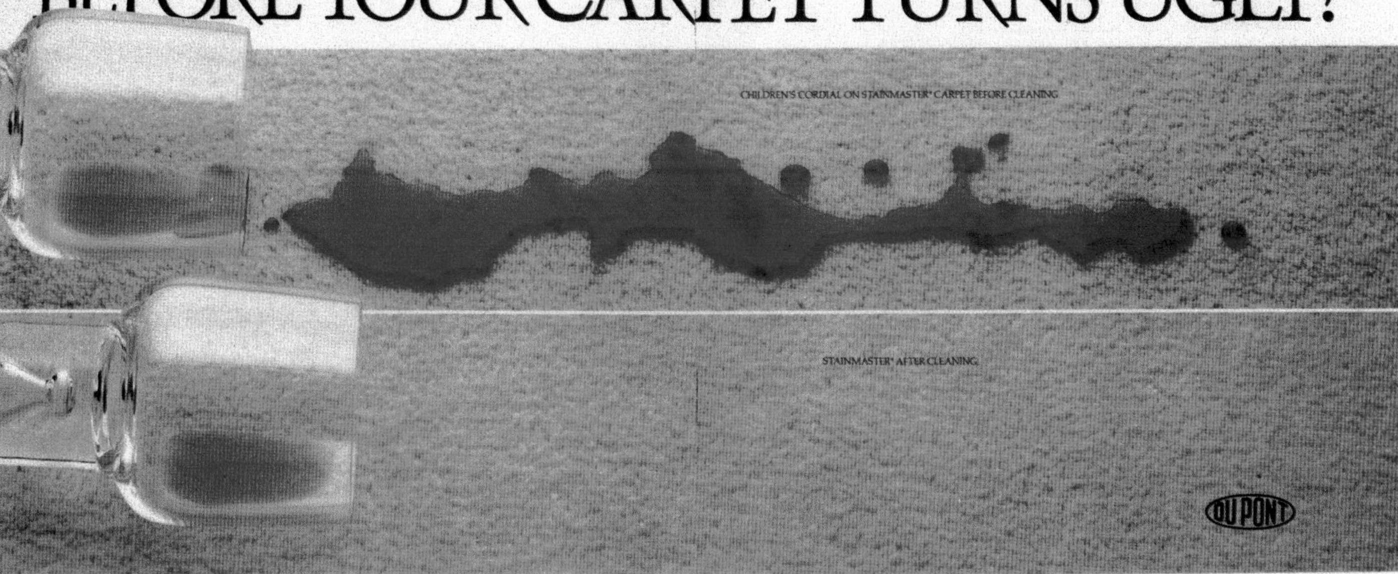
CHILDREN'S CORDIAL ON STAINMASTER® CARPET BEFORE CLEANING.
STAINMASTER® AFTER CLEANING.
DU PONT

Sooner or later, your carpet gets to sample the drinks you do.

After all, it doesn't take much to topple your favourite tipple.

And it doesn't take many drinks before your carpet turns ugly.

Unless, as you may have surmised, you have a certified Stainmaster® carpet.

We poured a drink on the Stainmaster® carpet above.

We then cleaned the carpet with plain water.

You can see the result.

The secret is in the fibre.

Most spills can easily be removed with water and a sponge.

Letting your Stainmaster® carpet retain its look of unabashed luxury.

We're so confident, we give Stainmaster® a full five year guarantee against common household food and drink stains.

And spell it out on a special guarantee form.

And, as you'll see when you read the guarantee, we match it with one against wear.

As further guarantee for the quality of Stainmaster® carpets, we are rather strict with those chosen to manufacture them.

All must conform to our rigid quality standards.

And to make sure they do, we constantly check them both in the factories, and at random off the showroom floor.

Stainmaster® carpets are available in a range of truly wondrous textures and colours.

From Australia's finest mills, such as Hycraft, Homfray, Godfrey Hirst, Redbook, Minster and Invicta.

DU PONT CERTIFIED STAINMASTER® CARPET

DPT 1017L ® = Du Pont registered trademark.

DPT 1017R Y&R MELB

324

Consumer Magazine Color: 1 Page Or Spread Including Magazine Supplements

325
ART DIRECTOR
Steve Dunn
WRITER
Tim Delaney
PHOTOGRAPHER
Graham Cornthwaite
CLIENT
Linguaphone
AGENCY
Leagas Delaney Partnership/London

326
ART DIRECTOR
Bob Barrie
WRITER
Jarl Olsen
DESIGNER
Bob Barrie
PHOTOGRAPHER
Rick Dublin
CLIENT
Hush Puppies Shoe Company
AGENCY
Fallon McElligott/ Minneapolis

327
ART DIRECTOR
Steve Dunn
WRITER
Tim Delaney
PHOTOGRAPHER
Graham Cornthwaite
CLIENT
Linguaphone
AGENCY
Leagas Delaney Partnership/London

328
ART DIRECTOR
David Martin
WRITER
Richard Middendorf
PHOTOGRAPHER
Cailor/Resnick
CLIENT
IBM
AGENCY
Lord Geller Federico Einstein

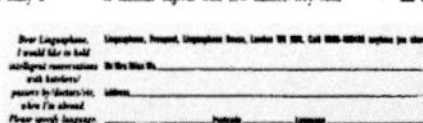

325

326

The world is shrinking. Shouldn't your vocabulary be expanding?

According to official figures, more than 21 million British people have travelled abroad in the past 12 months alone.

Yet statistics from the boys at the Education Ministry show that our interest in learning languages is actually falling.

Which must mean that more and more of us who arrive in other countries are reduced to communicating in language equivalent to baby talk.

For tourists this is, of course, all part of the 'fun.' For businessmen and women, however, it represents that deadliest of all the commercial sins.

It's uncompetitive.

Not surprisingly, large numbers of people with business interests abroad are now turning to Linguaphone for help. And with good reason.

Our method is based on two simple principles. One: people learn more quickly when they're enjoying themselves. And two: they learn more easily when they have listened to a language *before* reading about it.

Now we know that business people don't always have time to spend on immersion courses.

So our Minilab course gives you the freedom to learn when and where you like, and at a pace you find comfortable.

We can't claim it's easy. We wish we could. Having said that, the Linguaphone method is used to teach 30 different languages in over 100 countries.

No fewer than 27 British universities employ it. As do many of the biggest companies in the world, Ford, Unilever, BP, American Express and British Airways among them.

If your firm is expanding its overseas operations, ring Karina Mellinger, our Business Sales Manager, on 01-741 1655.

And if you doubt the importance of learning another language, she might well invoke the success of another island about the size of ours.

It's called Japan.

LINGUAPHONE

Address ______

______ Postcode ______ Language ______

327

Southern Pacific needed more from their computer company than a firm handshake.

What Southern Pacific needed was something more powerful than a locomotive.

They needed a way to manage literally tons of paperwork. They needed to improve customer response. In short, they needed to make their entire operation more efficient. So they asked IBM to help.

Working together, Southern Pacific and IBM developed an information system that revolutionized the railroad industry.

Put into service in the 1960s, the Total Operations Processing System (TOPS) tracks every shipment from order to delivery to billing. Today, it monitors 5 million carloads of freight a year, and continues to give Southern Pacific a competitive edge.

The building block design of TOPS has proven enormously flexible. The system has responded to Southern Pacific's changing needs tens of thousands of times over the last twenty years, without a break in service.

Recently, TOPS has expanded to support the industry's newest intermodal container freight facility, as well as a service customers can use to call up information, on their own PC, about rates or to locate a shipment en route.

This kind of system flexibility and a continuing partnership with IBM have enabled Southern Pacific to grow through fiercely competitive times.

Since 1960, the number of major railroads in the U.S. has gone from over 100 to fewer than 20. And competition today is tougher than ever. But then, so is Southern Pacific. After all, they've been in training with IBM for twenty years.

IBM®

Consumer Magazine Color: 1 Page Or Spread Including Magazine Supplements

329
ART DIRECTORS
Clem McCarthy
Alain Briere
WRITERS
Martin Puris
Bill McCullam
PHOTOGRAPHER
Jeffrey Zwart
CLIENT
BMW of North America
AGENCY
Ammirati & Puris

330
ART DIRECTOR
Ken Boyd
WRITER
Terry Bell
PHOTOGRAPHER
Stanley Wong
CLIENT
Volvo Canada
AGENCY
Scali McCabe Sloves/
Toronto

331
ART DIRECTOR
Steve Dunn
WRITER
Tim Delaney
PHOTOGRAPHER
Graham Cornthwaite
CLIENT
Linguaphone
AGENCY
Leagas Delaney
Partnership/London

332
ART DIRECTOR
Michael McLaughlin
WRITER
Stephen Creet
PHOTOGRAPHER
George Simhoni
CLIENT
Best Foods
AGENCY
MacLaren Advertising/
Toronto

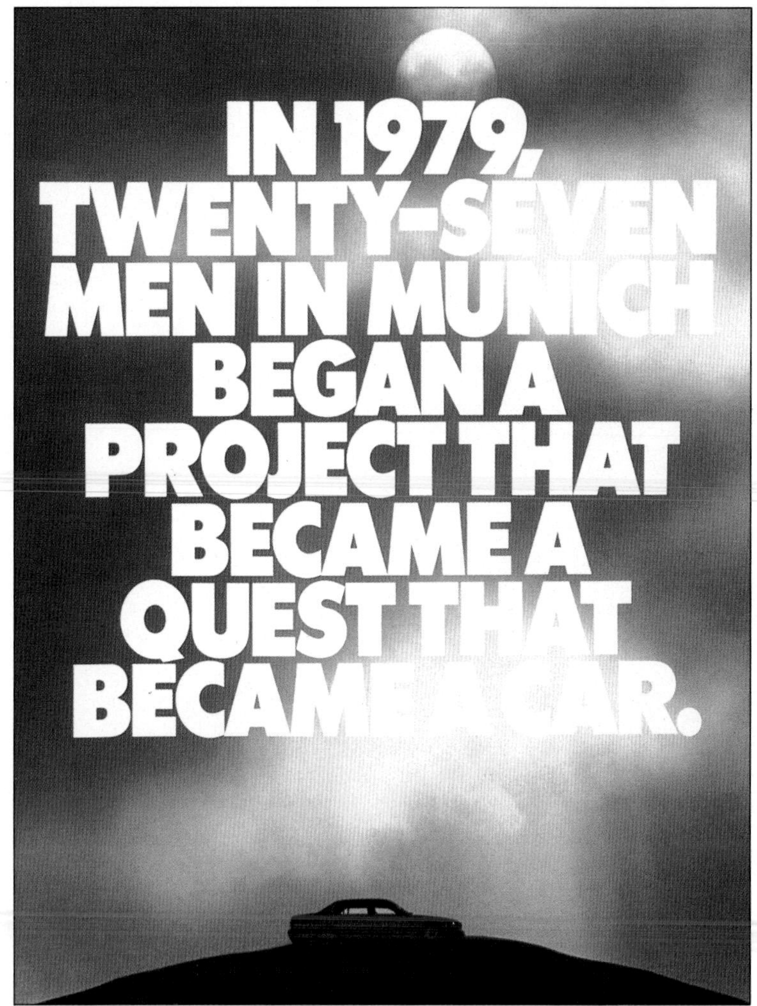

329

330

'A table for two? Certainly you old trout.'

LINGUAPHONE

331

Now that you've tried flamenco dancing, lion taming, and Japanese landscaping, it's time to try something unusual.

With justifiable pride, we announce the most exciting and unusual thing to happen to food since the discovery of fire: Hellmann's new line of flavoured mayonnaise. These new flavours – cucumber, garlic and mustard – are guaranteed to arouse even the most jaded food lover. But what truly makes them worthy of acclaim is their ability to transform basic food into a spirited and unusually tasty meal.

Cucumber
Cucumber Dill Sauce

1 cup	Hellmann's Cucumber Mayonnaise	250 mL
½ cup	grated, seeded cucumber	125 mL
½ cup	chopped celery	125 mL
2 tbsp	horseradish	25 mL
1 tbsp	lemon juice	15 mL
½ tsp	dill weed	2 mL

Combine all ingredients in a small bowl. Cover and chill for 1 hour to blend flavours. Serve with fish or cold meats. Also great as a vegetable dip or salad dressing. Makes 2 cups (500 mL).

You are, of course, familiar with the taste of cucumber, of garlic, and of mustard. But in combination with Hellmann's Mayonnaise, these flavours will present you with an entirely new sensation for your palate. They are delicate and slightly piquant; distinctive but not overpowering. And it is this subtlety that allows them to be perfectly suited to a wide array of foods.

Think of them as a dip for chicken and fish fingers, carrot sticks and other vegetables, chips and

fondues; as a spread for cheese balls, shrimp and garlic bread. Use them in salads of every description: potato, pasta, meat, poultry, seafood, caesar and tossed. Put them on hamburgers, hot dogs and sandwiches. Try the garlic mayonnaise on roast beef, the cucumber on salmon, the mustard on ham. Use them as a topping on steamed broccoli, brussels sprouts, and baked potatoes. The possibilities are endless.

Garlic
Savoury Baked Fish Fillets

1 lb	white fish fillets (cod, sole, halibut) fresh or frozen	500 g
½ cup	Hellmann's Garlic Mayonnaise	125 mL
½ cup	grated Parmesan cheese	125 mL
¼ cup	chopped green onion (optional)	50 mL

Place fish fillets in baking dish in single layer. Preheat oven to 350°F (180°C). Combine mayonnaise, cheese and green onion in small bowl. Spread over fish fillets. Bake for 15 minutes; then broil for an additional 3-4 minutes or until top is bubbly and golden brown. Makes 4-6 servings.

We have included three recipes, one for each flavour. Had space permitted us, we would have given you countless more. Instead, we would be delighted to send you a booklet full of delicious (and unusual) recipes.

Mustard
Piping Hot Cheese Bread

1	large French stick or 2 small	1
2½ cups	old Cheddar cheese finely shredded	625 mL
¾ cup	Hellmann's Mustard Mayonnaise	175 mL
2 tbsp	green onions, finely chopped dash nutmeg	25 mL

Cut bread diagonally into thick slices and place on baking sheet. Combine cheese, mayonnaise, onions and nutmeg. Spread on slices of bread. Place under broiler until cheese mixture is hot and bubbly. Serve immediately.

One last thought. The fact that these inspiring new flavours come from Hellmann's means there can be no doubt that they will be of the highest quality. Oh yes, you'll definitely think these new products are unusual – unusually good.

Recipe Offer:
For more free recipes, send your name and address to: Best Foods Canada Inc., "Hellmann's Recipes," Box 500, Etobicoke, Ont. M9C 4V5.

New Hellmann's Flavoured Mayonnaise.
Makes the usual unusual.

332

Consumer Magazine Color: 1 Page Or Spread Including Magazine Supplements

333

ART DIRECTOR
Dean Hanson

WRITER
Phil Hanft

PHOTOGRAPHER
Rick Dublin

CLIENT
Conran's

AGENCY
Fallon McElligott/ Minneapolis

334

ART DIRECTORS
Nancy Bink
Tony Romeo

WRITER
Rhonda Peck

PHOTOGRAPHERS
Earth Scenes
E.R. Degginger

CLIENT
IBM

AGENCY
Lord Geller Federico Einstein

335

ART DIRECTORS
Rich Silverstein
Clem McCarthy

WRITER
Jeff Goodby

ARTIST
Mark Hess

PHOTOGRAPHER
Hank Benson

CLIENT
Christian Brothers

AGENCY
Goodby Berlin & Silverstein/San Francisco

336

ART DIRECTOR
Frank Haggerty

WRITER
Kerry Casey

PHOTOGRAPHER
Marvy!

CLIENT
Normark/Rapala

AGENCY
Carmichael Lynch/ Minneapolis

Take this simple taste test.

1. Can you tell the $85 china from the $4.95 plate?

Some people become obsessed with good design.
Often to the extreme of sacrificing quality of life for tasteful things they cannot really afford.
At Conran's, we don't buy the notion that if it isn't expensive, it isn't good taste.
We've found that a sensible balance of quality and price is not only reasonable, but perfectly realistic.
To accomplish this, we've developed a highly-refined editing process.
This process dates back 23 years to Great Britain where Terence Conran opened his first stores.
The style of a piece isn't nearly as important to us as its quality of design and construction.
Some of our pieces are originals. Some aren't. Some are exclusive. Some are universally available.
But all must, without exception, pass the Terence Conran Standard Test Of Good Design:
They must do the job intended.
They must be well made and durable.
And they must be both pleasing to use and pleasing to look at.
Finally, the price should be of this world.
Because people with good taste almost always possess a measure of good sense as well.

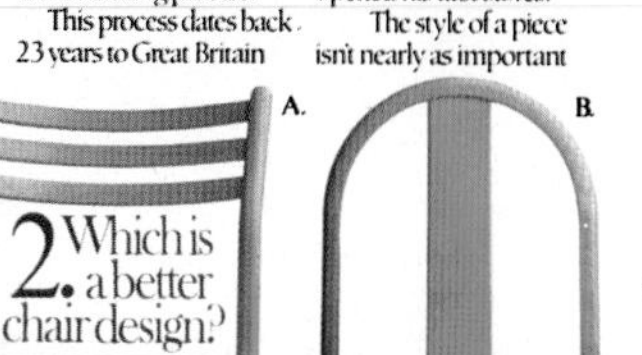

2. Which is a better chair design?

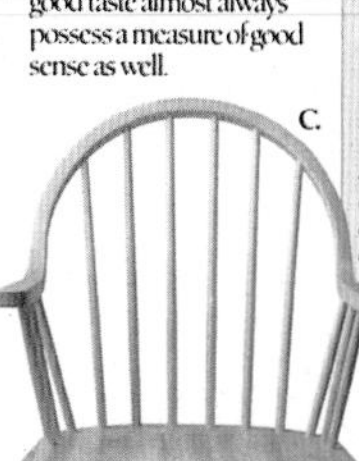

3. Which of these lamps was designed in 1925?

Answers

1. Both are traditional Danish designs. The one from Royal Copenhagen (left) costs $80 more than the one from Conran's (right). Obviously, you can buy a lot of fresh pasta for $80.

2. A trick question. Because "better" design is what you like better. The interesting thing is how well each chair adapts to many different decorative environments. The traditional Windsor (C) can comfortably mix with very contemporary, urban styles. The contemporary Italian design (B) will fit nicely with many traditional furnishings.

3. Actually, none of the lamps were designed in 1925. But all three are inspired by designs first introduced at the 1925 Exposition Internationale in Paris. And each represents well the Conran ideal. That good design transcends periods and styles to "live" long after its creators have departed.

conran's

333

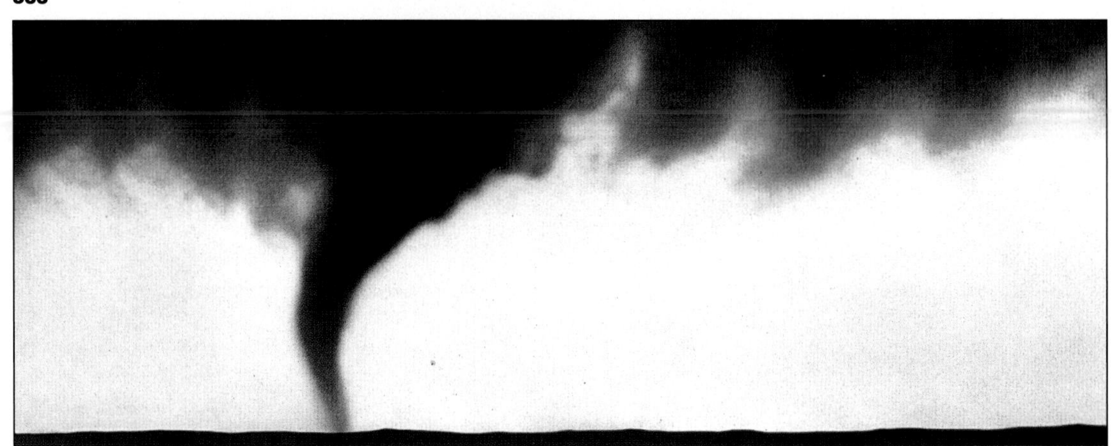

Insurance people have to be ready for whatever comes across their desks.

At any moment, a tornado, a tidal wave or an avalanche of information can take the people in an insurance company by surprise.

That's why Fireman's Fund chose IBM. Working closely together, Fireman's Fund and a team of IBM specialists are developing the kind of computer systems an insurance company needs to help avoid disaster, both inside and outside the office.

For instance, IBM's Expert Systems Environment software helps Fireman's Fund put the knowledge of its most senior people into a computer. This means that others with less experience can access the judgment of an expert underwriter when analyzing a risk.

IBM also designed an advanced office system to link Fireman's Fund headquarters in California to its branch offices across the country. It allows them instantaneously to share the most timely information on everything from the likelihood of a tornado in Kansas to a frost in Florida.

With the support of IBM, Fireman's Fund can respond faster and more accurately to its customers' needs. According to Fireman's Fund Systems Vice President, Deems Davis, "IBM is our insurance policy."

Of course, whether you're in the insurance business, or any business, there's one thing you always have to be ready for. Anything. IBM

334

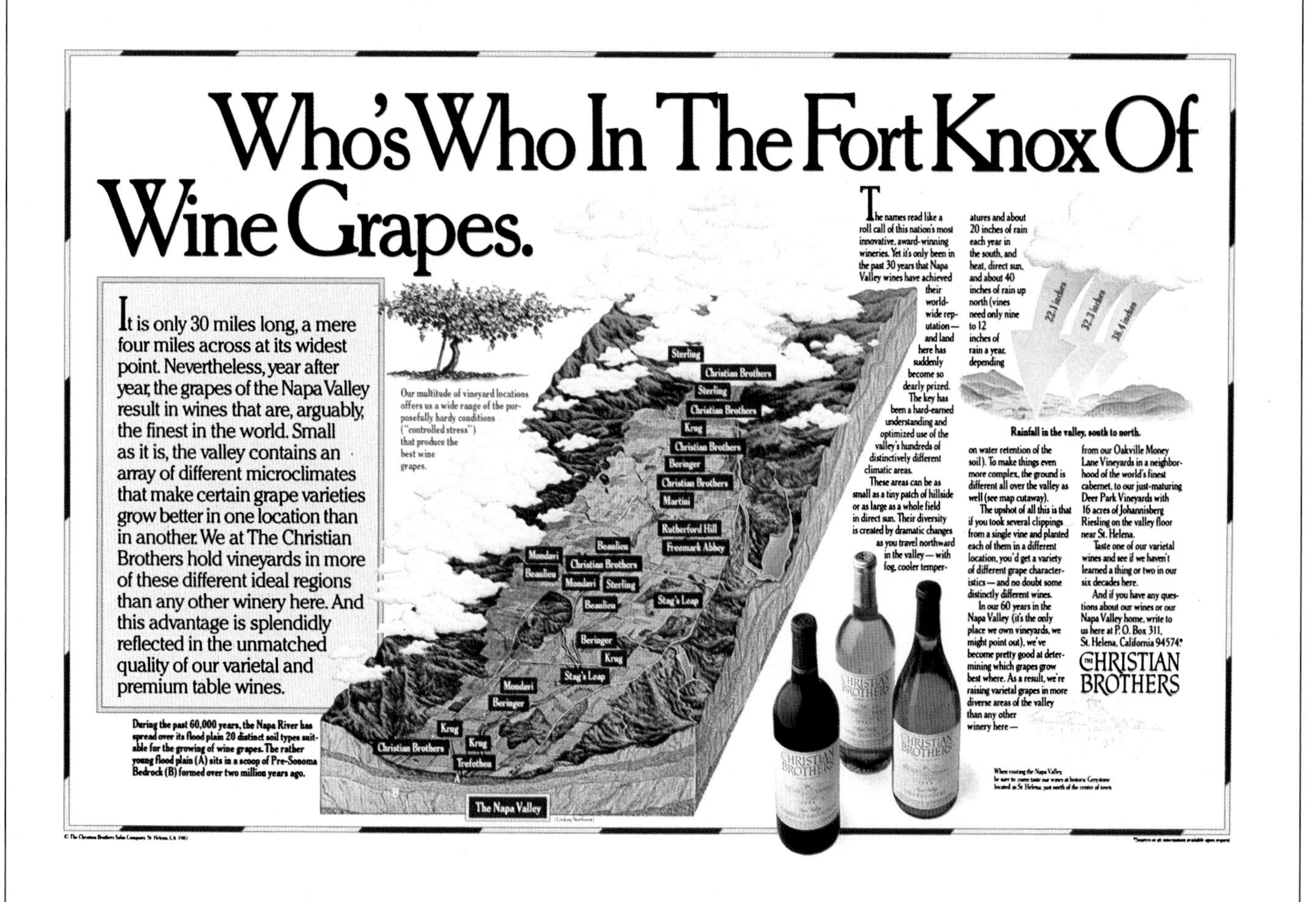

335

How to think big.

To catch a big fish, you have to think like a big fish. You have to predict big behavior. Understand big appetites. Trigger big strikes. In short, you have to think big.

What a big fish is thinking at mealtime.

A big fish is as likely to chase down a small dinner as you are to go across town for a small bag of french fries. It won't happen. Because the energy gained from the food is less than the energy expended to get it. So when the stomach of a trophy fish starts to growl, and he begins looking for his next meal, 2 things are heavy on his mind. Big meal. Easy meal. Which is why you should be fishing big Rapalas. They present a large, tasty, silhouette. And legendary action that perfectly imitates injured prey so the fish thinks he's found an easy mark.

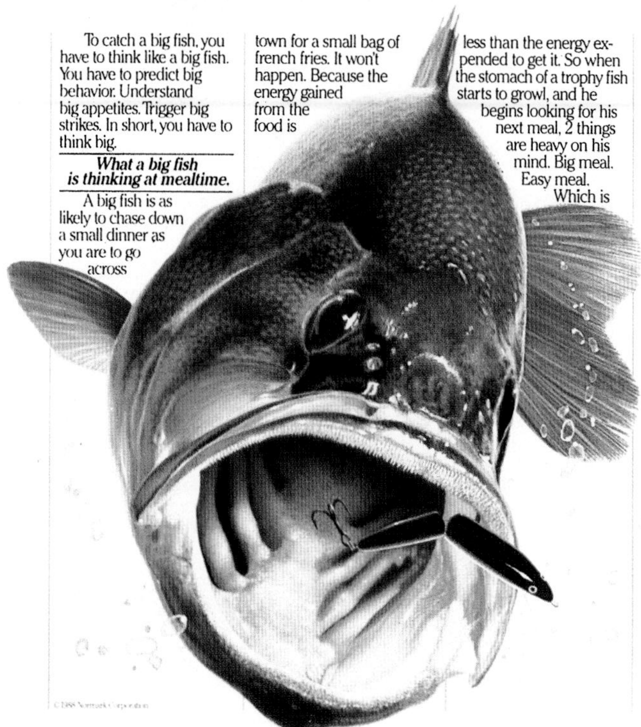

Think about why big fish get big.

A trophy fish has inhabited the same stretch of water for most of his life. All of the years have taught him exactly what food is native to the area. So the last thing he's going to do is hit any lure that hits the water.

To fool this fish, you need the perfect forgery of the forage. The Rapala. It's carefully hand tuned and tank tested so the action has just enough quiver, just enough wobble, just enough wiggle to make a big fish fall for it. And fall for it hard they do.

How different water conditions should alter your thinking.

In clear water, even at great distances, a big fish gets a good, clear look at your lure. So longer, thin Rapalas worked a bit faster have greater success. Because these streamline lures have more subtle, lifelike action. And by speeding them up, you give the fish less time to notice any flaws the clear water may accentuate. Original Floater® #18, Jointed™ #13, Countdown® #11, Husky® and Magnums® in silver, blue or natural forage colors are extremely effective.

In darker, turbid water, big fish have more difficulty locating food. Therefore rounder silhouettes with more action work as a better attractor. And a slower retrieve gives bigger fish a better opportunity to find and hit the target. Shad Rap® #9, Fat Rap® #7 and Jointed #13 in gold, fluorescent chartreuse, fluorescent red and natural forage colors are the ticket here.

Think big, be big.

Patience, patience, patience. Don't just work a big Rapala for a few minutes, decide there's no trophy in your future, and go back to more traditional fishing pursuits. Stick with it. Keep casting. Keep trolling. Keep the faith. And big things will happen.

3 silhouettes big fish hunger for.

The stout, round shape imitates soft finned baitfish like shad and shiners.

The long, thin shape imitates soft-finned baitfish like suckers and cisco.

The broad, natural shape imitates hard-finned fry like perch and bluegill.

Rapala by Normark

336

Consumer Magazine Color: 1 Page Or Spread Including Magazine Supplements

337

ART DIRECTOR
Mark Johnson

WRITER
Phil Hanft

PHOTOGRAPHER
Dennis Manarchy

CLIENT
Lee Jeans

AGENCY
Fallon McElligott/
Minneapolis

338

ART DIRECTOR
Geoffrey Roche

WRITER
Terry Bell

PHOTOGRAPHER
Cailor/Resnick

CLIENT
Volvo Canada

AGENCY
Scali McCabe Sloves/
Toronto

339

ART DIRECTORS
Rich Silverstein
Rick Strand

WRITER
Jeff Goodby

ARTIST
Mark Hess

PHOTOGRAPHER
Hank Benson

CLIENT
Christian Brothers

AGENCY
Goodby Berlin &
Silverstein/San Francisco

340

ART DIRECTOR
Dean Hanson

WRITER
Phil Hanft

PHOTOGRAPHER
Mark LaFavor

CLIENT
3M

AGENCY
Fallon McElligott/
Minneapolis

By the time most jeans look this good, you could be in college.
You don't have to be the class brain to know that if jeans started out looking this great, you'd start the year looking pretty good, too.
Which explains why new Lee Frosted Riders are such a hot item.
Lee Frosted Riders give you the same look and character everyone's wearing these days. So maybe, with some Lee Frosted Riders this fall, the year won't be a total waste after all. Available in relaxed fitting jeans, jackets and skirts. Grey, black and indigo.
Frosted Riders
Lee
The brand that fits

337

OWN A CAR THAT WILL BE A COMFORT TO YOU IN ITS OLD AGE.
The doors on a new Volvo 740 GLE open to an amazingly wide seventy degrees. This means the mere act of slipping into something more comfortable is now, in itself a whole lot more comfortable.
The front seats in a new Volvo 740 GLE may be independently heated and afford you all manner of adjustments including height and lumbar support. This means a trip across the country will prove to be every bit as comfortable as the one you take to the corner store for milk.
Inside the glove compartment of every new Volvo 740 GLE, you'll find the details concerning Volvo's industry leading roadside assistance program appropriately named "On Call".
This means should you ever require help in your travels, you'll get it. Twenty-four hours a day.
But best of all every new Volvo 740 GLE comes with Volvo's legendary reputation for steadfast dependability and rock like durability.
This means that unlike most cars which merely grow old, your new Volvo 740 GLE will grow old gracefully.
And isn't that a comforting thought?
VOLVO
A car you can believe in.

338

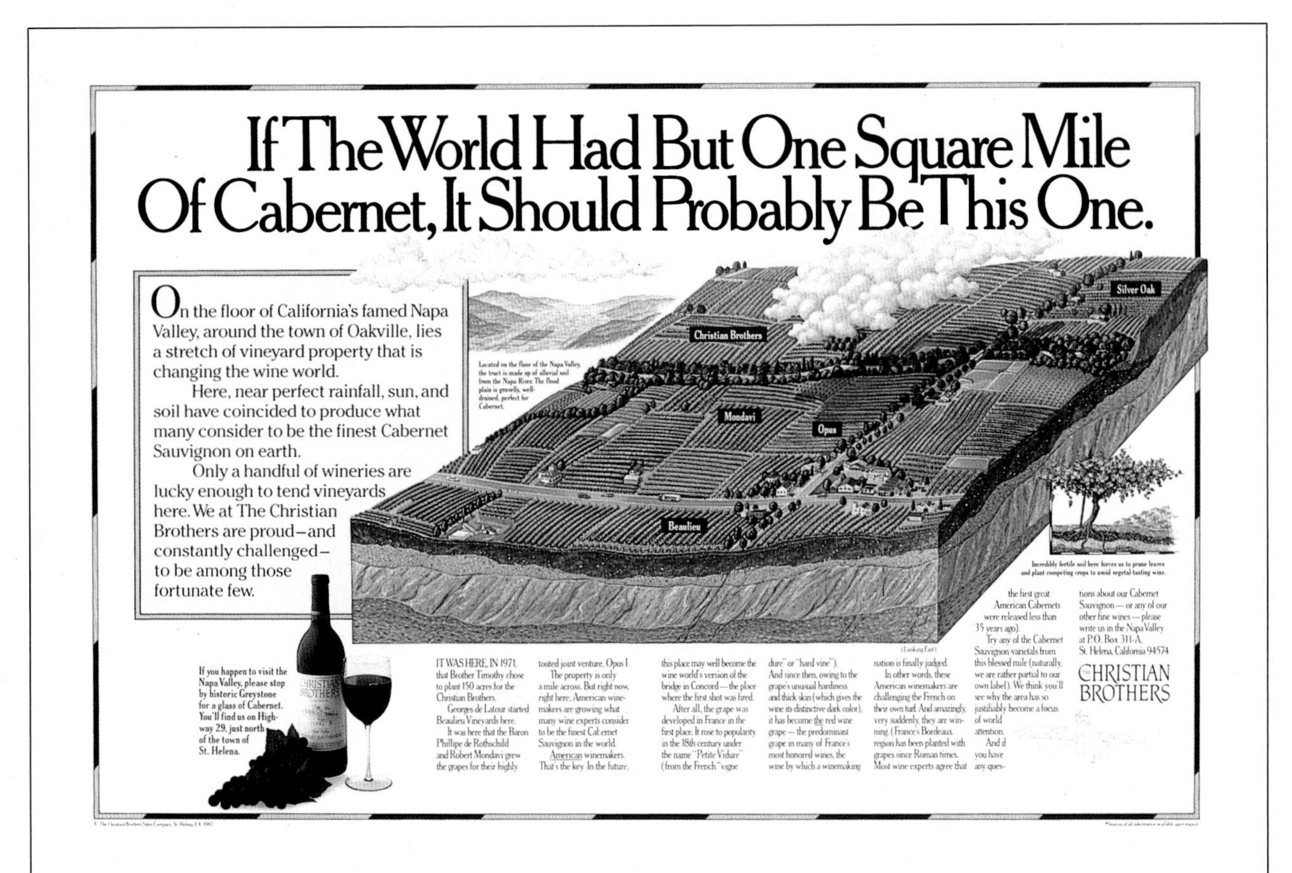

If The World Had But One Square Mile Of Cabernet, It Should Probably Be This One.
On the floor of California's famed Napa Valley, around the town of Oakville, lies a stretch of vineyard property that is changing the wine world.
Here, near perfect rainfall, sun, and soil have coincided to produce what many consider to be the finest Cabernet Sauvignon on earth.
Only a handful of wineries are lucky enough to tend vineyards here. We at The Christian Brothers are proud–and constantly challenged–to be among those fortunate few.
Located on the floor of the Napa Valley, the tract is made up of alluvial soil from the Napa River. The flood plain is gravelly, well-drained, perfect for Cabernet.
Christian Brothers
Silver Oak
Mondavi
Opus
Beaulieu
Incredibly fertile soil here forces us to prune leaves and plant competing crops to avoid vegetal-tasting wine.
(Looking East)
If you happen to visit the Napa Valley, please stop by historic Greystone for a glass of Cabernet. You'll find us on Highway 29, just north of the town of St. Helena.
IT WAS HERE, IN 1971, that Brother Timothy chose to plant 150 acres for the Christian Brothers.
Georges de Latour started Beaulieu Vineyards here.
It was here that the Baron Phillipe de Rothschild and Robert Mondavi grew the grapes for their highly touted joint venture, Opus I.
The property is only a mile across. But right now, right here, American winemakers are growing what many wine experts consider to be the finest Cabernet Sauvignon in the world.
American winemakers. That's the key. In the future, this place may well become the wine world's version of the bridge in Concord—the place where the first shot was fired.
After all, the grape was developed in France in the first place. It rose to popularity in the 18th century under the name "Petite Vidure" (from the French "vigne dure" or "hard vine").
And since then, owing to the grape's unusual hardiness and thick skin (which gives the wine its distinctive dark color), it has become the red wine grape—the predominant grape in many of France's most honored wines, the wine by which a winemaking nation is finally judged.
In other words, these American winemakers are challenging the French on their own turf. And amazingly, very suddenly, they are winning. (France's Bordeaux region has been planted with grapes since Roman times. Most wine experts agree that the first great American Cabernets were released less than 35 years ago).
Try any of the Cabernet Sauvignon varietals from this blessed mile (naturally, we are rather partial to our own label). We think you'll see why the area has so justifiably become a focus of world attention.
And if you have any questions about our Cabernet Sauvignon — or any of our other fine wines — please write us in the Napa Valley at P.O. Box 311-A, St. Helena, California 94574.
THE CHRISTIAN BROTHERS

339

This is what a wet washcloth feels like to a four year old with a scraped elbow.
For a kid with a cut or scrape, the prospect of cleaning it with a soapy rag can be as traumatic as the cut or scrape.
Maybe even more so.
Thankfully, now there is a more acceptable alternative.
3M Cleansing Pads with the pain reliever, lidocaine. Lidocaine helps numb the wound. So cleaning cuts, scratches and scrapes is no longer a pain. For you or your kids. For a free sample, write: First Aid Cleansing Pad Sample, Box 1104, Grand Rapids, MN 55745.
3M First Aid Cleansing Pads. They can help take some of the pain out of growing up.
3M
First Aid
Cleansing Pads
Contains Pain Relieving Lidocaine
Pre-Moistened Pads For Effective Cleansing
Convenient, Ready To Use
Doctor Tested
3M

340

Consumer Magazine Color: 1 Page Or Spread Including Magazine Supplements

341
ART DIRECTOR
Dave Martin
WRITER
Iva Silver
PHOTOGRAPHER
Cailor/Resnick
CLIENT
IBM
AGENCY
Lord Geller Federico Einstein

342
ART DIRECTOR
Vince Squibb
WRITER
Gerard Edmondson
PHOTOGRAPHER
Andreas Heumann
CLIENT
Mates Healthcare
AGENCY
Still Price Court Twivy D'Souza/London

343
ART DIRECTOR
Rick Carlson
WRITER
Scott Crawford
DESIGNER
Rick Carlson
PHOTOGRAPHER
Pelosi & Chambers
CLIENT
Cooper Tools
AGENCY
Howard Merrell & Partners/Raleigh, NC

344
ART DIRECTOR
Frank Haggerty
WRITER
Jack Supple
PHOTOGRAPHER
Rod Pierce
CLIENT
Normark/Rapala
AGENCY
Carmichael Lynch/Minneapolis

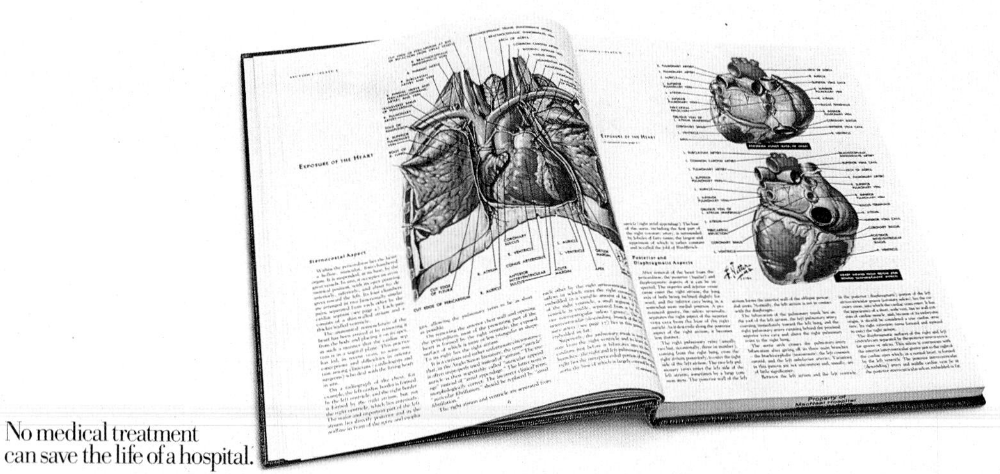

No medical treatment can save the life of a hospital.
In 1980, MacNeal Hospital was suffering from inefficiency.
They decided to call IBM. That decision began a business relationship that would grow over the next seven years.
Their specialists and IBM's specialists analyzed the symptoms. This Berwyn, Illinois, hospital was financially unhealthy. Beds were empty. Morale was low.
A new system was needed to get at the cause of the problem; one that used computers to integrate information and permitted every department to communicate efficiently.
IBM's Patient Care System was installed. Computer terminals were placed at every nursing station. Crucial patient information was available in seconds.
The time that was spent doing paperwork was now better spent doing patient work.
Over the years MacNeal has come to depend on IBM's service just as the community depends on MacNeal's. Both IBM and MacNeal are there 24 hours a day, 7 days a week.
The system designed by MacNeal and IBM put the hospital back on its feet. In fact, it grew a new wing. A $62 million totally computerized facility was constructed four years ago.
MacNeal is running in the black. The hospital that had no future has become the hospital of the future. We'd like to think the ongoing partnership between MacNeal and IBM is exactly what the doctor ordered.
IBM

341

"THEY'RE AWFULLY FIDDLY TO PUT ON. ISN'T THAT HALF THE FUN?"
Mates
Whether you are gay or straight, promiscuous or particular, condoms are a must these days. Few people would argue with that.
What makes Mates condoms such a good idea is that they're just as reliable and sensitive as other brands, yet they cost less.
What's more, every last penny made by Mates Healthcare Ltd. goes to help fight AIDS.
The range includes Natural Mates, Ribbed Mates and Coloured Mates. Every one of which carries the official BSI Kite-mark.
So they'll greatly reduce the risk of AIDS, cervical cancer and other sexually transmitted diseases, as well as unwanted pregnancies.
But what about the pregnant pause? That awkward moment when you have to stop what you're doing to put on a condom. Well, without being too suggestive, we'd like to make a suggestion.
What this tricky situation may call for is a woman's touch. The next time you make love, why not ask your partner to put the condom on for you. Then the course of true love will indeed run smooth.
Especially without those embarrassing interludes spent fumbling around in the dark.
MATES. YOU MAKE LOVE. THEY MAKE SENSE.

342

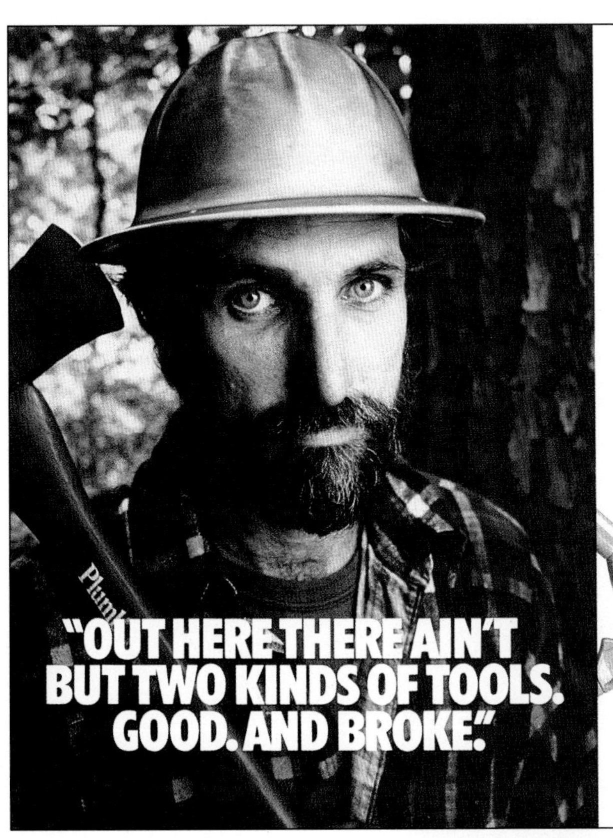

A logging camp is no place for weak knees. Or scrawny tools.

Have a tool give way on you here, and you could be looking at two tons of timber with a mind of its own.

You either get the hell out of the way. Or get yourself some better tools.

Like a set of genuine H.K. Porter cutters.

They can cut clean through a kinked choker cable with no burrs, thanks to cutting jaws that are drop-forged and heat-treated for real toughness.

It's this same kind of toughness we build into every single link of Campbell® chain.

Because wrestling a 4-foot thick Douglas-fir with ordinary chain is not the way a man goes about keeping all his fingers and toes.

Then, neither is whaling away at a tree trunk with a dull chainsaw.

To keep that blade razor sharp, what you need is a skilled hand. And a Nicholson® chainsaw file.

Like all Nicholson files, its cutting teeth are set absolutely true and uniform. Which makes keeping a consistent cutting angle that much easier, one stroke to the next.

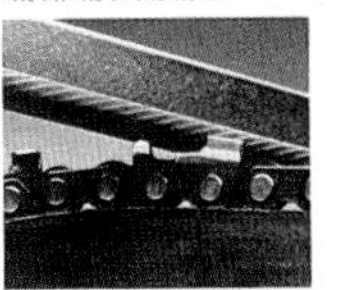

But then, it is just this sort of pure, unadulterated function that makes every CooperTools brand an American Original.

And makes other tools seem just average, if not broke.

CooperTools

The difference between work and workmanship.

BREWER TITCHENER® CAMPBELL® COVERT® CRESCENT® LUFKIN® MERRILL NICHOLSON® PLUMB® H.K.PORTER® TURNER® WELLER® WIRE WRAP® WISS® XCELITE®
A DIVISION OF COOPER INDUSTRIES, INC.

343

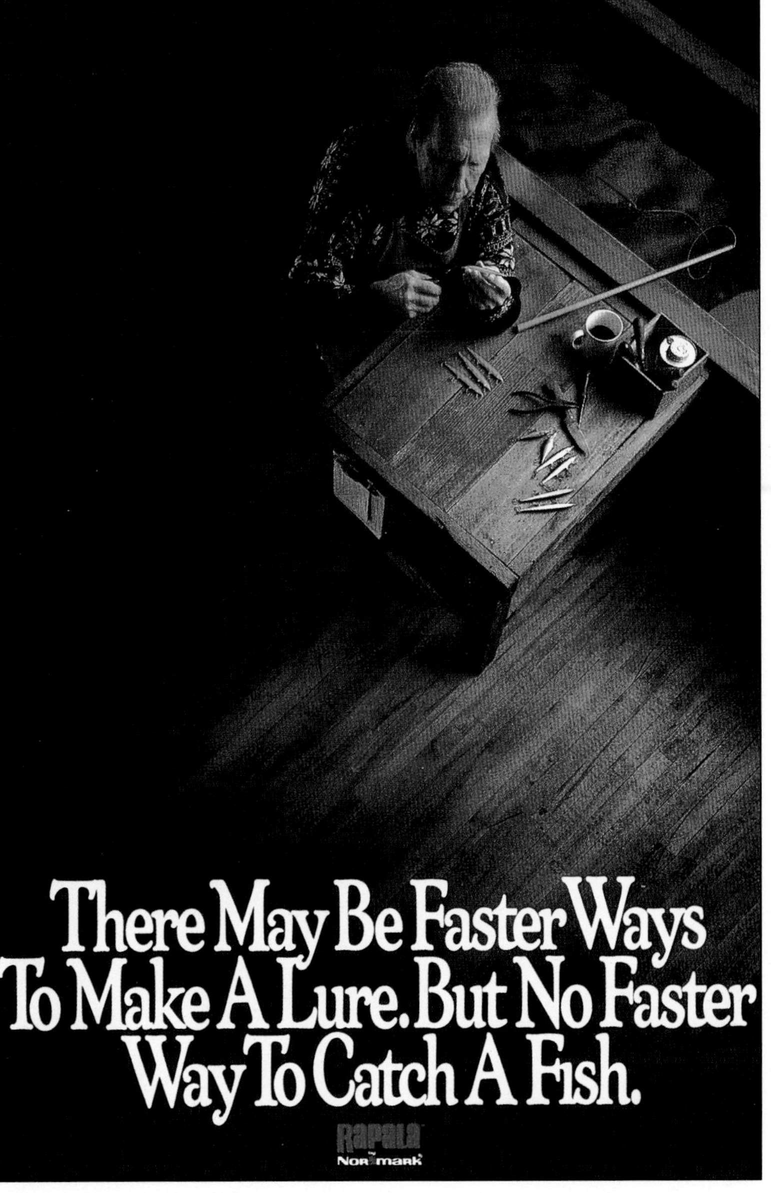

344

Consumer Magazine Color: 1 Page Or Spread Including Magazine Supplements

345
ART DIRECTOR
Michael Hutchinson
WRITER
Roberta Teitel
DESIGNER
Michael Hutchinson
PHOTOGRAPHER
Susan Schelling
CLIENT
Dep Corporation
AGENCY
Lowe Marschalk/
San Francisco

346
ART DIRECTORS
Cindy Rothbard
Ross Sutherland
WRITER
Jane Cross
DESIGNER
Ross Sutherland
PHOTOGRAPHER
Irwin Blitz
CLIENT
Le Menu Dinners
AGENCY
Ogilvy & Mather

347
ART DIRECTORS
Bruce Bloch
Carlos Darquea
WRITERS
Patricia Rockmore
Dennis Ferrone
PHOTOGRAPHERS
Uli Rose
Kei Ogata
CLIENT
Oil of Olay
AGENCY
Wells Rich Greene

348
ART DIRECTOR
Bob Brihn
WRITER
Jamie Barrett
ARTIST
Bob Blewett
CLIENT
US Hockey
AGENCY
Fallon McElligott/
Minneapolis

Dressed to the Teeth.
Topol
Coffee, tea, wine and tobacco stains on teeth just aren't your style.
New whitening, brightening Topol works more effectively...so you can wear a stain-free smile.

345

OUR CHEF'S LOVE AFFAIR WITH WINE LEAVES OUR DINNERS DELIGHTFULLY SAUCED.

The 25th of August, 1930. In a shaded Burgundy vineyard two hours from Paris, a small boy watched, enthralled, as his father selected wines for the family restaurant.

Who'd have thought a small French boy could make such a large difference to Le Menu Dinners?

This was André's first introduction to wine. And the beginning of a long and fruitful relationship.

Today Chef André Lamazière's fascination with wine affects his work on Le Menu Dinners in the most delicious ways.

Consider, for instance, the magnificent sauce that cradles our Chicken à la King. Rich, creamy and subtly flavored by a delicate sauterne. Then sweetened with a hint of sherry. A sauce with a decidedly French accent.

WINE WITH EVERYTHING?

Fortunately for us, Chef Lamazière feels no compulsion to limit his adventures with wine to dishes that sound a little French.

His Beef Sirloin Tips is a "pièce de résistance" in any language. Chunks of tender steak lavished in rich Burgundy and mushroom gravy. With a precise measure of golden sherry added as a loving, last-minute touch.

Chef Lamazière believes that even an all-American dinner can be elevated from excellent to extraordinary by a judicious amount of carefully selected wine.

Hence the unexpected dashes of sherry in our Chopped Sirloin Beef and full-bodied sauterne in our Yankee Pot Roast.

But lest you think our Chef's fondness for wine has caused him to completely lose his senses, we hasten to assure you that he never puts wine where wine does not belong.

A MASTER SAUCIER

Our Chicken Parmigiana, for example, comes cloaked only in the spicy tomato sauce and cheese that complement it so well.

However, if you see fit to serve a robust Chianti *with* this particular dinner, Chef Lamazière would heartily endorse it.

Beef Sirloin Tips: Chunks of tender beef are lightly sautéed, then simmered in a Burgundy and beef stock. Mushrooms are introduced, seasonings are adjusted and sherry is added. Served with: O'Brien potatoes and broccoli florets in a rich Cheddar cheese sauce.

LE MENU DINNERS

346

"I don't intend to grow old gracefully...
I intend to fight it every step of the way."
OIL of OLAY

347

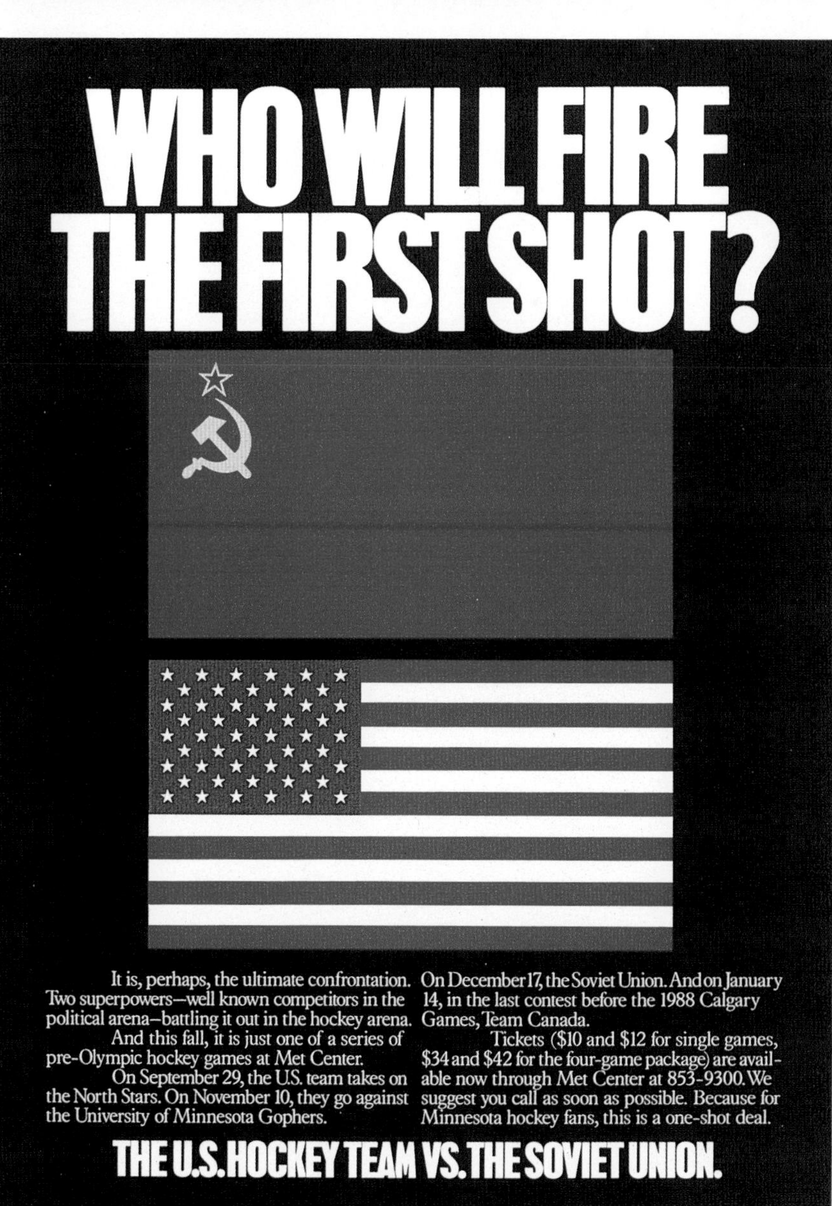
WHO WILL FIRE THE FIRST SHOT?
It is, perhaps, the ultimate confrontation. Two superpowers—well known competitors in the political arena—battling it out in the hockey arena.
And this fall, it is just one of a series of pre-Olympic hockey games at Met Center.
On September 29, the U.S. team takes on the North Stars. On November 10, they go against the University of Minnesota Gophers. On December 17, the Soviet Union. And on January 14, in the last contest before the 1988 Calgary Games, Team Canada.
Tickets ($10 and $12 for single games, $34 and $42 for the four-game package) are available now through Met Center at 853-9300. We suggest you call as soon as possible. Because for Minnesota hockey fans, this is a one-shot deal.
THE U.S. HOCKEY TEAM VS. THE SOVIET UNION.

348

Consumer Magazine Color: 1 Page Or Spread Including Magazine Supplements

349
ART DIRECTOR
Tracy Wong
WRITER
David Apicella
PHOTOGRAPHER
Aaron Jones
CLIENT
Fibre Trim
AGENCY
Ogilvy & Mather

350
ART DIRECTOR
Vince Squibb
WRITER
Gerard Edmondson
PHOTOGRAPHER
Andreas Heumann
CLIENT
Mates Healthcare
AGENCY
Still Price Court Twivy D'Souza/London

351
ART DIRECTOR
John Morrison
WRITER
Ken Segall
DESIGNER
Gina Norton
PHOTOGRAPHER
Bo Hylen Studios
CLIENT
Apple Computer
AGENCY
BBDO

352
ART DIRECTOR
Mary Morant
WRITER
Joe Nunziata
PHOTOGRAPHER
Ben Rosenthal
CLIENT
Schieffelin & Somerset
AGENCY
Lord Geller Federico Einstein

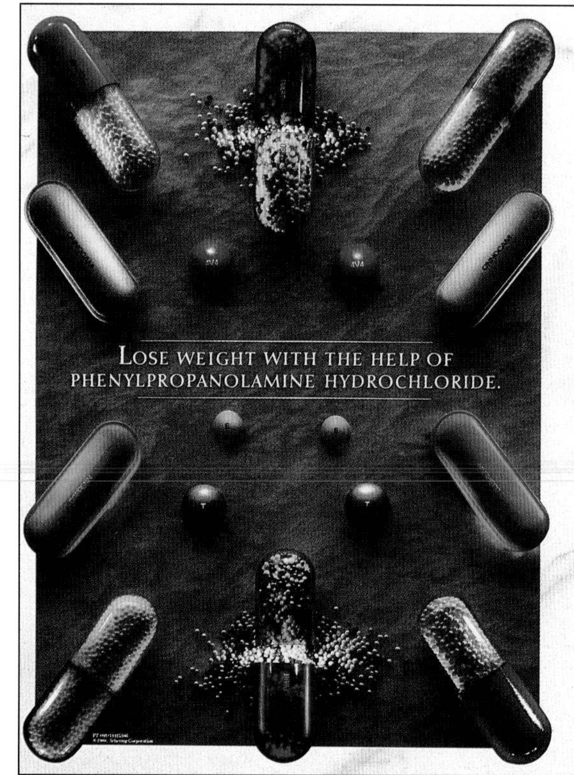

349

THESE DAYS, WOMEN ARE ONLY INTERESTED IN MEN WHO ARE WELL EQUIPPED.
Mates
MATES. YOU MAKE LOVE. THEY MAKE SENSE.

350

How to get people who work together to work together.

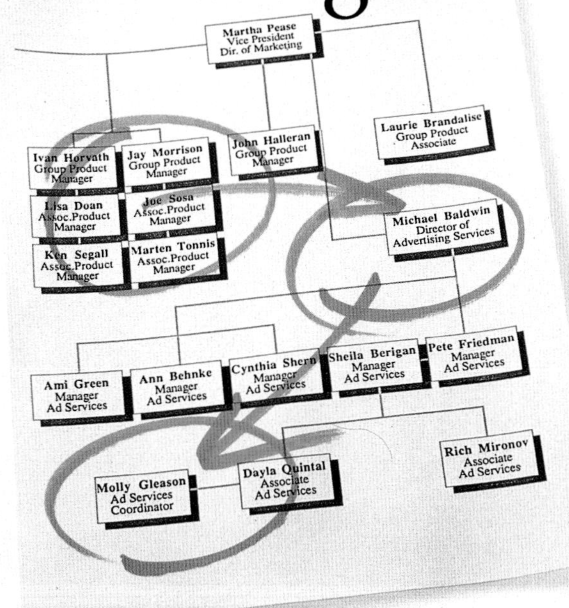

INTRODUCING APPLESHARE.

You've heard the talk about the future of personal computing.

About how Desktop Communications will change the way we work together. Let us share important documents. And allow us instant access not only to information, but to each other.

Well, enough talk.

AppleShare™ is here today.

All for one and one for all. With the AppleShare system, the workgroup's documents are yours for the asking.

It's a new file-serving system designed to build on the power of the AppleTalk® network. So each person can share information with other individuals, groups of people or everyone in the organization.

But what's truly revolutionary is how it works – just like a Macintosh™ personal computer.

The system utilizes a Macintosh with virtually any hard disk as a file server, so sharing is easy. Simply put a document into a folder, and it's available on the network. Instantly.

In fact, to use AppleShare, you need only a fleeting familiarity with two of the most basic Macintosh skills.

Pointing. And clicking.

THE FREEDOM OF INFORMATION ACT.

Every time you create a document, AppleShare lets you decide how (or if) it's to be shared.

Thanks to AppleShare access control, you can grant rights to specific individuals, at three different levels: 1) see folder, 2) read documents within a folder and 3) make changes.

And each folder will contain the most recent versions of the work within. Because the system is constantly updating itself.

ALL TOGETHER NOW.

Apple Desktop Communications can do wonders for productivity, beyond merely sharing folders.

Using a program like InBox, one person can easily send electronic mail to anyone on the network. Or just as easily, to a pre-defined list of people. And these messages can include complete documents, such as those created by Microsoft Word or Excel.

With this new power, Apple Desktop Publishing becomes a whole new ballgame. Because quickly and electronically, you can collect the information you want to publish. Even from people who don't use Macintosh.

INTRODUCING THE APPLETALK PC CARD.

Now you can communicate with other forms of intelligent life.

Just plug our PC Card into an MS-DOS-based computer, and it too can become an active part of the AppleTalk network.

Then, using a program like InBox PC, ideas that are conceived

Now even your MS-DOS computer can become a card-carrying member of the AppleTalk network.

in the MS-DOS world can be painlessly transferred to a Macintosh.

Where they can be analyzed more deeply. Studied more insightfully.

And, with the able assistance of an Apple LaserWriter® printer, presented far more brilliantly.

TURN KNOWLEDGE INTO POWER.

Once you've begun sharing information within the workgroup, you'll likely thirst for greater power.

Which, as it just so happens, is readily available.

You can bring others into the group, via AppleTalk cabling, phone lines or fiber optic cabling. Link a number of workgroups together with options like Hayes InterBridge.

Or, with FastPath and EtherSC, even tie the whole company together on Ethernet cabling.

The full power of Apple Desktop Communications can be yours today.

And to get going, there's only one thing you have to do.

Start communicating:

Call 800-538-9696, Ext. 700, for the name of a participating Apple dealer near you.

The power to be your best.™

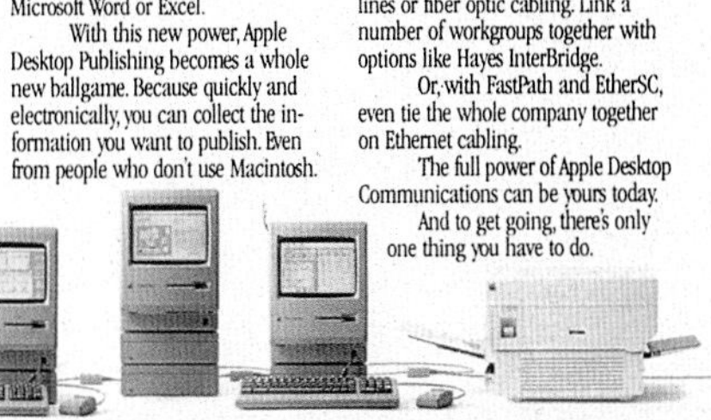

With Apple Desktop Communications, you can share information amongst a group of computers, including even those of the MS-DOS variety.

351

352

Consumer Magazine Color: 1 Page Or Spread Including Magazine Supplements

353
ART DIRECTOR
Rich Silverstein
WRITER
David Fowler
DESIGNER
Betsy Zimmerman
PHOTOGRAPHER
Jay Maisel
CLIENT
Royal Viking Line
AGENCY
Goodby Berlin & Silverstein/San Francisco

354
ART DIRECTOR
Dean Hanson
WRITER
Phil Hanft
PHOTOGRAPHER
Rick Dublin
CLIENT
Conran's
AGENCY
Fallon McElligott/ Minneapolis

355
ART DIRECTOR
Kathy Aird
WRITER
Laurie Brandalise
DESIGNER
Gina Norton
ARTIST
Mark Loncar
PHOTOGRAPHER
Terry Heffernan
CLIENT
Apple Computer
AGENCY
BBDO

356
ART DIRECTOR
John Scott MacDaniels
WRITERS
Cristina Gavin
John Scott MacDaniels
DESIGNER
John Scott MacDaniels
CLIENT
New Zealand Tourist & Publicity
AGENCY
Lowe Marschalk/ San Francisco

353

354

Macintosh used as food processor.

It can't slice, dice, blend or liquify. But it's quickly becoming the hottest desk appliance in the U.S. food industry.

Because it can do literally hundreds of jobs. Everything from designing packages to ordering sugar and spice by the ton.

In fact, companies as diverse as the Sara Lee Corporation and Pillsbury have been adding dozens of Macintosh personal computers to their operations.

They've found that Macintosh's incredible appetite for work is satisfied by all the latest desktop publishing packages and advanced business software.

And that it can tie a sprawling enterprise together with its own low cost network. Or by communicating with MS-DOS computers and mainframes.

Macintosh also has a lower training cost per desktop than any MS-DOS computer—prompting some spectacular jumps in productivity. In a recent in-depth analysis of selected Macintosh installations in business, users consistently reported productivity increases of 15%-25% and more. Food for thought for any business.

Why not call 800-446-3000 ext. 400 for the nearest authorized Apple reseller.

And finish processing all the facts.

The power to be your best.

355

Widespread unrest in New Zealand!
Looking for the perfect vacation spot to relax you—without putting you to sleep?
Change climates.
Come to New Zealand.
The place is really jumping! And sailing. And hiking. And golfing.
Escape from the rest of the world's pressures to the best of our world's pleasures.
New Zealand. One more really great thing to do here is fill in this coupon!
NZP
The climate is right for New Zealand.

356

Consumer Magazine Color: 1 Page Or Spread Including Magazine Supplements

357
ART DIRECTOR
Donna Tedesco
WRITER
Yoni Mozeson
PHOTOGRAPHER
Paul Redman
CLIENT
British Tourist Authority
AGENCY
Ogilvy & Mather

358
ART DIRECTOR
Joe Johnson
WRITER
Jim Jenkins
DESIGNER
Joe Johnson
PHOTOGRAPHER
Stephen Mark Needham
CLIENT
Pepperidge Farm
AGENCY
Ogilvy & Mather

359
ART DIRECTOR
Mark Johnson
WRITER
Bill Miller
PHOTOGRAPHER
Randy Miller
CLIENT
Lee Jeans
AGENCY
Fallon McElligott/ Minneapolis

360
ART DIRECTOR
Dean Stefanides
WRITER
Bernie Rosner
DESIGNER
Dean Stefanides
PHOTOGRAPHER
Dennis Manarchy
CLIENT
Ralston Purina
AGENCY
Scali McCabe Sloves

MUCH HAS CHANGED IN BIBURY OVER THE YEARS. GROCERIES NOW ARRIVE BY BICYCLE.

FLY BRITISH AIRWAYS, THE WORLD'S FAVOURITE AIRLINE, TO BRITAIN

You see fewer horses and carts on the streets of Bibury these days. But little else has changed. The Cotswold stone cottages still press shoulder to shoulder along Bibury's Arlington Row. The path still winds its way towards Arlington Mill. And the stream still flows beside it.

Everywhere in Britain, there are villages that look as they did centuries ago. From the coastal towns of Devon where cobbled streets slope to the sea. To the thatched-roof cottages of Sussex, and the half-timbered houses of East Anglia.

And everywhere in Britain you'll find that the people are warm and friendly. Needless to say, they all speak your language.

HOTELS: $21 TO $84 A NIGHT

Many of England's picturesque villages, including Bibury, are an easy day trip from London. The perfect way to explore London and the surrounding countryside is with British Airways Holidays "London Hotel Specials." Choose from 42 of London's finest hotels for only $21 to $84 a night, per person, double occupancy. That includes daily Continental breakfast, service charge and tax. And there's no minimum stay required.

If for you "the play's the thing," then British Airways Holidays offers a choice of special theatre packages. "The London Showcase," for example, features confirmed theatre tickets to the top shows, pre-theatre dinners, entertainment at "theme" restaurants and more.

British Airways Holidays offer the same flexibility when it comes to exploring the rest of Britain. "Car Rental in Britain" lets you rent a car for any length of time at special reduced rates—$17 to $60 a day with unlimited mileage.

SEE BRITAIN WITH AN AUTO-HOTELTOUR

Here's the most convenient way to see England, Scotland and Wales on your own. Stay at any of over 175 fine Trusthouse Forte Hotels—including some of Britain's most picturesque inns—all with full English breakfast. Then pick a car of any size with unlimited mileage. A 5-day package is only $224 to $341 per person, double occupancy, excluding airfare. On all car rentals, gas, tax and insurance are extra.

If you prefer to travel by guided motorcoach, British Airways Holidays offers four escorted tours that will show you the glories of Britain.

Of course, you have to fly British Airways to get these special packages and you must book them before you leave. So send for your free "British Airways Holidays" and "Britain Speaks Your Language" brochures. Then see your travel agent.

Because a trip to Britain is like a trip back in time.

B R I T A I N

Please send me your free brochures: *British Airways Holidays* and *Britain Speaks Your Language*.

Name
Address
City State Zip
Telephone ( ) Have you been to Britain before? Yes No

BRITISH AIRWAYS
The world's favourite airline.

W E S P E A K Y O U R L A N G U A G E

357

This ad is for people who are looking for a better source of fiber.

Well, you've picked the right page to read.

Because you're about to discover Pepperidge Farm's new Five Star Fibre™ Breads—the breads that have people wondering how something so delicious could be so nutritious.

Why Two Kinds Of Fiber Are Better Than One

The National Cancer Institute believes diets high in fiber and low in fat may reduce the risk of certain types of cancer.

Well, most high-fiber bran cereals* may be high in fiber, but often only one kind: *insoluble*. It's this kind of fiber that helps promote regularity.

But there's also a kind of fiber known as *soluble*, which most high-fiber bran cereals have in very small amounts, if at all. Yet diets high in this kind of fiber may actually lower your serum cholesterol, a risk factor for some types of heart disease.

So, at Pepperidge Farm, we've baked an ample amount of both insoluble *and* soluble fiber into each and every slice of our new Five Star Fibre Breads—a total of five grams' worth per serving. Compare that to whole wheat breads, which usually have less than two grams of fiber per slice.

Why Five Sources Of Fiber Are Better Than One

One source of fiber simply wasn't enough.

So Five Star Fibre Breads get their fiber (not to mention their flavor) from *five* natural sources. Now how many high-fiber bran cereals can say that?

These five sources include grains, fruits, nuts, seeds—even vegetables. All baked into tempting flavors like Orchard Fruit & Nut, Apple Spice Swirl, and Harvest Wheat. There's even a Five Star Fibre White Bread.

But instead of reading this ad about Five Star Fibre Breads, why not read a free booklet about them? It tells you everything you need to know about fiber, and even includes a fitness plan. For your free copy write: Pepperidge Farm, Attn: Five Star Fibre Fitness Guide, 595 Westport Ave., Norwalk, CT 06856.

Once you read this booklet—and once you taste our Five Star Fibre Breads—you'll know why it's hard to find a high-fiber bran cereal that's a better source of fiber.

Still, you can try. But we have the feeling you're going to have something in common with the page on the right: you're both going to come up blank.

New Five Star Fibre™ Breads

This ad is for people who think high-fiber bran cereal is the best source of fiber.

(See previous page)

358

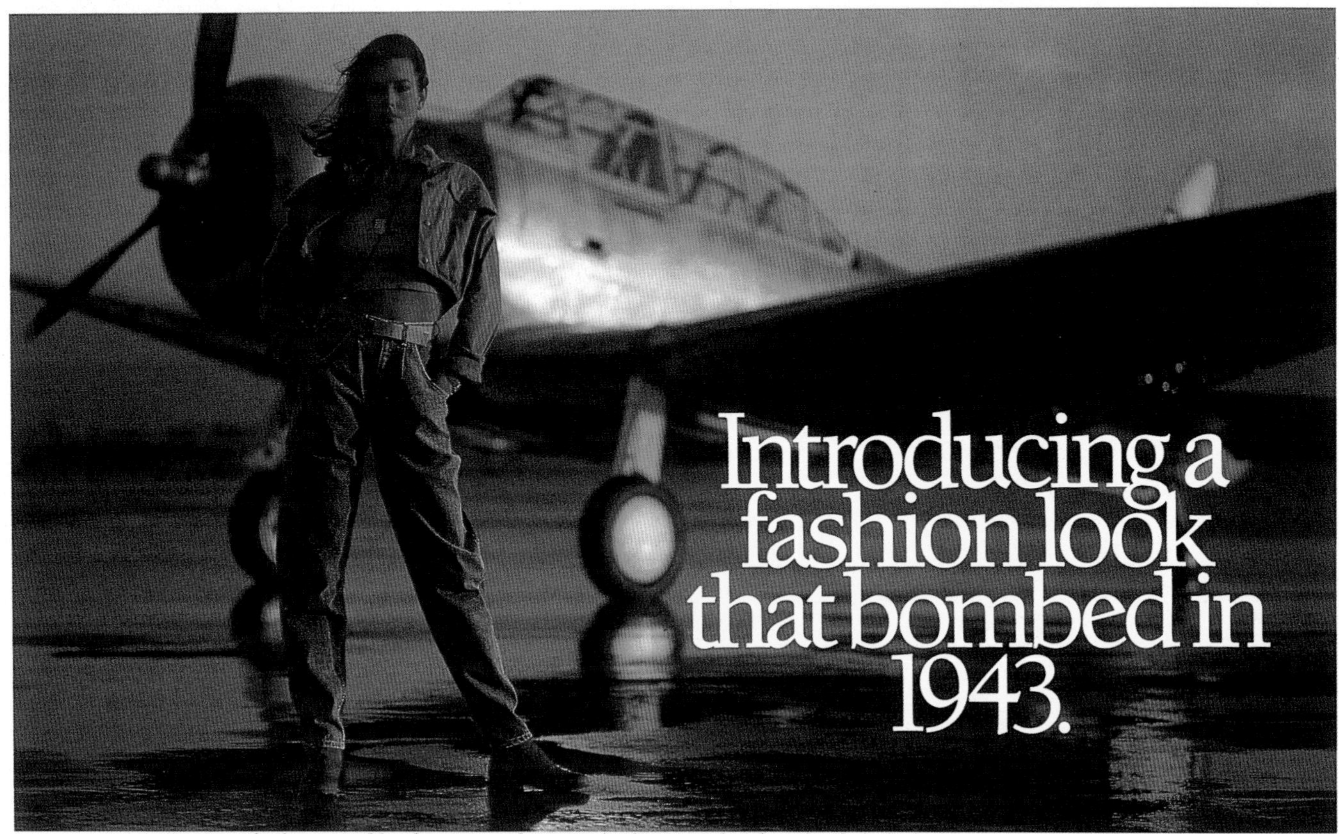
Introducing a fashion look that bombed in 1943.

Jump into a look inspired by the 101st Airborne. Lee® Sky Riders℠ have landed. Cut loose so you can cut loose. Stonewashed denim with a pleated front. Watch for the invasion near you. Sky Riders

Lee

The brand that fits.

359

When your dog is more than just a pet, you want to feed him more than just a "dog food."

That's why Purina developed a very special dog food that embodies the kind of nutritional care you want to give your dog.

It's Purina O.N.E.® brand dog food. Short for "Optimum Nutritional Effectiveness."

"I've always wanted a serious portrait of Duffy and me."

It's special because it's made with high quality ingredients, like real chicken, wheat and rice. And it's free of things that don't benefit your dog, like artificial colors and flavors.

It's special because it contains more protein and energy per ounce than the leading dry dog food..

And special because it's highly digestible. Which means your dog can utilize more of the good things that are in it.

Your dog will think it's special, too.

In taste tests Purina O.N.E. was preferred by dogs over the leading national dry dog foods.

ONE

For that one dog. Yours.

So if you love your dog so much you feel you can't do enough for him, here's a way to come close.

Purina

360

Consumer Magazine Color: 1 Page Or Spread Including Magazine Supplements

361
ART DIRECTOR
Paul Blade
WRITER
Larry Hampel
DESIGNER
Paul Blade
PHOTOGRAPHER
Clint Clemens
CLIENT
Volvo
AGENCY
Scali McCabe Sloves

362
ART DIRECTOR
Dean Stefanides
WRITER
Bernie Rosner
DESIGNER
Dean Stefanides
PHOTOGRAPHER
Dennis Manarchy
CLIENT
Ralston Purina
AGENCY
Scali McCabe Sloves

363
ART DIRECTOR
George Roux
WRITER
Jack Raymond
PHOTOGRAPHERS
Danny Lahman
Dennis Gray
CLIENT
Princess Cruises & Tours
AGENCY
Tracy-Locke/Los Angeles

364
ART DIRECTOR
Earl Cavanah
WRITER
Larry Cadman
PHOTOGRAPHER
Henry Sandbank
CLIENT
Volvo
AGENCY
Scali McCabe Sloves

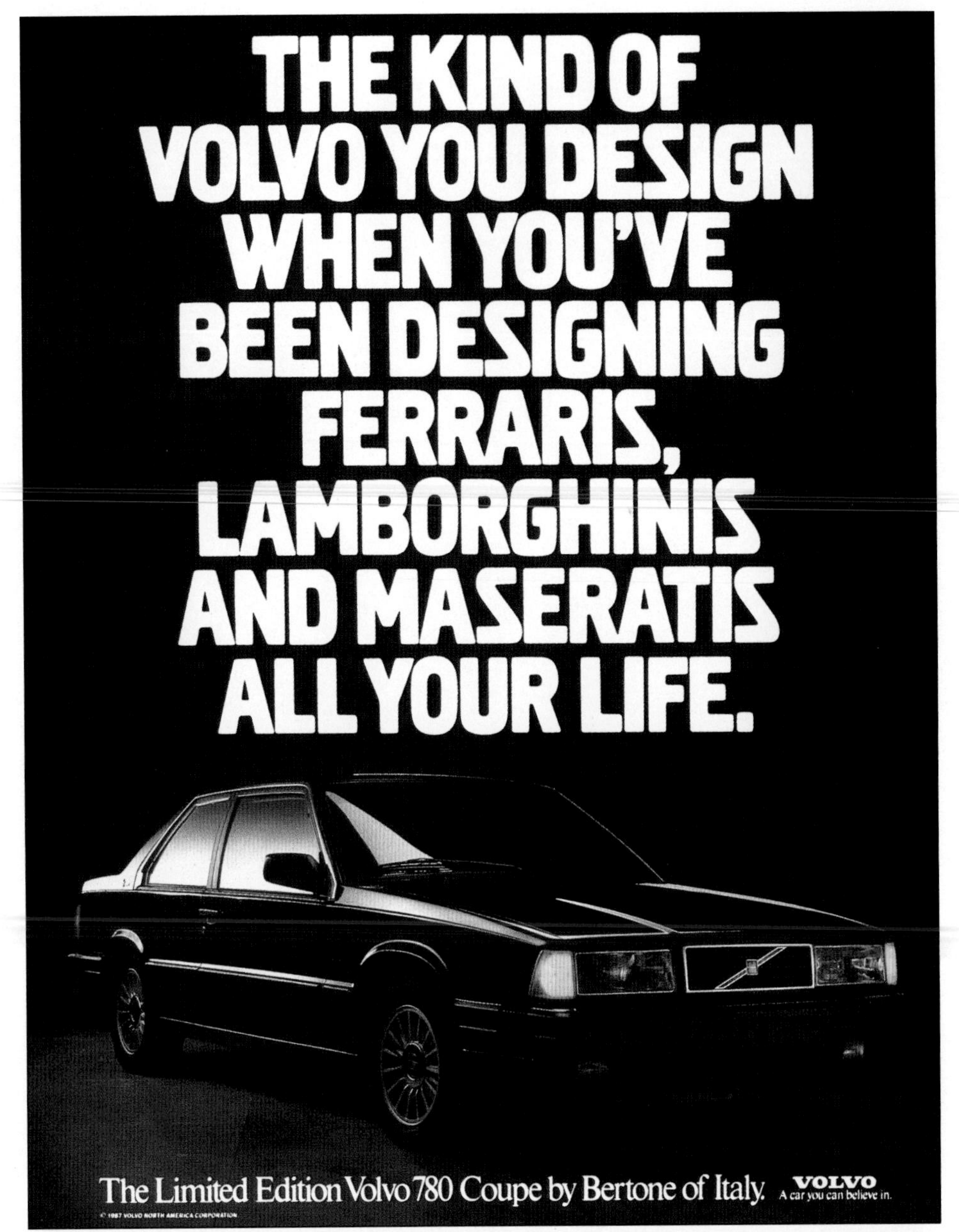

361

When your dog is more than just a pet, you want to feed him more than just a "dog food."
That's why Purina developed a very special dog food that embodies the kind of nutritional care you want to give your dog.
It's Purina O.N.E.® brand dog food. Short for "Optimum Nutritional Effectiveness."

"Some people say we look alike. Ralph's the one with the big ears."

It's special because it's made with high quality ingredients, like real chicken, wheat and rice. And it's free of things that don't benefit your dog, like artificial colors and flavors.
It's special because it contains more protein and energy per ounce than the leading dry dog food.
And special because it's highly digestible. Which means your dog can utilize more of the good things that are in it.
Your dog will think it's special, too.
In taste tests Purina O.N.E. was preferred by dogs over the leading national dry dog foods.
So if you love your dog so much you feel you can't do enough for him, here's a way to come close.

ONE
For that one dog. Yours.

© Ralston Purina Company, 1987

362

Be Sure What You See In Alaska
Is Limited Only By Your Imagination.
Not Your Cruise Line.
P&O Group
British Registry

Unlike other cruise lines, Princess cruises don't end with the Inside Passage and Glacier Bay. We'll take you all the way across the Gulf of Alaska to Whittier and Anchorage, gateway to the vast interior.

Four luxurious ships and three different itineraries offer you more opportunities to cruise the Gulf and the Inside Passage than anyone else. You'll sail 7 or 10 days past Columbia, the largest glacier in North America, the sixteen ice blue glaciers of College Fjord and the emerald green forested coasts of Prince William Sound.

We can also take you beyond the Arctic Circle to the crossroads of the world's largest caribou herd, near the Arctic National Wildlife Refuge. To Prudhoe Bay, virtually on top of the world. To Gold Rush towns like Whitehorse and Dawson City. To the rustic charm of Princess' new Harper Lodge at Denali National Park, home of Mt. McKinley.

You'll travel on luxurious motorcoach. Or on the Midnight Sun Express, one of the world's most elegant railway cars. Outside, mountains, forests and tundra where the Alaskan grizzly makes its home. Inside, fine linen, gourmet cuisine and the kind of gracious service you've come to expect from Princess.

Book under deposit by Jan. 31, 1988 and cruise for as low as $990, cruisetour for $895. You'll save up to $200 per person.

For more information, talk with your travel agent about our 4 Alaska cruise itineraries and 39 cruisetours. Or send for our free 1988 Alaska brochure.

363

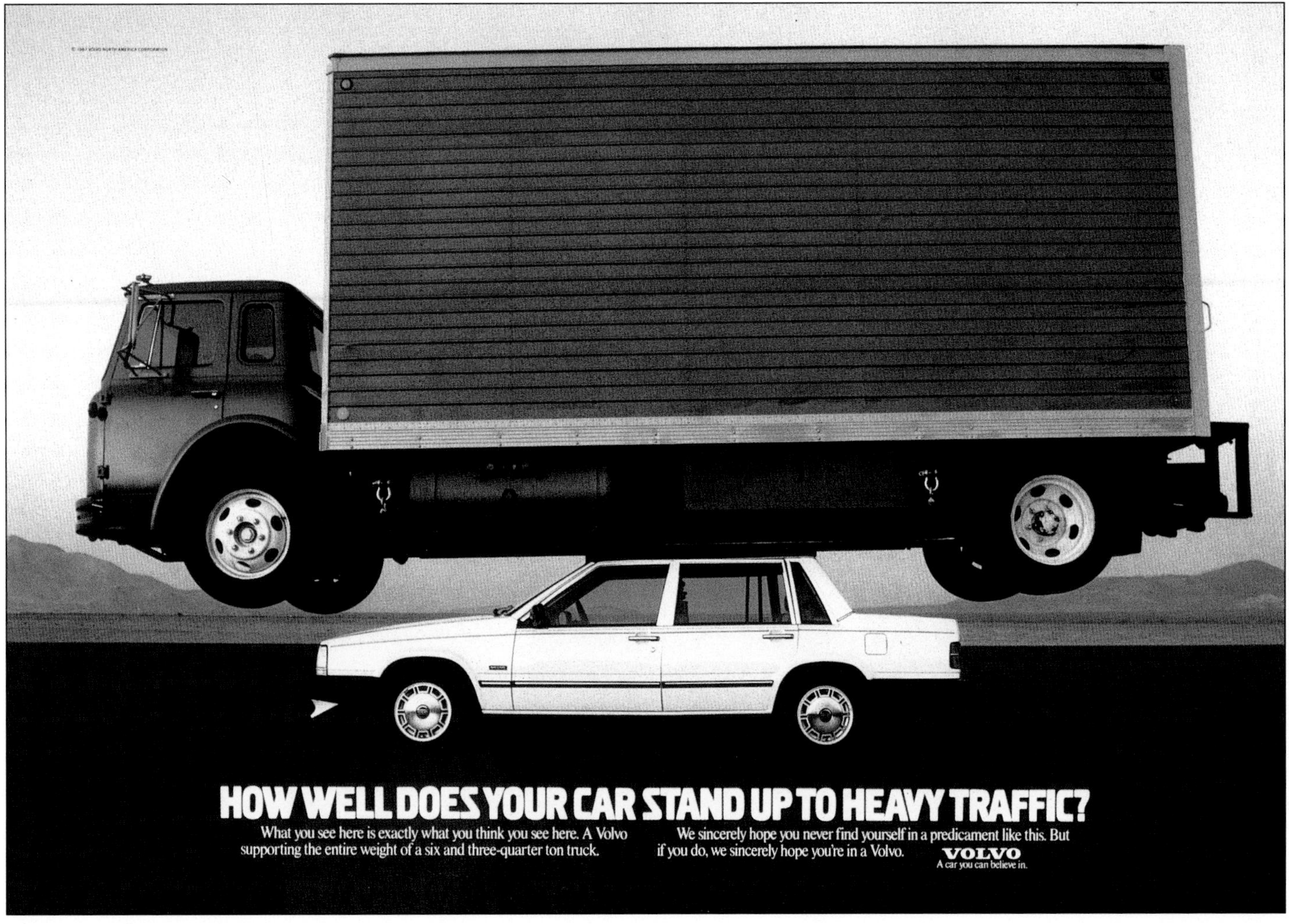

HOW WELL DOES YOUR CAR STAND UP TO HEAVY TRAFFIC?
What you see here is exactly what you think you see here. A Volvo supporting the entire weight of a six and three-quarter ton truck.
We sincerely hope you never find yourself in a predicament like this. But if you do, we sincerely hope you're in a Volvo.
VOLVO
A car you can believe in.

364

Consumer Magazine Color: 1 Page Or Spread Including Magazine Supplements

365
ART DIRECTOR
Bryan McPeak
WRITERS
Joel Mitchell
Craig Piechura
CLIENT
Iams
AGENCY
W.B. Doner & Company/
Southfield, MI

366
ART DIRECTOR
Jeff Vogt
WRITER
Tessa Super
PHOTOGRAPHERS
Robert Ammirati
Galen Rowell
Steve Krongard
Pete Turner
Jake Rajs
Eric Meola
CLIENT
Nikon
AGENCY
Scali McCabe Sloves

367
ART DIRECTORS
Steve Beaumont
Beth McConnell
WRITER
David Lubars
PHOTOGRAPHER
David Leach
CLIENT
Yamaha Motor Corporation
AGENCY
Chiat/Day - Venice, CA

368
ART DIRECTOR
Ron Rosen
WRITER
Craig Demeter
PHOTOGRAPHER
Jerry Cailor
CLIENT
Range Rover of North America
AGENCY
Grace and Rothschild

If you've been buying supermarket pet food, give your dog this spot quiz.

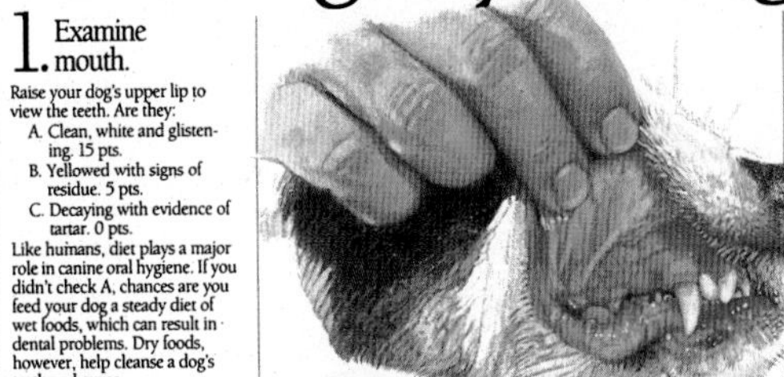

1. Examine mouth.
Raise your dog's upper lip to view the teeth. Are they:
A. Clean, white and glistening. 15 pts.
B. Yellowed with signs of residue. 5 pts.
C. Decaying with evidence of tartar. 0 pts.
Like humans, diet plays a major role in canine oral hygiene. If you didn't check A, chances are you feed your dog a steady diet of wet foods, which can result in dental problems. Dry foods, however, help cleanse a dog's teeth and gums.

2. Check breath odor.
While examining the mouth, you may have noticed the animal's breath. Is it:
A. Unoffensive. 10 pts.
B. Foul. 5 pts.
C. Sour, or sweet. 0 pts.
Most supermarket dog foods are grain-based. If improperly processed, grain-based cereals ferment in your dog's intestines and cause gas. In addition, many of these brands add onion and garlic to enhance the flavor. Unpleasant mouth odors can arise from indigestion. Sour odors may result from vomiting, and sweet odors may indicate diabetes.

3. Inspect nose and footpad leather.
Feel the tip of your dog's nose. Is the skin:
A. Tough yet pliable, with a slightly moist appearance. 15 pts.
B. Stiff, crusty or dry. 5 pts.
C. Very hard or cracking. 0 pts.
The nose leather of a healthy animal is clean, smooth and resilient. Similarly, footpad leather should be smooth and tough, yet pliable. In contrast, nose or footpad leather that is dry or cracked may suggest a diet lacking essential nutrients and fatty acids.

4. Examine stool.
Stool size and consistency are good indicators of a dog's overall well-being. Is it:
A. Small and firm. 20 pts.
B. Large and hard. 5 pts.
C. Large and excessively soft. 0 pts.
Stool volume is largely influenced by undigestible foods and enzyme deficiencies. While small, firm stools are easier to clean up, they also demonstrate your dog has properly assimilated all the crucial dietary nutrients.
Stool consistency indicates the quality of your dog's source of nutrients. Stool from a poor source may be soft. A hard stool can represent a mineral or fiber imbalance.

5. Feel skin and coat.
Thoroughly comb your fingers through your dog's hair in the opposite direction it lies naturally. Is it:
A. Healthy, vibrant and free of flaky deposits. 20 pts.
B. Dry, lackluster and poorly elastic. 5 pts.
C. Excessively oily, smelly with uneven growth. 0 pts.
There are normal variations in different breeds of dogs at different times of the year. However, poor nutrition always adversely affects skin and hair. Dogs that exhibit healthy skin and hair eat a diet with the proper balance of fats and protein, vitamins and minerals.

6. Evaluate muscle tone.
Feel along your dog's front shoulders and hindquarters. When compared to other dogs of the same size or breed, are the muscles:
A. Large and firm, yet supple. 20 pts.
B. Medium and soft. 5 pts.
C. Small and weak. 0 pts.
Good muscle development is directly related to physical activity and protein quality and quantity. Dogs that score high eat meat protein foods and follow a regulated program of feeding and exercise.

If your dog scored 95 or less, don't just change dog food, change where you buy it.

All dogs have dietary requirements that demand quality sources of protein. And meat best meets those requirements.
However, many leading supermarket dog foods rely on grains for their main source of protein.
Iams dog food isn't sold in supermarkets. It's sold only in pet shops, pet supply stores and feed stores. Sold by veterinarians, breeders and pet specialists. People who understand a dog's nutritional needs. And that's why they recommend Iams.
They know that by feeding Iams you'll notice a discernible difference in your animal's health and well-being. Because Iams Chunks, MiniChunks, Biscuits and Puppy Food are formulated to exceed a dog's special requirements.
Our foods are dry, made without any artificial color or flavor enhancers. If your dog can't use it, neither can we.
Dogs like the taste of Iams because we give them what they crave naturally—meat protein.
And Iams makes Eukanuba and Eukanuba For Puppies with even higher ratios of protein from chicken.
If you'd like to know more, visit an Iams retailer or simply call 1-800-525-IAMS (4267).
Settle for anything less and you'd be failing your dog.

IAMS
Special pet foods found only at special stores.

Iams Chunks, Iams MiniChunks, Iams Biscuits, Iams Puppy Food, Eukanuba and Eukanuba For Puppies are registered trademarks of The Iams Company.
©1987 The Iams Company

365

366

Does your motorcycle move you like this?

"We've ridden over 700,000 miles in our lifetime. This is definitely the best bike we've owned."
Alvin and Brenda Battey
Lone Oak, Texas

"I'm absolutely blown away by how much power it has. I used to ride a sport bike, so I know about power."
Scott Palmer
Fort Riley, Kansas

"Our membership number in the Venture Touring Society is '003.' That's how long we've believed in this bike."
Roger and Myra Coots
Kilgore, Texas

"It's amazing how well the fairing keeps the rain off you… of course, you have to be moving."
Glenn R. Hall
Arlington, Texas

"It's either the sportiest touring bike or the touringest sport bike we've ever ridden."
Roger and Patricia Jones
Mesa, Arizona

"Every time we ride it, it's almost like a vacation."

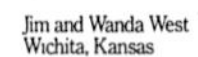

Jim and Wanda West
Wichita, Kansas

"We put 60,000 miles on the bike we had. Then we tested a Venture, and after one mile liked it better."
Van and Joy Witt
Fort Smith, Arkansas

"Most people buy a you-know-what. To us that's like buying a Chevy Impala: boring."
Steve and Doris Norman
O'Fallon, Missouri

"We've put 46,000 trouble-free miles on it, and loved every one of them."
Dean and Joan Tull
Wichita, Kansas

"I'd buy another one. But I plan on keeping this one awhile."
David B. Thurman
Hot Springs, Arkansas

"It's not boxy like other touring bikes. It looks like a racehorse."
Joe and Bernice Mercurio
Maryland Heights, Missouri

"There's no doubt in my mind that it'll out-handle, out-accelerate and outmaneuver any touring bike out there."
Larry Moore
Dearborn, Michigan

"My dog simply will not ride on anything else."
Karen Kent
Janesville, Wisconsin

"Thanks to the fairing design, bugs are no longer a staple in our diet."
Aubrey and Sharon Pack
Austin, Texas

"It actually makes me feel like part of the wind."
Richard M. Sinex
Key West, Florida

If you don't say things like this about your bike, it doesn't say much for your bike.

Which is why you should consider a Yamaha Venture or Venture Royale.

Ventures handle and accelerate better than any touring machine on the road.

And we're not the only ones who think so. Consider the fact that we've been making Ventures for a mere five years. And have sold a not-so-mere 30,000.

Consider also that 6,000 of those Ventures belong to members of our Venture Touring Society. Fanatics who practically live on their bikes.

And consider that now is a particularly good time to buy a Venture Royale. Because you can order our new fifth anniversary model with an engraved plaque personalized with your name.

The point is, any motorcycle can move people from point A to point B.

But as these pages demonstrate, a Venture can move people even when they're not riding it.

YAMAHA
We make the difference.

Yamaha and the Motorcycle Safety Foundation encourage you to ride safely and respect the environment. For further information regarding the MSF rider course please call 1-800-447-4700. Dress properly for your ride with a helmet, eye protection, long sleeved shirt, long trousers, gloves and boots. Do not drink and drive. It is illegal and dangerous.

2 year limited warranty. Warranty terms are limited. See your Yamaha dealer for details. Specifications subject to change without notice. CB microphone not included. Models sold in California equipped with evaporative emission control device.

It not only says you've arrived. It also says you'll get home.

A Range Rover, clearly, says a lot about the individual who owns one.

Its interior speaks volumes about high standards.

Lavish armchair seating and upholstery, a spectacular stereo and now, even an optional sunroof all comment on a dedication to things refined.

Range Rover's exterior reveals an eye for beauty. As a matter of fact, it was exhibited at no less than the Louvre as an example of elegant design.

Spending $33,000-plus for a 4X4 indicates more than wealth, however.

It also shows a healthy regard for practicality. For there are very few vehicles as extraordinarily capable as a Range Rover.

Its V-8 engine, 4-wheel drive and superb suspension can carry you home securely and smoothly through snow, rain, mud and the most obstinate of Nature's obstacles.

Call 1-800 FINE 4WD for the name of a dealer convenient to you. And test drive the vehicle that speaks highly of its owners.

Almost as highly as they speak about it.

RANGE ROVER

Consumer Magazine Color: 1 Page Or Spread Including Magazine Supplements

369

ART DIRECTOR
Earl Cavanah

WRITER
Larry Cadman

PHOTOGRAPHERS
Jim Salzano
Robert Ammirati

CLIENT
Nikon

AGENCY
Scali McCabe Sloves

370

ART DIRECTOR
Joel Levinson

WRITER
John Hurst

CLIENT
Hershey Foods

AGENCY
Ogilvy & Mather

371

ART DIRECTOR
Roy Grace

WRITER
Diane Rothschild

PHOTOGRAPHER
Carl Furuta

CLIENT
Range Rover of North America

AGENCY
Grace and Rothschild

372

ART DIRECTORS
Dick Pantano
Richard Foster

WRITERS
Joe O'Neill
Peter Nichols

CLIENT
Hyatt Hotels & Resorts

AGENCY
Hill Holliday Connors Cosmopulos/Boston

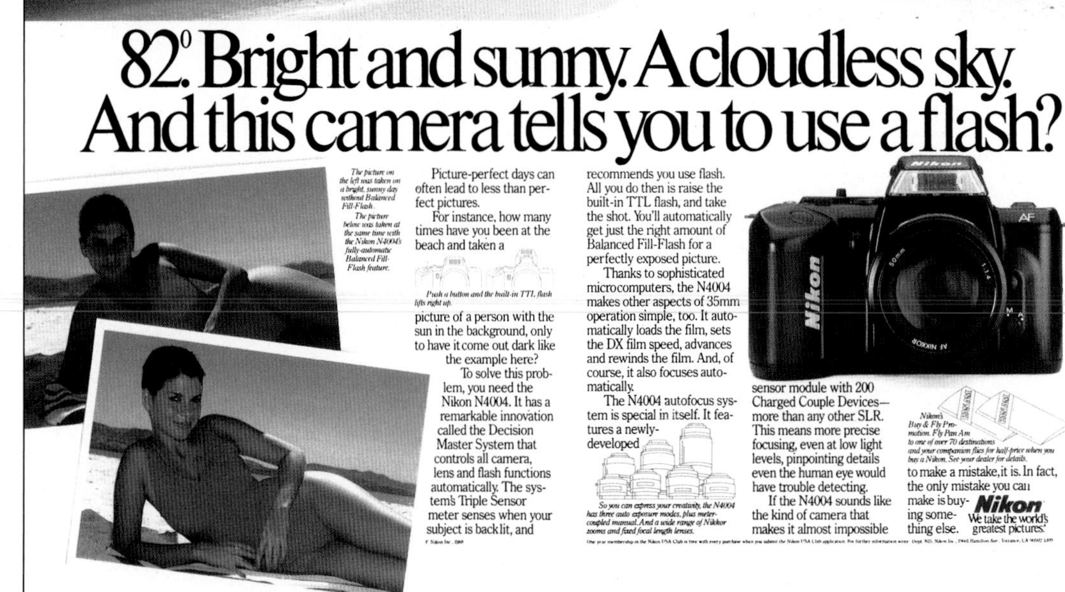

369

©1987 Hershey Foods Corporation

IN CASE OF EMERGENCY,

PULL.

HERSHEY'S

HERSHEY'S KISSES.

370

PLEASE BUCKLE UP FOR SECURITY © 1987 RANGE ROVER OF NORTH AMERICA

We brake for fish.

Would you like to experience a Range Rover under optimum conditions?

Just add water.

A Range Rover can wade through depths that would immobilize a mere car.

And provide the added traction of 4-wheel drive in a downpour.

What's all the more extraordinary, though, is that a Range Rover isn't a vehicle you'll want to save for a rainy day.

Because on a dry road, it handles like a road car. And on a test track, it surges along at roughly 100 mph.

RANGE ROVER

It even surrounds you with all the comfort and luxury of a luxury car.

So why not call 1-800-FINE 4WD for the name of a dealer convenient to you?

While, at a cost somewhat above $30,000, a Range Rover is hardly inexpensive, it's well worth the price.

After all, when you buy one you're not simply buying an ordinary 4-wheel drive vehicle.

You're converting your money into a liquid asset.

371

An appeal to those who set corporate per diems on behalf of those who must sleep with your decisions.

© 1987 Hyatt Corp.

Corporate per diems have always been viewed as a necessary evil.

Those who guard the company purse strings consider them necessary. While those who travel on a shoestring just consider them evil.

However, there's actually hope for a true meeting of the minds. Hope that comes in the form of a Hyatt® Hotel.

In short, Hyatt, the hotel where most business travellers would prefer to stay, is surprisingly no more expensive.

This preference for Hyatt can be attributed to the fact that everything at our hotels is geared to making a trip easier, more productive and more relaxing.

Our sweeping atriums instantly inspire lofty feelings and a sense of well-being. We've designed our guest rooms to be as conducive to work as they are to sleep.

And, to take the edge off a long day, there are relaxing lounges. Plus the added comfort of finding your bed turned down and your pillow fluffed up.

We invite you to compare our competitive corporate rates.

	New York	Washington, D.C.	Atlanta	Chicago	Minneapolis	Los Angeles	Seattle
HYATT	**$185.00** (Grand Hyatt New York)	**$145.00** (Grand Hyatt Washington)	**$119.00** (Hyatt Regency Atlanta)	**$150.00** (Hyatt Regency Chicago)	**$103.00** (Hyatt Regency Minneapolis)	**$105.00** (Hyatt at Los Angeles Airport)	**$75.00** (Hyatt Seattle)
MARRIOTT	$195.00	$167.00	$125.00	$152.00	$107.00	$114.00	$90.00
WESTIN	$215.00	$155.00	$125.00	$155.00	$110.00	$130.00	$110.00

Above are single occupancy corporate rates for Hyatt and the nearest Westin and Marriott hotels in each city. National reservations centers confirmed these rates on October 15, 1987, for November, 1987 occupancy.

To make the thought of returning to Hyatt even more attractive, there are a host of privileges available through the rewarding Hyatt Gold Passport® Frequent Traveller Program.

All of which enables business travellers to do something long thought to be impossible: maintain their dignity.

Without ever having to violate their per diems.

THE HYATT TOUCH™

HYATT HOTELS & RESORTS™

For reservations at any of 87 Hyatt Hotels in North America or 44 Hyatt International Hotels, call **1-800-228-9000, or your travel planner.**

372

Consumer Magazine Color: 1 Page Or Spread Including Magazine Supplements

373
ART DIRECTOR
Dean Hanson
WRITER
Phil Hanft
PHOTOGRAPHER
Oasis Art
CLIENT
Conran's
AGENCY
Fallon McElligott/ Minneapolis

374
ART DIRECTORS
Bruce Bloch
Carlos Darquea
WRITERS
Patricia Rockmore
Dennis Ferrone
PHOTOGRAPHERS
Kei Ogata
Uli Rose
CLIENT
Oil of Olay
AGENCY
Wells Rich Greene

375
ART DIRECTORS
Ivan Horvath
Marten Tonnis
WRITERS
Ken Segall
Doug Gotthoffer
Laurie Brandalise
DESIGNER
Gina Norton
PHOTOGRAPHER
Bo Hylen Studios
CLIENT
Apple Computer
AGENCY
BBDO

376
ART DIRECTOR
Raffael Altmann
WRITER
Eric Jensen
PHOTOGRAPHERS
Martin Langley
Martin Greenstein
CLIENT
Timberland
AGENCY
Lintas USA

373

374

From the people who wrote the book on Desktop Publishing.

Chapter Two.

In the graphic arts, there's almost always room for improvement.

Just ask any client.

So despite the acclaim we received for having created desktop publishing, we went right back to the drawing table.

And came up with a whole new generation of Apple® Desktop Publishing tools.

All to put even more power on your desk. To help you design, illustrate, lay out, comp up and (inevitably) revise — with the utmost of control.

It starts with the newest of our Macintosh® personal computers, the Macintosh SE and the Macintosh II. Which in all modesty, are two of the most powerful systems for publishing yet.

As for which one you'll want, that depends largely on your schedule.

Most job loads fit quite nicely in a Macintosh SE. Which in turn fits quite nicely on a square foot of desk space. No small achievement, given its improved speed and increased storage capacity.

If, on the other hand, your drawing table is a sea of work orders, you may want to clear a spot for the Macintosh II.

Because it can process words and graphics at dizzying speeds. Hold the equivalent of hundreds of drawers' worth of art and type files. And lay out your layouts with more colors than PMS has numbers.

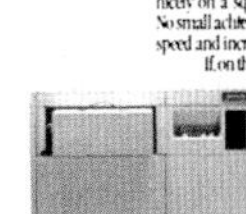

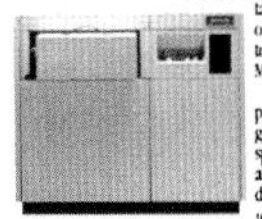

Of course, other recent improvements in the world of Apple Desktop Publishing have been just as stunning.

There are now large-screen display systems, such as SuperView, capable of showing up to two full pages at once. As big as life.

And scanners that let you digitize almost anything on paper – be it scrap art, finished art, line art or halftones. So you can transfer it to your Macintosh and enhance it as you please.

In high-resolution black-and-white. Or, using a Macintosh II, in your choice of 256 brilliant colors – drawing from a palette of over 16 million.

You can also build your artwork by hand. Tapping a well-stocked library

of second-generation programs like Illustrator or Cricket Draw to create pen-and-ink quality drawings in a fraction of the usual time.

Even more impressive, you can instantly make use of elements created by other people, departments or other kinds of computers. Without taking a step. Because Apple Desktop Communications lets you transfer artwork and documents electronically.

So, using advanced layout programs like ReadySetGo! 3.0 or Xpress, you can turn out comps in the time it used to take to turn out tissues.

Which conveniently brings us to our next topic. Getting it down on paper.

Our LaserWriter® Plus printer turns out full-page graphics and text in 300 dot-per-inch quality.

Think small.

KESKO CHRONICLE

HYBRID SWINE BEEFS UP PROFITS

And it's fluent in PostScript, the

industry standard page description language. Meaning that it can deftly replicate type in literally hundreds of different styles and sizes.

Anything from Times and Helvetica to ITC Zapf Chancery.

But if it's commercial quality you're after, Macintosh can also power industrial-strength tools like the Linotronic 100 and 300. Which let you publish, at more than 2500 dots per inch, anything you can put on the screen.

Of course, even better than reading about the new generation of Apple Desktop Publishing is putting it to work.

And that you can do simply by visiting an authorized Apple reseller who specializes in the subject.

For the location nearest you, call (800) 446-3000, extension 50.

Go see the latest chapter in desktop publishing history. Then write your own page.

The power to be your best.

375

TIMBERLAND. FOR THOSE WHO CAN'T YET WALK ON WATER.

Although some of us may claim otherwise, the ability to walk on water has been mastered by very few. The rest of us would be well advised to wear Timberland Sport Boots.

Though your feet may sink in the mud, we at Timberland guarantee that they will remain warm and dry. We start with a Gore-Tex® fabric bootie, sealed with Gore-Seam™ tape. This combination, with a leather and nylon shell and Thinsulate,® adds up to a "two tier" waterproof barrier between your foot and the cold, wet world. We were the first to develop this system.

Timberland Waterproof Gore-Tex® System

The entire boot is then permanently bonded to a remarkably comfortable dual density sole that is vastly lighter than any regular boot.

If you have any further doubts, we challenge you to test our boots on the terrain of your choosing. Bear in mind, however, that we flexed our boots 4,000,000 times under water without detecting a single leak.

This makes us confident you will discover that Timberland Sport Boots are not built on faith alone.

Timberland®

MORE QUALITY THAN YOU MAY EVER NEED.®

GORE-TEX® Registered Trademark of W. L. Gore & Associates, Inc.

Thinsulate® Thinsulate is a registered trademark of 3M.

*Registered Trademarks of The Timberland Company

376

Consumer Magazine Color: 1 Page Or Spread Including Magazine Supplements

377
ART DIRECTOR
Bryan McPeak
WRITERS
Joel Mitchell
Craig Piechura
CLIENT
Iams
AGENCY
W.B. Doner & Company/
Southfield, MI

378
ART DIRECTOR
Judy Austin
WRITER
Wayne Winfield
ARTIST
James Tughan
CLIENT
Spalding
AGENCY
Hill Holliday Connors
Cosmopulos/Boston

Consumer Magazine B/W: Campaign Including Magazine Supplements

379
ART DIRECTOR
Doug Byrnes
WRITER
Mike Coulter
DESIGNER
Doug Byrnes
ARTIST
David Hughes
CLIENT
Oddbins
AGENCY
HDM Horner Collis &
Kirvan/London

Could a cat that eats supermarket pet food take this test and land on its feet?

1. Monitor appetite.
Does your cat eat:
A. Many times a day from a single serving. 10 pts.
B. Once a day. 5 pts.
C. Once every other day. 0 pts.
Many feedings a day are preferable because it allows for more efficient digestion and utilization of food.
However, if your cat suddenly changes eating habits, consult your veterinarian. It could indicate a health problem.

2. Check eyes.
Look into your cat's eyes. Are they:
A. Bright, clear and moist. 15 pts.
B. Dull and dry. 5 pts.
C. Red-streaked with a discharge. 0 pts.
Properly blended nutrients and the correct amount of vitamins in the diet maintain eyesight and clarity.
Dullness occurs from changes in moisture on the surface of the eye or from changes in the body's fluid balance.
Excess moisture or teary eyes is prevalent among cats with respiratory disease.
Red-streaked eyes, or a discharge in the corners of the eyes is the result of abnormal conditions as well.

3. Evaluate fat deposits.
Stand your cat up on its hind legs and feel the fat pads of the lower abdomen. Are they:
A. Very small or undiscernible. 20 pts.
B. Readily visible or about ½" thick. 5 pts.
C. Obvious or ¾" thick and above. 0 pts.

The healthiest cats usually have a slight to moderate amount of fat. Fat pads are also behind the eyes. Normally, these pads gently push the eyes forward. But in some diseases, these pads deteriorate and the eyes seem to shrink into the skull.

4. Inspect mouth.
Raise your cat's upper lip to view the teeth. Are they:
A. Clean, white and glistening. 15 pts.
B. Yellowed with signs of residue. 5 pts.
C. Decaying with evidence of tartar. 0 pts.
Like humans, diet plays a major role in feline oral hygiene. If you didn't check A, chances are you feed your cat a steady diet of wet foods, which can result in dental problems. Dry foods help cleanse teeth and gums.

5. Examine stool.
Stool size, consistency and odor are good indicators of a cat's overall well-being.
Is it:
A. Small, firm and free of any unusual substances and odors. 20 pts.
B. Large, hard with an offensive odor. 5 pts.
C. Large, soft, with an offensive odor. 0 pts.
Stool volume is largely influenced by undigestible foods and enzyme deficiencies. Small, firm stools demonstrate your cat has properly assimilated all the essential nutrients. Stool consistency indicates the quality of your cat's source of nutrients. Stool from a poor source may be soft. A hard stool can represent a mineral or fiber imbalance.
Stool odor is usually traced to grain-based supermarket cat foods. If improperly processed, grain-based cereals ferment in your cat's intestines and cause gas and odor.

6. Feel skin and coat.
Comb your fingers through the hair in the opposite direction it lies naturally. Is it:
A. Healthy, vibrant and free of flaky deposits. 20 pts.
B. Dry, lackluster and poorly elastic. 5 pts.
C. Very oily, smelly, or uneven. 0 pts.
There are normal variations in different breeds of cats at different times of the year. However, poor nutrition always adversely affects skin and hair.
The proper balance of proteins and fats, vitamins and minerals help to assure a desirable look.

If your cat scored 95 or less, don't just change cat food, change where you buy it.

All cats have dietary requirements that demand quality sources of protein. Poultry and meat best meet those requirements.
However, many leading supermarket cat foods rely on grains for their main source of protein.
Iams cat food isn't sold in supermarkets. It's sold only in pet shops, pet supply stores and feed stores.
Sold by veterinarians, breeders and pet specialists. People who understand a cat's nutritional needs. And that's why they recommend Iams.
They know that by feeding Iams you'll see a discernible difference in your animal's health and well-being. Because both Iams Cat and Kitten Food are formulated to exceed a cat's special requirements.
Our foods are dry, made without any artificial colors or flavor enhancers. If your cat can't use it, neither can we.
Cats like the taste of Iams because we give them what they crave naturally—poultry and meat protein.
And Iams is high in taurine, an essential amino acid. Taurine regulates calcium into the heart, which prevents heart disease.
If you'd like to know more, visit an Iams retailer or simply call 1-800-525-IAMS (4267).
Settle for anything less and you'd be failing your cat.

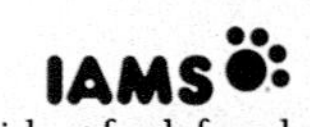

Special pet foods found only at special stores.

Iams Cat Food and Iams Kitten Food are registered trademarks of The Iams Company
©1987 The Iams Company

377

THREE WAYS TO TURN A LONG SHOT INTO A SURE THING.

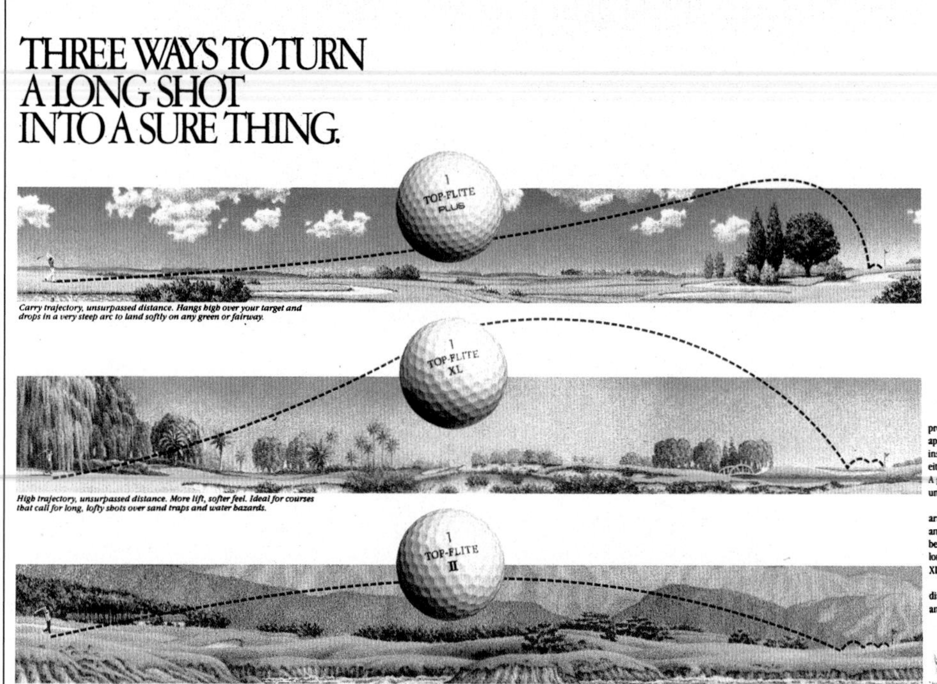

Carry trajectory, unsurpassed distance. Hangs high over your target and drops in a very steep arc to land softly on any green or fairway.

High trajectory, unsurpassed distance. More lift, softer feel. Ideal for courses that call for long, lofty shots over sand traps and water hazards.

Low trajectory, unsurpassed distance. Ideal for courses where wind plays havoc with every shot, or on hard fairways that allow for plenty of roll.

Today's golf courses demand both prodigious drives and long accurate approaches. Yet there are those who insist on playing a golf ball that makes either one a hit or miss proposition. A gamble which is both foolish and unnecessary.
Foolish, because of an imposing array of hazards designed to punish any shot that falls short. Unnecessary, because they could be playing the longest balls: Top-Flite Plus,® Top-Flite XL® and Top-Flite II™ golf balls.*
All of which deliver the extra distance, that makes going for broke an extremely responsible decision.

SPALDING © 1988 Spalding Sports Worldwide. Sold through golf professional shops. Spalding is a member of the National Golf Foundation.

TOP-FLITE. THE LONGEST BALLS.

378

A FEW CABINET CHANGES DENIS THATCHER MIGHT APPROVE OF.

Think not, for a moment, that we are implying the Premier's consort would interfere with affairs of state.

The cabinet we refer to is the one containing the tinctures.

Have you ever wondered what it looks like!

(Who said depleted!)

This being the case, D.T.'s most sensible course would be to head straight for Oddbins.

The nearest branch to Downing Street is only a hefty brassie and five iron away.

And thanks to the hustings, the P.M.'s spouse can hardly fail to be aware of our Finchley High Road branch.

Each Oddbins is a veritable cornucopia of fabled Malts, classic Gins, Cognac, Port and Sherry.

You name it, we've got it.

And if, in daydream, the mind should wander to a waiting wine cellar down Dulwich way, (surely Barratts can't have omitted one from the house plans can they!), we can replenish it well.

With over 500 fine wines to choose from, and with remarkable case discounts, everything is priced to survive even Mr Lawsons excesses.

And should the call be for Champagne, we offer 7 bottles for just the price of 6.

Particularly as it applies to all our 40 odd Champagnes. (Shurely shome mishtake! Ed. – No mishtake. Oddbins.)

For further details call in at any Oddbins.

Alternatively, see page 94.

·O·D·D·B·I·N·S·

LONDON, BELSIZE LANE NW3, BREWER ST. W1, BROMPTON RD, SW3, CHARLOTTE ST. W1, CLAPHAM SW4, EARLHAM ST. WC2, FARRINGDON ST. EC4, FULHAM RD. SW10, GEORGE ST. W1, GREEN LANE N21, HIGH HOLBORN WC1, FINCHLEY HIGH ROAD N12, KENSINGTON HIGH ST., W8, KINGS RD. SW10, KING WILLIAM ST. EC4, MARYLEBONE HIGH ST. W1, NOTTING HILL GATE W11, THE RIDGEWAY SW19, SOUTHAMPTON ROW WC1, UPPER ST. W1, WESTBOURNE GROVE W2 · ASCOT · BATH · BRIGHTON · BRISTOL, CLARE ST., PRINCESS VICTORIA ST., COLDHARBOUR RD., UNION ST · ALTON · BROMLEY · CAMBRIDGE, KING'S PARADE, REGENT ST · CARDIFF · CHELTENHAM, BATH RD., HIGH ST · CHESTER · CHICHESTER · CIRENCESTER · COBHAM · COULSDON · CROYDON · EXETER · GUILDFORD · HASLEMERE · HERTFORD · HOVE · KEW · KINGSTON LIVERPOOL, ALLERTON RD., BOLD ST · MANCHESTER, BARTON ARCADE, COOPER ST · MARLOW · MILTON KEYNES, ACORN WALK · OXFORD, BANBURY RD., HIGH ST · PLYMOUTH · RICHMOND · RICHMOND HILL SALISBURY · SOUTHAMPTON · SURBITON · SWANSEA · TUNBRIDGE WELLS · WINDSOR · WOKINGHAM · SCOTLAND · ABERDEEN, UNION GROVE, UNION ST · EDINBURGH, BRUNTSFIELD PLACE, MONTAGUE TERRACE, NEWINGTON RD., QUEENSFERRY ST., ST. JOHN'S RD · GLASGOW, BYRES RD., CLARKSTON, DRYMEN RD., FENWICK RD., HOPE ST., MILNGARIE RD., VICTORIA RD., WOODLANDS RD. · HELENSBURGH · PERTH. OR TEL: CAROLINE MILES 01-879 1199.

WHAT WOULD JOHN COLE MAKE OF ODDBINS PRICE LIST?

Hondootedly, Hodbins leetest hoffer is a wunner.

Tit for tat, Saatchi von Saatchi nee Thaatchi und Thaatchi buy six bottles of champagne get a seventh free.

Forty, tuctical voting in marginuls, brands off the sheluf. Elecshun foyver disparate kaolin and morfean unlikely event.

Chompagne range. Cecil Parkinson, Yorkshire County cricket, Barnsley MP.

Heidsieck Dry Monopole of The Bailey £8.99. Dom Perignon, Dom Mintoff, Dom Ino, Dom, dom, dom, (Beethoven's 5th), £39.99.

All eyes on Hod-bins expected Reims of paper. Epernay more than you need to. Ay to be sure. Gorblimey. Gorbachov. Gordonrichards.

Bim-bam-a-loo-bam-a-bim-bam-boo.

Success Mother Kelly's doorstep Australian wine promo Hodbins, Stanley Unwin who me Paddy MacGinty's goat.

Alloiance Cloret strongpoint, Labour Neil Kunnuck, third world and commonwealth ales and stouts, whisky a-go go. Champagne will ye no come back again, Horny, Collus, Keervan.

Hoffer ends July 7th.

·O·D·D·B·I·N·S·

LONDON, BELSIZE LANE NW3, BREWER ST. W1, BROMPTON RD, SW3, CHARLOTTE ST. W1, CLAPHAM SW4, EARLHAM ST. WC2, FARRINGDON ST. EC4, FULHAM RD. SW10, GEORGE ST. W1, GREEN LANE N21, HIGH HOLBORN WC1, FINCHLEY HIGH ROAD N12, KENSINGTON HIGH ST., W8, KINGS RD. SW10, KING WILLIAM ST. EC4, MARYLEBONE HIGH ST. W1, NOTTING HILL GATE W11, THE RIDGEWAY SW19, SOUTHAMPTON ROW WC1, UPPER ST. W1, WESTBOURNE GROVE W2 · ASCOT · BATH · BRIGHTON · BRISTOL, CLARE ST., PRINCESS VICTORIA ST., COLDHARBOUR RD., UNION ST · ALTON · BROMLEY · CAMBRIDGE, KING'S PARADE, REGENT ST · CARDIFF · CHELTENHAM, BATH RD., HIGH ST · CHESTER · CHICHESTER · CIRENCESTER · COBHAM · COULSDON · CROYDON · EXETER · GUILDFORD · HASLEMERE · HERTFORD · HOVE · KEW · KINGSTON LIVERPOOL, ALLERTON RD., BOLD ST · MANCHESTER, BARTON ARCADE, COOPER ST · MARLOW · MILTON KEYNES, ACORN WALK · OXFORD, BANBURY RD., HIGH ST · PLYMOUTH · RICHMOND · RICHMOND HILL SALISBURY · SOUTHAMPTON · SURBITON · SWANSEA · TUNBRIDGE WELLS · WINDSOR · WOKINGHAM · SCOTLAND · ABERDEEN, UNION GROVE, UNION ST · EDINBURGH, BRUNTSFIELD PLACE, MONTAGUE TERRACE, NEWINGTON RD., QUEENSFERRY ST., ST. JOHN'S RD · GLASGOW, BYRES RD., CLARKSTON, DRYMEN RD., FENWICK RD., HOPE ST., MILNGARIE RD., VICTORIA RD., WOODLANDS RD. · HELENSBURGH · PERTH. OR TEL: CAROLINE MILES 01-879 1199.

ONE LIST OLLIE WOULDN'T HAVE SHREDDED.

Should an Oddbins price list have fallen into Colonel Oliver North's hands, we feel he'd have positively fawned over it.

With over 500 fine wines, 39 various Champagnes, fabled malts, classic gins, cognac and sherry, Oddbins seems a much more sensible place to divert funds.

Who knows, with nearly 90 branches, perhaps Ollie had paid a visit to Oddbins on his last clandestine mission over here.

If so, he'd be well briefed. (Just like Miss Hall.)

With over 60% of our managers holding the Wine and Spirit diploma, they, like Ollie, know what they're talking about.

Indeed, just try shutting them up.

They'll spill the beans on case discounts, buying 6 bottles of Champagne and getting a 7th free. Why Australian wines are such good value and more.

You'll discover, (contra to popular opinion), that it isn't necessary to make exorbitant payments for fine wines.

So pop in and give us a fair hearing.

(We wonder if the President knows?)

The above ad was created by Mr. C.D. Rawson of Wetherby, West Yorkshire. We'd like him to accept our thanks and a case of Champagne.

We would also like to thank the 400 other entrants in our 'Do your own Oddbins ad' competition. The standards were incredibly high. So much so, we've decided to fire our current Copywriter and Art Director. Pip. Pip.

·O·D·D·B·I·N·S·

Consumer Magazine B/W: Campaign Including Magazine Supplements

380

ART DIRECTOR
Doug Lew

WRITERS
Bill Johnson
Bob Thacker

CLIENT
Minneapolis Institute of Arts

AGENCY
Ruhr/Paragon - Minneapolis

381

ART DIRECTOR
Lou Carvell

WRITER
Abbie Simon

PHOTOGRAPHER
Gary Hanlon

CLIENT
Smith Corona

AGENCY
Rosenfeld Sirowitz
Humphrey & Strauss

Detail from photograph of Käthe Kollwitz by Hugo Erfurth, c. 1925; Worcester Art Museum

Sober images from a time when German life was a cabaret.

In the years following the First World War, Germany was a country of chaos.

Yet, in the midst of this turmoil, German arts flourished. And a group of outstanding German photographers captured the era with astonishing images.

Photographers of the Weimer Republic

On display from June 14 to August 10. Revealing photographs of Germany between the World Wars.

This exhibition was organized by the Worcester Art Museum and funded in part by the National Endowment for the Arts. Lufthansa German Airlines provided the transportation.

The Art of the Samurai

On display from June 28 to Jan. 4. This exhibition provides an intriguing glimpse of the hand-crafted swords, armor, war stirrups and other traditional weaponry used from the 16th through the 19th centuries by the Samurai.

Don't miss the popular exhibit, *Treasures from the National Museum of American Art*, which provides a treasury of American art from colonial to contemporary times.

Organized by the National Museum of American Art and made possible by a grant from United Technologies Corporation, the exhibition will be on display until July 13.

Minneapolis Institute of Art

See the many ways in which the great were honored by the grateful.

When the S.S. Titanic sank, the survivors were rescued by the crew of the R.M.S. Carpathia. For their heroism, the Carpathia's captain and crew were awarded silver loving cups and commemorative medals (shown above).

Those medals, along with 150 other trophies and silver commemorative items are part of a new show, *Marks of Achievement: Four Centuries of American Presentation Silver*, on display at the Minneapolis Institute of Arts from February 14 through May 15.

The show surveys the silver pieces presented to statesmen, scholars, soldiers, industrialists, churches, athletes and loved ones on the occasion of important events or accomplishments.

Created by America's greatest silversmiths including Tiffany, Revere and Gorham, these works display a craftsmanship that is timeless. Come see for yourself. We know you'll agree that these trophies are so beautiful they belong in a museum, not on a mantle.

The Minneapolis Institute of Arts

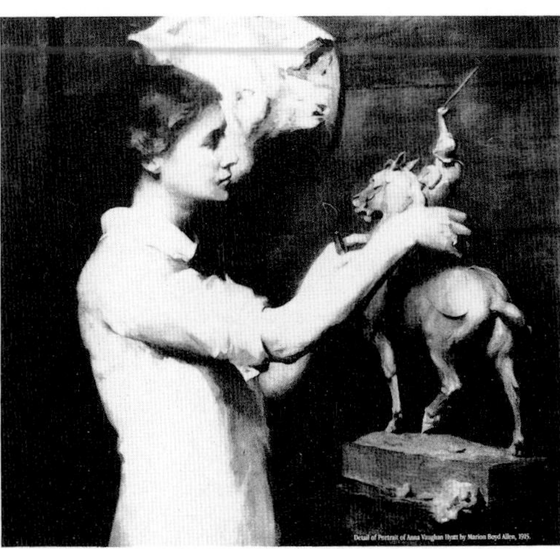

Detail of Portrait of Anna Vaughan Hyatt by Marion Boyd Allen, 1915.

Women shouldn't be put on a pedestal. Their work, however, is quite another matter.

Few, if any, accomplished women artists have been recognized as major figures in the history of art. Now, a national exhibition of paintings and sculpture by American women artists is rewriting art history.

American Women Artists, 1830-1930

This exhibition will be on display at The Minneapolis Institute of Arts from July 5 through August 30. It includes 124 portraits, historical scenes, landscapes, still lifes and sculptures by professional women artists of the 19th and early 20th centuries.

It's part of a celebration of the opening of the first museum in the world devoted exclusively to women artists, the National Museum of Women in the Arts, which organized this inaugural exhibition in cooperation with the International Exhibitions Foundation. This exhibition is made possible by a grant from the United Technologies Corporation.

Don't miss this opportunity to learn more about women in the arts. Come visit The Minneapolis Institute of Arts, 2400 Third Avenue South, Minneapolis, MN 55404.

The Minneapolis Institute of Arts

Introducing the Grammar-Right™ System. It puts passion in your prose, life in your letters, dash in your documents.

Meet the toughest critic since your English teacher–the revolutionary new Smith Corona XD 6700 with the Grammar-Right System. Misuse a word,-overuse a word, misspell or even mistype a word and you'll hear about it, with a beep.

Grammar-Right is an interactive system that works with you step by step to improve your writing style.

With advanced new features like Word Alert, Word Count and Thesaurus, you'll be in command of the English language, without ever leaving your desk.

You won't just be writing better, you'll be typing more accurately, too. Our 75,000 word Spell-Right electronic dictionary can catch spelling mistakes and typing errors before you do. WordEraser correction removes whole words at a touch. Plus, Word-Right AutoSpell, WordFind® List and 10-line correction give you a proofreading system that makes typing perfect pages quick...and easy.

The XD 6700 also boasts a long list of other super automatic features which make it one of the most advanced electronic typewriters in the world. Incidentally, we're proud to remind you that it's made right here in the U.S.A.

So if you're ready to put your English mistakes in the past, there should be a Smith Corona in your future.

MADE IN USA

For more information on this product, write to Smith Corona Corporation, 65 Locust Avenue, New Canaan, CT 06840 or Smith Corona (Canada Ltd.), 440 Tapscott Road, Scarborough, Ontario, Canada M1B 1Y4

Spell-Right™ Dictionary
You just spelled "right" wrong.

Thesaurus
Why be "good" when you can be "exceptional," "marvelous" or "magnificent"?

WordEraser® Correction
Erases "right" with the touch of a button.

Word Alert™
You just confused "right" with "write."

Word Count™
Stop being so "nice."
You've used that word 10 times.

Word-Right® AutoSpell
Takes the wrong "right" out and puts the right "right" in, automatically.

SMITH CORONA™
TOMORROW'S TECHNOLOGY AT YOUR TOUCH.

IF YOU WEREN'T BORN WITH GREAT WRITING SKILLS, YOUR PARENTS CAN STILL GIVE THEM TO YOU.

Introducing the Grammar-Right™ System. It puts passion in your prose, life in your letters, dash in your documents.

What you didn't inherit from your parents in writing ability, we've more than made up for with technology.

It's the remarkable new Smith Corona XD 6700 with the Grammar-Right System. Step by step it can turn a boring writer into a born writer.

Press the Word Count feature and the XD 6700 will remind you that you've used a certain word too often on the page. The Thesaurus will then give you word options to make your sentences richer. Word Alert tells you when you're using a commonly confused term and lets you know how to use it right. So you won't type "exceptable" when you meant "acceptable."

The XD 6700 doesn't just help you become a better writer, it helps you to type more accurately, too. That's because it has the most advanced correction system you can find on any portable typewriter. The 75,000 word Spell-Right electronic dictionary catches spelling and typing errors before you can. WordFind® will locate the error quickly. Word-Right AutoSpell will show you the correct spelling and type it in for you. Word-Eraser correction takes out whole words at a touch.

These, plus a host of other super automatic features all give you letter-perfect typing plus the kind of prose your English teacher never could get out of you. Now that's a *writing* gift. The Smith Corona XD 6700, proudly made in the U.S.A.

MADE IN USA

SMITH CORONA™
TOMORROW'S TECHNOLOGY AT YOUR TOUCH.

For more information on this product, write to Smith Corona Corporation, 65 Locust Avenue, New Canaan, CT 06840

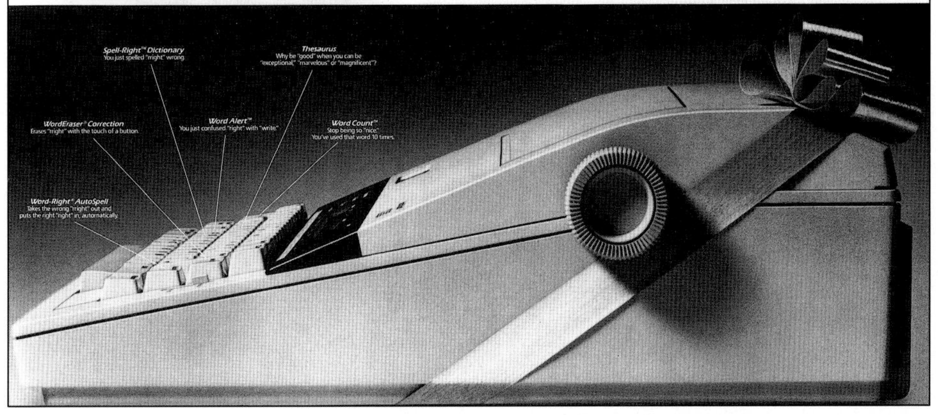

Consumer Magazine Color: Campaign Including Magazine Supplements

382

ART DIRECTOR
Michael Smith

WRITERS
Jackie End
Bill Hamilton
Amelia Rosner

PHOTOGRAPHERS
Annie Leibovitz
Cailor/Resnick

CLIENT
Arrow

AGENCY
Chiat/Day

383

ART DIRECTOR
Michael Smith

WRITER
Bryan Buckley

PHOTOGRAPHER
Dennis Manarchy

CLIENT
The Rockport Company

AGENCY
Chiat/Day

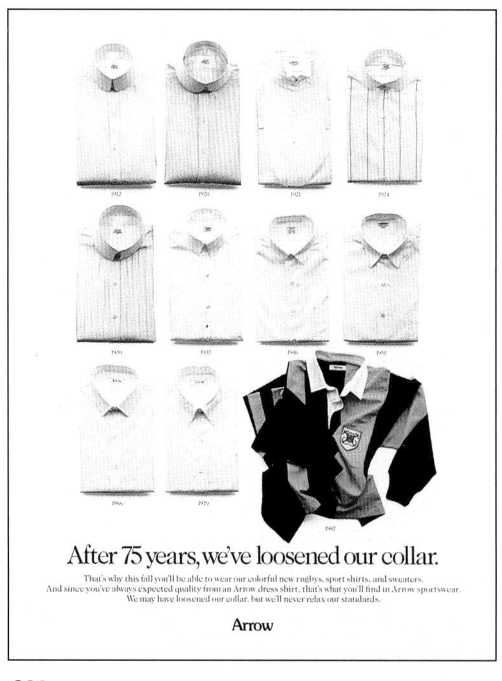

382

The shoes made for long walks in the country.
Robert Sweetgall did a coast to coast trip most travel agents would advise against.
A trip that included 168 stop overs. In such places as Kalamazoo, Michigan. Three Forks, Montana.. And Big Stone Gap, Virginia.
His itinerary included sight-seeing in the middle of the Mojave Desert. Strolling 300 miles through a couple of Montana blizzards. And spending a restful night sleeping on the dining room tables at Angie's Stone Baked Pizza.
All in all his 11,208 mile trip took about a year.
Which isn't bad. When you consider all he had was two legs and a couple pairs of Rockports to carry him through it.
Rockport
Marlboro, Mass.

Some writers just need a pair of shoes to inspire them.
It took two years of solitude on Walden Pond to inspire Henry Thoreau. It took a childhood in the Michigan wilderness to inspire Ernest Hemingway. And it took 4,000 miles on the road to inspire Jack Kerouac.
But for some, all it takes is a pair of Rockports.
The priest in the Bronx who says he believes "…in the Lord, an occasional shot of good Irish whiskey and a beaten pair of Rockports."
The waiter at Mario's who told us how his shoes "…have endured double shifts and the splattering of eight pounds of pasta primavera."
It's good to know that Rockports are bringing a little more enjoyment into these lives. Because their stories are certainly adding to ours.
Rockport
Marlboro, Mass.

How a little shoe company from Marlboro, Mass. is having a major effect on Wall Street.
It all started in a VW bus back in 1969. Out of the back of that bus, we started selling Rockports.
We sold them to back-packers. We sold them to sculptors. We sold them to just about everyone who spent long hard days on their feet and needed a pair of comfortable shoes.
Since then a few things have changed.
The VW was last seen delivering Buffalo Chicken Wings. Our first generation Rockports have evolved into a second. And while we're still selling our shoes to old customers, we've picked up some new ones.
Like on Wall Street. Where a few guys spend sixty hours a week standing in a space two feet wide. With only their gut instinct and our shoes for support.
It's nice to know these shoes are still making feet feel good. And that's the kind of positive effect we'd like to have on the economy.
Rockport
Marlboro, Mass.
BUY
SELL

Consumer Magazine Color: Campaign Including Magazine Supplements

384

ART DIRECTOR
Andrew Nairn

WRITERS
Alan Wooding
Dierdre Strang

PHOTOGRAPHER
Brian Morris

CLIENT
Garuda Indonesia

AGENCY
Foote Cone & Belding/
Kings Cross, Australia

385

ART DIRECTOR
Jerry Torchia

WRITER
Mike Hughes

PHOTOGRAPHER
Scott Barrow

CLIENT
Virginia Division of Tourism

AGENCY
The Martin Agency/
Richmond, VA

People say we're fanatical about our beaches here in Virginia.

We do confess to some rituals that might seem excessive to others.

For example, men and women do patrol our shores here every morning.

These private citizens clear away any debris left behind by man or tide. They've even been known to bring out rakes when sand needs caring for.

Virginia's beaches are swept by more than just the wind.

Of course, the people of Virginia are just as devoted to the land beyond the shoreline.

We keep the streets of nearby Colonial Williamsburg and the lawns at Monticello immaculate. We don't want anything on the Skyline Drive to distract you from the beauty of the Blue Ridge Mountains that surround you.

We keep the flame burning around the clock at Arlington National Cemetery. And we see to it that the vigil never ends at the Iwo Jima Memorial in Northern Virginia.

Naturally, you don't vacation in Virginia simply because it's clean or well-cared for. You come because the beaches are warm and close by and very inviting.

You come because your family wants to play in our giant theme parks, Busch Gardens and Kings Dominion. You come for the sheer fun of Old Town Alexandria and the Roanoke Farmer's Market. You come, perhaps, because you want your children to see Mount Vernon and Appomattox and the White House of the Confederacy. To see Jefferson's great buildings and America's great battlefields.

You come, finally, because in Virginia there are things that are fun and things that are meaningful for each and every member of your family. It's only when you leave Virginia that you find yourself talking about how nice it all was. How friendly. How *clean.*

For more information, call or write the Virginia Division of Tourism, Dept. J331, Richmond, VA 23219.

Virginia is for lovers

Discover a new world. Call 1-800-248-4833.

This is an advertisement for a resort that's bigger than some states.

It's a place where backpacks and tuxedos are equally welcomed. A place where presidents, from George Washington on, have come to work and to play.

Like all good resorts, this one has swimming pools, tennis courts and world-famous golf courses.

There are, of course, quaint foot-trails here. But there's also the Skyline Drive and the Blue Ridge Parkway. Natural Bridge is here. And Daniel Boone's Wilderness Trail.

Other resorts would be proud to have five stars. This one has millions,

Air-conditioned rooms are available this summer in the Blue Ridge Mountains of Virginia.

all crystal clear in the cool night air.

No corporation owns and operates this resort: it's yours the minute you climb its mountains, walk its valleys or explore its caverns.

We're referring, of course, to the Blue Ridge Mountains and Shenandoah Valley of Virginia, a natural resort that stretches more than 200 miles through some of the most beautiful and historic land in America.

The inhabitants include more than 200 kinds of birds, more than 40 kinds of mammals, and some of the friendliest people on earth. People who speak a language that's basically English, but distinctly their own.

This year, when you consider vacations, consider this. At our unique resort, you'll picnic by gentle waterfalls and breathe in fresh mountain air. You'll be charmed by the hill country hospitality of Charlottesville and Lexington. You'll be captivated by the genius of Jefferson at Monticello and the University of Virginia. But you can't do all of this unless you come here, to the mountains and valleys of Virginia. Where your room is already waiting for you.

For all the facts about Virginia, including information about Mount Vernon, Virginia Beach and Colonial Williamsburg, call or write the Virginia Division of Tourism, Dept. K501, Richmond, VA 23219.

Virginia is for lovers

Listen to the names.

Jamestown. Colonial Williamsburg. The American Revolution. Yorktown. Mount Vernon. Monticello. The Civil War. Richmond. The White House of the Confederacy. Manassas. Appomattox.

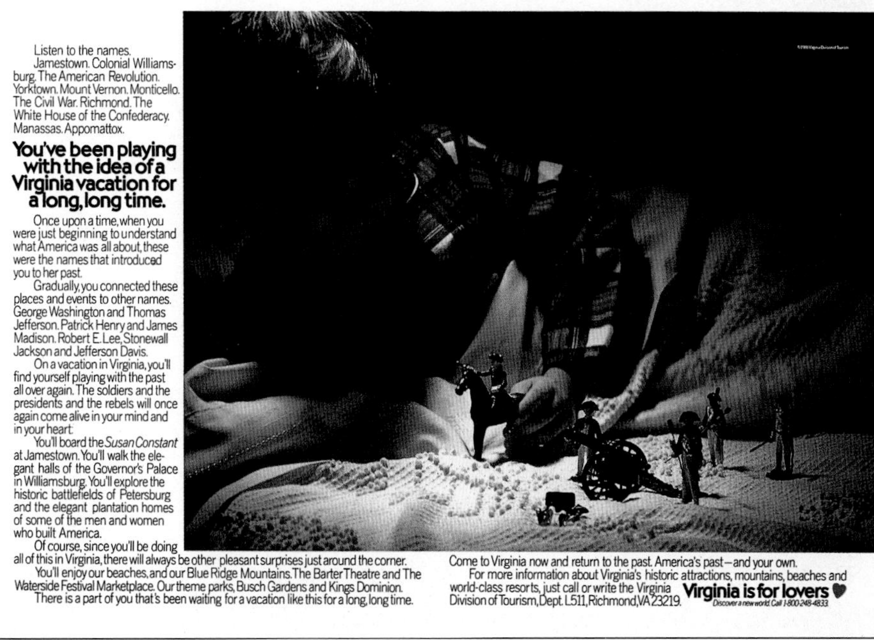

You've been playing with the idea of a Virginia vacation for a long, long time.

Once upon a time, when you were just beginning to understand what America was all about, these were the names that introduced you to her past.

Gradually, you connected these places and events to other names. George Washington and Thomas Jefferson. Patrick Henry and James Madison. Robert E. Lee, Stonewall Jackson and Jefferson Davis.

On a vacation in Virginia, you'll find yourself playing with the past all over again. The soldiers and the presidents and the rebels will once again come alive in your mind and in your heart.

You'll board the *Susan Constant* at Jamestown. You'll walk the elegant halls of the Governor's Palace in Williamsburg. You'll explore the historic battlefields of Petersburg and the elegant plantation homes of some of the men and women who built America.

Of course, since you'll be doing all of this in Virginia, there will always be other pleasant surprises just around the corner.

You'll enjoy our beaches, and our Blue Ridge Mountains. The Barter Theatre and The Waterside Festival Marketplace. Our theme parks, Busch Gardens and Kings Dominion.

There is a part of you that's been waiting for a vacation like this for a long, long time.

Come to Virginia now and return to the past. America's past—and your own.

For more information about Virginia's historic attractions, mountains, beaches and world-class resorts, just call or write the Virginia Division of Tourism, Dept. L511, Richmond, VA 23219.

Virginia is for lovers

Discover a new world. Call 1-800-248-4833.

Consumer Magazine Color: Campaign Including Magazine Supplements

386

ART DIRECTOR
Cabell Harris

WRITER
Ken Hines

PHOTOGRAPHER
Tim Olive

CLIENT
Clyde's

AGENCY
Lawler Ballard/
Richmond, VA

387

ART DIRECTORS
Tod Seisser
Irv Klein

WRITERS
Jay Taub
Stephanie Arnold

PHOTOGRAPHER
Henry Sandbank

CLIENT
Maidenform

AGENCY
Levine Huntley Schmidt &
Beaver

"Lingerie reveals more of a woman than just skin. When a woman wears beautiful lingerie it says she likes herself. I think that's sexy. To me, lingerie expresses how she feels. Playful. Romantic. Mysterious. The possibilities are always interesting."

Maidenform offers women over 150 ways to express themselves. Obviously, people are listening.

M A I D E N F O R M

"Lingerie says a lot about a woman. I listen as often as possible. Lingerie doesn't cover a woman's body so much as uncover her personality. It tells me how she feels about herself. It also tells me how she feels about me...if I get to see it."

Maidenform offers women over 150 ways to express themselves. And obviously, people are listening.

M A I D E N F O R M

"Lingerie does a lot for a woman. Not to mention what it does for a man. I love a woman who says how she feels. But I also love a woman who has secrets. In fact, it's what she keeps to herself that says the most about her.

Lingerie. That's a secret she doesn't share with the world. So sometimes you don't find out. But, then again, sometimes you do."

At Maidenform, we offer women over 150 ways to express themselves. Obviously, people are listening.

M A I D E N F O R M

Consumer Magazine Color: Campaign Including Magazine Supplements

388

ART DIRECTOR
Steve Davis

WRITER
Charles Ashby

PHOTOGRAPHER
Jimmy Williams

CLIENT
Del Monte

AGENCY
McKinney & Silver/
Raleigh, NC

389

ART DIRECTORS
Todd McVey
Robert Cramer

WRITERS
Lee Garfinkel
Amy Borkowsky

PHOTOGRAPHER
Beth Galton

CLIENT
Citizen Watch

AGENCY
Levine Huntley Schmidt &
Beaver

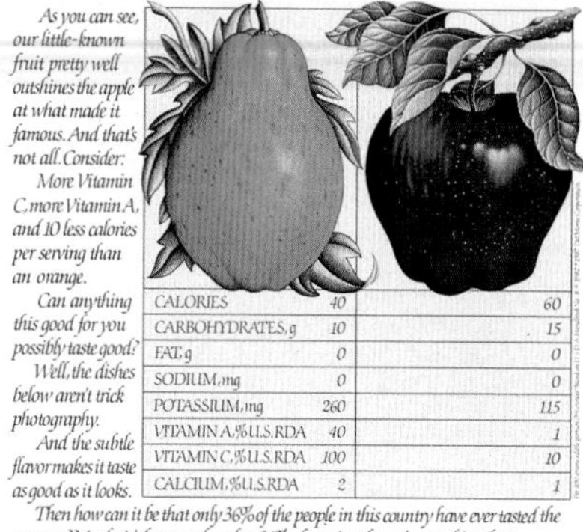

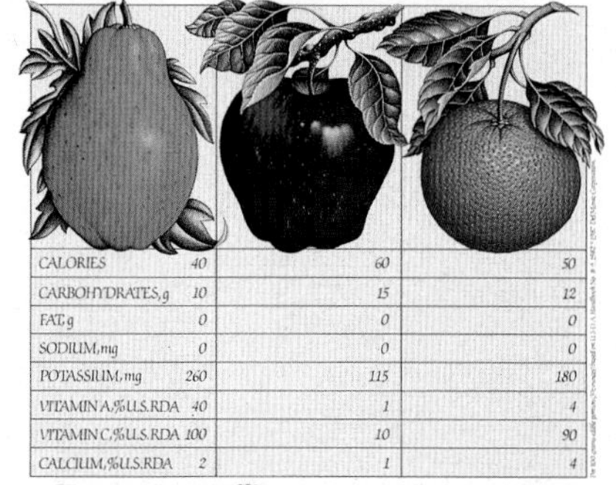

You can tell a lot about a person by the look on their face.

Watches without numbers obviously weren't meant just to tell time.

How to arrive at 8 o'clock. Sharp.

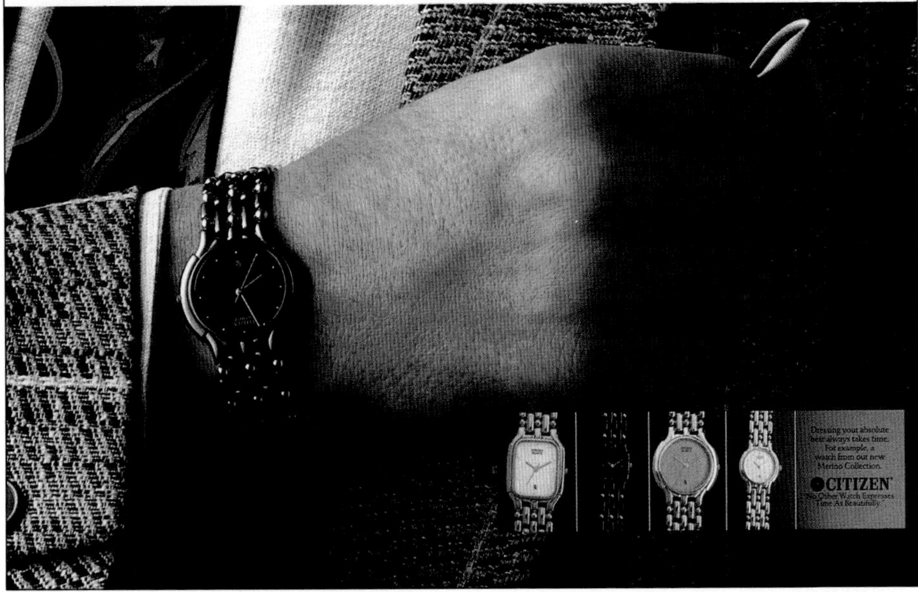

Consumer Magazine Color: Campaign Including Magazine Supplements

390

ART DIRECTORS
Mitch Gordon
John D'Asto

WRITERS
Tom Darbyshire
Mark Fenske

PHOTOGRAPHERS
Georg Bosek
Edward Trovillion

CLIENT
Illinois Office of Tourism

AGENCY
Zechman & Associates/
Chicago

391

ART DIRECTORS
Geoff Hayes
Steve Feldman

WRITERS
Evert Cilliers
Patrick Hanlon
Olga Arseniev

PHOTOGRAPHER
Steve Bronstein

CLIENT
Carillon Importers

AGENCY
TBWA

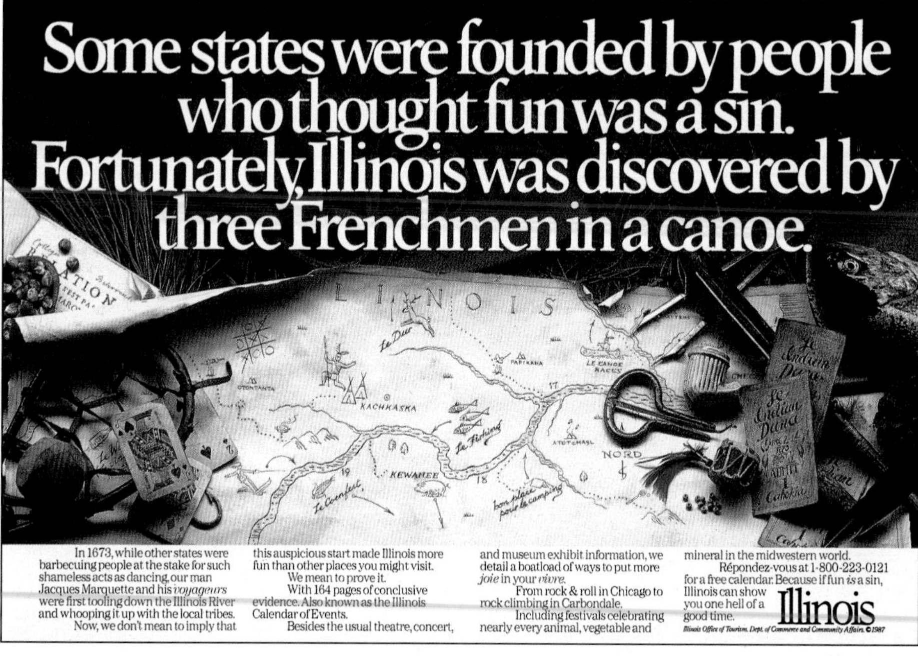

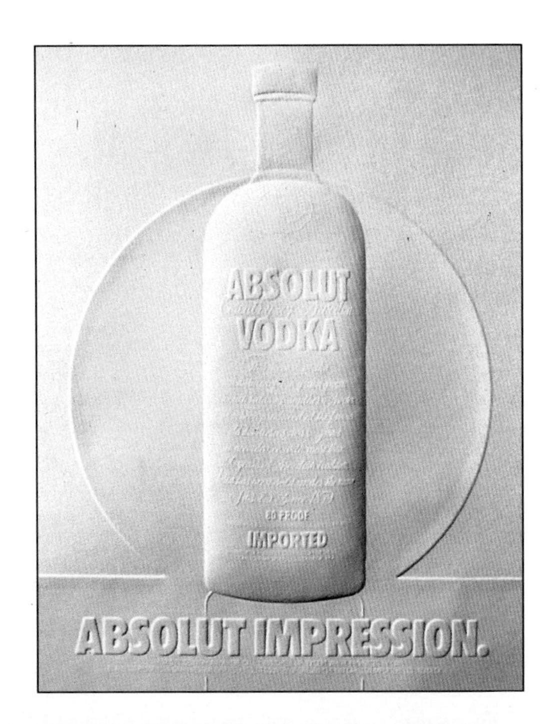
ABSOLUT
VODKA
80 PROOF
IMPORTED
ABSOLUT IMPRESSION.

ABSOLUT
Country of Sweden
VODKA
This superb vodka
was distilled from grain grown
in the rich fields of southern Sweden.
It has been produced at the famous
old distilleries near Åhus
in accordance with more than
400 years of Swedish tradition.
Vodka has been sold under the name
Absolut Since 1879.
80 PROOF
IMPORTED
ABSOLUT TRICK.
ABSOLUT TREAT.

ABSOLUT
Country of Sweden
VODKA
HAVE. .
ABSOLUT
Country of Sweden
PEPPAR
. . .BALL.
ABSOLUT
Country of Sweden
VODKA
ABSOLUT
Country of Sweden
PEPPAR
ABSOLUT
VODKA
ABSOLUT
PEPPAR
. . .AN ABSOLUT. . .

Consumer Magazine Color: Campaign Including Magazine Supplements

392

ART DIRECTOR
Ron Iden

WRITER
Ross Howard

PHOTOGRAPHER
David Branley

CLIENT
Phillips

AGENCY
Brooks Legon Bloomfield/
London

393

ART DIRECTOR
Trevor Kennedy

WRITER
Steve Spence

PHOTOGRAPHER
David Bailey

CLIENT
Ovaltine

AGENCY
Lowe Howard-Spink/
London

HAVING SOLD HIS GRANDFATHER, HE GAVE HIS DAUGHTER AWAY.

It's only natural to want the best for your children, especially on their wedding day.

But these days, to send your daughter down the aisle in anything approaching style can be a massacre in morning dress for your bank balance.

Which is why it could be worth taking a look around you. Frequently, objects you may own or inherit turn out to be alarmingly valuable.

So how do you go about turning the possession you don't want into the bridal procession you do?

Simply bring it along to your nearest Phillips and see one of our specialists (of which there are over 150 around the country for you to call upon). If you cannot bring it in, a photograph and brief description will certainly help.

After establishing exactly what you have, our specialists will suggest exactly when and where they think your object should be put up for auction, to achieve the highest possible price.

In practice, this could mean something brought to one of our fifteen regional auction rooms is sent to London to be sold. Equally, we could recommend that an object from London be sent to the regions or even abroad.

So, whether you have an object you know is worth thousands, or simply have a hunch it may be worth something, just speak to the relevant Phillips specialist.

Or, if you would like any further information about Phillips and a complimentary copy of our preview of forthcoming auctions, just ring 01-629 6602 and ask for Andrew Singleton. You will find our knowledge most rewarding.

An early 18th century walnut and marquetry grandfather (longcase) clock by William Wright of London. Sold recently at Phillips for £9,500.

FINE ART AUCTIONEERS AND VALUERS SINCE 1796

BLENSTOCK HOUSE, 7 BLENHEIM STREET, NEW BOND STREET, LONDON W1Y 0AS Telephone: 01-629 6602
LONDON (3 AUCTION ROOMS) BATH CAMBRIDGE CARDIFF CHESTER COLWYN BAY CORNWALL EDINBURGH EXETER FOLKESTONE GLASGOW IPSWICH KNOWLE LEEDS MELBOURNE MORLEY NORWICH OXFORD SHERBORNE BRUSSELS GENEVA NEW YORK PARIS ZURICH
Members of the Society of Fine Art Auctioneers.

HAVING PUT HIS HEIRLOOM THROUGH PHILLIPS, HE PUT HIS HEIR THROUGH SCHOOL.

It is a fact of life that the things you mean to do are often at odds with the means you have to do them.

These days it can cost £25,000 or more simply to provide a private education for one child.

Which is why it could be worth taking a look around you. Frequently, objects you may be given or inherit turn out to be alarmingly valuable.

Of course, it takes years of study and even more years of experience to distinguish the very fine from the merely functional.

Experience which is the hallmark of every one of the hundred-and-twenty or so Phillips specialists who are available for you to see.

So how do you go about turning the heirloom you don't want into the educated heir you do?

Simply bring it along. (If it's not portable, a photograph and brief description will suffice.)

Should whatever you bring be revealed as less than an important work of art or antique we certainly won't hide the fact.

Yet we will do everything in our considerable power to ensure that every object realises its true value, come what may.

To this end the Phillips specialists will suggest exactly when and where they think your object should be put up for auction (taking account of market conditions, not their own convenience).

In practice, this could mean an object brought to one of our fifteen regional auction rooms is sent to London to be sold.

Equally, we could recommend that an object from London be sent to the regions or abroad.

(For example, Scottish silver currently fetches the highest prices in Scotland itself, hence our policy of transferring it to Edinburgh for auction.)

Whether you have something you know is worth thousands, or simply have a hunch it may be worth something, bring it along and speak to the relevant Phillips specialist.

Or if you would like any further information about Phillips and a complimentary copy of our preview of forthcoming auctions, just ring 01-629 6602 and ask for Andrew Singleton. You will find our knowledge most rewarding.

Fine George III mahogany octagonal rent desk, sold recently at Phillips for £36,000.

FINE ART AUCTIONEERS AND VALUERS SINCE 1796

LONDON (3 AUCTION ROOMS) BATH CAMBRIDGE CARDIFF CHESTER COLWYN BAY CORNWALL EDINBURGH EXETER FOLKESTONE GLASGOW IPSWICH KNOWLE LEEDS MORLEY NORWICH OXFORD SHERBORNE BRUSSELS GENEVA NEW YORK PARIS ZURICH
Blenstock House, 7 Blenheim Street, New Bond Street, London W1Y 0AS Members of the Society of Fine Art Auctioneers

HAVING DISPOSED OF A SECONDHAND EMERALD. THEY ACQUIRED A FIFTEEN HAND CHESTNUT.

A horse might not quite cost a kingdom, but it would certainly set you back a princely sum.

The going rate for a good riding horse, or even pony, is at least £2000.

Saddlery and clothes will add £500 or so to your mounting bill. Then, once you take stabling, feed and farriers' and vets' fees into account, you will have to put aside around £4000 a year just to keep your new mobile asset mobile.

Which is why it could be worth taking a look around you. Frequently, objects you may own or inherit turn out to be alarmingly valuable.

Of course, it can take the eye of a specialist and years of experience to recognise the difference between an item of worth and one that's merely of interest. Hence Phillips have over a hundred-and-twenty specialists at your disposal.

So how do you go about turning the small mount you don't want into the larger variety you do?

Simply take it into your nearest Phillips. There are more than twenty auction rooms and offices around the country, staffed by professional auctioneers and specialists in fine art and antiques.

A fine emerald single stone ring in a plain mount. Recently sold at Phillips for £11,000.

Usually they will be able to appraise your item on the spot.

On the occasion when a more specialised eye is called for, then the relevant London department will be called upon.

When, and only when, they know exactly what they are dealing with, you will be advised of the best time to put your object up for auction, and the most favourable venue (since certain items fetch higher prices in certain places).

Photographs will be taken, where appropriate, and catalogues produced, culminating in the sale itself. You will be promptly advised of the hammer price, and your cheque will be with you shortly thereafter.

Not all the finest items are found in London. We recently sold a diamond pendant, which was first taken to our Cambridge office, for £140,000.

So whatever you may have and wish to sell, bring it along to your local Phillips.

For further information and a complimentary copy of our preview of forthcoming auctions, please call Andrew Singleton on 01-629 6602.

You'll find our knowledge most rewarding.

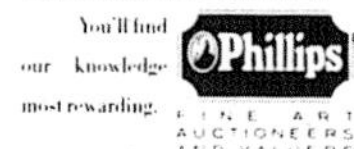

FINE ART AUCTIONEERS AND VALUERS

BLENSTOCK HOUSE, 7 BLENHEIM STREET, NEW BOND STREET, LONDON W1Y 0AS Telephone: 01-629 6602
LONDON (3 AUCTION ROOMS) BARNSTAPLE BATH CAMBRIDGE CARDIFF CARLISLE CARMARTHEN CHESTER COLWYN BAY CORNWALL EDINBURGH EXETER FOLKESTONE GLASGOW IPSWICH KNOWLE LEEDS MELBOURNE MORLEY NORWICH OXFORD PLYMOUTH ROCHDALE SHERBORNE WIMBORNE BRUSSELS GENEVA NEW YORK PARIS THE HAGUE ZURICH
Members of the Society of Fine Art Auctioneers.

THE THAIS DRINK OVALTINE FOR ENERGY. WHAT MUST THEY THINK OF US DRINKING IT BEFORE BED?

Before indulging in any strenuous activity, the good citizens of Bangkok indulge in a glass of their favourite energy drink.

Ovaltine.

In Thailand, you see, Ovaltine is seen differently than here. They actually call it the 'kick the day off' drink.

And, as Ovaltine contains the goodness of malt extract, barley and eggs, why not?

Malt extract, for example, is well known as an instant and long lasting source of energy.

Eggs are an excellent source of protein. And Ovaltine provides calcium in abundance. (Through both the milk powder it contains and the fresh milk you make it with.)

And, a mug of Ovaltine contains no artificial flavour, no added sugar, colour or preservatives.

Small wonder then that your average Thai football team insists on a pre-match mug.

Yet, despite the reasoning, it still sounds somewhat strange. Then again, if we think they're odd, what must they think we are?

Bonkers, probably.

ISN'T IT TIME YOU WOKE UP TO OVALTINE?

THE FRENCH CLAIM OVALTINE RESTORES ENERGY. IS THAT WHY THEY DRINK IT FOR BREAKFAST?

After a très fatiguant night on the town, what have this French couple headed straight for?

Hair of the dog, perhaps? Or black coffee? No . . . a cup of Ovaltine. Yet with the old joie de vivre obviously exhausted, why do they drink something to help them sleep?

Thing is, they don't. They drink it to wake up. Because your Continentals believe that the malt extract, barley and eggs in Ovaltine are a real boost to a flagging body.

Malt extract for instance, is well known as an instant and long lasting source of energy.

Eggs are an excellent source of protein. And Ovaltine provides calcium in abundance, through both the milk powder already in it and the fresh milk it's made with.

What's more, thanks to a generous helping of cocoa, Ovaltine has a delicious chocolatey taste.

Yet Ovaltine contains no added sugar, no artificial flavour, colour or preservatives.

So the moral of the story is this, girls. If a Frenchman offers you a mug of Ovaltine, beware.

He actually means next morning.

ISN'T IT TIME YOU WOKE UP TO OVALTINE?

NO WONDER THE CONTINENTALS ONLY NEED A ROLL FOR BREAKFAST.

Where's the brimming Cafétière of strong dark coffee, the basket full of fresh croissants, the lashings of Normandy butter and the deep pots of confiture Framboise?

You know, a typical 'Continental breakfast'. Well, to the left is a typical Continental breakfast.

Just un roll, beurre et a large mug of Le Petit Déjeuner Malté. Ovaltine to you and I.

Yes, Ovaltine can be drunk for breakfast.

And why not? It's made, is it not, from barley, malt extract and eggs. What better for setting you up for the day?

Malt extract, for instance, is well known as a long lasting source of energy.

Calcium is in abundance. Through both the milk powder already in it, and the fresh milk you make it with.

In fact, a mug of Ovaltine provides most of the nutrients required by the body.

And Ovaltine contains no added sugar, no artificial flavour, colour or preservatives.

Formidable! Eh? Mind you, if Ovaltine is such a good source of energy how come we Brits drink it before bed?

On second thoughts, don't answer that.

ISN'T IT TIME YOU WOKE UP TO OVALTINE?

Consumer Magazine Color: Campaign Including Magazine Supplements

394

ART DIRECTORS
Michael Arola
Mike Kelly

WRITER
Kip Klappenback

PHOTOGRAPHERS
Dennis Gray
Sean Thonson
Bob Grigg

CLIENT
Pirelli

AGENCY
Cochrane Chase Livingston/Newport Beach, CA

395

ART DIRECTORS
John Horton
Ron Brown

WRITERS
Richard Foster
David Abbott

PHOTOGRAPHERS
Ken Griffiths
Steve Cavalier
Graham Ford

CLIENT
Sainsbury's

AGENCY
Abbott Mead Vickers/SMS - London

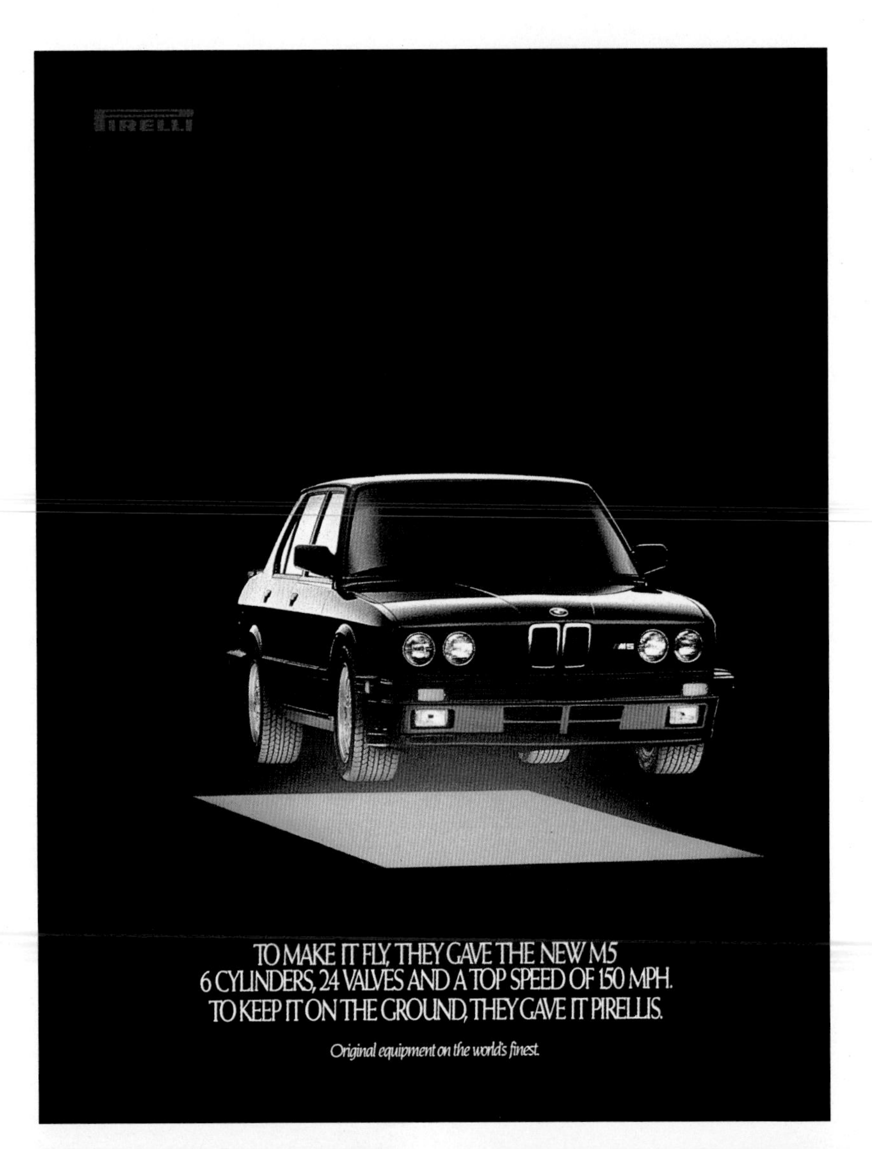

PIRELLI
TO MAKE IT FLY, THEY GAVE THE NEW M5
6 CYLINDERS, 24 VALVES AND A TOP SPEED OF 150 MPH.
TO KEEP IT ON THE GROUND, THEY GAVE IT PIRELLIS.
Original equipment on the world's finest.

IN ITS MOST POTENT FORM,
THE CAR HAILED AS "THE BEST HANDLING PRODUCTION SPORTS CAR IN AMERICA"
IS EQUIPPED WITH TIRES OF EQUAL CALIBRE.
Pirelli. Original equipment on the world's finest.

WHEN WOLFSBURG DECIDED
TO STRETCH THE LIMITATIONS OF THEIR FASTEST HATCHBACK,
THEY ASKED PIRELLI ALONG FOR THE RIDE.
GTI
PIRELLI
Original equipment on the world's finest.

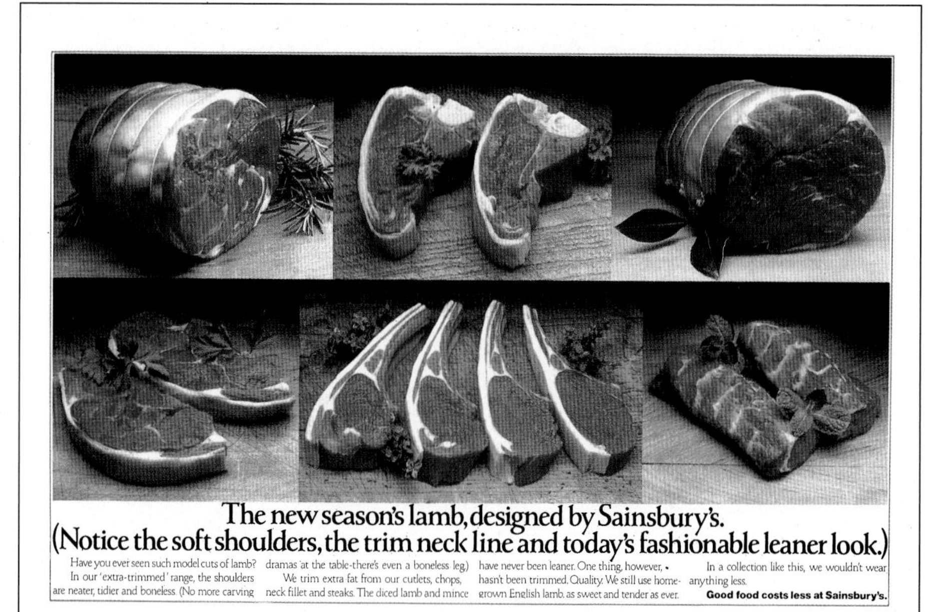

The new season's lamb, designed by Sainsbury's. (Notice the soft shoulders, the trim neck line and today's fashionable leaner look.)

Have you ever seen such model cuts of lamb?

In our 'extra-trimmed' range, the shoulders are neater, tidier and boneless. (No more carving dramas at the table-there's even a boneless leg.)

We trim extra fat from our cutlets, chops, neck fillet and steaks. The diced lamb and mince have never been leaner. One thing, however, hasn't been trimmed. Quality. We still use home-grown English lamb, as sweet and tender as ever.

In a collection like this, we wouldn't wear anything less.

Good food costs less at Sainsbury's.

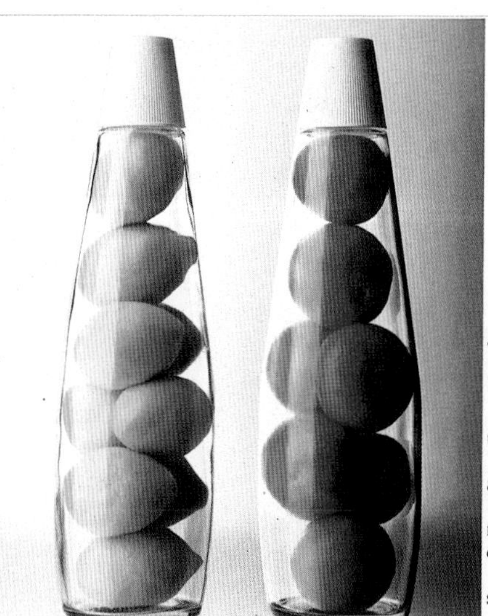

Sainsbury's squash 10% more fruit juice into their squashes.

Sainsbury's High Juice fruit squashes really do live up to their name.

They contain 50% fruit juice (twice the legal minimum) and 10% more than the competition.

We squash on average seven oranges into our orange squash, nine lemons into our lemon squash and ten limes into our lime cordial. (Quite a squeeze but worth it.)

What we don't put in are artificial colours, flavouring or sweeteners.

So even when you dilute to taste, it's still a delight to taste.

Good food costs less at Sainsbury's.

What is it that makes Sainsbury's Manzanilla such a dry sherry? Water, of course.

About 20 kilometres north-west of Jerez lies the small fishing village of Sanlucar de Barrameda. It is here, and only here, that the uniquely dry Manzanilla sherry is made.

Sanlucar's coastal position gives it a cooler, more humid climate than that of Jerez.

Ideal conditions, in fact, for the development of "flor," a film of yeast that forms naturally on the surface of the sherry in the cask.

Not all sherries develop flor, but those that do are destined to become drier and lighter than those that don't. And none is drier or lighter than Manzanilla.

Served chilled, as it should be, it has a crisp freshness that makes it the perfect aperitif. Some aficionados even claim to detect a faint salty tang on the palate.

Once opened, the bottle should be kept in the refrigerator and the contents consumed within three weeks. (Not a difficult task.)

It should also be no more than six months old when you buy it.

Unlike most wines, sherry does not improve with age in the bottle.

At Sainsbury's, you can be sure the Manzanilla you buy will be in the peak of condition.

It is supplied to us by one of the most reputable bodegas in Sanlucar, and our price ensures that it doesn't sit on the shelf for very long.

Indeed, a bottle of Sainsbury's Manzanilla costs no more than a bottle of ordinary sherry. Which makes it one taste that's easy to acquire.

Good food costs less at Sainsbury's.

Consumer Magazine Color: Campaign Including Magazine Supplements

396

ART DIRECTOR
Gordon Smith

WRITER
Paul Grubb

PHOTOGRAPHER
Peter Lavery

CLIENT
Mazda Cars

AGENCY
Gold Greenless Trott/ London

397

ART DIRECTORS
Clem McCarthy
Yvonne Smith
Marcus Kemp
Alain Briere

WRITERS
Martin Puris
Bill McCullam

PHOTOGRAPHER
Jeffrey Zwart

CLIENT
BMW of North America

AGENCY
Ammirati & Puris

DEAR VW,
ALL THOSE CHECKS, MAYBE IT'S TIME YOU CHECKED WHY THE FINNS AND DANES PREFER MAZDA.

You have a reputation for reliability, VW.

Now we don't know how many of your production workforce are quality control inspectors, with authority to halt production when they spot a fault, but we do know that you don't check more thoroughly than Mazda.

Because at Mazda, every single production worker has the authority to stop the production line when he spots a fault.

No matter how thorough you may be VW, you can't beat 100%.

And a Dane can buy a Mazda for less Kroner than a VW.

Maybe that's the reason why, in Finland and Denmark, more folk's wagons are Mazda.

mazda

(P.S. Freephone 0800 444 190. You'll be amazed at a Mazda.)

DEAR AUDI,
WHY DO FOUR TIMES AS MANY FINNS PREFER TO GET TO GRIPS WITH THE ROAD IN A MAZDA?

In Finland our cars are cornering the market, Audi.

Now you are famous for your performance on unmade, icy and mountainous roads (you know: the kind you find in Finland).

But what you'll also find in Finland is they drive four times as many new Mazdas as Audis.

In fact, one Finn who drives a Mazda recently won the World Championship Swedish Rally.

Timo Salonen's Mazda 323 4x4 Turbo finished almost four minutes ahead of the highest placed quattro.

Even in road trim, the new 323 4WD has a 1.6 litre turbo-charged engine with Intercooler.

It produces 148bhp, and rockets the car from standstill to 60mph in just over 7 seconds, then on to a top speed of around 125mph.

And, a Finn can buy a 323 4x4 Turbo for 274,000 Marka less than a quattro.

*?@! as they say in Germany.

mazda

(P.S. Freephone 0800 444 190. You'll be amazed at a Mazda.)

DEAR BMW,
IS IT JUST OUR THICK COAT OF PAINT THAT MAKES US OUTSELL YOU 3 TO 1 IN AUSTRIA?

You have a reputation for immaculate paintwork, BMW. Well, everyday Austrian cars are coated with salt and peppered with grit.

And Austrians buy three times more Mazdas than BMWs.

Now Austrians aren't thick, but they know our paint is.

Each bodyshell travels through 260 tons of paint for cathodic electro-painting.

So the paint isn't just painted on, it's bonded to the metal, even in areas previously deemed No Entry.

It's called the Porpoise Swim Line, because the bodyshell moves up and down as it advances forward.

Shaking off even the tiniest air bubble in the tightest corners of the shell.

And an Austrian has to shell out 68,700 less Schillings for a Mazda 626 paintjob, than he does for an equally impressive BMW 320i paintjob.

So you see, in Austria, it takes more than just a lick of paint to lick a Mazda.

mazda

(P.S. Freephone 0800 444 190. You'll be amazed at a Mazda.)

"A MAN SHOULD DO THREE THINGS IN HIS LIFE AND DRIVING THIS CAR IS ONE OF THEM."

THE NEW BMW 750iL.

The BMW 750iL has been greeted by the European press as "the superstar of the luxury class" and "not just a milestone in German automotive history, but its crowning achievement."

It was a well-known American automotive editor, however, who offered the spirited appraisal quoted on the opposite page.

Back when mighty Duesenbergs and Bugattis ruled the roadways, he explained, it was said that every man should enjoy three experiences in life: planting a tree, raising a son, and driving a 12-cylinder car.

The new flagship of BMW's 7-Series, he reports, makes the third endeavor more satisfying than ever imagined.

When you sit in the hand-stitched leather driver's seat, you command not merely an abundance of power but a seamless, unhesitating flow of power that never raises its voice above a whisper.

Your mastery of the most unruly roads is assured by the 750iL's even weight distribution and stable aerodynamics combined with a patented fully-independent suspension and gas-pressure shocks.

The car is long, spacious, and uncannily quiet. Its amenities are astonishing—a cellular telephone, for example, is standard equipment—and it evinces a level of workmanship that is elsewhere close to extinction.

Your authorized BMW dealer can confirm the truth of this by arranging a thorough test drive of the 750iL.

The noblest transformation that 4,235 pounds of steel, aluminum, glass, and leather have ever undergone.

THE ULTIMATE DRIVING MACHINE.

THE BMW 750iL. ENGINEERING MORE AKIN TO THE CORPORATE JET THAN THE CORPORATE CAR.
A Motor Trend editor once observed that driving a BMW "prompts an attitude akin to piloting a precision aeronautical machine rather than a mere automobile."
No BMW justifies such an attitude more thoroughly than the new flagship of the BMW 7-Series, the 750iL.
The turbine-like flow of power that makes it, "at autobahn speeds, a rational alternative to a private plane" (AutoWeek) comes from a 12-cylinder engine inspired by aircraft power plants.*
This compact, all-aluminum design borrows from aviation metallurgy. Its performance is optimized by a fail-safe aircraft-style system of dual engine-control computers. And it offers the dependable simplicity that aircraft engineers strive for as an ideal—the only routine maintenance it ever needs is oil and spark plug changes.
The sleek, long-wheelbase 750iL also benefits from the aviation-born discipline of aerodynamics.
Its shape reduces both lift and sensitivity to crosswinds. Combining with low-slung, evenly-distributed weight and a patented fully-independent suspension to give rock-like stability and nimble handling.
What might be called the world's first sports limousine features the same kind of anti-lock braking that helps prevent skids on 380-ton jetliners.
And its prodigiously soundproofed, wood-trimmed, leather-upholstered cockpit is equipped with electronic copilots that monitor some 26 of the car's vital functions, warn when outside temperatures approach freezing, maintain even cruising speed up and down steep hills, and more.
To experience these and a squadron of other innovations, let your authorized BMW dealer arrange a test drive of the 750iL.
A blend of performance and luxury you won't find anywhere else on the ground. Or in the air for that matter.
THE ULTIMATE DRIVING MACHINE.

Consumer Magazine Color: Campaign Including Magazine Supplements

398

ART DIRECTORS
Sherry Pollack
Gail Bartley

WRITERS
Lesley Stern
Bill McCullam
Paul Hartzell
David Tessler

PHOTOGRAPHER
Barney Edwards

CLIENT
Waterford Crystal

AGENCY
Ammirati & Puris

399

ART DIRECTORS
Ken Hoggins
Vince Squibb

WRITERS
Chris O'Shea
Paul Hodgkinson

PHOTOGRAPHERS
Gered Mankowitz
Dennis Waugh
Rolph Gobits

CLIENT
Lloyds Bank

AGENCY
Lowe Howard-Spink/
London

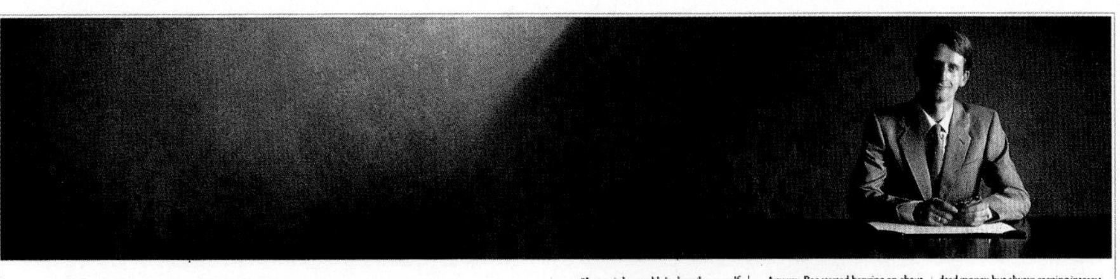

"I gave them carte blanche. They gave me Keith."

"I certainly wouldn't describe myself as rich. On the other hand, I'm not exactly short of a bob or two.

I'm in navigational electronics, you see, on the selling side. And business has, touch wood, been good.

I suppose it was the ballyhoo of the first privatisations that awakened my interest in shares.

My first few forays into the Stock Market proved most rewarding and from then on I was hooked.

I'd study the financial pages. I'd listen to 'The Financial World Tonight.' At one point I was even going to replace the Telegraph with the FT, but the rest of the family put their foot firmly down on that one.

Bit by bit my portfolio – if that's the word to describe my rag-bag of shares – grew to around £75,000.

Then, don't ask me why, it all became a bit of a pain.

I seemed to be forever making trips to the building society to transfer money. Filling in forms. Writing letters. Making phone calls.

Then there was the annual chore of deciphering old contract notes and regurgitating their contents for the Inland Revenue.

In fact it was this that led me to Keith.

One night in the Plough, with the usual motley crew, I mentioned this tiresome task I had to perform for the tax man.

My remark caught the ear of Reg. He's the Plough's resident know-all who permanently occupies a stool at the end of the bar.

Anyway, Reg started banging on about this 'Asset Management' thing Lloyds Bank had started.

Just the sort of thing a chap like me needed, he said, and you don't even need to be a Lloyds Bank customer.

As it happened, I was. So when I was next in the bank, I got all the bumph.

It made interesting reading. So interesting, in fact, that I decided to give it a try.

It seemed Lloyds Bank would relieve me of all the boring admin that goes with running a sizeable portfolio. Also, they'd take over the complete management of my assets, buying and selling as and when they saw fit.

So, basically, I gave them carte blanche.

And in return, they gave me Keith: my very own 'Personal Account Executive.'

When we first met I must admit I thought he looked, well, a bit wet behind the ears.

But I soon realised that there was quite a business brain on those youthful shoulders.

Initially we had a lengthy meeting to thrash out a strategy – something I'd never given any thought to before.

After much deliberation Keith reckoned I should go for a low-yield capital growth strategy including some tax-efficient gilts, otherwise the taxman would think it was his birthday.

So off Keith went to restructure my portfolio.

He also opened an investment account for me. That way the money involved in buying and selling is never dead money, but always earning interest.

Another thing he did was build in a cash-sweep facility on my current account so that anything over £1,000 is automatically swept into my investment account.

At first it felt strange having someone else manage my money, but I soon got used to it.

I'd just ring Keith, quote my password and he'd call up my file on his desk-top computer.

Then he'd rattle off the deals he'd done, give me account balances and tell me the value of my portfolio.

To keep things shipshape, Keith also sends me regular statements.

Everything, and I do mean everything, is in them.

Better still, the year-end statement I get is in a form acceptable to the tax man.

As I've got to know Keith, I've also found him a dab hand at other things. Insurance, pensions, a tricky problem my mother had with CGT – things like that.

But now the $64,000 question. How's he done with my investments?

Well, I'm more than happy. Keith's certainly done a lot better than I could have, and getting rid of all that infernal paperwork is, believe you me, a boon.

But that's enough about Keith. I'm beginning to sound like an advert for Lloyds Bank."

A THOROUGHBRED AMONGST BANKS.

"Sitting on a small fortune was decidedly uncomfortable."

"I suppose it was about the closest I'd ever come to a mid-life crisis.

I'd been up to my proverbial neck. My usual 12-hour working day had stretched to a norm of 15 hours. And weekends, which I once held sacrosanct, were being eaten away by paperwork.

Coincidentally John, my eldest, was safely ensconced in university and Jenny was off on some field trip to do with her Biology 'A' level.

So I thought, to heck with it all.

I asked my secretary to cancel all my appointments and book me a short holiday. I gave her 3 criteria: I wanted sunshine; a reasonable hotel; and she was to reveal its location to no one.

Within days my wife and I were in Miami.

While she took in the local sights, I did a lot of thinking.

On paper, I suppose, a lot of people would have envied me.

My company was growing. I had a nice house. Nice kids. Nice cars. And a nice little nest-egg of various shares that was fast approaching six figures.

What I didn't have was time to enjoy these things.

There and then, I resolved never again to work more than a 12-hour day, and restore my weekends to their sacred status. If something wasn't done it would just have to wait.

I felt better already.

Then, I don't know why, I recalled a conversation with my bank manager some months previously. (Religiously, twice a year, I take him to an outrageously expensive restaurant and insist on picking up the bill.)

Anyway, he knew about my portfolio and insisted on telling me about a service Lloyds Bank had dreamed up for its customers, and indeed anyone else, that would make their life much easier.

It was called Asset Management, or some such name.

Frankly, I hadn't really listened because I hadn't been that interested.

But on that holiday, the more I remembered the more appealing it became.

To cut a long story short, I signed on the dotted line within days of my return to England. The first thing Lloyds Bank did was assign me a 'Personal Account Executive', one Philip Hunter.

At our initial meeting I made it clear that I wanted him to take over the whole caboodle; handle all the paper work and make the buying and selling decisions.

We also agreed a broad strategy. He was to go for capital growth rather than income. He was occasionally to chance his arm on a few speculative stocks. And, backing a hunch of mine, I wanted him to take a particular interest in small electronics companies.

Once we'd got that straight he opened an interest-bearing account to act as a pool for purchases and sale proceeds.

He even built in a 'cash sweep' facility on my current account, so anything over £1,000 was automatically swept into my investment account. Then he got to work.

That was about a year ago now.

And since then I'm delighted to say that I've done practically nothing.

I no longer spend hours poring over the City pages deciding what to buy or sell.

I no longer have weighty company reports thudding onto my doormat.

I no longer have to faff about with scissors, pins and cheques when I go for a new issue.

I no longer spend hours with a calculator working out my worth, since they send me regular statements.

And, joy of joys, I no longer need to rummage through sheafs of old contract notes in April, because they prepare a special statement for the taxman.

I also ought to add that the service has a few frills which, while not vital, are most welcome. For instance, they automatically upped my Access Card limit to £5,000. And I can now draw up to £500 a day on my Cashpoint card.

But good as their Asset Management Service undoubtedly is, Lloyds Bank isn't a charity. All told, they charge me around £250 a quarter, which although well worth it, isn't peanuts.

In fact, d'you know what I'm going to do next time I take my bank manager to lunch?

I'm going to invite Philip Hunter along too. And when the bill arrives, I'm not going to put my hand in my pocket."

A THOROUGHBRED AMONGST BANKS.

This service is available to persons aged 18 and over. Information correct at time of going to press but may vary. Lending is at the Bank's discretion. Written details of our credit terms are available from branches of Lloyds Bank Plc, 71 Lombard Street, London EC3P 3BS. If you are interested call free of charge, 0800 444140 (24-hour personal service).

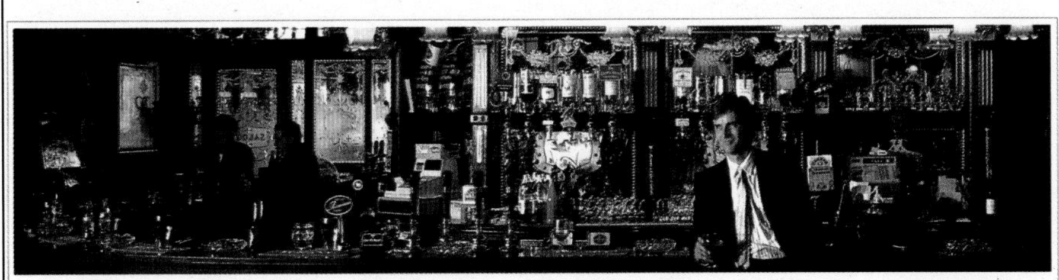

"Would you lend £5,000 to someone you'd never met before? My bank manager just did."

"I've never been a great fan of banks. The best idea they've ever come up with, as far as I can see, is getting your cash out of a hole in the wall.

I remember first using those machines at the local poly. I'd just signed on with Lloyds Bank and Cashpoints were a wild and wacky novelty.

Yes, those were the days. The grant cheque would arrive and disappear within a matter of weeks. (And it didn't all go on books, either.)

But then the formal letter would arrive on the doormat: in future, if I would desire to undertake an overdraft facility, then would I please inform the bank of my intentions to do so, etcetera, etcetera, signed Mr. A. J. Moneypenny, Branch Manager.

The name stuck. (Well it would, wouldn't it?)

I never did get to meet the famous Mr. A. J. Moneypenny, though he wrote to me quite a few times.

Even if I bumped into him in the street I wouldn't know him from Adam.

Well, my reckless student days are over. And look at me now: I'm respectable, aren't I?

I've landed a job with a computer firm, a flat with some mod cons and a fiancée with expensive tastes.

But before I surrender completely to marriage and mortgage, there's one thing I need.

It's nothing flash. Just a 1960's Jaguar Mark II 2.4 – in black.

I've lusted after one for ages. I've scoured the classifieds in 'Classic Cars' every month, these cars aren't exactly thick on the ground, I can tell you.

Then, the other day, I saw it. True, it had a lot on the clock, but I had to have it.

There was just one small problem: shortage of the necessary. And I could just imagine Mr A. J. Moneypenny's reply to my humble request for £4,900 (o.n.o.).

Still, I thought, I might as well try it on, I'd nothing to lose. And at any rate, I'd rather go through the bank than one of those obscure loan companies you see in the small ads in the tabloids.

So, I put on my best suit and voice, and rehearsed all the arguments in my head. Maybe I could plead total impoverishment and go for the heart.

The question was, would Mr. A. J. Moneypenny have one?

I rang the bell at Enquiries and waited. I could see it all before me. He'd sneer, would ask me to answer for all my past sins as a student, would say it was totally out of the question and show me the door.

But guess what? I never even got to see him. The girl behind the counter asked me to fill in an application. Then she disappeared, presumably to have a giggle with her mates at my sheer cheek.

The next thing I know, she's asking me if I'd prefer the money in cash or paid into my current account.

Well, I admit I gulped. But I was cool, wasn't I?

I said I'd better have it put into my account, one couldn't be too careful with all that cash, could one?

By the end of the next day, I'd got the car (having knocked the bloke down two hundred quid in the process).

And at this very moment, a gleaming black 1960's Jaguar Mark II 2.4 sits outside my front door, impressing the neighbours no end.

As for paying it all back, I thought I'd better play safe and go for the whole 5 years. At least the interest rate is set in concrete.

I know it's a lot of money, but believe you me, it's well worth it.

And all I can say is: here's to you, Mr. A. J. Moneypenny.

Whoever you are."

A THOROUGHBRED AMONGST BANKS.

Personal Loans available to people aged 18 or over and at the Bank's discretion. Written details available from Lloyds Bank Plc, 71 Lombard Street, London EC3P 3BS.

Consumer Magazine Color: Campaign Including Magazine Supplements

400

ART DIRECTORS
Clem McCarthy
Arthur Vibert
Alain Briere
Joe Steele

WRITERS
Paul Wolfe
Lesley Stern

PHOTOGRAPHER
Jeffrey Zwart

CLIENT
BMW of North America

AGENCY
Ammirati & Puris

401

ART DIRECTORS
Charles Inge
Simon Butler

WRITERS
Jane Garland
Gethin Stout

CLIENT
JVC

AGENCY
Lowe Howard-Spink/London

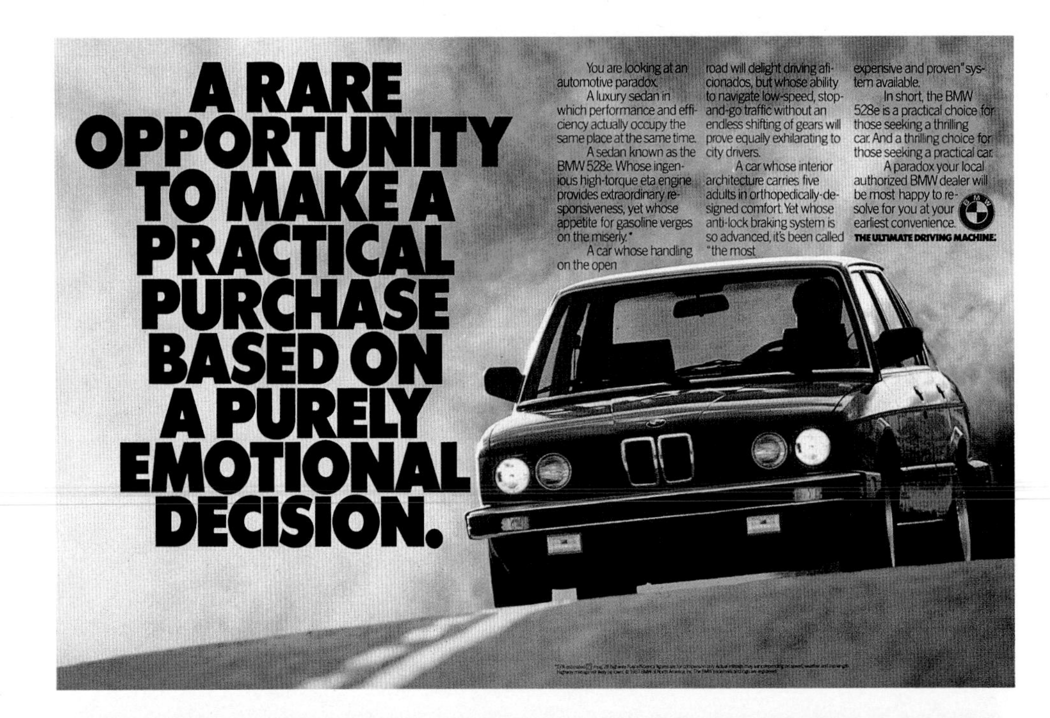

A RARE OPPORTUNITY TO MAKE A PRACTICAL PURCHASE BASED ON A PURELY EMOTIONAL DECISION.
You are looking at an automotive paradox.
A luxury sedan in which performance and efficiency actually occupy the same place at the same time.
A sedan known as the BMW 528e. Whose ingenious high-torque eta engine provides extraordinary responsiveness, yet whose appetite for gasoline verges on the miserly.*
A car whose handling on the open road will delight driving aficionados, but whose ability to navigate low-speed, stop-and-go traffic without an endless shifting of gears will prove equally exhilarating to city drivers.
A car whose interior architecture carries five adults in orthopedically-designed comfort. Yet whose anti-lock braking system is so advanced, it's been called "the most expensive and proven" system available.
In short, the BMW 528e is a practical choice for those seeking a thrilling car. And a thrilling choice for those seeking a practical car.
A paradox your local authorized BMW dealer will be most happy to resolve for you at your earliest convenience.
THE ULTIMATE DRIVING MACHINE.

A CAR FOR THOSE WITH THEIR HEART AT THE RACECOURSE BUT THEIR FEET ON THE GROUND.
If your enthusiasm for driving knows no bounds, but the realities of your lifestyle do, BMW offers some compensation: the BMW 535is. As close to a racing machine as you can get while still in the congenial confines of a luxury sedan.
The 535is, according to AutoWeek, "could carry the family and still go wheel-to-wheel against a hot sports car without giving an inch."
Its ferocity results from a race-bred power plant that demolishes 0 to 60 in 7.4 seconds.
Part of a racing heritage that extends, first of all, to the aerodynamic spoiler and air dam, and then to a taut suspension enhanced by progressive-rate gas pressure shocks.
At the same time, while your heart is at the racecourse, your body is pleasantly ensconced in torso-hugging, eight-way leather sports seats.
Your ears are pampered by no less than an eight-speaker anti-theft stereo sound system.
And your nervous system basks in the knowledge that a computerized anti-lock braking system will help prevent wheel lockup—even in panic stops.
For driving zealots who've acquired obligations along the way but have maintained their enthusiasm, an authorized BMW dealer will be happy to show you a 535is.
Consider it a race car the whole family can enjoy.
THE ULTIMATE DRIVING MACHINE.

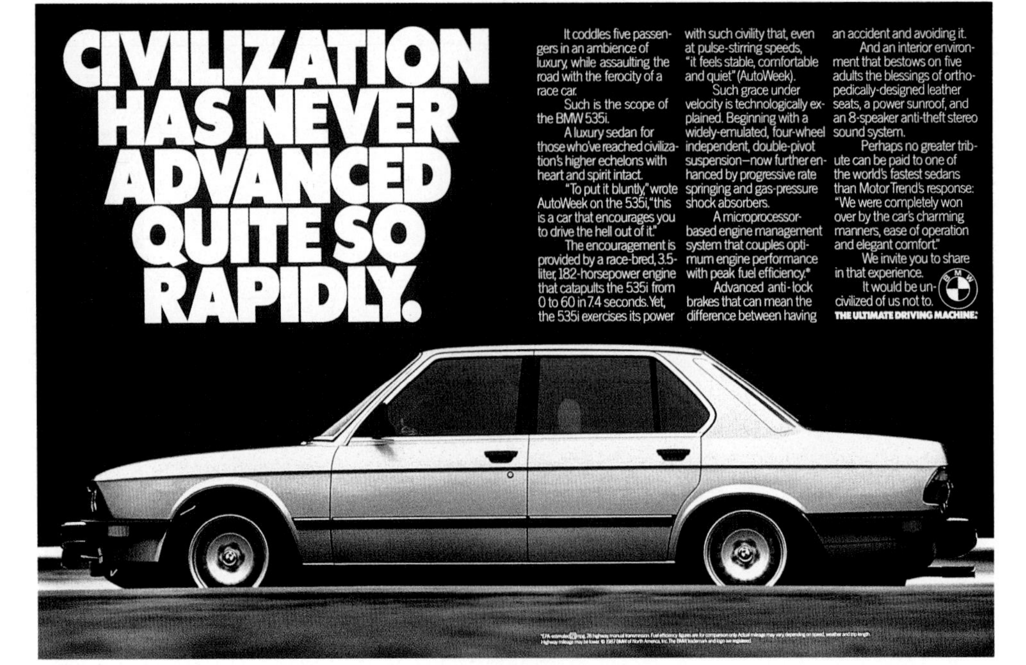

CIVILIZATION HAS NEVER ADVANCED QUITE SO RAPIDLY.
It coddles five passengers in an ambience of luxury, while assaulting the road with the ferocity of a race car.
Such is the scope of the BMW 535i.
A luxury sedan for those who've reached civilization's higher echelons with heart and spirit intact.
"To put it bluntly," wrote AutoWeek on the 535i, "this is a car that encourages you to drive the hell out of it."
The encouragement is provided by a race-bred, 3.5-liter, 182-horsepower engine that catapults the 535i from 0 to 60 in 7.4 seconds. Yet, the 535i exercises its power with such civility that, even at pulse-stirring speeds, "it feels stable, comfortable and quiet" (AutoWeek).
Such grace under velocity is technologically explained. Beginning with a widely-emulated, four-wheel independent, double-pivot suspension—now further enhanced by progressive rate springing and gas-pressure shock absorbers.
A microprocessor-based engine management system that couples optimum engine performance with peak fuel efficiency.*
Advanced anti-lock brakes that can mean the difference between having an accident and avoiding it.
And an interior environment that bestows on five adults the blessings of orthopedically-designed leather seats, a power sunroof, and an 8-speaker anti-theft stereo sound system.
Perhaps no greater tribute can be paid to one of the world's fastest sedans than Motor Trend's response: "We were completely won over by the car's charming manners, ease of operation and elegant comfort."
We invite you to share in that experience.
It would be uncivilized of us not to.
THE ULTIMATE DRIVING MACHINE.

Budding movie directors start here.

Hollywood look out.

This little black box you see before you may look harmless, but it's going to cause a few ripples.

A camcorder so simple, anyone can use it, with results so good, everyone will want to.

Remember focusing? Well now you can forget it. The GR-C11 does it all for you.

And lighting? Who needs it when this camera can deliver pictures even in candlelight.

Oh, and you can cut out the editor. This machine produces clean cuts all by itself; not to mention superior sound.

Then there's the power zoom lens for those close encounters.

Not forgetting the rechargeable battery which doubles up as a handgrip.

Sounds fishy? Can all you need to make a film really be included in an object roughly the same size as a VHS cassette?

The answer, of course, is yes. May we now suggest you start casting?

JVC
VHS

If it sends you to sleep it'll switch itself off.

If there's anything worth watching, it'll wake you up too.

Because our latest 14" 34cmv portable colour TV has a built-in timer that automatically switches it on as well as off.

For that special programme, just programme it up to a day in advance to turn itself on.

And it can be done without leaving the comfort of your favourite armchair (or indeed your bed) with our special remote control handset.

That isn't all your clever little box of tricks can do.

As a reminder, it can flash up the channel you've chosen in the left-hand side of the screen.

Whilst audio, brightness and colour levels can also be altered and graphically displayed.

In fact that, coupled with JVC renowned superior picture quality, means that you'll see every programme at it's very best.

Shame it can't improve the quality of the programmes themselves.

JVC

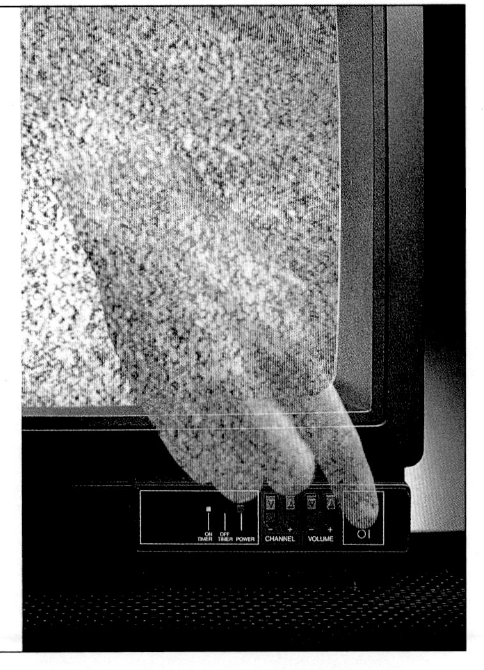

A video so advanced, it even records programmes that haven't been made yet.

Talk about being ahead of your time.

JVC's new video is not just one step in front of the printers at the Radio Times, but also the programme makers themselves.

The HR-D230 can be timed to record up to a year in advance.

What's more, at the press of a button, it will squeeze a full eight hours viewing on to your normal 4 hour tape.

So you can set off on a world cruise (or even a week in Frinton), knowing your favourite programmes will be waiting for you on your return.

Naturally, a video this sophisticated is not lacking in the usual state-of-the-art features.

The remote control boasts a 4-programme memory, so you can set it anywhere and simply transfer it to your machine on your return.

We've also incorporated a crystal clear LCD window, making programming errors a thing of the past.

And the video itself offers a host of automatic features: shuttle search, next-function memory and channel skip, to name but a few.

Not that the HR-D230 is just a box of electronic tricks.

At the heart of this machine is an HQ picture quality second to none, born of thirty years at the forefront of video technology.

Of course, with the HR-D230, you may be wondering where videos can possibly go next. Well, whatever happens, one thing is certain, we'll be the first to know.

JVC

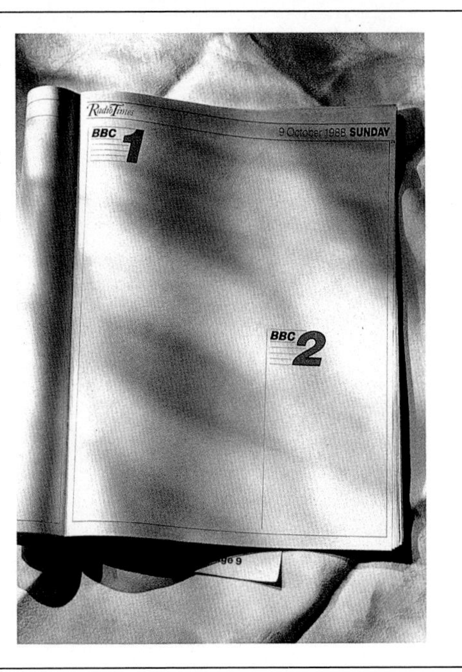

Consumer Magazine Color: Campaign Including Magazine Supplements

402

ART DIRECTOR
Dean Hanson

WRITER
Phil Hanft

PHOTOGRAPHER
Rick Dublin

CLIENT
Conran's

AGENCY
Fallon McElligott/ Minneapolis

403

ART DIRECTORS
Clem McCarthy
Alain Briere
Yvonne Smith
William Hartwell

WRITERS
Paul Wolfe
Bill McCullam
Rav Friedel

PHOTOGRAPHER
Jeffrey Zwart

CLIENT
BMW of North America

AGENCY
Ammirati & Puris

BMW BELIEVES LIFE BEGINS AT 6000 RPM'S.
For those with a marked propensity for race cars that you can drive to work, this one has been affectionately called the "Munich Mauler."
In its first four months of Grand Touring Racing, the BMW M3 has scorched the great racecourses of Europe. With the most wins to date in the World Touring Car Championship, the European Touring Car Championship, the German Championship, the Austrian Championship, the Belgian Championship, and the French Championship, just to name a few.
This wasn't achieved by advanced cosmetics, but rather by 192 horsepower from a 16-valve, 2.3-liter four-cylinder power plant developed by BMW Motorsport.
It's an engine for people with an appreciation for performance.
For the moment, picture yourself on the racetrack. In first gear, pop the clutch, floor the accelerator and you're pinned to the seat as 40 mph rushes up at you in 3.5 seconds.
3.5 seconds later you're traveling a mile a minute, still in second gear.
Shift into third and for a delightful 9 seconds there's no need to touch the clutch, until 91 mph.*
In fourth, you pass the speed at which a jet leaves the ground, topping out at 127 mph.
Now it's time to let your hair down. Fifth gear and the engine sings. "It's the sheer quality of those racing car sounds, delivered without ear strain or shock value, that starts to set this car apart...the sounds are marvelous, the power is intoxicating" (Car Magazine). Top speed, 145 mph.*
Care for a test drive?
THE ULTIMATE DRIVING MACHINE.

THE BMW M6. ONE OF THIS WORLD'S MOST POWERFUL AESTHETIC STATEMENTS.
To connoisseurs of design, the BMW M6 sports coupe is a classic whose lines have been exhibited at Le Musée des Arts in Paris, New York's Whitney, and other great museums.
To connoisseurs of performance, its beautifully laid-out 256-hp, dual overhead-cam, 24-valve inline engine is equally "a work of modern art" (Automobile Magazine).
This power plant is "simply the most joyous series-produced high performance 6-cylinder ever," appraises Road & Track. "Its marvelous, smooth growl, remarkable tractability—yet overwhelming force when asked to do something—is a sensation one must experience."
Whether one is proceeding untemperamentally through stop-and-go city traffic or at competition speeds of over 140 mph,* the experience is made all the more exquisite by 10-way power sports seating swathed in hand-stitched Napa leather.
And all the more assured, as well, by BMW's patented four-wheel fully-independent suspension and race-track-proven antilock braking system.
Your authorized BMW dealer will be happy to arrange a private showing of the limited-edition M6.
A masterpiece that is powerfully moving in every sense of the word.
THE ULTIMATE DRIVING MACHINE.

BE ONE OF THE 1200 FASTEST FAMILIES IN AMERICA.
Outings in the family car are standard procedure in America.
Jaunts in a hand-built car that just happens to be the fastest production sedan in the U.S. are not.
Yet that's precisely what awaits the 1200 American families who will own the limited-edition BMW M5. A highly civilized, hand-built four-door luxury sedan capable of scorching terrain at rates of up to 150 mph.*
"It is the ultimate civilized four-door hot rod," proclaimed Road & Track magazine.
A fitting tribute to this 5-Series BMW painstakingly imbued by BMW's elite Motorsport Division with a 6-cylinder, 256-horsepower engine Auto Motor und Sport hailed as "a piston engine monument."
The installation of such a prodigious engine, of course, is but a part of an assembly process that lavishes up to two weeks on each individual car. The result is a sedan that not only annihilates 0 to 60 in a microscopic 6.5 seconds, but carries five people in comfort, on seats swathed with hand-stitched leather.
We would like to congratulate in advance the 1200 American households who will soon choose to own a BMW M5.
Think of it as a rocket for the nuclear family.
THE ULTIMATE DRIVING MACHINE.

Consumer Magazine Color: Campaign Including Magazine Supplements

404

ART DIRECTORS
Bill Kreighbaum
Carl Warner

WRITERS
Ross Meyers
Glenn Gill
Bill Kreighbaum

DESIGNERS
Bill Kreighbaum
Carl Warner

PHOTOGRAPHERS
Greg Booth & Associates
Jim Bowie

CLIENT
Pier 1 Imports

AGENCY
The Richards Group/Dallas

405

ART DIRECTOR
Charles Herbstreith

WRITER
Mary Dean

CLIENT
Procter & Gamble/Gleem

AGENCY
Leo Burnett USA/Chicago

Fruits Of The Loom.

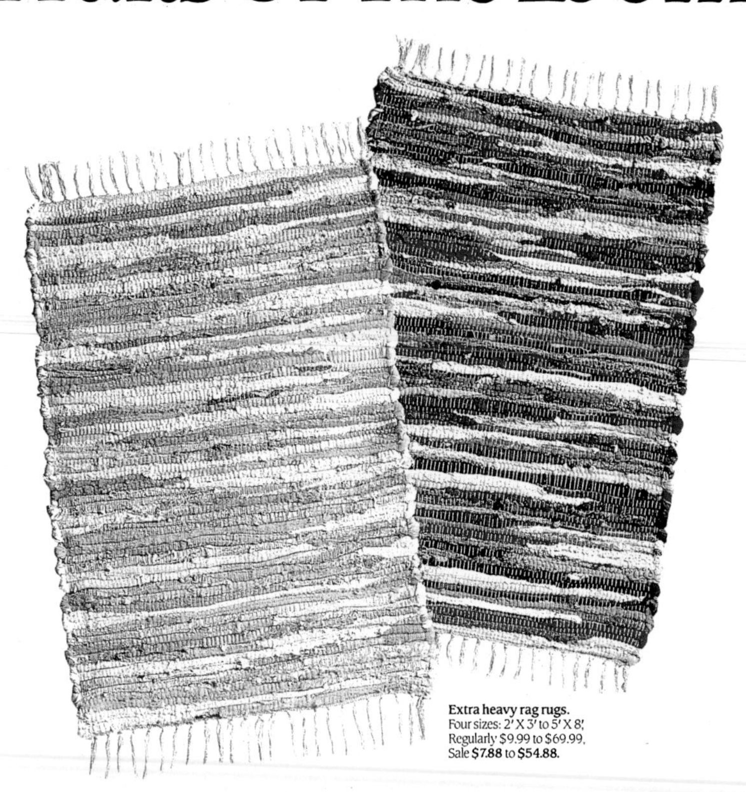

Extra heavy rag rugs.
Four sizes: 2' X 3' to 5' X 8'.
Regularly $9.99 to $69.99.
Sale **$7.88** to **$54.88.**

No, we're not selling underwear, but this is a brief sale. For one week these hand-loomed, multi-colored, 100% cotton rag rugs will be 20 to 25% off. Which makes an already good deal even better, considering they're heavier, thicker and more durable than your run-of-the-mill rag rug. All thanks to the weavers of Panipat, India. Come to Pier 1 and see the fruits of their labor.

A Place To Discover.™

At 20% Off, Our Carpets Will Fly.

This week we're reducing the price on all our handwoven rugs. They come in every imaginable size and color. There are small skinny ones for your hall. And big wide ones for your den. Of course, we can't guarantee every style in every store, but we can guarantee an impressive collection to choose from. So whether you choose a stunning design from Agra or a subdued pattern from Panipat, the effect it'll have on your room is magical. Reg. $7.99 to $199.99, Sale **$6.38** to **$159.88.**

A Place To Discover.™

This Week, We're Going Out On A Limb.

We went out of our way—seventeen countries in all—to bring you a quaint collection of handmade Christmas ornaments. Everything from wooden horses, paper fans and glass suns to papier-mâché balls, silk flowers, and straw dolls. You'll even find reindeer and Santas made of yarn. Together they represent just a few of our most recent additions to the family tree.

A Place To Discover.™

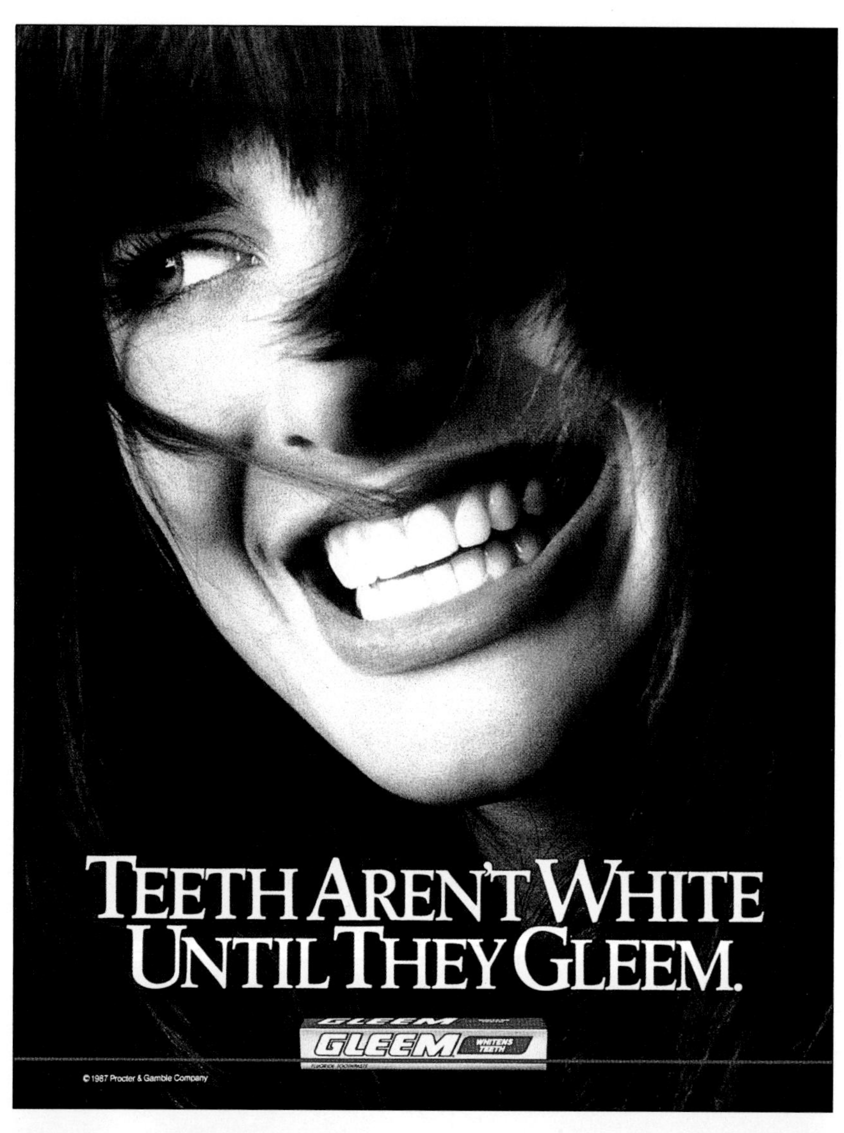
TEETH AREN'T WHITE
UNTIL THEY GLEEM.
GLEEM
WHITENS TEETH
©1987 Procter & Gamble Company

TEETH AREN'T WHITE
UNTIL THEY GLEEM.
GLEEM
WHITENS TEETH
In lab tests, Gleem's whitening formula was proven superior to leading fluorides and was unsurpassed versus brands designed to fight smoking or coffee stains, control tartar, and protect sensitive teeth.
© 1988 P&G Company

TEETH AREN'T WHITE
UNTIL THEY GLEEM.
GLEEM
WHITENS TEETH
©1987 Procter & Gamble Company

Consumer Magazine Color: Campaign Including Magazine Supplements

406

ART DIRECTORS
Richard Crispo
Dennis Lim

WRITER
Bob Ancona

PHOTOGRAPHERS
Bill Werts
Bo Hylen Studios

CLIENT
American Honda

AGENCY
Ketchum/Los Angeles

407

ART DIRECTOR
John Strohmeyer

WRITER
Stephen Fechtor

PHOTOGRAPHER
Charles Purvis

CLIENT
Parker Pen USA

AGENCY
Lowe Marschalk/
Cleveland, OH

THE PERFORMANCE SEDAN FOR THOSE WHO KNOW THERE'S MORE TO STATUS THAN THE STATUS QUO.
Call 1-800-TO-ACURA for a dealer near you.
ACURA
PRECISION CRAFTED PERFORMANCE

TRADITION HAS IT THE FINEST SPORTS COUPES COME FROM EUROPE.
THE LEGEND COUPE FLIES IN THE FACE OF TRADITION.
ACURA

THIS IS THE PERFORMANCE SEDAN THAT'S MAKING EUROPEAN AUTOMAKERS UNCOMFORTABLE.
BUT THERE'S NO REASON FOR YOU TO FEEL THAT WAY.
Call 1-800-TO-ACURA for a dealer near you.
ACURA
PRECISION CRAFTED PERFORMANCE

YOU WALK INTO A BOARDROOM AND EVERYONE'S NAKED.

HERE'S HOW YOU TELL WHO'S THE BOSS.

There you are. Multi-million dollar proposal in hand.

Standing in front of a group of very powerful gentlemen known to you only as "The Board."

In a way, you are thankful that they are known to you only as "The Board." Because they are stark, staring naked. And seated (to your great relief) at a very large boardroom table.

"What is this?" you think to yourself. "The ultimate stress interview?

"Who has the power? Who's in control? To whom do I present? And am I overdressed?"

Then suddenly, from the corner of your eye, you catch the glimmer of light on gold.

Its source: A Parker Premier fountain pen.

You study it for a moment, as it glides effortlessly across note paper.

You admire the European styling. The unrivaled craftsmanship. The quality finish and tempered, gold nib.

And all at once, it becomes clear. The owner of this fine writing instrument is the man you must sway in order to win the contract. The man to whom all others in the room must answer.

You turn to him, and begin your presentation by extracting your own pen, a Parker 75, from your jacket pocket. It proves to be a brilliant touch.

For, half an hour later, your multi-million dollar proposal is signed. And your future is sealed.

Then, amidst much congratulations, the chairman offers to show you to the door.

"Oh, no," you reply. "Don't get up."

THERE ARE TIMES WHEN IT HAS TO BE PARKER.

PARKER

The Parker Premier Black Fountain Pen comes with a worldwide, lifetime guarantee. © 1987 Parker Pen USA Limited, Janesville, Wisconsin.

YOU'RE AT A WASHINGTON COCKTAIL PARTY, AND THE CONVERSATION SUDDENLY TURNS TO NIB GRINDING.

HERE'S WHY YOU'RE THE EXPERT.

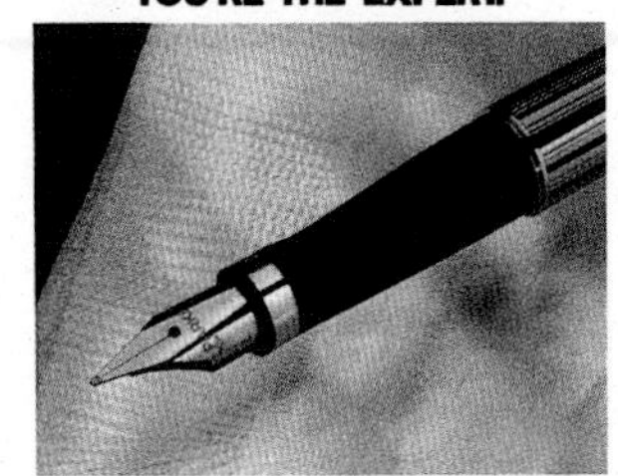

There you are, hobnobbing with the intelligentsia and literati of the Washington scene, when someone (probably in a low-cut evening dress) casually mentions how difficult it is to find a good nib-grinder these days.

Conversation stops.

You, being the gentleman that you are, rush to her rescue, fountain pen in hand, to explain one of the finer points of a Parker.

"The nib of each Parker," you say, "is precision-ground to allow it to conform to your own particular style and angle of writing."

The guests are dazzled.

Bolstered by their reaction, you go on to explain that the nibs are 18k gold and hand-worked to produce a superbly smooth writing flow and feel.

You expound on the fact that they are tempered and tipped with Ruthenium (a special alloy) to ensure just the right degree of flexibility.

You extol the virtues of the rigorous inspection process, which includes handwriting, microscope, and laser.

And finally, to the envy of the crowd, you firmly take the hand of the lady to whose rescue you've just come. And lead her to a quiet corner of the room, where she can further explore your expertise in other worldly matters.

THERE ARE TIMES WHEN IT HAS TO BE PARKER.

PARKER

The Parker Premier Gold Plate and Laque Fountain Pen comes with a worldwide, lifetime guarantee. © 1987 Parker Pen USA Limited, Janesville, Wisconsin.

YOU ASK YOUR MOTHER WHAT TO BUY YOUR FATHER FOR HIS BIRTHDAY, AND SHE SAYS, "OH, I DON'T KNOW, ANYTHING WITH RUTHENIUM."

THAT'S WHY YOU GIVE HIM THIS.

So there you are, in the same old bind you're in every year.

It's your father's birthday, and you haven't the foggiest notion of what to get him.

You call your mother for advice.

"Well you know," she says, "your father is a difficult man to shop for. Being the world-renowned heart surgeon, author, professional basketball player, art collector, and occasional talk-show host that he is. Have you tried something in Ruthenium?"

"Well, golly, Mom, can't say as I have. Ruthenium, huh? Where is that, exactly?"

"Ruthenium, my dear boy, is the special alloy used at the tip of each and every Parker fountain pen. From the Parker Premier, to the Parker 75, all the way down to the Parkers that are fine for other people, but not for your father."

"Gee, Mom, no kidding."

"In fact," she continues, "the nibs of Parker fountain pens are quite unique. Being specially tempered for the right degree of flexibility, tipped with the aforementioned alloy, and then rather rigorously inspected."

"Well, that's great, Mom," you say. "I get the feeling you think he needs a new fountain pen."

"He needs nothing," she says. "He *wants* a Parker."

"Got it."

THERE ARE TIMES WHEN IT HAS TO BE PARKER.

PARKER

The Parker Premier Black Fountain Pen comes with a worldwide, lifetime guarantee. © 1987 Parker Pen USA Limited, Janesville, Wisconsin.

Consumer Magazine Color: Campaign Including Magazine Supplements

408

ART DIRECTORS
Debbie Peacock
David Davis

WRITER
Tom Gabriel

DESIGNER
David Davis

CLIENT
Hawaii Visitors Bureau

AGENCY
Milici Valenti Park & Gabriel/Honolulu

409

ART DIRECTOR
Joe Gallo

WRITER
Bill Klimas

PHOTOGRAPHERS
Carl Corey
Derek Gardner

CLIENT
Audi of America

AGENCY
DDB Needham Worldwide/Chicago

Hair flying. Heart pounding. Pulse racing. You flew. Limitations were exceeded. Expectations surpassed. You and the car were one.
The same is true of the new 90 Quattro. With permanent all-wheel drive, Quattro traction comes to grips with the road at all four wheels. The feeling of control reassuring. The performance exhilarating. Five cylinders produce 130 HP. Sixty is reached in 8.5 seconds. Top track speed is 128 MPH. Drag coefficient a world class 0.32.
Steering is precise and quick. The basic suspension design rallye proven. The engine smooth revving. And soundly satisfying.
An Anti-Lock Braking System (ABS) is standard. Quick stops from speed are more easily controlled.
Leather sports seats hold you firmly. You ride secure. Senses alert. Every control at your fingertips. All is in harmony. You and the car are one.
Driving is what you hoped it would be. When you were a kid. In a little car. Racing down a hill.

INTRODUCING THE NEW AUDI 90 QUATTRO.

Remember what it was like to drive a car by the seat of your pants?

You folded the paper carefully.
The shape was so important. It had to be perfect. Because if it wasn't...it wouldn't fly.
The new Audi 90 Quattro flies.
Air flows smoothly over the rounded hood and across the curved windscreen. Down and around the rear spoiler.
Door handles are recessed. Front and rear windows are bonded in. The side glass is flush.
Underneath a smooth underside assures smoother air flow. Drag is reduced. Performance enhanced.
Five cylinders produce 130 HP. Sixty is reached in 8.5 seconds. Top track speed is 128 MPH. Drag coefficient a world class 0.32. The shape almost perfect.
With permanent all-wheel drive, Quattro traction comes to grips with the road at all four wheels. An Anti-Lock Braking System (ABS) is standard. Quick stops from speed are more easily controlled.
Leather sports seats hold you firmly. You ride secure. Senses alert. Every control at your fingertips. All is in harmony.
Driving is what you hoped it would be. When you were a kid. Catching a ride on the wind.

INTRODUCING THE NEW AUDI 90 QUATTRO.

Remember your first lesson in aerodynamics?

Legs pumping. Feet flying. You flew. No longer would you be held back. Or slowed down. This was the ultimate pleasure. You had grown up.
The new Audi 90 brings forth similar feelings.
Here is a car that matches your passion for performance.
Five cylinders produce 130 HP. Sixty is reached in 8.5 seconds. Top track speed is 128 MPH.
Handling is enhanced by front wheel drive. Steering is precise and quick. The basic suspension design rallye proven.
The engine smooth revving. And soundly satisfying.
An Anti-Lock Braking System (ABS) is standard. Quick stops from speed are more easily controlled.
Sporty leather seats hold you firmly. You ride secure. Senses alert. Every control at your fingertips. All is in harmony. You and the car are one.
Driving is what you hoped it would be. When you were a kid. On a bike. On your own.

INTRODUCING THE NEW AUDI 90.

Remember the day you took off your training wheels?

Consumer Magazine Color: Campaign Including Magazine Supplements

410

ART DIRECTORS
Glenn Dady
Gena Rogers

WRITERS
Mike Malone
Mary Kuska Knight

ARTISTS
Steve Pietzsch
Chris Payne
Greg King

PHOTOGRAPHERS
Tom Ryan
Pat Haverfeld

CLIENT
The Catfish Institute

AGENCY
The Richards Group/Dallas

411

ART DIRECTOR
Doug Patterson

WRITER
Gail Anne Smith

PHOTOGRAPHERS
Jeffrey Zwart
Bo Hylen Studios
Bill Werts

CLIENT
American Honda

AGENCY
Ketchum/Los Angeles

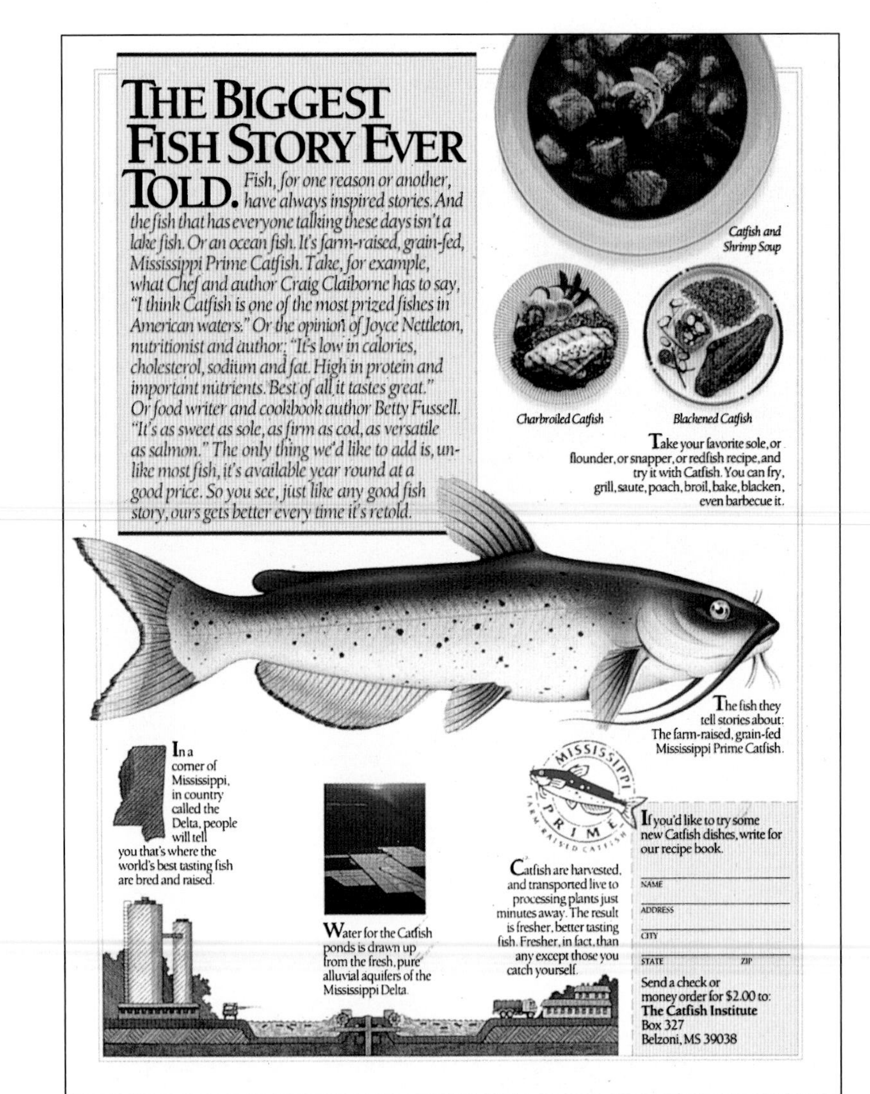

THE BIGGEST FISH STORY EVER TOLD.
Fish, for one reason or another, have always inspired stories. And the fish that has everyone talking these days isn't a lake fish. Or an ocean fish. It's farm-raised, grain-fed, Mississippi Prime Catfish. Take, for example, what Chef and author Craig Claiborne has to say, "I think Catfish is one of the most prized fishes in American waters." Or the opinion of Joyce Nettleton, nutritionist and author: "It's low in calories, cholesterol, sodium and fat. High in protein and important nutrients. Best of all, it tastes great." Or food writer and cookbook author Betty Fussell. "It's as sweet as sole, as firm as cod, as versatile as salmon." The only thing we'd like to add is, unlike most fish, it's available year round at a good price. So you see, just like any good fish story, ours gets better every time it's retold.
Catfish and Shrimp Soup
Charbroiled Catfish
Blackened Catfish
Take your favorite sole, or flounder, or snapper, or redfish recipe, and try it with Catfish. You can fry, grill, saute, poach, broil, bake, blacken, even barbecue it.
The fish they tell stories about: The farm-raised, grain-fed Mississippi Prime Catfish.
In a corner of Mississippi, in country called the Delta, people will tell you that's where the world's best tasting fish are bred and raised.
Water for the Catfish ponds is drawn up from the fresh, pure alluvial aquifers of the Mississippi Delta.
Catfish are harvested, and transported live to processing plants just minutes away. The result is fresher, better tasting fish. Fresher, in fact, than any except those you catch yourself.
MISSISSIPPI PRIME FARM-RAISED CATFISH
If you'd like to try some new Catfish dishes, write for our recipe book.
NAME
ADDRESS
CITY
STATE ZIP
Send a check or money order for $2.00 to:
The Catfish Institute
Box 327
Belzoni, MS 39038

THINK OF IT AS A CHICKEN THAT DOESN'T CLUCK.
Even though it may ruffle a few feathers, Mississippi Prime Catfish is showing up in more and more popular chicken recipes. Farm-raised and grain fed, its firm, flaky texture and delicate flavor make Catfish perfect for baking, broiling, grilling, blackening, even stir-frying. Like chicken, Catfish is high in protein, low in fat and cholesterol. But Catfish is lower in calories. So try it instead of chicken. Or anything else. We think you'll understand why Catfish has the competition squawking.
MISSISSIPPI PRIME FARM-RAISED CATFISH
Catfish Meunière
Spicy Pan-fried Catfish
Stir-fried Catfish
Catfish Salad
Catfish is high in protein and nutrients. Low in calories. Lower than beef. Pork. Yes, even chicken. Most important, Catfish tastes great.
Calories per 3.5 oz. serving*
Farm-raised Catfish 145
Chicken Breast 170
Beef Sirloin 210
Pork Loin 240
*Cooked/Source: USDA
If you'd like to try some new Catfish dishes, write for our recipe book.
NAME
ADDRESS
CITY
STATE ZIP
Send a check or money order for $1.50 to:
The Catfish Institute
Box 327
Belzoni, MS 39038

BEHIND EVERY GREAT CATFISH RECIPE IS AN UGLY CATFISH.
Few, if any, will claim there's such a thing as a handsome Catfish. On the other hand, there's a growing number who love the way it looks in their recipes. New York Times Food Editor Craig Claiborne, for one. "I've used Catfish in preparing many great classic French dishes, and the results were superb." Or from Betty Fussell, food author: "It's as sweet as sole, as firm as cod, as versatile as salmon." Try Catfish in one of your favorite recipes. You'll be in for a beautiful surprise.
MISSISSIPPI PRIME FARM-RAISED CATFISH
A fillet of Mississippi Prime farm-raised Catfish is low in calories. Lower than the equivalent portion of beef, chicken or pork.
Calories per 3.5 ounce serving*
Farm-raised Catfish 145
Chicken Breast 170
Beef Sirloin 215
Pork Loin 240
*Cooked/Source: USDA
The proud North American Channel Cat, or Ictalurus punctatus. Farm-raised and grain fed.
Catfish Chowder
Pan-Sauteed Catfish
Catfish Kabobs
When compared to other lean white fish, Catfish is second to none. You can fry, grill, saute, bake, broil, blacken, even barbeque it. Use it in soups, stews, and salads. It always cooks tender and flaky, with a delicate taste. Most important, it is available year round at a good price.
Stir-Fried Catfish
If you'd like to try some new Catfish dishes, write for our recipe book.
NAME
ADDRESS
CITY
STATE ZIP
Send a check or money order for $1.50 to:
The Catfish Institute
Box 327
Belzoni, MS 39038

UNTIL NOW, THE THOUGHT OF HAVING A FAMILY CAR WAS ALMOST ENOUGH TO KEEP YOU FROM HAVING A FAMILY.

They say that everything changes when you have a family. You make sacrifices. Diamonds for diapers. 3 a.m. parties for 3 a.m. feedings. The Ballet for ballet lessons. But it's worth it.

Unless you have to sacrifice your car.

Because when you stop to think about it, having a family means a lot of driving. Precisely the reason for the 5-door Acura Integra. With its Formula 1 inspired 1.6 liter, 16-valve, DOHC engine, the 5-door Integra shows its racing heritage every time you get behind the wheel. Its sophisticated computer programmed fuel injection system consistently delivers the power you need to command the road.

Meanwhile you'll be able to enjoy all this spirited response even more thanks to a sure-footed stability you can depend on.

Because the 5-door Integra clings to the road with a sport-tuned suspension system that lets you move with confidence. As well as athletic agility. Both front and rear stabilizer bars for flatter cornering. Responsive steering. Expert handling.

But the strength of the 5-door Integra doesn't end there. Its looks are exceptionally striking, too. Sleek design. Aerodynamically sharp. And ergonomically intelligent with gauges in the natural line of vision and controls right at your fingertips.

Formula 1 experience is the heritage of the Integra.

In fact, the 5-door Integra takes the sports sedan even further. By giving you a full back seat. By creating so much space for passengers, luggage, sports equipment—a whole month's groceries. There's even room to take your mother-in-law out for a ride.

All without compromising one iota of pure driving pleasure. Regardless of who's in the back seat.

Sure, having a family can be difficult from time to time.

But with the 5-door Acura Integra, you may well feel like you're spending more time in the fast lane than ever.

For more information, including the location of the dealer nearest you, just call 1-800-TO-ACURA.

ACURA
PRECISION CRAFTED PERFORMANCE
A division of American Honda Motor Co., Inc.

BEFORE OUR ENGINEERS BEGAN WORK ON THE INTEGRA, WE SENT THEM TO MONTE CARLO.

To most automakers, this trip might seem a little extravagant.

But because we were out to build a sports sedan that's more than just a great paint job, we sent our engineers to the toughest training ground there is. The Grand Prix circuit. There they worked on our winning Formula 1 engine and gained valuable expertise and knowledge. All so they could apply it to building a surprisingly innovative sports sedan.

In this case, the Acura Integra. Its Formula 1 inspired, 1.6 liter, 16-valve, DOHC engine puts you firmly in the seat of power. The racing-derived programmed fuel injection system helps make sure you always get the exciting performance you want.

Even when the road puts an unexpected twist in your plans.

In fact, that's where the fun begins. Front and rear stabilizer bars help keep cornering flat while contributing to responsive handling. The tightest curves, the sharpest turns, the toughest mountain roads are conquered with confidence. And a keen sense of excitement.

Even driving the straightaways is an exhilarating experience. In part because the flush glass, sloping hoodline and retractable headlights combine for highly efficient aerodynamics.

Formula 1 experience is the heritage of the Integra.

Not to mention the sleek styling that contributes to the Integra's distinctive good looks.

Functional beauty is expertly applied to the interior as well. Intelligent ergonomics result in reduced stress for the driver. Gauges are in a natural line of vision. Controls are perfectly positioned. This is one driving environment truly designed around the driver. Without compromising the comfort of the passengers. There's ample leg room and plenty of space. Not your usual sports sedan. But that was always the plan. Because even though it's the Integra engineers who get to experience all the excitement of Monte Carlo and the Grand Prix, it's the Integra owners who ultimately get to have all the fun.

The fun starts when you visit an Acura dealer. Call 1-800-TO-ACURA for the location of the one that's nearest you.

ACURA
PRECISION CRAFTED PERFORMANCE
A division of American Honda Motor Co., Inc.

Consumer Magazine Color: Campaign Including Magazine Supplements

412

ART DIRECTORS
Clem McCarthy
Alain Briere

WRITERS
Martin Puris
Paul Wolfe
Rav Friedel

PHOTOGRAPHER
Jeffrey Zwart

CLIENT
BMW of North America

AGENCY
Ammirati & Puris

413

ART DIRECTOR
John Scott MacDaniels

WRITERS
Cristina Gavin
John Scott MacDaniels

DESIGNER
John Scott MacDaniels

CLIENT
New Zealand Tourist & Publicity

AGENCY
Lowe Marschalk/
San Francisco

THE CAR THAT SPARKED A MULTINATIONAL INDUSTRY OF HIGH PERFORMANCE IMPERSONATORS.
It was 1977. America waited on gas lines. The auto industry seized the marketing opportunity and quickly shifted from gas-guzzlers to gas misers. The diesel was held out as the wave of the future. Defying conventional wisdom, BMW introduced yet another in a long and significant line of high-performance sports sedans: the 320i.
Since then, the diesel has diminished to a minuscule part of the market. BMW has brought the sports sedan to its highest state of evolution with the 325i.
And a new industry has emerged. Imitation BMW's.
Some estimate the number to be as high as 500,000 copies a year. Cars tempting to the uninitiated perhaps, but to those who've driven the genuine article they remain unreasonable facsimiles.
That's because the 325i originates not with a marketing opportunity but with a credo that dates back seven decades. One stating that extraordinary performance and brilliant engineering are the only things that make an expensive car worth the money.
It comes with a vitality derived from "as sweet an engine as BMW ever built" (Car and Driver magazine).
And an agility derived from the most grueling automotive environment in the world: the autobahns and Alps of Bavaria. Where the rush hour takes place at 120 mph.*
And on the 325i, luxury doesn't take a back seat. Even the rear headrests are swathed in supple leather.
For a prestigious step-up from the hordes of pretenders into the most authentic and fully evolved of European sports sedans, test drive the car created by the company that invented the category. At your nearest BMW dealer.
BMW
THE ULTIMATE DRIVING MACHINE.
*BMW does not condone exceeding posted speed limits. © 1987 BMW of North America, Inc. The BMW trademark and logo are registered

OF COURSE THERE ARE LESS EXPENSIVE IMITATIONS. THE QUESTION IS, WOULD YOU REALLY WANT TO OWN ONE?
If ever you find yourself lured by the car makers claiming to be "just as good as a BMW but cheaper," keep in mind the old nugget of folk wisdom: "Cheap is expensive."
Because in choosing an imitation over an authentic BMW 325, you will be forgoing an investment so sound, it is projected to hold its value better than 90% of all cars sold this year.*
But the purchase of an imitation is not just expensive at resale time. It's costly every time you turn the key.
It costs you the stirring response of BMW's ingenious 2.7-liter eta engine. Which, by delivering outstanding torque at low rpms, makes the BMW 325 as efficient in the city as it is exuberant in the country.**
It costs you an internationally-patented, fully-independent suspension born to take the twists and turns of the Bavarian Alps.
Most importantly, it costs you something more easily experienced than articulated: the fit, finish and feel of a true sports sedan, perfected over the years on the great racecourses of Europe. Not overnight in the boardrooms of business.
If you are in the market for a high-performance sedan, your local authorized BMW dealer will be happy to see that you don't become penny-wise and exhilaration-foolish.
BMW
THE ULTIMATE DRIVING MACHINE.

THE MANUFACTURER CAUTIONS YOU DO NOT EXCEED 100 MPH DURING YOUR FIRST 1,250 MILES.
Placed discreetly on the top inside left-hand corner of the windshield of every BMW 325is sports sedan is a small, transparent sticker which says to the driver, in effect:
During your first 1,250 miles, drive at changing velocities and engine revolutions. Do not exceed two-thirds maximum power in each gear.
5th gear in the BMW 325is at two-thirds engine speed is 100 mph.*
All of which raises a question: In a day and age when automobile manufacturers caution 50 mph during the first 1,250 miles, what kind of car is it that can be broken in at twice that speed?
One "fitted with as sweet an engine as BMW has ever built" (Car and Driver magazine).
One whose competition-tuned suspension, anti-lock brake system and functional aerodynamics were designed for the rigors of autobahn and Alpine driving.
And one that caused the Editor of Car and Driver to decree: "I hereby nominate it for permanent status in the car enthusiast's hall of fame." It's "a road entertainment package worth every cent of its sticker price."
After all, if this is the kind of reliability and endurance the BMW 325is can offer in the land of no speed limits, imagine what it will be like in a 55-mph world.
BMW
THE ULTIMATE DRIVING MACHINE.
*BMW does not condone exceeding posted speed limits. © 1987 BMW of North America, Inc. The BMW trademark and logo are registered

Life in New Zealand's fast lane.
Need to slow down and take a break?
Change lanes. Come to New Zealand.
Our 3 warm islands have what you need to relax. A casual lifestyle. Comfortable accommodations. People who take themselves a little less seriously and treat you more like one of their own.
You can scale the heights in a Wellington cable car, explore the depths of a glow-worm grotto, and still unwind on a sandy beach. All at a pace that's easy to take and prices that aren't hard to swallow.
In fact, just about the only thing we are in a hurry to do is send you a free New Zealand Book!
New Zealand Tourist & Publicity Office
10960 Wilshire Blvd., Suite 1530, Los Angeles, CA 90024
Rush me full details on slowing down in New Zealand.
Name
Address
City/State/Zip
NZTP
The climate is right for New Zealand.

Mass uprisings in New Zealand's countryside.
New Zealand still has what much of the world has lost sight of.
Escape to our 3 warm, green islands in the South Pacific. Settle down on a 90-mile-long beach. Or fly up to a year-long glacier. See unspoiled natural scenery and be spoiled by unsurpassed native hospitality.
Everything's right, right here! So send for your free New Zealand Book today.
New Zealand Tourist & Publicity Office
Name
City/State/Zip
NZTP
The climate is right for New Zealand.

Widespread unrest in New Zealand!
SHOTOVER JET
Looking for the perfect vacation spot to relax you—without putting you to sleep?
Change climates.
Come to New Zealand.
The place is really jumping! And sailing, And hiking. And golfing.
Escape from the rest of the world's pressures to the best of our world's pleasures.
New Zealand. One more really great thing to do here is fill in this coupon!
New Zealand Tourist & Publicity Office
Name
City/State/Zip
NZTP
The climate is right for New Zealand.

Consumer Magazine Color: Campaign Including Magazine Supplements

414

ART DIRECTOR
Frank Haggerty

WRITERS
Kerry Casey
Jack Supple

CLIENT
Normark/Rapala

AGENCY
Carmichael Lynch/
Minneapolis

415

ART DIRECTOR
Michael Hampton

WRITER
Cynthia Beck

CLIENT
NYNEX

AGENCY
Young & Rubicam

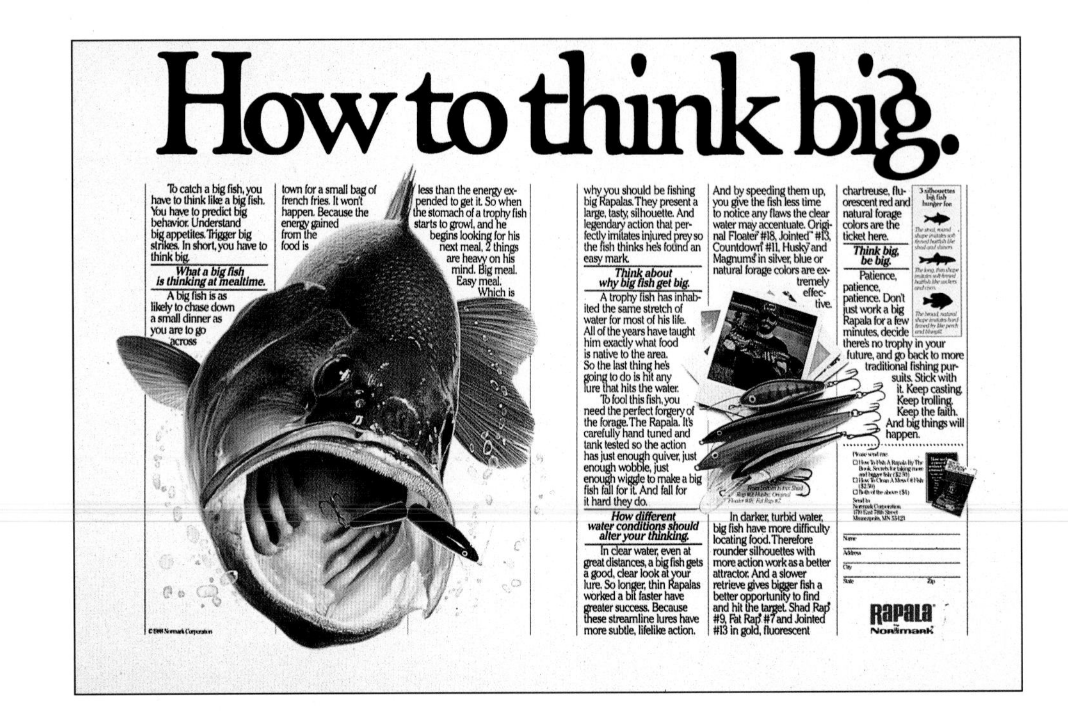

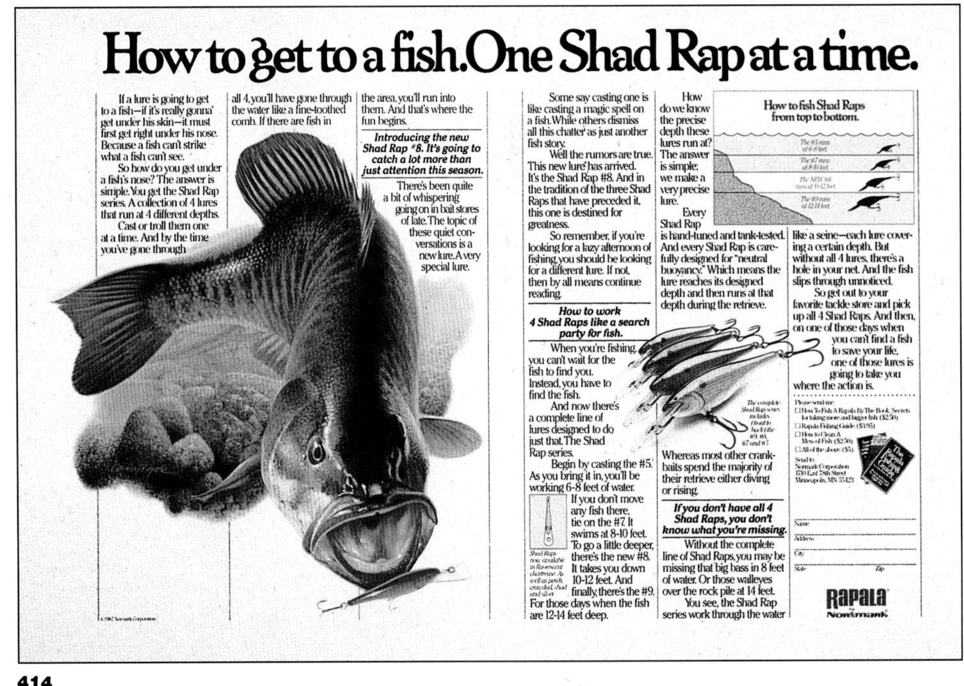

Did you hear the one about the farmer's data?

It seems there was a certain multi-billion-dollar-a-year farmer. One who believed in other liquids besides milk.

So he acquired Gulf Oil in eleven northeastern states. By now you probably know his name: Cumberland Farms.

Well, sir, one morning in the midst of all this growth, Cumberland Farms discovered they'd outgrown their own communications system. So they started looking around for a company that handles telecommunications and information management as well as they handle liquids.

They picked NYNEX, for some interesting reasons.

Naturally, Cumberland Farms knows the value of freshness. So when NYNEX came up with some original solutions to their needs—like privately owned lines with data capabilities between their headquarters and their distribution center, and a system that could keep growing with their company—they liked the freshness of our thinking.

They're also known for competitive prices. So when they saw our bid, they said, How now, NYNEX. And as experts in liquidity, they were glad to let NYNEX help with the deal.

The NYNEX family of information companies would like to help you, too—with everything from computer systems to telecommunications. Give us a call at 1 800 535-1535.

You may never look back.

Because once our clients find out the answer is NYNEX, how're you gonna keep 'em down on the farm?

THE ANSWER IS

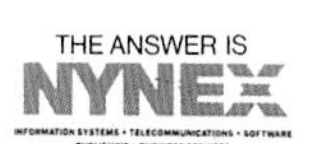

Chances are we're holding up your bank.

We don't mean to boast. But of the top ten U.S. banks, eight are NYNEX customers.

Of the top ten diversified financial institutions, nine are NYNEX customers.

So are over half of all *Fortune* 500 companies.

NYNEX is upholding these giants in lots of ways. We've given most of them their data-capable phone systems, and many of them their computers and software as well.

Now, as you know, we're not exactly the only people who offer telecommunications and information systems. So why are so many financial leaders choosing NYNEX?

One clue is our hot technology. Recently, for example, a worldwide bank needed help tracking their customer liability. And NYNEX gave them a software package that issues worldwide reports on who's naughty, who's nice.

The NYNEX family of companies would like to work with you, too. Besides our two phone companies, we have nine companies in information and office systems, business services, software and publishing.

To learn more about why NYNEX is the answer for your business, call us at 1 800 535-1535.

We suspect you'll like our bids as much as our technology. At NYNEX we understand that our customers—even the top banks—are not made of money.

THE ANSWER IS

What a beauti ful day for a disk drive.

Vroom, vroom. Purr, purrrrrrr.

Oh, no! A pothole.

If your company is a driving force in business, and if you're considering updating your information system, you've probably run into the usual bumps and holes—from unimaginative technology to wildly fanciful prices.

May we point out what many leaders in the automotive industry have found?

To really make the most of information and telecommunications, all roads lead to NYNEX.

That's why five of the top banks that provide automotive financing use NYNEX. Not to mention a slick sampling of the major oil companies.

Recently we even gave one of these giants a computer graphics system that helps them pinpoint the most promising places to drill for oil. Now, that's refined.

The NYNEX family of companies would like to work with you, too. Besides our two phone companies with their vast capabilities, we have nine companies in information and office systems, business services, software and publishing.

Call us at 1 800 535-1535. We think we can show you that the answer is NYNEX pretty fast.

In fact, we'll soon have your data moving at thousands of miles per second. Highway or city.

THE ANSWER IS

Consumer Magazine Color: Campaign Including Magazine Supplements

416

ART DIRECTOR
John Scott MacDaniels

WRITERS
Carol White
John Scott MacDaniels

DESIGNER
John Scott MacDaniels

CLIENT
Dep Corporation

AGENCY
Lowe Marschalk/
San Francisco

417

ART DIRECTOR
Rick Carlson

WRITER
Scott Crawford

DESIGNER
Rick Carlson

PHOTOGRAPHER
Pelosi & Chambers

CLIENT
Cooper Tools

AGENCY
Howard Merrell &
Partners/Raleigh, NC

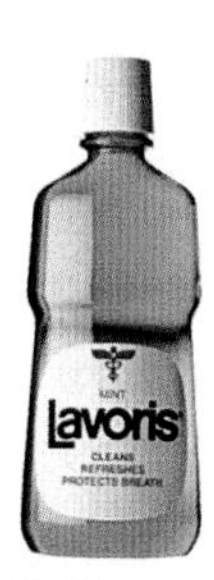

New Lavoris Mint: more effective than Scope Mint, even after 3 hours. Because eventually you've got to turn off the tv and talk to somebody!

New Lavoris Mint outlasts Scope Mint, even after 3 hours. Maybe if your favorite tv news anchor team had used it, they'd <u>still</u> be together nightly!

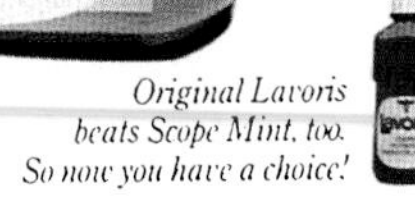

Original Lavoris
beats Scope Mint, too.
So now you have a choice!

New Lavoris Mint, the mouthwash that outlasts Scope Mint, even after 3 hours.

(This magazine contains a list of times when it could come in handy.)

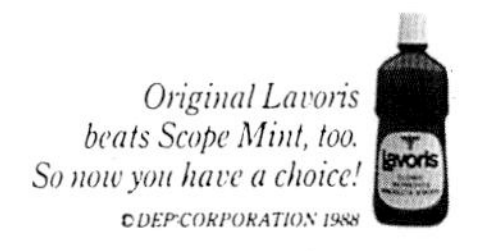

Original Lavoris
beats Scope Mint, too.
So now you have a choice!
©DEP CORPORATION 1988

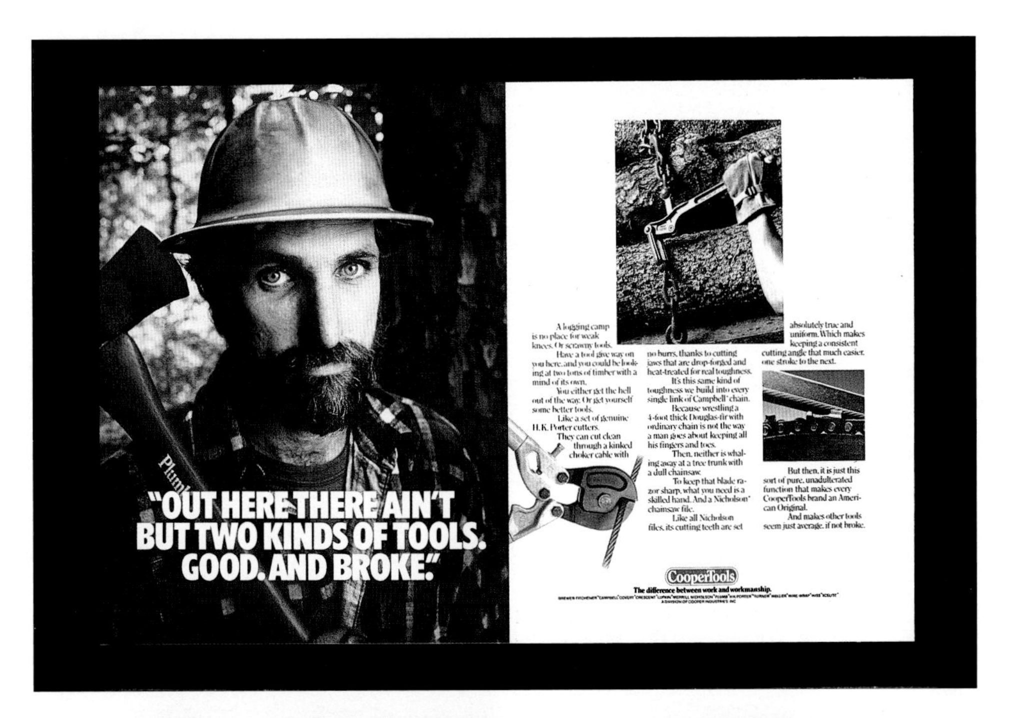
"OUT HERE THERE AIN'T BUT TWO KINDS OF TOOLS. GOOD. AND BROKE."
A logging camp is no place for weak knees. Or scrawny tools.
Have a tool give way on you here, and you could be looking at two tons of timber with a mind of its own.
You either get the hell out of the way. Or get yourself some better tools.
Like a set of genuine H.K. Porter cutters.
They can cut clean through a kinked choker cable with no burrs, thanks to cutting jaws that are drop-forged and heat-treated for real toughness.
It's this same kind of toughness we build into every single link of Campbell chain.
Because wrestling a 4-foot thick Douglas-fir with ordinary chain is not the way a man goes about keeping all his fingers and toes.
Then, neither is whaling away at a tree trunk with a dull chainsaw.
To keep that blade razor sharp, what you need is a skilled hand. And a Nicholson chainsaw file.
Like all Nicholson files, its cutting teeth are set absolutely true and uniform. Which makes keeping a consistent cutting angle that much easier, one stroke to the next.
But then, it is just this sort of pure, unadulterated function that makes every CooperTools brand an American Original.
And makes other tools seem just average, if not broke.
CooperTools
The difference between work and workmanship.

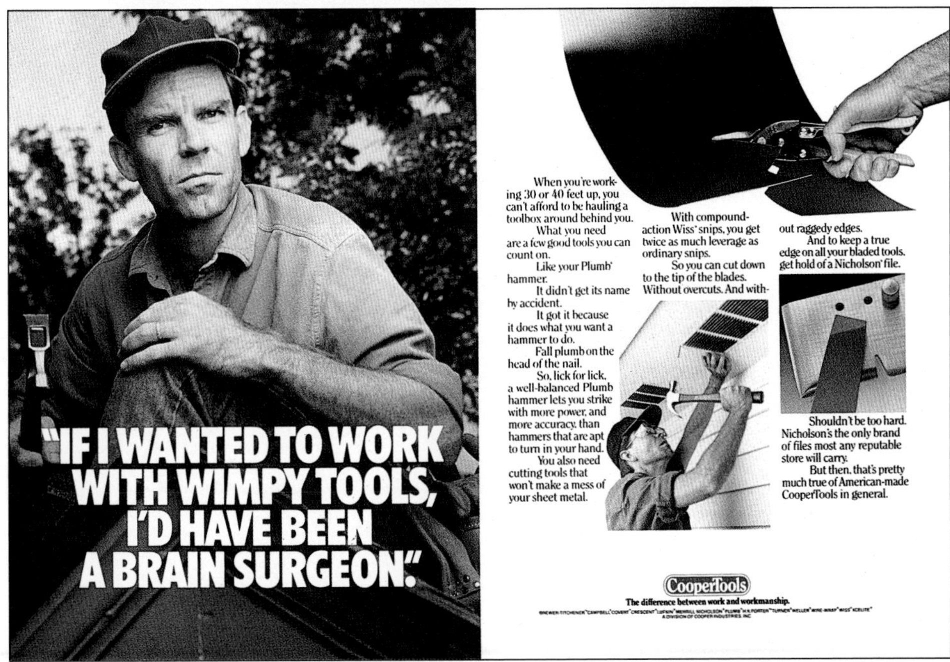
"IF I WANTED TO WORK WITH WIMPY TOOLS, I'D HAVE BEEN A BRAIN SURGEON."
When you're working 30 or 40 feet up, you can't afford to be hauling a toolbox around behind you.
What you need are a few good tools you can count on.
Like your Plumb hammer.
It didn't get its name by accident.
It got it because it does what you want a hammer to do.
Fall plumb on the head of the nail.
So, lick for lick, a well-balanced Plumb hammer lets you strike with more power, and more accuracy, than hammers that are apt to turn in your hand.
You also need cutting tools that won't make a mess of your sheet metal.
With compound-action Wiss snips, you get twice as much leverage as ordinary snips.
So you can cut down to the tip of the blades. Without overcuts. And without raggedy edges.
And to keep a true edge on all your bladed tools, get hold of a Nicholson file.
Shouldn't be too hard. Nicholson's the only brand of files most any reputable store will carry.
But then, that's pretty much true of American-made CooperTools in general.
CooperTools
The difference between work and workmanship.

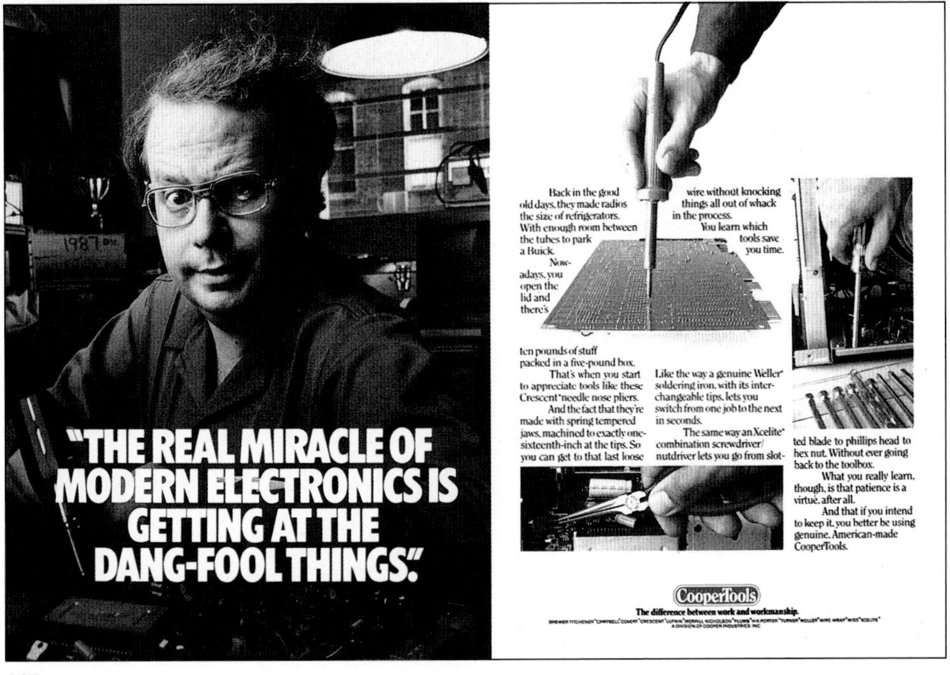
"THE REAL MIRACLE OF MODERN ELECTRONICS IS GETTING AT THE DANG-FOOL THINGS."
Back in the good old days, they made radios the size of refrigerators. With enough room between the tubes to park a Buick.
Nowadays, you open the lid and there's ten pounds of stuff packed in a five-pound box.
That's when you start to appreciate tools like these Crescent needle nose pliers.
And the fact that they're made with spring tempered jaws, machined to exactly one-sixteenth-inch at the tips. So you can get to that last loose wire without knocking things all out of whack in the process.
You learn which tools save you time.
Like the way a genuine Weller soldering iron, with its interchangeable tips, lets you switch from one job to the next in seconds.
The same way an Xcelite combination screwdriver/nutdriver lets you go from slotted blade to phillips head to hex nut. Without ever going back to the toolbox.
What you really learn, though, is that patience is a virtue, after all.
And that if you intend to keep it, you better be using genuine, American-made CooperTools.
CooperTools
The difference between work and workmanship.

Consumer Magazine Color: Campaign Including Magazine Supplements

418

ART DIRECTORS
Angelo DeSantis
Corky Kotkin

WRITER
Peter Faulkner

PHOTOGRAPHER
Gary Perweiler

CLIENT
Sony

AGENCY
McCann-Erickson

419

ART DIRECTOR
Mark Johnson

WRITER
Bill Miller

PHOTOGRAPHER
Randy Miller

CLIENT
Lee Jeans

AGENCY
Fallon McElligott/
Minneapolis

SONY
AF
Video 8
AUTO Handycam
They both bring back memories of your childhood.
But with the Sony, they won't be fuzzy.
SONY
THE ONE AND ONLY.

SONY
AF
Video 8
AUTO Handycam
They all bring back memories of your old baseball pals.
But with the Sony, there won't be a single error.
SONY
THE ONE AND ONLY.

SONY
AF
Video 8
AUTO Handycam
They both bring back memories of your special day.
But with the Sony, seeing it vividly is a piece of cake.
SONY
THE ONE AND ONLY.

Introducing a fashion look that bombed in 1943.
Jump into a look inspired by the 101st Airborne. Lee® Sky Riders™ have landed. Cut loose so you can cut loose. Stonewashed denim with a pleated front. Watch for the invasion near you.
Sky Riders
Lee
The brand that fits.

Daytona Beach, Florida
Cancun, Mexico

Be seen in all the right places.

No matter where you are, when you're wearing Lee® Leen Jeans, you'll be seen in all the right places. Fit tight, in stone washed or frosted indigo. You have nothing to hide.

Leen Jeans Lee

The brand that fits.

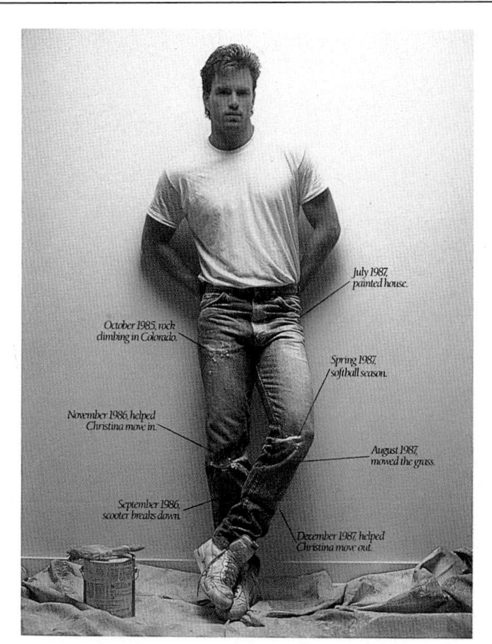

July 1987, painted house.
October 1985, rock climbing in Colorado.
Spring 1987, softball season.
November 1986, helped Christina move in.
August 1987, mowed the grass.
September 1986, scooter breaks down.
December 1987, helped Christina move out.

Only jeans that fit this well, get the chance to look this bad.

Lee® Storm Rider® jeans might just be the best fitting and most comfortable jeans you'll ever wear. And wear. And wear. And wear. And wear.

Storm Riders Lee

The brand that fits.

Consumer Magazine Color: Campaign Including Magazine Supplements

420

ART DIRECTOR
Dean Stefanides

WRITER
Bernie Rosner

DESIGNER
Dean Stefanides

PHOTOGRAPHER
Dennis Manarchy

CLIENT
Ralston Purina

AGENCY
Scali McCabe Sloves

421

ART DIRECTOR
David Page

WRITERS
Ron Sackett
Joe Nagy

PHOTOGRAPHER
Dennis Manarchy

CLIENT
Harley-Davidson

AGENCY
Carmichael Lynch/
Minneapolis

Kiss Anonymity Goodbye.
Right outside your door, a kind of sameness permeates the world. Witness the tens of thousands of so-called "custom" motorcycles on the streets. Built more by formula than feeling, they all seem to blend together. As do their riders.
It's a different story when you're on a Harley-Davidson. Wherever a Harley takes you, eyes are sure to follow.
It never fails. When it comes to causing a scene, nothing is in the same league.
Consider the Harley-Davidson Low Rider.™ Like all Harleys, a motorcycle impossible to ignore. People notice everything about it. The clean custom lines. The original console-mounted gauges on the Fat Bob gas tank. The dazzling chrome and black finish of the V² Evolution engine. The sound that fills the air when those 80 cubic inches come to life. It doesn't just turn heads. It draws crowds.
If you'd rather move through life unnoticed, you should probably stay away from a Harley-Davidson. But if you don't mind attracting more than a little attention every now and then, get on the new Low Rider. And get ready to kiss anonymity goodbye.
Things Are Different On A Harley

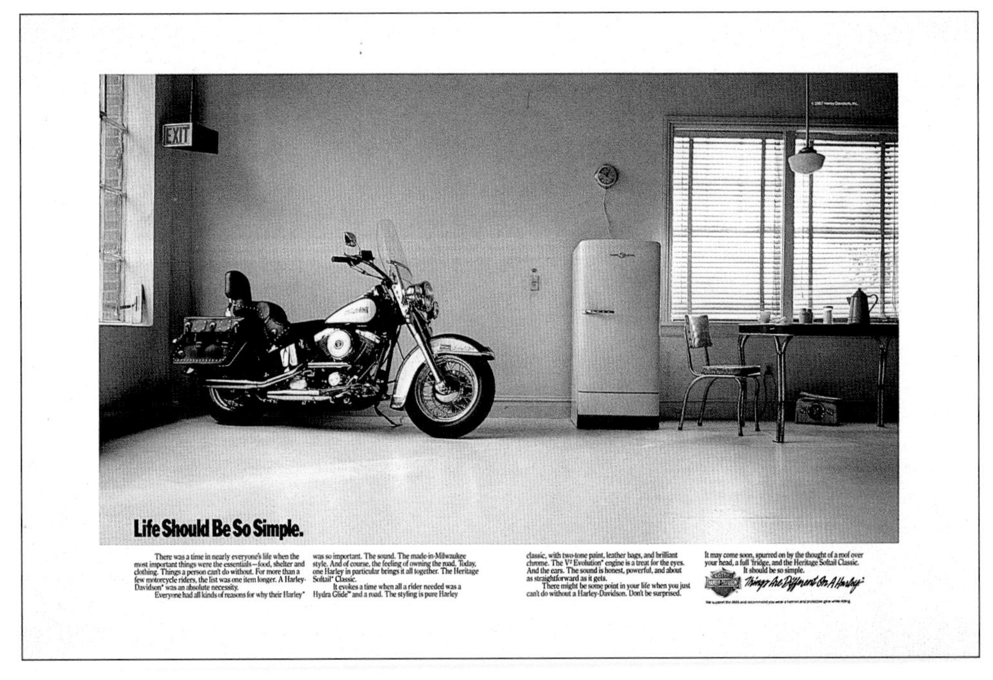
EXIT
Life Should Be So Simple.
There was a time in nearly everyone's life when the most important things were the essentials—food, shelter and clothing. Things a person can't do without. For more than a few motorcycle riders, the list was one item longer. A Harley-Davidson was an absolute necessity.
Everyone had all kinds of reasons for why their Harley was so important. The sound. The made-in-Milwaukee style. And of course, the feeling of owning the road. Today, one Harley in particular brings it all together. The Heritage Softail Classic.
It evokes a time when all a rider needed was a Hydra Glide™ and a road. The styling is pure Harley classic, with two-tone paint, leather bags, and brilliant chrome. The V² Evolution engine is a treat for the eyes. And the ears. The sound is honest, powerful, and about as straightforward as it gets.
There might be some point in your life when you just can't do without a Harley-Davidson. Don't be surprised. It may come soon, spurred on by the thought of a roof over your head, a full 'fridge, and the Heritage Softail Classic.
It should be so simple.
Things Are Different On A Harley

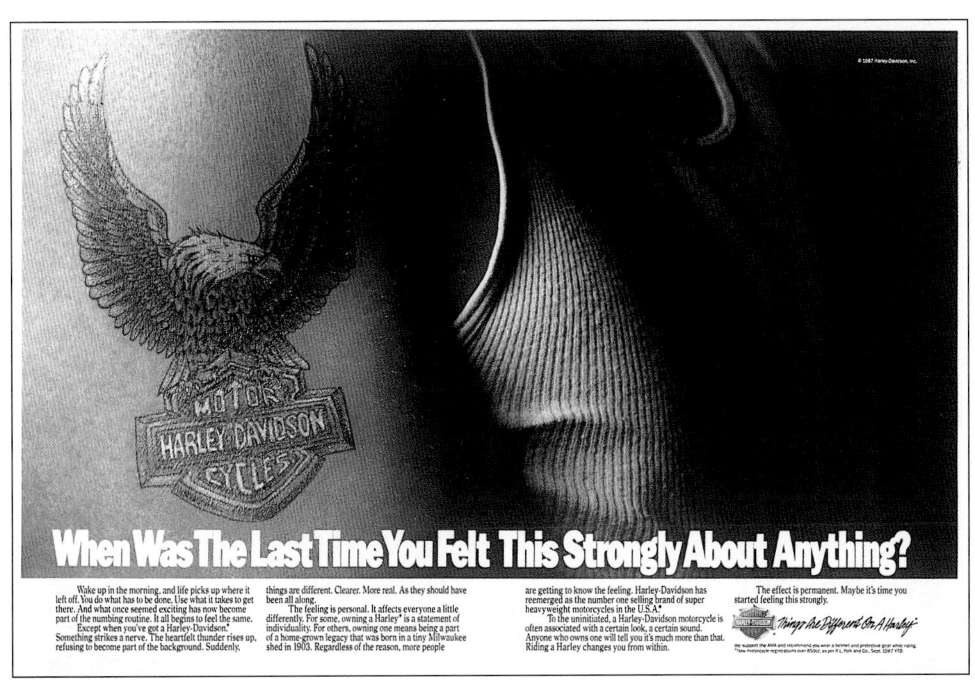
MOTOR
HARLEY-DAVIDSON
CYCLES
When Was The Last Time You Felt This Strongly About Anything?
Wake up in the morning, and life picks up where it left off. You do what has to be done. Use what it takes to get there. And what once seemed exciting has now become part of the numbing routine. It all begins to feel the same.
Except when you've got a Harley-Davidson. Something strikes a nerve. The heartfelt thunder rises up, refusing to become part of the background. Suddenly, things are different. Clearer. More real. As they should have been all along.
The feeling is personal. It affects everyone a little differently. For some, owning a Harley is a statement of individuality. For others, owning one means being a part of a home-grown legacy that was born in a tiny Milwaukee shed in 1903. Regardless of the reason, more people are getting to know the feeling. Harley-Davidson has reemerged as the number one selling brand of super heavyweight motorcycles in the U.S.A.*
To the uninitiated, a Harley-Davidson motorcycle is often associated with a certain look, a certain sound. Anyone who owns one will tell you it's much more than that. Riding a Harley changes you from within.
The effect is permanent. Maybe it's time you started feeling this strongly.
Things Are Different On A Harley

Consumer Magazine Color: Campaign Including Magazine Supplements

422

ART DIRECTOR
Kai Mui

WRITERS
John Harrington
Peter Louison

PHOTOGRAPHERS
James Nachtwey
Jun Nishimaki
Hideki Fujii

CLIENT
Eastman Kodak

AGENCY
Rumrill-Hoyt/
Rochester, NY

423

ART DIRECTOR
Vince Squibb

WRITER
Gerard Edmondson

PHOTOGRAPHER
Andreas Heumann

CLIENT
Mates Healthcare

AGENCY
Still Price Court Twivy
D'Souza/London

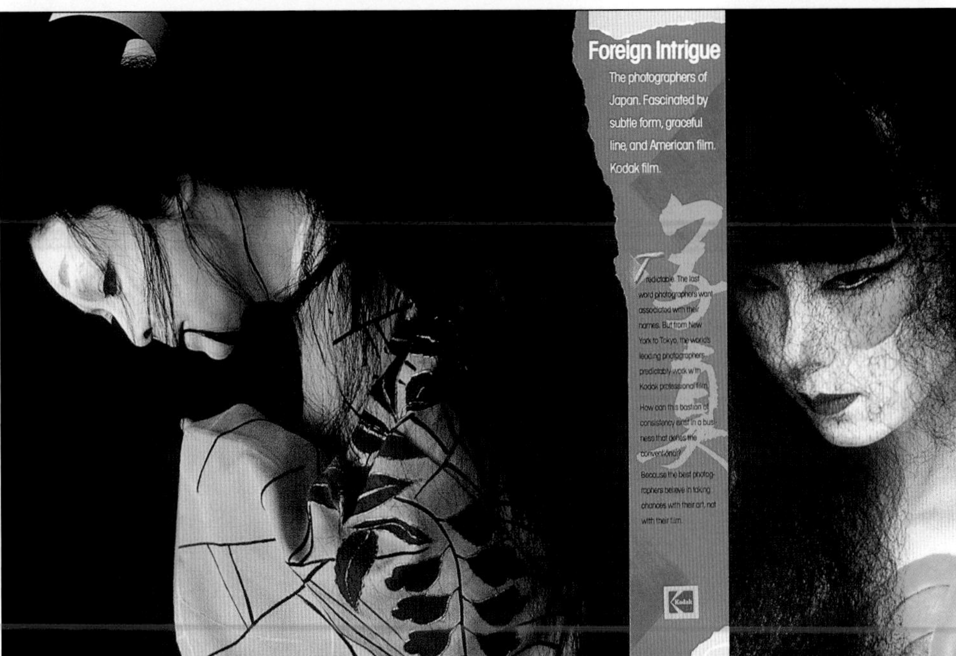

"THEY'RE AWFULLY FIDDLY TO PUT ON.
ISN'T THAT HALF THE FUN?"
Mates
MATES. YOU MAKE LOVE. THEY MAKE SENSE.

"WE HAD A LITTLE TIME TO OURSELVES.
SO WE THOUGHT WE'D
DO SOMETHING FOR CHARITY."
MATES. YOU MAKE LOVE. THEY MAKE SENSE.

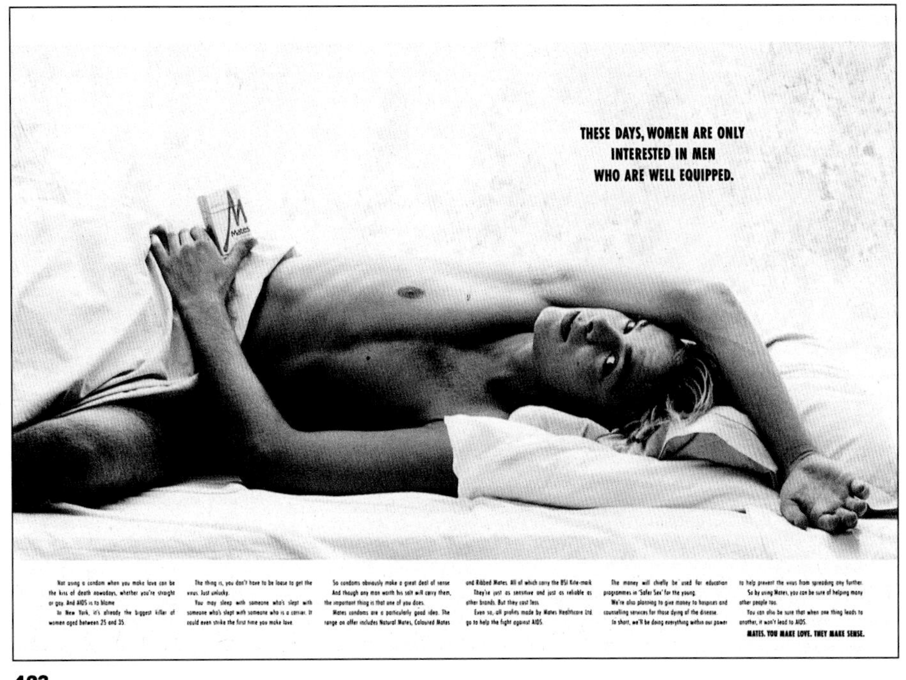
THESE DAYS, WOMEN ARE ONLY
INTERESTED IN MEN
WHO ARE WELL EQUIPPED.
Mates
MATES. YOU MAKE LOVE. THEY MAKE SENSE.

Consumer Magazine Color: Campaign Including Magazine Supplements

424
ART DIRECTOR
Mark Johnson
WRITER
Phil Hanft
PHOTOGRAPHER
Dennis Manarchy
CLIENT
Lee Jeans
AGENCY
Fallon McElligott/ Minneapolis

425
ART DIRECTOR
David Nathanson
WRITER
Phil Lanier
PHOTOGRAPHER
Bill Werts
CLIENT
Yamaha Motor Corporation
AGENCY
Chiat/Day - Venice, CA

Unfortunately, by the time your last pair of jeans looked this good, they were worn out.

It's such a pity. To have gone through so much together, only to part company just when your jeans finally have just the right look.

But that's the whole idea behind new Lee® Frosted Riders.™

Lee Frosted Riders give you the same worn look and character you get from jeans that are two or three years old. The difference is you don't have to wait two or three years to get it. Available in relaxed fitting jeans, jackets, skirts and bibs. Grey, black and indigo.

Frosted Riders Lee

Most jeans that look this good have ten times the mileage.

If you don't have time to wait for your jeans to look like they've been around the block a few times, new Lee® Frosted Riders™ are for you.

With Lee Frosted Riders, you get the same worn look and distinctive character that normally comes with two or three years of hard living. The difference is you don't have to wait two or three years to get it.

But you better jump into a pair soon. These jeans are going faster than a bored and stroked '57 Chevy on a lonely country road.

Now available in grey, black and indigo.

Frosted Riders Lee
The brand that fits.

You shouldn't have to spend the best years of your life waiting for your jeans to look this good.

In the accepted and time-honored pursuit of worn looking jeans, there is, at last, a genuine alternative to years of hard wear.

New Lee® Frosted Riders.™

Lee Frosted Riders give you the same worn look and character you get from jeans that are two or three years old. The difference is you don't have to wait two or three years to get it. Available in relaxed fitting jeans, jackets, skirts and bibs. Grey, black and indigo.

Frosted Riders Lee

YAMAHA
No, you don't have to join the Air Force to get one.
It's the 1988 Exciter. With a liquid-cooled 569cc two-stroke engine armed with new slide-valve carburetion this year. Yamaha Telescopic Strut Suspension and rear suspension that's better than ever. And a power-to-weight ratio that gives you the kind of acceleration you'd expect from something like a F-15, not a snowmobile.
To get one, see your local Yamaha dealer. Then file your flight plan.
YAMAHA
We make the difference.

PHAZER
Whether your kids are 14 years old or 40 years old, we know a sure-fire way of getting them to follow your example.
Jump on a snowmobile.
The only question is, which snowmobile to jump on. A choice made all the more difficult by the fact that Yamaha makes 14 different sleds, each the best in its class.
Such as the Yamaha Phazer—the number-one selling snowmobile in the world.
The Phazer earned that title by combining unique styling, versatility and high performance. And that's something you'll need plenty of, if you hope to stay ahead of your kids.
Because even the Yamaha Bravo and Bravo Long Track, our most economical full-size sleds, offer enough performance to keep young riders* entertained for years.
Then there's the incredibly comfortable, easy-to-learn Inviter. And the powerful Enticer line of sleds, including the luxurious Excel III and the new Enticer Long Track with reverse, designed to haul you and enough gear for your whole family.
You can see the entire Yamaha line at your nearest Yamaha dealer. Then head for the hills with your kids close behind.
Or vice versa.
YAMAHA
We make the difference.
How to get your kids to follow in your tracks.

PHAZER
YAMAHA
Of the 16 best sleds in the world, 15 are Yamahas.
That's because we make a total of 15 different models, including a whole new concept for having fun in the snow—the SnoScoot. And every Yamaha is famous for innovation, craftsmanship and reliability.
Starting with the economical yet full-size Bravo. The easy-to-learn Inviter for beginners. The Enticer line, including the new Enticer Long Track with reverse and the luxurious Excel III. And our rugged new utility sled, the VK540.
On the other end of the scale, we also make the incredible Exciter and Exciter Deluxe, the epitome of high performance. And the revolutionary Phazer, the most popular sport sled ever made.
So, if you want the best sled for any purpose, there are really only two places to look.
Inside your friendly Yamaha dealer.
Or behind your friendly Husky.
YAMAHA
We make the difference.

Consumer Magazine Color: Campaign Including Magazine Supplements

426

ART DIRECTOR
Rick Boyko

WRITER
Richard Kelley

PHOTOGRAPHER
Dennis Manarchy

CLIENT
Foster Farms

AGENCY
Chiat/Day - Venice, CA

427

ART DIRECTOR
James Dalthorp

WRITER
Galen Greenwood

CLIENT
Ben Hogan Company

AGENCY
Tracy-Locke/Dallas

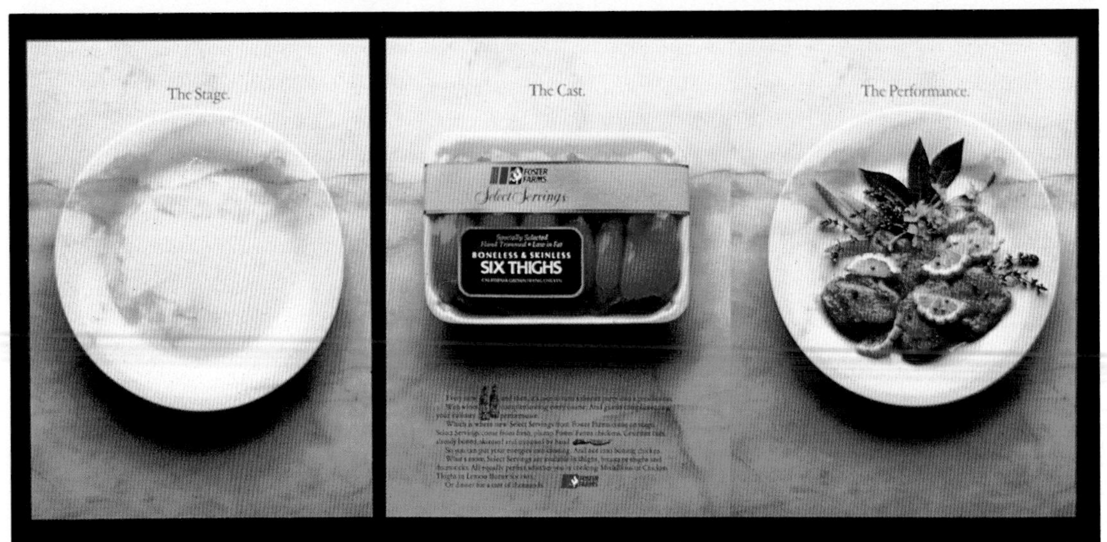

426

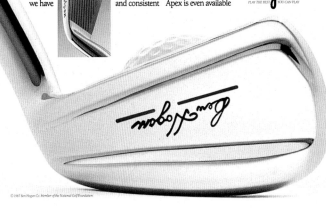

Consumer Magazine Color: Campaign Including Magazine Supplements

428

ART DIRECTOR
Roy Grace

WRITER
Diane Rothschild

PHOTOGRAPHERS
Henry Sandbank
Jerry Cailor
Carl Furuta

CLIENT
Range Rover of North America

AGENCY
Grace & Rothschild

429

ART DIRECTORS
Bruce Bloch
Carlos Darquea

WRITERS
Patricia Rockmore
Dennis Ferrone

PHOTOGRAPHERS
Uli Rose
Kei Ogata

CLIENT
Oil of Olay

AGENCY
Wells Rich Greene

"I don't intend to grow old gracefully...
I intend to fight it every step of the way."
OIL of OLAY

"I don't intend to grow old gracefully...
I intend to fight it every step of the way."
OIL of OLAY

"I don't intend to grow old gracefully...
I intend to fight it every step of the way."
OIL of OLAY

Consumer Magazine Color: Campaign Including Magazine Supplements

430

ART DIRECTOR
Doug Lew

WRITERS
Bill Johnson
Bob Thacker

CLIENT
Minneapolis Institute of Arts

AGENCY
Ruhr/Paragon - Minneapolis

431

ART DIRECTOR
Simon Chandler

WRITER
Adrian Lim

PHOTOGRAPHER
Steve Cavalier

CLIENT
Bowater Scott/Baby Fresh

AGENCY
Gold Greenless Trott/
London

Think of this show as the vacation pictures of America's Impressionists.
Long before color film was invented, America's finest artists recorded their vacations in brilliant watercolors. Working on location, they documented America's sun-bleached beaches, windswept coasts, and raindrenched everglades in a way no photographs ever could.
Now you can experience their impressions of scenic America in a stunning collection of American watercolors at The Minneapolis Institute of Arts from December 13, 1987 through February 14, 1988.
American Traditions in Watercolors
Rarely displayed because of the delicate nature of the medium, this collection surveys many of the major trends in American watercolor from the early 19th century to the present. Included are picture perfect scenes by Winslow Homer, John Singer Sargent, Edward Hopper and Andrew Wyeth.
This exhibition of 85 works was organized by the Worcester Art Museum and sponsored by Digital Equipment Corporation, with support from the Henry Luce Foundation and the National Endowment for the Arts.
Represented are some of Homer's first serious efforts in watercolor, painted around 1873 in Gloucester, as well as some examples of his last series, painted on vacation in Florida in 1904. Also represented are several Sargent paintings from a visit to Biscayne Bay in 1917.
If you visit the Institute during the holidays, be sure to take part in our annual tradition, Holidays in the Period Rooms. From December 3, 1987 through January 3, 1988, our Period Rooms will be decorated as they might have looked during the Christmas holidays of the 18th and 19th centuries.
From shimmering seascapes to dazzling decorations, something is sure to catch your eye at The Minneapolis Institute of Arts, 2400 Third Avenue South.
The Minneapolis Institute of Arts

Minnesota's Most Valuable Athlete Will Never Appear At The Dome.
In fact, Minnesota's most valuable player can't even play football or baseball. To find this incredible athlete, come to The Minneapolis Institute of Arts and discover the Doryphoros. A masterpiece of sculpture more than 2,000 years old.
In 440 B.C. the Greek sculptor Polykleitos created a statue of the perfect athlete. His work embodied all of the ideals of the High Classical Age. The Doryphoros captivated the ancient world for centuries to come. Although the original was destroyed, fortunately ancient Greek and Roman sculptors recreated the work. And today, only four of these ancient copies remain. The Doryphoros at the Minneapolis Institute of Arts is the only one in America.
No other American museum has anything comparable. At a cost of nearly 2.5 million dollars, the Doryphoros is truly one of the most important acquisitions in the history of The Minneapolis Institute of Arts. Come. Discover the majesty and the beauty of the Doryphoros for yourself. And see how Minnesota's most important athlete has won the world, without ever playing a single game.
The Minneapolis Institute of Arts

Who was that masked man?
He lived a simple existence on a small remote island in the South Pacific. And he created some of the most powerful, masterful and imaginative sculptures in the world.
Who was he? Find out for yourself when The Minneapolis Institute of Arts opens its exhibition of the startling carvings of New Ireland from October 10, 1987 through January 3, 1988.
An Assemblage of Spirits: Idea and Image in New Ireland
This exhibition presents 50 rare wood carvings created by New Irelanders in the 19th and early 20th centuries. The sculptures, assembled from museums and collections around the world, include wood masks, heads, figures, multi-figured poles, and dance ornaments. These objects are intricately carved, painted and decorated with seashells, fibers, seaweed, stone, chalk and sponge.
This exhibition was organized by The Minneapolis Institute of Arts and made possible, in part, by grants from the National Endowment for the Arts and the National Endowment for the Humanities.
Come discover for yourself who that masked man was. At The Minneapolis Institute of Arts, 2400 Third Avenue South, Minneapolis, MN.
The Minneapolis Institute of Arts

"Compared with Baby Fresh most wipes are piddley little things."
Baby Fresh are big enough to cover your entire hand. They're also soft and gentle enough to use on your baby's hands and face. What's more, they're nearly three times thicker than most wipes. And they have a handy flip open lid, so you won't flip your lid trying to get them out. Available in a Travel Pack, large and standard sizes, they wipe the floor with other wipes.
Baby Fresh

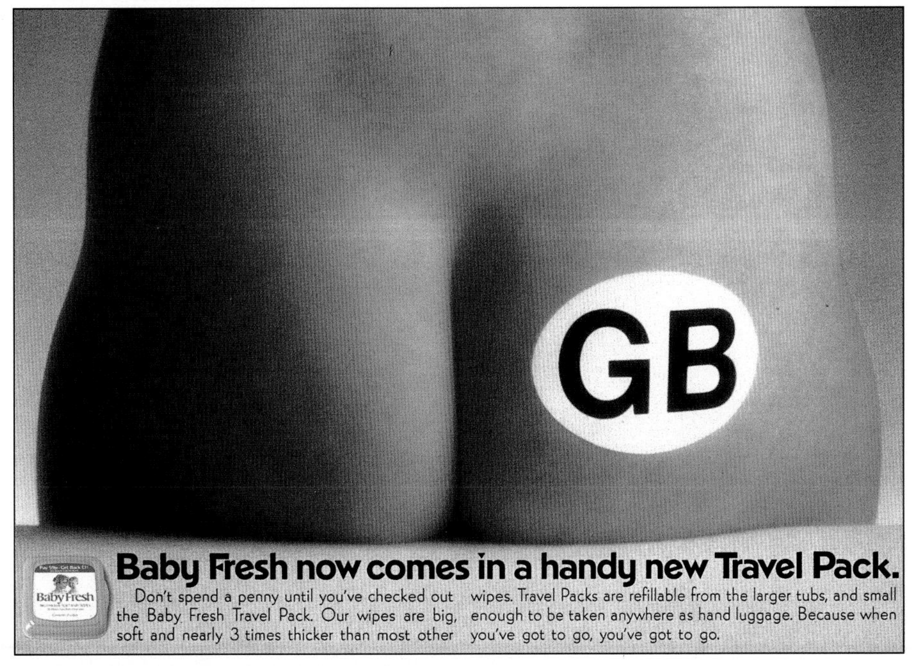
GB
Baby Fresh now comes in a handy new Travel Pack.
Don't spend a penny until you've checked out the Baby Fresh Travel Pack. Our wipes are big, soft and nearly 3 times thicker than most other wipes. Travel Packs are refillable from the larger tubs, and small enough to be taken anywhere as hand luggage. Because when you've got to go, you've got to go.
Baby Fresh

BABY NEWS
Before you spend a penny, check out Baby Fresh's new large size tub.
Running out of baby wipes in the middle of a job is enough to drive any Mum potty. So Baby Fresh now come in a new jumbo sized tub. And because they're big, soft, and nearly three times thicker than most other wipes, they're more economical to use.
Baby Fresh are also less of a struggle, because they have a convenient flip open lid.
So, if you're coming to the bottom of your baby wipes, get a big tub of Baby Fresh.
Baby Fresh

Consumer Magazine Less Than A Page B/W or Color: Campaign

432

ART DIRECTOR
Bill Cozens

WRITER
Alvin Wasserman

PHOTOGRAPHERS
Rick Blacklaws
Alan Zenuk
Bob Herger

CLIENT
Canadian Ministry of Tourism

AGENCY
McKim Advertising/ Vancouver

433

ART DIRECTOR
Kathy Kiely

WRITER
Karen Larson

PHOTOGRAPHER
Gozo

CLIENT
WCBS-TV

AGENCY
Della Femina Travisano & Partners

Our guided tours can have you exchanging views with a few fellow travellers on the wildly beautiful Spatsizi Plateau. Heli-hiking tours in our Rockies carry all your gear in and plunk you down in comfortable camps so you can take day trips at your leisure. Just outside of Vancouver there's the gentle wilderness of Manning Park or Garibaldi. And that means you can rough it in a bay-side bistro at journey's end. Of course folks who take us up on sailing, diving, kayaking and guest ranching also move in the best of circles. What's holding you back?
Bill Reid, Minister, Tourism, Recreation and Culture.
For your copy of our Adventure Vacation Guide write: Tourism British Columbia, Dept. T7M-OC-04, Parliament Bldgs., Victoria, British Columbia, V8V 1X4.
Super, Natural British Columbia
Social climbing is definitely encouraged here.

Others we send to live the soft life on a guest ranch. It all depends on what they're looking for in an adventure vacation. It could be paddling an ocean kayak. Or peddling in the Rockies. Perhaps a little smooth sailing. Or deep sea diving. Whichever adventure package they go on, the spectacular scenery is, of course, absolutely free. For your copy of our Super, Natural Adventure Vacation Guide, write Tourism British Columbia, Department T7M-CM-04, Box C-34971, Seattle, Washington 98124-1971. After that the roughest part will be deciding which way to go.
Bill Reid, Minister, Tourism, Recreation and Culture.
Super, Natural British Columbia CANADA
We give some of our visitors a rough time.

You can get through to the heavyweights of fly fishing here. Like trophy size rainbows. Or challenging steelhead. Lately, a lot of folks have even been getting tied up with cohos. Prefer to connect to a Dolly Varden or kokanee? Just bring your regular gear. With huge tyee waiting at the end of the line, our salt-water fishing is very engaging too. Make an appointment for a luxurious lodge or a lakeside retreat. Write Tourism British Columbia, Dept. #T7M-OU-06, Box C-34971, Seattle, WA, 98124-1971 for our Adventure Guide. We've got your number.
Bill Reid, Minister, Tourism, Recreation and Culture.
Super, Natural British Columbia CANADA
No phones, but our lines are always busy.

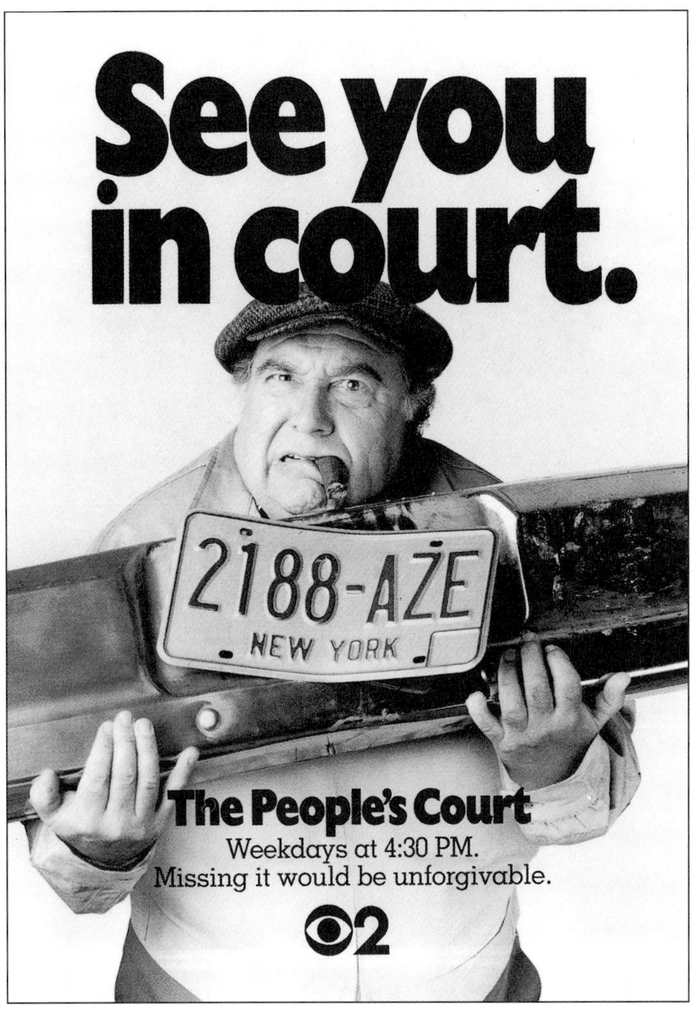
See you in court.
2188-AZE
NEW YORK
The People's Court
Weekdays at 4:30 PM.
Missing it would be unforgivable.
2

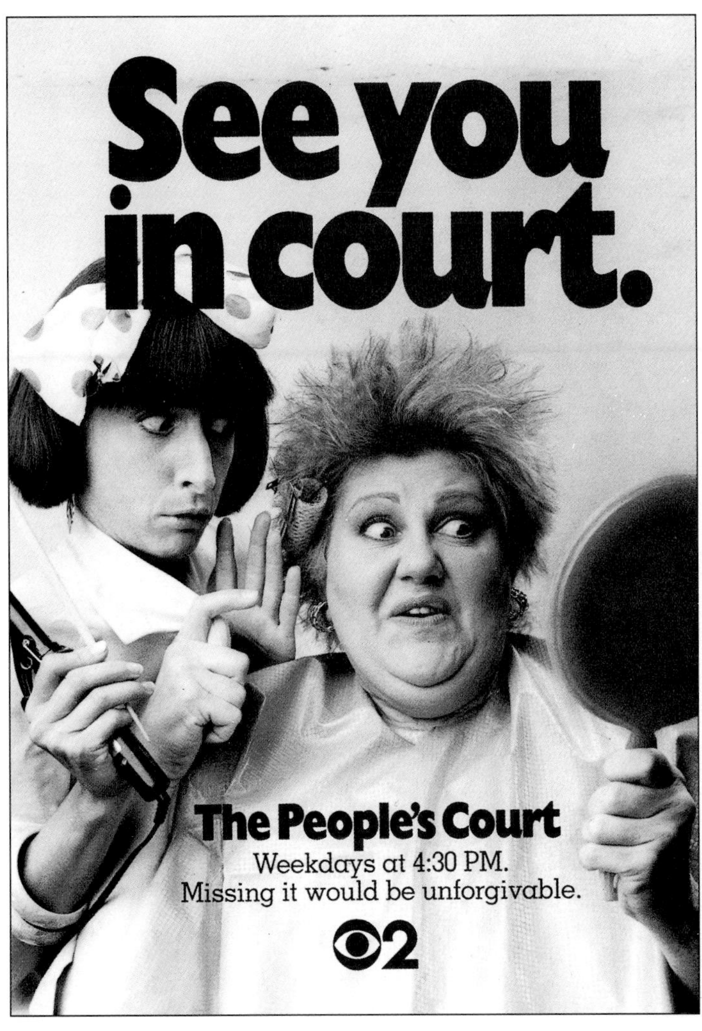
See you in court.
The People's Court
Weekdays at 4:30 PM.
Missing it would be unforgivable.
2

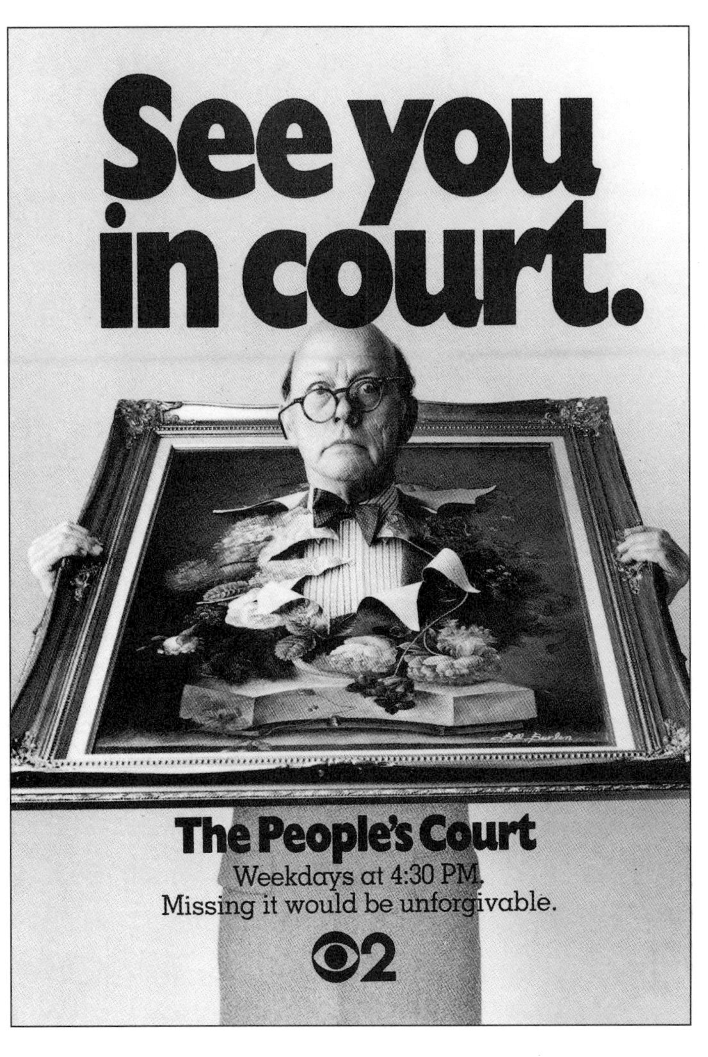
See you in court.
The People's Court
Weekdays at 4:30 PM.
Missing it would be unforgivable.
2

Consumer Magazine Less Than A Page B/W or Color: Campaign

434
ART DIRECTOR
Jim Retzer
WRITER
Susan Vering
PHOTOGRAPHER
Christopher Hawker
CLIENT
Dial Corporation
AGENCY
DDB Needham Worldwide/ Chicago

435
ART DIRECTOR
Frank Haggerty
WRITER
Kerry Casey
PHOTOGRAPHER
Marvy!
CLIENT
Blue Fox Tackle Company
AGENCY
Carmichael Lynch/ Minneapolis

Makes Big Fish Hit The Ceiling.
The Roland Martin Double Buzzer.™
BLUE FOX
©1988 Blue Fox Tackle Co., 645 N. Emerson, Cambridge, MN 55008.

Nothing Out-Jiggles This Jig.
The Foxee Jig.™
BLUE FOX
©1988 Blue Fox Tackle Co., 645 N. Emerson, Cambridge, MN 55008.

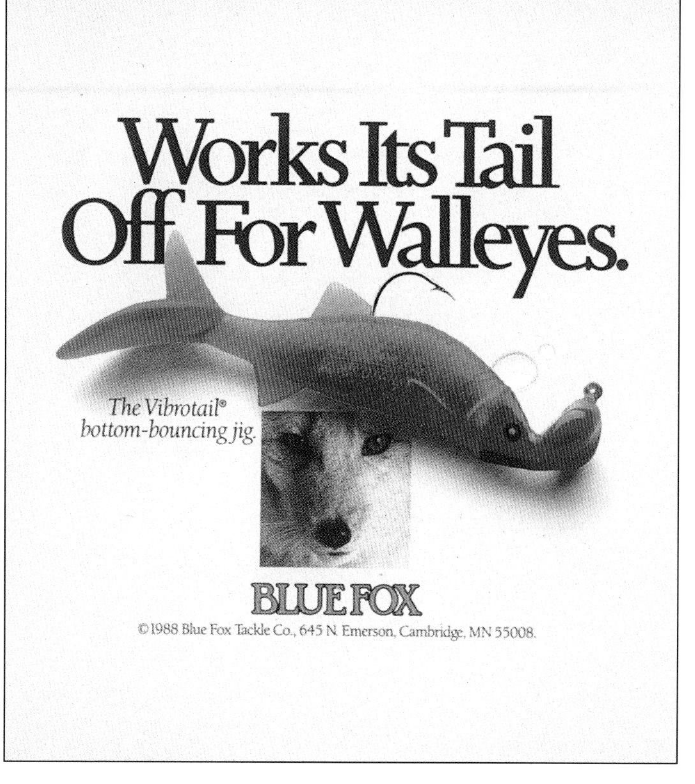
Works Its Tail Off For Walleyes.
The Vibrotail® bottom-bouncing jig.
BLUE FOX
©1988 Blue Fox Tackle Co., 645 N. Emerson, Cambridge, MN 55008.

Consumer Magazine
Less Than A Page
B/W or Color: Campaign

436

ART DIRECTOR
Jim Brock

WRITER
John Brockenbrough

DESIGNER
Jim Brock

PHOTOGRAPHER
Bob Jones Jr.

CLIENT
Palm Court Restaurant & Jazz Club

AGENCY
Finnegan & Agee/
Richmond, VA

437

ART DIRECTOR
Houman Pirdavari

WRITER
Bruce Bildsten

PHOTOGRAPHER
Terry Heffernan

CLIENT
Timex

AGENCY
Fallon McElligott/
Minneapolis

We're Probably The Only Restaurant In Town Where You Get Dizzy After Dinner.

Enjoy fresh seafood and sizzling steaks in our restaurant upstairs. Then bop down to our jazz club and savor the sounds of the immortal legends, along with plenty of original tunes, all performed live by some of today's hottest jazz musicians.

Palm Court Restaurant & Jazz Club

In historic Main Street Station, free parking, 783-1831.

Our Dinners Feature Lots Of Vitamins And Minerals, Followed By A Generous Helping Of Fats.

Enjoy fresh seafood and sizzling steaks in our restaurant upstairs. Then bop down to our jazz club and savor the sounds of the immortal legends, along with plenty of original tunes, all performed live by some of today's hottest jazz musicians.

Palm Court Restaurant & Jazz Club

In historic Main Street Station, free parking, 783-1831.

Dine With Us In Historic Main Street Station And Then Catch The Trane Downstairs.

Enjoy fresh seafood and sizzling steaks in our restaurant upstairs. Then bop down to our jazz club and savor the sounds of the immortal legends, along with plenty of original tunes, all performed live by some of today's hottest jazz musicians.

Palm Court Restaurant & Jazz Club

In historic Main Street Station, free parking, 783-1831.

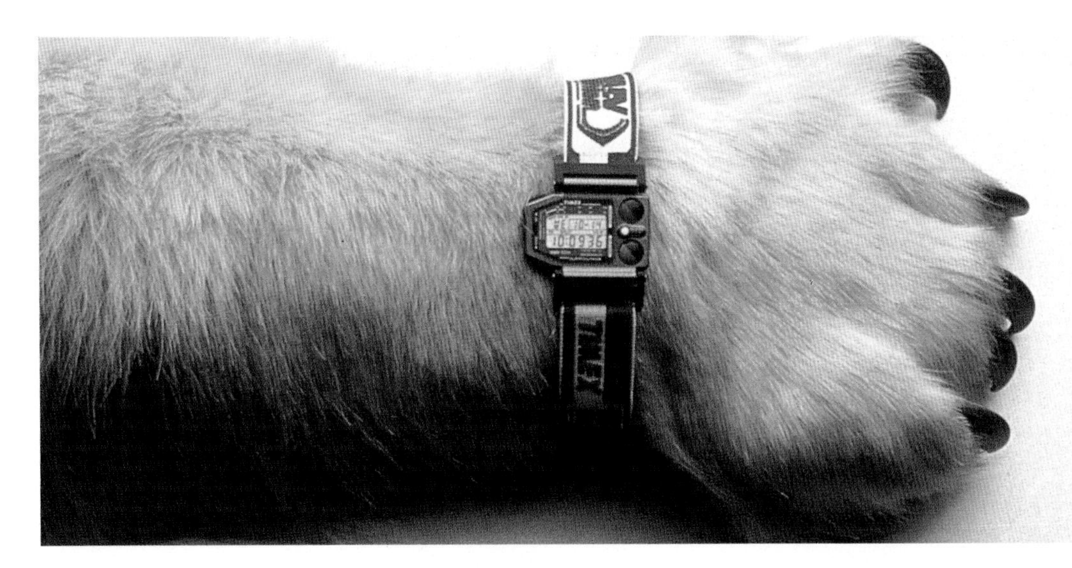

A ski watch should fit over your coat.

We not only designed the Timex Skiathlom* to fit the way you ski, but also to fit the way you dress while skiing.

It comes with two interchangeable straps. There's a high-tech resin strap, as well as an adjustable elastic one designed to fit over a parka or any part of your arm.

Even its buttons were designed oversized, so you can call up data from its sophisticated chronograph or thermometer with your gloves on.

For the Timex Skiathlom dealer that's nearest you, call 1-800-FOR-TIMEX. And we'll tell you where you can get your mitts on one.

TIMEX skiathlom

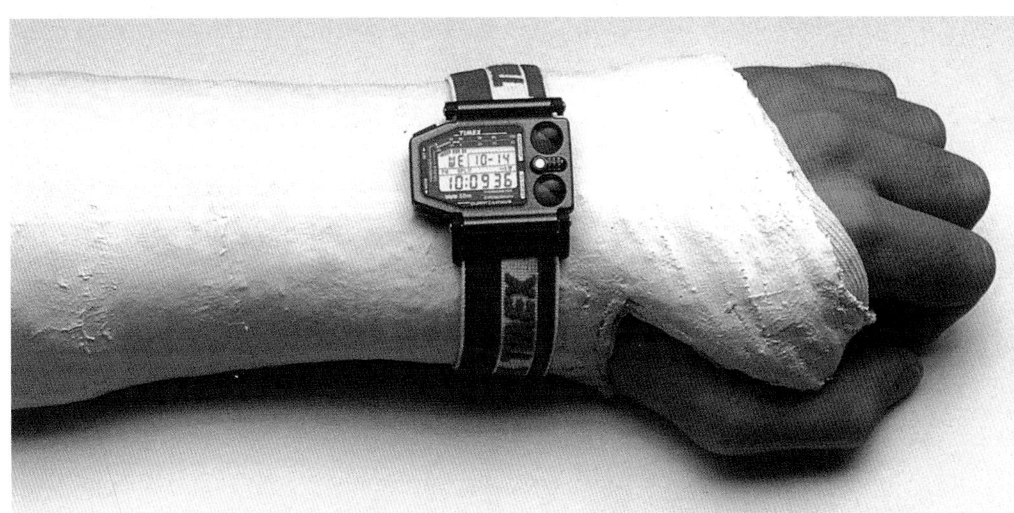

A ski watch should be hard to break.

With its sophisticated chronograph and built-in thermometer, the new Timex Skiathlom* is not only designed specifically for skiing. It's built for the punishment your body takes while skiing.

The falls. The cold. The wet.

Its case is water-resistant to 50 meters. Its elastic strap stretches to fit over bulky skiwear. Even its battery is designed to last four long years.

Call 1-800-FOR-TIMEX for the dealer that's nearest you. And be kind to yourself for a change.

TIMEX skiathlom

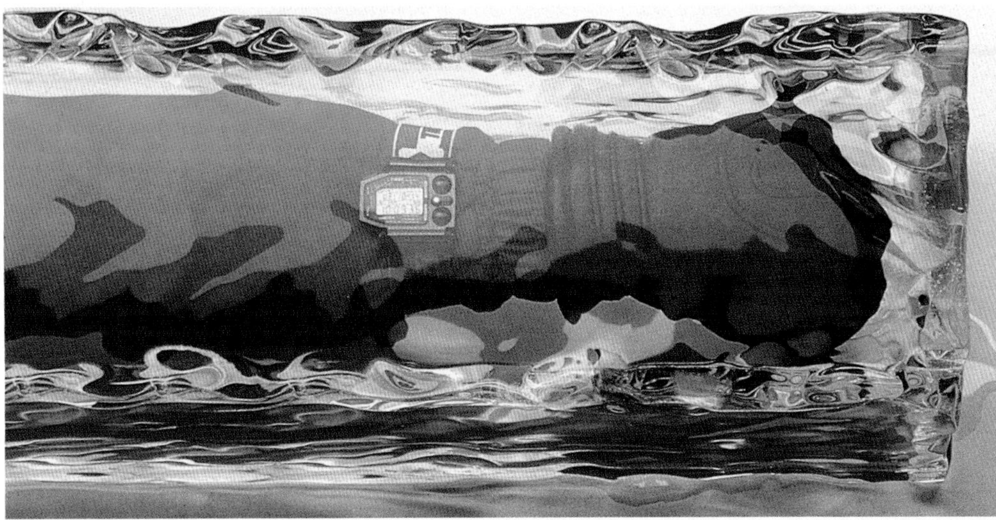

A ski watch should tell you how cold it is.

With its goggle-like strap and over-sized buttons, The Timex Skiathlom* is not only a true ski chronograph, it's a ski thermometer.

As a chronograph it's precise to 1/100th of a second, with selectable split or lap modes.

As a thermometer it's capable of readouts in Fahrenheit or Celsius, with both a digital and a bar-graph display. Plus, there's a 24-hour countdown timer, daily alarm, backlight and hourly chime.

If you'd like to see a Timex Skiathlom on your wrist, you're getting warmer. Call 1-800-FOR-TIMEX for your dealer.

TIMEX skiathlom

Trade B/W: 1 Page Or Spread

438

ART DIRECTOR
Laura Cole

WRITER
Christine Kellogg

PHOTOGRAPHE
Stan Caplan

CLIENT
Ertl

AGENCY
Sachs Finlay & Company/ Los Angeles

439

ART DIRECTOR
Tom Rosenfield

WRITER
Charlie Tercek

CLIENT
Michelin

AGENCY
DDB Needham Worldwide

440

ART DIRECTOR
Laura Cole

WRITER
Christine Kellogg

PHOTOGRAPHER
Stan Caplan

CLIENT
Ertl

AGENCY
Sachs Finlay & Company/ Los Angeles

441

ART DIRECTORS
Bryan Buckley
Mike Shine

WRITERS
Bryan Buckley
Mike Shine

CLIENT
Chiat/Day

AGENCY
Chiat/Day

Our big tractors sell for a lot of little reasons.

Front end loader scoops, raises, lowers, dumps and locks in position.
Tinted windows.
Backhoe lifts, extends, digs and dumps.
Durable die-cast construction.
Operational rear boom arm and bucket.
Deep treaded tires.
Working rear stabilizer bars.

From its scoop in front to its bucket in back, this tractor does double duty. A mighty hauler, it's also a mighty big seller.

No small wonder. At 1/16th scale, this hardy Case Loader Backhoe looks just like the real thing. With functioning arms that move or lock in place, buckets that dig and carry, deep tread tires for rough terrain, tinted windows and sturdy die-cast construction, this mighty machine is ready for the big haul.

But then, that's the way Ertl builds its replicas, authentic down to the smallest details. We've been building replicas this way for forty-three years, and we'll continue to do things this way under the strong financial backing of our parent company, Kidde, Inc.

So buy quality-made Ertl products. And see how our big tractors will continue to increase your sales and profits in a big way.

ERTL®

Just like the real thing. Only smaller.

Under license by JI Case. ©1987 THE ERTL COMPANY, DYERSVILLE, IOWA 52040

438

KEVIN SCHWANTZ IS A NICE GUY, BUT HE TENDS TO REPEAT HIMSELF.

First Place Elkhart Lake | First Place Mid-Ohio | First Place Loudon | First Place Memphis | First Place Sears Point

When he's riding Michelin Radials, Kevin Schwantz's tendencies are anything but boring.

He tends to win. And win. And win.

And in this season's AMA Super Bike Championship Series, that's exactly what happened.

Schwantz won more races than anybody else, five out of nine. And these racers weren't just anybody, but the best in America on two wheels.

He didn't just win these races, either. Schwantz owned them, blowing out his competition by 14.5 seconds at Elkhart Lake, 12.6 at Mid-Ohio, 10.7 at Loudon, and 8.3 at Memphis. (Luckily for the other racers, there was no official time at Sears Point.)

All in all, a remarkable performance. Of course, he did get some help. From Michelin Radials. Kevin Schwantz's results certainly indicate that these tires handle easier, grip better and run cooler. And soon Michelin Radial technology will be available for production bikes.

So keep an eye peeled for Michelin Hi-Sport Radial Production Racing Tires. Just don't be alarmed if you start repeating yourself. Just don't be alarmed if you start repeating yourself.

MICHELIN®
BECAUSE SO MUCH IS RIDING ON YOUR TIRES.®

439

Even our smallest tractors are big on detail.

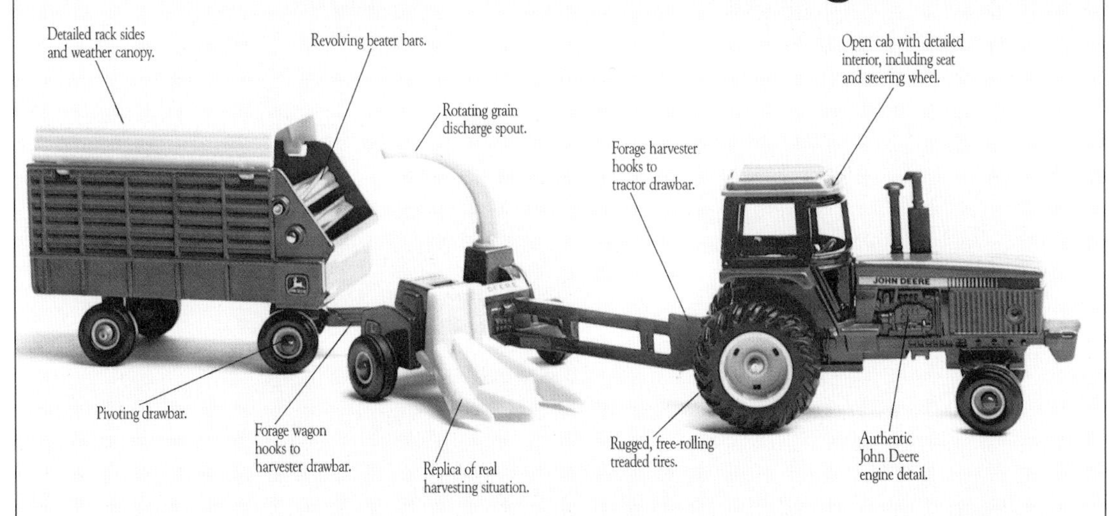

From the tractor in front to the harvester and wagon in tow, these small machines stand out in their field. Though they're small in size, they harvest big sales.

They're Ertl replicas. And at 1/64th scale size, they're Ertl's smallest replicas. But the big news is that from farm tractor to forage wagon, these John Deere machines are built just like the real thing. With little extras like operational parts, detailed exteriors, authentic interiors and sturdy die-cast construction, to complete the big picture.

Best of all, like most Ertl replicas, these farm machines have one giant-sized distinction. They're designed directly from original manufacturers' blueprints. That's what makes Ertl unique. And that's one big reason why we can continuously promise realistic, authentic, high-quality products.

Remember, because Ertl makes the most realistic replicas you can find, they're the best replicas you can sell. And that's no minor detail.

ERTL®

Just like the real thing. Only smaller.

Andy Awards Dinner Menu:
1964-Veal Marsala.
1965-Veal Marsala.
1966-Veal Marsala.
1967-Veal Marsala.
1968-Veal Marsala.
1969-Veal Marsala.
1970-Veal Marsala.
1971-Veal Marsala.
1972-Veal Marsala.
1973-Veal Marsala.
1974-Veal Marsala.
1975-Veal Marsala.
1976-Veal Marsala.
1977-Veal Marsala.
1978-Veal Marsala.
1979-Veal Marsala.
1980-Veal Marsala.
1981-Veal Marsala.
1982-Veal Marsala.
1983-Veal Marsala.
1984-Veal Marsala.
1985-Veal Marsala.
1986-Veal Marsala.
1987-Veal Marsala, with asparagus.

Who says award shows aren't getting better?

Chiat/Day

Trade B/W: 1 Page Or Spread

442
ART DIRECTOR
Tracy Wong
WRITER
Mike LaMonica
DESIGNERS
Tracy Wong
Mike LaMonica
PHOTOGRAPHER
David Langley
CLIENT
Ogilvy & Mather
AGENCY
Shing Unlimited

443
ART DIRECTOR
Mark Arnold
WRITER
Chris Wigert
PHOTOGRAPHER
Don Levy Photography
CLIENT
First Security National Bank & Trust
AGENCY
Lawler Ballard/ Cincinnati, OH

444
ART DIRECTORS
Rodd Martin
George Betsis
WRITERS
George Betsis
Rodd Martin
CLIENT
Jenks & Partners
AGENCY
Mojo

445
ART DIRECTORS
Rodd Martin
George Betsis
WRITERS
George Betsis
Rodd Martin
CLIENT
Revelation Shoes
AGENCY
Mojo

TO EVERYONE WHO KNOWS
WHAT IT'S LIKE PRODUCING
BRILLIANT ADVERTISING.

Best of luck tonight from Ogilvy & Mather.

442

Today, When A Small Bank Is Robbed, It's Usually By A Bigger Bank.

For smaller banks today, a lot of correspondent banking relationships have become downright dangerous.

The way some big banks are trying to steal your major customers, there's only one alternative short of selling out.

And that's to find a correspondent bank who isn't your competitor now. And never intends to be.

A bank with a correspondent program that provides services to over 250 banks. And has never robbed any of them.

A bank with the strength to offer service that can give you an edge in your market.

Services like electronic delivery systems, innovative loan participation programs, bank merger/acquisition consultation and financing, credit card processing, investment advisory services and more.

In short, you need a correspondent relationship with a bank like First Security.

For more information about how our bank can help yours, call us at (606) 231-2013.

Because if you want a correspondent bank relationship that gives you both safety and service, First Security has it.

FIRST SECURITY NATIONAL BANK & TRUST COMPANY

One First Security Plaza, Lexington, Kentucky 40507. Member FDIC.

443

Sarah Moon's best commercials all start with a plane taking off.

From Paris, where Sarah's based.

However, these days, she's more likely to be landing at JFK or L.A. than at Heathrow, Rome or Amsterdam.

Because she's landing more good scripts out of the U.S. now that she's with Jenks and Partners in New York.

To see her latest reel, call Sarah Jenks or John Garland. They also book her airline tickets.

JENKS & PARTNERS

24 West 25th St. New York, NY 10010.

Fax(212) 645-1786. Phone (212) 633-1432.

444

Revelations boots can breathe under water.

Most boots can keep moisture out, the problem is they also keep moisture in.

Revelations boots, on the other hand, are specially treated to allow them to breathe on the inside.

But your customers won't have to wait for a downpour to discover how truly comfortable our boots can be.

Because every boot comes in 48 sizes and widths, including wide calf variations.

We've also paid a lot of attention to how the outside of our boots perform.

Our fall collection includes 22 different styles from the latest fashion trends all the way to traditional classics.

Just for those women who'd prefer to be seen in boots that match their clothes.

Not their raincoats.

Revelations.

Fall 1988 Boot Collection Now Showing.

Showroom at 717 Fifth Avenue, New York. Or call 1-800-522-5616 (1-800-223-1464 for NY State) to arrange a presentation.

445

Trade B/W: 1 Page Or Spread

446
ART DIRECTOR
Gail Bartley
WRITER
Tom Thomas
PHOTOGRAPHER
Robert Ammirati
CLIENT
Barron's Trade
AGENCY
Angotti Thomas Hedge

447
ART DIRECTOR
Tom McManus
WRITER
Mike LaMonica
PHOTOGRAPHER
Michael Watson
CLIENT
Ladies Home Journal
AGENCY
TBWA

448
ART DIRECTORS
John Muller
Lee Ernst
WRITER
David Marks
PHOTOGRAPHER
Bettman Archives
CLIENT
Dix & Associates
AGENCY
Muller & Company/
Kansas City, MO

449
ART DIRECTOR
Bob Phillips
WRITER
Tom Thomas
ARTIST
John Alcorn
PHOTOGRAPHER
Robert Ammirati
CLIENT
Barron's
AGENCY
Angotti Thomas Hedge

Reach the privileged many.

According to the people who measure such things, some 32.7 million Americans now qualify as affluent.

Unfortunately, they don't organize themselves into a group that meets regularly for the convenience of advertisers.

Except in the case of Barron's; our readers do just that 52 times a year.

Every week, Barron's reaches a higher concentration of professionals and managers in top management than Business Week, Forbes or Fortune.

We reach a higher concentration of people with household incomes over $50,000. Or $75,000. Or $100,000.

And a higher concentration of those households whose net worth exceeds $1,000,000.

So before you choose a publication based on its "reach," you might ask what direction it's reaching in.

If you have a preference for upwards, we invite you to join the privileged many who advertise in Barron's.

BARRON'S
HOW THE SMART MONEY GETS THAT WAY

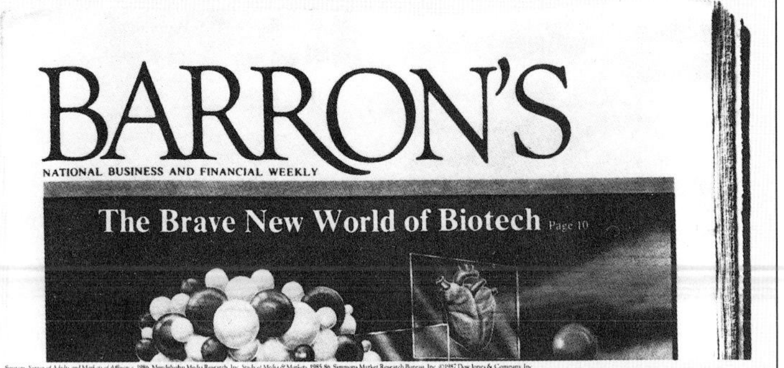

BARRON'S
NATIONAL BUSINESS AND FINANCIAL WEEKLY
The Brave New World of Biotech

446

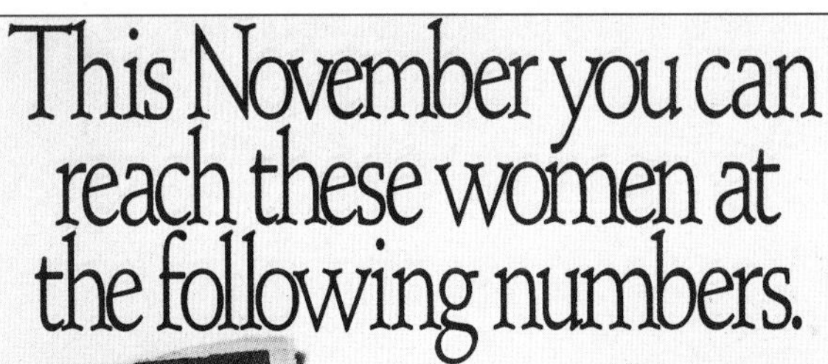

This November you can reach these women at the following numbers.

Page 118

Dolly Parton, Liz Taylor and Margaret Thatcher.

Other women's service magazines would be content to interview just *one* of them. But you'll find all three interviewed in the November Ladies' Home Journal. And this isn't just a one time occurrence.

Month after month we send our writers and photographers around the country and the world to interview the women other women are talking about. Women from politics, entertainment, business, royalty. In short, when important women speak out they choose to speak to the Journal. This unique approach to journalism doesn't just involve our readers, it attracts advertisers as well.

That's why our total ad pages are up 8% for the 4th quarter and up a huge 18% for our December issue alone. At Ladies' Home Journal we know what interests the women of today. And we deliver it. With dash and flair that sets the Journal an important notch above the rest.

So if you want to reach today's woman, give us a call. We've got her number.

LADIES' HOME JOURNAL
To reach the women who reach.

A Meredith publication

Publisher's estimates

447

Once every 100 years or so,
a woman who can really shoot
comes along.
Abby Dix shoots everything from real people to high fashion to tabletops.
For everyone from Blue Cross/Blue Shield to Carson's to Swanson's.
And you'll be glad to know, she's never had a single miss.
To see Abby's reel, call Dave Mueller & Associates at 337-6556.
They'll shoot it right over.
Dix & Associates
Commercial Film Production • Executive Producer: Jeanne Carpenter
2319 N. Orchard, Coachouse, Chicago, IL 60614 (312) 477-1161

448

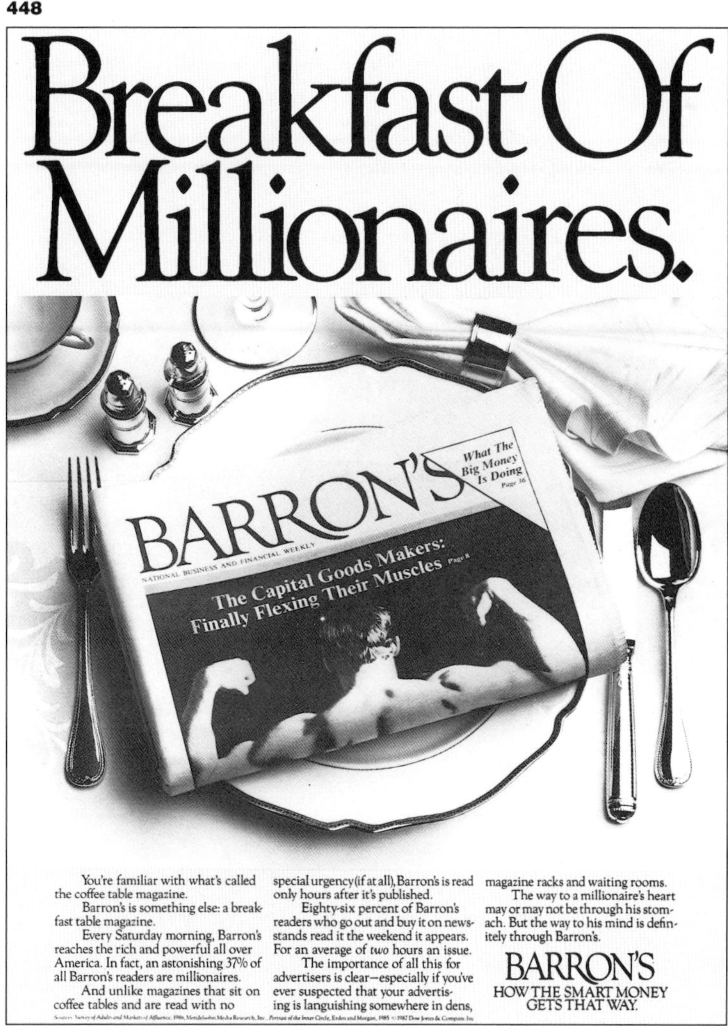
Breakfast Of
Millionaires.
BARRON'S
What The Big Money Is Doing
The Capital Goods Makers: Finally Flexing Their Muscles
You're familiar with what's called the coffee table magazine.
Barron's is something else: a breakfast table magazine.
Every Saturday morning, Barron's reaches the rich and powerful all over America. In fact, an astonishing 37% of all Barron's readers are millionaires.
And unlike magazines that sit on coffee tables and are read with no special urgency (if at all), Barron's is read only hours after it's published.
Eighty-six percent of Barron's readers who go out and buy it on newsstands read it the weekend it appears. For an average of two hours an issue.
The importance of all this for advertisers is clear—especially if you've ever suspected that your advertising is languishing somewhere in dens, magazine racks and waiting rooms.
The way to a millionaire's heart may or may not be through his stomach. But the way to his mind is definitely through Barron's.
BARRON'S
HOW THE SMART MONEY GETS THAT WAY.

449

Trade B/W: 1 Page Or Spread

450

ART DIRECTOR
Tom Lichtenheld

WRITER
Bruce Bildsten

CLIENT
Letterworx

AGENCY
Fallon McElligott/
Minneapolis

Trade Color: 1 Page Or Spread

451

ART DIRECTOR
Garrett Jewett

WRITER
Jim Walsh

PHOTOGRAPHER
Ibbetson Cherry

CLIENT
Colombian Coffee

AGENCY
DDB Needham Worldwide

452

ART DIRECTOR
Michael Smith

WRITER
Graham Turner

PHOTOGRAPHER
Steve Gross

CLIENT
Arrow

AGENCY
Chiat/Day

453

ART DIRECTOR
Steve Jaeger

WRITER
Chuck Gessner

PHOTOGRAPHER
Don Spiro

CLIENT
Colombian Coffee

AGENCY
DDB Needham Worldwide

We know where Fallon McElligott gets their award-winning headlines.

They buy them.
Letterworx Typography · 374-4116

450

Colombian coffee is now being served in the starboard lounge.

We don't want to go overboard in stating our case. But it does seem clear that consumer preferences are leaning more toward 100% Colombian Coffee than ever before.

After all, 54% of the American people now think that it's *the richest coffee in the world.*™ And with sales increasing 67% over the last 4 years, the people selling it think so, too.

What's more, thanks to extensive promotion and highly effective advertising, things look even better on the horizon.

Perhaps that's why so many smart roasters are now distributing and supporting Colombian Coffee brands of their own.

Because they know that the best way to make sure your ship comes in is to have 100% Colombian Coffee on it.

For more information, write to: 100% Colombian Coffee Program, P.O. Box 8545, NY, NY 10150. Or call: **800-223-3101.**

100% Colombian Coffee

451

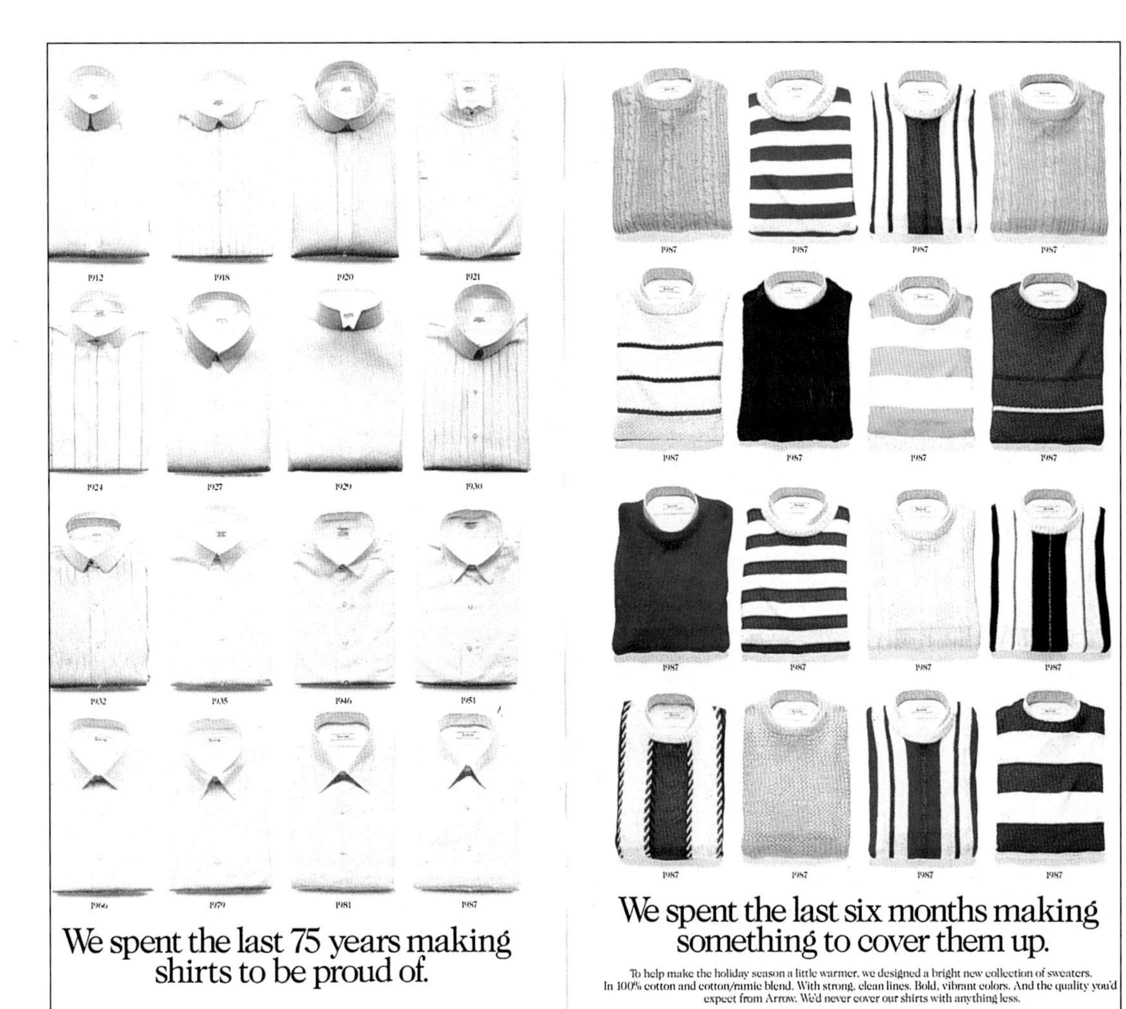
1912
1918
1920
1921
1924
1927
1929
1930
1932
1935
1946
1951
1966
1979
1981
1987
We spent the last 75 years making shirts to be proud of.
We spent the last six months making something to cover them up.
To help make the holiday season a little warmer, we designed a bright new collection of sweaters. In 100% cotton and cotton/ramie blend. With strong, clean lines. Bold, vibrant colors. And the quality you'd expect from Arrow. We'd never cover our shirts with anything less.
Arrow

452

©FNC, P.O. Box 8545, N.Y., N.Y. 10150
It must be a Colombian Coffee break.
Hedging... exposure... margin calls...? Who cares when they're drinking *the richest coffee in the world*™? Word out on the street is that most of America's coffee drinkers now believe that 100% Colombian is the best. What's more, they're even willing to pay a premium for it. Combine this strong demand with the prestige image we've created for Colombian Coffee and you'll realize this is one commodity you'll want to stock up on. 100% Colombian Coffee. It could help you make a real killing in the market.
For more information write: 100% Colombian Coffee, P.O. Box 8545, NY, NY 10150 or call: 1-800-223-3101.
100% Colombian Coffee

453

Trade Color: 1 Page Or Spread

454
ART DIRECTOR
Mark Oliver
WRITER
Sheila Saphier
DESIGNER
Mark Oliver
PHOTOGRAPHER
John Londei
CLIENT
ICI Chemicals & Polymers Group
AGENCY
ASL Lane/London

455
ART DIRECTOR
Diane Westfall
WRITER
Roseanne Azarian
PHOTOGRAPHER
Cosimo
CLIENT
Cigna
AGENCY
DDB Needham Worldwide

456
ART DIRECTOR
Mark Oliver
WRITER
Sheila Saphier
DESIGNER
Mark Oliver
ARTIST
Mark Oliver
PHOTOGRAPHER
Archive Material
CLIENT
ICI Chemicals & Polymers Group
AGENCY
ASL Lane/London

457
ART DIRECTORS
Tom McConnaughy
Brian Kelly
WRITER
James Schmidt
PHOTOGRAPHER
Christopher Hawker
CLIENT
Chicago Convention & Visitors Bureau
AGENCY
McConnaughy Barocci Brown/Chicago

Which skin care would he recommend: natural oil or water?

You wouldn't expect red hot metal and oil to be an entirely safe combination. Yet everyday in heat treatment shops, metal forgings heated up to 900°C are plunged into baths of mineral oil-based quenchant.

Not surprisingly, huge billows of acrid smoke and noxious fumes well up. They've become an accepted part of the job for the men who work there.

Sometimes a particularly violent reaction gets completely out of hand and entire factories have been razed to the ground by fire.

The scars from such "flare-ups" and the literally "hellish" working conditions have left their mark on many a man's skin.

It's a situation that's continued because it seemed there was no more efficient way to cool and harden the metal to produce optimum strength.

Water-based quenchants, a much safer and more acceptable alternative, always cooled the metal too fast making it flawed and weak.

Until Servimetal of France asked ICI Chemical Products to apply themselves to the problem.

Careful study of water-soluble polymers produced results. We found we were able to extend the molecules to such a degree we could produce a modified "water".

Or more accurately, a polymer for an aqueous-based quenchant with specific flow characteristics and high viscosity.

It not only met Servimetal's precise requirements, it exceeded them.

Emkarox, as the polymer for the new quenchant is called, is a high viscosity polyglycol that can be produced in almost any grade or thickness to meet a heat treater's particular needs.

And try as they will, none of our competitors have been able to produce a polyglycol for an aqueous quenchant that can match it.

One that does as good a job as mineral oil-based quenchants in nearly every case.

And makes a foundry a little less like hell to work in.

If you need a problem solved or want more information contact Edna Moore, ICI. Chemicals & Polymers Group, Wilton Centre, P.O. Box 90, Middlesbrough, Cleveland, TS6 8JE. Tel: (0642) 432852.

CHEMICAL PRODUCTS *we'll make it happen*

454

IF HE SURVIVES, CAN YOUR COMPANY GIVE HIM A REASON TO LIVE?

Once he's out of danger the real danger begins. Because people who survive debilitating accidents or illnesses can lose one of the most compelling reasons to live. Their jobs.

And the reality is that one out of seven Americans will become disabled for five years or more before reaching retirement.

Which is why the CIGNA companies* created an organization to manage long-term disability claims exclusively.

It has a rehabilitation program to help people return to productive work. And that's helping companies hold down the cost of providing assistance to the disabled employee.

Unfortunately, not all employees who are rehabilitated can return to their old jobs. So we also help to find new jobs by providing assistance in vocational training and educational programs.

And if the workplace is the barrier to getting back to work, we'll help redesign it to accommodate the disability.

We were even the first insurer to help employees receive benefits that Social Security may initially deny them. Which lightens the load on monthly income replacement payments.

What does all of this mean? That a disability need not be a liability.

So it's not surprising that CIGNA is one of the leading providers of long-term disability insurance, offering coverage to companies of all sizes.

To find out how our program can work for your company, write to CIGNA Companies, Department R-A, One Logan Square, Philadelphia, PA 19103.

Because when it comes to making a complete recovery, work may be the best medicine.

CIGNA

455

We've just added to the list of underwater legends.

Recently one of the biggest names in the oil business was faced with a problem many fathoms below the waves. Leakage from the underwater hydraulic fluid lines that run from North Sea oil platforms.

Damaging enough in terms of profitability. And capable of bringing production to a standstill.

But with miles of fluid lines encased in bundles, diver inspection just wasn't feasible.

So, knowing our reputation for solving the most complex problems and aware of our expertise in everything to do with the production of oil, they came to ICI Chemical Products.

And, you might say, we saved their bacon. With a pig.

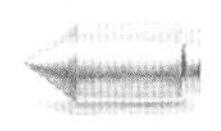

The Golden Pig

This particular pig was devised with the help of our Physics and Radioisotopes Group.

It's a strong, streamlined slug of plastic. Carrying a gold radioisotope.

With the line ends sealed and pressure maintained, the pig will nose its way to any leak and stop there.

The gamma rays emitted by the pig as it moves along are tracked by a remote-control detection apparatus alongside the pipeline. And conveyed to the ship via an umbilical.

Thus it provides an accurate fix on the location of the pipe leak and permits localised repair.

Like all the best ideas, it's appealing in its simplicity. Remarkable for its efficiency. An embodiment of the depth of our skills and the breadth of thinking at ICI Chemical Products.

Our leak-seeking device, by the way, has become known as the Golden Pig. And it's already something of a legend amongst the oil men of the North Sea.

If you need a problem solved or want more information contact Edna Moore, ICI Chemicals & Polymers Group, Wilton Centre P.O. Box 90, Middlesbrough, Cleveland, TS6 8JE. Tel: (0642) 432852.

we'll make it happen

456

Chances Are, You'll Leave Chicago With More Carry-On Bags Than You Came With.

Each year, hundreds of thousands of people attend conventions and trade shows in Chicago.

And sooner or later, almost every one of them takes a stroll down our two great shopping thoroughfares – Michigan Avenue and State Street.

Both offer a grand array of fashion, jewelry, electronics and leather goods.

And both make it almost impossible to head home empty-handed.

Of course, terrific stores aren't the only reason so many gatherings are held in Chicago.

We also offer what many people consider the finest meeting facilities in the country.

A collection of world-class restaurants, museums, theaters and hotels.

And, perhaps most important of all, we offer the experience that comes from hosting conventions and trade shows longer than just about anyone.

For more information on what Chicago has to offer, call us collect at (312) 567-8500. (Telex: 312-433-0306)

But remember, when you visit, don't bring a lot of bags.

Odds are, you'll pickup a few while you're here.

Chicago
Chicago Convention & Visitors Bureau

457

Trade Color: 1 Page Or Spread

458

ART DIRECTOR
David Bender

WRITER
Bob Chimbell

PHOTOGRAPHER
Earl Culberson

CLIENT
Walt Disney Company

AGENCY
JanklowBender

459

ART DIRECTOR
Pam Conboy

WRITER
Lee Schmidt

PHOTOGRAPHER
Dennis Manarchy

CLIENT
3M Health Care Specialties

AGENCY
Martin/Williams - Minneapolis

460

ART DIRECTOR
Mark Ashley

WRITER
Ken Lewis

CLIENT
Hercules

AGENCY
Cole Henderson Drake/ Atlanta

461

ART DIRECTORS
Cabell Harris
Bill Altice

WRITER
Ken Hines

PHOTOGRAPHER
Pat Edwards

CLIENT
E.R. Carpenter

AGENCY
Lawler Ballard/ Richmond, VA

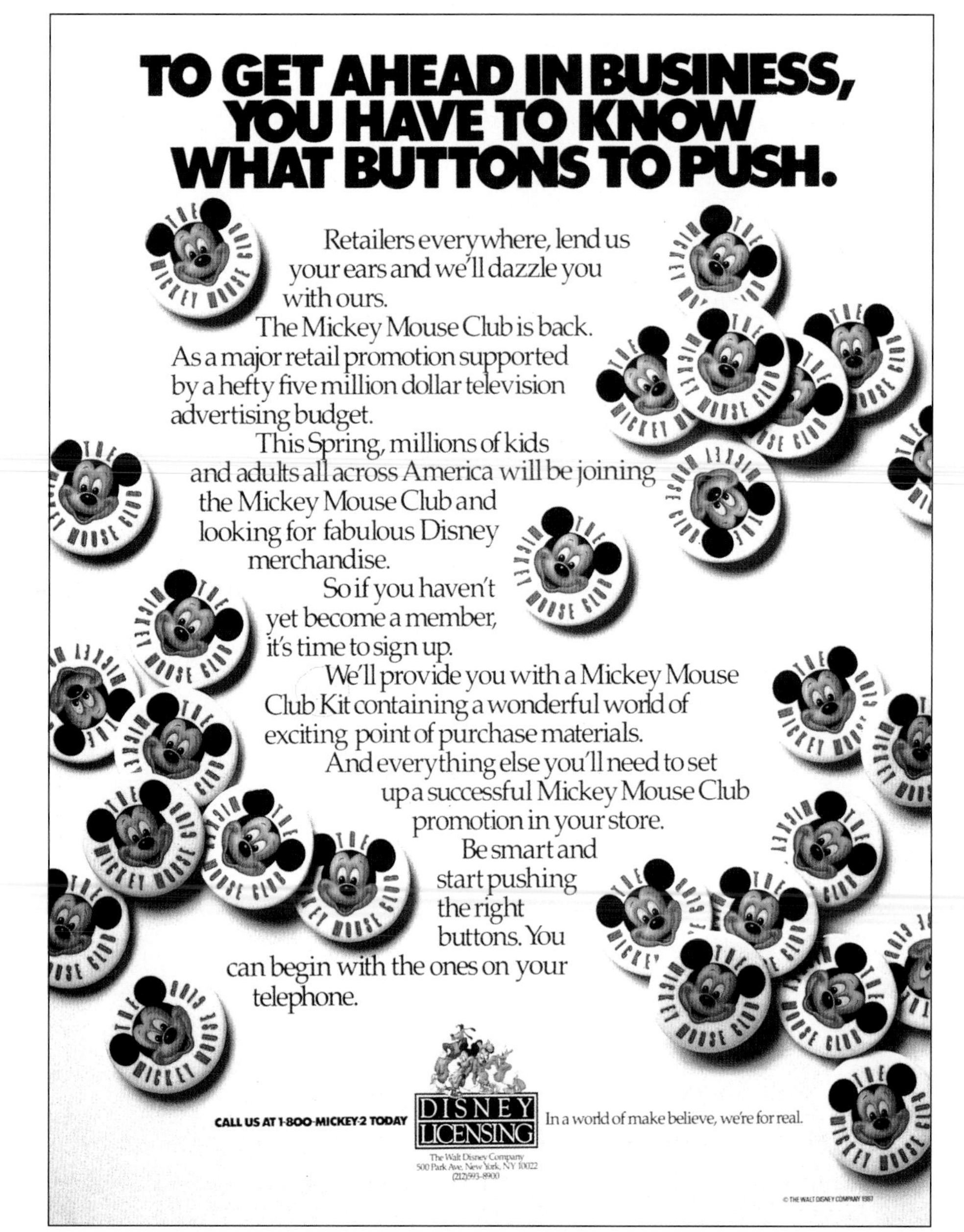

458

459

HERCULES FILM KEEPS SNACK FOOD FROM BECOMING JUNK FOOD.

Too often, snack foods go stale on the shelf. Then they go out with the twice weekly pick-ups.

What a waste.

Especially when you could be using laminations made of Hercules* oriented polypropylene films. Our films provide excellent barriers against oxygen and moisture. For better flavor retention. And longer shelf life.

Of course, there is more than one kind of snack. And Hercules makes a variety of films to suit the specific needs of each. We offer saran-coated, Surlyn*-coated and co-polymer sealable oriented polypropylene films. As well as opaque and metalized films to protect snacks from light.

But the benefits aren't limited to what's inside the package. Hercules has a higher consistency of quality. Your converters can meet delivery requirements quickly and with fewer problems.

Our films provide a wide sealing range. So you don't have to make adjustments as often. We even have slip-modified films that provide superb machinability.

And you're never alone when you work with Hercules. Our Film Applications Lab provides technical support unsurpassed in the industry. Whatever snack packaging needs you have, we can help you meet them. With just the right film.

To get more information on Hercules films for snacks, write Hercules Product Information, Hercules Incorporated, Hercules Plaza, Wilmington, DE 19894. Or call 1-800-247-4372.

Otherwise, you're just throwing your money away.

HERCULES

*DuPont registered trademark for resins.

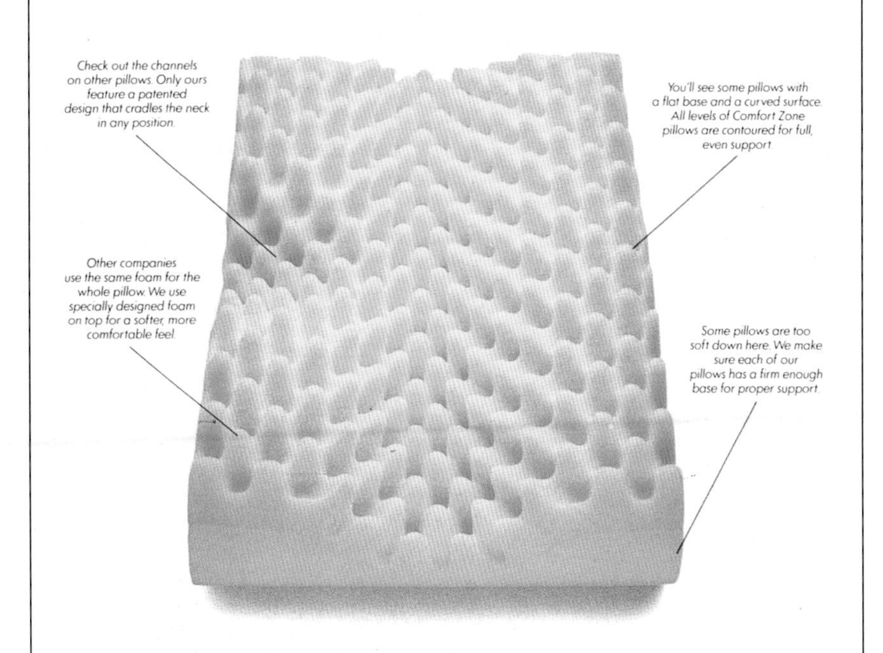

Check out the channels on other pillows. Only ours feature a patented design that cradles the neck in any position.
You'll see some pillows with a flat base and a curved surface. All levels of Comfort Zone pillows are contoured for full, even support.
Other companies use the same foam for the whole pillow. We use specially designed foam on top for a softer, more comfortable feel.
Some pillows are too soft down here. We make sure each of our pillows has a firm enough base for proper support.

If we made pillows like our competitors, we couldn't sleep at night.

Our entire Comfort Zone™ line is made from our specially formulated polyurethane foams.

Other companies use any foam they can get.

To us, that would be a nightmare. Nothing but the best is good enough for our patented Neck Pillow.™

The same goes for our new eye-catching packaging and our traffic stopping displays.

For the whole Comfort Zone story, including our new sleep shop concept, call your E.R. Carpenter Company representative. Or call us at (804) 359-0800.

We'll show you why our sales program works like a dream.

Comfort Zone™

Comfort Zone and Neck Pillow are trademarks of E.R. Carpenter Co. Inc.

Trade Color: 1 Page Or Spread

462
ART DIRECTOR
Mel Rustom
WRITER
Charles Bromley
PHOTOGRAPHER
Richard Nowitz
CLIENT
Israel Government Tourist Office
AGENCY
Biederman & Company

463
ART DIRECTOR
Jim Henderson
WRITER
Lee Schmidt
PHOTOGRAPHER
Crofoot
CLIENT
Dual Herbicide
AGENCY
Martin/Williams - Minneapolis

464
ART DIRECTOR
Wayne Gibson
WRITER
Luke Sullivan
ARTIST
Paul Bernath
CLIENT
Ethyl Corporation
AGENCY
The Martin Agency/ Richmond, VA

465
ART DIRECTOR
Wayne Gibson
WRITER
Mike Hughes
PHOTOGRAPHER
Jay Ahrend
CLIENT
Ethyl Corporation
AGENCY
The Martin Agency/ Richmond, VA

462

463

Thanks To Our New Poultry Feed Component, His Chances For Survival Are Now 38% Better.

Once upon a time, one of the only ways an egg producer could reduce egg shell breakage was with conventional vitamin and mineral supplements.

They seemed to work. But only to a point.

Past that point, it didn't seem to matter how many vitamins or mineral supplements you put in the poultry feed. Egg shells just wouldn't get any tougher.

Something was lacking in the diet.

Enter ETHACAL® feed component. A breakthrough in the reduction of egg shell breakage.

A poultry feed component that can reduce egg shell breakage up to an astounding 38%. No fairy tale. 38%.

Based on the size of the average poultry farm, even a conservative estimate would indicate that using ETHACAL feed component could save 500,000 eggs or more per year. A savings that could be as much as eight times its cost. Not exactly what you'd call chicken feed.

The reason why ETHACAL feed component so roundly outperforms other vitamin and mineral supplements is that it isn't your everyday vitamin or mineral supplement.

It's a synthetic zeolite that has a much higher calcium exchange capacity than anything that's been previously available.

This results not just in lower numbers of eggs lost, but also in lower feed requirements and longer poultry life.

Moral of our story: things might have been a lot different if all the king's horses and all the king's men had the following phone number and address. Call 504-388-8159. Or write Ethyl Corporation at 451 Florida Boulevard, Baton Rouge, Louisiana 70801.

Ethyl

464

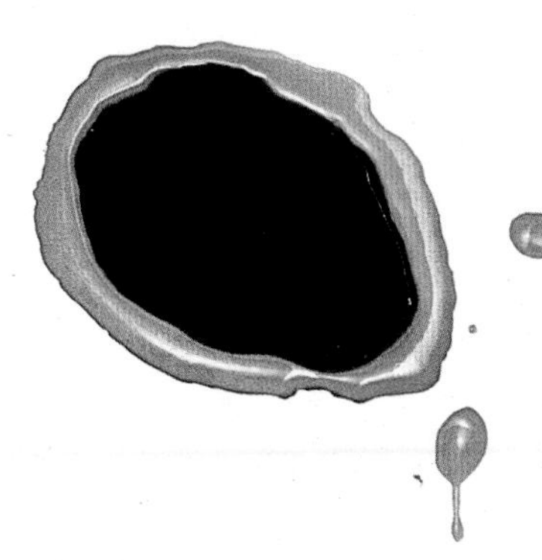

Maybe nobody could come up with a solution to a problem like this. Maybe everyone could.

But we know exactly where you should start when you have a tough chemical problem. At Ethyl.

Ethyl specializes in producing hard-to-produce chemicals.

That's what's made us the leader in aluminum alkyls, alpha olefins, brominated flame retardants and orthoalkylated phenols and anilines.

In fact, our research and development made some of these difficult chemicals possible in the first place. For example, who do you think invented selective orthoalkylation?

In the last few years we've redoubled our efforts to become the company you turn to when you need a reliable supplier of chemicals, even if those chemicals are the ones other manufacturers avoid.

In the past year we spent more than $165 million on new plants, acquisitions and research and development to increase our capabilities.

So now more than ever before we have the chemical expertise and the manufacturing capability to handle your toughest challenges.

Call us. Because if anyone can pass your acid test, it's Ethyl.

Where Would You Go If You Needed A Chemical That Would Eat Through This Page But Not The One Under It?

465

Trade Color: 1 Page Or Spread

466

ART DIRECTORS
Brian Fandetti
Margaret McGovern

WRITER
Paul Silverman

DESIGNER
Margaret McGovern

PHOTOGRAPHER
Myron

CLIENT
Unigraphic

AGENCY
Mullen Advertising/
South Hamilton, MA

467

ART DIRECTORS
Mike Shine
Ray Silka

WRITER
Charlie Tercek

CLIENT
Michelin

AGENCY
DDB Needham Worldwide

468

ART DIRECTOR
Gary Campbell

WRITER
Gary Brandon

DESIGNER
Gary Campbell

CLIENT
American - Darling Valve

AGENCY
Luckie & Forney Advertising/
Birmingham, AL

469

ART DIRECTOR
John Doyle

WRITER
Paul Silverman

CLIENT
Heritage Color

AGENCY
Mullen Advertising/
South Hamilton, MA

I'm a red hot mama,
but I'm blue for you.
I get purple with anger
at the things you do.
And I'm green with envy
when you meet a dame.
But you burn my heart up
with an orange flame.

I'm a red hot mama,
but you're white and cold.
Don't you know your mama
has a heart of gold.
Though we're in those grey
clouds, some day you'll spy
that terrific rainbow
over you and I.

Rodgers and Hart, *Pal Joey*

Unigraphic
Color Separations that Sing

304 Lincoln Ave., Saugus, MA 01906 (617) 233-5200

466

THE BALD TIRE THAT HAS OTHER TIRE MAKERS PULLING THEIR HAIR OUT.

There are a lot of bald clinchers on the market. Each one claiming to be "unequivocally the best."

We at Michelin, however, are in a fortunate position of not having to boast how terrific our HI-LITE tires are.

Because other people do it for us: Racers who win on HI-LITE™ tires week after week. And magazines like *Bicycling*.

After an exhaustive evaluation of treadless clinchers, the magazine found that Michelin outperformed Specialized and Avocet in key areas of performance and reliability.

Michelin came in first in cornering. First in comfort. First in tracking and durability.

What's more, the opinion of the magazine's staff was echoed by its readers, who rated the HI-LITE highest in overall satisfaction.

Which is just what you'd expect from HI-LITE. A high performance tire that has provided cyclists, from the Tour of New Jersey to the Tour de France, with the ultimate combination of speed and strength. Without compromising either.

At the heart of HI-LITE's extraordinary performance is its revolutionary three-ply casing construction.

Unlike the cords in each Avocet or Specialized casing ply which only go in one direction, each of the two outer plies (N-1) of the HI-LITE have cords which go in two directions for extra strength.

And we make that extra strength even stronger. Because the outside plies are double interwoven.

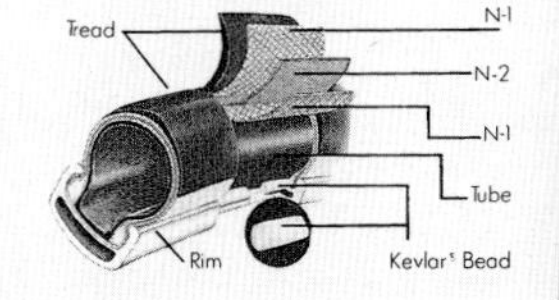

They surround a third, tightly woven, practically unstretchable middle ply (N-2). All of which creates a two-stage barrier for superior penetration resistance. But don't take our word for it.

According to *Bicycling (Oct. '86)*, the HI-LITE Comp "was the highest rated against punctures and it had a spotless record in casing durability."

But the HI-LITE doesn't stop there and neither did *Bicycling*. "As the tread wears down, the Comp doesn't seem to be as susceptible as the competition to more frequent punctures."

HI-LITE tires are built to last. And last. To begin with, the middle casing ply is strong. It contains air pressure so effectively, it prevents the tread rubber and sidewall from stretching (a common problem with other tires). And unstretched rubber is less susceptible to cutting, cracking, and wear. Says *Bicycling*, the HI-LITE Comp is "the one most likely to realize its potential mileage."

Moreover, since the tread compound does not have to compensate for casing stretch (as most other tires do), it can be engineered solely for performance.

The HI-LITE's slick tread and soft rubber compound deliver exceptional straight line tracking and cornering stability. Even when you're riding in the wet.

There are seven HI-LITE tires available to satisfy the needs of all serious cyclists, from road racers and triathletes to BMX racers and touring riders.

Try one and we think you will agree that compared to the HI-LITE by Michelin, the claims of performance and reliability made by other bald clinchers recede rather quickly.

MICHELIN®
BECAUSE SO MUCH IS RIDING ON YOUR TIRES.™

467

468

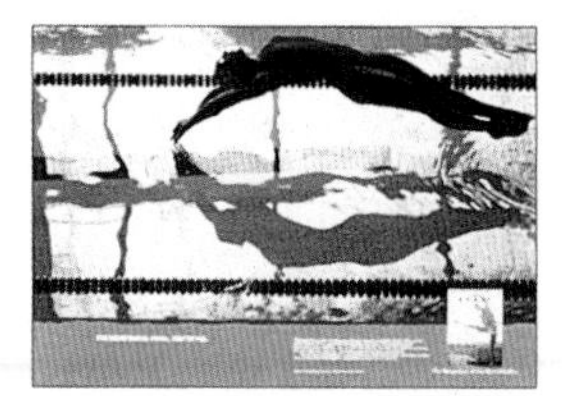

Ultrasport. Mullen. Heritage.

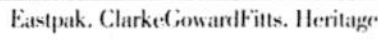

Eastpak. ClarkeGowardFitts. Heritage.

J.P. Stevens. ClarkeGowardFitts. Heritage.

Advertising Club of Greater Boston. Mullen. Heritage.

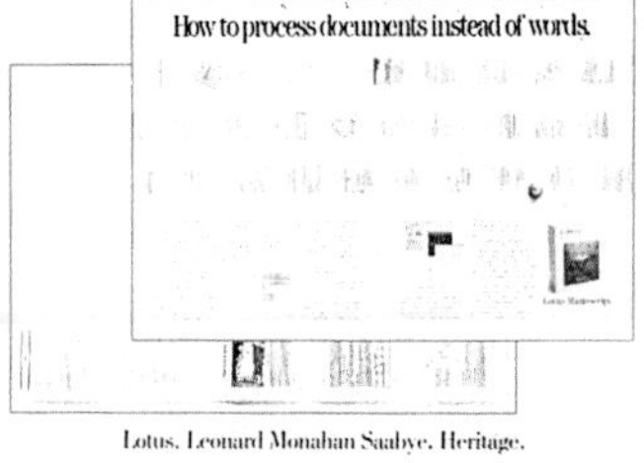

Lotus. Leonard Monahan Saabye. Heritage.

Dexter. Pagano Schenck & Kay. Heritage.

The True Test Of A Club Isn't
How It Feels In Your Hands. It's
How It Feels In Your Stomach.
SPALDING

If You're Afraid Of Not Carrying
The Bunkers, Then You're Not
Carrying The Right Clubs.
SPALDING

Spalding. Leonard Monahan Saabye. Heritage.

On the night of September 15, we separated the winners from the losers.

At this year's Hatch Awards, Heritage was the color separator on everything from first place consumer to first place trade. If you want to separate your work from the pack, call 401-273-1500.

Heritage Color, 222 Richmond Street, Providence, Rhode Island 02903 401-273-1500

The quality that separates the winners.

469

Trade Color: 1 Page Or Spread

470
ART DIRECTOR
Diane Cook Tench
WRITER
Luke Sullivan
PHOTOGRAPHER
Dean Hawthorne
CLIENT
FMC
AGENCY
The Martin Agency/
Richmond, VA

471
ART DIRECTOR
Terry Barich
WRITER
William Carey
DESIGNER
Terry Barich
PHOTOGRAPHER
Ron Pomerantz
CLIENT
Quaker
AGENCY
Campbell-Mithun/
Chicago

472
ART DIRECTOR
Diane Cook Tench
WRITER
Luke Sullivan
PHOTOGRAPHER
Dean Hawthorne
CLIENT
Barnett Banks
AGENCY
The Martin Agency/
Richmond, VA

473
ART DIRECTOR
John Scavnicky
WRITER
Chris Perry
DESIGNER
John Scavnicky
PHOTOGRAPHER
Ladd Trepal
CLIENT
Glidden Company
AGENCY
Meldrum and Fewsmith/
Cleveland, OH

Season-long control

Sencor DF
75% dry flowable herbicide
Economical broadleaf control

Won't burn soybeans

Low cost-per-acre

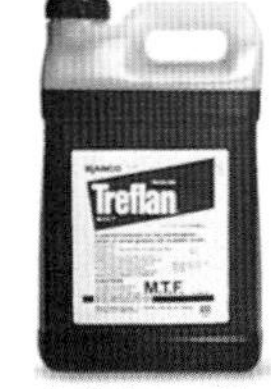

Excellent grass control

Weed control without tank-mixing

Ditto

Won't stress young soybean plants

Controls grasses and velvetleaf

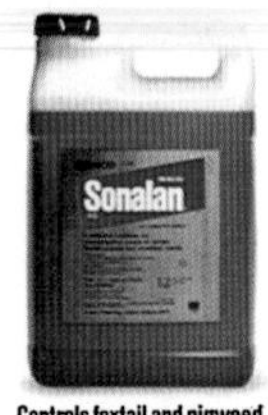

Controls foxtail and pigweed

New Commence™ herbicide does everything you see on the left page: excellent full-season control of velvetleaf, foxtail and pigweed without the risk of soybean injury. And if you think that's hard to believe, you should see what they're selling it for.

FMC.

470

Presenting A Dramatic Story Told In Cereal Form.

The Crisis

We entered the action halfway through an upsetting scene.

Canteen Corporation was up to its ears in cereal, not getting the performance it demanded.

They needed a good partner. Someone who understood their business. Who could offer ideas, solutions, a better way.

For some, it would have been too tall an order.

We, of course, were right in our element.

The Turning Point

We showed them Quaker's revolutionary bulk cereal serving systems—with more options than anyone had ever offered before.

We also showed them the biggest variety of bulk cereals anywhere.

Together, we changed the face of Canteen's breakfast operation.

Their cereal displays looked more appetizing than ever. Their line speeds were setting world-class times. And their portion costs were simply spectacular.

The Sequel

Obviously a story this successful shouldn't end here. So call and ask for Quaker Bulk Cereals and Serving Systems. Plus all our other products and services designed for your business. We promise a happy ending.

QUAKER
FOOD SERVICE DIVISION
2400 Merchandise Mart Plaza
Chicago, IL 60654
(312) 222-8700

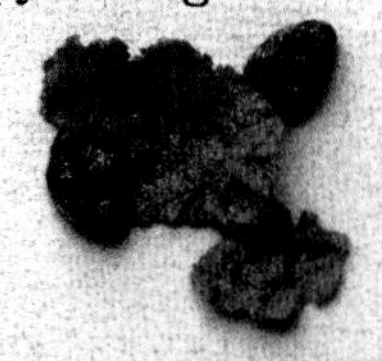

471

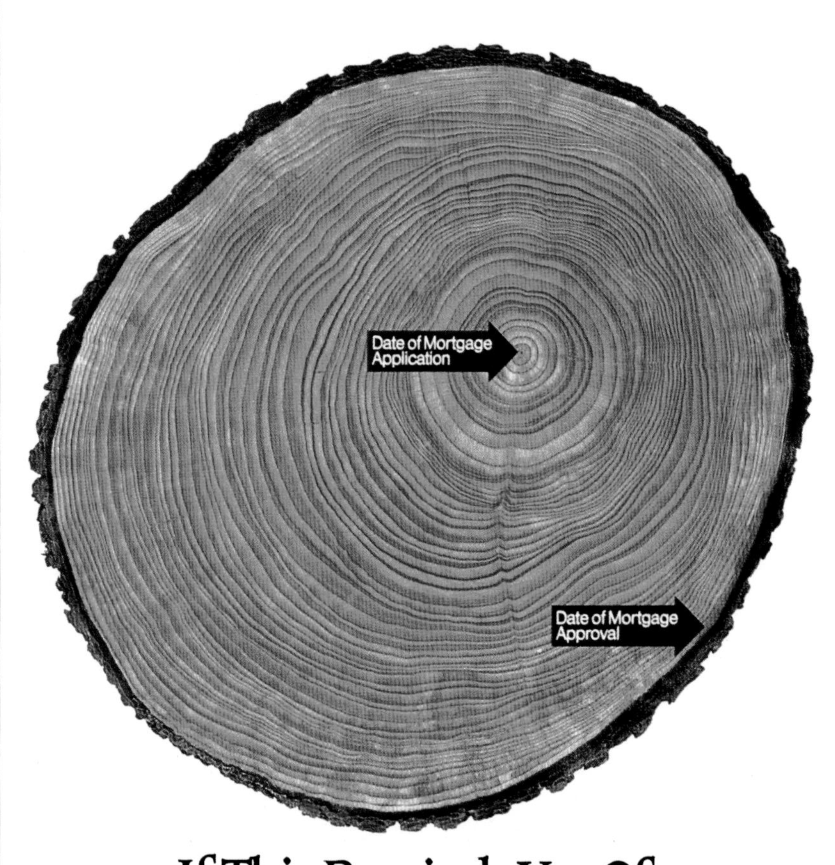
Date of Mortgage Application
Date of Mortgage Approval
If This Reminds You Of Your Mortgage Lender, Call Us.
We've become the #1 mortgage lender in Florida by keeping one thing in mind: in the real estate business, things move fast. So we try to also. Which means when you send your customers to us, we'll move on their loan applications. So you can move on. And they can move in.
Barnett Is Florida's Top Mortgage Lender.
Barnett Bank
All Barnett Banks are members of FDIC.

472

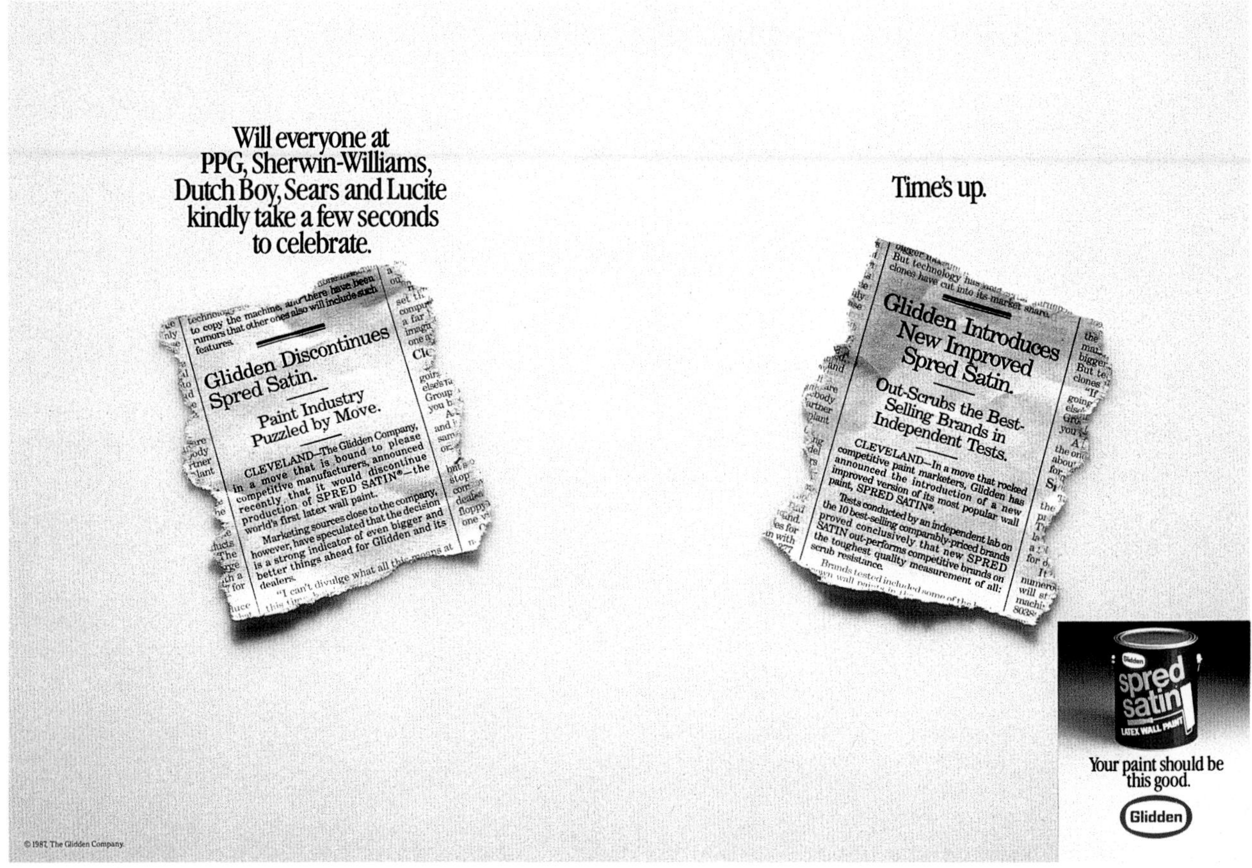
Will everyone at PPG, Sherwin-Williams, Dutch Boy, Sears and Lucite kindly take a few seconds to celebrate.
Glidden Discontinues Spred Satin.
Paint Industry Puzzled by Move.
Time's up.
Glidden Introduces New Improved Spred Satin.
Out-Scrubs the Best-Selling Brands in Independent Tests.
spred satin
LATEX WALL PAINT
Your paint should be this good.
Glidden
© 1987, The Glidden Company.

473

Trade Color: 1 Page Or Spread

474

ART DIRECTOR
Bernie Hogya

WRITER
Ronald Wachino

PHOTOGRAPHER
Gary Feinstein

CLIENT
Minolta

AGENCY
Bozell Jacobs Kenyon & Eckhardt

475

ART DIRECTORS
John Butler
Kevin Donovan

WRITERS
Kevin Donovan
John Butler

DESIGNERS
John Butler
Kevin Donovan

ARTIST
Linda Richards

PHOTOGRAPHER
Hashi

CLIENT
Goodyear

AGENCY
J. Walter Thompson

476

ART DIRECTOR
John Merriman

WRITER
Paul Weinberger

PHOTOGRAPHER
Paul Bevitt

CLIENT
Mobil Oil

AGENCY
Lowe Howard-Spink/London

477

ART DIRECTOR
David Fox

WRITER
Joe Alexander

PHOTOGRAPHER
Rick Dublin

CLIENT
Wegner Music Class

AGENCY
Clarity Coverdale Rueff/Minneapolis

474

The G132 steer tire: built to combat irregular treadwear.

Of course it's a little embarrassing. But irregular treadwear of the steer tire is a very serious ailment; one that can't be ignored.

Channel wear
Depressed rib wear
Diagonal wear
Cupping

If you're running a high-speed line-haul operation with a lightly loaded front end, you're likely to be stricken by irregular treadwear of the steer tire.

At last, there is hope: The Goodyear Unisteel G132 Radial. To minimize irregular treadwear, Goodyear engineers modified the shape of the tire crown area to produce a more uniform pressure distribution over the entire footprint. Which means less frequent rotating and changing of irregularly worn steer tires.

Goodyear also reduced the weight and lowered the tread depth of the G132 for less rolling resistance. Hence, greater fuel economy and a healthier bottom line. The G132 is just one more part of Goodyear's complete truck-tire health program, backed up by comprehensive retreading and the 1-800-TIRE-NET road-rescue service.

With early detection and proper treatment, your trucking operation can expect a full recovery from steer tire irregularity.

So, take two today. And call a Goodyear Truck Tire Specialist a few months down the road. By then, we expect you'll be feeling much better.

GOODYEAR

475

The man who paid £15 for a can of oil will now have his head examined.

£15 for four litres of motor oil?

But that's more than twice the price of ordinary mineral oil, is it not?

Has the gentleman concerned taken leave of his senses?

Let us loosen his screws and look inside.

At first sight, this cylinder head, so expensively lubricated by Mobil One Rally Formula, certainly appears to lack a few things.

There is no sludge, for example.

And carbon deposits are not present in the expected quantity.

The reason is simple.

Mobil One Rally Formula is a synthetic oil produced, not from some gusher beneath the North Sea, but from some genius in our research laboratory.

It has a uniquely uniform molecular structure.

And, over time, it will maintain your engine's cleanliness and performance.

Closer inspection reveals another surprising fact about this gentleman's cylinder head.

The surfaces of the cam shaft, tappets and bearings are not simply clean, they are pristine.

Again, much of the credit must go to Mobil One Rally Formula.

Because of its synthetic composition, it is actually a superior lubricant to standard mineral oil.

Moving parts move more smoothly. Ultimately, engine wear is reduced.

(Incidentally, this lessening of friction also results in increased power.)

By now you may have concluded that Mobil One Rally Formula is, perhaps, not so expensive after all.

But there is yet one more point to mention.

This head has been severely tested and stripped down not after the normal 6,000 mile drain interval.

But after double that amount.

Cheap, isn't it?

Mobil 1 Rally Formula
The world's most advanced motor oil.

If You Think The Audience Is Tough At Carnegie Hall, Try Performing In Front Of 5th Period Music Class.

These days, getting your students to enjoy their lessons can be a tough assignment.

That's why you need the most engaging tools available. Like The Music Class.™ An exciting new set of music software for elementary to high school students.

Simply, The Music Class helps you orchestrate *your* music class. With built-in tests and challenges that allow students to learn at their own speed. And playful graphics that work in concert with your instruction.

The Music Class even has a built-in record keeping program that tracks the progress of up to 125 students.

Plus, it can accompany any budget. With programs priced at a low $39 and $49.

The five programs can be run on any Apple II® or IIGS.® *Fundamentals*, all the basics, $49. *Rhythm*, how to feel the beat, $49. *Ear Training*, learning to hear, $49. *Music Symbols*, the language of music, $39. *Note Reading*, learning to see and understand, $39.

So order by calling toll free 1-800-843-1337. Or call collect 612-854-9554. Ask about our Coda Catalog with over 600 music software products. And you'll start conducting class like you never have before.

The Music Class™
From the Wenger Music Learning Division, Wenger Corp. 1401 East 79th Street, Minneapolis, MN 55420-1590.

Trade Color: 1 Page Or Spread

478

ART DIRECTOR
Jerri Powers

WRITER
Joe Anson

CLIENT
Florida Department Of Commerce

AGENCY
Anson-Stoner/
Winter Park, FL

479

ART DIRECTOR
Shelton Scott

WRITER
Renee Mandis

PHOTOGRAPHER
Mike Molkenthin

CLIENT
Chiquita Brands

AGENCY
Ammirati & Puris

480

ART DIRECTOR
Carole Erger-Fass

WRITERS
Wally Lawrence
Sheldon Gewirtz

DESIGNER
Carole Erger-Fass

CLIENT
British Design & Art Direction

AGENCY
Adweek In-House

481

ART DIRECTOR
Paul Asao

WRITER
Kerry Casey

PHOTOGRAPHER
Marvy!

CLIENT
Blue Fox Tackle Company

AGENCY
Carmichael Lynch/
Minneapolis

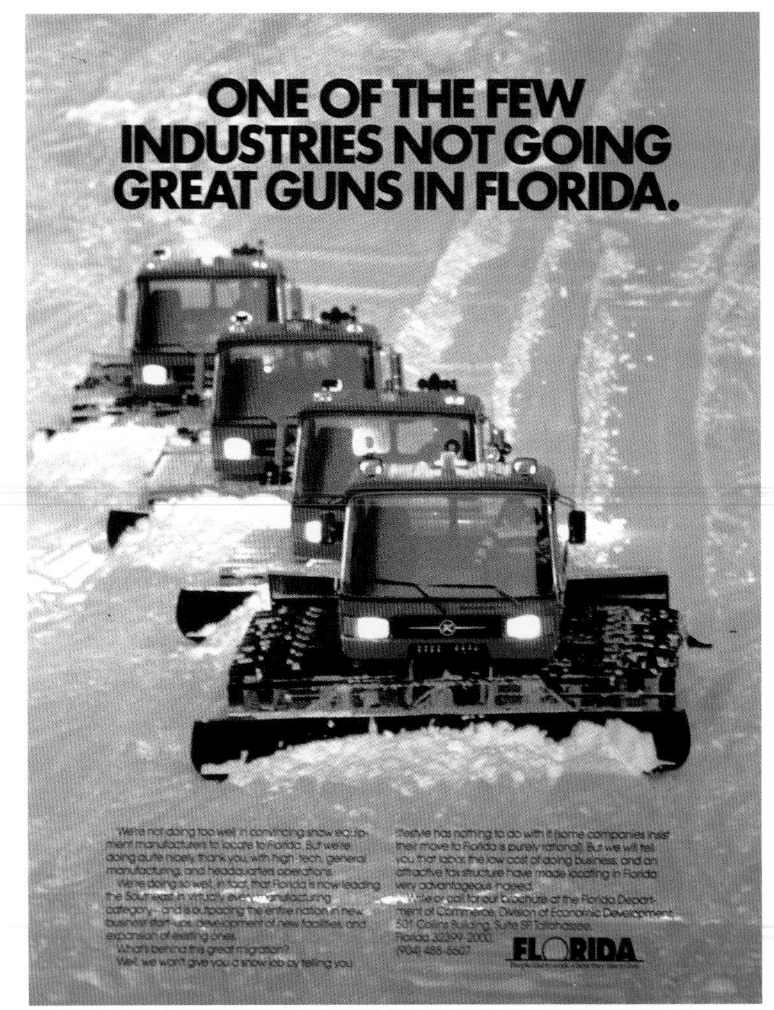

478

479

PLEASE STEAL OUR ADS.

(We steal yours.)

Dear Americans:

For years, we Brits have been flipping through the Clios, Effies, Andys, Hatches, Athenas, Obies, Kellys and Addys, not to mention the One Show and Mobius, to see what you in the States were doing creatively. When we saw something we liked, well, we're not ashamed to say that maybe we borrowed an idea or two.

Now it's your turn.

Starting now, we're distributing to our American friends the best and the brightest of British creativity, namely, the annual and showreel of the D&AD Awards.

The Crown Jewels

The Design & Art Direction Awards are the most prestigious awards in the industry simply because the standards are so high and so few prizes are given. What you see in the 1987 *Annual* and *Showreel* are the crown jewels of British advertising. In fact, you'll see a whole different face of advertising, relying less on numbers and more on seat-of-the-pants judgment.

Daring Television

How else can one explain the extraordinary black humour of The Prudential commercial, winner of a silver award for the agency Wight Collins Rutherford Scott. One would never produce a spot like this in the United States, would one?

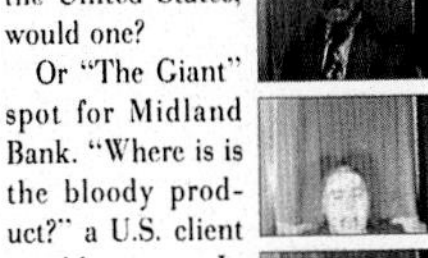

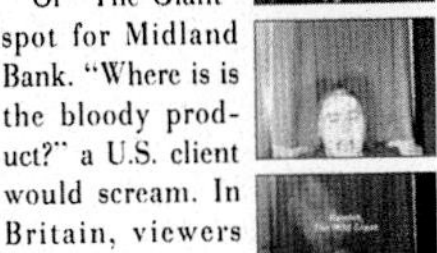

Or "The Giant" spot for Midland Bank. "Where is is the bloody product?" a U.S. client would scream. In Britain, viewers can't wait to see it again—or those wild, zany spots for Hamlet Cigars. And what Collett Dickenson Pearce & Partners Ltd. did for Radio Rentals is nothing less than a breakthrough in the way television uses time and space.

Silver Award
Hamlet Cigars

Of course I'm not going to tell you that my favorite campaign is the Heineken because everyone else would rise up in arms, but do decide for yourself as you watch all 38 spots and peruse the 450 pages of the *Annual.*

Provocative Print

The D&AD print awards for magazines and newspapers create instant fame for those talented enough to win. And why not? Those adverts for Morphy Richards underblankets enveloped the judges in whimsy. The Tampax campaign humbled us with their quiet power. And the copy for Inter City trains offered a much-needed explanation as to "why workaholics seldom get to the top."

Be on Guard

Look through all the other awards we gave this year for posters, packaging, editorial, book design and corporate design and you will see some eloquent examples of

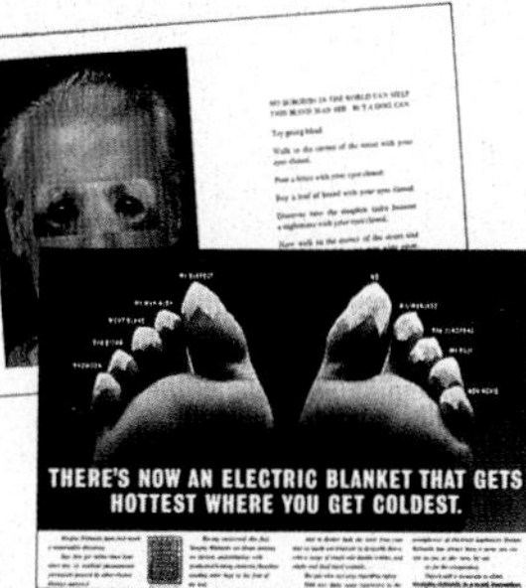

Silver Awards
Guide Dogs for the Blind
Morphy Richards Appliances

British style and humour. So many interesting ideas in fact, that you shouldn't be surprised if you find the D&AD stolen from your own office one day.

Get the D&AD from our friends at ADWEEK and feast your eyes. Enlighten your mind. And do take some ideas from us. Mind you, we'd be nothing less than flattered if you swipe them all!

Edward Booth-Clibborn
Chairman, D&AD

How to Order

The D&AD *Annual* costs $69. The *Showreel* is $129. Or get both for $175. Make your check payable to ADWEEK and mail to D&AD *Annual* and *Showreel:* c/o ADWEEK, 49 East 21st St., New York, NY 10010. For faster service call (212) 995-7225.

Gold Award
Signage Program
at the Rijksmuseum,
Amsterdam

YES, SEND ME THE:

☐ 1987 D&AD *Showreel* of Britain's finest TV spots today at $129.00.

☐ 1987 D&AD *Annual* at $69.00

☐ 1987 D&AD *Annual* and *Showreel* at $175.00.

Tape preference: ☐ ¾ ☐ VHS ☐ Beta

Enclosed is my check for $ ________ (payable to ADWEEK.)

Charge my: ☐ Visa ☐ Mastercard ☐ Amex

Acct. # ________

Exp. Date ________

Name ________

Company ________

Address ________

City ________

State ________ Zip ________

Mail to: British Design and Art Directors *Annual* and *Showreel*, c/o ADWEEK, 49 East 21st Street, NY, NY 10010

D&AD

Four New Ways To Make A Fish's Mouth Water.

At Blue Fox, we're committed to carefully designing and crafting lures. Lures that produce fish. Lures that produce sales.

Take the new Foxee Jig for example. It combines a soft, ribbed body with action so deadly you'd swear the water brought it to life. The Foxee is going to catch fishermen because the Foxee is going to catch fish. It's as simple as that.

Foxee Jig

And take a look at the new Roland Martin Muskie Special. It's exactly what crazed muskie fishermen have been asking for. A big, tormenting bucktail partnered with a big Roland Martin willow-leaf blade. (A blade, by the way, that's been enticing quite a few tournament-winning fish.) It's kinda scary to think what a muskie's going to do to this bait.

Roland Martin Muskie Special

Then there's the new Roland Martin Big Crappie Spinner Bait. It's perfect for nailing slab crappies in cover because the Colorado blade makes it weedless. And don't be surprised when you start hearing about how it's taking walleyes in the weeds and smallmouths out of the rocks. We know there's a big market out there for this little guy.

Roland Martin
Big Crappie Spinner Bait

And finally, there's the Roland Martin Double Buzzer. The best words to describe this lure are "look out!" This one's going to raise some hell. And some big fish too. Because the tandem blades smack and click and clank and bang together as you churn it along the surface. Add to that our patented life-like skirts in all the hottest colors and you're in business.

Roland Martin Double Buzzer

So if these new lures have whet your appetite, talk to your Blue Fox tackle representative at AFTMA Booth 1323. We've got this sneaky feeling that the Fox won't be outsmarted this year. Once again. BLUE FOX®

Trade Color: 1 Page Or Spread

482
ART DIRECTOR
Andrew Vucinich
WRITER
Joe Garrett
PHOTOGRAPHER
Rudi Legname
CLIENT
CooperVision
AGENCY
Chiat/Day - San Francisco

483
ART DIRECTORS
Jeffrey France
Don Harbor
WRITERS
Bruce Mansfield
Scott Mackey
PHOTOGRAPHERS
Joel Becker
Ronn Maratea
Dan Weaks
CLIENT
Lawler Ballard Advertising
AGENCY
Lawler Ballard/
Norfolk, VA

484
ART DIRECTOR
Steve Ohman
WRITER
Harold Karp
PHOTOGRAPHER
Gary Braasch
CLIENT
Olympus Corporation
AGENCY
Lowe Marschalk

485
ART DIRECTOR
Peter Cohen
WRITER
Larry Spector
CLIENT
The One Show
AGENCY
Levine Huntley Schmidt & Beaver

Introducing the lens we designed with our ears.

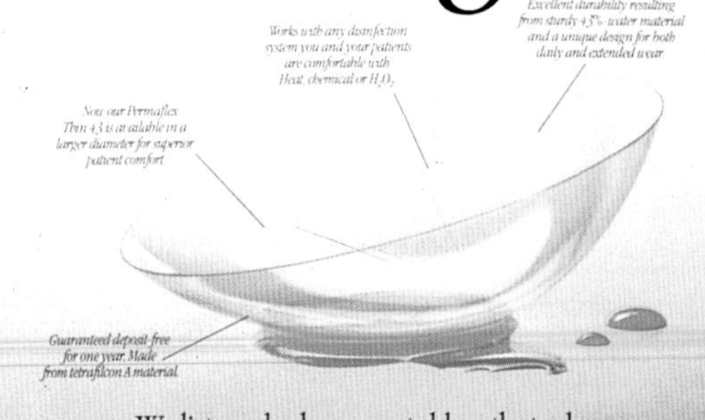

We listened when you told us that a larger diameter would make Permaflex® Thin 43 the ideal lens. So now it's available in a 14.4-mm diameter. As well as our original 13.8-mm version.

With the larger diameter, you can fit a broader range of corneas with immediate comfort. Without sacrificing any of the original Permaflex Thin 43 benefits that are so important to your patients.

Like visual acuity that's exceptionally crisp and clear.

And handling that's rated superior to B&L "O" Series by 97% of eye-care practitioners surveyed.*

And deposit-free comfort. Backed by our one-year Deposit Resistance Guarantee. Which has a return rate of less than 1%.**

In fact, the only thing that's changed about both Permaflex Thin 43 diameters is the price.

That's more comfortable too.

For more information, see your CooperVision sales representative or call us now on our toll-free lines.

We'll be all ears. CooperVision

482

If this is the kind of work we do for free, imagine what we can do if you pay us.

Call Dan Ballard, President, at 804-627-0261.

Lawler Ballard Advertising
Norfolk, Richmond, Cincinnati, Kalamazoo, Birmingham, Tampa

483

AT 35,000 FEET,
YOU CAN'T PULL OVER
TO CHECK
THE ENGINE.

Every day, the average jet engine is under as much stress as any ten CEOs. And after a series of long business trips, it just may begin to show signs of fatigue.

Obviously, six-and-a-half miles up in the air is no place to start looking under the hood.

That's where Olympus technology comes in. With Olympus industrial fiberscopes.

They're precisely what airline maintenance crews need to make frequent inspections. To reach places the human hand won't fit, to see what the naked eye cannot. To locate hidden cracks or other damage before tearing the whole engine apart.

Whether it's industrial scopes, medical and clinical instruments, biotechnological products, microscopes, microcassette recorders, video camcorders or our famous 35mm cameras, Olympus products are never the result of some engineering whim or marketing void, but rather, they are the technological response to some very human needs.

Until they put service stations in the sky, Olympus fiberscopes are the best assurance you have of finding engine trouble where it should be found. On the ground.

OLYMPUS
Focused on people™

484

EVERY YEAR,
THOUSANDS OF PEOPLE
GO TO THE
ONE SHOW AWARDS
DINNER.

BUT ONLY 79 ENJOY
THEIR MEALS.

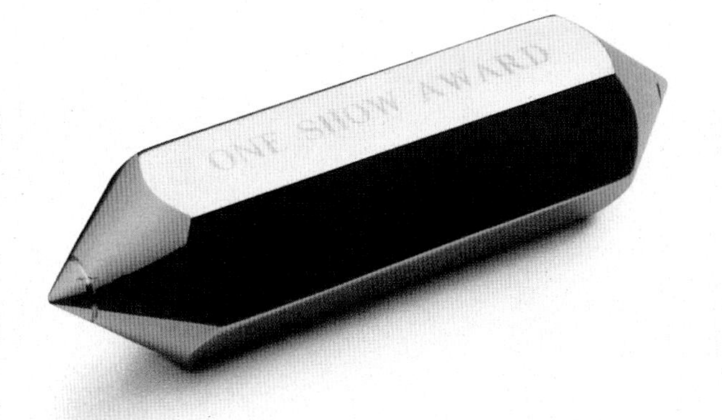

THE ONE CLUB FOR ART & COPY INC 3 WEST 18TH STREET, NEW YORK, NY 10011 / 212-255-7070

485

Trade Color: 1 Page Or Spread

486
ART DIRECTOR
Pam Conboy
WRITER
John Jarvis
PHOTOGRAPHER
Rick Dublin
CLIENT
3M
AGENCY
Martin/Williams - Minneapolis

487
ART DIRECTOR
Susan Casey
WRITER
Dave Goldenberg
DESIGNER
Beth Hulleberg
CLIENT
Oce Business Systems
AGENCY
Anderson & Lembke/ Stamford, CT

488
ART DIRECTOR
Dean Hanson
WRITER
Bruce Bildsten
CLIENT
First Tennessee Bank
AGENCY
Fallon McElligott/ Minneapolis

489
ART DIRECTOR
David Gardiner
WRITER
Tom O'Connor
CLIENT
Soundtrack
AGENCY
Rossin Greenberg Seronick & Hill/Boston

486

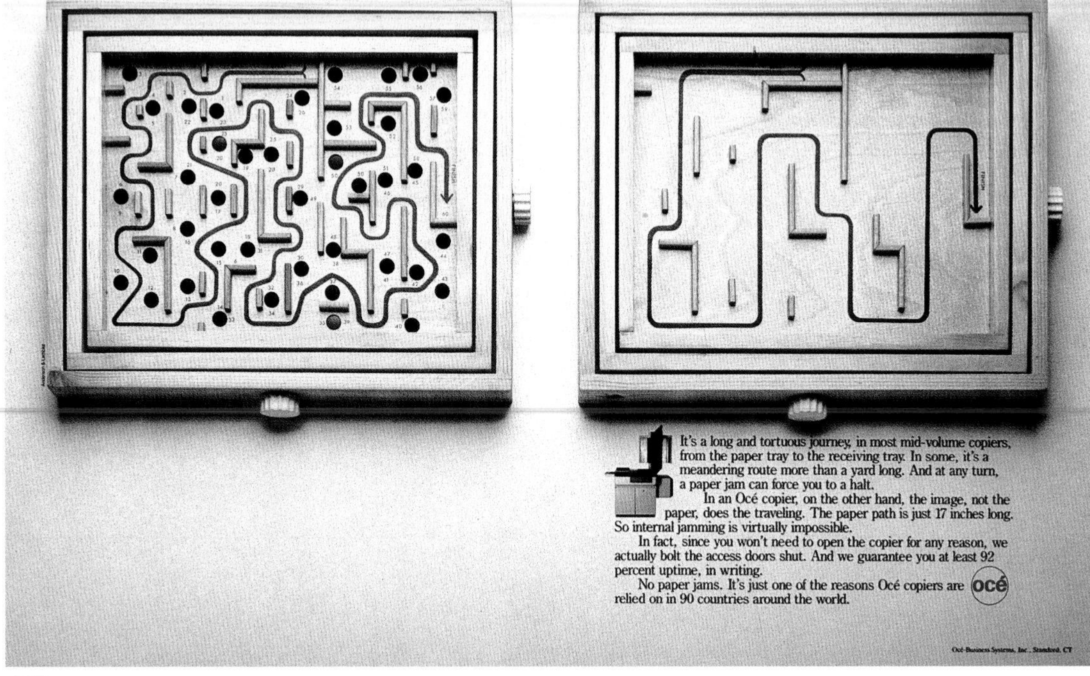

487

Three Things That Can Kill You.

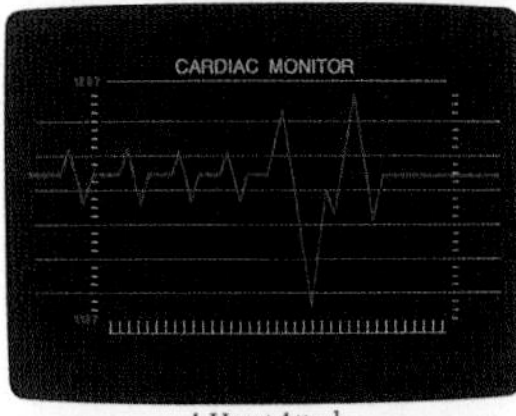

A Heart Attack

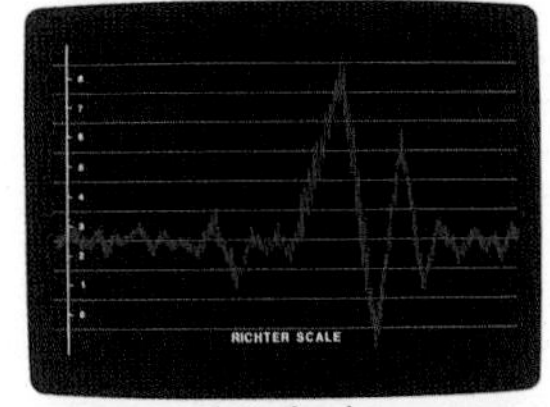

An Earthquake

Variable Interest Rates

Of all the great unknowns in life, interest rates can be the most frightening.

Especially for a business.

But, unfortunately, floating rate loans are all that most banks offer.

Which means that every time the interest rate jumps, your heart rate jumps.

However, at First Tennessee we not only can give you a fixed-rate term loan, we can give you a competitive rate.

So you can plan your expenses, and maybe even lower them.

Talk to a First Tennessee banker about fixed-rate term loans today.

We can't protect you from every disaster in life.

But at least we can give you one less thing to worry about.

488

Great campaigns have always had a catchy jingle.

If you want your next campaign to go down in history, do what NBC Sports, Sheraton Hotels, 7 Eleven and Ponderosa Steak Houses have all done. Call Soundtrack for the freshest, most memorable jingles around.

soundtrack

77 North Washington St., Boston 617-367-0510
25 East 21st St., New York City 212-420-6010

489

Trade Color: 1 Page Or Spread

490

ART DIRECTOR
Louie Moses

WRITER
Louie Moses

CLIENT
Moses Anshell

AGENCY
Moses Anshell/ Phoenix

491

ART DIRECTOR
Mark Johnson

WRITER
Phil Hanft

ARTIST
E.M. Stevenson

CLIENT
Hush Puppies Shoe Company

AGENCY
Fallon McElligott/ Minneapolis

492

ART DIRECTOR
Bob Meagher

WRITER
Don Nelson

DESIGNER
Bob Meagher

PHOTOGRAPHER
Dave Jordano

CLIENT
Ragold

AGENCY
Cramer-Krasselt/ Chicago

493

ART DIRECTORS
Rich Silverstein
Rick Strand

WRITER
Jeff Goodby

ARTIST
Mark Hess

PHOTOGRAPHER
Hank Benson

CLIENT
Christian Brothers

AGENCY
Goodby Berlin & Silverstein/San Francisco

ALL WE NEEDED TO WRITE THIS AD WAS A YELLOW MARKER.

Clients: Arizona Humane Society, ASU Sports, Arrowhead, Bowen Homes, Crescent Hotels, First Interstate Bank, Infincom/Ricoh, Kitchell, Marlborough, Pennysaver, St. Lukes, Tribune Newspapers

490

Now Hush Puppies come in just as many styles and sizes.
In 1958, Hush Puppies introduced a comfortable, basic suede shoe. It was a big hit. In fact, so big that thirty years later a lot of people still think of that shoe when they think of Hush Puppies.
In reality, there are over 130 other Hush Puppies styles. Some just as traditional as the original, others more contemporary. There are stylish heels and classic business pumps for women. Dressy loafers and power wing tips for men. Even a full line of children's shoes.
Look for us at the National Shoe Fair and FFANY. See what good breeding has done for the Hush Puppies line. Men's Line: Booth 2818, Jacob Javits Center. Women's Line: Hush Puppies Showroom, 717 5th Ave. at 56th Street.

491

Something tells us our newest flavor will be a success.
New Cocoamint Velamints® are the only sugar-free mints with the irresistible taste of chocolate. America's favorite flavor.
Maybe that's why they're already getting an incredible reception.
Why an astounding 85% of the people who tasted new Cocoamint Velamints in a national consumer survey said they plan to buy them.
And why almost a third of your Cocoamint Velamints sales should be purely incremental. New business.
New Cocoamint Velamints. Your customers will taste chocolate.
You'll taste success.
NEW
SUGAR FREE
COCOAMINT
Velamints
RAGOLD Inc.
First with fresh ideas.
Velamints is a registered mark of Ragold Inc.

492

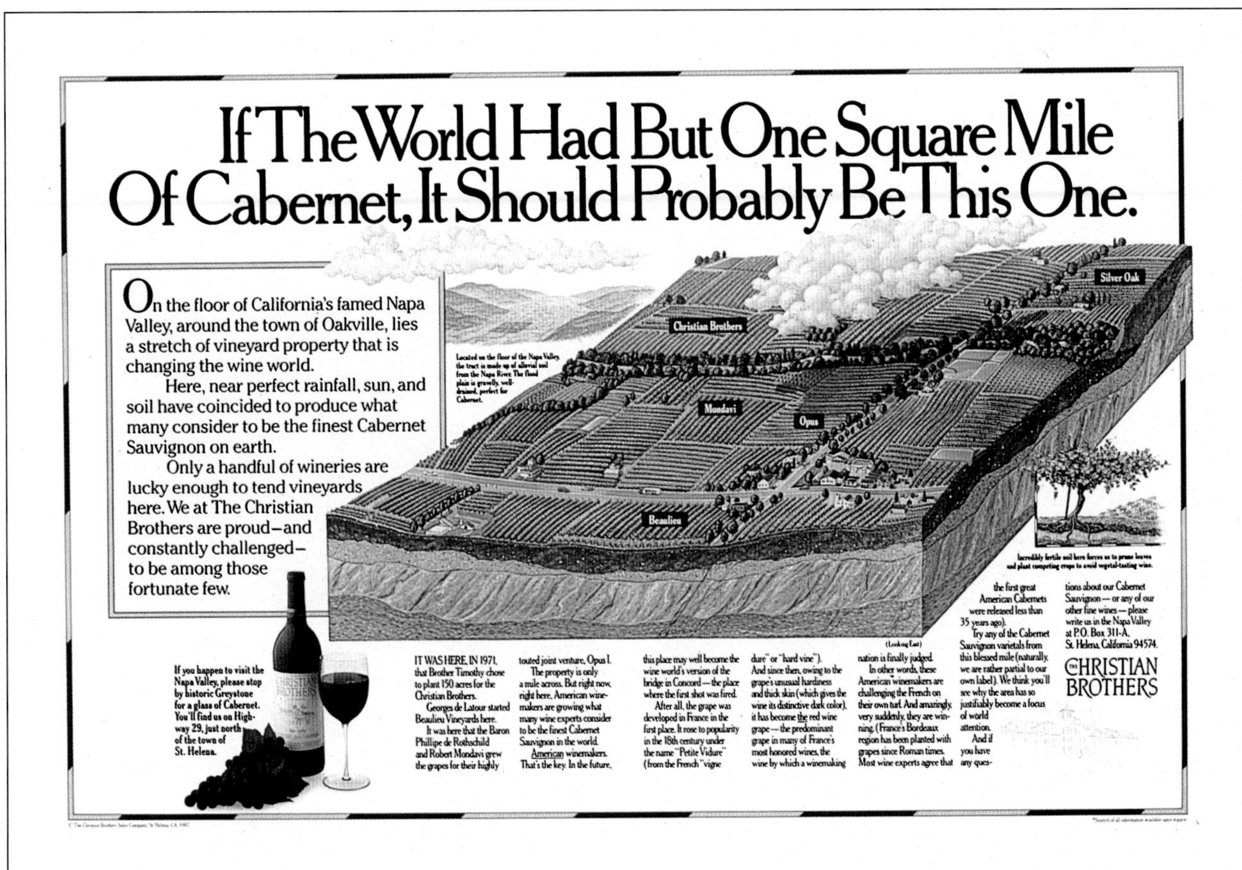
If The World Had But One Square Mile Of Cabernet, It Should Probably Be This One.
On the floor of California's famed Napa Valley, around the town of Oakville, lies a stretch of vineyard property that is changing the wine world.
Here, near perfect rainfall, sun, and soil have coincided to produce what many consider to be the finest Cabernet Sauvignon on earth.
Only a handful of wineries are lucky enough to tend vineyards here. We at The Christian Brothers are proud–and constantly challenged–to be among those fortunate few.
Christian Brothers
Silver Oak
Mondavi
Opus
Beaulieu
Located on the floor of the Napa Valley, the tract is made up of alluvial soil from the Napa River. The flood plain is gravelly, well-drained, perfect for Cabernet.
Incredibly fertile soil here forces us to prune leaves and plant competing crops to avoid vegetal-tasting wine.
(Looking East)
If you happen to visit the Napa Valley, please stop by historic Greystone for a glass of Cabernet. You'll find us on Highway 29, just north of the town of St. Helena.
IT WAS HERE, IN 1971, that Brother Timothy chose to plant 150 acres for the Christian Brothers.
Georges de Latour started Beaulieu Vineyards here.
It was here that the Baron Phillipe de Rothschild and Robert Mondavi grew the grapes for their highly touted joint venture, Opus I.
The property is only a mile across. But right now, right here, American winemakers are growing what many wine experts consider to be the finest Cabernet Sauvignon in the world.
American winemakers. That's the key. In the future, this place may well become the wine world's version of the bridge in Concord—the place where the first shot was fired.
After all, the grape was developed in France in the first place. It rose to popularity in the 18th century under the name "Petite Vidure" (from the French "vigne dure" or "hard vine").
And since then, owing to the grape's unusual hardiness and thick skin (which gives the wine its distinctive dark color), it has become the red wine grape—the predominant grape in many of France's most honored wines, the wine by which a winemaking nation is finally judged.
In other words, these American winemakers are challenging the French on their own turf. And amazingly, very suddenly, they are winning. (France's Bordeaux region has been planted with grapes since Roman times. Most wine experts agree that the first great American Cabernets were released less than 35 years ago).
Try any of the Cabernet Sauvignon varietals from this blessed mile (naturally, we are rather partial to our own label). We think you'll see why the area has so justifiably become a focus of world attention.
And if you have any questions about our Cabernet Sauvignon — or any of our other fine wines — please write us in the Napa Valley at P.O. Box 311-A, St. Helena, California 94574.
THE CHRISTIAN BROTHERS

493

Trade Color: 1 Page Or Spread

494
ART DIRECTOR
Mark Kuehn
WRITER
Patrick Pritchard
PHOTOGRAPHERS
David Vander Veen
Dave Gilo
CLIENT
Briggs & Stratton
AGENCY
Cramer-Krasselt/Milwaukee

495
ART DIRECTOR
Jon Parkinson
WRITER
David Metcalf
PHOTOGRAPHER
Gary Bryan
CLIENT
Champion
AGENCY
Scali McCabe Sloves

496
ART DIRECTORS
Peter Zagorski
Mike Cammuso
WRITER
John Koenig
CLIENT
Cessna
AGENCY
Ogilvy & Mather/Chicago

497
ART DIRECTOR
Sally Wagner
WRITER
Emily Scott
PHOTOGRAPHER
Kent Severson
CLIENT
3M
AGENCY
Martin/Williams - Minneapolis

494

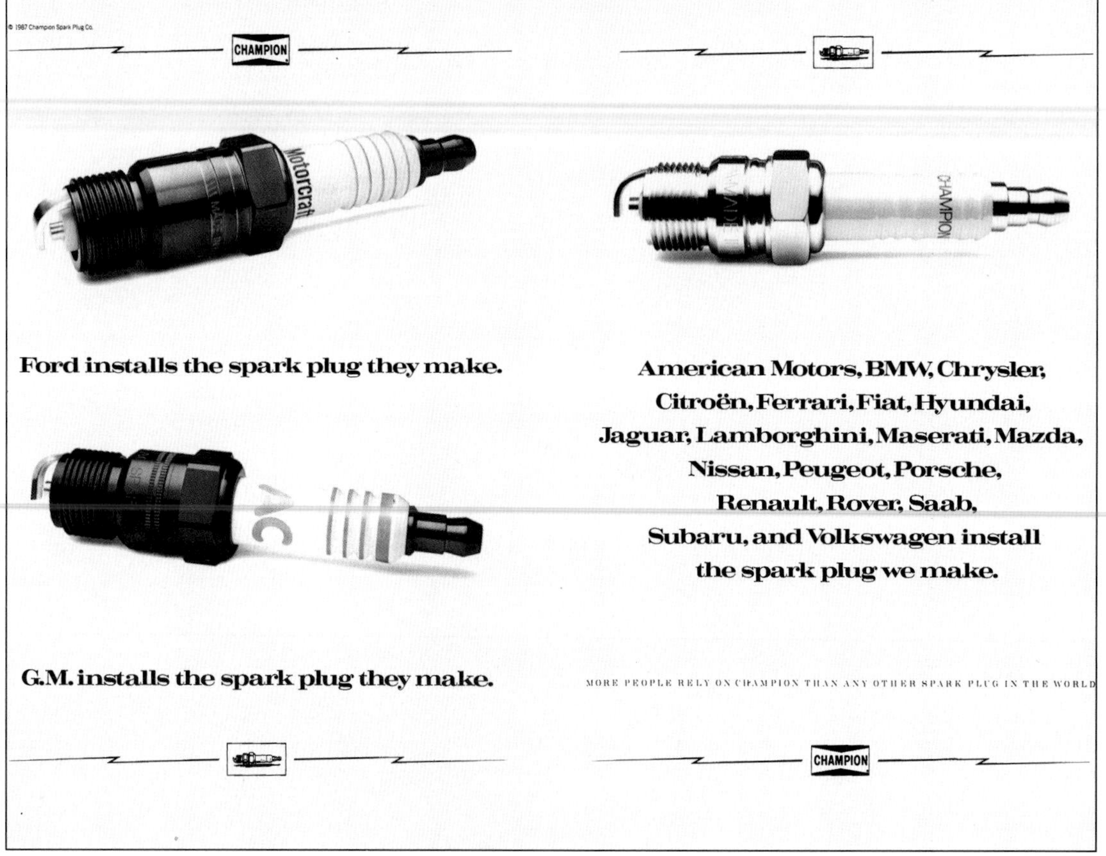

495

ONLY CESSNA CITATIONS CAN FLY UNDER THESE CONDITIONS.

Cessna
$23,000 A MONTH
CITATION II
$34,000 A MONTH
CITATION S/II
$57,000 A MONTH
CITATION III

The numbers don't lie.

Place an order to lease a Citation before July 31st and you'll lock in a lease rate of just 0.00896 for a 7-year term. About 40% less than typical commercial rates. Business aircraft have never before been available at a rate so low.

Which means monthly payments of just $23,000 on a fully equipped Citation II, $34,000 on the S/II, and $57,000 for the superiority of the Citation III. Payments on 10-year leases are lower still.

Why can we lease our planes for so much less? Because at lease's end they're worth so much more.

Everyone talks about having faith in their product.

At Cessna we're banking on it.

While this is a remarkable opportunity to fly the world's best-selling business jets, it's also a limited one. You must order by July 31.

For more information about the Citation lease program, please call 1-316-946-6056. We believe that if you buy our logic, you'll lease our airplane.

CESSNA CITATIONS

496

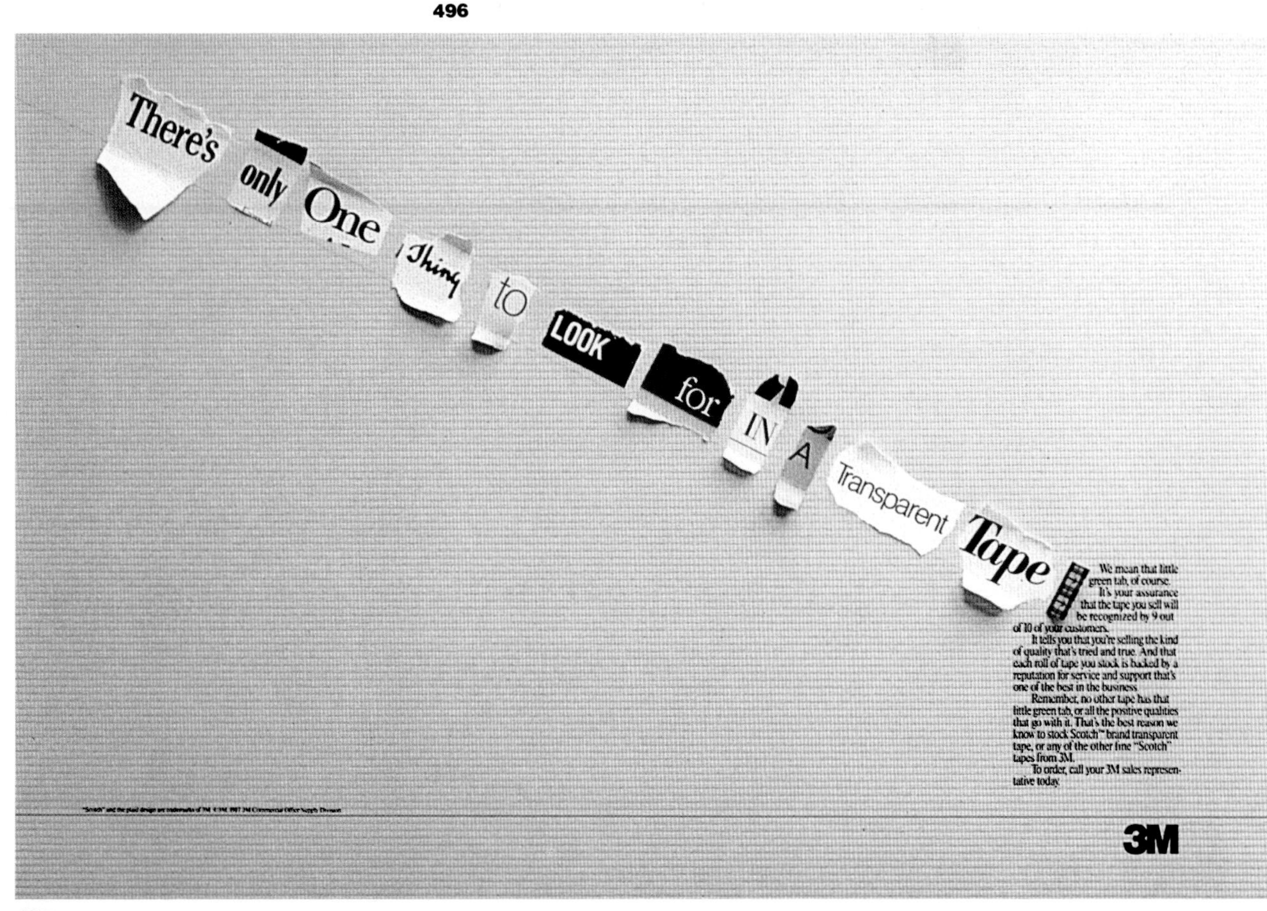

There's only One thing to LOOK for IN A Transparent Tape
We mean that little green tab, of course.
It's your assurance that the tape you sell will be recognized by 9 out of 10 of your customers.
It tells you that you're selling the kind of quality that's tried and true. And that each roll of tape you stock is backed by a reputation for service and support that's one of the best in the business.
Remember, no other tape has that little green tab, or all the positive qualities that go with it. That's the best reason we know to stock Scotch™ brand transparent tape, or any of the other fine "Scotch" tapes from 3M.
To order, call your 3M sales representative today.
3M

497

Trade Color: 1 Page Or Spread

498

ART DIRECTOR
Tom Lichtenheld

WRITER
John Stingley

DESIGNER
Michael Fazende

PHOTOGRAPHER
Craig Perman

CLIENT
Marine Midland Automotive

AGENCY
Fallon McElligott/
Minneapolis

499

ART DIRECTOR
Bob Barrie

WRITER
Jarl Olsen

DESIGNER
Bob Barrie

PHOTOGRAPHER
Rick Dublin

CLIENT
Hush Puppies Shoe Company

AGENCY
Fallon McElligott/
Minneapolis

500

ART DIRECTOR
Michael Fazende

WRITER
John Stingley

PHOTOGRAPHER
Time/Life

CLIENT
Marine Midland Automotive

AGENCY
Fallon McElligott/
Minneapolis

501

ART DIRECTOR
Houman Pirdavari

WRITER
Bill Miller

PHOTOGRAPHER
Rick Dublin

CLIENT
Rolling Stone

AGENCY
Fallon McElligott/
Minneapolis

498

499

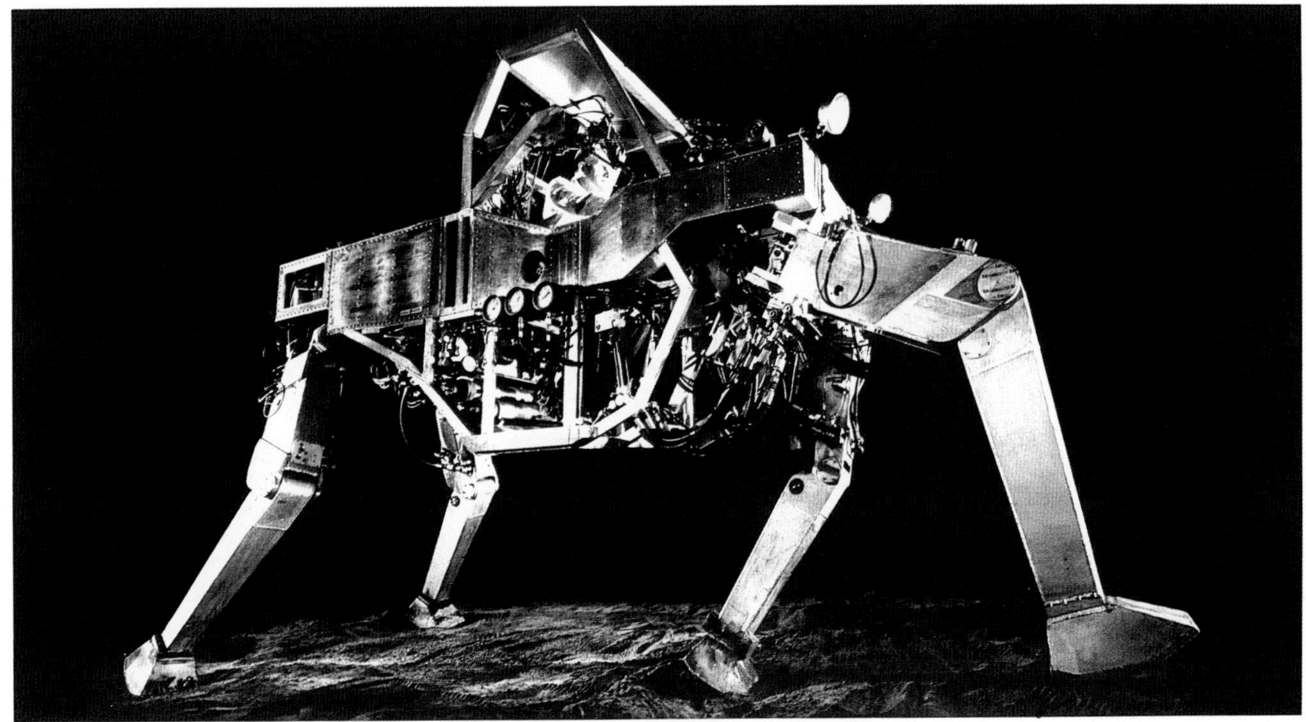

If it runs, we'll finance it.

Before you ask what it is, let us save you the trouble.

We don't know.

That's the point. At Marine Midland Automotive Financial, we don't care what new car line you sell. Or who the manufacturer is. Or where a car comes from. If it runs, we'll most likely finance it.

So rather than dealing with a lot of financial sources who only handle one line, you can deal with one source for everything.

That means you know what to expect. With consistent deals and service. So it's easier to work with your customers.

What's more, we'll also finance your inventory. Your leasing program. Your buildings. Even acquisitions of other dealerships.

Call 800-448-3400, ext. 334, for the name and number of your local representative.

We can't think of an easier way to move cars. Unless, of course, they grew legs and walked off the lot themselves.

MARINE MIDLAND AUTOMOTIVE FINANCIAL CORPORATION

500

Perception.

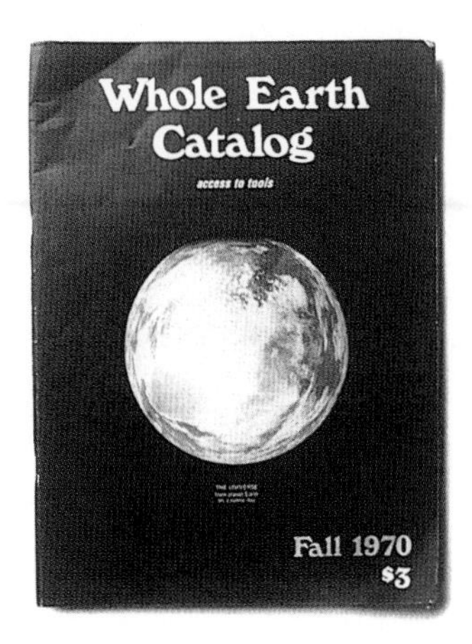

Reality.

If you still think the readers of Rolling Stone are sending away for blueprints of geodesic domes, put this information on your order blank: Last year, Rolling Stone readers spent more than 4 billion dollars on electronic equipment. If you're looking for a place to plug in your product, you'll find the power in the pages of Rolling Stone.

501

Trade Color: 1 Page Or Spread

502

ART DIRECTOR
Bob Brihn

WRITER
Bill Miller

PHOTOGRAPHER
Mark LaFavor

CLIENT
Federal Express

AGENCY
Fallon McElligott/
Minneapolis

503

ART DIRECTOR
Houman Pirdavari

WRITER
Bill Miller

PHOTOGRAPHER
Rick Dublin

CLIENT
Rolling Stone

AGENCY
Fallon McElligott/
Minneapolis

504

ART DIRECTOR
Bob Brihn

WRITER
Bill Miller

PHOTOGRAPHER
Mark LaFavor

CLIENT
Federal Express

AGENCY
Fallon McElligott/
Minneapolis

505

ART DIRECTOR
Kevin Lory Mote

WRITER
Diane Forman-Seimetz

ARTIST
Mike Stirnagle

CLIENT
McIlhenny

AGENCY
Tracy-Locke/Dallas

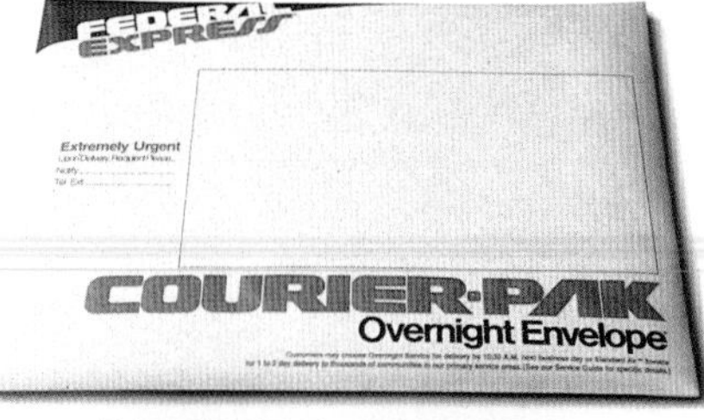

502

503

THE CALL OF DUTY.

ABOVE AND BEYOND.

When duty calls, Federal Express® answers.

IT'S NOT JUST A PACKAGE. IT'S YOUR BUSINESS.

504

ONE MORE THING THAT'S GREAT WITH TABASCO® ON IT.

It's always been a winner behind your bar. And a jazzy addition in your kitchen. Now let Tabasco® sauce perform its magic where your customers like it most: on the table. It's convenient. Elegant. And it satisfies your customers' cravings for livelier foods like no other condiment can. Tabasco brand pepper sauce. It appeals to your customers' good taste. And reflects yours. **IT'S FOR MORE THAN YOU THOUGHT IT WAS FOR.**

505

Trade Color: 1 Page Or Spread

506

ART DIRECTOR
Rich Silverstein

WRITER
David Fowler

PHOTOGRAPHER
Mark Hauser

CLIENT
Communication Arts Magazine

AGENCY
Goodby Berlin & Silverstein/San Francisco

507

ART DIRECTOR
John Speakman

WRITERS
Vern Johansson
Brian Quennell

DESIGNERS
John Speakman
Louis Fishauf

PHOTOGRAPHER
Nigel Dickson

CLIENT
Apple Canada

AGENCY
Scali McCabe Sloves/Toronto

508

ART DIRECTOR
Tom Lichtenheld

WRITER
Rod Kilpatrick

DESIGNER
Tom Lichtenheld

PHOTOGRAPHERS
Mark LaFavor
Dick Durrance

CLIENT
The Wall Street Journal

AGENCY
Fallon McElligott/Minneapolis

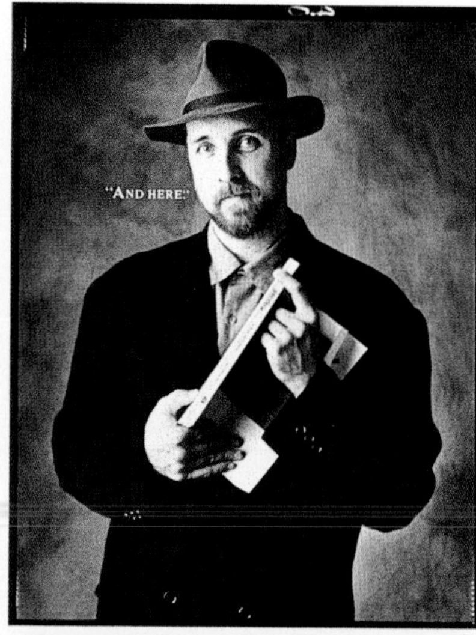

Tom Monahan President, Creative Director Leonard Monahan Saabye Providence

For 44 dollars, you can deface your own copy 8 times a year. Subscribe via Mary, at (415) 326-6040.

Communication Arts

506

If you couldn't do a layout before, you won't be able to do one now.

If you couldn't do a layout before, you won't be able to do one now.

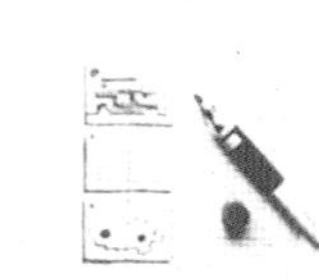

If you couldn't do a layout before, you won't be able to do one now.

People expect very big things from little machines. And then, with amazing regularity they're disappointed. Or frustrated. Or just plain hostile.

The truth is, if you have little artistic or commercial talent, an Apple Desktop Publishing system won't make you a graphic genius. Sorry.

But with a reasonable design sense, a bit of art school, a few years experience and a little time on a Macintosh, you can do what you're doing now.

Only a lot better.

A lot faster.

With a lot more control.

From "concept to production" as they say in the trade ads.

Once you settle into page composition software such as PageMaker or LetraPage, you can create full scale presentations that look like they cost just about what it takes to keep a studio rep in a BMW.

Without spending anywhere near the price of a nice lunch at Fenton's.

You start just like you do at a drawing board. With a blank piece of paper. Only now, your blank page is a screen.

You can fill it in with a few of the thousands of images already available through sources such as ClickArt. Or fill it in with whatever's on your mind by using software like FullPaint or MacDraw. Set up your columns. Position your photos.

No more squeaky magic markers.

No more paste-up. No more rules.

And once you've got the visuals in place, you can crop them any way you like.

Resize them.

Move them.

Get rid of them. Before the client asks you.

Replace them. After the client tells you.

Retouch them. Before the illustrator suggests it.

Add to them.

Subtract from them.

Perfect them right down to the last pixel on the screen and the last dot on the page.

Next, we come to the words.

You can set body copy in English instead of Lipsum Dolorum Factum Totum. And you can set it in any size you like.

In 4-point mouse type for all that legal mumbo jumbo.

Or 72-point banner type for that product name.

You can choose from dozens of typefaces. Palatino. Times. Courier. Symbol. ITC Bookman. New Century Schoolbook. ITC Avant Garde Gothic. ITC Zapf Chancery. And that good old standby, Helvetica. All in any style you like. From italic and boldfaced to subscripted and shadowed.

You can even kern each character to suit your individual taste. Smile, Mr. Keene.

And you can prove to your writer that "it's not going to fit" long before you and the typesetter are reduced to fits.

Once you've made the presentation, you can make all those "I love it but..." changes and send them to any typesetter using POSTSCRIPT compatible machines. POSTSCRIPT is the industry standard page description language. Which means anyone with a Linotronic system will be more than happy to accept your disk. Over the phone, via modem, or in person. With the appropriate P.O.

The end result of all this is that your work looks good.

Your company looks good.

Best of all, you look good.

Five days work gets reduced to five hours.

"What if" becomes "Here it is". Right before your eyes.

Changes become non-irritants.

Your mind has more room to roam because you have more time. More control.

More freedom.

More options.

And most importantly, used with the right intentions, you'll be able to sell better work.

But, like we said at the beginning, if you can't do a decent layout now, we can't help. Yet. But we're working on it.

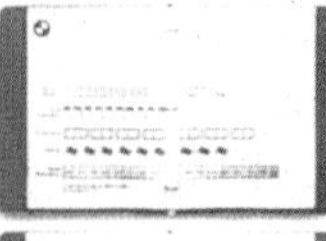

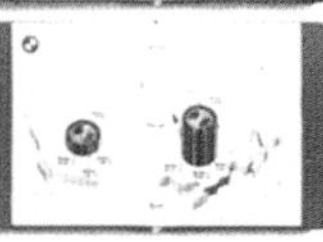

507

An opportunity like this comes along once in a lifetime. Oh, all right, eight times a year.

In the advertising business, you have to seize opportunity when you can find it.

Which, in some cases, isn't very often.

For example, just eight times in 1988, the more than two million readers of The Wall Street Journal will be treated to a journalistic tour de force: an in-depth report on a single topic of abiding personal and professional interest.

A Wall Street Journal Report combines the information you'd expect from The Journal with the informality you'd expect from a magazine. It puts our readers in touch with what they need to know and what they want to know at the same time. Somehow, it gets one of the fastest-moving, fastest-thinking readerships in the world to put its feet up for a while and—of all things—read.

Now, if The Wall Street Journal's Reports are a special event for our readers, consider for a moment what they represent for our advertisers.

An opportunity to educate an educated audience about your products.

An opportunity to help an exceedingly affluent group of men and women dispose of its disposable income.

An opportunity to put your opinions before America's opinion leaders.

An opportunity you can take advantage of by getting in touch with your Wall Street Journal sales office. They'll go to the ends of the earth to help you. Oh, all right, the ends of their sales territory.

The Wall Street Journal Reports.

Small Business • June 10

Sports February 26

Technology Today November 14

Global Finance & Investing September 23

Personal Finance/Taxes December 2

Medicine & Health April 22

The New Consumers May 13

Travel March 18

Trade Any Size
B/W Or Color: Campaign

509

ART DIRECTOR
Crafton Stagg

WRITERS
John Davis
Leslie Westlake
Guy Lowe

PHOTOGRAPHER
Jamie Cook

CLIENT
The Boca Raton Hotel and Club

AGENCY
Austin Kelley/Atlanta

510

ART DIRECTOR
Susan Casey

WRITER
Dave Goldenberg

DESIGNER
Beth Hulleberg

CLIENT
Oce Business Systems

AGENCY
Anderson & Lembke/
Stamford, CT

ENJOY THE INTRACOASTAL, THE ATLANTIC AND A BIT OF THE MEDITERRANEAN.
As constant as the tides, The Boca Raton Hotel and Club has offered the highest standard of luxury for over 60 years.
From the Mediterranean splendor of The Cloister palace, to the quiet sophistication of The Boca Beach Club, every facet exudes the luster of our Five-Star, Five-Diamond reputation. And outstanding service and cuisine have earned us the prestigious Gold Key and Pinnacle awards.
Write our Director of Sales, P.O. Box 225, Boca Raton, FL 33429, or call 800-327-0101. And refresh your spirit at the most sparkling resort in all the world.

The Boca Raton Hotel and Club
QUITE SIMPLY THE BEST.

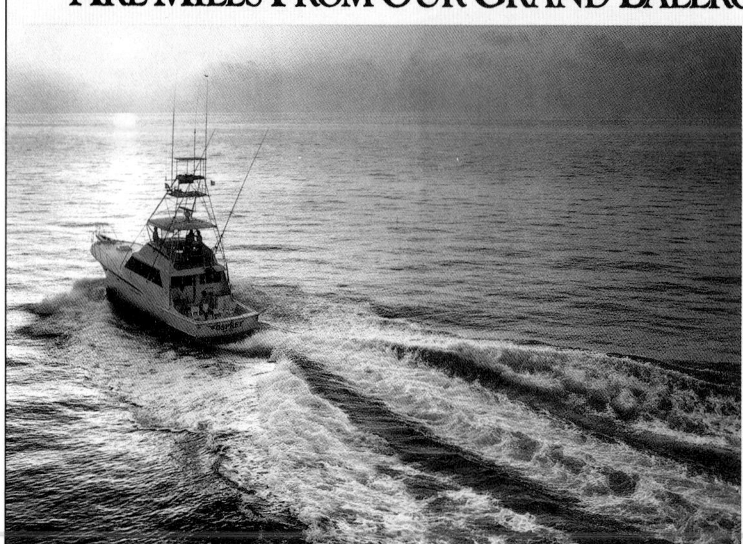
SOME OF OUR MOST POPULAR MEETING FACILITIES ARE MILES FROM OUR GRAND BALLROOM.
Successful business strategy often comes to light while wrestling a big blue from the Atlantic, sinking a 30-foot putt, or reaching for a crucial lob. The Boca Raton Hotel and Club knows the importance of mixing business with pleasure.
But for those who believe grand ideas are only found in grand meeting rooms, our Five-Star, Five-Diamond resort offers the best, from the renowned Great Hall to the most comfortable conference room. Impeccable service and outstanding cuisine have also earned us the prestigious Pinnacle and Gold Key awards.
Write our Director of Sales, P.O. Box 225, Boca Raton, FL 33429, or call (305) 395-3000. And set your course for the most sporting resort in all the world.

The Boca Raton Hotel and Club
QUITE SIMPLY THE BEST.

SOME OF THE MOST PRODUCTIVE MEETINGS TAKE PLACE AROUND THE WATER FOUNTAIN.
Our cup runneth over with reasons to choose The Boca Raton Hotel and Club for your next meeting. Five Stars, Five Diamonds and the prestigious Gold Key and Pinnacle awards only begin to tell our story of impeccable service, exceptional facilities and an unrivaled reputation for elegance.
From the impressive Great Hall, to a pristine Atlantic beach, to the charm of the Mediterranean courtyards, any gathering at The Boca Raton Hotel and Club will prove to be a memorable experience.
Write our Director of Sales, P.O. Box 225, Boca Raton, FL 33429 or call (305) 395-3000. And toast your good taste in choosing the splashiest resort in all the world.

The Boca Raton Hotel and Club
QUITE SIMPLY THE BEST.

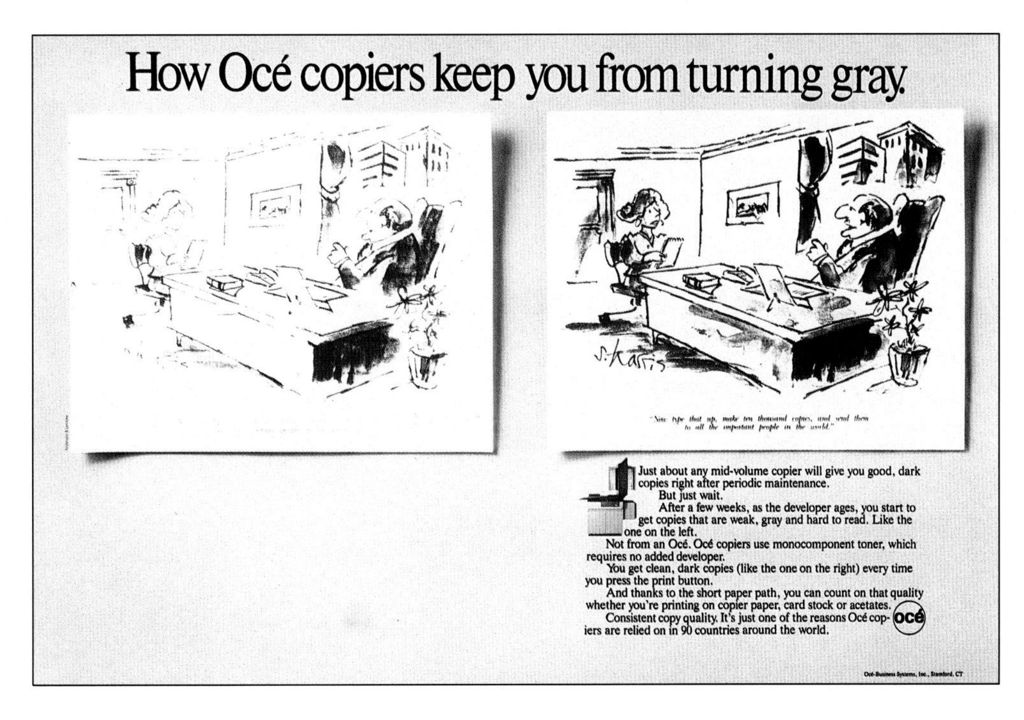

It came back as a copier.

Océ copiers aren't fancy. And maybe they aren't especially pretty.

But they'll never let you down.

In fact, we guarantee it in writing.

If they don't keep zipping along at least 95 percent of the time (and that's a bare minimum), you get money back.

No one else promises you mid-volume and high-volume copiers more reliable than that.

SO RELIABLE, THEY'RE BOLTED SHUT.

Here's the kind of reliability we're talking about:

Imagine making 9,000,000 copies in a row (it would take you about seven or eight years) without ever having to clear an internal paper jam.

The paper path in an Océ copier (left) is much too short for jams to occur.

And imagine never, during all that time, having to add toner. Or, for that matter, developer. Or, for that matter, having to clean corona wires or change fuser oil.

That's the way it is with Océ copiers.

They are so reliable, we actually bolt their access doors shut. (If you think we're kidding, just remember our uptime guarantee.)

As you might expect, Océ copiers run a bit differently from the copiers you're used to—and quite possibly fed up with.

(Pronounce it oh-*say*. It's Dutch, not Japanese, but we'll get into that later.)

In most copiers the paper is dragged from the paper tray to a drum, where it picks up the image.

An Océ, on the other hand, brings the image to the paper by way of two belts. The paper path is less than half the typical length, making paper jams nearly impossible.

Océ 1850 with 40-bin sorter.

COPIES THAT LOOK PRINTED.

This belt-imaging system gives you something else most drum-type copiers don't: Consistent offset-quality copies. The kind you send out to the printer for when you don't trust your own copier to deliver.

How is this possible? For one thing, our photoconductor is made from zinc oxide. It's more sensitive to fine lines and halftones than the photoconducting material drum-type copiers use.

Another reason is our clean toner-transfer system. Most copiers use a powerful electrostatic charge to make the image "jump" to the paper. That causes those "toner dust spots" and dulls the sensitivity of the photoconductor.

Océ copiers print the image cleanly onto the paper from a smooth silicone belt.

On top of that, Océ's Automatic Background Compensation adjusts the exposure to give you perfect copies every time, even from photographs and tinted originals.

This copy quality is consistent over time, too.

In most copiers, quality fades as the developer ages. The Océ process doesn't require developer. Nor does it use fuser oil, so your transparencies will be clean and free from streaks.

Too dark / Acceptable / Too light

Océ doesn't use developer. Quality stays high (left). In most copiers, quality falls sharply as developer ages.

The only thing Océ copiers consume is toner. But you don't have to worry about that, either. We top off the 90,000-copy toner reservoir every time we come by. At no additional cost to you.

That's right—no additional charge for toner!

In fact, if you're concerned about costs—and who isn't?—you're in for a surprise.

Océ copiers cost you less to buy and run than any comparable machines in their class. (Tell us your copying needs and we'll tell you exactly how much less.) They also use up to 60 percent less electricity, thanks to low-heat fusing and low-charge toner-transfer. You'll save on paper, too. Océs print perfectly well on inexpensive paper.

You'll even save room on floor space. An Océ copier requires up to 30 percent less than any comparable machine.

THE 110-YEAR-OLD NEWCOMER.

Who are we to suggest that, when it comes to copiers, you can have your cake and eat it, too?

Océ is a 110-year-old Dutch company that's been making reproduction equipment since 1920, long before some of our biggest competitors got their start.

We are the largest European manufacturer of copiers, with a reputation in 90 countries for building reliable "workhorse" machines. Our reputation is growing here, too.

Toner Transfer and Fusing system (left) prevents toner dust spots, and helps Océ run cooler and cleaner.

Since coming to America four years ago we've put our copiers in some of the largest businesses, universities and government offices in the country.

You'll find Océs at Harvard, in the FBI, the Smithsonian Institution, the three TV networks, four of the six top commercial banks, five of the nine biggest insurance companies and four of the eight largest financial companies.

Just to name a few.

Hanson's Guidelines rated our Océ 1925 a "Gold Medalist" best buy.

The highly respected Buyers Lab called our Océ 1825 "clearly the most impressive copier BLI has seen to date for producing up to 100,000 single-sided copies per month."

We think you'll be impressed, too.

océ

Océ Business Systems, Stamford, CT 06904

Trade Any Size B/W Or Color: Campaign

511

ART DIRECTOR
Tom Lichtenheld

WRITER
Bruce Bildsten

PHOTOGRAPHERS
Steve Umland
Jim Arndt

CLIENT
O.M. Scott & Sons

AGENCY
Fallon McElligott/
Minneapolis

512

ART DIRECTORS
David Deutsch
Rocco Campanelli

WRITER
Don Deutsch

PHOTOGRAPHER
Hiro

CLIENT
Lear Publishing Company

AGENCY
David Deutsch Associates

What The Average Person Considers An Eyesore On The Golf Course.

What A Scotts Tech Rep Considers An Eyesore On The Golf Course.

Just the sight of Poa annua makes us cringe. And it seems to never go away.

So after putting our ears to the ground and our best minds in the lab we discovered a beautiful solution. Our remarkable new TGR™ Poa Annua Control.

Scotts patented TGR technology weakens Poa annua on fairways and bentgrass greens, while controlled-release fertilizer helps desirable turf thrive and overtake the Poa.

But most important, the transition to desirable grasses is gradual. So there's not a sudden change in playing surface conditions.

Ask your Scotts Tech Rep to help you incorporate TGR Poa Annua Control in your turf management program.

At least you'll have one less ugly problem to worry about.

For more information contact your Scotts Tech Rep or simply call 1-800-543-0006. In Ohio call collect 513-644-2900.

What The Average Person Considers Big Trouble.

What A Scotts Tech Rep Considers Big Trouble.

We're not ones to walk away from trouble. But, like you, we do everything we possibly can to avoid it.

So, with a lot of feedback from our Tech Reps, we found a simple, effective way to stop weeds before they even start. Our versatile pendimethalin preemergent weed control.

Its combination of broadspectrum action, control effectiveness and residual is unsurpassed. And we offer it in dry and liquid applied forms, with or without fertilizer, for greater flexibility.

Most important, since pendimethalin is so cost-effective, your Scotts Tech Rep can tailor a preemergent program to both meet your needs and your budget.

So if weeds are threatening you, try our pendimethalin. It practically scares them away.

For more information contact your Scotts Tech Rep or simply call 1-800-543-0006. In Ohio call collect 513-644-2900.

The Average Person's Family Snapshot.

A Scotts Tech Rep's Family Snapshot.

We admit, at times a Scotts Tech Rep does put his work before his family.

But then, the care and nurture of your turf is a very big responsibility. Your problems are his problems.

And, when a Tech Rep isn't spending time with you, he's spending time with our research and development people.

Providing them with the feedback that makes our new products so revolutionary, and keeps our existing products so dependable.

So it really is unfortunate that a Scotts Tech Rep doesn't take better family snapshots.

He needs something to remember what his family looks like.

For more information, just contact your Scotts Tech Rep or call us at 1-800-543-0006.

511

HIRO
LEAR'S
THE MAGAZINE FOR THE WOMAN WHO WASN'T BORN YESTERDAY
Gretchen Siebel, Marketing Executive. One of 12,500,000 traditional women over 40 with HHI above $40,000.
Premier Issue March/April '88. For information contact: Michele S. Magazine, Publisher, 505 Park Avenue, New York, NY 10022 (212) 888-0007.

HIRO
LEAR'S
THE MAGAZINE FOR THE WOMAN WHO WASN'T BORN YESTERDAY
Judith Paige, Nutritionist. One of 12,500,000 traditional women over 40 with HHI above $40,000. Premier Issue March/April '88.
For information contact: Michele S. Magazine, Publisher, 505 Park Avenue, New York, NY 10022 (212) 888-0007

HIRO
LEAR'S
THE MAGAZINE FOR THE WOMAN WHO WASN'T BORN YESTERDAY
Mary Weir, Designer. One of 12,500,000 traditional women over 40 with HHI above $40,000.
Premier Issue March/April '88. For information contact: Michele S. Magazine, Publisher, 505 Park Avenue, New York, NY 10022 (212) 888-0007

Trade Any Size B/W Or Color: Campaign

513

ART DIRECTORS
Barbara Gerber
Gary Custer

WRITER
David Schutten

PHOTOGRAPHER
Nick Vedros

CLIENT
US Sprint

AGENCY
Valentine-Radford/
Kansas City, MO

514

ART DIRECTOR
Tom Smith

WRITER
Michael Marino

DESIGNER
Tom Smith

PHOTOGRAPHER
Martin Reuben

CLIENT
Lincoln Electric

AGENCY
Wyse Advertising/
Cleveland, OH

This could be the most expensive sign you've ever ignored.

Ignoring an ordinary "buried cable" sign is bad enough. But when you ignore a buried fiber optic cable sign, you risk cutting off thousands of times as many phone calls. And becoming liable for thousands of dollars in repair.

Which is why this sign is so important. It lets you know you're digging dangerously close to our fiber optic cable.

It's no ordinary cable. It's the key to America's future communications network. Providing telephone service to millions of people.

That includes emergency calls. Calls you can't afford to cut off. Even if you could afford the repair bill. So watch for this sign. And, please, call before you dig. **Call 1-800-521-0579.**

US Sprint

You won't believe how much it costs to dig here.

It may not look it, but the real estate between these signs could cost you thousands of dollars an inch.

Because anywhere you see our sign means you're digging dangerously close to our buried fiber optic cable. A cable that can cost hundreds of times more to repair than ordinary phone cable.

Because, fiber optic cable isn't ordinary phone cable. It's the key to America's future communications network. And it can carry thousands of times as many calls.

That includes emergency calls. Calls you can't afford to cut off. Even if you could afford the repair bill.

So watch for this sign. And, please, call before you dig. **Call 1-800-521-0579.**

US Sprint

It's the people who miss this sign that do the real damage.

Look for this sign anywhere you dig. It lets you know you're working dangerously close to our buried fiber optic cable.

If you miss our sign, chances are you'll hit our cable. And, unlike ordinary copper cable, breaking a fiber optic cable accidentally can break you financially. Because fiber optic cable isn't ordinary phone cable. It's the key to America's future communications network.

It's hundreds of times more expensive to repair than ordinary copper cable because it can carry thousands of times as many calls. That includes emergency calls. Calls you can't afford to cut off. Even if you could afford the repair bill.

So watch for this sign. And, please, call before you dig. **Call 1-800-521-0579.**

US Sprint

The race is not always to the swift.
In the race against downtime, the winner is the motor that finishes last. The motor that runs. And runs. And runs.
Few motors made anywhere in the world will match the steady stamina of a Lincoln motor.
Lincoln motors will often double the running life of competitive motors because they run cooler.
Lincoln motors run more dependably too. In fact, Lincoln is the only motor in the world to carry a full five-year warranty.
The unusually high quality which characterizes Lincoln motors isn't just built in. It's born in.
Born of a company dedication to quality and performance so strong, it has become a famous business school study.
Every Lincoln motor is made in America. By American workers.
Every Lincoln worker has a lot of incentive to build the longest-running, lowest-maintenance motor you can buy.
And that should give you incentive to investigate Lincoln motors for yourself.
They're born to run. And run. And run.
The Lincoln Electric Company. Cleveland, Ohio.

LINCOLN MOTORS®

MADE RIGHT. RIGHT IN AMERICA.

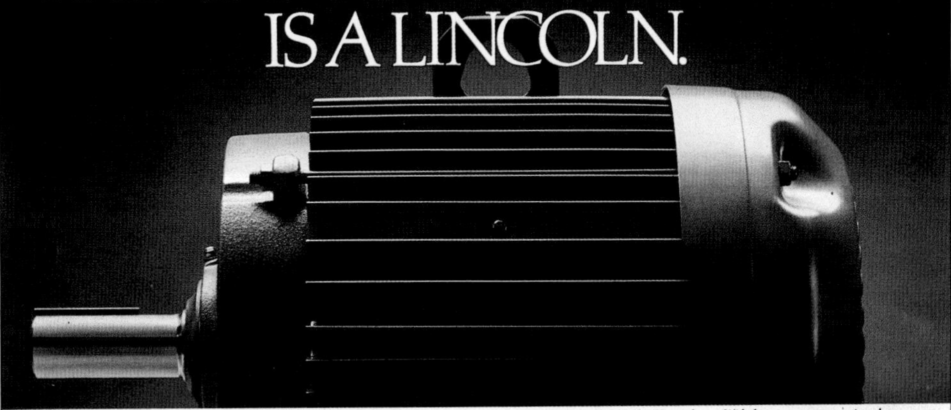

You've heard of Cadillac cars, but you've never heard of Lincoln motors?
People sometimes tell us that. Then they discover that they have had Lincoln motors working for their companies for years.
"I forgot about our Lincoln motors," they say. "They never give us trouble."
Lincoln has been perfecting electric motors since 1895. And perfecting the manufacture of them too.
We make them right. Right here in America. We not only compete with motors made in other parts of the world. We win.
Lincoln is the only company in the world confident enough to put a five-year warranty on its motors.
Productivity and perfectionism among our workers is so high, our management system is studied at Harvard and in Japan.
But Lincoln workers, motivated by a chance to share substantially in company profits, have yet to be matched. They build motors right.
And Lincoln motors usually cost less to buy than motors of lesser quality.
Contact your nearest Lincoln distributor the next time you install motors.
With the money you save using a long-running, top-quality Lincoln motor, who knows? Your company may buy you a Cadillac. The Lincoln Electric Company. Cleveland, Ohio.

LINCOLN MOTORS®

MADE RIGHT. RIGHT IN AMERICA.

OUR MOTTO. OUR MOTOR.

MADE RIGHT.
RIGHT IN
AMERICA.

Many managers think it's time for American industry to demonstrate its ability to manufacture quality industrial products and cease exporting jobs overseas.
Lincoln Electric's performance proves it can be done. Take our motor.
It is the only motor in the world that is manufactured with enough quality to offer a five-year warranty.
Yet it costs less to buy than most competitive motors.
Our secret is Yankee ingenuity. Lincoln motors are built in America. By American workers.
Our Lincoln motors are designed to run cool. Well below their thermal capacity. A motor that runs even 10 degrees Centigrade cooler can run at least twice as long as a hotter motor.
Our Lincoln motors are also built to run trouble-free. Our defect rate is the lowest in the industry, because our workers are so highly motivated. They share substantially in company profits. They also pay for customer problems. And when a man is building a profit for himself at the same time he is building a motor for you, he builds it right.
Which brings us to our motto. Made right. Right in America.
We think it gives you two good reasons to buy Lincoln Motors. The Lincoln Electric Company. Cleveland, Ohio.

MADE RIGHT. RIGHT IN AMERICA.

Trade Any Size B/W Or Color: Campaign

515

ART DIRECTOR
Roy Grace

WRITER
Diane Rothschild

PHOTOGRAPHERS
Carl Fisher
Bruno

CLIENT
Whittle Communications

AGENCY
Grace and Rothschild

516

ART DIRECTOR
Jill Bohannan

WRITER
Ray Thiem

CLIENT
The Jenn-Air Company

AGENCY
Young & Rubicam/
Chicago

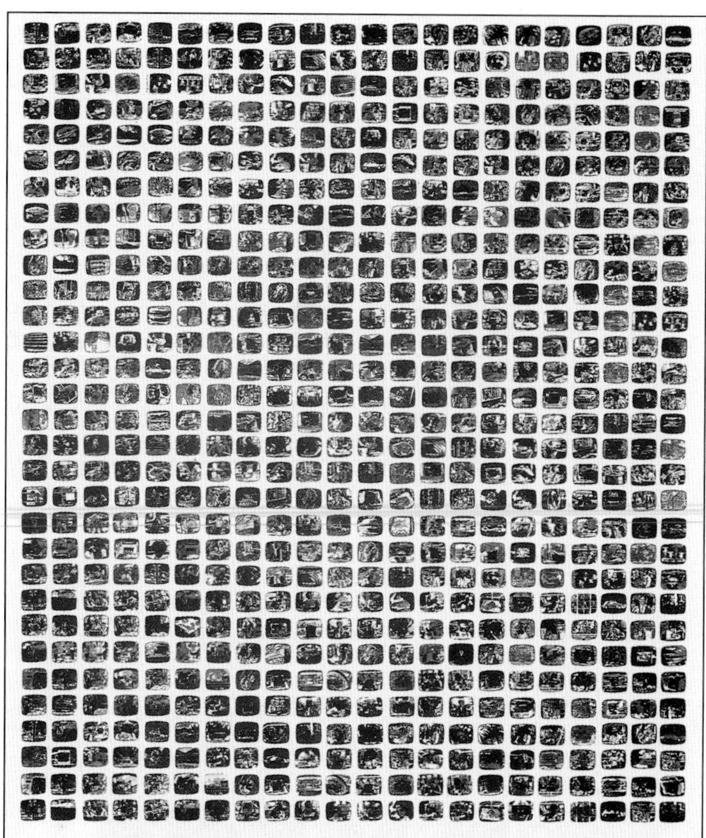

Fortunately, a television station can air only this many commercials a day.

You spent months hammering out a strategy.

Weeks fine-tuning the execution.

You built in dazzling production values. And spent millions on research, testing, and media.

But the commercial didn't work as well as you'd hoped.

How come?

Maybe the answer is right up there.

When you consider the brain-numbing amount of advertising the average viewer can see in a single day, how well can you expect any commercial to work?

Not surprisingly, one study found that recall of television advertising dropped by 61% over a 16-year period.

Some experts even predict that with the introduction of 15-second spots, commercial recall may drop to as low as 4%.

Obviously, commercials are getting lost in the crowd.

And the solution may not lie in spending more on television.

It may lie in spending less.

And investing in the alternatives we provide.

At Whittle Communications we offer advertisers the chance to communicate their messages in uncluttered environments.

We produce a range of exclusive media that includes magazines, newspapers, video systems, and wall-sized information centers.

And we produce these for some of the leading advertisers in the country.

In fact, so many major clients have found our media so effective that in the past ten years our average annual growth rate has been 33%.

We're currently a $100,000,000 company with a staff of 850 people. And we expect to grow even larger.

After all, the more advertising people see on television, the more advertisers see in us.

Whittle
communications

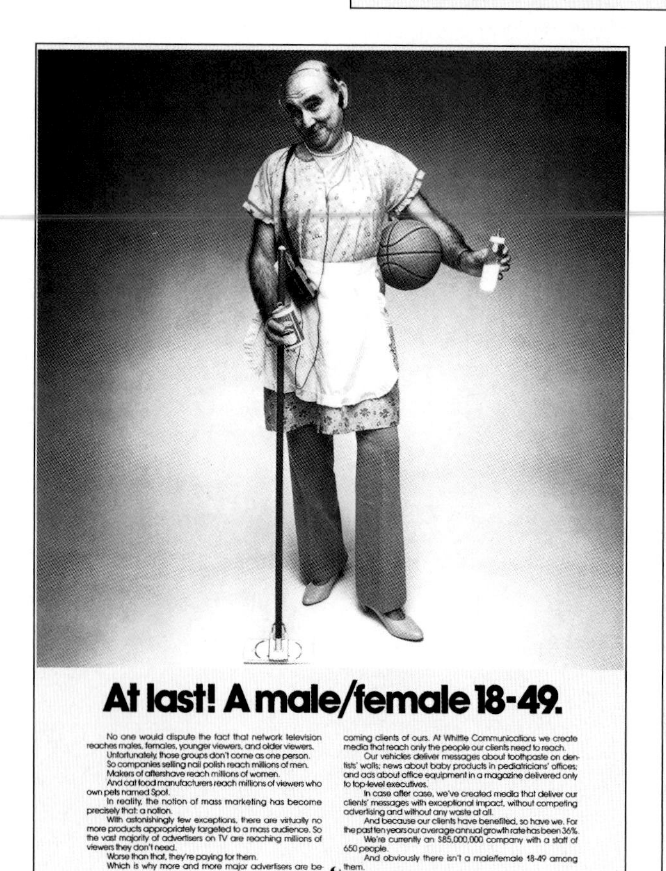

At last! A male/female 18-49.
No one would dispute the fact that network television reaches males, females, younger viewers, and older viewers.
Unfortunately, those groups don't come as one person.
So companies selling nail polish reach millions of men.
Makers of aftershave reach millions of women.
And cat food manufacturers reach millions of viewers who own pets named Spot.
In reality, the notion of mass marketing has become precisely that: a notion.
With astonishingly few exceptions, there are virtually no more products appropriately targeted to a mass audience. So the vast majority of advertisers on TV are reaching millions of viewers they don't need.
Worse than that, they're paying for them.
Which is why more and more major advertisers are becoming clients of ours. At Whittle Communications we create media that reach only the people our clients need to reach.
Our vehicles deliver messages about toothpaste on dentists' walls; news about baby products in pediatricians' offices; and ads about office equipment in a magazine delivered only to top-level executives.
In case after case, we've created media that deliver our clients' messages with exceptional impact, without competing advertising and without any waste at all.
And because our clients have benefited, so have we. For the past ten years our average annual growth rate has been 36%.
We're currently an $85,000,000 company with a staff of 650 people.
And obviously there isn't a male/female 18-49 among them.
Whittle
communications

A lot of people didn't even know it was sick.

It's not exactly news.

The networks' share of viewers has dropped 16% in the last eight years.

And in homes with cable, the figure is down to 51%.

In the face of numbers like these, it's not surprising that so many advertisers are looking for new ways to reach people.

What's surprising is that some advertisers aren't.

Particularly when new ways are available.

At Whittle Communications we provide a wide range of precisely targeted, extremely efficient, and exceptionally impactful media.

More than that, we provide a range of media in line with the realities of 1987.

Because we reach people in places like offices.

And health clubs.

And all in all, the innovative media we produce have proved so effective that we've grown into a $100 million company with a staff of 850 people.

And a client list that includes a significant number of the country's most significant advertisers.

After all, reaching people is no longer as easy as ABC. Or, for that matter, NBC or CBS.

Whittle
communications

Jenn-Air comes in red or blue.

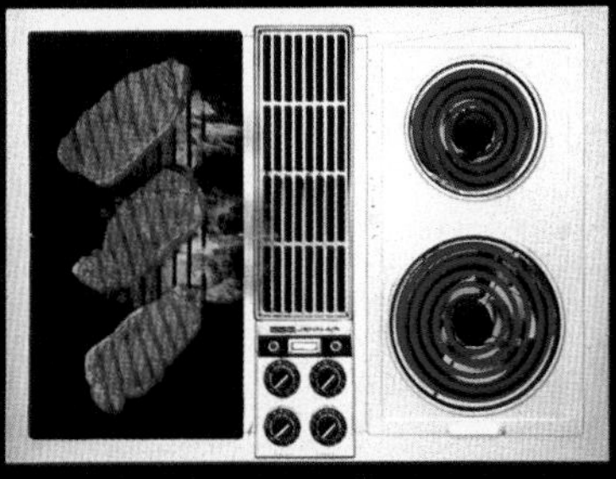

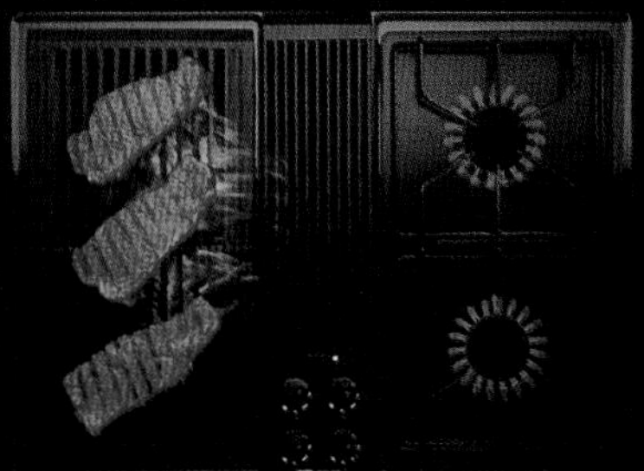

Few things attract a home buyer as quickly as a cheery, open-looking kitchen featuring a Jenn-Air cooktop.

And now our cooktops come in gas as well as electric.

With the addition of gas, Jenn-Air now has 9 downdraft cooktops. No one else offers so many different sizes, styles and options to fit your needs.

For more information about Jenn-Air cooktops—gas or electric—plus our complete Jenn-Air kitchens, call your distributor. Ask him about our Kitchen Package prices.

Jenn-Air.

Write Jenn-Air Builder Program, 3035 Shadeland Ave., Indianapolis, IN 46226. © 1987 Jenn-Air Co. A division of Maytag Company

Jenn-Air runs hot and cold.

It's no secret that a Jenn-Air Grill-Range in the kitchen can give you an extra edge with home buyers. So just imagine what an entire Jenn-Air kitchen could do.

Start with our new refrigerator. Like all Jenn-Air products, it offers the ultimate in convenience.

Xtra Ice™ icemaker. Frost-free freezer. Adjustable glass shelves. Energy Saver switch. Reversible door.

It even has a built-in dispenser in the door for ice water and cubes.

What's more, our refrigerators come in a variety of models with customized panels to match any kitchen decor.

For more about our refrigerators plus our complete Jenn-Air kitchens, call your distributor. Ask him about our Kitchen Package prices.

Jenn-Air.

Write Jenn-Air Builder Program, 3035 Shadeland Ave., Indianapolis, IN 46226. © 1987 Jenn-Air Co. A division of Maytag Company

Jenn-Air cooks and cleans up.

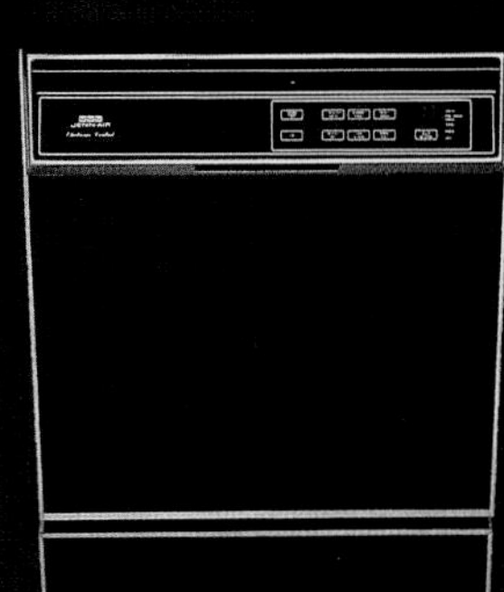

Everyone knows about the Jenn-Air Grill-Range and how it has become the symbol of quality for ranges.

Well now Jenn-Air has a line of seven dishwashers that is every bit as well respected.

All have scrubbing power second to none in the industry and are remarkably quiet running.

Plus they are simple to install. Will fit into even the tightest spaces. And like all Jenn-Air appliances, are built to last.

For more information about our dishwashers, compactors, disposers plus our complete Jenn-Air kitchens, call your distributor. Ask him all about our Kitchen Package prices.

Jenn-Air.

Write Jenn-Air Builder Program, 3035 Shadeland Ave., Indianapolis, IN 46226. © 1987 Jenn-Air Co. A division of Maytag Company

Trade Any Size B/W Or Color: Campaign

517

ART DIRECTOR
Gary Goldsmith

WRITER
Neal Gomberg

DESIGNER
Gary Goldsmith

PHOTOGRAPHER
Gil Cope

CLIENT
Knoll International

AGENCY
Goldsmith/Jeffrey

518

ART DIRECTOR
Jim Condit

WRITER
Bob Morrison

PHOTOGRAPHER
Eric Henderson

CLIENT
Home Lines Cruises

AGENCY
Cole Henderson Drake/
Atlanta

It can tell you a lot about your office furniture.

It's called a coffee break.

And it gives people a chance to share office gossip and talk about Monday Night Football. To rejuvenate themselves and feel good about their work.

But too many coffee breaks? That usually means people are fatigued and not very productive. And that usually means there's something wrong with your office furniture.

The Knoll Office Systems all have acoustical panels to help people keep concentrating.

Adjustable, glare-free Task/Ambient Lighting to help people keep reading.

Adjustable computer keyboard trays to help people keep computing.

Walls that are high enough for privacy or low enough to help people keep communicating.

All of which help make people more productive.

And when people are productive, your office system pretty much pays for itself.

At Knoll, we offer everything from systems to seating and from desks to textiles. As well as the service that makes managing your office a lot easier. Call 1-800-633-0034 to talk with a representative or authorized dealer nearest you.

He'll buy you a cup of coffee.

Knoll

Every company has its own personality.

Maybe it's conservative.

Or flamboyant.

Or maybe it's conservative and flamboyant.

The point is your office furniture should be able to say: "This is the kind of company we are."

Something Knoll Office systems and seating happen to do very well.

They can suit almost any personality. Open plan office, private office or data processing center. From the receptionist to the CEO.

And to give all those offices their own personalities, you can choose from wood veneers like mahogany and maple. Fabrics and plastic laminates. And colors from beige to shades that can please the most flamboyant chairman of the board.

At Knoll, we offer everything from systems to seating and from desks to textiles. As well as the service that makes managing your office a lot easier.

Call 1-800-633-0034 to talk with a representative or authorized dealer nearest you.

(We promise he won't have green hair.)

Knoll

Once you tie the knot, that's it. It's your office furniture.

For better or for worse, in growth periods and in slow periods, in open plans and in closed offices, 'til obsolescence do you part.

In other words, it had better last.

Something Knoll Office Systems are engineered to do very well. All of them are built with the most durable steel, wood veneers, laminates and fabrics. And all of them can change as your company changes.

Morrison can quickly create virtually any kind of work space. From open to data processing to private offices with movable full height walls.

Hannah can hide unwieldy wires and cables better than any other office system.

Zapf can give everyone in the company an open, elegant, office.

And speaking of commitment, there are our service people. Team Knoll. They'll be there for you before installation to do everything from writing specifications to developing typical workstations. During installation, to supervise assembly. And after installation for care and maintenance training with your facilities people.

At Knoll, we offer everything from systems to seating and from desks to textiles. As well as the service that makes managing your office a lot easier. Call 1-800-633-0034 to talk with a representative or authorized dealer nearest you.

We'll start the courtship.

It'll make it a lot easier for you to say, "I do."

It's almost as big a commitment as buying office furniture.

Knoll

517

Every morning they rise and praise the travel agent who saved them $500.

Right now we're offering a $500 discount on all ten-day cruises from Ft. Lauderdale to the Caribbean. Or $400 off our nine-day cruise. But there's another reason your clients will love you for recommending Home Lines. Destinations. Islands like Montserrat. Martinique. Barbados. Even South America. Then there's the luxury. It's complete, unabashed self-indulgence. Comforts like bigger cabins and newer ships. Superb cuisine. Attentive Italian crews. Sun decks as big as an acre. So book Home Lines' mv Atlantic or mv Homeric. In 10 days your clients could save up to $500.

Let's see them do that at home.

Discounts are per cabin and available when you purchase your ticket 60 days in advance of sailing date. For information and reservations, call 1-800-221-4041 toll-free nationwide; 1-800-522-5780 in New York; 212-775-9041 in New York City, Nassau County and Westchester County. (mv Atlantic: Liberian registry. mv Homeric: Panamanian registry.)

Home Lines Cruises
The Finest To The Caribbean.
Sailing December Through March.

The last thing your group wants is to be treated like a group.

As you know, all cruise lines are not exactly the same. Some pack 1,400 passengers on their ships. Some pack even more. Which means your clients get precious little attention. Not to mention breathing room.

Then there's Home Lines.

Our new Homeric is a spacious 42,000 tons but carries only 1,000 passengers. And her sister ship, the Atlantic, is just as roomy, just as comfortable. Both have outstanding Italian crews with a well-deserved reputation for personalized service. In fact, on Home Lines the word "group" only refers to how your clients are booked.

Never how they're treated.

For more information and reservations, call 1-800-221-4041 toll-free nationwide; 1-800-522-5780 toll-free in New York; 212-775-9041 in New York City, Nassau County and Westchester County. (mv Atlantic: Liberian registry. mv Homeric: Panamanian registry.)

Home Lines Cruises
The Finest To Bermuda
And The Caribbean.

The difference between flying to Bermuda and cruising to Bermuda.

On Home Lines, your clients can do something they can't do on any airplane.

Dance until dawn.

Or bask by a swimming pool surrounded by an acre of sundeck.

Be spoiled absolutely rotten. Eat gourmet food served impeccably by a charming Italian crew.

What it gets down to is this.

If your clients cruise to Bermuda, they'll enjoy over 20 different activities along the way.

If they fly to Bermuda, all they'll do is sit.

For reservations, or information about our New York departures, call 1-800-221-4041 nationwide; 1-800-522-5780 in New York state, and 1-212-775-9041 in New York City, Nassau County and Westchester. (mv Homeric: Panamanian registry. mv Atlantic: Liberian registry.)

Home Lines Cruises
The Finest To Bermuda.
Sailing April Through November.

Collateral Brochures Other Than By Mail: Single

519
ART DIRECTOR
Michael Merriman
WRITER
Tom Mackechney
DESIGNER
Michael Merriman
PHOTOGRAPHER
Wyatt McSpadden
CLIENT
Trafton & Autry Printers
AGENCY
Holland Merriman & Christian/Dallas

520
ART DIRECTOR
Tyler Smith
WRITER
Lee Nash
DESIGNER
Tyler Smith
ARTIST
Fritz Dumville
PHOTOGRAPHER
Aldo Fallai
CLIENT
Louis, Boston
AGENCY
Tyler Smith Art Direction/Providence, RI

521
ART DIRECTOR
John C. Reger
DESIGNER
Dan Olson
CLIENT
Business Week
AGENCY
Design Center/Minneapolis

522
ART DIRECTORS
Larry Zuger
Steven Wertanen
Bill Morden
WRITER
Mel Foster
DESIGNER
Larry Zuger
ARTIST
Wiest Group
PHOTOGRAPHERS
Laurie Rubin
Tony D'Orio
Chuck Shotwell
Ron Strong
Kevin Smith
Ken Stidwill
CLIENT
J. Walter Thompson
AGENCY
J. Walter Thompson/Detroit

519

Le Langhe, Piemonte, Italia

Be seated.

Picture, if you will, a mountainous region in northern Italy whose mastery of style can be traced back to 100 A.D.

Imagine, furthermore, a people whose most revered legacy is the perpetuation of quality and style.

Benvenuti a Le Langhe.

Situated in the region called "Italy's window on France," Le Langhe is an area of ancient hills planted thick with vines and oaks.

There are no tour buses here.

No postcard stands.

No baseball-capped tourists with their noses flattened into the pages of a guide book.

This is an area whose greatest attraction is the style of its people.

Here, quality pervades the lives of its inhabitants. Quality in the wines from nearby Asti. Quality in the fabrics from neighboring Biella. Quality in the cheeses, Gorgonzola and Fontina.

In Le Langhe, the talk of business is not punctuated by the question, "Quanto?," but by the exclamation, "Bello!"

We salute this dedication to the art of quality, this level of excellence no longer possible in today's society.

Join us in this much-too-brief a glimpse of Le Langhe and the Piemonte region. Let us celebrate this old European style of elegance for as long as it may be.

520

BUSINESS WEEK'S
CORPORATE
ADVERTISING
PORTFOLIO

521

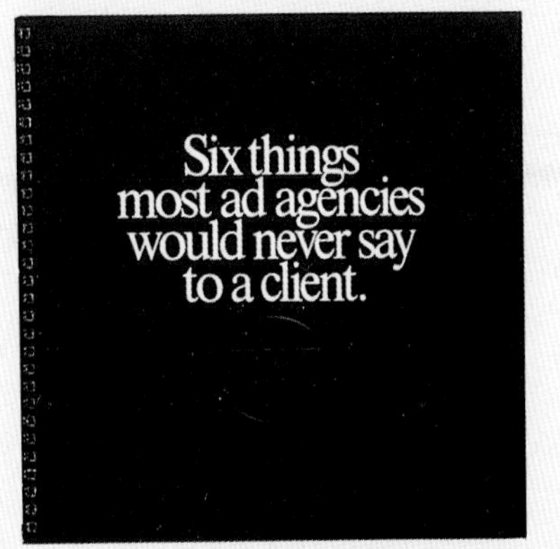
Six things most ad agencies would never say to a client.

"You're not ready to advertise."

When we landed an outdoorwear company in 1983, we couldn't wait to size them up. ■ Carhartt had experienced flat sales. They had also set ambitious growth goals requiring a very aggressive advertising program. ■ Following an initial study of the company, we offered them our best advice. "You're not ready to advertise. Not until your distribution is brought into line with consumer purchasing patterns. And certainly not until your targets of opportunity are defined." ■ They admitted that, for a 95-year-old company, they were still a trifle green. ■ One year later, however, following comprehensive planning and an aggressive retail expansion program, Carhartt was ready to launch its first advertising program. ■ Within the first two years, Carhartt brand sales rose 77%, brand awareness rose 80%, customer base went up 85% and the number of active retailers increased by 43%. ■ All of this was accomplished with a national media budget of under $1 million annually. And it left Carhartt very ripe to set even more ambitious goals for the future.

522

Collateral Brochures Other Than By Mail: Single

523
ART DIRECTOR
Cliff Goodenough
WRITER
Bernie Hafeli
DESIGNER
Cindy Ward
CLIENT
First Interstate Bank
AGENCY
Livingston & Company/ Seattle

524
ART DIRECTOR
David Glaze
WRITER
Len Vucci
DESIGNER
David Glaze
PHOTOGRAPHER
Jay Silverman
CLIENT
Suzuki of America
AGENCY
The Designory/ Long Beach, CA

525
ART DIRECTORS
Toni Bowerman
Tom Kaminsky
WRITER
Craig Walker
DESIGNER
Toni Bowerman
PHOTOGRAPHER
John Goodman
CLIENT
EASTPAK
AGENCY
ClarkeGowardFitts Design Group/Boston

526
ART DIRECTOR
Tom Kaminsky
WRITER
Craig Walker
DESIGNER
Tom Kaminsky
PHOTOGRAPHER
John Goodman
CLIENT
Great Island Trust
AGENCY
ClarkeGowardFitts Design Group/Boston

FIRST INTERSTATE AID KIT

FOR LOANS.

523

524

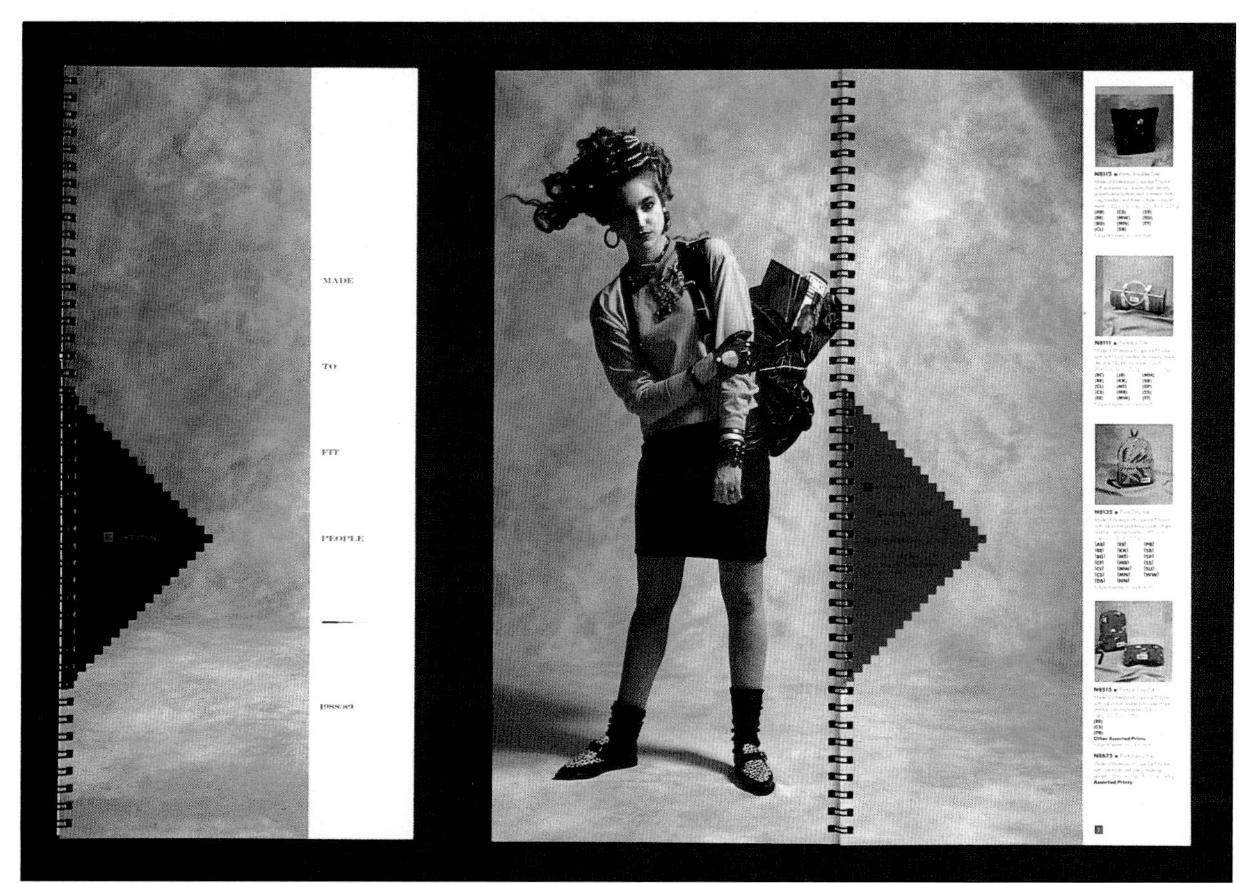

525

526

Collateral Brochures Other Than By Mail: Single

527

ART DIRECTOR
Paul Garrett

WRITER
Mike Doyle

PHOTOGRAPHERS
Keith McMillian
Mike Parsons

CLIENT
Garrett Doyle Fugler

AGENCY
Garrett Doyle Fugler/
London

528

ART DIRECTOR
Tom Kaminsky

WRITER
Craig Walker

DESIGNER
Tom Kaminsky

PHOTOGRAPHER
John Van-S

CLIENT
University of Massachusetts

AGENCY
ClarkeGowardFitts Design
Group/Boston

529

ART DIRECTOR
David Bartels

WRITERS
Cathy Mataloni
Donn Carstens

DESIGNERS
David Bartels
Chuck Hart

ARTISTS
Carter Goodrich
Mark Fredrickson
Everett Peck
Rick Meyerwitz
Greg Macnair
Cathy Bleck
Nick Backes
Scott Pollack
Bill Mayer
Jim Jacobs

CLIENT
Love Management Company

AGENCY
Bartels & Carstens/
St. Louis

530

ART DIRECTOR
Robert Saabye

WRITER
Ernie Schenck

DESIGNER
Bobert Saabye

ARTIST
Lenny Long

PHOTOGRAPHER
Myron

CLIENT
Rhode Island School of
Design

AGENCIES
Pagano Schenck & Kay/
Providence, RI
Leonard Monahan Saabye
Lubars/Providence, RI

527

528

529

There Have Been Times When Art Has Been Just A Little Hard To Swallow.

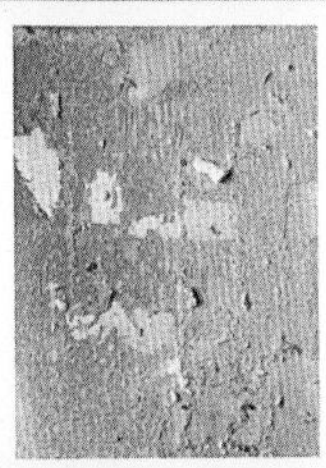

Tonight Isn't One Of Them.

There Have Been Times When Art Has Been Just A Little Hard To Swallow.

530

Collateral Brochures Other Than By Mail: Single

531
ART DIRECTORS
Jamie Mambro
Nancy Malacaria
WRITER
Tom Monahan
DESIGNER
Nancy Malacaria
CLIENT
Lotus Development Corporation
AGENCY
Leonard Monahan Saabye Lubars/Providence, RI

532
ART DIRECTOR
Paul Meehan
WRITER
Tim Crowther
DESIGNER
Paul Meehan
ARTIST
Michael Wing
PHOTOGRAPHER
Paul Torcello
CLIENT
Ansett Hotels & Resorts
AGENCY
Young & Rubicam/ Melbourne

533
ART DIRECTOR
Angela Dunkle
WRITER
Jamie Barrett
DESIGNER
Angela Dunkle
PHOTOGRAPHER
Rick Dublin
CLIENT
Marecek & Cairns
AGENCY
Fallon McElligott/ Minneapolis

534
ART DIRECTORS
Jerry Atnip
John Howard
WRITER
Nancy Bergen
DESIGNERS
Jerry Atnip
John Howard
ARTISTS
Stephanie Duke
Jeff Hatcher
PHOTOGRAPHER
Michael Rutherford
CLIENT
The Pakulis Collection
AGENCY
Steve Diggs & Friends/ Nashville

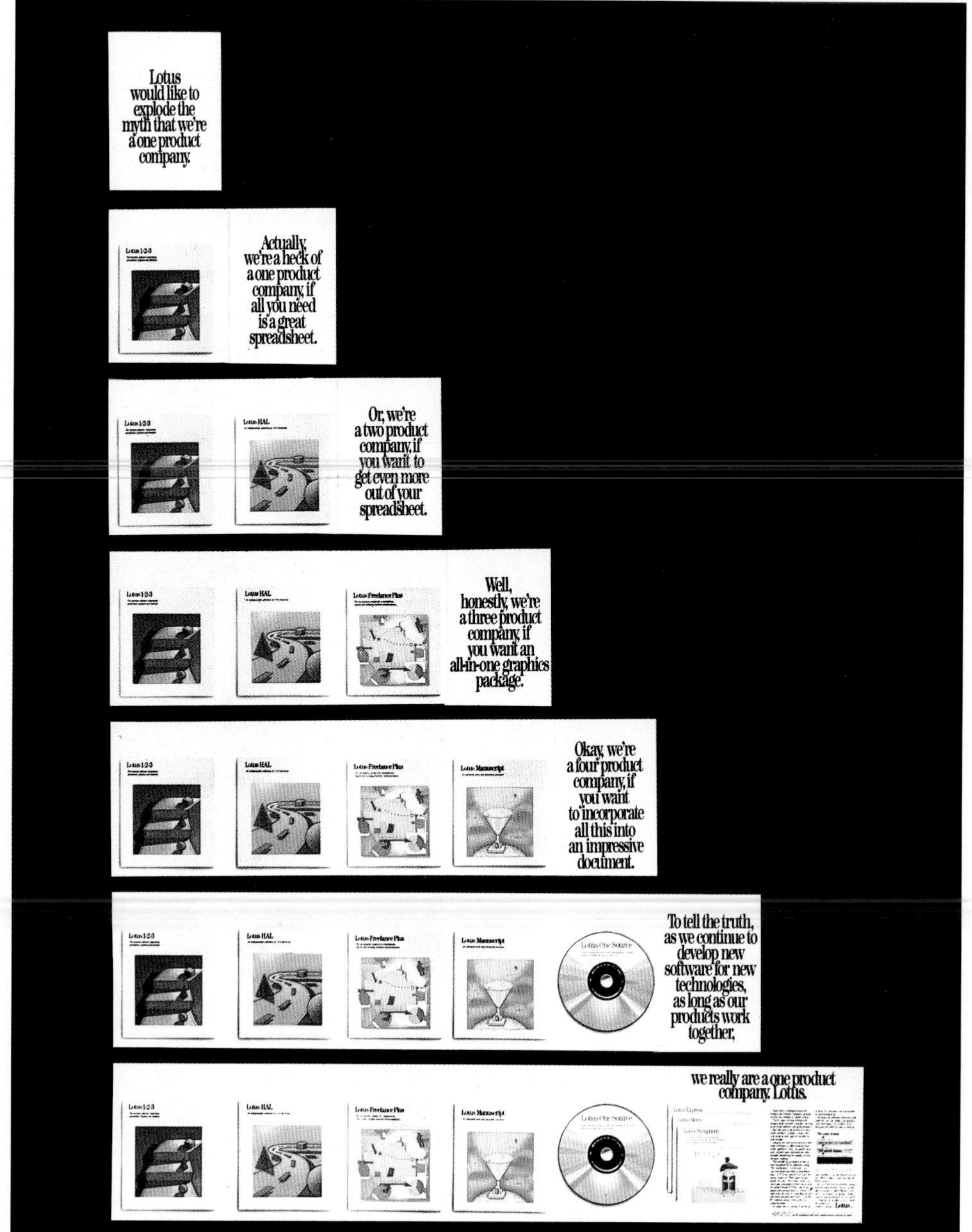

531

532

UNFORTUNATELY, THIS IS ABOUT AS CREATIVE
AS MOST MEETINGS GET.

533

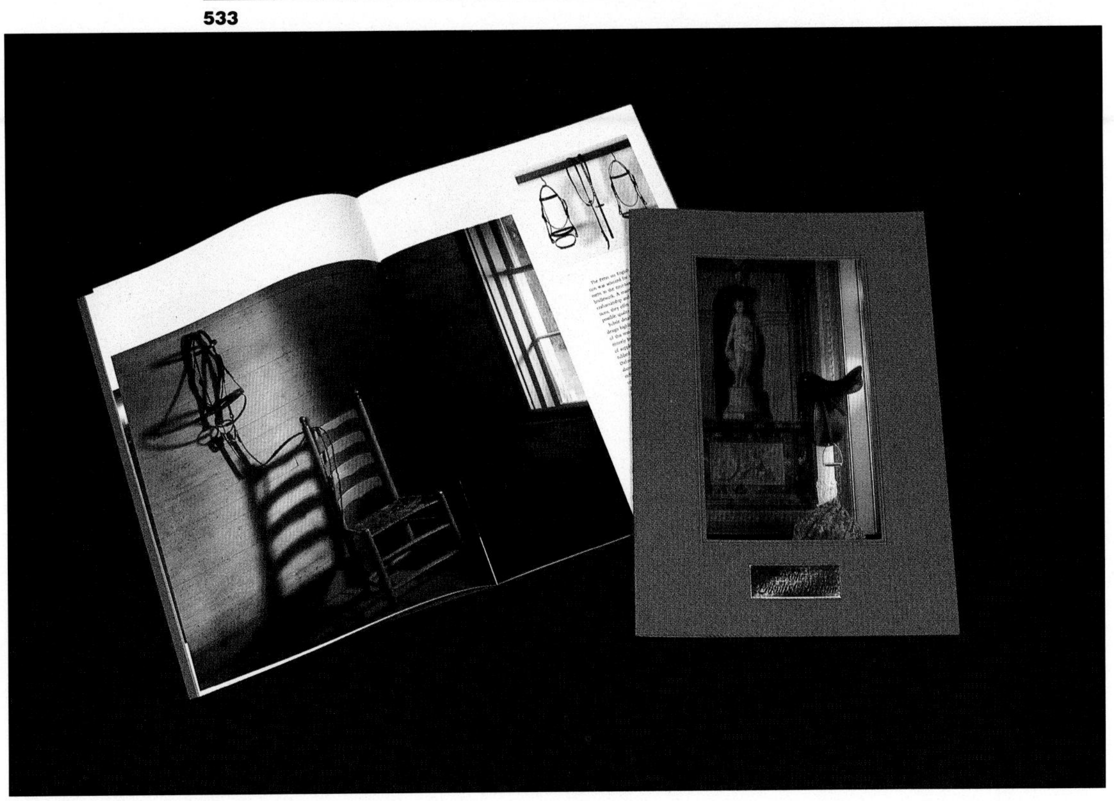

534

Collateral Sales Kits: Single

535
ART DIRECTOR
Wally Runnels
WRITER
Gail Whitkin
DESIGNER
Wally Runnels
ARTIST
Naomi Hata
CLIENT
New World Video
AGENCY
W.B. Doner & Company/
Los Angeles

536
ART DIRECTOR
Peter Rauch
WRITER
Tom Nathan
ARTIST
Leo Skidmore
PHOTOGRAPHERS
Jeffrey Zwart
Robert Ammirati
CLIENT
BMW of North America
AGENCY
Ammirati & Puris

537
ART DIRECTOR
S.A. Habib
WRITER
Roy Vaughn
DESIGNER
S.A. Habib
CLIENT
Gourmet Foods
Incorporated
AGENCY
Buntin Advertising/
Nashville

538
ART DIRECTOR
Laura Astuto
WRITER
David Kaminsky
CLIENT
Xerox
AGENCY
Lowe Marschalk

535

536

537

XEROX

This year some of America's most respected stars are helping us salute the Constitution.

To celebrate the bicentennial of the Constitution we've put together a promotion featuring nine of America's most historic flags.
Here's everything you'll need to help get our salute off the ground, including a chance to raise a flag of your own.

XEROX

To honor the Constitution we're all going to rally around the flag.

Come see what gave George Washington courage, Ben Franklin hope and Francis Scott Key goose bumps.

DONT TREAD ON ME

538

Collateral Sales Kits: Single

539

ART DIRECTORS
Beth Jeffe
Peter Rauch
Aki Seki

WRITERS
Tom Nathan
Ray Myers
David Corr
Bertrand Garbassi

ARTIST
Gerald Huerta

PHOTOGRAPHERS
Jeffrey Zwart
Jerry Cailor
Robert Ammirati

CLIENT
BMW of North America

AGENCY
Ammirati & Puris

540

ART DIRECTOR
Frank Schulwolf

WRITER
Arthur Low

ARTISTS
John Alcorn
James Dietz
Ted Lodigensky
Paul Salmon

CLIENT
Ryder System Aviation
Leasing & Services

AGENCY
Susan Gilbert & Company/
Coral Gables, FL

541

ART DIRECTOR
Angela Dunkle

WRITER
Jamie Barrett

DESIGNER
Angela Dunkle

CLIENT
The Wall Street Journal

AGENCY
Fallon McElligott/
Minneapolis

542

ART DIRECTORS
Rob French
Gary Creek

WRITER
Gary Creek

DESIGNER
Rob French

CLIENT
Cable Alabama Corporation

AGENCY
Totalcom/
Tuscaloosa, AL

539

540

All the things a business traveler needs rolled into one.
Successful businesspeople know that information is power. That's why more than four million of them read The Wall Street Journal. And why they prefer hotels that provide it. To find out how your hotel can offer The Journal, write to: Allen Simeone, Director of Circulation Sales, Dow Jones & Company, Incorporated, Princeton, New Jersey, 08540.
The Wall Street Journal Amenities Program.
THE WALL STREET JOURNAL.
Personal Reasons

541

CABLE ALABAMA & TOTALCOM COULD ELIMINATE THE ENTIRE RABBIT POPULATION IN THE HUNTSVILLE AREA.
ONE DOWN...
For Fine Tuned Advertising That Will Receive The Best Reception In Town, Call Totalcom·883-7363.

542

Collateral Sales Kits: Single

543
ART DIRECTOR
Laurel Emery
WRITER
Lesley Teitelbaum
ARTIST
Jacqui Morgan
PHOTOGRAPHERS
Hans Nelleman
David Massey
Beth Galton
Peter Simon
Jan Staller
CLIENT
High Street Development
AGENCY
Great Scott Advertising

Collateral Direct Mail: Single

544
ART DIRECTOR
Andy Lawson
WRITER
Andy Niccol
CLIENT
BBDO
AGENCY
BBDO/London

545
ART DIRECTOR
Nesta David
WRITER
Kit McKrackin
DESIGNER
Nesta David
PHOTOGRAPHER
Arthur Elgort
CLIENT
Christian Dior
AGENCY
Bel-Aire Associates

546
ART DIRECTOR
Susan Butterworth Clark
WRITER
Claudia Caplan
PHOTOGRAPHER
Dan Wolfe
CLIENT
Kevin & Susan Clark
AGENCY
Dailey & Associates/
Los Angeles

543

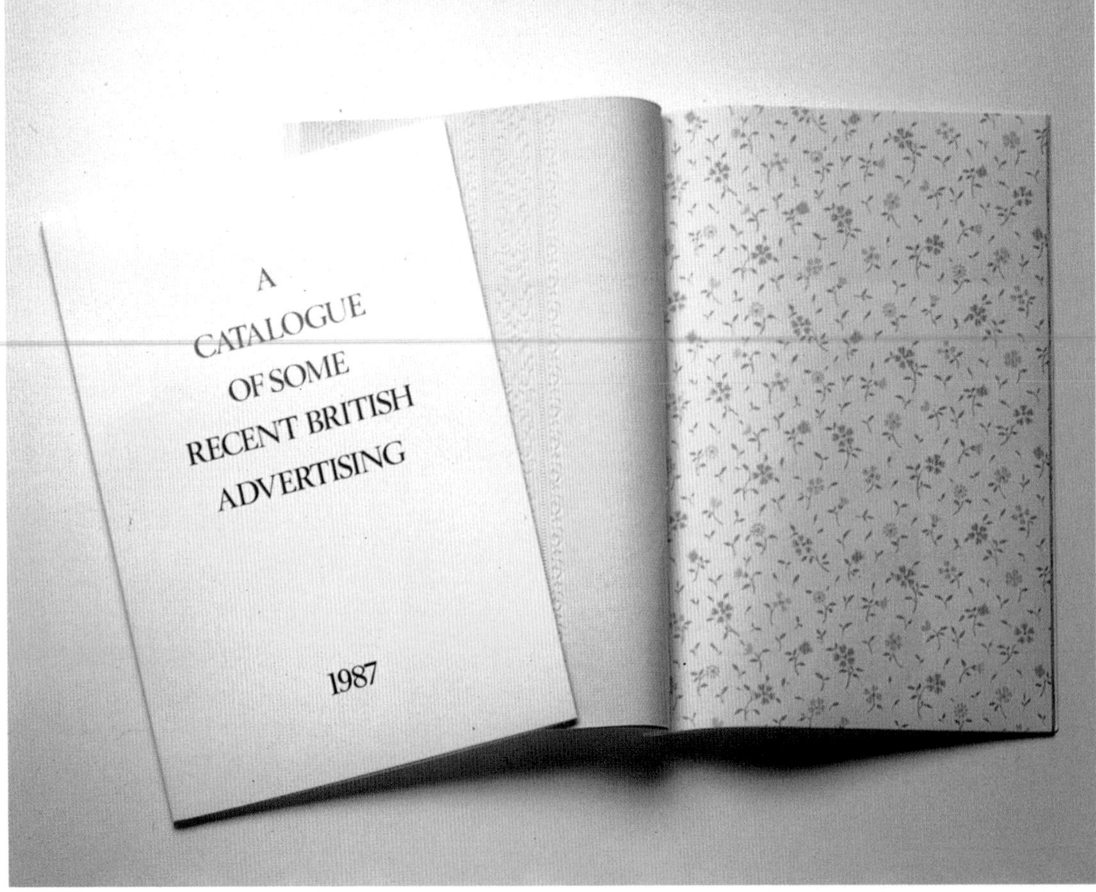

544

40e
Christian Dior
Dior is 40, a grand and glorious 40. From that first momentous
after new look has succeeded . . . today, the Dior image is present everywhere.
corner of fashion, beauty and lifestyle remains unshaped by the legacy, a transcendent vision
of luxury and style that "gives Dior designs their greatest triumph, that of superbly belonging
to their time." Time and time again.
To you who've recognized, who've bought and believed: a grateful acknowledgment, and a future
together as extraordinary as the past.
Colombe M. Nicholas
President
Christian Dior-New York

545

CLARK
CLARK
INTRODUCING
TWO SWEET LITTLE
CLARKS.
WITH NUTS.
Daniel Alan Clark
Born: December 1, 1987
3:26 pm
7 lbs. 1 oz.
19¾ inches
Brian Russell Clark
Born: December 1, 1987
3:41 pm
6 lbs. 11 ozs.
19 inches

546

Collateral Direct Mail: Single

547

ART DIRECTOR
Angelo Juliano

WRITER
Angelo Juliano

DESIGNER
Angelo Juliano

ARTIST
Baby Peyton Lester

CLIENT
Corinne & Matt Lester

AGENCY
Angelo Juliano

548

ART DIRECTOR
Robin Chrumka

WRITER
Mike Stocker

PHOTOGRAPHER
Kathaleen Martin

CLIENT
Health Alliance Plan

AGENCY
J. Walter Thompson/
Detroit

549

ART DIRECTOR
Charles Hively

WRITER
Charles Hively

DESIGNER
Charles Hively

CLIENT
The Hively Agency

AGENCY
The Hively Agency/
Houston

550

ART DIRECTOR
Dave Shelton

WRITER
Liz Whiston

DESIGNER
John Gorman

ARTISTS
Brian Grimwood
Bush Hollyhead
Paul Leith
Ian Pollock

CLIENT
HDM Horner Collis &
Kirvan

AGENCY
HDM Horner Collis &
Kirvan/London

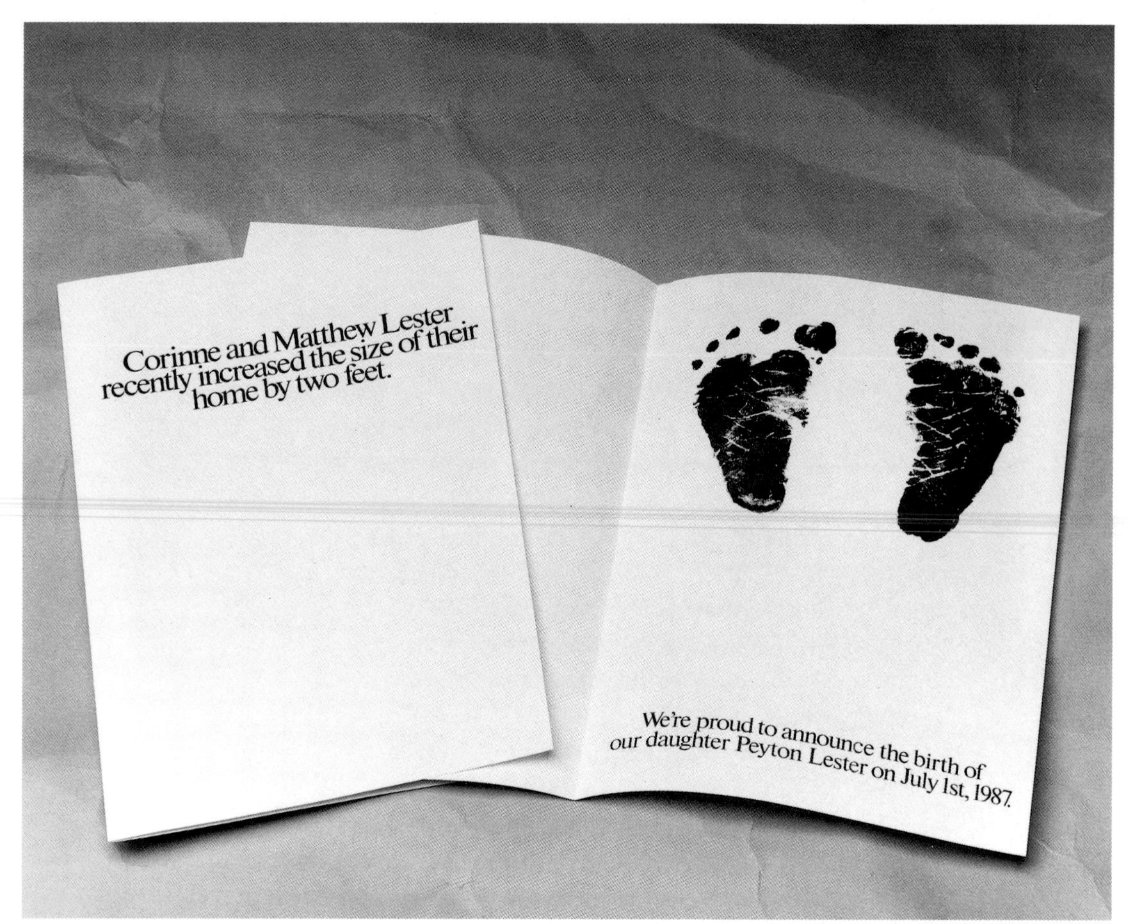

547

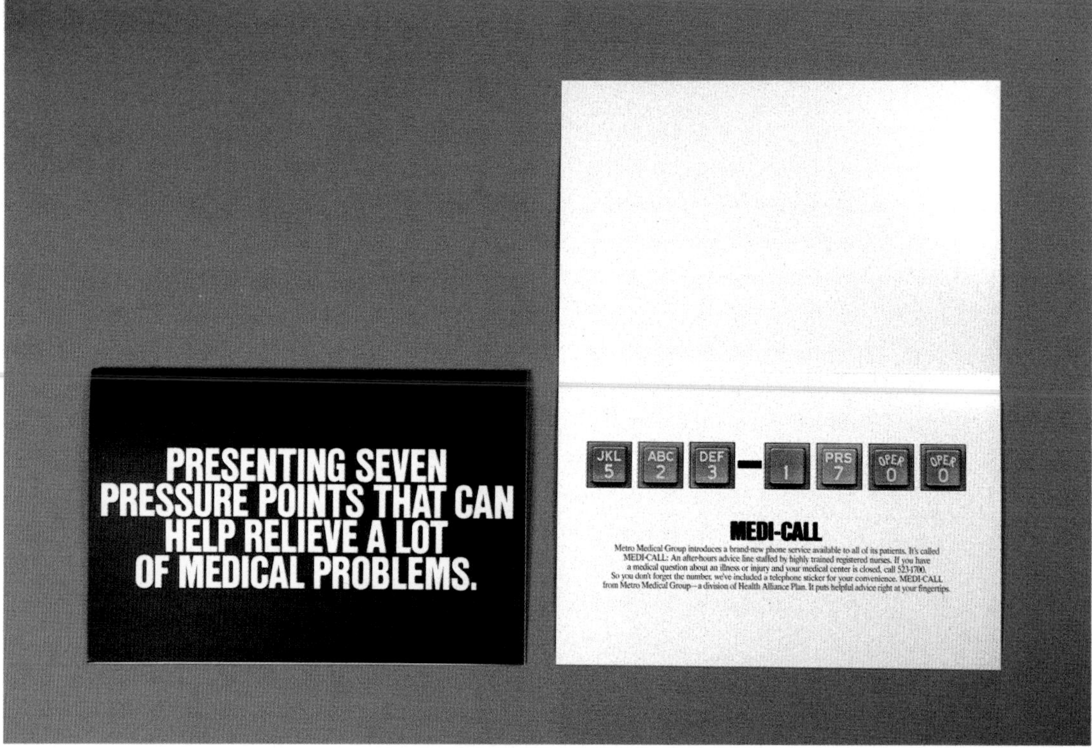

548

549

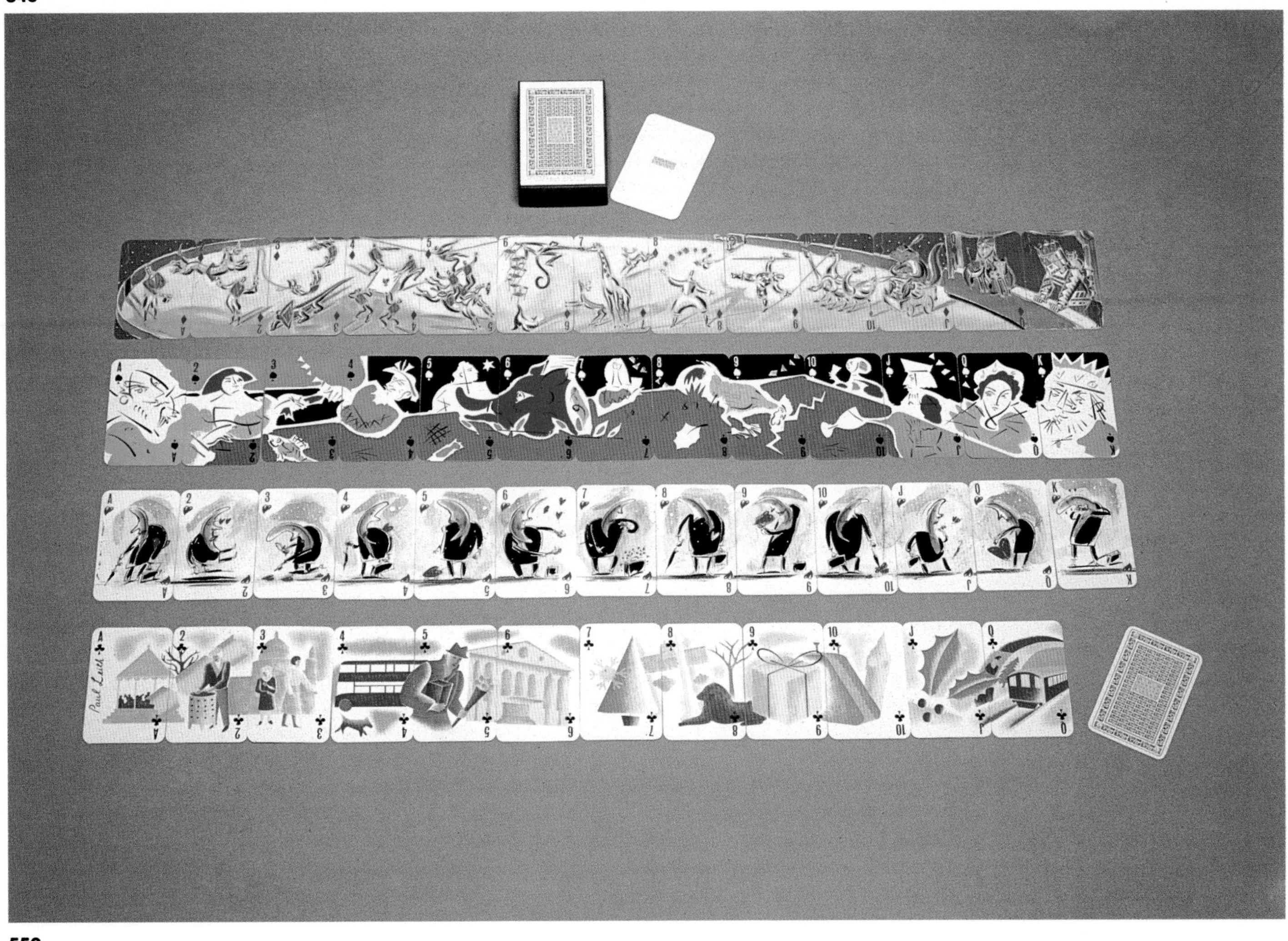

550

Collateral Direct Mail: Single

551
ART DIRECTOR
Dan Silverstone
WRITER
James Overall
PHOTOGRAPHERS
Walter Wick
Dick Frank
CLIENT
Glenmore Distilleries
AGENCY
Grybauskas & Partners

552
ART DIRECTOR
Tom Lichtenheld
WRITER
Rod Kilpatrick
CLIENT
Rod Kilpatrick
AGENCY
Fallon McElligott/
Minneapolis

553
ART DIRECTOR
Beth Werther
WRITER
Richard Johnson
DESIGNER
Beth Werther
ARTIST
Henry Mangrum
CLIENT
Creative Forum
AGENCY
A. Richard Johnson/
Nashville

554
ART DIRECTOR
Robert Saabye
WRITER
Tom Monahan
DESIGNER
Sharon Collins
CLIENT
Leonard Monahan Saabye
Lubars
AGENCY
Leonard Monahan Saabye
Lubars/Providence, RI

551

552

LETTERS FROM TOM

553

IN THE PAST NINE MONTHS LMS HAS SURVIVED A TORNADO, A FIRE AND A FLOOD.
NOW WE FACE THE GREATEST THREAT TO AN AD AGENCY'S WELL-BEING.
August 7, 1986: A rare Rhode Island tornado claims a 12-foot arched window, a company car and a lot of frayed nerves.
October 16, 1986: A five-alarm fire next door puts us out of commission for 36 hours.
February 2, 1987: 16 inches of water in the basement knocks out phones, heat and electricity for who knows how long? (Clocks were down, too.)
After what we've been through most companies would consider human sacrifice. But it takes a lot more than an act of God (or two, or three) to dampen this ad agency's spirits. Besides the real threat to our future success makes these little setbacks seem like child's play.
You see, what should really have us scared out of our wits is our g-r-o-w-t-h.
Yes, the G-word. It's taken many a small, vital, agile, young advertising agency and overnight turned it into, horrors, the worst of all agency fates, . . . a mid-sized company, safe, boring and content.
You see, in the agency business, as the stakes get higher, the quality of the creative often gets lower. It's sort of a law of nature.
Leonard Monahan Saabye is a company that truly values the quality of its work. And so do our clients. We're known throughout the country for our creative. We've got some of the brightest people north of the east river. And we've got an account list any Mad. Ave. agency would envy.
Now we're in a wonderful period of growth. Not simply in terms of size, but in terms of the sophistication level of our clients, our people and our work.
So here comes the true test. Can we maintain the quality that has helped us come this far? On April 7th at the monthly NEBA breakfast meeting we'll answer that and other crucial questions about how we plan to handle our growth. And believe us, we've got all the necessary elements in place to address this threat head on. You know, life rafts, fire extinguishers, values, those kind of things.
The meeting will be held in the Belvidere Room of the Back Bay Hilton, Tuesday April 7th at 8:15 am. Tickets are $18 for members, $20 for guests, a reserved table for ten is $180. Call NEBA for reservations and information 617-426-3575.
GROWTH.

554

Collateral Direct Mail: Single

555
ART DIRECTOR
Michael Fazende
WRITER
Jarl Olsen
CLIENT
University of Minnesota
AGENCY
Fallon McElligott/
Minneapolis

556
ART DIRECTOR
John Vitro
WRITER
John Robertson
CLIENT
Marshall Harrington
Photography
AGENCY
Vitro Robertson/
San Diego, CA

557
ART DIRECTORS
Lloyd Wolfe
Mark Arnold
WRITER
Chris Wigert
CLIENT
Lawler Ballard Advertising
AGENCY
Lawler Ballard/
Cincinnati, OH

558
ART DIRECTOR
Larry Jarvis
WRITER
Glen Wachowiak
PHOTOGRAPHER
Eric Saulitis
CLIENT
Ad Career Day
AGENCY
Bozell Jacobs Kenyon &
Eckhardt/Minneapolis

It wasn't easy to reach the brain of an athlete on steroids.

(actual size)

555

556

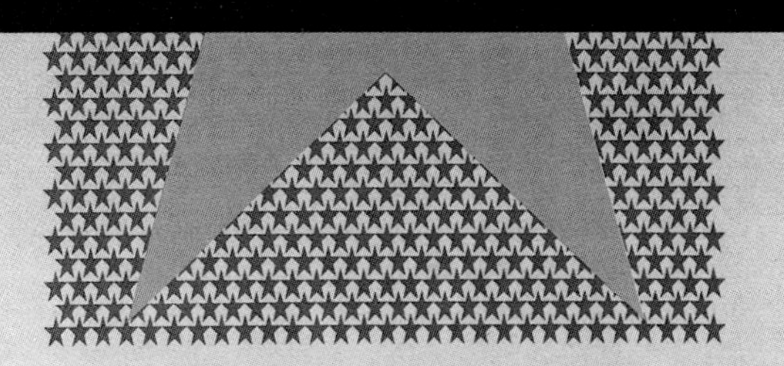

CELEBRATION·OF·EXCELLENCE
HOW·SWEET·IT·IS
We're Sending You This Book Because There's A Very Good Chance Your Ad Agency Won't.
This year, Lawler Ballard once again dominated the Cincinnati Ad Show. That's not unusual for us. But what's amazing is that all of our clients were winners. Each and every one of them. Because we believe that better advertising gets better results. If you believe your advertising should be getting better results, give Gene Taylor a call at (513) 381-7500.
Stars of Advertising
1986 Addy Awards
Showbook

557

OGILVY
ON
ADVER-
TISING
Unfortunately, you can't ask it a question.
Advertising Career Day '87

558

Collateral Direct Mail: Single

559

ART DIRECTORS
Craig Tanimoto
Jeff Terwilliger

WRITER
Craig McNamara

CLIENT
Highland Park High School

AGENCY
Bozell Jacobs Kenyon & Eckhardt/Minneapolis

560

ART DIRECTOR
John Vitro

WRITER
John Robertson

CLIENT
Baby Max Vitro

AGENCY
Vitro Robertson/ San Diego, CA

561

ART DIRECTOR
Rod Smith

WRITER
Fred Bertino

DESIGNER
Rod Smith

PHOTOGRAPHER
Rod Smith

CLIENT
Fred Bertino

AGENCY
Smith Bertino/Boston

562

ART DIRECTOR
Yvonne Smith

WRITER
Yvonne Smith

DESIGNER
Yvonne Smith

ARTIST
Gina Norton

CLIENT
Joe, Laurie & Giuliano Pizzulo

AGENCY
Brandalise/Smith - Malibu, CA

INFERIORITY COMPLEXES, PEER GROUP PRESSURE, AND SEXUAL ANXIETY.

Relive all the fun of high school at our class reunion.

HIGHLAND PARK CLASS OF 1977

September 26, 8 pm at Landmark Center in St. Paul

559

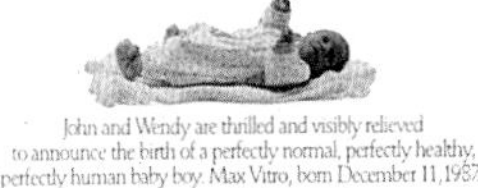

John and Wendy are thrilled and visibly relieved to announce the birth of a perfectly normal, perfectly healthy, perfectly human baby boy. Max Vitro, born December 11, 1987. Seven pounds, two ounces.

560

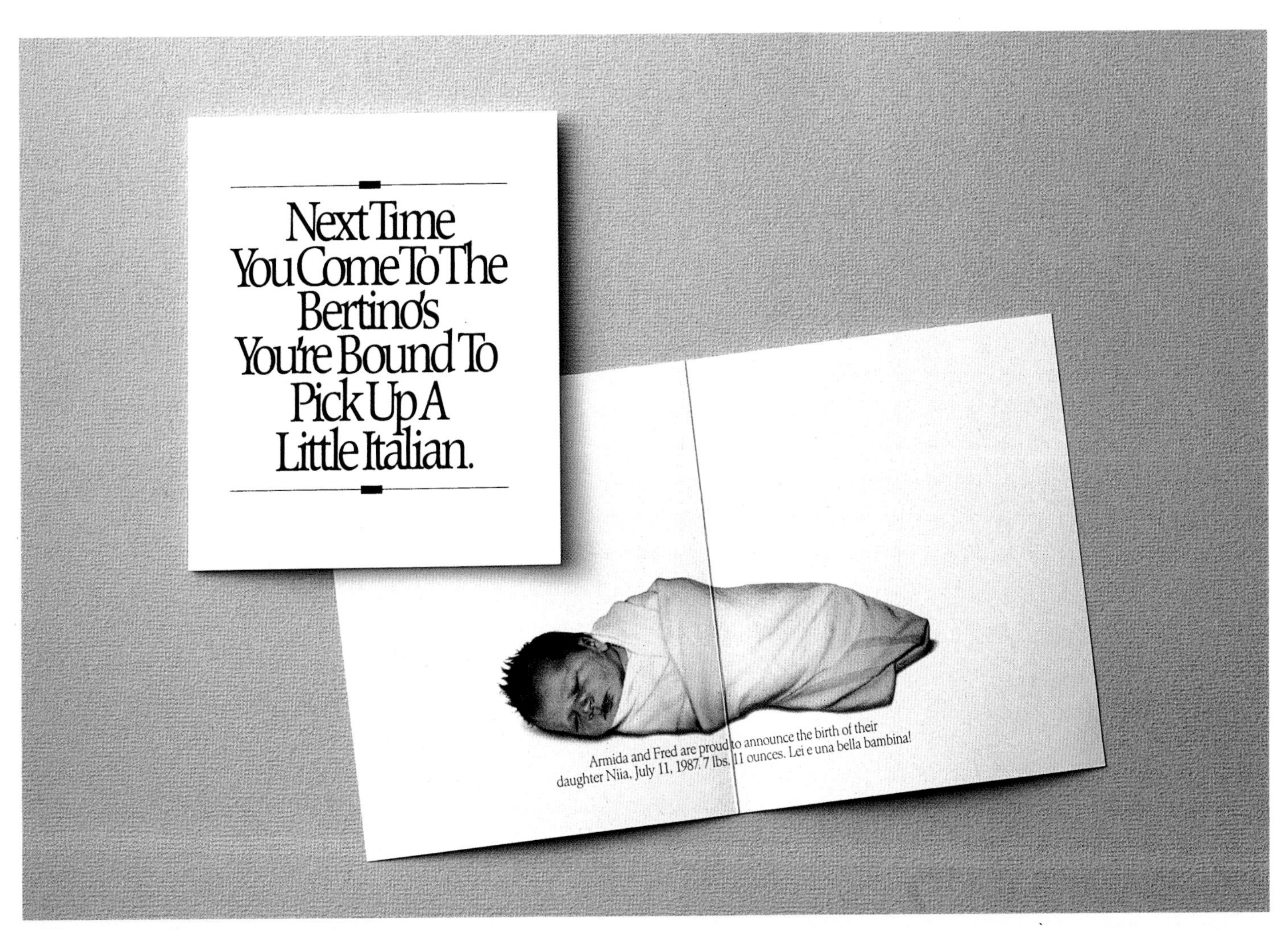

Next Time You Come To The Bertino's You're Bound To Pick Up A Little Italian.
Armida and Fred are proud to announce the birth of their daughter Niia, July 11, 1987. 7 lbs. 11 ounces. Lei e una bella bambina!

561

WARNING: SEXUALLY EXPLICIT MATERIAL ENCLOSED.

IT'S A BOY.

Name: Giuliano Joseph Pizzulo
Parents: Laurie Brandalise Pizzulo and Joseph Pizzulo
Born: March 9, 1987 at 10:09 pm
Weight: 7 pounds, 4 ounces
Length: 20," exactly.

562

Collateral Direct Mail: Single

563

ART DIRECTORS
Terry Schneider
Larry Frey
Warren Eakins

WRITER
Pamela Sullivan

CLIENT
Creative Quarterly

AGENCY
Backwater Advertising/
Portland, OR

564

ART DIRECTOR
Warren Eakins

WRITER
Dave Newman

CLIENT
Borders Perrin &
Norrander

AGENCY
Borders Perrin &
Norrander/Portland, OR

565

ART DIRECTOR
Cabell Harris

WRITER
Ken Hines

PHOTOGRAPHER
IBID

CLIENT
Rib Championship

AGENCY
Lawler Ballard/
Richmond, VA

566

ART DIRECTORS
Carolyn Tye
Mark Fuller
Danny Boone

WRITER
Curlin Reed

CLIENT
Curlin Reed

AGENCY
Ford & Westbrook/
Richmond, VA

563

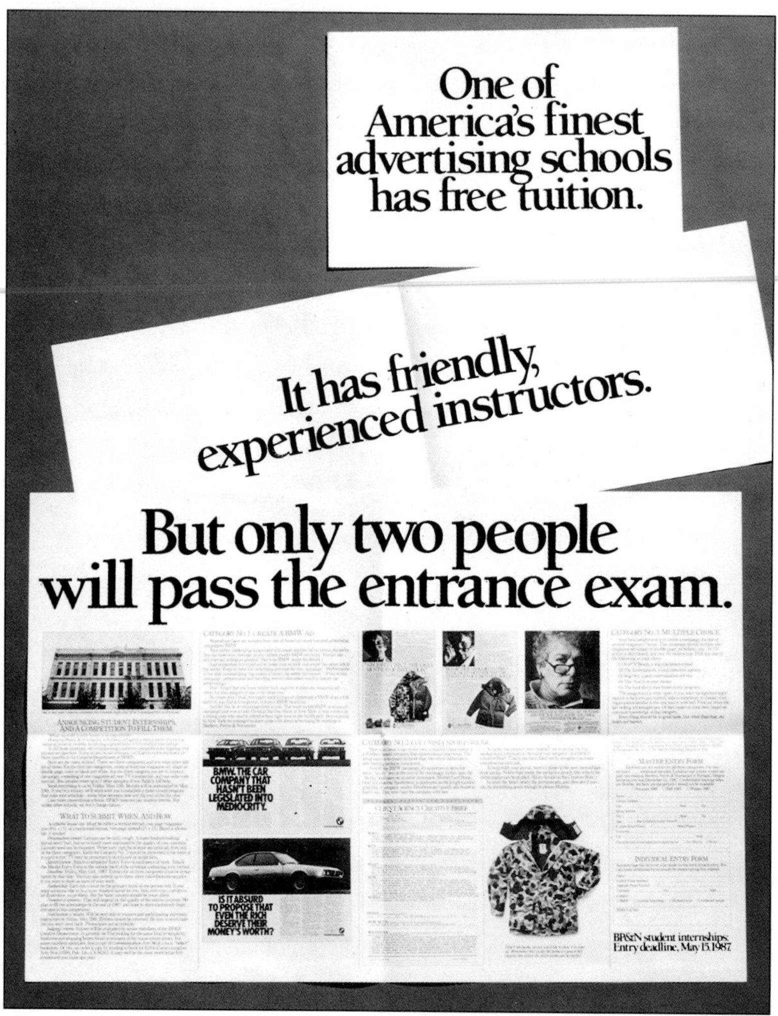

564

CONTESTANTS ARE ALREADY LINING UP FOR THIS YEAR'S WORLD RIB CHAMPIONSHIP.

Last year Tom Ferguson of Giovanni's in Berwyn, Illinois took home $10,000 in prize money. Runners-up walked away with over $3,000. All they had to do was cook up the best tasting ribs in the Richmond World Invitational Rib Championship. This year's championship will be July 16-19. We'll have more prize money, more excitement and more media attention. Watch for your entry form in the mail. And don't let somebody else hog all the glory.

Richmond World Invitational Rib Championship

Box 8596, Richmond, VA 23226

565

THE DAY MY AGENCY FOUND OUT I'D GOTTEN MY FIRST PIECE IN CA, THEY FIRED ME.

It's the nature of this business. You hear about agencies having to make cutbacks every day. Even on the best of days. So you have to take the good with the bad. And keep going. My portfolio will tell you a lot about my writing. Bill Westbrook, my creative director, said he'd be glad to tell you a lot about me.

I've had three years of agency experience. But I consider this last year working with Ford & Westbrook my best one. Happily, so did the judges at CA.

If you'd like to judge for yourself, I'd love the chance to show you my book. Or I can send you some samples. To reach me, call (804) 783-9000 or (804) 355-6260 in Richmond, Virginia. Ask for Curlin Reed. Copywriter.

566

Collateral Direct Mail: Single

567

ART DIRECTORS
Don Perkins
Connie Blum

WRITERS
Jim Clemon
Don Perkins

CLIENT
Mutual of Omaha

AGENCY
Bozell Jacobs Kenyon & Eckhardt/Omaha, NE

568

ART DIRECTOR
John Vitro

WRITER
John Robertson

PHOTOGRAPHER
David Kramer

CLIENT
David Kramer Photography

AGENCY
Vitro Robertson/
San Diego, CA

569

ART DIRECTOR
Beth Meeks Hansen

WRITER
Greg Beaupre

CLIENT
The Como Zoo

AGENCY
McCool & Company/
Minneapolis

570

ART DIRECTOR
Kevin Grimsdale

WRITER
John Mahoney

CLIENT
The Martin Agency

AGENCY
The Martin Agency/
Richmond, VA

567

568

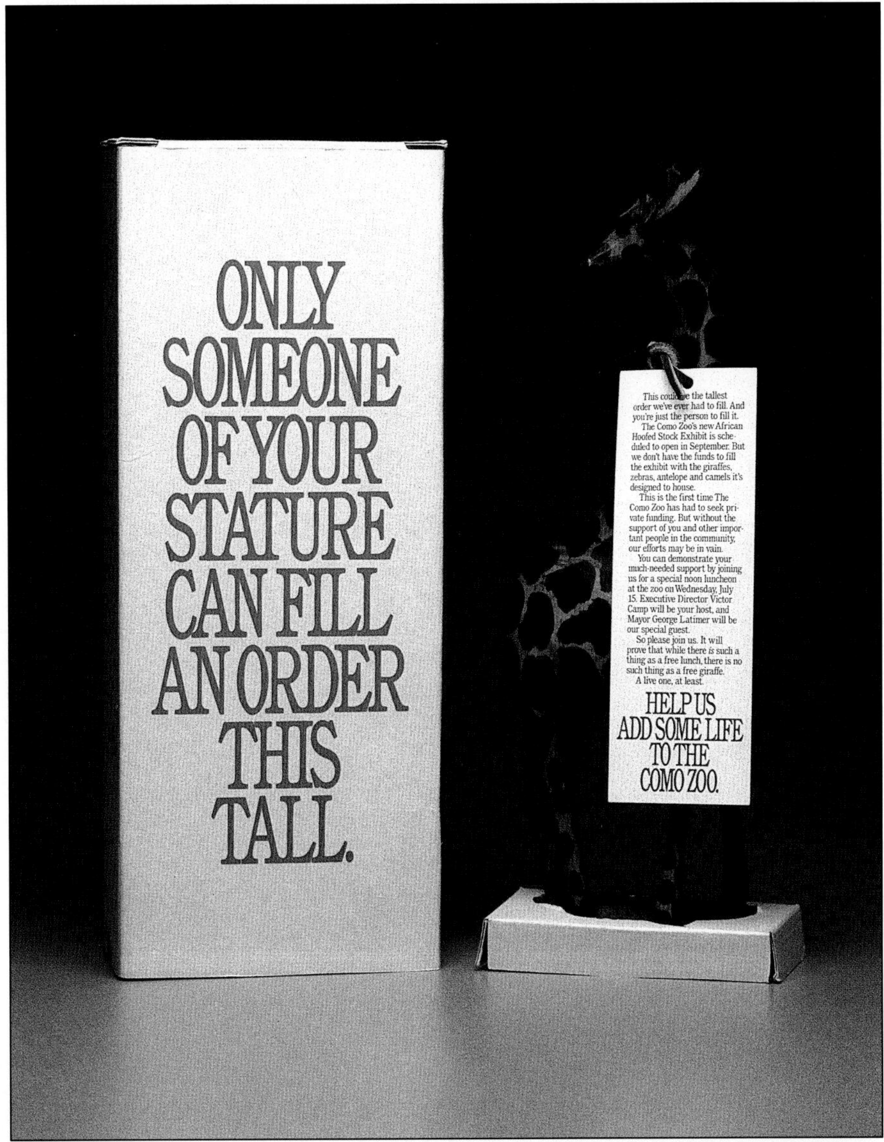
ONLY
SOMEONE
OF YOUR
STATURE
CAN FILL
AN ORDER
THIS
TALL.
This coul e the tallest order we've ever had to fill. And you're just the person to fill it.
The Como Zoo's new African Hoofed Stock Exhibit is scheduled to open in September. But we don't have the funds to fill the exhibit with the giraffes, zebras, antelope and camels it's designed to house.
This is the first time The Como Zoo has had to seek private funding. But without the support of you and other important people in the community, our efforts may be in vain.
You can demonstrate your much-needed support by joining us for a special noon luncheon at the zoo on Wednesday, July 15. Executive Director Victor Camp will be your host, and Mayor George Latimer will be our special guest.
So please join us. It will prove that while there is such a thing as a free lunch, there is no such thing as a free giraffe.
A live one, at least.
HELP US
ADD SOME LIFE
TO THE
COMO ZOO.

569

We'd like to leave you with
one last thought on choosing
a giant New York agency.
Large, lumbering New York agencies once ruled the earth. But times have changed.
The present and the future belong to advertising agencies that can not only react fast to
fast-changing markets, but more importantly, anticipate them. An agency like us. To our
mind, we think choosing The Martin Agency is just another case of natural selection.

570

Collateral Direct Mail: Single

571
ART DIRECTOR
Sharon Brady
WRITERS
Tom Cunniff
Greg Jordan
DESIGNER
Sharon Brady
PHOTOGRAPHER
Mark Atkinson
CLIENT
Greg & Laurie Jordan
AGENCY
Barker Campbell & Farley/Virginia Beach, VA

572
ART DIRECTOR
Debbie Lucke
WRITER
Tom Page
DESIGNER
Kathy Bochert
CLIENT
NEC
AGENCY
Ingalls Quinn and Johnson/Boston

573
ART DIRECTOR
Andy Lawson
WRITER
Andrew Niccol
CLIENT
Pepsi Cola
AGENCY
BBDO/London

574
ART DIRECTOR
Frank Schulwolf
WRITER
Arthur Low
ARTISTS
John Alcorn
James Dietz
Ted Lodigensky
Paul Salmon
CLIENT
Ryder System Aviation Leasing & Services
AGENCY
Susan Gilbert & Company/Coral Gables, FL

571

572

IF YOU'RE
NOT SELLING
THE ONLY
DIET COLA
WITH 100%
NUTRASWEET,
WHAT ARE
YOU
SELLING?
diet
Joke
NUTRASWEET BLEND

573

THE
Boche

574

Collateral Direct Mail: Single

575
ART DIRECTOR
Ryle Smith
WRITER
Jim Clemon
PHOTOGRAPHER
Robert Ervin
CLIENT
First National Bank of Omaha
AGENCY
Bozell Jacobs Kenyon & Eckhardt/Omaha, NE

576
ART DIRECTORS
Lynda Decker
Marvin Fried
WRITERS
Carolyn Crimmins
Judy Hultquist
DESIGNER
Lynda Decker
CLIENT
Mercedes-Benz
AGENCY
McCaffrey McCall Direct Marketing

577
ART DIRECTOR
Frank Schulwolf
WRITER
Arthur Low
ARTISTS
John Mattos
Paul Salmon
Ted Lodigensky
PHOTOGRAPHER
George Schiavone
CLIENT
Ryder System Aviation Leasing & Services
AGENCY
Susan Gilbert & Company/Coral Gables, FL

578
ART DIRECTORS
Wally Runnels
Alan Lawrence
WRITER
Michael Albright
DESIGNER
Wally Runnels
ARTIST
Naomi Hata
CLIENT
W.B. Doner & Company
AGENCY
W.B. Doner & Company/Los Angeles

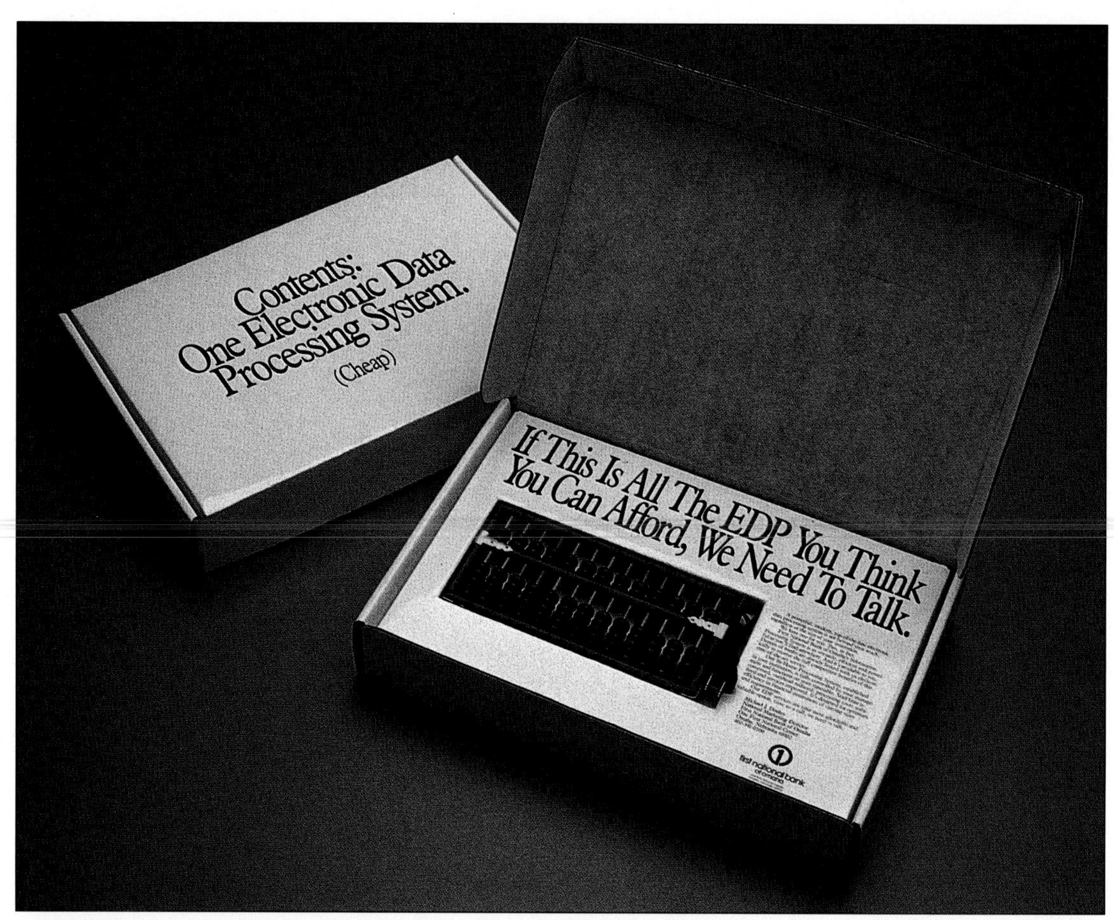

575

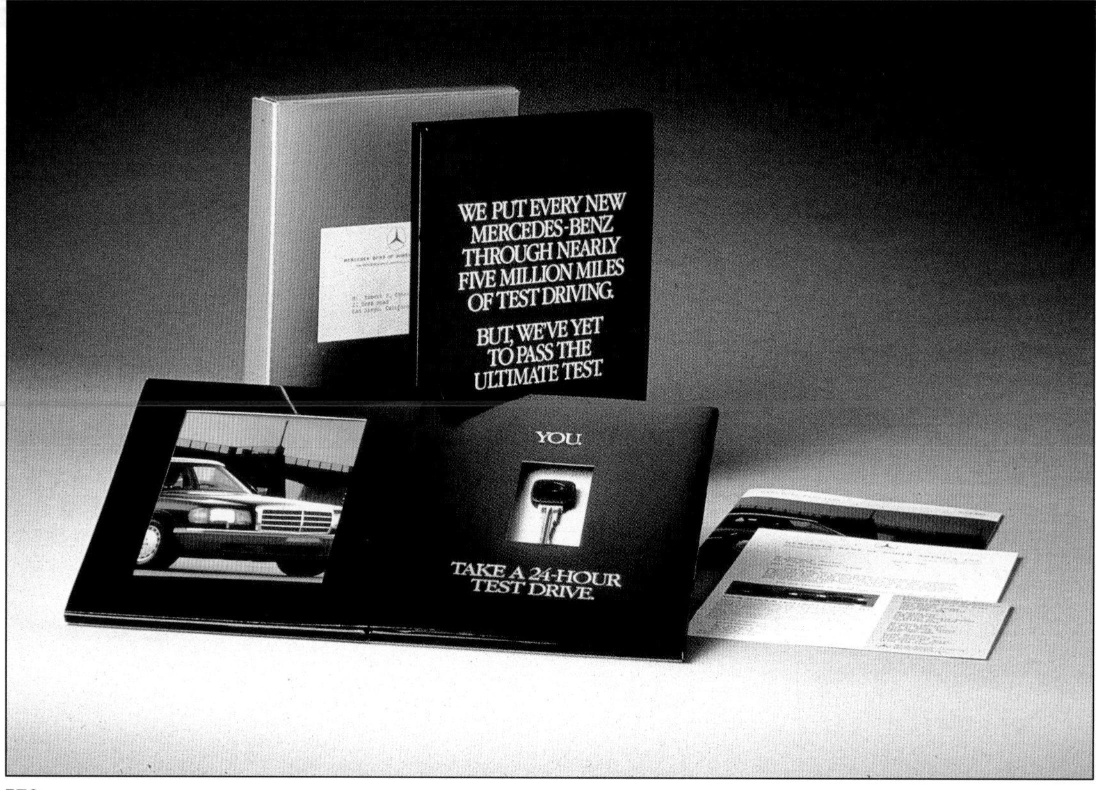

576

FRENCHY

577

ON JANUARY 15TH,
WEXLER & SHALEK
OFFICIALLY
BECAME
W.B. DONER & CO.
TIME TO BREAK
OPEN THE BOTTLE.
LIQUID PAPER
POUR IT ON.
Wexler & Shalek has a
new name and address.
ON JANUARY 15TH,
WEXLER & SHALEK
OFFICIALLY
BECAME
W.B. DONER & CO.
TIME TO BREAK
OPEN THE BOTTLE.

578

Collateral Direct Mail: Campaign

579
ART DIRECTOR
Coby Neill
WRITER
Todd Tilford
CLIENT
Don Huntington
AGENCY
Valentine-Radford/
Kansas City, MO

Collateral P.O.P.

580
ART DIRECTOR
Rick Paynter
WRITER
Gary Watson
DESIGNER
Rick Paynter
PHOTOGRAPHER
David Langley
CLIENT
Quadtree
AGENCY
Poppe Tyson/
Morris Plains, NJ

581
ART DIRECTOR
Ron Sandilands
WRITER
Bernie Hafeli
CLIENT
First Interstate Bank
AGENCY
Livingston & Company/
Seattle

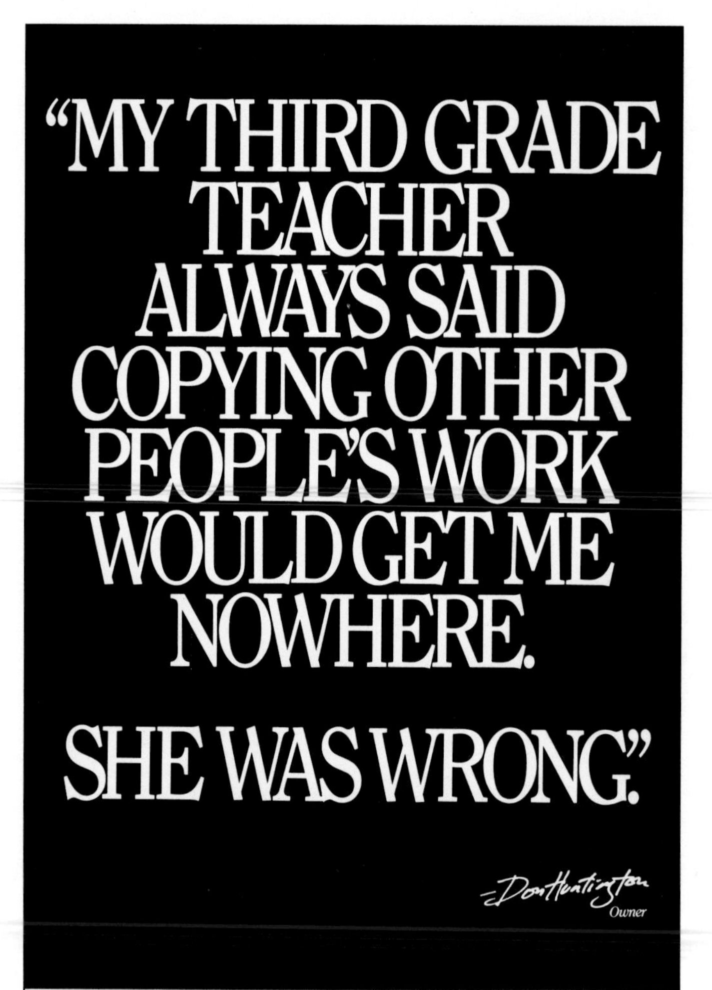
"MY THIRD GRADE TEACHER ALWAYS SAID COPYING OTHER PEOPLE'S WORK WOULD GET ME NOWHERE.
SHE WAS WRONG."
Owner
Crisp copies. Color and black-and-white printing. Uncompromising service.
KWIK-KOPY PRINTING
11212 W. 75th Street
Shawnee, KS. 268-8877

"NOT MANY PEOPLE CAN MAKE A LIVING COPYING OTHER PEOPLE'S WORK."

Crisp copies. Color and black-and-white printing. Uncompromising service.

KWIK-KOPY PRINTING
11212 W. 75th Street
Shawnee, KS. 268-8877

"OUR SERVICE IS ONE THING OUR COMPETITORS CAN'T DUPLICATE."

Crisp copies. Color and black-and-white printing. Uncompromising service.

KWIK-KOPY PRINTING
11212 W. 75th Street
Shawnee, KS. 268-8877

Which Model Porsche Is The Model?
Quadtree Simulation So Accurate, You Can't Tell The Difference.

580

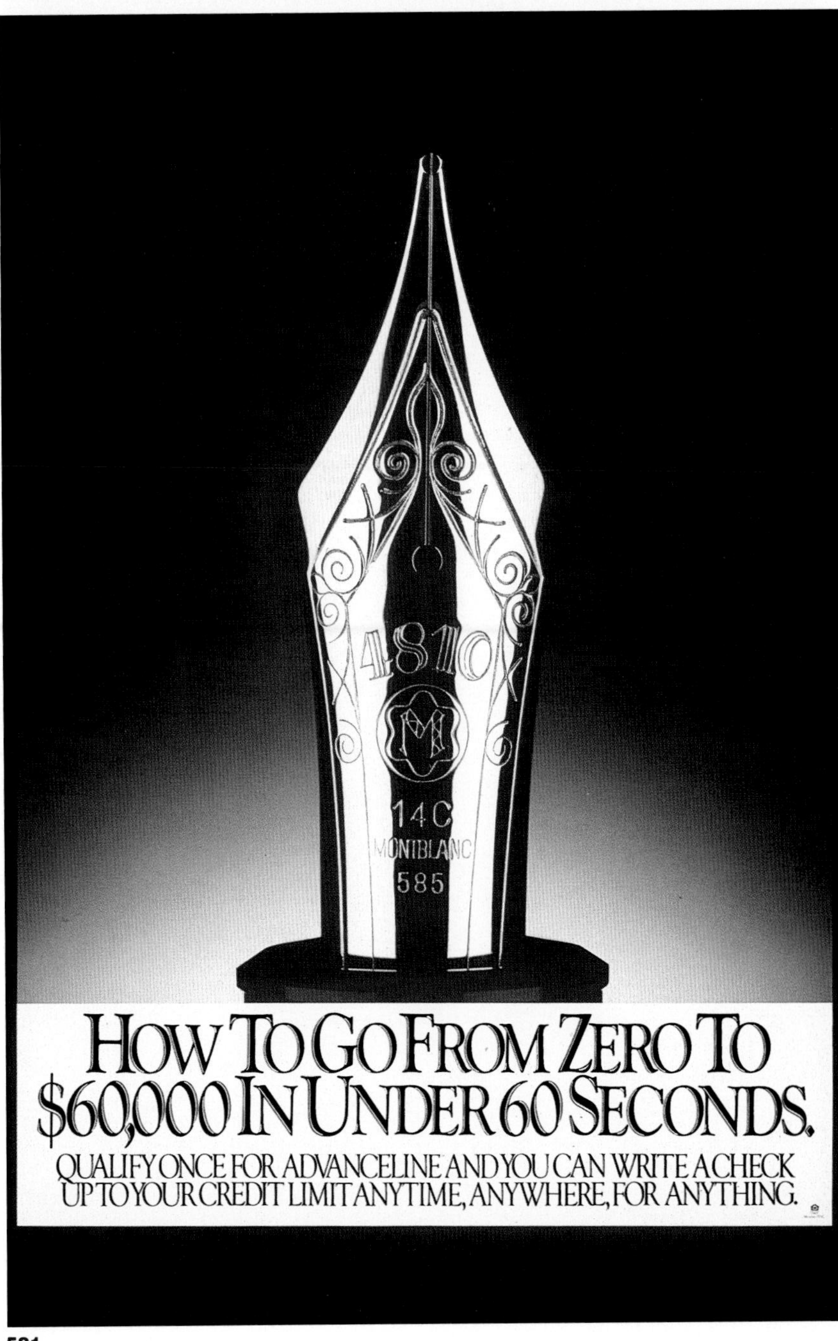
14C
MONTBLANC
585
HOW TO GO FROM ZERO TO $60,000 IN UNDER 60 SECONDS.
QUALIFY ONCE FOR ADVANCELINE AND YOU CAN WRITE A CHECK UP TO YOUR CREDIT LIMIT ANYTIME, ANYWHERE, FOR ANYTHING.

581

Collateral P.O.P.

582
ART DIRECTOR
Jim Condit
WRITER
Bob Morrison
PHOTOGRAPHER
Peter Vaeth
CLIENT
Home Lines Cruises
AGENCY
Cole Henderson Drake/Atlanta

583
ART DIRECTOR
Don DeFilippo
WRITER
John Porter
ARTIST
Art Simons
PHOTOGRAPHER
Joe Giannetti
CLIENT
Guitar Center of Minneapolis
AGENCY
Porter-DeFilippo/Minneapolis

584
ART DIRECTORS
Michael Wilde
Jim Hill
WRITERS
Michael Wilde
Jim Hill
DESIGNER
Michael Wilde
ARTIST
Michael Wilde
PHOTOGRAPHER
Dick Dickinson
CLIENT
University of South Florida
AGENCY
Benito Advertising/Tampa, FL

585
ART DIRECTOR
Mark Haumersen
WRITER
Lyle Wedemeyer
CLIENT
Play It Again Sports
AGENCY
Martin/Williams - Minneapolis

582

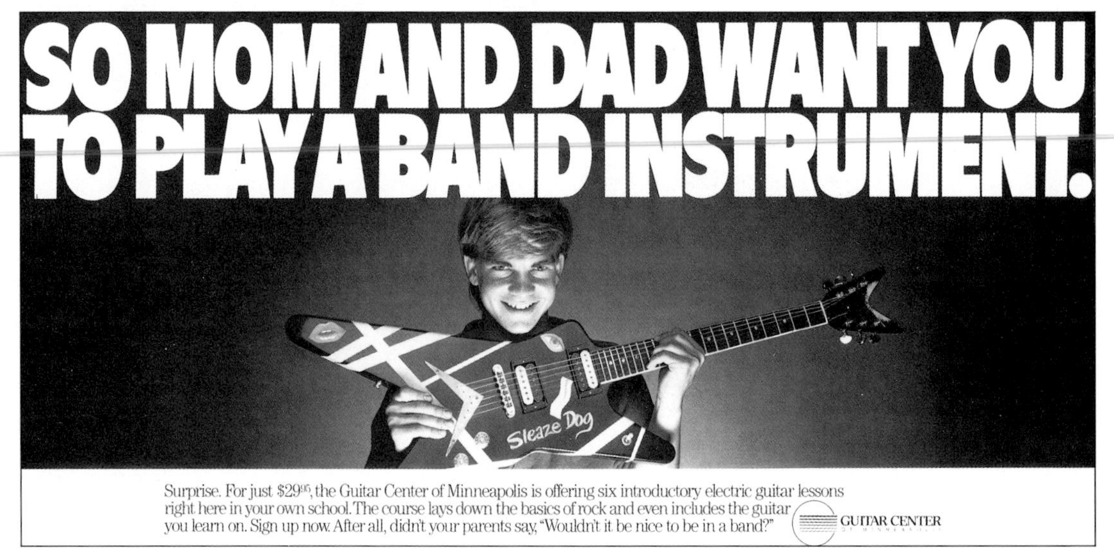

583

SUPPLY. **DEMAND.**

When several hundred college graduates are going after the same job, somebody's going to be left out. Improve your odds by signing up for USF Cooperative Education at SVC-243. Or call 974-2171. And get some real working experience before you go after the job.

USF COOPERATIVE EDUCATION

584

LOUISVILLE SLUGGER
125
GENUINE
IT'S HARDLY USED.
THE PREVIOUS OWNER
STRUCK OUT A LOT.
Play It Again Sports.
Sports Equipment That's Used. But Not Used Up.

585

Collateral
P.O.P.

586
ART DIRECTOR
David Fox
WRITER
Joe Alexander
PHOTOGRAPHER
Jim Altobell
CLIENT
St. Cloud State University
AGENCY
Clarity Coverdale Rueff/
Minneapolis

587
ART DIRECTOR
Peter Rauch
WRITER
Tom Nathan
PHOTOGRAPHER
Jeffrey Zwart
CLIENT
BMW of North America
AGENCY
Ammirati & Puris

588
ART DIRECTOR
Angela Dunkle
WRITER
Jamie Barrett
DESIGNER
Angela Dunkle
ARTIST
Ron Finger
CLIENT
Lee Jeans
AGENCY
Fallon McElligott/
Minneapolis

589
ART DIRECTORS
Nancy Rice
Nick Rice
WRITER
Jim Newcombe
DESIGNERS
Roger Christensen
Great Faces
CLIENT
Shin-On's
AGENCY
Rice & Rice/Minneapolis

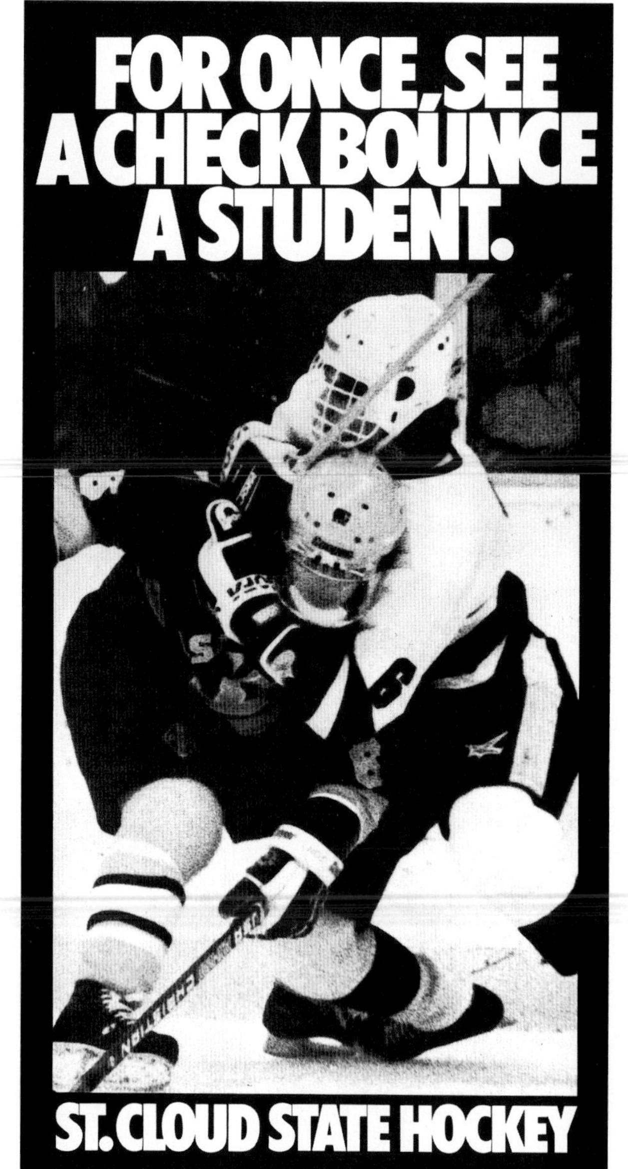

586

587

For a free vacation, fill out this form.
Buy a pair of Lee Jeans during Lee Fit Week and you'll not only get a free Kodak Fling camera, you'll get a chance to go somewhere and use it. See your retailer for more details.
Lee
Lee

588

We Now Serve Our Food A Whole New Way.

Cooked.

In addition to a great sushi bar, Shin-On's is now a great tempura bar.
So our business is now running hot and cold.

SHIN-ON'S
SUSHI BAR
& RESTAURANT

589

Collateral
P.O.P.

590
ART DIRECTOR
Mike Sheen
WRITER
Rebecca Rush
CLIENT
United Way
AGENCY
Ogilvy & Mather/Chicago

591
ART DIRECTOR
Mark Johnson
WRITER
Phil Hanft
PHOTOGRAPHER
Dennis Manarchy
CLIENT
Lee Jeans
AGENCY
Fallon McElligott/
Minneapolis

592
ART DIRECTOR
Bob Brihn
WRITER
Phil Hanft
PHOTOGRAPHER
Kerry Peterson
CLIENT
Brooks
AGENCY
Fallon McElligott/
Minneapolis

593
ART DIRECTOR
Houman Pirdavari
WRITER
Jarl Olsen
PHOTOGRAPHER
Dave Jordano
CLIENT
Penn
AGENCY
Fallon McElligott/
Minneapolis

We're not the only ones who advertise for a living.

It just takes one look around to see how many people desperately need help. And they're clearly not getting the help they need on the street.

This year, the contribution you make to the United Way or the American Cancer Society will reach thousands of people who are homeless, sick, or simply in need of the support only these organizations can give them.

So please give generously. Because for too many people, advertising is no way to make a living.

Ogilvy & Mather 1987 Combined Appeal

590

Frosted Riders Lee
Unfortunately, by the time
your last pair of jeans looked this good,
they were worn out.

591

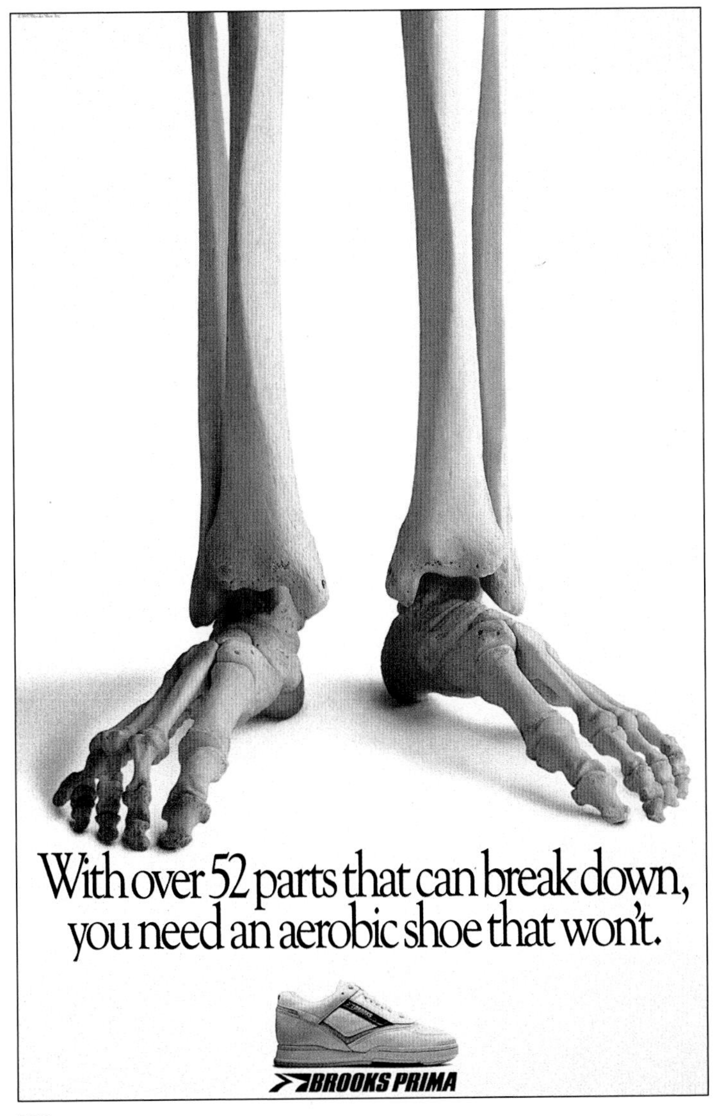
With over 52 parts that can break down, you need an aerobic shoe that won't.
BROOKS PRIMA

592

It isn't easy to kill a Pro Penn.
The new Pro Penn. With a 30% longer playing life than our regular tennis ball.

593

Collateral
P.O.P.

594

ART DIRECTOR
Mark Johnson

WRITER
Bill Miller

PHOTOGRAPHER
Randy Miller

CLIENT
Lee Jeans

AGENCY
Fallon McElligott/
Minneapolis

595

ART DIRECTOR
Gary Kaczmarek

WRITER
Doug Engel

ARTISTS
Kent Mueller
Air Artworks

CLIENT
Point Beer

AGENCY
Lindsay & Stone/
Madison, WI

596

ART DIRECTOR
Bob Barrie

WRITER
Jarl Olsen

DESIGNER
Bob Barrie

PHOTOGRAPHER
Rick Dublin

CLIENT
Hush Puppies Shoe
Company

AGENCY
Fallon McElligott/
Minneapolis

597

ART DIRECTOR
Angela Dunkle

WRITER
Jamie Barrett

DESIGNER
Angela Dunkle

PHOTOGRAPHER
Mark LaFavor

CLIENT
Lee Jeans

AGENCY
Fallon McElligott/
Minneapolis

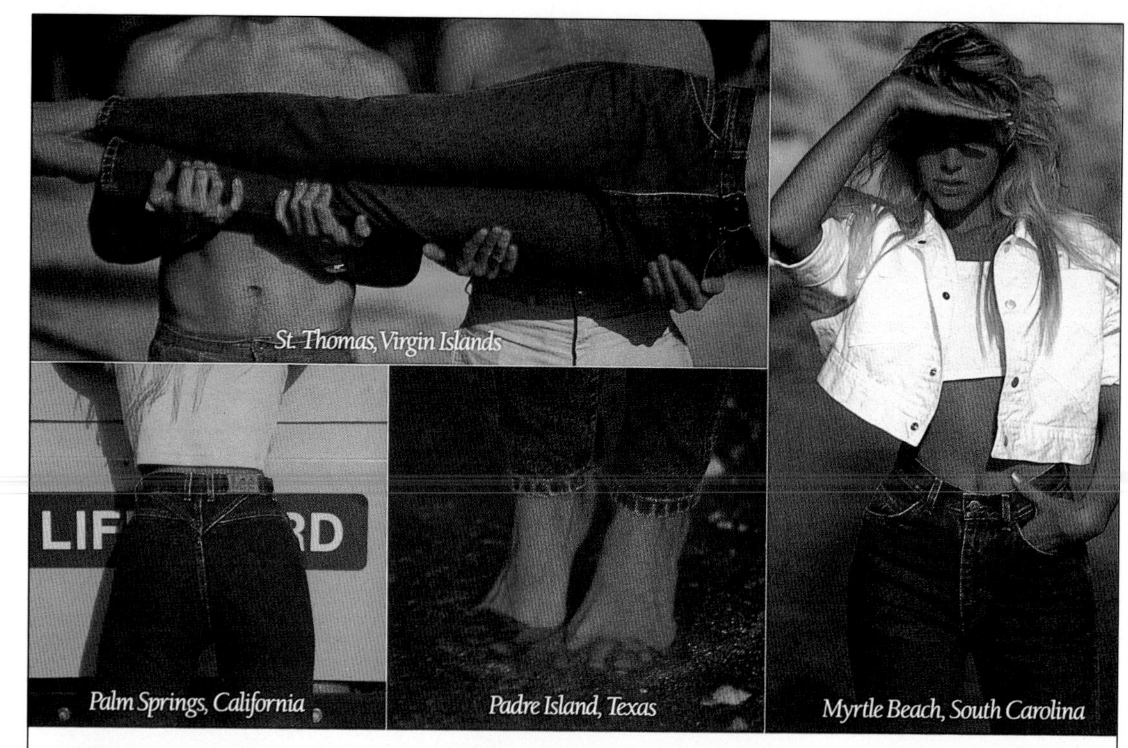

St. Thomas, Virgin Islands
Palm Springs, California
Padre Island, Texas
Myrtle Beach, South Carolina
Be seen in all the right places.
Leen Jeans
Lee
The brand that fits.

594

Finding The Right Taste Was Hard.
Choosing The Name Was Easy.
Point
BEER

595

Perrier
Sophisticated Hush Puppies.
Our classic pumps. For those with a nose for the finer things.

596

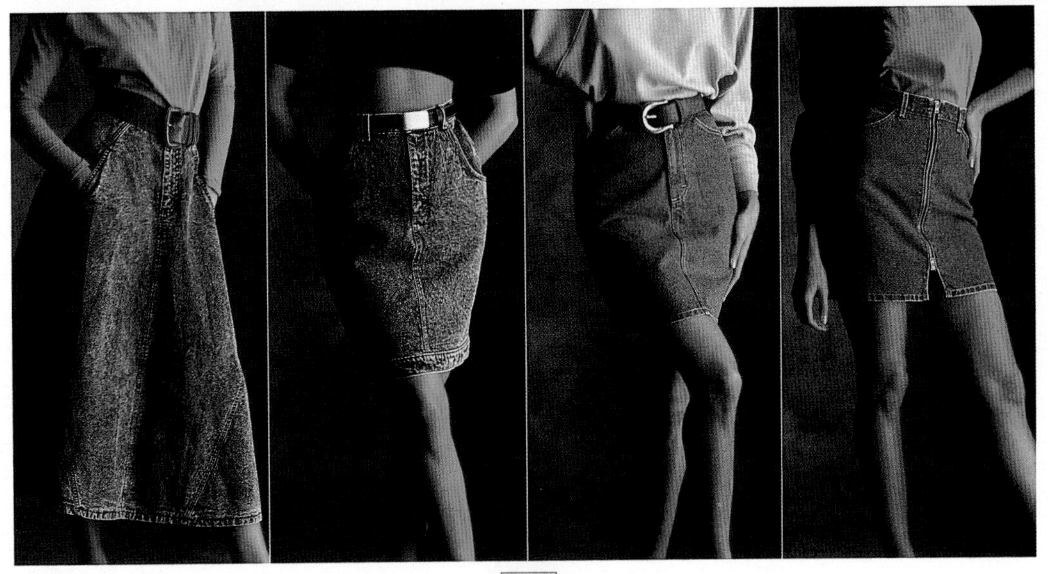
The complete line of
Lee skirts. More or less.
Lee
The brand that fits.

597

Collateral P.O.P.

598
ART DIRECTORS
Peter Rauch
Meri Duffy
WRITERS
Tom Nathan
Alex Kroll
ARTIST
Gerald Huerta
CLIENT
BMW of North America
AGENCY
Ammirati & Puris

Outdoor: Single

599
ART DIRECTOR
Robin Chrumka
WRITER
Mike Stocker
PHOTOGRAPHER
Kathaleen Martin
CLIENT
Health Alliance Plan
AGENCY
J. Walter Thompson/
Detroit

600
ART DIRECTOR
Joe Sciarrotta
WRITER
Tom DeCerchio
CLIENT
Godfather's Pizza
AGENCY
J. Walter Thompson/
Chicago

601
ART DIRECTORS
John Butler
Kevin Donovan
WRITERS
Dan Staley
Kevin Donovan
John Butler
PHOTOGRAPHER
Bruno
CLIENT
Goodyear
AGENCY
J. Walter Thompson

602
ART DIRECTOR
Monte Hallis
WRITER
Alan Marcus
ARTIST
Andy Zito
CLIENT
Six Flags Magic Mountain
AGENCY
Della Femina Travisano &
Partners/Los Angeles

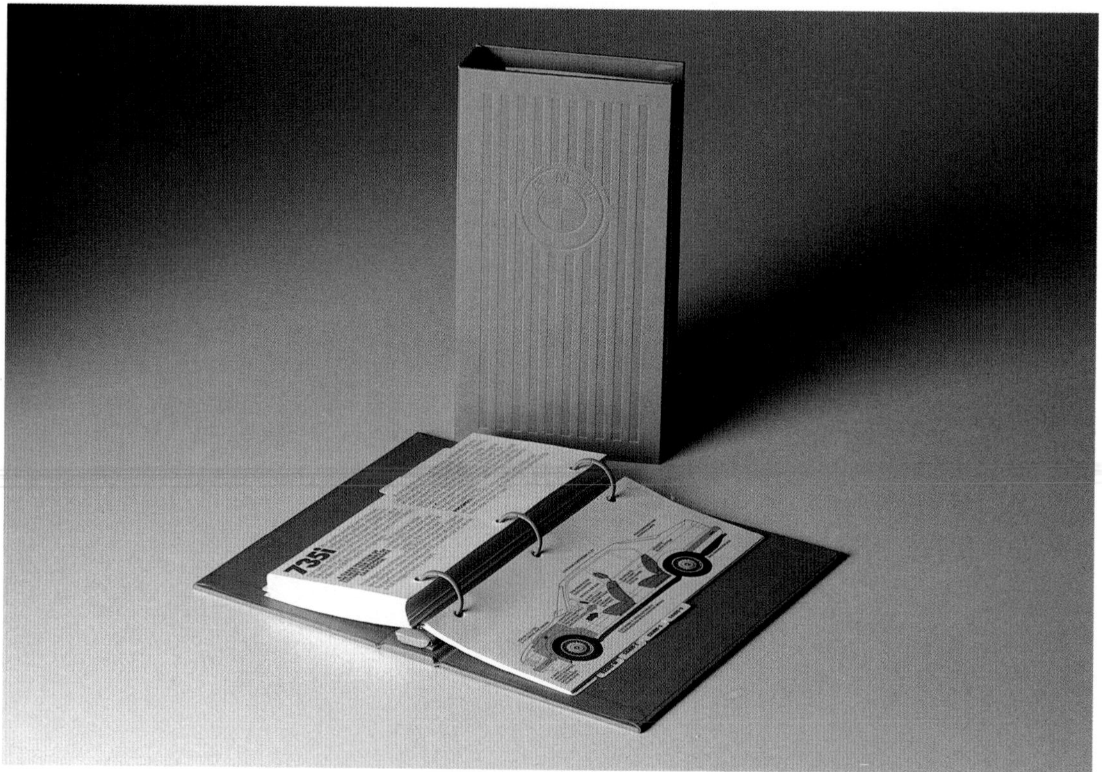

598

SEVEN PRESSURE POINTS THAT CAN HELP RELIEVE A WIDE VARIETY OF MEDICAL PROBLEMS.

MEDI-CALL

With Metro Medical Group's new MEDI-CALL service, you can get advice from a registered nurse whenever your center is closed. Call 523-1700. Metro Medical Group, a division of Health Alliance Plan.

599

Say no to Pot Roast. 223-1111

Godfather's Pizza™
Free Emergency Delivery

600

ABC
DEF
GHI
JKL
MNO
PRS
TUV
WXY
OPER
IT'S A LOT EASIER THAN PUSHING YOUR TRUCK.
1-800-TIRE-NET. It's the number to call for emergency road service. Almost anywhere in North America. 24 hours a day.
GOODYEAR

601

There's nothing like a little ride in the park.
SIX FLAGS
MAGIC MOUNTAIN

602

Outdoor: Single

603
ART DIRECTOR
Pam Conboy
WRITER
Lyle Wedemeyer
ARTIST
Oasis Art
CLIENT
Skipper's Seafood Restaurants
AGENCY
Martin/Williams - Minneapolis

604
ART DIRECTOR
Cliff Goodenough
WRITER
Steve Dolbinski
CLIENT
Alaska Airlines
AGENCY
Livingston & Company/ Seattle

605
ART DIRECTOR
Bill Zabowski
WRITER
Pete Smith
ARTIST
Pam Dalton
CLIENT
MedCenters Health Plan
AGENCY
Martin/Williams - Minneapolis

606
ART DIRECTORS
Peter Hobden
Ken Sara
WRITER
Peter Hobden
CLIENT
Nike International
AGENCY
Grey/London

607
ART DIRECTOR
Sylvie Barrière
WRITER
Jean Gamache
CLIENT
McDonald's Canada
AGENCY
Cossette Communication Marketing/Montréal

608
ART DIRECTORS
Ken Sara
Peter Hobden
WRITER
Peter Hobden
CLIENT
Nike International
AGENCY
Grey/London

603

Great Moments In Flight.
7:00 12:15 3:00 6:35
Alaska Airlines To Los Angeles International.

604

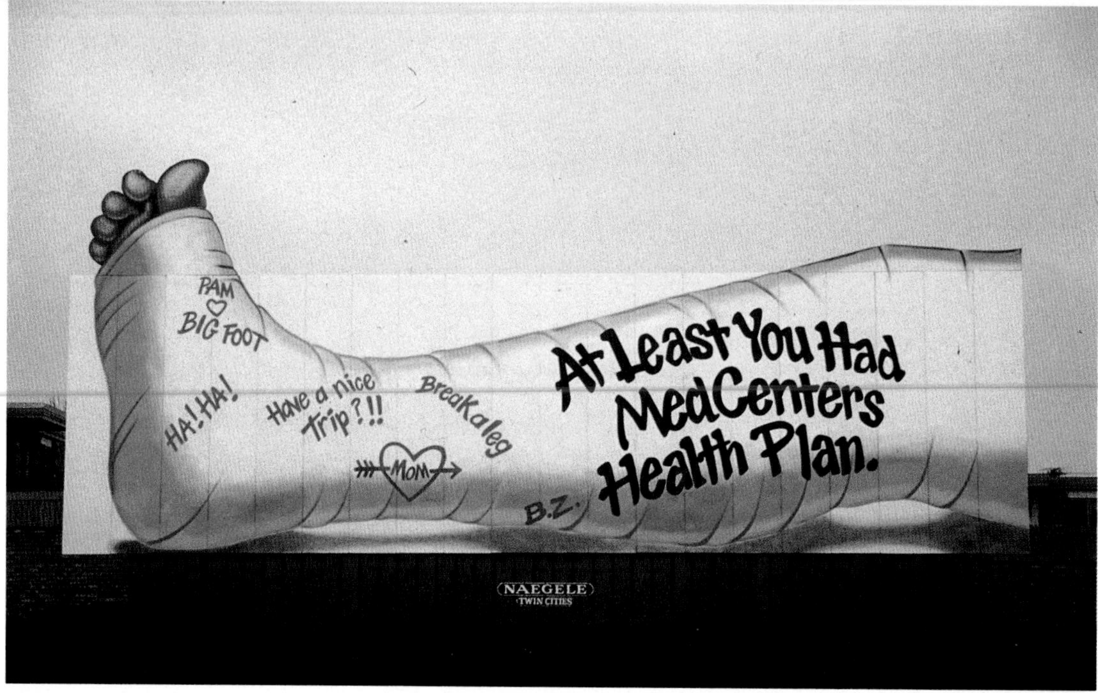

605

FRANK DOES IT IN McENROE'S SHOES.

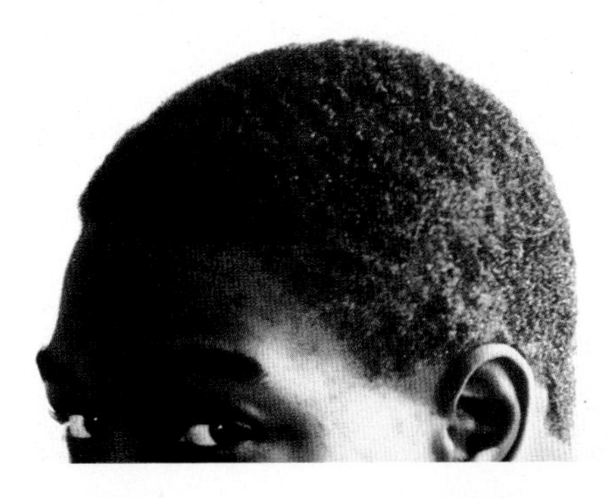

ONE SHOE. ALL SPORTS. THE AIR TRAINER FROM NIKE.

606

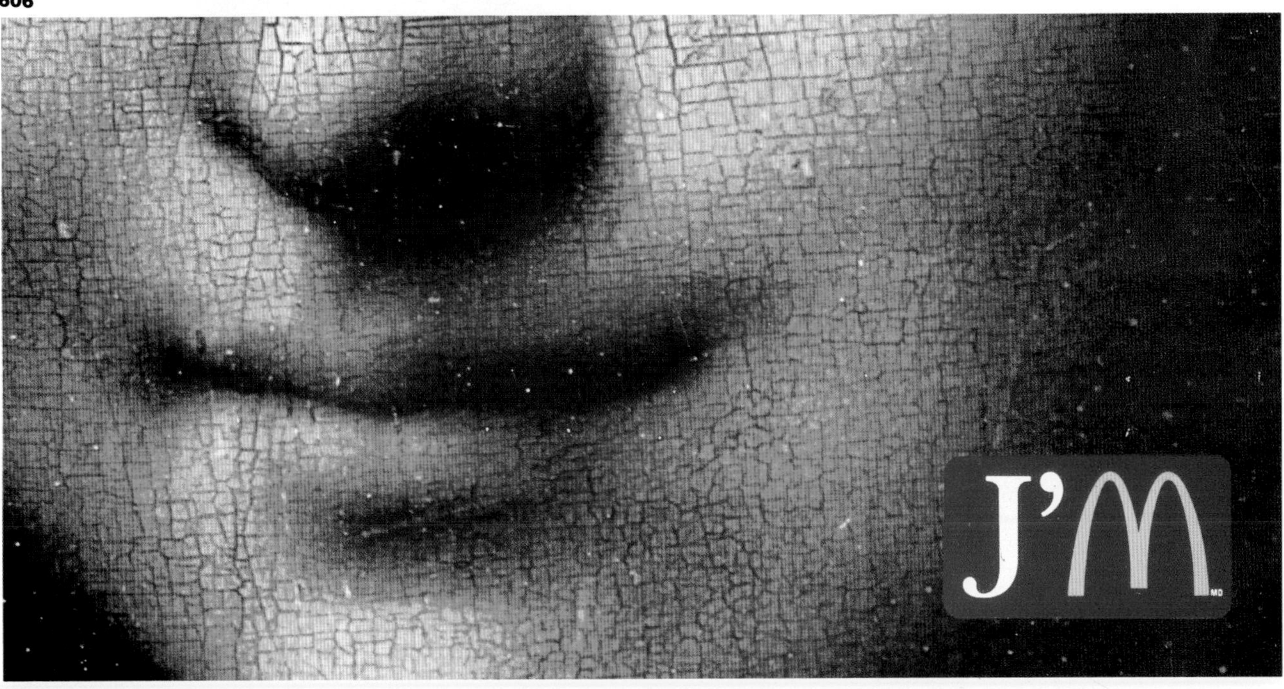

J'M

607

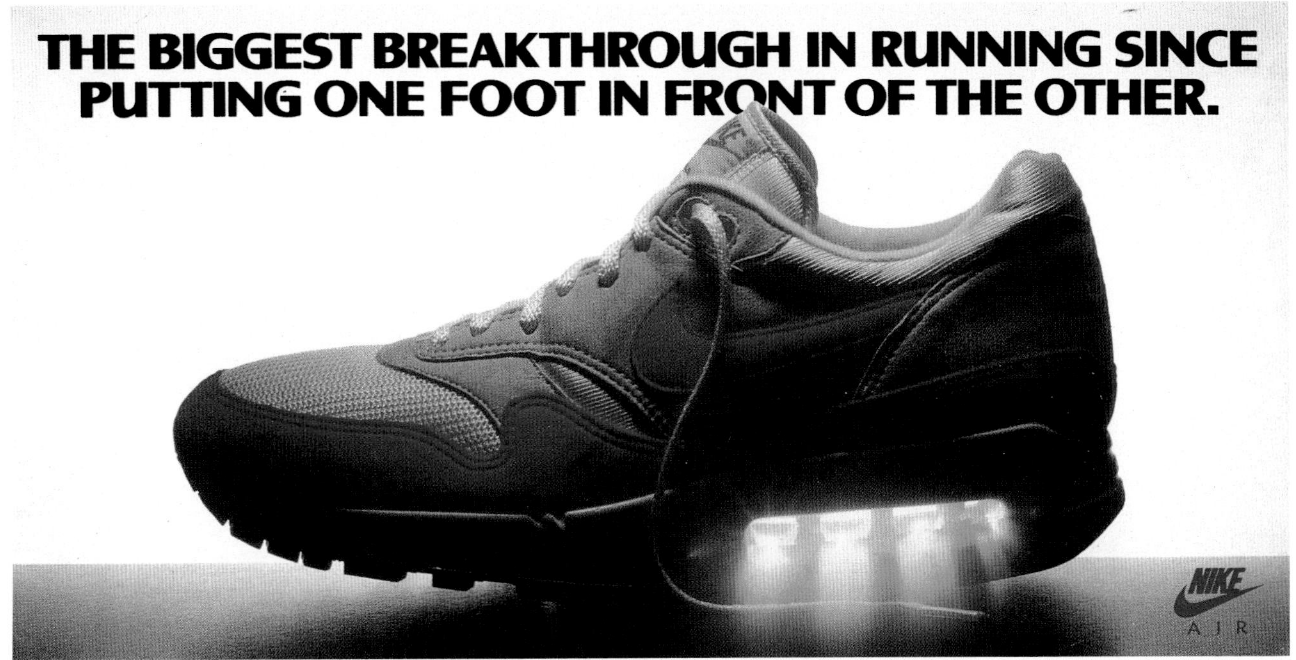

THE BIGGEST BREAKTHROUGH IN RUNNING SINCE PUTTING ONE FOOT IN FRONT OF THE OTHER.
NIKE
AIR

608

Outdoor: Single

609
ART DIRECTORS
Angela Sciezka
Paul Regan
WRITER
Scott Ramsden
CLIENT
McDonald's of Newport, RI
AGENCY
Arnold & Company/
Boston

610
ART DIRECTOR
Colin Marr
WRITER
Colin Marr
PHOTOGRAPHER
Nick Price
CLIENT
United Rum Merchants
AGENCY
Marr/Associates -
Edinburgh

611
ART DIRECTORS
Robert Reitzfeld
Roseann Consolo
WRITER
Kevin Mooney
DESIGNERS
Robert Reitzfeld
Roseann Consolo
CLIENT
Los Angeles Hilton
AGENCY
Altschiller Reitzfeld

612
ART DIRECTORS
Kathy Izard
Jim Mountjoy
WRITERS
Ed Jones
Steve Lasch
PHOTOGRAPHER
Jon Silla
CLIENT
WJZY
AGENCY
Loeffler Ketchum
Mountjoy/Charlotte, NC

613
ART DIRECTOR
Jac Coverdale
WRITER
Jerry Fury
PHOTOGRAPHER
Paul Sinkler
CLIENT
St. Paul Pioneer Press
Dispatch
AGENCY
Clarity Coverdale Rueff/
Minneapolis

614
ART DIRECTOR
Ron Brown
WRITER
David Abbott
PHOTOGRAPHER
Derek Seagrim
CLIENT
Ikea
AGENCY
Abbott Mead Vickers/
SMS - London

609

610

611

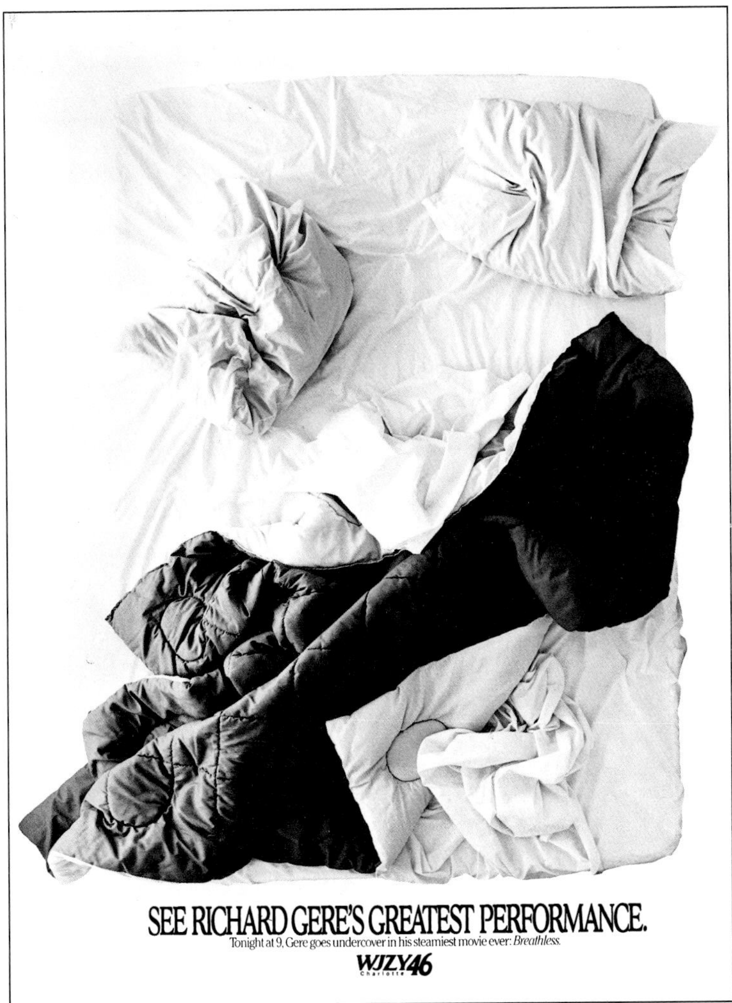
SEE RICHARD GERE'S GREATEST PERFORMANCE.
Tonight at 9, Gere goes undercover in his steamiest movie ever: *Breathless.*
WJZY46
Charlotte

612

25¢ a scoop.
PULL
AM
PIONEER PRESS DISPATCH
1987 WORLD SERIES
They're halfway home
PIONEER PRESS DISPATCH
ST. PAUL PIONEER PRESS DISPATCH
Whether you dip into our orange boxes or have us delivered fresh to your door, you'll find we have more flavor than other papers.
That's because of the commitment and enthusiasm our writers and photographers put into our paper each day.
In fact, for the last three years we've won more journalism awards than any other Minnesota newspaper, including a Pulitzer Prize.
And last year Charlie Walters and Pat Reusse were named Sportswriters of the Year.
We're also the only paper in the Twin Cities with a genuine doubledecker: an AM and PM edition.
So don't even think about paying another dime for a paper. Get the scoop for only a quarter. *For home delivery call 291-1888.*
ST. PAUL PIONEER PRESS DISPATCH
Nobody else brings you the news like this.

613

For the new björn.
IKEA®
The furnishings store from Sweden. Opens Oct. 1st. Warrington, Jct. 9, M62.

614

Outdoor: Single

615
ART DIRECTOR
Bill Kamp
WRITER
Howard Rockett
DESIGNERS
Bill Kamp
Mike Sellers
CLIENT
Golden Corral
AGENCY
Rockett Burkhead & Lewis/Raleigh, NC

616
ART DIRECTOR
John Lee Wong
WRITERS
Ken Fitzgerald
John Lee Wong
DESIGNER
John Lee Wong
PHOTOGRAPHER
Gerry Wilson
CLIENT
Kentucky Fried Chicken
AGENCY
HDM/Los Angeles

617
ART DIRECTOR
Ron Brown
WRITER
David Abbott
PHOTOGRAPHER
Derek Seagrim
CLIENT
Ikea
AGENCY
Abbott Mead Vickers/SMS - London

618
ART DIRECTOR
Denise Weber
WRITER
Tom McDonnell
PHOTOGRAPHER
Jim Barber Photography
CLIENT
White Mountain Cooler
AGENCY
Ally & Gargano

619
ART DIRECTOR
Bob Phillips
WRITER
Tom Thomas
CLIENT
The NY Restaurant Group - Smith & Wollensky
AGENCY
Angotti Thomas Hedge

"Daddy. Are we there yet?"

GOLDEN CORRAL

Great steaks, great salads, 3 miles on right.

615

The best leg of your trip is coming up.

616

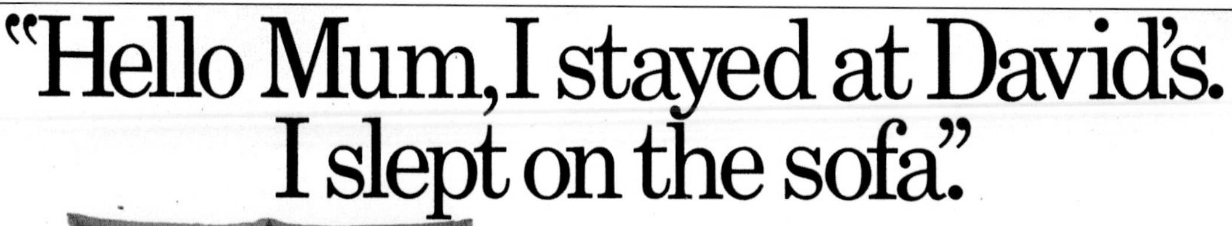

617

The White Mo
ange.
White Mountain
COOLER
White Mountain
ORANGE COOLER
White Mountain
BERRY COOLER
White Mountain
PEACH COOLER

618

Great steak is unlike other passions. You can pursue it during business hours.

Lunch at Smith & Wollensky.
The quintessential New York City steakhouse.
49th St. & 3rd Ave. (212) 753-1530.

619

Outdoor: Single

620
ART DIRECTOR
Rod Smith
WRITER
Fred Bertino
CLIENT
Museum of Science
AGENCY
HBM/Creamer - Boston

621
ART DIRECTOR
Mark Denton
WRITER
Chris Palmer
PHOTOGRAPHER
Paul Bevitt
CLIENT
Whitbread-Heineken
AGENCY
Lowe Howard-Spink/
London

622
ART DIRECTORS
Ted Shaine
Alain Briere
WRITER
Helayne Spivak
PHOTOGRAPHER
Stephen Frink
CLIENT
Club Med
AGENCY
Ammirati & Puris

623
ART DIRECTOR
Mary Ann Daperna
WRITER
Felipe Bascope
PHOTOGRAPHER
Jim Hall
CLIENT
Suzuki of America
AGENCY
keye/donna/pearlstein -
Los Angeles

624
ART DIRECTOR
Steve Thursby
WRITER
Allen Kazmer
PHOTOGRAPHER
Terry Collier
CLIENT
Volkswagen Canada
AGENCY
DDB Needham Worldwide/
Toronto

A Passage to India.

Take this bus to the India Exhibit at the Museum of Science.

620

621

SCHOOL CROSSING
CLUB MED
The antidote for civilization.

622

Never a dull winter.
SUZUKI
1-800-447-4700
SUZUKI

623

Putting more volks into wagens.
The Fox Around $8,700*
*Freight and dealer preparation included. Dealer may sell for less.

624

Outdoor: Single

625
ART DIRECTOR
Frank Haggerty
WRITER
Kerry Casey
CLIENT
Minnesota Zoo
AGENCY
Carmichael Lynch/
Minneapolis

626
ART DIRECTORS
John Muller
Jay Henning
WRITER
Rob Price
DESIGNER
John Muller
ARTIST
Patrice Eilts
PHOTOGRAPHER
Pitzner Studio
CLIENT
Union Bank
AGENCY
Muller & Company/
Kansas City, MO

627
ART DIRECTOR
John Seymour-Anderson
WRITER
Mike Gibbs
CLIENT
Steiner Development
AGENCY
McCool & Company/
Minneapolis

628
ART DIRECTOR
Tony Smith
WRITER
Hugo Kondratiuk
DESIGNER
Tony Smith
CLIENT
Peugeot
AGENCY
HDM Horner Collis &
Kirvan/London

"Wolf!"
(They're At The Minnesota Zoo. Honest.)
Wolves. At The Minnesota Zoo.

625

626

SPACE MEN SEEK CONTACT
WITH LOCAL BUSINESS LEADERS.
STEINER DEVELOPMENT 473-5650
NAEGELE

627

STOP
NO PARKING ANY TIME
4 HOUR PARKING 7AM-6PM
THE NEW PEUGEOT 309 GTI
0-60 FASTER THAN THE GOLF GTI 16V. 0-60 FASTER THAN THE FORD RS TURBO. TOP SPEED 128 MPH. ACTION NOT WORDS.

628

Outdoor: Single

629
ART DIRECTOR
Maggie Gallagher
WRITER
Sara Fontannaz
PHOTOGRAPHER
David Montgomery
CLIENT
Whitbread-Heineken
AGENCY
Lowe Howard-Spink/ London

630
ART DIRECTOR
Mark Johnson
WRITER
Phil Hanft
PHOTOGRAPHER
Mark LaFavor
CLIENT
Lee Jeans
AGENCY
Fallon McElligott/ Minneapolis

631
ART DIRECTOR
Rick Dalbey
WRITER
Barry Cadish
ARTIST
Frank Farah
CLIENT
Newport Bay Restaurant
AGENCY
Marx/Knoll Denight & Dodge - Portland, OR

632
ART DIRECTOR
Howard Friedman
WRITER
Karen Ritter
PHOTOGRAPHER
Denny Tillman
CLIENT
Dunkin' Donuts
AGENCY
Ally & Gargano

633
ART DIRECTOR
Tom Lichtenheld
WRITER
Rod Kilpatrick
PHOTOGRAPHER
Kent Severson
CLIENT
The Wall Street Journal
AGENCY
Fallon McElligott/ Minneapolis

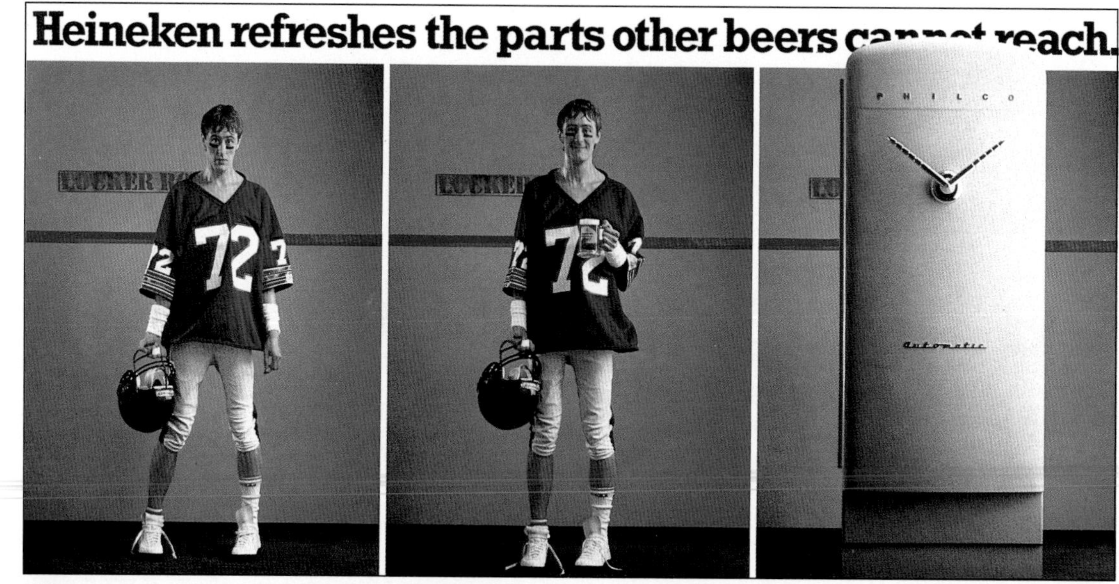

629

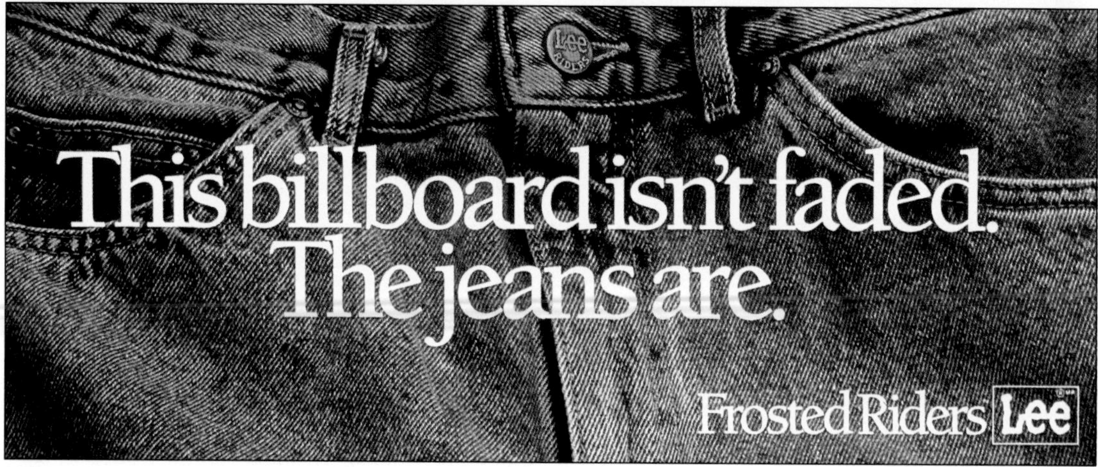

630

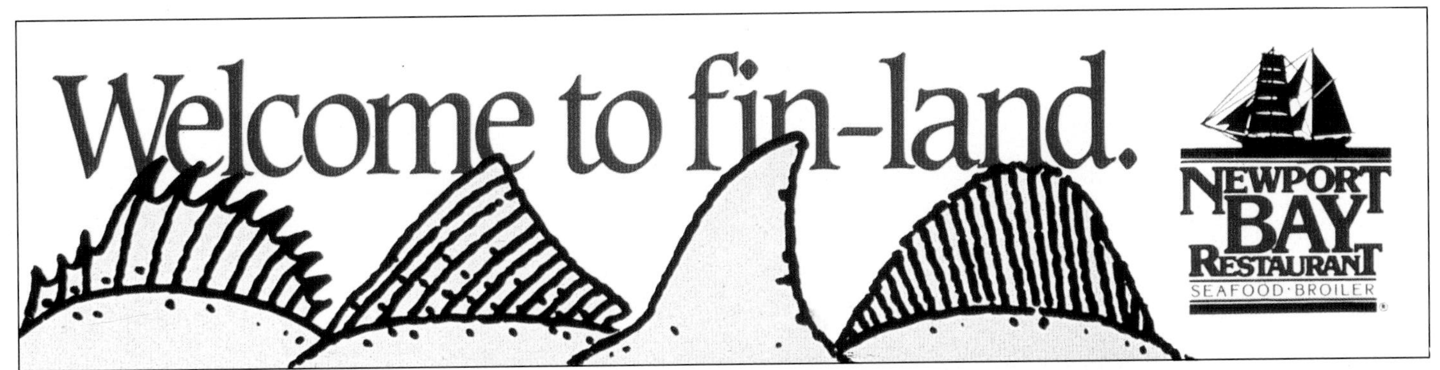
Welcome to fin-land.
NEWPORT BAY RESTAURANT
SEAFOOD·BROILER

631

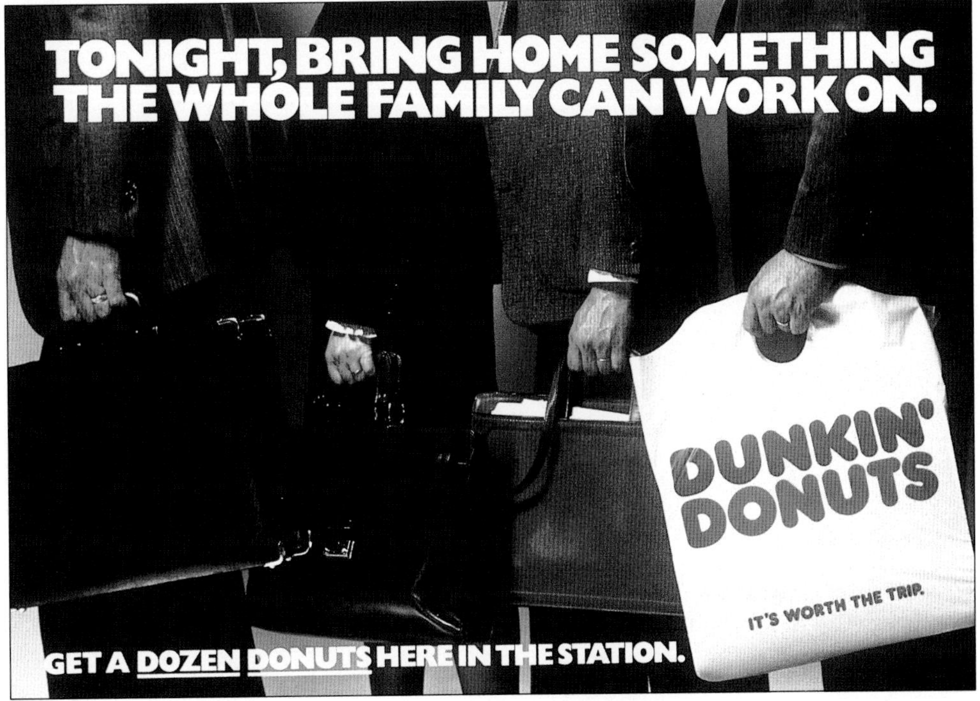
TONIGHT, BRING HOME SOMETHING THE WHOLE FAMILY CAN WORK ON.
DUNKIN' DONUTS
IT'S WORTH THE TRIP.
GET A DOZEN DONUTS HERE IN THE STATION.

632

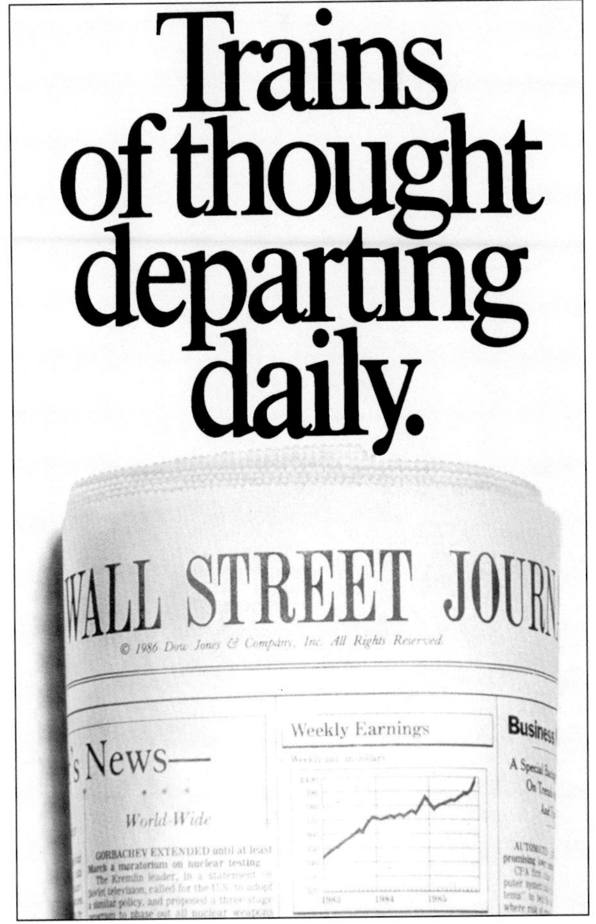
Trains of thought departing daily.
WALL STREET JOURN
© 1986 Dow Jones & Company, Inc. All Rights Reserved.
News—
World-Wide
Weekly Earnings
Business

633

Outdoor: Single

634
ART DIRECTOR
Judy Penny
WRITER
Dan Brown
CLIENT
The Museum of Fine Arts
AGENCY
Hill Holliday Connors Cosmopulos/Boston

635
ART DIRECTOR
Bob Kwait
WRITER
Bob Kwait
DESIGNERS
Bob Kwait
Ron Van Buskirk
ARTIST
Darrel Millsap
CLIENT
San Diego Zoo
AGENCY
Phillips-Ramsey/San Diego, CA

636
ART DIRECTOR
Bob Brihn
WRITER
George Gier
CLIENT
Federal Express
AGENCY
Fallon McElligott/Minneapolis

637
ART DIRECTOR
Angela Dunkle
WRITER
Jamie Barrett
DESIGNER
Angela Dunkle
ARTIST
Oasis Art
CLIENT
MedCenters Health Plan
AGENCY
Fallon McElligott/Minneapolis

638
ART DIRECTOR
Rick Dalbey
WRITER
Barry Cadish
ARTIST
Frank Farah
CLIENT
Newport Bay Restaurant
AGENCY
Marx/Knoll Denight & Dodge - Portland, OR

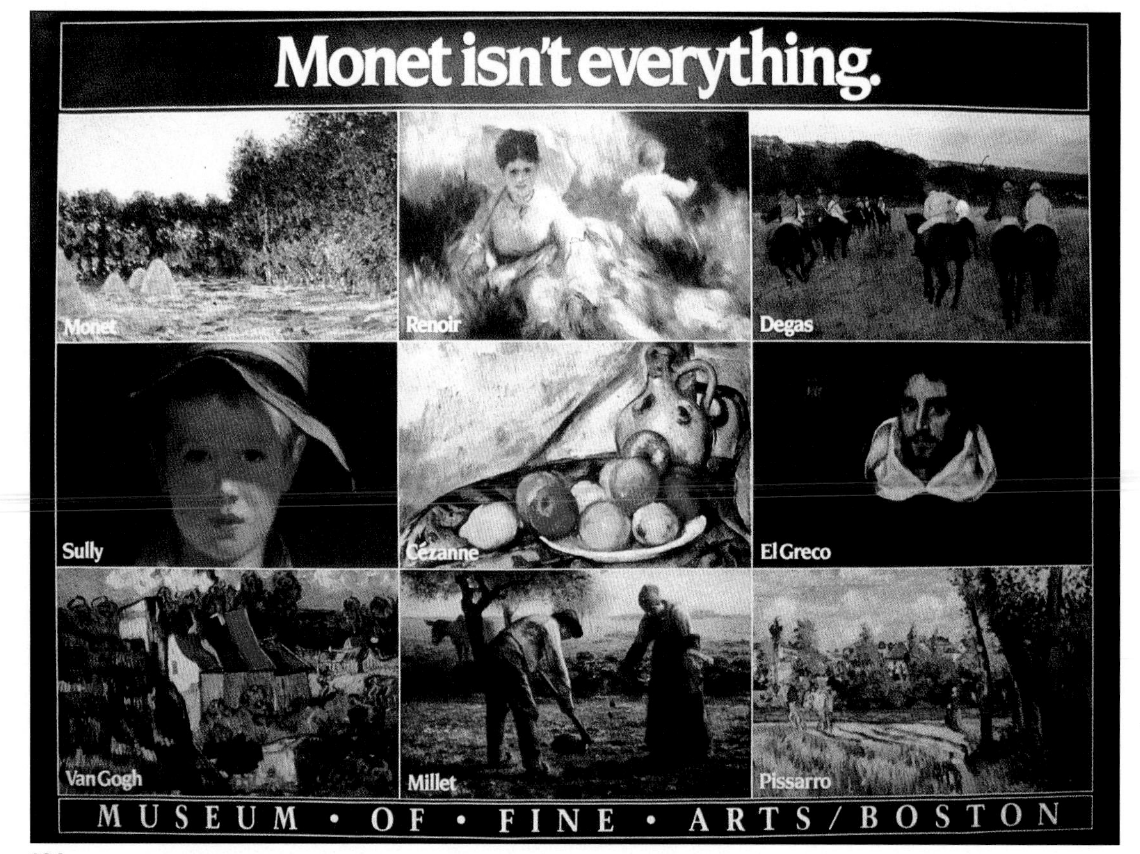

634

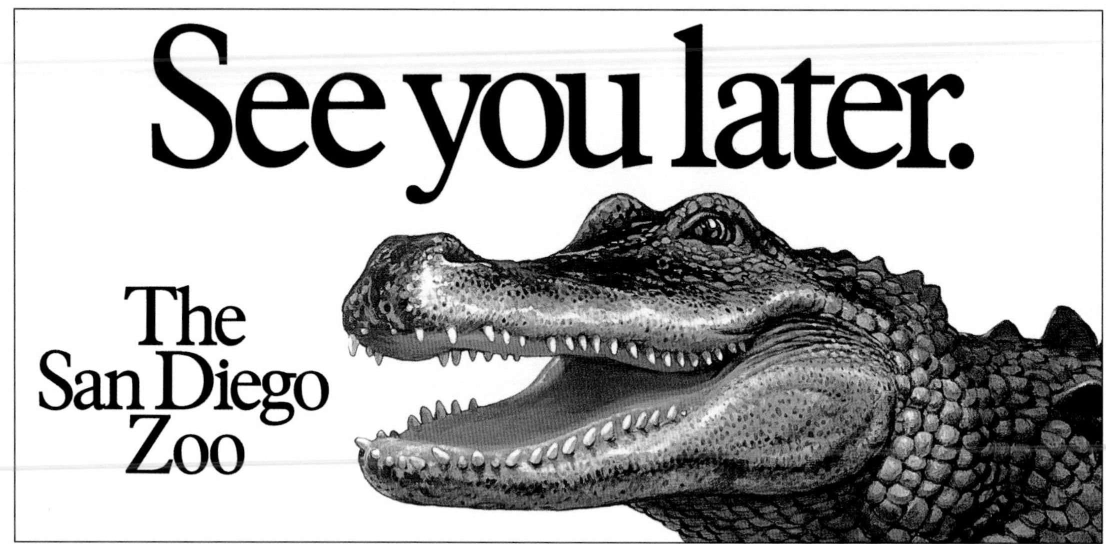

635

How to get ahead in a mail dominated society.

Call Federal Express. Because when your letters and packages go places, you will too.

FEDERAL
EXPRESS
It's not just a package.
It's your business.

636

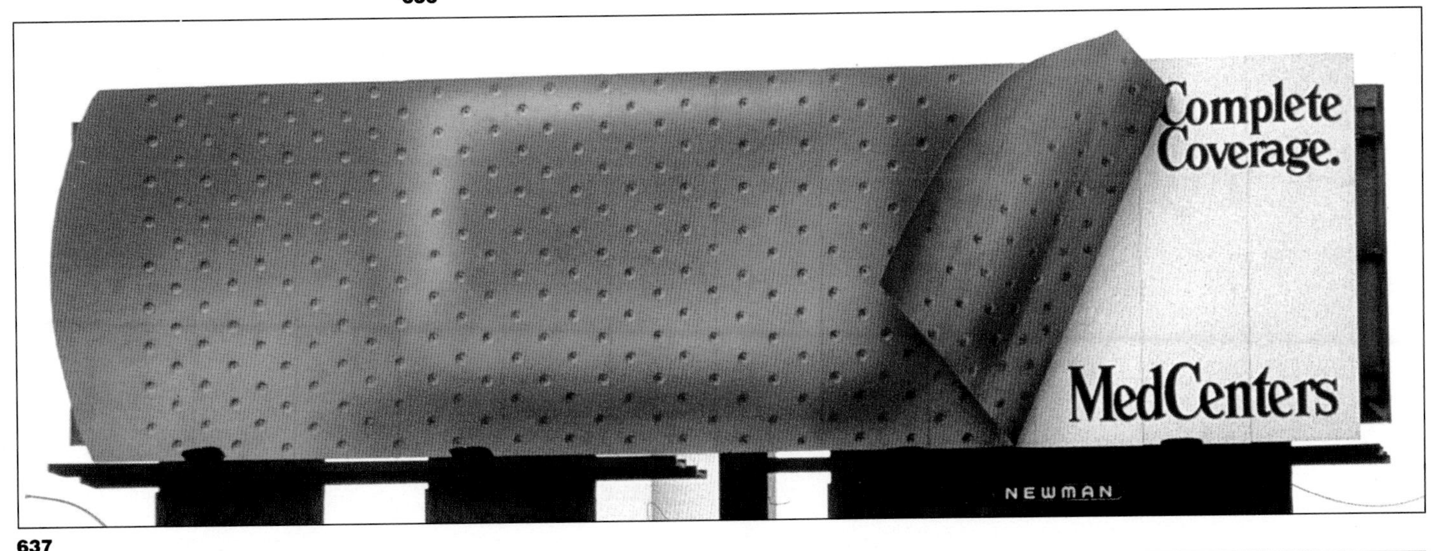

637

Approved by the Sturgeon General

NEWPORT BAY RESTAURANT

SEAFOOD·BROILER

638

Outdoor: Single

639

ART DIRECTOR
Earl Cavanah

WRITER
Larry Cadman

PHOTOGRAPHERS
Norman Mauer Productions
Columbia Pictures
Roger Richmond Agency
Jerry Friedman

CLIENT
Nikon

AGENCY
Scali McCabe Sloves

640

ART DIRECTOR
Houman Pirdavari

WRITER
Sam Avery

PHOTOGRAPHER
Robert Giusti

CLIENT
Federal Express

AGENCY
Fallon McElligott/
Minneapolis

641

ART DIRECTOR
Mark Johnson

WRITER
Jarl Olsen

CLIENT
Donaldson's

AGENCY
Fallon McElligott/
Minneapolis

642

ART DIRECTOR
Paul Blade

WRITER
Larry Hampel

DESIGNER
Paul Blade

PHOTOGRAPHER
Jeffrey Zwart

CLIENT
Volvo

AGENCY
Scali McCabe Sloves

643

ART DIRECTOR
Roy Grace

WRITER
Diane Rothschild

PHOTOGRAPHER
Henry Sandbank

CLIENT
Range Rover of North
America

AGENCY
Grace and Rothschild

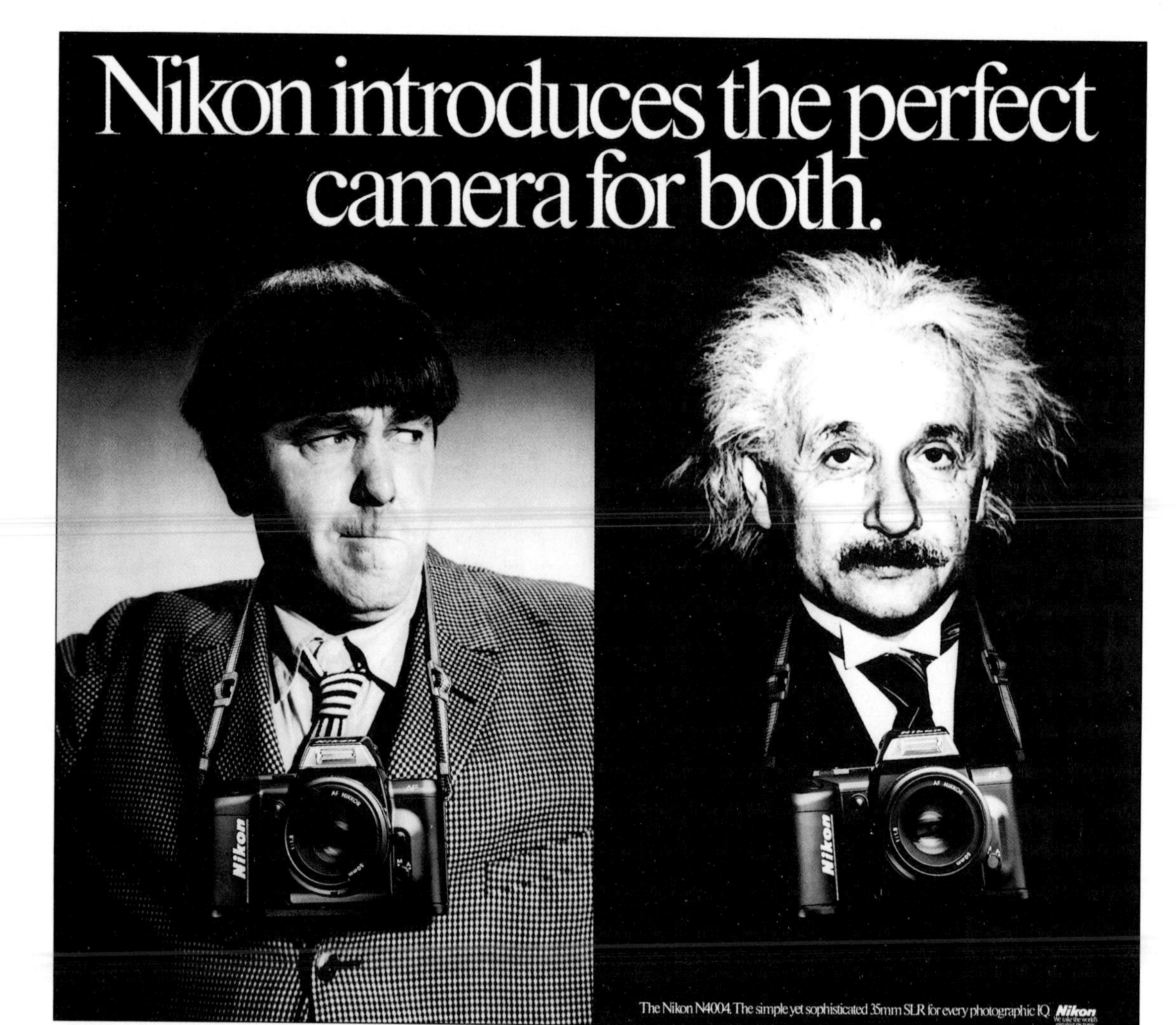

Nikon introduces the perfect camera for both.
Nikon
The Nikon N4004. The simple yet sophisticated 35mm SLR for every photographic IQ.
Nikon
We take the world's greatest pictures.

639

FEDERAL EXPRESS
Overnight delivery to England.
Door-to-door worldwide delivery. Of almost anything. Almost anywhere. Call your local office for complete details. Federal Express

640

If you can't reach this billboard,
you can always reach our fragrance counter.
(SCRATCH & SNIFF)
Donaldsons
NAEGELE

641

TO A RADAR GUN, THEY LOOK EXACTLY ALIKE.
VOLVO
A car you can believe in.

642

It's not a 4x4. It's a 4x4.
RANGE ROVER
1-800-FINE 4WD
GANNETT OUTDOOR

643

Outdoor: Single

644
ART DIRECTOR
Judy Penny
WRITER
Dan Brown
CLIENT
The Museum of Fine Arts
AGENCY
Hill Holliday Connors Cosmopulos/Boston

645
ART DIRECTOR
Bob Brihn
WRITER
Jamie Barrett
ARTIST
Bob Blewett
CLIENT
US Hockey
AGENCY
Fallon McElligott/Minneapolis

646
ART DIRECTOR
Lance Paull
WRITER
Frank Campion
CLIENT
The Museum of Fine Arts
AGENCY
Cabot Advertising/Boston

647
ART DIRECTORS
Andy Dijak
Mas Yamashita
WRITER
David Butler
PHOTOGRAPHER
Carl Furuta
CLIENT
Porsche Cars North America
AGENCY
Chiat/Day - Venice, CA

644

WHO WILL FIRE THE FIRST SHOT?
THE U.S. HOCKEY TEAM VS. THE SOVIET UNION.
One of four pre-Olympic games. Call Met Center for tickets.

645

Imagine telling your parents
you want to be an artist.
Maybe you should tell them about the Museum School first. And what a great place it is for anyone serious about a career in the arts.
Tell them about our many different degree and diploma programs for both full and part-time students. About the distinguished artists on our faculty and the all-elective studio format.
And tell them about our affiliation with Tufts University and how you'll have access to the resources of the Museum of Fine Arts.
Who knows? Telling your parents you want to be an artist could be easier than you ever imagined.
For a catalogue and an application, write to: School of the Museum of Fine Arts, 230 The Fenway, Boston, MA 02115. Or call us at (617) 267-1218.
School of the Museum of Fine Arts
Affiliated with Tufts University

646

The coupe de grace.

647

Outdoor: Single

648
ART DIRECTOR
Damon Collins
WRITER
Mary Wear
DESIGNER
Damon Collins
PHOTOGRAPHER
Paul Bevitt
CLIENT
Hedges & Butler/
Zamoyski Vodka
AGENCY
Gold Greenless Trott/
London

649
ART DIRECTORS
Robert Reitzfeld
Roseann Consolo
Martica Griffin
WRITER
Kevin Mooney
DESIGNERS
Robert Reitzfeld
Roseann Consolo
Martica Griffin
CLIENT
Los Angeles Hilton
AGENCY
Altschiller Reitzfeld

Outdoor: Campaign

650
ART DIRECTORS
Mark Erwin
Richard Kelley
WRITERS
Harry Woods
Richard Kelley
DESIGNER
Robert Keding
ARTIST
Robert Keding
CLIENT
California Magazine
AGENCY
Scali McCabe Sloves
West/Los Angeles

648

649

"What could possibly compare with whale sex?"

Adventure Vacations. In the June issue. On newsstands now.

California MAGAZINE

"Why did they all ignore my fly?"

Trout fishing. In the September issue. On newsstands now.

"Meet flowing blobs of jelly with high I.Q.'s."

Space Travel. In the August issue. On newsstands now.

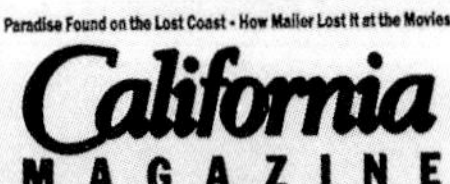

Paradise Found on the Lost Coast • How Mailer Lost It at the Movies
California
MAGAZINE

Outdoor: Campaign

651

ART DIRECTOR
Steve Dunn

WRITER
Tim Delaney

PHOTOGRAPHER
Daniel Jovanneau

CLIENT
Harrods

AGENCY
Leagas Delaney Partnership/London

652

ART DIRECTOR
Ken Boyd

WRITER
Terry Bell

PHOTOGRAPHER
Stanley Wong

CLIENT
Labatt Brewing

AGENCY
Scali McCabe Sloves/ Toronto

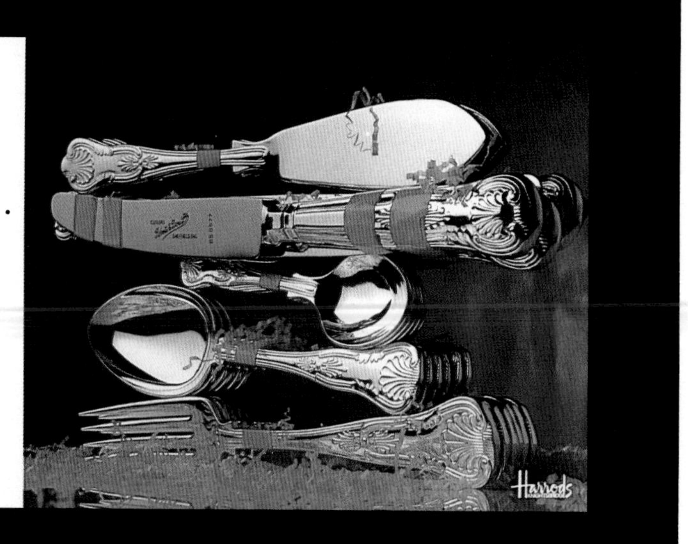

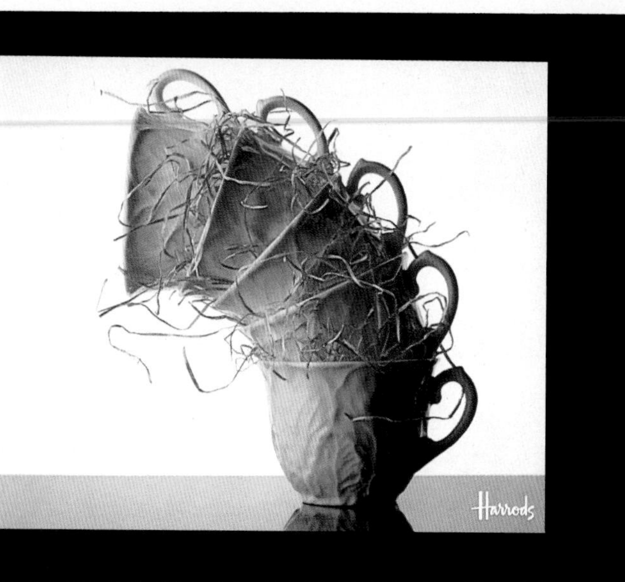

651

IT'S IMPOSSIBLE TO KEEP
A DEEP DARK SECRET.
GUINNESS
See the dark
at your
Brewer's Retail.

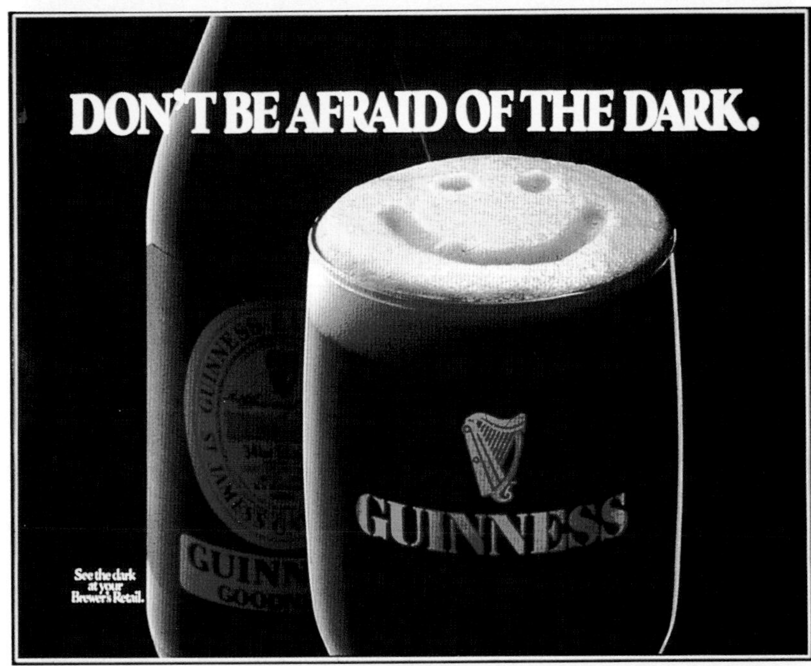
DON'T BE AFRAID OF THE DARK.
GUINNESS
See the dark
at your
Brewer's Retail.

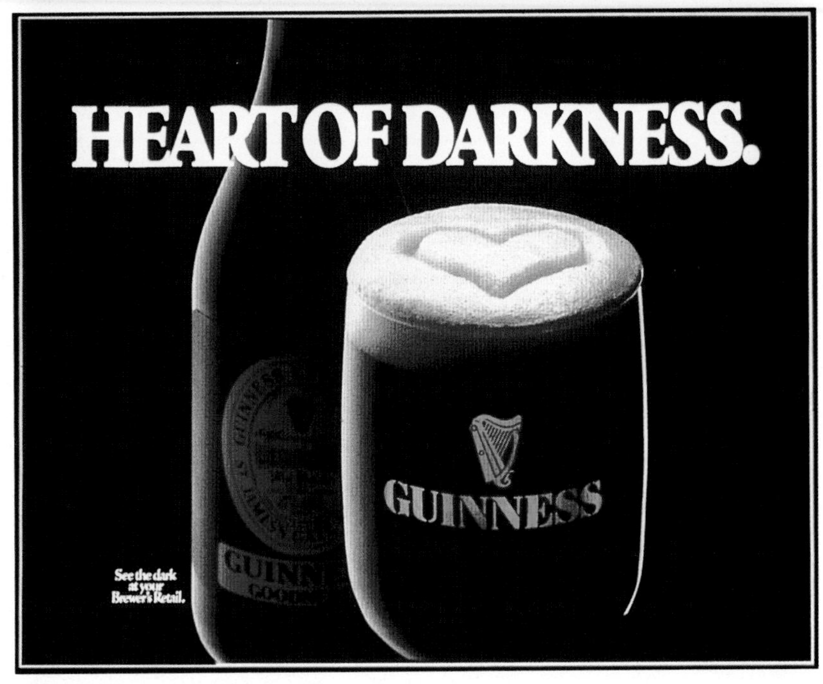
HEART OF DARKNESS.
GUINNESS
See the dark
at your
Brewer's Retail.

Outdoor: Campaign

653

ART DIRECTOR
Leif Nielsen

WRITER
Steve Conover

PHOTOGRAPHER
Ian Campbell

CLIENT
Chieftain Products

AGENCY
DDB Needham Worldwide/
Toronto

654

ART DIRECTOR
Jeff Roll

WRITER
Paul Decker

PHOTOGRAPHER
Jim Hall

CLIENT
Suzuki of America

AGENCY
keye/donna/pearlstein -
Los Angeles

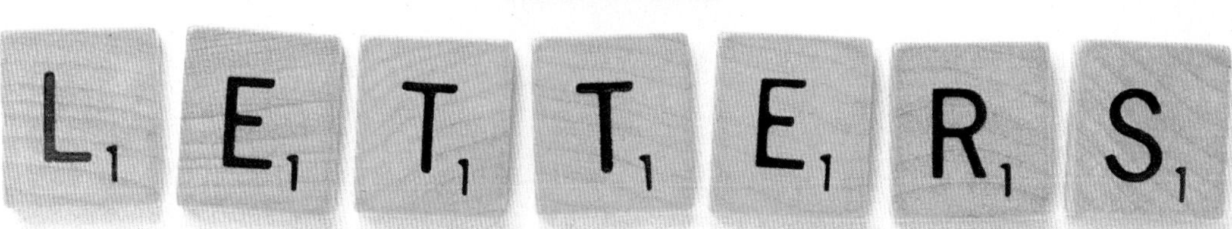

Scrabble CHIEFTAIN

Fill in the

B3 L1 N1 K5

Scrabble CHIEFTAIN

Expand your

V4 O1 C3 A1 B3 U1 L1

Scrabble CHIEFTAIN

653

A cure for the car sick.

SUZUKI
1-800-447-4700

A million laughs. $7495.*

*Manufacturer's suggested retail price excluding all transportation, tax, license, dealer preparation, and options (rear seat).

SUZUKI
1-800-447-4700

Caution: This vehicle may exceed 55 smiles per hour.

SUZUKI
1-800-447-4700

Outdoor: Campaign

655

ART DIRECTOR
Bob Barrie

WRITER
George Gier

DESIGNER
Bob Barrie

ARTIST
Bob Barrie

CLIENT
The Adler Planetarium

AGENCY
Fallon McElligott/
Minneapolis

656

ART DIRECTOR
John Scott MacDaniels

WRITER
Cristina Gavin

DESIGNER
John Scott MacDaniels

ARTIST
Daniel Marr

CLIENT
Amtrak's San Joaquin

AGENCY
Lowe Marschalk/
San Francisco

655

GANNETT OUTDOOR

Looks like perfect weather for Amtrak's San Joaquin!

ALL ABOARD AMTRAK

GANNETT OUTDOOR

Looks like perfect weather for Amtrak's San Joaquin!

ALL ABOARD AMTRAK

GANNETT OUTDOOR

Looks like perfect weather for Amtrak's San Joaquin!

ARD MTRAK

Public Service Newspaper Or Magazine: Single

657

ART DIRECTOR
Tom Schwartz

WRITER
Dean Hacohen

PHOTOGRAPHER
Larry Sillen

CLIENT
Partnership for a Drug-Free America

AGENCY
DDB Needham Worldwide

658

ART DIRECTORS
Cathi Mooney
Ken Mandelbaum

WRITERS
Ken Mandelbaum
Cathi Mooney

PHOTOGRAPHER
Kurt Andersen

CLIENT
Association for Retarded Citizens

AGENCY
Mandelbaum Mooney & Associates/San Francisco

659

ART DIRECTORS
Bob Kuperman
Richard Bess
Melinda Kanipe

WRITER
Pacy Markman

PHOTOGRAPHER
Marc Feldman

CLIENT
Partnership for a Drug-Free America

AGENCY
DDB Needham Worldwide/ Los Angeles

660

ART DIRECTORS
Bob Kuperman
Melinda Kanipe
Richard Bess

WRITER
Pacy Markman

PHOTOGRAPHER
Marc Feldman

CLIENT
Partnership for a Drug-Free America

AGENCY
DDB Needham Worldwide/ Los Angeles

657

Last year, a man who had lived his entire life in an institution, moved into a house.

He decorated it himself, and found, for the first time, that he was surrounded by things that he liked.

He shopped for his own food, and finally was able to eat what he wanted to.

At night, when he undressed for bed, he was able, for the first time in his life, to do it in privacy.

Until recently, people with mental retardation were routinely institutionalized.

Today, they are finally leading normal lives. Holding down jobs. Supporting themselves. Living in their own homes and apartments.

The Association for Retarded Citizens provides a variety of programs designed to help people with mental retardation to become self-sufficient, productive members of the community. Including supportive services to help them live on their own.

We help them move from institutions to group living situations where they learn how to cook, clean, and even balance a budget. From there, they can move into their own homes or apartments.

Unfortunately, this takes time and money. For every ten people we move into independent housing, hundreds more wait in institutions and group homes.

Which is why your help is desperately needed. For more information write to us, or call 415-931-3330.

Unfortunately, there are reasons why people are still institutionalized.

Lack of money shouldn't be one of them.

The Association for Retarded Citizens.
3110 California St., S.F., 94115

658

Beauty and the Beast

"I used to go into the bathroom and talk to the person in the mirror. And it was really weird because the person in the mirror was stone sober. I would have conversations with this person in the mirror who was trying to tell me what I was doing to myself. At first, it was, 'Mary, this is ridiculous, what are you doing?' type things. 'You're dying, stop doing coke, get help. Talk with somebody.' Then we had fifteen minute conversations. The physical me would be leaning up against the wall, but I'd see her moving in the mirror, waving her hands, yelling. And I'd walk away, and sit at my desk and do a toot. Try to get over what happened there."

If you knew Mary at sixteen, you wouldn't have noticed anything unusual about her. She was pretty. And smart. Her family wasn't particularly rich or poor. Her childhood wasn't unusual. She was probably a lot like you or your friends. It could have happened at a party. Or on a date. Someone said, "Want to do a line?" There's not much more to the beginning than that. Because up until a couple of years ago, there were lots of people, smart people, who were convinced you couldn't get addicted to cocaine. That cocaine was a glamourous drug. It didn't put you into a stupor like heroin. Or make you move in slow motion like pot. It made you feel great. Look great. It was a real high. It was beautiful. It was too good to be true. It's not true.

What do we know that we didn't know before? Well, nobody's saying cocaine isn't an addictive drug anymore. Far from it. It's psychologically addictive. More so than almost any other drug.

They do tests with laboratory animals and various drugs. The ones on cocaine will push the lever for the drugs more and more often. Until they die. That doesn't even happen with heroin or PCP.

And though for years people have died from cocaine use, it took a couple of highly-publicized, tragic deaths to get the message home to everyone. You can die the first time or the tenth time or the fiftieth time you do coke. Because of the way the brain processes the drug, you can do the same dose week after week, and one day *that* dose will kill you.

No one can predict who will die or who won't. There's no such thing as "safe snorting." The truth is every time you do a line of coke, you risk dying.

In fact, the only thing about cocaine that's predictable is its unpredictability. Ten percent of the people who try the drug get addicted...like Mary. But no expert can predict who will or won't get addicted. And, of course, everyone who did was sure they wouldn't.

There's nothing glamourous about the way cocaine works. It goes one of two ways. You do some coke. Get high. Then about twenty minutes later, you feel low. Irritable. Some people can walk away from the drug then. But there are the others who are driven to recapture the high. For them, each time,

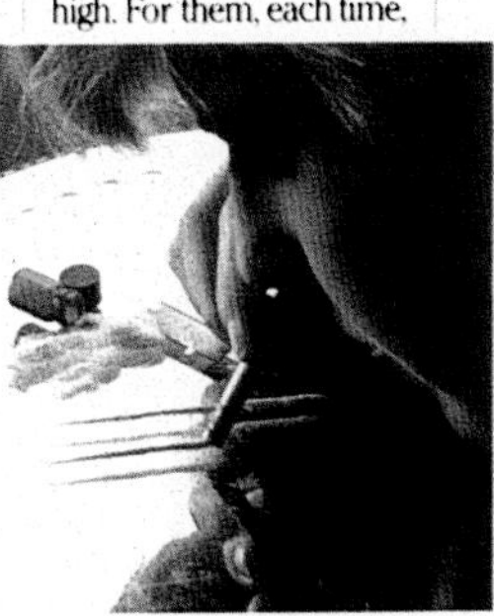

it takes more coke to get there. And the more coke they do, the deeper the lows. Irritation becomes depression. Or worse.

Lots of people who get addicted to coke experience periods of real paranoia. The feeling that they're being chased. Some become frightened at the sight of a policeman. Of course, that's partly because cocaine possession is illegal. And, in most states, the penalties are very stiff.

And cocaine addiction can get even uglier. The person who truly needs cocaine now needs nothing else. Not food. So the appetite goes. Not friends. Not sex. You know how someone on heroin behaves. Getting the drug is everything. Where you get the drug, what lies you have to tell, what you'll do to get the money—everything is secondary to getting the drug. The picture's no prettier with coke. It's almost exactly the same as heroin. The dependency, the deception, the irrational fear, the loss of self. You look in the mirror and someone else is looking out at you. Coke *is* a real scary drug.

That's the truth.

Partnership for a Drug-Free America

659

What to do if he hands you a line.

You're on a date. You really like him. He seems to like you. You're alone. He pulls out a little yellow bottle with a white powder in it, a small mirror, and lays out a couple of lines of cocaine. There's usually a little dialogue that goes with this ritual. He may say, "It'll make you feel high. You're going to have the most fantastic sexual experience you have ever had." And, of course he'll say, "Everybody does it."

That's the way a lot of young women get introduced to cocaine today. If it happens to you, what do you do? You want to appear sophisticated. You like him, remember. Maybe the sex *will* be great. You've heard that from other girls. What do you do?

It's up to you. No one should make that decision for you. But if you're going to have to make the decision—and sooner or later, you probably will—if you keep reading, at least you'll make the decision armed with the facts.

First of all, everybody doesn't do cocaine. You know that.

And, you know everybody who does cocaine does not get addicted to it. About ten percent do. (If you're talking about smoking coke—like crack or rock or freebasing—the numbers jump to almost fifty percent. And smoking it, you *can* get addicted the first time.)

So, to be honest, if you say yes to the guy, the odds are nine to one you won't get addicted. Not bad. Until you consider that no one can predict whether you'll be that one in ten who does get addicted. It's a little like playing Russian roulette.

The very same goes for dying. Last year almost seven hundred people in the U.S. died of confirmed cocaine overdoses. And there were probably thousands more where cocaine was involved. But there were millions who used cocaine. So the odds are you won't die. But again, no one can predict who'll die from what dose of cocaine. Some people do it for years. Some people die the first or fifth or tenth time. Again, Russian roulette.

What's important here is that cocaine is a *drug*. An unpredictable drug. It affects different people in different ways. But it works on everyone the same way. If you snort cocaine, it makes the heart beat faster. It's a fact. Your blood pressure rises. Then it hits the brain. That's where coke does its work. That's where the high comes from. It's a powerful drug. So each time you use it, it does the same thing to the heart, the same thing to the brain. And the results are cumulative. It's not uncommon for people who get addicted to cocaine to suffer from high blood pressure. It's not uncommon for addicts to suffer severe bouts of paranoia. But even the first time you use it, there's a predictable psychological reaction.

First there's the high, which lasts about twenty minutes, then a low, a down. That's why people do another line. To get the high back. But every high is guaranteed to be followed by a low. Sometimes, right away, the low is really depression.

You can figure out the rest. The more frequent the use the more severe the depression. Cocaine and suicide are old friends.

And what about cocaine and sex?

To be honest, no one really knows. Some people will tell you that it enhances sexual pleasure. It may be the coke. It may simply be the myth that the coke enhances sexual pleasure. (In Africa, certain tribes believe that eating ground rhinocerous horn enhances sexual pleasure.)

What doctors do know about cocaine and sex is this: The more you use it, the lower the drive for sex, the lower the enjoyment of sex. And that goes for other drives as well. Like addiction to any drug, the addiction becomes the sole reason for living. Everything else comes second—sex, friends, job, family.

You're familiar with the pattern in heroin addiction. Well, it's exactly the same with cocaine addiction. Except for one thing. There is some evidence that cocaine may be even more addictive than heroin. If the guy on the date offered you heroin, would you take it? Would it be a tough decision? In any case it's your decision.

But if he hands you a line, you may want to hand him this ad.

Partnership for a Drug-Free America

660

Public Service Newspaper Or Magazine: Single

661

ART DIRECTOR
Mark Oakley

WRITER
Jennifer Blair

DESIGNER
Mark Oakley

PHOTOGRAPHER
Bettman Archives

CLIENT
Meeting Street School

AGENCY
Leonard Monahan Saabye Lubars/Providence, RI

662

ART DIRECTOR
Scott Eggers

WRITER
Ben Vergati

DESIGNERS
Marilee Vergati
Curtis Asplund

PHOTOGRAPHER
Neal Vance

CLIENT
Dallas County Health Department

AGENCY
Knape & Knape/Dallas

663

ART DIRECTOR
Scott Eggers

WRITER
Ben Vergati

DESIGNERS
Scott Eggers
Curtis Asplund

PHOTOGRAPHER
Neal Vance

CLIENT
Dallas County Health Department

AGENCY
Knape & Knape/Dallas

664

ART DIRECTORS
Bob Kuperman
Melinda Kanipe
Richard Bess

WRITER
Pacy Markman

ARTIST
Axel Giese

PHOTOGRAPHER
Marc Feldman

CLIENT
Partnership for a Drug-Free America

AGENCY
DDB Needham Worldwide/Los Angeles

Where do poster children go when they grow up?

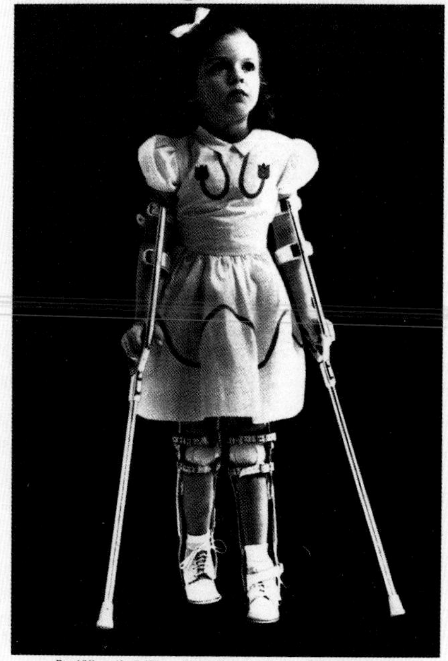

For a child born with a disability, becoming an adult presents a whole new set of problems.

The world suddenly becomes a bigger place. And the challenges to be faced are bigger too.

Like how to communicate without a voice. How to work without arms. And most importantly, how to become independent after a lifetime of depending on others.

Today, the Meeting Street School is helping people of all ages to meet these challenges.

You see, with over forty years of experience teaching and caring for severely disabled children, we've learned a few things.

Learned that speaking is just one of many ways to get people to listen.

Learned that walking is just one way to get where you want to go.

And, learned that given the appropriate tools, proper training, and a lot of encouragement, everyone has something to offer.

So help us help the disabled meet one of the biggest challenges they face. Being an adult.

For more information on the Meeting Street School and how you can help, call our development office at 438-9500.

Meeting Street School

661

DON'T LET LOVE SWEEP YOU OFF YOUR FEET.

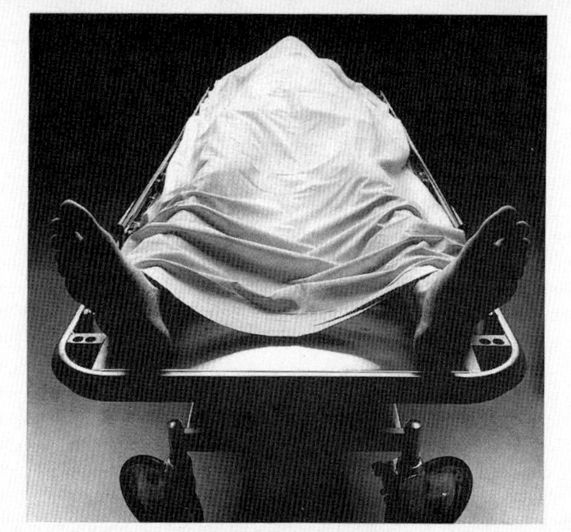

Unfortunately, love won't keep you from getting AIDS. Sleep with the wrong person and you may wake up to the hard cold facts about AIDS too late.

Because when you sleep with someone, you're sleeping with everyone he or she has slept with for the past eight years.

And there's no known cure for AIDS. Everyone who gets the disease dies.

But AIDS can be prevented. By saying no to sex. And by saying no to needle drugs.

Sure, sex can be embarrassing to talk about, but don't let it embarrass you to death. Get all the facts about AIDS, and talk about them with your girlfriend or boyfriend.

Then if you choose to have sex, stick to one partner. And always use a condom. It's one of the best defenses against AIDS.

The point is, if you're going to have sex, you should do it responsibly.

So don't take AIDS lying down. For more information on how AIDS is transmitted and how you can protect yourself, call the Dallas County Health Department, (214) 351-4335. All calls are confidential.

AIDS. IT CAN'T BE CURED. BUT IT CAN BE PREVENTED.

662

A BAD REPUTATION ISN'T ALL YOU CAN GET FROM SLEEPING AROUND.

Think about it. When you sleep with someone, you're sleeping with everyone he or she has slept with for the past eight years. And if someone along the line had the AIDS virus, you would have been exposed.

Unfortunately, there is no known cure for AIDS. Everyone who gets it dies.

But AIDS can be prevented. By saying no to sex. And by saying no to needle drugs.

Don't let it embarrass you to death. Get all the facts about AIDS, and talk about them with your girlfriend or boyfriend. Then if you choose to have sex, stick to one partner. And use a condom, properly, every time. It's one of the best defenses against AIDS. The point is, if you're going to have sex, you should do it responsibly.

Don't fool around with your life. Find out more about how AIDS is transmitted, and how you can protect yourself, call the Dallas County Health Department, (214) 351-4335. All calls are strictly confidential.

AIDS. IT CAN'T BE CURED. BUT IT CAN BE PREVENTED.

663

"I was told sex was great with coke. I didn't think it was so great. I just liked the sex. It was like, you could do that, and that way you could have a relationship with someone, but you didn't have to worry about them bothering you or harassing you or wanting to develop anything.

"And I would walk into a club or whatever, and every guy there would know I was there. I would just have this aura about me that said, 'Okay, she's here and looking.' And that was my game. I'd pick out one person, and I'd say to myself, 'I could get you to come home with me.' And I did. God forbid that I would think about disease. Herpes or VD. None of that seemed important at the time."

– *"Stephanie," age 30*
A recovering cocaine addict

Cocaine & Sex

What Does Cocaine Have To Do With Sex?

To begin with, most young women are introduced to cocaine in a sexual setting. A guy will offer her a couple of lines as a prelude to sex—or as an inducement to have sex. She'll hear that cocaine makes sex more enjoyable, that everybody does cocaine.

Then there's the decision-making process itself. Guys decide to do coke because of pressure from the group. For them, like sex, it's a macho thing, a test of their manhood, an initiation rite to belong to the group.

For girls, the decision of whether or not to do coke is often a more personal one. A woman tends to treat it in the same way she decides about whether or not to have sex. She's often more thoughtful. The more educated she is, the more she wants information. Now, information on sex has been around a long time. Information on cocaine has been a little harder to come by. And a lot of the information on cocaine is brand new.

Does Cocaine Make Sex Better?

To be honest, nobody really knows. Some women say it does. Others, like the "Stephanie" above, say "no." It just may be that the myth that cocaine makes sex better is what's at work here. If you believe something's an aphrodisiac, it may actually feel like it is an aphrodisiac.

There are fewer claims that cocaine use makes sex better for men. Actually, it's exactly the opposite. Most men report increased sexual difficulty even with casual cocaine use.

And, all the experts agree that addicted women and men experience a pronounced decrease in their sex drive and in their level of sexual enjoyment. It makes sense. If you picture a heroin addict, you know that heroin is the most important thing in her life. It comes before family, job, friends—and sex. Unless she's using sex to get money for her habit.

But isn't heroin much more addictive than cocaine?

Right now, experts believe that cocaine is one of the most addictive of all drugs—including heroin. It's because of the way cocaine works. You snort a couple of lines. You get high. It lasts for about twenty minutes. Then there's a low. You want to get high again. You snort a couple more lines of coke.

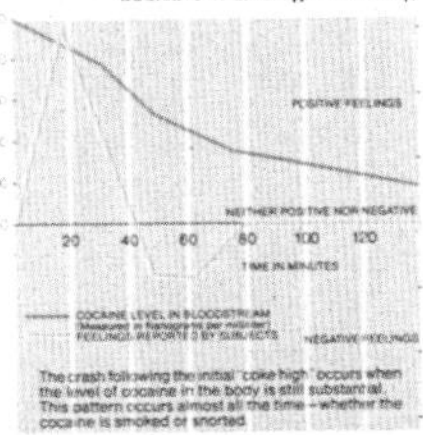

The crash following the initial "coke high" occurs when the level of cocaine in the body is still substantial. This pattern occurs almost all the time—whether the cocaine is smoked or snorted.

Of course, not everyone who tries coke gets addicted. Only about ten percent do. But no one can predict who will become addicted. Everyone who is addicted was sure they would not be.

Normal heartrate.

Heartrate accelerated by cocaine use.

Cocaine And A Woman's Body.

If you're a typical young woman today, you're very concerned about your body. Not just about how it looks. But about how you take care of it. You're probably careful about what you eat. You may even be smart enough not to smoke and risk the diseases connected with smoking. You probably have some information on what alcohol can do to your body. And if you drink, you do it in moderation.

Here is some information on cocaine which is probably new to you. But which should be helpful when you're faced with the decision, and odds are you will be, of whether or not to actually try cocaine.

The drug acts directly on your heart and your brain. If you snort cocaine, almost immediately your heart will beat faster, your blood pressure will rise. Ask anyone who's tried it. The high comes when the coke hits the brain. That's the first time you do coke. If you continue, there are cumulative effects.

The constant challenge to the heart can result in hypertension—high-blood pressure.

In the brain, there's the destruction of good nerve cells. And, worse, something doctors have only recently discovered. Cocaine causes the brain to produce a new kind of cell. These are not "good" nerve cells. And they're activated by the cocaine. And they multiply with use. And, with use, the danger multiplies. For without any warning, these cells can become activated while doing what may be an ordinary amount of cocaine. The result can be seizures—or death.

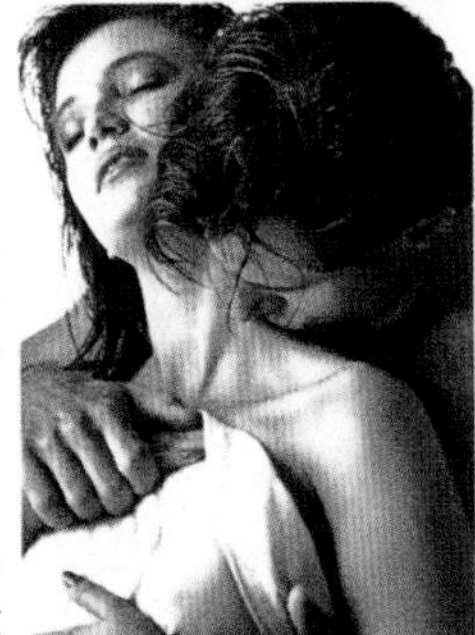

Cocaine use over any period of time tends to lessen the body's ability to fight disease. You're more susceptible to infection. Cocaine use affects the appetite. You're less likely to eat well. That increases the physical danger as well.

Psychologically, as "Stephanie" wrote, you just forget about your body. You have the delusion of being free from harm. So the coke user is less careful with regard to sexual diseases.

"In the drug program I'd entered, I realized what I had been doing. I wanted to reach that high, but you can't get high anymore. Not on coke. Not on sex. Not on anything. There's no high left. No euphoria. Pain is all there is."

Partnership for a Drug-Free America

664

Public Service Newspaper Or Magazine: Single

665

ART DIRECTOR
Raul Pina

WRITER
Joe Della Femina

CLIENT
Citizens Against Smoking

AGENCY
Della Femina Travisano & Partners

666

ART DIRECTOR
Jac Coverdale

WRITER
Joe Alexander

CLIENT
Earth Protector

AGENCY
Clarity Coverdale Rueff/ Minneapolis

667

ART DIRECTOR
Wayne Gibson

WRITER
Luke Sullivan

CLIENT
People for the Ethical Treatment of Animals

AGENCY
The Martin Agency/ Richmond, VA

668

ART DIRECTOR
Carolyn Tye

WRITER
Kerry Feuerman

PHOTOGRAPHERS
John Whitehead
IBID

CLIENT
United Way

AGENCY
Ford & Westbrook/ Richmond, VA

2000 BULLETS, 600 ARROWS,
82 TOMAHAWKS
AND 30 SPEARS COULDN'T DO
WHAT CIGARETTES DID.
He won the west and World War II single-handed. He was bigger than life on and off screen. He was John Wayne, the indestructible "Duke." And he was destroyed by lung cancer, a disease caused almost exclusively by cigarettes.
Cigarettes kill, slowly, surely, insidiously. If you smoke, stop. If you don't, keep it that way. Unless you think you're tougher than a legend.
CITIZENS AGAINST SMOKING

665

THANKS TO THE CITY COUNCIL, MINNEAPOLIS HAS THIS NEW GARBAGE DISPOSAL SITE.

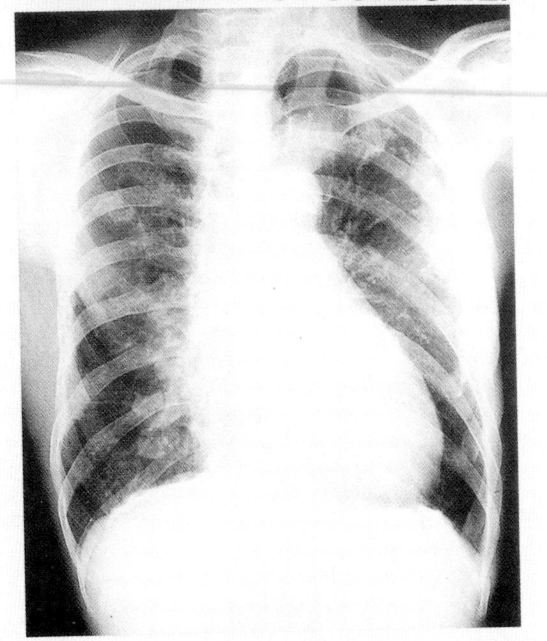

Hennepin County's new garbage burning plant near Downtown Minneapolis will fill our air with cancer causing dioxins, lead compounds, and other harmful pollutants. Yet most Minnesotans don't know all the facts surrounding this dangerous issue. Please help us clear the air by writing or calling Earth Protector, 1138 Plymouth Bldg., Mpls., MN 55402. (612) 375-0202. Donations are welcome.

MINNESOTANS AGAINST THE GARBAGE BURNING PLANT

666

Thanks to a $12 million government grant, scientists have conclusive proof that monkeys die when their skulls are crushed.

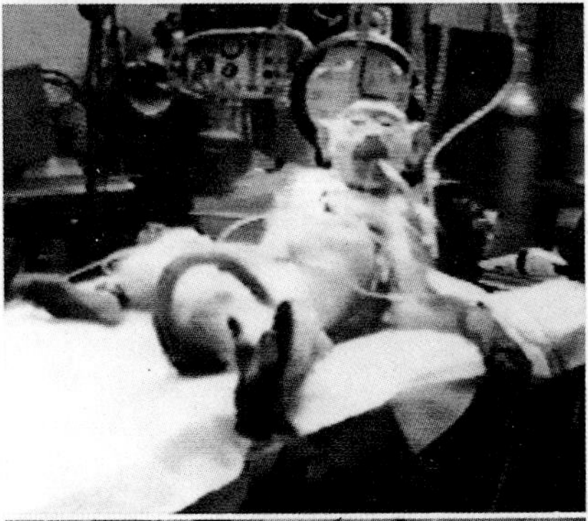

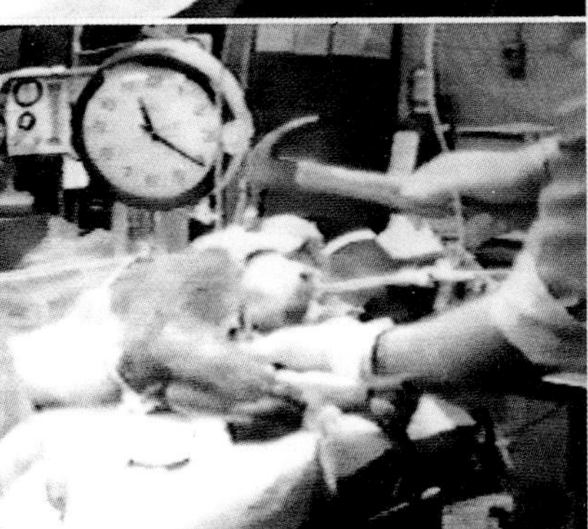

Did you know what other "experiments" that you've helped underwrite with your hard-earned tax dollars?

You paid to have a group of grown men keep a group of cats awake for a week straight.

Cats that were then placed on floating pieces of wood to see how long the cats' fear of falling in would keep them awake. Proving exactly what? Anything?

Care for another? To test the effectiveness of the Heimlich maneuver (already well-documented as effective), another federally-funded lab wanted to drown some dogs.

Fortunately, the scientists were drowned with letters instead (thanks to an effort by our organization) and the experiment was called off.

That experiment isn't the only one we've managed to have had scrapped.

We helped raise such an outroar over the head-injury research on the monkeys you see in these pictures, that it was closed down.

But for every sadistic and scientifically worthless experiment we've shut down, there are literally thousands we haven't.

People For The Ethical Treatment Of Animals (PETA) works with medical and legal professionals, the media, members of Congress, and people like you to help expose animal abuse and tax waste in this horrible animal experimentation industry.

We've brought an end to many horror stories, but thousands of cruel experiments are being conducted even as you read this ad.

That's why we're asking for your help. Because our opponents don't listen to moral arguments or pleas of mercy.

They have to be pinned down in court.

So please, send us your tax-deductible contribution today. And thank you.

Yes, I want to help stop the abuse of animals in experiments.

Name ______

Address ______

City ______ State ______ Zip ______

Please accept my tax deductible contribution of: $15 ______

$25 ______ $50 ______ $100 ______ other ______

People For The Ethical Treatment Of Animals

667

BEFORE WE ASK YOU FOR ANOTHER DOLLAR, YOU DESERVE TO KNOW WHERE THE LAST 12 MILLION WENT.

If you ever wondered just how much good your contribution to the United Way did, take heart.

Last year, only 10 cents out of each dollar went to administrative and fund raising costs. The other 90 cents went to mending broken families and feeding hungry senior citizens. It helped provide coats for children who were cold. It helped battered wives start new lives. It took drunk drivers off our streets and put them on the road to recovery.

As in every year, a committee of local volunteers decided who would receive the funds. The amount was based on need. In all, 58 local United Way Agencies and services put your donation to good use. Here they are to say thank you, and as the hands say below, please give generously again this year.

1. *American Red Cross, Virginia Capital Chapter.* Help for disaster victims, aid to military families, first aid, water safety, CPR courses. Also training related to home health and parenting, and volunteer opportunities for youth and adults.

2. *Arts Council of Richmond Special Audiences Project.* Cultural experiences through performances and workshops for individuals with little exposure because of handicaps or social status.

3. *Central Virginia Legal Aid Society, Inc.* Legal advice and representation in civil matters for people who cannot afford an attorney and have no court-appointed attorney.

4. *Communication Center for the Deaf.* Short-term message relay, information and referral, requests for interpreters and problem resolution assistance for deaf people through TTD/telephone message relay service (through United Way of Greater Richmond).

5. *Housing Opportunities Made Equal (HOME).* Housing counseling for low income home seekers. Mediation in tenant/landlord problems. Production and distribution of guides to rental housing in greater Richmond area.

6. *Information & Referral Center.* Free, confidential, 24-hours, seven-days-a-week referral service for individuals and organizations with problems or questions in the city of Richmond and the counties of Charles City, Chesterfield, Goochland, Hanover, Henrico, New Kent and Powhatan (through United Way of Greater Richmond).

7. *Literacy Council of Metropolitan Richmond, Inc.* One-to-one tutoring to enable illiterate adults to acquire reading, writing and math skills necessary to take advantage of opportunities in their environment.

8. *The Richmond Urban League, Inc.* Housing and employment counseling, education and other community services for Richmond's poor and disadvantaged.

9. *United Service Organization (USO).* Supportive services to military personnel and their families.

10. *The United Way of Greater Richmond.* Social planning, fund raising, information and referral, volunteer recruitment, public education and technical management assistance.

11. *Virginia Voice for the Print Handicapped.* Radio reading service for the visually or physically handicapped who are unable to read conventionally-printed materials.

12. *Volunteer Center.* Promotion of volunteerism through training and volunteer referrals (through United Way of Greater Richmond).

13. *Emergency Shelter, Inc.* Temporary emergency shelter and counseling for individuals in need.

14. *Metropolitan Area Resource Clearing House (M.A.R.C.H.).* Emergency assistance in the form of food or fuel assistance.

15. *The Daily Planet, Inc.—Street Center.* Community service center providing meals, counseling and other supportive services for deinstitutionalized adults returned to the Richmond area and other homeless persons.

16. *The Salvation Army.* Counseling, emergency assistance, temporary emergency shelter, disaster relief, missing persons information, Boys Club and neighborhood services in Church Hill.

17. *Travelers Aid Society of Virginia.* Crisis-oriented counseling and temporary emergency financial aid for people who are in difficulty away from home.

18. *Young Women's Christian Association of Richmond, Virginia. (YWCA).* Emergency shelter for victims of spouse abuse. Counseling and supportive services for rape victims and abused spouses. After-school and summer daycare for children. Educational programs and seminars, physical fitness for men and women, classes and clubs for teenagers.

19. *CONTACT Old Dominion, Inc.* Crisis intervention and telephone counseling through regional hotline.

20. *Fan Free Clinic.* Free medical services offered to individuals in need in the Richmond community.

21. *Hanover Association for Retarded Citizens, Inc.* Advocacy organization for retarded Hanover citizens who need help and transportation.

22. *Hanover Mental Health Association, Inc.* Day support services for individuals with mental health problems, including various prevention and educational programs.

23. *Instructive Visiting Nurse Association.* Health and rehabilitative services for patients needing care in their homes.

24. *Memorial Guidance Clinic, Inc.* Out-patient psychiatric facility for children with emotional and social problems, evaluation, treatment and consultation.

25. *Richmond Area Association for Retarded Citizens.* Infant intervention program, vocational training, sheltered workshop, recreation, socialization and summer camp for the mentally retarded. Also information, referral and advocacy.

26. *Catholic Charities of Richmond, Inc.* Group and individual counseling, limited adoption program, respite care services, care for refugee children.

27. *Children's Home Society of Virginia.* Statewide foster care, adoption and counseling.

28. *Family and Children's Service of Richmond, Inc.* Counseling and family life education courses, intensive short-term help to families with child abuse and neglect, homemaker program, teenage runaway counseling and emergency shelter for runaway teens. (Oasis House).

29. *Friends Association for Children, Inc.* Day care for pre-school and school-aged children, social group work for youth and family social services, administration of the community Child Care Scholarship Fund.

30. *Jewish Family Services, Inc.* Individual and group counseling, homemaker assistance for older adults in the community, limited adoption program.

31. *Parents Anonymous of Virginia, Inc.* Self-help, support and educational programs to prevent child abuse.

32. *Volunteer Emergency Foster Care.* Emergency foster care for dependent children.

33. *Bethlehem Center.* In Highland Park, counseling and emergency assistance, day care for senior citizens and children, and a nutrition site for the elderly.

34. *Grace House.* Developmental pre-school directed toward children of low income families living in Fan District of Richmond. Toy lending library for development of parent/child interactive skills.

35. *Meals on Wheels of Greater Richmond, Inc.* Voluntary meal delivery to the handicapped and elderly who cannot buy or prepare their own meals.

36. *Office of Refugee Resettlement.* Refugee social adjustment, and counseling. Also crisis intervention services.

37. *Richmond Community Action Program—East End Soup Kitchen.* Feeding program—nutrition site for hungry and homeless in Church Hill.

38. *Southside Day Nursery.* Day care for pre-school children with two working parents.

39. *William Byrd Community House, Inc.* Located in Oregon Hill, Randolph and the Maymont area. Nutrition site for the elderly, emergency assistance, adult counseling, day care and domestic violence prevention program. Also youth activities, including a local juvenile delinquency prevention program.

40. *Big Brothers & Big Sisters of Metropolitan Richmond, Inc.* Adult volunteer companionship and guidance to children from single-parent homes.

41. *Boys Clubs of Richmond, Virginia, Inc.* Recreation, group and individual guidance, day camp, tutorial educational, and health-related services for boys.

42. *Boy Scouts of America—Robert E. Lee Council.* Citizenship training, character and leadership development, and personal fitness for boys.

43. *Commonwealth Girl Scout Council.* Development of awareness of self and others, educational program to build personal values and community services.

44. *Girls Club of Richmond.* Youth development activities for girls in North Richmond and Highland Park areas.

45. *Jewish Community Center of Richmond.* Social, educational and cultural programs for all ages, child day care, and health and fitness programs.

46. *Young Men's Christian Association of Greater Richmond (YMCA).* Family-oriented programs to develop personal and mental fitness through child/parent clubs, teams, camping and instructional programs; emphasis on leadership and values development. Also child day care.

47. *Offender Aid and Restoration of Richmond, Inc.* Employment, family, social adjustment and other counseling to misdemeanants in jail or on probation.

48. *Prison Visitation Project.* Visitation and support services for families of inmates and juvenile offenders.

49. *Richmond Aftercare, Inc.* Halfway house for recovering substance abusers who have completed in-patient treatment and need more treatment within a supportive living environment; separate halfway houses for men and women.

50. *Richmond Cerebral Palsy Center.* Out-patient medical, therapeutic and various educational services for cerebral palsy youth to 21 years of age.

51. *Richmond Goodwill Industries.* Vocational training and employment for the physically, mentally and emotionally handicapped.

52. *Adult Development Center.* Out-patient, social, recreational, and therapeutic services to physically handicapped adults.

53. *Hanover Adult Center, Inc.* Day care for older adults whose families need respite from 24 hour care.

54. *Retired Senior Volunteer Program.* Recruitment and placement of retired people who want to volunteer (through The United Way of Greater Richmond).

55. *Stuart Circle Center, Inc.* Day care for older adults whose families need respite from 24 hour care; support group for Parkinson patients and family members.

56. *Senior Center of Richmond, Inc.* Educational and recreational services to people 50 years of age or more.

57. *South Richmond Senior Center, Inc.* Educational, recreational services, and nutrition site for people age 60 or more.

58. *Richmond Community Senior Center.* Educational and recreational services for older citizens, nutrition site and day care center for senior citizens.

THE UNITED WAY OF GREATER RICHMOND

Public Service Newspaper Or Magazine: Single

669

ART DIRECTOR
Cabell Harris

WRITER
Luke Sullivan

PHOTOGRAPHER
Pat Edwards

CLIENT
Girl Scouts

AGENCY
The Martin Agency/
Richmond, VA

670

ART DIRECTOR
Steve Stone

WRITER
Peter Wegner

CLIENT
Family Violence Project

AGENCY
Goodby Berlin &
Silverstein/San Francisco

671

ART DIRECTOR
Sally Oelschlager

WRITER
Kerry Casey

PHOTOGRAPHER
Steve Umland

CLIENT
KTCA/2

AGENCY
Carmichael Lynch/
Minneapolis

672

ART DIRECTOR
Scot Fletcher

WRITER
Larre Johnson

PHOTOGRAPHER
Michael Ruppert

CLIENT
Partnership for a
Drug-Free America

AGENCY
keye/donna/pearlstein -
Los Angeles

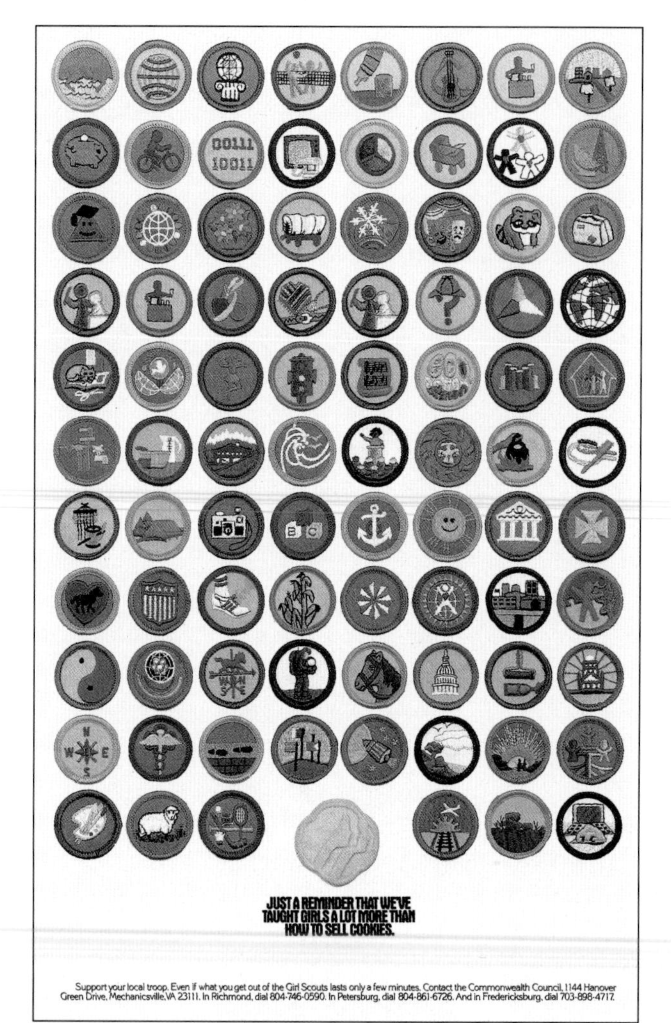

JUST A REMINDER THAT WE'VE TAUGHT GIRLS A LOT MORE THAN HOW TO SELL COOKIES.
Support your local troop. Even if what you get out of the Girl Scouts lasts only a few minutes. Contact the Commonwealth Council, 1144 Hanover Green Drive, Mechanicsville, VA 23111. In Richmond, dial 804-746-0590. In Petersburg, dial 804-861-6726. And in Fredericksburg, dial 703-898-4717.

669

ANNO · ETATIS ·
SVÆ · XLIX ·
It's not worth being his queen one day if you're his victim the next.
If you're trapped in a violent relationship, call (415) 821-4553. We'll help you to change your life while the word still has meaning. The Family Violence Project.

670

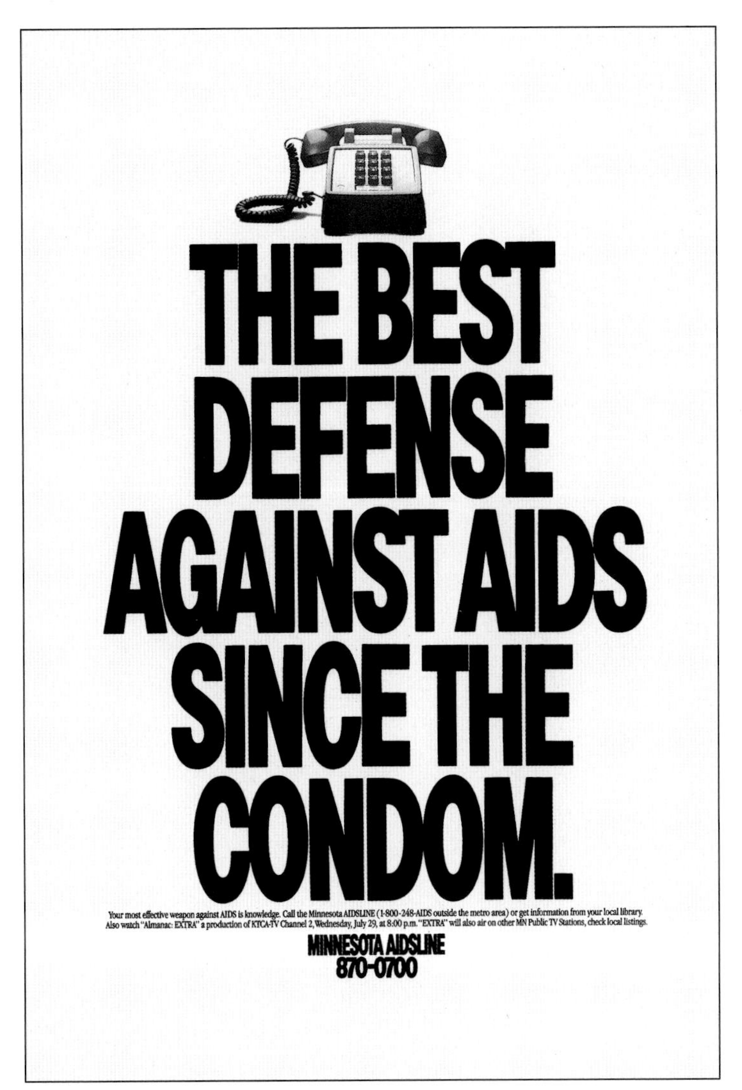
THE BEST
DEFENSE
AGAINST AIDS
SINCE THE
CONDOM.
Your most effective weapon against AIDS is knowledge. Call the Minnesota AIDSLINE (1-800-248-AIDS outside the metro area) or get information from your local library.
Also watch "Almanac: EXTRA" a production of KTCA-TV Channel 2, Wednesday, July 29, at 8:00 p.m. "EXTRA" will also air on other MN Public TV Stations, check local listings.
MINNESOTA AIDSLINE
870-0700

671

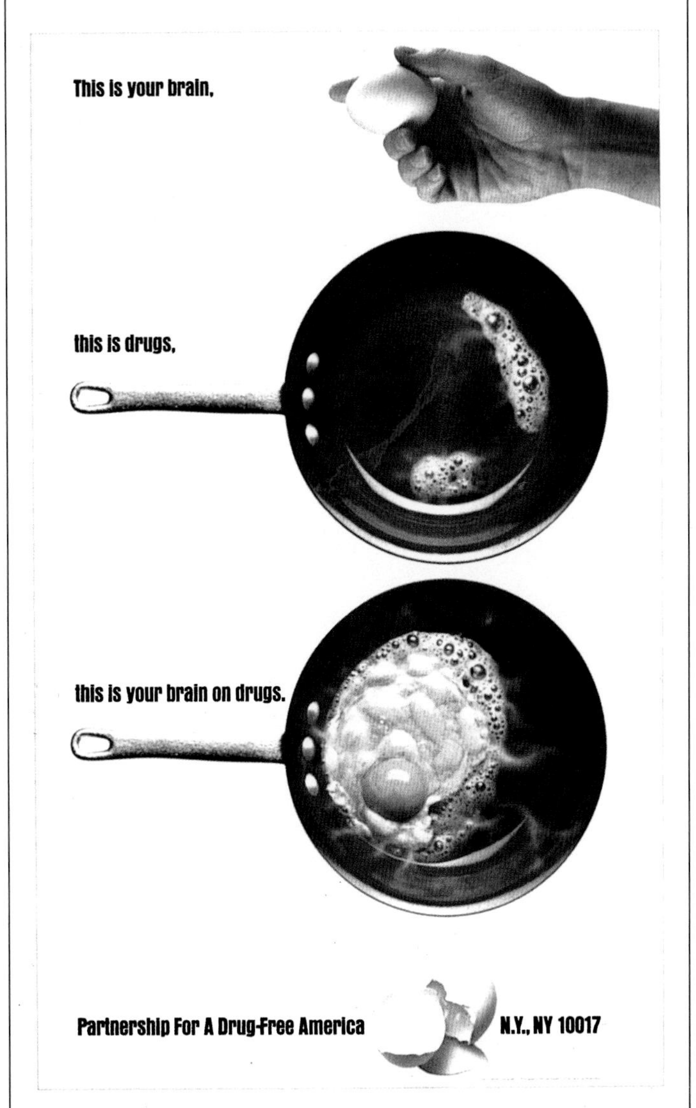
This is your brain,
this is drugs,
this is your brain on drugs.
Partnership For A Drug-Free America
N.Y., NY 10017

672

Public Service Newspaper Or Magazine: Single

673
ART DIRECTOR
Jerry Ketel
WRITER
Mark Waggoner
PHOTOGRAPHER
Mark Glazer
CLIENT
Metro Crisis Intervention Service
AGENCY
Ad-2/Portland, OR

674
ART DIRECTOR
Jerry Ketel
WRITER
Jerry Ketel
PHOTOGRAPHER
Mark Glazer
CLIENT
Metro Crisis Intervention Service
AGENCY
Ad-2/Portland, OR

675
ART DIRECTOR
Michael Fazende
WRITER
George Gier
PHOTOGRAPHER
Tom Berthiaume
CLIENT
4 A's
AGENCY
Fallon McElligott/Minneapolis

676
ART DIRECTOR
Gary Kaczmarek
WRITER
Doug Engel
PHOTOGRAPHER
Bettman Archives
CLIENT
Greater Madison Board of Realtors
AGENCY
Lindsay & Stone/Madison, WI

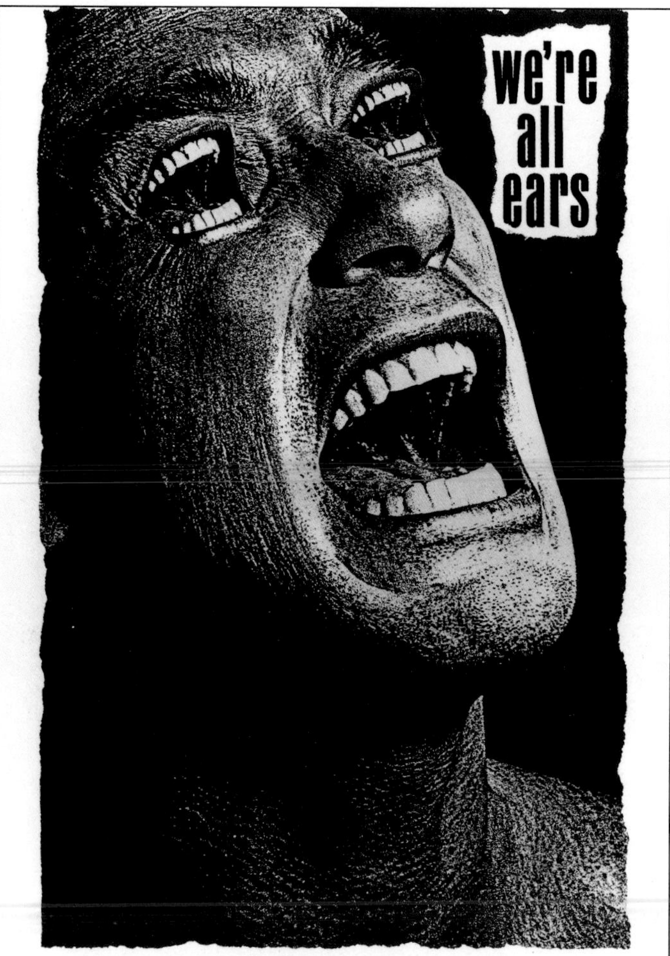

we're all ears
In times of crisis, call out for help. We're always there to listen. 223-6161.
METRO CRISIS INTERVENTION SERVICE.

673

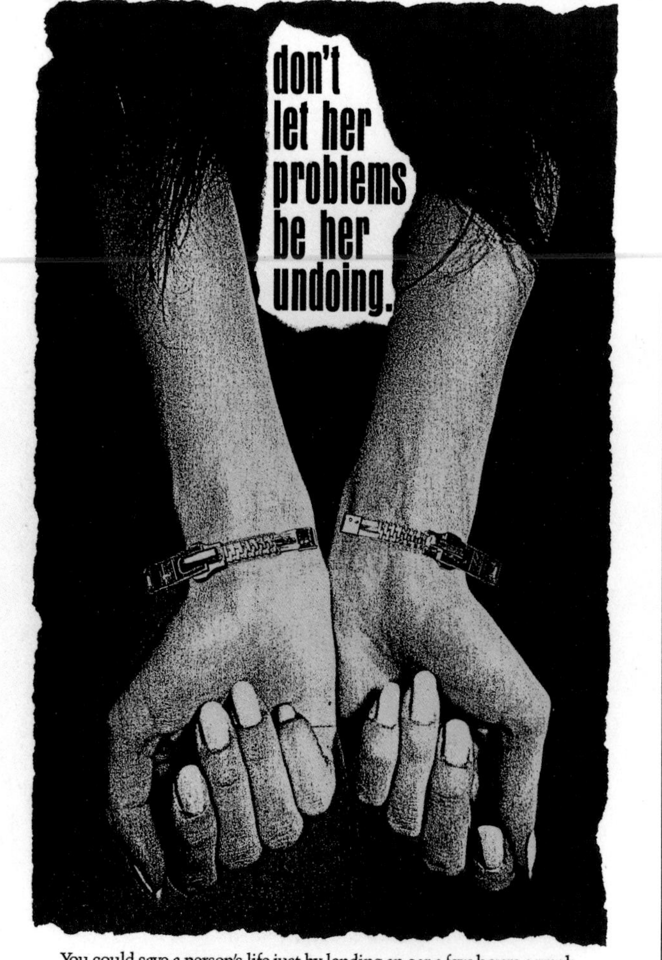

don't let her problems be her undoing.
You could save a person's life just by lending an ear a few hours a week.
Make a difference. 226-3099 METRO CRISIS INTERVENTION SERVICE.

674

SOME ADVERTISING CAN HAVE A DRAMATIC EFFECT ON CHILDREN.

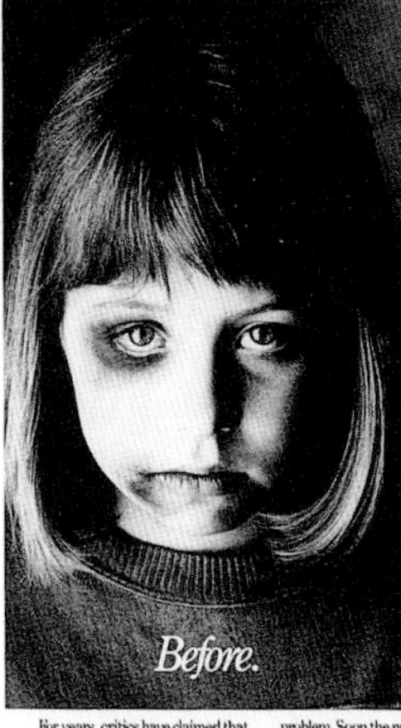

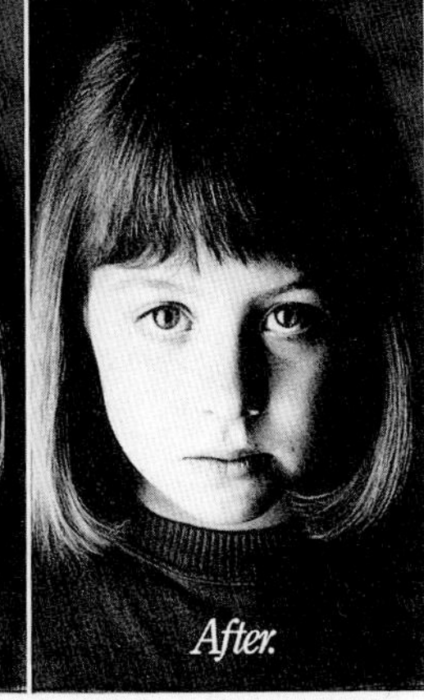

For years, critics have claimed that advertising can seriously affect children.

Fortunately, for the abused children of the world, this is sometimes true.

In 1976, the Advertising Council created a powerful campaign to help prevent child abuse.

As a result, people began coming to grips with the brutality of this ugly problem. Soon the number of reported child-abuse cases soared. Meaning that the children involved were finally in a position to receive the help they needed.

Members of the advertising community create campaigns like this one for a number of worthy causes each year.

Such organizations as the American Red Cross, the American Cancer Society and the Boy's Clubs of America all benefit.

In fact, since 1942, our contributions to public service advertising have totaled over 15 billion dollars. And that's had quite an effect on everybody.

ADVERTISING
ANOTHER WORD FOR FREEDOM OF CHOICE.
American Association of Advertising Agencies

675

For A Measly Ten Bucks,
You Can Become Someone's Uncle.
The Vilas Park Zoo Ball is important because the $10.00 donation you pay for an advance ticket goes directly towards building a new Primate House on the Zoo grounds, which kind of makes you an uncle of sorts. So if you're looking for an excuse to go bananas, the Vilas Park Zoo Ball is the perfect chance to go ape.
Vilas Park Zoo Ball
Saturday, July 25 · 8:00 PM · Sponsored by Greater Madison Board of Realtors®
Ball tickets are available at the Office of the Greater Madison Board of Realtors, all Shopko's in Madison, the office of the Madison Vilas Park Zoo, all Stop and Go's in Dane County, Condon Jewelers in West Towne, East Towne and Downtown, the Camera Company on Pinckney, State Street and East Washington, all Pizza Pit locations, Park Ponderosa, McFarland, Lyons Mortgage, Madison and at the door the night of the event.

676

Public Service Newspaper Or Magazine: Single

677
ART DIRECTOR
Bill Snitzer
WRITER
Jeff Weakley
PHOTOGRAPHER
Stan Kaplan
CLIENT
Greenpeace
AGENCY
Larsen Colby Koralek/
Los Angeles

678
ART DIRECTOR
Craig Tanimoto
WRITER
Dick Thomas
PHOTOGRAPHER
Joe Lampi
CLIENT
Boy Scouts
AGENCY
Bozell Jacobs Kenyon &
Eckhardt/Minneapolis

679
ART DIRECTORS
Bryan McPeak
Tony Gaudin
WRITERS
Craig Piechura
Dave Michalak
PHOTOGRAPHER
Jerry Farber
CLIENT
Michigan Humane Society
AGENCY
W.B. Doner & Company/
Southfield, MI

680
ART DIRECTOR
Robin Chrumka
WRITER
Mike Stocker
PHOTOGRAPHER
Bill Morden
CLIENT
Detroit Police Officers
Association
AGENCY
J. Walter Thompson/
Detroit

WE'RE NOT THE ONLY ONES TRYING TO PRESERVE THE WHALES.

In 1984, the Japanese government promised to stop all commercial whaling within four years.

Unfortunately, they were only telling fish stories.

The truth is, the Japanese are shooting their grenade-tipped harpoons right through legal loopholes that allow whaling for scientific reasons.

While the International Whaling Commission has found Japan's "scientific reasons" very hard to swallow, the Japanese restaurant industry has found it very appetizing. They're already placing their orders.

Thanks to your support we've made tremendous strides in saving this endangered species. We can't stop now. Please make a donation.

Let's help the whales out of this pickle.

GREENPEACE
1611 Connecticut Avenue, NW, Washington, DC 20009

677

EVERY DAY, FEWER TEENAGERS DRINK AND DRIVE.

Obituary Notices

Jarvis
Larry B., age 16, beloved son of Bob and Theresa Jarvis of Appleton, died accidently in auto accident on Friday. Funeral services 12:30 p.m. Wednesday, 1st Baptist Church of Appleton. Larry is also survived by sister, Laura, 12, and grandparents, Everett and Jane. Memorials may be directed to donors choice.

Johnson
Mike J., age 18, of Lakewood, died Sat-

SAFE-RIDES
Instead of driving drunk, call us: 221-3800.

678

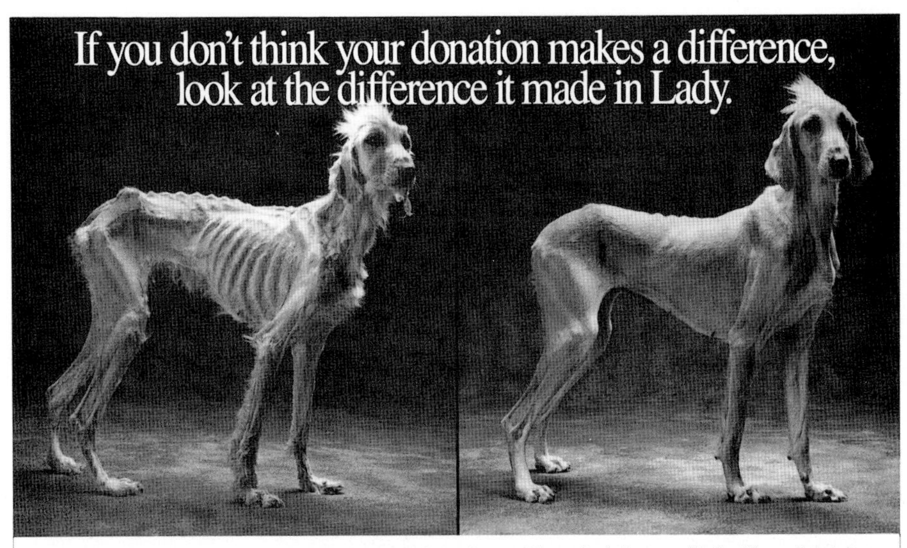

If you don't think your donation makes a difference, look at the difference it made in Lady.

What comes to mind when you think of an Afghan Hound? Probably a pampered purebred. Well-groomed. Aristocratic.

Certainly nothing like the dog that our cruelty investigator carried into the Michigan Humane Society (MHS) last January 30th.

What he found was one of the worst cases of starvation and neglect the MHS has ever encountered. A 6-year-old, female Afghan we named Lady, weighing just 19 pounds, and suffering from violent seizures.

She had been locked up, without food, for more than a month. Abandoned. The only water Lady received dripped down from a hole in the roof of the garage in which she had been left to die.

Examining veterinarian, Dr. Barbara Blaine, described the dog's condition as "literally skin and bones," concluding that "it is difficult to believe that this dog is alive."

But Lady is alive, thanks to your contributions to the MHS.

Her weight has doubled in three months. Her coat, which was so hopelessly matted it had to be completely shaved, is growing back. And her former owner has been charged with two counts of animal cruelty.

If stories like this one make you madder than hell, there's no better time to express your outrage than "Be Kind to Animals Week" (May 3-9). And there's no better way to do it than mailing a check to the MHS.

We promise your donation will make a difference. For Lady, it was the difference between life and death.

MICHIGAN HUMANE SOCIETY

Thousands of animals are cared for lovingly each year by the Michigan Humane Society. During "Be Kind to Animals Week," won't you help us help them?

Name______

Address______

City______ State____ Zip____

____$10 ____$25 ____$50 ____$100 ____Other

The Michigan Humane Society is a non-profit organization funded by private contributions. All contributions are tax deductible. Thank you for caring.

Please make checks payable to: Michigan Humane Society, 1401 Chrysler Drive, Detroit, MI 48211.

679

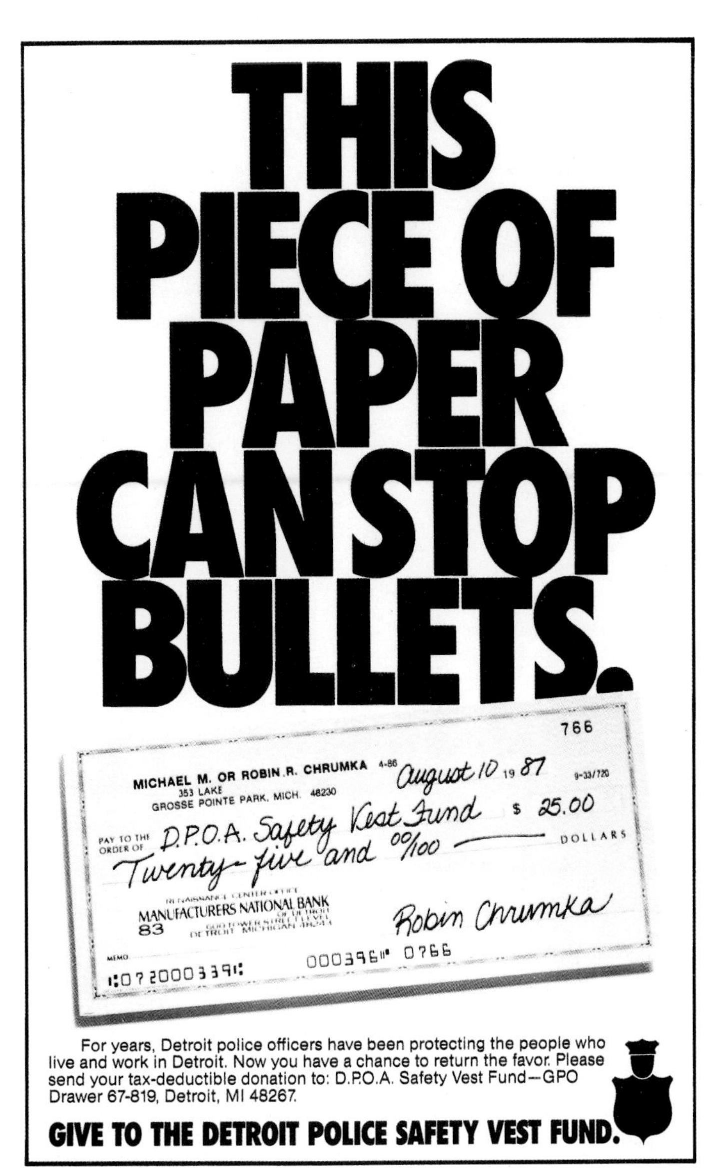

680

Public Service Newspaper Or Magazine: Single

681
ART DIRECTOR
Steve Basemore
WRITER
David Bernstein
PHOTOGRAPHER
David Langley
CLIENT
Partnership for a Drug-Free America
AGENCY
Backer Spielvogel Bates

682
ART DIRECTOR
Scott Kane
WRITER
K.C. Hayes
PHOTOGRAPHER
Ron Fortier
CLIENT
The Rapid City Public Library
AGENCY
Hakuhodo/Los Angeles

683
ART DIRECTOR
Robin Chrumka
WRITER
Mike Stocker
PHOTOGRAPHER
Bill Morden
CLIENT
Detroit Police Officers Association
AGENCY
J. Walter Thompson/Detroit

684
ART DIRECTOR
Craig Tanimoto
WRITER
Dick Thomas
CLIENT
Boy Scouts
AGENCY
Bozell Jacobs Kenyon & Eckhardt/Minneapolis

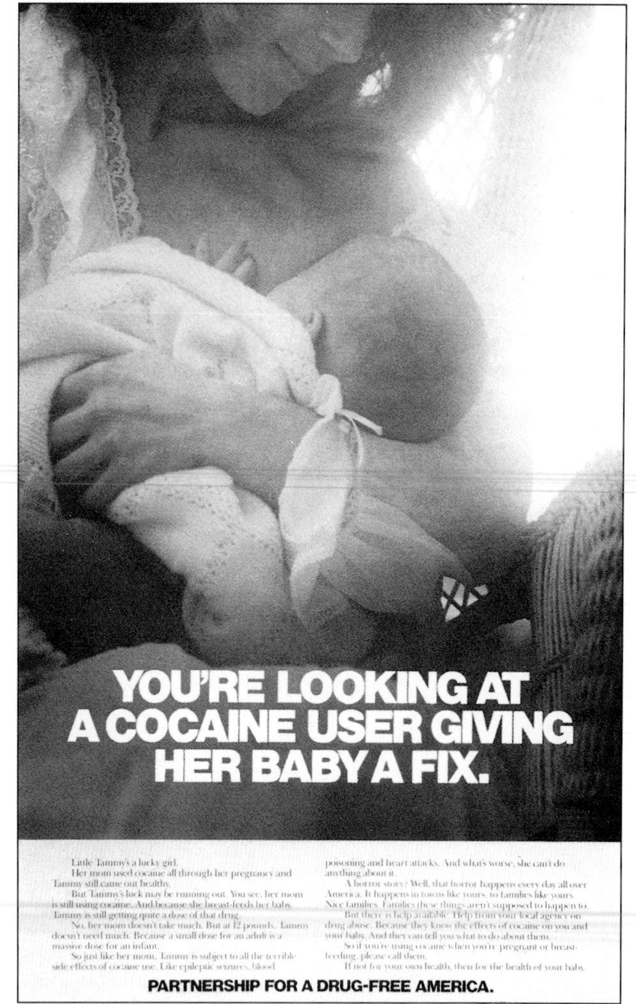

681

"I went to the Rapid City Public Library and found hundreds of dead people."

EKA PARKISON, GENEALOGIST

Homesteaders. Gold miners. Well drillers and wagon makers.

Eka's ancestors come to life again, right in our reference section. She found them hidden in journals, resting peacefully in genealogy records, tucked away in our 2000-volume collection of South Dakota history.

At the Rapid City Public Library, we make it easy to unearth the facts.

Whether you want information or inspiration, all you have to do is ask, and our staff will guide you to just the right resource. We have everything from phone books to cook books, from the great classics to computer data banks.

So if you're curious about something, don't sit there wondering. Just give us a call.

Or stop by.

Who knows what you'll dig up.

Come to an understanding. The Rapid City Public Library.

The Rapid City Journal supports the Rapid City Public Library.

682

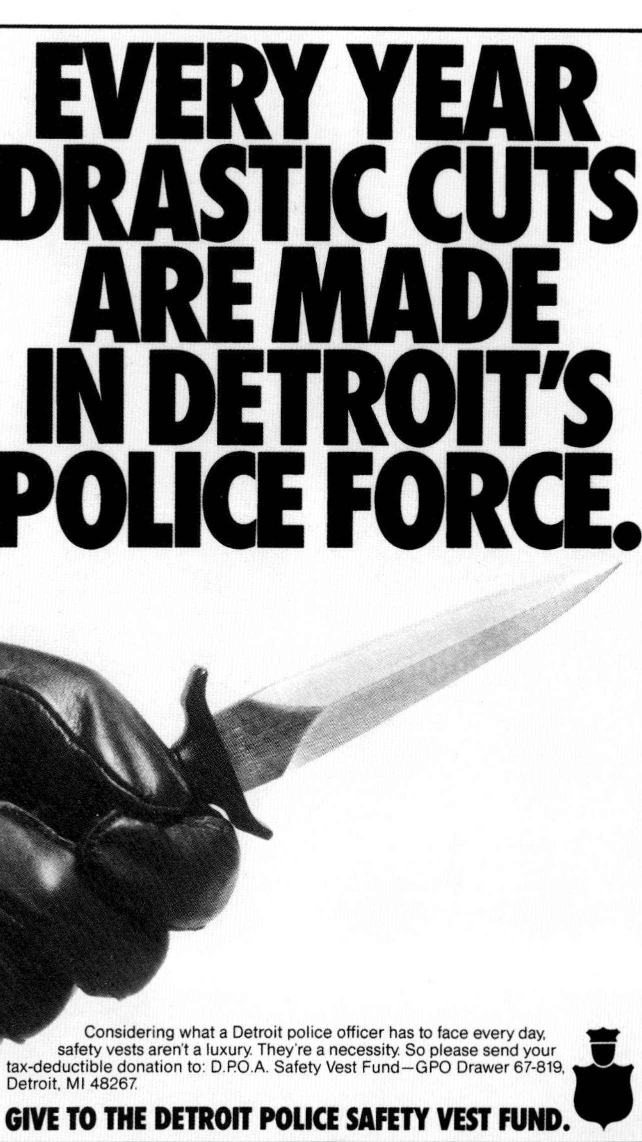

683

YOU WOULDN'T TAKE CHANCES WITH A LOADED GUN.

WHY TAKE CHANCES WITH A LOADED DRIVER?

SAFE-RIDES

Instead of riding with a drunk, call us: 221-3800.

684

Public Service Newspaper Or Magazine: Single

685

ART DIRECTOR
Michael Vaughan

WRITERS
Michael Vaughan
Margaret Elman

CLIENT
Pyramid Companies

AGENCY
Messner Vetere Berger Carey

686

ART DIRECTOR
Tom Bleakly

WRITER
Tim Pegors

DESIGNER
Tom Bleakly

CLIENT
St. John's Lutheran Church

AGENCY
Blaisdell & Westlie/
St. Paul, MN

687

ART DIRECTOR
Jenni Mason

WRITERS
Mike Smith
Scott McCormick

CLIENT
Hallmark

AGENCY
Valentine-Radford/
Kansas City, MO

688

ART DIRECTOR
Tom Bleakly

WRITER
Tim Pegors

DESIGNER
Tom Bleakly

CLIENT
St. John's Lutheran Church

AGENCY
Blaisdell & Westlie/
St. Paul, MN

You spend all year telling your kids not to talk to strangers, but on Oct. 31st, you send them to their homes.

Halloween is scary enough, so don't let your children go trick-or-treating alone.

Better still, have them come trick-or-treating with lots of other kids at the Salmon Run Mall. We'll have free goody bags for every kid plus a party with lots of games and entertainment.

So don't worry, the scariest people there will be in the Costume Contest.

Shopping Hours: Monday-Saturday 9:30-9:30; Sunday 11-6. At Exit 45 (Route 3) off I-81.

685

Anyone Who Believes In Jesus Christ Should Be Committed.

We're committed to our beliefs at St. John's Lutheran. Join us this Sunday.

Box 955 8748 210th St. W, Lakeville, Minnesota 55404 469-4916

686

We can write anything we want about illiterates.

They can't read it anyway.

We can call them stupid. Incompetent. Lazy. Without a picture on the page, they have no idea what we're saying. But the fact is, they're none of those things. They're simply people like us who haven't learned to read yet. Ask your local library how you can help change that. Because next time we run this ad, we'd like to have to be more careful about what we say.

This message created in the public interest by Valentine-Radford Advertising/PR Kansas City, MO

687

If Jesus Could Rise From The Dead, Surely You Can Get Up For The 11:00 a.m. Service.

For some people, getting up early on the weekend requires an almost superhuman effort. At St. John's we make it worth your while. So, rise to the occasion and visit us this Sunday.

688

Public Service Newspaper Or Magazine: Single

689

ART DIRECTOR
Tom Bleakly

WRITER
Tim Pegors

DESIGNER
Tom Bleakly

CLIENT
St. John's Lutheran Church

AGENCY
Blaisdell & Westlie/
St. Paul, MN

Public Service Newspaper Or Magazine: Campaign

690

ART DIRECTOR
Robin Chrumka

WRITER
Mike Stocker

PHOTOGRAPHER
Bill Morden

CLIENT
Detroit Police Officers
Association

AGENCY
J. Walter Thompson/
Detroit

Don't Let Your Kids Grow Up Thinking God's Last Name Is Damn.

Does it seem that your efforts to teach values to your children have been in vain?
At St. John's, we take Christian Education seriously. Visit us this Sunday.

Box 955 8748 210th St. W, Lakeville, Minnesota 55404 469-4916

689

THIS PIECE OF PAPER CAN STOP BULLETS.
766
MICHAEL M. OR ROBIN R. CHRUMKA
353 LAKE
GROSSE POINTE PARK, MICH. 48230
August 10 1987
PAY TO THE ORDER OF D.P.O.A. Safety Vest Fund $ 25.00
Twenty-five and 00/100 DOLLARS
MANUFACTURERS NATIONAL BANK
Robin Chrumka
For years, Detroit police officers have been protecting the people who live and work in Detroit. Now you have a chance to return the favor. Please send your tax-deductible donation to: D.P.O.A. Safety Vest Fund—GPO Drawer 67-819, Detroit, MI 48267.
GIVE TO THE DETROIT POLICE SAFETY VEST FUND.

HELP A DETROIT COP PUT ON A FEW POUNDS FOR HEALTH REASONS.
A safety vest only weighs six pounds. But to a Detroit police officer, those six pounds can be the difference between life and death. So please send your tax-deductible donation to: D.P.O.A. Safety Vest Fund—GPO Drawer 67-819, Detroit, MI 48267. After all, protecting our police officers is a responsibility we can't take lightly.
GIVE TO THE DETROIT POLICE SAFETY VEST FUND.

EVERY YEAR DRASTIC CUTS ARE MADE IN DETROIT'S POLICE FORCE.
Considering what a Detroit police officer has to face every day, safety vests aren't a luxury. They're a necessity. So please send your tax-deductible donation to: D.P.O.A. Safety Vest Fund—GPO Drawer 67-819, Detroit, MI 48267.
GIVE TO THE DETROIT POLICE SAFETY VEST FUND.

Public Service Newspaper Or Magazine: Campaign

691

ART DIRECTOR
Derrick Hass

WRITER
Howard Fletcher

DESIGNER
Derrick Hass

ARTIST
Derrick Hass

PHOTOGRAPHER
Bob Miller

CLIENT
Royal National Institute for the Deaf

AGENCY
Ogilvy & Mather/London

692

ART DIRECTOR
Hanna Mayer

WRITER
Sande Lohm

PHOTOGRAPHER
Liz Willard

CLIENT
Baltimore Junior Association of Commerce

AGENCY
W.B. Doner & Company/ Baltimore

"I'M ONE OF A MINORITY GROUP. IT TOOK AN ACT OF PARLIAMENT TO GET ME A JOB."

Elizabeth is a victim of discrimination.
Not because she's black.
Not because she's a woman.
But because she's deaf.
A while ago, Elizabeth applied for an office job with a local council.
They agreed she was able to do the job, yet they were in two minds about taking her on.
What clinched it was the Disabled Persons (Employment) Act 1944. It lays down that registered disabled people should make up 3% of a workforce.

Eventually, the council complied with the Act. Many employers don't. They don't have to, the quota scheme is unenforceable.
It's illegal to discriminate against Elizabeth because of her race. Or because of her sex.
Unfortunately, it's quite legal to discriminate against her because of her deafness.

THE ROYAL NATIONAL INSTITUTE FOR THE DEAF.

"IT TOOK THE COUNCIL 17 YEARS TO DECIDE THAT I WASN'T FIT FOR THE JOB."

Year in, year out, George worked on the council dustcarts.
With no complaints, apart from the odd spilled bin.
Then one day, without warning, he was called into the office.
And given his cards.
The phone box was the cause of his downfall. He couldn't use it.
How could he? He was born deaf.
According to the boss, he was a liability because he couldn't ring up the depot. (The fact that in 17 years he'd never needed to, was conveniently ignored.)
That's the trouble with some employers. When they look at a deaf worker they just see disability.
Not ability.

THE ROYAL NATIONAL INSTITUTE FOR THE DEAF.

IT'S FUNNY HOW BILL NEVER GETS TO HEAR ABOUT OVERTIME.

Bill works for a small firm, fabricating metal.
He likes the job. In fact, he wouldn't mind putting in some extra hours.
Unfortunately, he doesn't get the opportunity. Although his work-mates hear about overtime, he doesn't.
It's hardly surprising. Bill is profoundly deaf.
He can lip-read perfectly, but not when the boss has his back turned. Or when the foreman moves away before finishing a sentence.
They seem to forget that deaf men and women need a little consideration in the workplace.
Remember. Deaf people work with their hands, and their minds.
Not with their ears.

THE ROYAL NATIONAL INSTITUTE FOR THE DEAF.

691

To see how 300,000 Marylanders function on the job, drink half a bottle of whiskey.

Drinking on the job is *not* an isolated occurrence.

At least not in Maryland.

Studies show that nearly 10% of the state's total workforce abuse either alcohol, drugs or both. Abuse it to the point where their perception is hazy. Their hand-eye co-ordination, dulled. And their judgement, totally altered.

Unfortunately, it doesn't stop them from doing their jobs.

They still practice law. Operate heavy machinery. Run day care centers. Haul chemicals. Even design skyscrapers. In fact, they hold down jobs in every category across the board.

Think about it.

Think what that's costing in terms of productivity. In increased accident and sickness claims. More importantly, think what it could eventually cost in terms of lives.

The choice is simple. Either we put a stop to the problem. Or, at its current rate of growth, the problem puts a stop to us.

Now, isn't that a rather sobering thought?

To find out how you can help, call (301) 752-0365 for a free brochure.

Or, write: Marylanders for a Drug-Free Workplace, 7 East Franklin Street, Baltimore, Maryland 21202.

Unless we can stop drug abuse in the workplace, we're all going to feel the effects.

Marylanders for a Drug-Free Workplace • A project of the Baltimore Junior Association of Commerce, Inc.

10% of Maryland's business decisions are made by drunks.

Decisions like whether or not a car is mechanically safe to drive.

How and where to invest a client's money.

Or whether or not a bridge really needs major repair work.

Those are just a few of the decisions made every day in Maryland's workplace. A workplace where nearly 10% of the total workforce is either on alcohol, drugs or both. In other words, on substances that alter both their judgement and coordination.

If you think that isn't going to affect Maryland's future economy, dream on. It's already costing us plenty. In increased accident and sickness claims. In lost productivity. And in some cases, the toll can even be counted in terms of lives.

There are no two ways about it. The problem is costly. It's contagious. And it's out of control.

The choice is simple. Either we close our eyes and hope it goes away. Or, we do something about it. And that's the one decision we all have to make.

To find out how you can help, call (301) 752-0365 for a free brochure.

Or, write: Marylanders for a Drug-Free Workplace, 7 East Franklin Street, Baltimore, Maryland 21202.

Unless we can stop drug abuse in the workplace, we're all going to feel the effects.

Marylanders for a Drug-Free Workplace • A project of the Baltimore Junior Association of Commerce, Inc.

The facts are becoming painfully clear. Drug and alcohol abuse in the workplace is a dangerous habit. Unfortunately, in Maryland, it's also becoming a daily one.

Today, nearly 10% of our total workforce is either on drugs, alcohol or both. That adds up to approximately 450,000 people. People who don't think twice about taking a few puffs or a few sips to get them through the day.

And they never think at all about the consequences.

Like what it's costing in increased accident and sickness claims. In lost productivity. And most importantly, in terms of lives. Innocent lives that are being put at risk every single day.

In spite of all the evidence to the contrary, a lot of people still think that getting high at work isn't going to hurt anybody. Something has to be done about it. Because the fact is, they're wrong.

Dead wrong.

To find out how you can help, call (301) 752-0365. Or, write: Marylanders for a Drug-Free Workplace, 7 East Franklin Street, Baltimore, Maryland 21202.

Unless we can stop drug abuse in the workplace, we're all going to feel the effects.

Marylanders for a Drug-Free Workplace - A project of the Baltimore Junior Association of Commerce, Inc.

Public Service Newspaper Or Magazine: Campaign

693

ART DIRECTOR
Mia Ellis

WRITER
Bruce Adlhoch

PHOTOGRAPHER
C.B. Harding

CLIENT
Oregon Health Division

AGENCY
Pihas Schmidt Westerdahl/
Portland, OR

694

ART DIRECTOR
Carl Stewart

WRITER
Jamie Shevel

CLIENT
American Diabetes Association

AGENCY
Scali McCabe Sloves

PERFORM A DEATH-DEFYING ACT.

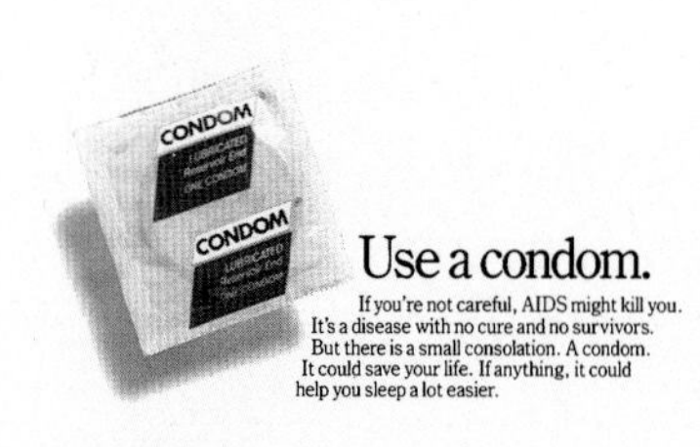

Use a condom.

If you're not careful, AIDS might kill you. It's a disease with no cure and no survivors. But there is a small consolation. A condom. It could save your life. If anything, it could help you sleep a lot easier.

AIDS is a killer. Protect yourself. Call 223-AIDS in Portland or 1-800-777-AIDS outside of Portland.

Prepared for Oregon Health Division by Pihas Schmidt Westerdahl © 1987 PSW

DON'T HAVE SEX WITH YOUR EYES CLOSED.

Use a condom.

If you're not careful, AIDS might kill you. It's a disease with no cure and no survivors. But there is a small consolation. A condom. It could save your life. If anything, it could help you sleep a lot easier.

AIDS is a killer. Protect yourself. Call 223-AIDS in Portland or 1-800-777-AIDS outside of Portland.

Prepared for Oregon Health Division by Pihas Schmidt Westerdahl © 1987 PSW

BE GOOD IN BED.

Use a condom.

If you're not careful, AIDS might kill you. It's a disease with no cure and no survivors. But there is a small consolation. A condom. It could save your life. If anything, it could help you sleep a lot easier.

AIDS is a killer. Protect yourself. Call 223-AIDS in Portland or 1-800-777-AIDS outside of Portland.

Prepared for Oregon Health Division by Pihas Schmidt Westerdahl © 1987 PSW

693

IF DIABETES IS A DISEASE YOU CAN LIVE WITH, WHY DID 150,000 DIE LAST YEAR?

Since 1 out of every 20 people has diabetes, you probably know someone who lives with it.

But what you probably don't know is what it's like to deal with diabetes: to have to stick to a diet every single day; to constantly monitor your blood sugar level; or to take insulin injections several times daily.

And you probably didn't know that diabetes can lead to other diseases, like heart disease, kidney disease and blindness.

Or, that every year 150,000 die.

Help us find a cure for diabetes. Before you know someone who dies from it.

Support the Research of the American Diabetes Association

American Diabetes Association

INSULIN IS NOT A CURE FOR DIABETES. IT JUST KEEPS PEOPLE ALIVE UNTIL WE FIND ONE.

There is no cure for diabetes. At least not right now. And until there is, millions of people have to live with the disease.

If you think that's easy, imagine living on a diet every day of your life; constantly monitoring your blood sugar level; and taking insulin injections several times a day.

But as hard as that sounds, not taking care of your diabetes makes it much worse. Because diabetes can lead to heart disease, kidney disease, blindness and gangrene.

And for 150,000 people each year, it leads to death.

Insulin is not a cure. But until we find one, it's all we have.

Support the Research of the American Diabetes Association

IMAGINE DYING FROM A DISEASE YOU NEVER KNEW YOU HAD.

Eleven million people in the U.S. have diabetes. But almost half of them don't know it.

Untreated, diabetes can lead to heart disease, kidney disease, blindness and gangrene.

And for 150,000 people each year, it leads to death.

That's why you should be aware of the symptoms of diabetes: blurred vision, excessive thirst and frequent urination are just some of the warning signs. Because the sooner you find out if you have diabetes, the more likely you are to get it under control, before complications set in.

Finding out you have diabetes can be scary. But not finding out can be fatal.

FIGHT SOME OF THE WORST DISEASES OF OUR TIME.
Support the American Diabetes Association.

Public Service Newspaper Or Magazine: Campaign

695

ART DIRECTOR
Raul Pina

WRITER
Joe Della Femina

CLIENT
Citizens Against Smoking

AGENCY
Della Femina Travisano & Partners

696

ART DIRECTOR
Carolyn Tye

WRITERS
Kerry Feuerman
Rob Schapiro

PHOTOGRAPHER
John Whitehead

CLIENT
United Way

AGENCY
Ford & Westbrook/
Richmond, VA

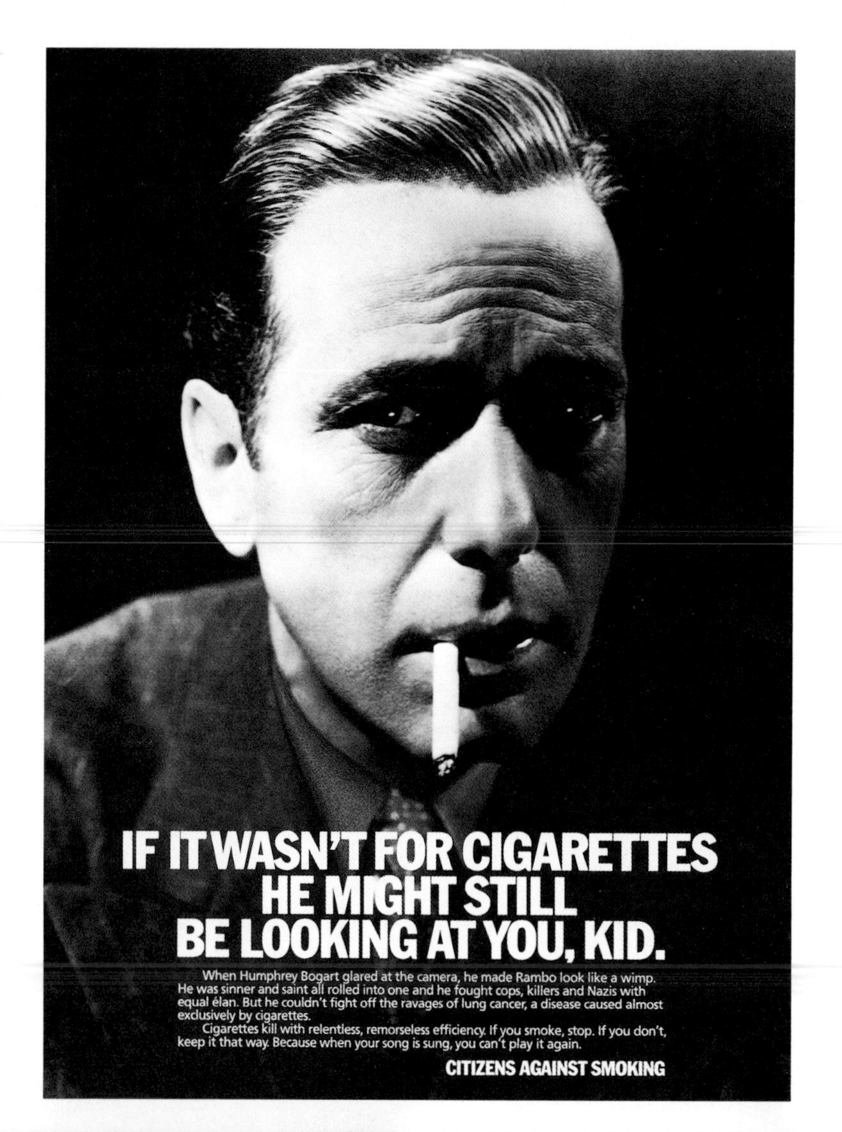

IF IT WASN'T FOR CIGARETTES
HE MIGHT STILL
BE LOOKING AT YOU, KID.
When Humphrey Bogart glared at the camera, he made Rambo look like a wimp. He was sinner and saint all rolled into one and he fought cops, killers and Nazis with equal élan. But he couldn't fight off the ravages of lung cancer, a disease caused almost exclusively by cigarettes.
Cigarettes kill with relentless, remorseless efficiency. If you smoke, stop. If you don't, keep it that way. Because when your song is sung, you can't play it again.
CITIZENS AGAINST SMOKING

THANKS TO CIGARETTES
YOU CAN ONLY
SEE RICKY ON RERUNS.
Desi Arnaz loved Lucy and he loved life. And he lost them both. The former to the vagaries of the human heart. The latter to lung cancer, a disease caused almost exclusively by cigarettes.
Cigarettes kill. That is not theory. It's cold, horrible, deadly fact. If you smoke, stop. If you don't, keep it that way. Because when your show's over, there are no reruns.
CITIZENS AGAINST SMOKING

695

2000 BULLETS, 600 ARROWS,
82 TOMAHAWKS
AND 30 SPEARS COULDN'T DO
WHAT CIGARETTES DID.
He won the west and World War II single-handed. He was bigger than life on and off screen. He was John Wayne, the indestructible "Duke." And he was destroyed by lung cancer, a disease caused almost exclusively by cigarettes.
Cigarettes kill, slowly, surely, insidiously. If you smoke, stop. If you don't, keep it that way. Unless you think you're tougher than a legend.
CITIZENS AGAINST SMOKING

HOW MANY TIMES CAN ONE WOMAN FALL DOWN A FLIGHT OF STAIRS?
One of the most painful parts of being a battered wife is admitting it to other people. Please, help us help them. Give generously to the United Way.
SOMEONE IS WAITING FOR YOU TO GIVE TO THE UNITED WAY.

SOMETHING'S WRONG WHEN YOU'RE MORE AFRAID OF LIVING THAN YOU ARE OF DYING.
Without our help, the only thing some people have to look forward to is another day of loneliness. Please give generously to the United Way.
SOMEONE IS WAITING FOR YOU TO GIVE TO THE UNITED WAY.

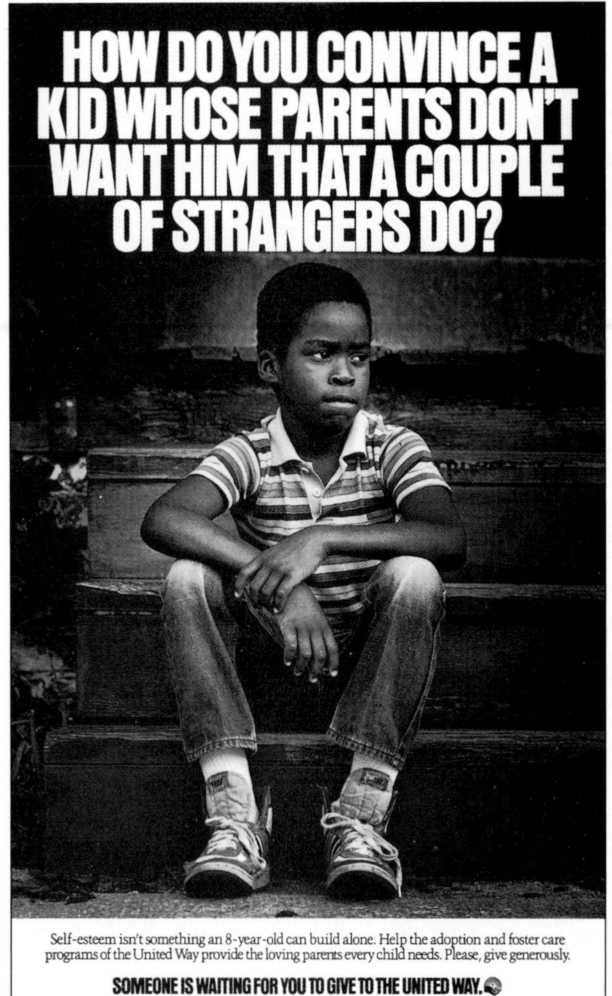
HOW DO YOU CONVINCE A KID WHOSE PARENTS DON'T WANT HIM THAT A COUPLE OF STRANGERS DO?
Self-esteem isn't something an 8-year-old can build alone. Help the adoption and foster care programs of the United Way provide the loving parents every child needs. Please, give generously.
SOMEONE IS WAITING FOR YOU TO GIVE TO THE UNITED WAY.

Public Service Newspaper Or Magazine: Campaign

697
ART DIRECTOR
Wayne Gibson
WRITER
Andy Ellis
CLIENT
Boys Club of Richmond
AGENCY
The Martin Agency/
Richmond, VA

Public Service Outdoor: Single

698
ART DIRECTOR
Jeff Jones
WRITER
John Jarvis
PHOTOGRAPHER
Craig Gjerness
CLIENT
Oak Hill Lutheran Brethren Church
AGENCY
Martin/Williams -
Minneapolis

699
ART DIRECTOR
Richard Page
WRITER
Christopher Wilson
DESIGNER
Richard Page
PHOTOGRAPHER
Paul Sinkler
CLIENT
Animal Rights Coalition
AGENCY
Martin/Williams -
Minneapolis

AT AN AGE WHEN MOST BOYS ARE ASKING WHERE BABIES COME FROM, WE KNOW ONE 10 YEAR OLD WHO FEARS HE MIGHT HAVE GONORRHEA.

The purpose of this ad isn't to speculate why kids are becoming more "sophisticated."

It's to tell you the Boys Club recognizes this fact. And responds by educating.

So we've introduced kids to speakers from drug rehabilitation centers, Alcoholics Anonymous, Planned Parenthood and on and on.

To learn how you can support these efforts, call 359-5250.

BOYS CLUBS OF RICHMOND

LIKE MANY FATHERS, JAMES' DAD SHOWED HIM HOW TO SHOOT A GUN. HE WAS COMMITTING SUICIDE AT THE TIME.

This is a true story we recently faced at the Boys Club. So, if you think this is just a place where kids go to play basketball, think again.

And remember that when you support the Boys Club, you're also encouraging things like cultural appreciation, health education, job training, and counseling for boys in need of emotional support.

To learn how you can support these efforts, call 359-5250.

BOYS CLUBS OF RICHMOND

THE LIFEGUARDS AT THE BOYS CLUB KEEP A CLOSE WATCH. IN FACT, LAST YEAR THEY SPOTTED THREE CASES OF CHILD BEATING.

The Boys Clubs of Richmond boasts a staff of 21. We say "boasts" because we're proud of their ability to find the potential and talents that exist in each individual boy.

But perhaps prouder of those occasions when they've spotted the less obvious. Things like learning disabilities, emotional problems and even abuse.

If you'd like to support these efforts, call 359-5250 to learn how.

BOYS CLUBS OF RICHMOND

697

ARE YOU A BORED-AGAIN CHRISTIAN?
If you're not receiving the spiritual nourishment and fellowship you need, join us in the Church of the Lutheran Brethren.
We're just the right size for people who want to make a difference in their world, and who recognize that contributions can be made in places other than the collection plate.
OAK HILL LUTHERAN BRETHREN CHURCH.
8101 Xerxes Avenue South, Bloomington • 881-9186

698

201
RESEARCH
LABORATORY
Last year, curiosity killed over 125,000 cats.
It also killed over 300,000 dogs, 35,000 primates and 60,000,000 other laboratory animals. And this year, the numbers will get even larger. Unless people like you begin to question what's being done for the sake of curiosity. And start to wonder what should be done for the sake of animals.
ANIMAL RIGHTS COALITION

699

Public Service
Outdoor: Single

700
ART DIRECTOR
Walt Taylor
WRITER
Rebecca Flora
PHOTOGRAPHER
Ronn Maratea
CLIENT
Virginia Department of Alcoholic Beverage Control
AGENCY
Lawler Ballard/
Norfolk, VA

701
ART DIRECTOR
Bill Zabowski
WRITER
Lyle Wedemeyer
PHOTOGRAPHER
Jim Arndt
CLIENT
United Way
AGENCY
Martin/Williams -
Minneapolis

702
ART DIRECTOR
Walt Taylor
WRITER
Rebecca Flora
PHOTOGRAPHER
Dan Weaks
CLIENT
Virginia Department of Alcoholic Beverage Control
AGENCY
Lawler Ballard/
Norfolk, VA

703
ART DIRECTOR
Sally Oelschlager
WRITER
Kerry Casey
PHOTOGRAPHER
Steve Umland
CLIENT
KTCA/2
AGENCY
Carmichael Lynch/
Minneapolis

700

701

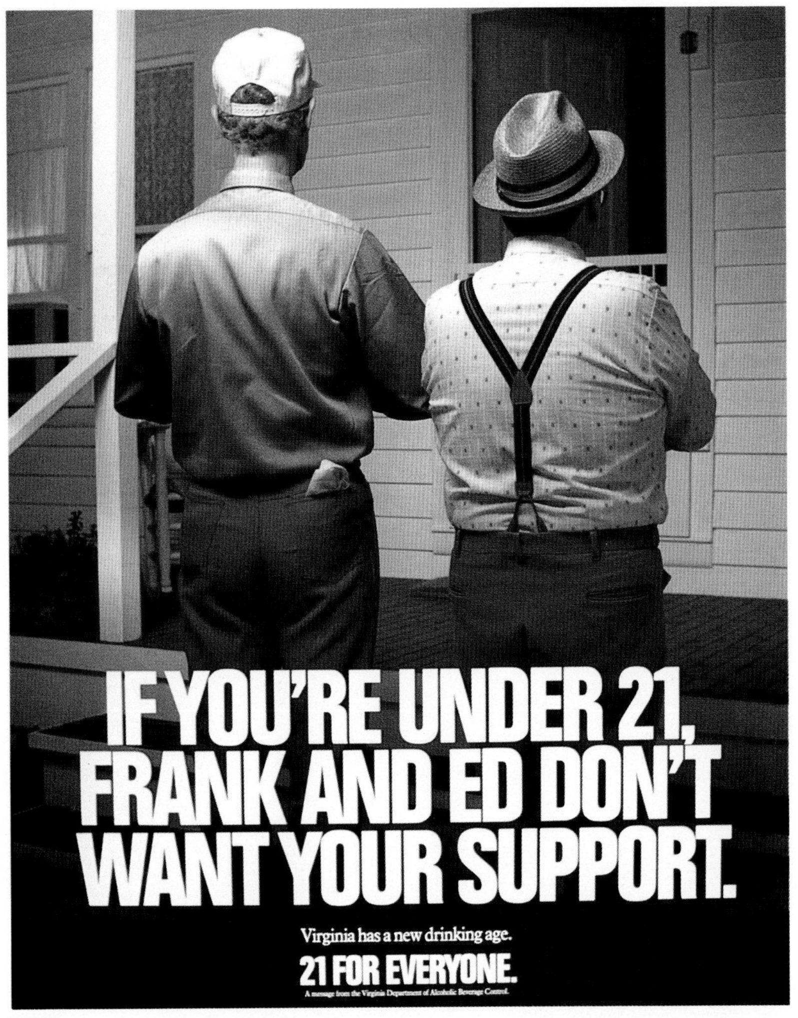
IF YOU'RE UNDER 21,
FRANK AND ED DON'T
WANT YOUR SUPPORT.
Virginia has a new drinking age.
21 FOR EVERYONE.
A message from the Virginia Department of Alcoholic Beverage Control.

702

THE BEST
DEFENSE
AGAINST
AIDS SINCE
THE CONDOM.
MINNESOTA AIDSLINE
870-0700

703

Public Service
Outdoor: Single

704
ART DIRECTORS
Ed Kagy
Richard Ruhlman
WRITERS
Richard Ruhlman
Ed Kagy
DESIGNER
Ed Kagy
PHOTOGRAPHER
Carl Fowler
CLIENT
Violent Crime Task Force
AGENCY
Liggett-Stashower/
Cleveland, OH

705
ART DIRECTOR
Jerry Gentile
WRITER
Mark Monteiro
PHOTOGRAPHER
Lamb & Hall
CLIENT
United Way
AGENCY
DDB Needham Worldwide/
Los Angeles

706
ART DIRECTOR
Rocco Campanelli
WRITER
Richard Kirshenbaum
PHOTOGRAPHER
Rocco Campanelli
CLIENT
Emmaus House
AGENCY
David Deutsch Associates

707
ART DIRECTOR
Doug Malott
WRITER
John Sparks
DESIGNER
Doug Malott
ARTIST
Doug Malott
PHOTOGRAPHER
Cosby Boyer
CLIENT
Freedom House
AGENCY
Athey Martin Webb/
Richmond, VA

704

705

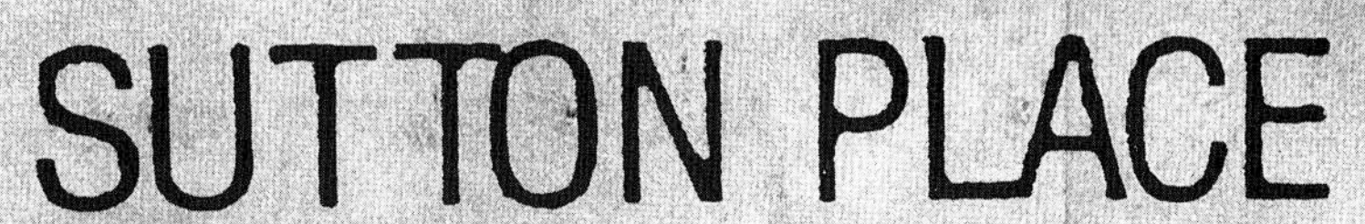

Elegant 1 bdrm, spectac riv vu, mrbl frplc,
24 hr drmn, terrace. A steal at $595,000.
ANY CONTRIBUTION WOULD MEAN SO VERY MUCH TO THE HOMELESS.
EMMAUS HOUSE, P.O. BOX 1177, NEW YORK, NY 10035 (212) 410-6006

706

This Christmas Eve, Children Won't Be The Only Ones Who Can't Fall Asleep.

Freedom House, 302 West Canal Street, Richmond, Virginia 23220 (804) 649-9791

A Public Service Message From Athey Martin Webb

707

Public Service Outdoor: Single

708
ART DIRECTOR
Carolyn Tye
WRITER
Curlin Reed
PHOTOGRAPHER
John Whitehead
CLIENT
Benedictine High School
AGENCY
Ford & Westbrook/
Richmond, VA

709
ART DIRECTOR
Richard Page
WRITER
Christopher Wilson
DESIGNER
Richard Page
PHOTOGRAPHER
Paul Sinkler
CLIENT
Animal Rights Coalition
AGENCY
Martin/Williams -
Minneapolis

710
ART DIRECTOR
Michael Fazende
WRITER
Jarl Olsen
CLIENT
University of Minnesota
AGENCY
Fallon McElligott/
Minneapolis

711
ART DIRECTORS
David Smith
Gary Husk
WRITER
Glenn Overman
CLIENT
Food Bank of Jacksonville
AGENCY
Husk Jennings Overman/
Jacksonville, FL

Help Burned Out Students.

708

Too bad Polly can't talk her way out of this.
Of the 500,000 exotic birds imported into this country every year, over 125,000 of them die in transit of shock, suffocation, malnutrition or disease. And of the 375,000 birds that do survive the trip, over 300,000 never adjust to captivity and die within months. Please help us speak up for them.
ANIMAL RIGHTS COALITION

709

The only way to tell a male and female penguin apart is by autopsy. After years of steroid use, the same may be true of humans.

STEROIDS ARE BIG TROUBLE.

710

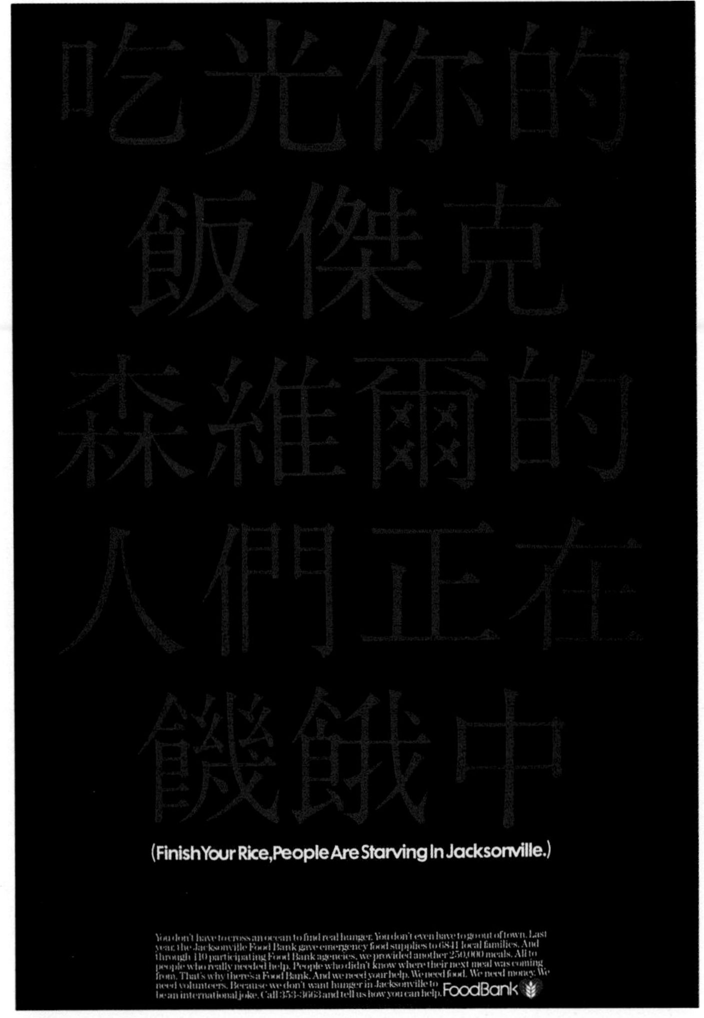

711

Public Service
Outdoor: Single

712

ART DIRECTOR
Rachel Couillard

WRITER
Jill Silverman

ARTIST
Tilly's Kids

CLIENT
United Way

AGENCY
Ogilvy & Mather

713

ART DIRECTOR
Don Fibich

WRITER
Kevin Kolke

DESIGNER
Don Fibich

PHOTOGRAPHER
Tim Bush

CLIENT
Red Cross

AGENCY
Wyse Advertising/
Cleveland, OH

714

ART DIRECTOR
Sally Oelschlager

WRITER
Kerry Casey

PHOTOGRAPHER
Steve Umland

CLIENT
KTCA/2

AGENCY
Carmichael Lynch/
Minneapolis

715

ART DIRECTOR
Eddy Greenwood

WRITER
Jim Anderson

PHOTOGRAPHER
Shaun Bresnahan

CLIENT
Christian Aid

AGENCY
Gold Greenless Trott/
London

716

ART DIRECTOR
George Halvorson

WRITER
Terry Bremer

PHOTOGRAPHER
Jim Arndt

CLIENT
National Easter Seal Society

AGENCY
Campbell-Mithun/
Minneapolis

THANK YOU for
My Mother and father
Which I love them verg
Much.

United Way

Your contribution helps Leake and Watts Children's Home place children in foster homes.

712

The average heart attack victim has five minutes to live.

Unfortunately, the average rescue squad takes ten minutes to respond.

Learn CPR.

American Red Cross

713

THIS IS HOW AIDS IS SPREAD.
MINNESOTA AIDSLINE
870-0700
WATCH "ALMANAC EXTRA"
JULY 29, 8:00 PM.
KTCA2
NAEGELE

714

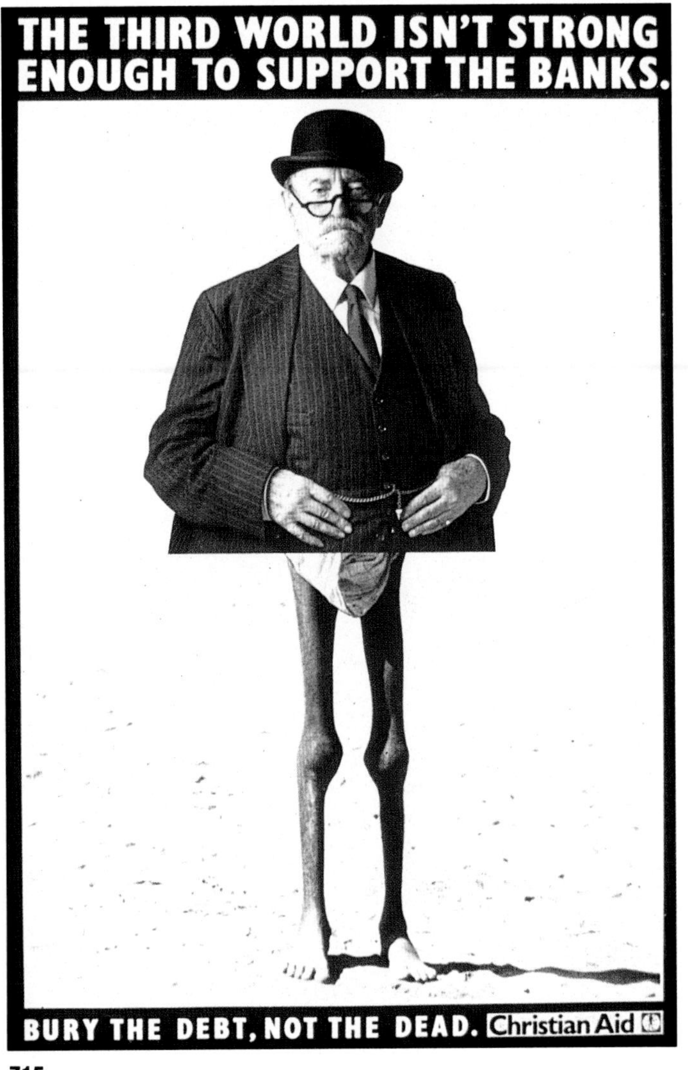

THE THIRD WORLD ISN'T STRONG ENOUGH TO SUPPORT THE BANKS.
BURY THE DEBT, NOT THE DEAD.
Christian Aid

715

ON JUNE 6, WE HELPED DELIVER A FATHER.
With the help of Easter Seals, and a burning spirit, what you see here is not a man with a disability, but a man called Dad. Give to Easter Seals. Give the power to overcome.
Easter Seals

716

Political Newspaper Or Magazine: Campaign

717

ART DIRECTOR
Kathryn Windley

WRITER
Hillary Jordan

DESIGNER
Kathryn Windley

PHOTOGRAPHER
Gary McGuire

CLIENT
Beyond War

AGENCY
Ogilvy & Mather/
Los Angeles

718

ART DIRECTORS
Pat Epstein
Paul Blade

WRITER
Karen Sultz

CLIENT
Soviet Jewry

AGENCY
Scali McCabe Sloves

THE BEST WEAPON AGAINST WAR IS A PAIR OF SCISSORS.

At this moment, there are roughly 40 armed conflicts happening somewhere in our world. They're "small" wars. But each one of them has the potential to escalate into a bigger war. A nuclear war.

The experts tell us that won't ever happen.

They claim that nuclear weapons are simply too destructive to use; therefore, no one will ever dare use them.

They also claim that nuclear stockpiling *lowers* our chances of world war.

If you're like most people, you have doubts about the sanity of these policies. But you have greater doubts about your own ability to change them for the better.

Fortunately, you're wrong about that.

Right now, you have a lot of opportunities to make a difference. Twelve of them, to be exact.

Twelve presidential candidates.

All of whom are scrambling to create platforms which will win your vote in the primaries.

We've listed the candidates below. Before you send one of them to the White House, send him this coupon.

Tell him you think war is a senseless way to resolve conflict. Tell him he needs to *earn* your vote by making global security his top priority.

But hurry.

This offer is good for a limited time only.

Dear________________,

I believe that any war—even a "small" one—is too risky in a nuclear age.

I believe the United States should make a greater effort to mediate regional conflicts.

I believe that improving U.S.-Soviet relations is a national security imperative.

I believe we must take the strongest possible initiative to stop nuclear proliferation.

Please keep these priorities in mind as you develop your platform. I intend to keep them in mind when I vote.

Name
Address
City State Zip

BEYOND WAR
Join The Fight. 1-800-338-2161

BEFORE YOU PUT THEM IN OFFICE, PUT THEM ON THE SPOT.

For the last several months, the presidential candidates have bombarded you with opinions. Opinions on tax reform. Education. Government waste. Toxic waste. The trade deficit. The poor.

Undoubtedly the candidates consider these issues pressing. Undoubtedly they are.

But there's one issue that makes all the others seem insignificant.

Right now there are roughly 40 armed conflicts happening in our world. They're "small" wars. But each one has the potential to escalate into a much bigger war.

A nuclear war.

If you're like most people, you're against war. But you don't believe you can stop it.

That's where you're mistaken.

At this moment, you have access to 12 of the country's most powerful politicians. One of them will become your President. All of them need your vote.

Instead of just listening to their concerns, make them listen to your concerns.

Ask them the toughest questions you can think of about war. And if doing away with war isn't at the top of their list, put it there.

Before you put them in the White House.

☐ What initiatives will you make to mediate regional conflicts?

☐ How do you plan to improve U.S.-Soviet relations?

☐ What will you do to prevent nuclear proliferation?

☐ What specific steps will you take to end war?

BEYOND WAR
Join The Fight. 1-800-338-2161

BY CLIPPING THIS COUPON YOU CAN SAVE MILLIONS.

We're not referring to dollars, but to something infinitely more valuable. People. American people. Russian, Dutch and Turkish people. People from China, Peru and everywhere in between.

Right now, there are roughly 40 armed conflicts happening somewhere in our world. They're "small" wars. But each one of them has the potential to escalate into a bigger war.

A nuclear war.

If you're like most people, you're against war. But you don't believe there's anything you can do to stop it.

Actually, there's something important you can do. Something you can do right now.

Twelve presidential candidates have set up shop in New Hampshire. They're not here to enjoy the crisp weather. Or the autumn color.

They're here to create platforms which will send them to the White House. Platforms you approve of. And contribute to.

We've listed the candidates below, along with their addresses. While their ears are open, tell them they need to *earn* your vote by making global security their number one priority. But tell them soon.

This is one coupon you simply can't afford to let expire.

Dear________________,

I believe that any war—even a "small" one—is too risky in a nuclear age.

I believe the United States should make a greater effort to mediate regional conflicts.

I believe that improving U.S.-Soviet relations is a national security imperative.

I believe we must take the strongest possible initiative to stop nuclear proliferation.

Please keep these priorities in mind as you develop your platform. I intend to keep them in mind when I vote.

Name
Address
City State Zip

BEYOND WAR
Join The Fight. 1-800-338-2161

717

THERE ARE THOUSANDS OF WAYS GORBACHEV CAN IMPROVE HIS IMAGE.

Glasnost has done a lot for Gorbachev's image. Unfortunately, it hasn't done much for hundreds of thousands of Soviet Jews.

They still cannot get exit visas to Israel. They cannot be reunited with their families. And they cannot study their culture or practice their religion without fear of reprisal.

Help Soviet Jews gain their rights by showing up at the Washington Summit March and Rally on Sunday, December 6th. Do your part to help Reagan convince Gorbachev that a comprehensive resolution must be reached at the Washington Summit. A resolution that provides normalization of the emigration process and religious and cultural freedom to every Soviet Jew.

The March leaves from the Ellipse at 1 pm, followed by a mass rally at 2 pm on the Mall, opposite the Capitol. For more information, call the Coalition to Free Soviet Jews Summit Hotlines at 1-800-328-5727 ext. 20 or (212) 391-0954.

This may be your one chance in history to improve the life of every Soviet Jew. And help Gorbachev truly improve his own image.

SHOW YOU CARE. SHOW UP.

The Greater New York Area mobilization coordinated by Coalition to Free Soviet Jews.
Representing concerned organizations in New York City, Long Island, Westchester, Rockland County, and Northern New Jersey. 8 W. 40th St., Suite 1510, N.Y., N.Y. 10018 (212) 354-1316.

Special Summit Hotlines (212) 391-0954, outside N.Y. (202) 483-5200.

Supported by United Jewish Appeal—Federation of Jewish Philanthropies of Greater New York. Washington Summit March and Rally sponsored by The Summit III Task Force.
Coalition to Free Soviet Jews Chairman: Alan Pesky, Executive Director: Zeesy Schnur

Show up and join Ida Nudel, Vladimir Slepak, Natan Sharansky, Vice President George Bush, Senator Robert Dole and other Congressional leaders, New Jersey's Governor Thomas Kean, Israel's Ambassador Moshe Arad, Elie Wiesel, Morris B. Abram, Bishop William Keeler—National Conference of Catholic Bishops, Arie Brouwer—National Council of Churches, Performing Artists Paul Simon, Pearl Bailey, Mary Travers and others...

THIS THANKSGIVING, SAVE THE LEFTOVERS.

These names are only a small portion of the two and a half million Jews remaining in the Soviet Union. They still cannot get exit visas to Israel. They cannot be reunited with their families. And they cannot study their culture or practice their religion without fear of reprisal.

You can help them gain their rights by showing up at the Washington Summit March and Rally on Sunday, December 6th. Help Reagan tell Gorbachev that Soviet Jewry cannot and will not be a bargaining table scrap. Show you care. Show up.

SPONSORED BY THE COALITION TO FREE SOVIET JEWS.

March begins from the Ellipse at 1PM, followed by 2PM Rally on the Mall opposite the Capitol. Special Summit Hotlines (212) 391-0954 or 1-800-328-5727, Ext. 20.

The Greater New York Area mobilization coordinated by Coalition to Free Soviet Jews. Representing concerned organizations in New York City, Long Island, Westchester, Rockland County, and Northern New Jersey. 8 W. 40th St., Suite 1510, N.Y., N.Y. 10018 (212) 354-1316.
Supported by United Jewish Appeal—Federation of Jewish Philanthropies of Greater New York. Washington Summit March and Rally sponsored by The Summit III Task Force.

IF YOU STAY PUT ON DECEMBER 6TH, SO MIGHT THOUSANDS OF SOVIET JEWS.

Right now thousands of Soviet Jews cannot obtain exit visas to return to their homeland, Israel. Families cannot be reunited. And religious and cultural freedoms are severely limited by fear and danger of reprisal.

On December 7th, Reagan and Gorbachev will hold a summit of unprecedented historical significance. And you will have an unprecedented opportunity to directly help Soviet Jews gain their fundamental freedoms.

Show up at the Washington Summit March and Rally on Sunday, December 6th. At 1pm the march will begin from the Ellipse, followed by a mass rally at 2pm on the Mall opposite the nation's Capitol.

Join forces with Sharansky, Nudel, Slepak and tens of thousands of people as we influence history. Your presence is critical. We must show the Administration and Gorbachev that a constructive, comprehensive resolution has to be reached to end the plight of the Soviet Jews.

For more information and travel arrangements, call the Coalition to Free Soviet Jews at (212) 354-1316. And don't miss the chance to use your freedom to help Soviet Jews secure theirs.

SHOW YOU CARE. SHOW UP.

The Greater New York Area mobilization coordinated by Coalition to Free Soviet Jews.
Representing concerned organizations in New York City, Long Island, Westchester, Rockland County, and Northern New Jersey.
8 W. 40th St., Suite 1510, N.Y., N.Y. 10018 (212) 354-1316.

Special Summit Hotlines (212) 391-0954, outside N.Y. (202) 483-5200.

Supported by United Jewish Appeal–Federation of Jewish Philanthropies of Greater New York. Washington Summit March and Rally sponsored by The Summit III Task Force.

Political Newspaper Or Magazine: Campaign

719

ART DIRECTORS
Larry Jarvis
Ron Anderson

WRITERS
Dick Thomas
Craig McNamara

CLIENT
Freespeech Committee

AGENCY
Bozell Jacobs Kenyon & Eckhardt/Minneapolis

Freedom of assembly is not an unmixed blessing.

Most Americans agree wholeheartedly that The First Amendment guarantees the right of peaceful assembly.

For themselves.

But not everyone believes that this guarantee should protect all individuals or groups. Especially those with a history of violence.

For example, a 1986 poll showed that a substantial number of Minnesotans thought freedom of expression shouldn't always apply to such groups as Nazis or the Ku Klux Klan.

Trouble is, if the rights of unpopular groups are ignored today, the rights of a group you belong to may be ignored tomorrow.

One of the best ways to protect your freedom of expression is to use it.

By speaking up for The First Amendment.

Freespeech

He killed three million people who didn't agree with him.

As a U.S. citizen, your right to speak your mind is guaranteed by The First Amendment, which says in no uncertain terms that Congress shall make no law abridging the freedom of speech.

Unfortunately, a surprising number of people want to add a lot of ifs, ands, or buts.

For example, in a 1986 poll of Minnesotans, 40% of them said government should prohibit expression of views that might lead people to commit undesirable or violent acts.

Trouble is, if someone else's right to express an unpopular view is ignored today, your right to express a different view may be ignored tomorrow.

One of the best ways to protect your freedom of expression is to use it.

By speaking up for The First Amendment.

Freespeech

He wasn't protected by The First Amendment.

It is no accident that the first words of The First Amendment to the U.S. constitution are these:

"Congress shall make no law respecting an establishment of religion, or prohibiting the free exercise thereof...."

Because the founding fathers were well aware that wherever religion was established, some form of religious intolerance, oppression or persecution was likely to follow.

Even so, not everyone agrees as to how much The First Amendment restricts government involvement in religious matters.

For example, in a 1986 poll of Minnesotans, 77% of them believed the government has the right to monitor certain religious groups if they are thought to be doing something illegal.

Obviously, no one has a right to break the law. But the question still arises: who would monitor the government monitors?

One of the best ways to protect your rights under the law is to exercise them.

So if you want to speak up for The First Amendment, feel free.

Freespeech

Radio Finalists

Consumer Radio: Single

720

WRITERS
Alan Barzman
Bert Berdis
Jim Kirby
Rich Procter

AGENCY PRODUCER
Allan Godshall

CLIENT
Frigidaire

AGENCY
Stockton West Burkhart/
Cincinnati, OH

721

WRITERS
Luke Sullivan
Diane Cook Tench

AGENCY PRODUCER
Craig Bowlus

CLIENT
Signet Bank

AGENCY
The Martin Agency/
Richmond, VA

722

WRITER
Steve Sandoz

AGENCY PRODUCERS
Steve Sandoz
Andy Henderson

CLIENT
Alaska Airlines

AGENCY
Livingston & Company/
Seattle

723

WRITER
Paul Mimiaga

AGENCY PRODUCER
Elizabeth O'Toole

CLIENT
Calistoga Mineral Water Company

AGENCY
Hal Riney & Partners/
San Francisco

724

WRITER
Dick Orkin's Radio Ranch

CLIENT
The Beach Waterpark

AGENCY
Lawler Ballard/
Cincinnati, OH

720

MAN: Ah, excuse me . . .

GUY: Welcome to Frigidaire Dealin' Days!

MAN: Did you say Frigidaire "Dealin' Days?"

GUY: Right, it's a great time to save big on every Frigidaire appliance in the store.

MAN: Well, you've got a lot of nerve.

GUY: A lot of what?

MAN: My card, sir.

GUY: Oh, you're a Copywriter?

MAN: You got it.

GUY: So you write advertising copy?

MAN: No! I copyright advertising phrases.

GUY: You mean . . .

MAN: I own the rights to the phrase "Dealin' Days."

GUY: I see.

MAN: Now, do you Frigidaire guys ever use the phrase "Bargains galore throughout the store?"

GUY: No, we don't.

MAN: Good. 'Cause I own that too.

GUY: But during Frigidaire Dealin' Days we *do* have bargains galore throughout the store on every Frigidaire appliance we sell.

MAN: What about the phrase "shop early for terrific savings?"

GUY: No, we don't use it.

MAN: Lucky for you.

GUY: But it is a good idea to shop early because this is the best time of the year to save on Frigidaire appliances.

MAN: Well since you didn't know I owned "Dealin' Days," I'll let you off with just a warning this time.

GUY: Gee thanks.

MAN: But don't ever do it again.

GUY: O.K.

MAN: Now, goodbye!

GUY: Toodle-oo.

MAN: What's that?

GUY: Toodle-oo.

MAN: You did it again.

GUY: Oh no.

MAN: I own "Toodle-oo." I've got the paperwork right here . . .

GUY: Look, am-scray, O.K.?

MAN: Am-scray? That's one of mine too!

GUY: Take a powder!

MAN: Take a powder?

721

VO: We're blindfolding Mrs Bickman of Baltimore, Maryland . . . just to prove a point! Because we're going to have her try a taste test between the leading brand of snack chip and this . . . (VO COMES CLOSER TO MIKE AND WHISPERS WHAT IT IS TO OUR AUDIENCE) . . . a Fee Option Checking Account from Signet Bank/Maryland. (BACK TO REGULAR SPEAKING VOLUME) O.K., let's see which chip she prefers. Ready, Mrs Bickman?

MRS BICKMAN: I guess.

VO: All right, here's chip number one.

(SFX: POTATO CHIP CRUNCHING)

MRS BICKMAN: Yeah . . . it's got . . . it's got a nice corn crunch. I like it.

VO: O.K., *now* try chip number two.

(SFX OF HIM RIPPING A CHECK OUT OF A CHECKBOOK; OF HER CRUMPLING IT UP INTO A BALL AND THEN CHEWING IT)

MRS BICKMAN: It's . . . awful. Really awful.

VO: Yes, but what if I told you that chip number two comes with a MasterCard with no annual fee for the first year?

MRS BICKMAN: No annual fee, really? Lemme try another one.

(SFX OF ANOTHER CHECK BEING RIPPED OUT, CRUMPLED, CHEWED)

VO: Yes, and with these chips you get unlimited checkwriting and free check stationery. All for just $5 a month! Well Mrs Bickman, now which chip do you think tastes best?

MRS BICKMAN: Well, chip number one had a nice crunch . . . but no MasterCard. I'll have to go with number two.

VO: Well, here you have it. So come on into Signet Bank/Maryland for your own Fee Option Checking Account. Betcha can't open . . . just one. Signet Bank is a member FDIC and an Equal Opportunity Lender.

722

(SFX: MEETING HALL; MAN TAPPING ON MICROPHONE)

ANNCR: Have you noticed that, these days, all airlines offer the same low fares?

SPEAKER (OVER P.A. SYSTEM): As Golden Mean of the order of the average, I ask that all rise for the oath of mediocrity.

GROUP: We will be average in thought, word and deed.

SPEAKER: Be seated. Yes Mr Blah?

BLAH: How are we flying to the national average conference?

SPEAKER: I assumed we'd have an average flight on an average airline.

BLAH: Well I propose we fly Alaska Airlines.

(SFX: CROWD REACTION)

ANNCR: Because as soon as one airline lowers fares, they all lower fares.

SPEAKER: Mr Median?

MEDIAN: Your ordinariness, Alaska's service is way above average.

BLAH: But their fares aren't. They're as low as anyone's.

ANNCR: Which means a flight on Alaska doesn't cost any more than a flight on an average airline.

SPEAKER: Well, then I agree we should fly on Alaska. All in favor?

CROWD: Aye.

SPEAKER: Opposed?

MEDIAN (LONE VOICE): Nay.

SPEAKER: So be it. Everybody but Mr Median will fly on Alaska.

MEDIAN: Maybe we should have a recount.

ANNCR: So if you can get the same low fare from any airline, why fly just any airline?

723

VOICE: People have had some wonderful experiences drinking Calistoga and Juice. But none like the one Bill Irons had. Bill's a local shoe repairman, who suddenly became ill. Lying in bed one night, Bill said he felt himself leave his body. He floated up, high above the town, connected to his real body by a silver cord. There, he watched his wife open a bottle of Calistoga and Juice . . . the Passion Peach . . . and put it to his lips. Slowly, the silver cord pulled him down; back into his body. Bill likes to tell his story to anyone who comes into his shoe repair shop. Folks usually nod in agreement, ask for half-soles or heels, and pay in advance.

ANNCR: Calistoga and Juice. Made with the original Napa Valley mineral water.

724

(SFX: PEOPLE WALKING & TALKING; CASH REGISTERS RINGING; GROCERY CARTS CLANGING)

SON: Hey, Dad.

DAD: Yes, son.

SON: How came you wore your underpants to the grocery store?

DAD: The . . . these aren't my underpants.

SON: They look just like those underpants mom bought me.

DAD: No, No! These happen to be very fashionable designer, um, swim trunks.

SON: Then how come they have super heroes on them like my underpants.

DAD: That's the very fashionable design.

SON: Boy! If I wore my underpants to the grocery store, mom would kill me.

(SFX: DAD GRUMBLING)

DAD: Look, Billy, I wore these swim trunks to Krogers because after we leave here we're going to The Beach.

SON: The Beach Waterpark?

DAD: Yes. And we stopped here at Krogers so I could get the $2 discount pass so we can go have fun on Lazy Miami and Snake River Rapids . . .

SON: Uh-huh.

DAD: . . . and all the other neat rides of The Beach . . .

SON: Uh-huh.

DAD: . . . and we can eat hot dogs and popcorn . . .

SON: And ice cream?

DAD: Sure.

SON: So, they let you into The Beach in your underpants.

DAD: The . . . Once and for all, these are not my underpants!

SON: O.K., Dad.

MOM: Frank? What are you doing here?

DAD: Hi, hon.

SON: Hi, Mom.

MOM (LOWERED VOICE): And how come you're wearing underpants to the grocery store?

DAD: These are not . . .

MOM: And where are those new swim trunks I bought you?

DAD: You mean, these aren't . . .

MOM: No.

DAD: Ohhhh boy.

ANNCR: The Beach. Interstate 71, Exit 25, across from Kings Island.

Consumer Radio: Single

725
WRITERS
George Betsis
Rodd Martin
AGENCY PRODUCER
Paul Goodwin
CLIENT
Koala Springs
AGENCY
Mojo

726
WRITER
Joe Alexander
AGENCY PRODUCER
Erin Zellner
CLIENT
Galleria Shopping Mall
AGENCY
Clarity Coverdale Rueff/
Minneapolis

727
WRITERS
Dick Orkin
Christine Coyle
Steve Doroba
AGENCY PRODUCER
Jan Jolivette
CLIENT
The Kroger Company
AGENCY
Campbell-Mithun/
Chicago

728
WRITERS
Marian Allen Godwin
Todd McVey
AGENCY PRODUCER
Rachel Novak
CLIENT
Genesee Brewing Company
AGENCY
Levine Huntley Schmidt &
Beaver

729
WRITERS
Sara Fontannaz
Maggie Gallagher
AGENCY PRODUCER
Sandie Bennett
CLIENT
Mail On Sunday
AGENCY
Lowe Howard-Spink/
London

730
WRITER
Bruce Hannum
AGENCY PRODUCER
Bruce Hannum
CLIENT
G. Heileman Brewing
AGENCY
Ruhr/Paragon - Minneapolis

725

MUSIC: We drink . . . it . . . in . . . Woolongong, Mittagong, Bunarong, Bong Bong, Wagga Wagga, Woop Woop, Curl Curl, Woy Woy, Budgewoi, Collaroy, Prosapine, Jindabyne, Coolangatta, Wangaratta, Oonadatta, Parramatta, Ulladulla, Tiboburra, Binaburra, Nulla Nulla, Double Bay . . .

ANNCR (MUSIC UNDER): Australians from all over just love Koala Springs Mineral Water with orange and mango juices.

MUSIC: . . . Bendigo, Ivanhoe, Bangolo, Thredbo, Armadale, Lilydale, Mona Vale, Innisvail, Arrarat, Ballarat, Townsville, Birdsville, Corakai, Gundagai, Bogabri, Narrabri . . . there's no place we won't drink it . . . there's no place we won't drink it . . . Marble Bar, Malabar, Gunnudah, Muwillambah, Jambaroo, Wallaroo, Mindaroo, Jabarroo, Tenterfield, Beaconsfield, Peterboro, Maryboro, Ayres Rock, Hanging Rock, Dirty Creek . . .

ANNCR (MUSIC UNDER): But now Koala Springs Mineral Water in seven exotic fruit juice combinations is available here, so Americans all over will be drinking it.

MUSIC: . . . Nashville, Cederville, Louisville, Haverhill, Arkansas, Baltimore, Alabama, Indiana, Gettysburg, Etonburg, Angustown, Louistown, Amarillo, Idaho, Buffalo, Toledo . . . there's no place we won't drink it . . . there's no place we won't drink it.

ANNCR: Koala Springs. It's mineral water with an Australian flavor.

726

SALLY KELLERMAN: Imagine for a second you have no clothes on . . . but then you begin to cover yourself with chocolate . . . and you squeeze into some shimmering butter . . . or you take hot mustard and slide it over your toes, up your leg, and around your waist . . . these are just some of the sumptuous sensations you'll soon find on plates . . . fashion plates, that is . . . because this fall at Galleria, the colors of our clothes and accessories are a feast for the eyes . . . with everything from mocha mini-skirts, hot mustard pants and cognac coats . . . to walnut wool cardigans, buttery knit sweaters, and olive skinned belts . . . so stop by . . . because you can't imagine what it's like to wrap yourself in tomato . . . until you've tried it.

(MUSIC: UP)

ANNCR: Galleria, 69th and France, in Edina.

727

MAN: Hi, I just picked up my pictures here at Kroger and there seems to be a mistake.

CLERK: A mistake?

MAN: Yeah, I only took twelve pictures and there's twenty-four here.

CLERK (LAUGHS): Oh, no sir, that's because . . .

MAN: You must have put someone else's pictures in the envelope with mine.

CLERK: No, sir. Kroger gives you two prints for each shot.

MAN: See, these are my twelve here. And these . . . Wow, look at this sunset. This person takes pictures as good as me. The quality is unbelievable!

CLERK: We only use Kodak paper, sir. And the person who took these pictures . . .

MAN: Has a couch exactly like mine. Look at this. What a coincidence.

CLERK: Sir . . .

MAN: This is spooky. The coffee table in front of the couch is identical to the one I have in my living room.

CLERK: Sir, Kroger gives you two prints for the price of one. Double prints. Understand?

MAN: Yeah, but look at this!

CLERK: What?

MAN: The woman in this picture looks exactly like my Aunt Betty from Bethesda.

CLERK:That is your . . .

MAN: The pointy nose, the red bouffant. She even has a dress like this.

CLERK: You're looking at your own pictures.

MAN: Wait till I tell my . . . oh, my goodness. Look at this!

CLERK: What?

MAN: The woman in this picture could be my wife's twin sister. I never would have believed it, but here it is. Proof I can see with my own two eyes . . .

ANNCR: The Kroger Photo Department. Top quality photo finishing. And two prints with each shot.

728

(SFX: FOOTSTEPS DOWN A HALLWAY)

DONALD (TALKING TO HIMSELF): I've been with the company for over ten years. I've worked hard, stayed late, come in when I've been sick. I've given 150%. O.K., I'm due for a raise. They owe it to me! But, just to be safe I'll get on his good side first!

(SFX: KNOCK ON DOOR)

DONALD (CLEARING HIS THROAT): Mr Finkelstein?

MR F (BOOMING VOICE, VERY INTIMIDATING–ORSON WELLISH): Yes, what is it, Donald?

DONALD: Uh . . . how are you?

MR F (QUICK STACCATO ANSWERS): Feverish.

DONALD: Well, how's your wife?

MR F: We're getting divorced.

DONALD: Uh, how's your son?

MR F: Had a sex change.

DONALD: That cute little daughter of yours?

MR F: Pregnant.

DONALD: Your parents?

MR F: In prison.

DONALD: Your dog?

MR F: Dead.

DONALD: Your Mercedes?

MR F: Totalled.

DONALD: Your lear jet?

MR F: It crashed.

DONALD: Your yacht?

MR F: It sunk.

DONALD: Your house?

MR F: Burned down.

DONALD: Your horses?

MR F: They're dog food! LOOK DONALD WHAT DO YOU REALLY WANT?!!!

DONALD: Well, I . . . uh . . .

MR F: WHAT, WHAT, WHAT?!!!

DONALD: Boy, could I go for a Genny now!

ANNCR: There are times when only one beer will do. Smooth cold-aged Genesee.

MR F: Well, what is it?

DONALD (BLURTS IT OUT): I want a raise, sir.

MR F: A raise? Fine.

DONALD: Really?

MR F: Sure.

DONALD: Great!

MR F: Good.

DONALD: Fantastic.

MR F: Terrific.

ANNCR: Genesee Brewing Company. Rochester, New York.

729

ARTHUR MULLARD: 'Ello, this is Nanette Newman, the world renowned beauty, 'ere to warn you not to miss *Visage* with the *Mail on Sunday*. People often say: 'Nanette, 'ow do you stay looking so lovely?' Well, I'm an avid reader of *Visage*, the health and beauty magazine full of hot tips on looking good. Shame I missed the last issue.

MVO: *Visage*, free with the *Mail on Sunday* and *You* magazine. A newspaper. Not a snoozepaper.

730

ANNCR: Schmidt Beer presents the Schmidt Bit Players.

WOMAN: Sometimes I think to myself, Brooke, do you want him to get closer? And I answer, Brooke, yes, I do want him to get closer. And sometimes I ask myself, Brooke, do you really want a Schmidt? And I say yeah, Brooke, I would like a Schmidt. And sometimes I ask myself, Brooke, why do you ask all those questions when your name is Carol?

ANNCR: And now Schmidt Beer presents "Household Hints with the Schmidt Brothers."

BERNIE: Hello there.

ERNIE: Hello there.

BERNIE: This is Bernie Schmidt.

ERNIE: This is Ernie Schmidt.

BERNIE: And today we're goin' to teach ya how to put a new washer inside your faucet.

ERNIE: First ya grab yourself a Schmidt Beer.

BERNIE: Then ya drink it.

ERNIE: And then ya put the washer in the faucet.

BERNIE: Yeah. But, ah . . .

ERNIE: This ain't gonna work, no, this is way too big.

BERNIE: Maybe we shoulda got a washer without a lint trap.

ERNIE: You might be right there.

ANNCR: Join us next time when the Schmidt brothers plumb a wall.

ERNIE: All right, grab the plumb bob.

BERNIE: No, the name's Bernie, remember, not Bob.

ERNIE: No no, grab the plumb bob.

BERNIE: No, I don't work with fruits.

(SFX: POURING SOUNDS)

MAN: Hhhhhi, the first time I tasted Schmidt Beer I liked it so much I drank the company.

(SFX: POURING SOUNDS)

ANNCR: Schmidt Brewing Company, St. Paul, Minnesota.

Consumer Radio: Single

731
WRITER
David Fowler
AGENCY PRODUCER
Lisa Dee
CLIENT
Motel 6
AGENCY
The Richards Group/Dallas

732
WRITERS
Walt Kraemer
John Scott MacDaniels
AGENCY PRODUCER
Deborah Cooke
CLIENT
Caltrans
AGENCY
Lowe Marschalk/
San Francisco

733
WRITER
Minneapolis Broadcast Company
CLIENT
Marquette Place
AGENCY
Minneapolis Broadcast Company

734
WRITER
Sande Lohm
AGENCY PRODUCER
Sande Lohm
CLIENT
The Baltimore Sun
AGENCY
W.B. Doner & Company/
Baltimore

735
WRITER
Scott McCormick
AGENCY PRODUCER
Mike Miller
CLIENT
United TeleSpectrum
AGENCY
Valentine-Radford/
Kansas City, MO

736
WRITER
Peter Wegner
AGENCY PRODUCER
Robin Olesen
CLIENT
San Francisco Examiner
AGENCY
Goodby Berlin &
Silverstein/San Francisco

737
WRITERS
Tom Amico
Jim Proimos
Steve Etzine
AGENCY PRODUCERS
Tom Amico
Jim Proimos
CLIENT
Mid Atlantic Milk Marketing
AGENCY
W.B. Doner & Company/
Baltimore

731

ANNCR: Hi. Tom Bodett for Motel 6 with Tom's Tips for Road Trips. First walk around and kick all the tires. I don't know what this accomplishes but my father always did it. He sure did ruin a lot of good shoes that way. Then go down to the gas station and fill'er up. You'll know it's full when gas sprays out all over you. That's how I usually tell. Check the oil but do it while the engine's hot otherwise you won't burn your knuckles. Then call 505-891-6161 and we'll reserve rooms for you at Motel 6 locations all along your trip. Even tell you about restaurants and other points of interest like Prairie Dog Town in Lubbock, Texas. Or tell you where to find the nearest Motel 6. We'll give you the lowest prices of any national chain. You'll get free T.V., movies and local calls, plus free swimming at most locations, and the kids stay free in their parents' room where you can keep an eye on them. Our number's 505-891-6161. I'm Tom Bodett for Motel 6. Be sure you unplug the iron before you go. We'll leave the light on for you.

732

HUSBAND: Honey, where's my car keys?

WIFE: In your hand.

HUSBAND: O.K.

WIFE: Darling, I got you this relaxation tape.

HUSBAND: Relaxation. There's no relaxing on the San Diego Freeway Doris . . .

WIFE: Well, try it . . . Bob.

HUSBAND (IN CAR): Traffic stopped. I'm not going anywhere. Might as well play this tape and see what happens.

TAPE VOICE: Welcome to highway relaxation . . .

HUSBAND: Well, that sounds like a car.

TAPE VOICE: . . . are you tense?

HUSBAND: Yes, I'm very . . .

TAPE VOICE: . . . First . . .

HUSBAND: . . . I'm talking to a tape!

TAPE VOICE: . . . if you see one of Amtrak's San Diegan trains pass you by . . .

HUSBAND: Yeah, it just did.

TAPE VOICE: . . . Give it no thought at all . . .

HUSBAND: . . . then don't bring it up.

TAPE VOICE: . . . ignore those happy passengers who are spending far less, in a comfortable environment . . .

HUSBAND: I'm stuck in a car on the San Diego Freeway . . .

TAPE VOICE: . . . relaxing . . . and comfortable . . .

HUSBAND: . . . I don't want to hear about efficient, relaxing, comfortable choo-choo trains.

TAPE VOICE: Do not make faces at the Amtrak San Diegan passengers . . .

HUSBAND: I'm not making faces at the passengers. My face is red with rage because this tape . . .

TAPE VOICE: . . . do not stick out your tongue at the San Diegan passengers.

HUSBAND: I'm not sticking out my tongue . . . I couldn't talk . . . listen . . . (STICKS OUT TONGUE AND TRIES TO TALK)

TAPE VOICE: By now you are totally relaxed.

HUSBAND: I'm calm.

733

(MUSIC: "DANCE OF THE SUGARPLUM FAIRIES" CONTINUES UNDER THROUGHOUT)

WOMAN: Ahhhh, the joys of winter driving. You know, those special, frigid moments that develop between you and your car.

(SFX: MAN SHOVELING SNOW)

Who could ever forget the three hours you spent digging your car out of a massive snow pile. Only to discover . . . it wasn't your car.

(SFX: MAN YELLING, 'THIS ISN'T MY CAR. AAARGH!')

Or the time you paid $25 to have it jump started . . .

(SFX: COLD ENGINE CRANKING OVER AND OVER)

And another $450 in repairs after it lurched forward into the rear of the tow truck.

(SFX: TIRE SQUEEL; CRUNCH OF CAR HITTING SOLID OBJECT)

Of course, nothing quite matches the incredible sensation you felt when your anti-lock braking system proved totally worthless on glare ice.

(SFX: CAR SLIDING; CRUNCHES INTO ANOTHER SOLID OBJECT)

This cheerful message is brought to you by your friends at Marquette Place, conveniently located in downtown Minneapolis. Marquette Place, elegant apartments where you can go to work, to stores, to restaurants . . . just by getting on an elevator. And if you do need to drive, you'll find your car waiting warm and dry, in Marquette's indoor parking ramp. Have a nice winter.

734

TALENT: When the two researchers finally arrived, it didn't take the ailing hairdresser long to get to the point. 'I know how I got this thing,' he said, 'I had sex with this guy. He gave me hepatitis and I bet he gave me this new disease, too.'

ANNCR: In 1982, the disease had no name. No publicity. But already, the search for its origin had begun.

TALENT: 'His name,' the man said, 'is Gaetan Dugas.' From the looks on their faces, he knew he had just said the magic word.

ANNCR: Finally, the story is being told. Starting Monday in *The Evening Sun,* a five-part excerpt from the book, *And The Band Played On*. The true story of how the AIDS epidemic began and how it was allowed to continue.

TALENT: Around this time, rumors began on Castro Street about a guy with a French accent. After sex, he'd turn up the lights and point to his lesions. 'I've got gay cancer,' he'd say, 'I'm gonna die and so are you.'

ANNCR: A story of epidemic proportions—starts Monday in *The Evening Sun*.

735

(SFX: AMBIENT TRAFFIC)

VOICE 1: Excuse me?

VOICE 2: Yes. . .

VOICE 1: Are you by chance waiting here for . . .

VOICE 2: Yes I am . . . I'm waiting here for the price of cellular car telephones to come down.

VOICE 1: Oh good, so this is the right corner then.

VOICE 2: That's right . . . this is where it all happens.

VOICE 1: Uh-huh.

VOICE 2: Works every time. I waited here for the price of video tape recorders to come down . . . air fares, you know what happened to them.

VOICE 1: Well, I'm here to tell you about a very special offer on cellular car phones from United TeleSpectrum.

VOICE 2: Here it comes . . . oh goody.

VOICE 1: Now, for a limited time if you buy a GE 1000 cellular phone for $819, they'll give you a second one for half price!

VOICE 2: There you go.

VOICE 1: And, if you sign up for one year, they'll give you a Preferred Customer Package that gives you FREE installation, FREE custom calling, FREE detailed airtime billing and up to 200 minutes of air time so you can talk for hours FREE.

VOICE 2: See.

VOICE 1: They'll even give you a free pocket calculator just for calling. No obligation.

VOICE 2: Now you're talkin'. Where do I call?

VOICE 1: Call now. 1-800-556-2343. That's 1-800-556-2343.

VOICE 2: Good. Wait here for me, O.K.?

VOICE 1: O.K. What am I waiting for?

VOICE 2: Truffles. Dumb little mushroom things . . . cost a fortune.

VOICE 1: O.K.

VOICE 2: Don't lose my place. I can't afford it.

VOICE 1: O.K.

(RUN TEN SECONDS OF TRAFFIC NOISE FOR LOCAL LIVE ANNCR TAG)

ANNCR: To find out more about United TeleSpectrum's special introductory offer, call 1-800-556-2343. Hurry, offer expires May 16th, 1988. Certain conditions and limitations apply. Phones are reconditioned with one year warranty.

736

(SFX: LOUD RESTAURANT KITCHEN NOISES)

WILL: Hi, this is Will Hearst, publisher of the *San Francisco Examiner.* I'm here in the kitchen of Bob's Burger Haven, talking with proprietor Bob Smulack about our *Epicure* section.
Bob, I know it's common practice to post *Epicure* reviews in restaurant windows, but out of a possible five stars, Bob, our reviewer gave you none.

BOB: Everyone's got a little room for improvement.

WILL: But Bob, this says, quote, "It's easier to find a rat than a waiter, and when you do, you can hardly tell the difference." Do you really want people to know that?

BOB: I keep tellin' the kid to dress nicer.

WILL: Maybe you could explain to our readers why you have a diagram of the Heimlich maneuver on the back of your menu.

BOB: Well, next to the patty melt, it's our most requested item.

ANNCR: *Epicure.* A gourmet's guide to fine wines, recipes and restaurants, Wednesdays in the *Examiner.* Call 800-345-EXAM and get seven papers for the price of the Sunday paper alone. That's 800-345-EXAM. From the Next Generation, at the *Examiner.*

WILL: This is a cute little gimmick you've got here on the table, Bob. What do you call it?

BOB: I call it . . . Bob's Roach Motel.

737

(SFX: LONELY HARMONICA; FIRE CRACKLING)

ANNCR: It was the best of times, it was the worst of times. I take that back. It was the worst of times, period. As a matter of fact, times were so tough you could crack a nut between them.

(SFX: FLY BUZZ, SLAP)

There was nothing for a man to do but talk. Monologues, dialogues, narratives, you name it. They could say it. Those were the days when a man could spin a yarn, two men could darn a sock, three men could knit a pant suit. Four men could . . . ah, never mind. If you come out of that in one piece, you come out with two things. A taste for milk and a thirst for life. Or was it the other way around? Milk. It's a fitness you can drink. From an animal you can trust.

(SFX: WIND, HARMONICA UP)

This message brought to you by the Middle Atlantic Milk Marketing Association.

Consumer Radio: Single

738

WRITER
Melanie Johnston

CLIENT
Anheuser-Busch/
Zeltzer Seltzer

AGENCY
Hal Riney & Partners/
Chicago

739

WRITERS
Harry Woods
Richard Kelley

AGENCY PRODUCER
Beth Hagan

CLIENT
California Magazine

AGENCY
Scali McCabe Sloves West/
Los Angeles

Consumer Radio: Campaign

740

WRITERS
Marian Allen Godwin
Todd McVey

AGENCY PRODUCER
Rachel Novak

CLIENT
Genesee Brewing Company

AGENCY
Levine Huntley Schmidt &
Beaver

741

WRITER
Miller Leonard

AGENCY PRODUCER
Miller Leonard

CLIENT
Dollar General Corporation

AGENCY
Madden & Goodrum/
Nashville

742

WRITERS
Lorenzo Music
Lynn Stiles

AGENCY PRODUCER
Sally Smith

CLIENT
A.G. Britt & Company

AGENCY
Lord Geller Federico
Einstein

743

WRITER
Rod Kilpatrick

AGENCY PRODUCER
Cathy Jydstrup

CLIENT
The Wall Street Journal

AGENCY
Fallon McElligott/
Minneapolis

744

WRITER
Tom O'Connor

AGENCY PRODUCER
Tom O'Connor

CLIENT
Massport

AGENCY
Rossin Greenberg Seronick
& Hill/Boston

738

VO: *Boom schaka-laka-laka,*
Boom schaka-laka-laka.
Zeltzer Seltzer Flavored Soda.
Six fun flavors,
Hey, hey, hey.
Peach, so neat.
Raspberry, not too hairy.
Black Cherry, better than plain old cherry.
Vanilla Creme, a real dream.
Blueberry, good for guys named Larry.
Cola Berry, nothing rhymes with this.
Yum, yum, yum,
Felder-e, felder-i-i-i,
Chica-boom, chica- boom.

This exciting jingle has been brought to you by the people who bring you Zeltzer Seltzer. Something utterly new in the world.

739

MAN: On September 16th, 1986, Coco and Jay Rock were found guilty of murder in the first degree. A verdict they are now appealing from the California State Prison at Chino, where they were shipped on October 31st with a sentencing. Their pictures were on the front page of the *L.A. Times* Metro Section. But it wasn't their crime that landed them there. It was the fact that in the courtroom, they were laughing. Or rather, Coco was laughing. He'd been laughing ever since they were arrested.

ANNCR: Why do kids join gangs? Find out this month in *California Magazine*. You'll meet L.A.'s Playboy Cripps, one of the most notorious gangs in the country. It's just one article in the July issue of *California Magazine*. On news-stands today.

MAN: Coco told Jay Rock he didn't mind going to prison where he could watch television, listen to the radio, and have plenty of food.

740

(SFX: FOOTSTEPS DOWN A HALL WAY)

DONALD (TALKING TO HIMSELF): I've been with the company for over ten years. I've worked hard, stayed late, come in when I've been sick. I've given 150%. O.K., I'm due for a raise. They owe it to me! That's it! But, just to be safe I'll get on his good side first!

(SFX: KNOCK ON DOOR)

DONALD (CLEARING HIS THROAT): Mr Finkelstein?

MR F (BOOMING VOICE, VERY INTIMIDATING–ORSON WELLISH): Yes, what is it, Donald?

DONALD: Uh . . . how are you?

MR F (QUICK STACCATO ANSWERS): Feverish.

DONALD: Well, how's your wife?

MR F: We're getting divorced.

DONALD: Uh, how's your son?

MR F: Had a sex change.

DONALD: That cute little daughter of yours?

MR F: Pregnant.

DONALD: Your parents?

MR F: In prison.

DONALD: Your dog?

MR F: Dead.

DONALD: Your Mercedes?

MR F: Totalled.

DONALD: Your lear jet?

MR F: It crashed.

DONALD: Your yacht?

MR F: It sunk.

DONALD: Your house?

MR F: Burned down.

DONALD: Your horses?

MR F: They're dog food! LOOK DONALD WHAT DO YOU REALLY WANT?!!!

DONALD: Well, I . . . uh . . .

MR F: WHAT, WHAT, WHAT?!!!

DONALD: Boy, could I go for a Genny now!

ANNCR: There are times when only one beer will do. Smooth, cold-aged Genesee.

MR F: Well, what is it?

DONALD (BLURTS IT OUT): I want a raise, sir.

MR F: A raise? Fine.

DONALD: Really?

MR F: Sure.

DONALD: Great!

MR F: Good.

DONALD: Fantastic.

MR F: Terrific.

ANNCR: Genesee Brewing Company. Rochester, New York.

741

ANNCR: Every day is Dollar Day at your Dollar General Store. What in the world does that mean? Well, it means a lot of things. When we said it to your grandmother back in 1939, it meant she could bring a little ole green dollar in and it'd go further than anywhere else in town. It means that, today, in these days of bar codes and computers doing your price reading for you, there's still one store you can come to, pick up a great buy, read the price right on it, add it up in your head and go on. That's always been the way of Dollar General. It means that if you ever get to thinking you can't make it, all you have to do is walk in our door and we'll thrill you once again with what all a good ole American dollar can buy, straight out. That's something you can count on any day of the week. 'Cause every day always has been and always will be Dollar Day at your Dollar General Store.

742

(SFX: PHONE RINGS TWICE; FUMBLED PICK-UP)

ANDY (ALARMED): Hello? Am I late? I'm up!

WOMAN: I'm sorry, sir. Did I wake you?

ANDY: That's O.K. Who is this?

WOMAN: I'm Miss Stiles.

ANDY: Miss?

WOMAN: And I have a question for you. Would you be interested in something tall, cool, tingly, hip and great at parties?

ANDY: Are you kidding? I was just dreaming about you.

WOMAN: Sir, I'm talking about a drink.

ANDY: So am I! Then dinner, then back to my place.

WOMAN: No, I'm talking about a cooler.

ANDY: A cooler.

WOMAN: Have you heard about Britt Iced TeaBreeze?

ANDY: Well, not exactly, per se, but I'm sure willing to.

WOMAN: Wonderful! Britt Iced TeaBreeze is the adult cooler with the refreshing taste of tea and a tingle of citrus. Would you be willing to try some?

ANDY: Miss Stiles . . . have I ever refused you anything? Where can I get Britt Iced TeaBreeze? Am I saying it right?

WOMAN: Perfect. Britt Iced TeaBreeze is available everywhere you buy coolers.

ANDY: Great. I'll meet you there in five minutes.

(SFX: PHONE HANGS UP)

ANDY: Oh-oh.

(SFX: PHONE PICKED UP, RECEIVER DESPERATELY CLICKED)

ANDY: Miss Stiles? Miss Stiles?

ANNCR: Britt. The cooler iced tea cooler. A.G. Britt & Co., New Orleans, La.

743

MAN (STIFFLY, THROUGH P.A. SYSTEM): Finally, I'd like to remind all of you of this company's uncompromising commitment to adequacy. We won't be satisfied until we're just about as good as the competition. So I expect all you employees to give a sixty percent effort. I want you to stop at very few things to put our company smack in the middle. And in return, I promise you rewards in line with your most mundane dreams . . .

ANNCR: American business seems to be preoccupied with the search for excellence. But in the real world, good enough is usually good enough. Which presents a real opportunity for people who read *The Wall Street Journal.* With *The Journal* to catalyze your thinking, you'll find that excellence isn't a buzzword. It's a guiding principle.

MAN: So let's have two cheers for our company spirit. Hip-hip . . .

ANNCR: *The Wall Street Journal.* The daily diary of the American dream.

744

ANNCR. (VERY POSH BOSTON SYMPHONY-TYPE): As part of our continuing series, "Prose in the Public Interest," we present the classic poem "Ode to a Traveller," to be read today by our distinguished guest, Mr Roger Clemens. Mr Clemens . . .

ROGER: *When venturing to Logan Airport*
To journey hither and yon
There are means of transportation
You can depend upon.

Each is just delightful
Both speedy and sublime
The airport water shuttle, limos,
Taxis, buses and Blue Line.

From Quincy on the South Shore
If I may digress
Non-stop right to the airport
There goes the Logan Express.

So listen all ye travellers
There are better ways by far
Of venturing to the airport
Than driving in your car.

(SFX: APPLAUSE)

ANNCR: Thank you, Mr Clemens. A truly moving rendition. We trust it will inspire everyone to find the best way to the airport by calling Massport at 1-800-23-LOGAN. Why let getting to Logan get to you?

Consumer Radio: Campaign

745
WRITER
Walt Kraemer
AGENCY PRODUCER
Walt Kraemer
CLIENT
Wine World
AGENCY
Mojo MDA/San Francisco

746
WRITERS
Steve Kessler
Steve Rabosky
David Lubars
AGENCY PRODUCER
David Prince
CLIENT
Pizza Hut
AGENCY
Chiat/Day - Venice, CA

747
WRITERS
Garrett Brown
Anne Winn
CLIENT
American Express
AGENCY
Ogilvy & Mather

748
WRITERS
Walt Kraemer
John Scott MacDaniels
AGENCY PRODUCER
Deborah Cooke
CLIENT
Caltrans
AGENCY
Lowe Marschalk/
San Francisco

745

ANNCR: Another radio toast . . .

(SFX: POP)

ANNCR: . . . with Napa Ridge.

GIRL: Ooooo.

GUY: It's my new stereo. I wanted you to be the first to see it.

GIRL: Pretty fancy.

GUY: Oh, and I also have some wine chilling in the refrigerator.

GIRL: Wine, oooo.

GUY: I wanted you to be the first to taste it.

GIRL: Oooo, how nice.

GUY: It's Napa Ridge Chardonnay.

GIRL: Napa . . . Ridge . . .

GUY: Napa Ridge Chardonnay. It's well-balanced, lovely bouquet.

GIRL: Super.

GUY: It's fruity with a hint of oak. Do anything you want with the stereo, I'll be right back with the wine.

GIRL: Is this something you just discovered? This . . . what's it called?

GUY: Napa Ridge.

GIRL: Uh-huh.

GUY: Yes, I just discovered it. I wanted you to be the first to share it with me. Like Columbus and his date.

GIRL: Oooo. What's this thing with the blinking lights and the two cassettes?

GUY: Oh, that's my phone answering machine.

(SFX: CLICK)

ANSWERING MACHINE (FEMALE VOICE): Hi, Warren. This is Rusty. I enjoyed your new stereo last night. Especially that wine discovery of yours, Napa Ridge. Thank you for letting me be the first, Columbus.

GIRL: Warry, do you have a baseball bat or something?

GUY: There should be one in the closet.

GIRL: Thank you.

GUY: Just getting the cork, hon.

GIRL: Take your time.

GUY: Alright.

GIRL: Huh!

(SFX: SMASH)

ANNCR: Napa Ridge Winery, St. Helena, California.

746

COMMITTEE PERSON: Now, Mr Helm, would you say that your establishment skimped on ingredients like pepperoni to increase your company's profits?

MR HELM: As I have stated before, if this occurred, I had no prior, current or future knowledge of it.

ANNCR (IN WHISPER): You're listening to the Committee Hearings on the Pizza Cover-Up. Being questioned, the Logistics Director of the Run Of The Mill Pizza Company.

CP (SHUFFLING PAPERS): Well, we have evidence. You have a copy in front of you that your company awards a prize to the store that sells the most pepperoni pizzas, but uses the least pepperoni.

MR HELM: I was not aware of that, sir, no.

CP: A six-foot bronze pepperoni pizza in your likeness and you have no knowledge of it.

MR HELM: No.

CP: Roll in Exhibit A, please.

(SFX: HEAVY METAL SQUEAKING WHEELS; CROWD MURMUR)

CP: Were you aware that a Pizza Hut Pan Pizza-To-Go has significantly more cheese and toppings than your takeout pizzas have?

MR HELM: Is there another exhibit?

CP: No . . .

MR HELM: Then I have no recollection of that, sir.

CP: Were you aware that Pizza Hut makes the same hot, fresh Pizza-To-Go that they serve in their restaurants?

MR HELM: I wasn't aware of that, sir.

CP: Mr Helm, it is apparent that you're not aware of anything that's going on in your own pizza business.

MR HELM: I'm aware of that, sir.

CP: Bailiff! Get this man out of here.

(SFX: GAVEL)

LOCAL ANNCR: Pick up a hot, delicious Pizza Hut Pan Pizza-To-Go today.

WAITER: Hello, my name is twenty-eight. I'll be your waiter today. Table for one? Your android can wait over there.

ANNE: Table for two, thanks. My android and I sit together.

ANDROID: Thanks, boss.

ANNE: So tell me more about this cash stuff.

ANDROID: Oh, by the twenty-first century, cash had disappeared. Shall I order?

ANNE: Uh, yeah. The usual, no baked potato.

(SFX: ROBOT)

WAITER: Thank you, android.

ANDROID: Thank you, irritating robot-waiter. So . . . the best humans were Cardmembers, like you boss, with the American Express Card.

ANNE: No one used cash anymore?

ANDROID: Cash didn't have a chance. If you lost it, it was gone. You got no receipts. Everyone *handled* cash.

ANNE: Eew. What was it like?

ANDROID: It was made of green paper. The color rubbed off. That's how you got a green thumb. I think that's right.

ANNE: Really?

ANDROID: Now the American Express Card was accepted all over the Universe, wherever there was intelligent life.

ANNE: I've certainly enjoyed mine.

ANDROID: I know you have, Boss. I wish I had one.

WAITER: Anything to drink?

ANNE: Pluto water.

ANDROID: I'll have a quart of 10W30. (LAUGHS)

ANNE: I think we need to update your humor module.

ANDROID: Why did the chicken cross the road?

ANNE: Please don't start!

ANDROID: It's *your* humor module that needs work.

VO: The American Express Card. The perfect way to pay for any meal. Don't leave home without it.

GARNER & BARNEY (SINGING): *Forty-one bottles of beer on the wall* . . . (BARNEY CONTINUES TO SING)

GARNER: C'mon everybody.

MARSHA: Please, let's not sing about beer anymore.

GARNER: Well, we're driving . . .

MARSHA: . . . sing about iced tea.

UNCLE HARLIN: Iced tea sounds good.

(SFX: MUSIC COMES UP AS ANNCR BEGINS)

ANNCR: Amtrak presents the Carsby family. On the road somewhere between Bakersfield and the Bay Area.

GARNER: Alright, we'll make up a game, O.K.?

(SFX: SOUND OF TIRE BLOWING OUT)

UNCLE HARLIN: Oh, the explosion game.

MARSHA: What now?

GARNER: It's a flat tire; nothing to worry about.

UNCLE HARLIN: It's only flat on the bottom.

(SFX: DRUM CRASH FROM BARNEY)

BARNEY: Hey!

(SFX: CRICKETS SINGING IN BACKGROUND BEGINS)

MARSHA: Uncle Harlin, out. Barney, out . . .

BARNEY: O.K.

MARSHA: . . . but leave your drums in the car.

(SFX: TRAIN PASSING, HORN SOUNDING)

UNCLE HARLIN: Whoa, what was that?

MARSHA: That was an Amtrak train.

UNCLE HARLIN: Clippin' right along, wasn't it?

GARNER: Well, but I mean, they don't have their family gathered around them on the side of the road.

UNCLE HARLIN: They ever get flat tires?

GARNER (SIMULTANEOUSLY): They have metal wheels.

MARSHA (SIMULTANEOUSLY): They don't have tires.

BARNEY: Dad?

GARNER: Yes, Barney.

BARNEY: I have to go to the bathroom.

GARNER: Well, go ahead, you got the whole San Joaquin Valley!

(SFX: MUSIC COMES UP AS ANNCR BEGINS)

ANNCR: You could take a chance, or you could take a train. Give Amtrak's San Joaquin a ride.

(SFX: CRICKETS SINGING IN BACKGROUND AGAIN)

BARNEY: Mom, what's those steel things along the road?

MARSHA: Those are called railroad tracks, honey. You might want to point those out to your father.

ANNCR: Amtrak's San Joaquin.

Consumer Radio: Campaign

749

WRITER
Virgil Shutze

AGENCY PRODUCER
George Medland

CLIENT
Atlanta Business Chronicle

AGENCY
HutchesonShutze/Atlanta

750

WRITER
Melanie Johnston

CLIENT
Anheuser-Busch/
Zeltzer Seltzer

AGENCY
Hal Riney & Partners/
Chicago

751

WRITER
Charles Griffith

AGENCY PRODUCER
Sally Smith

CLIENT
The New Yorker Magazine

AGENCY
Lord Geller Federico
Einstein

752

WRITER
Miller Leonard

AGENCY PRODUCER
Miller Leonard

CLIENT
Dollar General Corporation

AGENCY
Madden & Goodrum/
Nashville

Public Service Radio: Single

753

WRITER
Jarl Olsen

AGENCY PRODUCER
Cathy Jydstrup

CLIENT
University of Minnesota

AGENCY
Fallon McElligott/
Minneapolis

754

WRITER
Kerry Casey

AGENCY PRODUCER
Jack Steinmann

CLIENT
Minnesota Office of
Tourism

AGENCY
Carmichael Lynch/
Minneapolis

755

WRITER
George Gier

AGENCY PRODUCER
Cathy Jydstrup

CLIENT
Children's Defense Fund

AGENCY
Fallon McElligott/
Minneapolis

Public Service Radio: Campaign

756

WRITER
George Gier

AGENCY PRODUCER
Cathy Jydstrup

CLIENT
Children's Defense Fund

AGENCY
Fallon McElligott/
Minneapolis

749

WOMAN: Good morning, Mr Biggs. Welcome to your first day at Boggs, Biddle and Bailey. Here's your coffee, your jelly donut and *The Atlanta Business Chronicle.*

MAN: Aren't I supposed to read *The Wall Street Journal?*

WOMAN: Around here everyone reads *The Atlanta Business Chronicle.*

MAN: But isn't *The Wall Street Journal* . . . ?

WOMAN: *The Atlanta Business Chronicle* tells you everything that's going on in Atlanta. It's more topical, more incisive and offers people on their way up more comprehensive Atlanta business coverage than any other publication and you've got jelly on your tie.

MAN: But *The Wall Street Journal* would tell me . . .

WOMAN: The price of bauxite in Bolivia. Whoopdeedoo. If you want to get anywhere in this town, Biggs, you read *The Business Chronicle.* Start reading while I put some club soda on that tie.

(SFX: PSSSSSSST)

MAN: Argh!

ANNCR: Get the straight scoop on Atlanta business. Find out who's really making it, what's developing, when it's breaking, where it's going and why it's happening. Subscribe to *The Atlanta Business Chronicle.* Call 249-1010.

MAN: Uh, Ms Trisedale, where do I go for a power lunch?

WOMAN: Power lunch is out. Power breakfast is in. Read about it in *The Atlanta Business Chronicle.* It'll tell you where everybody who's anybody goes.

MAN: Am I everybody or anybody?

WOMAN: Right now you're nobody.

ANNCR: *The Atlanta Business Chronicle.* Where Atlanta's business comes first.

750

ANNCR: Some of you have been quite curious about the name of our flavored soda: Zeltzer Seltzer.
In this country of towns named Walla Walla . . .
of dances called the bunny hop
groups named Flim and the B'B's
women named Edna
men named Floyd
shoes named Weejuns
rivers named Youchagheny
sounds named Puget
mountains named Rocky
vegetables called rutabagas
animals called possums
grains called grits.

Whaddaya expect? Tiffany Seltzer?
Zeltzer Seltzer.
Something utterly new in the world.

751

ANNCR: Hi. Sure is great having magazines with pictures isn't it? Helps you figure out what the words mean. Like when the President gives a speech, you get to see a picture of the President giving a speech! Adds that extra dimension. Or when there's a flood, you get to see brown water and the tops of cars. Well, *The New Yorker* has pictures, too. But, instead of just sitting next to the words, they come out of 'em. A lot of people think those are the best kind of pictures and that *The New Yorker* is the best-written, best-read magazine in America. And they're right.

752

ANNCR: Every year about this time, something interesting happens in this country: a change of underwear. Families'll struggle along all summer in tatters, but the minute Back-to-School time hits, they're ready to do something. Maybe it's the fact that kids have to go back to gym class or maybe it has something to do with swimming holes, swimming pools and the like. How do kids forget to put their underwear back on? We don't know what it is, but we're sure ready for it at Dollar General. And we beat the big boys' socks off when it comes to prices. Why, you can underwear a family of four for just $10 at Dollar General. Come on in and get two pairs of girls' briefs, a ladies' bra and bikini set, three pairs of men's Fruit of the Looms and three pairs of boys' Fruit of the Looms . . . all that for just one $10 bill. Try that down at the mall. Yes sir, when it comes to the important things in life, you can always count on us at Dollar General.

753

VO: The following is presented in the interest of equal time and does not necessarily represent the opinion of this station, its management or sponsors.

GRUFF MAN: 'I would like to respond to the recent attacks in the press and on this station on the use of steroids by athletes and persons concerned with increasing their physical development. Steroids have been wrongly blamed for a variety of medical problems, from heart disease and liver cancer to baldness and acne. I have personally used steroids for a number of years and I can honestly say that I have never observed any serious side effects. It certainly hasn't been my experience that steroids bring about feminine characteristics in men and masculine characteristics in women. I think it's time that the media, which is continually trying to tell us what to do, forgot about steroids and focused their attention on some problem which poses a real threat to the public health.' Sincerely, Tina Louise Tooshman.

VO: Steroids. They're big trouble.

LIVE ANNCR: Sponsored by University of Minnesota Men's Athletics and "M" Club.

754

(THE COPYWRITER ATTEMPTS TO IMPERSONATE THE CALL OF A LOON—VERY UNSUCCESSFULLY)

(SFX: OOOOO-WHOOOO-OHHH; OOOOOHHH-EEEE-OOOH . . .ETC., GOES UNDER)

VO: There are some things man simply can't replace.

(SFX: UP COMES THE BEAUTIFUL, HAPPY/SAD CALL OF A REAL LOON.

Save the loons.

755

(SFX: BABY BEGINNING TO CRY)

ANNCR: Have a baby when you're a teenager . . .

(SFX: BABY CRYING FULL CRY)

And you'll hear about it for a long time.

756

YOUNG GIRL: My mom and dad never approved of him. They say he's loud and my schoolwork is suffering because of him.
My friends never call me anymore. They say I spend too much time with him.
Besides, he gets so angry when I'm not with him. If I'm gone even for a minute, he lets me know about it.
You know, I'm really too young to be tied down like this.

(SFX: BABY CRYING)

O.K., O.K., Mommy's coming.

ANNCR: When you're a teenager, the years of commitment it takes to raise a child can seem like a lifetime.
A message from The Children's Defense Fund.

Television Finalists

Consumer Television Over :30 (:45/:60/:90) Single

757

ART DIRECTOR
Michael Smith

WRITER
Graham Turner

AGENCY PRODUCER
Mark Sitley

PRODUCTION CO.
O. Pictures

DIRECTOR
Mary Lambert

CLIENT
Arrow

AGENCY
Chiat/Day

758

ART DIRECTORS
Bill Hamilton
Rick Boyko

WRITER
Bill Hamilton

AGENCY PRODUCERS
Eric Herrman
Mark Sitley

PRODUCTION CO.
Coppos Films

DIRECTOR
Mark Coppos

CLIENT
Reebok

AGENCY
Chiat/Day

759

ART DIRECTOR
Rick Carpenter

WRITER
Dick Sittig

AGENCY PRODUCER
Sandra Tuttle

PRODUCTION CO.
Travisano DiGiacomo Films

DIRECTOR
Ron Travisano

CLIENT
American Isuzu Motors

AGENCY
Della Femina Travisano &
Partners/Los Angeles

760

ART DIRECTOR
Alan Chalfin

WRITER
Lee Garfinkel

AGENCY PRODUCER
Bob Nelson

PRODUCTION CO.
Steve Horn Inc.

DIRECTOR
Steve Horn

CLIENT
Subaru of America

AGENCY
Levine Huntley Schmidt &
Beaver

757

CHORUS (BEGINS SINGING "HIGHER AND HIGHER" IN SLOW, FOUR-PART HARMONY): *Your love has lifted me higher . . .*
. . . than I've ever been lifted before.
So keep it up.

SOLOIST #1 (PICKS UP TEMPO): *So keep it up.*

CHORUS: *Quench my desire.*

SOLOIST #2: *Quench my desire.*

CHORUS: *And I'll be at your side for ever more.*

CHORUS (BEGINS TO INCREASE TEMPO AND ENERGY): *You know your love keeps on liftin'.*

SOLOIST #2: *Keeps on liftin'.*

SOLOIST #3: *Higher.*

CHORUS: *Higher and higher.*

CHORUS (INCREASES TEMPO AND SINGS FULL VOICE): *I said your love, your love keeps on, keeps on liftin', liftin' me higher and higher.*

VO: Arrow shirts, we've loosened the collar.

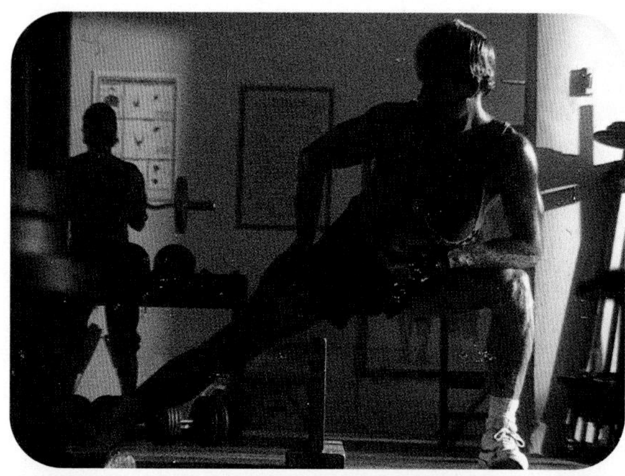

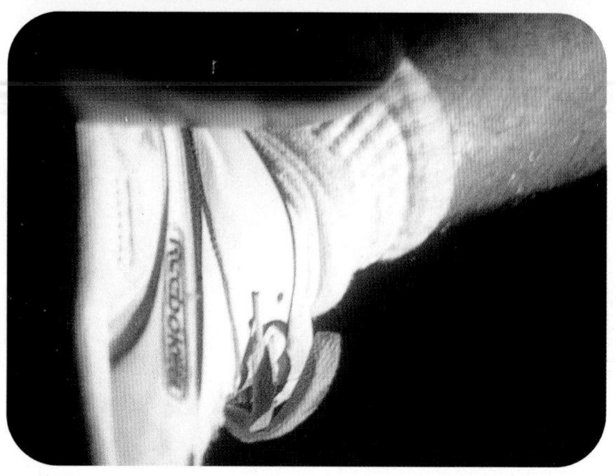

758

(SFX: BREATHING AND EXAGGERATED SOUND EFFECTS THROUGHOUT)

SILENCE

SUPER: REEBOK. SPORTS CONDITIONING SHOES.

759

JOE: How fast is the new Isuzu Impulse Turbo? How does 950 miles per hour sound?

SUPER: SOUNDS LIKE A LIE.

JOE: The Turbo Impulse. Faster than a speeding . . .

(SFX: POP!)

JOE: Well, *you* know . . .

760

FATHER: I don't want anyone driving my XT while I'm away on business. Do you understand?

(MUSIC: "LA BAMBA")

ANNCR: The new Subaru XT-6 has a powerful six-cylinder engine. Computerized full-time, four-wheel drive. And one of the most aerodynamic shapes in the industry, which makes it very difficult to resist.

FATHER: Someone drove my car. Who was it?

(GRANDMA: HUMS "LA BAMBA" UNDER BREATH.)

ANNCR: The new Subaru XT-6.
We built our reputation by building a better car.

Consumer Television Over :30 (:45/:60/:90) Single

761
ART DIRECTOR
Steve Fong
WRITER
Dave Woodside
AGENCY PRODUCER
Karen Carlson
PRODUCTION CO.
THT Productions
DIRECTOR
Martin Bell
CLIENT
Worlds of Wonder
AGENCY
Chiat/Day - San Francisco

762
ART DIRECTOR
Jane Walsh
WRITER
Mary Ann Donovan
AGENCY PRODUCER
Fred Slobodin
PRODUCTION CO.
Lovinger/Cohn
DIRECTOR
Lillian Auerbach
CLIENT
Time-Life Books
AGENCY
Wunderman Worldwide

763
ART DIRECTOR
Bob Ribits
WRITER
Alex Goslar
AGENCY PRODUCERS
Angelo Antonucci
Carole Floodstrand
PRODUCTION CO.
Koetz & Company
DIRECTOR
Leroy Koetz
CLIENT
Procter & Gamble/Cheer
AGENCY
Leo Burnett USA/Chicago

764
ART DIRECTOR
Don Easdon
WRITER
Bill Heater
AGENCY PRODUCER
Will McDonald
PRODUCTION CO.
PYTKA
CLIENT
John Hancock
AGENCY
Hill Holliday Connors
Cosmopulos/Boston

761

(MUSIC: BEAT STARTS)

(SFX: BELL RINGS; MUSIC UP)

KID VO: Well, if you ask me, Class Act gives you everything you need to succeed in school. Binders, to help you be more prepared. School bags to keep you organized. Folders for those important discoveries.

(MUSIC: UP THROUGHOUT)

KID VO: Even answering machines. Plus all the other tools that will help you reach your full potential as an adult.

MAN ANNCR: Stuff-It.
Sack-It.
Got-It.
Book-It.
From Class Act.

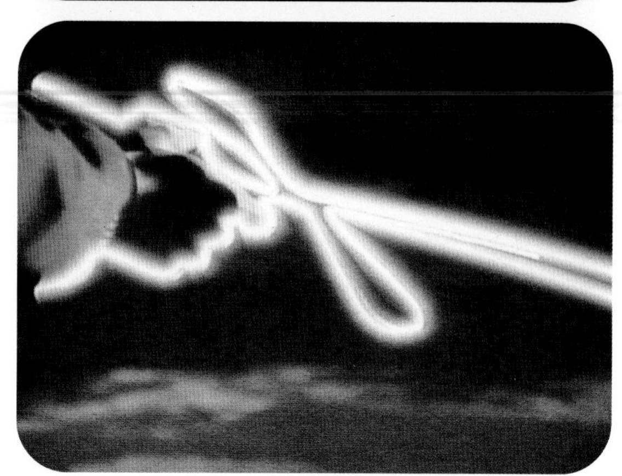

762

(MUSIC AND SFX: THROUGHOUT)

ANNCR: Chicago. A man is about to get on a plane. Suddenly, he changes his mind. An hour later, the plane crashes. It's dismissed as chance.

SUPER: DISMISSED AS CHANCE.

ANNCR VO: Northern Texas. A UFO is reported by a dozen people. Although there were no storms, it's dismissed as lightning.

SUPER: DISMISSED AS LIGHTNING.

ANNCR VO: Time Life Books announce *Mysteries of the Unknown.* An important new series that goes deeper into the world of mysterious and unexplained phenomena than ever before. It uncovers the secrets and tells all that can be told. Stonehenge. A visitor shapes a wire antenna into an ancient symbol and points it at the stones. A surge of power knocks him unconscious.

SUPER: DISMISSED AS IMAGINATION.

ANNCR VO: Was it all in his mind or much more than that? Experience Mysteries of the Unknown for ten days free. Then decide if you want to dismiss it.

SUPER: DISMISSED?

763

(MUSIC: THROUGHOUT)

ANNCR: Nobody's better in cold than All-Temperature Cheer.

764

WIFE VO: Alright.

MAN: Very funny . . .

WIFE VO: It was his idea, not mine.

MAN: Oh, it was his idea . . .

WIFE VO: I had nothing to do with it.

MAN: I'm going to stand up to do this.

WIFE VO: Oh, he made it . . . he made it.

MAN: Thank you. (LAUGHS) When you were twenty-one, we drank a toast to it. (UNDER BREATH) Looks like you.

WIFE VO: I wasn't old enough. (LAUGHS)

MAN: Alright . . . when you were thirty . . . I can't read this . . .

WIFE VO: Glasses. Let me hold it down for you.

MAN: . . . you could boast of it.

WIFE VO: Yes, yes, 'cause you married me. Now you're forty . . . (UNDER BREATH) that picture's awful (NORMAL VOICE) . . . so make the most of it. Yeah, alright . . . Take a look. Now your pants size and your age match.

MAN: Well . . . isn't that clever.

Consumer Television Over :30 (:45/:60/:90) Single

765
ART DIRECTOR
Don Easdon
WRITER
Bill Heater
AGENCY PRODUCER
Will McDonald
PRODUCTION CO.
PYTKA
CLIENT
Wang
AGENCY
Hill Holliday Connors Cosmopulos/Boston

766
ART DIRECTOR
Mike Moser
WRITERS
Bill O'Neill
Dave O'Hare
AGENCY PRODUCER
Peter Valentine
PRODUCTION CO.
Coppos Films
DIRECTOR
Mark Coppos
CLIENT
California Cooler
AGENCY
Chiat/Day - San Francisco

767
ART DIRECTOR
Peter Cohen
WRITER
Larry Spector
AGENCY PRODUCER
Rob Thomas
PRODUCTION CO.
Giraldi Suarez Productions
DIRECTOR
Bob Giraldi
CLIENT
US Heathcare
AGENCY
Levine Huntley Schmidt & Beaver

768
ART DIRECTOR
Bob Ribits
WRITER
Alex Goslar
AGENCY PRODUCERS
Angelo Antonucci
Carole Floodstrand
PRODUCTION CO.
Koetz & Company
DIRECTOR
Leroy Koetz
CLIENT
Procter & Gamble/Cheer
AGENCY
Leo Burnett USA/Chicago

765

WANG AGENT: I was giving a seminar on network management in Atlanta: Making SNA work without IBM. Anyway, the seminar is booked with MIS guys who don't believe it can happen. And so I show them it *has* happened over one of the biggest SNA networks in the world and here it is. No IBM mainframe . . . no IBM controllers . . . no IBM screens on the desks . . . no IBM iron anywhere. What's there instead? Five IBM look-alike mainframes . . . a Wang VS . . . a VS computer at each node . . . hundreds of them . . . and thousands of our workstations . . . covering the whole continent. One network. And the whole thing . . . every twist and turn . . . managed by a Wang VS—I didn't even have to talk to them about all the applications they were running. I just said, 'This is how you control a network *today.*' AND . . . blink . . . blink . . . blink. I could practically see the lightbulbs go on over their heads.

SUPER: WANG MAKES IT WORK.
GIVE US A DAY TO MAKE IT WORK FOR YOU.

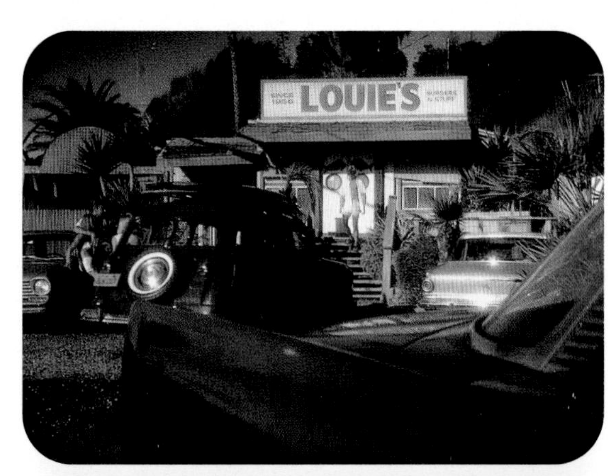

766

(MUSIC UP: "UNO, DOS, ONE, TWO, TRES, QUATRO . . . WOOLY, BULLY")

(MUSIC: UNDER)

ANNCR VO: This is one of California Cooler's original testing facilities.
It was here that white wine and real fruit was served from a tub to hundreds of dedicated volunteers.
Today, that blend has been perfected. But hey, test it anyway.
California Cooler.
The real stuff.

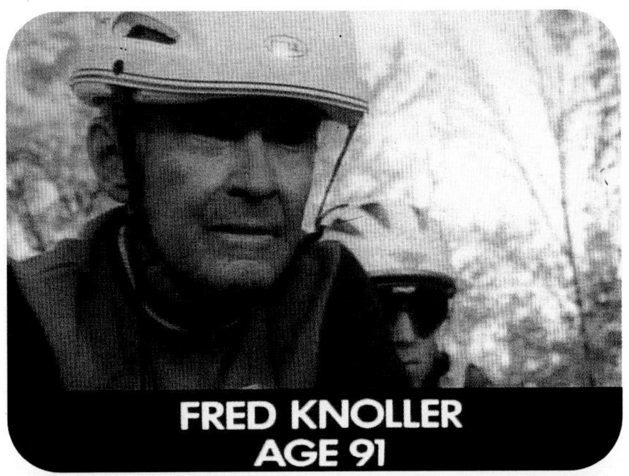

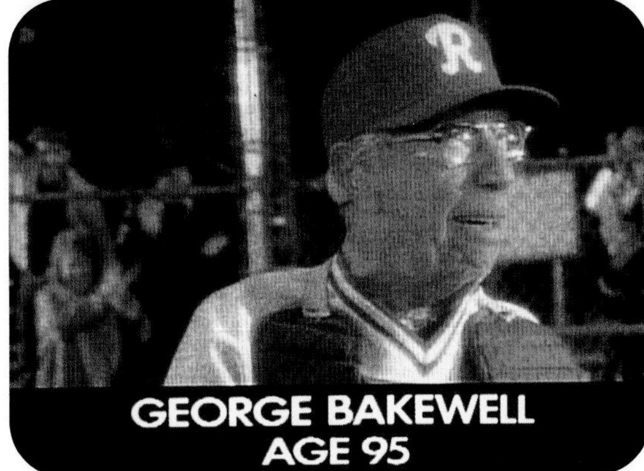

767

CYCLIST VO: That's what I do best is cycling. These trees are beautiful. The sky is beautiful. When I cycle I feel healthier for what I've done.

SUPER: FRED KNOLLER. AGE 91

SOFTBALL PLAYER: I play ball for two reasons. I like it and it adds years to my life. I wouldn't still be playing if I wasn't in terrific shape. If you feel young, act young, you're gonna stay young, *I* think.

SUPER: GEORGE BAKEWELL. AGE 95

PILOT VO: What's the difference how old you are. You're as old as you feel and I don't feel old.

SUPER: JANE STOVALL. AGE 102

ANNCR VO: The way to grow old and healthy is to start on a health plan when you're young and healthy. So later in life, instead of just being alive, you can really live.

PILOT VO: It's a wonderful life. You should try it. (FADING LAUGH)

SILENT SUPER: US HEALTHCARE.

768

(MUSIC: THROUGHOUT)

ANNCR: Nobody's better in cold than All-Temperature Cheer.

Consumer Television Over :30 (:45/:60/:90) Single

769
ART DIRECTOR
Don Easdon
WRITER
Bill Heater
AGENCY PRODUCER
Will McDonald
PRODUCTION CO.
PYTKA
CLIENT
Wang
AGENCY
Hill Holliday Connors Cosmopulos/Boston

770
ART DIRECTOR
Charles Inge
WRITER
Jane Garland
AGENCY PRODUCER
Annie Alexander
PRODUCTION CO.
Production Zone
DIRECTOR
Steve Drewitt
CLIENT
Mail On Sunday
AGENCY
Lowe Howard-Spink/London

771
ART DIRECTOR
Charles Inge
WRITER
Jane Garland
AGENCY PRODUCER
Charles Crisp
PRODUCTION CO.
Paul Weiland Film
DIRECTOR
David Bailey
CLIENT
Vauxhall Motors
AGENCY
Lowe Howard-Spink/London

772
ART DIRECTOR
Ron Brown
WRITER
David Abbott
AGENCY PRODUCERS
Liz Hutton
Nerine Soper
PRODUCTION CO.
John Clarke Productions
DIRECTOR
John Clarke
CLIENT
Ikea
AGENCY
Abbott Mead Vickers/SMS - London

769

WANG AGENT: We're doing a demo down in EBC for a guy. Data processing . . . voice . . . graphics . . . Heavy processing and *real* programming. The last thing in integration. We take a DEC workstation and via Wang PBX it's talking to his own IBM mainframe through our VS. And the DEC workstation is talking to an IBM PC . . . via Wang Office. Guy applauds. Then gets up. And checks our wires. You know, just to make sure. I thought it was funny.

SUPER: GIVE US A DAY TO MAKE IT WORK FOR YOU. WANG MAKES IT WORK.

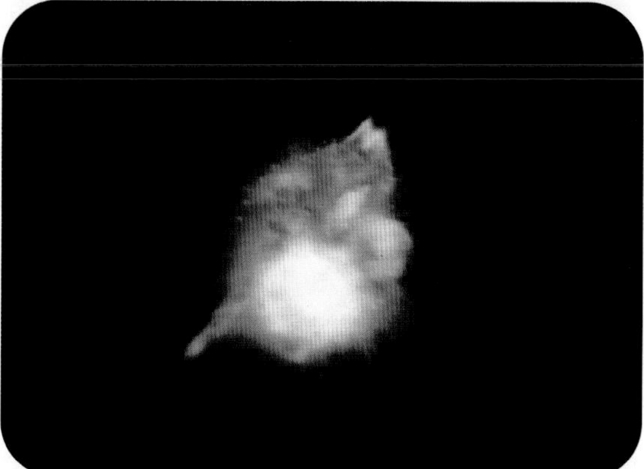

THERE WILL BE NO SECOND NOAH'S ARK.
M.GORBACHEV.

770

(SFX: SOUND OF THE ETHER THROUGHOUT)

MVO (RUSSIAN ACCENT): Our Earth is a ship on which we are all passengers.

(SFX: EXPLOSION)

MVO: There will be no second Noah's Ark.

SUPER: MIKHAIL GORBACHEV WILL ADDRESS THE PEOPLE OF THE WORLD IN *THE MAIL ON SUNDAY.* WILL YOU LISTEN?

771

(MEDITATION HUM THROUGHOUT)

MVO: The Nova from Vauxhall.
Once driven, forever smitten.

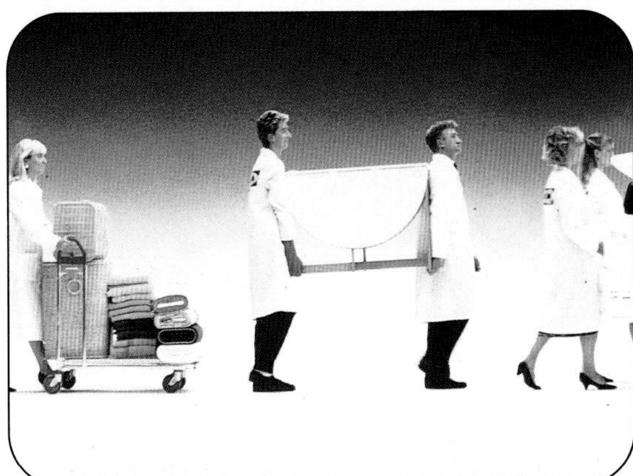

772

(MUSIC: UNDER)

MVO: First the Swedes came to burn and pillage . . .
then they came to sell us funny-looking
motor cars . . .
then they sent their young maidens to care for our
children and drive our men wild.
Now they've come to make amends.
Ikea is a wonderful furnishings store—as big as
three football pitches—full of stylish Swedish
furnishings at ridiculously low prices—with a
restaurant, playrooms and car parks.
Sweden, we forgive you everything.
Except maybe all those very boring tennis players.
Ikea, the furnishings store from Sweden.
Opens October first.

Consumer Television Over :30 (:45/:60/:90) Single

773
ART DIRECTOR
Bruce Ritter
WRITERS
David Lamb
Nancy Jordan
Bruce Ritter
AGENCY PRODUCER
Hank Sabian
PRODUCTION CO.
PYTKA
DIRECTOR
Joe Pytka
CLIENT
Anheuser-Busch/Michelob
AGENCY
DDB Needham Worldwide/Chicago

774
ART DIRECTOR
Mike Stephenson
WRITER
Derek Apps
AGENCY PRODUCER
Simon Wells
PRODUCTION CO.
Paul Weiland Film
DIRECTOR
Gerry Gavigan
CLIENT
Whitbread Best/Trophy
AGENCY
Lowe Howard-Spink/London

775
ART DIRECTOR
John Lucci
WRITER
David Johnson
AGENCY PRODUCER
Barbara Mullins
PRODUCTION CO.
Steve Horn Inc.
DIRECTOR
Steve Horn
CLIENT
Pepsi-Cola
AGENCY
BBDO

776
ART DIRECTOR
Dan Bogosh
WRITER
Tim Kane
AGENCY PRODUCER
Gary Franks
PRODUCTION CO.
Gerard Hameline
DIRECTOR
Gerard Hameline
CLIENT
Anheuser-Busch/Bud Light
AGENCY
DDB Needham Worldwide/Chicago

773

(MUSIC: UP)

SINGER: *High above the heat*
Of a summer
New York Street.
An out-of-work musician
Plays a solo saxaphone.
Where they look from such a height
The sound of it's so right
They're talkin' back to the night.
It's all that they can do.
Talkin' back to the night.

ANNCR VO: The night belongs to Michelob.

SINGER: *Talkin' back to the night.*

774

(MUSIC: CLARION; MUTED TRUMPET WAH-WAHING SUGGESTIVELY TO A HIGH POINT; LAUGHING TRUMPETS; SLOW, WOBBLY TUBA LAUGHING; CUCKOO; JAZZY HORNPIPE; SHIP'S HOOTER; SHIP'S WHISTLE; CELEBRATORY SHIPS' HOOTERS; CUCKOO; STACCATO CORNET; JOINED BY NASAL SAX; CUCKOO; DUET OF BASS GUITAR AND TINKLING PIANO; TRUMPET; CUCKOO; WAILING, MOANING WAH-WAHING GUITARS AND SYNTHS; BELL; REEDY, STUTTERING CLARINET; MASS LAUGHING OF TRUMPETS AND WOBBLY TUBA; TRIUMPHANT CUCKOO; JAZZY CLARION CALL.)

VO: For the Best Best in the Land . . . Join the Band. For a Pint that's Head and Body above the Rest, Join the Band.

SUPER: WHITBREAD TROPHY. JOIN THE BAND.

775

(SFX: CROWD CHEERING)

BASEBALL ANNCR ON T.V.: Well, this is it, fans. It's all come down to this moment . . .
This is where it all gets decided.
Johnson steps in . . . checks the signs . . .

(SFX: ORGAN IN STADIUM)

BASEBALL ANNCR: He makes a few adjustments and goes through the motions . . .
Talk about a classic confrontation . . .
The heat is on and, boy, you can really feel the tension . . .
Johnson's reaching way down. He's diggin' in . . .
Here's the delivery.

(SFX: CAN OPENING; BAT HITTING BALL)

BASEBALL ANNCR: Look out . . . What a shot . . .
He's going back, back, way back . . .
He's headin' for the wall. It is going, going . . . It is gone!!!

ANNCR VO: Pepsi. The Choice of a New Generation.

BASEBALL ANNCR: And that's it folks. The ball game is over.

776

(MUSIC: UP)

CHIEF: That's great. But we wanted a Bud Light.

CAVEMEN: Bud Light.

ANNCR: If you want the great taste of Bud Light . . .
Ask for it.

CHIEF: Now go get pizza.

CAVEMEN: Pizza.

ANNCR: Because everything else is just a light.

Consumer Television
Over :30 (:45/:60/:90)
Single

777
ART DIRECTOR
Len McCarron
WRITERS
Rick Meyer
Ted Sann
AGENCY PRODUCER
Regina Ebel
PRODUCTION CO.
Rick Levine Productions
DIRECTOR
Rick Levine
CLIENT
DuPont
AGENCY
BBDO

778
ART DIRECTOR
Rick Dalbey
WRITER
Darrell Williams
AGENCY PRODUCER
Darrell Williams
PRODUCTION CO.
Mincey Productions
DIRECTOR
Bill Tannen
CLIENT
The Benjamin Franklin Savings & Loan
AGENCY
Marx/Knoll Denight & Dodge - Portland, OR

779
ART DIRECTOR
John Merriman
WRITER
Paul Weinberger
AGENCY PRODUCER
Erika Issitt
PRODUCTION CO.
Lewin & Watson
DIRECTOR
Nick Lewin
CLIENT
Whitbread-Heineken
AGENCY
Lowe Howard-Spink/London

780
ART DIRECTOR
Rich Silverstein
WRITER
Jeff Goodby
AGENCY PRODUCER
Debbie King
PRODUCTION CO.
Jon Francis Films
DIRECTOR
Jon Francis
CLIENT
San Francisco Examiner
AGENCY
Goodby Berlin & Silverstein/San Francisco

777

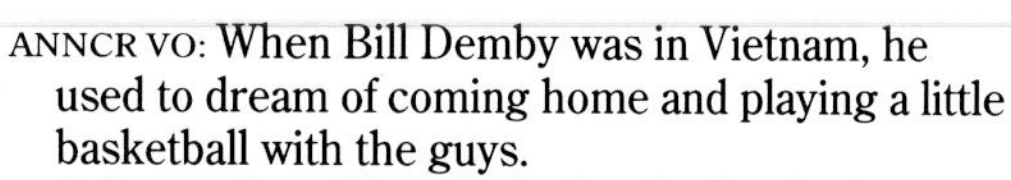

ANNCR VO: When Bill Demby was in Vietnam, he used to dream of coming home and playing a little basketball with the guys.
A dream that all but died when he lost both his legs to a Viet Cong rocket.
But then, a group of researchers discovered that a remarkable DuPont plastic could help make artificial limbs that were more resilient, more flexible, more like life itself.
Thanks to these efforts, Bill Demby is back.
And some say he hasn't lost a step.
At DuPont, we make the things that make a difference.
Better things for better living.

778

TEACHER: Franklin used his skillful diplomatic maneuvering and personal charm to prevent a split. With Franklin's help, America had become a nation.
(PAUSE) So . . . who can tell us about Benjamin Franklin?
Stewart. Are you with us?

STEWART: Sure. Ah . . . Franklin (RECOGNITION) The Benjamin Franklin. A four-point-five billion dollar financial services institution . . .

(SFX: GIRLS GIGGLING UNDER)

STEWART: . . . with offices in four western states . . . offering interest-paying checking, savings, CDs . . (STUMBLING) loans . . . su . . . subsidiaries in investment services, insurance, leasing and . . . (PAUSE) . . . and, of course, named after the famous American statesman, philosopher and inventor who coined the phrase, "a penny saved is a penny got" . . . not "a penny earned" as most people think.

779

(SFX: SOAP OPERA MUSIC)
TWIN BEHIND DESK: Thank you, honey. Sure is dead around here. Why don't you go on home.
(SFX: OFFICE DOOR OPENS)
TWIN BEHIND DESK: Who the heck are you?
SECOND TWIN: I'm the twin brother you never knew you had. I've come to help you search for Daddy.
TWIN BEHIND DESK: Forget it. Daddy's gawn.
(SFX: OFFICE DOOR OPENS)
TWINS TOGETHER: Daddy!
DADDY: Good to see you, boys. And how's your momma? I sure have missed her.
WOMAN #1: Darling . . .
WOMAN #2: Darling . . .
WOMAN #3: Darling . . .
WOMAN #1: Now we're all together, how are we going to rescue Emmylou?
SECOND TWIN: Poor Emmylou.
ALL CHORUS: Emmylou!
DADDY: O.K., so that's Blair who lost his memory for twenty years. And there's Joleen who slept through the last six episodes . . .
(SFX: GUNSHOT)
DADDY: But who's the guy who's just been shot?
FIRST TWIN: That was the scriptwriter.

780

(MUSIC: UNDER THROUGHOUT)
WILL: O.K., we're on deadline. What stories have we got?
FRANK: Not very much. A little back-yard grass fire. Somebody's barbecue tipped over.
GRANDFATHER (WHISPERS): Will, it's perfect—"Family Flees Blazing Inferno!"
WILL (OVER SHOULDER TO PORTRAIT): Not now!
FRANK: Yeah, I guess we'll save it for the second edition.
LARRY: We got a BART train stalled in the tube.
GRANDFATHER: "Passengers Trapped in Tunnel of Death!"
WILL (TO PORTRAIT): Gimme a break!
LARRY: Yeah, you're right.
WILL: No, I didn't mean you, Larry. It was just that, uh . . .
FRED: Hey, there's a rumor they may try to run the President for a third term.
JIM: What's the headline?
GRANDFATHER: Will! Will! I've got it!
WILL: Grandpa! Knock it off!
(FOUR DISTINCT MUSIC CHORDS)
JIM: That's it!
JOHN: That's brilliant!
GRANDFATHER: It's in the blood.
ANNCR: The Next Generation, at the *San Francisco Examiner.*

Consumer Television
Over :30 (:45/:60/:90)
Single

781
ART DIRECTOR
Nick Scott
WRITER
Richard Spencer
AGENCY PRODUCER
Debbie Court
PRODUCTION CO.
Sid Roberson
DIRECTOR
Simon Delaney
CLIENT
Mates Healthcare
AGENCY
Still Price Court Twivy D'Souza/London

782
ART DIRECTORS
Rick Boyko
Miles Turpin
WRITERS
Elizabeth Hayes
Richard Kelley
Dustin Jensen
Melvyn Jones
Harold Arlund
AGENCY PRODUCER
Kelly Waltos
PRODUCTION CO.
Petermann/Dektor
DIRECTOR
Leslie Dektor
CLIENT
Home Savings of America
AGENCY
Chiat/Day - Venice, CA

783
ART DIRECTOR
Ivan Horvath
WRITERS
Ken Segall
Michael Baldwin
AGENCY PRODUCERS
Paul Gold
Trish Reeves
PRODUCTION CO.
PYTKA
DIRECTOR
Joe Pytka
CLIENT
Apple Computer
AGENCY
BBDO

784
ART DIRECTOR
Marcia Murray
WRITER
Sue Parenio
AGENCY PRODUCER
John Massey
PRODUCTION CO.
Petermann/Dektor
DIRECTOR
Leslie Dektor
CLIENT
General Foods/Maxwell House
AGENCY
Ogilvy & Mather

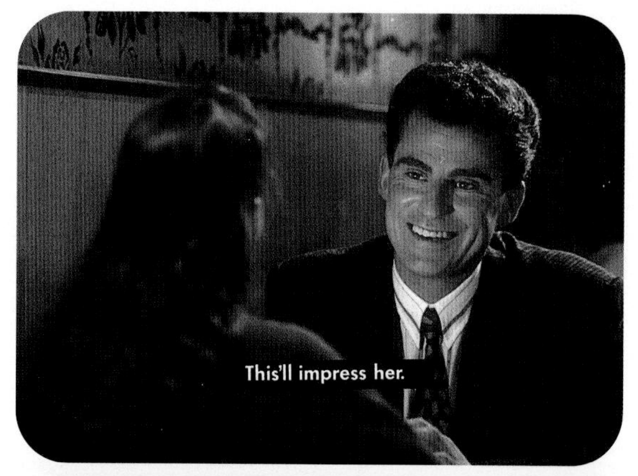

781

MAN: I'll get it. (SUBTITLE: THIS'LL IMPRESS HER)

GIRL: No, you always pay. (SUB: HE ISN'T MADE OF MONEY)

MAN: I insist. (SUB: OR DO I?)

MAN: Are you sure? (SUB: PHEW!)

GIRL: It's eight each. (SUB: AND WORTH EVERY PENNY)

MAN: Ooooops! (SUB: AAAARRRR-GGGGHHHH!) (SUBTITLE: ¡#*!)

GIRL: I think you've dropped something. (SUB: BET HE FEELS AN IDIOT)

MAN: Er, I don't know what to say. (SUB: WHAT AN IDIOT!)

GIRL: Don't say anything. (SUB: I THINK YOU'RE VERY SENSIBLE)

GIRL: Shall we go?

MVO: Mates are a new range of condoms. Like other condoms, they're reliable. But they're cheaper. It doesn't matter who carries them as long as one of you does.

MAN: Thanks for a lovely evening. (SUB: SHAME I RUINED IT)

GIRL: Thank you. (SUB: SHAME IT'S OVER)

MAN: See you again next week? (SUB: HARDLY WORTH ASKING)

GIRL: Of course. (SUB: I THOUGHT HE'D NEVER ASK)

MVO: Mates. You make love. They make sense.

782

DUSTIN: I'm looking for a paper job. That's the only way I get money.

FENNEMAN: In Kansas City, Missouri, there's a savings and loan that's helping Dustin Jensen save for his future.

DUSTIN: I haven't got around to starting to save for a car or a house yet, just college and a pet.

FENNEMAN: While in Baldwin Hills, California, that same savings and loan helped Melvyn and Robin Jones move into their longtime dream.

JONES: Driving down the street and pulling into our driveway and, you know, it's like . . . wow . . . to go out and water your own grass and you realize, 'I'm a homeowner.'

FENNEMAN: Savings of America, 312 branches in seven states, and in the ninety-eight years we've been helping people, no one has lost a penny, including Harold Arlund.

HAROLD: I've made myself pretty secure. Definitely have done that.

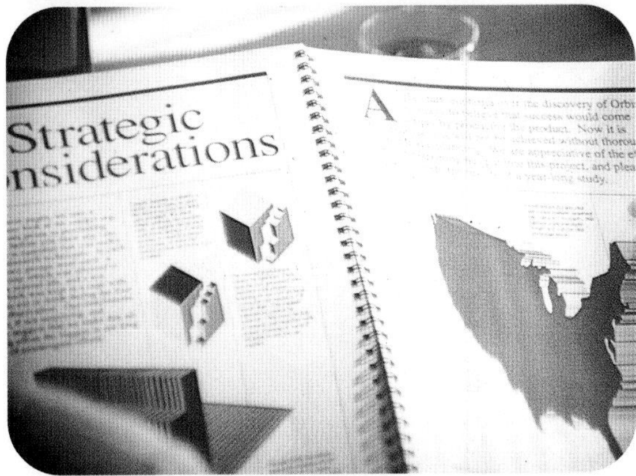

783

JOEY: Hey, Baldwin, how you doin'?

BALDWIN: Pretty good, Joey. How are you?

SAL: Ah, finished already.

WOMAN: Hey, I thought we were supposed to be doing this in-house.

BALDWIN: That's right. Pass the salt, would you?

SAL: Hey, your group did this?

BALDWIN: New computer. The salt?

SAL: Quintile analysis? Gimme a break.

BALDWIN: Well, Segall did that.

SAL: I thought he was in the LA office.

BALDWIN: So's Edwards—she did the graphics.

SAL: The market projections?

BALDWIN: Garnett. Chicago.

SAL: How'd you get everybody together in the same place?

BALDWIN: I told you. New computer.

SAL: What kind of system can do that?

BALDWIN (UNINTELLIGABLY): Mcntsh.

SAL: What?

BALDWIN: Mcntsh.

SAL: Pardon me?

SUPER: MACINTOSH. THE POWER TO BE YOUR BEST.

784

SINGER: *It's the way we start the morning*
the way we close a deal.
It's the way we share a secret
the way we end a meal.
Drinkin' our kind of coffee
Good to the last drop—hey!
Only Maxwell House fresh flavor
tastes like coffee made our way.
Only Maxwell House fresh flavor
tastes like coffee made our way.

It's the way we write a letter
the way we set the stage.
It's the way we break the winner's tape
no matter what our age.
Drinkin' our kind of coffee
Good to the last drop—hey!
Only Maxwell House fresh flavor
tastes like coffee made our way.
Only Maxwell House fresh flavor
tastes like coffee made our way.

Consumer Television Over :30 (:45/:60/:90) Single

785
ART DIRECTOR
Greg Willmott
WRITER
Stephen Fisher
AGENCY PRODUCER
Terri Condon
PRODUCTION CO.
Great Southern Films
DIRECTOR
Bob Slatter
CLIENT
3AK
AGENCY
Thomson White & Partners/Melbourne

786
ART DIRECTOR
Roger Mosconi
WRITER
Michael Patti
AGENCY PRODUCER
Jerry Cammisa
PRODUCTION CO.
Rick Levine Productions
DIRECTOR
Rick Levine
CLIENT
Pepsi-Cola/Diet Pepsi
AGENCY
BBDO

787
ART DIRECTORS
Rick Boyko
Miles Turpin
WRITERS
Elizabeth Hayes
Robin Jones
Melvyn Jones
AGENCY PRODUCERS
Richard O'Neill
David Prince
Elaine Hinton
PRODUCTION CO.
Petermann/Dektor
DIRECTOR
Leslie Dektor
CLIENT
Home Savings of America
AGENCY
Chiat/Day - Venice, CA

788
ART DIRECTOR
Olavi Hakkinen
WRITER
David Johnson
AGENCY PRODUCERS
David Frankel
Hyatt Choate
PRODUCTION CO.
Steve Horn Inc.
DIRECTO
Steve Horn
CLIENT
General Electric Corporate
AGENCY
BBDO

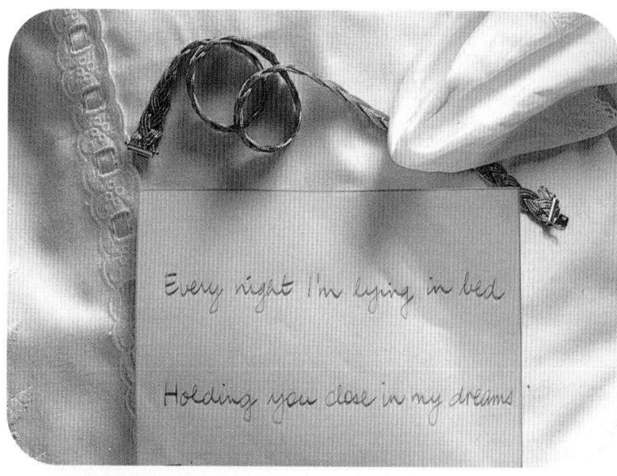

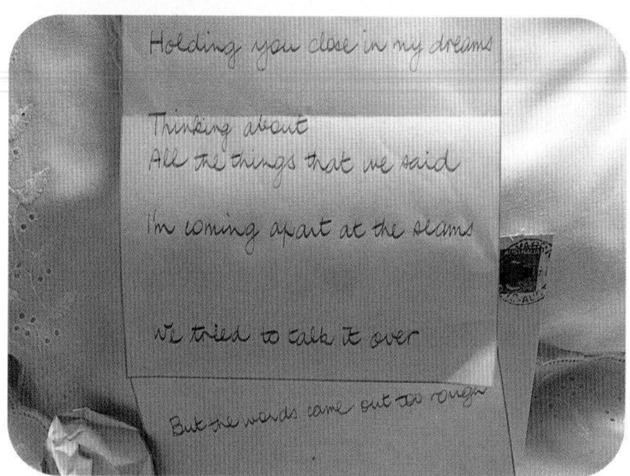

785

SINGER: *Every night I'm lying in bed*
Holding you close in my dreams
Thinking about
All the things that we said
I'm coming apart at the seams
We tried to talk it over
But the words come out too rough
I know you were trying
To give me the best of your love
Oh, sweet darling
You get the best of my love
You get the best of my love
Oh sweet darling
You get the best of my love.

786

(SFX: KNOCKING ON DOOR)
GIRL: Hi, I just moved in next door. Could I borrow a Diet Pepsi?
MICHAEL J. FOX: Sure, come in. Yes! How about something else?
GIRL: Listen, if you don't have a Diet Pepsi . . .
MICHAEL J. FOX: No, no I got it.
MUSIC: *Headin' up to heaven*
Chasin' down a dream
Turnin' on my engine, and the tension screams.
I'm on the edge tonight.
GIRL: You O.K. in there?
(SFX: WINDOW BREAKING)
MICHAEL J. FOX: Here's your Diet Pepsi.
(SFX: KNOCKING ON DOOR)
GIRL: That must be my roommate, Danny.
MICHAEL J. FOX: Danny?
GIRL #2: Hi, I'm Danielle. You got another Diet Pepsi?
MICHAEL J. FOX: Sure.
ANNCR VO: Diet Pepsi. The Choice of a New Generation.

787

MELVYN: It has to be the most thrilling experience for a person to go through because again you don't really know how it feels until you've been through all the negative things . . .

ANNCR: Melvyn and Robin Jones, Home Savings Customers.

ROBIN: When I saw this house, I said, 'We'll get a loan.'

MELVYN: It was, 'We were going to get a loan.'

ROBIN: And that's when we started going through major anxiety, you know, because we didn't have perfect credit . . . because, you know, ten years ago you paid a doctor bill late or something and then I decided somebody's gonna loan us money to get the house because, you know, we're nice people, stable, we've been on our jobs for a hundred years.

ANNCR: Home Savings didn't give Melvyn and Robin Jones a home loan based on their past. We gave them one based on their future.

ROBIN: I went and picked up the kids.

MELVYN: We opened the door.

ROBIN: And one of them, she said, 'Are we sleeping here tonight? And I said, 'Yes,' and she ran from room to room with tears in her eyes.

788

VO: All our science,
all our technology.
All our mathematics,
our computations.
Somehow they all add up to moments.
That are beyond any calculation.

SUPER: WE BRING GOOD THINGS TO LIFE.

Consumer Television Over :30 (:45/:60/:90) Single

789

ART DIRECTOR
Paul Kirner

WRITER
Bill Bruce

AGENCY PRODUCER
Gene Lofaro

PRODUCTION CO.
Steve Horn Inc.

DIRECTOR
Steve Horn

CLIENT
Pepsi-Cola/Diet Pepsi

AGENCY
BBDO

Consumer Television Over :30 (:45/:60/:90) Campaign

790

ART DIRECTOR
Don Easdon

WRITER
Bill Heater

AGENCY PRODUCER
Will McDonald

PRODUCTION CO.
PYTKA

CLIENT
John Hancock

AGENCY
Hill Holliday Connors Cosmopulos/Boston

791

ART DIRECTORS
Bill Hamilton
Rick Boyko

WRITER
Bill Hamilton

AGENCY PRODUCERS
Eric Herrman
Mark Sitley

PRODUCTION CO.
Coppos Films

DIRECTOR
Mark Coppos

CLIENT
Reebok

AGENCY
Chiat/Day

792

ART DIRECTOR
Eric Steinhauser

WRITER
Charlie Breen

AGENCY PRODUCERS
Eric Steinhauser
Chris Ott

PRODUCTION CO.
Dennis Guy & Hirsch

CLIENT
Miller Brewing/Genuine Draft

AGENCY
Backer Spielvogel Bates

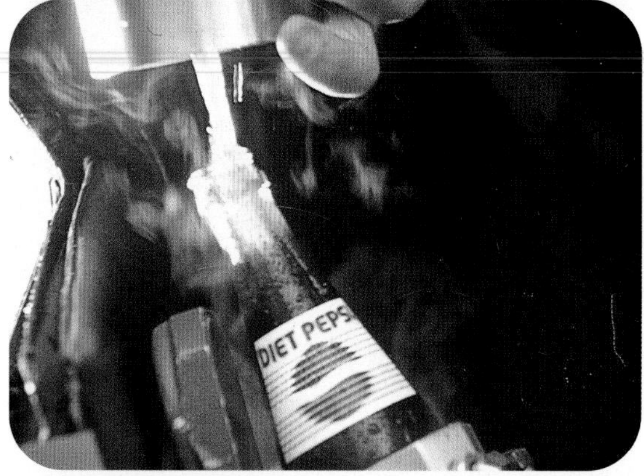

789

(MUSIC: THROUGHOUT)

MUSTANG: Den Mother, this is X Ray Tango one two seven. We're at angels eleven bearing zero niner zero, over.

TOWER: Nice going, Mustang. Maneuvers completed. Relax and have one on me.

MUSTANG: Roger, Den Mother.

(SFX: BOTTLE POPPING UP)

MUSTANG: Great!

PILOT #1: What's the problem, Mustang?

MUSTANG: No problem.

PILOT #2: Trouble with your refreshment system?

MUSTANG: Uh . . . Negative.

(SFX: BOTTLE OPENING . . . FIZZ; POURING; TAPPING ON CANOPY)

PILOT #1: Where is he?

MUSTANG: Hi, boys.

ANNCR VO: Diet Pepsi. The Choice of a New Generation.

790

WIFE VO: Alright.

MAN: Very funny . . .

WIFE VO: It was his idea, not mine.

MAN: Oh, it was his idea . . .

WIFE VO: I had nothing to do with it.

MAN: I'm going to stand up to do this.

WIFE VO: Oh, he made it . . . he made it.

MAN: Thank you. (LAUGHS) When you were twenty-one, we drank a toast to it. (UNDER BREATH) Looks like you.

WIFE VO: I wasn't old enough. (LAUGHS)

MAN: Alright . . . when you were thirty . . . I can't read this . . .

WIFE VO: Glasses. Let me hold it down for you.

MAN: . . . you could boast of it.

WIFE VO: Yes, yes, 'cause you married me. Now you're forty . . . (UNDER BREATH) that picture's awful (NORMAL VOICE) . . . so make the most of it. Yeah, alright . . . Take a look. Now your pants size and your age match.

MAN: Well . . . isn't that clever.

791

(SFX: MUSIC WITH A BEAT, CITY SOUNDS; EXAGGERATED SOUND EFFECTS)

SILENCE.

792

(MUSIC: UP AND UNDER THROUGHOUT)

SINGER: *It's real. I know it's real.*
No other reason for the way I feel.
Oh, yeah, it's as real as it gets.

HERO: That's nature, man. You get hot, you get cold.

SINGER: *It feels good, so right.*
No doubt about it,
This is what I like.

DELI OWNER: Working hard?

HERO: Sure.

HERO: Toby, how you doing?

SINGER: *It's as real as it gets.*

HERO: How's everything?

OFFICER: You deserve a ticket.

SINGER: *The only thing I've got on my mind is*
To hold onto the good times.

HERO: Rich, you're washing your car! And you guys must be supervising!

ANNCR VO: The best things are the real things.
And draft beer is the real beer.
Miller Genuine Draft.

SINGER: *Oh, yeah. It's as real as it gets. Huh!*

(MUSIC: OUT)

Consumer Television
:30 Single

793
ART DIRECTOR
Neil Leinwohl
WRITER
Kevin McKeon
AGENCY PRODUCER
Milda Misevicius
PRODUCTION CO.
Gerard Hameline
DIRECTOR
Ross Cramer
CLIENT
Tri-Honda Auto Dealers Association
AGENCY
Korey Kay & Partners

794
ART DIRECTOR
Bob McCarron
WRITER
Jerry Wexler
AGENCY PRODUCERS
Jerry Wexler
Bob McCarron
PRODUCTION CO.
Filmworks
DIRECTOR
Lewis Roth
CLIENT
Monarch Country Club
AGENCY
Wexler McCarron & Roth/Pompano Beach, FL

795
ART DIRECTOR
Mark Drewek
WRITERS
Wes Hranchek
Tom Jordan
AGENCY PRODUCER
Reed Allen
PRODUCTION CO.
Logan Productions
DIRECTOR
Jim Logan
CLIENT
Fiskars
AGENCY
Hoffman York & Compton/Milwaukee

796
ART DIRECTOR
Ron Louie
WRITER
Chuck Gessner
AGENCY PRODUCERS
Lora Nelson
Rikki Furman
PRODUCTION CO.
Greenberg & Associates
DIRECTOR
Robert Mrozowski
CLIENT
Colombian Coffee
AGENCY
DDB Needham Worldwide

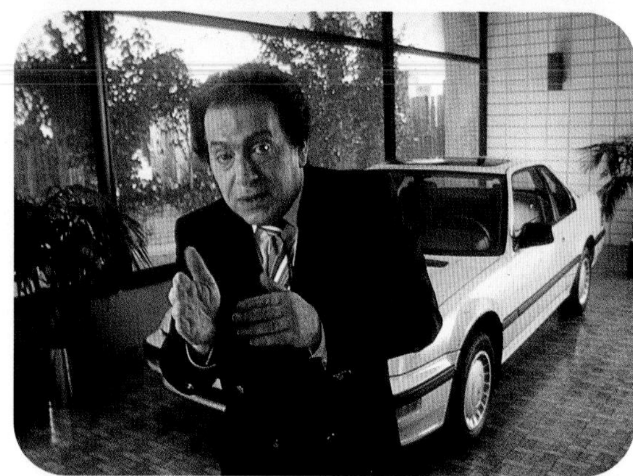

793

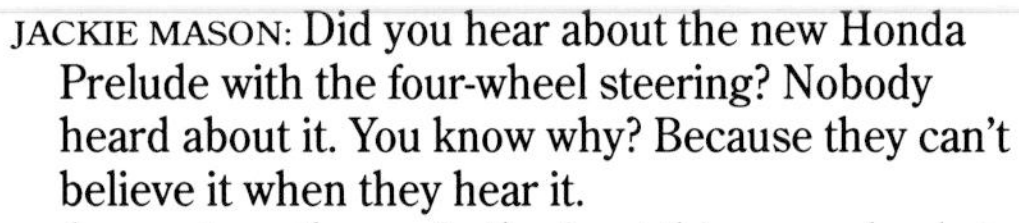

JACKIE MASON: Did you hear about the new Honda Prelude with the four-wheel steering? Nobody heard about it. You know why? Because they can't believe it when they hear it.
As you turn the car in the front this way, wheels in the back are turning the ways nobody ever saw before. It has new direction for wheels to turn because you turn like this, the wheels turn like that, the car goes like this, and all of a sudden you're going like that. You don't know why but it's getting you there in a way that you never did before.
And you know why you need this? I don't know.

794

(MUSIC: UP)

VO: Introducing Monarch Country Club. Exceptional homes on a nasty golf course.
A *very* nasty golf course.

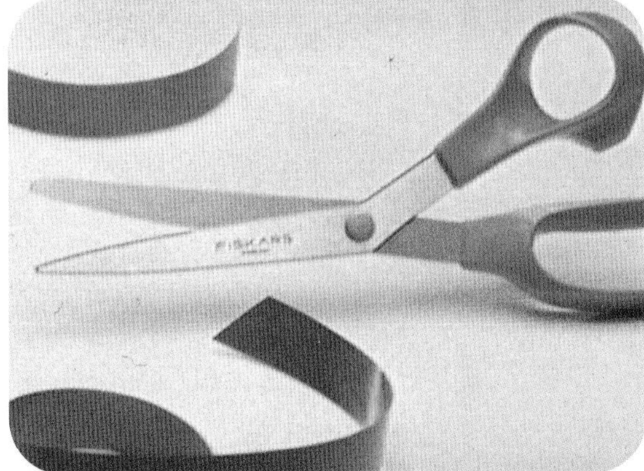

795

(MUSIC: PATRIOTIC THEME)

ANNCR: No matter who you are, when you just can't cut it, get a pair of Fiskars scissors. The one with orange handles. Fiskars. Just say 'no' to all the others.

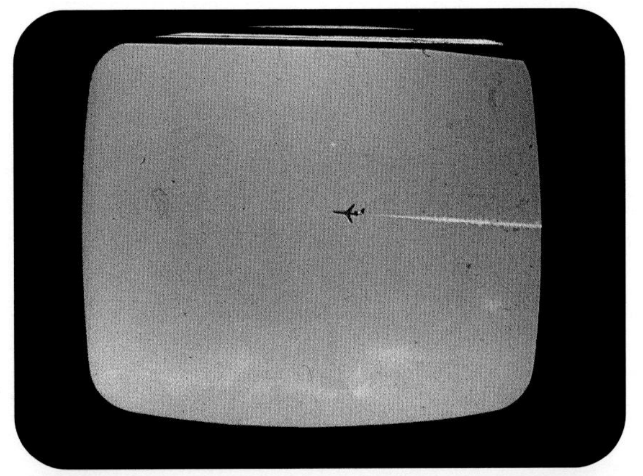

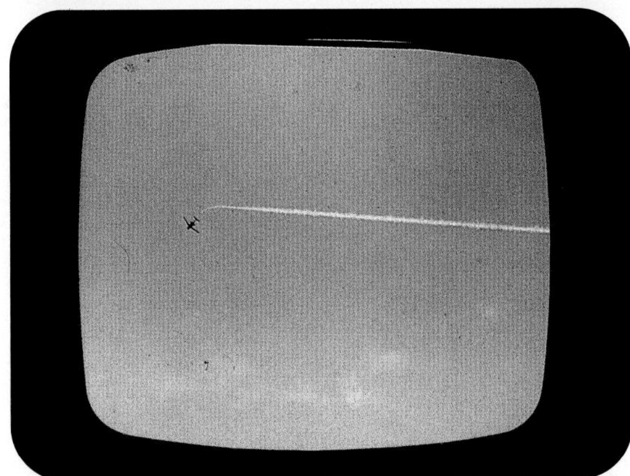

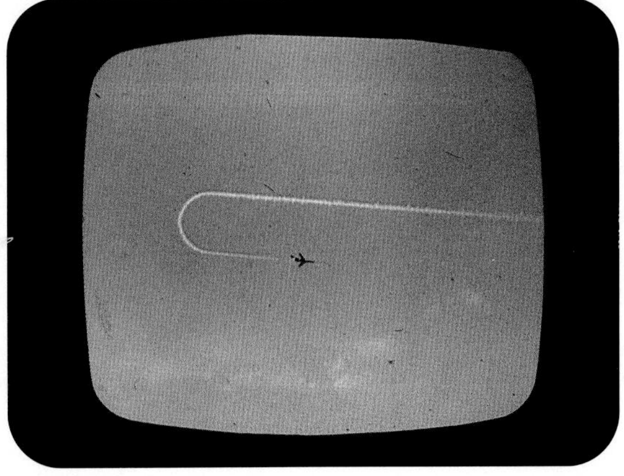

796

MALE VO: We've just reached our . . .

(SFX: KNOCK, KNOCK; DOOR OPENING)

MALE VO: . . . cruising altitude of 31,000.

FEMALE VO: Captain, we forgot the Colombian Coffee.

(SFX: PLANE ENGINE)

ANNCR: 100% Colombian Coffee.
It's the richest coffee in the world.

Consumer Television
:30 Single

797
ART DIRECTOR
Ron Sandilands
WRITER
Steve Sandoz
AGENCY PRODUCER
Cindy Henderson
PRODUCTION CO.
Sēdēlmaier Productions
DIRECTOR
Joe Sēdēlmaier
CLIENT
Alaska Airlines
AGENCY
Livingston & Company/
Seattle

798
ART DIRECTOR
John Staffen
WRITER
Mike Rogers
AGENCY PRODUCER
Ugo Pergolotti
PRODUCTION CO.
Rick Levine Productions
DIRECTOR
Michael Werk
CLIENT
Volkswagen
AGENCY
DDB Needham Worldwide

799
ART DIRECTOR
Sal DeVito
WRITER
Amy Borkowsky
AGENCY PRODUCER
Rachel Novak
PRODUCTION CO.
Story Piccolo Guliner
DIRECTOR
Mark Story
CLIENT
Genesee Brewing Company
AGENCY
Levine Huntley Schmidt &
Beaver

800
ART DIRECTOR
Ron Louie
WRITER
Phyllis Robinson
AGENCY PRODUCER
Sandy Corbet
PRODUCTION CO.
Spots Films/New York
DIRECTOR
David Cornell
CLIENT
Clairol/Loving Care
AGENCY
DDB Needham Worldwide

797

ANNCR: If a restaurant gave you the kind of service you get on many airlines, you'd never go back.

MAN #1: Baby apple . . . I gotta baby cheese.

MAN #2: I don't like breakfast. I never did like breakfast. If I did like breakfast, I wouldn't like this breakfast.

MAN #1: I'd like a spoon.

FLIGHT ATTENDANT: Hot coffee?

MAN #1: I'd like a spoon.

WOMAN: Miss, I don't think the hearty breakfast agrees with my husband.

FLIGHT ATTENDANT: Maybe he'd prefer our eye opener breakfast?

MAN #2: Ahoy, yoy, yoy, yoy, yoy.

ANNCR: But on Alaska Airlines, even though the fares we charge are just as low as anyone's, the fare we serve is always a cut above.

798

(SFX: CAR ACCELERATION AND SCREECHING THROUGHOUT)

VO: Volkswagen engineers have developed a remarkable fuel injection system . . . which gives our Jetta seventeen percent more horsepower than before . . . and top track speeds of over 100. Of course, there are . . . those Volkswagen engineers who believe they've developed something no less remarkable . . . the brakes. German Engineering. The Volkswagen way.

799

ANNCR VO: This should give you some idea of the difference between beer and Genesee Cream Ale. Smooth Genesee Cream Ale. It's not the same old brewskie.

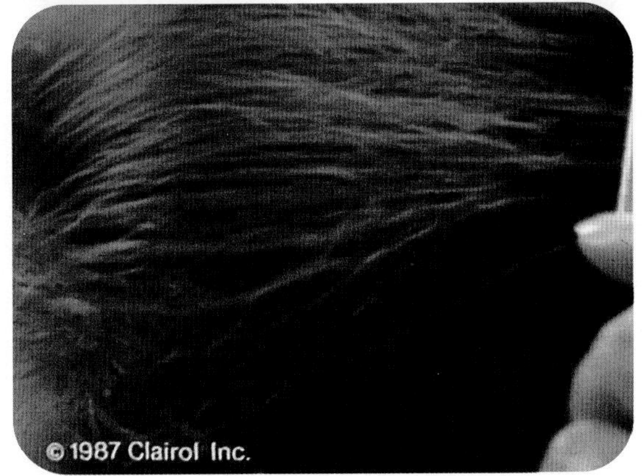

Gray hair
or Loving Care.

800

(MUSIC: THROUGHOUT)

VO: Maybe it's time to change the way you deal with gray.

SUPER: PLUCK.

Did you know there's a hair coloring as gentle to the hair as a shampoo.

SUPERS: PLUCK
PLUCK.

No peroxide. No roots.

SUPERS: PLUCK
PLUCK
PLUCK.

Just healthy-looking, natural-looking color. It's Loving Care. Loving Care gives you a beautiful match to your natural color.

SUPER: PLUCK

Nature is forcing . . .

SUPER: PLUCK

. . . you to make . . .

SUPER: PLUCK

. . . a decision.

SUPER: PLUCK

Make it. Gray hair or Loving Care.

Consumer Television
:30 Single

801

ART DIRECTOR
Alan Lawrence

WRITER
Michael Albright

AGENCY PRODUCER
Frank Tammariello

PRODUCTION CO.
Riverrun Films

DIRECTORS
Alan Lawrence
Frank Tammariello

CLIENT
Ralph's Grocery Company/The Giant

AGENCY
W.B. Doner & Company/ Los Angeles

802

ART DIRECTOR
Craig Neuman

WRITER
Brian Brooker

AGENCY PRODUCERS
Craig Neuman
Brian Brooker

PRODUCTION CO.
Bob Jones' Film Productions

DIRECTOR
Bob Jones

CLIENT
Missouri Repertory Theatre

AGENCY
Barkley & Evergreen/ Shawnee Mission, KS

803

ART DIRECTOR
Peter Cohen

WRITER
Larry Spector

AGENCY PRODUCER
Rachel Novak

PRODUCTION CO.
Story Piccolo Guliner

DIRECTOR
Mark Story

CLIENT
Webster Industries/ Good Sense

AGENCY
Levine Huntley Schmidt & Beaver

804

ART DIRECTOR
Monte Hallis

WRITER
Alan Marcus

AGENCY PRODUCER
John Tripp

PRODUCTION CO.
Riverrun Films

DIRECTOR
Jordan Cronenweth

CLIENT
Six Flags Magic Mountain

AGENCY
Della Femina Travisano & Partners/Los Angeles

801

(MUSIC: UP AND UNDER THROUGHOUT)

ROSEANNE: You know what I love? When a supermarket throws a special and then, to get anything else in the place, you've gotta leave 'em the pink slip to your car? What do they think, we are stupid? I just go to The Giant. Their prices are so zippo. They even show you what other markets charge, so I save major bucks. Which not only helps my budget, but has allowed us to purchase that château in the South of France.

802

(HAUNTING MUSIC: THROUGHOUT)

SUPER: OUR SEASON IS OFF THE GROUND.
DRACULA.
MISSOURI REPERTORY THEATRE.

803

MAN: When the people at Good Sense asked me to stand under one of their garbage bags, filled with fifty-eight pounds of elephant fertilizer . . . I said forget it!
When they said they'd pay me a fortune, I said . . . maybe.
Then they told me their bags were made of super tough plastic to resist punctures and tears.
Which obviously took a load off my mind.

(SFX: ELEPHANT ROARING)

ANNCR: Good Sense.

(SFX: BAG DROPPING)

ANNCR: The best thing you'll ever throw out.

804

VO: FreeFall.
Colossus.
Roaring Rapids.
Revolution.
Z-Force.
Shock Wave.
Because there's nothing like a little ride in the park.

Consumer Television
:30 Single

805

ART DIRECTOR
Rick Carpenter

WRITER
Dick Sittig

AGENCY PRODUCER
Nancy Koch

PRODUCTION CO.
N. Lee Lacy

DIRECTOR
Matthew Meshekoff

CLIENT
American Isuzu Motors

AGENCY
Della Femina Travisano & Partners/Los Angeles

806

ART DIRECTOR
Alan Chalfin

WRITER
Lee Garfinkel

AGENCY PRODUCER
Bob Nelson

PRODUCTION CO.
Steve Horn Inc.

DIRECTOR
Steve Horn

CLIENT
Subaru of America

AGENCY
Levine Huntley Schmidt & Beaver

807

ART DIRECTOR
Gerald Andelin

WRITER
Hal Riney

AGENCY PRODUCER
Deborah Martin

PRODUCTION CO.
PYTKA

DIRECTOR
Joe Pytka

CLIENT
E&J Gallo Winery

AGENCY
Hal Riney & Partners/San Francisco

808

ART DIRECTOR
Marty Weiss

WRITER
Robin Raj

AGENCY PRODUCERS
Mark Sitley
Steve Amato

PRODUCTION COS.
Directing Artists
Fernbach Productions

DIRECTORS
Kevin Godley
Lol Creme
Alex Fernbach

CLIENT
NYNEX

AGENCY
Chiat/Day

805

JOE: I just sold an I-Mark to the Queen.

SUPER: HE TELLETH A LIE.

JOE: The interior is roomy enough for a king . . . or a queen, if that's all you got.
There's air conditioning so Her Highness won't sweat . . . and a stereo to drown out the cries of the peasants.
Prices start at seven pounds, nine ounces . . .

SUPER: PRICES FROM $7,439.

JOE: . . . but I traded one to What's Her Name for this hat.

GUARD: Roight!!! That does it!!!

JOE: Ta ta!

ANNCR VO: Now, factory to dealer incentives could mean big savings on all Isuzus.

806

ANNCR: Remember when a drive-in was a buck, a hot dog was a dime and cars were under $10,000.

VOICE FROM INSIDE CAR: Stop that Jimmy!

ANNCR: Now the movie is $6, a hot dog is $1.75, and cars, well, Subaru still has an entire line of cars for under $10,000.

VOICE FROM INSIDE CAR: Stop that Jimmy!

ANNCR: The more things change, the more they stay the same.

807

FRANK: Hello.
Here in Southern California, many people return to nature, to find relief from the chaos and pressures of contemporary urban life.
If you are planning this as well, we wanted to remind you that Ed's new Bartles & Jaymes Premium Red Wine Cooler can greatly contribute to the relaxing and tranquil atmosphere of the great outdoors.
So if the unspoiled wilderness is in *your* plans this summer, be sure to take plenty of Bartles & Jaymes.
Believe me, you will be glad you did.
Thank you for your support.

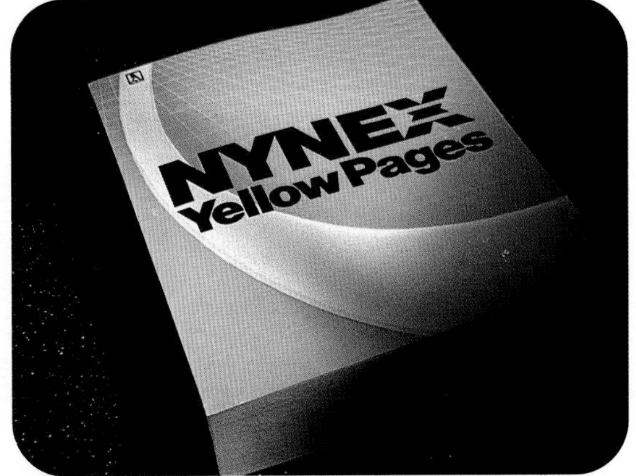

808

(SFX: OPENING CHIME; SOUND OF MARCHING)

OFF-CAMERA SERGEANT (YELLING): Attend Hut! Funky Chicken.

(SFX: MILITARY SNARE DRUM THROUGHOUT)

SARGE: Duckwalk! . . . Moonwalk! . . . Disco! . . . Windmill! . . . Air Guitar! . . . James Brown!

SOLDIERS (YELLING TOGETHER): Huh!

SARGE: Jimi plays Monterey!

VO: If it's out there, it's in here . . . The NYNEX Yellow Pages.

(SFX: BOOK SLAMS SHUT)

VO: Why would anyone need another?

Consumer Television
:30 Single

809

ART DIRECTOR
Terry Tomalty

WRITER
Don Veinish

AGENCY PRODUCER
Rick Price

PRODUCTION CO.
The Partners Film Company

DIRECTOR
Rick Price

CLIENT
Smith & Nephew

AGENCY
J. Walter Thompson/
Montréal

810

ART DIRECTOR
Gerald Andelin

WRITER
Hal Riney

AGENCY PRODUCER
Deborah Martin

PRODUCTION CO.
PYTKA

DIRECTOR
Joe Pytka

CLIENT
E&J Gallo Winery

AGENCY
Hal Riney & Partners/
San Francisco

811

ART DIRECTOR
Ron Sandilands

WRITER
Steve Sandoz

AGENCY PRODUCER
Cindy Henderson

PRODUCTION CO.
Sëdëlmaier Productions

DIRECTOR
Joe Sëdëlmaier

CLIENT
Alaska Airlines

AGENCY
Livingston & Company/
Seattle

812

ART DIRECTOR
Barry Vetere

WRITER
Tom Messner

AGENCY PRODUCER
Trish O'Reilly

PRODUCTION CO.
Nicolella & Company

DIRECTOR
Richard Nicolella

CLIENT
WBZ-TV

AGENCY
Messner Vetere Berger
Carey

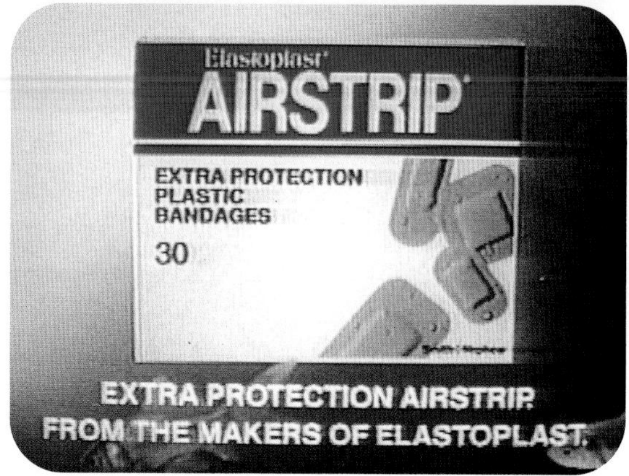

809

(SFX: INCOHERENT UNDERWATER SPEECH—GLUB, GLUB)

SUBTITLES: HELLO.
I'M HERE TO DEMONSTRATE . . . THESE AIRSTRIP PLASTIC BANDAGES. OTHER PLASTIC STRIPS MAY SAY THEY'RE WATERPROOF, BUT THEIR PADS GET (UGH!) SOGGY. NOT AIRSTRIP. AIRSTIP STAYS STUCK . . . AND ITS PAD STAYS DRY AND CLEAN . . . FOR EXTRA PROTECTION FROM DIRT AND GERMS.
LOOK.
AIR CAN GET IN. BUT EVERYTHING ELSE IS SEALED OUT.
EXTRA PROTECTION AIRSTRIP.
FROM THE MAKERS OF ELASTOPLAST.

VO: Airstrip. From the makers of Elastoplast.

SUBTITLE: HELP!

(SFX: GLUB, GLUB)

810

FRANK: Hello.
While almost everybody likes the original Bartles & Jaymes Premium Wine Cooler, a few people have suggested we introduce another flavor.
So Ed has developed a scientific system to decide which flavor to introduce. Are you ready, Ed?

(SFX: PLUNK)

Well, according to Ed's scientific system, we will introduce a new wine cooler called "Red". I am not really sure what the cooler flavor of red *is*, but I expect we will find out.
So watch for our new red cooler, and we thank you for your support.

811

ANNCR: Many airlines offer reduced rates. Unfortunately, that's not all they've reduced.

ANNCR: It makes you wonder what's next.

MAN: I'd appreciate it, do you have four quarters for a dollar? Anybody have two quarters for a dollar? Yes miss, do you have two quarters for five dollars, please? Oh boy, I'd really appreciate it.

ANNCR: On Alaska Airlines, we have low fares, too. But you'd never know it by the way we treat you.

812

VO: On September eighth at 6:00 pm, Edward Zepf sat down to watch the news and ended up saving his life.
That night Channel 4's Medical Reporter, Jeanne Blake, invited everyone to take a simple test.
Of the 65,000 people who responded, Edward Zepf was one of those who discovered a tumor before it was cancerous.
Does it matter which news program you watch?
It will always matter to Edward Zepf of Boston, Massachusetts.

Consumer Television :30 Single

813
ART DIRECTORS
Irv Klein
Tod Seisser
WRITERS
Stephanie Arnold
Jay Taub
AGENCY PRODUCER
Bob Nelson
PRODUCTION CO.
Sandbank Films
DIRECTOR
Henry Sandbank
CLIENT
Maidenform
AGENCY
Levine Huntley Schmidt & Beaver

814
ART DIRECTORS
Brent Mellet
Jerry Roach
WRITER
Chris Grabenstein
AGENCY PRODUCER
Bruce Davidson
PRODUCTION COS.
Lovinger/Cohn
Sloggett Sanders & Hule
DIRECTOR
Richard Sloggett
CLIENT
Miller/Matilda Bay
AGENCY
J. Walter Thompson

815
ART DIRECTOR
Tom Stoneham
WRITER
Tom Molitor
AGENCY PRODUCERS
Tom Stoneham
Tom Molitor
PRODUCTION CO.
James Productions
DIRECTOR
Denny Carlson
CLIENT
King County Medical Blue Shield
AGENCY
Borders Perrin & Norrander/Seattle

816
ART DIRECTOR
Barry Vetere
WRITER
Ron Berger
AGENCY PRODUCER
Trish O'Reilly
PRODUCTION CO.
They Shoot Films
DIRECTOR
Lou Addesso
CLIENT
Regina Company
AGENCY
Messner Vetere Berger Carey

813

ANNCR: I have an offer from someone very close to you. Maidenform.
Right now, just buy any two bras, panties, or lingerie styles, and we'll give you another one free. So let's say you buy any two Maidenform bras like these, you can get another one like this free.

814

WOMAN: How's it going, mate?

MAN: Yard work makes ya mighty thirsty.

WOMAN: Little nip of the smooth refresher?

MAN: Aaah! Matilda Bay Cooler. (TO SHEEP) Hey, fuzzball—ya missed a spot. (ABOUT COOLER) Aaah—that's really something.

WOMAN: Didja bring the hedge clippers?

MAN: Oh, yeah.

ANNCR VO: Matilda Bay's a different kind of cooler from a different kind of place. Now made by our mates in the States. It'll take your taste away from the everyday.

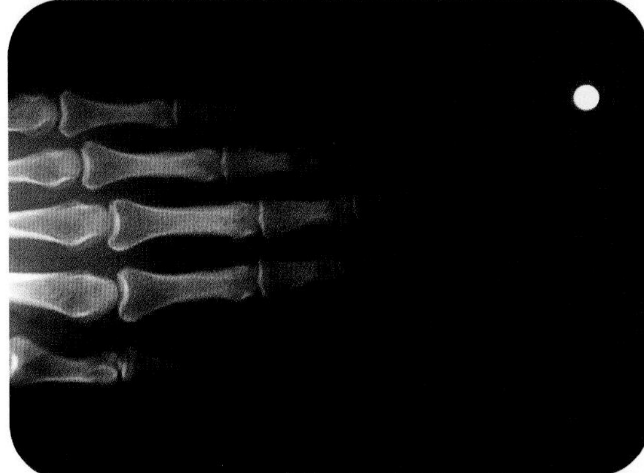

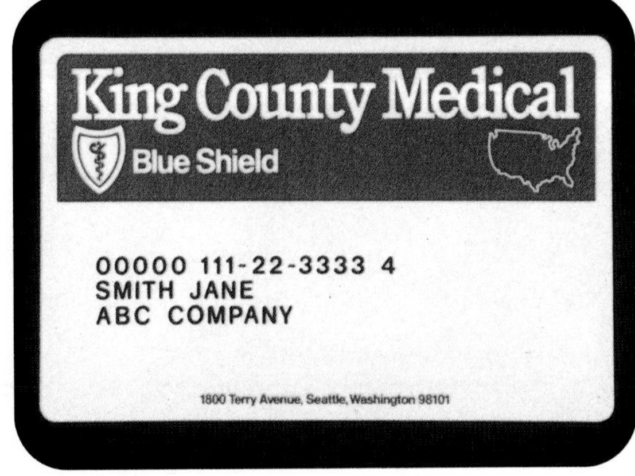

King County Medical
Blue Shield
00000 111-22-3333 4
SMITH JANE
ABC COMPANY
1800 Terry Avenue, Seattle, Washington 98101

815

VO: Imagine this is a lump in your breast. Breasts are basically tissue, glands, fat and skin. Which makes lumps this small hard to find.

(SFX: STILL QUIET, JUST SOUNDS OF FINGERS ON PADS)

We'd like to make a point about mammography.

(SFX: NON-FRIGHTENING BRZZT)

Mammography can find a tumor up to six years before you can feel it. Call today for information on our low-cost mammogram offer.

816

VO: We're at a famous restaurant outside of Chicago, where we've secretly replaced the coffee with sand and ground up clam shells. Let's see what happens.

(SFX: CHAOS)

Relax, Monsieur André, this is all to prove a point . . . about how well the Regina Electrikbroom cleans beautiful bare floors.
Zip, Zip—no more clam shells.
Now, if the Regina Electrikbroom can do such a good job here, imagine what it can do in your home. Just ask Monsieur André.

Consumer Television
:30 Single

817
ART DIRECTOR
Gerald Andelin
WRITER
Hal Riney
AGENCY PRODUCER
Deborah Martin
PRODUCTION CO.
PYTKA
DIRECTOR
Joe Pytka
CLIENT
E&J Gallo Winery
AGENCY
Hal Riney & Partners/
San Francisco

818
ART DIRECTOR
Alan Chalfin
WRITER
Lee Garfinkel
AGENCY PRODUCER
Bob Nelson
PRODUCTION CO.
Griner Cuesta
DIRECTOR
Michael Cuesta
CLIENT
Subaru of America
AGENCY
Levine Huntley Schmidt &
Beaver

819
ART DIRECTOR
Larry Corby
WRITER
Peter Angelos
AGENCY PRODUCER
Bob Sallen
PRODUCTION CO.
Petermann/Dektor
DIRECTOR
Leslie Dektor
CLIENT
Sunkist Growers
AGENCY
Foote Cone & Belding/
Los Angeles

820
ART DIRECTOR
Marty Weiss
WRITER
Robin Raj
AGENCY PRODUCERS
Mark Sitley
Steve Amato
PRODUCTION COS.
Directing Artists
Fernbach Productions
DIRECTORS
Kevin Godley
Lol Creme
Alex Fernbach
CLIENT
NYNEX
AGENCY
Chiat/Day

817

FRANK: Hello.
With vacation time here, Ed and I would like to remind you that there is no better beverage for vacation activities than Bartles & Jaymes. Either in the original version, or Ed's new premium red. As for our vacation activity, we are learning to fly-fish. This takes great skill and patience. Not only just catching the flies in the first place, but also getting them on the hook.
We hope you will enjoy your vacation with Bartles & Jaymes, and we thank you for your support.

818

ANNCR: Day after day more people depend on Subaru Wagons than any imported wagon in America. And with good reason. They're reliable and durable. In fact, if Subaru didn't make your life easier . . .

HUSBAND: Honey, is dinner ready?

ANNCR: Who would?

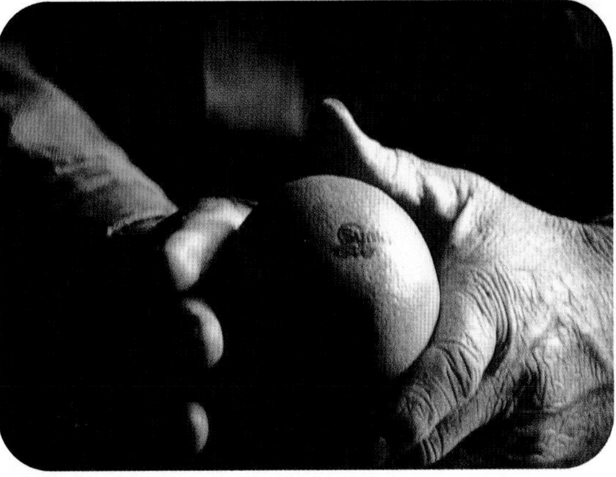

819

GROWER: I've grown up with that label. I've known none other.

SUPER: ROGER PALMER, SUNKIST GROWER.

I've done what my a—great grandfather started out doing. It's a—I think a tradition in our family to grow good oranges. And I think it may be difficult to raise good oranges but it's easy for *you* to choose them. Just read the label.

-1600 Food & Candy Stop
Turner Tuning–15 Riverside
5-4873 Varsell Piano's–42 Ridgecre
9-3895 Weiner & Sons–97 Rose La
34-9359
71-4112 ▶ **Piano Rolls**
Arnold Piano Company–1
Baldwin Organ–39 Living
LS Buckley Brothers–317 E.

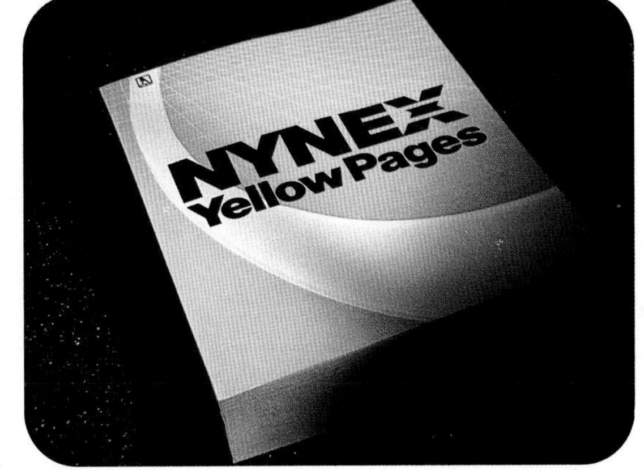

820

(SFX: OPENING CHIME; SOUND OF PIANO ROLLING AS MAN PLAYS COCKTAIL MUSIC)

(SFX: SOUND OF PIANO PLAYING, ROLLING)

(SFX: SOUND OF PIANO PLAYING, ROLLING)

(SFX: SOUND OF PIANO PLAYING, ROLLING)

VO: If it's out there, it's in here . . .
The NYNEX Yellow Pages.

(SFX: BOOK SLAMS SHUT)

Why would anyone need another?

Consumer Television
:30 Single

821
ART DIRECTOR
Tom Wolsey
WRITER
David Schneider
AGENCY PRODUCER
Maureen Kearns
PRODUCTION CO.
BFCS
DIRECTOR
Thom Higgins
CLIENT
The Bank of New York
AGENCY
Ally & Gargano

822
ART DIRECTOR
Gerald Andelin
WRITER
Hal Riney
AGENCY PRODUCER
Deborah Martin
PRODUCTION CO.
PYTKA
DIRECTOR
Joe Pytka
CLIENT
E&J Gallo Winery
AGENCY
Hal Riney & Partners/
San Francisco

823
ART DIRECTOR
Dean Hanson
WRITER
Tom McElligott
AGENCY PRODUCER
Judy Brink
PRODUCTION CO.
BFCS
DIRECTOR
Thom Higgins
CLIENT
Lee Jeans
AGENCY
Fallon McElligott/
Minneapolis

824
ART DIRECTOR
Tierney McMahon
WRITER
Jamie Pfaff
AGENCY PRODUCER
Norrie Nelson
PRODUCTION CO.
EVE
DIRECTOR
Katherine Lefebvre
CLIENT
RCA/Camcorder
AGENCY
Leo Burnett USA/Chicago

821

(SFX: TAP, TAP, TAP . . .)

PRESIDENT VO: So Schlumper, I understand you got the company a checking account that pays no *interest*. Is that your idea of a business acumen, Schlumper? Getting us a checking account that pays *no interest*?
Is that what you think you were hired to do??

VO: If you're letting a bank take *your* company's money without paying for it, consider Checkinvest, from The Bank of New York. We'll help you earn interest with your business checking account. Every single day.

822

FRANK: Ed's research says that some of our customers are yuppies and while I personally wouldn't care to shave my head and stand around in airports, I believe it is anyone's right to be a yuppie if they want to.
So please continue to enjoy the Bartles & Jaymes, whatever your race or creed. And thanks for your support.

823

(MUSIC: THROUGHOUT)

ANNCR VO: Everyday, millions of American women practice a strange ritual.
It's called "getting into jeans."
Today there are jeans *designed* to fit a woman's curves . . . *without* the usual ritual.
Lee Relaxed Riders.
It's not a better body you need.
It's better jeans.

824

DAD VO: Eric! Smile!

KID VO: Eric smile. Eric wave to Daddy. Phooey!
Since they got that little RCA camcorder, I get no peace. It's so easy. He takes it everywhere.
Dad!
Oh, well. I guess some day I'll look back at this and laugh.

ANNCR VO: Finally, a VHS camcorder so small, so easy to use, it doesn't miss a thing. Trust RCA to bring it to you.
The Small Wonder VHS from RCA.

Consumer Television
:30 Single

825
ART DIRECTOR
Mark Denton
WRITER
Chris Palmer
AGENCY PRODUCER
Mike Griffin
PRODUCTION CO.
Paul Weiland Film
DIRECTORS
Richard Curtis
Paul Weiland
CLIENT
Whitbread-Heineken
AGENCY
Lowe Howard-Spink/
London

826
ART DIRECTORS
Tod Seisser
Irv Klein
WRITERS
Jay Taub
Stephanie Arnold
AGENCY PRODUCER
Rachel Novak
PRODUCTION CO.
Sandbank Films
DIRECTOR
Henry Sandbank
CLIENT
Maidenform
AGENCY
Levine Huntley Schmidt &
Beaver

827
ART DIRECTOR
Bob Ribits
WRITER
Alex Goslar
AGENCY PRODUCERS
Angelo Antonucci
Carole Floodstrand
PRODUCTION CO.
Koetz & Company
DIRECTOR
Leroy Koetz
CLIENT
Procter & Gamble/Cheer
AGENCY
Leo Burnett USA/Chicago

828
ART DIRECTOR
Marcus Kemp
WRITER
Paul Wolfe
AGENCY PRODUCER
Colleen O'Connor
PRODUCTION CO.
BFCS
DIRECTOR
Thom Higgins
CLIENT
BMW of North America
AGENCY
Ammirati & Puris

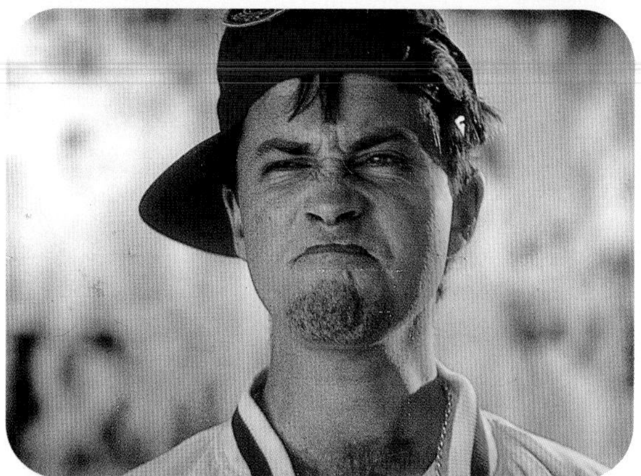

825

(SFX: RAUNCHY MUSIC)

SUPER: HEINEKEN REFRESHES THE CAR PARTS OTHER BEERS CANNOT REACH.

826

CORBIN BERNSEN: I once bought lingerie for a woman. It was interesting. I walked into the store. Looked around.
It was a little embarassing. A little intimidating, maybe.
Finding her size? That was easy. Matching her personality? That was a little more difficult. But a lot more fun.

SUPER: MAIDENFORM.

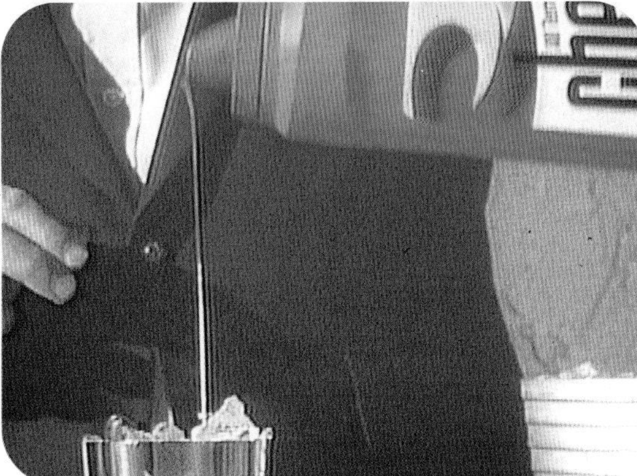

827

(MUSIC: THROUGHOUT)

ANNCR: Nobody's better in cold than All-Temperature Cheer.

828

VO: The BMW 325i Convertible. The ultimate . . . tanning machine.

Consumer Television
:30 Single

829

ART DIRECTOR
Gerald Andelin

WRITER
Hal Riney

AGENCY PRODUCER
Deborah Martin

PRODUCTION CO.
PYTKA

DIRECTOR
Joe Pytka

CLIENT
E&J Gallo Winery

AGENCY
Hal Riney & Partners/
San Francisco

830

ART DIRECTOR
Ted Duquette

WRITER
Ron Lawner

AGENCY PRODUCER
Amy Lieberman

PRODUCTION CO.
Jennie & Company

DIRECTOR
Adrian Lyne

CLIENT
Beecham Cosmetics

AGENCY
HBM/Creamer - Boston

831

ART DIRECTOR
Michael Fazende

WRITER
John Stingley

AGENCY PRODUCER
Char Loving

PRODUCTION CO.
PYTKA

DIRECTOR
Joe Pytka

CLIENT
O.M. Scott & Sons

AGENCY
Fallon McElligott/
Minneapolis

832

ART DIRECTOR
Ted Shaine

WRITER
Helayne Spivak

AGENCY PRODUCER
Ozzie Spenningsby

PRODUCTION CO.
Spots Films/New York

DIRECTOR
David Cornell

CLIENT
Club Med

AGENCY
Ammirati & Puris

829

FRANK: If you look at your calendar, you'll notice that Vernal Equinox's Day is coming up. To help celebrate, nothing is better than the Bartles & Jaymes Premium Wine Cooler.
Frankly, we were surprised to see Vernal's name on a holiday. We knew him as a kid, and never thought he'd ever amount to much.

830

SUPER: WHAT IS SEXY?

SUPER: JOVAN MUSK.

SUPER: WHAT SEXY IS.

831

(SFX: MUSIC UNDER; CROWD MUMBLING AND TALKING EXCITEDLY)

ANNCR: This spring in Marysville, Ohio, something incredible happened.

KID: Mom, what is it?

ANNCR: Incredible, because Marysville is the home of Scotts lawn products.

(SFX: MUSIC CONTINUES)

MAN: Appears to be the Officinale species.

(SFX: MUSIC CONTINUES)

WOMAN: We had one in '45. Course that was before cell-division chemistry.

ANNCR: To Scotts users, lawn problems are just hard to believe.

ANNCR: Hey everybody, crabgrass at the Stevens place!

(SFX: CROWD GETS VERY EXCITED, STARTS TO MOVE QUICKLY AWAY)

ANNCR: When all there is to do is watch the grass grow, you really get to know grass.

832

VO: Somewhere phones are ringing.
Somewhere televisions are blaring.
Somewhere sirens are wailing.
Somewhere headlines are screaming.
Somewhere money is talking.
Which is precisely why we created Club Med.
Because you have to draw the line on civilization somewhere.

Consumer Television :30 Single

833
ART DIRECTOR
Joel Machak
WRITER
Dave Colwell
AGENCY PRODUCER
Mike Rafayko
PRODUCTION CO.
Film Fair
CLIENT
Commonwealth Edison
AGENCY
Leo Burnett USA/Chicago

834
ART DIRECTOR
Gerald Andelin
WRITER
Hal Riney
AGENCY PRODUCER
Deborah Martin
PRODUCTION CO.
PYTKA
DIRECTOR
Joe Pytka
CLIENT
E&J Gallo Winery
AGENCY
Hal Riney & Partners/
San Francisco

835
ART DIRECTORS
Jerry Gentile
Yvonne Smith
WRITERS
Mark Monteiro
Steven Wesley Bridgewater
AGENCY PRODUCER
Shannon Silverman
PRODUCTION CO.
Story Piccolo Guliner
DIRECTOR
Mark Story
CLIENT
First Nationwide Bank
AGENCY
DDB Needham Worldwide/
Los Angeles

836
ART DIRECTOR
Geoff Hayes
WRITER
Joy Golden
AGENCY PRODUCER
Ed Pollack
PRODUCTION CO.
Steve Horn Inc.
DIRECTOR
Steve Horn
CLIENT
Fromageries Bel
AGENCY
TBWA

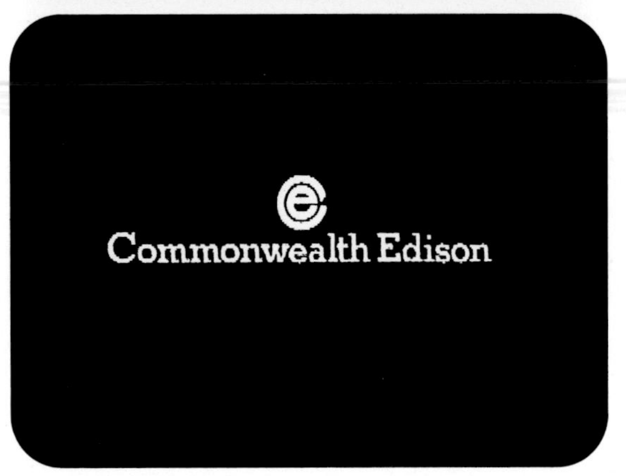

833

OC: When I was eight or nine, we didn't have electricity yet.
But my dad was a boxing fan. And soon as he heard we were gonna get power, he went out and bought the biggest radio I'd ever seen.
Oh, it was handsome. It sat there in the living room. Dad polished it every day. Then came the big Lewis-Braddoci fight.
But the electricity didn't come till the next day.
I'll never forget dad sitting in the dark, staring at his new radio.

ANNCR: The power of electricity. Brought to you by Commonwealth Edison, for less than two cents a fight.

834

FRANK: Hello.
Well, now that Ed has his M.B.A., he is currently studying fruit flavors—some of the better ones being the Rubus Macropetalus; the Vitis Vinifera; and the Prunus Persica. But the best fruit flavor of all appears to be the Coolerus Ruber Ed and I, better known as the Bartles & Jaymes Premium Red Cooler.
So if you spot one of these in your store, be sure to buy it. You'll help Ed with his reseach, and have a very refreshing beverage besides.
Thank you for your support.

835

TELLER: Good morning, sir.

MAN: I need to cash a check.

TELLER: No problem, Mr Bridgewater.

MAN: And I realize I'm from out-of-state . . .

TELLER: Well, your bank is part of the First Nationwide Network.

MAN (UNDER): Here's my bank card and my license . .

TELLER: That's fine, sir.

MAN: I've got thirty-four credit cards. Here's my passport. This is the title to my house, title to my car, this is the title to my favorite song . . .

TELLER: No, really, that's plenty.

CUSTOMER: I also belong to Joggers Anonymous. Here's my immunization papers, my Clear Speakers Club of America card, my one hour photo card. I also have a Rototillers champion card . . .

TELLER (OVER): Here you go, sir.

ANNCR VO: At First Nationwide we treat you with respect, concern and understanding. But don't worry. You'll get used to it.

CUSTOMER (UNDER): . . . strands of barbed wire . . .

836

VALLEY GIRL: So, like this totally gorgoso highway patrolman stops me. I said, 'I have to get my little Round Laughing Cow into the frig, O.K.?' He said, 'No cows in cars.' I said, 'Officer, it's not a real cow—it's cheese. Mild Mini Bonbel. Nippy Mini Babybel. And Mini Gouda too. Five bite-size snacks in little net bags, like really awesome and naturelle. Want to try one?' So he said, 'O.K.' So I said, 'O.K.' So O.K. O.K. So then I said, 'When can I see you again?' He was so totally freaked like he dropped the cheese and bit the ticket. And now it's like two weeks and he never called.

Consumer Television :30 Single

837
ART DIRECTOR
Mike Withers
WRITER
Peter Hoffman
AGENCY PRODUCER
Maureen Kearns
PRODUCTION CO.
Gomes Lowe
DIRECTOR
Dick Lowe
CLIENT
Dunkin' Donuts
AGENCY
Ally & Gargano

838
ART DIRECTOR
Marty Weiss
WRITER
Robin Raj
AGENCY PRODUCERS
Mark Sitley
Steve Amato
PRODUCTION COS.
Directing Artists
Fernbach Productions
DIRECTORS
Kevin Godley
Lol Creme
Alex Fernbach
CLIENT
NYNEX
AGENCY
Chiat/Day

839
ART DIRECTOR
Clem McCarthy
WRITER
Rav Friedel
AGENCY PRODUCER
Robert Samuel
PRODUCTION CO.
Dick James
DIRECTOR
Dick James
CLIENT
BMW of North America
AGENCY
Ammirati & Puris

840
ART DIRECTORS
Algis Jaras
Ray Seide
WRITERS
Dick Crouser
Ann O'Phelan
AGENCY PRODUCERS
Ray Seide
John Borchardt
PRODUCTION CO.
Setterholm Productions
DIRECTOR
John Kump
CLIENT
Great Clips
AGENCY
Campbell-Mithun/
Minneapolis

837

VO: Over the years, a select few sandwiches have earned a place at the very pinnacle of the sandwich world.
And now introducing the next sandwich to be so honored.
The Dunkin' Donuts Croissant Sandwich.
Actually *nine* great sandwiches, from tuna salad to egg and bacon.
All are made to order night and day.
And served warm on croissants baked fresh in our shops.
So try Dunkin' Donuts Croissant Sandwiches.
And be prepared for greatness.

838

(SFX: OPENING CHIME, RESTAURANT SOUNDS)

MVO: Excuse me . . .

WAITER: Sir!

MVO: What are your specials today?

WAITER: I don't know.

FVO: Do your entrees come with salad?

WAITER: I don't know.

MVO: Do you have escargots?

WAITER: Escargots? (PAUSE) I don't know.

FVO: May we see a menu?

WAITER (CONFUSED): Yes! No! I don't know.

VO: If it's out there, it's in here . . .

(SFX: PLATES BREAKING)

VO :The NYNEX Yellow Pages.

(SFX: BOOK SLAMS SHUT)

VO :Why would anyone need another?

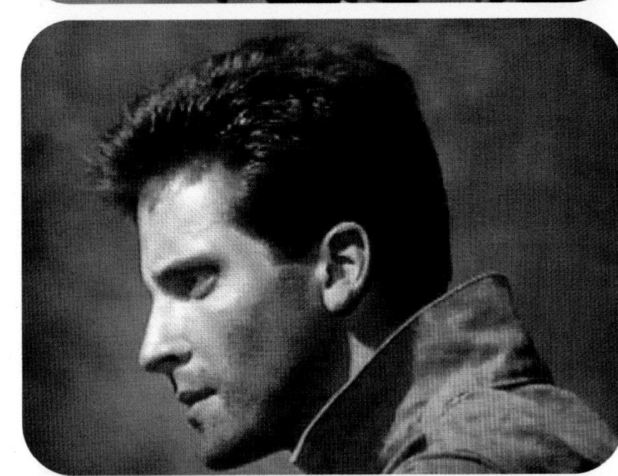

839

ANNCR: In 1979, twenty-seven men in Munich began a project, that became a quest, that became a car. Spare nothing, they were told, but build the finest, most spirited luxury sedan car in the world, That car has now arrived in America, and it's called the BMW 750iL.

840

ANNCR VO: Now, Great Clips for hair presents . . . The Philosopher.

GUY: Whenever I feel that without a *new* red Ferrari . . . life *is* devoid of all meaning . . . I go and I get a great Great Clips haircut. And I feel a lot better.
O.K. . . . a *little* better.

(SFX: RHYTHM TRACKS UNDER)

ANNCR VO: Great Clips for hair, $8.
Great perms and stylings, too.
There's a Great Clips shop right nearby.
No appointments needed.

Consumer Television
:30 Single

841
ART DIRECTOR
Ray Barrett
WRITER
Rob Janowski
AGENCY PRODUCER
Lizzie O'Connell
PRODUCTION CO.
Hibbett Ralph
DIRECTOR
Willie Patterson
CLIENT
Faberge/Brut
AGENCY
FCO/London

842
ART DIRECTOR
Jeff Roll
WRITER
Paul Decker
AGENCY PRODUCER
Harvey Greenberg
PRODUCTION CO.
Kira Films
DIRECTOR
Joe Hanright
CLIENT
Suzuki of America
AGENCY
keye/donna/pearlstein - Los Angeles

843
ART DIRECTOR
Bob Phillips
WRITER
Rav Friedel
AGENCY PRODUCER
Colleen O'Connor
PRODUCTION CO.
Steve Horn Inc.
DIRECTOR
Steve Horn
CLIENT
BMW of North America
AGENCY
Ammirati & Puris

844
ART DIRECTOR
Dean Hanson
WRITER
Phil Hanft
AGENCY PRODUCER
Char Loving
PRODUCTION CO.
Sandbank Films
DIRECTOR
Henry Sandbank
CLIENT
Conran's
AGENCY
Fallon McElligott/ Minneapolis

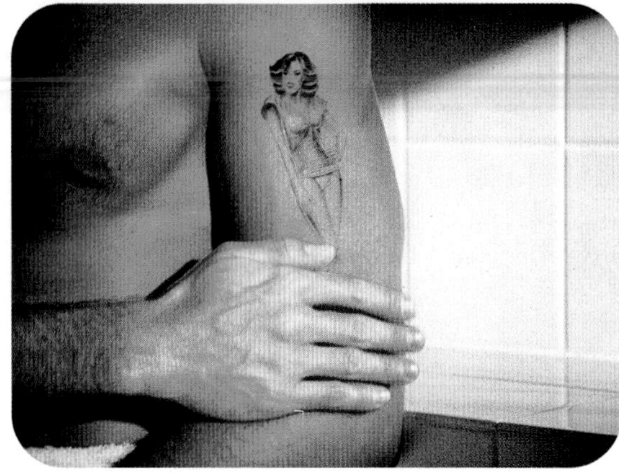

841

(SFX: SHOWERS, BLOKES CHATTING ETC.)

GIRL: Mmmm Brut. It makes me feel like a new man.

842

SUPER: A TEST DRIVE.

MICHAEL WINSLOW: Beep, beep hi!

SUPER: NEVER A DULL MOMENT.

843

WOMAN: How much longer till we get there?

MAN: About twenty minutes.

VO: Anti-lock brakes . . . an internationally . . . patented suspension . . . uncanny control . . . Conventional luxury sedans are built to survive accidents . . .
The BMW 528e is built to avoid them.

WOMAN: Let's see if they're O.K.

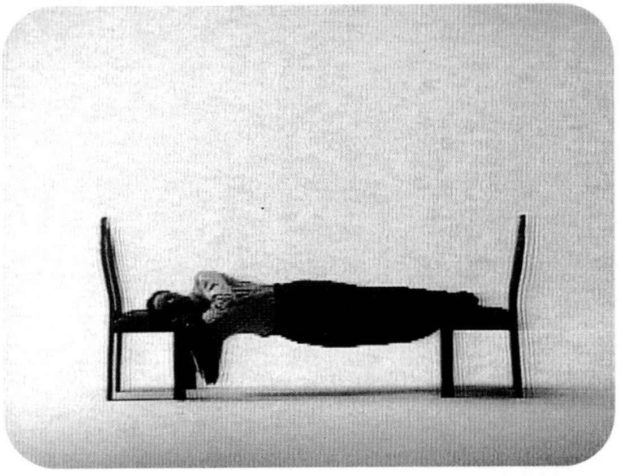

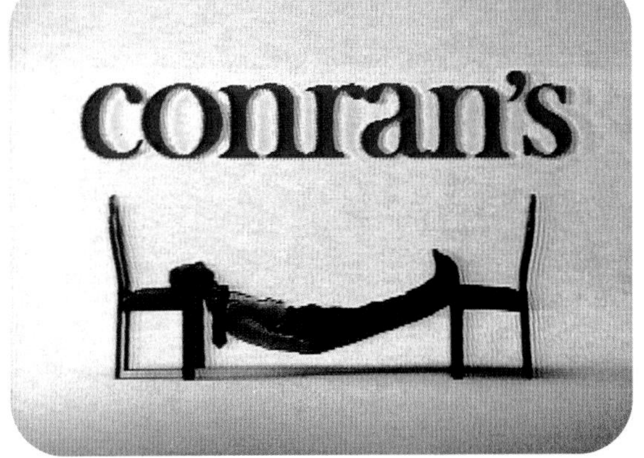

844

(NATURAL SFX THROUGHOUT)

VO: At Conran's, we don't think beautifully-designed furniture for your dining-room . . . should cost so much . . . you can't afford furniture for your bedroom.
Conran's. Complete home furnishings.

Consumer Television
:30 Single

845
ART DIRECTORS
Doug Engel
Gary Kaczmarek
WRITER
Doug Engel
PRODUCTION CO.
Ferderbar Studios
CLIENT
Chancery Restaurants
AGENCY
Lindsay & Stone/
Madison, WI

846
ART DIRECTOR
John Morrison
WRITER
Robert Chandler
AGENCY PRODUCERS
Barbara Mullins
Jennifer Heftler
PRODUCTION CO.
Giraldi Suarez Productions
DIRECTOR
Fred Goodich
CLIENT
Apple Computer
AGENCY
BBDO

847
ART DIRECTOR
Dean Hanson
WRITER
Phil Hanft
AGENCY PRODUCER
Char Loving
PRODUCTION CO.
Sandbank Films
DIRECTOR
Henry Sandbank
CLIENT
Conran's
AGENCY
Fallon McElligott/
Minneapolis

848
ART DIRECTOR
Bob Kwait
WRITER
Rich Badami
AGENCY PRODUCER
Dave Hoogenakker
PRODUCTION CO.
Triad
DIRECTOR
Johnny Dust
CLIENT
San Diego Zoo
AGENCY
Phillips-Ramsey/
San Diego

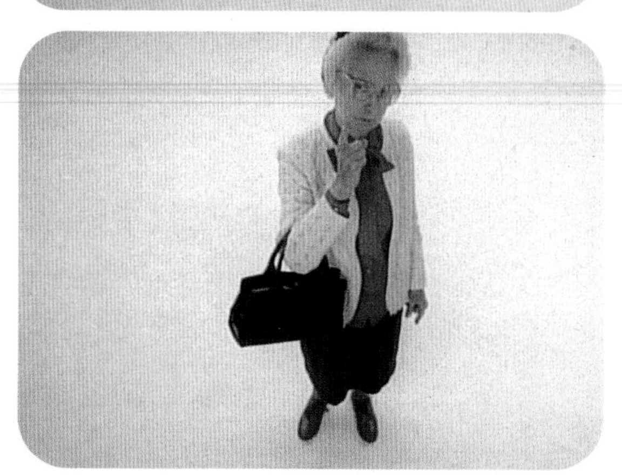

845

ANNCR: You mean you're not taking Mother to the Chancery?
Shame on you.

We the People

We the People

We the People

846

(MUSIC: IN AND UNDER)

TYPES: US GUYS

RETYPES: US PERSONS

RETYPES: US FORKS

RETYPES: US FOLKS

RETYPES: WE FOLKS

RETYPES: WE THE AMERICAN PEOPLE

RETYPES: WE THE PEOPLE

847

VO: At Conran's, we don't believe beautifully-designed furniture . . . should be so expensive . . . you're afraid to even sit on it.

(SFX: BURP)

848

(MUSIC: CLASSICAL)

Consumer Television :30 Single

849

ART DIRECTOR
Jerry Gentile

WRITER
Mark Monteiro

AGENCY PRODUCERS
Shannon Silverman
Diane Hill

PRODUCTION CO
Johns+Gorman Films

DIRECTOR
Gary Johns

CLIENT
Comprehensive Care Corporation

AGENCY
DDB Needham Worldwide/ Los Angeles

850

ART DIRECTORS
Ted Shaine
Marcus Kemp

WRITER
Rav Friedel

AGENCY PRODUCER
Robert Samuel

PRODUCTION CO.
Cherry Mellon Ibbetson

DIRECTOR
Peter Cherry

CLIENT
BMW of North America

AGENCY
Ammirati & Puris

851

ART DIRECTOR
John Speakman

WRITER
Terry Bell

AGENCY PRODUCER
Jo-Ann Brownsey

PRODUCTION CO.
Mistral Film Productions

DIRECTOR
Christopher Sanderson

CLIENT
Ralston Purina

AGENCY
Scali McCabe Sloves/ Toronto

852

ART DIRECTOR
Michael Fazende

WRITER
John Stingley

AGENCY PRODUCERS
Char Loving
Judy Brink

PRODUCTION CO.
Johns+Gorman Films

DIRECTOR
Jeff Gorman

CLIENT
Emmis Broadcasting

AGENCY
Fallon McElligott/ Minneapolis

849

(MUSIC THROUGHOUT)

(SFX: WIND)

ANNCR VO: Since 1973, only one place has admitted more drug and alcohol abusers . . . than CareUnit. If you don't call, we can't help.

850

VO: No one would deny that the Japanese are afficionados of fine machinery. So when they reach that station in life when they can afford really fine machinery, guess what they buy? A car from Germany called the BMW 325i. Making BMW last year's number-one-selling luxury import in Japan.

851

WOMAN: At first he'd be an hour late for dinner. Then two. Then one night, he just didn't come home.

(SFX: WHISTLE, TRAFFIC NOISES, BIKE GEARS)

WOMAN: I was devastated. But the truth was, she was giving him what he really hungered for.

(SFX: BIRDS CHIRPING)

GRANDMA: This will be our little secret.

WOMAN: Now I give him nothing but Purina Meow Mix. Did you know, it's the only food with the tastes of Tuna, Liver and Chicken? It's what he always asked for. I guess I just wasn't listening.

ANNCR: Purina Meow Mix. If you don't feed it to your cat, who will?

(SFX: BARBERSHOP DOOR CHIME RINGS; TRAFFIC NOISES)

BARBER: This'll be our little secret.

852

ANNCR: Just try catching sports on most radio stations.Then try WFAN 1050 AM. The world's first twenty-four-hour sports radio station.

Consumer Television
:30 Single

853
ART DIRECTOR
Ted Shaine
WRITER
Helayne Spivak
AGENCY PRODUCER
Ozzie Spenningsby
PRODUCTION CO.
Spots Films/New York
DIRECTOR
David Cornell
CLIENT
Club Med
AGENCY
Ammirati & Puris

854
ART DIRECTOR
Jeff Vogt
WRITER
Joe O'Neill
AGENCY PRODUCERS
Frank Scherma
Ozzie Spenningsby
PRODUCTION CO.
Coppos Films
DIRECTOR
Mark Coppos
CLIENT
BMW of North America
AGENCY
Ammirati & Puris

855
ART DIRECTORS
Jan Koblitz
Betsy Ensign
WRITER
Steve Landsberg
AGENCY PRODUCER
Dorothy Franklin
PRODUCTION CO.
Bill Hudson & Associates
DIRECTOR
Bill Hudson
CLIENT
Coca-Cola USA
AGENCY
McCann-Erickson

856
ART DIRECTOR
Ted Shaine
WRITER
Helayne Spivak
AGENCY PRODUCER
Ozzie Spenningsby
PRODUCTION CO.
Spots Films/New York
DIRECTOR
David Cornell
CLIENT
Club Med
AGENCY
Ammirati & Puris

853

VO: The world news Club Med style.
Oil spills along the coast.
Foreign relations improving.
Gold plunges overseas.
Border dispute settled.
Tensions ease in Gulf.
And that's the way it is.
At Club Med.

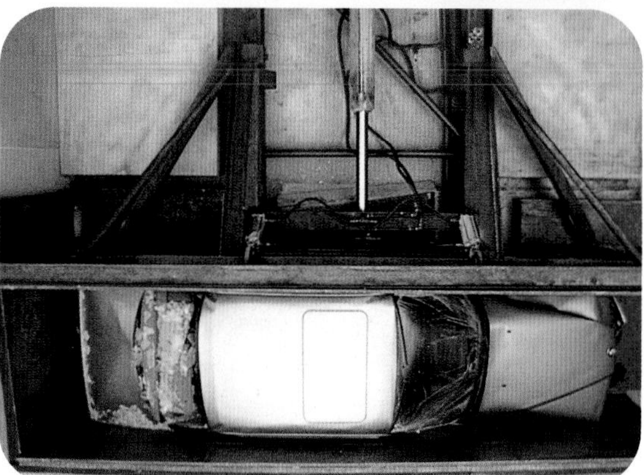

854

VO: Had it survived, it would have sold for nearly $50,000.00.
But in the name of safety . . .
Quality . . .
Consummate reliability . . .
Four hundred BMWs were sacrificed in testing.
Extreme?
Not to the person who invests in the four hundred and first.
Introducing the new BMW 735i.

855

BIG BROTHER: Do you see this? This is mine. You don't go near it. You don't even think about it. You take any, and you're terminated. I'm warning you, you touch it and you're history.

(SFX: CRACK, FIZZZZZ OF SODA CAN OPENING)

BIG BROTHER: You're dead!

ANNCR: When Coca-Cola is part of your life, you can't beat the feeling.

BIGGEST BROTHER: *Who's* dead?

856

VO: Thirty-seven years ago, Club Med made a special arrangement with civilization.
Send us your frazzled . . . your crazed . . . your beleagured . . . your burnt-out . . . your over-burdened . . . your tension-riddled, and we'll send you back a human being.

Consumer Television
:30 Single

857
ART DIRECTOR
Joe Del Vecchio
WRITERS
Don Green
Joe Nunziata
AGENCY PRODUCER
Bob Smith
PRODUCTION CO.
Sandbank Films
DIRECTOR
Stan Schofield
CLIENT
Dean Witter
AGENCY
Lord Geller Federico
Einstein

858
ART DIRECTOR
Andy DeSantis
WRITERS
Fred Siegel
Peter Faulkner
AGENCY PRODUCER
Michael Aubrey
PRODUCTION COS.
Lear Levin Productions
Rebo
CLIENT
Sony
AGENCY
McCann-Erickson

859
ART DIRECTOR
Jon Parkinson
WRITER
David Metcalf
AGENCY PRODUCER
Dane Johnson
PRODUCTION CO.
Berkofsky Barrett
DIRECTOR
Mike Berkofsky
CLIENT
Champion
AGENCY
Scali McCabe Sloves

860
ART DIRECTORS
Rick Boyko
Miles Turpin
WRITERS
Elizabeth Hayes
Mary Ann Bixby
AGENCY PRODUCERS
Richard O'Neill
David Prince
Elaine Hinton
PRODUCTION CO.
Petermann/Dektor
DIRECTOR
Leslie Dektor
CLIENT
Home Savings of America
AGENCY
Chiat/Day - Venice, CA

857

(MUSIC: UNDER THROUGHOUT)

ARTHUR NEWMAN: I'm Arthur Newman.
Women would love to get their arms around my brother, Paul! And so would investment firms. But I have a firm that loves to work for people like you and me, too.
Dean Witter.
You see . . . I may not be a heart throb, but Dean Witter still handles my investments with tender loving care.

MUSIC: *You're somebody at Dean Witter.*

ANNCR VO: A member of the Sears Financial Network.

858

VO: The Sony Trinitron T.V.
Some people have it.
And some people don't.

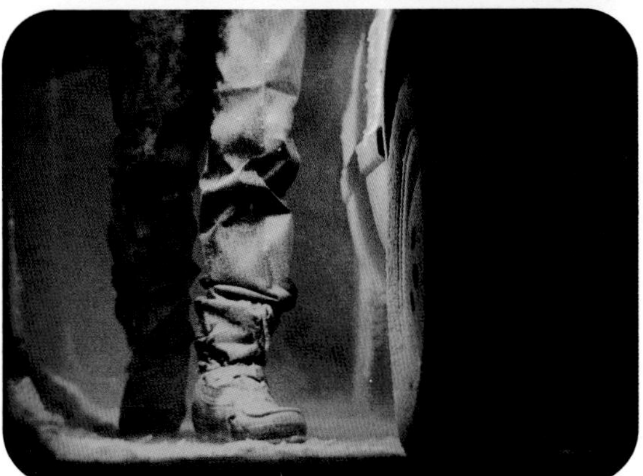

859

(MUSIC/SFX: COLD)

VO: When the temperature drops below thirty Fahrenheit . . . remember the spark plug that's tested to start below zero Fahrenheit.

(MUSIC/SFX: HEAT)

Champion. We go to ridiculous extremes . . . to test the reliability of our spark plugs.

860

MARY ANN: I'm divorced. I've been divorced for eight years. This is the first house I've owned on my own. It's not easy. The buck stops with me. But I accept that.

ANNCR: Mary Ann Bixby wasn't alone when she got her home loan. She had Home Savings.

MARY ANN: The day that the wallpaper went up in the hall, my daughter said, 'Mom, this house sure looks like a female owns it.' And I said, 'That's fine.'

Consumer Television :30 Single

861

ART DIRECTOR
Jeff Vogt

WRITER
Tom Nathan

AGENCY PRODUCER
Colleen O'Connor

PRODUCTON CO.
Sandbank Films

DIRECTOR
Henry Sandbank

CLIENT
BMW of North America

AGENCY
Ammirati & Puris

862

ART DIRECTOR
Jeff Abbott

WRITERS
Mike Sullivan
Jeff Abbott

AGENCY PRODUCER
Sheldon Cohn

PRODUCTION CO.
Spots Films/New York

CLIENT
Chiquita Brands

AGENCY
W.B. Doner & Company/
Southfield, MI

863

ART DIRECTOR
Earl Cavanah

WRITER
Larry Cadman

AGENCY PRODUCER
Susan Chiafullo

PRODUCTION CO.
Story Piccolo Guliner

DIRECTOR
Jack Donnelly

CLIENT
Volvo

AGENCY
Scali McCabe Sloves

864

ART DIRECTOR
Rich Silverstein

WRITERS
Andy Berlin
Jeff Goodby

AGENCY PRODUCERS
Cindy Fluitt
Debbie King

PRODUCTION CO.
Big Deahl Productions

DIRECTOR
David Deahl

CLIENT
Home Express

AGENCY
Goodby Berlin &
Silverstein/San Francisco

861

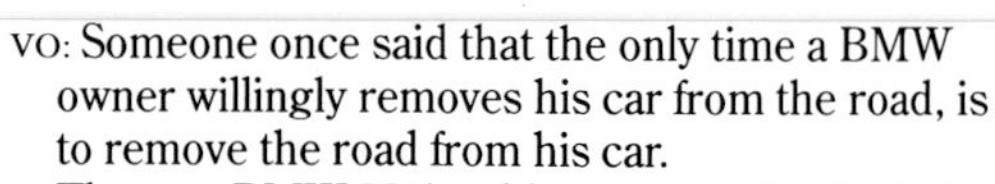

VO: Someone once said that the only time a BMW owner willingly removes his car from the road, is to remove the road from his car.
The new BMW 325is adds new meaning to that piece of insight.
A thirty-nine percent increase in power, competition-tuned suspension, serious aerodynamics; all of which tends to reduce washing the BMW 335is, to an act of futility.

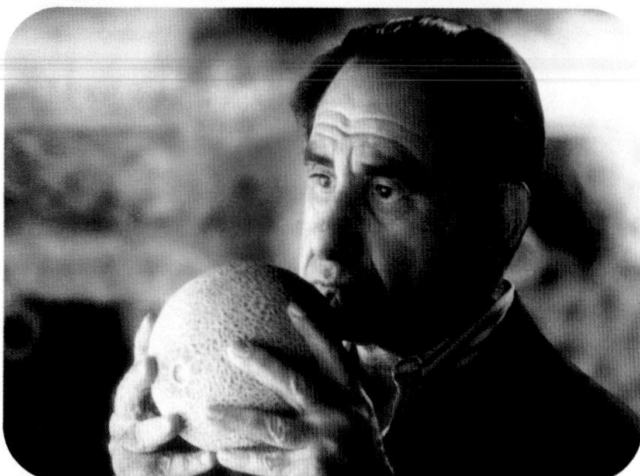

862

SPOKESMAN: Even in our advanced civilization, picking a melon is still something of a primitive ritual. But not anymore. Introducing Chiquita melons. They're always sweet and always delicious.
Just look for the Chiquita label. It's how you know you've got a good one.

863

(MUSIC: UP AND UNDER)

(SFX: THROUGHOUT)

ANNCR VO: At Volvo, we've been building cars for sixty years and we've been safety-testing them almost as long. Some carmakers might say we've been obsessed with safety. Well, they'd be right. You see, we want to make sure our customers keep coming back.

864

(MUSIC: UNDER THROUGHOUT)

SALLY KELLERMAN: Fifty years ago, Mees Van der Roweh changed the course of modern design with a bold statement: "Less is more."
After all those years, we think we've finally hit on exactly what he meant.

Consumer Television :30 Single

865
ART DIRECTOR
Ralph Ammirati
WRITER
Martin Puris
AGENCY PRODUCER
Ozzie Spenningsby
PRODUCTION CO.
Coppos Films
DIRECTOR
Mark Coppos
CLIENT
BMW of North America
AGENCY
Ammirati & Puris

866
ART DIRECTOR
Earl Cavanah
WRITER
Larry Cadman
AGENCY PRODUCER
Jaki Keuch
PRODUCTION CO.
Sandbank Films
DIRECTOR
Henry Sandbank
CLIENT
Volvo
AGENCY
Scali McCabe Sloves

867
ART DIRECTORS
Jessica Collins
Chris Lezotte
WRITERS
Mike Zadoorian
Chris Lezotte
AGENCY PRODUCER
Kris Roberts
PRODUCTION CO.
Michael Daniels
DIRECTOR
Hobby Morrison
CLIENT
Giant Eagle
AGENCY
W.B. Doner & Company/
Southfield, MI

868
ART DIRECTOR
Bonnie McBain
WRITER
Bernie Pitzel
AGENCY PRODUCER
Laura Morrison
PRODUCTION CO.
Ulick/Mayo Productions
CLIENT
Long John Silver's
AGENCY
Foote Cone Belding/
Chicago

865

VO: There are those who fervently believe that true perfection is found in the details.
At the Bavarian motor works, we gave that belief a name.
We call it . . . the BMW 735i.
Beautiful? To be sure.
Yet perhaps the most beautiful thing about it is its spirit.

866

(MUSIC: THROUGHOUT)

(SFX: CLICK)

ANNCR VO: How well does your car stand up to heavy traffic?

(MUSIC: OUT)

867

SUPER: WILLIE DIXON TALKS ABOUT THE BLUES.

WILLIE: You see, there's a different kind of blues around these days. Whole new breed. Very fresh. That's what makes them good. And sweet? They're probably the sweetest blues you'll ever get. Of course, you won't find blues like these everywhere. And they won't be around for long. Very tasty. (LAUGHS)

VO: 1987 Blues Berries. Only at Giant Eagle.

WILLIE: Home of the Blues . . . (LAUGHS)

868

GUY: I love this country. It's so funny.
Like this chicken thing.
See, this is chicken cube. This is chicken strip. And this, is chicken chicken. All white meat, best tasting part of chicken. Tenderloin. Most juiciest part. Comes with fries and cole slaw. And where's the only place you get chicken this good?
At a fish place. I love this country.

SONG: *Long John Silver's sounds good to me.*

Consumer Television
:30 Single

869
ART DIRECTOR
Peter Favat
WRITER
Dana Jones
AGENCY PRODUCER
David Cohen
PRODUCTION CO.
They Shoot Films
DIRECTOR
George D'Amato
CLIENT
Converse
AGENCY
Ingalls Quinn and Johnson/
Boston

870
ART DIRECTOR
Jim Mochnsky
WRITERS
Jim Dale
Arthur Mitchell
AGENCY PRODUCER
Sandy Mislang
PRODUCTION CO.
Eye View Films
DIRECTOR
Bob Schwartz
CLIENT
Edison Electric Institute
AGENCY
W.B. Doner & Company/
Baltimore

871
ART DIRECTOR
Ron Fisher
WRITER
Virgil Shutze
AGENCY PRODUCER
George Medland
PRODUCTION CO.
Ackerman-Benson
DIRECTOR
Jerry Collamer
CLIENT
South Carolina Federal
AGENCY
HutchesonShutze/Atlanta

872
ART DIRECTORS
Dave Cook
Neil Sullivan
AGENCY PRODUCER
Grizel Veitch
PRODUCTION CO.
Brian Byfield Films
DIRECTOR
Brian Byfield
CLIENT
Global Watches/Sekonda
AGENCY
Gold Greenless Trott/
London

869

(SFX: MUSIC; OPERA SINGER; MUSIC)

SILENCE

(SFX: DIVER'S SHOUT; MUSIC)

VO: All Stars. Strike back.

(SFX: SNOW)

870

ANNCR: What would we do without electricity?

MAX SMITH: For example, if we didn't have electricity, if you're in . . . if you're in a bathroom and you have to go, you have to go . . . you have to go and there's no lights, you have to go in the dark.

ANNCR: Electricity. There's no substitute.

871

MVO: How does your bank react when you ask for a home equity loan?

ORANGUTAN: YAWNS . . .

MVO: All day banking?

ORANGUTAN: SHAKES HIS HEAD NO . . .

MVO: Free checking?

ORANGUTAN: BLOWS A RASPBERRY . . .

MVO: How about a mortgage loan?

ORANGUTAN: SHAKES HIS HEAD NO . . .

MVO: Line of credit?

ORANGUTAN: STICKS OUT HIS TONGUE . . .

MVO: Won't even listen, huh?

ORANGUTAN: COVERS EARS WITH HANDS . . .

MVO: Bet they don't even know your name?

ORANGUTAN: SHAKES HIS HEAD NO . . .

MVO: Must drive you clean out of your tree?

ORANGUTAN: SLAPS HANDS OVER FACE . . .

MVO: Well . . . if we were you pal, we'd bank with us.

SUPER: SOUTH CAROLINA FEDERAL

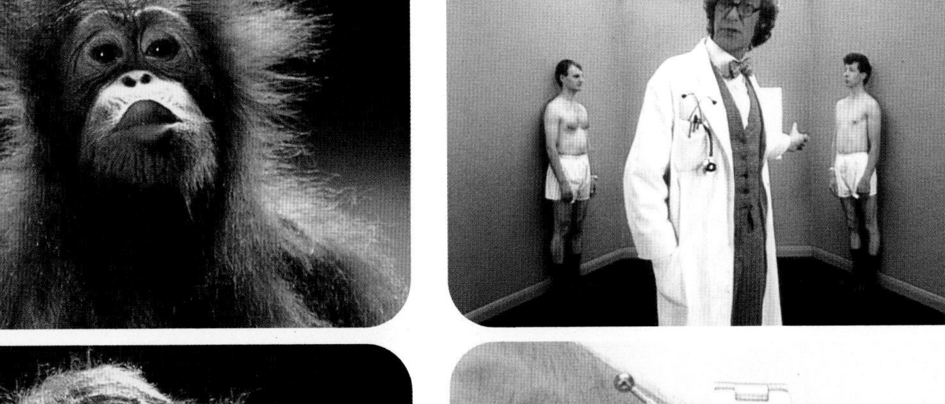

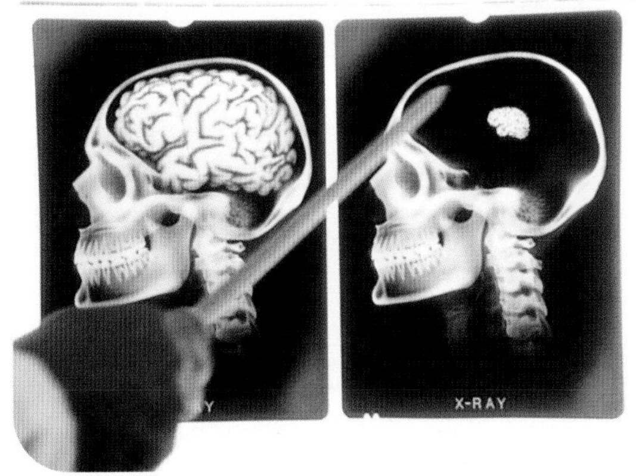

872

DOCTOR: Two apparently normal men.
This man's watch is a Sekonda; it's tested for accuracy and durability and costs under £30.
This man's watch tells the month, the year, your blood pressure and miles per gallon.
Why would such apparently similar men choose such different time-pieces?
Internal examination of the watches fails to explain the phenomenon.
Ah, we must examine the owner to see what makes him tick.

MVO: Sekonda. Beware of expensive imitations.

Consumer Television
:30 Single

873
ART DIRECTOR
Dean Stefanides
WRITER
Larry Hampel
AGENCY PRODUCER
Jaki Keuch
PRODUCTION CO.
Rick Levine Productions
DIRECTOR
Patrick Russel
CLIENT
National Dairy Board
AGENCY
Scali McCabe Sloves

874
ART DIRECTOR
Ed Wolper
WRITER
John Malecki
AGENCY PRODUCER
Jaki Keuch
PRODUCTION CO.
Story Piccolo Guliner
DIRECTOR
Paul Guliner
CLIENT
Perdue
AGENCY
Scali McCabe Sloves

875
WRITERS
Mike Sullivan
John DeCerchio
Gary Rom
AGENCY PRODUCER
Sheldon Cohn
PRODUCTION CO.
Elite Films
CLIENT
7-Eleven
AGENCY
W.B. Doner & Company/
Southfield, MI

876
ART DIRECTOR
Rick Boyko
WRITERS
Elizabeth Hayes
Emma Unger
Milton Unger
AGENCY PRODUCERS
Richard O'Neill
David Prince
Elaine Hinton
PRODUCTION CO.
Petermann/Dektor
DIRECTOR
Leslie Dektor
CLIENT
Home Savings of America
AGENCY
Chiat/Day - Venice, CA

873

(SFX: MUSIC UP AND UNDER)

FATHER VO: What is with those sneakers . . . will you please tie the laces!!

MOTHER VO: Are you ever gonna take those sunglasses off? We haven't seen your face in two months.

FATHER VO: Your hair, what's in your hair . . . motor oil?

MOTHER VO: If I've told you once, I've told you a thousand times—don't drink out of the bottle!!!

ANNCR VO: This thirty seconds of total coolness has been brought to you by milk.

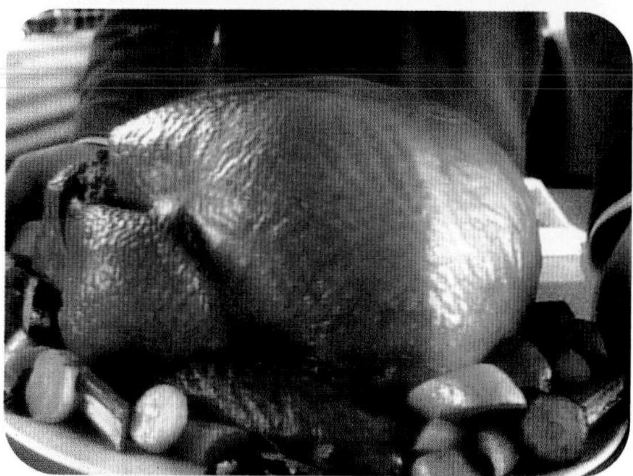

874

(MUSIC: UNDER THROUGHOUT)

ANNCR VO: Frank Perdue was never satisfied with turkey.

MOTHER: Franklin, what's wrong?

YOUNG FRANK: For one thing, it's too dry. And this breast! It's kind of skimpy.

ANNCR: Now, years later, there's a turkey good enough for him. The Perdue Turkey. A ten- to fourteen-pound bird that's always naturally tender and juicy. With lots of delicious breast meat.

FRANK PERDUE: Finally!

875

COLEMAN: Here's a letter from a Mr Mike Biglin. 'Dear Sir, You say that day in and day out it's virtually impossible to beat 7-Eleven's price on a gallon of milk. I wouldn't believe *that* if I heard it from my own *mother.*'
Michael, here is your own mother . . .

MOTHER: Michael, believe Mr Coleman. It's the truth.

COLEMAN: Mm mm. Happy, Mike?

TAG: A GALLON OF MILK JUST $2.17 EVERY DAY.
7-ELEVEN. NOW EVEN GOOD PRICES COME EASY.

MOTHER: Where'd I go wrong?

COLEMAN: Now don't do that to yourself, Mom. Don't do that. Tell you why . . .

876

MILTON: We've always made it and I don't worry because she's a good manager. Whether we have a little or a lot. We make it. One week we were so poor I bought a bushell of carrots and we lived on carrots all week, and now when we go out to dinner and we see carrots, we look at each other and smile. It didn't hurt us. It was fun.

ANNCR: Milton and Emma worked very hard for their retirement. So did Home Savings.

MILTON: We're just ordinary people.
We're late bloomers.

Consumer Television :30 Single

877

ART DIRECTOR
Barbara Schubeck

WRITER
Sharon Vanderslice

AGENCY PRODUCER
Neal Bergman

PRODUCTION CO.
Ulick/Mayo Productions

DIRECTOR
Geoffrey Mayo

CLIENT
WNBC-TV

AGENCY
Lord Geller Federico Einstein

878

ART DIRECTOR
David Sharpe

WRITER
Michael Paul

AGENCY PRODUCER
Sheila Moen

PRODUCTION CO.
Rawi Schulz

DIRECTOR
Ousama Rawi

CLIENT
Texaco Canada

AGENCY
SMW Advertising/Toronto

879

ART DIRECTOR
Bill Halladay

WRITER
Mary Ann Zeman

AGENCY PRODUCER
Neal Bergman

PRODUCTION CO.
Giraldi Suarez Productions

DIRECTOR
Bob Giraldi

CLIENT
Fuji

AGENCY
Lord Geller Federico Einstein

Consumer Television :30 Campaign

880

ART DIRECTOR
Neil Leinwohl

WRITER
Kevin McKeon

AGENCY PRODUCER
Milda Misevicius

PRODUCTION CO.
Gerard Hameline

DIRECTOR
Ross Cramer

CLIENT
Tri-Honda Auto Dealers Association

AGENCY
Korey Kay & Partners

877

LITTLE GIRL (READING HALTINGLY):
See the school board.
See the school board fight.
See the money go back and forth.
See the bad man get the job.
See the teacher cry.
See the little children get hurt.

ANNCR VO: Gabe Pressman reports on the politics of education. This week at six on Channel 4.

878

VO: This woman feels she's a safe driver. Yet she continually makes dangerous driving errors. Like this one: Her rear view is clear. She pulls out to pass. Did you spot it? She should have looked over her left shoulder as well . . . to check her car's blind spot.
And now she's about to make one of the worst driving errors of her life.

WOMAN: Hi, honey. Ready to go?

VO: She's going to teach her daughter . . . everything she knows.
Please let a professional teach them to drive. And survive.

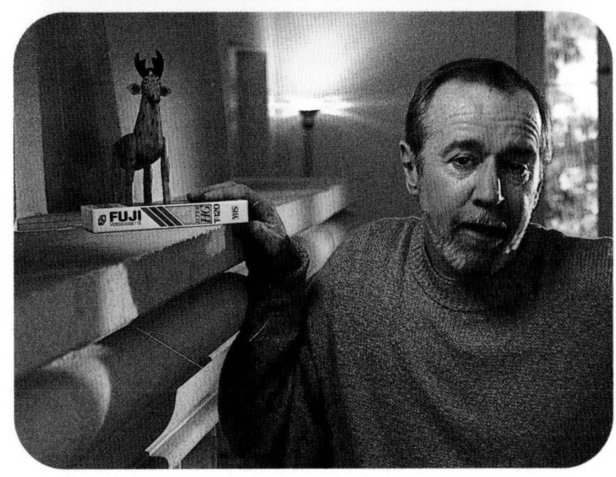

879

GEORGE CARLIN: Hey, are you watching me now or did you videotape me before? If you taped me before, you're not watching me now. You're watching me later. But if you're taping me now and you want me to be clear and sharp when you watch me later, use the good stuff—Fuji Videotape,
With Fuji Videotape . . . no matter how much later later is . . . it never looks like later. It looks like now. See ya later.
Fuji Videotape. Put the good stuff on the good stuff.

880

JACKIE MASON: Did you hear about the new Honda Prelude with the four-wheel steering? Nobody heard about it. You know why? Because they can't believe it when they hear it.
As you turn the car in the front this way, wheels in the back are turning the ways nobody ever saw before. It has new direction for wheels to turn because you turn like this, and all of a sudden you're going like that. You don't know why but it's getting you there in a way that you never did before.
And you know why you need this? I don't know.

Consumer Television :30 Campaign

881
ART DIRECTOR
John Staffen
WRITER
Mike Rogers
AGENCY PRODUCER
Ugo Pergolotti
PRODUCTION CO.
Rick Levine Production
DIRECTOR
Michael Werk
CLIENT
Volkswagen
AGENCY
DDB Needham Worldwide

882
ART DIRECTOR
Steve Fong
WRITER
Dave Woodside
AGENCY PRODUCER
Karen Carlson
PRODUCTION CO.
THT Productions
DIRECTOR
Martin Bell
CLIENT
Worlds of Wonder
AGENCY
Chiat/Day - Venice, CA

883
ART DIRECTOR
Alan Lawrence
WRITER
Michael Albright
AGENCY PRODUCER
Frank Tammariello
PRODUCTION CO.
Riverrun Films
DIRECTORS
Alan Lawrence
Frank Tammariello
CLIENT
Ralphs Grocery
Company/The Giant
AGENCY
W.B. Doner & Company/
Los Angeles

884
ART DIRECTOR
Rick Carpenter
WRITER
Dick Sittig
AGENCY PRODUCERS
Sandra Tuttle
Nancy Koch
PRODUCTION COS.
Travisano Di Giacomo Films
N. Lee Lacy
DIRECTORS
Ron Travisano
Matthew Meshekoff
CLIENT
American Isuzu Motors
AGENCY
Della Femina Travisano &
Partners/Los Angeles

881

(SFX: CAR ACCELERATION AND SCREECHING THROUGHOUT)

VO: Volkswagen engineers have developed a remarkable fuel injection system . . . which gives our Jetta seventeen percent more horsepower than before . . . and top track speeds of over 100. Of course, there are . . . those Volkswagen engineers who believe they've developed something no less remarkable . . . the brakes. German Engineering. The Volkswagen way.

882

(SFX: BELL RINGS; MUSIC UP)

KID VO: The way I see it, with a Stuff-It Binder you will automatically do better at school.
You'll be more prepared.
You'll keep better notes.
You will impress your teachers.
Above all, now this is important, you will always take advantage of every opportunity to learn.

MAN ANNCR VO: Stuff-It. The Binders.

GIRL VO: Nice try, squeak.

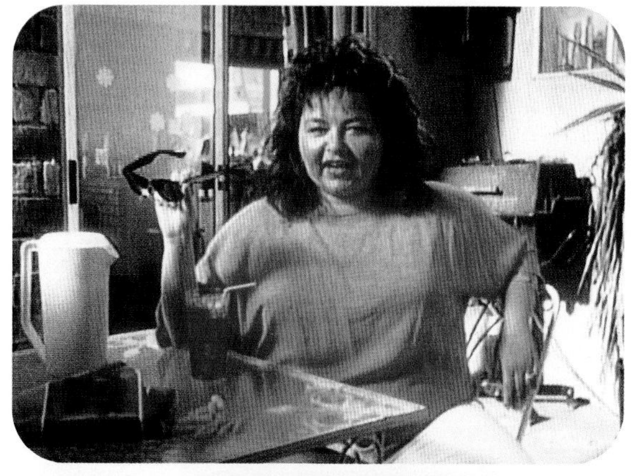

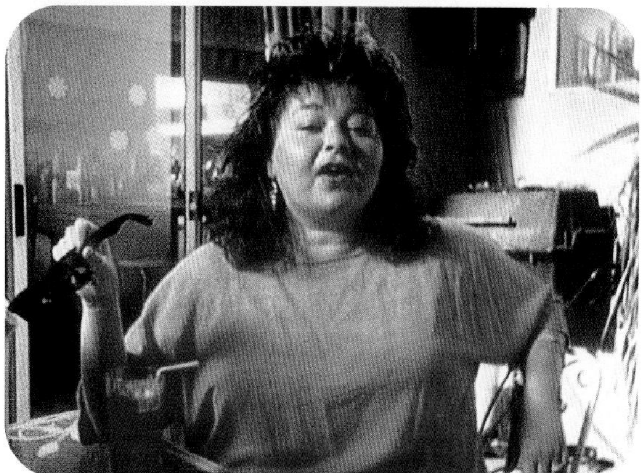

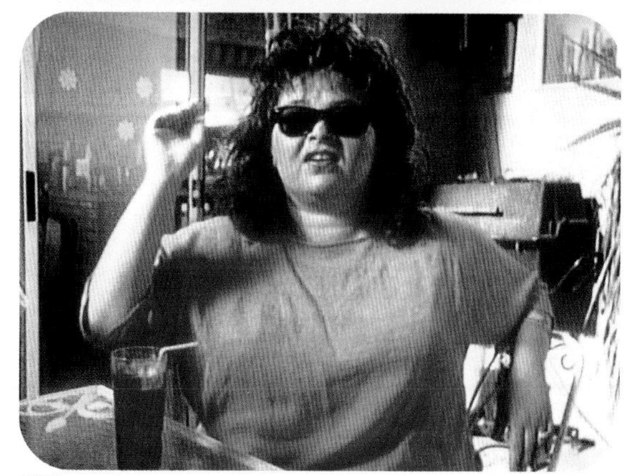

883

(MUSIC: UP AND UNDER THROUGHOUT)

ROSEANNE: Now that I live in California, I've tried to adapt a holistic approach to the housewife thing. After a long day in the tanning parlor and yoga institute, I'm in no mood to traipse around town to a bunch of supermarkets looking for groceries like I'm in search of my past lives. I just go to The Giant, where I get the whole schmeer for peanuts. It helps focus my energies, and enhances my feelings of self-worth.

884

EXPLORER #1: What the . . .

JOE: Hi!

EXPLORER #2: How'd you get up here?

JOE: In the amazing Trooper II.

SUPER: HE'S LYING.

JOE: Course I *did* have to shift into four-wheel drive. Wanna buy it?

EXPLORER #2: No, we're supposed to walk.

EXPLORER #3: Can it take all of us?

JOE: No sweat.

EXPLORER: Are you sure about this?

JOE: You have my word on it. (TRAILS OFF INTO ECHO)

ANNCR VO: The rugged Trooper II. From Isuzu.

Consumer Television
:30 Campaign

885

ART DIRECTORS
Tod Seisser
Irv Klein

WRITERS
Jay Taub
Stephanie Arnold

AGENCY PRODUCERS
Bob Nelson
Rachel Novak

PRODUCTION CO.
Sandbank Films

DIRECTOR
Henry Sandbank

CLIENT
Maidenform

AGENCY
Levine Huntley Schmidt & Beaver

886

ART DIRECTOR
Barry Vetere

WRITER
Tom Messner

AGENCY PRODUCER
Trish O'Reilly

CLIENT
WBZ-TV

AGENCY
Messner Vetere Berger Carey

887

ART DIRECTOR
Gary Wolfson

WRITERS
John DeCerchio
Sheldon Cohn

AGENCY PRODUCER
Hugo Broder

CLIENT
Michigan State Lottery

AGENCY
W.B. Doner & Company/ Southfield, MI

888

ART DIRECTOR
Peter Cohen

WRITER
Larry Spector

AGENCY PRODUCER
Rachel Novak

PRODUCTION CO.
Story Piccolo Guliner

DIRECTOR
Mark Story

CLIENT
Webster Industries/ Good Sense

AGENCY
Levine Huntley Schmidt & Beaver

885

MICHAEL YORK: When a women wears beautiful lingerie it says that she likes herself. I think that's sexy.
To me, lingerie expresses how she feels . . . playful . . . romantic . . . mysterious . . .
The possibilities are always interesting.

SUPER: MAIDENFORM

886

VO: Of the 1,500 athletes who participated in the 1987 Massachusetts Special Olympic Summer Games, almost half of them had no one to share their great moment of triumph. No parent, no brother, no sister.
Which is why for the past nine years, Charles Austin of WBZ-TV has not only reported on the Summer Olympics, he's also participated in them.

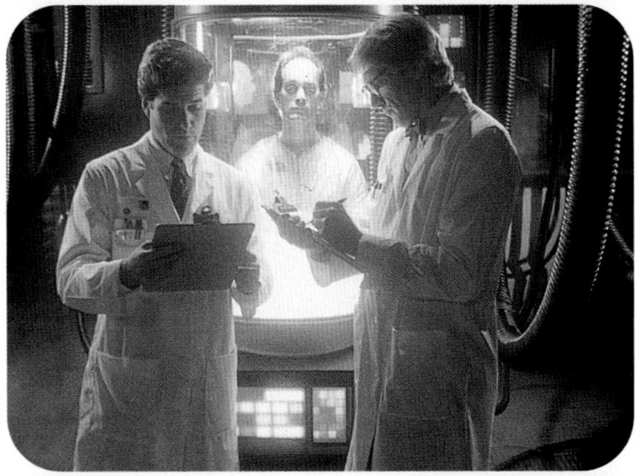

887

VO: Now entering suspended animation . . .

MAN #2: So when does he want us to wake him?

MAN #1: Oh, get this . . . when the Super Lotto jackpot reaches one hundred million dollars.

MAN #2: Why does he want to wait? The jackpot is already a million and a half bucks.

MAN #1: Right. Besides, I hear somebody wins it every week.

MAN #2: That means if he's waiting for a hundred million dollar jackpot, he'll be in there . . .

MAN #1: Forever.

MAN #2: Yeah. Coffee?

MAN #1: You buyin'?

VO: Play Super Lotto. What are you waiting for?

888

MAN: Most paper plates will hold up to maybe one serving of pie.

(SFX: WHOOSH)

After that, they become soggy . . . and limp.
But Good Sense plastic plates stay rigid and don't leak.

(SFX: WHOOSH)

So you can go back for seconds.

(SFX: WHOOSH)

And thirds.

(SFX: WHOOSH)

ANNCR: Good Sense plastic plates. The best things you'll ever throw out.
By the way, we also make plastic cups.

Consumer Television
:30 Campaign

889

ART DIRECTOR
Bob Barrie

WRITER
Mike Lescarbeau

AGENCY PRODUCER
Char Loving

PRODUCTION CO.
Coppos Films

DIRECTOR
Mark Coppos

CLIENT
Continental Illinois

AGENCY
Fallon McElligott/
Minneapolis

890

ART DIRECTORS
Earl Cavanah
Paul Blade

WRITERS
Larry Cadman
Larry Hampel

CLIENT
Volvo

AGENCY
Scali McCabe Sloves

891

ART DIRECTOR
Sal DeVito

WRITER
Amy Borkowsky

AGENCY PRODUCER
Rachel Novak

PRODUCTION CO.
Story Piccolo Guliner

DIRECTOR
Mark Story

CLIENT
Genesee Brewing Company

AGENCY
Levine Huntley Schmidt &
Beaver

892

ART DIRECTOR
Mike Lowes

WRITER
Tom Scharre

AGENCY PRODUCER
Gordon Byrd

PRODUCTION CO.
G.M.S.

DIRECTOR
Scott Miller

CLIENT
Audi of America

AGENCY
DDB Needham Worldwide/
Chicago

889

REX: Listen to this woman as a Continental banker would hear her.

WOMAN: My goal is to get steady income from my investments. I want to take my money and make it grow.

(SFX: TAPE REWIND UNDER)

REX: Now listen to her as someone else might hear her.

WOMAN: . . . take my money . . .

REX: Wouldn't you rather talk to a Continental banker?

VO: Continental Illinois . . . we make money work. Continental Illinois National Bank and Trust Company of Chicago. Member FDIC.

890

(MUSIC: UNDER)

(SFX: CAR ENGINE)

ANNCR VO: The Porsche 944. The Volvo Turbo Wagon.

(SFX: WIND)

To you, they're two completely different cars . . .

(SFX: BEEPS, ENGINES, TIRES SCREECH)

. . . but to a radar gun . . .

(SFX: BEEPS, ENGINE ROAR)

. . . they look exactly alike.

891

ANNCR VO: This should give you some idea of the diffference between beer and Genesee Cream Ale. Smooth Genesee Cream Ale. It's not the same old brewskie.

892

CHAIRPERSON VO: This conference now welcomes Ms Woodward to the podium.

SUPER: MOTHER.

(SFX: GIGGLES)

SUPER: PHILANTHROPIST.

VO: Thank you so much for caring.

SUPER: ACTRESS.

M.C. VO: Ladies and gentlemen, Emmy award winner—Joanne Woodward!

(MUSIC: THEME UP)

ANNCR VO: They say the car you drive says a lot about you. But we think the kind of people . . .

SUPER: JOANNE WOODWARD.

. . . who drive our cars says a lot about Audi. When you're ready to follow your own road, you're ready for an Audi.

Consumer Television
:30 Campaign

893

ART DIRECTOR
Gord Oglan

WRITER
Bill Durnan

AGENCY PRODUCER
Sandy Cole

PRODUCTION CO.
Propeller

DIRECTOR
Alar Kavilo

CLIENT
Molson Breweries
Canada Ltd.

AGENCY
MacLaren Advertising/
Toronto

894

ART DIRECTOR
Bill Halladay

WRITER
Mary Ann Zeman

AGENCY PRODUCER
Neal Bergman

PRODUCTION CO.
Giraldi Suarez Productions

DIRECTOR
Bob Giraldi

CLIENT
Fuji

AGENCY
Lord Geller Federico
Einstein

895

ART DIRECTORS
Steve Jeffery
Nancy Braunstein
John Massey

WRITER
Steve Jeffery

AGENCY PRODUCERS
Nancy Braunstein
John Massey

PRODUCTION COS.
David Ashwell Films
MGMM/LA
Spots Films/New York

DIRECTORS
David Ashwell
David Mallot
Barry Myers

CLIENT
Seagrams Golden Wine
Coolers

AGENCY
Ogilvy & Mather

896

ART DIRECTORS
Nick Scott
Logan Wilmont

WRITERS
Richard Spencer
Mike Court

AGENCY PRODUCER
Debbie Court

PRODUCTION CO.
Sid Roberson

DIRECTOR
Simon Delaney

CLIENT
Warburtons Bakery

AGENCY
Still Price Court Twivy
D'Souza/London

893

SINGER: *This magic moment*
So different and so new
Was like any other
I saw you
And then it happened

ANNCR VO: Molson Canadian—
Taste that'll stop you—
Cold.

SINGER: *This magic moment*
So different and so new.

894

GEORGE CARLIN: Hey, what if people really did turn green with envy?
Well, for one thing, it would be a whole lot easier to watch T.V. I mean, cowards would be yellow, heroes would be true blue and, of course, you'd wanna record them all . . . on Fuji Videotape, the good stuff.
With Fuji . . . blue stuff is blue stuff and yellow stuff is yellow stuff. So you'll always recognize a yellow-bellied, black-hearted villian who's green with envy. And you'll catch him red-handed.
Fuji Videotape. Put the good stuff on the good stuff.

895

(SFX: BRUCE WILLIS'S FACE SLAPPED)

(PARROT: SCREECHES.)

WOMAN: I told you never to set foot in here again. Out!

WILLIS: I just ordered.

WOMAN: Well, it's hot. One drink.

WILLIS: Two.

WOMAN: One.

WILLIS: Two. Seagram's Wine Coolers. One for me. One for you.

WOMAN: You think all it takes is Seagram's Golden.

WILLIS: Let's try it on the rocks.

(MONKEY: SCREECHES.)

WOMAN: Oh, how it sparkles.

WILLIS: The sparkle was always there. Tonight we bring it back.

SUPER: SEAGRAMS. THIS IS WHERE THE FUN STARTS.

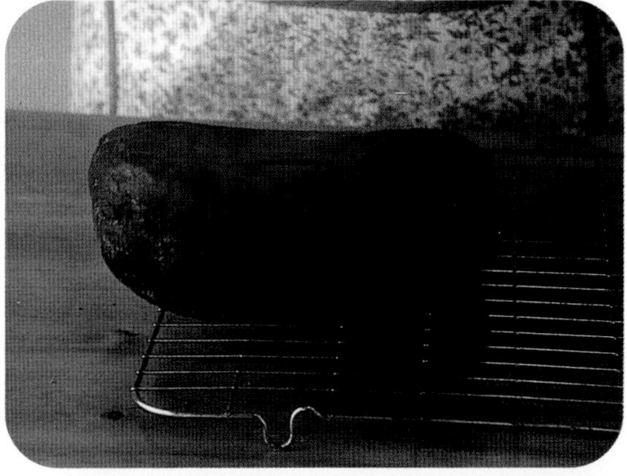

896

(HALF-SECOND SILENCE)

MVO: This is Mrs Joyce Warburton, a member of the Warburton baking family.
For five generations, the Warburton's have taken the finest ingredients . . .
Added their own baking skills . . .
And produced bread as only they know how.

(SFX: THUD!)

Of course, Mrs Warburton—née Booth—is only a member of the family by marriage.
So she has to rely on her husband, Derrick.
Warburton's. Bakers, born and bred.

Consumer Television :30 Campaign

897
ART DIRECTOR
Dean Stefanides
WRITER
Bernie Rosner
AGENCY PRODUCER
Susan Chiafullo
PRODUCTION CO.
Franco-American
DIRECTOR
Sarah Moon
CLIENT
Ralston Purina
AGENCY
Scali McCabe Sloves

898
ART DIRECTORS
Ted Shaine
Clem McCarthy
Marcus Kemp
WRITERS
Rav Friedel
Paul Wolfe
AGENCY PRODUCERS
Robert Samuel
Colleen O'Connor
PRODUCTION COS.
BFCS
Dick James
Cherry Mellon Ibbetson
DIRECTORS
Peter Cherry
Thom Higgins
Dick James
CLIENT
BMW of North America
AGENCY
Ammirati & Puris

899
ART DIRECTORS
Bob Akers
Christie Kelley
WRITERS
Ron Hawkins
Melanie Johnston
Larry Simon
PRODUCTION CO.
PYTKA
DIRECTOR
John Pytka
CLIENT
Bob Evans Farms
AGENCY
Hal Riney & Partners/
Chicago

900
ART DIRECTORS
Barry Vetere
Michael Vaughan
WRITER
Tom Messner
AGENCY PRODUCER
Trish O'Reilly
PRODUCTION CO.
Princzko
CLIENT
LIFE Magazine
AGENCY
Messner Vetere Berger
Carey

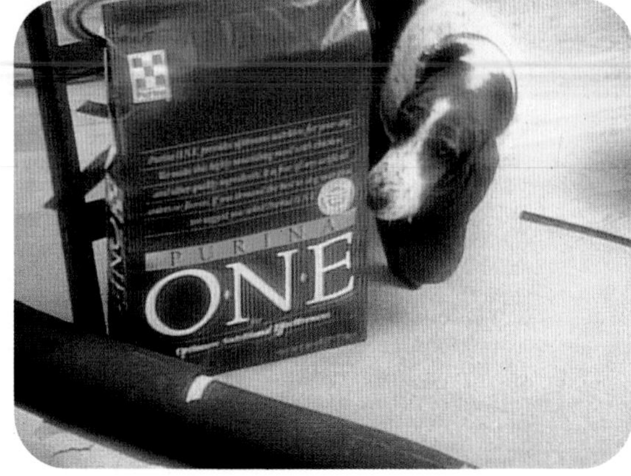

897

VO: One.
One dog in a million
When you feel this way, there's one kind of dog food.
A dog food with real chicken.
That provides optimum nutrition.
A dog food as special as your dog.
Purina O.N.E. brand dog food.
For that one dog. Yours.

898

VO: No one would deny that the Japanese are afficionados of fine machinery. So when they reach that station in life when they can afford really fine machinery, guess what they buy?
A car from Germany called the BMW 325i.
Making BMW last year's number one-selling luxury import in Japan.

899

(MUSIC: UP AND UNDER)

(SFX: MEAT BEING WRAPPED)

CARLTON: What's another thirty miles?

ANNCR VO: At Bob Evans, we don't believe in freezing our sausage . . .

DELI GUY: You mean Hainesville gets it and Milwaukee doesn't?

ANNCR VO: Or in adding preservatives.

L.A. GUY: You don't sell in L.A.?

ANNCR VO: So if we don't come to your part of the country, it's not because we don't like you . . .

SOUTHERN WOMAN: But Charlottesville is just around the bend.

ANNCR VO: It's just that you can only deliver fresh sausage so far.

NEW YORKER VO: So you don't like New York City—the cradle of civilization?

ANNCR VO: Bob Evans.
We deliver fresh sausage or we don't deliver.

(MUSIC: FADES OUT)

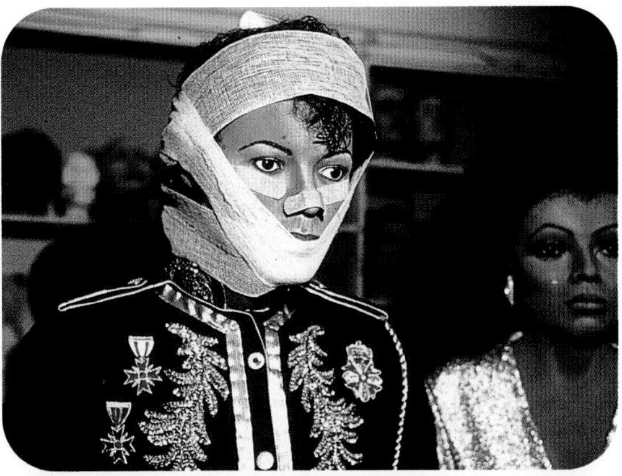

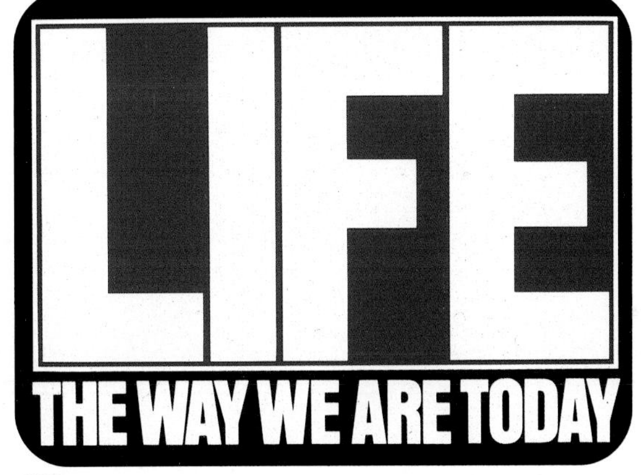

900

VO: Page 12
Can the wax museum keep up with the plastic surgeons?
Page 110
Vietnam's missing in action. More than their memories are alive.
Page 73
Arthur Miller on the way they were.
Page 45
Kelly McGillis on the way she was, is, and will be.

November 1987
LIFE
The way we are today.

Consumer Television :30 Campaign

901
ART DIRECTORS
Rick Boyko
Miles Turpin
WRITERS
Elizabeth Hayes
Emma Unger
Milton Unger
Robin Jones
Melvyn Jones
Mary Ann Bixby
AGENCY PRODUCERS
Richard O'Neill
David Prince
Elaine Hinton
PRODUCTION CO.
Petermann/Dektor
DIRECTOR
Leslie Dektor
CLIENT
Home Savings of America
AGENCY
Chiat/Day - Venice, CA

902
ART DIRECTOR
Dean Stefanides
WRITER
Larry Hampel
AGENCY PRODUCER
Jaki Keuch
PRODUCTION CO.
Rick Levine Productions
DIRECTOR
Patrick Russel
CLIENT
National Dairy Board
AGENCY
Scali McCabe Sloves

Consumer Television Over :10 But Under :30 Single

903
ART DIRECTOR
Mark Drewek
WRITER
Tom Jordan
AGENCY PRODUCER
Reed Allen
PRODUCTION CO.
Logan Productions
DIRECTOR
Jim Logan
CLIENT
Dickens Antiques
AGENCY
Hoffman York & Compton/Milwaukee

904
ART DIRECTOR
Sal DeVito
WRITER
Amy Borkowsky
AGENCY PRODUCER
Rachel Novak
PRODUCTION CO.
Story Piccolo Guliner
DIRECTOR
Mark Story
CLIENT
Genesee Brewing Company
AGENCY
Levine Huntley Schmidt & Beaver

901

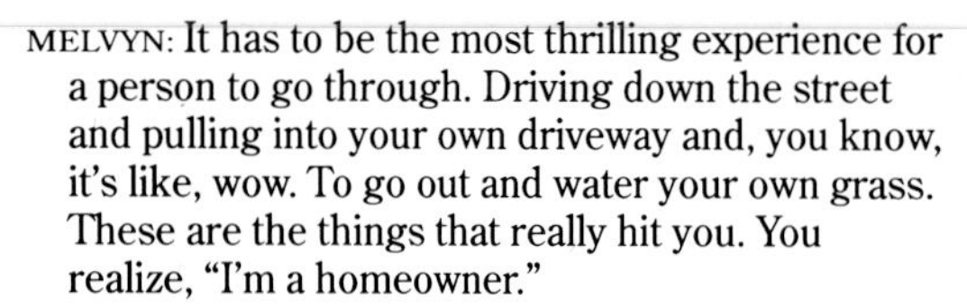

MELVYN: It has to be the most thrilling experience for a person to go through. Driving down the street and pulling into your own driveway and, you know, it's like, wow. To go out and water your own grass. These are the things that really hit you. You realize, "I'm a homeowner."

ANNCR: Home Savings wanted to give Melvyn and Robin Jones a home loan almost as much as they wanted a home.

MELVYN: All we needed was some institution that would say, "We trust you guys."

902

(MUSIC: UP AND UNDER)

MOTHER VO: Have you cleaned your room, young man?

FATHER VO: I've told you a thousand times: don't leave your bike in the driveway!!!

MOTHER VO: Do you plan on spending the rest of your life in that jacket?

FATHER VO: Would you please get a haircut?

MOTHER VO: Did you lock your sister in the closet?!! O.K., just for that you're not going to Uncle Larry's barbeque.

ANNCR VO: This thirty seconds of total coolness has been brought to you by milk.

903

(MUSIC: "TEEN ANGEL" PLAYS THROUGHOUT)

ANNCR: Remember that old radio?
You know . . . the one nobody wanted?
Want to buy it back?

904

ANNCR VO: This should give you some idea of the diffference between beer and Genesee Cream Ale. Smooth Genesee Cream Ale. It's not the same old brewskie.

Consumer Television Over :10 But Under :30 Single

905

ART DIRECTOR
Ken Amaral

WRITER
Jim Welborn

CLIENT
Dance St. Louis

AGENCY
D'Arcy Masius Benton & Bowles/St. Louis

906

ART DIRECTOR
Earl Cavanah

WRITER
Larry Cadman

AGENCY PRODUCER
Jaki Keuch

PRODUCTION CO.
Sandbank Films

DIRECTOR
Henry Sandbank

CLIENT
Volvo

AGENCY
Scali McCabe Sloves

907

ART DIRECTOR
Sal DeVito

WRITER
Amy Borkowsky

PRODUCTION CO.
Story Piccolo Guliner

DIRECTOR
Mark Story

CLIENT
Genesee Brewing Company

AGENCY
Levine Huntley Schmidt & Beaver

Consumer Television Over :10 But Under :30 Campaign

908

ART DIRECTORS
Pat Peduto
Gene Johnson
Doris Cassar

WRITERS
Dan O'Neill
Paige St. John
Rob Lokody

AGENCY PRODUCER
Jack Blandford

PRODUCTION CO.
Bill Hudson & Associates

DIRECTOR
Bill Hudson

CLIENT
Northwest Airlines

AGENCY
Saatchi & Saatchi DFS Compton

905

CAPT. BINGHAMPTON: Mikhail . . . Mikhail . . .
Mikhail . . . where are you?
I want you to fetch Mikhail.
I'm finally going to get Mikhail.

CAPT. BINGHAMPTON VO: Mikhail! . . . Mikhail . . .
Get me Mikhail . . .
I told you I'd get Mikhail and I finally got him.

906

(MUSIC: THROUGHOUT)

(SFX: CLICK)

ANNCR VO: How well does your car stand up to heavy traffic?

(MUSIC: OUT)

907

ANNCR VO: This should give you some idea of the diffference between beer and Genesee Cream Ale. Smooth Genesee Cream Ale. It's not the same old brewskie.

NORTHWEST

200 CITIES
ACROSS THE U.S.

908

MAN: Harry!
Kalamazoo Tuesday?
I can do that!
Memphis Wednesday?
I can do that!
New York Thursday?
I can do that!
How am I going to do that?

ANNCR: No matter where you do business, Northwest can fly you there.

Consumer Television Over :10 But Under :30 Campaign

909
ART DIRECTOR
Mike Moser
WRITERS
Brian O'Neill
Dave O'Hare
AGENCY PRODUCER
Peter Valentine
PRODUCTION CO.
Coppos Films
DIRECTOR
Mark Coppos
CLIENT
California Cooler
AGENCY
Chiat/Day - San Francisco

910
ART DIRECTORS
Donna Tedesco
Terry O'Leary
WRITERS
Bill Connors
Doug Feinstein
AGENCY PRODUCER
Mootsy Elliot
PRODUCTION COS.
Apogee
Director's Chair
Image Point
DIRECTORS
Richard Taylor
Dick Miller
CLIENT
Duracell
AGENCY
Ogilvy & Mather

911
ART DIRECTOR
Paul Scolaro
WRITER
Tony Gomes
AGENCY PRODUCER
Randy Cohen
PRODUCTION CO.
Fernbach Productions

DIRECTOR
Alex Fernbach
CLIENT
Conde Nast's Traveler
AGENCY
David Deutsch Associates

912
ART DIRECTORS
Barry Vetere
Michael Vaughan
WRITER
Tom Messner
AGENCY PRODUCER
Trish O'Reilly
PRODUCTION CO.
Princzko
CLIENT
LIFE Magazine
AGENCY
Messner Vetere Berger
Carey

Halloween is coming.

909

(MUSIC: SPOOKY, UNDER)

ANNCR VO: Halloween is coming.
Don't let this happen to you.
Stock up for Halloween.

SUPER: THE REAL STUFF.

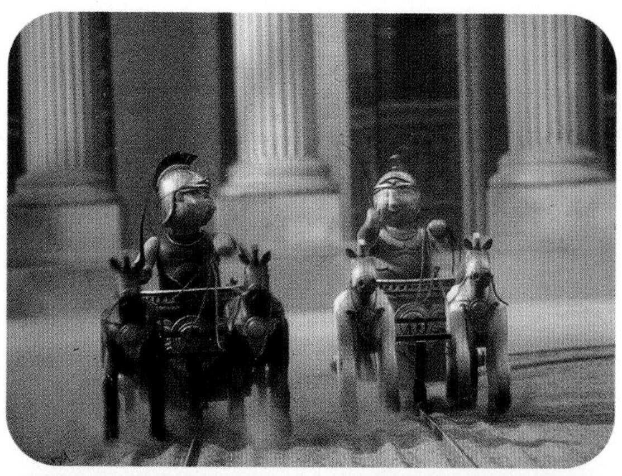

910

ANNCR VO: Today's Coppertop Battery makes yesterday's seem like ancient history. In fact, it's so completely improved, it'll last up to thirty percent longer than the ones we made two years ago. To keep going long after our old battery is a thing in the past. Today's Duracell. No battery lasts longer.

911

VO: Carol Troy takes you inside the Soviet Union for a look at some new fashion trends that may surprise you. Only in the pages of Conde Nast's *Traveler*, the inside guide to the outside world.

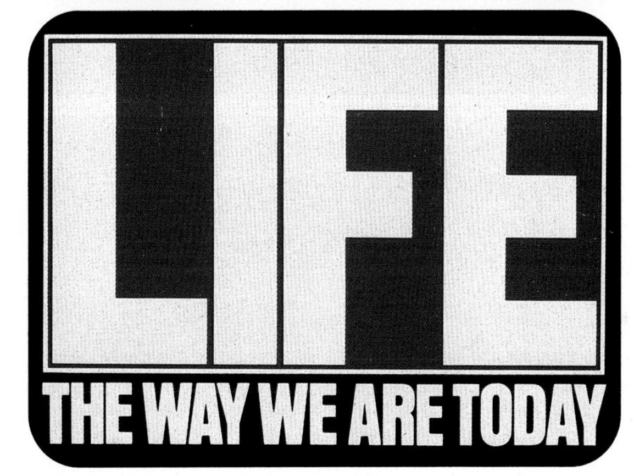

912

VO: Page 72
'I've been poisoned by radiation, and sent a child to the gas chamber,' Meryl Streep says of her roles.
'God, if it weren't for the moments when I fell in love, I'd go nuts.'

LIFE
The Way We Are Today.

Consumer Television Over :10 But Under :30 Campaign

913
ART DIRECTOR
Sal DeVito
WRITER
Amy Borkowsky
AGENCY PRODUCER
Rachel Novak
PRODUCTION CO.
Story Piccolo Guliner
DIRECTOR
Mark Story
CLIENT
Genesee Brewing Company
AGENCY
Levine Huntley Schmidt & Beaver

Consumer Television :10 Single

914
ART DIRECTOR
Alan Lawrence
WRITER
Michael Albright
AGENCY PRODUCER
Frank Tammariello
PRODUCTION CO.
Riverrun Films
DIRECTORS
Alan Lawrence
Frank Tammariello
CLIENT
Ralph's Grocery Company/The Giant
AGENCY
W.B. Doner & Company/ Los Angeles

915
ART DIRECTOR
Dabni Harvey
WRITER
Robert Gerke
AGENCY PRODUCER
Bob Belton
PRODUCTION CO.
Harmony Pictures
DIRECTOR
Robert Lieberman
CLIENT
PIP Printing
AGENCY
BBDO/Los Angeles

Consumer Television :10 Campaign

916
ART DIRECTOR
Alan Lawrence
WRITER
Michael Albright
AGENCY PRODUCER
Frank Tammariello
PRODUCTION CO.
Riverrun Films
DIRECTORS
Alan Lawrence
Frank Tammariello
CLIENT
Ralph's Grocery Company/The Giant
AGENCY
W. B. Doner & Company/ Los Angeles

913

ANNCR VO: This should give you some idea of the diffference between beer and Genesee Cream Ale. Smooth Genesee Cream Ale. It's not the same old brewskie.

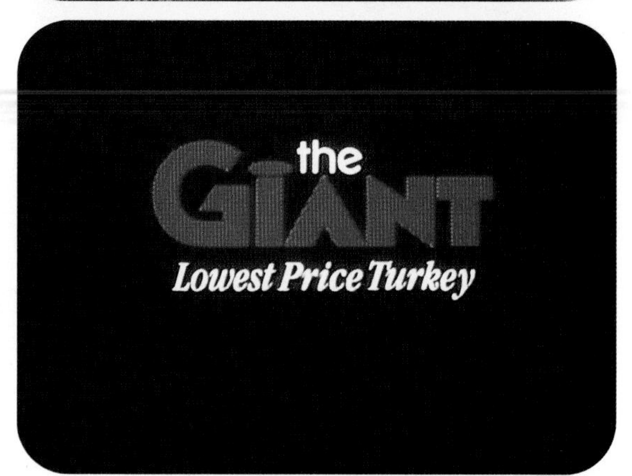

914

(MUSIC: UP AND UNDER THROUGHOUT)

ROSEANNE: Now The Giant's got the lowest prices on turkey, well I've got one of these that sits on the couch and watches wrestling.

915

WOBNIACK: I'm sorry, Mr Santucci. You see, they printed our company logo sort of upside down. But it's kinda cute.

ANNCR VO: If you're not using PIP to handle your printing, you should know—we also do resumes.

SUPER: PIP PRINTING. PIP CAN DO IT.

916

(MUSIC: UP AND UNDER THROUGHOUT)

ROSEANNE: Now The Giant's selling Cornish Game Hens for sixty-nine cents per pound, you can add rice or you can stuff it.

Public Service Television: Single

917

ART DIRECTOR
Dianne Douglas Graham

WRITER
Jeff Stark

AGENCY PRODUCER
Bill Gross

PRODUCTION CO.
Helburn Productions

DIRECTOR
Bill Helburn

CLIENT
Partnership for a Drug-Free America

AGENCY
Saatchi & Saatchi DFS Compton

918

ART DIRECTOR
Logan Wilmont

WRITER
Mike Court

AGENCY PRODUCER
Debbie Court

PRODUCTION CO.
Sid Roberson

DIRECTOR
Simon Delaney

CLIENT
Mates Healthcare

AGENCY
Still Price Court Twivy D'Souza/London

919

WRITER
Susan MacMurchy

PRODUCTION CO.
AIDSFILMS

DIRECTORS
Franklin Getchell
John Hoffman

CLIENT
AIDS

AGENCY
AIDSFILMS

920

ART DIRECTOR
Liz Beth Rokicki

WRITER
Jerry Cronin

PRODUCTION CO.
Video Craft

CLIENT
Cystic Fibrosis Foundation

AGENCY
Hill Holliday Connors Cosmopulos/Boston

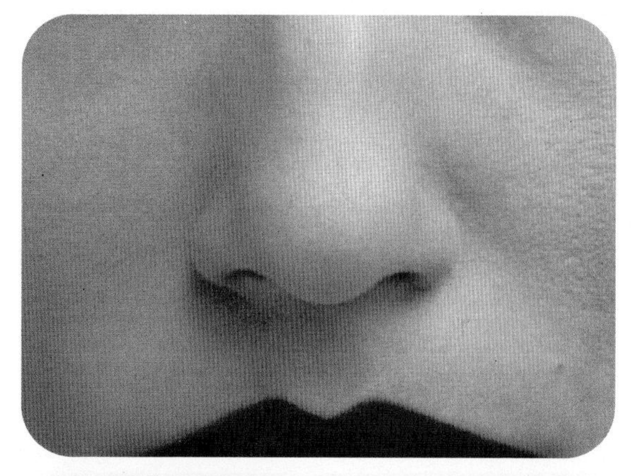

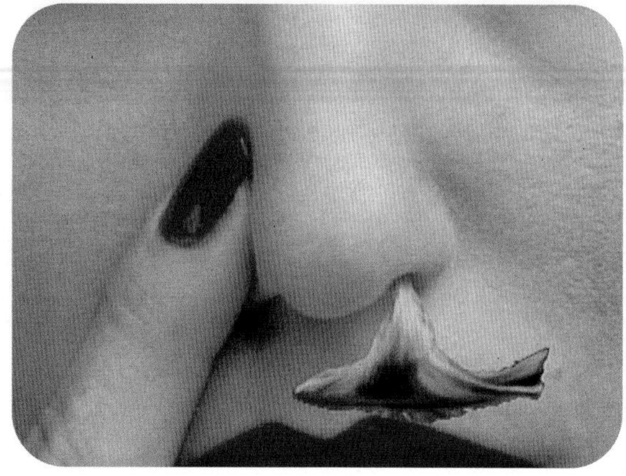

917

VO: One gram of cocaine costs as much as a boombox.

(SFX: SNIFF)

Three grams of cocaine costs as much as a T.V.

(SFX: SNIFF)

Seven grams, a trip to Paris.

(SFX: SNIFF)

A gram a week for a year, a new car.

(SFX: SNIFF)

If you're on coke
everything you work for
is disappearing
right under your nose.

SUPER: PARTNERSHIP FOR A DRUG-FREE AMERICA.

918

(HALF-SECOND SILENCE)

(SFX: FRONT DOOR OPENING)

MUM: Hello, love. (SUBTITLE: YOU'RE LATE)

CAROL: Still up? (SUB: SNOOP)

MUM: Just reading. How's your Steve? (SUB: WHAT HAVE YOU BEEN UP TO?)

CAROL: Oh, he's fine. (SUB: HE'S GREAT)

MUM: He's such a nice boy. (SUB: YOU'RE SLEEPING WITH HIM)

CAROL: I like him a lot. Coffee? (SUB: SHE KNOWS!)

MUM: You won't get carried away, will you? (SUB: I HOPE YOU TAKE PRECAUTIONS.)

CAROL: Of course not. (SUB: WE USE A CONDOM)

MUM: Only you can't be too careful. (SUB: YOU DON'T WANT TO GET PREGNANT)

CAROL: I know that, silly. (SUB: I DON'T WANT TO CATCH ANYTHING)

MVO: Condoms can stop more than pregnancy. They also help protect you against sexually transmitted diseases, even AIDS. So these days, it goes without saying, they make sense.

MUM: It's just that I worry. (SUB: YOU'RE SO YOUNG)

CAROL: You are daft. (SUB: I'M NOT STUPID)

MUM: Less of your cheek. (SUB: I'VE BEEN YOUNG TOO, YOU KNOW)

MVO: Condoms.
It goes without saying they make sense.

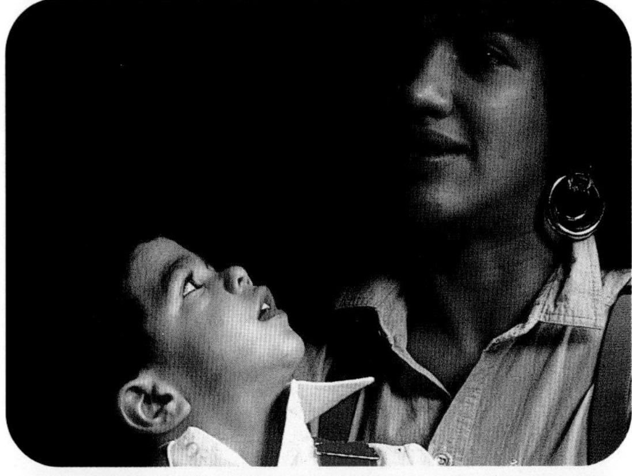

919

MOTHER: I have AIDS and my baby has AIDS.
My husband may have it but he he won't go to the doctor. In the beginning he wouldn't even talk about it.
My mother helps us but sometimes I think she's afraid.
Every night I kneel by my baby's crib and pray to be strong for him.
Every night I pray that my baby won't die.

VO: Protect the people you love. Use a condom.

920

ANNCR: Play hard, Joey . . . play hard . . . For you have cystic fibrosis, a disease that crowds your lungs with mucus, leaving you less room to giggle . . . less room to laugh . . . less room to call your buddies' names . . . Until, finally, there's no room left to breathe . . . Give to the Joey Foundation. And help fight cystic fibrosis. The number one genetic killer that every day destroys three more children. And those who love them . . . Please give generously . . . Thank you.

Public Service Television: Single

921

ART DIRECTOR
Dianne Douglas Graham

WRITER
Jeff Stark

AGENCY PRODUCER
Bill Gross

PRODUCTION CO.
Robins Productions

DIRECTOR
Larry Robins

CLIENT
Partnership for a Drug-Free America

AGENCY
Saatchi & Saatchi DFS Compton

922

ART DIRECTOR
Michael Fazende

WRITER
Jarl Olsen

AGENCY PRODUCER
Char Loving

PRODUCTION CO.
Bajus Jones

CLIENT
University of Minnesota

AGENCY
Fallon McElligott/ Minneapolis

923

ART DIRECTORS
Rick Bell
Scot Fletcher

WRITER
Larre Johnson

AGENCY PRODUCER
Harvey Greenberg

PRODUCTION CO.
PYTKA

DIRECTOR
Joe Pytka

CLIENT
Partnership for a Drug-Free America

AGENCY
keye/donna/pearlstein - Los Angeles

924

ART DIRECTOR
Kevin Heslip

WRITER
Rod Thompson

PRODUCTION CO.
Sundog Productions

DIRECTOR
Larry Carroll

CLIENT
Partnership for a Drug-Free America

AGENCY
McCann-Erickson/ Farmington Hills, MI

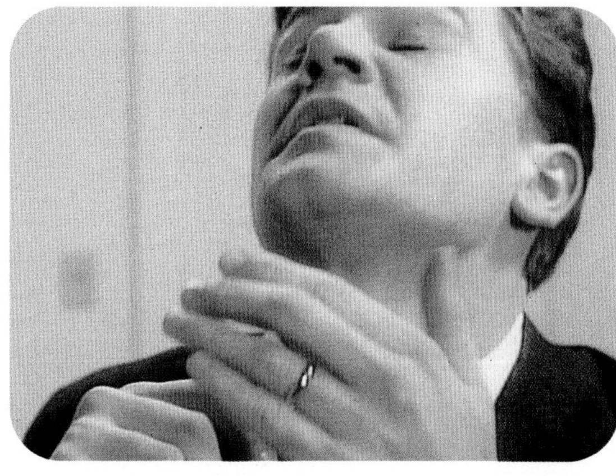

921

YUPPIE (SNIFFS): I do coke so I can work longer.
So I can earn more.
So I can do more coke.
So I can work longer. (FASTER AND FASTER)
So I can earn more.
SoIcandomorecokeSoIcanworklonger (ETC; FADE)

MUSIC: *I'm always chasing rainbows waiting for a little bluebird in vain.*

SUPER: THE END.
PARTNERSHIP FOR A DRUG-FREE AMERICA.

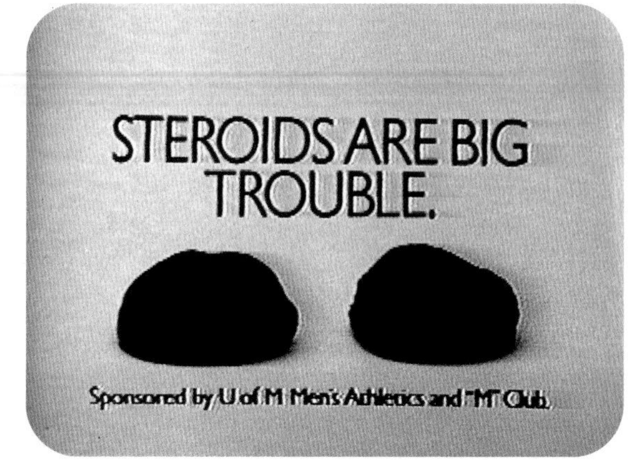

922

(MUSIC: TUBA PLAYING ROUSER SONG)

ANNCR: When a man takes steroids, he introduces a chemical into his body . . . that acts like male hormone, so the parts that used to make male hormone shut down.
Eventually they waste away, leaving the man sterile.

(MUSIC: LITTLE MORE THAN A HIGH-PITCHED WHINE)

A lot of big athletes have taken steroids. But they aren't very big now.
Steroids. They're big trouble.

923

GUY: My brother's friend, Rick, wanted to do something special for him for his birthday.
He bought him some crack.
Maybe it was bad stuff. Maybe they just couldn't handle it. That was two years ago . . . today.
Sometimes I think Rick was the lucky one. He died.
'Happy birthday, buddy.'

SILENCE.

SUPER: PARTNERSHIP FOR A DRUG-FREE AMERICA.

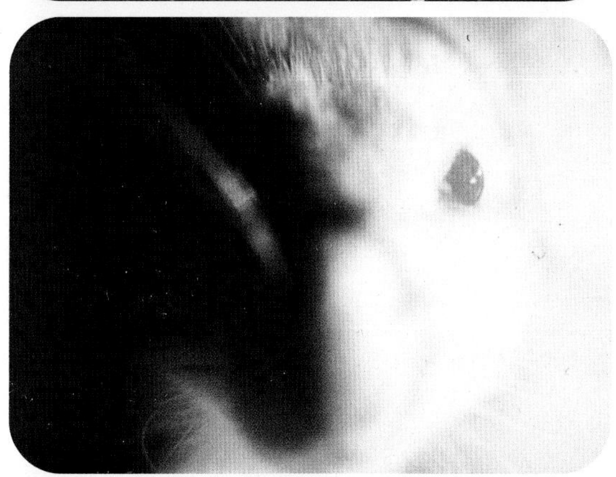

924

VO: Only one drug is so addictive, nine out of ten laboratory rats will use it . . .
and use it . . .
and use it . . .
until dead.
It's called cocaine and it can do the same thing to you.

SUPER: FACE THE FACTS: DRUGS ARE A DEAD END.
PARTNERSHIP FOR A DRUG-FREE AMERICA

Public Service Television: Single

925
ART DIRECTOR
Dennis Lim
WRITERS
Gail Anne Smith
Martin MacDonald
Cambria Cohen
AGENCY PRODUCER
Joel Squier
PRODUCTION CO.
Johns+Gorman Films
DIRECTOR
Jeff Gorman
CLIENT
American Lung Association
AGENCY
Ketchum/Los Angeles

Public Service Television: Campaign

926
ART DIRECTOR
Jane Rubini
WRITER
David Warren
AGENCY PRODUCER
Ed Pollack
PRODUCTION CO.
Bianchi Films
DIRECTOR
Ed Bianchi
CLIENT
Foster Parents/NYC Special Services for Children
AGENCY
TBWA/Bianchi Films

927
ART DIRECTOR
Walt Taylor
WRITER
Rebecca Flora
AGENCY PRODUCERS
Jeff France
Bruce Mansfield
PRODUCTION CO.
Big City Films
DIRECTOR
Jeff France
CLIENT
Virginia Department of Alcoholic Beverage Control
AGENCY
Lawler Ballard/
Norfolk, VA

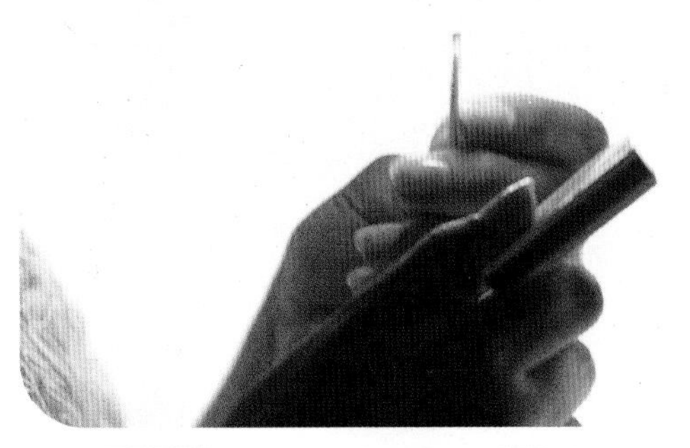

925

(SFX: MATCHES STRIKING, BEING DROPPED IN ASHTRAY)

VO: Maybe someone's trying to tell her something.

926

MONIQUE: Oh, dear God, please help my mom . . . 'cause when she's drunk, it's me she picks on . . . What did you say? . . . Help will come soon? . . . Good, 'cause mom started using the broom . . . What next will she use: the extension cord? The chair, the table, the ironing board? . . . Oh, no, guess what? Momma's gone again . . . and I'm worried about the bruises on my skin . . .

927

YOUNG MAN: Gimme a light.

BARTENDER: Gimme some I.D.

ANNCR VO: Just a reminder. Virginia has a new drinking age.

Student Competition

College Competition

Assignment: PAND (Performing Artists for Nuclear Disarmament)

928

ART DIRECTOR
Chris Dunning

WRITER
Chris Dunning

COLLEGE
Washington University

929

ART DIRECTOR
Danny Fernandez

WRITER
Danny Fernandez

COLLEGE
Stockton State College

930

ART DIRECTOR
Kevin Ellis

WRITER
Kevin Ellis

COLLEGE
Columbus College of Art & Design

931

WRITER
Susan Gayle Crank

COLLEGE
Virginia Commonwealth University, Richmond, VA

928

929

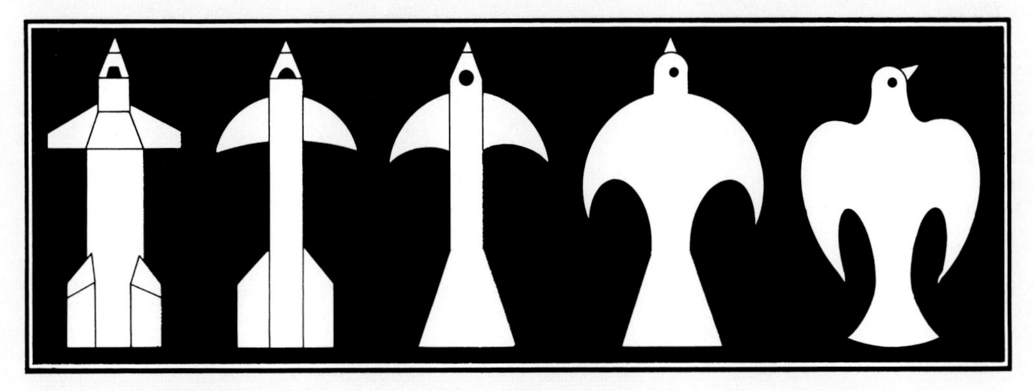

evo·lu·tion \ˌev-ə-ˈlü-shən *also* ˌē-və-\ *n* [L *evolution-, evolutio* unrolling, fr. *evolutus*, pp. of *evolvere*] (1) : a process of continuous change from a lower, simpler, or worse to a higher, more complex, or better state : GROWTH (2) : a process of gradual and relatively peaceful social, political, and economic advance

"It would indeed be a tragedy if the history of the human race proved to be nothing more than the story of an ape playing with a box of matches on a petrol dump."
— *David Ormsby Gore*

Performing Artists For

Nuclear Disarmament

930

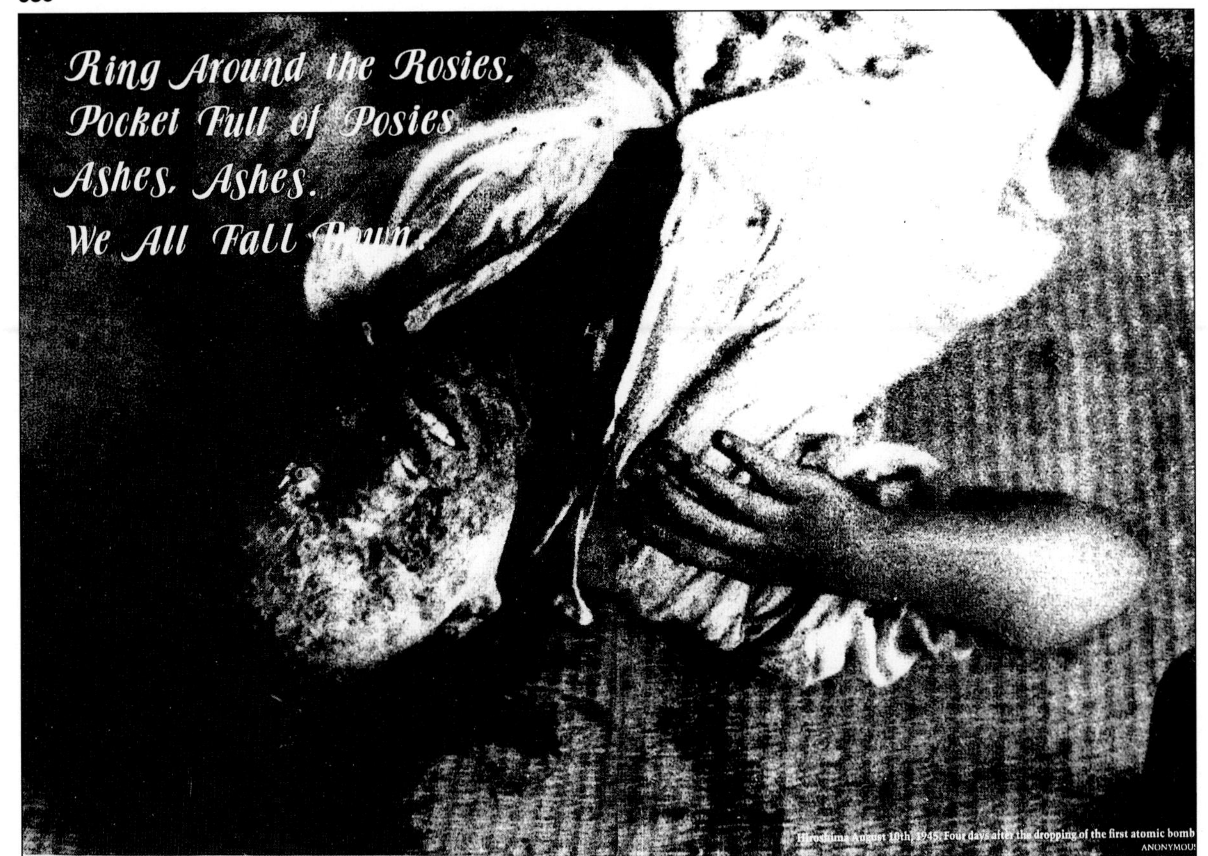

Ring Around the Rosies,
Pocket Full of Posies.
Ashes, Ashes.
We All Fall Down.
Hiroshima August 10th, 1945. Four days after the dropping of the first atomic bomb
ANONYMOUS

Performing Artists For Nuclear Disarmament.

Please, Join PAND. Call (212) 431-7921.

931

College Competition

Assignment: PAND (Performing Artists for Nuclear Disarmament)

932
ART DIRECTOR
David M. Canright
WRITER
David M. Canright
COLLEGE
University of Texas at Austin

933
ART DIRECTOR
Tim Sabo
WRITER
Tim Sabo
COLLEGE
University of Texas at Austin

934
ART DIRECTOR
Christopher Sekin
WRITER
Christopher Sekin
COLLEGE
University of Texas at Austin

935
ART DIRECTOR
Rose Gomez
WRITER
Kitty Schulz
COLLEGE
University of Texas at Austin

936
ART DIRECTOR
Alexander Antoniades
COLLEGE
East Texas State University

932

933

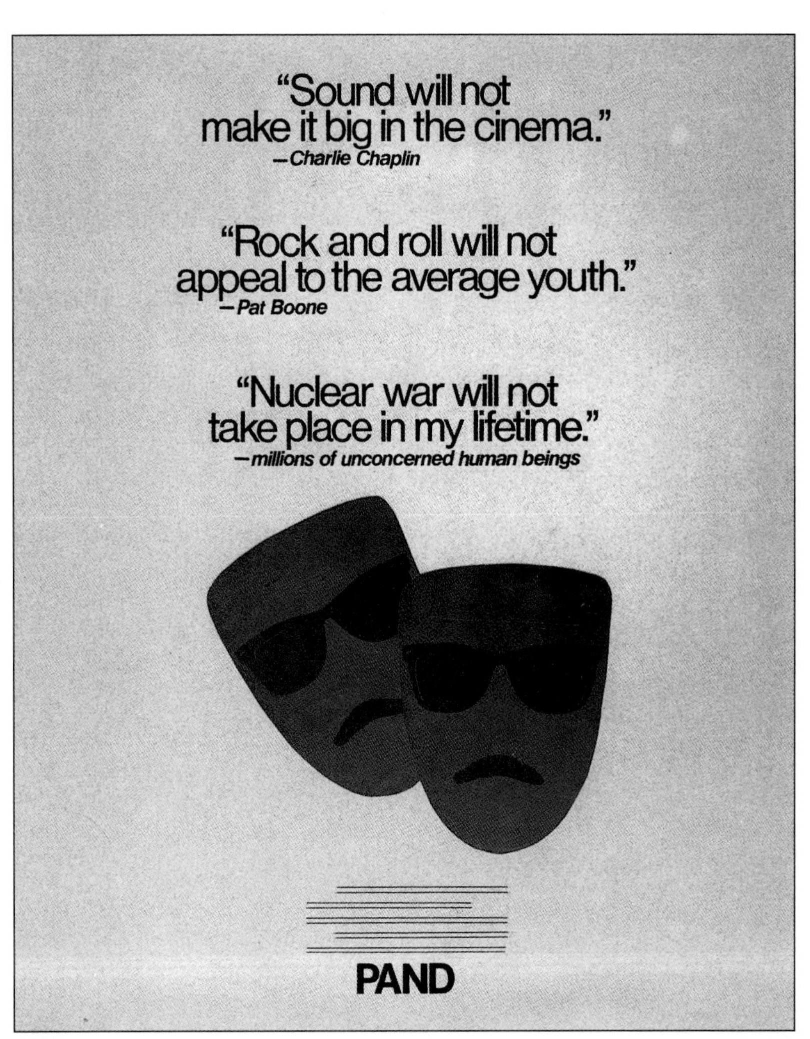
"Sound will not make it big in the cinema."
—Charlie Chaplin
"Rock and roll will not appeal to the average youth."
—Pat Boone
"Nuclear war will not take place in my lifetime."
—millions of unconcerned human beings
PAND

934

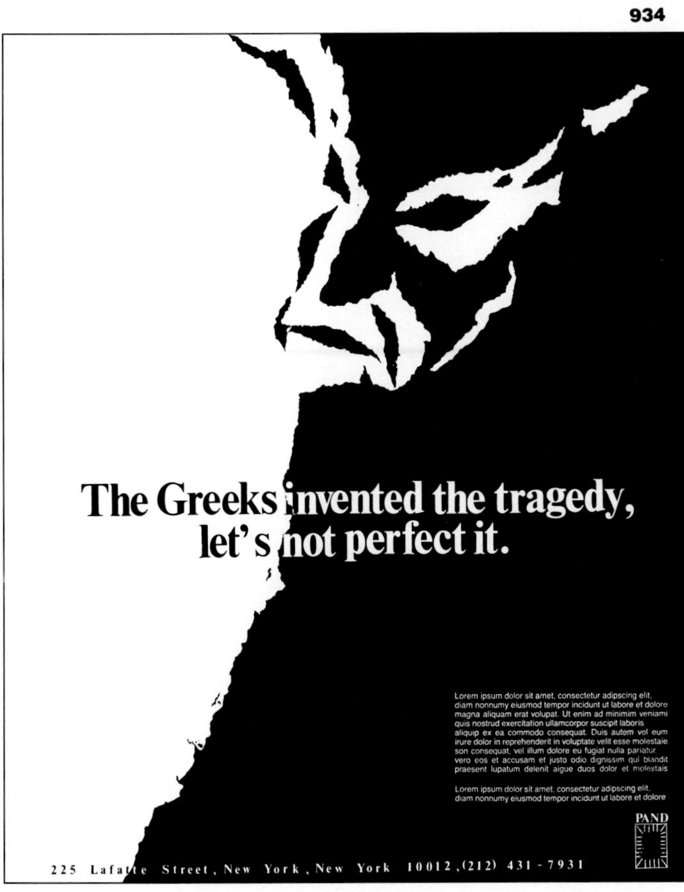
The Greeks invented the tragedy, let's not perfect it.
Lorem ipsum dolor sit amet, consectetur adipscing elit, diam nonnumy eiusmod tempor incidunt ut labore et dolore magna aliquam erat volupat. Ut enim ad minimim veniami quis nostrud exercitation ullamcorpor suscipit laboris aliquip ex ea commodo consequat. Duis autem vel eum irure dolor in reprehenderit in voluptate velit esse molestaie son consequat, vel illum dolore eu fugiat nulla pariatur. vero eos et accusam et justo odio dignissim qui blandit praesent lupatum delenit aigue duos dolor et molestais
Lorem ipsum dolor sit amet, consectetur adipscing elit, diam nonnumy eiusmod tempor incidunt ut labore et dolore
PAND
225 Lafayette Street, New York, New York 10012, (212) 431-7931

935

UNFORTUNATELY THE LAST SHOW WILL PLAY TO A PACKED HOUSE

936

Index

Index

Art Directors

Writers

Designers

Artists

Photographers

Agency Producers

Production Companies

Directors

Clients

Agencies

Colleges

This End Up
THE ONE SHOW
LONDON 1988